*The Engineering Handbook
of Smart Technology for
Aging, Disability, and
Independence*

The Engineering Handbook of Smart Technology for Aging, Disability, and Independence

Edited by

Abdelsalam (Sumi) Helal
Professor, University of Florida, Gainesville, FL, USA

Mounir Mokhtari
Associate Professor, Institut National des Télécommunications, Évry, France

Bessam Abdulrazak
Assistant Professor, Université de Sherbrooke, Québec, Canada

WILEY

A John Wiley & Sons, Inc., Publication

Copyright © 2008 by John Wiley & Sons, Inc. All rights reserved.

Published by John Wiley & Sons, Inc., Hoboken, New Jersey
Published simultaneously in Canada

No part of this publication may be reproduced, stored in a retrieval system, or transmitted in any form or by any means, electronic, mechanical, photocopying, recording, scanning, or otherwise, except as permitted under Section 107 or 108 of the 1976 United States Copyright Act, without either the prior written permission of the Publisher, or authorization through payment of the appropriate per-copy fee to the Copyright Clearance Center, Inc., 222 Rosewood Drive, Danvers, MA 01923, (978) 750-8400, fax (978) 750-4470, or on the web at www.copyright.com. Requests to the Publisher for permission should be addressed to the Permissions Department, John Wiley & Sons, Inc., 111 River Street, Hoboken, NJ 07030, (201) 748-6011, fax (201) 748-6008, or online at http://www.wiley.com/go/permission.

Limit of Liability/Disclaimer of Warranty: While the publisher and author have used their best efforts in preparing this book, they make no representations or warranties with respect to the accuracy or completeness of the contents of this book and specifically disclaim any implied warranties of merchantability or fitness for a particular purpose. No warranty may be created or extended by sales representatives or written sales materials. The advice and strategies contained herein may not be suitable for your situation. You should consult with a professional where appropriate. Neither the publisher nor author shall be liable for any loss of profit or any other commercial damages, including but not limited to special, incidental, consequential, or other damages.

For general information on our other products and services or for technical support, please contact our Customer Care Department within the United States at (800) 762-2974, outside the United States at (317) 572-3993 or fax (317) 572-4002.

Wiley also publishes its books in a variety of electronic formats. Some content that appears in print may not be available in electronic formats. For more information about Wiley products, visit our web site at www.wiley.com.

Library of Congress Cataloging-in-Publication Data

The engineering handbook of smart technology for aging, disability, and independence / edited by Abdelsalam (Sumi) Helal, Mounir Mokhtari, Bessam Abdulrazak.
    p. cm.
  Includes index.
  ISBN 978-0-471-71155-1 (cloth)
  1. Self-help devices for people with disabilities. 2. Older people with disabilities. 3. Technology and older people. I. Helal, Abdelsalam A., 1959- II. Mokhtari, Mounir. III. Abdulrazak, Bessam.
  RM950.E56 2008
  617'.033—dc22
                                              2008009568

Printed in the United States of America

10 9 8 7 6 5 4 3 2 1

Contents

Foreword	xi
Preface	xiii
Author Biography	xvii
Contributors	xix
Introduction to the Book *Sumi Helal, Mounir Mokhtari, Bessam Abdulrazak, and Mark Schmalz*	1
PART I DEFINITIONS, CLASSIFICATIONS, AND POLICIES	**27**
1. Technology for Successful Aging and Disabilities *Amol Karmarkar, Eliana Chavez, and Rory A. Cooper*	29
2. International Policy Context of Technologies for Disabilities: An Analytic Framework *Rene Jahiel*	49
3. Technology for Individuals with Disabilities: Government and Market Policies *Katherine D. Seelman*	61
4. Assistive Technology and the International Classification of Functioning, Disability, and Health *Jerome E. Bickenbach*	81

5. Technology for Integration of Students with Disabilities in Higher Education — 101
Marci Kinas Jerome, Kristine Neuber, Brianna Stegall, Anna Emenova, and Michael Behrmann

6. ISO 9999 Assistive Products for Persons with Disability: Classification and Terminology — 117
Ir. Theo Bougie

PART II USERS, NEEDS, AND ASSISTIVE TECHNOLOGY — 127

7. Low-Tech Assistive Technology — 129
Kathleen Laurin and Jill Sherman Pleasant

8. People with Visual Disabilities — 143
John Gill and Linda Jolliff

9. Assistive Devices for People with Visual Impairments — 163
John Gill

10. Assistive Devices for People with Hearing Loss — 191
Matthew H. Bakke

11. People with Cognitive Disabilities — 203
Mary Kay Rizzolo and David Braddock

12. Assistive Devices for People with Cognitive Impairments — 217
Hélène Pigot, Jérémy Bauchet, and Sylvain Giroux

PART III HUMAN–MACHINE INTERACTION AND ALTERNATIVE COMMUNICATION — 237

13. Computer Access in the Workplace — 239
Karen Milchus and Carrie Bruce

14. Platforms and Operating System Accessibility — 263
Barry Feigenbaum and Kip Harris

15. Voice Interactive Systems — 281
Rudzionis Algimantas, Kastytis Ratkevicius, and Vytautas Rudzionis

16. The Communication Assistant (Alternative Communication) — 297
Leanne L. West

17. Wearable Systems Design Issues for Aging or Disabled Users — 317
Maribeth Gandy, Tracy Westeyn, Helene Brashear, and Thad Starner

18. Tactile Displays   **339**
Stephen A. Brewster, Steven A. Wall, Lorna M. Brown, and Eve E. Hoggan

PART IV   ASSISTIVE ROBOTICS   **353**

19. Assistive Robotics for Independent Living   **355**
Bessam Abdulrazak and Mounir Mokhtari

20. Mobile Platform-Based Assistive Robot Systems   **375**
Zeungnam Bien, Kwang-Hyun Park, Myung Jin Chung, Dae-Jin Kim, Jin-Woo Jung, Pyung-Hun Chang, and Jin-Oh Kim

21. Robot Therapy at Elder Care Institutions: Effects of Long-term Interaction with Seal Robots   **405**
Takanori Shibata and Kazuyoshi Wada

22. Prostheses: Human Limbs and Their Artificial Replacements   **419**
Richard F. ff. Weir

PART V   USER MOBILITY   **437**

23. Wheelchairs within the Context of Smart House Design   **439**
Dimitar Stefanov

24. People with Special Needs and Traffic Safety   **459**
Nahid Shahmehri, Ioan Chisalita, and Johan Åberg

25. Blind Navigation and the Role of Technology   **479**
Nicholas A. Giudice and Gordon E. Legge

26. Walker Systems   **501**
Andrew Rentschler

27. Accessible Public Transportation Services in America   **519**
Katharine M. Hunter-Zaworski

28. Transportation Services in Europe   **535**
Isabelle Dussutour

29. Transportation Services in Asia   **549**
Joseph Kwan and Eric Tam

PART VI   TECHNOLOGIES FOR SMART ENVIRONMENTS   **567**

30. Modeling the Well-Being of Older People   **569**
Andrew Sixsmith

CONTENTS

31. Context Awareness — 585
Jadwiga Indulska and Karen Henricksen

32. Middleware for Smart Spaces — 607
Daqing Zhang, Tao Gu, and Manli Zhu

33. Safety, Security, Privacy and Trust Issues — 619
Abdallah M'hamed

34. Automated Medication Management Devices — 631
R. J. Davies, Christopher Nugent, D. D. Finlay, N. D. Black, and D. Craig

35. Virtual Companions — 645
Nahid Shahmehri, Johan Åberg, and Dennis Maciuszek

36. Textile Sensing and e-Textiles (Smart Textiles) — 673
Rita Paradiso, Nicola Taccini, and Giannicola Loriga

PART VII SMART ENVIRONMENTS AND CYBERINFRASTRUCTURES — 693

37. The Gator Tech Smart House: A Programmable Pervasive Space — 695
Sumi Helal, Raja Bose, Steven Pickles, Hicham Elzabadani, Jeffrey King, and Youssef Kaddourah

38. Health Application and Telecare — 711
Mathijs Soede, Frank Vlaskamp, and Charles Willems

39. Immersive Telecare for Assisting People with Special Needs — 727
Sumi Helal and Bessam Abdulrazak

40. Smart Systems in Personal Transportation — 737
Aaron Steinfeld

41. Tools for Studying Novel Proactive Healthcare Applications for Places of Living — 749
Stephen Intille and Kent Larson

42. Algorithms for Smart Spaces — 767
Diane J. Cook, G. Michael Youngblood, and Gaurav Jain

PART VIII EMERGING STANDARDS, GUIDELINES, AND DESIGN METHODS — 785

43. User-Sensitive Design for Older and Disabled People — 787
Alan Newell

44. **Universal Design/Design for All: Practice and Method** *Edward Steinfeld*	803
45. **Design for Well-Being** *Andreas Larsson and Tobias Larsson*	819
46. **Technology Evaluation within Healthcare and Social Care** *Suzanne Martin, George Kernohan, Bernadette McCreight, and Christopher Nugent*	833
47. **Usability in Designing Assistive Technologies** *Jean-Claude Sperandio and Marion Wolff*	855
48. **Smart Home and Health Telematics: Standards for and with Users** *Milan Erbes*	867
49. **ICT Standardization for the Elderly and People with Disabilities in Japan** *Hajime Yamada*	907
Index	921

Foreword

The disability and aging fields are dynamic. We are in a transition period, moving away from an old vision for disability to a new one. Older adults and people with disabilities were viewed as dependent and in need of consistent professional guidance. Increasingly, they are viewed as people with abilities, much like other people. The old model of disability focused solely on the individual level, and on approaches to disablement only at the body level. The new model of disability is universal, integrative and expansive. Technology innovation and the international human rights movement have provided much of the energy driving transition to a new integrative model of disability and aging. *The Engineering Handbook of Smart Technology for Aging, Disability and Independence* provides a comprehensive introduction to the new model and related challenges for research and development.

The integrative model is embodied in the World Health Organization's (WHO) International Classification of Functioning, Disability and Health (ICF), adopted in 2001. Disablement is approached at the body, functional, social and environmental levels. The ICF components, body, activities, participation and environment, are in dynamic relationship to one another, therefore, generating interesting challenges for research and development (R&D) and measurement. Assessment measures assume a real world context of school, family and employment.

The integrative model is participatory. Participation of end users and stakeholders has implications for R&D and the education and training of professionals. Throughout the world, people with disabilities and older adults have an expressed preference to live as independently as possible in their communities. As the *Handbook* illustrates, they often need technological supports to realize their everyday living objectives. End users of technology will be more involved in the planning and implementation of studies that generate quality of life outcomes. The technology development process must become proactive in initiating participatory design that receives feedback from end users, industry and regulators. Engineering curricula must be adapted to teach our students about the integrative model of disability, participatory design and the importance of social factors such as end user acceptance and stakeholder markets and regulation.

Breakthroughs in biomedical and technological sciences and their applications are ongoing. Applications have improved the quality of life for some but not all older adults and people with disabilities. Human rights advocacy for full citizenship and community inclusion have permeated the international arena. The World Health Organization has estimated the disability population as approximately one billion, mostly living in lower resource countries. Without commitment to accessibility, affordability, availability and usability, technology will not benefit the many around the world that need it to pursue active lives, to study, to work and live in their communities.

The *Handbook* sets out a framework in which engineering innovation is complemented by exploration of contextual factors such as human rights, standards, policy and the role of international organizations. While the engineering community may grasp the potential of technology to improve quality of life, it also has an important role in the realization of the new vision for older adults and people with disabilities through its education and advocacy within the technical community. Engineering innovation must be further harnessed to effect social good.

KATE SEELMAN

2008

Preface

Aging and disability have begun to impact our quality of life. Elderly people and those living with disabilities [people with special needs (PwSN)] are loosing their independence and overall wellbeing. The growing PwSN population is too large to be cared for through traditional government programs. The cost associated with such programs and the lack of a skilled caregiver workforce makes it very difficult to meet the needs of this segment of the population. It is therefore inevitable that we resort to technology in our search for solutions to the costly and challenging problems facing PwSN.

This handbook presents a broad overview of multidisciplinary research and development aiming at achieving independence and wellbeing for PwSN. The book covers the user population, the various impairments and disabilities, and state-of-the-art assistive technology, ranging from simple assistive devices to comprehensive assistive environments. A unique aspect of this book is presenting the readers with a uniform and coherent treatment of a large number (over 50) of cross-disciplinary, diverse research topics—all centered around PwSN.

AUDIENCE

This book has been designed for two audiences. The first includes professionals, researchers, and students seeking an understanding of the PwSN population and their needs, and the existing body of research and practice focusing on improving PwSN wellbeing and independence. This audience spans several engineering disciplines, including computer science engineering, electrical engineering, biomedical engineering, and rehabilitation engineering. It also spans geriatricians, occupational therapists, physical therapists, clinical and health psychologists, behavioral scientists, and physicians.

The second audience comprises anyone who has interest in assistive technologies for people with special needs and wants to know what is currently available, and what will be possible in the near and more distant future. This group includes but is not limited to the public health policymakers, health services professionals, national and state funding agencies, government health departments, and specialized institutions. This audience also includes the PwSN themselves.

BOOK ORGANIZATION

The book is divided into eight parts, each consists of several chapters. The purpose of each part is summarized below:

Part I: Definitions, Classifications, and Policies. This part presents the most important definitions related to disabilities and aging and the technologies dedicated to this population. It also discusses policy-related issues.

Part II: Users, Needs, and Assistive Technology. This part addresses user needs for the elderly and people with disabilities. It covers the various user populations, including statistics, such as population size, growth rate, government spending on population programs, research and development (R&D), and health, among other statistics. This part also introduces devices and systems developed for PwSN in support of communicating, writing, reading, studying, among other things.

Part III: Human–Machine Interaction and Alternative Communication. This part addresses research experiences focused on improvement of the human–machine interaction in terms of aging and disabilities. It also covers innovative systems, generic interfaces, systems adaptations, and virtual reality. This part also covers speech prosthesis, talking calculators, and tactile or voice output measuring devices. Communication boards or books, multilevel voice output devices with levels, dynamic displays, icon sequencing, among other systems are also discussed.

Part IV: Assistive Robotics. This part discusses robotic solutions and the latest advances in assistive devices. Such systems can now, or will in the future, serve many of the "personal assistance" needs of older persons with disabilities. This part covers robots that assist people in daily life tasks (eating and drinking, applying makeup, etc.), robots for therapy, robots for training, and robots for sport rehabilitation.

Part V: User Mobility. This part discusses user mobility issues and solutions that could help users overcome their lost mobility. It also addresses issues and approaches to driver safety, testing, and remediation, and the role of technology in enabling mobility and providing alternatives transportation systems. Finally, this part outlines many domains related to user mobility such as new wheelchair designs, smart wheelchairs, driving dilemmas, and adaptation of public transportation systems.

Part VI: Technologies for Smart Environments. This part discusses technologies that enable the creation of smart environments. It covers: home networking, home automation, middleware technologies, service infrastructures, context-aware frameworks, tracking, behavior analysis, among others technologies.

Part VII: Smart Environmants and Cyberinfrastructures. This part discusses the integration of advanced technologies into the daily life of user environments (home, work, public places, public administrations, etc.) that enable the creation of an assistive environment. It also addresses issues and approaches to smart technology applications. This part also covers the use of Information and Communication Technology (ICT) and services to promote organizational performance and quality of life, telehealth applications and patient monitoring, information, and education.

Part VIII: Emerging Standards, Guidelines, and Design Methods. This part discusses methods related to designing products that fit the user's needs and capacities. It also discusses new tools and concepts, and other issues related to the provision of usable and accessible technology that promotes independent and safe living. This part also discusses emerging standards and guidelines to build accessible devices, tools, and environments.

HOW TO USE THIS BOOK

The book is a compendium of a broad set of research areas, all centered around PwSN. The main intended use of the book is as a field reference for "one-stop shopping" by researchers and practitioners. The book has been organized into parts to enable readers to use it as a supplemental material in many courses on engineering and the health professions. Policymakers, governments, and health service professionals can use the book as a source for the latest information on PwSN and the related technologies available to them.

We hope that you find the book both valuable and interesting.

SUMI HELAL

University of Florida

MOUNIR MOKHTARI

Institute Nationale de Télécommunications

BESSAM ABDULRAZAK

Université de Sherbrooke

Author Biography

ABDELSALAM (SUMI) HELAL, Ph.D., is a Professor in the Computer and Information Science and Engineering Department (CISE) at the University of Florida (UF), Gainesville. His research interests span the areas of pervasive computing, mobile computing, as well as networking and Internet computing. He directs the Mobile and Pervasive Computing Laboratory and leads several government-funded research projects on "Smart Homes" and "Health Telematics for Successful Aging and Personal Health." He is cofounder and director of the Gator Tech Smart House, a UF experimental home for applied pervasive computing research in the domain of elder care. Additionally, he is founder, president, and CEO of Phoneomena, Inc., a mobile application and middleware company, and founder and president of Pervasa, Inc., a UF startup focused on platform and middleware products for sensor networks.

Dr. Helal is a cofounder and an editorial board member of the *IEEE Pervasive Computing* magazine. He is the editor of the magazine's column on "Standards, Tools and Emerging Technologies". He is also the networking area editor for the *IEEE Computer* magazine. He has published over 200 books, book chapters, journal articles, and conference or workshop papers. He is a senior member of the Institute of Electrical and Electronics Engineers (IEEE) as well as a member of the Association for Computing Machinery (ACM) and the USENIX Association. Dr. Helal received his B. Eng. degree from Alexandria University, Egypt, and his Master's and Ph.D. degrees in computer science from Purdue University, West Lafayette, Indiana.

MOUNIR MOKHTARI, Ph.D., is an associate professor at the Institut TELECOM (ex GET/INT), France. He obtained his Master's degree from Paris 12 Val de Marne University, France, in 1992, and a Master's of Research degree in networking from INT in 1994. He collaborated with Pierre and Marie Curie University and INSERM Laboratory to obtain his Ph.D. degree in computer science in 1997. His research activity focuses mainly on human-machine interaction, rehabilitation robotics, and health telematics. Dr. Mokhtari, who is leading several European and national projects, is the head and founder of Handicom Lab (Handicap Engineering and Communication Lab, which was founded in 1999).

BESSAM ABDULRAZAK, Ph.D., is an assistant professor of computer and information science engineering at the University of Sherbrooke, Quebec, Canada. Previously, he was a postdoctoral candidate at the University of Florida, Gainesville, and before that, at Telecom-SudParis, France. He received his Ph.D. degree in computer science from Telecom-SudParis; M.S. degree in robotics from Paris VI, France; and B.Sc./Ing degree from USTHB, Algeria. His research interests include ubiquitous and pervasive computing, ambient intelligence, smart spaces, assistive technologies, and rehabilitation robotics.

Contributors

BESSAM ABDULRAZAK, Université de Sherbrooke, Département d'Informatique, Faculté des Sciences, Sherbrooke, Québec, Canada

JOHAN ÅBERG, Laboratory for Intelligent, Information Systems, Department of Computer and Information Science (IDA), Linköpings Universitet, Linköping, Sweden

RUDZIONIS ALGIMANTAS, Kaunas University of Technology, Siaures, Kaunas, Lithuania

MATTHEW H. BAKKE, Gallaudet University, Department of Hearing, Speech and Language Sciences, Washington, DC, USA

JÉRÉMY BAUCHET, University of Sherbrooke, Département d'Informatique, Faculté des sciences Sherbrooke, Sherbrooke Québec, Canada

MICHAEL BEHRMANN, George Mason University, Helen A. Kellar Center for Human Disabilities, University Drive, Washington, DC, USA

JEROME E. BICKENBACH, Department of Philosophy, and Faculties of Law and Medicine, Queen's University, Kingston, Ontario, Canada

ZEUNGNAM BIEN, Department of Electrical Engineering and Computer Science, Guseong-dong, Yuseong-gu, Daejeon, Republic of Korea, South Korea

ND BLACK, Faculty of Engineering, University of Ulster, Northern Ireland

IR. THEO BOUGIE, Bougie Revalidatie Technologie, Postbus, The Netherlands

RAJA BOSE, CSE Building, CISE Department, University of Florida, Gainesville, FL, USA

DAVID BRADDOCK, Coleman Professor in Psychiatry and Executive Director, Coleman Institute for cognitive Disabilities, University of Colorado, Discovery Drive, Boulder, CA, USA

HELENE BRASHEAR, TSRB/IMTC, Atlanta, GA, USA

STEPHEN A. BREWSTER, Department of Computing Science, University of Glasgow, Glasgow, United Kingdom

LORNA M. BROWN, Department of Computing Science, University of Glasgow, Glasgow, United Kingdom

CARRIE BRUCE, Georgia Institute of Technology, CATEA/Georgia Institute of Technology, Atlanta, GA, USA

PYUNG-HUN CHANG, Department of Mechanical Engineering, KAIST, Guseong-dong, Yuseong-gu, Daejeon, South Korea

ELIANA CHAVEZ, VA Pittsburgh Healthcare System, Pittsburgh, PA, USA

IOAN CHISALITA, Laboratory for Intelligent Information Systems, Department of Computer and Information Science (IDA), Linköpings Universitet, Linköping, Sweden

MYUNG-JIN CHUNG, Department of Electrical Engineering and Computer Science, KAIST, Guseong-dong, Yuseong-gu, Daejeon, South Korea

DIANE J. COOK, School of Electrical Engineering and Computer Science, Washington State University, Pullman, WA, USA

RORY A. COOPER, VA Pittsburgh Healthcare System, Pittsburgh, PA, USA

D CRAIG, Queens University of Belfast, Northern Ireland

RJ DAVIES, Faculty of Engineering, University of Ulster, Northern Ireland

ISABELLE DUSSUTOUR, Mission ITS, Conseil Général des Côtes d'Armor, place du Général de Gaulle, Saint Brieuc, France

HICHAM ELZABADANI, CSE Building, CISE Department, University of Florida, Gainesville, FL, USA

ANNA EMENOVA, George Mason University, Helen A. Kellar Center for Human Disabilities, Fairfax, VA, USA

MILAN ERBES, av. du General Leclerc, Bourg la Reine, France

BARRY FEIGENBAUM, IBM Research, Human Ability and Accessibility Center—IBM Research, Austin, TX, USA

DD FINLAY, Faculty of Engineering, University of Ulster, Northern Ireland

MARIBETH GANDY, TSRB/IMTC, Atlanta, GA, USA

JOHN GILL, Royal National Institute of the Blind, London, United Kingdom

SYLVAIN GIROUX, University of Sherbrooke, Département d'Informatique, Faculté des sciences Sherbrooke, Sherbrooke Québec, Canada

NICHOLAS A. GIUDICE, University of California, Santa Barbara, Department of Psychology, Santa Barbara, CA, USA

TAO GU, Institute for Infocomm Research, I2R, Heng Mui King Terrace, Singapore

KIP HARRIS, IBM Accessibility Center, Austin, TX, USA

SUMI HELAL, CSE Building, CISE Department, University of Florida, Gainesville, FL, USA

KAREN HENRICKSEN, School of Information Technology and Electrical Engineering, The University of Queensland, Brisbane, Australia

EVE E. HOGGAN, Department of Computing Science, University of Glasgow, Glasgow, United Kingdom

KATHARINE M. HUNTER-ZAWORSKI, National Center for Accessible Transportation., Apperson Hall, Oregon State University, Corvallis, OR, USA

JADWIGA INDULSKA, School of Information Technology and Electrical Engineering, The University of Queensland, Brisbane, Australia

STEPHEN INTILLE, Massachusetts Institute of Technology (MIT), Cambridge, MA, USA

RENE JAHIEL, University of Connecticut-International Health Policy Research, Hartford, CT, USA

GAURAV JAIN, Department of Computer Science and Engineering, University of Texas at Arlington, Arlington, TX, USA

YOUSSEF KADDOURAH, CSE Building, CISE Department, University of Florida, Gainesville, FL, USA

MARCI KINAS JEROME, Helen A. Kellar Institute for Human Disabilities, George Mason University, Washington, DC, USA

JIN-WOO JUNG, Human-Friendly Welfare Robot System Engineering Research Center, Kaist, Guseong-dong, Yuseong-gu, Daejeon, Republic of Korea

AMOL KARMARKAR, VA Pittsburgh Healthcare System, Pittsburgh, PA, USA

GEORGE KERNOHAN, School of Nursing, University of Ulster, Jordanstown Campus, Shore Road, Newtownabbey, Co. Antrim, Northern Ireland

JEFFREY KING, CSE Building, CISE Department, University of Florida, Gainesville, FL, USA

DAE-JIN KIM, Human-Friendly Welfare Robot System Engineering Research Center, KAIST, Guseong-dong, Yuseong-gu, Daejeon, Republic of Korea

JIN-OH KIM, Department of Information and Control Engineering, Kwangwoon University, Wolgye-dong, Nowon-gu, Seoul, Republic of Korea

JOSEPH KWAN, The Jockey Club Rehabilitation Engineering Centre (REC), Hong Kong Polytechnic University, Hong Hom, Kowlooon, Hong Kong, SAR

KENT LARSON, Massachusetts Institute of Technology (MIT), Cambridge, MA, USA

ANDREAS LARSSON, Division of Computer Aided Design, Luleå University of Technology, Sweden

TOBIAS LARSSON, Division of Computer Aided Design, Luleå University of Technology, Sweden

KATHLEEN LAURIN, Arizona Technology Access Program, Northern Arizona University, Phoenix, AZ, USA

GORDON E. LEGGE, University of Minnesota, Minneapolis, MN, USA

GIANNICOLA LORIGA, Milior SPA, Prato, Pistoiese, Prato, Italy

DENNIS MACIUSZEK, Department of Computer and Information Science (IDA), Linköpings Universitet, Linköping, Sweden

SUZANNE MARTIN, School of Health Sciences, University of Ulster, Jordanstown campus, Newtownabbey, Co. Antrim, Northern Ireland

BERNADETTE McCREIGHT, School of Sociology and Applied Social Studies, University of Ulster, Jordanstown campus, Shore Road, Newtownabbey, Co. Antrim, Northern Ireland

ABDALLAH M'HAMED, Institut National des Télécommunications, rue Charles Fourier, Évry, France

KAREN MILCHUS, Georgia Institute of Technology, CATEA/Georgia Institute of Technology, Atlanta, GA, USA

MOUNIR MOKHTARI, Institut National des Télécommunications, rue Charles Fourier, Évry cedex, France

KRISTINE NEUBER, George Mason University, Helen A. Kellar Center for Human Disabilities, University Drive, Fairfax, VA, USA

ALAN NEWELL, Queen Mother Research Centre, Applied Computing, University of Dundee, Dundee, Scotland

LINDA JOLLIFF, Royal National Institute of the Blind, London, United Kingdom

CHRISTOPHER NUGENT, School of Computing and Mathematics, Faculty of Engineering, University of Ulster, Jordanstown Campus, Newtownabbey, Co. Antrim, Northern Ireland

STEVEN PICKLES, CSE Building, CISE Department, University of Florida, Gainesville, FL, USA

RITA PARADISO, Presently on leave at Milior s.p.a., Prato, Italy, Milior SPA, Prato, Pistoiese, Prato, Italy

KWANG-HYUN PARK, Department of Electrical Engineering and Computer Science, KAIST, Guseong-dong, Yuseong-gu, Daejeon, Republic of Korea

HÉLÈNE PIGOT, University of Sherbrooke, Département d'Informatique, Faculté des sciences Sherbrooke, Sherbrooke, Québec, Canada

KASTYTIS RATKEVICIUS, Kaunas University of Technology, Kaunas, Lithuania

ANDREW RENTSCHLER, CED Accident Analysis, Jacksonville, FL, USA

MARY KAY RIZZOLO, Department of Disability and Human Development (DHD), College of Applied Health Sciences, University of Illinois at Chicago (UIC), Chicago, IL, USA

VYTAUTAS RUDZIONIS, Vilnius University of Technology, Kaunas, Lithuania

KATHERINE D. SEELMAN, University of Pittsburgh, School of Health and Rehabilitation Sciences, Pittsburgh, PA, USA

MARK SCHMALZ, University of Florida, Gainesville, FL, USA

NAHID SHAHMEHRI, Laboratory for Intelligent Information Systems, Department of Computer and Information Science (IDA), Linköpings Universitet, Linköping, Sweden

JILL SHERMAN PLEASANT, University of Montana Rural Institute, Missoula, MT, USA

TAKANORI SHIBATA, Ministry of Economy, Trade and Industry (METI), Tsukuba, Japan

ANDREW SIXSMITH, Division of Primary Care, University of Liverpool, Liverpool, United Kingdom

MATHIJS SOEDE, iRv, Institute for Rehabilitation Research, -Kenniscentrum voor Revalidatie en handicap-, Zandbergsweg, Hoensbroek, The Netherlands

JEAN-CLAUDE SPERANDIO, University of Paris, Laboratoire d'Ergonomie Informatique, Paris Cedex, France

THAD STARNER, TSRB/IMTC, Atlanta, GA, USA

DIMITAR STEFANOV, University of Coventry, Priory Street, Coventry, United Kingdom

BRIANNA STEGALL, George Mason University, Helen A. Kellar Center for Human Disabilities, Fairfax, VA, USA

AARON STEINFELD, Robotics Institute, Carnegie Mellon University, Pittsburgh, PA, USA

EDWARD STEINFELD, State University of New York at Buffalo, School of Architecture and Planning, Buffalo, NY, USA

NICOLA TACCINI, Milior SPA, Prato, Pistoiese, Prato, Italy

ERIC TAM, The Jockey Club Rehabilitation Engineering Centre (REC), Hong Kong Polytechnic University, Hong Hom, Kowlooon, Hong Kong, SAR

FRANK VLASKAMP, iRv, Institute for Rehabilitation Research, -Kenniscentrum voor Revalidatie en Handicap-, Zandbergsweg, Hoensbroek, The Netherlands

KAZUYOSHI WADA, Tokyo Metropolitan University, Tokyo, Japan

STEVEN A. WALL, Department of Computing Science, University of Glasgow, Glasgow, United Kingdom

RICHARD F. FF. WEIR, Northwestern University, Rehabilitation Engineering Research Center and Prosthetics Research Laboratory, Chicago, IL, USA

LEANNE WEST, Georgia Institute of Technology, Atlanta, GA, USA

TRACY WESTEYN, TSRB/IMTC, Atlanta, GA, USA

CHARLES WILLEMS, iRv, Institute for Rehabilitation Research, -Kenniscentrum voor Revalidatie en handicap-, Zandbergsweg, Hoensbroek, The Netherlands

MARION WOLFF, University of Paris, Laboratoire d'Ergonomie Informatique, Paris Cedex, France

HAJIME YAMADA, Department of Economics, Toyo University Hakusan, Bunkyo Tokyo, Japan

G. MICHAEL YOUNGBLOOD, Department of Computer Science and Engineering, University of Texas at Arlington, Arlington, TX, USA

DAQING ZHANG, Institute for Infocomm Research, I2R, Heng Mui Keng Terrace, Singapore

MANLI ZHU, Institute for Infocomm Research, I2R, Heng Mui Keng Terrace, Singapore

Introduction to the Book

Sumi Helal and Mark Schmalz
University of Florida, Gainesville, FL

Mounir Mokhtari
Institut National des Télécommunications, Évry, France

Bessam Abdulrazak
Université de Sherbrooke, Québec, Canada

According to the World Health Organization (WHO), there are between 750 million and 1 billion people with special needs (PwSN) in our world today. This includes the growing elder population and people living with disabilities. In 2002 it was estimated that 20% of the US population and 13% of the European population are PwSN. In the United States, over 35 million Americans (12% of the population) are over the age of 65. This 65+ population is expected to double by 2030. In fact, the oldest population (85+) is the most rapidly growing segment of our population. In 1900 there were only 100,000 persons 85+; in 2000, there were 4.2 million; in 2050, there will be 21 million (Fig. I.1). The significance of these numbers is that there is a strong correlation between elders' disability and age; at least 62% of elders 85+ have difficulty with one or more core activities of daily living. Consider dementia alone and how it degrades the quality of life for elders, adversely impacting their independence. Approximately 10% of people age 65+ have cognitive impairments that impair functional abilities. Alzheimer's disease is the most common cause of dementia in persons over 65, causing progressive decline in abilities.

Aging and disability pose challenging and costly problems needy of urgent solutions that cannot be solved by traditional government programs alone. This book focuses on technology and its promise in promoting independence for people with special needs. The use of devices, computers, robots, and other established assistive technology (AT) can potentially increase the autonomy of PwSN, by compensating for physical limitations and circumventing difficulties with normal activities of daily living (ADL).

The Engineering Handbook of Smart Technology for Aging, Disability, and Independence,
Edited by A. Helal, M. Mokhtari and B. Abdulrazak
Copyright © 2008 John Wiley & Sons, Inc.

2 INTRODUCTION TO THE BOOK

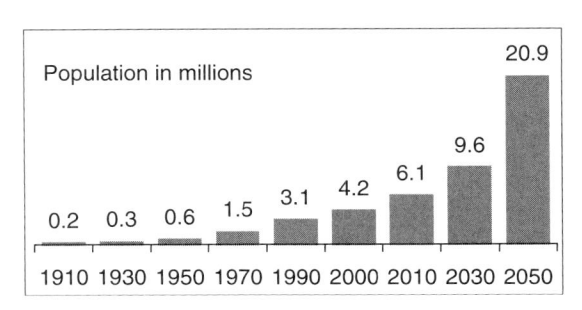

FIGURE I.1 Population aged 85+, 1910–2050.

I.1 THE POPULATION

Numerous researchers have attempted to define the concept of *disability* in diverse historical or geographic settings, with regard to attributes or modulating factors such as impairment, health condition, and individual–environment interaction. Since the 1960s, numerous such attempts have led to significantly varying definitions. The first *international classification of impairment, disease, and handicap* (ICIDH) [1] developed by the World Health Organization (WHO), which has been used worldwide for more then twenty years, defines a handicap as "a disadvantage for a given individual, resulting from an impairment or a disability, that limits or prevents the fulfillment of a role that is normal for that individual" [1].

The Disabled People's International (DPI) organization defines *disability* as "the loss or limitation of opportunities to take part in the normal life of the community on an equal level with others due to physical and social barriers" [2].

People with disabilities (also referred to as *disabled persons*) are "persons who are atypical in body, intellect, or emotions and who are categorized by society as disabled by a process of examination, explanation for their difference, and legitimization of their role in society and the resources that society puts at their disposal" [3].

The WHO revision of the ICIDH, the *International Classification of Functioning, Disability and Health* (ICF), provides a handicap with medical and contextual dimensions. Further, the handicap is seen as a result of an interaction between personal characteristics (health condition) and social and environmental factors [4].

I.1.1 Handicap and Wellbeing

Wellbeing or quality of life is an important concern for PwSN, who, like every person, is seeking to be well, happy, healthy, and prosperous. PwSN have several important components of wellbeing. A key activity is independent living with convenient access to goods and services, as well as being socially active and enjoying self-esteem and dignity. In modern societies, PwSN can attain some components of wellbeing such as access to services using assistive technology (AT). Other components, such as freedom of navigation and travel, are much more difficult because of environmental obstacles encountered by the disabled.

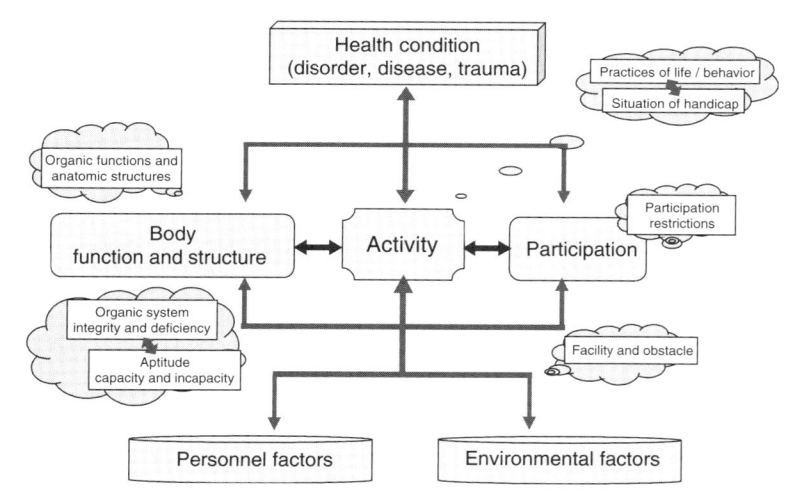

FIGURE I.2 International classification of functioning, disability, and health (ICF).

I.1.2 Handicap and the International Classification of Functioning, Disability, and Health (ICF)

The World Health Organization (WHO) ICF addresses the situation of being handicapped, in a diverse way. The WHO classification adopts a functional approach [4], focusing on the level of health and functional capacity, without limiting consideration to the deficiency–incapacity–disadvantage chain, where handicap results from physical deficiency or disease [1]. Since an individual's functioning and disability occurs in a social and environmental context, ICF also includes environmental factors.

In summary, ICF combines two approaches: medical and social. The *medical* approach is traditional, where the handicap is perceived as an endogenous congenital problem, or as a direct consequence of a disease or disorder that requires medical care. The *social* approach focuses on the patient's environment. Here, a handicap is perceived as a problem created by society or the individual's environment, where the handicap represents incomplete social integration of the handicapped individual.

Social classification stresses models of human operation (Fig. I.2), where a handicap results from dynamic interaction between a patient's health condition (diseases, trauma, wounds, etc.) and other contextual factors. Examples of contextual factors include personal and environmental factors, which are considered concurrently. To summarize, the ICF defines a person with a disability as "a person with one or more impairments, one or more activity limitations, one or more participation restrictions or a combination" [4].

I.1.3 Needs of People with Special Needs (PwSN)

Analyzing the human beings, Maslow has identified five categories of needs, with different priority levels (Fig. I.3), in the following order: survival (physiological), safety, social needs, esteem, and self-actualization (fulfillment). Maslow's model is also valid for PwSN, whose needs are similar to those of ordinary persons. Nevertheless, many of

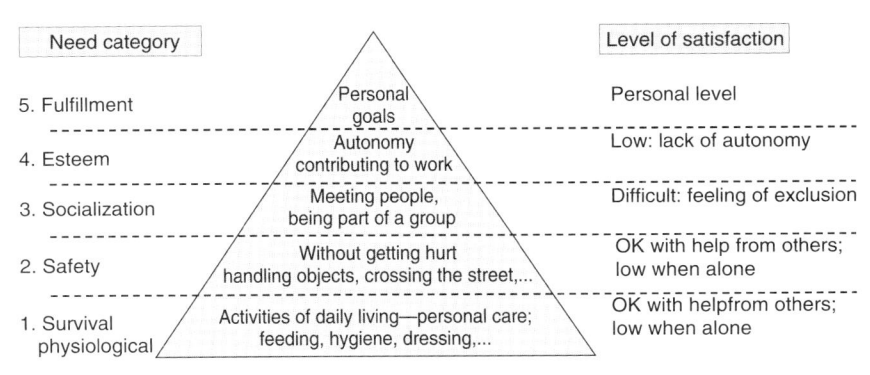

FIGURE I.3 Maslow pyramid model, which enabled the structuring of user needs.

these needs are not fulfilled, so PwSN seek to fulfill these need and reach a state of well-being. Initially, PwSN attempt to fulfill the first level of needs (*survival*). The survival needs are formed by the physiological needs and include the biological requirements for feeding, performing hygiene, sleeping, ADL, and so on. When PwSN fulfill their survival needs, they will look for situations that keep them *safe*, before moving up the chain and fulfill their needs to be part of *society* and to *achieve* [5].

As an example of needs in terms of safety, consider a person with visual impairment who wishes to cross the street safely. In contrast, for the elderly, safety might represent the ability to obtain emergency help after falling and not being able to stand again. Social need is a key element that PwSN would like to develop continuously [6]. For example, a person with a hearing impairment suffers from a diminution of social contact, while someone with a motor disability feels excluded from social activities.

The third level of the pyramid relates to *esteem*, both *self-esteem* and *being favorably recognized* by others. Esteem is often related to the capability of achieving things, contributing to a work activity and being autonomous. In particular, PwSN in a dependent situation feel the need for increased autonomy, as well as the opportunity to prove their worth to themselves and others through work or other activities [6].

I.1.4 Types of Impairment

PwSN live with impairments that impact their abilities to conduct activities of daily living (ADL). An impairment can limit or restrict one or more ADLs, including moving from one place to another (e.g., navigation, locomotion, transfer), maintaining a position (e.g., standing, sitting, sleeping), interacting with the environment (e.g., controlling systems, gripping objects), communicating (e.g., speaking, writing, hand gestures), feeding (chewing, swallowing, etc.), and perceiving the external world (by movement of the eyes, the head, etc.).

Many older persons face one or more impairments. Their situation is often similar to that of people with disabilities. Their needs are similar to those people with multiple handicaps with a decrease in the muscular, vision, hearing and cognitive capacities [7].

A review of all impairments and handicaps of PwSN is not possible in a single chapter. We briefly describe the most common and known handicaps and impairments.

I.1.4.1 Motor and Physical Disabilities

Motor disability is any condition that affects a person's ability to perform motor tasks (moving and manipulating objects); limits the person's ability to navigate the environment; limits or precludes mobility; or significantly impacts gross motor function such as walking, running, skipping, tying shoelaces, crawling, sitting, and handwriting. Motor disabilities may result in *mobility* incapacities, including movement restriction; *motor* incapacities, including limitation in moving, coordinating, or controlling movement of the body; and *dexterity* incapacities, including limitation in moving, controlling, or coordinating movement in the arms, wrists, hands, or fingers in order to perform tasks.

Various motor disabilities result from congenital conditions, injury, accidents, or diseases such as progressive neuromuscular disease. The best-known motor disabilities include limb amputation, arthritis (rheumatoid arthritis and osteoarthritis), cerebral palsy, clubfoot, cystic fibrosis, paralysis, multiple sclerosis, muscular dystrophy, paralysis, Parkinson's disease, poliomyelitis (polio) and its aftereffects, spina bifida, and stroke.

Incapacities, limitations, and abilities vary widely even within the same group of disabilities. However, common problems are related to difficulty in performing activities of daily living. The ADL scales or functional motor testing can be used to measure disability in motor function. In other words, the degree of motor *handicap* is determined by the extent to which the disability affects the person's social, professional, and family roles [8]. A person with a motor disability may use assistive technology (AT) equipment such as a wheelchair, an assistive walking device, crutches, or a limb prosthesis in order to navigate and manage the ADL. The individual may need special tools such as an ergonomically designed desk or table in lieu of a standard office desk.

I.1.4.2 Vision Impairment and Visual Disabilities

Vision impairment may result in a restricted field of vision or a diminished ability to see sharpness of detail, read standard-size print, determine color or depth perception, see contrasts, adjust to changes in light or glare, or locate objects [9]. Vision loss can affect a person's activities of daily living (ADL), leisure pursuits, education, vocation, and social interaction. The severity of vision loss and the resulting limitations vary with such factors as age of onset, support systems available, and coping strategies [10].

Visual impairment is related to difficulty in ADL performance and to decline in health and psychosocial status [11]. Assistive devices are available to maximize remaining visual ability. Approximately 8.6% of the population over 18 years of age in the United States, experience problems with vision despite corrective measures [12], with a higher incidence among the elderly people [13].

Vision impairment in older people has been documented and described by numerous investigators [14–16]. Older people constitute a heterogeneous population, which makes it difficult to determine the exact number of persons who are blind or have a severe visual impairment. However, one study estimated that 82 out of 1000 older individuals have a serious visual impairment [17]. Another study projected that by 2020, there will be approximately 54 million blind people over age 60 worldwide [18].

Most elders with vision impairment are not totally blind, but have partial or weak vision, often due to conditions such as macular degeneration. Advances in ophthalmic surgery and more effective medical control of eye diseases have contributed to the greater proportion of older persons who have impaired vision versus total blindness. The sharp increase in the 65+ age group has also contributed to a steady increase in the number of persons with useful partial sight. Although a person with a visual impairment may retain usable vision, loss of sight requires spending more time and effort in accomplishing tasks [7].

I.1.4.3 Hearing Impairment

Hearing loss can result from exposure to excessively loud noise over time, from hypertension and neurological diseases such as stroke, or from the side effects of medications. The three major types of hearing loss are conductive, sensorineural, and central. Many older people experience "mixed hearing loss," a combination of conductive and sensorineural impairments.

Conductive hearing loss occurs when sound waves cannot reach the inner ear; the impact of conductive hearing loss is similar to wearing earplugs. Hearing aids are often quite effective for persons with conductive hearing loss. Sensorineural hearing loss relates to damage to the cochlea and surrounding hair cells—the cells that send electrical signals to the brain. Many people refer to sensorineural hearing loss as "nerve deafness"; one common type among older persons is *presbycusis*, which first causes inability to hear high-pitched sounds, and later, over time, results in degenerative loss of hearing acuity. *Tinnitus* is also a sensorineural disorder, causing ringing or buzzing in the ears and affecting more than 90% of persons age 65+. *Central hearing loss* relates to damaged of nerves leading to the brain or damage to the brain itself. Stroke and traumatic brain or vascular disorders can result in central hearing loss [7].

Hearing impairment is one of the five most common chronic conditions of aging. One of three persons over age 64 has some degree of hearing impairment. The prevalence among older persons is expected to increase as currently more people age 45–64 have reported hearing loss than have those 65 and older. Many assistive devices are available for persons with hearing impairment, but hearing loss is often so gradual that many elders accept it as simply a normal process of aging and do not seek medical assistance. Hearing loss adversely affects communication, and decreased communication can in turn result in isolation and depression [19]. Hearing loss can affect safety and health in other ways as well, such as failing to hear a fire alarm or inability to clearly understand a pharmacist's directions for taking medications.

I.1.4.4 Communication Disabilities

A *communication disability* is any incapacity, condition, or disease that affects a person's ability to interact and communicate. It may result in limitation in understanding, receiving, or producing a communication.

People with a communication disability cannot adequately comprehend or express ideas, experiences, knowledge, and feelings. They cannot easily express themselves, understand others, or build relationships. Difficulties of people with communication disability may include difficulties in understanding and "finding the right words"; producing, ordering, and discriminating between speech sounds; applying rules about how words, phrases, and sentences are formed to convey meaning; and using and understanding language in different social contexts [20].

The best-known communication disabilities include *speech disorders*, such as esophageal speech or stuttering; *autism*, which is a developmental defect that affects understanding of emotional communication; *aphasia*, which is loss of the ability to produce or comprehend language; *expressive language disorder*, which affects speaking and understanding where there is no delay in nonverbal intelligence; *mixed receptive–expressive language disorder*, which affects speech, understanding, reading, and writing where there is no delay in nonverbal intelligence; *dyslexia*, which is a defect of the systems used in reading; and *dyscalculia*, which is a defect of the systems used in communicating numbers or impairment in mathematical ability. The communication disabilities also include *blindness* and *deafness* [21].

I.1.4.5 Cognitive Disabilities

Dementia is a broad term used to describe a decline in intellectual functioning that results in cognitive impairment in areas that include language, memory, visuospatial skills, personality, and cognition [22]. Alzheimer's disease is a common form of dementia in people over 65 [23]. Cognitive impairment resulting from stroke [transient ischemic attack (TIA)] is the second most frequently occurring type of dementia [24]. The major characteristic of Alzheimer's disease is a progressive decline in cognitive function. Cognitive skills include orientation, insight, attention, memory, abstract thinking, calculating, problem solving, and organization [25]. Dementia is not a normal part of the aging process. However, approximately 10% of people over the age of 65 have cognitive impairments that affect their functional abilities [26].

With impaired cognitive function, a person may experience confusion, disorientation, limited attention span, memory impairment, and decreased learning ability [27]. Other common symptoms of Alzheimer's disease include language disorders, apraxia, visuoconstructive difficulty, and difficulty with abstract thinking [28,29].

As Alzheimer's disease progresses, it affects a person's independent function. For example, a person may become disoriented, fail to recognize familiar faces, or be unable to match names with faces. In some cases, the person may experience hallucination. A person's ADL are influenced by impaired cognition. Limited performance in instrumental activities will occur first, including shopping, money management, meal preparation, household chores, and communication. A person with Alzheimer's disease will experience a gradual decline in ability to meet their safety, self-care, household, leisure, social interaction, and vocational needs. Eventually, the person will lose the ability to perform basic activities of daily living, including eating, dressing, toileting, grooming, bathing, and locomotion.

I.2 THE DEMOGRAPHICS

The number of PwSN living in a disadvantaged setting is increasing significantly. The number of people with disability is estimated at around 13% in Europe (Table I.1) and around 15% in the United States (Table I.2). Table I.1 gives the population per country per disability for four European countries. Table I.2 gives an extensive account of the population divided between males and females and across various age groups. It further breaks down the population based according to the type of disability (e.g., physical, sensory, or mental).

In practice, handicaps have diverse origins: medical (surgery, infection and drugs), traffic accidents (bicycle, motorcycle, and automobile accidents), industrial accidents, sport-related accidents (ski, horse, motocross, hang glider, paraglide, dive, rugby, etc.), genetic (myopathy; muscular dystrophy, etc.), nutritional (poison, junk-food consumption), and failed suicide attempts, to name only a few.

For instance, in 2000 in France, the causes of motor handicaps were as follows: 49% traffic accidents (71% car accidents and 29% motorcycle accidents), 21%

TABLE I.1 Handicaps in Europe in 2000

Country	Lower Limbs	Upper Limbs	Motor	Visual	Additive	Mental
France	3,162,000 (5.1%)	1,054,000 (1.7%)	4,216,000 (6.8%)	1,116,000 (1.8%)	1,488,000 (2.4%)	1,178,000 (1.9%)
Netherlands	758,960 (5.3%)	257,760 (1.8%)	1,016,720 (7.1%)	157,520 (1.1%)	286,400 (2.0%)	329,360 (2.3%)
Spain	2,286,000 (5.8%)	748,942 (1.9%)	3,034,942 (6.7%)	788,360 (2.0%)	1,064,286 (2.7%)	906,614 (2.3%)
UK	4,819,000 (7.9%)	1,586,000 (2.6%)	4,450,000 (10.5%)	1,830,000 (3.0%)	2,867,000 (4.7%)	1,708,000 (2.8%)

[a]*Source:* Royal National Institute of the Blind (RNIB), 2002.

TABLE I.2 Handicaps in United States in 2002[a]

Population	Male #	Male %	Female #	Female %	Total #	Total %
Total 5–15 years old	22,810,520	100.00	21,775,627	100.00%	44,586,147	100.00
With a disability (any type)	1,833,676	8.0	1,052,858	4.8%	2,886,534	6.5
With a physical disability	287,382	1.26	230,545	1.06%	517,927	1.16
With a sensory disability	303,997	1.33	249,730	1.15%	553,727	1.24
With a mental disability	1,547,386	6.78	783,005	3.60%	2,330,391	5.23
With a self-care disability	244,662	1.07	154,801	0.71%	399,463	0.90
Total 16–64 years old	92,647,138	100.00	95,394,171	100.00%	188,041,309	100.00
With a disability (any type)	11,130,352	12.0	11,659,947	12.2%	22,790,299	12.1
With a physical disability	6,236,494	6.73	7,369,862	7.73%	13,606,356	7.24
With a sensory disability	3,054,203	3.30	2,255,939	2.36%	5,310,142	2.82
With a mental disability	4,135,685	4.46	4,262,419	4.47%	8,398,104	4.47
With a self-care disability	1,703,475	1.84	2,114,433	2.22%	3,817,908	2.03
With an agoraphobic[b] disability	2,399,008	2.59	3,219,736	3.38%	5,618,744	2.99
Total 65–74 years old	8,400,634	100.00	9,959,175	100.00%	18,359,809	100.00
With a disability (any type)	2,522,501	30.0	3,033,823	30.5%	5,556,324	30.3
With a physical disability	1,826,085	21.74	2,460,184	24.70%	4,286,269	23.35
With a sensory disability	1,048,912	57.44	822,068	8.25%	1,870,980	10.19
With a mental disability	610,827	58.23	718,133	7.21%	1,328,960	7.24
With a self-care disability	423,825	69.39	637,071	6.40%	1,060,896	5.78
With an agoraphobic disability	593,272	139.98	1,043,194	10.47%	1,636,466	8.91
Total ≥75 years old	6,443,495	100.00	9,957,223	100.00%	16,400,718	100.00
With a disability	3,155,326	49.0	5,352,226	53.8%	8,507,552	51.9
With a physical disability	2,248,362	34.89	4,177,169	41.95%	6,425,531	39.18
With a sensory disability	1,647,831	25.57	2,187,959	21.97%	3,835,790	23.39
With a mental disability	961,300	14.92	1,698,005	17.05%	2,659,305	16.21
With a self-care disability	739,990	11.48	1,556,725	15.63%	2,296,715	14.00
With an agoraphobic disability	1,194,770	18.54	2,946,977	29.60%	4,141,747	25.25

(continued overleaf)

TABLE I.2 (*Continued*)

	Male		Female		Total	
Population	#	%	#	%	#	%
Grand Total						
Total ≥5 years old	130,301,787	100.00	137,086,196	100.00	267,387,983	100.00
With a disability	18,641,855	14.31	21,098,854	15.39	39,740,709	14.86
With a physical disability	10,598,323	8.13	14,237,760	10.39	24,836,083	9.29
With a sensory disability	6,054,943	4.65	5,515,696	4.02	11,570,639	4.33
With a mental disability	7,255,198	5.57	7,461,562	5.44	14,716,760	5.50
With a self-care disability	3,111,952	2.39	4,463,030	3.26	7,574,982	2.83
With an agoraphobic disability	4,187,050	3.21	7,209,907	5.26	11,396,957	4.26

[a] *Symbols*: # — number; % — percent.
[b] In the context here, *agoraphobia* means Fear of goind outdoors or outside one's home.
Source: US Census Bureau, 2005.

industrial accidents, 16% sport-related accidents (including ski, horse, motocross, hang glider, paraglide, dive, rugby), and 9% failed suicide attempts.

Furthermore, most developed nations are becoming societies of the aged (Table I.3). For example, the elderly population is estimated at >15% of the total population in Europe (Table I.3 and Fig. I.4). In the United States, over 34.5 million people are over age 65 (13%), while a relatively high number (approximately 40.5%) struggle with one or more disabilities (Table I.2).

The number of older Americans has increased by approximately 12% since the mid-1990s. Unfortunately, this increase is expected to escalate by 34% by 2028, and to double by 2038.

It is important to note that there is a strong correlation between age and disability among the elderly (Fig. I.5). In the United States, at least 44.9% of elders between the ages of 65 and 69, and 62% of elders over 85 have difficulty with one or more core activities of daily living (US Census Bureau, 2002). (The incidence and characteristics of PwSN are discussed further in Chapter 2.)

I.2.1 Worldwide Interest in Disability

Fortunately, there exist numerous national, regional, and international teams, taskforces, and organizations working in areas related to aging, disability, and assistive technology. Most of these international organizations were formed to address the reconstruction of devastated nations, and prevention of economic instability following World War II. The focus and objectives of these organizations have evolved in response to international conditions; today, many international organizations, including the World Health Organization (WHO), the United Nations (UN), the World Bank (WB), and the World Trade Organization (WTO), have programs related to disability issues.

In addition to large international organizations, local, regional, governmental, and nongovernmental organizations (NGOs) and agencies or committees, such as the European

TABLE I.3 Estimation Number of Elderly People Worldwide

Region	Year	≥85 (%)	≥75 (%)	≥65 (%)
Asia	2000	0.8	1.9	6.0
	2015	1.4	2.8	7.8
	2030	2.2	4.6	12.0
North Africa/Near East	2000	0.6	1.4	4.3
	2015	0.9	1.9	5.3
	2030	1.3	2.8	8.1
Sub-Saharan Africa	2000	30.0	0.8	2.9
	2015	0.4	1.0	3.2
	2030	0.6	1.3	3.7
Europe	2000	3.3	6.6	15.5
	2015	5.2	8.8	18.7
	2030	7.1	11.8	24.3
North America	2000	3.3	6.0	12.6
	2015	3.9	6.4	14.9
	2030	5.4	9.4	20.3
Latin America/Caribbean	2000	0.9	1.9	5.5
	2015	1.5	2.8	7.5
	2030	2.4	4.6	11.6
Oceania	2000	2.3	4.4	10.2
	2015	3.1	5.2	12.4
	2030	4.4	7.5	16.3

Source: US Census Bureau, 2000.

Union (EU), the North America Free Trade Agreement (NAFTA), the Central America Free Trade Agreement (CAFTA), the Asian and, BRIC (Brazil, Russia, India, and China) groups, Disabled Peoples International (DPI), the International Disability Alliance (IDA), International Disability Policy Research (IDPR), the National Science Foundation (NSF), and the (US) National Institute on Disability and Rehabilitation Research (NIDRR), maintain keen interest in disability issues. The activities of these organizations varies among humanitarian aid, policy development and negotiation, regulation and law, financing acquisition of assistive technology, and supporting disability-related research.

Academic research and development pertaining to disability and related technology issues has grown significantly. Various events have been dedicated to PwSN and assistive technology (AT). This includes conferences such as the Rehabilitation Engineering Society of North America (RESNA), the Association for the Advancement of Assistive Technology in Europe (AAATE), REHACARE, as well as the International Society for Augmentative and Alternative Communication (ISAAC). Additional events are more specialized, such as the International Conference on Rehabilitation Robotics (ICORR), the International Conference on Smart homes and health Telematics (ICOST), and the International Conference on Computers Helping People with Special Needs (ICCHP).

I.3 ASSISTIVE TECHNOLOGIES (AT)

Surgery, generic therapy, rehabilitation, human assistance, and the use of assistive technology (AT) help disabled people cope with their handicaps. *Surgery* (medical

12 INTRODUCTION TO THE BOOK

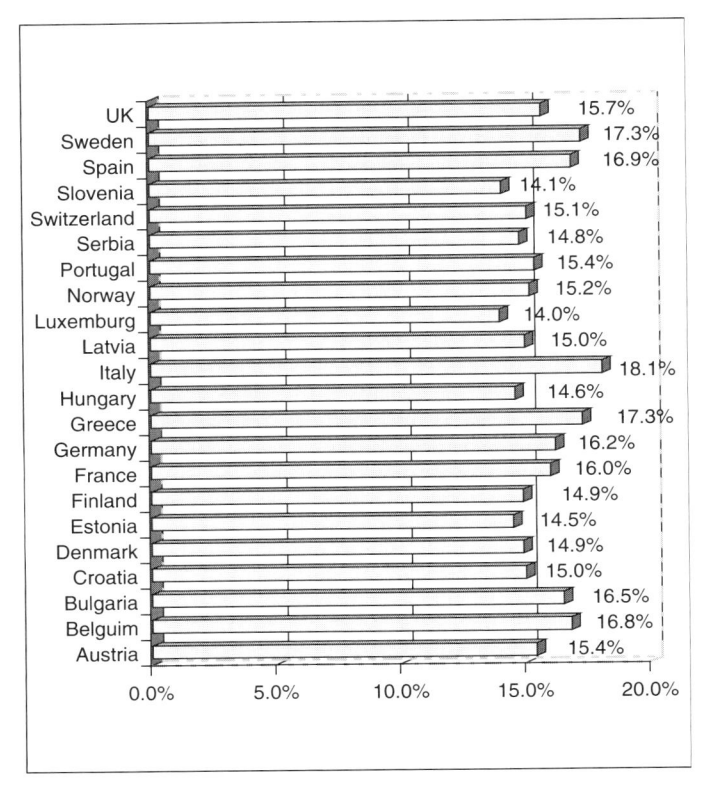

Country	%
UK	15.7%
Sweden	17.3%
Spain	16.9%
Slovenia	14.1%
Switzerland	15.1%
Serbia	14.8%
Portugal	15.4%
Norway	15.2%
Luxemburg	14.0%
Latvia	15.0%
Italy	18.1%
Hungary	14.6%
Greece	17.3%
Germany	16.2%
France	16.0%
Finland	14.9%
Estonia	14.5%
Denmark	14.9%
Croatia	15.0%
Bulgaria	16.5%
Belguim	16.8%
Austria	15.4%

FIGURE I.4 Percentage of population over age 65 in Europe.

intervention) helps decrease deficiency and, in some cases, restores capability. *Genetic therapy* attempts to remediate genes responsible for a given disease or disorder. Although promising in concept, genetic therapy is in its infancy and, as yet, has no broad application. *Rehabilitation* develops and adapts residual capabilities, while *human assistance* aids PwSN in their daily living activities. Unfortunately, such assistance is not always available and not necessarily cost-effective. AT can increase the autonomy, independence, and quality of life for PwSN and can also enable the integration of social, professional, and environmental aspects of life for PwSN populations.

I.3.1 AT and Daily Living of PwSN

Assistive technology affords PwSN greater equality of opportunity, by enhancing and expanding their communication, learning, participation, and achievement with higher levels of independence, wellbeing, and quality of life. Such assistive technologies are essential for helping PwSN with severe physical, sensorial, or mental limitations to become more independent, and to improve their quality of life. Typically, AT works by compensating for absent or nonfunctional skills, by maintaining or enhancing existing abilities. PwSN utilize AT to enhance the performance of their daily living tasks, including communication, vision, hearing, recreation, movement, seating and mobility, reading, learning, writing, and studying, as well as controlling and accessing their environment.

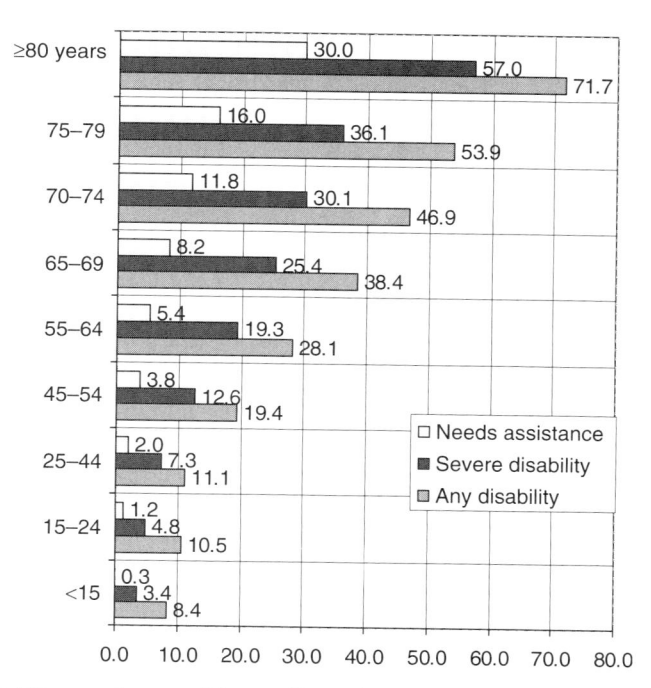

FIGURE I.5 *Disability prevalence and the need for assistance by age in the United States (US Census Bureau, 2002).*

Assistive Technology varies from low-tech devices such as a cane or adapted loop, to high-tech systems such as assistive robotics (Chapter 19) or smart spaces (Chapters 38 and Part VII). Currently, most popular technologies for PwSN are simple; or examples of mobility-enhancing equipment include wheelchairs, communication via mobile telephones and computers, and voice-activated smart devices to enhance environmental control. Advances in communication and information technologies further support the development of new, more complex technologies such as utilization of smart wheelchairs (Chapter 23), assistive robots (Chapter 19), and smart spaces (Chapter 38).

I.3.2 AT Definitions

Assistive technology encompasses all systems that are designed for PwSN, and that attempt to compensate the handicapped. This includes robotic telemanipulators, wheelchairs, or navigation systems for the blind. AT also includes systems that restore personal functionality, such as external prostheses and orthoses.

There are various organizational definitions for assistive technology:

The international standard ISO 9999 defines AT (referring to AT as "technical aid") as "any product, instrument, equipment or technical system used by a disabled person, especially produced or generally available, preventing, compensating, monitoring, relieving or neutralizing the impairment, disability or handicap" [30].

In the United States, the Technology Act [31] and Assistive Technology Act [32] define an AT device as "any item, piece of equipment or product system, whether acquired commercially, modified, or customized, that is used to increase, maintain, or improve functional capabilities of individuals with disabilities." These Acts also define a *assistive technology service* as "any service that directly assists an individual with a disability in the selection, acquisition, or use, of an assistive technology device."

The Older Americans Act [33] defines AT as "technology, engineering methodologies, or scientific principles appropriate to meet the needs of, and address the barriers confronted by, older individuals with functional limitations."

In Europe, the European Commission (EC) defines AT as "products, devices or equipment that are used to maintain, increase or improve the functional capabilities of people with disabilities" [34].

The World Health Organization (WHO) defines an Assistive Device as "Equipment that enables an individual who requires assistance to perform the daily activities essential to maintain health and autonomy and to live as full a life as possible. Such equipment may include, for example, motorized scooters, walkers, walking sticks, grab rails and tilt-and-lift chairs"

WHO also defines assistive technology as "An umbrella term for any device or system that allows individuals to perform tasks they would otherwise be unable to do or increases the ease and safety with which tasks can be performed" [35].

I.3.3 AT and ICF

Assistive technologies have demonstrated promise in helping PwSN enhance their performance of daily activities, which is the core of ICF. In practice, AT intervenes at the following levels of the classification scheme portrayed in Figure I.2: environmental factors, personal factors, health condition, participation, and activity.

A person might not be "disabled" if his or her physical, sensorial, or mental limitations or impairments are compensated, and if disabilities related to *environmental factors* are eliminated. The assistive technologies discussed in this book provide the majority of compensation for limitations or impairments. In particular, AT bridges the gap between a person's functional abilities, or lack thereof, and salient requirements for performing daily tasks and maintaining social or cultural activities. For example, a wheelchair is an AT that compensates for lack of mobility. Similarly, an optical magnifying device is an AT that helps a person read, thus compensating visual limitations. In terms of an environment, a "smart house" assists PwSN in accessing and controlling their environments, thus compensating for multiple limitations.

Additionally, AT significantly enhances a PwSN's ability to cope with her or his situation, which helps bridge the gap between disability limitations and social participation.

Maintenance of good health is also important for people with disabilities. Assistive technologies can support PwSN who have health problems by helping them to maintain their state of health. For example, therapeutic robots and prosthesis for rehabilitation, assistance in feeding, medication administration systems, and reminders to eat or take medication offer simple but effective help for disabled or elderly people.

In general, AT reduces the environmental obstacles (*environmental factors*), assists people in their daily living activities, allows them to live independently, and helps them maintain a high quality of life. Additionally, AT enhances capacities and socioeconomic integration (*personal factors*) of PwSN, helps disabled persons maintain good health (*health condition*), and helps them remain socially active. Thus, AT augments personal performance levels, increasing the PwSN's *participation* in the immediate environment as well as major *activities* of life.

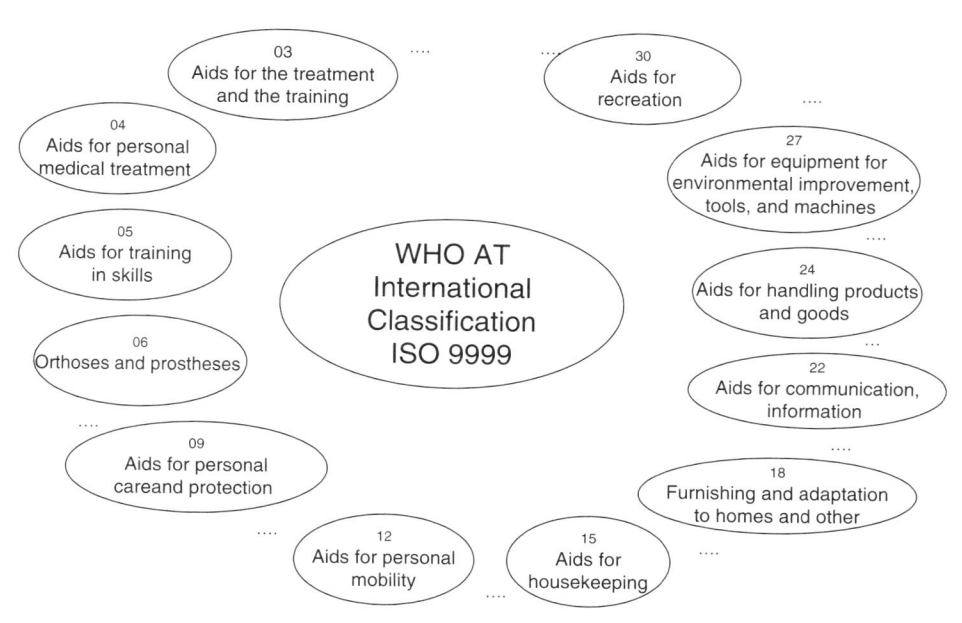

FIGURE I.6 Categories of AT: ISO 9999 international classification system.

I.3.4 AT Classification

Assistive technologies have been evolving toward increasingly adaptive systems, capable of supporting PwSN in diverse environments (e.g., home, office, leisure). A large number of these AT systems are categorized according to specific classification schemes (Taxonomies); the most widely used are the WHO international standardization [4] and ISO 9999 classification [35] (Fig. I.6). ISO 9999 is widely accepted as a national standard, which classifies AT on the basis of functional and environmental divisions, as well as principal identified needs.

ISO 9999 focuses on AT mainly for individual use by a person with a disability who needs assistance for performing daily activities. Thus, we next consider ISO categories most relevant to the smart technology for aging, disability, and independence, using ISO 9999 codes (further details are given in Section I.3.5):

Category 04: Aids for Personal Medical Treatment. This AT category includes products for respiratory, circulation, light, and dialysis therapy; abdominal hernia care; and administering medicines. It also includes equipment and materials for cognitive physical, physiological, and biochemical testing, sterilizing materials, stimulators, products for thermal (hot or cold) treatment, pressure-sore prevention (*antidecubitus*), perceptual training, visual training, spinal traction, and movement training, as well as strength and balance training.

Category 05: Aids for Training in Skills. These assistive technologies provide help with training, for example, training of communication (alternative and augmentative communication; communication techniques—Braille, sign language, etc.), manual dexterity training for handling objects (products, goods, input devices, etc.), and skills training (cognitive, basic, etc.), and vocational training, as well as training in daily living activities. Also covered are education in various subjects, for example, in the arts and social skills. This category also includes products for communication therapy and continence training.

Category 06: Orthoses and Prostheses. This category includes upper/lower-limb orthoses (controlled by the person's body or an external power supply) and prostheses of the upper and lower limbs and other organs (spinal, hair, or breast replacement; ocular and facial prostheses; etc.). This category also includes functional neuromuscular (electrical) stimulators (FNSs), hybrid orthotic systems, and orthopedic footwear.

Category 09: Aids for Personal Care and Protection. Assistance for personal care and protection include clothes and shoes, as well as AT for clothing and dressing, eating, cooking, toileting, and washing including showering and bathing. This category also includes assistive technologies for manicure and pedicure, hair care, dental care, facial care, skin care, skin protection, and skin cleaning. Further assistance is provided in the form of urine diverters, collectors, products for urine absorbtion and devices to prevent involuntary urine and/or feces leakage. Finally, this category includes products for measuring human physical and physiological performance, as well as metrics and assistance in sexual activities.

Category 12: Aids for Personal Mobility. This category includes AT for personal mobility, as well as AT for carrying objects (e.g., transporting luggage belonging to a disabled persons). Also included are walking aids handled by a patient using one arm (cane, crutches, etc.), walking aids manipulated with two arms (e.g., walker or frame), specially designed automobiles, together with systems for loading a wheelchair onto or inside a car, adapted vehicles such as strollers or wheeled walking frames, and wheelchairs and their accessories (shelves, racks, etc.). Further assistive technologies in this category include human-driven and human-powered aids for transferring patients (e.g., transfer boards and carpets, rung and cable ladders), turning or moving patients (e.g., cushions for raising and turning patients), aids that support the patient when rising (e.g., chairs with a seat that moves upward), assistance with orientation [white canes, global positioning satellite (GPS) systems, etc.].

Category 15: Aids for Housekeeping. This AT category supports patients in their performance of domestic activities, including products for preparing food and drink (nonskid mat, weight measurement scales or balances, special knives, etc.), eating and drinking (e.g., plates, glasses, cutlery), house cleaning, and making or maintaining textiles or textile-based products (scissors, measuring tape, sewing devices, etc.).

Category 18: Furnishing and Adapting Homes and Other Premises. This AT category includes furniture for work or leisure (e.g., chairs with or without casters), furniture accessories, and appliances or fixtures for work or leisure environments (e.g., residential, professional, or educational spaces). Also included are special-purpose tables, lighting fixtures and support equipment, and products that support various seating activities (e.g., seats that elevate or support people with disabilities), as well as beds, including barriers or suspension brackets attached to the bed. A further subcategory includes support devices such as handrails, grab bars, and supporting handles, safety gates, doors, windows, and means for opening or closing curtains, as well as AT for adjusting the height or attitude of furniture, equipment that supports access to vertically organized objects, and general safety equipment for the home or other premises.

Category 22: Aids for Communication, Information. Assistive technologies for communication include assistance with reading, writing, seeing (spectacles, weak-vision aids, special lens mounts, contact lenses, etc.), electro-optical AT such as reading machines or video enlargers, computers with special input/output devices, typewriters, and electronic components such as voice synthesis devices. Also included in this category are word processors; manual drawing and writing devices (e.g., rulers, pencils); nonoptical AT for reading (e.g., page turners); audio videorecorders, including earphones and microphones; television and video transmission and reception equipment, including decoders for captioned programs; telephones; and AT for telephony such as camera phones, sound and video amplifiers and processors; as well as systems for sound transmission (infrared earphones, microphones, etc.) and assistance with face-to-face communication (e.g., voice generators and amplifiers). Further equipment in this category includes audio devices (e.g., intraauricular hearing aids, artificial pinnae, glasses with built-in audio amplifiers, tactile transducers for audio signals, and implantable hearing aids). Finally, there are safety technologies such as assistance with generating and receiving cautionary information (e.g., warning signals for doors, traffic, and approaching objects), personal warning systems (e.g., panic buttons, patient safety alarms) A further category supports the needs of the blind, for example, speaking books, and books and other reading materials printed with raised characters such as those printed in Braille.

Category 24: Aids for Handling Products and Goods. Persons with disabilities, as well as people with normal capabilities, require assistance in handling containers, as well as operating or controlling various devices. In the context of disability, AT in this category is used to compensate for or replace the function of an arm or hand with or without fingers (e.g., assistance for gripping, sliding, or rotating objects). This category also includes AT for extended reach, positioning, carrying, transporting, and telecontrolling (controlling by telephone remotely, from a distance; manual or electric grippers, extension cables, etc.), fixed-location devices such as nonskid mats and carpets or low-friction mats for sliding objects. On a larger scale, this category of AT also includes industrial transportation vehicles, conveyors, and cranes, which can be used by all individuals.

Category 27: Aids for Environmental Improvement, Including Tools and Machinary. This category includes all AT for environmental improvement, including manually operated tools, measuring instruments, machines, powered tools and their attachments, as well as special furniture for work environments such as workbenches or tool cabinets.

Category 30: Aids for Recreation. This category includes toys, games, and musical instruments; AT for exercise and sport; and photography equipment for emulsion film or digital video. Also included are recreational equipment for hunting and fishing; tools, materials, and equipment for handicrafts, indoor/outdoor gardening, traveling, camping, and caravanning; smoking equipment; and instruments or tools for pet care.

The reader will notice some overlap between categories, such as low-friction mats that help with the transport of objects via sliding. In practice, borders between various categories in ISO 9999 are difficult to determine, because a given type of

AT can be applied in different ways. Thus, in Section I.3.5, we classify AT on the basis of technology types in relation to a person's daily needs.

I.3.5 AT and User Needs: A Classification Scheme

To help the reader navigate this handbook, we provide a set of tables below that summarize research and techniques, and link existing assistive technologies to the handicaps and impairments that they address, and to the book chapters that cover these technologies (see Tables I.4–I.8).

I.3.6 AT and the Marketplace

Markets for assistive technologies follow the general marketing rule that products introduced into a market influence the demand and growth of markets for such products. In practice, AT products can either represent a barrier to demand or become an engine of demand. This relationship between PwSN and AT in the marketplace follows one of two strategies: (1) trivialization or (2) specialization, which are discussed as follows:

> *Specialization* is based on the development of products or services that are adapted for PwSN. In practice, the AT industry considers PwSN populations as solvent autonomous markets. Developed products are adapted for PwSN needs, so the satisfaction of each target population or subpopulation is good, thereby supporting further product development or adaptation. Nonetheless, the market for such AT is not growing quickly, owing to (1) development costs, (2) high price of the final product, and (3) generally low income of people with disabilities. The exception to this rule is products for elderly retired people, which have significantly higher incomes and a much larger market.
>
> *Trivialization* considers PwSN as an augmentation of the market for devices used by people without disabilities. In this strategy, industry does not target PwSN populations directly. Instead, the products for PwSN are of standardized type, that is, generic with multipurpose capabilities. Given requirements for safety and comfort, these products and services are designed to be modified or adapted to meet PwSN needs. This strategy targets a much larger market but does not consider user satisfaction among PwSN.

I.3.7 AT and Design Methods

Given the requirements of functionality, safety, and comfort, the design of AT for PwSN requires both excellent engineering capacities and relevant knowledge about PwSN characteristics. Product developers must be fully aware of needs, wants, and capabilities of PwSN populations, as well as limitations associated with each handicap. Numerous design methods have been suggested to assist in the process of AT development. Most widely known are user centered design and universal design, which are discussed as follows:

> *User-centered design* is a set of techniques and processes that enable developers to focus on users, within the design process. In practice, users are involved in the development process, depending on their skills and experience, and their interaction

TABLE I.4 People with Motor Disabilities

Impairment	Needs and Barriers		Technologies	
	Less Common	More Common	Less Common	More Common
Upper-limbs deficiencies/dexterity	Survival Feeding (food preparation, eating, drinking) Hygiene (brushing teeth, hairdressing, shaving) Dressing Manipulation of objects	Survival Hygiene (toileting, bathing, laundry) Housekeeping — home cleaning (Chapter 7) Safety Safety Technologies (Chapter 33) Safety of environment Self-care and medication management (medication times; pillbox; effects; procedure);	Robotics [telemanipulation (Chapter 19), feeding systems (Chapter 19), hygiene systems (Chapters 19, 20), systems for playing games (Chapters 19, 20), bookholders] Speech technology [audio technology for input/output (I/O) and control (Chapters 9, 15), writing translators (Chapters 9, 15), text-to-speech translators (Chapter 13)] Prosthesis [artificial arms (Chapter 22)]	Lift systems (Chapters 20, 34) Robotics [robotic therapy (Chapters 21, 40)] Mobile systems [phones, wearable electronics (Chapters 16, 17)] Computers (Chapters 13–15) Augmentative and Alliterative Communication (including I/O Interfaces) [adaptable/configurable interfaces (Chapters 13, 14, 19, 20), speech technologies] Feeding Systems [robots (Chapters 19, 40)]
Lower-limb deficiencies	Survival Feeding (food preparation) Social needs Mobility Navigation, including go-through doors, moving from one place/room to another and negotiating stairs (Chapter 7)	Social needs Socialization (Chapter 7) Communication and interaction with environment Access to information technology (Chapters 13, 14) Transportation, including driving car, access to public transit services (Chapters 7, 24)	Walking assistance [walker system (Chapter 26), ambulatory systems (Chapter 26)] Mobility aids [wheelchair (Chapter 23), scooters, adapted-design cars] Prosthesis [artificial limbs (Chapter 22)]	Hygiene systems, including toileting, bathing, dressing, cleaning up, house cleaning (Chapters 19, 20, 34) Socialization and Entertainment Tools [special games (Chapters 19, 20), virtual companions (Chapter 35), videoconferences] Transportation [public transportation facilities (Chapters 24, 27–29), driving]

TABLE I.4 (Continued)

Impairment	Needs and Barriers		Technologies	
	Less Common	More Common	Less Common	More Common
Lift	Social needs Change position, including get in/out of bed, chair, shower, bathtub (Chapter 7)	Education Access to public administration, facilities (government authorities, banks, public services) Recreation and leisure (Chapter 7) Shopping Esteem Independence Employment (Chapter 7)	Lift systems [transfer systems (Chapter 20), lift chairs]	Organizers and reminder assistants [medication reminder/management (Chapters 24, 34, 40)] Smart environments (Parts VI,VII) [home control (Chapter 9), adapted living facilities, adult-care home/residential facilities, assisted-living facilities] Tele care systems [mentoring, tracking systems (Chapters 13, 40)] Physical and Occupational therapy tools [robotic therapy (Chapter 21)] Shopping tools (Internet access) Education Tools
Stability, balance, orientation	Social needs Navigation (Chapter 7)		Walking assistance [walker systems (Chapter 26), ambulatory systems (Chapter 26)] Navigation systems (Chapters 7, 20, 23, 24)	

TABLE I.5 People with Visual Disabilities

Impairment	Needs and Barriers	Technologies — Less Common	Technologies — More Common

Low vision	Survival
	  Feeding (food preparation)
	  Housekeeping — home cleaning (Chapter 7),
	Safety
	  Safety Technologies (Chapter 33)
	  Safety of environment
		I/O Interfaces [loops (Chapter 13), lighting (Chapter 9)];	Mobile systems [phones, wearable electronics (Chapters 16, 17)]
			Computers (Chapters 13–15)

Color blindness (Chapter 9)		configurable screen color and contrast (Chapter 13);	Augmentative and alliterative communication (including I/O interfaces) [adaptable/configurable interfaces (Chapters 13, 14, 19, 20), tactile interfaces (Chapters 7, 9, 13), vibrotactile displays (Chapter 19), reading screen, speech technologies]
Blindness vision loss	Reading notices Self-care and medication management	IO Interfaces: Braille computer terminals (Chapter 9)	Speech technology [audio technology for I/O interfaces and control (Chapters 9, 15), writing translators (Chapters 9, 15), text–speech translators (Chapter 13)]

Tube vision	Social needs
	  Navigation, positioning, and orientation (Chapter 9)
	  Socialization (Chapter 7)
	  Access to information technology (Chapters 13, 14)
	  Communication and interaction with environment
	  Access to public administration and facilities (government authorities, banks, public services)
	  Employment (Chapter 7)
	  Recreation and leisure (Chapter 7)
	  Shopping
	Esteem
	Independence
		IO Interfaces Loop (Chapter 13), Lighting (Chapter 9)	Navigation systems [mobility, positioning, and orientation aids (Chapters 9, 24)]
			Feeding systems [food preparation (Chapters 9, 40)]
			Socialization and entertainment tools [special games (Chapters 19, 20), virtual companions (Chapter 35), videoconferences]
			Transportation [public transportation facilities (Chapters 24, 27–29)]
			Organizer and reminder assistants [medication reminder/management (Chapters 24, 34)]
			Entertainment aids [interactive digital TV (Chapter 9)]
			Smart environments (Parts VI, VII) [home control (Chapter 9)]
			Telecare systems [mentoring, tracking systems (Chapters 13, 40)]
			Shopping tools (Internet access)
			Education tools
			Internet (Chapter 9)

TABLE I.6 People with Hearing Disabilities

Impairments	Common Needs & Barriers	Technologies Less Common	Technologies More Common
Deafness/ hearing loss	Safety, Safety Technologies (Chapter 33)	Prosthesis [digital hearing aids (Chapter 10), voice output–communication aid (VOCA) (Chapter 16)]; additive prosthesis (Chapter 13)	Mobile systems [phones, other wearable electronics (Chapters 16, 17)]
	Self-care		Computers (Chapters 13–15)
			Augmentative and alliterative communication (including I/O Interfaces) [Adaptable/configurable interfaces (§13, §14, §19, §20), tactile interfaces (§7, §9, §13), Vibro-tactile displays (§19), Reading screen, Speech technologies]
Weak hearing	Social needs, Access to information technology (Chapters 13, 14)	I/O Interfaces [Noise reduction and control (Chapters 10, 13), amplified telephones (Chapter 10)]	Speech technology [audio technology for output (§9, §15), Text - speech translator (§13), Configurable hearing aids (§10)]
	Communication and interaction with environment Recreation and leisure (Chapters 7)	Speech technology [noise reduction and control (Chapters 10, 13), amplified telephones (Chapter 10)] Speech therapy tools	Organizer and Reminder Assistants {Medication reminder/management (§24, §34)}
			Socialization and Entertainment tolls {Special games (§19, §20), Virtual Companions (§35), videoconferences, Captioned TV, Interactive digital TV (§9)}
	Shopping		Communication Aids {TTY (§10), TRS: Telecommunications Relay Service (§10), VCO: Video Relay Service (§10), IP relay (§10), VRS: Voice carryover (Chapter 10)
	Access to public administration and facilities (government authorities, banks, public services)		Transportation [public transportation facilities (Chapters 24, 27), special signalization]
	Esteem Independence Employment (Chapter 7) Socialization (Chapter 7)		Smart environments (Parts VI, VII) [home control (Chapter 9)] Shopping tools (Internet access) Education tools

TABLE I.7 People with Cognitive Disabilities

Impairments	Needs and Barriers	Technologies
	Survival,	
Cognition	Hygiene (toileting, bathing, laundry)	Mobile systems [phones, wearable electronics (Chapters 16, 17)]
Memory loss	Feeding (food preparation, eating, drinking)	Computers (Chapters 13–15)
Forgetfulness	Remembering (Chapter 12)	Socialization and entertainment tools [special games (Chapters 19, 20), virtual companions (Chapter 35), videoconferences]
	Housekeeping — home cleaning (Chapter 7)	Augmentative and Alliterative communication (including I/O interfaces) [adaptable/configurable interfaces (Chapters 13, 14, 19, 20)]
	Safety,	
	Safety Technologies (Chapter 33)	Organizer and reminder assistants [for timekeeping, medications, appointments, hygiene, etc. (Chapters 11, 12), electronic organizers, medication reminder/management (Chapters 24, 34), procedure assistants (Chapters 12, 40)]
	Safety of environment	Transportation [public transportation facilities (Chapters 24, 27, 28, 29)]
	Self-care and medication management	
	Social needs,	
	Socialization (Chapter 7)	Communication aids [communicators (Chapter 12), pagers (Chapter 12), multimedia procedure assistants (Chapter 12), large-screen programmable phones, electronic information organizers (Chapters 11, 12), electronic mail (Chapter 12)]
	Navigation (Chapter 9)	Orthotics [cognitive orthotics (Chapter 12)]
	Access to information technology (Chapters 13, 14)	Smart environments (Parts VI, VII) [home control (Chapter 9)]
	Education	Shopping tools (Internet access)
	Communication and interaction with environment	Education tools
	Shopping	
	Esteem	
	Independence	
	Employment (Chapter 7)	
	Recreation and leisure (Chapter 7)	

is facilitated by a domain expert. The intensity of this involvement varies with the stage of research and product development. Often, the developed AT meets PwSN satisfaction. However, this design method is expensive in terms of resources and time expended by engineers and domain experts. It is also difficult to recruit

TABLE I.8 People with Communication Disabilities

Impairments	Needs & Barriers	Technologies

Can be multiple deficiencies including:
Speech mechanism problem
Language processing
Hearing
Vision
Motor skills
	Safety
	  Safety Technologies (Chapter 33)
	  Self-care and medication management
	Social needs
	  Socialization (Chapter 7)
	  Access to information technology (Chapters 13, 14)
	  Communication and interaction with environment
	  Access to public administration and facilities (authorities, banks, public services)
	  Shopping
	  Recreation and leisure (Chapter 7)
	  Problems with speech, writing
	Esteem
	  Independence
	  Employment (Chapter 7)
		Mobile systems [phones, wearable electronics (Chapters 16, 17)]
		Computers (Chapters 13–15)
		Augmentative and alliterative communication (including I/O interfaces) [adaptable/configurable interfaces (Chapters 13, 14, 19, 20), tactile interfaces (Chapters 7, 10, 13), vibrotactile displays (Chapter 19), reading screen, speech technologies, augmentative–alliterative communication (AAC) (Chapters 7, 16)]
		Socialization and entertainment tools [special games (Chapters 19, 20), virtual companions (Chapter 35), videoconferences]
		Medication organizers [medication reminder/management (Chapters 24, 34, 40)]
		Speech technology [audio technology for I/O interfaces and control (Chapters 9, 15), writing translators (Chapters 9, 15), text–speech translators (Chapter 13)]
		Translators
		Transportation [public transportation facilities (Chapters 24, 27)]
		Smart environments (Parts VI, VII) [home control (Chapter 9), pervasive computing, context awareness, middleware]
		Shopping tools (Internet access)
		Education tools

potential end users and to interact with them, especially when these end users are older people, or people with disabilities (see also Chapter 34).

Universal design (also called *design for all*) is the design of products and environments to be usable by all people, to the greatest extent possible, without the need for adaptation or specialized design [36]. Here, the design process is guided and constrained by a number of objectives: accessibility, adaptability, transgenerational applicability, and/or universal applicability or appeal. Universal design does not emphasize differences among PwSN, or between PwSN and the general population. Instead, the ideas of adapting products, services, or the environment are extended to users at large. In practice, products are developed to meet the needs of average users. If a user differs significantly from the average population (e.g., a person with a significant handicap), then the product will provide poor user satisfaction (see also Chapter 45).

I.4 CONCLUSION

The majority of people with special needs suffer from social and professional exclusion. This is because the majority of the world cannot deal financially with the related problems and their growing scale. All agree that the use of technology could provide scalable and economical means to addressing issues of aging and disability. However, more research and development activities are needed to bring assistive technology to maturation and cost-effectiveness. We hope that this handbook provides the value intended by its editors, which is to bridge disciplines in a language that can be understood by all. So, we hope that engineers develop a better and more accurate understanding of PwSN problems, as they propose to solve them. We also hope that professionals such as geriatricians, rehabilitation specialists, occupational therapists, and clinical psychologists will learn more about technology to be able to better support engineers develop successful, cost-effective solutions collaboratively.

REFERENCES

1. Wood P: *International Classification of Impairments, Diseases and Handicaps*, WHO, Geneva, 1980.
2. DPI: Disabled People's International: *Proc 1st World Congress*, Singapore, 1982.
3. DePoy E, Gilson SF: *Rethinking Disability. Principles for Professional and Social Change*, Brook Cole, Belmont, CA; 2004.
4. WHO: *International Classification of Functioning, Disability and Health*, World Health Organization, Geneva, 2001.
5. Wikipedia, Website free encyclopaedia, ≪/fr.wikipedia.org≫.
6. Penaud C, Mokhtari M, Abdulrazak B: Technology usage for dependant people: Towards the right balance between user needs and technology, in Miesenberger K, Klaus J, Zagler W, Burger D, eds, *Computers Helping People with Special Needs*, Springer, Proc 9th *Int Conf Computers Helping People with Special Needs (ICCHP)*, Paris, July 2004, pp 898–905.
7. Mann W, Helal S: Technology and chronic conditions in later years: Reasons for new hope, in Wahll H, Tesch-Romer C, Hoff A, eds, *New Dynamics in Old Age—Individual, Environmental and Societal Perspectives*, Baywood, 2007.
8. *WHO International Classification of Impairments, Disabilities and Handicaps*, World Health Organization, Geneva, 1980.
9. Marmor MM: Age-related eye diseases and their effects on visual function, in Faye EE, Stuen CS, (eds), *The Aging Eye and Low Vision*, The Lighthouse, New York, pp 11–21.
10. Bailey LL, and Hall A: *Visual Impairment: An Overview*, American Foundation for the Blind, New York; 1990.
11. Wallhagen MI, Strawbridge WJ, Shema SJ, Kurata J, Kaplan GA: Comparative impact of hearing and vision impairment on subsequent functioning, *J Am Geriatr Soc.* **49** (2001).
12. Pleis JR, Coles R: *Summary Health Statistics for U.S. Adults: National Health Interview Survey*, 1999, US Dept Health and Human Services, Centers for Disease Control and Prevention, National Center for Health Statistics. US Government Printing Office, 2003.
13. Long RG, Crews JE, Mancil R: Creating measures of rehabilitation outcomes for people who are blind and visually impaired: The FIMBA project, *J Blind Visual Impair* **94** (5): 292–306 (2002).
14. Clark M, Bond M, Sanchez L: The effect of sensory impairment on the lifestyle activities of older people, *Austral J Aging* (1999).

15. Wahl HW, Oswald F, Zimprich D: Everyday competence in visually impaired older adults: A case for person-environment perspectives, *Gerontologist* **39**(2): 140–149 (1999).
16. West CG, Gildengorin G, Haegerstrom-Portnoy G, Schneck ME, Lott L, J. Bradyn J: Vision and driving self-restriction, *J Am Geriat Soc*; **51**: 1348–1355 (2003).
17. Adams PF, Benson V: *S Current estimates from the National Health Interview Survey, 1989*, National Center for Health Statistics, Vital Health Statistics 10(176), US Government Printing Office, 1990.
18. WHO: *Blindness and Visual Disability: Part 5: Seeing ahead: Projections into the Next Century*, Fact Sheet 146, World Health Organization, Geneva, Feb 1997.
19. Arlinger S: Negative consequences of uncorrected hearing loss: A review, *Int J Audiol* **42**: 17–20 (2003).
20. I CAN organization: www.ican.org.uk.
21. Wikipedia encyclopedia: www.wikipedia.org.
22. Glickstein J: *Therapeutic Interventions in Alzheimer's Disease: A Program of Functional Skills for Activities of Daily Living and Communication*, Aspen Publishers, Gaithersburg, MD, 1997, pp 235–240.
23. National Institute on Aging: *Progress Report on Alzheimer's Disease: Taking the Next Steps*, NIH Publication 00–4859, Washington, DC, 2000.
24. Butin DN: Helping those with dementia to live at home: An educational series for caregivers, *Phys Occup Ther Geriatr* **9**(3–4): 69–82 (1991).
25. Abreu BC, Toglia JP: Cognitive rehabilitation: A model for occupational therapy, *Am J Occup Ther* **41**(7): 439–448 (1987).
26. Beck JC, Benson DF, Scheibel AB, Spar JE, Rubenstein LZ: Dementia in the elderly: the silent epidemic." *Ann Int Med* **97**(2): 231–241 (1982):
27. Poole J, Dunn W, Schell B, Barnhart JM: Statement: Occupational therapy services management of persons with cognitive impairments, *Am J Occup Ther*, **45**(12): 1067–1068 (1991).
28. Aho K, Harmsen P, Hatano S: Cerebrovascular disease in the Community: Results of WHO collaborative study, *Bull WHO*, **58**: 113–130 (1980).
29. Pynoos J, Ohta RJ: In-home interventions for persons with Alzheimer's disease and their caregivers, *Phys Occup Ther Geriat* **9**(3/4): 83–92 (1991).
30. ISO 9999: *Technical Aids for Persons with Disabilities—Classification and Terminology*, 2002.
31. US Technology–Related Assistance for Individuals with Disabilities Act of (1988), PL (Public Law) 100–407, Section 3.
32. US Assistive Technology Act of 1998, PL 105–394.
33. US Older Americans Act of 1965, 42 USC (US Code), Title I.
34. European Commission: *Access to Assistive Technology in the European Union*, European Commission Directorate-General for Employment and Social Affairs, Unit E, 4, 1–188, 2003.
35. *Assistive Products for Persons with Disabilities—Classification and Terminology*, International Standard, ISO 9999, 3rd ed, 2002.
36. Connell B, Jones M, Mace R, Mueller J, Mullick A, Ostroff E, Sanford J, Steinfeld E, Story M, Vanderheiden G: *The Principles of Universal Design*, The Center of Universal Design (www.design.ncsu.edu), 1997.

PART I

Definitions, Classifications, and Policies

1

Technology for Successful Aging and Disabilities

Amol Karmarkar, Eliana Chavez, and Rory A. Cooper
VA Pittsburgh Healthcare System

Although technology acceptance or rejection is dependent on a combination of several factors, it is not possible to accurately weigh these factors to determine the highest predictor for acceptance or rejection of an assistive technology (AT) device. Optimal use of AT devices depends on a combination of variables, including personal and environmental factors, the device in itself, the service delivery factor, and the social factor. Usability of the devices also depends on the training that the user receives. Inadequacy in training may lead to unfamiliarity with the use of the device, which in turn may result in restricted use or nonuse of the device. Three types of acceptances related to AT can be described as reluctant acceptance, grateful acceptance, and internal acceptance. *Reluctant acceptance* occurs when the individual is accepting the device only as a "necessity" or a medium for completing activities of daily living (ADL). In *grateful acceptance*, the device is viewed as a part of life and considered as one of the "assets." With this type of acceptance, AT is a medium for overcoming functional deficits occurring as a result of the disability. *Internal acceptance* is the highest category among the levels of acceptance of AT devices, where individuals view the devices as a part of themselves. The AT device in this case is considered by users as a medium for overcoming their physical impairments and a replacement for the impaired part of their bodies [1].

The acceptance or rejection of AT devices in turn is affected by several factors. These factors have a strong common component, namely, the temporal effect. The temporal component influences the usability of a device. The usability, nonusability, or both, of a device, is determined by a dynamic relationship between several variables including

The Engineering Handbook of Smart Technology for Aging, Disability, and Independence,
Edited by A. Helal, M. Mokhtari and B. Abdulrazak
Copyright © 2008 John Wiley & Sons, Inc.

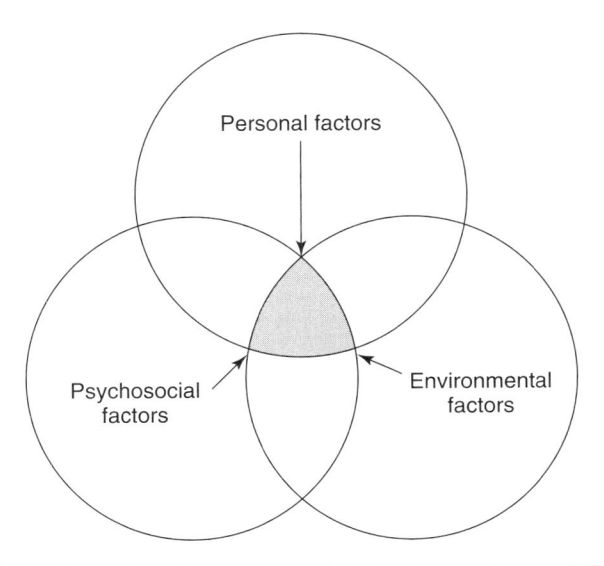

FIGURE 1.1 Interaction between different factors for acceptance of AT devices.

personal, environmental, psychosocial, and economical factors. The interaction between these factors continually changes across the time domain, which directly affects acceptance/rejection of AT device (Fig. 1.1).

Another factor that increases the usability of an AT device is the perception about the advantages and disadvantages of the AT devices. If the (perceived) benefits outweigh the (perceived) disadvantages, then, there are higher chances of that device to be utilized. On the contrary, if the (perceived) disadvantages outweigh the (perceived) benefits of the device, there are higher chances that the device will no be used.

Personal factors, including motivation, cooperation, optimism, good coping skills, and the ability to learn or adapt to new skills, work in a combination for the user [2]. In the older population, all the abovementioned factors diminish gradually. Therefore, acceptance of AT devices can be a challenge in this population, which, in turn, may result in suboptimal use of AT devices for functional independence.

A review article [3] indicated a relationship between (1) the type and degree of impairment and the severity of illness and (2) the use of AT devices. A variation in the number of AT devices used was observed in people with varying disorders within the aging population. The overall trend indicated a positive relationship between the severity of disorders and the number of AT devices used by the older people [3]. The usability of AT devices also depends on environmental accessibility. The presence of environmental barriers can limit acceptance of the devices. For instance, consider an elderly individual, living in a two-story house, who has been prescribed a power wheelchair for functional mobility. There is a ramp to enter the house. The second floor, where the individual spends most of his time during a day, however, is not accessible. In this situation, the use of the power wheelchair inside the house will be limited by the presence of an environmental barrier. Acceptance of AT in older adults is also determined to a large extent by views of society. An example of this is the higher acceptability of home modifications, such as grab bars in the bathroom and a high-rise commode; than that of a mobility device such as a cane or a walker. The latter are considered to be indicative of a significant disability [4].

1.1 INADEQUATE TRAINING

The Department of Health and Human Services (HHS) mentioned inadequate training of use of AT for elderly population as one of the significant barriers in decreasing usability of the devices [5]. In acute-care settings such as hospitals, the reduced length of stay limits the time availability for occupational/physical therapist to provide adequate education about the use of AT devices during discharge. This results in elderly individuals going home with different types of AT devices, but having limited knowledge regarding the use and maintenance information about these devices. Ineffective follow-up care after discharge from hospitals also results in hesitance to use AT devices at home, causing rejection or abandonment of the devices. Lack of standardization across various settings specialized in prescription of AT, and the variable training time allocated and emphasized across different settings, also leads to inconsistent levels of acceptance. Evidence is pointing at the benefits of providing training of AT in improving effectiveness of use and in prevention of primary and secondary injuries associated with inappropriate use. However, the existing research focuses primarily on effectiveness of training for operating manual wheelchairs. Also, very few studies related to aging and AT mentioned training as an important component for improving acceptance of use of the devices. Chiu and Man [6] indicated greater improvement in the functional independence, higher satisfaction with the AT devices as well as a higher usage of AT devices, among the elderly individuals who received a home based training program after getting discharge from the hospital, as compared to other groups of elderly individuals who did not receive home based training program [6].

Following are some of the guidelines that can be helpful in providing training for older individuals regarding use of AT devices:

1. *Client and Family Involvement.* Along with client involvement in selection and finalizing AT devices, an immediate family member's involvement is also beneficial. This could be effective with elderly people being discharged from hospitals or skilled nursing facilities and returning home, where the device will be used. A smooth transition from hospital to home could be facilitated by involvement of one or more family members.
2. *Follow-Up Care.* Status of elderly people after being discharged from the care setting and receiving the device from a specialized clinic is not monitored effectively. If communication is maintained between providers and consumers, with responses to questions about the use of AT for specific purposes within the home environment, it could provide the encouragement required for continuing the use of AT devices.
3. *Instructions and Training in Context of Use.* Elderly individuals usually receive training in use of AT devices in an environment completely different from the environment where the devices will be used. Transference of skills from one environment to the other sometimes is not very efficient, resulting in increased level of frustration and ultimately to nonuse of the device. On the contrary, if

emphasis is placed from the start on transferring skills and cross-training for all environments, transition of AT use will be more effective.

1.2 TECHNOLOGY REJECTION

Technology abandonment has been a critical issue that has a negative impact on the user's daily living and also on the clinical practice. Because of the intricate nature of the prescription procedure, the cost could accumulate; thus premature rejection of the prescribed AT devices could be an expensive business for the healthcare services. Phillips and Zhao [7] raised this issue for the first time in their descriptive article about factors related to rejection of AT. The study indicated that a change in the needs of people was the most important factor. The easier it was to obtain an AT device, the greater was the likelihood that it would be rejected. The higher was the performance of an AT device, the lower was the rejection rate. If the users' opinions were considered in the AT service delivery process, there were higher rates of device retention.

1.3 IMPROVING MATCH BETWEEN PERSON, ASSISTIVE TECHNOLOGY, AND ENVIRONMENT

Several factors need to be considered prior to prescription of the AT device, with some of the more important ones listed below:

- Inclusion of end users in design, feature selection, and evaluation process of AT devices.
- Sharing information between providers and clients, and taking feedback for determining match between users and AT.
- In the event that client is not satisfied with original loaner equipment, provision for replacement with newer equipment. This process can reduce wastage of human and system resources if a client is not willing to use a particular type of prescribed AT device.
- Consideration of time factor—effective use of AT device could be a time-consuming procedure, which needs to include all factors where an AT device will be used. Also, this process must be adapted by the user in the physicosocial environment where it will be used.

1.4 TECHNOLOGY FITTING

When providing a mobility device, it is essential to conduct a careful and methodical evaluation of a potential mobility user with clinical input from trained professionals. An assistive technology practitioner (ATP) should consider several steps before providing an AT device. The matching person–technology (MPT) assessment process is one means for providing a more personal approach to matching person and technology. The MPT components include the environments in which the person uses the technology, the individual's characteristics and preferences, and the functions and features of the technology.

Characteristics within these three components can each influence technology use either positively or negatively. If there are too many negative influences, the chances of the technology being successfully used are greatly reduced. In fact, the technology itself can appear perfect for a given need, but if the user does not possess the appropriate personal characteristics or does not receive the needed support, that perfect technology may go unused or may be used inappropriately. The steps in a successful MPT assessment are as follows:

1. *Client Evaluation.* The nature and progression of the disease should be well understood and considered. Joint range of motion, especially at the hips and knees, as well as pelvic and spinal alignment, will determine the proper configuration and postural supports of an AT device. Sensory and central processing skills should also be evaluated. The risk for and presence of skin breakdown needs to be considered, for example, for proper seat cushion selection. Each cushion has advantages and disadvantages that need to be carefully considered. Pressure mapping is typically used as part of the routine screening or evaluation procedure to determine whether individuals are at risk of developing pressure sores. Pressure mapping (Fig. 1.2) is often used for relative comparison between different types of cushions and wheelchair setups to assist in the selection of such equipment. They are also useful as biofeedback to the individual regarding weight shift and pressure relief abilities and strategies [8]. Inappropriate seat cushion provision can lead to costly and fatal pressure sores as well as affect the user's postural alignment and ability to transfer in and out of the chair [9]. Features such as tilt-in-space and backward-reclining systems need to be considered for people who cannot physically adjust or reposition to reduce the potential for postural deformities, discomfort, and skin breakdown [10]. When considering manual wheelchair propulsion, an ATP should also consider the stress being applied to the upper extremities, which has been associated with upper-extremity repetitive strain injuries [11]. An external

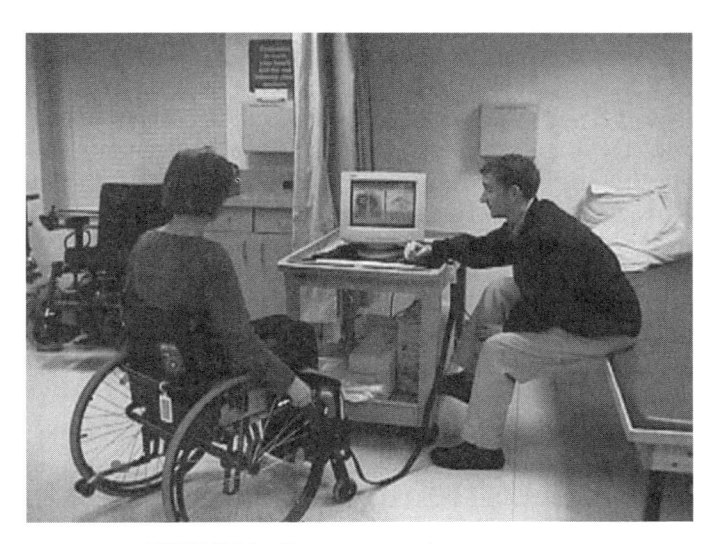

FIGURE 1.2 Pressure-mapping assessment.

FIGURE 1.3 A SmartWheel.

    device called SmartWheel (Fig. 1.3) had been introduced in a clinical setting to measure forces at the wheelchair during wheelchair propulsion. A SmartWheel is an instrument that can be easily attached to most standard manual wheelchairs [12]. *Simulation* is an assessment process in which the AT team observes the dynamic interaction between the client and the AT equipment.

2. *Driving Abilities.* The appropriate mobility device needed, whether a manual wheelchair, a scooter, or a power wheelchair, needs careful evaluation. For example, a power wheelchair—a heavy piece of equipment capable of reaching high speeds—can cause serious damage, injury, and even death in a collision. Therefore, the ATP must carefully assess a candidate's ability to operate the equipment, especially when the candidate has cognitive or perceptual deficits. People with these deficits should not necessarily be prohibited from the use of a power wheelchair; however, they may require training to learn to operate the device.

3. *Environmental Accessibility Evaluation.* A home-and-work assessment is often needed to ensure that the device will be compatible. Few power wheelchairs can be carried upstairs, or through narrow doorways, or made to negotiate tight turns in a hallway or bathroom. A proper assessment involves taking the device to the user's home, surveying the environment for accessibility, and having the potential user get into the device and drive it where needed within the course of a routine day. The home assessment should also involve having the candidate complete specific tasks. This includes transferring to various surfaces, reaching for objects, cooking, pulling up to a table or work surfaces, and completing any other important activity.

4. *Transportation Accessibility Evaluation.* The physical capabilities of the person to manage the device must be considered. For example if a power wheelchair or scooter must be transported, the person who will be conducting the task should have an opportunity to stow the device to verify that the operation is feasible. A consumer who will use an accessible vehicle, such as a van with a lift or ramp,

will need to drive the device into the vehicle, maneuver it into an appropriate position for securement or transfer to another seat, and then exit the vehicle. It is crucial to consider a device that has the appropriate attachment points to ensure optimal safety during transportation [13].

1.4.1 Client Training and Equipment Delivery Model

Equipment delivery must include careful attention to final adjustment and to proper training in the equipment's safe and effective. Even though the equipment was previously specified in detail, it is important for the ATP to be present during the final fitting to verify that the seating goals and objectives have been achieved. ATP help is important to make prescriptive decisions during the fine-tuning of the adjustable components [14].

During the final fitting, training and delivery of the equipment should be done. The client must be properly trained in the use of the equipment. This training should include instruction in proper sitting, postural adjustment, weight shift, propulsion, chair maneuverability, transfers, soft-tissue protection procedures, vehicular transportation of the equipment, and operation of all components of the equipment [14].

1.4.2 Client Follow-Up

Delivery of the equipment is not the end of the process. Assessment of the effectiveness of the equipment should continue throughout the duration of use. The frequency and extent of the follow-up visits should be determined according to each client's needs [14]. To accomplish a thorough follow-up assessment, the team should review the seating (or equipment) goals and objectives, as well as the prescriptive approaches that were recorded during the client's prior assessment. With that information in mind, the team should screen the client's needs, identifying any changes or additions that would effect a change in the client's equipment. Any changes in the client's abilities or demands on the social or physical environment should be reassessed [14].

1.5 DEVELOPMENT AND TECHNOLOGY TRANSFER

1.5.1 Participatory Action Design (PAD)

The PAD model describes a process of developing products (AT product) in this instance. The process starts with identification of users' needs. There are several ways of doing this: through focus groups, with an open-ended discussion moderated by a person from a design team, getting feedback from users through surveys and questionnaires about specific requirements and possible solutions. All of this information is put together, which will help in identifying various features of conceptual products. These data are also helpful in comparing two options of a product feature, and determine advantages or disadvantages of each. The next step includes development of a mock-up system, where all these features are incorporated together, to have a product design. All the features of the product, are then compared to benchmarks available, ensuring that the designed feature are at par with the industry standard. However, since all this is done on paper or in a computer-aided design (CAD) system, actual performance cannot be measured until the next step. The prototype is built up after this step, and it includes all the features discussed above. After this, a comparison is made with the standards for the product. Product efficacy is usually determined by doing a durability–reliability testing of the product. Standards, which will be discussed in greater depth in the next section, can be used to determine the level of durability of the developed product. Durability testing typically determines the ability of individual components of a particular device to withstand repeated use by the end user. Following incorporation of the changes as suggested by the efficacy testing, the product is submitted for the Food and Drug Administration (FDA) approval process. The FDA approval process is an extensive procedure, with the main emphasis on ensuring safety to the end users. Unfortunately, with AT devices very few, especially mobility-related, products undergo the FDA approval process. The clinical effectiveness of AT devices could be established in several phases. Typically, four phases of testing are involved to determine clinical effectiveness: (1) conducting a focus group of clinicians, end users, and manufacturers, who provide feedback on benefits and disadvantages of that product; (2) testing the product using an unimpaired population; (3) using case studies, where a small number of (potential) end users are tested on the device, as the outcomes for determining clinical effectiveness could include physical capacity measure and or functional performance measure; and (4) testing a large group of potential end users, for generalization to the entire population who will eventually be using the device. The most intricate step in this entire process is establishing insurance coverage for a particular product. This involves either formulation of a common code for the device and establishing a fee schedule for the device (Fig. 1.4).

PAD is the form of research design that accounts for the needs and opinions of the end users and tries to implement that in designing of a product. Several features of a PAD are

- Consideration of end users as partners right from the beginning of the design process
- Feedback at all stages of development, which can lead to constant modification of the desired product
- Problem breakups in small parts, starting to find solutions for a smaller problem and working the way upward (i.e., bottom–up approach to problem solution)

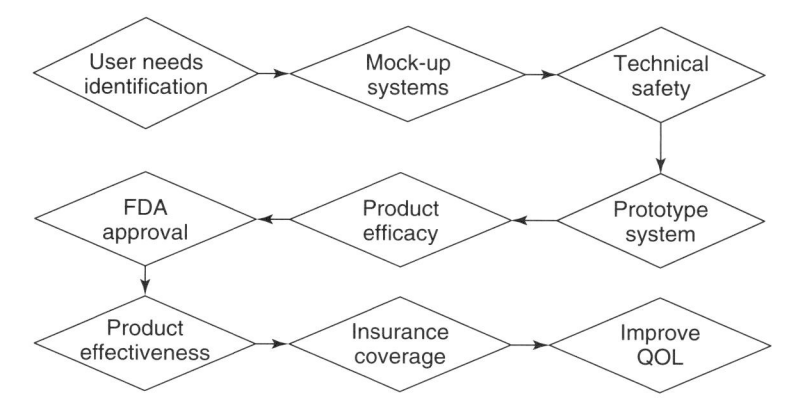

FIGURE 1.4 *Participatory action design model (QOL — quality of life).*

1.5.2 Quality Assurance

As mentioned above standards are those benchmarks against which a product or a service could be compared. Standards are also useful for determining durability of a product and comparing several products available on the market, so as to prescribe the most durable, reliable, and cost-effective AT device to consumers. Unlike that of the body implant industry, where standards are the crucial prerequisite for FDA approval, AT devices do not mandate meeting a minimal-standards requirement prior to prescription. The scenario is changing, with the wheelchair industry following standards testing for determining quality of their product. In 1979 the American National Standard Institute (ANSI), together with the Rehabilitation Engineering Society of North America (RESNA), formulated testing standards for wheelchairs, commonly known today as *ANSI/RESNA standards*. The standards are applicable to all forms of wheelchairs—manual, power, and scooters—with some differences, which depend on the feature that has to be tested. These standards are developed and continuously refined by the workgroups, who change their parameters according to constant shifts in the manufacturing quality and user requirements. There are several sections of standards for wheelchair performance testing; one of the most critical standards is the durability test. The durability performance test, which is also known as the *fatigue strength test*, determines the average life of a wheelchair under certain testing conditions and generalizes this to the end user's daily use of the wheelchair. The durability test has two separate components: the double-drum test and the curb drop test (Figs. 1.5 and 1.6):

The double-drum test needs to be conducted before the curb drop test. In the former, a 100-kg dummy is placed on a chair, which is set up on two drums, with drive wheels placed on one drum and castors on the other drum. The speed of rear drum is 1 m/s, which is set 5–7% slower than the front drums. The purpose of this test is to simulate the commonly encountered road hazards by a wheelchair user. The standard for this testing indicates a value of 200,000 cycles, which is the minimum requirement for the wheelchairs to pass the test, without any major mechanical failure. The curb drop test

FIGURE 1.5 Double-drum testing.

FIGURE 1.6 Curb drop testing.

is designed to simulate traversal over uneven terrains, especially going up and down small curbs. A 100-kg dummy is set on the wheelchair, which is lifted 5 cm above ground level and then dropped. This is repeated until there is any major failure of the system. The ANSI/RESNA standards for this test are 6666 drops. The numbers selected for the fatigue strength test, typically represents a 3–5 years of functioning life for a wheelchair.

These standards could be utilized in several possible ways to improve quality of the AT device itself and deliver services to consumers:

- *Ensuring Safety.* These tests mimic the performance tests conducted in the automobile industry, with a purpose of providing quality products to consumers.
- *Product Comparisons.* The standards could be utilized in comparing the products for providing the best available care to consumers. Pearlman et al. [15] compared product efficiency of three types of power wheelchairs with Medicare codes: K0010 (nonprogrammable), K0011 (programmable), and K0014 (programmable with customized seating). The study found that determination of the cumulative survival level, which was based on the fatigue strength tests using ANSI/RESNA standards, was significantly higher for the K0011 and K0014 chairs than for the K0010 ones. The study suggested prescription of more durable wheelchairs despite higher cost upfront, to have longer life expectancy, which can ultimately ensure greater patient safety [15].
- *Cost Analysis.* Although this could be done in a very crude form, the cost efficiency of a particular product could be determined by comparing the life expectancy of the product and cost.

1.5.3 Total Quality Management (TQM) and Continuous Quality Improvement (CQI)

The commonly used lingo in the management field emphasizes TQM and CQI, for any industry related to providing services. *Total quality management* is defined as a process of constant accomplishment of clients' satisfaction through a continuous improvement (in quality of products and services). *Continuous quality improvement*, on the other hand, is a constantly changing process for adapting to newer demands and needs of the end users and bring changes in the product and/or service delivery in order to establish a TQM. The CQI process is very crucial for maintaining and improving optimal use of AT devices by an end user and also prevents premature abandonment. Several steps are involved in this process (see Fig. 1.7).

Several other recommendations suggested in the literature could be applicable for ensuring TQM and CQI in the AT devices prescription–delivery process:

1. *Client Needs and Values.* The process should be customized according to clients' needs and values. With client as a source of control, the process should account for the clients' needs and requirements. This will enforce creativity for clinicians to provide AT to clients, and bring in new designs and solutions. Clinicians should also have the expertise for anticipating future needs of clients and consider them before making a final choice. For example, in progressive diseases, clients may not be able to foresee their future needs. In this situation, clinicians may need to factor in those aspects.
2. *Communication.* This is key to maintaining quality. The communication should be between client, clinicians, engineers, and manufacturers. In the communication process, there should be sharing of knowledge among the team, which will help the client make decisions and ensure quality. The system should be transparent, allowing sharing of all advantages and hazards associated with a particular product that will help the client make an informed decision. With an aging population, denial of disability could be a potential barrier for acceptance of technology. Open dialogues within the team may help people understand their limitations and make appropriate decisions.

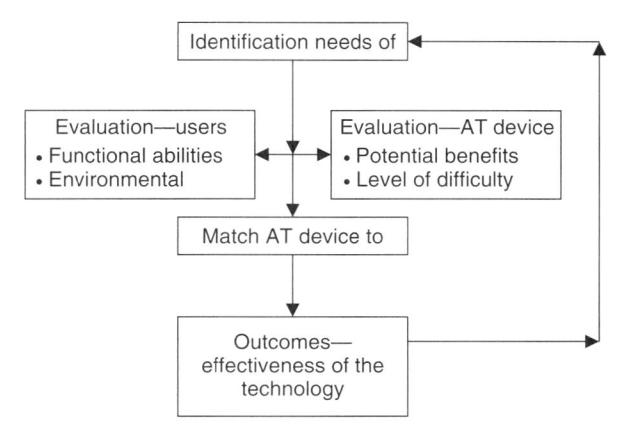

FIGURE 1.7 CQI model for AT device delivery process (adapted from Ref. 12).

3. *Evidence as a Basis for All Decisionmaking Processes.* With vast availability of free information on the Internet, there could be mixed evidence about a particular technology. Clinicians need to act as a filtering mechanism, accepting best available evidence and discarding falsifying statements about a product. Clinicians also need to learn to make best use of available evidence for all decisionmaking processes and also push for new evidence for bringing quality of care up continuously.
4. *Client Safety.* This should be the priority of providing any form of healthcare, including AT devices. Analyses of the entire system should be conducted regularly to prevent occurrence of systematic and/or random errors. Again, clinicians and others involved in the AT delivery process should be accountable for acceptance of mistakes and encourage free discussion of the same for prevention in the long run.

1.6 SERVICE DELIVERY MODELS

There is a basic process for delivery of services to the client, and several steps are involved in this process [2]. The first step is referral and intake. The client or a close relative or friend or a healthcare professional will have identified the need for AT and will contact an ATP to make a referral. The service provider gathers basic information and determines whether there is a match between the type of services he or she provides and the identified needs of the client.

Once the criteria for intake have been met, the evaluation phase begins. A more detailed specification of the client's AT needs is determined. Following a thorough identification of the client's needs, the client sensory, physical, and central processing skills are evaluated. Understanding the disease process and prognosis and the client's current skill level are also identified. These are the gaps between abilities and goals that AT devices are supposed to fill. At this stage, the ATP will review the evidence-based practice literature and will bring her or his own expertise to narrowing the number of devices that will be discussed with the client. Next, advantages and disadvantages of the AT devices will be clearly explained to the client. The client's opinion is essential in the AT selection process [16]. The client knows his or her assets, needs, and limitation and is the best individual to make the final selection. Therefore, technologies that match the needs and skills of the client are identified, and a trial evaluation is performed. At this point, a home evaluation should be performed if there is a need. If the AT is fulfilling the client's goal and his/her environment, the AT should be ordered, and a letter stating the medical necessity should be written. This medical necessity letter should describe the client's current condition, level of function, daily living situation, and equipment features, including advantages and cost benefits of the equipment. The medical necessity letter must justify the importance and benefit of the AT device to purchasing agencies. The ATP should be aware of funding sources available to the client. Although funding is important, the results of the AT evaluation should be based first on the client's need and second on the funding.

When funding is secured, the client proceeds with intervention in the implementation phase. In this phase, the equipment that has been recommended, ordered, modified, and/or set up is delivered to the client. Initial training on the basic operation of the device and ongoing training strategies for using the device are also performed at this stage. After the AT device has been delivered, the AT provider should periodically reevaluate the degree of integration of the initial device into the user's life. The client should be able to use her/his available skills to achieve the desired goals within the immediate environment with the AT device chosen. It is also important to update the AT device to a more appropriate system when needed by the user if improved products appear in the marketplace.

The AT delivery process is dynamic and requires an interdisciplinary team, where several professionals should be involved. The client, family member(s), and caregivers should be considered team members. Research into consumer dissatisfaction and disuse of AT suggest that device abandonment could be reduced if consumers are actively involved from start to finish in the development process [2]. Therefore, the AT process delivery outcome would be a result of the team, client, and family effort and will impact the client's independence and quality of life.

1.7 CLIENT-CENTERED APPROACH

Assistive technology services are provided via consultation, in which an ATP is called to address the AT needs of a client. Several people may be involved with the client, including family members, teachers, vocational counselors, and therapists. The AT and intervention are more successful when these significant others are identified and involved at the beginning of the process. It is essential that the assessment and intervention be a collaborative process. The role of the ATP is to educate consumers of the choices available, to enable the client to make decisions related to the AT in an informed manner. The challenge for the ATP is to do this without unduly influencing the client's choice. The value of this approach is that the client and the ATP inform each other throughout the process and develop a shared mutual responsibility for the outcome. The ATP should initiate the collaborative process by identifying significant others as a part of the intake referral procedure. The success of the AT system depends on coordination and teamwork among all the individuals involved with the client. In a client-centered approach, the client's input is important to the success of the AT process [2].

1.8 REIMBURSEMENT AND PAYMENT

A commonly used analogy in the US healthcare system is a "pie" with different types of healthcare services competing against each other to get a large "piece of the pie." All services, including AT, are significantly affected by the constant increase in the cost of healthcare. Provision of the AT services is, to a large extent, controlled by the availability of the funding source. As the insurance structure in United States does not support uniformity in terms of coverage of AT from person to person, this could sometimes be a major barrier in providing quality of services to clients. Provision of AT consists of several steps, such as assessment, AT provision, follow-up, and repair and maintenance. The cumulative cost of the entire process could be significant; in most cases insurance companies are the only available option for getting a piece of AT equipment, rather than the person paying individually for the services. As mentioned earlier, because of the high cost of the services, a combination of several types of insurance agencies—public as well as private—is required in order to get a piece of AT. For several years, the requirements for AT funding have also changed drastically. There has been an increase in the need of third-party reimbursement agencies for documentation and evidence. AT practice, therefore, which was traditionally based on the expertise of an occupational or physical therapist, now requires need for evidence-based practice to support the decisionmaking of a prescribed piece of AT equipment. Impact of evidence-driven AT service reimbursement practice has a significant impact on the following:

- Assessment procedure, which now demands time-related cost-efficiency from clinicians
- Documentation, justifying the need for that particular piece of equipment and its advantages over the other lower-cost options available
- Developing standards for different types of AT that are undergoing constant revision and changes, such as the American National Standard Institute (ANSI)/Rehabilitation Engineering Society of North America (RESNA) standards for wheelchairs, for providing a benchmark of care
- Prescription that accounts for clinical practice guidelines, and the client's needs and preferences, to reduce the possibility of abandonment of the prescribed device
- Service delivery in a timely and cost-effective manner
- Follow-up care, including repair and maintenance of the prescribed device, to improve long-term use and minimize frequent replacement of the entire instrument

1.8.1 Funding Sources

A wide variety of funding options are available for provision of AT services in the United State. The common objective in provision of AT services is based on medical necessity of the client. A common definition of medical necessity, despite the variability in interpretation by different insurance agencies as proposed by Center for Medicare Medicaid Services (CMS), is "Services that are proper and needed for the diagnosis or treatment of medical condition meet the standards of good medical practice and are not mainly for the convenience of [the] health professional" [17].

Funding sources for AT include the following:

1. *Medicare.* Established in 1965, Medicare is the largest payer for AT services throughout the United States. Some of the eligibility criteria for Medicare are (a) age >65 years and receiving monthly Social Security benefits; (b) age <65 years and receiving Social Security Disability Income (SSDI), (c) age <65 years with a diagnosis of amyotrophic lateral sclerosis (ALS), (d) diagnosis of end-stages renal diseases, and (e) age >18 years acquiring disability before age 22 years. AT devices, which are referred to as "durable medical equipment" (DME) by Medicare, are covered by Medicare Part B, and are defined as equipment that is used primarily to serve medical necessity, can withstand repeated use, and is seldom useful to a person in the absence of an injury and illness. AT devices that are funded through Medicare Part B are designed for use by clients in the home environment with the ability of substituting (lost) body functions. Medicare funding generally works in combination with funding by other insurance agencies, with Medicare paying approximately 80% of the cost of the AT device and the insurance company (or clients themselves) covering remaining 20%. A medical justification letter identifying need for that particular piece of AT equipment is an essential prerequisite for Medicare funding.

2. *Medicaid.* Medicaid provides medical coverage for individuals with limited income and individuals with disabilities who meet the income eligibility guidelines. Medicaid is a state-governed program. Therefore, the eligibility criteria differ from one state to the other. Eligibility criteria for Medicaid are (a) a person enrolled in a government benefits program such as Supplemental Security Income (SSI), (b) a person with a significant disability receiving SSDI and meeting income eligibility criteria, (c) the parent of a disabled child (age <21 years) who meets SSDI and income guidelines, and (d) person previously receiving SSI but who is now working. Medicaid pays for AT that is medically necessary, and should be under the fee schedule. If the device does not have a fee schedule or if its cost exceeds the amount of fee schedule, a prior authorization is required. Medicaid is always referred to as the "payer of last resort," meaning that a person is eligible to apply through Medicaid for AT if other insurance agencies have denied provision of that service.

3. *Office of Vocational Rehabilitation (OVR).* OVR is a federally funded state-governed program that helps individuals with disabilities to resume and retain employment. The goal of provision of AT devices through OVR is to meet the vocational needs of individuals with disabilities. The wide range of AT services funded by OVR includes work evaluation, work training, and job placement, by funding AT devices from mobility aids to workstation modifications.

4. *Veterans Administration (VA).* This is a federally funded program that provides healthcare benefits, including AT, to eligible individuals. Enrollment in the VA system is required prior to determination of benefit eligibility. VA administers several programs for providing AT, ranging from mobility devices to work modifications to transportation system modifications.

5. *Workers' Compensation.* Workers' compensation is a state-run insurance program that provides health benefits to those who incurred employment-related injuries and/or diseases. AT includes equipments and home modifications, which a person receives with a physician's prescription and prior authorization for that device through a service provider, which is typically a private insurance company.

6. *Education.* Education-based programs are governed by local school districts in order to provide appropriate public education to a child with a disability. A child (age <21 years) with a disability is deemed eligible for the special education program [viz., an Individualized Education Program (IEP)] if it is determined that utilization of the AT device is necessary for that child to complete his or her school-related activities both at home and at school.

7. *Private Health Insurance.* Reimbursement of AT services differs significantly among private insurance providers. However, they follow the same guidelines as that of Medicare, and medical necessity is the basis for the justification of AT-related services.

1.8.2 The Funding Procedure for AT Devices

In spite of variation in funding processes for reimbursement of AT-related services, there are some common rules, and the following steps apply in seeking funding for all AT-related services:

1. *Identification of Insurance Source.* Even though the best practice should never be based on the type of insurance that a client has, a thorough evaluation of this resource is essential. Since the objectives of different insurance agencies differ, this understanding can help achieve a fit between the insurance agency's objectives and the client's objectives.
2. *Procedural Coding.* The Center for Medicare and Medicaid Services (CMS) has developed a common procedural coding system (HCPCS) and constantly revised codes for different AT devices and AT-related services. These codes are very critical since they define the specific purpose that an AT [durable medical equipment (DME)] device serves and also indicates specific service utilization. The main purpose of these codes is to enable clinicians to bring uniformity to their billing. Understanding these codes is also crucial for writing a better justification letter, showing a match for a person's need by prescribing a specific AT device.
3. *Justification Letter.* Irrespective of the type of insurance agency involved, a justification letter is the most important component of the AT funding procedure. The purpose of a justification letter is to provide a rationale for providing a particular AT device or ordering AT-related services that can (a) meet medical necessities for that person, (b) compensate for the functional limitation, and (c) be the best and least cost option.
4. *Appeal Process.* This is the process that follows a denial of a requested AT service or piece of equipment. Although the appeal procedure differs for different insurance carriers, it is mediated through a clinician. Several steps are involved in the appeal process, such as identification of reasons for denial and providing reasons supporting the decision. Sometimes a request for personal appeal can be granted, where a clinician can represent the case through an attorney in a courthouse. [12,2,17,18]

1.9 CONSUMER EMPOWERMENT

In more recent decades, society has placed an increasing value on quality of life (QOL) issues and has supported the development of rehabilitative services and products [14]. The United States has experienced the passage of several significant pieces of state and federal legislation and an increase in federal dollars spent for rehabilitative product research and development, as well as a public expectation that federal and state governments should provide financial assistance for those who need seat mobility equipment (or assistive technology) [7]. Some of the landmark legislations are the following:

1. The Rehabilitation Act of 1973, which authorized the expenditure of federal funds for the training persons with mental and physical disabilities for competitive employment. Through this Act, individuals with disabilities could not be excluded from or discriminated against in programs conducted by federal agencies, programs receiving federal financial assistance, federal employment, or employment practices of federal contractors. For the first time in US history, the civil rights of individuals with disabilities were protected by law.
2. There were changes in state residential institutions (during the 1970s and 1980s), with transfer of persons who previously lived in large state facilities to smaller group homes that were often located within residential communities.

3. The Fair Housing Act of 1988 was intended to increase housing opportunities of individuals with disabilities. This legislation allows individuals with disabilities to make modifications of existing buildings, if the modifications are necessary to enable a disabled person to live functionally. It also requires that new multifamily housing with four or more units be designed and built to allow access for individuals with disabilities. Despite new guarantees of civil rights and educational laws, individuals with disabilities did not achieve broad civil rights until the passage of the American with Disabilities Act (ADA).

4. The American with Disabilities Act (ADA) in 1990, a landmark federal antidiscrimination law, ensures equal access to employment opportunities, public accommodations, and state/local services. With this act, Congress identified the full participation, inclusion, and integration of individuals with disabilities into mainstream society as a national goal. Public places, such as government buildings, libraries, restaurants, and universities, must be accessible for people with disabilities. The ADA law applies to private sector as well as state and local government. The ADA titles are listed here:

   ADA Title I—Employment. This provision prohibits discrimination in employment. Employers should provide reasonable accommodation to individuals with physical and mental limitations.

   ADA Title II PART A—State and Local Government Activities. Requires that state and local governments five provide individuals with disabilities equal opportunity to benefit from all of their programs, services, and activities, such as public education, employment, transportation, recreation, healthcare, social services, courts, voting, and public meetings. State and local government are required to follow specific architectural standards in the new construction and alteration of their buildings.

   ADA Title II PART B—Public Transportation. Public transportation services, such as buses and public rail transit (subways) must comply with requirements for accessibility. Paratransit services should be provided for individuals who are unable to use the regular transit system independently.

   ADA Title III—Public Accommodations. This prohibits provision exclusion, segregation, and unequal treatment of disabled individuals in public places.

   ADA Title IV—Telecommunication. This provision ensures address, telephone, and television access for people with hearing and speech disabilities.

In addition to the enactment of legislation, there has been a gradual shift from the medical model to the social model. Increasingly, disability is perceived as a social problem, not a medical problem, as before. The social model does not deny the problem of medical impairment, but identifies disability as matter of participation in society. It is not individual limitations, which are the major cause of disability, but society's failure to provide appropriate services [19]. Another social change that affects the delivery of seating (or assistive technology) services is consumers' growing demand to be informed [14]. Increasingly, they demand to know about the treatment and products that are being recommended, and they demand their right to choose. They want to be active participants in the development of their healthcare plans. Such changes in the role of the consumer in turn modify the role of the AT practitioner from decisionmaker to information resource, guide, and partner. Current trends suggest that therapists should empower clients by providing them with information and helping them make wise choices. These services acknowledge the importance of the therapeutic interaction between the therapist and the client and highlight the client's active participation in the prescription of the seating (or assistive technology) process [14].

1.10 FUTURE TECHNOLOGY

The use of technology has demonstrated promise in assisting elderly individuals achieve independence [20]. Currently, assistive technology most commonly applied includes mobility (powered wheelchairs), communication, and environmental control. Several researches on technology devices are still in development. Examples of those technologies are (1) smart wheelchairs, (2) smart walkers, (3) wheelchair-mounted robotic arms, and (4) smart houses.

Older adults with cognitive impairment or individuals with poor vision can benefit from a device called the "smart wheelchair" [20]. A smart wheelchair consists of either a standard power wheelchair base to which a computer and a collection of sensors have been added, or a mobile robot base to which a seat has been attached. Users can choose different operation modes (e.g., line follower, door passage, obstacle avoidance, navigation) through one switch according to their individual situations and needs [20]. There are different types of wheelchair navigation systems; smart walkers can assist elderly individuals who have both mobility and visual impairment. The goal of these devices is to provide obstacle avoidance and navigation as well as to prevent falls and provide postural stability among frail elderly [21].

Wheelchair-mounted robotic arm (WMRA) technology has been an area where the use of computer-integrated controls is applied. Currently, a robotic arm can be installed on a fixed workstation [22], mounted on a mobile platform, or attached to a wheelchair [23]. WMRA provides disabled individuals with tools to independently perform activities of daily living (ADL) and vocational support tasks that would otherwise require assistance from others. Typical tasks of robotic manipulation aids include manipulating and moving objects, assistance in eating and drinking, and controlling communication devices and environment control units. Such a manipulation aid is usually controlled by its operator by a joystick, keypad, voice-command, or other input device [24].

Communication devices and environmental control units are common applications of computer integrated technology, which provides more options for individuals who have minimal physical control and increases their level of independence and productivity. A base environment control system has been built to assist people with severe disabilities in controlling their home environments. The concept of a smart house for people with disabilities is becoming popular and exciting [25]. In a smart house, an elderly person or an individual suffering from a physical disability is able to control a device in another part of the house. The smart house can also facilitate communications and enhance both personal and building security. Communication technologies in a smart house keep people with disabilities in touch with careers and loved ones, and also provide the means to reduce the number of journeys to stores or banks. Smart houses can be realized by using a central control bus, which can be implemented by cable, infrared receivers, or radio. The bus connects all sensors and all actuators in the smart house. A computer connected to a bus system with a serial interface is designed to control the bus [25].

As we have shown, elderly individuals can benefit tremendously from assistive devices to perform essential functions in their daily lives. Assistive devices are essential to help people with severe physical limitation to become more independent and to improve their quality of life.

REFERENCES

1. Barker DJ, Reid D, Cott C: Acceptance and meanings of wheelchair use in senior stroke survivors, *Am J Occup Ther*, **58**:221–30 (2004).
2. Cook AM, Hussey SM: *Assistive Technologies: Principles and Practice*, 2nd ed, Mosby St. Louis 2002.
3. Louise-Bender Pape T, Kim J, Weiner B: The shaping of individual meanings assigned to assistive technology: a review of personal factors, *Disab Rehab*, **24**:5–20 (2002).
4. Gitlin LN: Assistive technology in the home and community for older people: Psychological and social considerations, in Scherer MJ, ed, *Assistive Technology: Matching Device and Consumer for Successful Rehabilitation*, 1st ed, American Psychology Association, Washington DC, 2002.
5. Elliot R: *Assistive Technology for the Frail Elderly: An Introduction and Overview*, University of Pennsylvania, Philadelphia, (1991).
6. Chiu WY, Man DWK: The effect of training older adults with stroke to use home-based assistive devices, *Occup Ther J Res (Occup Partic Health)*, **24**:113–20 (2004).
7. Phillips B, Zhao H: Predictors of assistive technology abandonment, *Assist Technol*, **5**:36–45 (1993).
8. Shapcott N, Levy B: By the numbers. Making the case for clinical use of pressure measurement mat technology to prevent the development of pressure ulcers, *Teamrehab*, 16–9 (1999).
9. Brienza DM, Karg PE, Geyer MJ, Kelsey S, Trefler E: The relationship between pressure ulcer incidence and buttock-seat cushion interface pressure in at-risk elderly wheelchair users, *Arch Phys Med Rehab*, **82**:529–33 (2001).
10. Sprigle S, Sposato B: Physiologic effects and design considerations of tilt-and-recline wheelchairs, *Ortho Phys Ther Clin N Am*, **6**:99–122 (1997).
11. Boninger ML, Souza AL, Cooper RA, Fitzgerald SG, Koontz AM, Fay BT: Propulsion patterns and pushrim biomechanics in manual wheelchair propulsion, *Arch Phys Med Rehab*, **83**:718–23 (2002).
12. Cooper RA: *Wheelchair Selection and Configuration*, Demos, New York, 1998
13. Van Roosmalen L, Hobson DA, Karg P: Preliminary evaluation of wheelchair occupant restraint system usage in motor vehicles, *J Rehab Res Devel*, **39**:83–93 (2002).
14. Buning ME, Angelo JA, Schmeler MR: Occupational performance and the transition to powered mobility: a pilot study, *Am J Occup Ther*, **55**:339–44 (2001).
15. Pearlman JL, Cooper RA, Karnawat J, Cooper R, Boninger ML: Evaluation of the safety and durability of low-cost nonprogrammable electric powered wheelchairs, *Arch Phys Med Rehab*, **86**:2361–70 (2005).
16. Batavia AI, Hammer GS: Toward the development of consumer-based criteria for the evaluation of assistive devices., *J Rehab Res Devel*, **27**:425–36 (1990).
17. Center for Medicare and Medicaid Services: *Certificates of Medical Necessity*, US Department of Health and Human Services, Washington DC, 2006.
18. Inst of Disabilities: *Pennsylvania's Initiative on Assistive Technology (PIAT)*, Temple University, Philadelphia, 2006.

19. Albrecht GI, Seelman KD, Bury M: *Handbook of Disabilities Studies*, Thousand Oaks: Sage Publication, California, 2001.
20. Cooper RA: Inteligent control of power wheelchairs, *IEEE Engineering in Medicine and Biology Magazine*, **15**:423–31 (1998).
21. Rentschler AJ, Cooper RA, Blasch B, Boninger ML: Intelligent walkers for the elderly: Performance and safety testing of the VA-PAMAID robotic walker, *J Rehab Res Devel*, **40**:423–32 (2003).
22. Hillman M, Pullin G, Gammie A, Stammers C, Orpwood R: Development of a Robot arm and workstation for the disabled, *J Biomed Eng*, **12**:199–204 (1990).
23. Hillman M, Pullin G, Gammie A, Stammers C, Orpwood R: Clinical Experience in Rehabilitation Robotics, *J Biomed Eng*, **13**:239–43 (1991).
24. Prior SD, Warner PR: Wheelchair-mounted robots for the home environment, *Proc IEEE/RSJ Int Conf Intelligent Robots and Systems*, 1993, pp. 1194–1200.
25. Allen B: An integrated approach to smart house technology for people with disabilities, *Med Eng Phys* 203–206 (1996).

2

International Policy Context of Technologies for Disabilities: An Analytic Framework

Rene Jahiel

University of Connecticut-International Health Policy Research

2.1 INTRODUCTION

Policy refers to a course of action (or inaction) adopted by a government or other power [1]. It is embodied in laws, regulations, directives, agreements, or other binding relationships. Disability policies are policies that affect disabled people or disabling environments, regardless of whether they are directly aimed at such. Disabled people have special needs along with the same rights as other people, and they need special goods or services that have created a disability industry [2]. Thus, disability policy can be analyzed from the perspective of demand (of disabled persons for assistive devices and other goods, services, rights, or recognition) and supply (by governments and private corporations for assistive devices and other goods, services, rights, and recourses for grievance). Policies affecting disability consumers or suppliers are distributive (i.e., who gets what), regulatory (i.e., what rules have to be followed), and criminal (what actions get one in trouble with the law). International disability policy research (IDPR) deals with policies that are enforced directly by nations, that are negotiated among nations, and that depend on corporate and banking interests. IDPR is still a very young discipline, which is only beginning to emerge from international health policy research, at a time when the

---

The Engineering Handbook of Smart Technology for Aging, Disability, and Independence,
Edited by A. Helal, M. Mokhtari and B. Abdulrazak
Copyright © 2008 John Wiley & Sons, Inc.

medical model of disability is being replaced by a more complex model including social as well as individual aspects of disability and disablement [3].

This chapter first describes the population and international dimensions of IDPR, then presents a framework for the development of IDPR, and finally discusses some areas in need of further research with regard to assistive devices.

2.2 THE POPULATION DIMENSION AND THE DEMAND SIDE

Disability is described by some personal characteristics (i.e. impairments) and some features of interaction of the person with the social and physical environment [4]. *Disabled persons* are persons who are atypical in body, intellect, or emotions and who are categorized by society as disabled by a process of examination, explanation for their difference, and legitimization of their role in society and the resources that society puts at their disposal [5]. This definition highlights the great variability of the concept of disability in different historical or geographic settings, with regard to impairments and with the individual–environment interaction that modulates disability.

Policies are constructed by the groups with enough power to set a given course of action or inaction. Since there are far more nondisabled persons than disabled persons in the population, the prevailing norms and values tend to reflect those of the majority. Most of a society's policies are set by nondisabled persons for nondisabled persons [6]. In terms of dominant, repressed and emerging structural interests [7], the dominant structural interests are those of nondisabled persons and disabled persons are part of a repressed structural interest in most countries. However, in relatively recent times, organizations of people with disabilities together with disability professionals and members of the disability industry have joined to form an emerging structural interest with considerable impact on disability policies.

Disability policies have been categorized by Drake [6] into several models of what the policy does for the population with disabilities. In the *negative policy model* the state actively denies the human rights of people with disabilities. In the *laissez-faire model* the state lets people with disabilities fend for themselves or with the help of their families. In the *piecemeal approach model* the state makes incomplete responses to disablement, without a comprehensive strategic plan. In the *maximal policy model* the state has developed a strategic approach to identify and respond to the several disadvantages caused by disability that are seen to arise from the personal characteristics of people with disabilities. In the *social or rights-based policy model* the state accepts that disablement is a product of the society and environment designed by nondisabled people for nondisabled people and that it has a responsibility to serve all its citizens by actions directed to the environment as well as the person. Many poor and industrially developing countries follow the laissez-faire model. Transitional and many industrially developed countries usually follow the piecemeal model. The maximal policy model is found in a few rich Western industrialized countries. No state has yet fully implemented a social or rights-based model, despite many national and international declarations affirming these rights.

The demand side of disability has three parameters: need, political demand, and economic demand. *Need* refers to a presumably objective estimate of what has to be done to provide people with disabilities with a given status in society, depending on that society's disability policy model. *Political demand* refers to what people with disabilities and their families or representative government demand from the state in terms of subsidies and special services and goods, rights, and equalization of chances. *Economic demand* refers to what people with disabilities or the state are capable of paying and willing to pay for disability services and goods. Demand also includes supplier-induced demand.

2.3 SUPPLY SIDE AND INTERNATIONAL DIMENSION

2.3.1 Supply Side

The supply side consists of the nations, their governments, industrial companies and distributors, banks, and real estate. Supply-side policies deal with transfer of and commerce in goods and services; local development of industries producing goods or services; and the training, licensing, and monitoring of professional and nonprofessional workers who serve people in situations of disability.

2.3.2 International Dimension: Nations

The old dichotomy between industrially developed and developing countries or between rich and poor nations is now valid only at the extreme ends of the distribution of these features, because many nations have intermediate positions. The richest group of nations consists of the 30 members of the Organization for Economic Cooperation and Development (OECD), which are Western industrialized nations, Japan, South Korea, Mexico, and Turkey. The "Asian tigers" include small, rich East Asian nations (Singapore, Taiwan, and Thailand) Brazil, Russia, India, and China (BRIC) constitute an important group of large transitional nations with very rapid economic growth, with growth rates in gross domestic product (GDP) or stockmarket indices much higher than those of OECD nations [8]. Spanish-speaking American nations form another group of nations that are united by their language and culture, current social activism, and improving economic status. The Moslem Crescent consists of nations from Morocco to the west to Indonesia in the east that are united by a common Moslem culture and whose economic status ranges from very rich to very poor. Finally, sub-Saharan African nations include the poorest and least economically advanced countries and those with the highest rates of disability. Other groupings include the European Union, and a small group with advanced disability policies, the Scandinavian countries.

2.3.3 International Dimension: Transnational Organizations

Transnational organizations that unite groups of nations on the basis of economic agreements, contracts, or laws, formed during 1945–1948, in the aftermath of World War II (WWII), to help in the reconstruction of devastated nations and prevent economic dislocations such as the ones that created the setting for WWII in the 1930s. Their objectives have evolved since then in relation with changing international conditions. The main ones are the United Nations (UN), the World Health Organization (WHO), the World Bank (WB), and the World Trade Organization (WTO).

2.3.3.1 United Nations

The United Nations (UN) is the principal international organization with regard to the rights of persons in situations of disability. Its approach to rights is based on the Universal

Declaration on Human Rights [9]. It has had more specific declaration of rights of various groups of people in situations of disability, including its Resolution 3447 in 1975 on the rights of disabled persons [10]. Declarations of rights are not policies but documents that contribute to cultural change over a period of years and serve as supports and sometimes catalysts for policies.

Several UN commissions or other entities followed up with various statements delving further into the responsibilities of nations to ensure that the rights of disabled persons can be exercised in various sectors of social activities. One of the most consonant with modern social concepts of disability is the Madrid Declaration [11].

The focal point for the development of the UN mission to guide nations in disability policy is in the Division for Social Policy and Development of the UN Secretariat in New York, with its Enable series of programs, including the World Programme of Action Concerning Disabled People in 1982 [12], its Standard Rules on the Equalization of Opportunities for Persons with Disabilities in 1993 [13]. The Rule on Support Services is directly relevant to assistive technology, as it enjoins states to ensure provision of assistive devices and equipment, personal assistance, and interpreter services; to support the development, production, distribution, and servicing of assistive devices; to stimulate the development of simple and inexpensive devices using local material and local production facilities; and to recognize that all persons needing assistive devices should have financial access to them, free of charge or at a low affordable price.

This led in 2001 to an Ad Hoc Committee on a Comprehensive and Integral International Convention on the Protection and Promotion of Rights and Dignity of Persons with Disabilities, which held its seventh session in 2006 [14] and is (at the time of writing) near to achieving a consensus among nations. A convention that has been agreed on represents a commitment of states on principles for disability policies, and it is an important stepping stone for states to develop much more comprehensive disability policies in tune with contemporary concepts of disability, including policies on disability technology.

The UN is also doing regular statistical studies on disability. The UN Economic and Social Commission for Asia and the Pacific has done a survey on production and distribution of assistive devices in nations of East and South Asia and the Pacific, including a regional review [15] and reports on individual states [16].

2.3.3.2 The World Health Organization

The World Health Organization's (WHO's) health programs have already had a major effect on the prevention of disability; one may cite the prevention of poliomyelitis in the prevention of neuromotor disabilities or of trachoma in the prevention of blindness. Since the mid-1980s, WHO has developed not only a classification system but a conceptual approach to disability that has had major influence, with the ICIDH [17] and its successor, the International Classification of Functioning, Disability and Health [4]. The ICF standardization of assessment of detailed features of disability is significant with regard to disability policies, specifically, that it will provide a more standardized and controlled gauge of need, as well as a map of the present concepts of disability that are likely to influence policies [18].

2.3.3.3 The World Bank

The World Bank was founded in 1946 in order to help reconstruct and develop nations in Europe and elsewhere that had been devastated by WWII. In more recent years it has focused on programs for poor nations. It raises funds through private financial markets and receives regular donations from the world's wealthy countries. It provides recipient countries with loans, credits, grants, and technical assistance. Its approach has evolved several times [19]. Up to the 1960s it focused on large investments in physical capital and infrastructure economic growth as the route to development. In the 1960s and 1970s, it shifted to meeting people's basic needs (nutrition, health, education, family planning) as a precondition to economic and social development. In the 1980s and 1990s, in changes that paralleled the political culture of the times, the World Bank shifted to a politicoeconomic restructuring that would favor privatization, shrinkage of the public sector, trade liberalization with open markets, and economic management as tools. It is in the same period that, along with WHO, it developed. a disability-adjusted life-years (DALYs) as a tool for an economic measure of the global impact of disability and of the success of health interventions [20], which has been vigorously criticized by the disability community because it implies a "reduced value" of lives lived with a disability, equates disability with an illness, and does not take into account either the great productivity of many disabled persons in our society or the fact that disability has a social environmental component in the interaction of individual and society that determines it. Finally, it promotes prevention at the expense of inclusion [21].

There was also great opposition to the "structural adjustment" programs for their role in increasing the disparity between rich and poor, causing unemployment and closing needed public health programs. Since 2000 the academic approach to development has emphasized the need to expand the freedoms that people enjoy [22]. The World Bank (WB) shifted to a more empirical approach to understanding poverty, in several studies of "voices of the poor" [23] and to a somewhat more multidimensional approach to alleviation of poverty and development, which included health, nutrition, and education as well as various economic decisions regarding the debt of poor countries and recognition of the role of corruption in the failure of previous programs.

Furthermore, for the first time WB made a significant effort to understand poverty [24], with a commissioned report [25] and an assessment of disability in WB programs [26,27]. Also in 2002, the WB appointed its first Adviser on Disability and Development, Judith Heumann, a well-known specialist in disability who had been a cofounder of the World Institute on Disability. Since then, the WB has conducted studies to assess the number of people with disability in the areas it serves and the relationships of disability to its programs. That should pave the way for a more systematic approach to disability and development.

2.3.3.4 *The World Trade Organization*

The World Trade Organization (WTO), like the WB, had its origins in meetings at Bretton Woods in the reconstruction of Europe following WWII. But its ambitious initial project for an international trade organization was rejected by the negotiating nations, and a more modest project emerged, for control over trade in some goods, the General Agreement on Trade and Tariffs (GATT). The main purpose of GATT was to decrease in trade barriers among nations, chiefly by lowering tariffs over numerous commodities in several "rounds" of negotiations, named after the first city or nation of its meetings. In the 1980s and 1990s, following the political changes already referred to for WB, GATT and WB adopted under the leadership of the United States and United Kingdom a set of economic policies known as the "Washington consensus" that advocated deregulation, privatization, shrinkage of public services, and low inflation. The evolution of GATT into the WTO in 1994 gave these policies a structural basis. WTO expanded functions include a General

Agreement on Trade in Services (GATS) that covers financial, health, insurance, educational, and other services; an Agreement on Trade-Related Aspects of Intellectual Property Rights (TRIPPS), which covers patents, copyrights, trademarks, industrial designs, and other issues; an Agreement on Technical Barriers to trade (TBT) that reduces barriers to trade that derive from technical standards and regulations on safety and quality of products; and an Agreement on the Application of Sanitary and Phyto-sanitary standards (SPS) that reduces barriers to trade resulting from certain health-related regulations.

Clearly, the impact of WTO on assistive technology can be very important, with good as well as bad effects. For instance, harmonization of standards may raise the standards of some poor countries but may inhibit the development of local industries in other poor countries, and it might impose standards that conflict with a country's culture or modus vivendi of maintaining life under poverty. GATT does not have uniformly lowered tariffs, but tariffs on certain goods continue to be protected. High tariffs may serve as a barrier to the import of devices into a poor country, while low tariffs may make a country's own products less competitive than foreign ones and depress the sales of these products in the native country. GATS may flood a country with services from global corporations and thus limit the local development of such services. TRIPPS can be of major importance. The advanced technology products that are protected by patents or other instruments are produced mainly in technologically advanced rich countries, and their cost may not be affordable to most of the population in poor countries; a more recent example in the news was about medications for human immunodeficiency virus (HIV). TRIPPS allows some accommodation for this problem, but seldom goes far enough. As some countries, especially those of the BRIC group, develop (or already have) high capacity to produce these advanced technologies, problems have already developed in adhering to standards of protection of property rights of the Western nations, and they are bound to increase. In general, WTO, as well as WB, are supported by monies from rich industrialized countries, prominent among which are the United States, and, notwithstanding the mission of helping development, these countries are first and foremost concerned with their interest and the maintenance of a status quo that is in their favor, no matter how exploitative it often is of the poor countries. There is little likelihood that the poor countries will soon have enough power to oppose these trends. However, the BRIC countries and possibly some other South American and Asian countries are expected to successfully compete and overtake the Western countries economically and technologically in a matter of years, and it will be interesting to see what the influence of these countries (with relatively recent memories of poverty) may be on trade practices and development.

2.3.3.5 Other Organizations

Several other transnational organizations negotiate and/or impose specific practices, regulations, and restrictions on their member nations. Examples are the European Union and its member nations; the North American Free Trade Agreement (NAFTA) among the United States, Canada, and Mexico; the Central American Free Trade Agreement (CAFTA) among the United States and five Central American countries; and Mercosur (Mercado Comun del Sur), a very rapidly enlarging organization of Latin American States [29]. There is no space to discuss these agreements here, but many of the principles discussed in Section 2.3.3.4 would apply to these entities as well. However, an important difference with WTO in the relationships within each of these blocks is that they are composed of nations that are, if not equal in economy and technology to those of the WTO programs, at least much more similar economically, technologically, and culturally.

2.4 A FRAMEWORK FOR IDPR

This framework is constructed along longitudinal and cross-sectional dimensions in order to account for the full paths of international disability policy development and to allow more frequent use of quantitative research. Until now, most disability policy research has emphasized case studies, surveys across nations, and historical studies. A more systematic approach to the entire process of policy development, implementation, and assessment is feasible with contemporary science, and the proposed framework provides one step toward it.

The longitudinal dimension, or vertical axis (Fig. 2.1), provides landmarks for following an intervention from its initiation to its eventual effects on situations of disability. At each stage in the vertical axis, the cross-sectional dimension includes the various forces that determine the outcome of that stage

2.4.1 Vertical Axis (Longitudinal Dimension)

Figure 2.1 shows the longitudinal course of development and implementation of a policy. The course of action represented by a policy is usually developed by privileged groups in society who have contacts with the networks embodying the social forces needed

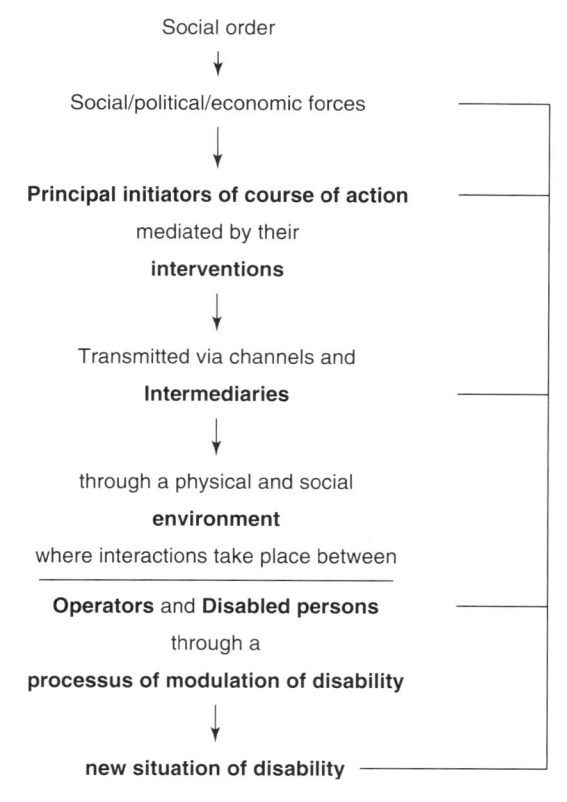

Social order
↓
Social/political/economic forces
↓
Principal initiators of course of action
mediated by their
interventions
↓
Transmitted via channels and
Intermediaries
↓
through a physical and social
environment
where interactions take place between
Operators and **Disabled persons**
through a
processus of modulation of disability
↓
new situation of disability

FIGURE 2.1 General analytical framework: vertical axis.

for informing their decisionmaking and granting them the power to initiate a course of action; those are referred to as "initiators" here. Once the initiators have triggered a course of action by their intervention, it is usually transmitted through several relays or intermediate persons or organizations down to the level of the environment where the policy action took place. At that level, the last intermediary person or organizations (I referred to as "operators" here) interact (or fail to interact) with people affected by the policy, particularly people with disabilities. That interaction may involve a process of change or modulation of the environment, the person, or the environment–person relationship that leads to a new or modified situation of disability. Alternatively, it may lead to no change and the maintenance of the status quo. Feedback loops, shown on the right side of the figure, may take place at several levels.

2.4.2 Cross-Sectional Dimension

The initiators, intermediaries, environment, and operator and disabled persons are subject to various forces from several social sectors, categorized here as government, industry and banking, professions, media, local community, family, and organizations of advocates for disabled persons. These forces may originate in general social affairs or in the feedback reaction or support shown in Figure 2.1. The pattern may be different at different levels along the Figure 2.1 axis.

2.4.3 Descriptive Studies

These studies describe the sequences of events along the vertical axis or in the interaction with forces in the cross-sectional dimension at each level. At this early stage of its development descriptive studies are very important. They provide the knowledge about variables and parameters without which analytic studies would be very limited.

2.4.4 Analytical Studies

When potentially significant variables have been identified in descriptive studies, four types of quantitative studies may be done with regression analysis or other statistical methods. Four types of regression studies are needed to capture the whole policy process, each with its own units of analysis and variables. The first has the initiators as units of analysis (e.g., decisionmakers at WHO or WB), social forces as explaining variables (e.g., participating national governments, donor corporations), and the interventions as explained variables (e.g., a decision to provide a loan to a country or to change a tariff). The second set has intermediaries as units of analysis (e.g., the people in the agency or in the recipient country who are responsible for carrying the intervention); the explaining variables would be the interventions of the initiators as well as other forces affecting the intermediaries directly. The explained variables would be the environmental changes that take place as a result of the actions of the intermediaries (e.g., loss of funds secondary to corruption, or development of a black market). The third set has the environmental unit (e.g., a location, a service) as a unit of analysis; the explaining variables are the actions of the intermediaries, and the explained variables are the modified intervention that reaches the operators and the people with disabilities as well as side effects that may be significant to them. In the fourth set, the unit of analysis would be the operators (agents who engage in interactions with disabled persons in executing the program). The explaining variables will be the actions of the intermediaries, the actions of the disabled persons, and various environmental factors; and the explained variables would be the changes that occur in the situation of disability. A similar set of studies would have the disabled persons as units of analysis and the same explaining and explained variables as in the preceding example.

2.5 RESEARCH AREAS FOR INTERNATIONAL DISABILITY TECHNOLOGY POLICY RESEARCH

There has been relatively little research on the international policy aspects of disability technology, in comparison with the relatively large amount of research on the population dimension of disability policy and on general international technology policy. Some of the latter, for instance, on pharmaceuticals, is relevant to disability; however, the focus of this last section will be assistive technology.

The first point that needs to be made is that there is a great variety of technological aids and devices, as illustrated by the chapters of this book, of different levels of complexity and sophistication and cost, while the large majority of disabled people who live in the poor countries and even some transitional ones (as well as many poor people elsewhere) have access only to the least developed products. Many people in the poor areas might do much better with the higher forms of technology, although many people in these areas may not need the higher forms of technology, and many people in affluent countries might do just as well with less advanced technology. There is a need to bring more order in this process. Possibly, a first step might be to develop a classification of assistive devices along a model analogous to the one used in the WHO. International Classification of Functioning, Disability and Health (ICF). This would include a classification of assistive devices relative to their enabling function (analogous to the body function and structural component of the ICF classification), a scoring of each item of technology according to its enabling power (this would be analogous to the severity qualifiers in ICF), a classification of societal activities that would require various levels of complexity of the devices (there is there a rough analog of the activity/participation component of ICF), and a classification of cultural or political factors that might facilitate or impede use of the technologies. (analogous roughly to the environment component of ICF).

A second area is the elucidation of the causal factors involved in the career of a policy from its inception to its impact (or lack thereof) on people with disabilities, along the lines discussed in relation to Figure 2.1. There is a great deal of conflict about interpretations of what is happening to international disability policies including those related to technology. Transparency is badly needed, and a systematic research program as discussed in relation to Figure 2.1 would go a long way to provide this transparency in a manner that may be acceptable to all parties.

Similar studies would be particularly important with regard to BRIC. These countries may well be the leaders in disability technology and in IDPR in the next decade or two, and they are building on a relatively clean slate. They may well be the leaders in the large-scale development of universal design.

Finally, IDPR on technology transfers among countries of similar political economy and culture (as in the European Union, BRIC, or Mercosur). The growth of these blocs since the mid-1970s is at least as significant as the growth of GATT at an earlier stage. Studies on standardization of products, harmonization of services, protection of both intellectual property and competitive innovation, tariffs and other barriers, and facilitative environments may be easier to do in these international settings than the others and serve a models for studies in other settings.

This leaves the poor countries of sub-Saharan Africa. Resolution of internecine wars, much increased debt forgiveness policies, global corruption watch, massive investments in some critical health problems such as HIV-AIDS, progress toward women's liberation, investment in free education at all levels, and widely available primary healthcare services might be needed before significant progress can be seen. Interventions to overcome disability and help disabled people to be an important productive force in the economy of the country would also be an important part of such a set of requirements, and assistive technologies and universal design would be a key to the success of such interventions.

REFERENCES

1. Heclo H: Review article: policy analysis, *Br J Polit Sci* **2**:83–102 (1972).
2. Albrecht G: *The Disability Business. Rehabilitation in America*, Sage, Santa Monica, CA, 1992.
3. Barnes C, Mercer G, Shakespeare T: *Exploring Disability. A Sociological Introduction*, Blackwell, Oxford, UK, 1999.
4. WHO: *International Classification of Functioning, Disability and Health*, World Health Organization, Geneva, 2000.
5. DePoy E, Gilson SF: *Rethinking Disability. Principles for Professional and Social Change*, Brook Cole, Belmont, CA, 2004.
6. Drake RF: *Understanding Disability Policies*, Macmillan Press, London, 1999.
7. Alford R: *Health Care Politics. Ideological and Interest Group Barriers to Reform*, Univ Chicago Press, 1975.
8. Authers J. (2006) The short view, *Financial Times* p 19 (April 13, 2006).
9. UN: *The Universal Declaration on Human Rights* (resolution 217A), United Nations, New York, 1948.
10. UN: *A Compendium of Declarations on the Rights of Disabled Persons*, United Nations, New York, 1988.
11. The Madrid Declaration: *Non Discrimination Plus Positive Action Results in Social Inclusion*, 2003 (available at http://www.madriddeclaration.org/dec/MADRID_DECLARATION_EN-final.htm; last accessed 4/25/06).
12. UN: *World Programme of Action Concerning Disabled Persons*, UN Resolution 37/52, annex, Dec 3, 1982, United Nations, New York, 2006.
13. UN: *The Standard Rules on the Equalization of Opportunities for Persons with Disabilities*, UN Resolution 48/96, annex, Dec 20, 1993, United Nations, New York, 2006.
14. UN: Ad hoc Committee on a Comprehensive and Integral International Convention on the Protection and Promotion of the Rights and Dignity of Persons with Disabilities, 2006 (papers accessible at http://www.un.org/esa/socdev/enable/rights/adhoccom.htm or http://www.un.org/esa/socdev/enable/rights/ahc/documents.htm).
15. UN: Economic and Social Commission for Asia and the Pacific, Production and distribution of assistive devices for people with disabilities, Part I, *Proc Technical Workshop on the Indigenous Production and Distribution of Assistive Devices, Regional Review*, United Nations, New York, 1997.

16. UN: Economic and Social Commission for Asia and the Pacific, Production and distribution of assistive devices for people with disabilities, Part II, *Proc Technical Workshop on the Indigenous Production and Distribution of Assistive Devices, Regional Review*, United Nations, New York, 1997.
17. WHO: *International Classification of Impairments, Disabilities and Handicaps*, World Health Organization, Geneva, 1980.
18. Bickenbach JE, Chatterji S, Badley EM, Ustun TB: Models of disablement, universalism, and the international classification of impairments, disability, and handicap, *Soc Sci Med* **48**:1171–1187 (1999).
19. Ruger JP: The changing role of the World Bank in public health, *Am J Public Health* **95**:60 (2005).
20. Murray CJL, Lopez AD: *The Global Burden of Disease*, World Bank, Washington, DC, and Harvard School of Public Health, Cambridge, MA, 1996.
21. Groce N, Chamie M, Me A: *Measuring the Quality of Life: Rethinking the World Bank's Disability Adjusted Life-Years*, Rehabilitation-International, 1998 (accessible at http://www.rehab-international.org3publications/rivoli49/measuring quality.html).
22. Sen A: *Development as Freedom*, Knopf, New York, 1999.
23. Narayan D, Chambers M, Shah MK, Petesch P: *Voices of the Poor: Crying Out for Change*, Oxford Univ Press, New York, 2000.
24. World Bank: *Partnership in Development: Progress in the Fight against Poverty*, World Bank, Washington, DC, 2004.
25. Metts Rl: *Disability Issues: Trends and Recommendations for the World Bank*, Social Protection Discussion Paper 0007, World Bank, Washington, DC, 2000.
26. Stienstra D, Fricke Y, D'Aubin A, Research Team Canadian Center on Disability Studies: *Baseline Assessment: Inclusion and Disability in World Bank Activities*, World Bank, Washington, DC, 2002.
27. Stienstra D, Walters C, Grant H, Huang H-M, Troschuk I: *Women with Disabilities: Accessing Trade*, 2004 (last updated 12/13/04; accessible at http://www.swc-cfc.gc.ca/pubs/pubspr/0662367391/index_e.html; last accessed 4/25/06).
28. Shaffer ER, Waitzkin H, Brenner J, Jasso-Aguilar R: Global trade and public health, *Am J Public Health* **95**:23–34 (2005).
29. Mercosur, 2000 (accessible at http://en,wikipedia.org/wiki/Mercosur, or at http://www.mercosur.int/).

3

Technology for Individuals with Disabilities: Government and Market Policies

Katherine D. Seelman
University of Pittsburgh

> The National Science and Technology Policy Organization and Priorities Act of 1976 has just about everything in it that would be useful, except the word "handicapped" ... add a focus on the special needs of the handicapped to be served by new scientific and engineering technological developments.
>
> —Irving P. Schloss

3.1 INTRODUCTION

In the quotation above, Irving P. Schloss [1,2], on behalf of the American Foundation of the Blind in 1976, made a plea to have the newly adopted US science and technology framework serve the innovation needs of people with disabilities. His request was not met. As a result, science and technology policy, like so much of disability policy, has been developed mostly on separate tracks [3,4]. One track is for the mainstream population and the other, for people with disabilities.

The Engineering Handbook of Smart Technology for Aging, Disability, and Independence,
Edited by A. Helal, M. Mokhtari and B. Abdulrazak
Copyright © 2008 John Wiley & Sons, Inc.

3.2 PURPOSE

This purpose of this chapter is to present and analyze US policy related to technology that supports individuals with disabilities who are age 18 or older. Policy analysis will consider whether existing policy is in alignment with consumer preferences and related needs for innovation as well costs and benefits to the public. Younger and older individuals with disabilities have a widely expressed preference to move beyond the confines of health services policies [5,6]. Research findings indicate that people with disabilities, especially those under 75 years of age, prefer policies that allocate technology resources that will more fully support them in the mainstream of their communities rather than in institutions. While this population is segmented by age, need, and to some extent preference, the disability population has identified housing as one shared critical issue.

Preference for participation in the mainstream of social institutions is beginning to be reflected in epidemiologic studies of factors that determine health [7] as well as disability classifications [8], paradigms [9], and in technology itself. Emerging technologies, such as pervasive computing and smart devices, have applications in housing and in the community that can support consumer preferences for independence. Policy issues involve the cost and benefits of allocating significant public resources to institutional living and acute care rather than community living and social integration; disincentives to work for those of working age; and technology-related questions of risk, safety, efficacy, usability, accessibility, and privacy. Health, demographic, and other characteristics of the user populations constitute important data for policy decisionmakers as they allocate resources to certain population segments within the older adult and disability populations to the detriment of others.

3.3 POLICY CONTEXT

Technology for individuals with disabilities is embedded in a complex policy context. Policy itself is not easy to categorize. Discrimination law plays an important role and is a factor in categorizing policy. Discrimination takes many forms such as exclusion from services, failure to make reasonable accommodations, and problems related to accessibility.

The policy section reflects the somewhat circuitous evolution of policy from benefits, to services to environmental access with some evidence of increasing interest in innovation. Law, policy, and programs related to technology have been organized into the following categories: (1) mainstream law such as the National Science and Technology Policy Organization and Priorities Act described, in the introductory chapter quotation [1,2]; (2) mainstream benefits such as Medicaid, which may provide assistive technology (AT) reimbursement coverage; (3) antidiscrimination law, such as the Rehabilitation Act of 1973 [10] and the Americans with Disabilities Act of 1990 (ADA) [10] covering employment and other services, as well as environmental access policies for special populations; (4) technology-specific laws such as the Decoder Circuitry Act of 1990 [10] and the Telecommunications Act of 1996 [10], which support technology adaptations, environmental access, and universal design as a means of integration into mainstream social institutions; and (5) policy implications of emerging technologies such as telehealth, pervasive computing, and smart technology. Definitions of assistive technology (AT), environmental access, and emerging technologies are presented in the following sections.

3.4 POLICY STUDIES

Policies related to technology for older adults and people with disabilities have been the subject of many studies and have been organized and described in charts and tables [11,12]. They often concentrate on public income and health benefit programs such as Social Security Disability Insurance (SSDI) and Medicare and Supplemental Security Income (SSI) and Medicaid. The Centers for Medicare and Medicaid Services (CMS) within the US Department of Health and Human Services, for example, makes important Medicare reimbursement decisions about durable medical devices such as wheelchairs, after determining that these devices meet a standard of medical necessity. Health policy and civil rights policy are often in conflict because the former uses a medical standard and the latter uses a social integration standard to allocate resources. Nonetheless, income and health programs have large budgets and are critically important to individuals with disabilities because they provide reimbursement and other benefits. In contrast, the ADA and many other policies related to AT and environmental access do not have budgets so that costs of research and development (R&D), employment accommodations, manufacture, and delivery are absorbed by the private sector. These costs involve adoption and use of AT and modification and construction of buildings, public spaces, and transportation and information systems.

A comprehensive policy overview suggests that terms such as *durable medical equipment* (DME) used by CMS and even AT are increasingly inadequate to describe the sweep of innovation and the medical, functional, and social integration needs of the disability population. A focus on benefits and service policies alone is inadequate to meet the challenge of technology needs of older adults, individuals with disabilities, and their providers and caregivers.

3.5 TECHNOLOGY DEFINITIONS, CLASSIFICATIONS, AND PARADIGMS

3.5.1 Assistive Technology (AT)

While definitions of AT are integrated into a number of pieces of legislation such as the Technology Related Assistance for Individuals with Disabilities Act (hereafter referred to as the *Tech Act*) of 1988 and the Older Americans Act of 1965 [13,14], there is no internationally accepted standard definition or term for AT. AT is characterized by personal adaptations and customization to the body condition of the intended user. AT definitions tend to support function and social activities for people with mobility, sensory, or cognitive disabilities. AT includes a wide range of devices such as special computer input devices, hearing aids, and screen readers for the blind. However, mainstream devices with special-use applications, such as a personal digital assistant (PDA), which is used as a memory prompter, face reimbursement problems because they are not devices dedicated only to special needs.

An international standard, ISO 9999, defines a technical aid (for disabled persons) as "any product, instrument, equipment or technical system used by a disabled person, especially produced or generally available, preventing, compensating, monitoring, relieving or neutralizing the impairment, disability or handicap" [15]. Studies of AT by the US Department of Commerce and the European Commission (EC) define assistive technology with more of a focus on function [16,17]. The EC defines AT as follows: "AT refers to products, devices or equipment that are used to maintain, increase or improve the functional capabilities of people with disabilities" [17].

In the United States, technical aids are frequently referred to as *AT* or *assistive devices*. The definition of AT is usually based on the Tech Act. The Tech Act defines an AT device as "any item, piece of equipment or product system, whether acquired commercially, modified, or customized, that is used to increase, maintain, or improve functional capabilities of individuals with disabilities" [13]. The Older Americans Act defines AT as "technology, engineering methodologies, or scientific principles appropriate to meet the needs of, and address the barriers confronted by, older individuals with functional limitations" [14]. AT is not recognized as a benefit category by CMS. However, durable medical equipment (DME) is recognized as a benefit category, and a medical necessity standard is applied to DME. The Tech Act, the Older Americans Act, and CMS-administered health programs of Medicare and Medicaid are service-related and do not provide subsidies or incentives for device research and development (R&D), manufacture, and marketing [18,19].

3.5.2 AT, Orphan Technology, and Universal Design

AT is also characterized by small and fragmented markets and is sometimes referred to as "orphan technology" when the market size is under 200,000 [20,21]. Markets are routinely configured on the basis of availability of third-party payments. AT companies are often without the means to invest in R&D for next-generation products. Assistive technology products may enter the market late, sometimes to compensate for lack of universally designed mainstream products that could accommodate a broader range of function.

In the 1980s the US architect Ron Mace introduced the notion of universal design and defined it as "an approach to design that incorporates products as well as building features which, to the greatest extent possible, can be used by everyone" [22]. The concept of universal design has generated a movement around the world to develop products that are designed for the broadest range of function. However, technology design occurs at the R&D stage, but user involvement in participatory design is not a norm in product development.

Harry Knops, past president of the Association for the Advancement of Assistive Technology in Europe, highlighted design for diversity as an objective in shaping future AT solutions [23]. He identified the following as a family of AT solutions: (1) mainstream consumer goods, (2) design for all, (3) development of optimal accessibility features, (4) plug-in accessibility systems, and (5) standalone AT. While Knops did not rank these solutions, the standalone AT solution, which most closely approximates AT devices, might well be the least desirable solution and a target for absorption by the other solutions. Perhaps even more so than those of Europe and the United States, Japan's AT market strategies seem to be influenced by the sharp growth in its aging population. Japan has approached the small market problems associated with AT by focusing on the manufacturing and market stages of technology development and diffusion. Japan has been making widely available "common-use products" [24]. Common-use products are used by a broad range of users and thus create a larger market than do traditional AT devices.

3.5.3 Environmental Access and Emerging Technology

There are no widely accepted definitions of environmental access and emerging technologies. *Environmental access* is used here to refer to technology that provides reasonable accommodations and accessibility that lead to social integration of people with disabilities, such as lifts in buses. Environmental access is more associated with large-scale systems such as transportation and mainstream products such as PDAs. *Emerging technologies* are advanced mainstream technologies, such as telehealth, pervasive computing, and smart devices that can collect, process, and transmit information; communicate; move; execute tasks; and learn. Existing and potentially emerging technology applications include smart houses and remote health monitoring. Their availability as supports for people with disabilities will depend on "emerging" policy and market factors.

3.5.4 Disability Classifications and Disability Paradigms

A 2003 epidemiology study on health determinants in life expectancy reports an important shift from studying the quantity of remaining life to studying the quality of remaining life, from a focus on mortality to morbidity determinants, including socioeconomic, political, and cultural factors [7]. This study references the World Health Organization's International Classification of Functioning, Disability and Health (ICF) [8] in part because the ICF framework includes morbidity determinants that support individual function such as AT. Epidemiology has been traditionally associated with the World Health Organization's International Classification of Disease and a paradigm of disability that is reductive to medical conditions. The medical paradigm of disability has been instrumental in the formation of policy, as the following section illustrates.

3.6 LEGACY OF DISCRIMINATION

As the quotation introducing this chapter [1] indicates, the science and technology interests of individuals with disabilities have a history of being somewhat segregated from the mainstream of US science and technology efforts. Institutions with a mission in science policy and basic R&D such as the White House Office of Science and Technology Policy, the federal laboratories, the National Science Foundation, and the National Institutes of Health (NIH) have had limited involvement in Rehabilitation Science and engineering R&D that supports independent living [3]. Small agencies and programs, such as the National Institute on Disability and Rehabilitation Research (NIDRR) in the Department of Education, Rehabilitation Research and Development Centers in the Department of Veterans Affairs, and the National Center for Medical Rehabilitation Research (NCMRR) within NIH, have been more directly involved in rehabilitation and engineering applications targeted to functional supports, environmental accessibility and community integration. In the absence of a disability presence in large, well-financed basic research, many products conceptualized at the R&D stage are not designed for use within the functional range of individuals with disabilities [25].

3.6.1 Human Factors and Participation in R&D

Human factors is a field involving research into human psychosocial, physical, and biological characteristics and working to apply that information with respect to the design, operation, or use of products or systems for optimizing human performance, health, safety, and/or habitability. Human factors in AT development are not always identical to factors considered in the development and use of mainstream consumer products, the design for which is guided by the profile of the typical, average consumer. The significance of the inclusion of human factors in the design process cannot be overestimated. As medical devices, for example, increasingly move from clinical locations to the home, they will have to meet safety and efficacy criteria for usability by lay caregivers and consumers. Human factors, participatory design, and engineering psychology data are crucial to the development and implementation of criteria for fair, accessible, and usable evaluation and testing by such federal agencies as the US Food and Drug Administration (FDA) [26].

Unlike the cultural norms of rehabilitation engineering research, business culture and norms guiding basic and even applied research do not seem to support user involvement. Business norms present a significant barrier to the introduction of human factors that would influence the product design process to represent the range and diversity of function common to people with disabilities.

The NIH, the FDA, and the private sector use established methods of evaluation to test the safety and efficacy of technology. They include case studies, consensus development, randomized controlled trials (RCTs), and economic analysis as well as metrics that measure safety and efficacy [26]. Of these methods, only case studies and consensus development are concerned with social, ethical, and legal dimensions of devices. For many years, RCTs discriminated against women and minorities who were excluded because they did not meet the profile of average, typical subjects. Women's health groups and Congress brought pressure on NIH and FDA to address these biases. Apparently both NIH and FDA complied, but FDA took less aggressive action. The population of older adults and people with disabilities is large and has well-honed advocacy tools with which to bring about cultural change but has not targeted R&D.

3.7 POPULATION SIZE, DEMOGRAPHICS, AND AT USER TRENDS

Size, value, health, and demographic characteristics of the disability population provide important information on which to base current and future technology policy decisions and market investments. When older adults are counted as part of the population of people with disabilities, the size of the population generates heightened interest in disability issues by government policymakers and targeted industries. Although the adult disability market is segmented by age and by need [11,12], a large voting block with considerable purchasing power or dependence on federal outlays can influence political decisions and market investments.

3.7.1 Age

The adult disability population can be divided into the following age segments: (1) 21–65, (2) 65–84, and (3) 85+ years. The growth of the older population has mostly outpaced the total population and the population under 65 [27,28]. Segment 3 of the 65+ population is growing most rapidly. While age is not necessarily an indicator of disability, research shows that the incidence and prevalence of disability increase with age and conditions may vary by age. For example, people who are over 85 are at highest risk for Alzheimer's disease (AD), with women making up a larger proportion of AD patients than men, at an average lifetime cost per patient of $174,000 [27]. In general, research findings show that the average costs of services associated with maintaining an elderly person at home throughout the entire course of disability (i.e., older persons who develop disabilities while in the community) are estimated at about $174,000 [29]. The average expected lifetime costs of care for maintaining a nursing home resident in the community rather than in a nursing home is estimated to be only slightly higher, at $179,000. Nursing home residents are typically more disabled, and they also have shorter life expectancies than do individuals with disabilities living at home. Tracking and monitoring technology are examples of technologic responses to preferences for enhanced independence and community integration and related issues of potential risks and threats to safety.

While the average age of onset of spinal cord injury (SCI) is rising and the number of SCI older adults is increasing, males between the ages of 25 and 40 are at high risk [30]. Not including lost wages, the average lifetime cost of a person 25 years old at time of severe tetraplegia is $2,801,647 and a person with paraplegia, $936,088. Enhanced independence and social integration of SCI adults would greatly benefit from innovation in the workplace, housing, and AT adaptation.

Clearly, AD and SCI are associated with high public costs. However, the cost difference between community and institutional care may not be significant so that decision criteria for the allocation of public resources may broaden to include individual choice and investments in innovation. Still another cost, the cost to public programs of not returning to work or early retirement, may also be an incentive to provide more support for an accessible workplace.

3.7.2 Assets, Income, and Poverty

According to findings from research supported by the American Association of Retired Persons (AARP), since 1989 the differences in net worth by age is striking [31,32]. While mean net worth increased over the 9-year period for all age groups, the changes in median net worth were negative for all age groups under 55 and positive for all those above age 55. Moreover, the annual average increases in median net worth were substantial only for families headed by a person over age 65. Between 1989 and 1998, aggregate debt burdens increased among families headed by a person aged 50 or older within each age subgroup.

The medium household income of working-age persons with disabilities increased from $34,200 in 2003 to $34,300 in 2004 [28]. The poverty rate of working-age people with disabilities increased from 23.3% in 2003 to 24.1% in 2004. Poverty rates differ by gender and race, with women, particularly those of minority background, the poorest [27,28]. Federal public assistance programs spent $226 billion in 2002 on working-age people with disabilities, including cash or in-kind benefits or 2.2% of the nation's GDP and 11.3% of all federal outlays [33]. These expenditures mostly provided benefits, such as income support and healthcare.

3.7.3 Employment

While advancements in medicine, rehabilitation, technology, and civil rights laws may suggest that the impact of impairment on employment would lessen, actual rates of employment continue to be low among individuals with disabilities under 65 [34]. The employment rate of working-age people with disabilities decreased from 37.9% in 2003 to 37.8% in 2004, while the employment rate of people without disabilities increased from 77.6% in 2003 to 77.8% in 2004 [28]. Labor force participation rates of men over 65 have increased from 17.5% in 2000 to 18.6% in 2003 and women over 65, from 19.4% to 22.7%. Retiree healthcare benefits may play a major role in decisions about when to retire [11], and income and health benefits are also important factors in decisions about employment for those under 65.

These trends show that older adults living today have limited assets that could be used for purchase of emerging technologies that support independence. However, younger adults and future generations may have limited purchasing power and be burdened by debt. These trends also show a need to address potential and existing public costs related to the support of people who are over 85 and younger people with disabilities who do not have sufficient access to the workplace.

3.8 ASSISTIVE TECHNOLOGY TRENDS

This section explores findings about usage trends drawn mostly from studies by AARP [35] and from a national study in 2005 released by the National Institute on Disability and Rehabilitation Research (NIDRR) of AT users age above age 18 that includes a summary of a number of other surveys and studies of AT [36]. According to the NIDRR study, AT use was not related to gender, age, race, or impairment level. Respondents with higher levels of education were the most likely users. The prevalence of AT and IT use at school and at work was 36%; use at home was 49%, and use in the community was 50%. Most of the assistive devices enhanced mobility, such as crutches and wheelchairs. However, hearing aids and, oxygen tanks were also the most frequently used devices. Most respondents said that AT made them more productive, but 24% reported that AT did not substantially reduce their dependence on other people. Almost 40% of respondents said that they paid for AT or IT themselves or with help from a family member, and a similar percentage relied on a third-party payer, such as private health insurance, Medicare, or Medicaid, to pay for the needed AT or IT. Other studies indicate that even a larger percentage of payments come from consumers and their families [10].

3.8.1 Home Modification

Home modifications studies typically include older adults and show how the use of these modifications increases independence by accommodating functional limitations [36]. Most respondents indicated that they wanted to remain at home, and many respondents were concerned about paying for the modifications. Kitchens and bathrooms were reported as having the greatest problem areas. Study findings suggest that a family member and friends pay for most modifications. The need for home modifications and universally designed homes are among the key policy implications of a report released in 2003 by AARP on independent living and disability [5].

3.8.2 Education

There are limited studies on technology use in secondary education. However, those that do exist seem to indicate that institutions of higher education have higher rates of environmental accommodations than technology and adaptive equipment accommodations [36].

3.8.3 The Workplace

Studies show that assistive technology in the workplace is a major problem for individuals with disabilities [37]. Using equipment and access are the two most frequently mentioned problems. In a 2006 study in southwestern Pennsylvania, older workers found especially attractive benefit programs that included assistive technology and ergonomics [38]. Telecommuting may also be a potential solution for those who have transportation challenges [39].

While AT use is widely acknowledged to support people in conducting of their lives, findings suggest that policy is not aligned with the need for AT. Insufficient resources exist for research and development, availability of training, reimbursement and accessibility of housing, the workplace and the Internet.

3.9 POLICY RELATED TO TECHNOLOGY FOR ADULTS WITH DISABILITIES

This section presents technology-related mainstream and special population law, policy and programs as well as exploring policy implications of emerging technology that may have the potential to be supportive of independence and community integration. Policies are explored in terms of consumer preferences to live in the community, related costs and benefits considerations and finally for implications related to innovation and markets. While taxation policy has not been presented, US tax policy has been used as an incentive or as a funding tool for individuals with disabilities, employers, and businesses to make AT more affordable and available [40].

3.9.1 Mainstream Science and Technology Policy

According to *Enabling America,* a study of federal rehabilitation science and engineering, total federal spending on programs emphasizing rehabilitation-related research represented $147 million or about 0.2% of the 1995 federal R&D budget [41]. While this percentage continues to be representative of federal allocations, there are other signs that the federal government, in particular the White House, is becoming more involved in technology innovation for adults with disabilities across the age span. In 1997, the White House National Economic Council hosted a meeting to discuss industry involvement in an accessible Internet [3]. Subsequently, the National Science Foundation and NIDRR funded the World Wide Web Accessibility Initiative (WAI) [42], an international Program Office of the World Wide Web Consortium with a mission of removing accessibility barriers. The WAI approach to Web accessibility has revolved around three interrelated initiatives: content accessibility of Websites, usability of Web browsers and media players, and Web authoring tools and technologies to support production of accessible content and sites.

In 2005, the White House joined the Department of Veteran's Affairs (VA) and a broad range of federal agencies and the private sector in hosting the White House/VA Conference on Emerging Technologies [43]. The purpose of the conference was to bring together researchers, funders, policymakers, and government leaders to talk about innovation, collaboration, and barriers to the development of rehabilitation technology. Eric Dishman of Intel, who is chairman of the Center for Aging Services Technology (CAST), was particularly complementary of the support of the White House Office of Science and Technology. Established in 2003, CAST has become a national coalition of more than 400 technology companies, aging services organizations, research universities, and government representatives [44].

3.9.2 Benefits Policy

A wide range of benefits are available to veteran-eligible military members who leave the service after retirement or after their military obligations have been met [11,45]. For civilians, the Social Security Act, which was signed into law in 1935, provides the framework for US civilian benefits policy [11,46]. As the brief description below indicates, both military and civilian benefits cover AT devices or durable medical equipment and related services if the client meets eligibility requirements. Veteran's benefit programs are more supportive of technologies that improve functioning and serve as long-term social supports than are civilian benefits programs.

3.9.2.1 Benefits for Veterans

Veteran benefits include medical, dental, and health services; training and rehabilitation services; and home loans. Veterans with some specific disabilities can receive funds to help pay for specially adapted housing or adapting a vehicle. The VA may fund assistive devices for inpatient or follow-up outpatient care. For example, the VA can purchase and fund hearing aids, wheelchairs, artificial limbs, or orthopedic shoes for disabled veterans.

3.9.2.2 Benefits for Civilians: Social Security

Within the framework of the Social Security Act, "social security" is based on a concept of providing income and health maintenance programs for families in such instances as retirement, disability, poor health, or death [47]. In general, a person must pay into the Social Security system by working and allowing a certain amount of income to be deducted from earnings. People over 65 and some disabled people under 65 are covered under Medicare health insurance established in 1965.

To be considered disabled under Social Security law, a person must have a physical or mental condition that prevents employment or performance of any substantial gainful work. The condition must be expected to last for at least 12 months or to result in death. If the disability is severe, the worker is eligible for Social Security Disability Insurance (SSDI), which was established in 1956. Under certain conditions recipients may maintain Medicare coverage while working. People seldom return to work, due in part to fear of loss of cash benefits and health insurance and, if a work attempt fails, reluctance to undergo the lengthy and complex process of reapplication. Social Security Administration programs do not directly purchase, rent, or lease adaptive technologies [11].

Proof-of-disability requirements are considered major disincentives to return to work and still another example of a lag between early disability policy, which focuses more on medical conditions, and later disability policy, such as the ADA, which focuses more on social integration. Disincentives to employment contribute to the poverty rate of individuals with disabilities and to the huge federal outlays for public assistance programs described in Section 3.7.2 (above).

3.9.2.3 Social Security and Medicare

Medicare is a healthcare program that routinely requires research and clinical evidence of medical necessity to support durable medical equipment (DME) coverage. CMS policy also imposes in-the-house restrictions on the use of devices so that reimbursement decisions are, in part, based on evidence of marginal ambulation. Medicare coverage is most intensive in personal DME for activities of daily living (ADL) such as bathing, toileting, and transferring, but does not include housing modifications.

Medicare has made minor adjustments to coverage to meet the need for functional supports. On January 1, 2000, the Medicare National Coverage Decision for Speech Generating Devices was enacted by the Centers for Medicare and Medicaid Services (CMS) [48,49]. Computer-based and dedicated PDA-based augmentative–alternative communication (AAC) devices would be covered when they have been modified to only run on AAC software. When coverage criteria are met and medical necessity has been demonstrated, funds for speech-generating devices (SGDs) are available. However, CMS policy definitions of the types of technology considered for funding and the categories for SGDs are not based on the state of the art, or full capabilities and range of AAC technology [50]. CMS policy fails to acknowledge the significance of language. SGDs are language tools and not technology tools. This results in frequent conflict between CMS policy and the ethics of AAC professionals. Outcome data support the importance of interfacing SGDs with mainstream and off-the-shelf technology (e.g., cell phones, computers) and using SGDs to support tasks and activities other than speech output communication (computer emulation, email, environmental controls, etc.).

It is instructive to note that the American Medical Association (AMA) develops DME coding for CMS. In 2004, the AMA adopted a common procedural terminology (CPT) code for AT services that is also highly restricted [49]. The AMA's CPT manual supports the WHO International Classification of Disease, which is medically focused, and has no bridge to the International Classification on Functioning, Disability and Health.

3.9.2.4 Social Security and Social Security Disability Insurance
Social Security Disability Insurance (SSDI), which has wage caps, may allow some impairment-related work expenses to be deducted as costs against wages. They include items such as medical or prosthetic devices, residential modifications, and special transportation [51].

3.9.2.5 Social Security and Supplemental Security Income
Another program administered by the Social Security Administration for low-income individuals is Supplemental Security Income (SSI), established in 1972. SSI is not based on work credits. Eligibility is based on age (65 or older), income guidelines, and disability at any age for persons who earn below a specific income. SSI beneficiaries must meet the same inability to work requirements as do Social Security beneficiaries.

3.9.2.6 Social Security and Medicaid
Medicaid is the health insurance plan for SSI recipients. Medicaid is a state–federal partnership with a core set of benefits and others that states can agree to cover such as AT. Under certain conditions Medicaid eligibility for SSI recipients can be continued if the recipients engage in substantial gainful employment. Medicaid is the larges public coverage for AT. While state Medicaid plans vary in their coverage of AT, roughly 80% of plans cover some AT [11]. Medicaid does not cover most cognitive AT, transportation AT, or home modifications.

The Social Security Act authorizes multiple waiver and demonstration authorities to allow states flexibility in operating Medicaid programs [52]. Each authority has a distinct purpose, and distinct requirements. Medicaid waivers represent an important effort to cover and coordinate a range of services in the community for persons who otherwise would be living in institutions. CMS has indicated that "adaptive aids that are not covered under a State Plan, as well as communications devices can often be covered under Medicaid section 1915(c) waivers, other waivers or demonstrations" [11,53].

Two SSI programs subsidize certain AT for some persons with disabilities. A "plan for achieving self support" (PASS) allows a person to use income or resources to achieve a work goal. This money is set aside under a PASS program and is not counted in the eligibility evaluation and may increase SSI income. Impairment-related work expenses (IRWEs) were discussed in Section 3.9.2.4 as a way to reduce countable income below the limit. IRWE criteria for SSDI recipients would quality as IRWE for SSI purposes [51].

3.9.2.7 The Ticket to Work and Work Incentives Improvement Act

Health and income policy is strongly associated with the medical paradigm of disability. There have been attempts to lessen the impact of proof-of-disability restrictions on work. The Ticket to Work and Work Incentives Improvement Act of 1999 provides individuals with disabilities the option of maintaining Medicare coverage while working [54]. It encourages the states to adopt the option of allowing individuals with disabilities to purchase Medicaid coverage that is necessary to maintain employment.

3.10 SERVICES, ENVIRONMENTAL ACCESS, AND DISCRIMINATION LAW

This section focuses not only on discrimination-related services law, policy, and programs, such as the Older Americans Act, The Tech Act, the Fair Housing Amendments Act, and the Rehabilitation Act, but also on civil rights law, especially the Americans with Disabilities Act. Section 3.11 emphasizes legislation, policies and programs that are technology-specific.

3.10.1 Discrimination

Discrimination [55,56] can take many forms such as exclusion from services, failure to make reasonable accommodations, and problems related to inaccessibility. Adoption by Congress of discrimination laws was especially intense during the 30-year period from the 1970s through the 1990s. These laws address services, accommodations, and access in areas such as employment, transportation, voting, air travel, higher education, and fair housing. However, this legislation often requires that individuals seek judicial remedies. Litigation may not be a desirable path. Lawyers often cannot recap costs because of low monetary awards. Therefore, few lawyers are available to take these cases [55]. The litigation experience from Title I of the ADA, which addresses employment discrimination, indicates that plaintiffs fare poorly. Title I involves employment-related reasonable accommodations such as accessible facilities, and acquisition or modification of equipment or devices. Related court cases generated by discrimination law are not within the purview of this chapter.

3.10.2 Older Americans Act of 1965

The Older Americans Act of 1965 (OAA) [11] is administered by the Administration on Aging within the Department of Health and Human Services. OAA provides a comprehensive array of community-based services. Title III, Part B provides grants that include housing services to repair, renovate, and adapt houses to meet accessibility needs. Unlike the Rehabilitation Act, OAA does not have a budget line to support Rehabilitation Science and engineering R&D.

3.10.3 Rehabilitation Act of 1973

The Rehabilitation Act of 1973 [57,58] is administered by the Office of Special Education and Rehabilitative Services in the US Department of Education [57,58]. The Act has been amended over the years and reflects changing policy emphases over time. Definitions of disability and other terms within the Rehabilitation Act have been adopted in other pieces of legislation such as the Fair Housing Act. Title II addresses research and training carried out by the National Institute on Disability and Rehabilitation Research (NIDRR). Among its various programs, NIDRR supports an extensive network of Rehabilitation Research Engineering Centers and the Worldwide Web Accessibility Initiative.

Title I addresses vocational rehabilitation (VR) services funded by federal and state matching grants. While the program is administered by the Rehabilitation Services Administration (RSA) on the federal level, state VR agencies have considerable latitude in administering their programs. Eligibility is based on evidence that the potential client has a disability that interferes with the ability to work. VR agencies provide a wide range of services, including restoration of physical functioning, housing modifications, transportation, and the provision of AT as long as the AT is related to a vocational goal. Some VR agencies have special programs for older adults. In 2002, rehabilitation technology expenditures totaled roughly $96 million [11]. However, VR's apparent inability to successfully serve SSDI and SSI beneficiaries has been an issue for both RSA and SSA [59].

Title V of the Rehabilitation Act addresses rights and advocacy. Section 502 establishes the Architectural and Transportation Barriers Compliance Board, hereafter referred to as the *Access Board*, which has responsibility for development and compliance of a number of important guidelines, standards, and requirements under legislation such as the Architectural Barriers Act of 1968 [60], the ADA, and Section 255 of the Telecommunications Act.

Section 504 requires that services, programs, and activities, including information services, of a covered entity that receives federal funds must be accessible to and usable by people with disabilities [57,58]. Each federal agency has its own set of Section 504 requirements that apply to its own program, and each agency is responsible for enforcing its own regulations. Section 504 may also be enforced by private lawsuits. Section 508 requires that employees and citizens with disabilities have comparable access to electronic and information technology [61]. While Section 508 is within Title V—rights and advocacy—it is also a procurement policy. The US government is a large purchaser of electronic and information technology and has established procurement procedures for the purchase of accessible equipment.

3.10.4 Housing and the Fair Housing Amendment Act of 1988

Several programs within the Department of Housing and Urban Development (HUD) and the US Department of Agriculture provide lower-income individuals and those with disabilities with affordable housing and housing modification [11]. However, the Fair

Housing Amendments Act [62] is more expansive. FHA prohibits discrimination against people with disabilities. The regulations prohibit discrimination by a person in the business of selling or renting dwellings and include private owners as well as real estate agents and brokers. Landlords of rental properties must permit renters to make modifications to increase accessibility. These modifications are done at the renter's expense, and the renter has to restore the property to premodified conditions. Multifamily dwellings built for first occupancy after 1991 must meet certain accessibility standards. Private owners of single-family dwellings are for the most part exempt from FHA. Regulations also include the concept of reasonable accommodations, developed under Section 504 of the Rehabilitations Act of 1973. FHA provides a broad set of strong remedies for individuals who can prove that they are victims of disability-related discrimination. Much of the litigation is related to the ability of local government to exercise control over group living arrangements. These arrangements are often used as an economical alternative to nursing homes.

3.10.5 The Technology-Related Assistance for Individuals with Disabilities Act of 1988 as Amended and the Assistive Technology Act of 1998

The Technology-related Assistance for Individuals with Disabilities Act of 1988 authorized systems change grants to the states to increase access to AT devices and services within education, employment, and the community [36]. Since the enactment of the Tech Act in 1988, a total of over $475 million in federal funds have been appropriated.

3.10.6 The Americans with Disabilities Act of 1990

The earliest and most prominent broad-based statutes barring disability discrimination were Sections 501, 503, and 504 of the Rehabilitation Act. They prohibited federal agencies and those doing business with the government from discriminating against qualified individuals with disabilities on the basis of disability. The Americans with Disabilities Act prohibited the majority of public and private sector employers, administrators, managers, and owners of public accommodations and others from discriminating against people with disabilities. These antidiscrimination laws have had considerable and continuing impact on accessibility, the technology marketplace, and social integration.

3.11 POLICY RELATED TO ENVIRONMENTAL ACCESS AND UNIVERSAL DESIGN

An accessibility–usability–universal design thread runs throughout US legislation. The laws reflect the evolution of environmental access from a focus on the built environment, to the telecommunications environment for people with hearing impairments to the telecommunication environment across mainstream population and disability populations.

3.11.1 The Architectural Barriers Act of 1968

The Architectural Barriers Act of 1968 is the oldest federal legislation addressing accessibility. It requires that buildings and facilities that are designed, constructed, or altered with federal funds or leased by a federal agency, comply with federal standards for physical accessibility. Regulations and compliance are the responsibility of the Access Board.

3.11.2 Telecommunications Systems and Universal Design

Four laws reflect early efforts to make the telephone system and television more accessible. They also illustrate applications of universal design to broaden the range of use of mainstream telecommunication equipment and systems. In 1982, Congress passed the Telecommunications for the Disabled Act, which requires that workplace telephones used by persons with hearing aids and emergency phones be hearing-aid-compatible [63]. In 1988, Congress passed the Hearing Aid Compatibility Act, which required most telephones manufactured or imported into the United States to be compatible for use with telecoil-equipped hearing aids [64]. The Telecommunications Accessibility Enhancement Act of 1988 [65] allowed the General Services Administration to ensure that the federal communications system was fully accessible for hearing- and speech-impaired individuals. To address accessibility to television for those with hearing impairment [10], Congress enacted the Television Decoder Circuitry Act of 1990. This legislation required closed caption circuitry or a computer chip to be part of all televisions with screens 13 inches or larger manufactured for sale and use in the United States.

3.11.3 Telecommunications Act of 1996

Section 255 and Section 251(a)(2) of the Communications Act of 1934 as amended by the Telecommunications Act of 1996 require manufacturers of telecommunications equipment and providers of telecommunication services to ensure that such equipment and services are accessible and usable by persons with disabilities, if readily achievable. Thee amendments ensure that individuals with disabilities have access to a broad range of products and services such as telephones, cell phones, pagers, and call waiting [66]. The Internet and electronic mail (email) are not currently covered. The Federal Communications Commission (FCC), an independent federal agency in Washington, DC, enforces the Telecommunications Act. Accessibility complaints can be filed with the FCC, but lawsuits are not authorized, and there is no provision for damages. The following quote is a comment on the significance of the Telecommunications Act [67]:

> This was the first product design law to attempt to drive the market to create accessible products. It is not a traditional civil rights law since it is an accessible design law that does not depend on the filing of a complaint for its requirements to be enforced.

The costs of environmental access and universally designed technologies have been absorbed largely by the private sector and to some extent the public. While the environment is increasingly more accessible, new technologies, such as the Web, which are not covered by current law, continue to create lags that may be compensated for by AT or orphan technology peripheral devices or adaptations.

3.12 EMERGING TECHNOLOGIES

Emerging technologies, such as telehealth, pervasive computing, and smart technologies hold promise for addressing consumer preferences for independence and community-based living. However, they face formidable policy challenges, many of which have implications for private-sector investment in R&D, manufacturing, and marketing.

3.12.1 Telehealth

Telehealth [68,69] involves the collection and transfer of electronic data using a variety of telecommunications technology, including telephone lines, the Internet, and satellites. While telehealth has its origins in telemedicine, it also has broader applications for individuals with disabilities in activities such as vocational rehabilitation, job coaching, remote transmission of sign language interpretation, and text for deaf and hard of hearing individuals. Policy barriers to wide-scale introduction and use of telehealth include interoperability, safety, development of clinical practice protocols, reimbursement, licensure, privacy, security, and cost of using advanced telemedicine applications. Applications that would benefit consumers and caregivers, such as those with AD and SCI, include home health monitoring, including behavioral health, enhancing social networks, and the availability of clinical expertise in underserved locations.

3.12.2 Pervasive Computing and Smart Technologies

Pervasive computing is a term referring to computers that are mobile or embedded in the environment and connected to an increasingly ubiquitous network structure [70,71]. Policy challenges include standards development to connect a variety of devices, systems, and sensors that make up a multimodal, rather than a single-computer, environment. Older adults, individuals with disabilities, and caregivers may be concerned about design of inclusive product interfaces so that the digital divide is not further expanded. They may be concerned about intellectual property rights related to the ubiquitously generated information that may bar further design for accessibility, and they may perceive these technologies as threats to privacy [72]. Like telehealth, smart technologies may collect information that is essentially private using sensors and other monitoring and tracking devices [72–74]. In turn, US lawmakers and regulators may respond with requirements for embedded privacy technology and policies and procedures such as informed consent. Pervasive computing has applications in most human activities, including healthcare, smart houses, and work environments. Workstations equipped with pervasive computing technology, for example, may follow the worker's gaze and respond to the user's focus by shifting applications. This kind of innovation has the potential to enable those with SCI and other mobility and dexterity limitations to navigate the work environment.

3.13 CONCLUSIONS

Innovation opportunities are themselves pervasive but not without risk for potential investors. Government policy could provide taxation and low-cost loan and special contracting arrangement incentives, as well as mount more demonstration projects such as smart houses. These incentives would mitigate some risks and costs such as delays in product design to market time, increase in design-associated costs, costs of ensuring that the technology meets technical, reliability, safety, and functional requirements.

Commitment of government R&D resources, especially those of the National Science Foundation, is appropriate to basic research in technology independence, quality of life, and social integration. However, government policy would have to expand its disability-related focus from benefits and services to R&D, manufacturing, and marketing.

The older adult and disability population does not and is not projected to have significant purchasing power so financing innovation will turn on enhanced government subsidies and identification of other markets [27,28,31–33,75]. The Center for Aging Services (CAST), which has attracted considerable interest in and out of government, is a national coalition of technology companies that may serve as a model for capturing national and international markets in independence-enhanced technology for health, housing, information, and employment.

REFERENCES

1. Schloss IP: *Report of the Panel on Research Programs to Aid the Handicapped*, Government Printing Office, Washington, DC, 1976.
2. National Science and Technology Policy, Organization, and Priorities Act of 1976, PL 94–282.
3. Seelman KD: Science and technology: Is disability a missing factor? in Seelman KD, Albrecht G, Bury M, eds, *Handbook of Disability Studies*, Sage, Thousand Oaks, CA, 2001.
4. *IT R&D: Incorporating Accessibility for People with Disabilities. President's Information Technology Advisory Committee*, May 18, 2000, National Coordination Office for Information Technology Research and Development, 2002 (available online at http://www.itrd.gov/ac/pitac-18may00/accessibility/assess-seelman.pdf, 5/20/02).
5. Gibson MJ: *Beyond 50.03: A Report to the Nation on Independent Living and Disability*, AARP Policy Institute, April 2003 (retrieved 3/06 from http://www.aarp.org/research/housing).
6. Rich R, Erb CT, Rich RA: *Critical Legal and Policy Issues for People with Disabilities*, 2002 (retrieved 3/06 from http://papers.ssrn.com/sol3/papers).
7. Myers GC, Lamb VL, Agree EM: Patterns of disability change associated with the epidemiologic transition, in Robine J-M et al, eds, *Determining Health Expectancies*, Wiley-InterScience, 2003, pp 59–74 (retrieved 3/06 at http://www3.interscience.wiley.com/cgi-bin/bookhome/104546511/?CRETRY=1&SRETRY=0).
8. World Health Organization: *International Classification of Functioning, Disability and Health*, World Health Organization, Geneva, 2001.
9. Seelman KD: Trends in rehabilitation and disability: Transition from a medical model to an integrative model, *Encyclopedia of Special Education*, Third Edition, Cecil R. Reynolds & Elaine Fletcher-Janzen Ed, V. 3, pp. 2060–2066 2006.
10. The Rehabilitation Act of 1973, as amended; 29 USC, Americans with Disabilities Act of 1990; 42 USC §§ 12101 et seq, Decoder Circuitry Act of 1990, PL 101–431, Telecommunications Act of 1996, PL 104–104.
11. Freiman MP, Mann WC, Johnson J, Lin S, Locklear C: *Public Funding and Support of Assistive Technologies for Persons with Disabilities*, Nr.2006–04, AARP Public Policy Institute, 2006 (retrieved 3/06 from http://www.aarp.org/ppi).
12. Rehabilitation Engineering Research Center on Mobile Wireless Technologies for Persons with Disabilities: (August 2003 Update). *Policy and Regulatory Assessment: Factors Influencing Aoption of Wireless Technologies: Key Issues, Barriers and Opportunities for People with Disabilities*, Aug 2003 update (retrieved 3.06 from http://www.wirelessrerc.gatech.edu/).
13. US Technology-Related Assistance for Individuals with Disabilities Act of 1988, PL 100–407, Section 3.

14. Older Americans Act of 1965, 42 USC, Title I.
15. International Standards Organization: *ISO 9999 Technical Aids for Persons with Disabilities—Classification and Terminology*.
16. US Department Commerce, *Technology Assessment and the U.S. Assistive Technology Industry*, Bureau of Industry & Security Office of Strategic Industries and Economics, Washington, DC, 1–107, 2003 (retrieved Oct 2004 from http://www.bxa.doc.gov/DefenseIndustrialBasePrograms/OSIES/DefMarketResearchRpts/assisttechrept/).
17. European Commission: *Access to Assistive Technology in the European Union*, European Commission Directorate-General for Employment and Social Affairs Unit E4, 1–188, 2003.
18. US Congress Office of Technology Assessment: *Technology and the Handicapped*, Government Printing Office, Washington, DC, 1982 (retrieved 3/06 from http://www.wws.princeton.edu/ota/).
19. Rogers EM: *Diffusion of Innovations*, The Free Press, New York, 1995.
20. Brandt CD: Availability and accessibility of the nation's research infrastructure: The transfer of assistive technology by federal laboratories, *J Technol Transf* **28**(3/4):197–205 (2003).
21. Seelman KD: Universal design and orphan technology: Do we need both? *Disabil Stud Q* **25**(3) (summer 2005).
22. Iwarsson S, Stahl A: Accessibility, usability and universal design—positioning definitions of concepts describing person–environment relationships, *Disab Rehab* **25**(2):57–66 (Jan 2003).
23. Knops HThP: Shaping the future with assistive technology, in *Assistive Technology—Shaping the Future*, Assistive Technology Research Series 11, IOS Press, Amsterdam, 2003.
24. Kyoyo-Hin Foundation: *Kyoyo-Hin White Paper 2001* (retrieved 10/04 from http://kyoyohin.org/eng/index.html).
25. Seelman KD: Technology for full citizenship: Challenges for the research community, in *Accessibility and Usability Considerations for Medical Instrumentation*, Jack M. Winters & Molly Follette Story Ed CRC Press, Boca Raton, FL; Taylor & Francis, London, 2006 pp 307–317.
26. Cohen AB, Hanft RS: *Technology in American Health Care: Policy Directions for Effective Evaluation and Management*, Univ Michigan Press, Ann Arbor, 2004.
27. He W, Sengupta M, Velkoff VA, DeBarros KA: US Census Bureau, Current Population Reports, P23–209, *65+ in the United States: 2005*, US Government Printing Office, Washington, DC, 2005, pp 1–254.
28. Rehabilitation Research and Training Center on Disability Demographics and Statistics: *2004 Disability Status Reports*, Cornell Univ Ithica, NY, (retrieved 3/06 from www.DisabilityStatistics.org).
29. Cohen MA, Weinrobe M, Miller J, Ingoldsby A: *Independent Living: Becoming Disabled after Age 65: The Expected Lifetime Costs of Independent Living*, AARP Policy Research Institute, 2005 (retrieved 3.06 from http://www.aarp.org/research/housing-mobility/indliving/2005_08_costs.html).
30. Spinal Cord Injury Information Network (retrieved 3/06 at http://www.spinalcord.uab.edu/show.asp?durki=21446).
31. Gist J: *Income Distribution and Wealth Distribution in 1998: Findings from the Survey of Consumer Finances*, AARP Research Report, April 2000 (retrieved 3/06 from http://www.aarp.org/research/assistance/incomedist/aresearch-import-322-DD44.html#Age).
32. *Deeper in Dept: Trends among Midlife and Older Americans*, AARP Research Report, April 2000 (retrieved 3/06 from http://www.aarp.org/research/assistance/incomedist/aresearch-import-322-DD44.html#Age).

REFERENCES

33. Goodman NJ, Stapleton DC: *Federal Program Expenditures for Working-age People with Disabilities*, Research Report. (retrieved June, 2008 http://dps.sagepub.com/cgi/content/abstract/18/2/66 *J Disabil Policy Stud* (retrieved 3/06 from http://papers.ssrn.com).
34. Levine DI: *Reinventing Disability Policy*, Institute of Industrial Relations Working Paper Series Working Paper 65, 1997, pp 1–20 (http://papers.ssrn.com).
35. http://www.aarp.org/ppi.
36. Carlson D, Ehrlich N, US Department of Education National Institute on Disability and Rehabilitation Research: *Assistive Technology Use and Need by Persons with Disabilities in the United States*, Washington, DC, 2005 (available online at http://www.edpubs.org).
37. Butterfield TM, Ramseur JH: Research and case study findings in the area of workplace accommodations including provisions for assistive technology: A literature review, *Technol Disab* **16**:201–210 (2004).
38. Three Rivers Workforce Investment Board and Carnegie Mellon Center for Economic Development: *Managing the Changing Workfoce in Southwestern Pennsylvania: A Closer Look at Issues Related to Our Region's Aging Workforce*, April 2006, p 23.
39. Stapleton DC, Burkhauser RV, eds: *The Decline in Employment of People with Disabilities: A Policy Puzzle*, The Upjohn Institute for Employment Research, Kalamazoo, MI, 2003.
40. Mendelsohn S, Sheldon JR: The federal tax law as a subsidy for assistive technology, *Proc Bridges to Better Advocacy Conf*, Austin, TX, April 21–22, 2005 (retrieved 3/06 from http://www.nls.org/conf2005/tax%20law%20and%20AT.htm).
41. Brandt EN, Pope AM, eds: *Enabling America: Assessing the Role of Rehabilitation Science and Engineering*, National Academy Press, Washington, DC, 1997.
42. World Wide Web Accessibility Initiative, available online at http://www.w3.org/WAI/.
43. Executive Office of the President and US Department of Veteran's Affairs. *Proc White House/VA conf Emerging Technologies*, Oct 13–14, 2004. Bookshop Baltimore - Book number: 10696 at http://www.antiqbook.com/boox/balt/10696.shtml
44. Center for Aging Services Technologies, (http://www.agingtech.org/about.aspx).
45. Veterans benefits (http://usmilitary.about.com/od/theorderlyroom/l/blvetbenefits.htm).
46. The Social Security Act of 1935 as amended currently codified as 42 USC §901.
47. http://en.wikipedia.org/wiki/Social_Security_Administration.
48. Golinker L: *Update on Medicare Reimbursement for AAC Devices*, 2001 (lgolinker@aol.com).
49. http://www.cms.hhs.gov/MedHCPCSGenInfo/.
50. Hill K, Rupp T, Tucci M: (2004). *AAC Outcomes and Persons with ALS and Visual problems*, poster presented at the 2004 ASHA Annual Convention, Philadelphia, Nov 2004.
51. Sheldon JR: *Work Incentives for Persons with Disabilities under the Social Security and SSI Programs*, 2002 (retrieved 3/06 from http://www.nls.org).
52. http://www.cms.hhs.gov/MedicaidStWaivProgDemoPGI/.
53. US Department of Health and Human Services, Centers for Medicare & Medicaid Services, State Medicaid Director Letter SMDL #03-006, July 14, 2003.
54. Ticket to Work and Work Incentives Improvement Act, PL 106–170.
55. Colker R, Milani AA: *Everyday Law for Individuals with Disabilities*, Paradigm Publishers, Boulder, CO, 2005.
56. US Department of Justice, Civil Rights Division Disability Rights Section: *A Guide to Disability Rights Laws*, 2005 (retrieved 3/06 from http://www.usdoj.gov/crt/ada/cguide.htm).
57. http://www.ed.gov/about/offices/list/osers/index.html.
58. http://www.access-board.gov/enforcement/Rehab-Act-text/intro.htm.

59. Statement by Judith E. Heumann, Assistant Secretary Office of Special Education and Rehabilitative Services (retrieved 3/06 from http://www.ed.gov/offices/OLCA/jhmnn.html).
60. Architectural Barriers Act of 1968, 42 USC §§ 4151 et seq.
61. Retrieved 3.06 from http://www.section508.gov/index.cfm?FuseAction=Content&ID=3.
62. Fair Housing Act Amendments of 1988, PL 100–430.
63. Telecommunications for the Disabled Act of 1982, PL 97–410.
64. Hearing Aid Compatibility Act of 1988, PL 100–394.
65. Telecommunications Accessibility Enhancement Act of 1988, PL 100–542.
66. Regulations retrieved 3/06 from http://www.accessboard.gov/telecomm/html/telfinal.htm).
67. Retrieved 3/06 from http://www.webaim.org/coordination/law/us/telecom/.
68. Office for the Advancement of Telehealth (retrieved 3/06 from http://telehealth.hrsa.gov/).
69. http://www.ntia.doc.gov/reports/telemed/execsumhtm.
70. Retrieved 3/06 from National Institute of Standards and Technology from http://www.nist.gov/pe2001.
71. Pervasive computing gets organized, *Comput World* (retrieved 3/06 from http://www.computerworld.com/printhis/2003/0,4814,77369,00.html).
72. Retrieved 3/06 from European Digital Rights from http://www.edri.org/edrigram/number3.23/ubiquitous.
73. Internet Society Wireless Location Privacy: *Law and Policy in the U.S., EU and Japan* (retrieved 3/06 from http://www.isoc.org/briefings/015/index.shtml).
74. *Oatfield Estates*, retrieved 3/06 from http://www.elite-care.com/main-oatfield-tech.html
75. Century Foundation: *Public Policy in Older America: A Century Foundation Guide to the Issues*, Century Foundation Press, New York, 2006.

4

Assistive Technology and the International Classification of Functioning, Disability, and Health

Jerome E. Bickenbach

Queen's University Kingston, Ontario, Canada

4.1 DISABILITY AND ENVIRONMENT

In May 2001, the World Health Assembly of the World Health Organization (WHO) unanimously endorsed the *International Classification of Functioning, Disability and Health* (ICF), and member states were urged "to use the ICF in their research, surveillance and reporting as appropriate." Although on the face of it, ICF is a health classification or terminology, at its conceptual heart of the ICF is the revolutionary notion that disability is a complex phenomena that arises from an interaction between attributes of the person and the overall physical, human-built, attitudinal, and social environment in which the person lives and acts.

The term "revolutionary" mentioned above applies for politicians and policymakers but is also a commonplace for therapists and other disability service providers, as well as a hard reality for persons with disabilities themselves. Unaccommodating workplaces, inaccessible buildings, and the lack of appropriate assistive technology (AT) are not merely predictors of disability; they *create* disability. That is the lesson of the ICF. If all we knew were medical or diagnostic information about a person's functional status,

---

The Engineering Handbook of Smart Technology for Aging, Disability, and Independence,
Edited by A. Helal, M. Mokhtari and B. Abdulrazak
Copyright © 2008 John Wiley & Sons, Inc.

we could only guess at the nature and extent of their disabilities. It is the person's environment that determines disability.

Occupational and physical therapists know this intuitively, even when the focus of their therapeutic interventions is physiological or biophysical. In the realm of theory, ICF's revolutionary notion arose at least as early as the 1940s when social psychologists began suggesting "interactional" theories of human functioning (see the review in Ref. 1), accounts that were compiled and greatly extended by researchers such as Bronfenbrenner [2] and gerontologist M. Powell Lawton, who suggested an "ecological model" for exploring the interplay between individuals and their environments—physical, personal, and social [3,4]. For their part, disability study scholars have long recognized, and organized their own research in light of "ecological" or "environmental" theories of disability creation [5].

As the AT literature amply demonstrates, this theoretical insight into the nature of disability is also very much at the heart of the theory and practice of assistive technology (see, e.g., Refs. 6 and 7). The view that disability status is jointly determined by the person's physical status and environmental constraints, demands, or degree of environmental facilitation is also integral to the universal design and enabling environment approaches for the built environment [8] and is to the matching person–technology (MPT) strategy for AT [9–12].

Given that they appear to share basic premises, AT research and the ICF are made for each other. Although relatively new to the research scene, the ICF is already being taken up both as a statistical and epidemiologic tool and as a theoretical model of disability in a wide variety of contexts. AT is no exception. It has been argued that the ICF presents a holistic, biopsychosocial framework that is congenial to AT practice [13,14], and the components of the classification (body structure and function, activity and participation, and environmental and personal factors) are precisely the elements involved in AT assessment and intervention, making ICF a useful framework for AT outcomes research. Finally, since ICF speaks in a language that crosses disciplines, it is useful for both researchers and practitioners in the multidisciplinary field of AT [15,16].

Some of the burgeoning literature and research projects that are making the link between AT and ICF are reviewed below. Beforehand, it is important to be clear about what ICF is (and is not), its structure and theoretical building blocks, how it came to be, and its primary and projected uses. ICF is not only an international standard; it is a fundamental statistical and scientific tool that has direct, and potentially far-ranging policy applications with resource allocation consequences. But ICF is also easily misunderstood.

Not a few people in the disability community have expressed concerns about a scientific "model of disability" that, in the hands of policy developers, might be used to undermine hard-fought political and social gains. After all, disability is, in part, "socially constructed" and so, they argue, socially manipulated. If the very definition of disability embodies personal experience and political action, why cede this over to a scientific tool from the WHO?

For their part, researchers and scientists might be wary of a putatively scientific instrument based on a theoretical model in which social attitudes, values, and other elusive and unquantifiable phenomena become fundamental determinants of disability. How does ICF preserve the essential scientific preconditions of objectivity and rigor?

4.2 ICF: BACKGROUND AND DEVELOPMENT

From its inception, the World Health Organization has recognized that reliable and timely information about the health of populations is a critical input into the development and implementation of health policy. Since 1947, member nations have been required by WHO's constitution to report "causes of death" or mortality statistics in terms of WHO's *International Statistical Classification of Diseases and Related Health Problems* (ICD-10). Although useful for measuring life expectancy, these data did not capture the overall health status of living populations. Missing is information about nonfatal health outcomes, that is, levels of functioning and disability in all areas of life. Health, from WHO's perspective, is a matter of the condition of one's life, not merely the cause of one's death.

But why must information about functioning and disability be part of our conception of the health status of individuals and population? The answer is a matter of basic epidemiology. We know from many studies that medical diagnosis alone does not predict health service needs, length of hospitalization, level of care required, intervention, or AT requirements [17,18]. Nor is the presence of a disease or disorder an accurate predictor of social participation, receipt of disability, or other social benefits, work performance, return-to-work potential, or likelihood of social integration. Diagnosis on its own does not give us the information that we need for health planning and management purposes, nor does it provide us the evidence base for social policy planning. What is missing is information about the lived experience of health, data about the level and extent of functioning and disability.

There is also an increased recognition among social planners and service agencies of the theoretical insight about disability creation already mentioned. The take-home message of this insight is that reductions in the incidence and severity of disability in a population can be brought about by either enhancing the functional capacity of the individual or improving performance by modifying features of the social and physical environment in which the person lives. Yet, to properly analyze the impact of these different kinds of interventions, we need a way of classifying domains of areas of life as well as the environmental factors, such as AT, that can improve performance.

To capture all of this important health information, WHO returned to a tool it had released for field trial purposes in 1980, the *International Classification of Impairments, Disabilities and Handicaps* (ICIDH). Responding to international demand from WHO's worldwide network of collaborating centers, an ICIDH revision process was begun in 1993. Over the next 8 years, collaborating center and governmental and nongovernmental organizations—including groups representing persons with disabilities—engaged in a step-by-step systematic development of a revised version of the ICIDH. After initial drafts were produced and reviewed by experts, a series of field trials were begun to look into the cross-cultural and linguistic applicability of the model and classificatory structure and language of the ICIDH-2. The rationale of the ethnographic methodologies and an analysis of the 15-country field trials has been published [19]. The final draft, now renamed the *International Classification of Functioning, Disability and Health* (ICF), was put on the agenda of the 54th World Health Assembly and endorsed in May 2001.

4.3 PRINCIPLES BEHIND THE ICF

The ICF is a classificatory tool for functioning and disability; its principal purposes are, as far as WHO is concerned, to establish an international language for consistent and comparable health, and health-related, data, from either clinical or survey sources. Although not itself an assessment instrument, it provides a complete, structured, and operationalized terminology that allows existing health and functional assessment tools to be correlated or crosswalked, and on which new assessment or measurement tools can be constructed. But ICF also provides a conceptual model of functioning and disability that has a broad variety of potential uses in data management, electronic health recording, clinical assessment, health systems management and performance assessment, outcomes measurement, policy and legal development, and research.

Given that the terminological and codification functions of the ICF classifications, which in turn determine the practical detail of how ICF is put together, are structured by ICF's conceptual model, it is appropriate to start with the theory of ICF before moving on to the practical detail. More importantly, as just mentioned, ICF's model of functioning and disability can be abstracted and used in a myriad of ways: ICF purports to explicate the concept of disability itself, so that is where any description of ICF must begin.

It is convenient to set out ICF's conceptual picture of functioning and disability as a set of principles. These principles are hardly novel and each has long been in the disability literature in one form or another. Constructing "models of disability," indeed, is something of a cottage industry among academics and practitioners alike, and the publication and increased use of ICF will likely not affect the rate at which new models are suggested.

But ICF's model differs from others in the literature in three, crucial respects: (1) the ICF model is not a mere rhetorical flourish or political slogan—it is fully operationalized in the form of a series of classification; (2) the ICF model is not restricted to a disease condition or syndrome—it is, first and foremost, about human functioning (and only derivatively about human disfunctioning) across all aspects of human life; and (3) the ICF model is the product of an international, intersectorial, and interdisciplinary consensus, and has been subjected to the most extensive field testing that has ever been attempted.

4.3.1 Disability is a Multidimensional Notion

Almost everyone who writes on disability these days acknowledges that "disability" is ambiguous and has various meanings depending on the context. Much confusion is generated when people incautiously use the term in a medical, rehabilitation, AT, social policy, or legal context, without clearly specifying what aspect of the overall notion they have in mind. Most careful researchers have noted that, roughly, "disability" refers to either difficulties in the functioning of parts of the body, limits in an individual's inherent capacity to perform actions, or difficulties in actually performing simple or complex actions and behaviors that are fully integrated in the physical and social context in which the person lives.

This three-way distinction is at the heart of the ICF model. Unlike its predecessor, however, ICF is principally a classification of positive (or neutral) functioning, and the three levels are identified: (1) body functions and structures, (2) activities, and (3) participation. Disability arises derivatively from these notions, in cases where there are

TABLE 4.1 ICF Levels of Functioning and Disability

Functioning
Body functions are physiologic functions of body systems (including psychologic functions)
Body structures are anatomic parts of the body such as organs, limbs, and their components
Activity is the execution of a task or action by an individual
Participation is involvement in a life situation

Disability
Impairments are problems in body function or structure such as a significant deviation or loss
Activity limitations are difficulties an individual may have in executing activities
Participation restrictions are problems an individual may experience in involvement in life situations

---

problems at the body level (impairments of body or structure), or activity limitations or participation restrictions. Table 4.1 gives the ICF levels with definitions.

The ICIDH term "handicap"—although it had the virtue of conveying the essential message that the difficulties a person faces are created by external (i.e., handicapping) factors—was abandoned early in the revision process because it is incorrigibly negative, if not insulting, in usage. Although possibly an English-only phenomena (the French *handicapée* apparently lacks negative connotations and in any event is retained in the French version of ICF), it was felt that the wholly positive term "participation" fit better with the spirit of the revision.

The three levels of disability do not exhaust the overall model since, without some context, neither functioning nor disability can exist. Hence, the ICF model includes contextual factors, divided into two subcomponents: environmental factors and personal factors. There is a classification of environmental factors in the ICF, but there is no corresponding classification of personal factors as yet (see Table 4.2).

Although naturally enough, neither the WHO nor anyone else can successfully dictate how terms in ordinary language are used, within the ICF "disability" refers to all three levels, not to any particular one exclusively. Therefore, care must be taken, if relying on the ICF, to specify which level or levels of functioning one is identifying by the ambiguous term "disability." Far too often in academic literature writers, whose concern

TABLE 4.2 ICF Contextual Factors

Contextual Factors
Contextual factors represent the complete background of an individual's life and living and can have a positive or negative influence on the individual's performance as a member of society, on the individual's capacity to execute actions or tasks, or on the individual's body function or structure

Environmental Factors
Environmental factors make up the physical, social, and attitudinal environment in which people live and conduct their lives

Personal Factors
Personal factors are the particular background of an individual's life and living, and comprise features of the individual that are not part of a health condition or health states; these factors may include gender, race, age, other health conditions, fitness, lifestyle, habits, upbringing, coping styles, social background, education, profession, past and current experience (past life events and concurrent events), overall behavior pattern and character style, individual psychological assets, and other characteristics.

is with one level of functioning will insist that is the level where disability "really exists." Thus those who assume what is usually called the "medical model" argue that disability is "really" a matter of body level disfunctioning, or impairment, whereas those who adopt one of the many versions of the "social model" of disability may argue that disability "really" is the disadvantages resulting from an unaccommodating, stigmatizing, or discrimination environment, or participation restrictions. Both sides are correct in that they are talking about disability, but both are wrong when they assume that the aspect of disability they highlight is all there is to the complex phenomena [20].

4.3.2 Disability is Interactional

The second principle of the ICF model is the theoretical insight with which we started, that disability, in all three levels, is an outcome of a complex interaction or relationship between intrinsic features of the person and features of the external context or environment in which he or she lives and acts. Since paradigmatically, human functioning is the subject matter of our concept of health, a person's health status is an essential component of ICF's overall model of functioning and disability. Health is an intrinsic feature of the human body, health—as opposed to health determinants—is an attribute of the person, which concerns the level and kind of functioning the person exhibits, both at the body level (muscle strength) and the level of capacity to person acts and behaviours (watching, walking, communicating). All of this, of necessity, occurs in a context—the world or environment.

So, environmental factors are an essential component of ICF's understanding of functioning and disability. This said, it is plain that the role of the environment in the creation of impairments and activity limitations is different from its role in the creation of participation restrictions. With Impairments, we at most assume the environmental effect of fundamental features of the physical world—light, gravity, temperature. With limitations on our capacity to perform actions, Environmental Factors of more complexity are involved (height of tables, walking surfaces, shape of objects).

But with participation restrictions, the environment—in all its multitude of forms, physical, interpersonal, and social—is almost entirely responsible for the restriction. When we notice the failure of a person to perform a complex set of actions such as being a parent, going to school or performing the task of a job, especially when we have evidence of the person's capacity to execute the actions, then we must look to the environment for answers. Is this person being prevented by the attitudes of others? Does this individual have the right assistive devices? Does the worksite have design features that accommodate the person?

But if features of the environment can *restrict or have no effect* on how a person with an impairment or activity limitation can perform in daily life, other features can *enhance* the level of performance. Environmental factors, in short, function either as barriers to performance (worsening the potential performance level of an individual with an impairment) or as facilitating (enhancing that potential). The actual impact of an environmental factor on participation can be determined only individually and by observation; a facilitator for one individual may be a barrier for another. Yet there are some classes of factors—and AT is obviously one—that are designed, and typically always function, as environmental facilitators.

Putting the principles of complexity and interaction together suggests the visual representation of the ICF model in Figure 4.1.

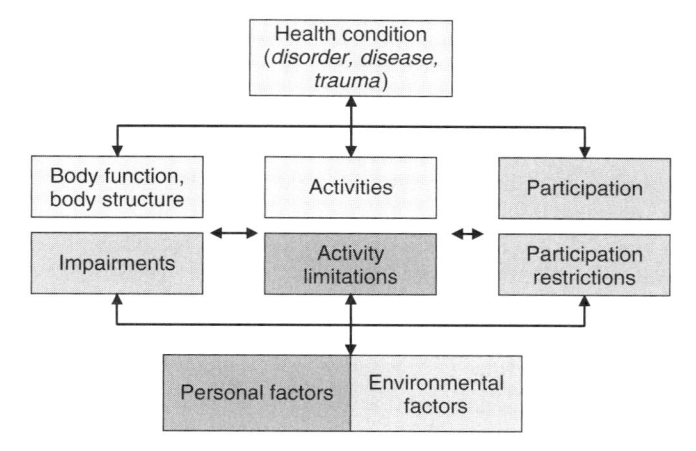

FIGURE 4.1 The ICF model of functioning and disability.

Like most diagrams, Figure 4.1 can be misleading. The general aim of the diagram is to display the interaction between intrinsic features of the person—in particular the underlying health condition—and contextual factors, in particular environmental factors. At the same time, the arrows ought not to be read as causation. The principal objection to the model in the old ICIDH was that it implied that impairments caused disabilities that in turn caused handicaps [20,21]. The drafters of the ICF wanted to clearly reject that implication. To be sure, there are predictable relationships between the levels of functioning and disability, but only research can tell us what these relationships are; for the same reason, only research will illuminate what undoubtedly are complex relationships between contextual factors and the levels of disability [22].

The point here is methodological and fundamental. ICF has been carefully drafted not to make assumptions about what causes what in the creation of disability at all levels. The ICF is *etiologically neutral*, in the sense that it does not presume any causal connections between disease conditions and disabilities. Such connections of course exist, but it is not for the model to posit them. The model is not "hardwired" so that we can determine, without evidence, either that the underlying health condition or the environment is the most prominent causation element in disability creation. Only evidence about particular cases—not a priori theory—can answer that question. In a sense, therefore, ICF is *theory-neutral* as an explanation of disability. It provides a logical structure for research about disability, without predetermining the answers that research gives.

4.3.3 Disability is Universal

The ICF offers a model of human functioning and disability, not a model of disability as the identifier of (or label for) a separate, minority group of people. The ICF is not a classification of people at all; it is a classification of states of functioning. The ICF recognizes that decrement of functioning, or disability, is not a "special" circumstance; it is a universal feature of the human condition. Over the course of the lifespan, the chances of living without any kind or level of functional decrement are virtually nil. No human has a complete repertoire of physiologic functions or capabilities, suitable for every physical and social environment. The range of variation in human abilities is vast, and the complete absence of disability is a limiting case of theoretic interest only. Disability, in short, is epidemiologically universal, and in this sense it is normality for human beings.

Universalism is not merely a scientific principle; it is also political strategy. Sociologist and disability advocate Irving Zola observed that "an exclusively special needs approach to disability" is at best a short-term strategy and what is needed for the long term "are more universal policies that recognize that the entire population is 'at risk' for the concomitants of chronic illness and disability." What disability advocates need is a political strategy that "demystifies the specialness of disability." "Only when we acknowledge the near universality of disability and that all its dimensions (including the biomedical) are part of the social process by which the meanings of disability are negotiated will it be possible fully to appreciate how general public policy can affect this issue" [23].

A similar comment was made by WHO's Director General Dr. Gro Harlem Brundtland when ICF was endorsed in 2001 [24]:

> ICF thus "mainstreams" the experience of disability and recognises it as a universal human experience. By shifting the focus from cause to the full range of lived experiences it places all health conditions on an equal footing allowing them to be compared using a common metric—the ruler of health and disability. From emphasizing people's disabilities, and labelling people as "disabled," we now focus on the level of health and functional capacity of all people.

4.3.4 Functioning and Disability are Continuous, not Categorical

This principle is a correlate of universality, but deserves separate mention. Social policy aimed at persons with disabilities—everything from pensions to antidiscrimination laws—implicitly requires recipients of benefits to qualify as disabled. These laws and policies, in short, impose a template on the social world that neatly divides people into two groups: those with disabilities and those without. The rationale for this practice in policy terms is obvious; scientifically it is arbitrary. Functional limitation is not an all or nothing matter, levels of disability fall on a continuum of severity, from none or negligible, to mild, moderate, and severe. The ICF model reflects this truism.

To be sure, and certainly in the case of impairments, the ICF includes an exhaustive set of domains of functioning and structure—the separate categories in the classifications—and presumes population norms or statistically based thresholds in terms of which an observed level of functioning or structure is identified as a decrement of function or structure, and so an impairment. For *activities* and *participation*, these thresholds are obviously far more controversial and contentious since they amount to a claim of what constitutes "normal" levels of activity (subject always to the assumption that the person's wishes to perform the action or exhibit the behavior in question; one who chooses not to work, when one could work, does not have a participation restriction).

The important point, though, is that the ICF does not supply population norms for any level of functioning, it is a classification, not an assessment tool. The model of the ICF does not determine a priori who has a disability and who does not. The ICF model treats disability as a universal human phenomenon, not a categorical trait of a discrete group of people. As such, the ICF must be used in conjunction with purpose-built and evidence-based assessment and measurement tools that determine in a scientific and therapeutic context that is open to scrutiny and potential revision. Increasingly these tools are informed by the lived experience of persons with functional decrements, for they are ultimately the experts.

Since 2005, an extensive international exercise tapping into multidisciplinary, professional and consumer consensus has yielded "core sets" of ICF categories for specific diseases and disorders [13]. This preliminary effort is the first step toward an evidence-based consensus on thresholds and other therapeutic contact points. This is vital research that builds on the ICF model (to identify the levels of disability and environmental factors relevant to the core set of terms) as well as its terminology and classificatory structure.

4.3.5 Etiologic and Terminologic Neutrality

Finally, and as already mentioned, ICF's model makes no a priori claims about antecedent biomedical causes of decrements of functioning. The ICF makes it possible—primarily through the media of its classifications—to describe the lived experiments of a person with depression, or diabetes, or arthritis. The ICF does not tells us what functional decrements someone will have if this person has a particular health condition, that is, for us to find out by observation and interview. The ICF model imposes a structure on our observations, reminding us to consider the full range of someone's lived experience, particularly the impact of the person's physical and social environment. The rest is left to the user.

Etiologic neutrality is reflected in the language of the ICF classifications as *terminologic neutrality*. Subject to unavoidable features of our language (there is no neutral term for "pain" for example), the classifications are expressed in neutral terms describing functions, rather than negative terms identifies as problems or difficulties. Wording domain names in neutral language also gives the classification the power to describe both positive and negative aspects of each domain of functioning and disability.

An important corollary of etiologic neutrality is that neither in the model nor in the details of the classifications is a distinction drawn between "physical" and "mental" disabilities. The inability to carry out the activities related to moving around a marketplace and shopping for oneself is a disability, which may be associated with a mental illness such as agoraphobia, or a debilitating physical condition such as arthritis. Nothing is gained—and only discriminating stereotyping is achieved—by tying particular activity limitations or participation restrictions directly and irrevocably to mental or physical medical conditions. Such linkages as there are should be based on solid evidence, not presupposition.

Such are the governing principles of ICF's conception of human functioning and disability. Historically, the ICF model is a modification of the so-called social model of disability, or as it is often also called the *environmental* or *ecologic model* [1,5]. Environmental factors are essential components of the ICF model. In interaction with body functioning and capacity levels intrinsic to the person, environmental factors are responsible for the actual performance, or lack of performance, of actions in a person's life. At the same time, unlike some versions of the social model that insist that disability itself is a product of social perceptions, the ICF model identifies objectively determined decrements in functioning and capacity as one of the important senses of the term "disability." As it merges the insights of both the social and the medical models of disability, without failing victim to the weaknesses of either, the ICF model is called the "biopsychosocial" model of disability [25].

There are some intriguing implications of these principles. Taking the principles of universality and continuity together, as already mentioned, implies that disability is normality. Any attempt to create a threshold of disability, a bright line between "the disabled" and the "nondisabled" is socially constructed, and thus politically negotiable.

The principles of complexity and interaction provide important insights into intervention strategies. First, the point of all interventions is to increase participation (not merely deal with body function decrements), so it is in this domain that our therapeutic outcome measurements should be derived. "Fixing" the person, by means of biomedical intervention (surgery, medication, rehabilitation, or skills development) may certainly increase levels of participation. But for many chronic conditions, corrective interventions have limited effect and participation can be increased only through environmental changes, including the provision of usable aids and assistive devices.

In short, our intervention strategy must always look in two directions: corrective functional limitation in the person, and altering the person's environment so as to facilitate performance. Whether a strategy of correction or of environmental facilitation or a combined strategy is the most effective in increasing participation cannot be determined without evidence. More importantly, we cannot just assume as a society that it is economically more efficient to fix the individual with a disability than make facilitating modifications to the person's environment, when it may well be the other way around.

Much more can be said about the implications of the underlying principles of ICF model on our understanding of human functioning and disability, and a substantial body of multidisciplinary academic and professional literature has explored these implications for nearly a decade now. The AT community—both researchers and practitioners—have made their contributions to this discussion, and have found the ICF model to be congenial to the theory and practice of AT. Before reviewing trends in AT research and practice using ICF, we should not forget that ICF is far more than a model of functioning and disability.

4.4 ICF AS CLASSIFICATION AND INTERNATIONAL LANGUAGE OF FUNCTIONING AND DISABILITY

The structure of ICF's four classifications and terminologies was the result of nearly a decade of international expert consultation, iterative drafting, consensus conferences, cultural application research (the details of which are reported by Üstün et al. [19]), input from specialized taskforces and international groups representing medical and rehabilitative professionals as well as persons with disabilities. The story has been told in several places [17,18]. WHO's intentions were to create an exhaustive terminology for health and disability statistics that would also have clinical and policy applications. The field testing (and eventual translation into dozens of languages) was aimed at producing an international language for comparative statistics.

As already noted, WHO's own use of ICF lies in the area of international health information, for which consistency and comparability across countries is essential. Despite the enormous effort, it is understood that the 2001 edition of ICF will inevitably need to be updated from time to time, and a committee composed of representatives of WHO collaborating centers around the world has been set up for this purpose.

The four component classifications of the ICF are (1) body function, (2) body structure, (3) activities and participation, and (4) environmental factors. Classifications 1 and 2 are directly parallel (e.g., Chapter 2 of *body functions* deals with sensory functions, while Chapter 2 of *body structures* deals with the structures of the eyes, ears, etc.). Each classification is arranged hierarchically with up to four embedded levels (the chapter heading is the first level). Thus, an item at the fourth level will be subsumed under a third-level term, which itself is subsumed under a second-level term. The first-level terms, or chapter headings, divide the universe of the classification into discrete and nonoverlapping, but mutually exhaustive divisions. The chapters of each of the four classifications are listed in Table 4.3.

Each item or category is provided with an alphanumeric code and is given with a short operational definition. The code number identifies the unique place of each item within the classification (with the initial letters b, s, d, and e representing the classifications *body function*, *body structure*, *activities and participation*, and *environmental factors*,

TABLE 4.3 ICF Classifications: First Level

Body functions
  Chapter 1   Mental functions
  Chapter 2   Sensory functions and pain
  Chapter 3   Voice and speech functions
  Chapter 4   Functions of the cardiovascular, hematologic, immunologic, and respiratory systems
  Chapter 5   Functions of the digestive, metabolic, and endocrine systems
  Chapter 6   Genitourinary and reproductive functions
  Chapter 7   Neuromusculoskeletal and movement-related functions
  Chapter 8   Functions of the skin and related structures

Body structures
  Chapter 1   Structures of the nervous system
  Chapter 2   The eye, ear, and related structures
  Chapter 3   Structures involved in voice and speech
  Chapter 4   Structures of the cardiovascular, immunologic, and respiratory systems
  Chapter 5   Structures related to the digestive, metabolic, and endocrine systems
  Chapter 6   Structures related to the genitourinary and reproductive systems
  Chapter 7   Structures related to movement
  Chapter 8   Skin and related structures

Activities and participation
  Chapter 1   Learning and applying knowledge
  Chapter 2   General tasks and demands
  Chapter 3   Communication
  Chapter 4   Mobility
  Chapter 5   Self-care
  Chapter 6   Domestic life
  Chapter 7   Interpersonal interactions and relationships
  Chapter 8   Major life areas
  Chapter 9   Community, social, and civic life

Environmental factors
  Chapter 1   Products and technology
  Chapter 2   Natural environment and human-made changes to environment
  Chapter 3   Support and relationships
  Chapter 4   Attitudes
  Chapter 5   Services, systems, and policies

respectively). The next number in the code identifies the first level, or chapter; the next pair of numbers represents the place of the item at the second level, and so on to the fourth level. Second-level items are provided with inclusions (alternative or more specific terms that are to be included under the item name) and exclusions (other item names found in the classification that are distinct from the item in question); and all items are provided with definitions. For illustration, Figure 4.2 displays an edited version of one item from *body functions*, namely, b210, and includes one of the third-level items subsumed under it (b2101), and three of the fourth-level items subsumed under it (b21020, b21021, and b21022).

Chapter 2
Sensory functions and pain

This chapter is about the functions of the senses, seeing, hearing, tasting, and so on, as well as the sensation of pain.

Seeing and related functions (b210-b229)

b210 Seeing functions

Sensory functions relating to sensing the presence of light and sensing the form, size, shape, and color of the visual stimuli.

Inclusions: visual acuity functions; visual field functions; quality of vision; functions of sensing light and colour, visual acuity of distant and near vision, monocular and binocular vision; visual picture quality; impairments such as myopia, hypermetropia, astigmatism, hemianopia, colorblindness, tunnel vision, central and peripheral scotoma, diplopia, nightblindness, and impaired adaptability to light

Exclusion: perceptual functions (b156)

....

b 2102   Quality of vision

Seeing functions involving light sensitivity, color vision, contrast sensitivity, and the overall quality of the picture.

b 21020   Light sensitivity

Seeing functions of sensing a minimum amount of light (light minimum), and the minimum difference in intensity (light difference)

Inclusions: functions of dark adaptation; impairments such as nightblindness (hyposensitivity to light) and photophobia (hypersensitivity to light)

b 21021   Color vision

Seeing functions of differentiating and matching colors

b 21022   Contrast sensitivity

Seeing functions of separating figure from ground, involving the minimum amount of luminance required

FIGURE 4.2   ICF b210.

Additional materials in annexes of the ICF provide basic instructions for coding—for either clinical purposes or general data collection and collation—including application of the qualifiers for each classification that serve a variety of functions, depending on the classification. Different users will, of course, employ the ICF classifications, coding structures, or terminology in different ways, depending on need. Survey developers have no need for items below the first or perhaps second levels; clinicians may need to add on additional, more detailed, items at the fifth or subsequent levels. Once again, flexibility has been the guide in the development of the ICF classifications.

The potential applications of ICF for AT practitioners are as various as they are for any other health professional. The basic ICF function of data coding—for consistent and comparable data across episodes of care and other data-collecting points—are fundamental to the structure of the ICF and so are well tested. ICF coding has been used in a wide variety of contexts around the world. Clinical applications of ICF tend to embed the terminology in other instruments that supply the assessment and measurement functions that ICF does not provide. Research and policy applications of the ICF are limited only by the imagination of the researcher, or the needs of the policy developer. Since 2005, the AT community has cautiously turned to the ICF to see if it can be of assistance. Although the ICF is a young tool, a considerable range of AT applications have already found their way into research and practice.

4.5 OTHER ICF APPLICATIONS

4.5.1 Applications of ICF for AT Research and Practice

The ICF and its earlier, field-tested ancestors ICIDH-2 Beta 1 and Beta 2, all caught the attention of AT researchers and practitioners. Fortunately, during the revision process that began in 1995, the Centers for Disease Control and Prevention made it possible for the proposed *environmental factors* classification to be independently developed and field-tested. Because of this support, WHO was able to enlist the support of, and garner input from, a variety of international experts in AT, universal design, and other "environmental" expertises. Some of these experts let the AT community know of ICF developmental activities [6], and ongoing AT research endeavors, such as those of the Consortium on Assistive Technology Outcomes Research (CATOR) [26] could incorporate the ICF into their work, even before ICF was officially approved by the World Health Assembly in 2001. Since that time, at its annual meeting the North American Collaborating Center on the ICF (NACC)—part of the original network of international collaborating centers WHO used for field-testing purposes—has regularly featured presentations by AT specialists, (such as Arthanat and Lenker [27], Lenker and Jutai [15], Scherer [16], Scherer and Sax [28], and Smith and Longenecker [29]).

A review of the not-inconsiderable literature since 2001 falls naturally into two broad groups: applications of ICF's conceptual model of disability to AT practice and research, and applications of ICF classifications for outcomes research, data management and AT use, and survey development. This closely parallels the emerging literature and trends in ICF application around the globe. There has been a great deal of work, across a multitude of health and health-related disciplines and professions in which the model of ICF is used as a structure for instruments (assessment tools, surveys, or questionnaires), for intervention strategies, for coordinating multidisciplinary teams across episodes of care, for health systems and health data system management. In this work, the ICF is very much in the background. ICF's model is flexible and relatively theory-neutral and thus compatible with a wide variety of applications. On the other hand, ICF has been taken up—once again by a myriad of health and health-related professions—as a common language for collecting, codifying, and organizing health and disability data, arising from clinical encounters, surveys, questionnaires, and censuses. The promise of the ICF terminology and classification system—particularly its ability to be crosswalked to existing terminologies, assessment tools, and surveys—is slowly being realized.

4.5.2 AT Applications of the ICF Conceptual Model

One of the first AT organizations to embrace the ICF model was the Association for the Advancement of Assistive Technology in Europe (AAATE). At their annual meeting in 2002, President Renzo Andrich [30] remarked that the ICF makes it clear that disability should be viewed "as an attribute of a given individual, but rather [as] a situation that may affect any individual in case a gap exists between individual capabilities and environmental factors, and this gap restricts the quality of life and hinders fullest exploitation of the individual's potential in society" [31]. According to this concept, AT bridges that gap, thereby facilitating and enhancing the person's performance levels, and increasing participation. The ICF model, Andrich continued, points us in the direction of holistic "assistive solutions" in which AT, operating at the individual level to compensate for functional limitations, must be integrated with other environmental modifications to the built environment, transport and mobility infrastructure, communications, and other categories [31].

Other AT writers have been more cautious, seeing the advantages of the ICF model for integrating AT interventions into the overall health and health-related service picture [32], while at the same time pondering the conceptual linkages of the key concepts in person–environment relationships with the components of the ICF model [33]. Some authors have chosen to fit the ICF model into broader frameworks—the "enablement perspective" [14] or "rehabilitation problem-solving" [34]—where AT provision finds a prominent place.

Most commonly though, for those in the AT field who have investigated ICF, the basic affinities between AT and ICF have been too obvious not to warrant comment: ICF offers a holistic and biopsychosocial framework, incorporating the three dimensions (body function and structure, activity and participation) that are also elements of AT assessment and intervention [27]. The ICF model structures a common language that cuts across disciplines, which is attractive to the multidisciplinary field of AT [35]. Moreover, the *environmental factors* part of the ICF model include all of the physical, social, and cultural factors that, AT writers insist, are relevant to AT assessment in the *products and technology* chapter of the classification [7]. In addition, features of the individual relevant to AT interventions, such as socioeconomic status, age, education level, and coping abilities, are included as personal factors. In short, it is a simple task to map on the scope of AT assessment and intervention onto the ICF model (which in turn can be expressed in ICF classification and terminology).

Lenker et al. [35] have also argued that the ICF model comports well with the three best-established AT assessment strategies: the semistructure interview format of the Canadian Occupational Performance Measure (COPM) [36], the individual prioritized problem assessment (IPPA) structured assessment and goal-setting process [37], and the matching person–technology (MPT) assessment framework, with its battery of instruments designed to match individual capacities to AT devices according to the person's needs and other environmental factors [38]. Of the three, MPT has been at the center of considerable activity involving the ICF. Research funded by the US National Institute for Disability and Rehabilitation Research has helped to make the conceptual affinity between the MPT strategy and ICF model practically significant generally [9], and specifically in planning for individuals with cognitive disabilities [11,12], and for measuring participation levels [16].

The ICF model has also been studied by researchers attempting to place AT interventions into a more secure, theoretical structure. Gitlin [38], taking a broader look at research in home environments for the elderly, has argued that "the environmental perspective" can be fruitfully integrated into the wider ICF model (see also Iwarsson [39]). One promising theoretical consequence of this would be measure the role of AT in "bridging the participation gap"; [21] that is, the difference in levels or quality of participation between those with, and those without, disability. The ICF model provides the framework for measurement participation gaps, opening the door to research that determines the impact of particular AT, for specified activity limitations and in specific participation contexts—say, for example, the impact of AT for people with arthritis experiencing mobility limitations in the workplace [22].

An area of ongoing AT research involves ways of assessing the usability of, and client satisfaction with, devices and technology provided to increase the person's performance. The ICF model has proved to provide an ideal basis for structuring assessment instruments and evaluation questionnaires [39,40]. A closely related endeavor is that of linking AT usability, or the psychosocial impact of AT, onto some measure of overall quality of life. That there should be correlations between AT use and quality of life is obvious, but it is more challenging to be precise about the nature of the AT impact on quality of life, and even more challenging to develop valid and reliable measures of this impact. One such tool, the psychosocial impact of assistive devices scale (PIADS), has been developed specifically for sensitivity to the ICF dimension of participation [41–43].

4.5.3 AT Applications of ICF Classifications and Terminology

One of the earliest and most obvious applications of the ICF involved correlating or crosswalking the terminology in the *environmental factors* classification with ISO 9999 (*Technical Aids for Persons with Disabilities—Classification and Terminology*) [44] and other AT classifications and terminologies [28,45]. The advantages of using ICF in this manner is that AT terminologic standards can be linked, not merely to the ICF *environmental factors* classification, but to *body function* and *structure* classifications, and from there to the specific impairment for which the AT is intended, and, finally, from there to the areas of participation the individual's performance in which the AT will enhance. The US Interagency Committee on Disability Research has opted to use ICF classifications to organize information about AT research funded by the US Department of Education [46].

However, the area in which the ICF has been most often used is in the development and validation of AT outcomes. The case for the need for AT outcome measures was forcefully made by Fuhrer et al. [47], who argued that in a field such as AT, a discipline whose hallmark is a commitment to addressing consumers' goals, evidence-based practice entails an emphasis on outcomes that will measure the impact of AT on users' daily lives. An essential criteria of adequately of any such measure, furthermore, is that it comports with highly elaborated, worked-out, and tested frameworks and terminologies, in particular that of the ICF.

A more active role for ICF as a taxonomy for use in AT outcomes research, suggested by Lenker and Jutai [15], has been discussed in more detail by Jutai et al. [48]. An adequate taxonomy is needed to classify the outcomes intended for the use of any assistive device in a manner that properly captures, and distinguishes, the family of outcomes that are relevant. The CATOR framework for conceptually modeling outcomes, incorporating ICF concepts and terminologies, identifies classes of outcomes that are most directly related to user needs and objectives. These classes of outcomes are effectiveness, social significance, device satisfaction, psychological functioning, and subjective well-being. Since these are irreducible and heterogeneous outcomes (with complex causal relationships between each), it is essential that background terminology be both exhaustive (in order to capture all the desired outcomes) and consistent (to avoid category overlap and confusion). As ICF sets out objective categories of human functioning, it is an ideal source of terminology for outcomes research. The organizing principles for the classifications are well described, the classifications are exhaustive yet nonredundant and the key concepts are empirically differentiated, and consistent.

This said, the limitations of the ICF are also apparent when put to service in outcomes research [49]. The ICF is a very general health classification designed to be flexible in order to serve the widest spectrum of potential users as possible. It does not identify, or even locate, temporal or causal connections, connections that are necessary when making predictions about outcomes. The ICF makes no claim about priority of outcomes, or how one set of environmental factors may, or may not, influence others, or indeed how any factor influences performance levels. Finally, although all AT is, in principal, included in *environmental factors*, the level of detail in that classification is inadequate for precise description of AT.

Still, as it is a general classificatory tool, ICF will invariably fail to provide the essential layer of detail that some applications demand. All of the classifications, not merely the *environmental factors* classification, are lacking in the kind of detail that specialists demand, certainly in clinical contexts. The hierarchical, branching structure of ICF classifications is perfectly compatible with the addition of more detail at the "stems" of each "branch." Specialists are invited to provide that level of detail. The ICF is also compatible with the addition of causal linkages and other conceptual additions, In short, for those instances—and AT outcomes research is clearly one—where the ICF does not give users all that they need, ICF must be augmented with other instruments, in order to fully integrate ICF with research and practice.

4.6 CONCLUSION

For many reasons, conceptual, and historical, ICF and AT theory and practice are closely aligned. It is natural for the AT practitioner and researcher to turn to the ICF for assistance. It is part of the core message of the ICF model of functioning and disability that environmental factors such as AT have the potential of reducing the impact of an impairment on a person's performance in all areas of human existence—and it is an article of faith among AT developers and providers that this technology can reduce, if not eliminate, disability. The physical, built, attitudinal and social environment in which a person lives; the products and services that are available; and the overall cultural, political, and social environment all contribute in ways either positive or negative to the situations and circumstances of living that we label "disability." Clearly, ICF and AT are on the same wavelength, and the future is bright for collaboration and synergy.

REFERENCES

1. Bickenbach JE: *Physical Disability and Social Policy*, Univ Toronto Press, Amsterdam: IOS Press 1993.
2. Bronfenbrenner U: *The Ecology of Human Development, Experiments by Nature and Design*, Harvard Univ Press, Cambridge, MA, 1979.
3. Lawton MP, Simon B: The ecology of social relationships in housing for the elderly, *Gerontologist* **8**:106–115 (1968).
4. Lawton MP, Nahemow L: Ecology and the aging process, in Eisdorfer C, Lawton MP, eds, *The Psychology of Adult Development and Aging*, American Psychological Association, Washington, DC, 1973, pp 619–674.
5. Amundson R: Disability, handicap, and the environment, *J Soc Phil* **9**:1–16 (1992).
6. Gray DB, Quatrano LA, Lieberman ML: Moving to the next stage of assistive technology development, in Gray DB, Quatrano LA, Lieberman ML, eds, *Designing and Using Assistive Technology: The Human Perspective*, Paul H Brookes, Baltimore, 1998, pp 299–309.
7. Cook AM, Hussey SM: *Assistive Technologies Principles and Practice*, Mosby, St. Louis, 2002.
8. Steinfeld E, Danford GS, eds, *Enabling Environments: Measuring the Impact of Environment on Disability and Rehabilitation*, Kluwer Academic, New York, 1999.
9. Scherer MJ, ed: *Assistive Technology: Matching Device and Consumer for Successful Rehabilitation*, APA Books, Washington, DC, 2002.
10. Scherer MJ: The change in emphasis from people to person: Introduction to the special issue on assistive technology, *Disab Rehab* **24**(1–3):1–4 (2002).
11. Scherer MJ: *Living in the State of Stuck: How Technology Impacts the Lives of People with Disabilities*, 4th ed, Brookline Books, Cambridge, MA, 2005.
12. Scherer M: Assessing the benefits of using assistive technologies and other supports for thinking, remembering and learning, *Disab Rehab* **27**(13):731–739 (2005).
13. Stucki G, MJ, eds, ICF core sets for the acute hospital and early post-acute rehabilitation facilities *Disab Rehab* (special issue) **27**(7/8) (2005).
14. Goldstein DN, Cohn E, Coster W: Enhancing participation for children with disabilities: Application of the ICF enablement framework to pediatric physical therapist practice, *Pediatr Phys Ther* **16**(2):114–120 (2004).
15. Lenker JA, Jutai JW: Assistive technology outcomes research and clinical practice: What role for ICF? *8th North American Collaborating Center Conf ICF*, Toronto, 2002.
16. Scherer M: Measuring participation and the disability experience with the assistive technology device predisposition assessment, *5th North American Collaborating Centre Meeting*, Toronto, 2004.
17. Üstün TB, Chatterji S, Kostansjek N, Bickenbach JE: The World Health Organization's International Classification of Functioning, Disability and Health (ICF) and functional status information in health record, *Health Care Financ Rev* **24**(3):77–88 (2003).
18. Üstün TB, Chatterji S, Bickenbach J et al: The International Classification of Functioning, Disability and Health: A new tool for understanding disability and health, *Disab Rehab* **25**(11/12):565–571 (2003).

19. Üstün TB, Chatterji S, Bickenbach JE, Trotter II RT, Saxena S: *Disability and Culture: Universalism and Diversity*, Hogrefe and Huber, Bern, 2000.
20. Bickenbach JE, Chatterji S, Badley EM, Üstün TB: Models of disablement, universalism and the ICIDH, *Soc Sci Med* **48**(9):1173–1187 (1999).
21. Bickenbach JE: ICIDH-2 and the role of environmental factors in the creation of disability, in Buhler C, Knops H, eds, *Assistive Technology on the Threshold of the New Millennium*, Amsterdam: IOS Press 1999, pp 7–12.
22. Wang PP, Badley EM, Gignac M: Exploring the role of contextual factors in disability models. *Disabil Rehabil*, **28**(2):135–40 (2006).
23. Zola IK: Toward the necessary universalizing of a disability policy, *Milbank Q* **67**:401 (1989).
24. WHO: Bruntland speech on ICF, 2002 (http://www3.who.int/icf/icftemplate.cfm).
25. WHO: Introduction, in *International Classification of Functioning, Disability and Health (ICF)*, World Health Organization, Geneva, 2001.
26. Consortium on Assistive Technology Outcomes Research (CATOR) (http://www.atoutcomes.com/pages/welcome.html).
27. Arthanat S, Lenker J: Evaluating the ICF as a framework for clinical assessment of persons for assistive technology device recommendation, *10th Annual Meeting of North American Collaborating Center on ICF*, Halifax, Nova Scotia, Canada, 2005.
28. Scherer MJ, Sax C: Cross mapping the ICF to a measure of assistive technology (AT) predisposition and use, *ICF NACC Conf*, Rochester, MN, 2005.
29. Smith RO, Longenecker Rust K: Matching assistive interventions to the ICF, *5th North American Collaborating Centre Meeting*, Toronto, 2004.
30. Andrich R: AAATE 2003 Opening Speech (Dublin, Ireland) (http://www.aaate.net/uploaded/54/aaate_conference_2003_openingspeech_president.doc).
31. AAATE position paper: *A 2003 View on Technology and Disability* (http://www.aaate.net/docs/aaate_positionpaper_2003.doc).
32. Blake DJ, Bodine C: An overview of assistive technology for persons with multiple sclerosis, *J Rehab Res Devel* **39**(2):299–312 (2002).
33. Iwarsson S, Staehl A: Accessibility, usability and universal design—positioning and definition of concepts describing person-environment relationships, *Disab Rehab* **25**(2):57–66 (2003).
34. Steiner WA, Ryser L, Huber E, Uebelhart D, Aeschlimann A, Stucki G: Use of the ICF model as a clinical problem-solving tool in physical therapy and rehabilitation medicine, *Phys Ther* **82**:1098–1107 (2002).
35. Lenker JA, Scherer MJ, Fuhrer MJ, Jutai JW, DeRuyter F: Psychometric and administrative properties of measures used in assistive technology device outcomes research, *Assist Technol* **17**(1):7–22 (2005).
36. The Canadian Occupational Performance Measure (COPM), Law M, Baptiste S, Carswell A, McColl MA, Polatajko H, Pollock N (http://www.caot.ca/copm/).
37. Wessels R, Persson J, Lorentsen O et al: IPPA: Individually prioritized problem assessment, *Technol Disab* **14**(3):141–145 (2002).
38. Scherer MJ, Craddock G: Matching person & technology (MPT) assessment process (reliability and validity), *Technol Disab* (special issue: *Assessment Assist Technol Outcomes, Effects Costs*) **14**:125–131 (2002).
39. Iwarsson SA: Long-term perspective on person–environment fit and ADL dependence among older Swedish adults, *Gerontologist* **45**:327–336 (2005).
40. Melander-Wikman A, Jansson M, Gard G: The MobiHealth Usability Evaluation Questionnaire, *eHealth Int* **2**(1) (2005) (http://www.ehealthinternational.net/).

Scherer MJ: Outcomes of assistive technology use on quality of life, *Disab Rehab*, **18**:439–448 (1996).

41. Day H, Jutai J: Measuring the psychosocial impact of assistive devices: The PIADS, *Can J Rehab*, **9**:159–168 (1996).
42. Day H, Jutai J, Woolrich W, Strong G: The stability of impact of assistive devices, *Disab Rehab*, **23**:400–404 (2001).
43. Day H, Jutai J, Campbell KA: Development of a scale to measure the psychosocial impact of assistive devices: Lessons learned and the road ahead, *Disab Rehab*, **24**(1–3):31–37 (2002).
44. International Standards Organization (ISO): ISO 9999, *Technical Aids for Persons with Disabilities—Classification and Terminology*, 2002, (and further updates available at http://www.iso.org/iso/en)
45. Bougie Ir T: The use of the ICF and ISO9999 for expressing intended use of assistive technology, *Meeting of WHO Collaborating Centres for Family of International Classifications*, Cologne, Germany, Oct 19–25, 2003
46. US Department of Education, ICDR: *Compendium of Assistive Technology Research: A Guide to Currently Funded Research Projects*, Washington, DC, 2004.
47. Fuhrer MJ, Jutai JW, Scherer MJ, Deruyter F: A framework for the conceptual modelling of assistive technology device outcomes, *Disab Rehab* **25**(22):1243–1251 (2003).
48. Jutai JW, Fuhrer MJ, Demers L, Scherer MJ, DeRuyter F: Toward a taxonomy of assistive technology device outcomes, *Am J Phys Med Rehab* **84**:294–302 (2005).
    Day H, Jutai J, Campbell KA: Development of a scale to measure the psychosocial impact of assistive devices: Lessons learned and the road ahead, *Disabil Rehabil*, **24**(1–3):31–37
49. Gray DB, Hendershot GE: The ICIDH-2: Developments for a new era of outcomes research, **81**, Supplement 2 *Arch Phys Med Rehab*, **81** (Suppl 2):S10–S14 (2000).
50. Gitlin LN: Conducting research on home environments: Lessons learned and new directions, *Gerontologist* **43**:628–637 (2003).
51. Scherer MJ, Glueckauf R: Assessing the benefits of assistive technologies for activities and participation, *Rehab Psychol* **50**(2):132–141 (2005).

5

Technology for Integration of Students with Disabilities in Higher Education

Marci Kinas Jerome, Kristine Neuber, Brianna Stegall, Anna Emenova, and Michael Behrmann

George Mason University

5.1 INTRODUCTION

The last quarter-century (i.e., the timespan since 1983) has opened many doors for individuals with disabilities as more and more persons with sensory, physical, learning, and intellectual disabilities have begun to take advantage of postsecondary education. Whether they attend 2-year community colleges or 4-year universities or whether they earn a college degree or take coursework targeted toward further development of vocational skills, they are extending their learning experiences the same way their peers do after graduating from high school. The college experience is a significant time for all young adults, providing the opportunity to mature and become independent in the years following high school.

To a large extent these opportunities are the result of federal and state policy development and implementation for persons with disabilities. Section 504 of the Rehabilitation Act of 1973 established the rights of students with disabilities to attend institutions of higher education (IHEs) early on since most IHEs received federal funding and discrimination on the basis of disability was prohibited. Section 504 evolved into the Americans with Disabilities Act (1990, 1997) [1], which requires that public and private organizations provide reasonable accommodations to persons with disabilities and provided specific rights to computers and telecommunications equipment to not only students but also faculty and staff in higher education. The Technology Related Assistance Act of 1988

The Engineering Handbook of Smart Technology for Aging, Disability, and Independence,
Edited by A. Helal, M. Mokhtari and B. Abdulrazak
Copyright © 2008 John Wiley & Sons, Inc.

(now the Assistive Technology Act of 1998 and 2004) provided definitions of assistive technology devices and services that have been used by the ADA and other federal and state laws, including the Individuals with Disabilities in Education Act (IDEA) of 1990 and which is now the Individuals with Disabilities in Education Improvement Act of 2004. The IDEA began as the Education for All Handicapped Children's Act of 1975 (PL 94-142) and was passed because there were nearly 2 million children with disabilities in the United States who were not allowed to attend public schools. As a result of this law, children with disabilities are guaranteed a free appropriate public education in the least restrictive environment. The problem in K–12 (kindergarten through 12th grade) education is actually in determining what the word "appropriate" means versus what is the "best" or "ideal" service.

As children with disabilities reach the age of majority (18) and graduate from high school (under IDEA they have the right to stay in school through the age of 21), they leave a world of mandatory services and enter the world of eligibility where the rights to services are not guaranteed and the concepts of "reasonable accommodations" comes into play. Under IDEA, services are mandatory for individuals whose disabilities adversely affect on their education, including assistive technology (AT). Under ADA, in higher education, the student has the right not to be discriminated against, but must be their own advocates and ask for support services. In higher education, assistive technology may be available, provided it is determined to be a "reasonable accommodation" for the student.

Technology is increasingly important to succeed in our society—in work, at play, at home, and in the community as well as in our efforts in lifelong learning. Whether using online banking or an ATM, sending your mother an email, purchasing a theater ticket on the Internet, or preparing an analysis and report for work, access to appropriate technology is ubiquitous. Fortunately, there are a broad range of assistive technologies that enable persons with disabilities to access those technologies, or to meet everyday functional needs. Students with impaired speech can use augmentative communication devices, students with vision impairments can use screen readers to access computers, students with hearing impairments can have speech translated to sign through signing avatars, students with physical disabilities have mobility devices to enable them to move around the school campus, and students with intellectual or learning disabilities have organizational and memory tools to assist them in completing their work. Assistive technology is improving at the same or better rate than other technologies, and our imaginations pose the only limit to finding new and creative solutions that enable everyone who wants to attend postsecondary institutions to do so. We must continue to strive to develop policies and services to enable these students to benefit from higher education.

5.2 UNIVERSITY POLICY: RIGHTS AND SERVICES FOR STUDENTS WITH DISABILITIES

Since the mid-1970s there decades has been a dramatic growth in the numbers of students with disabilities entering higher education. The percentage of students with disabilities enrolled in postsecondary institutions has tripled since 1978 [2]. The percentage of freshman who reported a disability ranging from hearing impairment, orthopedic, learning, visual impairment and blindness among others, rose from 3% in 1978 to 9% in 1998. In addition, 50% of students with disabilities enrolled persist to complete a degree or certificate [3].

This growth can be partially attributed to several laws passed to ensure equal rights and opportunities for students with disabilities. These laws include provisions to ensure access and services in the area of assistive technology. Section 504 of the Vocational Rehabilitation Act of 1973 [4], the Americans with Disabilities Act of 1990 [1], and most recently Section 508 of the Vocational Rehabilitation Act Ammendments of 1998 [5], mandating access to Web-based materials for people with disabilities, have all contributed to greater access to assistive technology at higher-education institutions.

5.2.1 Brief Discussion of Laws

Section 504 of the Vocational Rehabilitation Act of 1973 was the first civil rights law that protected people with disabilities from discrimination at the postsecondary level, stating that "No otherwise qualified individual with a disability in the United States shall, solely by reason of her or his disability be excluded from participation in, be denied the benefits of, or be subjected to discrimination under any program or activity receiving federal financial assistance" [4]. The main focus of Section 504 was to ensure that people with cognitive, sensory as well as mobility limitations, could access federally funded programs and services. Section 504 covers areas including admissions, academic adjustments, housing, and financial aid in addition to nonacademic services. The regulations under Section 504 list a number of academic adjustments that may be made, including AT equipment and services, referred to as "auxiliary aids" (34 CFR §104.44). Auxiliary aids such as software programs, videomagnifiers, or braille embossers may be used to provide access to materials in alternative formats such as electronic text, large print, and Braille.

The American with Disabilities Act (ADA) of 1990 [1] extended the provisions under the Vocational Rehabilitation Act of 1973 to the private sector including private institutions of higher education and privately owned businesses. The ADA also provides protection against discrimination in the areas of physical access to facilities, employment practices, and telecommunications [1]. Since the passage of ADA in 1990, postsecondary institutions have seen a dramatic increase in resources and courses taught online. While the question of accessibility of electronic materials was raised in ADA, it provides no specific guidelines or standards for services or materials delivered online [6]. This issue was addressed more recently through Section 508 of the Vocational Rehabilitation Act, which mandates that electronic and information technology is (or should be) accessible. This law currently covers institutions that receive federal funding; however, many public institutions fall into this category. In addition, several states and IHEs have begun to develop their own policies regarding Web accessibility to ensure that their programs are accessible to students with disabilities as defined in Section 504. Section 508 provides specific guidelines and standards that are applicable to the six areas of technology: software applications and operating systems; Web-based information and applications; telecommunication products; video and multimedia products; self-contained, closed products (e.g., fax machines and kiosks); and desktop and portable computers [5]. In compliance with Section 508, federal agencies must develop, procure, maintain, or use electronic and information technology that meets very specific standards and is accessible by both disabled and nondisabled people unless it imposes an undue burden on the agency.

5.2.2 Organizational Structure

The abovementioned laws help guide services provided to both students and employees with disabilities at postsecondary institutions. Typically there are two entities primarily responsible for ensuring compliance with these laws: (1) disability support services that provide assistance to students and instructional faculty and (2) the 504/ADA compliance officer, who is typically located in an office on campus devoted to ensuring equity and diversity in programs and hiring practices. This office is often called the *Office of Equity and Diversity Services* (OEDS).

5.2.2.1 Disability Resource Center

Students who choose to disclose their disabilities and are found eligible are supported through an office on campus often referred to as *Disability Support Services* (DSS). DSS is responsible for providing direct services to students and instructional faculty. Services include determining student's eligibility for services, collaboration with students to determine the nature of reasonable accommodations, developing institutional policies and procedures, and working closely with faculty to ensure the provision of academic adjustments and auxiliary aids for students with disabilities [7].

The transition from K–12 to higher education can be challenging for students with disabilities. The framework of legal support significantly shifts from the responsibility of the educational agency to the responsibility of the individual with a disability. In K–12 education students are entitled to a free and appropriate public education. Services are recommended and guided by a team of educators and the student's parents. Once the student moves on to college, services are no longer guaranteed. Instead, students must act as their own advocates and self-identify themselves and their need for accommodations.

The fact that they received services in K–12 education does not automatically make them eligible for services at the postsecondary institution. At the postsecondary level, a person with a disability is one who: "(1) has a physical or mental impairment that substantially limits one or more major life activities, (2) has record of such an impairment, or (3) is regarded as having such an impairment. Major life activities include walking, seeing, hearing, speaking, breathing, learning, working, caring for oneself, and performing manual tasks." [42 U.S.C. § 12102(2), 1990] [1].

Students are entitled to reasonable accommodations under ADA. There are two basic types of accommodations available to qualified students: academic adjustments and auxiliary aids and services. Academic adjustments such as extended time for tests, exams administered in a separate room, and course substitutions, modify the academic program to meet the needs of students with disabilities. Recorded and electronic books and lectures, sign language interpreters, and assistive technology devices such as braille notetakers are just some examples of auxiliary aids and services [8].

Accommodations are determined according to the student's disability but should not cause "substantial" changes and adjustments in the existing program and/or significant alterations of the course standards and expectations [9]. There are times when faculty may refuse to provide prescribed accommodations if they believe that the accommodation will significantly alter the academic integrity of the course. Accommodation disputes are most often handled by disability support services staff who suggest the ways to accommodate the students, and/or find a compromise between a reasonable accommodation and the significant alteration to the program. If a compromise cannot be reached through a meeting with the professor, the dispute would likely be elevated and handled by the 504/ADA Compliance Officer through the Office of Equity and Diversity Services.

5.2.2.2 Office of Equity and Diversity Services

All postsecondary institutions are required to have an office or an individual responsible for compliance of mandates specified under Section 504 of the Vocational Rehabilitation Act and the Americans with Disabilities Act [10]. Small institutions may combine this position with the direct services offered through disability support services. Larger institutions, like George Mason University, house this position within an office that ensures equitable practices, affirmative action, and protection from sexual harassment. At George Mason University this office is referred to as the *Office of Equity and Diversity Services* (OEDS). The main responsibilities of the Section 504/ADA Compliance Officer are diverse and wide-ranging, including responsibility for developing processes for compliance and overseeing the evaluation and implementation of those processes.

While the disability services office provides direct services to students with disabilities, the 504/ADA coordinator oversees the overall compliance for the university, including student services, barrier removal provisions for accessible transportation, training and information dissemination, and tracking and processing complaints and grievances related to compliance with disability law. In addition, the 504/ADA Compliance Officer works with Human Resources to ensure equitable hiring processes, and determining eligibility and appropriate accommodations for employees with disabilities.

5.3 THE PROCESS FOR OBTAINING ASSISTIVE TECHNOLOGY SERVICES: A CASE STUDY

By 1998, 98% of 2-year and 4-year postsecondary educational institutions provided at least minimal support and accommodations to students with disabilities [11]. Although the laws mandate these services at all postsecondary institutions, the provisions of services vary from one institution to another. To provide an example, we will discuss the process at George Mason University. Disability Support Services are provided through the Disability Resource Center (DRC). The DRC currently serves slightly over 1000 students with disabilities. The total student enrollment at the university is approximately 30,000. These students have a wide variety of disabling conditions. Students with learning disabilities represent the largest group of disabled students on campus (35%) of the total number. Students with ADD/ADHD, students with emotional and psychological disorders and those with medical needs represent other relatively large groups. There are also students with head or brain injuries and visual, hearing, and mobility impairments. The mission of DRC is "to facilitate equal access to university programs, events, activities, and services for students with students."

Once students are deemed eligible for services, they meet with a counselor who helps them identify the need for accommodations in each course for which they are registered. If they require accommodations for a course, a faculty contact sheet is completed listing each accommodation for the course. The student is then required to sign the form and take it to the professor for signature, preferably at the beginning of the course. Accommodations listed on this form often include assistive technology such as recorded lectures; electronic books; use of an assistive listening device; and use of software such as screen reading, voice recognition, and spelling and grammar checking. The form may also explain that a sign language interpreter will be present in the class. Other types of accommodation may include extended time for projects or exams.

5.3.1 Assistive Technology Initiative

One of the most common forms of accommodation offered to students is in the form of computer-based assistive technology. Postsecondary institutions are required to provide these accommodations in a timely manner on request. Advancements in this field have provided an unlimited array of software and devices to students with disabilities. Assistive technology services at the postsecondary level generally fall into four distinct areas: (1) consultation and screening for individual accommodations, (2) campuswide access, (3) creation of accessible text, and (4) Web accessibility. Many universities have an individual who is primarily responsible for ensuring access to computer-based assistive devices and software on campus. In most cases this position is located in the disability resource center.

At George Mason University, assistive technology services are provided through a separate office that works in partnership with both the Disability Resource Center and the Office of Equity and Diversity Services. The program resides at the Kellar Institute for Human disAbilities which is part of the College of Education and Human Development (CEHD). Providing services through the CEHD has allowed the university to use equipment located in the Assistive Technology Lab, which is primarily an instructional lab for students enrolled in the doctoral, master's, and certificate programs in assistive technology. The Assistive Technology Initiative is a model program designed to leverage resources in order to provide the most comprehensive services to students and employees.

5.3.2 Consultation and Screenings for Individual Accommodations

Students who are eligible for services through the Disability Resource Center are referred to the ATI for a screening to determine appropriate AT accommodations. A wide range of assistive technology software and devices are available to students, ranging from simple graphic organizers for students with learning disabilities, screen-reading/enlarging software for students with visual impairments, to advanced technologies such as single-switch access and eye-gaze technology for students with significant physical disabilities. Recommendations are sent back to the DRC to be added to the faculty contact form. Ongoing support is provided to the student in regard to training and technical support for recommended equipment and software. Employees with disabilities are afforded the same services but must be referred by the Office of Equity and Diversity Services.

5.3.3 Campuswide Access

Campuswide access to assistive technology also falls under the responsibility of the ATI. The ADA specifies that effective access to computers and services must be provided during the same hours they are available to all students [10]. Therefore, it is essential that accessible computers be located in academic computer labs, libraries, and other areas open to students on weekends and overnight hours. The ATI provides technical support and training to individuals responsible for all areas where assistive technology is located.

5.3.4 Creation of Accessible Text

A large number of students served through the disability resource center have disabilities that affect their ability to read print materials (i.e., visual impairment, learning disabilities, and physical disabilities). The ATI provides eligible students access to textbooks and other printed materials in an accessible format, such as electronic text that can be read by the computer through synthesized speech. Textbooks that cannot be purchased on CD from the publisher are scanned using a high-speed scanner and optical character recognition (OCR) software. In addition, short documents such as worksheets and exams can be translated and created in Braille through the services of the ATI.

5.3.5 Web Accessibility

Another important area of accommodation is Web-based course materials and university resources. With the dramatic increase in online courses and resources such as online registration, assistive technology services extends to ensuring that university-operated Websites are accessible according to guidelines specified in Section 508 of the Vocational Rehabilitation Act. Other universities may choose to follow guidelines developed by the World-Wide Web Consortium (W3C). Ensuring that Websites are accessible is a complicated and time-consuming process because of the number of Websites constructed and the dynamic nature of information on the Web. The ATI helps to develop and maintain appropriate policies and provides direct consultation with the university Web team as well as regular training sessions and awareness activities to Webmasters, faculty, and staff across all campuses.

With the advances in assistive technology it appears that there are limitless ways to accommodate students in the classroom and in university-sponsored programs. However, it is important to remember that the purpose of accommodations, whether AT aids or modifications to programs, are provided to level the playing field, not provide an advantage to the student with a qualifying disability.

5.3.6 Summary

Several laws have been developed to enable students with disabilities to participate in higher education. The number of students with disabilities pursuing degrees in IHEs is steadily increasing although still lacking in comparison to the general student population. For students, the transition from a protected environment afforded through the K–12 education system to the postsecondary environment can be difficult as they learn to advocate for themselves. However, several services and safeguards are in place through the disability support services and the Office of Equity and Diversity Services to help students and employees with disabilities obtain appropriate and reasonable accommodations. Access to assistive technology software and devices is mandated through provisions identified in Section 504 of the Vocational Rehabilitation Act and the Americans with Disabilities Act. With the influx of online courses, the issue of Web accessibility has surfaced. Many universities have begun to develop policies and plans to ensure that courses and resources are accessible through the use of assistive technology. With continued commitment to compliance with established disability legislation and the continued advancement and promise of assistive technology, the future is bright for students with disabilities at postsecondary institutions.

5.4 DISTANCE EDUCATION TECHNOLOGY IN HIGHER EDUCATION

College campuses nationwide are embracing the integration of distance education technology into many of their undergraduate and graduate courses. Although often used as a generic term, *distance education* encompasses a variety of technologies, including email, course Websites, course management tools, and video- and audioconferencing. Today, *distance education* can refer to the use of technology as an organizational and communication tool to enhance a traditional course where an instructor and students gather together in a physical location, to supersede the physical location so that students and the instructor can meet virtually in real time instead of on campus, or to eliminate the need for a traditional class by designing self-paced student course modules that require little to no instructor interaction.

Both students and instructors have pushed the demand to incorporate more distance education technology in college courses. For students, the greatest benefits include the time and money saved in travel and parking and the flexibility to participate, interact, and complete assignments based around their busy family, work, and social lives. Instructors appreciate the same flexibility; however, they also value the pedagogic benefits of utilizing distance education technology in their courses.

There are several benefits to teaching using distance education technology. Although initially time-consuming, instructors who teach online or use technology-interactive elements must be extremely organized and prepared in advance of class. Willis [12] identifies that teaching with distance education has several other advantages, including the ability reach a more diverse group of learners, inviting guest speakers who would otherwise not be available because of distance or time, and increasing interaction among students, including those from various social, cultural, economic, and experiential backgrounds.

5.4.1 Distance Education Technology for Students and Instructors with Disabilities

For college students with disabilities the trend to include more distance education options opens many new doors of opportunity. Depending on their disability, students may find it challenging to travel to campus and access the campus facilities, to access course lectures, materials, and handouts, and to be an active participant with other classmates and the instructor in a traditional face-to-face class. The ability to access course materials ahead of time via a course Website, to participate in online discussions with classmates and the instructor, and/or to participate at home instead of traveling to campus afford many individuals with disabilities the chance to be productive and active learners when it was otherwise impossible or arduous. Furthermore, utilizing distance education creates new opportunities for faculty with disabilities, eliminating many of the same barriers that students with disabilities encounter in face-to-face courses. For example, an instructor who is hearing impaired or has a speech disorder may prefer to teach an online course because it is more efficient to communicate through email, asynchronous chats, and annotated lecture slides.

Unfortunately, the same technology that makes it easier and more efficient for some individuals to take college courses at the same time creates access barriers for many people, in particular those with disabilities. Many people are familiar with the term "digital divide." To participate in online courses or use distance education technology components, students need to have access to the required technology such as a reliable high-speed Internet connection. For individuals with disabilities there is often a "second digital divide" [13]. Although people with disabilities may have all the technology tools to needed participate in classes, because of accessibility barriers of the distance education technology, they cannot make full use of the technology tools, services, and information.

5.4.1.1 Accessibility Barriers

Accessibility barriers depend on disability and at times contradict each other; what may be beneficial for one disability is not for another. Burgstahler [14] describes the access barriers for different disability groups.

5.4.1.1.1 Vision Individuals who are blind use screen reader technology to access the computer. Screen readers use a synthesized voice to read the information on the computer to the user, including the Internet. Since screen readers cannot read graphics, complex tables, flash, and frames without proper accessible markup, individuals struggle with many online learning components. Students who are blind may have difficulty in accessing course Websites to download lectures and handouts and to participate in synchronous course components such as real-time chat and electronic whiteboards because they are not screen-reader-accessible. Although companies such as Macromedia and Blackboard are committed to developing accessible solutions [15], the barriers still exist today.

For individuals with low or limited vision the access barriers are not as severe, but they still they may have difficulty navigating Websites and course materials if the materials are not available in large print or if the page becomes cluttered or overwhelming with the use of screen magnification software. Although a screen magnifier will enlarge the font or graphics to an appropriate size for the individual to see and participate, the user also looses the ability to see the whole screen at the same time and must scroll from side to side and up and down to view the entire content. The user inevitably is slowed down by the technology. Although the individual can physically participate in online chat and whiteboard discussions, the learning experience may not be beneficial to them because they cannot always be active and effective participants in this medium.

5.4.1.1.2 Hearing For individuals who are deaf and/or hard of hearing, audio and video components pose the greatest barrier. In face to face classes, deaf students often read lips and/or use an interpreter to acquire the information and participate in discussions. Yet, courses that utilize live audio- and videoconference components or Web-based media clips are difficult for students because they are seldom captioned and the video quality is such that it is difficult, if not impossible to read lips. Emerging technologies include real-time voice recognition captioning and signing avatars that can be used in conjunction with live video and audio components. In the future these may increase accessibility for many individuals.

5.4.1.1.3 Motor Individuals who have motor impairments with limited or no use of their hands utilize alternative keyboard and mouse technology to navigate the computer, including the Internet. Similar to blind individuals who use screen readers, people with motor impairments rely on the use of keyboard shortcuts to access online course materials and communication tools. As discussed previously, the same technology that is inaccessible to screen readers is also inaccessible to individuals who use alternate access methods.

5.4.1.1.4 Cognition and Learning Unlike other disability groups, individuals with cognitive and learning disabilities face few physical access issues but still often struggle in distance education courses. Online courses tend to include a lot of text and information, and if not properly organized on course Website and management systems, students may be confused and feel overwhelmed. The organization strategies they use in face-to-face classes may be different in an online learning environment. Furthermore, because individuals with learning and cognitive disabilities often have difficulty with reading, writing, and spelling participating in fast-paced real-time components such as synchronous chats may not be conducive to their learning style.

5.4.1.2 Universal Design for Learning

Many universities are quick to develop online courses and incorporate distance education technology into their courses without considering the needs of those students with disabilities. Students with disabilities often find distance education components challenging, and universities may need to go to great lengths to provide accommodations and accessibility options for students. Yet, in reality many students struggle with distance education technology components because for some it is a lack of access to the technology and materials while for others it is a new learning environment and requires them to develop and embrace a new style of learning. Therefore, universities need to adopt principles of universal design when developing online courses and interactive components.

Universal design was initially used in architecture in reference to accessible building design that could benefit all individuals such as automatic door openers and curb cuts. Universal design is the "design of products and environments to be usable by all people, to the greatest extent possible, without the need for adaptation or specialized design" [16]. Principles of universal design are currently utilized for print materials for individuals with disabilities such as the availability of course textbooks in digital format. Digital format allows individuals who are blind or have print disabilities to fully access course materials using the computer or other mobile technology to have the text read aloud. These same principles should be applied when developing online courses and selecting distance education components prior to course instruction to ensure that all enrolled students can access the technology and participate as active learning.

5.4.1.3 Providing Alternatives

Unlike print media, developing accessible and universally designed distance education technology proves to be more challenging because the content is more dynamic. As stated previously, although many technology developers such as Macromedia and Blackboard strive to produce accessible tools for individuals with disabilities, the truth is that what is accessible for one student may still pose a barrier for another even if designed with accessibility in mind. The second issue is that even though the technology system may be accessible to individuals with disabilities, how the instructor utilizes those tools within the course may still present barriers. For example, the instructor may use the Blackboard Web-based course management tool to post lecture notes and handouts in an online course. While Blackboard has improved their system to be accessible with screen readers, a student who is blind may still be unable to access the course materials because the instructor posted the files in a format that was not accessible to the student's screen reader.

One crucial component in making distance education technology accessible to individuals with disabilities is to provide options and alternatives.

5.4.1.3.1 Handouts and Resources

Most course materials are now designed electronically and are readily available to email students and to post on course Websites. However, not all file formats, including Microsoft PowerPoint, Adobe Acrobat, and Macromedia Flash, are accessible for individuals with disabilities, especially individuals who are blind. There are several online resources to assist instructors in designing and converting these files into an accessible format. However, the key strategy is to provide electronic materials in multiple formats to ensure access to all students, including students who may not own a specific software program needed to access that file, and also to ensure that AT tools can access the file for individuals with disabilities. The same principle holds true for multimedia files such as videoclips used during instruction. For instance, if the videoclip cannot be closed-captioned for a student who is deaf, then the instructor can provide a transcript of the video for the student to read.

5.4.1.3.2 Interactive Tools Maintaining interactivity is a key element in any quality distance education program. Currently, several strategies and tools are available to increase interactivity between both the students and the instructor and among students. These tools include both real-time synchronous interaction such as live video- and audio-conferencing, chatrooms, and whiteboards and any time-asynchronous interaction such as discussion boards and email. In general, there are more accessibility issues with synchronous components because many of the available technology tools are still inherently not accessible to assistive technology devices. Although developers are continually working to improve accessibility as they develop new products and updates, progress is still slow. Instructors must be mindful that synchronous course components may pose challenges to students in their courses and, like resource materials, must provide alternatives and options to ensure meaningful participation, for instance, giving students working in an online group the option to work in real-time chatroom or to participate in a phone or audioconference.

5.4.2 Summary

Distance education technology offers great flexibility and options for both students and instructors in higher education. For individuals with disabilities, the integration of distance education technology presents both new opportunities and hurdles in receiving a quality education. Universally designed distance education components should be selected to maximize accessibility and usability by all students. To ensure accessibility, instructors need to provide options and alternatives to students with disabilities, including providing materials in multiple formats and providing options to participate in course instruction and activities as a active and engaged learner. Ultimately, students should not be penalized because of technology barriers.

5.5 POSTSECONDARY OPPORTUNITIES FOR STUDENTS WITH INTELLECTUAL DISABILITIES

With the Individuals with Disabilities Education Act of 1997 and its increased emphasis on age appropriateness and inclusion, increasing numbers of students with disabilities are completing high school with the expectation of attending a postsecondary institution. This expectation is not limited to students with learning, physical, or sensory disabilities. Students with intellectual disabilities share this expectation, and 13% attend postsecondary institutions [17]. The Division on Developmental Disabilities of the Council for Exceptional Children released a position statement supporting the inclusion of young adults with mental retardation in age-appropriate settings, in particular, those students ages 18–22

[18]. Students with intellectual disabilities have traditionally been excluded from higher education. While their siblings graduated high school and went on to college, they often remained in high school until the age of 22, when they would transition into a community day program or supported employment. A number of institutions of higher education now offer programs for young adults with intellectual disabilities to participate in the college experience while also furthering their functional academic and vocational skills.

Neubert et al. [19, p. 156] define postsecondary programs as ones "that provide education or vocational training to individuals with [mental retardation] or other [severe disabilities] within two or four year colleges or universities, or adult education programs." There are currently over 90 programs [20] incorporated into or affiliated with 2- and 4-year colleges and universities across the country for students with intellectual disabilities and severe learning disabilities. These programs vary in their target audience and program design. They interpret the college experience in varying degrees of authenticity and inclusion. Programs range from self-contained to full-inclusion programs in the college experience. Self-contained programs focus on life skills and functional employment skills, while partially integrated programs offer social opportunities for students to interact with nondisabled peers and occasionally enroll in college courses, although not necessarily for credit. In full-inclusion programs students receive large amounts of individualized support and are fully integrated in classes, although again, not always for credit. Any of these programs may culminate in certificates of completion, college credit, and/or an associate's degree, depending on the program and the student's abilities. Some of these programs offer dual enrollment with public secondary schools to provide age-appropriate placement while students continue to receive services under the Individuals with Disabilities Education Improvement Act of 2004. While the number of programs remains relatively small, research has shown that postsecondary education can improve employment chances for individuals with disabilities [21–23].

5.5.1 Technology Integration

Burgstahler [24] explains that instructional and assistive technologies have the potential to increase students' personal independence, employment options, and community participation. Consequently, the availability of technology in postsecondary settings is of critical importance, particularly considering many students with mental retardation who could benefit from assistive technology do not have access to it in K–12 settings [25]. The independent nature of postsecondary environments supports the authentic inclusion of technology. It is also an environment better prepared to handle the inadequacies of available technology. For example, there are limited choices of age-appropriate software to support adult acquisition of basic literacy skills [26]. Unlike families and K–12 public schools, colleges and universities are often in a unique position in that they have the intellectual, temporal, and technologic resources to develop appropriate software.

Burgstahler [24] explains that much of the possible success for students with disabilities in postsecondary education will relate to their access to and use of technology in these experiences. Instructional technology is typically utilized in traditional postsecondary programs, as witnessed with the use of PowerPoint presentations and existence of computer labs. For students with intellectual disabilities, instructional technology functions as assistive technology, supporting them in activities that would not be possible otherwise. Postsecondary programs can incorporate instructional technology and assistive technology in numerous ways to support students' independence and employment aspirations.

5.5.2 Case Study: Learning into Future Environments

George Mason University's Learning into Future Environments (LIFE) program is a postsecondary program for young adults with intellectual disabilities housed at a 4-year institution. The LIFE program illustrates successful integration and the value of technology in programs for students with intellectual disabilities in a postsecondary education setting. It incorporates technology across content and courses, teaching functional academic, employment, and independent living skills. In this program students email mentors and friends, participate in Fantasy Football Leagues, and use Palm Pilots. As society becomes increasingly technologically-driven, the LIFE program teaches its students basic skills to operate common technologies.

5.5.2.1 Employment Skills

Research has shown that postsecondary education experiences improve chances of competitive employment for individuals with disabilities [17]. Consequently, employment skills are interwoven throughout the program. Many of the activities and internships geared toward fostering these skills involve the use of technology. Students learn and apply email and data entry skills. For example, students enter data for professors and maintain the technical assistance library database. In addition to data entry skills, the LIFE students learn social skills needed for employment. The use of videocameras, with their visual and auditory feedback, raises students' awareness of their behavior, promoting appropriate behavior and self regulation [27]. They learn to operate cell phones: checking messages, saving telephone numbers, and setting alarms. With cell phones, they practice leaving voicemail messages. The immediate feedback from the replay features supports students' efforts toward clarity in diction and word choice, both of which are important when contacting family, friends, and employers.

Similar to using cell phone alarms, some students have begun using Palm Pilots to help stay organized and timely. Preliminary research on the use of Palm Pilots to improve task completion with individuals with mental retardation has been promising. It can provide visual and auditory prompts to walk individuals through tasks, reducing their reliance on others [28]. Palm Pilots allow for differentiated applications and supports. Davies et al. [28] found that Palm Pilots were perceived favorably by users, perhaps in part because of their widespread use by the general public. While Palm Pilots and computer programs support the independence of individuals with mental retardation, the software programs were specifically designed for this population [26,28,29]. Much of the commercially available software for these devices is too complex for successful use by individuals with intellectual disabilities. Consequently, LIFE faculty spend time adapting traditional software for student use.

The LIFE program's expectations and curriculum facilitate authentic use of technology, promoting the attainment of employment skills. Traditional postsecondary education involves more freedom and responsibility than secondary education. These differences are replicated by the LIFE program. Students are expected to schedule and manage travel across the university, attending classes and social events independently. They are expected to arrive on time to classes, internships, and appointments, as they would be in employment situations. The use of technology assists LIFE students in fulfilling their responsibilities. The LIFE program uses technology to build social and task related skills needed for employment.

5.5.2.2 Academic Skills

The LIFE program works to further students' academic skills, which will also help improve their chances for future employment. There is a focus on functional communication, reading, writing, and math. Complementing work on vocational skills, students learn to maintain a checkbook through the use of a spreadsheet template modeled after a checkbook register. Use of computer programs has been found effective in assisting individuals with intellectual disabilities in managing their money [29]. Electronic books read with a talking word processor serve as resources for developing auditory comprehension, another valuable skill in employment and life. Some students utilize voice recognition programs as writing tools. Others develop communication, writing skills, and sight word vocabularies through the use of software such as Cloze Pro and Clicker 5. The LIFE program in many cases introduces and/or reintroduces students to technology that will help them throughout their adult lives. Technology serves as a tool, strengthening the academic skills fostered in the program.

5.5.2.3 Leisure Skills

Use of computers by individuals with intellectual disabilities is often limited to academic endeavors [25]. However, in the LIFE program students have the opportunity to develop technology-based leisure skills. Surfing the Web, a leisure activity for many individuals, is also enjoyed by the students. Unlike many individuals with mental retardation who have limited access to the Internet [26], LIFE students learn safe Internet practices with the benefit of supervised guidance. Furthermore, students have become proficient with the basic features of cardmaking software, digital cameras, and graphics programs. They will soon add the use of videocameras to this list.

LIFE students utilize the technology skills they acquire to participate in typical college activities. They will use the videocameras in conjunction with their theater production. They have access to all social activities at the university, from music groups, to basketball games, to lunch in the student union building. Students use the Internet to locate upcoming activities and digital cameras to document their experiences. The LIFE students often use their email to arrange lunch engagements with other students. The LIFE program utilizes technology to support student participation in age-appropriate leisure activities.

5.5.3 Summary

Higher education now provides more opportunities for students with intellectual disabilities to live the "college experience." Technology, integrated into these programs, assists students with further developing academic, social, employment, and leisure skills. Postsecondary institutions often place more responsibility on students and have the resources to develop technology, providing both the expectations and the tools to assist students with intellectual disabilities in living as independently as possible. As students with disabilities continue to attend postsecondary institutions in higher numbers, technology is expected to play an increasing role in their college experience.

REFERENCES

1. Americans with Disabilities Act of 1990: 42 USCA, § 12101 et seq (retrieved 2/26/06 from http://uscode.house.gov/download/pls/42C126.txt).

2. US Department of Education, National Center for Education Statistics: *Enrollment in Postsecondary Institutions, Fall 2001 and Financial Statistics, Fiscal Year 2001* (retrieved 2/26/06 from www.nces.ed.gov/programs/quarterly/vol).

3. Stodden RA, Conway MA, Chang KBT: Findings from a study of transition, technology and postsecondary supports for youth with disabilities: Implications for secondary school educators, *J Spec Educ Technol* **18**(4):29–43 (2003).

4. Vocational Rehabilitation Act of 1973: PL 93-112, USC 29, § 794a (retrieved 1/26/06 from http://uscode.house.gov/download/pls/29C16.txt).

5. Vocational Rehabilitation Amendments: Section 508, PL 105-220, USC 29, § 794d (retrieved 1/26/06 from http://uscode.house.gov/download/pls/29C16.txt).

6. Edmonds C: Providing access to students with disabilities in online distance education: Legal and technical concerns for higher education, *Am J Distance Educ* **18**(1):51–62 (2004).

7. Gamble G: *An Analysis of Disability Support Services in Higher Education*, Univ Alabama, ERIC Document Reproduction Service ED445445, 2000.

8. Wolanin T, Steele P: *Higher Education Opportunities for Students with Disabilities: A Primer for Policymakers*, Institute for Higher Education Policy, Washington, DC, 2004.

9. Thomas S: College students and disability law, *J Spec Educ* **33**(4):248–265 (2000).

10. Friend GF, Judy B, Reilly V: *The ADA Coordinator's Guide to Campus Compliance*, LRP Publications, Horsham, PA, 2002.

11. US Department of Education, National Center for Education Statistics (NCES): *An Institutional Perspective on Students with Disabilities in Postsecondary Education,* 1999 (retrieved 1/26/06 from http://nces.ed.gov/pubsearch/pubsinfo.asp?pubid=1999046).

12. Willis B: *Distance Education: A Practical Guide*, Educational Technology Publications, Englewood Cliffs, NJ, 1993.

13. Burgstahler S: Distance learning: Universal design, universal access, *Educ Technol Rev* **10**(1) (2002) (retrieved 3/07/06 from http://www.aace.org/pubs/etr/issue2/burgstahler.cfm).

14. Burgstahler S: Real connections: Making distance learning accessible to everyone, 2006 (retrieved 3/7/06 from Univ Washington, Disabilities, Opportunities, Internetworking, and Technology (DO-IT) Website: http://www.washington.edu/doit/Brochures/Technology/distance.learn.html).

15. National Center of Disability and Access to Education (NCDAE): *Technology Fact Sheets*, 2005 (retrieved 3/07/06 from http://www.ncdae.org/tools/index.cfm).

16. Mace R: *What Is Universal Design?* (retrieved 3/07/06 from North Carolina State Univ Center for Universal Design Website: http://design.ncsu.edu/cud/univ_design/ud.htm).

17. Wagner M, Newman L, Renee C, Levine P: *National Longitudinal Transition Study 2: Changes over Time in the Early Postschool Outcomes of Youth with Disabilities*, 2005 (SRI Project P11182), SRI International, Menlo Park, CA, 2005.

18. Smith TEC, Puccini IK: Position statement: Secondary curricula and policy issues for students with mental retardation, *Educ Train Mental Retard Devel Disab* **30**(4):275–282 (1995).

19. Neubert DA, Moon MS, Grigal M, Redd V: Post-secondary educational practices for individuals with metal retardation and other significant disabilities: A review of the literature, *J Voc Rehab* **16**:155–168 (2001).

20. Univ Massachusetts, Boston, Institute for Community Inclusion, University of Hawaii, Center on Disability Studies, & Federation for Children with Special Needs: *ThinkCollege.net* (retrieved 1/26/06 from http://thinkcollege.net/programs/index.php).

21. Gilmore D, Schuster J, Zafft C, Hart D: Postsecondary education services and employment outcomes within the Vocational Rehabilitiation System, *Disab Stud Q* **21**(1) (2001) (retrieved 1/23/06 from http://www.dsq-sds.org/_articles_pdf/2001/Winter/dsq_2001_Winter_08.pdf).

22. National Council on Disability and Social Security Administration: *Transition and Post-School Outcomes for Youth with Disabilities: Closing the Gaps to Post-Secondary Education and Employment*, NCDSSA, Washington, DC, 2000.
23. Zaft C, Hart D, Zimbrich K: College career connection: A study of youth with intellectual disabilities and the impact of postsecondary education, *Educ Train Devel Disab* **39**(1):45–53 (2004).
24. Burgstahler S: The role of technology in preparing youth with disabilities for postsecondary education and employment, *J Spec Educ Technol*, **18**(4) (2003).
25. Wehmeyer ML: Assistive technology and students with mental retardation: Utilization and barriers, *J Spec Educ Technol* **14**(1):48–58 (1999).
26. Wehmeyer ML, Smith SJ, Palmer SB, Davies DK: Technology use by students with intellectual disabilities: An overview, *J Spec Educ Technol* **19**(4):7–21 (2004).
27. Embregts PJ: Using self-management, video feedback, and graphic feedback to improve social behavior of youth with mild mental retardation, *Educ Train Devel Disab* **38**(3):283–295 (2003).
28. Davies DK, Stock SE, Wehmeyer M: Enhancing independent task performance for individuals with mental retardation through use of handheld self-directed visual and audio prompting system, *Educ Train, Mental Retard Devel Disab* **37**(2):209–218 (2002).
29. Davies DK, Stock SE, Wehmeyer ML: Utilization of computer technology to facilitate money management by individuals with mental retardation, *Educ Train Mental Retard Devel Disab*, **38**(1):106–112 (2003).

6

ISO 9999 Assistive Products for Persons with Disability: Classification and Terminology

Ir. Theo Bougie
Bougie Revalidatie Technologie, The Netherlands

6.1 INTRODUCTION TO ISO 9999

The International Organization for Standardization (ISO) is a worldwide federation of national standards bodies (ISO member bodies) [1,2].

International Standard ISO 9999 establishes a classification of assistive products, which are specially produced or generally available for persons with disabilities. Assistive products (including software) are classified according to function. The classification scheme consists of three hierarchical levels—classes, subclasses, and divisions—and the codes consist of three pairs of digits each. As in other classification schemes, codes, titles, explanatory notes, inclusions, exclusions and cross-references are given for each hierarchical level. Besides the explanatory text and the classification itself, a conversion table between the previous edition and a revised edition of the standard and an alphabetical index are provided in order to facilitate the use and improve the accessibility of the classification.

With finalization of the fourth revision of ISO 9999 (in 2007), the title was changed from *Technical Aids for Persons with Disabilities—Classification and Terminology* to

---

The Engineering Handbook of Smart Technology for Aging, Disability, and Independence,
Edited by A. Helal, M. Mokhtari and B. Abdulrazak
Copyright © 2008 John Wiley & Sons, Inc.

Assistive Products for Persons with Disability—Classification and Terminology. Hence *technical aids* are referred to as *assistive products*.

6.2 SCOPE OF ISO 9999

This international standard establishes a classification of assistive products, specially produced or generally available, for persons with disabilities.

Assistive products used by a disabled person that require assistance by another person for their operation or administration are included in the classification.

The following items are specifically excluded from ISO 1999:

- Items used for the installation of assistive products
- Solutions obtained by combinations of assistive products that are individually classified in this international standard
- Medicines
- Assistive products and instruments used exclusively by healthcare professionals
- Nontechnical solutions, such as personal assistance, guide dogs, or lip reading
- Implanted devices
- Financial support

This standard includes the following classes:

04 Assistive products for personal medical treatment
05 Assistive products for training in skills
06 Orthoses and prostheses
09 Assistive products for personal care and protection
12 Assistive products for personal mobility
15 Assistive products for housekeeping
18 Furnishings and adaptations to homes and other premises
22 Assistive products for communication and information
24 Assistive products for handling objects and devices
27 Assistive products for environmental improvement, tools, and industrial machinery
30 Assistive products for recreation

6.3 CONSTRUCTION OF ISO 9999

The classification consists of three hierarchical levels, termed *classes, subclasses*, and *divisions*, successively. Each class, subclass, or division consists of a code, a title, and, if necessary, an explanatory note and/or reference to other parts of the classification.

Explanatory notes are used to clarify the content of the class, subclass or division. Inclusions and/or exclusions are used to provide examples. References are used for two purposes:

- To distinguish different classes, subclasses, or divisions
- For information, such as references between related products

In general, references are made to the lowest possible level.

6.4 CODING SYSTEM OF ISO 9999

The code consists of three pairs of digits. The first pair of digits indicates a class; the second pair, a subclass; and the third pair, a division.

For practical reasons, in this standard the classes are indicated by one pair of digits only (deleting two pairs of zeros), and subclasses are indicated by two pairs of digits (deleting one pair of zeros). The code determines the position of the class, the subclass, or the division, respectively, in the classification.

The digits for the codes were originally designated with intervals of three. In subsequent revisions, the intervening digits have been used to introduce new classes, subclasses, and divisions without significantly modifying the classification.

In revisions, codes that were originally used to classify items have been omitted from the classification and are not used to classify new items that have been added to the classification.

6.5 OTHER CLASSIFICATION CHARACTERISTICS OF ISO 9999

All titles in the classification are in the plural form (see Fig. 6.1).
Titles at the three hierarchical levels are characterized as Follows:
Titles at class level generally describe a broad area of functions, such as "assistive products for housekeeping." Class-level titles describing a specific product are used only when the term is broadly applied or when the function of the product is incorporated in the name, for example, "orthoses and prostheses."

Alphabetical and analytical index
- communication and information 22
- communication software 22 36 15
- communication therapy 05 03
- communication training 05 03
- communication with pictures/drawings (training) 05 06 27
- compasses 12 39 12
- component boxes 27 09 06
- compressed air suits 04 06 03
- compression garments 04 06 03
- compression units 04 06 12
- computer joysticks 22 39 09
- computer terminal tables 18 03 03
- computers 22 36
- computers (accessories) 22 36 18
- concept development (training) 05 12 12
- connecting units (urine collection) 09 27 18

FIGURE 6.1 Some ISO 9999 classification.

Titles at subclass level describe a special function, for instance, "assistive products for reading," within the broad area covered by the class, such as "assistive products for communication and information."

Titles at division level refer to particular products, such as "book support and bookholders," covered by the subclass, for example "assistive products for reading."

In cases where an assistive product is used by persons with a specific disability, or is age- or gender-specific, the title used may refer only to that group.

6.5.1 Classification Rules

6.5.1.1 General Rules

A class is equal to the sum of its subclasses, and a subclass is equal to the sum of its divisions.

In general, parts of assistive products, accessories to assistive products, individually adapted assistive products, and individual adaptations in homes and other premises are included in the assistive products with which they are associated.

Parts, accessories, and adaptations are separately classified when they are associated with a group of assistive products. In these cases, they are classified as closely as possible to the group of assistive products with which they are associated; an example is "12 07 Accessories for assistive products for walking."

The classification is organized in such a manner that all assistive products can be classified without being tested or measured. A classification of hypothetical assistive products is avoided.

The classes are created in such manner that they don't overlap with respect to the broad functions described for other classes. The subclasses are created so as to avoid overlap between the specific functions of other subclasses, and the divisions are created so as to avoid overlap between products in other divisions.

6.5.1.2 Rules for Specific National Applications

Classes 00, 01, 02, and 90 through 99 and the associated subclasses and divisions are reserved for national applications.

A fixed-position code, 89, is reserved at all levels for assistive products that are categorized as "other."

In addition, further levels may be added to any part of the classification to serve national or local purposes (e.g., see Fig. 6.2).

6.5.2 Group 22: Assistive Products for Communication and Information

A special group of the classification deals with assistive devices for communication and information. This group was fully reorganized in the 2007 issue of the ISO Standard (fourth revision), due to new technologies and other functions of information and communication technology (ICT) and computer technology for disabled people.

Following the general characteristics of the ISO 9999 standard and the way products are classified, the subdivision of Group 22 is based on the execution of human activities and the role that assistive devices can play to support or enable those functions. It includes modern technologies (PC, PDA, etc.) and also classical solutions such as assistive devices for reading books and bookholders (e.g., see Fig. 6.3).

Of course, the solutions for providing input to and output from computers are part of the classification.

```
06 03  Spinal orthoses

Devices that are designed to modify body structures and body functions of the
spine
            The device may be custom-fabricated, i.e., designed to meet the
            functional needs of the individual user, or prefabricated, i.e.,
            designed to meet particular functional requirements. The
            prefabricated devices are adjustable, i.e., need adjustment for the
            individual user, or ready to use, i.e., need no adjustment for the
            individual user
            Assistive products for abdominal hernia care; see 04 12
06 03 03    Sacroiliac orthoses (pelvic orthosis)
            Devices that encompass the pelvis including the sacral region
06 03 04    Lumbar orthoses
            Devices that encompass the lumbar region of the trunk
06 03 06    Lumbosacral orthoses
            Devices that encompass the whole or part of the lumbar and sacroiliac
            regions of the trunk
```

FIGURE 6.2 Example of an ISO 9999 classification addendum.

```
22      Assistive products for communication and information
    ■   22 03   Assistive products for seeing
    ■   22 06   Assistive products for hearing
    ■   22 09   Assistive products for voice production
    ■   22 12   Assistive products for drawing and writing
    ■   22 15   Assistive products for calculation
    ■   22 18   Assistive products for handling audio, visual, and video
                information
    ■   22 21   Assistive products for face-to-face communication
    ■   22 24   Assistive products for telephoning (and telematic
                messaging)
    ■   22 27   Assistive products for alarming, indicating, and signaling
    ■   22 30   Assistive products for reading
    ■   22 33   Computers and terminals
    ■   22 36   Input devices for computers
    ■   22 39   Output devices for computers
```

FIGURE 6.3 Communication/information-related assistive devices covered by ISO 9999.

6.5.3 Other Product-Related Standards

Additional standards, specifically related to assistive technology products, are listed in Figure 6.4.

6.5.4 Relation to the WHO Family of International Classifications

In 2004 the ISO 9999 standard was accepted as a member of the WHO Family of International Classifications [3] (WHO-FIC) [4]. The WHO-FIC consists of high-quality classifications for relevant sectors in the health system, included in order to stimulate use of the standard ISO 9999.

The ISO 9999 uses the terminology of the International Classification of Functioning Disability and Health (ICF, WHO, 2001). The ICF is a complete, up-to-date survey

> **Product-related ISO standards on assistive technology**
>
> Besides ISO 9999 Classification of Assistive Products ISO is involved in a number of more product-related standards.
> The following ISO (sub)committees active:
> - TC168 — Prostheses and Orthoses
> - TC168/WG1/WG2 — Terminology and Classification on Prostheses and Orthoses
> - TC168/WG3 — Test Methods of Prostheses and Orthoses
> - TC168/WG5 — Prostheses and Orthoses
> - TC173 — Assistive Products for Persons with Disability
> - TC173/SC1 — Wheelchairs
> - TC173/SC3 — Aids for Ostomy and Incontinence
> - TC173/SC4/WG2 — Braille, Tactile Reading and Writing
> - TC173/SC6 — Hoists for Transfer of Persons
> - TC173/WG1 — Walking Aids
>
> For a complete survey, refer to www.iso.org. For classification issues the target oriented (sub)committees have the lead and provide input for ISO/TC173/SC2. Main task of TC173/SC2 is to set the rules for the classification, to complete it, to promote it and to consider the link and relation with other relevant classification and terminology activities.

FIGURE 6.4 *Some additional AT product-related ISO 9999 standards.*

of human functioning and contains body functions and structures, human activity and participation domains, and environmental factors. The ICF includes chapters on body functions such as speech and talking as well as a chapter on communication in the *activities and participation* classification.

A separate document is currently under development by the ISO/TC173/SC2 that includes cross-references between ISO 9999 and ICF at the level of individual ISO 9999 codes. Any code from ISO 9999 refers to one or more ICF codes. A mapping of ISO 9999 codes versus ICF environmental factors is also available. This reference table was published on the Internet in mid-2006 [5].

The reference table and mapping list create links, for instance, between ICF body functions such as speech and related ISO 9999 assistive devices such as products for voice production (Subgroup 22.09).

6.6 HISTORY OF ISO 9999

The ISO 9999 standard originated in the early 1970s. Prior to then, issues regarding technical aids for persons with disabilities were tackled mainly at the national level, by national legislation and regulations with national systems for the provision of aids and national industries [6]. Inherent to this national structure was a listing of products that could be reimbursed at the national level.

In 1978 the Nordic Classification [7] was adopted as a starting point for the development of ISO 9999. The first issue of ISO 9999 in 1978 generally reflected this Nordic Classification.

With the development of policies on the inclusion of persons with disability in society, recognizing disability as an issue belonging to minority groups as well as the globalization of society, interest in ISO 9999 topics at the international level was increasing. In North America the ADA act [8] was developed. The European Commission made disability movement manifest—after a series of isolated projects—in the HELIOS programs [9]; HANDYNET—a European information system on technical aids—was a substantial part of HELIOS. HANDYNET was initially based on a need for a multilingual classification as a retrieval tool. ISO 9999 was applied by HANDYNET in the multilingual system. In order to enhance the retrieval, HANDYNET exerted significant effort in ISO 9999 in translation into all languages used in European countries and organized a collection of experiences and comments for upgrading of the standard.

The technical assistance industry was also interested in an international market. The US and European market developed smoothly in parallel in the direction of open markets. This policy was intended for the open European market, stimulated by the adoption of a Medical Devices Directive [10] by the European Commission that included medical devices for handicapped people. This European Directive obliged national governments to implement national legislation from 1998 on to adopt and stimulate the working of an open economic market of technical aids (AT devices).

Relevant qualifiers for an international market are international standards and common terminology. The standardization bodies were increasingly urging ISO to begin standardization work on technical aids. This was resulting in the establishment of Technical Committee ISO/TC173 on technical aids for the disabled in 1973. More or less in parallel, Europe (CEN) and USA (ANSI) followed with their own standardization committees. A broad spectrum of medical devices was a topic for standardization, such as walking aids, hoists and lifts, wheelchairs and scooters, and prostheses and orthoses, with a specific committee (ISO/TC168).

The interest in a classification of assistive devices on a functional basis as well as the introduction of a common terminology has existed from the initial launching of ISO/TC173. The decision to establish a subcommittee on classification and terminology was made by ISO/TC173 in 1973. This subcommittee forms the formal basis for an ISO standard on classification and terminology, termed *ISO 9999 Technical Aids for Persons with Disabilities—Classification and Terminology*.

ISO/TC173/SC2—the "owner" of the original ISO 9999 standard—took from the beginning on care for upgrades through the known process of revisions of a standard. In the ISO standards environment, a revision or update of any standard usually occurs at 5-year intervals, with questions as to whether the a revision or update is actually needed. This procedure resulted in new versions of the standard in 1992 (first revision), 1998 (second revision), and 2002 (third revision). The fourth revision was finalized during 2007.

From 1992 on, ISO 9999 was also adopted as the European CEN standard through a closely linking mechanism for mutual updates and maintenance work [11]. ISO 9999 has the lead; any change in CEN 9999 follows any change in ISO 9999.

Early in 2006 the national standardization bodies (members of ISO) of the following countries were designated as "P members" [12] of ISO/TC173/SC2: Austria, Denmark, Finland, France, Germany, Israel, Italy, Japan, Korea, Norway, The Netherlands (including its secretariat), Romania, Serbia and Montenegro, Spain, Sweden, and the United Kingdom. Additionally, a number of national standardization were designated as "O members": [13] Brazil, China, Iceland, India, and Poland.

In conformity with ISO rules, liaisons exist between number of ISO and IEC committees as well as international organizations.

The ISO 9999 classification of assistive products for persons with disability—"classification and terminology"—is adopted as a national standard in the following countries: Denmark, France, Germany, The Netherlands, Spain, Colombia, and the United Kingdom [14].

6.7 MAIN APPLICATION AREAS OF ISO 9999

Within the regular revision process of the standard, the TC173/SC2 committee decided in 2001 to collect data on use of the standard and to ask users for suggestions and comments in order to improve the classification [15]. A written inventory was set up and distributed among the national standardization bodies who were asked to collect information in their countries. The primary users each received a copy of the inventory and were asked to fill it out. The completed questionnaire was returned by 15 national standardization bodies and 18 user institutions.

The results indicated that the standard was used in different countries for different purposes. Examples are use intended for

- *Legislative and regulatory purposes*—for example, listing of assistive devices for provisional and reimbursement reasons.
- *Standardization work*—for instance, the scope of ISO and CEN standards on assistive devices is expressed on the basis of the standard.
- *Administrative purposes*—such as registering and coding devices on store for future provision
- *Information dissemination on assistive devices*—the main (digitalized) information systems in EU countries make use of the standard (e.g., www.dmi.dk, www.hi.se/sida, www.handy-wijzer.nl, www.rehadat.de). The classification was translated at the beginning of its existence for that purpose within the framework of the HANDYNET project for practical use in the European information system in the national languages of Denmark, Finland, France, Germany, Greece, Italy, Japan, The Netherlands, Norway, Portugal, Spain, and Sweden.
- *Research and development (R&D)*—research projects focusing on usability and user experience use the standard for collecting and structuring research data.

6.8 THE FUTURE OF ISO 9999

The fourth revision of ISO 9999 was completed in early 2007 with the presentation of the new standard. Following ISO procedures, another next revision may be expected by 2010 or 2012. In the meantime the ISO/TC173/SC2 will prepare this next revision by collecting comments and proposals.

For this future revision, a new working group will be established by ISO/TC173/SC2, starting with an inventory on new developments that could be of concern for ISO 9999.

Some of the following issues might be addressed in the next revision:

- Whether ISO 9999 contains sufficient detail on the specific functions of the individual user of an assistive device. Some users of the standard are planning at the national level a fourth or even a fifth or sixth classification level in order to enable use of the standard in assessment procedures (need for detailed structures and classification schemes; e.g., the Cliq project [16] and the Nordic Foundation project [17]).

- How to deal with the fact that modern assistive devices have an increasing number of functions, such as a PDA, and whether it is necessary to keep the rule to have only one (main) code per assistive product.
- Determining the design for all ISO 9999 products with respect to the needs of the target group: the consumers, the disabled persons, who will use the AT devices.

NOTES AND REFERENCES

1. ISO 9999 was prepared collaboratively by Technical Committee ISO/TC 173, *Assistive Product for Persons with Disability*; Subcommittee SC 2, *Classification and Terminology*; and Technical Committee CEN/TC 293, *Technical Aids for Disabled Persons*, Secretariat ISO/TC173/SC2; see www.nen.nl.
2. International standards are usually prepared by ISO technical committees. Each member body interested in a subject for which a technical committee has been established has the right to be represented on that committee. International organizations—governmental and nongovernmental—in liaison with ISO, also take part in the work. ISO collaborates closely with the International Electrotechnical Commission (IEC) on all matters of electrotechnical standardization.
3. See http://www.rivm.nl/who-fic.
4. See http://www.who.int/classifications/related/en/index.html.
5. See http://www.rivm.nl/who-fic.
6. See http://www.hi.se/English/heart.shtm for information on the HEART study; (Horizontal European Activities on Rehabilitation Technology), a large-scale study for the European Commission funded by the technology and informatics for disabled and elderly (TIDE) program running from 1993 to 1995 executed by a broad consortium of national institutes working on rehabilitation technology.
7. The Nordic Classification was a common classification used in Denmark, Norway, and Sweden to classify the technical aids that were on their national markets and could be subject of national provisional systems.
8. In the United States and North America the Americans with Disabilities Act (ADA) became operational in 1990. This Act gave rights on accessibility of the society for all citizens, including those with disabilities; see http://www.usdoj.gov/crt/ada/adahom1.htm.
9. HELIOS is an acronym of *Handicapped people in Europe Living Independently in an Open Society*; the HELIOS 1 and HELIOS 2 programs ran from 1984 to 1992. A result of HELIOS was the establishment of the European Platform on Disability (EDA); see http://www.edf-feph.org/.
10. European Directive on Medical Devices MDD, 1993, 93/42/EEC.
11. ISO and CEN can decide on mutual updating of their standards through the so-called Vienna Agreement. This means that one of the two organizations takes the lead—in this case ISO—and executes maintenance and updates of its standard in the usual way. Periodically the other organization accepts the result of that work and implements it as the new standard.
12. "P member," in terms of standards work, denotes *participant*, meaning a member who is actively involved in the maintenance and control of the standard.

13. "O member," in terms of standards work, denotes *observer*, meaning a member who is not actively involved in the maintenance and control of the standard but has the right to vote at particular stages of the standards work.
14. This classification was based on an inventory of ISO/TC173/SC2 among users of ISO 9999 in 2002.
15. These data were collected from an inventory of ISO/TC173/SC2 among users of ISO 9999 in 2002.
16. The Cliq project, which originated in the Netherlands, has developed a classification of assistive devices on the functioning and intended use of the device from the user's perspective and based on ISO 9999. *Cliq* stands for *CLassification Implements Quality*; see also www.cliq.nl.
17. Nordic Foundation for a Classification; see description by Thomas Lyhne at tly@hmi.dk; 2004, DMI.

PART II
Users, Needs, and Assistive Technology

7

Low-Tech Assistive Technology

Kathleen Laurin
Northern Arizona University

Jill Sherman Pleasant
University of Montana Rural Institute

7.1 INTRODUCTION

Technology significantly influences the way most of us go about the business of living. It is embedded in the multiple activities we engage in on a daily basis and influences the way in which we function in our homes, workplaces, and communities. It has changed the way we work, learn, communicate, relax or pursue recreational activities, travel, and shop. For example we cook food in a microwave oven, use cell phones and computers for communication, listen to music on devices the size of a credit card, shop by using the Internet, and travel by using global positioning systems that direct us to our destinations. Not surprisingly, technology also has the power to change and improve the lives of older adults who experience loss of functional abilities associated with the aging process and/or specific medical conditions. When technology is applied in this manner, it is identified as *assistive technology* (AT) and/or *assistive devices*.

Assistive technology was legislatively defined in the Technology-Related Assistance for Individuals with Disabilities Act of 1988 as "any item, piece of equipment, or product system, whether acquired commercially off the shelf, modified, or customized, that is used to increase, maintain, or improve functional capabilities of individuals with disabilities" [1]. Assistive technology (AT) includes thousands of devices and products—ranging from

---

The Engineering Handbook of Smart Technology for Aging, Disability, and Independence,
Edited by A. Helal, M. Mokhtari and B. Abdulrazak
Copyright © 2008 John Wiley & Sons, Inc.

simple to complex items—that enable people to be more productive and independent in daily living activities such as communication, self-care, mobility, recreation, learning, and employment (Table 7.1). In other words, assistive technologies are tools that can improve an individual's ability to perform specific tasks, increase functional capabilities, and become or remain more safely independent. As noted in the definition above, an item does not necessarily have to be designed and fabricated as an assistive device, but often becomes one simply by virtue of its application. For example, mainstream technology such as electronic organizers, also known as *personal digital assistants* (PDAs), can assist individuals with memory, organization, and/or learning difficulties to plan, sequence, and remember important daily events.

Assistive technology devices work by either maintaining or enhancing an individual's existing abilities or by compensating for absent or nonfunctional skills. Video magnification products such as a closed-circuit television (CCTV) allow a person with limited vision to use his/her remaining eyesight by enlarging words and pictures to a more readable or recognizable size. When enhancement is not possible, assistive technology can offer an alternative way to accomplish a task. Use of a vibrating alarm clock (substitution of vibration for sound) will enable a person who is deaf or severely hard of hearing to wake up at the time desired each morning. Captioning technology—computer-assisted real-time translation (CART)—allows individuals who are deaf and hard of hearing to understand what is going on around them by providing a written transcript of the words spoken during a meeting, training session, or group presentation. Access to a computer through alternative keyboards, mouse options, and software choices is now a reality for people with limited hand function due to pain, weakness, or paralysis. Wheelchairs, power scooters, ramps, wheelchair lifts, and hand controls for cars are examples of assistive technologies that improve the ability to move around and travel independently for people whose mobility is compromised by arthritis, stroke, Parkinson's disease, diabetic peripheral neuropathies, and other physically challenging conditions. Assistive technologies not only increase the independence of the individual but also reduce the need for caretaker assistance [2].

Devices are typically considered as either basic low technology or high technology. Low technology (low tech) is generally regarded as devices that are relatively simple in design, easy to use without the need for intensive training, low cost, and readily available. Low-tech items include simple gadgets (often called "gizmos"), small appliances, and universally designed products such as the OXO Good Grips™ line of kitchen utensils and tools that are found in retail establishments and are marketed to the general population. Conversely, high-technology devices differ by being more complex in their design, usually require training and/or skill acquisition, are more expensive, and commonly lack the range of choice of low-technology devices because of a more limited market. High-tech items are often electronically based such as dynamic augmentative communication devices, computer applications, power controls for wheeled mobility, and electronic aids for daily living such as those used for hands-free environmental control. Technological advances have provided many options and continue to grow rapidly. Nonetheless, basic technology will continue to be a valuable solution for individuals who experience limitations due to aging, chronic conditions, and/or disability.

The aging and disability demographics of the United States underscore the need for readily available assistive technology devices and services. In the United States, the

TABLE 7.1 Examples of Major Life Activity Domains and Tasks

		Mobility				
Self-Care	Home Management	Home	Community	Communication	Productive Work	Recreation and Leisure
Bathing	Childcare	Enter/exit home	Access public facilities, e.g., stores, offices, religious sites, transportation	Face-to-face conversation	Paid work	Crafts
Dressing	Cleaning	Get in/out of bed or chair			Volunteer activities	Going to movies
Eating	Laundry	Get in/out of shower or tub		Telephone use Computer use		Hobbies Hunting/fishing
Grooming	Meal preparation					
Self-administering medication	Personal finances			Access Internet		Listening to music
Toileting	Shopping	Get on/off toilet Go from room to room	Drive a car Get in/out of a car Move from place to place within a building	Write		Playing cards Reading Socializing Sports Watching TV
		Negotiate stairs				

131

aging population showed tremendous growth during the twentieth century. In 1900, only 3.1 million Americans were age 65 and older; by 2003 that number reached almost 36 million people. During that same timespan the number of people age 85 and older grew from 100,000 to 4.2 million [3]. These numbers will increase drastically as the "baby boom" generation (defined as those born between 1946 and 1964) ages. Thus the population increase of older adults is expected to grow significantly between 2010 and 2030, by which time the number of seniors is expected to reach 70 million people [3]. The probability of having a disability increases with age. The 1997 US Census Bureau report on Americans with Disabilities found that 44.9% of those between the ages of 65 and 69 reported a disability. That percentage continued to increase for each successive 4-year span and cumulated at 73.6% for those age 80 and over [4]. According to the US Census Bureau, in 1997 19.7% of the population had some level of disability and 12.3% had a severe disability [5]. However, in 1990 only 5% of the population reported using assistive devices [6]. The 1994 National Health Interview Survey on Disability (NHIS-D) reported that for those over the age of 65 the most widely used devices were for mobility, followed by those for hearing and vision [7,8]. The survey did not include devices used for daily living activities. Given these aging demographics, it is expected that the demand for health and social services as well as accessible housing options will continue to increase [9]. For many, assistive technology and/or modifications to their environments will allow individuals to maintain a greater level of independence, thus reducing their reliance on other services.

7.2 ASSESSMENT AND SELECTION CONSIDERATIONS

Many simple, low-tech devices can be bought in stores, through catalogs, and on the Internet without a physician prescription or any professional guidance whatsoever. Regardless of price and technical complexity, to be useful, assistive technology must match the individual's specific needs, do the job for which it is intended, be compatible with the environments in which it will be used, and be available and affordable to the person who needs it [10]. It is also critical that the individual view the device positively and be amenable to incorporating it into his or her activities [11].

There are several conceptual models or frameworks for assistive technology assessment that focus on the relationship between the person, technology, and environment. These include the matching person–technology (MPT), human–activity–assistive technology (HAAT), and human–environment–technology interface (HETI) models [12–14]. The AT assessment process requires consideration of multiple factors, and these models provide a structure in which to organize and address these numerous variables. Although a formal AT assessment might not be used when considering low-technology options, it is imperative when helping a person select assistive technology that every effort is made to ensure that the choice will meet the individual's needs. In order to accomplish this, it is important to address six key areas that will have considerable influence over whether the technology is appropriate and available to the user: (1) the person's functional limitations, (2) the person's residual abilities and skills, (3) the tasks and activities that the person needs and wants to perform (the user's perspective), (4) the environments and contexts in which the activities and device use will take place, (5) the desired features and characteristics of the device, and (6) funding considerations.

7.2.1 Functional Limitations

Functional limitations refer to the sensory (hearing, vision, and touch), physical (strength, movement, coordination, dexterity), and/or cognitive (memory, concentration, judgment, information processing, etc.) deficits that limit a person's ability to successfully engage in and carry out daily activities in the domains of self-care, home management, mobility (at home and in the community), communication, productive work, and recreational pursuits. These limitations can occur as a result of congenital or developmental disorders, illness, disease, and/or trauma. They can affect multiple systems and are more common in people over age 65 [15].

When helping an individual make a choice about assistive technology, it is important to be knowledgeable regarding the etiology and pathology of the underlying medical condition. It is essential to understand whether the functional limitations are temporary or permanent, and if the disability will remain fairly stable or whether further deterioration and loss of function should be anticipated. These factors can influence whether a short- or long-term solution is needed. For example, it is reasonable to expect that an inability to walk because of knee replacement surgery is temporary, while an inability to walk as a result of a leg amputation may be permanent. Both situations may require the use of mobility aids such as a walker, wheelchair, and toilet grab bars. However, the person with the amputation is likely to have an ongoing need for these types of devices as well as more complex technology in the form of a prosthetic leg.

7.2.2 Residual Abilities and Skills

Residual abilities and skills refer to what the individual is still capable of doing despite a functional limitation. It may mean that the person has some degree of usable vision despite being considered legally blind, or that the person has good upper-body strength and balance despite a diagnosis of spinal cord injury with paralysis below the waist. *Intact upper-body abilities* mean that the person is likely to need simpler, less costly assistive technology to transfer in and out of the wheelchair to the bed, toilet, car, and so on. Cerebral vascular accidents (strokes) often result in upper-extremity paralysis on one side of the body; however, the functional limitations may be somewhat mitigated if the dominant extremity has not been affected—allowing the person to retain the skills of writing and manipulating objects.

7.2.3 Desired Tasks and Activities

These are the activities, tasks, and respective task subcomponents that people need or desire to engage in as part of their daily routines and lifestyle choices. It is essential to explore with these individuals what they actually do on a daily or even weekly basis and the order of their priorities. It is important to understand that technology—assistive or otherwise—may not be easily accepted by individuals who have yet to internally integrate and pragmatically acknowledge the need to alter and modify their activities and environments [16]. For example, a person used to bathing in a tub may be resistant to using a shower chair and handheld shower nozzle, perceiving it as an unwelcome change to a longstanding routine.

7.2.4 Environments and Contexts

It is important to address not only the physical environment (location, space, indoors vs. outdoors, etc.) but also the less tangible, but equally important contexts for device use based on factors related to culture and social circumstances. Cultural beliefs, ethnic identity, education, family roles, self-image, and self-efficacy are variables that must be considered in order to support device acceptance and use by the person with a disability and the family members or caretakers [14,17–19].

7.2.5 Features and Characteristics of the Device

Device features and characteristics are important variables related to the acceptance and use of technology. In addition to providing the specific technical features that address the user's functional limitations, the device's ease of use, appearance, weight, portability, reliability, and adaptability all influence use and acceptance [18]. Maintenance and repair of the device as well as time and skill needed to learn to operate the device are additional considerations that should not be overlooked.

7.2.6 Availability/Affordability

Although financial considerations should not drive the assessment process, cost certainly can be a factor affecting the type of assistive technology that the person ultimately receives. Items that are considered to be "medically necessary" typically require a prescription written by a physician and therefore may be covered in part or in total by public or private health insurance plans. Assistive technology that supports a vocational or educational goal may be funded by those respective state agencies if appropriate criteria are met. In situations covered by the Americans with Disability Act, assistive technology, in the form of a reasonable accommodation, may be available without cost to the individual. For example, movie theaters have an obligation to provide free assisted-listening systems for use during performances as a reasonable accommodation for persons who are hard of hearing, and employers may be required to provide AT to enable an employee to perform job duties. If a third-party funding source is not available, consumers will have to decide whether the desired equipment is affordable through their own personal or family financial resources. Because the funding issue is complex and often a barrier to assistive technology (AT) acquisition, professionals who provide evaluation and assessment services or offer guidance to consumers on selection of AT devices should be familiar with the range of AT funding options that exist nationally and in their particular geographic regions.

7.3 BASIC COMPENSATORY CONSIDERATIONS FOR LOW-TECH AT MODIFICATIONS

Reducing functional limitations through low-tech assistive technology involves selecting and trying products that make it easier for the person to perform the task(s) or offers a new or modified way of accomplishing the same activity. Use of AT devices may be more effective when employed in conjunction with modified strategies and approaches to the task. For example, discussing the benefits of sitting while performing dressing and grooming tasks is a strategy to combat fatigue or balance problems. Incorporating the use of a dressing stick or sock aid while the person is sitting models the suggested strategy and adds tools that compensate for problems with reaching and bending, thus fostering independence.

7.3.1 Physical Limitations

When the individual has functional limitations related to impairments in strength, movement, coordination, dexterity, or use of only one hand, the objective is to look for AT products with features that compensate for these particular problems. Desirable characteristics may include lightweight design; products that slide or glide to reduce the need to lift; mechanisms that extend a person's reach; device components that enhance stability, offer larger surface area, or provide increased friction; or clamping/gripping mechanisms. A vast array of low-tech examples for self-care and home management activities are available and include the following examples, presented for illustrative purposes only:

- Rubber handle knobs and faucet grip covers—allow handles, knobs, or faucets to be activated with less effort for gripping and twisting.
- Spill Not™ jar and bottle opener—opens jars and bottles with one hand.
- Rocker knife—useful for cutting meat and vegetables with a curved bladed knife with one hand.
- Drinking straw holder—fits over a glass or cup and holds the straw stationary for those who have limited use of their hands.
- Built-up handled cooking and eating utensils—provide a larger gripping surface for people who have limited use of their hands due to injury or conditions such as arthritis.
- Dishes with raised edges for better scooping—people who have use of only one arm often find that a raised-edge dish enables them to push or scoop food onto their eating utensils with less spillage.
- Weighted utensils—provide more control by reducing hand tremor.
- Eyedrop dispenser—eliminates eye blinks, ensures that drops are delivered to the eye.
- Long-handled brushes (hairbrushes, back brushes, scrub brushes, etc.)—when movement is restricted at shoulders, hips or knees, long-handled devices make reaching easier with less stretching or bending.

7.3.2 Vision Loss

When the individual has functional limitations due to impaired vision, the objective is to enhance residual visual abilities by using compensatory strategies and identify assistive technology devices that provide increased lighting, higher contrast, enlarged text and images, and auditory and or tactile feedback in places of visual cues.

- Color-coded, large-number measuring spoon set—this is an inexpensive kitchen tool that makes it easier to identify correct measurements for cooking.
- Talking kitchen food scale—the weight of food items is spoken aloud.

- Talking pillbox organizer—a device useful not only for people with limited sight, but also for people with memory problems or confusion.
- Magnifier tweezers or nail clippers—a magnifier on the end of the tweezers or clipper enhances the visibility of the area being groomed.
- Check-writing guides—assist people who have low vision to write checks. The guide fits over a standard check and enables the user to simply fill in the blanks.
- Vibration triple-mode timer–stopwatch with large, bold numbers—can be used by people with low vision and/or hearing loss as a timer or memory aid.
- Large-number thermostat—makes it easier to read and adjust household temperature controls.
- Talking calculators—are an inexpensive way for people with limited vision to use a calculator. Talking calculators state the calculations out loud.
- Clip-on PDA magnifier—personal digital assistants are very useful devices for memory, scheduling, and notetaking, but for many the screen is too small. This magnifier makes the screen contents easier to read.

7.3.3 Hearing Loss

When the individual has functional limitations due to impaired hearing, the objective is to use compensatory strategies and identify assistive technology devices that amplify sound, reduce background noise, improve acoustics, substitute text and graphics for speech, and replace auditory signals with those that provide vibration or light in place of sound. Examples include

- Vibrating or flashing kitchen timers—substituting light or vibration for sound, a flashing or vibrating timer alerts the individual that the set time period has elapsed.
- Vibrating alarm clock—attached device vibrates under pillow.
- Flashing smoke detectors—a bright strobe light flashes as the alarm sounds.
- Captioned TV—all television sets made after July 1993 have the built-in ability to provide captioned TV (where speech is displayed as text at the bottom of the screen). The option is usually found in the television menu.
- Assistive listening devices—by law, all movie theaters must supply headphones (free of charge) with volume control for people who are hard of hearing. Wireless headphones with volume control for television viewing are available, as are a variety of assisted listening devices for noisy environments such as restaurants, to hear speakers during meetings or group activities, for private conversations with physicians or clergy, and for financial transactions.

7.3.4 Cognition

Aging in and of itself can affect cognitive abilities. Additionally, conditions such as Alzheimer's disease, cerebral vascular accidents (strokes), and head injuries due to falls may cause cognitive difficulties such as confusion, memory loss, and/or forgetfulness. Examples of memory aids include

- Calendars with large squares that incorporate colorful markers and/or stickers
- Phones with large squares for pictures and programmable numbers

- Electronic organizers
- Pill organizer and alarm
- Vibrating medication watch
- Orientation clock that notes the time, date, and day of the week
- Organizers such as a basket to keep items like keys, eyeglasses, remote control devices, and magazines or books in a consistent location
- Safety alerts that sound an alarm—can be used anywhere such as when someone opens a door or is in the kitchen near the stove

7.3.5 Communication

Communication is a very broad area of human activity that impacts the individual's ability to both remain independent and create and maintain social networks, especially in today's technology-driven society. Communication impairments can be related to deficits (alone or in combination) in speech mechanisms, language processing, hearing, vision, and motor skills. Common medical conditions affecting communication abilities—either temporarily or permanently—include cerebral vascular accidents, amyotrophic lateral sclerosis, Parkinson's disease, brain tumors, dementias, throat or tongue cancer, conditions requiring the use of ventilators, and/or with tracheotomy tubes and developmental disabilities such as cerebral palsy and autism. The resultant functional limitations associated with these conditions can impinge on the following communication modalities: face-to-face conversation, speaking on the telephone, writing, keyboarding, and other computer use.

7.3.5.1 *Speech*

Persons with speech impairment may benefit from the use of augmentative–alternative communication (AAC) devices and systems. Also know as speech generating devices these include a very broad range of simple to complex technology designed to supplement a person's verbal communication abilities or provide an alternative to oral communication when the individual cannot produce intelligible speech. Examples of low-tech, compensatory communication aids include providing the person with paper and pens; using dry erase markers and writing surfaces; creating communication boards that utilize pictures, letters, words, or phrases; and providing simple voice output devices that record digitized speech to produce a limited amount of spoken messages. Decisions about suitability for and type of augmentative communication device or system should be determined in consultation with appropriate professionals such as speech–language pathologists with expertise in this area.

7.3.5.2 *Telephone Usage*

With the federal regulations that require manufacturers of telecommunication equipment to incorporate accessibility features into their devices, there is now a vast array of commercially available landline and cellular phone technology that supports telephone use by persons with disabilities. Sound amplification, flashing lights that signal a ringing phone, voice-activated dialing capability, enlarged buttons, and captioned speech are examples of accessibility features. Many states offer accessible telephones and TTYs (text telephones) and other related equipment at no cost to qualified persons with disabilities.

Funded through surcharges on phone bills, these funds support the Telephone Relay Services and Telecommunications Equipment Distribution Programs. While equipment offered and eligibility requirements vary from state to state, people served typically include those who are deaf, hard of hearing, and both deaf and blind (deafblind). Some states include persons who are speech- disabilities or have mobility-impairments. While most states focus on providing telephone and alerting devices, some states also include augmentative communication devices and Internet access.

7.3.5.3 Writing

When handwriting is compromised by a physical condition, there are many low-tech products to choose from, including adapted pens, paper variations, adapted writing guides, and portable word processors. When hand and grip strength are reduced, switching to a felt-tip, gel pen or one with a built-up (embossed) surface requires less force and may be less fatiguing to the writer. Persons who experience tremors and shakiness may find that their handwriting legibility improves when they use a writing guide or template that provides a defined boundary for staying within the lines. This is a solution that is also applicable to persons with vision impairment and is especially helpful for signing checks and legal documents. Portable word processors can replace the need for extensive writing, and note taking. They can be particularly valuable for educational and employment needs. However, printing from these devices usually requires an interface with a computer or printer. Inexpensive digital recorders offer an alternative to writing, but still allow the user to capture and remember necessary information.

7.3.6 Mobility

The ability to move freely is often compromised by age-related changes, chronic conditions, and/or disability. Mobility may be affected by limitations related to balance, strength, flexibility, range of motion, ability to bear weight, activity tolerance, muscle tremors or spasms, and/or paralysis. Fortunately, there is a wide spectrum of products designed to assist individuals with mobility limitations. These options provide an individual with a greater level of independence and enable them to safely navigate within their home and community environments. The following discussion provides a brief overview of basic mobility options, including grab bars, standing poles, canes, and walkers. Because of their wide availability and soaring popularity, an overview of powered scooters is also included.

7.3.6.1 Grab Bars, Handrails, and Standing Poles

Grab bars and handrails assist individuals by providing balance and stability and enable users to capitalize on their available strength. These devices can provide support for movement from a standing to sitting position and vice versa. Handrails should be installed according to building code requirements for navigating stairs and ramps, but can also be installed in other living space areas in order to assist an individual who may have trouble with balance or walking. Grab bars are most commonly installed in bathrooms, but are also useful in other areas where a person may need leverage or balance assistance when moving from one position to another. Grab bars are available in a variety of materials and colors as well as shapes and sizes. They can be mounted either vertically, horizontally, or at an angle. It is critical that these devices be properly and securely mounted to the wall framing and not simply attached to the wall surface with screws or anchors. Grab bars can also be mounted to the floor and/or other permanent objects, but again, it is essential they be correctly installed [20]. In commercial applications, installation should be done according to the Americans with Disabilities Act Accessibility Guidelines (ADAAG) as well as local building codes. In residential applications, ADA guidelines provide a good reference, but customization to best meet the needs of the individual should be considered. For example, mounting height adjustments according to the individual's height may be necessary. Standing poles are vertical poles that most often go from floor to ceiling but can also be attached to a wall. They can assist an individual to get in and out of bed or be placed in the livingroom next to a chair or sofa. These items are available from hardware stores, plumbing supply stores, medical supply stores, and a variety of specialty suppliers who offer stock and custom-made options.

7.3.6.2 Ambulatory Aids

Some of the most common ambulatory aids used by the aging population include canes and walkers. Canes are designed to assist individuals with balance and stabilization and are also used by those who have low vision or are blind. Long white canes are specifically designed to aid persons with blindness or low vision in navigating the environment by providing tactile and auditory cues [13]. When selecting a cane for orientation and mobility related to loss of vision, it is best to consult with an eye care specialist who is knowledgeable about orientation and mobility. Canes designed to assist with physical mobility are available with a variety of options and can be purchased at many retail locations. Canes have four main parts: shaft, handle, base, and tip. Canes shafts can be constructed of aluminum, graphite, carbon fiber, or traditional wood, and can be hand-crafted from exotic hardwoods. Some shafts are collapsible and fold to a small size when not in use. Handle options include numerous styles such as straight, curved, ball-topped, crook, t-shaped, ergonomic, and customized. Bases can consist of a single-point base or a multipoint base (often referred to as a "quad base") that provides for greater stability. Tips can be made of metal, rubber, or composite materials and are available in many shapes and sizes, including sharp multipoint tips for walking on ice. In order to ensure successful use, maximize safety, and minimize secondary conditions related to improper fit and style, it is best to consult with a qualified occupational or physical therapist for best selection [21].

Walkers are most beneficial for individuals with significant balance problems and/or difficulty with gait. As with canes, there are multiple designs that include those without wheels and two-wheeled, three-wheeled, and four-wheeled designs. Those without wheels are often referred to as "rigid" or "pickup walkers" and require the individual to have enough upper-extremity strength to lift and move the device [22]. The two-wheeled walker is equipped with wheels on the front legs and rigid legs on the back, which allows an individual to roll the device forward, but still offers stability when used properly. Three-wheeled designs incorporate two back legs and one forward, creating a triangular shape that collapses for easy transport. Four-wheeled walkers offer the easiest glide of most options but also require the greatest control. All wheeled walkers have a variety of hand-brake options. Other options include baskets for carrying items and seats for resting [22]. As with other mobility devices, selection and fit should be done with assistance from a qualified professional.

Other devices that assist with mobility include transfer boards that allow an individual to slide from one place to another such as from a wheelchair to a car seat. The Car

Caddie™ attaches to the frame of most vehicles and assists an individual by providing balance and/or leverage during entry into or exit from the vehicle.

Although battery-operated scooters would not be considered low-technology devices because of their price and mechanical complexity, they are mentioned in this discussion because they have become readily available and are very functional as well as stylish. Most major retailers provide scooters as an accommodation for those who need them in order to shop in their stores. Scooters are designed for different environments and applications and are available in a variety of styles and colors. Some are lightweight and designed to disassemble easily for easy transport. Three-wheeled scooters offer the tightest turning radius and greatest maneuverability. Four-wheeled scooters are the most stable and designed for outdoor travel. Scooters also differ in terms of their power drive systems (front-wheel versus rear-wheel), types and size of batteries, and control features such as steering and braking. Options include the type and style of seating and armrests, lights, horns, power display, and onboard battery chargers. Once used exclusively by those who needed mobility assistance, they are now being used by the general population for convenience. As with other devices, when market demand increases, the product continues to evolve, improve, and become less expensive to purchase.

7.3.7 Recreation and Leisure

Since historical times, recreation and leisure have been very important activities that provide individual enjoyment as well as social interaction. Plato, the ancient Greek philosopher, proclaimed that "you can discover more about a person in an hour of play than in a year of conversation." Functional limitations can pose challenges to engaging in recreation and leisure activities, but there are a variety of assistive devices that can promote participation in both active and sedentary activities.

Examples of outdoor recreation activities that individuals have engaged in through the use of assistive devices and accessible environments include, but are not limited to, biking, snow skiing, water skiing, golfing, boating, hunting, fishing, swimming, horseback riding, camping, hiking, bowling, and gardening. For example, specialized devices for fishing, such as electric reels for casting and reeling in, are designed to ease the individual's grip on the rod. For golf, the BACKTEE™ eliminates the stooping and bending activities associated with teeing up a ball by attaching to any standard golf grip and assisting with placing a tee into the ground, picking up a ball and placing it on the tee, and picking up the tee itself. For gardening there are a variety of modified handtools that compensate for lack of gripping ability, hand strength, and/or wrist strength as well as items that mitigate mobility issues related to bending, stooping, and reaching. There are also a variety of handtools designed for easy gripping and reduced force and various gloves and cuffs that assist with gripping and holding functions as well as those that dampen vibration for mechanical and shop-related activities.

For more sedentary activities such as card games, there are devices that will shuffle the cards, devices that will hold a hand of cards, and large-print or Braille cards for those who have trouble seeing them. Many board games such as scrabble, checkers, chess, and dominos are available in large-print versions. Magnifiers, needle threaders, small clamps, and electric scissors can be used for sewing, needlecraft, and tye flying. Devices for reading include magnifiers, bookholders, and page turners.

7.3.8 Employment

Because of economic status concerns and the rising cost of inflation, many individuals continue to work beyond the age of retirement. In addition, the Bureau of Labor statistics reported that 24.8% of the population over age 65 engaged in volunteer activities [23]. Often assistive technology can be the key to enabling an individual to continue to be productive in the work environment. Many of the solutions discussed earlier such as assistive technologies for hearing and vision can be essential accommodations in the workplace. There are many inexpensive solutions for completing tasks such as filing, operating office equipment, lifting or moving objects, assembly, and other work-related tasks. For example, a desktop lazy Susan provides easy access to desktop items for those with a limited range of motion, and a reacher can be used to pick up and grasp items that are not within easy reach. Often a simple modification in the work environment such as raising or lowering a workstation, providing a cart to move items, providing seating to eliminate the need for standing, using clamps for holding items, or using a headset or speaker phone, can provide an employee or volunteer with an alternative way to complete a task.

7.4 CONCLUSION

The rapid and ongoing advances in mainstream technology have been bolstered by America's penchant for gadgets. Consumer demand for items that assist or simplify a variety of life activities and a technology-sophisticated baby boomer population have contributed to the existence of diverse, reasonably affordable, and readily available low-tech products. These products can support a higher level of participation and independence for persons with disabilities and those with functional limitations associated with the aging process.

REFERENCES

1. Technology-Related Assistance for Individuals with Disabilities Act of 1988, PL 100-147, Aug 19, 1988, Section 3.1.
2. Mann WC: The potential of technology to ease the care provider's burden, *Generations* 25(1):44–49 (2001).
3. Federal Interagency Forum on Aging-Related Statistics: *Older Americans 2004: Key Indicators of Well-Being*, Federal Interagency Forum on Aging-Related Statistics, US Government Printing Office, Washington, DC, Nov 2004 (http://www.agingstats.gov/chartbook2004/default.htm).
4. Houtenville, AJ: *Disability Statistics in the United States*, Ithaca, NY; Cornell Univ Rehabilitation Research and Training Center, 2006 (www.disabilitystatistics.org, posted 5/15/03; accessed 2/19/06).
5. McNeil JM: *Americans with Disabilities: 1997*, Current Population Report P70-73, US Government Printing Office, Washington, DC, 2001.
6. Jans L: Use of Assistive Technology: Findings from National Surveys, assistive technology data collection project, InfoUse, Berkeley, CA, 2000 (retrieved from http://www.infouse.com/atdata/csun_text.html).
7. Jones ML, Stanford JA, Arc M: People with mobility impairments in the United States today and in 2010, *Assist Technol* 8(1):43–53 (1996).

8. National health Interview Survey on Disability (NHIS-D), Table 1. Number of Persons Using Assistive Technology by Age of Person and Type of Device: United States, 1994 (retrieved from http://www.cdc.gov/nchs/about/major/nhis_dis/ad292tb1.htm).
9. LaPlante ME, Hendershot GE, Moss AJ: The prevalence of need for assistive technology devices and home accessibility features, *Assist Technol Disab* **6**:17–28 (1997).
10. Sherman J: *Assistive Technology and Aging: Tools for Independence*, Arizona Technology Access Program (retrieved from http://www.nau.edu/ihd/AzTap; undated).
11. Gitlin LN: Why older people accept or reject assistive technology [electronic version], *Am Soc Aging* **XIX**(1) (1995).
12. Scherer MJ: *Matching Person and Technology*, 1996 (available from Marcia Scherer, 486 Lake Road, Webster, NY 14580, USA, http://members.aol.com/IMPT97/MPT.html).
13. Cook A.M, Hussey SM: *Assistive Technologies Principles and Practice*, 2nd ed, Mosby, Sacramento, CA, 2002.
14. Smith R: Technological approaches to performance enhancement, in Christiansen C, Baun C, eds, *Occupational therapy: Overcoming Human Performance Deficits*, Slack, Thorofare, NJ, 1991, pp 47–788.
15. Gitlin LN: Assistive technology in the home and community for older people: Psychological and social considerations, in Scherer MJ, ed, *Assistive Technology: Matching Device and Consumer for Successful Rehabilitation*, American Psychological Association, Washington, DC, 2002, pp 109–122.
16. Vash CL, Crewe NM: *Psychology of Disability*, 2nd ed, Springer, New York, 2004.
17. Rintala DH: Gender and ethnoracial differences in the ownership and use of technology, in Scherer MJ, ed, *Assistive Technology: Matching Device and Consumer for Successful Rehabilitation*, American Psychological Association, Washington, DC, 2002, pp 95–107.
18. Scherer MJ: Matching consumer with appropriate assistive technologies, in Olsen DA, DeRuyter F, eds, *Clinician's Guide to Assistive Technology*, St. Louis, MO: Mosby, St. Louis, 2002, pp 3–13.
19. Scherer MJ: *Living in the State of Stuck: How Assistive Technologies Affect the Lives of People with Disabilities*, Brookline Books, Cambridge, MA, 1993.
20. Stanford JA, Arch M, Megrew MB: An evaluation of grab bars to meet the needs of elderly people, *Assist Technol* **7**(1):36–47 (1995).
21. Mann WC, Granger C, Hurren D, Tomita M, Charvat B: An analysis of problems with canes encountered by elderly persons, *Phys Occup Ther Geriatr* **13**(1/2):25–49 (1995).
22. Mann WC, Hurren D, Tomita M, Charvat B: An analysis of problems with walkers encountered by elderly persons, *Phys Occup Ther Geriatr* **13**(1/2):1–23 (1995).
23. Bureau of Labor Statistics: *Volunteering in the United States, 2005*, USDL 05-2278, 2005 (retrieved from http://www.bls.gov/news.release/volun.nr0.htm).

8

People with Visual Disabilities

John Gill and Linda Jolliff
Royal National Institute of Blind People, London, United Kingdom

The popular image of a blind person is of someone who is young, is totally blind, reads Braille, is musical, is happy, loves animals, and has bionic hearing. However, reality is somewhat different—the visually impaired population is far from homogeneous and has very varied needs and aspirations.

8.1 DEMOGRAPHICS

The World Health Organization [1] estimates that

- Globally, in 2002 more than 161 million people were visually impaired, 124 million of whom had low vision and 37 million of whom were blind. However, refractive error as a cause of visual impairment was not included, which implies that the actual global magnitude of visual impairment is greater.
- Worldwide for each blind person, an average of 3.4 people have low vision, with country and regional variation ranging from 2.4 to 5.5.
- Visual impairment is unequally distributed across age groups. More than 82% of all people who are blind are 50 years of age and older, although they represent only 19% of the world's population. Because of the expected number of years lived in blindness (blind years), childhood blindness remains a significant problem, with an estimated 1.4 million blind children below age 15.

The Engineering Handbook of Smart Technology for Aging, Disability, and Independence,
Edited by A. Helal, M. Mokhtari and B. Abdulrazak
Copyright © 2008 John Wiley & Sons, Inc.

- Available studies consistently indicate that in every region of the world, and at all ages, females have a significantly higher risk of being visually impaired than do males.
- Visual impairment is not distributed uniformly throughout the world. More than 90% of the world's visually impaired live in developing countries.

The Department of Health [2] statistics for the UK are

- On March 31, 2003, 157,000 people were registered as blind people (England).
- On March 31, 2003, 155,000 people were registered as partially sighted (England).
- Of all registered blind people who had an additional disability, 25% were also recorded as deaf or having a hearing impairment. About a quarter of these people were blind and deaf, while three-quarters were blind with a hearing impairment (England).
- Of all registered partially sighted people who had an additional disability, 23% were also deaf or had a hearing impairment. A third of these people were partially sighted and deaf, while two-thirds were partially sighted with a hearing impairment (England).
- In total, 56% of all blind people and 61% of all partially sighted people who had an additional disability were also recorded as having a physical disability (England).

There are about 1 million people in the UK who could be registered as "blind" or "partially sighted," and the number is growing every year with the increase in life expectancy. The total would be far greater if one were to include those who cannot read fine print without spectacles—and this includes most people over 50. In this book the term "visually impaired" is used to describe those people whose vision is such that they could be registered as blind or partially sighted. Most visual impairment is acquired late in life; about 2% are under the age of 16, 10% are between 16 and 59, and 88% are over 60 years old.

This association between age and loss of vision has a number of consequences. Less than 2% of visually impaired people can read braille, but 75% have sufficient residual vision to read a newspaper headline. Also, a significant proportion have at least one other impairment; for instance, 35% of those with a visual impairment also have a hearing impairment.

In a person aged 60 with "normal" eyesight, about one-third as much light reaches the retina as when they were 20. Therefore, older people often have problems operating controls when there is low illumination. Older people adapt at a slower rate to changes in the ambient illumination, which can be problematic when the illumination on a control panel is greatly different from what is being viewed or controlled.

8.2 EYE CONDITIONS

8.2.1 Aniridia

Aniridia is a rare congenital eye condition causing incomplete formation of the iris. This can cause loss of vision, usually affecting both eyes.

FIGURE 8.1 *The human eye.*

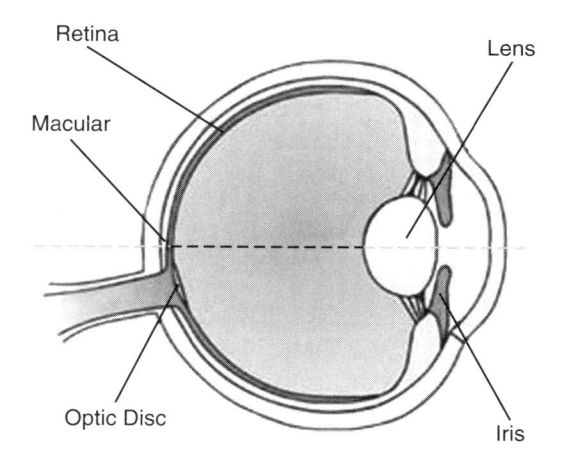

Light enters the eyes through the lens and produces an image on the retina. The highest concentration of visual receptors is at the macular.

In aniridia, although not entirely absent, all that remains of the iris, the colored part of the eye, is a thick collar of tissue around its outer edge (Fig. 8.1). The muscles that open and close the pupil are entirely missing. The appearance of a "black iris" is the result of the really enormous pupil.

There is no single cause for this eye condition that falls roughly into two groups, one of which is hereditary and the other of unknown origin. Aniridia can result from autosomal dominant or autosomal recessive inheritance or may occur on its own.

Autosomal dominant individuals in this group will be unlikely to have additional health or developmental problems and may have normal or poor vision. Autosomal dominant problems result when one of a pair of matched genes is normal while the other carries the abnormality. There is a 50% chance of inheritance in each such pregnancy. Usually several individuals in successive generations will be affected.

Autosomal recessive inheritance carries a risk of accompanying learning disabilities. Autosomal recessive problems arise when both parents carry the abnormal gene, although they are unaffected. There will be a 25% inheritance risk in each pregnancy. Usually this only affects siblings within a single generation.

The effects will vary considerable between individuals and differing causes. Rarely aniridia may be associated with a tumor of the kidney called *Wilm's tumor*. This type is sporadic, although it has been associated with chromosomal disorder and may increase risk of other developmental flaws. Wilm's tumor can normally be treated very successfully.

Some babies with aniridia might be sensitive to light, while others might experience clouding of the lens, so it is important to seek advice about protecting your baby's eyes, should the eye specialist feel that these conditions may arise.

Aniridia may be associated with other eye conditions such as nystagmus, glaucoma, corneal disease, cataract, lens sublaxation (dislocation), macula, and optic nerve disease.

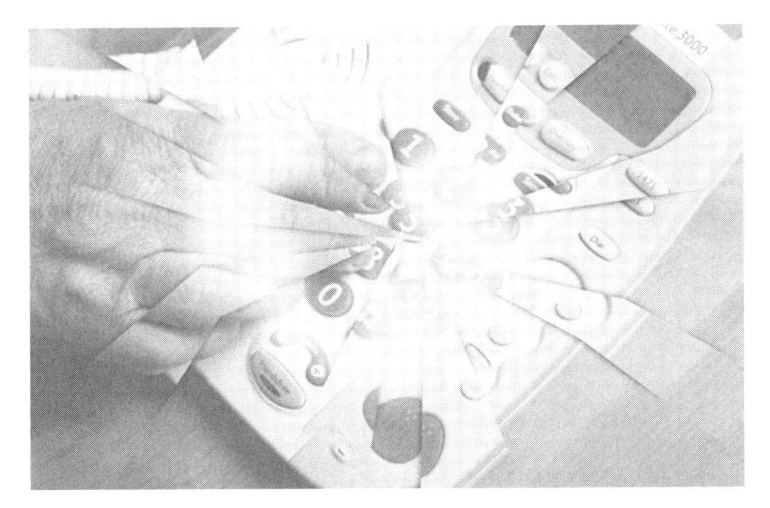

FIGURE 8.2 Cataract.

8.2.2 Cataracts

In 2002, cataracts represented 47.8% of the total causes of blindless globally [1].

The lens is a clear tissue found behind the iris, the colored part of the eye. The lens helps to focus light on the back of the eye—the retina—forming an image. A *cataract* is a clouding of the lens. The vision becomes blurred because the cataract is like frosted glass. There is often a change in color vision such that colors may become washed out or faded. Figure 8.2 is a simulation of how someone with cataracts might see the telephone.

Cataracts can form at any age, but most develop as people get older. In younger people they can result from conditions such as diabetes, following ingestion of certain medications, and alongside other longstanding eye problems.

8.2.2.1 Laser Surgery Following Cataract Operations

Within a few months, sometimes years, following a cataract operation people can again have vision difficulties. Sight can become blurred, or problems with bright lights and glare can develop. This is due to a thickening of the back of the lens capsule. Medically this is known as *posterior lens capsule opacification*. Usually this can be dealt with quite simply. Using a laser, the ophthalmologist can make a hole in part of the capsule so that the light can once again pass directly to the back of the eye. This can improve vision in the vast majority of cases. The procedure is called *YAG laser capsulotomy*. Synthetic yttrium aluminum garnet (YAG) is used in an infrared laser in this type of surgery. For most people there is an immediate improvement in sight within a few minutes of treatment, with vision improving again once the dilating drop has worn off, but for some people it can take a few days for the sight to become clear again.

8.2.3 Colorblindness

Sharpe et al. [3] state:

- The most common forms of colorblindness are inherited and are associated with the inability to discriminate red and green wavelengths (also termed *red-green colorblindness*). They arise from alterations in the genes located on the X chromosome, which encode the midlength-wave (green) and long-wave (red) sensitive photopigment molecules.
- Because these defects are inherited as recessive traits, the incidences are much higher in UK males (∼8.0%), who possess a single X chromosome, than in females (∼0.5%), who possess two X chromosomes.
- Incidences of red-green color deficiencies vary between human populations of different racial origin. The highest rates are found in Europeans and the Brahmans of India (∼8% of males) and Asians (∼4%); the lowest in Africans (∼2.5%) and the aborigines in Australia (∼2%), Brazil, North America (∼2.0%), and the South Pacific Islands (∼1.0%)

Colorblindness is the reduced ability to distinguish between certain colors or wavelengths of light. To see colors properly, light-detecting photoreceptor cells, called *cones*, are needed in the retina of the eye. Three different types exist, each containing a different photopigment: the short-wave (S, sometimes called "blue"), midlength-wave (M, sometimes called "green")- and long-wave (L, sometimes called "red") sensitive cones. These have distinct, spectral sensitivities, which define the probability curve of photon capture as a function of wavelength. The absorbance spectra of the S-, M-, and L-cone photopigments overlap considerably, but their wavelengths are of maximum absorbance in different parts of the visible spectrum. If one or more of these types of cells is faulty, then colorblindness results.

Colorblindness is normally diagnosed through clinical testing, and a number of tests have been devised. The most common test is the use of special test plates called "pseudoisochromatic" plates or "color confusion plates". The plates are made up of a series of spots of varying hues and lightnesses, with a central number or letter standing out from the background. Those with defective vision are unable to distinguish these figures or will see a different figure resulting from the different appreciation of the hues. By changing the figure and background colors, one can identify the basic types of defective color vision. Other more specific tests, such as the anomaloscope, can pinpoint the more subtle defects in color vision and provide a more accurate classification.

There is no cure for colorblindness; however, certain techniques can be used to help discriminate between colors, including handheld filters, tinted spectacles, and monocular contact lenses. However, such devices must be used with caution. For instance, wearing a colored filter over one eye reduces luminance, and can actually diminish color discrimination and visual acuity, induce visual distortions, alter stereopsis, and impair depth perception. Indeed, a review of the research on whether tinted lenses or filters improve visual performance in weak vision concluded that they actually worsen color vision. It should be emphasized that improving test scores on specialized color vision tests is not the same thing as curing colorblindness.

Phenotypically, there are three main types of inherited colorblindness, resulting from alterations in the cone photopigments: (1) anomalous trichromacy (when one of the three cone pigments is altered in its spectral sensitivity, but trichromacy or normal three-dimensional color vision is not fully impaired), (2) dichromacy (when one of the cone pigments is missing and color is reduced to two dimensions), or (3) monochromacy (when two or all three of the cone pigments are missing and color and lightness vision is reduced to one dimension).

The most common, hereditary colorblindnesses are known as *red-green color vision deficiencies*, which are associated with disturbances in either the L-cone photopigment (protan defects, where protanomaly is the alteration form and protanopia is the loss form) or M-cone photopigment (deutan defects, with deuteranomaly as the alteration form and deuteranopia as the loss form). Generally, the loss forms are more severe than the alteration forms, with some people not able to tell green and red apart and others able to make some discriminations (Figs. 8.3–8.6).

Tritan defects affect the S cones, which are often referred to as *yellow-blue disorders*, but the term *blue-green disorder* is more accurate because there is diminished ability to discriminate colors in the short- and midlength-wave regions of the spectrum. Tritan defects arise from alterations in the gene encoding the S-cone photopigment and are autosomal dominant (linked to chromosome 7) in nature. Incidences are equivalent in males and females. In the UK, the frequency of inherited tritan defects has been estimated as being as low as 1:13,000–1:65,000. Tritanopia is the loss form of tritan defects. Like

FIGURE 8.3 Colorblindess — normal.

FIGURE 8.4 Colorblindness — protanopic.

FIGURE 8.5 Colorblindness — deuteranopic.

FIGURE 8.6 Colorblindness — tritanopic.

many autosomal dominant disorders, it is complicated by frequent incomplete manifestation. Tritanomaly, the alteration form, has never been satisfactorily documented.

Although congenital tritan defects are rare, the most frequently acquired color vision defects, whether due to aging or to choroidal, pigment epithelial, retinal, or neural disorders, are the acquired blue-yellow defects. These are similar, but not identical, to tritan defects. Unlike tritan defects, which are assumed to be stationary, acquired defects are usually progressive and have other related signs, such as associated visual acuity deficits.

Total colorblindness or monochromacy occurs when a person has only a single functioning cone class (blue or S-cone monochromacy, green or M-cone monochromacy, or red or L-cone monochromacy) or has no functioning cones (complete achromatopsia or rod monochromacy). These forms of colorblindness are extremely rare.

Red-green colorblindness is hereditary and is passed via the X chromosome. Women, who have two X chromosomes, are rarely colorblind. However, ~15% of them are carriers (i.e., they inherit an X chromosome carrying an abnormal photopigment gene array from one parent) and may share in part in the colorblindness that they pass on to their sons, owing to a process of dosage compensation known as *X-chromosome inactivation of lyonization*. As carriers, they have a 50% chance of having a colorblind son, and a 50% chance of having a daughter who is a carrier.

If a girl inherits one of the affected X chromosomes from her mother (who must be a carrier) and an affected X chromosome from her father (who must therefore be colorblind), she will also be colorblind. However, this set of circumstances is rare.

The less common forms of colorblindness arise from other factors, including cortical trauma, cerebral infarction, disorders of the ocular media of the eye, fundus detachment, progressive cone dystrophies, macular degeneration, vascular and hematologic diseases, glaucoma, optic nerve disorders, diabetes, multiple sclerosis, and toxic agents (e.g., lead, tobacco, alcohol) that affect the retina or the optic tracts.

8.2.4 Diabetic Retinopathy

Diabetes is the leading cause of blindness in people of working age in the UK [4]. Twenty years after diagnosis, nearly all people with type 1 diabetes will have some form of retinopathy [5] and 60% of people with type 2 diabetes will have some degree of retinopathy [5]. In 2002, diabetic retinopathy represented 4.8% of the total causes of blindness globally [1].

Diabetes can affect the eye in a number of ways. The most serious eye condition associated with diabetes involves the retina, and, more specifically, the network of blood vessels lying within it (Fig. 8.7).

Estimates suggest that nearly 1 person in 25 in the UK is affected by diabetes mellitus, a condition indicating that, because of a lack of insulin, the body cannot cope normally with sugar and other carbohydrates in the diet. Diabetes can start in childhood, but more often begins in later life. It can cause complications that affect different parts of the body, including the eye. There are two different types of diabetes mellitus:

Type 1 Diabetes. This can also be referred to as *insulin-dependent diabetes mellitus* (IDDM). This type of diabetes commonly occurs before the age of 30 and is the

FIGURE 8.7 Diabetic retinopathy.

result of the body producing little or no insulin. Type 1 is controlled by insulin injections.

Type 2 Diabetes. This can also be referred to as *non-insulin-dependent diabetes mellitus* (NIDDM). This type of diabetes commonly occurs after the age of 40. In this type of diabetes the body does produce some insulin, although either the amount is insufficient or the body is not able to make proper use of it. This type of diabetes is generally controlled by diet or tablets, although some people in this group will use insulin injections.

Diabetic retinopathy is usually graded according to how severe it is. The three main stages are

Background Diabetic Retinopathy. This condition is very common in people who have had diabetes for a long time. Vision will be normal with no threat to sight. At this stage the blood vessels in the retina are very mildly affected, although they may bulge slightly (microaneurysm) and may leak blood (hemorrhage) or fluid (exudates). The macula area of the retina mentioned earlier remains unaffected.

Maculopathy. With time, if the background diabetic retinopathy becomes more severe, the macula area may become involved. This is called *maculopathy*. If this happens, central vision will gradually worsen. It may be difficult to recognize people's faces in the distance or to see detail such as small print. The amount of central vision that is lost varies from person to person.

Maculopathy is the main cause of loss of vision and may occur gradually but progressively.

It is rare for someone with maculopathy to lose all their sight.

Proliferative Diabetic Retinopathy. As the eye condition progresses, it can sometimes cause the blood vessels in the retina to become blocked. If this happens, new blood vessels form in the eye. This is called *proliferative diabetic retinopathy*, and is nature's way of trying to repair the damage to replenish the retina's blood supply.

Unfortunately, these new blood vessels are weak. They are also in the wrong place—growing on the surface of the retina and into the vitreous gel. As a result, these blood vessels can bleed very easily and cause scar tissue to form in the eye. The scarring pulls and distorts the retina. When the retina is pulled out of position, this is called *retinal detachment*. In addition

- Proliferative retinopathy is rarer than background retinopathy.
- The new blood vessels will rarely affect vision, but their consequences, such as bleeding or retinal detachment, may cause vision to worsen. Visual loss in this case is often sudden and severe.
- Eyesight may become blurred and patchy as the bleeding obscures part of the vision.
- Without treatment, total loss of vision may occur in proliferative retinopathy.
- With treatment, sight-threatening diabetic problems can be prevented if caught early enough. However, laser treatment will not restore vision already lost.

Temporary blurring may occur as one of the first symptoms of diabetes, although it may also occur at any time when the diabetes is not well controlled. It is due to a swelling of the lens of the eye and will clear without treatment soon after the diabetes is brought under control again.

Cataracts, a clouding of the lens of the eye, may develop, causing the vision to become blurred or dim because light cannot pass through the clouded lens to the back of the eye. This is a very common eye condition that develops as people age, but a younger person *with* diabetes may develop cataracts sooner than an older person *without* diabetes. The treatment for cataracts involves an operation to remove the cloudy lens, which is usually then replaced by a plastic lens, helping the eye to focus properly once again.

8.2.5 Glaucoma

Glaucoma of some form is found in about 2% of the population over the age of 40. It can also affect children and young adults, although much less frequently [6]. It is estimated that more than 500,000 people suffer from glaucoma in England and Wales alone, with more than 70 million people affected across the world [6]. In 2002, glaucoma accounted for 12.3% of the total causes of blindness globally.

Glaucoma is the term for a group of eye conditions in which the optic nerve is damaged at the point where it leaves the eye. This nerve carries information from the light-sensitive layer in the eye, the retina, to the brain, where it is perceived as a picture.

The eye needs a certain amount of pressure to keep the eyeball in shape so that it can work properly. In some people, the damage is caused by raised eye pressure. In others, eye pressure may be within normal limits but damage may occur because of weakness in the optic nerve. In most cases both factors are involved but to a varying extent. Eye pressure is largely independent of blood pressure.

A layer of cells behind the iris (the colored part of the eye) produces a watery substance, called *aqueous fluid*. The fluid passes through a hole in the center of the iris (called the *pupil*) to leave the eye through tiny drainage channels. These channels are located within the angle between the front of the eye (the cornea) and the iris and return the fluid to the bloodstream. Normally, the fluid produced is balanced by the fluid draining out, but if it cannot escape, or too much is produced, then the eye pressure will rise. (The aqueous fluid has nothing to do with tears.)

If the optic nerve is subjected to excessive pressure, it can be injured. How much damage there is will depend on how much pressure there is and how long it has lasted, and whether there is a poor blood supply or other weakness of the optic nerve. A severely high pressure will damage the optic nerve immediately. A lower level of pressure can cause damage more slowly; in such cases, vision would gradually be lost if the condition is not treated.

There are four main types of glaucoma.

8.2.5.1 Chronic Glaucoma

The most common type is chronic (slow-onset) glaucoma, primary open-angle glaucoma (POAG) in which the aqueous fluid can enter the drainage channels (open angle), but they slowly become blocked over many years. The eye pressure rises very slowly and painlessly, thus obscuring the problem, but the field of vision gradually becomes impaired.

Several factors increase the risk of chronic glaucoma:

Age—chronic glaucoma becomes much more common with increasing age. It is uncommon below the age of 40 but affects 1% of people over this age and 5% over 65.

Race—people of African-Caribbean origin have about 4 times the risk of POAG as do whites.

Shortsightedness—people with a high degree of shortsightedness (myopia) are more prone to chronic glaucoma. Diabetes is believed to increase the risk of developing this condition.

The danger with chronic glaucoma is that the eye may seem perfectly normal. There is no pain and eyesight will seem to be unchanged, but vision is being damaged.

The early loss in the field of vision is usually in the shape of an arc a little above and/or below the center when looking "straight ahead." This blank area, if the glaucoma remains untreated, spreads both outward and inward. The center of the field is affected last, and eventually the person experiences the sensation of looking through a long tube; this condition is called "tunnel vision." In time even this sight would be lost.

8.2.5.2 Acute Glaucoma

Acute (rapid-onset) glaucoma is much less common in Western countries. This happens when there is a sudden and more complete blockage to the flow of aqueous fluid to the eye. This occurs because a narrow "angle" closes to prevent fluid from reaching the drainage channels. This can be quite painful and will cause permanent vision damage if not treated promptly.

In acute glaucoma the pressure inside the eye rises rapidly. This is because the periphery of the iris and the front of the eye (cornea) come into contact, preventing the aqueous fluid from reaching the tiny drainage channels in the angle between them. This is sometimes called *closed-angle glaucoma*.

The sudden increase in eye pressure can be very painful. The affected eye becomes red; the sight deteriorates and may even black out. There may also be nausea and vomiting. In the early stages misty rainbow-colored rings around white lights (often referred to as "halos") may be seen.

Acute glaucoma may not always be severe. Sometimes people have a series of mild attacks, often in the evening. Vision may seem "misty" with colored rings seen around white lights, and there may be some discomfort in the eye.

8.2.5.3 Secondary and Developmental Glaucoma

There are two other main types of glaucoma. When a increase in eye pressure is caused by another eye condition, this is called *secondary glaucoma*. There is also a rare but potentially serious condition in babies called *developmental* or *congenital glaucoma*, which is caused by malformation in the eye.

8.2.6 Macular Degeneration

It is estimated that there are over 500,000 people with macular conditions in the UK [7]. Macular degeneration is the most common form of visual impairment in the UK and throughout the developed world [7]. In 2002, age-related macular degeneration represented 8.7% of the total causes of blindness worldwide [1].

The eye is shaped like a ball. The pupil, close to the front, is the opening, which allows light to enter the eye. Just behind the pupil is the lens, which focuses the light on the retina at the back of the eye. The retina is a delicate tissue, that converts the light into images and sends them to the brain. The macula is a small area at the very center

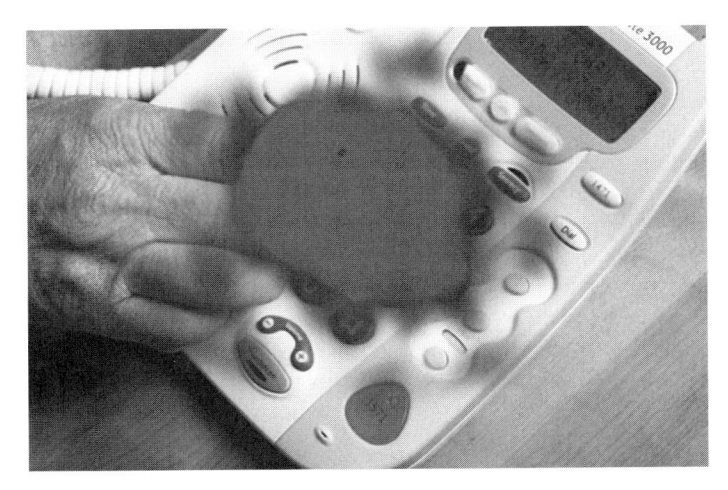

FIGURE 8.8 Macular degeneration.

of the retina. The macula is very important and is responsible for what we see straight in front of us, allowing us to see fine detail for activities such as reading and writing, as well as our ability to see color (Fig. 8.8).

Sometimes the delicate cells of the macula become damaged and stop working, and there are many different conditions that can cause this. If it occurs later in life, it is called *age-related macular degeneration*, (AMD).

Broadly speaking, there are two types of macular degeneration or AMD, usually referred to as "wet" and "dry." This is not a description of what the eye feels like but what the ophthalmologist (eye specialist) can see when looking at the macula.

"Wet" AMD results in a buildup of fluid under the retina. This causes bleeding and scarring, which leads to sight loss. It can develop quickly and sometimes responds to laser treatment in the early stages. It accounts for only about 10% of all people with AMD.

"Dry" AMD is the most common form of the condition. It develops very slowly, causing gradual loss of central vision. Many people find that the vision cells simply stop working, similar to the colors fading in an old photograph. There is no medical treatment for this type. However, aids such as magnifiers can be helpful with reading and other small detailed tasks.

AMD usually involves both eyes, although one may be affected long before the other. This sometimes makes the condition difficult to notice at first because the sight in the "good" eye is compensating for the loss of sight in the affected eye.

In the early stages the central vision may be blurred or distorted, with objects appearing in an unusual size or shape and straight lines appearing wavy or fuzzy. This may happen quickly or develop over several months. The affected person may be very sensitive to light or actually see lights, shapes, and colors that are not there. This may cause occasional discomfort. AMD is not painful.

Because AMD affects the center of the retina, people with the advanced condition will often notice a blank patch or dark spot in the center of their range of sight. This makes reading, writing, and recognizing small objects or faces very difficult.

8.2.7 Nystagmus

No accurate figures are available on the prevalence of nystagmus, but it is etimated that between 1:1000 and 1:2000 people have some form of the condition [8]. The prevalence of nystagmus is estimated at 1:1000–1:3000 people. In the UK, that would work out to somewhere between 20,000 and 60,000 people. A nystagmus register is currently being created that will hopefully provide a more accurate estimate in the near future [9].

Nystagmus is characterized by an involuntary movement or shaking in one or both eyes. When experienced in both eyes, the movement (called *oscillations*) may occur independently or simultaneously. Oscillations may be horizontal, vertical, rotary (circular), or a combination of these. Degree of movement can vary with changes in focal distance, with direction of gaze, and depending on whether one (monocular) or both (binocular) eyes are in use.

There are a number of different categories of oscillations, the nomenclature of which is usually based on the direction or type of oscillation. *Jerk nystagmus* consists of a slow movement in one direction followed by a very rapid movement in the opposite direction. It is comparable to watching a series of telephone poles from the window of a moving train. As the eyes focus on one pole, they move slowly in one direction. When the pole moves out of the field of view, the eyes snap forward in the opposite direction until they meet the next pole. People with congenital jerk nystagmus usually have reduced visual acuity, which is caused by the nystagmus. *Pendular nystagmus* refers to a slow rhythmic movement of the eyes. There is no obvious discrepancy between the speeds of the movement back and forth. Pendular nystagmus is almost always associated with severely reduced visual acuity. It is believed that pendular nystagmus is caused by the visual impairment (the opposite is the case for jerk nystagmus). The visual impairment must develop in early infancy to result in pendular nystagmus. With pendular nystagmus, the degree of movement can vary depending on where the eye is pointing.

Other categories include downbeat nystagmus, upbeat nystagmus, torsional (rotary) nystagmus, horizontal nystagmus, seesaw nystagmus, gaze-evoked nystagmus (which appears when the patient is looking in a particular direction), and periodic alternating nystagmus (which consists of an alteration between different types of oscillations).

All categories of nystagmus can be associated with abnormal head posture. In some cases the head is held at an unusual angle to minimize the movement of the eye(s). In other cases (e.g., spasmus nutans), the nystagmus is accompanied by a nodding of the head. The nodding is merely associated with the condition and is not believed to be a compensatory measure. Spasmus nutans is seen only in very young children (less than 6 years old).

The degree of vision impairment experienced by different people with nystagmus varies from a slight blurring of vision to being registered blind. With the exception of people with other underlying eye conditions, the majority of people with nystagmus are partially sighted and not completely blind.

The causes of nystagmus are wide and varied. Nystagmus can be congenital (present at birth) or acquired (as a result of, e.g., disease or injury).

Eye movement is controlled by three different mechanisms:

1. *Fixation* is the subtle compensatory mechanism that ensures that the eyes remain fixed and focused on an object.
2. The *vestibuloocular reflex* keeps the viewed object centered when the position of the head is changed.

3. The *neural integrator* enables the person's gaze to remain fixed on a certain object, overcoming the eye's natural response to return to a relaxed position.

Disruption of any of these three mechanisms can result in nystagmus. Nystagmus can also be associated with

- Retinitis pigmentosa (a hereditary degenerative disease of the retina that leads to loss of vision)
- Albinism
- Glaucoma
- Cataracts
- Multiple sclerosis and other demyelinating diseases
- Disorders or malformation of the craniocervical (head–neck) junction
- Lesion(s) (abnormal damage or growth or loss of function) in one or more areas of the brain
- Lesion(s) in the inner ear
- Heat stroke
- Head trauma
- Encephalitis
- Syphilis
- Drugs
- Alcohol

Examples of characteristics associated with nystagmus are (one or more of these may be present)

- Diplopia (seeing double)
- Blurred vision
- Abnormal head posture
- Head nodding
- Vertigo
- Tinnitus (a buzzing, ringing, or whistling sound in one or both ears)
- Deafness
- Myokymia (quivering or rippling of resting muscles)

Examples of problems faced by a person with nystagmus will include those typical of any vision impairment, such as

- Difficulty in reading or complete inability to read text
- Difficulty in or complete inability to distinguish between colors
- Difficulty in finding specific location of functions (e.g., difficulty locating buttons on a ticketing machine or difficulty locating the card slot on an ATM)

Similarly, in cases where the person also has tinnitus or deafness, problems will include those typical of a hearing impairment. These may include difficulty in or inability to hear audio instructions or signals.

Additionally, the abnormal head posture associated with nystagmus may pose a difficulty in reading; however, people who have nystagmus over a long period of time learn to adapt to the condition. This characteristic may pose a problem in situations where one is required to hold one's head still (e.g., having a photograph, a facial recognition scan, or an iris scan taken).

The characteristic head nodding of, for example, spasmus nutans will pose a problem for reading and will also make it difficult to hold the head still. However, it should be noted that this characteristic is seen only in very young children (<6 years old).

One type of congenital jerk nystagmus, called *latent nystagmus*, is apparent only when one eye is covered. With this particular condition, a technology or system that requires the use of one eye (i.e., that with a monocular eyepiece) may be problematic.

Similarly, in some cases of nystagmus, the condition is apparent only when the eyes are pointed in a particular direction. Familiarity with their conditions may enable people to compensate for this problem themselves.

Difficulties arise when a person with nystagmus is required to look in a number of different directions (e.g., from a keyboard to a screen) and/or at a number of different distances (e.g., from a timetable held in the hand to an information screen located further away). The person may therefore require more time to complete an action. This will be a particular problem when a machine or system has an automatic time-out function.

As with other vision impairments, small text and text consisting of all capitals will pose problems. This also applies to moving text (e.g., an information screen with scrolling text). All three of these categories of text are associated with difficulty in focusing.

The location of text (e.g., instructions) is very important to people with nystagmus, who often need to bring their faces quite close to the text in order to read it.

8.2.8 Retinitis Pigmentosa (RP)

The British Retinitis Pigmentosa Society [10] estimates that over 25,000 families in the UK have RP, and on a world scale the number runs into millions; and 1 in 80 of the population carry the gene responsible for RP.

Retinitis pigmentosa (RP) is the term for a group of hereditary eye disorders. These disorders affect the retina, which is the light-sensitive tissue lining the back of the eye, in which the first stages of sight take place. In RP, sight loss is gradual but progressive. It is unusual for people with RP to become totally blind, as most retain some useful vision well into old age.

The retina in the eye serves a similar purpose to a film inside a camera. Light is focused by a lens at the front of the camera onto a light-sensitive film at the back, to form a picture. In a similar way, light entering the eye is focused onto a light-sensitive tissue that lines the inside of the eye at the back. This tissue is the retina.

The retina consists of two main layers, a thin one called the *pigment epithelium* and a thicker one, made up of many layers of cells, called the *neural retina*. One particular layer in this neural retina contains many millions of cells called *photoreceptors*, which are able to respond to light. A few million cells called *cones* are concentrated in the central portion of the retina. These allow us to see fine detail and color. Away from the central portion of the retina are about 120 million cells, which are mostly rod cells. They enable us to see when light is dim and provide peripheral vision outside the main line of sight.

When light is focused onto these rods or cones, a small electrical charge is generated (the amount depends on the amount of light), and this charge passes down the optic nerve to the brain. As each of these cells receives a slightly different amount of light and sends a different electrical pulse, the brain is able to assemble a picture.

It is now known that many different inherited defects cause RP. In all RP-related conditions, however, the ability of the retina to respond to light is affected. The problem can be in many parts of the retina such as the rod or cone cells, or in the connections between the cells of the retina.

There are three ways in which RP can be inherited:

Autosomal Dominant Inheritance. This is the pattern of inheritance where RP is known to exist in a family, affecting both males and females. The probability of RP being passed from an affected parent to a child is exactly 50%.

Autosomal Recessive Inheritance. There will seldom be any known history of RP in the family, but if two carriers who show no obvious symptoms have a child, there is a 25% chance that he or she will have RP.

X-Linked Inheritance. This is a pattern of inheritance where only males develop the disease but female members of a family are carriers. Some carriers can develop a mild form of RP. For example, if a man has X-linked RP, his sons will not develop RP, but all of his daughters will become carriers. These daughters will each have a 50% chance of producing an affected son and a 50% chance of producing daughters who will be carriers.

This inheritance pattern is sometimes difficult to identify in a family where there have been no sons for several generations, as the faulty gene could have passed down a line of female carriers and then suddenly affected a male child.

There is no hard-and-fast rule, but in most cases the early symptoms of RP develop between the ages of 10 and 30. The most common first symptom is difficulty in seeing in poor light, for example, outdoors at dusk, or in a dimly lit room. A second symptom is reduction of the visual field, in which sight is lost from the sides, or from above and below. This is often referred to as "tunnel vision," meaning that the rod cells, and some of the outer cone cells, have been affected first.

In some RP-related conditions central vision is lost first. The first signs of this are difficulty in reading print or carrying out detailed work. All RP conditions are progressive, but the speed at which deterioration takes place varies from one person to another.

In many types of RP, glare from bright lights is an increasing problem, although some people do not experience this until the more advanced stages. Many people with RP develop cataracts. Cataracts are a clouding of the lens at the front of the eye. They usually occur around middle age in people with RP. When they have reached a certain stage, an eye specialist may recommend their removal. The lens is then either replaced with an implant, or specially made spectacles are prescribed.

After the operation, the patient will still have RP, but if the retina has not deteriorated too far, a limited amount of vision will be restored. This is the most common origin of the "miracle cure" stories that appear from time to time in the press.

RP is just an eye condition but there are other conditions that people with RP can inherit. One example of this is Usher syndrome, where people develop the dual disability of hearing loss and retinitis pigmentosa.

8.2.9 Best's Disease

Best's disease, also known as *Best's vitelliform macular dystrophy*, is a hereditary form of progressive macular dystrophy. Sight loss can be variable, but, like other macular problems, Best's disease threatens central vision in one or both eyes.

8.2.10 Charles Bonnet Syndrome

Charles Bonnet syndrome (CBS) is a term used to describe the situation when people with sight problems start to see things that they know aren't real. Sometimes called "visual hallucinations," the things people see can take all kinds of forms from simple patterns of straight lines to detailed pictures of people or buildings. These can be enjoyable or sometimes upsetting. Charles Bonnet syndrome affects people with sight difficulties and usually only people who have lost their sight later in life. It can affect people of any age, however, usually appearing after a period of worsening sight. The visual hallucinations often cease within a year to 18 months.

8.2.11 Coats' Disease

Coats' disease (after George Coats, British ophthalmologist), also known as *exudative retinitis*, is a progressive condition of the retinal capillaries that occurs in children and young adults, usually males. Typically commencing during the first decade of life, it progresses gradually and affects central vision, usually in only one eye.

8.2.12 Coloboma

A *coloboma* is a gap or fissure in part of the structures of the eye. This gap can occur in a range of areas and be large or small. The most common form of gap is caused by an imperfect closure of a cleft, present in the womb but usually closed by birth. This gap can occur in the eyelid, iris, lens, choroid, or optic disk.

8.2.13 Congenital Cataracts

A *congenital cataract* is an opacity (cloudiness) in the lens of the eye that is present at, or develops shortly after, birth.

8.2.14 Corneal Dystrophy

Corneal dystrophies form a group of rare disorders that usually affect both eyes. They may be present at birth, but more frequently develop during adolescence and progress gradually throughout life. Some forms are mild; others, severe.

8.2.15 Corneal Graft

When a damaged cornea cannot be improved by other treatment, a corneal graft may be performed (corneas are removed from the eyes of people who have died). Corneal grafts may improve sight, alleviate pain, and, in the case of ruptured corneas, repair perforations.

8.2.16 Dry Eye

Tears serve to lubricate the eye and are produced around the clock, but when insufficient moisture is produced, stinging, burning, scratchiness, and other symptoms are experienced and may be referred to as "dry eye," *keratitis sicca*, *keratoconjunctivitis sicca* (KCS), or *xerophthalmia*.

8.2.17 Genetic Eye Disease

Genetic eye disease occurs when the DNA in a gene is faulty, and gives rise to a protein that does not work properly. Because the same protein may be used in many different tissues of the body, a single genetic disease may give rise to a number of disabilities, for example, blindness and deafness. There are many different types of genetic eye disease, and collectively they are the most common cause of sight loss in children and young people.

Retinitis pigmentosa is the best-known genetic eye disease. Many cases of severe eye disease in children such as microphthalmos (small eye), cataract, glaucoma, and retinoblastoma (an eye tumor occurring in childhood) can be caused by genetic defects. Many genetic diseases that affect several body systems also affect the eye, such as Marfan's syndrome, neurofibromatosis. It is increasingly recognized that many adult eye diseases such as cataract, glaucoma, and diabetes are modified by a person's genetic makeup.

8.2.18 Hemianopsia

Hemianopsia, sometimes called *hemianopia*, is blindness in half of the visual field. This loss can be caused by a variety of medical conditions, of which stroke is among the most commonly experienced.

8.2.19 High-Degree Myopia

"Shortsightedness," or *myopia*, is a vision problem resulting from excessively long growth of the eyeball, or a steeply curved cornea. High-degree myopia (sometimes known as *pathologic myopia* or *degenerative myopia*) is a chronic, degenerative condition that can create problems because of its association with degenerative changes at the back of the eye.

8.2.20 Macular Dystrophy

Macular dystrophy is a hereditary condition in which there is a degeneration of the retinal receptors in the region of the macula. There are separately identified macular dystrophies; the most common are Best's disease, Stargardt's macular dystrophy, and bull's-eye maculopathy. They tend to appear earlier in life and cause a reduction in central vision.

8.2.21 Macular Hole

A *macular hole* is a small hole in the macula in the center of the retina. Macular holes usually affect only one eye, although there is a 10% (1:10) chance that the other eye will eventually be affected.

8.2.22 Posterior Vitreous Detachment

Posterior vitreous detachment (PVD) is a common condition that occurs in about 75% of people over the age of 65. As people age, the vitreous, a jelly-like substance inside the eye changes.

8.2.23 Retinal Detachment

Retinal detachments often develop in eyes with retinas weakened by a hole or a tear. This allows fluid to seep underneath, weakening the attachment so that the retina becomes detached. When detached, the retina cannot compose a clear picture from the incoming rays and vision becomes blurred and dim.

8.2.24 Retinopathy of Prematurity

If an infant is born prematurely, with the retinal blood vessel development incomplete, problems occur. Abnormal blood vessels may develop, which can subsequently lead to bleeding and scar tissue formation. This may then stretch the retina, pulling it out of position. Visual loss may result.

8.2.25 Stargardt's Macular Dystrophy

Stargardt's macular dystrophy is an inherited condition that affects the macula. Conditions involving the macula affect central vision. Although there may be considerable sight loss, in some cases to levels where registration would be offered, total loss of sight is rare.

8.2.26 Temporal Arteritis or Giant Cell Arteritis

Giant cell arteritis, *temporal arteritis*, and *cranial arteritis* are terms that can be used when diagnosing an inflammatory disease affecting the medium-sized arteries, more specifically the many arteries that supply the head and eyes. *Arteritis* is a condition that can cause sudden loss of sight in one eye. Arteritis may be generalized or confined to one area. When the condition is generalized, the term *giant cell arteritis* is more likely to be used, but when the effects are limited to the arteries in the scalp, it is more likely that the terms *temporal* or *cranial arteritis* will be used.

8.2.27 Thyroid Eye Disease

Thyroid eye disease (TED) is also known as *dysthyroid ophthalmopathy*, *Basedow's disease, endocrine exophthalmos*, *ephthalmopathy*, *Graves' disease*, or *thyrotoxic* or *thyrotrophic exophthalmos*. The thyroid gland lies in the neck in front of the windpipe and helps maintain normal body metabolism. Association between disease of the thyroid gland and exophthalmos, an abnormal protrusion or bulging forward of the eye, has been recognized for over a century; however, although exophthalmos is easily recognized, the pathology is still unclear.

8.2.28 Uveitis

If the eye is considered as a hollow, fluid-filled, three-layered ball, then the outer layer is the *sclera*, a tough coat, the innermost is the retina, the thin light-gathering layer, and the middle layer is the uvea. The *uvea* is made up of the iris, the ciliary body, and the choroid. When any part of the uvea becomes inflamed, then it is called *uveitis*. There are many different types of uveitis. This is because: The Uvea is made up of different parts. So, if the iris is affected, the condition and its treatment could be totally different from the situation when the choroid is affected. The inflammation in the uvea very often affects other parts of the eye such as the retina, and so a variety of other problems can be present to complicate the picture. Also, in a large number of medical conditions (e.g., Behcet's disease, sarcoidosis, and toxoplasmosis, to name only three), uveitis may appear as only one of many other symptoms of the disease.

ACKNOWLEDGEMENT

The section on color vision was written with the help of Professor Lindsay Sharpe, Professor of Vision Science, University of Newcastle.

REFERENCES

1. WHO: Magnitude and Causes of Visual Impairment, Fact Sheet 282, World Health Organization, Nov 2004 (www.who.int/mediacentre/factsheets/fs282/en/index.html).
2. Department of Health, UK: *Registered Blind and Partially Sighted People Year Ending 31 March 2003, England*, (www.dh.gov.uk/assetRoot/04/07/23/38/04072338.pdf).
3. Sharpe LT, Stockman A, Jägle H, Nathans J: Opsin genes, cone photopigments, color vision, and color blindness, in Gegenfurtner KR, Sharpe LT, eds, *Color Vision: From Genes to Perception*, Cambridge Univ Press, 1999, Chapter 1, pp 1–51.
4. Kohner E, et al: Report of the Visual Handicap Group, *Diabet Med* 13(Suppl 4):S13–S26 (1996).
5. *Diabetes UK* (www.diabetes.org.uk).
6. IGA: *Introduction to Glaucoma*, International Glaucoma Association (IGA) (www.glaucoma-association.com/nqcontent.cfm?a_id=243&=fromcfc&tt=article&lang=en&site_id=176).
7. MDS: *What is Macular Degeneration?* Publications & Information, Macular Disease Society (www.maculardisease.org/template.asp?section=000500030002).
8. Nystagmus Network UK (www.nystagmusnet.org/).
9. University of Leicester, UK (www.le.ac.uk/).
10. British Retinitis Pigmentosa Society (www.brps.org.uk/).

9

Assistive Devices for People with Visual Impairments

John Gill
Royal National Institute of Blind People, London, United Kingdom

By the year 2028 or so, there will be an increase in the number of people over retirement age, a decrease in the number of people paying income tax, and an increase in the expectation concerning quality of life by older people. All this has implications for the appropriate use of technology to assist people to live independently for longer.

Since over half of visually impaired persons in the UK live alone, they have to cope with cooking, housework, taking medication, and personal care. In addition, they may want to maintain their gardens and join in social activities such as sports. A variety of ingenious devices have been developed to assist with specific activities.

9.1 APPLICATION AREAS

9.1.1 Domestic Appliances

In the past the controls on most domestic appliances (e.g., washing machines, cookers, and central heating controllers) could be modified for a blind person by adding embossed markings to the control panel. However, the change from electromechanical controls to dynamic visual displays has meant that other solutions must be found, and it has not been economically viable to modify each device individually to give speech output (Fig. 9.1).

The Engineering Handbook of Smart Technology for Aging, Disability, and Independence,
Edited by A. Helal, M. Mokhtari and B. Abdulrazak
Copyright © 2008 John Wiley & Sons, Inc.

FIGURE 9.1 Cooker control.

9.1.2 Packaging

Developments for the general public are not always to the advantage of visually impaired persons. For instance, the standardization of packaging means that aerosol containers of oven cleaner and hairspray can feel the same. One small step was the introduction of an embossed triangle on packaging of dangerous substances (Fig. 9.2). A few items are specially designed to be easy to differentiate by touch to help blind persons; for instance, the banknotes in the UK are of different sizes depending on denomination.

9.1.3 Food Preparation

The essential aspect is for a blind cook to be well organized. There are a number of techniques, ways of doing things, such as for cutting and peeling vegetables. In addition devices, such as talking weighing scales, can help. However, many problems remain. Opening tamperproof packaging can be very difficult. Graphics and indicators on controls can be very difficult to see, especially if they are small or use low contrast colors.

9.1.4 Medicines

For many older people, taking medicines is part of everyday life. Often there are problems in differentiating tablets and in accurately measuring liquids. A number of devices have been developed, but most are difficult to use by someone with poor manual dexterity or

FIGURE 9.2 Tactile danger warning on packages containing hazardous substances.

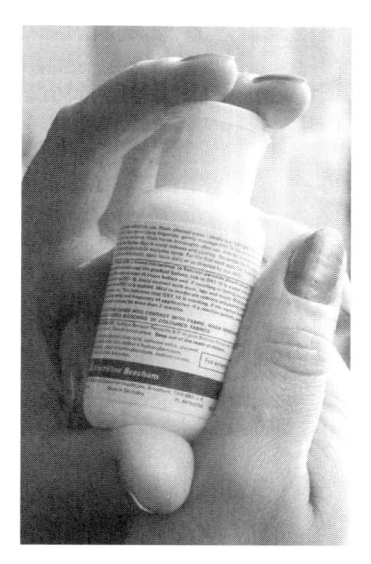

FIGURE 9.3 Medicine bottle.

hand tremor. Labels are often in small print with poor visual contrast (Fig. 9.3). It is somewhat surprising that the labels on eyedrop bottles are often difficult to read despite the probability of the user having impaired vision.

9.1.5 Shopping

The increase in out-of-town supermarkets has resulted in the gradual demise of local shops. This change has been to the disadvantage of many visually impaired persons who benefited from the personal service that the local shops could offer. In supermarkets it can be difficult to find the right products, and even harder to determine the price. There have been a number of proposals for using the barcode to help visually impaired people sort their groceries at home. The barcode gives the product number, so it would be necessary to have a databank to relate this number to the product name and label information. As yet the cost of providing such a service is too high, but this could change in the next few years.

9.1.6 Smart Housing

The interconnection of devices in the home has been held back by the lack of a consensus on appropriate standards, but this may be partly resolved in the foreseeable future by such systems as Bluetooth. However, the television set may become the central display for such a system, and therefore it is essential that allowance be made by the designers for people who have difficulty in reading the screen or understanding the process.

A simple smart house might give an audible warning of any windows left open when someone locks the front door from the outside. Also it could provide warnings about a cooker left on, show who is at the door, and allow remote adjustment of heating, for example. In addition, it is possible to connect the internal system to a telecommunication link to provide remote assistance or telemedicine. The reason for the great interest in this area is the realization of the economic necessity for as many people as possible to live independently for as long as possible. The cost of the technology involved in smart housing is modest when compared with the cost of residential care.

9.1.7 Television

Television is today's main medium for information and entertainment. Indirect controls are now the standard interface for most systems, and these can be difficult to use by people with weak vision (Fig. 9.4).

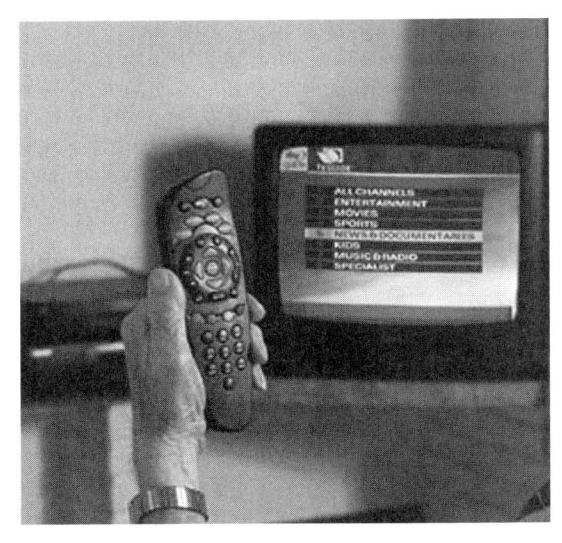

FIGURE 9.4 *Television remote control.*

9.2 MOBILITY AND ORIENTATION

The environment in which we live is becoming increasingly complex. Even a journey across a city by bus requires a range of skills, including

- Being able to avoid obstacles on the pavement
- To walk in the right direction
- To safely cross the road
- To know when you have reached a destination (e.g., have found the correct bus stop).
- To know which is the right bus
- To pay the correct fare
- To find a vacant seat
- To know when to alight from the bus

These tasks may seem trivial, but for someone with no useful vision, they are skills which have to be learned. Even for someone with weak vision, all these tasks are less easy than for someone with normal sight.

9.2.1 Electronic Mobility Aids

Since the mid-1970s, engineers have devoted considerable resources to developing electronic systems to help a blind person avoid obstacles. The most common approach has been to use ultrasonics; as with radar, the range is obtained from the length of time it takes for a pulse to be reflected back to the transceiver. Other systems have used lasers or infrared. Many of the devices only provided information about the range of the nearest object; a "picture" could be created by moving the sensor from side to side. Other devices have attempted to give a more complete image of the environment but at the expense of providing an excessive amount of information to the blind user.

The main problems are not in designing the electronic circuitry for a satisfactory electronic mobility aid but in

- Identifying the optimum information needed for independent pedestrian travel
- Displaying this information to the blind persons in a nonvisual format (usually by auditory or vibratory signals)
- Manufacturing the device at a reasonable price
- Training blind persons in the use of the device

The capacities of the senses of hearing and touch are very small compared to that of the visual channel for a human. Therefore, selecting and processing the information to make best use of the nonvisual channels is not a simple task. The sensors in future devices are likely to involve more than one modality (e.g., both a videocamera and an ultrasonic transceiver) in order to obtain the necessary data that can be processed to produce an accurate image of the immediate environment. However, the research that has been done on the automatic processing of satellite pictures and the research on neural networks offer hope that significant advances could be made in the near future.

FIGURE 9.5 Embossed map.

9.2.2 Embossed Maps

For a blind person, the problem of getting about is not merely the risk of walking into objects. One problem is that of knowing the layout of the environment; here, an embossed map can help (Fig. 9.5). However, embossed maps are not easy to produce or interpret since simply embossing a sighted map seldom leads to an intelligible embossed map.

The problem of converting a sighted graphical representation to an embossed one can be illustrated by the problem of indicating direction. Visually, direction is often shown as an arrow on a line. An embossed arrow gives a sense of direction at only one point on the line, and the symbol is unfamiliar to many blind people. However, a line sawtooth in cross section provides an indication of direction over the whole length of the line, and it is easy to associate the symbol with the meaning since the line is smooth in one direction and rough in the other.

Computer-aided design systems have been developed to speed up the process of producing embossed maps and diagrams. However, there is still much work to be done on the design of the maps and on methods of tactual reading.

9.2.3 Orientation Systems

Even with an embossed map and a mobility aid, it is still very easy for a blind person to get lost. A number of electronic orientation aids have been developed, but few have been widely used because of the cost of modifying the environment. One type of system uses infrared (IR) transmitters mounted at street corners; the IR signal is modulated so that a receiver, held by the blind person, gives out an audible message. These systems can also be used to indicate the status of traffic lights. Similar radio-based systems have been used in some countries, but the advent of Bluetooth is likely to dramatically reduce the cost of installing such systems.

A different concept is for the blind person to carry a tag similar to the ones used in shop security systems. Thus machines can detect the presence of a blind person within

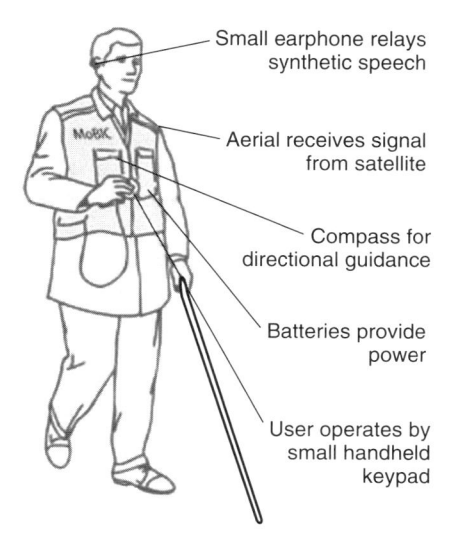

FIGURE 9.6 *The MoBIC system.*

a few meters and modify that person's behavior (e.g., produce a speech message). The tag or smart card can be precoded, which could indicate that the person would prefer messages in an alternative language.

9.2.4 Positioning Systems

Satellite navigation systems, such as the global positioning system (GPS), can be used to determine one's position to a few meters. However, this requires line of sight to three or four satellites, which means being outdoors and not close to tall buildings. This position is given simply as latitude and longitude, so it needs to be integrated with a detailed digital map of the area. Just such a system was successfully developed by the MoBIC project (Fig. 9.6); this prototype system gave blind pedestrians their position within 2 m, but for only 75% of the time. The problem was loss of line of sight to sufficient satellites or loss of the differential radio signal. However, it proved the technical feasibility and helped identify the problems in designing the human–machine interface for blind users.

An alternative method of finding one's position is possible from mobile telephony by determining the relative signal strengths at different base stations. With the next generation of mobile systems, this has been further developed to provide sighted users with information related to their locality (e.g., the location of the nearest cash dispenser or Chinese restaurant). The advantage of the mobile telephony system is that it does not require line of sight to satellites, but the accuracy may not be as good as that of GPS. But, as always, the price charged to blind people for the equipment and using the service will be a significant factor in determining its takeup.

9.3 ACCESS TO INFORMATION

It is a myth that vision is a finite commodity and that using it means that it will fail sooner. When conventional spectacles give insufficient correction, weak-vision aids can be used. These devices include simple handheld magnifiers, stand-mounted magnifiers, and spectacle-mounted and handheld telescopes. In general, the higher the power of magnification, the smaller the field of view and the shorter the working distance (i.e., the space between the aid and the material to be viewed).

9.3.1 Closed-Circuit Television

Closed-circuit television systems enable the individual to select the appropriate magnification combined with image enhancement (i.e., improved contrast) and image reversal (e.g., white print on a black background) (Fig. 9.7). There are also headborne devices with automatic focusing that can be used at any distance, but the price of these devices is high.

9.3.2 Lighting

Lighting is probably the single most important factor in facilitating reading by older people. In general, older people benefit from high levels of illumination, but the problem is to obtain these levels without the user suffering from glare. The illumination on a surface is inversely proportional to the square of the distance from the luminaire. Therefore, bringing a reading lamp to a third of the distance will provide 9 times as much light on the reading material. Many people benefit from simple solutions such

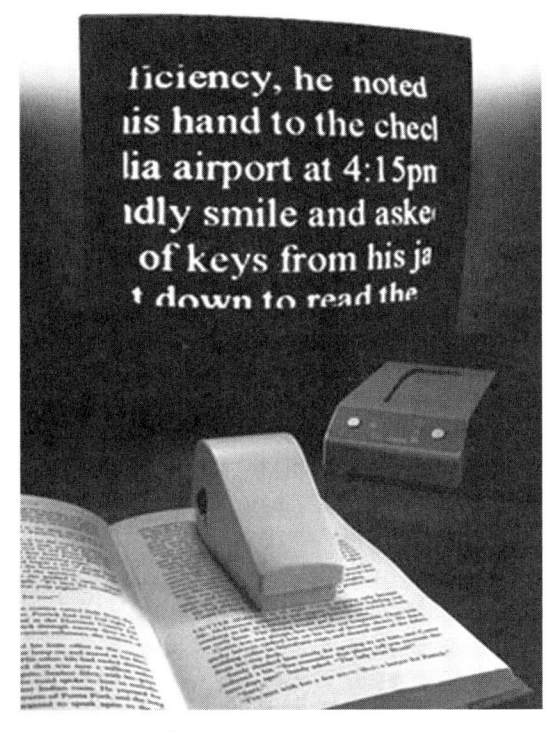

FIGURE 9.7 Closed-circuit television reading system.

as replacing a conventional bulb in a reading lamp with a spotlight bulb of the same wattage; this results in 7 times as much illumination on the reading material.

9.3.3 Audio Technology

One of the most useful aids for a blind person is a tape recorder since it requires few special skills to record or to listen to the material. However, there are a number of problems such as controlling the speed of playback and indexing. If the speed of a tape recording is increased, the pitch also increases, making it difficult to understand (it sounds like Donald Duck). However, increased, research done many years ago by the Royal Navy on communicating with deep-sea divers breathing helium led to electronic circuitry to compensate for this frequency shift; the helium gives the divers a very high-pitched voice. There is still no satisfactory solution to indexing on an ordinary compact cassette.

9.3.4 Digital Technology

However, digital technology offers the possibility of combining text and audio, and incorporating sophisticated searching and indexing facilities. For reading an audio novel, the main advantages of digital technology would be improved audio quality. For a cookbook, the new technology could offer facilities such as direct links to nutrition information. For an academic reference book, the possibilities become even greater as long as the publisher had the resources to incorporate the extra facilities. The future of electronic books for the general population is surrounded by considerable hype. However, US legislation has forced the main developers to consider the needs of visually impaired persons. So it is hoped that these developments will lead to an increase in accessible literature for blind people.

An important aspect of this digital technology is the ability to transfer data over high-speed telecommunication links. For instance, the asynchronous digital subscriber line (ADSL) works over ordinary telephone lines but could transfer a typical audio novel in under 20 min using MP3 compression techniques; this might be economically attractive if the telecommunication network operators were to offer inexpensive call charges during the night for visually impaired persons. The precedent for such charging could be the free postage of material for blind people offered by the postal service. Third-generation mobile telecommunication systems offer speeds up to 2 Mbit/s when in the vicinity of a transmitter, so this could be another method for delivering talking books to blind individuals.

9.3.5 Braille

The best-known communication system for blind people is Braille, which was developed by the French inventor Louis Braille in 1853. A combination of six dots can only have 64 different configurations. This presents a problem in that many more than 64 different characters are used in modern printed texts; so, at times, more than one Braille character is needed to represent one print character. A Braille book is typically 20 times as bulky as the print edition. Therefore, a form of shorthand is employed that uses 189 abbreviations and contractions, giving a space saving of about 25%. For computer use, it is becoming common to use an eight-dot Braille system that can represent 256 characters using only a single cell.

Since there is a shortage of skilled transcribers, computer systems are often used to translate text into contracted Braille, which is then output on a special embosser. The algorithms for this translation are not simple since the rules governing the use of contractions depend on pronunciation and meaning. For example, there is a contraction for "mother" that can be used as part of a longer word provided it does not bridge a syllable boundary as in "chemotherapy."

Since one of the greatest deprivations caused by blindness is lack of privacy, the provision of bank statements in Braille has been a very popular service for over 25 years. This system can be totally automated since bank statements are in a fixed format. Layout is more problematic for mathematics and music. Since Braille mathematics is written on one line, the conversion of the layout on the printed page to a meaningful form in Braille is far from trivial. Braille music is also significantly different in layout from sighted music notation since the Braille reader has to read linearly.

There are about 13,000 people in the UK who regularly read Braille. (*Note*: this should be compared to the one million people whose vision is such that they could be registered as blind or partially sighted.) For these people it is a very useful communication medium since it can be written as well as read by a blind person. This level of readership, which is typical of developed countries, is partly attributable to the difficulty in learning a new method of communication by people who lose their vision later in life. Another factor is that diabetic retinopathy is a significant cause of visual disability among those of working age, and diabetes usually adversely affects the sense of touch.

9.3.6 Tactile Graphics

The increasing use of graphics in printed books, particularly school textbooks, introduces problems. Although many diagrams can be converted to an embossed form, the process of reading by touch means that a diagram has to be tactually scanned and a mental image built of the whole diagram; this is the reverse of visual reading, where one looks at the overall picture and then reads the detail.

9.3.7 Reading Machines

Some years ago NASA (the US National Aeronautics and Space Administration) had a problem with communicating with astronauts during liftoff. The problem was of information overload using visual and auditory communication. Therefore they investigated the use of tactual communication; the project failed, but the research formed the basis of a reading aid for blind persons. The Optacon used a handheld camera connected to 144 piezoelectric elements that produced a vibratory image of the print character; the task of recognizing the character was left to the human. Its use has been limited by the low reading speed (typically 40 words per minute after extensive training).

Systems designed to recognize printed characters have been developed for inputting text to computers. Such systems have immediate application for visually impaired persons since the information can be output in synthetic speech, on a Braille display, or in large characters on a screen. None of these systems can read handwriting satisfactorily.

A facsimile (fax) machine can be used to transmit handwritten text to a central office where a human reads it back over the telephone. With the decreasing cost of fax machines, this technique is looking increasingly attractive as a means for providing a remote reading service.

9.3.8 Speech Technology

More recent developments in speech technology have led to significant improvements in quality and accuracy, and a reduction in prices. This is important for people with disabilities since speech technology can be used for interpersonal communication, access to information, and control of the environment.

Although the intelligibility of the available speech synthesis systems is quite high for a number of languages, there is evidence that significantly better quality should be achievable. Research is focused on naturalness, prosody, and flexibility (e.g., different voices). Other important research areas are modeling of emotions and speech synthesis from the meaning of the text.

Speech recognition is difficult because

- The basic units of speech are hard to recognize.
- Continuous speech adds more difficulties.
- Speaker and environmental differences are very important.
- There is insufficient knowledge about the human language understanding process.

Speech dialog systems, in which speech synthesis and recognition are used in a human–machine dialog, have been demonstrated for applications such as bank cash dispensers and hands-free voice dialers on public telephones. These systems are for the general public and therefore have to cope with significant variances between individual speakers. Current systems are limited to vocabularies of a few hundred words, but laboratory prototypes exist with vocabularies of a few thousand words.

If the system is designed for an individual speaker, then accuracy dramatically improves, large vocabularies can be used, and the cost reduces to a modest level. Speech synthesis is a stable technology, but speech recognition is still substantially inadequate when compared with human capabilities, particularly in noisy environments. Research on speech processing has had a significant impact on the design of cochlear implants as well as digital hearing aids. However, there is a need for better understanding of user needs and matching these needs to appropriate research and development. There is also a need to use current knowledge in practical situations to evaluate potential benefits.

9.3.9 Computers

Since the late 1980s, the most important change for many blind people has been the advent of the personal computer. With text-based operating systems, such as the disk operating systen (DOS), a blind person could access information with almost the same ease as a sighted person. The output from the computer could be in synthetic speech, a transitory Braille display or large characters on the monitor. Many visually impaired people use their personal computers just for word processing. This gives them the ability to check what they have typed and to correct any errors.

9.3.9.1 Graphical User Interfaces

However, the introduction of the graphical user interface, of which Windows is the best known example, introduced a range of new problems (Fig. 9.8). Early versions of Windows were partly inaccessible and required the blind person to have an understanding of the structure of the operating system. More recent versions of Windows have been

FIGURE 9.8 The graphical user interface.

more accessible because Microsoft has built in more accessibility features, but even so it is still not as easy as DOS for a blind person to use. Some blind people only use DOS, but most new software is not available in a DOS version.

9.3.9.2 The Internet

Email, since it is text-based, has been very useful for many blind people since it is relatively easy to learn and use. The World Wide Web offers exciting possibilities for accessing large quantities of information, but there are problems. First, the blind user needs a suitable browser. The main problem is that many Websites use graphics such that they are not meaningful when accessed by a text-based browser (e.g., with speech or Braille output). Guidelines have been produced for how to design accessible Websites, but these guidelines are widely ignored by commercial organizations. So some Websites are accessible, but these tend to be ones belonging to government departments. The popular commercial Websites, such as those for home shopping and home banking, are still largely inaccessible.

9.4 MULTIPLE IMPAIRMENTS

The number of people over retirement age in Europe is likely to increase by over 1% per year for the next two decades (i.e., until 2028 or so). With this increase in the aging population, there has been an increase in the number of people with a visual impairment in addition to some other impairment. The effects of multiple impairments varies considerably from one individual to the next, but can be summarized as the multiplication rather than the addition of the separate impairments. Often a multiple impairment limits the range of devices appropriate for an individual. For instance, someone with low vision and a hand tremor is likely to find a stand-mounted magnifier more satisfactory than a handheld magnifier.

However, there is an acute shortage of devices specially designed for this increasingly large group of people. In times of war, the incidence of multiple impairments among young people rises significantly. It is not just soldiers, but also civilians, including children, who are affected by landmines.

The proportion of children who have multiple impairments, rather than just a visual impairment, has risen since improvements in medicine have meant that fewer babies are being born with a single impairment, coupled with improved survival rates for babies with multiple impairments. The result has been that schools for blind children have had to adapt to cope with handling children with multiple impairments.

However, these demographic changes have not been reflected in the activities of those undertaking research and technologic development. This may be, in part, attributable to the difficulties of studying groups that are far from homogeneous. Also, commercial suppliers of devices have found it more difficult to sell devices to this group of customers.

The implication is that devices should be configurable or adaptable to meet the needs of the individual. Systems that are programmable, such as mobile phones, are easier to adapt to provide a range of user interfaces.

9.4.1 Deafblindness

The term *deafblind* is used in this handbook to individuals having combined loss of hearing and sight to such degree that they cannot make immediate use of the same facilities used by those with impaired hearing or sight alone. This definition, therefore, includes people who have a combination of severe hearing loss and low vision. Using this definition, there are about 250 deafblind persons per million of the population in the UK.

To be useful to a deafblind person, a device does not necessarily have had to be designed specifically for the deafblind. However, more and an increasing number of devices designed for blind people employ audio output, such as synthetic speech, so there are fewer inexpensive devices with tactual output. For instance, the number of electronic calculators with Braille output is falling since the cost of synthetic speech output has reduced dramatically. These trends have been to the advantage of blind people but have significantly reduced the choice available to deafblind persons.

9.4.2 Signals and Alarms

A number of alarm clocks with raised markings on the dial and an electrically activated vibrator for the alarm are available on the market. The vibrators are typically small electric motors with eccentric weights. Clockwork vibrators are not used in any of the standard products; the reason for this is not clear. The vibrator does not need to be directly connected by a wire to the clock—it can be triggered by a low-power radio signal. This means that the vibrator can be worn on the body (e.g., like a wristwatch).

The simplest doorbell signalers involve a pushbutton being connected to an electrical device that then transmits a signal to activate a vibrator worn by the deafblind person. Sometimes the transmission is done via a closed-loop aerial; this has a number of disadvantages including the high cost of installing the aerial and that the device operates only in the immediate vicinity of the loop. These systems are being superceded by radio devices. The input to the system is not necessarily a pushbutton; it is possible to use an IR detector or a pressure pad under the carpet.

A sound indicator is an electronic device that transmits a vibratory signal when it picks up an audio signal (e.g., a telephone bell) above a preset level. Usually the vibratory signal lasts for a fixed minimum time, and the amplitude of the vibration is usually constant (i.e., independent of the amplitude of the input signal). Some devices can be tuned to pick up audio signals only at or about a fixed frequency; this is useful in minimising the number of times the device is activated by picking up the wrong audio signal.

9.4.3 Other Low-Technology Devices

A small number of devices have been modified to give vibratory output—for example, a liquid level indicator, a light probe, and typing aids. These are numerically very few because the development and manufacturing costs are high for a small national market.

9.4.4 Access to Information Technology

It was the advent of the personal computer with Braille or magnified visual output that opened up opportunities for a significant increase in access to information by deafblind people. Software for producing large characters on the monitor is relatively inexpensive, but Braille displays have remained expensive.

The basic mobile telephone has been of limited use to deafblind people. However, the introduction of Universal Mobile Telecommunications System (UMTS) offers exciting possibilities if the services are affordable. For instance, the ability to transmit pictures of one's location relative to a service center and receive textual replies could greatly assist a deafblind pedestrian in an unfamiliar environment. However, not all technologic developments are to the advantage of deafblind people. With analog television it is possible to obtain braille output of teletext, which gives basic access to the news. As yet, it has not been possible to obtain a suitable output from digital teletext.

The Internet provides an alternative method for obtaining the news and other information. However, current systems for accessing the Web are not sufficiently user-friendly for many deafblind persons to use unassisted.

Although technology could greatly increase access to information and the ability of deafblind people to participate in society, this is unlikely to happen unless there is a significant and ongoing investment in developing new devices and systems and making them available at affordable prices.

9.5 INCLUSIVE DESIGN

Increasingly, blind people need to be able to use equipment designed for the general public; this includes ticket-selling machines at unstaffed railway stations, cash dispensers [automatic teller machines (ATMs)], and public telephones. In the foreseeable future, inability to use such systems is likely to increase the divide between the blind and sighted populations; these systems could include next-generation mobile phones, interactive television, and electronic purses.

Therefore, it is essential that equipment for use by the general public be designed for access by as many people as is reasonably possible. With the increasing aging population, this must include people with presbyopia as well as those with a combination of different impairments.

The "inclusive design" message has had limited practical impact on the area of information and communication systems and services. This is despite the considerable effort expended by various groups around Europe. In the case of cash dispensers, the companies manufacturing the equipment see their customers as the banks purchasing their equipment. Even though they may have incorporated inclusive design features in their range of terminals, it is to no avail if the bank is not interested in offering it to their customers. Within the bank it may be a technical department which is responsible for selecting equipment for the bank, but it will be the local branches who have direct contact with disabled customers and who may provide a modicum of training in the use of the cash dispenser. Unfortunately, local branch staff are unlikely to be aware of the technologic possibilities for improving the accessibility of the equipment.

At the policy level it may be sufficient to specify that the equipment and services be accessible to as many people as is reasonably possible. However, this leaves open many questions, including the meanings of the terms "accessible." and what is "reasonable" Also, it does not cover the often crucial question as to who pays for any additional costs such as training.

The development of guidelines for inclusive design of systems and services in the area of information and communication technologies is seriously hampered by the sparcity of sound scientific data about the needs of people with disabilities. What data does exist is all too often based on inadequate sample sizes or inappropriate methodology. This is an area that is perceived to be low on academic content.

Industry wants guidelines for pandisability, but this will require greater collaboration between all the relevant organizations representing the different disability groups. With new equipment and services that are in only the early stages of specification, such as third-generation mobile communications, it is difficult to be precise. However, if the influencing is left to the stage when it is clear what features will be incorporated, it is often too late to get anything significant changed.

Information for product designers may be detailed design guidelines (e.g., the maximum height and angle of a display so that it can be read by a wheelchair user). However, this approach is possible only for established technology for which detailed design guidelines exist. In other cases it will be necessary to provide generic guidelines backed up by recommendations on how to test prototypes with a cross section of potential users. For telecommunication designers the problems are shortage of time and lack of an established system for evaluating with disabled users. This is an area where user organizations could take a more active role in providing speedy evaluation of prototype systems and services.

9.5.1 New Technology

The development time in telecommunications has been decreasing, which means that the time between proposal of the project and finalization of the specifications is short. Also, secrecy is considered essential by many commercial organizations. Therefore, the possibility of having direct contact with the product specifier at the right moment is remote. So, in practice, it is essential to provide the information, or a signpost to it (e.g., a Web address), in advance and hope that the recipient remembers it at the relevant moment. This can be easier if the company has a design checklist that includes questions on the accessibility of the product by disabled users.

Policy documents from the European Commission are written in a special language that is difficult to understand by the uninitiated; only relatively recently have some of the organizations representing disabled people taken on staff with the skills to interpret these documents. However, these organizations seldom have the technical expertise to understand some of the implications. Therefore, there needs to be some form of collaboration between those who understand the language and the regulatory issues, those who have a good grasp of the technology, and those with lobbying skills.

9.5.2 Standardization

Standards are crucial in the telecommunication industry, where there is a rigorous, but sometimes slow, process for developing standards. In the television industry, the process is somewhat different in that the technical standards are frequently determined by bodies made up of only industry representatives and there is no policy for involving consumers. The situation is different again in computer software, where the commercially dominant players set the de facto standards with apparently no consultative process. This means that convergence will involve a clash of cultures as well as the more obvious problems of integrating three different groups of technology.

Standardization is slow, time-consuming, lacks academic content, and sometimes has limited direct commercial benefit. Academics shun the area since it does not produce research publications. Industry is hesitant about inclusive design standards work since they can see no short-term commercial benefit.

Industry and many government departments feel it is the role of the organizations of disabled people to assist with the implementation and awareness phases. However, the disability organizations have often expressed the view that they should be paid to do this work.

Since governments now see the primary purpose of standards as facilitating trade, the role of the consumer has become somewhat uncomfortable. Therefore, legislation or mandatory regulation would appear to be the only practical way of requiring commercial organisations to adopt inclusive design principles. However, the current trend is toward minimizing regulatory control, and European legislation does not appear likely in the near future.

9.6 PUBLIC TERMINALS

The solutions to some of the problems of people with disabilities may appear trivial to a nondisabled person, but they can nevertheless have a major effect on the usability of a piece of equipment or access to a service. For instance, many people would like a notch in the facia of the terminal so that they can lean their walking sticks against the terminal without the sticks falling over. Other problems require more complex modifications, but often solutions are available but not implemented.

9.6.1 Consistent User Interface

For many disabled and elderly users, the most important aspect is consistency in the user interface of public terminals; this is particularly important for visually, intellectually, and cognitively impaired users.

With public terminals, the user may use it only occasionally and has probably been provided with minimal training in using it (Fig. 9.9). What is perceived as "logical" by

FIGURE 9.9 Public access terminal.

the average user may be different from what seems "logical" to the designer, so it is essential to test any new user interface with a cross section of potential users (including disabled and elderly people).

9.6.2 Allowing a Choice of Interface

To select a preferred interface such as audio instructions or large characters on the screen, the user could simply press a button or otherwise select from a menu on the screen; this is likely to increase the time taken to undertake a transaction if there are more than a few options. Another possibility is to store the user's preferences on a central computer and implement them as soon as the PIN (personal identification number) has been entered.

For card-operated terminals, it is possible to store the information on the user's card (the coding of user requirements is specified in the European standard EN1332-4), and this is in many ways more desirable than storing private information about a user on a central database. With a magnetic stripe card there is very limited spare capacity for storing this information (but this method has been used for storing the user's preference for displayed language), but a smart card (containing an electronic chip) has fewer restrictions on storage capacity and thus appears to be ideal for this purpose.

Many disabled users would like to be able to select and store their preferred interface whenever they use their cards at public access terminals. It is essential that information be stored on a card only with the consent of the user.

9.6.3 Locating a Terminal

For a blind person, it can be difficult to find the terminal in an unfamiliar environment. One possibility is to use a contactless smart card, carried by the blind person, to trigger an audible signal from the terminal at a distance of a few meters.

9.6.4 Audio Interaction

Public access terminals can incorporate audio prompts in the form of "beeps" to indicate an action. It is recommended that new equipment provide a more sophisticated solution of using audio leadthrough in the form of a verbal set of instructions. Audio leadthrough can assist people with visual or cognitive impairments (and first-time users). Message content should be chosen very carefully since a message that might be acceptable to the users for the first few times they hear it may become unacceptable when they hear it for the hundredth time. Many users with impaired hearing, who can hear only lower frequencies, can more easily hear a male voice than a female one.

If audio output is used to provide private information to the user, it should be through a telephone handset located at the terminal or through a headset connected through a standard minijack to the terminal; however, it is essential that the position of the jack socket be standardized. If a handset is provided, inductive coupling and amplification should also be incorporated.

9.6.5 Card Orientation

Blind persons, and many elderly persons, have problems in inserting the card in the correct orientation; this is a particular problem on cards that are not embossed. However, there is a European standard for an orientation notch (EN1332-2) in the card (Fig. 9.10)

9.6.6 Braille

Braille instructions on outdoor terminals have limited value in cold weather since tactual sensitivity is dramatically reduced with decreasing temperature. The estimated number of Braille readers in Europe is less than 200,000, so, although useful for some blind users, Braille is not a total solution for all visually impaired users.

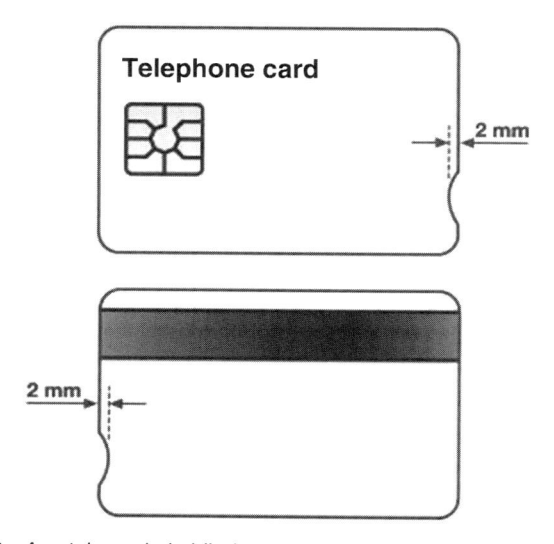

FIGURE 9.10 A notch can help blind users insert the card in the correct orientation.

9.6.7 Reading Screens

People who wear bifocals find it difficult to read the screen of most public access terminals, since neither lens gives a focused image for the distance between their eyes and the screen. In addition, many people leave their spectacles in the car or do not wear them in public. So the number of people who have problems in reading the screen is much more than those considered "blind" or "visually impaired," who constitute about 1.5% of the population.

People with weak vision should not be prevented from getting their faces close to the screen. However, it is possible to increase the size of the characters on the screen for individual customers who require this facility. This can be done by selecting this option from a menu or preferably by storing this information on the customer's card. With touchscreen systems, it could be arranged that holding one's finger in the top left corner for at least 2 s indicates that one would like double-size characters on the screen. Ambient light, such as from an illuminated sign above the terminal, can cause problems if it results in glare or reflections from the screen.

Moving text on a screen can be very difficult to read for someone with even a mild sight impairment, so it should be avoided whenever possible.

9.6.8 Speech Output

Digitally stored speech can give very good audio quality, but it is effectively limited to prestored messages. Full-vocabulary synthetic speech is often difficult to understand for the naive user, particularly one having a hearing impairment. Nonconfidential information can be output on a loudspeaker, but the volume should be a function of the current ambient noise level; this is less of a problem with handsets or headphones.

One technological possibility would be for a disabled user to have a hand control unit with an IR or radio link to the terminal. Although Bluetooth may become the standard interface, there is still a problem in persuading service providers to fit it to all terminals (which would include retrofitting to existing terminals).

9.6.9 Text on Screens

Displayed text should use simple, large, bold fonts in upper- and lowercase characters. Displayed messages should be simple in sentence structure and use natural language, and any graphical symbols (such as icons) should be accompanied by text. Information that is sensitive and private to the cardholder should not be visible to any other person; screen filters, which act like a slatted blind and restrict the user to be directly in front of the screen, improve privacy, but often at the expense of visual quality. Users may wish to display information with a large character size, but they should be made aware of the privacy problem.

9.6.10 Keypads

Standard layout of keypads is essential for visually impaired people and highly desirable for other users. To help blind persons, there should be a single raised dot on the number 5 key. However, this does not solve the problem of the existence of two common layouts for the numeric keys (i.e., the telephone and the calculator layouts); it is recommended that the telephone layout be used exclusively on public access terminals (Fig. 9.11).

FIGURE 9.11 *Inconsistent layout of keypads can be problematic for blind users.*

Ideally, keys should be internally illuminated when the terminal is waiting for input from that keypad. There should be some form of feedback on key input (e.g., a beep and/or tactual indication). Tactile feedback can be provided by a gradual increase in the force, followed by a sharp decrease in the force required to actuate the key, and a subsequent increase in force beyond this point for cushioning.

9.6.11 Allowing More Time

Many elderly people and those with cognitive impairments do not like to be rushed or to think that they are likely to be "timed out" by the machine, so it is necessary to allow such people to use the terminal at their own pace; this requirement could be stored on the user's card.

9.6.12 Touchscreens

To help elderly people and those with hand tremors, key fields should be as large as possible and separated by a "dead area". There should be high contrast between touch areas, text, and background color. Avoid using a pretty picture as background—it is a menace to anyone with poor vision or someone reading the screen under difficult conditions (e.g., in bright sunlight).

For blind users, one possibility is to arrange that holding one's finger in a specified corner of the screen for at least 2 s initiates speech output (this must *not* be the same corner used to request large characters on the display), or tapping twice in the corner. Another method would be to store this requirement on the user's card.

Touchscreens can be triggered by either insertion or withdrawal of the fingertip. With the latter system, it is technically possible for users to pass their fingertips over the screen and get speech output describing the active area that they are touching at the time. Then the system is triggered only by withdrawing the fingertip from over an active area.

9.6.13 Printed Receipts

To aid visually impaired users, receipts should have a minimum font size of 12 point with a clear typeface with upper/lowercase text, but 16 point would be preferable if space permits. It is important that the print have good contrast on opaque paper with a minimum of background pattern. A common complaint is poor print quality on receipts, which can be a result of the printer ribbon not being replaced regularly.

9.7 CONVERGENT SYSTEMS

There has been much speculation about the impact of the coming together of computing, telecommunications, and broadcasting, but as yet it has had little practical effect. However, this is expected to in the near future, opening up new possibilities for services to help visually impaired people. It is difficult to predict what new services will be available since the limitations will be mainly commercial viability rather than technical feasibility.

9.7.1 Mobile Phones

Mobile telephones increasingly require the user to read a small liquid crystal screen to operate many of the functions in the phone. Although the phones incorporate increasingly powerful microprocessors, manufacturers have not seen a commercial opportunity in providing models that incorporate speech output of the messages normally displayed on the screen. However, there are some indications that this may change because motorists are seen as a significant market segment.

The *wireless application protocol* (WAP) can be used for financial transactions such as reloading an electronic purse. Extra functionality to suit visually impaired users could be built into the terminals, but this in itself is unlikely to provide full access to services. Therefore, it will be necessary to modify the server or proxy server. The *WAP user agent profile specification* covers aspects of the technical interface, and the *user preference profile* concerns content selection (e.g., the user is interested in receiving sports scores); neither of these profiles covers the needs of people with disabilities.

General packet radio service (GPRS) is a high-speed packet data technology that will permit data transmission speeds of up to 100 kbit/s over the global system for mobile communications (GSM) network. This is well suited for frequent transmission of small amounts of data. However, it could be overtaken by the Universal Mobile Telecommunications System (UMTS).

UMTS is the next generation of mobile telecommunications system that will have seamless operation between terrestrial and satellite links. It will provide high-speed access to the Internet with data rates of up to 2 Mbit/s for a stationary terminal, less when on the move. It will include packet data transmission with the potential to adjust bandwidth on demand for asymmetric traffic. In the UK the network licenses have been sold by the government for vast sums (the first five licenses sold for over $44 billion), which will have to recouped from the users.

UMTS will permit the transmission of video. For instance, a blind person might send a picture to a service center where a sighted person could give instructions on how to reach the desired destination. Another possible use for UMTS would be to download talking books during the night; a typical novel would take about 20 min to download using MP3.

9.7.2 Electronic Purses

For some time prepayment cards have been in general use for applications such as public telephones. These disposable cards are loaded with a fixed amount of value, which are then decremented during use. The next development was to make the cards reloadable, which can be done at specialized terminals or automated teller machines (ATMs; cash dispensers). Then it was only a small step for the cards to be used for more than a single application; these cards are called *electronic purses*.

However, these systems vary significantly depending on the type of organization operating the service. Historically the banking organizations have placed great importance on security, whereas public transport operators have been more concerned to minimise the time taken to complete the transaction.

Some electronic purse systems offer the facility to transfer funds between the card and the customer's bank account using a screen phone. Screen phones can be modified to be accessible by blind people, so this method of loading a card could be the preferred mode for many blind and partially sighted users.

For visually impaired persons, the main problems with electronic purse systems relate to the user interface. In particular many of the devices, such as balance readers and electronic wallets, have poor contrast visual displays, which also pose problems for many elderly persons (Fig. 9.12). One possibility would be to have special versions of the balance readers and wallets for those who cannot read the standard versions. Such a special wallet/balance reader might include

- High-contrast display with larger characters (or speech output)
- Larger buttons with clear visual markings and tactual feedback
- A funnel opening to help guide the card into the reader

A significant aspect of electronic purses is that the user does not need to have a bank account or even be creditworthy. This is likely to make electronic purses the preferred method of remotely paying for shopping by many older visually impaired persons.

FIGURE 9.12 A wallet for an electronic purse.

Another attraction for this group of customers is that as soon as the transaction has taken place, they can check the remaining balance on their electronic purse; unlike credit or debit cards, there is no risk of an unexplained item appearing on a future statement.

9.7.3 Interactive Digital Television

Interactive television is attracting considerable investment as it is seen as a significant step in selling new services to customers who may not be computer users. The UK government envisages that it will be a major method of interaction between the public and the government by 2013 or so.

Traditional television can be characterized as one-to-many, whereas the Internet would be characterized as many-to-one. As yet interactive television is frequently just an enhanced one-to-many system with uncertainty as to how to satisfactorily also be a many-to-one system.

Some systems offer email, which is proving popular among those who do not have access to a computer or have no inclination to use one. Currently there are no facilities for enlarging the text or changing colors, which presents problems for many visually impaired users.

In the UK, home shopping has taken off faster on interactive television than on the Web; this is attributed to the fact that viewers are less anxious about credit card fraud through the television set than the Internet.

9.7.4 Convergence

In the future, the remote control for the television might be a mobile phone, connected by Bluetooth, into which is inserted the electronic purse to pay for goods and services.

9.8 FUTURE RESEARCH

In the near future, there are likely to be improvements in the medical prevention and treatment of eye conditions, but the increase in the aging population will probably mean that the net effect is that there will be a larger number of people with visual impairments. Many older visually impaired persons have seen little benefit from the advances in the area of assistive technology. If they use assistive technology, beyond conventional weak-vision aids, it will usually be the low-technology low-priced devices to assist in daily living.

A major problem has been in transferring prototypes from the laboratory into products generally available at affordable prices. Unless new funding mechanisms are developed to facilitate this process, few visually impaired people will benefit from the scientific and technological research being done on their behalf.

Universities discourage research on "simple" devices because there appears to be little academic content. Industry seldom perceives a significant commercial market for these devices; therefore. This means that this area has been left largely to nonprofit organizations.

What is needed are studies of the problems faced by visually impaired people, and the development of novel inexpensive devices to meet these needs. This will require imagination as well as a knowledge of appropriate production processes. Last, but not least, all this needs to be linked to a marketing strategy that reaches the potential consumers. For too long, visually impaired people have had to make do with poorly designed products.

Another aspect is the desirability of developing products that are attractive to nondisabled users. It is worth noting that the fountain pen, typewriter, and long-playing record were originally developed for use by blind people.

There is a particular need for devices for people with more than one impairment. The problem is that this is a far from a homogeneous group, so it is likely to involve developing devices that are adaptable.

Many research workers find it easier to study the needs of people who are totally blind since it is difficult to do an accurate comprehensive functional assessment of someone with low vision. This has been particularly noticeable in the area of research on electronic mobility devices. There has also been a tendency to look for purely technological solutions to human problems.

9.8.1 Vision Enhancement

An area of research that appears promising is vision-enhancing systems in which the user is presented with a display with enhanced contrast of the objects in the near field. Such a system would use a body-mounted camera and a head-up display. The existing devices are too expensive, and the usability aspects need to be improved. Also, such a system could be designed to partly compensate for loss of color discrimination.

9.8.2 Cortical Stimulation

Research is being done on connecting a videocamera to the human brain. One approach was to implant a number of electrodes in the brain; this proved problematic, so more recent research has concentrated on methods of stimulating the optic nerve. This research is important but is unlikely to produce systems that are widely available within the next ten years.

9.8.3 Vision Substitution

Vision substitution can involve converting a video signal to a nonvisual form, which can be auditory, tactual, or some combination of the two. Since both the auditory and tactual channels have far lower information capacity than does the visual channel, it is necessary to process the signal from the cameras before it is sent to the nonvisual display. Ideally this processing should include edge detection and object recognition. With increasingly powerful wearable computers, vision substitution systems look very promising if the appropriate algorithms can be developed.

9.8.4 User Interfaces

The ability to modify the user interface will be crucial if new systems are to be accessible to visually impaired people. In particular, such a facility will be essential in areas such as interactive television and the next generation of mobile communications.

9.8.5 Wireless Coding

Systems such as Bluetooth, are expected to permit communication between devices such as mobile phones, televisions, central heating controllers, and assistive devices. However, this is insufficient since there also needs to be a standard method of coding information to be sent to and from assistive devices.

9.8.6 Orientation Systems

It is in the area of orientation systems that exciting but practical developments can be expected in the near future. This may involve a combination of satellite and mobile telephony technology coupled with an electronic map accessed over a UMTS link. However, it will be important that service delivery, including training, be developed at the same time.

9.8.7 Graphics

A major research area relates to graphical representations. The trend for systems for sighted people is for the increasing use of graphics, but research on nonvisual presentations is lagging far behind. For people with low vision, more research is needed on how to optimally present visual graphics; this may involve transposing colors for people who are colorblind.

9.8.8 The Internet

The World Wide Web is partly accessible for users who have to rely on nonvisual output. However new modes of presentation and the rate of development could mean that access will become more difficult. This is a serious problem since the Web has the potential for significantly narrowing the gap between blind and sighted people regarding access to information.

9.8.9 Virtual Reality

In the longer term, technologic developments in other fields could benefit those working with visually impaired persons. For instance, virtual reality technology could provide realistic simulations of visual defects, including fields, acuity, color discrimination, and effects of illumination; in addition, multiple impairments could be simulated. Such a system might be useful for evaluating proposed public buildings.

Virtual reality technology allows people with sensory disabilities to perceive what they might not otherwise be able to since it can gather information in a sensory modality in which they are impaired and deliver it to one where they are not. It also has the potential to be used as a training aid for skills such as spatial coordination and orientation.

As intriguing as virtual reality is, the enabling technology is still crude (Fig. 13). Major technologic hurdles exist in the area of tracking a person's motion and position in a nonintrusive way, in displaying high-definition stereo color images of the scene covering the user's peripheral vision and, in the area of image generation, speed for a smooth and realistic animation of the scene. Tactile output and the construction of physical images, to support the visual images in virtual environments, require further development to produce realistic sensations.

FIGURE 9.13 *Virtual reality system.*

Over the next decade (i.e., by 2018 or so), there will be exciting possibilities for improving the quality of life for visually impaired people, but there are hurdles to be overcome to ensure that the appropriate research is undertaken and the results of this research reach the potential consumers.

FURTHER READING AND INFORMATION

Publications

Gill J M Financial Services and Visually Disabled Persons. ISBN 0 901797 65 0, Sept 1991.

Gill J M Non-visual Screen Representations. In Issues in Telecommunications for People with Disabilities. ISBN 92 826 3128 1, 1991.

Gill J M A Vision of Technological Research for Visually Disabled People. ISBN 0 9516611 4 0, March 1993.

Gill J M Access to Graphical User Interfaces by Blind People. ISBN 1 85878 004 7, October 1993.

Gill J M The Forgotten Millions: Access to Telecommunications for People with Disabilities. ISBN 92 826 7399 5, March 1994.

Gill J M The Design of Man-Machine Interfaces for Use by Visually Disabled People. International Technical Aids Seminar for the Visually Disabled, July 1995. www.tiresias.org/publications/reports/japan.htm

Gill J M The Forgotten Customers: One in Ten have Difficulty with Packaging. Food, Cosmetics and Drug Packaging, August 1995. www.tiresias.org/publications/reports/packag.htm

Gill J M & Currie K Smart Cards and Terminals. In Roe P R W (ed) *Telecommunications for All*. COST 219, October 1995.

Gill J M Telecommunications: The Missing Links for People with Disabilities. ISBN 92 827 5115 5, February 1996.

Gill J M An Orientation and Navigation System for Blind Pedestrians. ISBN 1 86048 008 X, April 1996. www.tiresias.org/publications/reports/mobicgl.htm

Gill J M(ed) Mobility of Blind and Elderly People Interacting with Computers. ISBN 1 86048 006 3, April 1997.

Gill J M Access Prohibited? Information for Designers of Public Access Terminals. ISBN 1 86048 014 4, May 1997, revised March 1998. www.tiresias.org/publications/pats

Gill J M (ed) Domestic Telecommunication Terminals: Access by People who are Blind or have Low Vision. COST 219 UK Group, December 1997.

Gill J M, Silver J, Sharville C, Slater J & Martin M Design of a Typeface for Digital Television. Third Tide Congress, Helsinki, June 1998. In Placencia Porrero I & Ballabio E *Improving the Quality of Life for the European Citizen*. IOS Press, ISBN 90 5199 406 0, 1998.

Gill J M The Use of Electronic Purses by Disabled People: What are the Needs? ISBN 1 86048 017 9, August 1998. www.tiresias.org/publications/epurse

Gill J M (ed) Guidelines for the Design of Screen and Web Phones to be Accessible by Visually Disabled Persons. ISBN 1 86048 018 7, December 1998. www.tiresias.org/publications/reports/webphone.htm

Gill J M Approaches for Influencing the Design of New Telecommunication Systems and Services. International Conference on Smart Homes and Telematics, February 1999. www.tiresias.org/publications/reports/approach.htm

Gill J M Design Features of Terminals to Improve Accessibility by Visually Impaired Persons. Vision 99 Conference, July 1999. www.tiresias.org/publications/reports/terminal.htm

Gill J M & Shipley A D C Telephones: What Features do Disabled People Need? ISBN 1 86048 020 9, August 1999. www.tiresias.org/phoneability/telephones

Gill J M Which Button? The Design of User Interfaces for People with Visual Impairments. ISBN 1 86048 023 3, August 2000. www.tiresias.org/publications/controls

Gill J M Priorities for Technological Research for Visually Impaired People. Visual Impairment Research, ISSN 1388-235X, Vol **7**, Nos 2-3, August-December 2005, pp 59-62.

Roe P R W, Sandhu J S, Delaney L, Gill J M & Mercinelli M User Needs: Consumer Overview. In Roe P R W (ed) *Telecommunications for All*. COST 219, October 1995.

Shipley A D C & Gill J M Call Barred? The Inclusive Design of Wireless Systems. ISBN 1 86048 024 1, 2000. www.tiresias.org/phoneability/wireless.htm

Silver J H, Gill J M & Wolffsohn J S W Text Display Preferences on Self-Service Terminals by Visually Disabled People. ISBN 1 86048 001 2, November 1994. www.tiresias.org/publications/reports/atm.htm

Websites

Trace Center, Univ Wisconsin: www.trace.wisc.edu

Tiresias, RNIB Scientific Research Unit: www.tiresias.org

COST 219: www.tiresias.org/cost219ter

10

Assistive Devices for People with Hearing Loss

Matthew H. Bakke

Gallaudet University

People with hearing loss are a very diverse population, and thus have a broad spectrum of communication needs. Factors that determine those needs include hearing loss type, degree, and configuration, age at onset of hearing loss (either before, during, or after learning spoken language), age, communication modality (spoken language vs. American Sign Language), culture, lifestyle (including entertainment, travel, hobbies, etc.), employment, and many others. Because the needs of the population are quite variable, people with hearing loss and the professionals who advise them are faced with many technology choices. This chapter gives a brief overview of the technologies that are currently available for people with hearing loss. For the purposes of this discussion, the technologies are categorized according to user need: personal hearing systems, wide-area assistive technologies, alerting and warning devices, and technologies for telecommunications access.

10.1 PERSONAL HEARING SYSTEMS

10.1.1 Hearing Aids

The most generally used and ubiquitous personal hearing system is the hearing aid. A hearing aid is designed to amplify ambient sounds and deliver the amplified signals to the impaired ear. Because hearing loss results in a loss of sensitivity to soft sounds, gain is provided so that the sounds become loud enough to be heard. However, gain cannot be uniformly applied across all speech frequencies because hearing loss typically affects different frequency regions differently. Nor should gain be provided in the same way for input signals of all levels, or else many of the sounds of daily life would be made so loud as to be intolerable to the user. As it happens, people with sensory hearing loss, which results from a loss of sensory hair cells in the cochlea and is the most common type of hearing loss, are subject to a phenomenon known as *recruitment*, which can be briefly described as an abnormal growth of loudness. In other words, while softer sounds may be inaudible, louder sounds are perceived to be as loud as they would be without the presence of hearing loss. Thus, hearing aids must control the amount of gain provided for input signals of differing amplitude and frequency.

10.1.1.1 Hearing Aid Configurations

There are several *styles* of hearing aids, differing in size, shape, and coupling to the ear. Arranged according to size from larger to smaller, they are as follows: body, behind-the-ear, in-the-ear, in-the-canal, and completely-in-the-canal hearing aids.

Body hearing aids are the oldest style, rarely found in today's market. Consisting of a body-worn case with a microphone, a cord, a button receiver, and an earmold, this style of hearing aid minimizes acoustic feedback in the case of profound hearing loss where gain is substantial. It also has the virtue of being easier to manipulate, having larger batteries and controls. A *behind-the-ear* (BTE) hearing aid consists of a head-worn case that houses the microphone and electronics and fits behind the *pinna* of the external ear, and a tone hook that connects to acoustic tubing, which in turn connects to an earmold. This configuration is most common in people with more severe or profound hearing loss because of their gain requirements and the problem of acoustic feedback. The greater distance (relative to an in-the-ear or in-the-canal style of aid) between the amplified signal and the microphone of the hearing aid helps reduce the likelihood of feedback. This type of hearing aid has the virtue of being larger, so that those with visual and fine-motor limitations may find it easier to manage. The larger size is also a disadvantage for many users who have cosmetic concerns about the hearing aid's visibility. In contrast, *in-the-ear* (ITE), *in-the-canal* (ITC), and *completely in-the-canal* (CITC) hearing aids are much smaller and fit entirely into the *concha* (ITE) or ear canal (ITC or CITC), obviating the need for a separate earmold. The case is custom-made to fit snugly and form a seal between the ear canal and the outside air, in order to control feedback. The microphone is typically placed on the face of the hearing aid, and thus is placed in a natural position at the entrance of the ear canal. While these smaller-sized hearing aids are valued for their reduced visibility, there is a cost in increased possibility of feedback due to the proximity of the microphone to the amplified signal from the hearing aid.

10.1.1.2 Digital Hearing Aids

For many years, hearing aids have been essentially miniature amplifiers with electronic circuits designed to amplify, filter, and control the levels of signals. However, since the development of computer chips that are very small, powerful, efficient, and able to operate at low voltages, digital hearing aids have become the industry standard. Such aids contain computer circuits that convert sound into numerical representations that can be transformed mathematically and converted back into sound for delivery to the ear. Digital hearing aids provide for greater flexibility and adaptability in fitting, permitting more precise frequency shaping as well as the implementation of complex signal-processing algorithms. They also allow hearing aids to have multiple memories, enabling users to select among two or more different fittings that have been specially tuned for specific environments such as noisy restaurants, telephone calls, and children's voices. A problem with digital hearing aids is their complexity. It is a challenge for an audiologist to achieve the "best fit" for hearing aids in which a large number of variables are at play. For this reason, digital hearing aids are typically marketed with software that implements fitting strategies unique to the features of the particular hearing aid. Audiologists are faced with the challenge of having multiple software applications, often from different hearing aid companies. Thankfully, there is a standard computer interface that was developed by a consortium of hearing aid companies that permits audiologists to work with multiple brands using the same hardware interface, known as NOAH.

10.1.1.3 Frequency Selectivity

As mentioned earlier, hearing loss affects different frequency regions of hearing differently. Typically, hearing in the higher-frequency regions tends to be more affected than in lower-frequency regions, although this is not always the case. At first blush, it may seem logical to provide gain that is equivalent to the hearing loss and therefore to "mirror" the hearing loss with amplification. In practice, however, this is not desirable because of recruitment. Much hearing aid research in the early years of electronic hearing aids was focused on how much gain to provide at each frequency for maximum speech perception performance and comfort (an excellent review is provided by Dillon [1, Chapter 9]). Various prescriptive formulas have been worked out and over time have become more complex as hearing aid technology has become more sophisticated. Digital hearing aids are fit by audiologists using software in which one or more prescriptive formulas have been implemented. In some cases these formulas are based on hearing thresholds and in others on loudness judgments.

10.1.1.4 Loudness Control

Because of recruitment, loudness must be controlled in hearing aids to prevent discomfort. Loudness control is also necessary to prevent possible additional damage to hearing, as well as to maximize speech intelligibility. Hearing aids often use amplitude compression, also known as *automatic gain control* (AGC) or *automatic volume control* (AVC), to adjust the growth of loudness and limit output. Simple AGC circuits control gain across all frequencies simultaneously, but because an individual's hearing loss, and therefore recruitment, may be different in different frequency regions, multichannel hearing aids have been developed in which different AGC characteristics are applied to two or three separate bands of frequency. Adaptive compression circuits have been used in advanced hearing aids. Such circuits are designed to modify their temporal parameters (attack time, release time) depending on the characteristics of the incoming sound. Thus, sounds with rapid changes in amplitude, such as impulsive sounds, are treated differently by the circuit than are sounds that change their amplitude more slowly, resulting in improved user comfort.

10.1.1.5 Noise Reduction

Consumers' most common complaints about their hearing aids involve their performance in backgrounds of noise [2]. Many attempts at reducing the effects of noise have been made, but single-microphone noise reduction in hearing aids has been largely unsuccessful improving speech understanding in noise [3]. Currently there is a great deal of interest in directional-microphone hearing aids, which are most sensitive to sounds coming from the front and suppress sounds from the rear and sides. Their design is based on the assumption that users will want to hear best in the direction in which they are looking, and that noise sources will be more likely to arise from other directions. This may not always be the case, since listening situations can vary greatly. In some situations, users may prefer to have an omnidirectional pattern so that they can monitor the environment in all directions; in other situations users may prefer a highly directional pattern in order to improve the signal-to-noise ratio (SNR) of the desired speech. Current hearing aids are often equipped with switches that permit the user to choose a directional pattern that suits the situation.

10.1.2 Cochlear Implants

In the case of people with hearing loss so severe that hearing aids provide only limited or no benefit, cochlear implants are now an option. While hearing aids amplify and deliver sound to an impaired inner ear, cochlear implants bypass the cochlea and directly stimulate the neurons of the auditory system with electrical pulses that result in auditory sensations. A cochlear implant system consists of both external and internal components. Externally worn components include a microphone, a speech processor, and a head-worn transmitter; internal components include a receiver/stimulator that is placed behind the ear and fixed to the skull and a connected electrode array that is threaded into one of the ducts (the scala tympani) of the cochlea. Naturally, a surgical procedure is required to put the internal components in place. This usually takes place on an outpatient basis, and after a period of healing of about one month, the external components are fit and the stimulation is turned on. While early cochlear implants consisted of head-worn microphones and body-worn speech processors, contemporary cochlear implants have very small processors that are worn behind the ear, like hearing aids. Sound is picked up by the microphone, which is typically mounted at the ear, similar to a behind-the-ear hearing aid. The sound is then processed by the speech processor, and the processed signal is transmitted across the skin to the internal receiver via a head-worn transmitter. The internal receiver accepts the signal from the transmitter, and performs the final operation: that of sending trains of electrical pulses to the assigned electrodes in the array. The array consists of a number of electrodes arranged tonotopically along the cochlea, representing frequencies from low (at the end of the array, deepest into the cochlea) to high (toward the entry point of the array).

It can take many months or years for an individual to gain full benefit from a cochlear implant, although there is much variability in patient outcomes. Some people appear to receive immediate and substantial benefits, such as being able to talk on the telephone, while others receive only limited benefit even after many years. There are many factors that are related to outcomes with cochlear implants, including age at onset of deafness, duration of deafness before implantation, number of surviving neurons in the cochlea, and many others, some of which are not well understood. Candidacy for a cochlear implant is largely determined by these considerations as well as the level of residual hearing [4]. The Food and Drug Administration (FDA) has established candidacy guidelines for adults and children for each of the approved devices. Cochlear implant stimulation is limited in its ability to reproduce sound sensations, and even those who may perform well in terms of speech understanding may have great difficulty appreciating music [5]. One reason for this is the fact that unlike natural hearing, cochlear implant stimulation is an extracted coded signal that is generated by the speech processor of the implant. The function of the speech processor is to convert the audio signal into a set of instructions for stimulating the electrodes in the array. The instructions vary according to the speech-processing strategy that is chosen and the individual's sensitivity to electrical stimulation. When fitting the cochlear implant, an audiologist measures the user's sensitivity by conducting a behavioral evaluation of thresholds for just-detectible and most comfortable levels of electrical stimulation for each electrode in the array. The patient's threshold and comfort levels are stored in the speech processor and used in the process of encoding sound into electrical stimulation of the electrode array.

In representing speech, it is important to provide detailed spectral and temporal information. The speech processor provides spectral information to the user by filtering the signal into several frequency bands, extracting the envelope of the signal in each band and using it to modulate a series of electrical pulses that are delivered to a corresponding electrode along the array. Temporal information is provided through rapid sampling of the signal and updating of the stimulation at the electrodes. The relative value to speech understanding of these two parameters in cochlear implants is not fully understood. Different speech processing strategies emphasize temporal and spectral information to differing degrees. Each of the strategies now being used has been successful in helping many users understand speech, although adults who are fit with cochlear implants appear to be quite definite about which strategy they prefer [6].

There are several different speech processing strategies, and they differ in their availability according to the implant manufacturer. Each implant offers two or more options from which the user, guided by the audiologist, chooses one that sounds most acceptable and yields the best speech understanding. On initial stimulation, more than one option is made available because the speech processors contain two or more memories in which different strategies may be stored. Very young children clearly do not have the ability to make this decision, so the choice of the first strategy to try is most often made on the basis of the experience of the cochlear implant center and the audiologist. During a trial period, the child's responses to sound will be assessed by parents, teachers, and the implant team, with changes made as required.

10.2 WIDE-AREA ASSISTIVE LISTENING

(Plomp, 1978; Nabelek, 1993) Speech perception performance of people using cochlear implants deteriorates substantially with background noise [7] as people with hearing loss have an increased susceptibility to the effects of noise and distance. For this reason, assistive listening systems have been developed to help manage problems caused by reverberation and ambient noise found in many environments such as theaters, places of worship, schools, auditoriums, and arenas. The basic principle is simple—a microphone is placed close to the desired sound source (e.g., on the speaker's lapel) and coupled to an individual's ear (as when using a headphone), hearing aid, or cochlear implant. While hardwired connections may still be used in some situations, generally ALDS use three different wireless media to transmit and receive signals: magnetic induction [induction loops (ILs)], frequency-modulated (FM) radiofrequencies, and infrared light (IR).

10.2.1 Hardwired Systems

The simplest and least expensive assistive listening system available is a hardwired personal amplifier, which consists of a microphone, an amplifier and a transducer. An example of such a system is the Pocketalker, produced by Williams Sound (www.williamssound.com). The virtue of such systems is their simplicity and low cost. They can serve as general-use amplifiers for situations in which hearing aids are not available. They also serve as assistive listening systems when the microphone is placed in proximity to the sound source and connected by a wire to the amplifier and the listener. This can be particularly useful in noisy restaurants or other noisy conditions, as well as in emergency situations. An example of the latter is that of a person with a hearing loss in a hospital without his or her hearing aid. A Pocketalker may be used as a temporary measure to help facilitate communication with caregivers and physicians. Such systems have an additional advantage when confidentiality is important, such as in counseling situations. Whereas wireless systems broadcast information so that it could possibly picked up by others, a hardwired system is completely private.

10.2.2 Magnetic Induction

The first application of magnetic induction to assistive hearing was intended to facilitate telephone listening. Early telephone handsets created magnetic fields around the earpiece as an unintended byproduct. Telecoils in hearing aids were designed to pick up the modulations of the magnetic field and present the signal to the user. Telephones that work in this way with hearing aids are said to be hearing aid–compatible. Both wireline (landline) and wireless (mobile) telephones manufactured for sale in the United States are required to be hearing aid compatible.

Magnetic induction has been widely applied in group listening systems. In such "loop systems," a loop of wire is placed around a room (floor or ceiling height). The desired signal (from a microphone or other sound system) is amplified and passed through the loop, setting up a modulated magnetic field. Hearing aid wearers switch their hearing aids to telecoil mode (T) or telecoil/microphone (TM) mode to hear the signal. For users who do not have hearing aids with telecoils, magnetic induction receivers are available that can be used with headphones.

Magnetic induction can also serve as an interface between other assistive technologies and a hearing aid or cochlear implant that has a telecoil. A neck loop or silhouette can be used for this purpose. A neck loop is a kind of miniature teleloop system; a loop of wire is worn around the neck connected by a plug (typically a 3.5-mm miniphone plug) to any audio device that has a compatible socket, such as an MP3 player, radio, television, or FM/IR assistive device. A silhouette is similar in function, although it substitutes the loop of wire with a thin wafer, shaped like a behind-the-ear (BTE) hearing aid that sits on the ear in proximity to the hearing aid. A wire connects the silhouette to any input device with a compatible socket.

A significant advantage of magnetic induction is that no receiver is needed for a user with a hearing aid or cochlear implant equipped with a telecoil. It solves many listening problems of hearing aid or cochlear implant wearers, and can be found on most telephones. Unfortunately, not all hearing aids in the United States are dispensed with a telecoil, which limits the usefulness of teleloop systems. Magnetic induction systems do not provide privacy, and the signals have a tendency to spill over to adjacent rooms. Interference is an additional problem that sometimes arises to bedevil hearing aid users. Sources include some kinds of lighting, cathode ray tubes (CRTs), backlit displays on telephones, and other electrical appliances and devices. Unfortunately, the only solutions available when confronted with magnetic interference is to identify and turn off the source of the interference, or move to another location.

10.2.3 FM Systems

Frequency-modulated systems act as miniature independent radio transmitters, broadcasting the desired signal to the audience. The signals may be live speech or music picked up by a microphone, or other signals such as soundtracks, that are connected via line input to the FM transmitter from an existing public address system. The user must have a receiver that is tuned to the same frequency channel as the transmitter. FM systems use the same radio signal as commercial FM radio, but they use specific frequency bands (72–75 MHz and 216–217 MHz) that are essentially unregulated and used for personal radio in the United States (*Code of Federal Regulations*, 47 CFR 2.106). The maximum permissible power of an assistive listening system is 80 mV/m at 3 m, which can be effective between 300 and 500 ft. Somewhat greater operating distances are possible with the 216–217-MHz band. Such devices are low in power and not likely to interfere with other permitted users in the same channels (e.g., paging devices, emergency vehicles). No priority is given to assistive listening devices; in the event of interference, a user must switch to another channel within the same frequency band.

An advantage of FM is the fact that the coverage is fairly uniform over the effective range. While interference from other sources of radio energy is possible, such problems are not common and can be dealt with by changing the frequency of transmission. A disadvantage of FM transmission is the ease with which it can be received, making public performances more susceptible to pirating. There have been reports of performers not agreeing to use FM systems for this reason. For the same reasons, when private information is being exchanged, FM is not the technology of choice.

10.2.4 Infrared Systems

Infrared systems use light outside the visible spectrum (∼700–1000 nm) as a medium for transmission. Channels are band-limited to reduce interference from other sources of light and heat. The light carrier is modulated by a subcarrier frequency, usually 95 kHz, although this can vary among systems. A transmitter encodes the desired audio signal and sends it to the emitter (an array of light-emitting diodes), which beams the light to the receivers in the audience. An infrared receiver always has a lens and a photodetecting diode that is capable of picking up the IR light signal. An optical filter on the lens helps reduce interference. The receiver demodulates the subcarrier and the audio signal is retrieved and amplified for listening. Direct line of sight is usually required for IR to work effectively (as in a television remote control). Bright sunlight will interfere with the signal and add static, although some systems are quite successful in reducing light interference.

In situations where privacy is important, infrared offers a good choice because the transmission can be contained within the room, unlike FM or magnetic induction systems, in which there is considerable spill-over of the signal into surrounding areas. This makes infrared particularly appealing to the entertainment industry.

10.2.5 Captioning

For some time closed captioning has been well established in televisions in the United States, and has benefited people with and without hearing loss as witnessed by the use of closed captioning for televisions in noisy bars and restaurants. In 1990, the

Television Decoder Circuitry Act (PL 101-431) mandated that televisions greater than 13 inches manufactured for sale in the United States have built-in circuits for decoding closed captions. In the years since 1990, the number of programs offering closed captions has increased. Current Federal Communications Commission (FCC) regulations require that "as of January 1, 2006, all 'new' English language programming, defined as analog programming first published or exhibited on or after January 1, 1998, and digital programming first aired on or after July 1, 2002, must be captioned, with some exceptions" (http://www.fcc.gov/cgb/consumerfacts/closedcaption.html). Captions not only present the text of words spoken in a given program but also provide auditory contexts such as "leaves rustling" or "rain pelting on a roof." This distinguishes captions from other forms of subtitling, such as those used in foreign films, for example. As television migrates to its digital form in the United States, closed captions will have more user-defined features available such as font size and background color.

Captioning in movie theaters is far less common than closed captioning in televisions, probably because of objections to showing open captions. Typically there have been special performances at off-peak hours when people with hearing loss can take advantage of the benefit of captioned movies. Rear-window captioning is a system of captioning that takes advantage of reflected captions that appear in reverse at the back of a theater. These captions are reflected off a clear plexiglass device that is attached to the seat and positioned by the person wanting captions. Thus, a form of "closed captioning" can be made available in public venues.

Real-time captioning is provided by trained reporters using specialized chord keyboards such as those used by court reporters. When connected with captioning software, the stenographer code generated by the keyboards is rapidly converted to readable text that can be used in providing captions in real time. Such systems are used for television news programming as well as for live events such as lectures and symposia. More recently, captions have been made available remotely by the use of a telephone line and a computer that is connected to the Internet. Such remote real-time captioning has made it possible for deaf and hard-of-hearing people to participate effectively in conference telephone calls without the use of sign language interpreters.

10.3 ALERTING AND WARNING SYSTEMS

When important warning and alerting information needs to be conveyed to people with severe or profound hearing loss, it is often necessary to use visual or vibratory alerting signals in place of (or supplementary to) auditory alerts. There are many devices on the market that serve this function in various situations: wakeup, doorbell and door knock alerts, telephone/fax/TTY rings, fire and burglar alarms, child monitoring, and oven timing. Some systems use a microphone to pick up signals in the environment. An example is a child monitoring system. Such a system allows the parent to place a transmitter with a built-in microphone in a child's room. A receiver in another part of the house activates a light when a sound occurs in the baby's room so that the parents can respond and check to see that the child is all right. It is also possible to use closed-circuit television in the home so that the child can be monitored visually without an adult having to enter the room. Such technologies are often available in mainstream electronics stores and are not particularly expensive. Other devices rely on signals that are generated by the telephone, doorbell, or other signaler in the home. Relays that are connected to doorbells or telephones, for example, can flash lights in the home. Patterns of flashing can indicate whether the light is indicating a phone call or a doorbell ring. Many systems are now wireless, and can be easily installed in the home. Body-worn pagers can be activated in addition to, or in place of, flashing lights; and some manufacturers are providing modular home alerting systems that are quite comprehensive. Specialized equipment of this type can be easily searched for and purchased on the Internet, but it is often difficult for people to install such devices themselves. It can be difficult to locate installers who have experience and knowledge about the installation of such devices for people with hearing loss. Finally, audible wakeup alarms are often ineffective for people with hearing loss. Even with substantial residual hearing, a person with hearing loss may not be able to hear alarm clocks or clock radios with sufficient reliability. Multifunction alarm clocks are available that can provide alternative alarm sounds (e.g., low-frequency signals that may be heard in the presence of high-frequency hearing loss), bed vibrators, and flashing lamps.

10.4 TELECOMMUNICATIONS ACCESS

Since the invention of the telephone, voice telecommunication has been a critical feature of modern life. This has presented a major obstacle to telecommunications access for people with hearing loss. Special amplified telephones are designed to render voice communications audible to people with hearing loss, and text telephones have been used to provide access to those for whom remote voice communication is impossible. More recent developments in computer networking and the growth of the Internet have improved the picture substantially. Email and instant messaging, particularly with portable wireless devices, have become ubiquitous in the deaf community. More recent developments in broadband Internet connectivity have made video telephony practical, permitting the use of visual communication systems like sign language and speechreading over a telephone connection.

10.4.1 Amplified Telephones

For people with sufficient residual hearing to allow for voice communication over telephone lines, mainstream telephones may not provide sufficient gain for comfortable listening. Often obtaining an amplified headset for a telephone, or purchasing an amplified telephone, can resolve the problem. Such telephones are currently available from special providers of assistive technology as well as in mainstream electronics stores. Their essential function is to amplify the incoming signal so that it can be heard by the user who may or may not be using a hearing aid or cochlear implant.

An alternative to an amplified phone for those whose personal hearing system has a telecoil is to use the "T" setting on a hearing aid or cochlear implant with a hearing aid compatible telephone. This was discussed above in the section on magnetic induction (Section 10.2.2). Use of the telecoil has the additional virtue of blocking out acoustic noise in the environment when one talks on the phone. Since cellular telephone providers are now required to provide hearing aid compatible phones, albeit on a limited basis (by September 16, 2006, the five largest wireless carriers had to make five hearing aid–compatible phones available; by February 18, 2008 all wireless carriers had to make 50% of their phones hearing aid–compatible), this advantage can be great when speaking on the phone in public places. However, hearing aid and cochlear implant users need to be careful when purchasing wireless telephones to ensure that there is no interference from the wireless transmitter in the phone. An ANSI standard (ANSI C63.19) has been developed to help ensure compatibility and guide the user when purchasing a wireless telephone. Nevertheless, the burden is still on the purchaser to be sure that the wireless telephone works for him or her.

10.4.2 TTY

Also known as *telecommunication device for the deaf* (TDD), the TTY (an acronym related to the teletypewriter) is the more popular term for the American text telephone. This technology was commonly used in the past, but has begun to be superseded in the deaf community by mobile email and paging devices that better meet the communication needs of deaf people and are briefly discussed below. Nevertheless, the TTY remains important because it is the only completely reliable way a deaf or hard of hearing individual can directly call emergency services (911). Furthermore, they can be used with relay services (described below) for communication with hearing individuals over mainstream telephones; and they can be used in mode known as VCO or voice carryover (described below, in Section 10.4.3.2) for those who wish to communication using their own voice. TTY devices, including VCO phones, are available for sale by companies that specialize in assistive devices for deaf and hard-of-hearing people.

The growth of the World Wide Web has had a great impact on the ability of deaf and hard-of-hearing people to communicate using a mainstream service such as email and instant messaging. The increase in the use of mobile email technologies such as mobile text messaging and email access has likewise revolutionized the way that deaf and hard-of-hearing people can interact and communicate with others. The advent of these services, which do not constitute assistive technology but rather are mainstreamed technologies used by a large segment of the population, have resulted in a decrease in the use of TTY. As mentioned above, however, emergency services have not kept up with this trend, and TTYs are still recommended for reporting emergencies to 911.

10.4.3 Relay Services

10.4.3.1 Telecommunications Relay Service (TRS)

Deaf and hard-of-hearing people who rely on text telecommunications need to be able to communicate with hearing people using mainstream telephones. For this reason, the United States and many other countries have made telecommunications relay service (TRS) available around the clock. This service is provided by communication assistants who are equipped with both a TTY and voice telephone. Any telephone or TTY user can call the relay service, and the communication assistant will relay the conversation between a voice caller and a TTY caller.

10.4.3.2 Voice Carryover (VCO)

Voice carryover (VCO) and two-line VCO are variations of TRS aimed at deaf and hard-of-hearing people who prefer to voice for themselves. In VCO, the deaf or hard-of-hearing caller can use his or her own voice for communication, and the communication assistant will type the hearing caller's words on a TTY. In two-line VCO, both callers can hear the other's speech, but the TTY user can also read the words as they are spoken. Another option for callers is called *captioned telephone service*. Like VCO, it is designed for users who wish to speak and listen for themselves, but require the additional support of captioning. A telephone is used that has text capabilities, and the communication assistants speak into a voice recognition system, which translates the words into text. The text is displayed on the telephone's text display so that the user can refer to it during the conversation.

10.4.3.3 IP Relay

The use of IP relay has increased. This technology has the advantage of being usable with a computer or other device with Internet capability rather than a TTY. A caller contacts the relay center via a Webpage, and a voice call is placed by the communication assistant, who voices the caller's text for the hearing party and enters the hearing party's part of the conversation into text.

10.4.3.4 Video Relay Service (VRS)

Video relay service (VRS) has also expanded greatly, and for obvious reasons is very popular among those who use American Sign Language for communication. The basis for the operation of the system is a video camera device coupled with a television or computer, which uses a high-speed Internet connection to transmit video images with sufficient detail for ASL to be effectively used. The VRS caller can contact the relay center through a Website (when using a computer) or through the video equipment attached to a television set. The caller communicates using ASL to a sign language interpreter, who places a voice call to the hearing party. The conversation takes place in real time and without text between the ASL user and the hearing party through the interpreter. It permits the full use of ASL, including facial expression, gesture, and body language and is thus more comfortable than text for an ASL communicator. Like other forms of relay service, there is no cost for the service, and the service should not be used to make emergency calls. For maximal safety, these should be made using a TTY and calling 911. This is because the communication assistant may not know the location of the caller or be able to direct the call to the appropriate emergency service.

10.5 FURTHER INFORMATION

A Website for further information about the NOAH hearing aid programming hardware and software can be found at http://www.noah3.com/

A very comprehensive introduction of cochlear implants by Dr. Philipos C. Loizou can be found at http://www.utdallas.edu/~loizou/cimplants/tutorial/.

The three Cochlear Implant Companies with FDA approved devices on the American market have a great deal of information about cochlear implants available on their Websites:

Cochlear Corporation: http://www.cochlearamericas.com/

Advanced Bionics Corporation: http://www.bionicear.com/

Med-El Corporation: http://www.medel.com/

The FCC has very informative reviews of various captioning and telecommunication technologies for deaf and hard of hearing consumers in its consumer facts Webpages:

Closed Captioning: http://www.fcc.gov/cgb/consumerfacts/closedcaption.html
Hearing Aid Compatibility: http://www.fcc.gov/cgb/consumerfacts/hac.html
Telecommunications Relay Service: http://www.fcc.gov/cgb/consumerfacts/trs.html
Internet Protocol Relay: http://www.fcc.gov/cgb/consumerfacts/iprelay.html
Video Relay Service: http://www.fcc.gov/cgb/consumerfacts/videorelay.html

The US Access Board has published bulletins on its Website that explain assistive hearing technologies for consumers, installers, and providers of this equipment: http://www.access-board.gov/adaag/about/bulletins/als-index.htm.

The Rehabilitation Engineering Research Center on Hearing Enhancement has published its final report to the US Access Board, *Large Area Assistive Listening Systems (Als): Review And Recommendations*: http://www.hearingresearch.org/publications_and_presentations.htm.

REFERENCES

1. Dillon H: *Hearing Aids*, Boomerang Press, Turramurra, Australia (distributed in the USA by Thieme, New York), 2001.
2. Bakke MH, Levitt H, Ross M, Erickson F: *Large Area Assistive Listening Systems (ALS): Review and Recommendations*, Final Report to US Architectural and Transportation Barriers Compliance Board (US Access Board), Lexington School for the Deaf/Center for the Deaf, Rehabilitation Engineering Research Center on Hearing Enhancement, New York, 1999 (retrieved 5/19/06 from http://www.hearingresearch.org/publications_and_presentations.htm).
3. Dillon H, Lovegrove R: Single-microphone noise reduction systems for hearing aids: A review and an evaluation, in Studebaker GA, Hochberg I, eds, *Acoustical Factors Affecting Hearing Aid Performance*, 2nd ed, Allyn & Bacon, Needham Heights, MA, 1993, pp 353–372.
4. UK Cochlear Implant Study Group: Criteria of candidacy for unilateral cochlear implantation in postlingually deafened adults I: Theory and measures of effectiveness, *Ear Hearing* **25**(4):310–335 (2004).
5. Leal M, Shin Y, Laborde M, Calmels M, Verges S, Lugardon S, Andrieu S, Deguine O, Fraysse B: Music perception in adult cochlear implant recipients, *Acta Otolaryngol* **123**(7):826–835 (2003).
6. Waltzman S: State of the science in assistive hearing devices for people who are hard of hearing, State of the Science Conf Assistive Technologies for People with Hearing Loss, May 11, 2001, Graduate Center, City Univ New York, 2001.
7. Stickney GS, Zeng F, Litovsky R, Assmann P: Cochlear implant speech recognition with speech maskers, *J Acoust Soc Am* **116**(2):1081–1091 (2004).
8. Plomp R: Auditory handicap of hearing impairment and the limited benefit of hearing aids., *J Acoust Soc Am* **63**:533–549.
9. Nabelek AK: Communication in noisy and reverberant environments, in Studebaker GA, Hochberg I, eds, Acoustical Factors Affecting Hearing Aid Performance, 2nd ed, Allyn & Bacon, Needham Heights, MA, 1993, pp 15–28.

11

People with Cognitive Disabilities

Mary Kay Rizzolo
University of Illinois at Chicago (UIC)

David Braddock
University of Colorado

Technology is playing a growing role in the lives of people with disabilities. However, people with cognitive disabilities still lag substantially behind all other groups in the utilization of technology. Technology promotes independence, productivity, and quality of life, but attitudinal barriers often create low expectations of the benefits of technology for persons with cognitive disabilities. This chapter first portrays the magnitude of the population of persons with cognitive disabilities worldwide—highlighting prevalence trends in both the developing and developed countries (Sections 11.1 and 11.2). We then discuss more recent international civil rights initiatives designed to increase social and economic opportunities for persons with disabilities. The role that technology might play in helping people with disabilities and their caregivers access these new opportunities is discussed in the Section 11.3, which describes four types of technology with great potential for use by people with disabilities.

11.1 COGNITIVE DISABILITY IN THE DEVELOPED WORLD

Cognitive disability entails a substantial limitation in one's capacity to think, including conceptualizing, planning, and sequencing thoughts and actions, remembering, interpreting subtle social cues, and understanding numbers and symbols. Cognitive disabilities

---

The Engineering Handbook of Smart Technology for Aging, Disability, and Independence,
Edited by A. Helal, M. Mokhtari and B. Abdulrazak
Copyright © 2008 John Wiley & Sons, Inc.

204 PEOPLE WITH COGNITIVE DISABILITIES

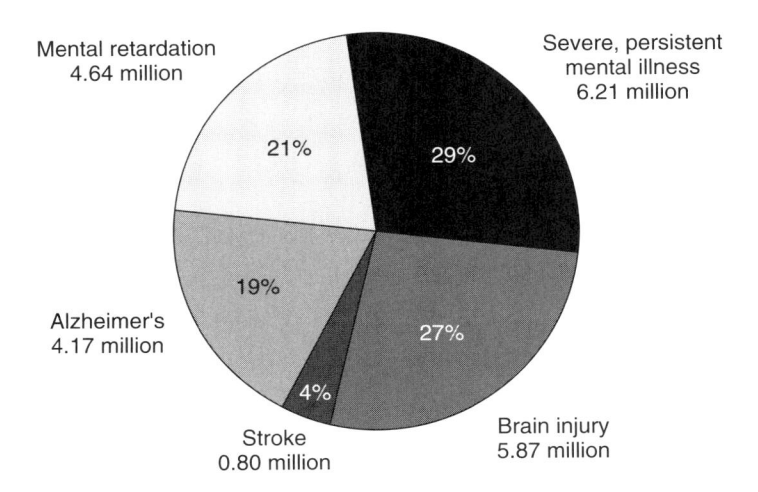

FIGURE 11.1 Cognitive disability in the united states, 2004, preliminary data [2].

include intellectual disabilities and can also stem from brain injury, Alzheimer's disease and other dementias, severe and persistent mental illness, and, in some cases, stroke [1] (see Fig. 11.1 [2]).

More than 21 million persons[1] in the United States were estimated to have a cognitive disability in 2003 ([2], Kelly-Hayes et al. [3], Office of Special Education Programs [4], 2002, and the US Surgeon General [5]). The number of persons with Alzheimer's disease and related dementias is expected to increase rapidly as the nation's population ages. Currently, 12% of the US general population is aged 65 or older. Census Bureau demographers anticipate that this percentage will grow steadily until 2028 or so, finally leveling off at 22% of the US population in 2030. Problems loom even larger in countries such as Japan and Germany, where the aging cohort is projected to approximate one-third of their general populations by the year 2040.

Using Delphi consensus techniques, Ferri and colleagues [7] determined that there were 23.4 million persons worldwide in 2001 with Alzheimer's disease and related dementias. They further speculated that more than 4.6 million new cases will be diagnosed each year, rising to over 81 million cases by 2040. Of the 23.4 million persons with Alzheimer's and related dementias in 2001, 40% were living in developed countries [7]. Similarly, while the *incidence* of stroke in developed countries is declining because of decreased smoking and better blood pressure management, the *absolute number* of persons with stroke is rising because of aging of the population [8].

11.2 COGNITIVE DISABILITY IN THE DEVELOPING WORLD

The vast majority of the global population (82%) resides in the developing nations of the world. However, relatively little is known about the numbers of persons with disabilities—especially cognitive disabilities—in these countries [9]. The World Health

---
[1]This figure does not include an additional 2.8 million children receiving special education services with "learning disabilities."

Organization has estimated that 600 million people worldwide are living with disability [10]. However, epidemiologists note that this figure is merely a computation using a 10% prevalence rate applied to global population estimates [9]. Fujiura and Rutkowski-Kmitta note that "the better perspective on counting disability is to interpret measurement operations as imperfect proxies that capture only a fraction of the complex reality that is disablement" [11, p. 39]. Yet, human rights advocates recognize the role statistics on disablement play in guiding and monitoring disability policy and programs globally, and in equalizing opportunities for persons with disabilities [12].

Although precise statistics on the number of persons with cognitive disabilities in the developing world are unavailable, researchers have offered estimates based on population figures. Olness [13], for example, speculates there are approximately 780 million children with cognitive limitations in the developing world due to malnutrition, iron-deficiency anemia, parasitic infections, and genetic and metabolic diseases resulting in brain impairment. Moreover, children in low income countries often have limited access to medical treatment and rehabilitative services, including assistive technologies [14]. Epidemiologic prevalence studies provide widely varying rates in developing countries—some as high as 20.3 per 1000 persons in Bangladesh [15]. See Fujiura et al. [9] for a more comprehensive discussion of population statistics on intellectual disabilities in the developing world.

Updated WHO Global Burden of Disease data for 2002 also give us an indication of the enormity of the population of persons with other cognitive disabilities worldwide. For example, over 25 million people worldwide are reported to experience schizophrenia, and 28 million have bipolar disorder [16]. More than 24 million people are estimated to have Alzheimer's disease and other dementias, and this number is expected to rise dramatically; today, approximately 60% of persons with dementia live in developing countries—this percentage is projected to rise to 71% by 2040 [7]. This is nearly a fourfold increase in the number of persons with dementia in the developing world—from approximately 14 million persons to over 57 million.

While epidemiologists can only provide rough estimates of the numbers of persons with various cognitive disabilities worldwide, information on public spending for this population is even less readily available. Public-sector disability services in developing countries are typically extremely modest programs based on rehabilitation and educational models imported from developed nations. Such programs are often supplemented by disability services offered through community-based rehabilitation programs (CBRs) financed by United Nation development agencies, such as the International Labour Organization (ILO), UNESCO, the World Health Organization (WHO), and nongovernmental organizations (NGOs).

Mental health services in the developing world are particularly inadequate. The World Health Organization [17] found that almost 40% of the countries worldwide did not have a data collection system or any epidemiologic studies for mental health reporting. Many low-income countries rely on development agencies and NGOs owing to a lack of public-sector infrastructure for providing more comprehensive disability services and supports. For example, in Cambodia, only 10 inpatient psychiatric beds are funded for the entire country of 12 million people [18]. The WHO's ATLAS survey [17] found that the median number of psychiatric beds in low-income countries was 0.24 per 10,000 persons in the general population. This compares to median figures of 7.5 beds per 10,000 in high-income countries. It is interesting to note that, to date, the WHO has not completed an ATLAS study specifically focused on intellectual and developmental disabilities. The chronic lack of financial commitments translates into exceedingly limited programmatic opportunities for persons with mental disabilities in developing countries. The almost nonexistent resource base frequently translates into abusive mental health and intellectually disability facilities, as documented in Mexico, Turkey, and Paraguay and disclosed by human rights groups like Mental Disability Rights International [19]. It should be pointed out, however, that degrading and illegal conditions in mental institutions in highly developed nations such as the United States were rampant as recently as in the 1960s [20].

11.3 CIVIL RIGHTS FOR PERSONS WITH COGNITIVE AND OTHER DISABILITIES

Several international human rights initiatives have been adopted to promote social and economic opportunities for persons with disabilities. In 1994, the United Nations General Assembly unanimously adopted the Standard Rules on the Equalization of Opportunities for Persons with Disabilities (Standard Rules) [21]. The Standard Rules are not legally enforceable internationally, but they do provide basic international standards for programs, laws, and policy on disability [22]. The Standard Rules grew out of earlier pressure from international disability interests to promote greater participation by people with disabilities in society. This philosophy was initially expressed in the 1971 Declaration of the Rights of Mentally Retarded Persons [23], the 1975 Declaration of the Rights of Disabled Persons [24], and the more comprehensive statement expressed in the 1982 World Program of Action Concerning Disabled Persons [12]. The European Union (in 1996) has also adopted general disability policies similar to the UN's World Program of Action. At the national level, since the early 1990s, more than 40 countries have enacted domestic disability laws, most of them antidiscrimination in nature [25]. Australia adopted the Disability Discrimination Act of 1993 outlawing discrimination on the basis of disability, and the constitutions of Canada, Germany, Austria, Finland, and Brazil have been similarly amended. Constitutional changes have also been adopted in South Africa, India, Malawi, Uganda, and the Philippines [22,26]. These actions are representative of the more recent flurry of legislative activity on a worldwide basis to promote the rights of people with disabilities.

On December 13, 2006, a convention on the rights of persons with disabilities was adopted, elevating the international stature of disability as a human rights issue. The international convention on disability is "the first human rights convention conducted since the 1989 agreement on the rights of the child" [27]. As of May 14, 2007, there were 92 convention signatories and one ratification (Jamaica). The convention recognizes that all individuals with disabilities are entitled to human rights and fundamental freedoms and recognizes that disability results from barriers (both physical and attitudinal) in society and the environment [22, p. ix]:

> The emerging global commitment to equalizing opportunities for disabled people implies much more than a simple commitment to traditional anti-discrimination principles. It also implies a commitment to removing and preventing social and environmental barriers that have traditionally restricted access for people with disabilities to social and economic opportunities. Fulfillment of this commitment, therefore, requires an expansion of disability

policies and strategies to include not only traditional rehabilitation and anti-discrimination measures, but also affirmative strategies to prevent and remove social and environmental barriers.

Increasing the physical and social participation of persons with disabilities enhances both social and economic opportunities. Metts [22], an economist, estimated that the global population of persons with all disabilities is between 235 and 549 million, with an associated loss of gross domestic product (GDP) of $1.3–$1.9 trillion. Economic costs are incurred through lost productivity of unemployed persons with disabilities and unemployment of caregivers who forfeit outside employment to provide care.

In fiscal year (FY) 2004, total US public spending for all disability services and income maintenance reached approximately $448 billion (Fig. 11.2), for 46 million recipients [2]. Of this $448 in consolidated spending by federal, state, and local units of governments, an estimated 30–35% financed services for individuals with cognitive disabilities [2]. However, notwithstanding this seemingly substantial level of expenditure, according to Fujiura [28], 90% of individuals with intellectual and developmental disabilities in the United States received "nonfunded" long-term care services from informal caregivers such as family members. Only 10% were in the formal publicly funded system. Fujiura et al. [29] estimated that families spent an additional $6300 per year in 1990 dollars ($9247 in adjusted 2004 dollars) on out-of-pocket expenses for their adult child with a developmental disability.

Moreover, while individuals with dementia are significant consumers of formal healthcare, one estimate of the annual cost of informal care (e.g., unpaid family caregivers) in the United States totaled $18 billion in 1998 ($21.7 in adjusted 2004 dollars) [30]. Informal care provided to elderly Americans with depressive symptoms represented an additional cost of $9 billion in 1998 ($10.8 in adjusted 2004 dollars) [31].

A key to accessing these new civil rights–based social and economic opportunities for people with disabilities, as well as their caregivers, will be the use of technology. For example, home-based technologies to assist with the support and monitoring of persons with disabilities could provide many caregivers with greater opportunities to

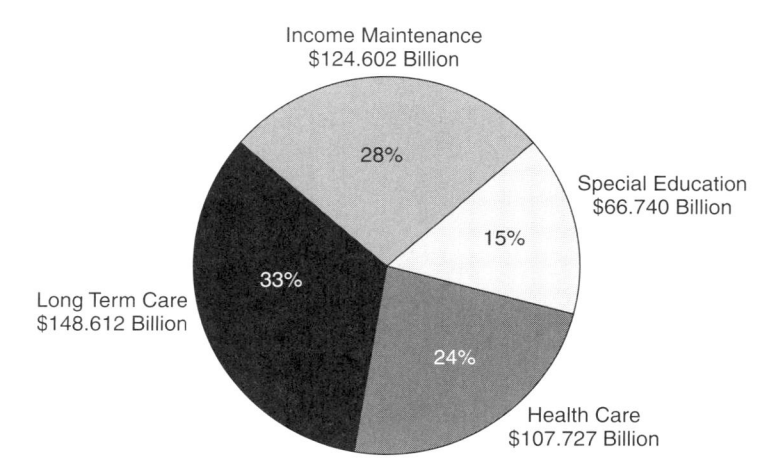

FIGURE 11.2 Cognitive disability in the United States, 2004, preliminary data (continued) [2].

seek employment outside the home. In Section 11.4, we discuss present and emerging technologies and their relevance to disability.

11.4 TECHNOLOGY USE BY PERSONS WITH COGNITIVE DISABILITIES

Three general categories of technologies exist that can be used by persons with cognitive disabilities: assistive technologies, electronic and information technologies, and "universally designed technologies" [32,33]. In our conclusion, we also discuss a fourth category—"smart home technology"—which has significant implications for long-term care support.

11.4.1 Assistive Technologies

The term "assistive technology device" is defined in the US Technology-Related Assistance for Individuals with Disabilities Act of 1988 [Public Law (PL) 100-407] and the Assistive Technology Act of 1998 (PL 105-394) (29 USC 2201) as "any item, piece of equipment, or product system, whether acquired commercially, modified or customized, that is used to increase, maintain, or improve functional capabilities of individuals with disabilities" [Title 29, Chapter 31, § 3002(a)(3)]. The term "assistive technology service" is defined in these acts as "any service that directly assists an individual with a disability in the selection, acquisition, or use, of an assistive technology device" [Title 29, Chapter 31, § 3002(a)(4)].

Persons with cognitive disabilities utilize assistive technologies to enhance functioning in activities of daily living, control of the environment, positioning and seating, vision, hearing, recreation, mobility, reading, learning and studying, math, motor aspects of writing, composition of written material, communication, and computer access. Technologies range from low-tech devices, such as pictorial communication boards or adapted eating utensils, to high-tech devices, including adapted software and voice output devices with speech synthesis [34]. Until relatively recently, when the term "technology" was used in conjunction with "cognitive disability," it most likely referred to these assistive technology devices.

11.4.2 Electronic and Information Technologies

The US Clinger Cohen Act of 1996 [35] defines information technology as any "equipment or interconnected system or subsystem of equipment, that is used in the automatic acquisition, storage, manipulation, management, movement, control, display, switching, interchange, transmission, or reception of data or information." The US Rehabilitation Act of 1998 [36] identifies electronic and information technologies (EIT) as the same as information technology "except EIT also includes any equipment or interconnected system or subsystem of equipment that is used in the creation, conversion, or duplication of data or information." Thus, the term EIT also includes products such as telephones, information kiosks, transaction machines (such as ATMs), the Internet, and multimedia.

State-of-the-art electronic and information technologies have rarely been adapted for people with cognitive disabilities—even though they have the potential to assist persons with cognitive disabilities, and those with age-related cognitive decline, to achieve greater independence, productivity, and quality of life [37–41]. Personal support technologies

(PSTs), such as personal digital assistants (PDAs), for example, can be preprogrammed by parents or caregivers to prompt individuals with cognitive disabilities to perform a wide variety of well-defined vocational and independent living tasks [42]. Specialized PDA software is currently available for enabling individuals with developmental and other cognitive disabilities to manage personal schedules with much greater independence [43], for helping direct individuals during their work tasks [42,44], and for assisting with activities of daily living [45,46]. PDAs can also interface with wireless communication protocols to track and monitor an individual's daily activities, and provide prompts to the individual as needed to complete educational or work tasks [44,47,48].

Electronic and information technologies also have the potential to assist in the prevention of certain cognitive disabilities. For example, health education campaigns have been effective in Finland and Japan in improving lifestyle choices and reducing cholesterol levels. Japan's campaign resulted in a reduction in stroke rates by over 70% [49]. The use of technology-based educational programs could facilitate this outreach. One international study found that the lifetime cost per person after experiencing a stroke was between $59,000 to $230,000 US dollars [50].

Early intervention utilizing electronic technologies may be beneficial for persons with Alzheimer's in nurturing the development of strategies for dealing with memory difficulties. Research has demonstrated the ability of individuals with Alzheimer's disease to retain previously learned motor skills throughout the course of their disease. However, acquiring and retaining new skills has proven to be more challenging for these individuals, and often requires constant repetition and practice [51]. Developers must take into account these limitations when designing cognitive technologies for persons with more advanced stages of Alzheimer's disease or related dementias [33, p. 294]:

> While E&IT products and services can, indeed, serve the same purpose of addressing functional limitations as AT devices, such devices are not developed with that narrow intent, but instead are aimed at addressing broader goals for technology to enhance productivity, automating routine tasks, improving the flow of information, streamlining and improving communication and so forth. It is, in many ways, the explosion of activity in this ... category of technology that has created both the opportunity for technology to significantly improve the quality of life for people with and without disabilities and, as such, created the aforementioned digital divide.

Many users with cognitive disabilities are limited in their use of existing technologies because of design characteristics incompatible with their learning styles. Wehmeyer and his colleagues [32,33] have provided a comprehensive analysis of the primary factors of cognitive ability and their associated impacts on technology use by people with cognitive disabilities. For example, problems with speech articulation may impact the use of technologies that rely on speech input, while screen clutter may prove distracting for users with limited visual perception. Use of picture-based cues, limited options, and touchscreens are just some of the features designers can utilize to facilitate technology use by persons with memory or learning difficulties [3,33].

11.4.3 Universally Designed Technologies

The previous section discussed adapting technologies for use by persons with cognitive disabilities. Another approach is to promote universal design principles to enable people with cognitive disabilities to utilize technologies available to the general public. Universal design intends that products—especially software and computers—provide an interface that is suitable for *all* potential users, including persons with disabilities. Web standards, such as user agent accessibility guidelines [52], federal US regulations (e.g., Section 508) and public/private initiatives, such as the World Wide Web Accessibility Initiative (WAI) of the World Wide Web Consortium (W3C), promote access to software and the Internet for people with disabilities. But how does one define accessibility? Elbert Johns, Director of TheArcLink (as cited by Rizzolo et al. [53]), has suggested the importance of clearly defining the principal components of "accessibility" as this term pertains to people with developmental disabilities and their use of information technology. Specifically, he notes that for information to be accessible to a person with a developmental disability, it must (1) decrease the dependence on rote memory as a tool for recalling information, (2) use as many complementary formats as possible (visual, audio, multigraphic), (3) reduce the need for the recipient to utilize complex organizational skills for comprehension, and (4) be presented in a vocabulary or reading level that approximates the level of the recipient. More intuitive, user-centered, computing interfaces are necessary to increase accessibility and empower persons with cognitive disabilities to use common technologies such as the Internet and personal computers [3,33].

Metts [22] identified the "provision of cost-effective assistive technologies" as one of the key principles nations must adopt to promote the physical and social inclusion of people with disabilities. This will be especially critical for individuals with cognitive disabilities who lag substantially behind all other groups in our society in the utilization of technology. A growing digital divide exists between persons with and without disabilities. Kaye [54] found that almost 60% of persons with disabilities have never used a computer compared to less than 25% of persons without disabilities [55]. This discrepancy also exists in computer ownership. Fewer than 24% of people with disabilities own a computer, compared to over 50% of persons without disabilities [55]. Furthermore, fewer than 10% of persons with disabilities have access to the Internet compared to 38% of persons without disabilities. People with cognitive disabilities are extremely underserved in accessing assistive technologies, compared not only to nondisabled citizens but also to persons with physical and sensory disabilities, themselves an underserved group [56].

A study by Wehmeyer [57] assessed the use of personal computers by adults with intellectual disability in the United States; 33% of families reported a computer in their homes. In over 70% of these households, the individual with intellectual disability used the computer for communication, education, budgeting, leisure, or work-related purposes. The majority of families, however, did not own a personal computer, although many believed their family member could benefit from computer access. Reasons given for not having a computer were cost, lack of training, complexity of the computer, "lack of assessment of technology need," and lack of information on the benefits of a computer [57, p. 48]. Wehmeyer [58] found higher rates of access to computers among *students* with intellectual disability. Over 83% of respondents indicated that they had access to a computer either at home or at school, and used the computer for educational activities, leisure activities, and communication.

In 2001, the National Down Syndrome Society [59] conducted a survey of all attendees at its annual conference to determine utilization rates of computers and other electronic devices. In total, 66% of family members and professionals indicated that their family members with Down's syndrome used a computer. Of those identified as using a computer, only 30 individuals used a Web browser and only 2, an adapted browser. Approximately 20% of individuals reported using an email program, although none of these programs were specifically adapted for persons with cognitive disabilities. Only a handful of individuals used technology-based prompting systems, such as a PDA, to provide cues at home, school, or work [59].

11.5 CONCLUSION

Gary Albrecht, in his article on rationing health care to disabled people [60], describes the "the weak bargaining position that disabled persons hold as consumers" [60, p. 654]. Until people with cognitive disabilities are viewed as a profitable consumer group, many technologies will simply not be developed and/or marketed on a large enough scale to accommodate the different learning styles and abilities of persons with such disabilities. The increasing numbers of people with age-related cognitive disabilities, particularly those in highly developed societies such as Japan, the United States, and western Europe, are creating a larger consumer market for cognitive technologies. Interest in developing and marketing new technologies that accommodate this group is likely to increase significantly.

The assistive technology industry is, in fact, growing. According to a US Department of Commerce survey [34], 359 companies manufacturing assistive technologies reported sales of $2.87 billion in 1999, up 21.8% from 1997 sales. Market projections suggest that emerging neuroscience technologies, like brain–machine interfaces permitting brain control of robot arms or computers, will be a $3.6 billion industry by 2008 [61].

In addition, over the next 10–15 years (from the time of this writing) "smart home technologies" are likely to spread widely throughout long-term care residential settings for people with cognitive disabilities in the United States and in the rest of the developed world. Smart home technology can help address the rapidly growing demand for long-term care services and supports and the accompanying need for tens of thousands of additional staff. Increased life expectancy, general population growth, and the aging of family caregivers are also contributing to the rapidly increased demand for long-term care for persons with cognitive disabilities such as intellectual disabilities and Alzheimer's.

There are, for example, approximately 500,000 persons with intellectual disabilities in the United States alone currently living in out-of-home residential settings [62]. Smart Home Technologies are already being utilized in numerous residences for people with intellectual disabilities in two states—Indiana and Wisconsin. Technologies employed in the homes include (1) pan–tilt–zoom cameras for centralized monitoring of high-risk areas such as the kitchen; (2) motion, temperature, carbon monoxide, and door break sensors along with floor pressure pads; (3) personal emergency response systems; (4) PDAs customized for activities of daily living (ADL) support; (5) selective access to appliances; and (6) security/safety systems. Also, Elite Care Corporation near Portland, Oregon is pioneering smart home development for aging populations using Web-based care information systems (www.elite-care.com). Over the next decade and beyond, emerging technology-related residential care systems for people with cognitive disabilities are likely to feature increasingly sophisticated predictive modeling and cognitive assistance capabilities. The careful evaluation and refinement of such emerging human services technologies—from both benefit/cost and consumer self-determination standpoints—will be the most crucial determinants of their widespread adoption.

REFERENCES

1. Braddock D, Rizzolo MC, Thompson M, Bell R: Emerging technologies and cognitive disability, *J Spec Educ Technol* **19**(4):49–56 (2004).
2. Braddock D: *National Study of Disability Finance (Preliminary Data)*, Dept Psychiatry, Univ Colorado, Boulder, 2006.
3. Kelly-Hayes M, Robertson JT, Broderick JP, Duncan PW, Hershey LA, Roth EJ., Thies WH, Trombly CA: The American Heart Association stroke outcome classification, *Stroke* **29**:1274–1280 (1988).
4. US Department of Education: 25th Annual Report to Congress on Implementation of the Individuals with Disabilities Education Act., Office of Special Education and Rehabilitative Services, Office of Special Education Programs, Washington, DC, 2003.
5. US Department of Health and Human Services: *Mental Health: A Report of the Surgeon General*, US Department of Health and Human Services, Substance Abuse and Mental Health Services Administration, Center for Mental Health Services, National Institutes of Health, National Institute of Mental Health, Rockville, MD, 1999.
6. Braddock D: Aging and developmental disabilities: Demographic and policy issues affecting American families, Statement before the Senate Special Committee on Aging, Senate Special Committee on Aging, Washington, DC, 1998.
7. Ferri CP, Prince M, Brayne C, Brodaty H, Fratiglioni L, Ganguli M, Hall K, Hasegawa K, Hendrie H, Huang Y et al: Global prevalence of dementia: A Delphi consensus study, *Lancet* **366**:2112–2117 (2005).
8. World Health Organization: *The Atlas of Heart Disease and Stroke*, WHO, Geneva, 2004.
9. Fujiura GT, Park HJ, Rutkowski-Kmitta V: Disability statistics in the developing world: A reflection on the meanings in our numbers, *J Appl Res Intellect Disab* **18**(4):295–304 (2005).
10. World Health Organization: *International Consultation to Review Community-Based Rehabilitation (CBR)*, WHO, Geneva, 2003.
11. Fujiura GT, Rutkowski-Kmitta V: Counting disability, in Albrecht G, Seelman K, Bury M, eds, *Handbook of Disability Studies*, Sage, Thousand Oaks, CA, 2001, pp 69–96.
12. United Nations: *World Program of Action Concerning People with Disabilities*, New York, 1982.
13. Olness K: Effects on brain development leading to cognitive impairment: A worldwide epidemic, *Devel Behav Pediatr* **24**(2):120–130 (2003).
14. Durkin M: The epidemiology of developmental disabilities in low-income countries, *Mental Retard Devel Disab Res Rev* **8**(3):206–211 (2002).
15. Durkin MS, Khan NZ, Davidson LL, Huq S, Munir S, Rasul E, Zaman SS: Prenatal and postnatal risk factors for mental retardation among children in Bangladesh, *Am J Epidemiol* **152**(11):1024–1033 (2000).
16. World Health Organization: *The World Health Report 2004: Changing History*, WHO, Geneva, 2004.
17. World Health Organization: *Mental Health Atlas 2005*, WHO, Geneva, 2005.
18. Miller G: The unseen: Mental illness's global toll, *Science* **311**(5760):458–461 (Jan 2006).

19. Mental Disability Rights International: *Initiative for Inclusion: Kosovo*, 2006 (retrieved 3/22/06 from http://www.mdri.org/projects/initiativeinclusion.htm).
20. Blatt B, Kaplan F: *Christmas in Purgatory*, Allyn & Bacon, Boston, 1967.
21. United Nations: *The Standard Rules on the Equalization of Opportunities for Persons with Disabilities*, New York, 1994.
22. Metts RL: Disability Issues, Trends and Recommendations for the World Bank, report prepared for the World Bank, 2000.
23. United Nations General Assembly Resolution 2856 (XXVI), *On the Declaration on the Rights of Mentally Retarded Persons*, New York, 1971.
24. United Nations General Assembly Resolution 3447 (XXX), *On the Declaration on the Rights of Disabled Persons*, New York, 1975.
25. Kanter A: The globalization of disability rights law, *Syracuse J Int Law Commerce* **30**:241 (2003).
26. Kanter A: The globalization of disability rights law, University of Illinois at Chicago, 2006.
27. United Nations: Press Conf Disabilities Convention, 2006 (retrieved 3/22/06 from http://www.un.org/News/briefings/docs/2006/060203_Disabilities_PC.doc.htm).
28. Fujiura GT: Demography of family households, *Am J Mental Retard* **103**(3): 225–235 (1998).
29. Fujiura GT, Roccoforte JA, Braddock D: Costs of family care for adults with mental retardation and related developmental disabilities, *Am J Ment Retard* **99**(3):250–261 (1994).
30. Langa KM, Chernew ME, Kabeto MU, Herzog AR, Ofstedal MB, Willis RJ, Wallace RB, Mucha LM, Straus WL, Fendrick AM: National estimates of the quantity and cost of informal caregiving for the elderly, *Journal of General Internal Medicine* **16**:770–778 (2001).
31. Langa KM, Valenstein MA, Fendrick AM, Kabeto MU, Vijan S: Extent and cost of informal caregiving for older Americans with symptoms of depression, *Am J Psychiatr* **161**:857–863 (2004).
32. Wehmeyer M, Smith SJ, Palmer SB, Davies DK: Technology use by students with intellectual disabilities: An overview, *J Spec Educ Technol* **19**(4):1–25 (2004).
33. Wehmeyer M, Smith SJ, Palmer SB, Davies DK, Stock SE: Technology use and people with mental retardation, *Int Rev Res Mental Retard* **29**:291–337 (2004).
34. Technology and Medicine Division (TAM) of the Council for Exceptional Children and the Wisconsin Assistive Technology Initiative, 2003, *Assistive Technology Consideration* (retrieved 11/21/04 from http://www.ideapractices.org/resources/tam/index.html).
35. Clinger-Cohen Act of 1996, PL 104-106, Division E, 1996.
36. US Rehabilitation Act of 1998, PL 105-220 [29 USC § 794 (d)], 1998.
37. Bowles C: World's first brain prosthesis, NewScientist.com, 3/12/03 (retrieved 11/21/04 from http://www.eurekalert.org/pub_releases/2003-03/ns-twf031203.php).
38. Eisenberg A: A chip that mimics neurons, firing up the memory, *New York Times*, June 20, 2002 (retrieved 11/21/04 from http://www.nytimes.com/2002/06/20/technology/circuits/20NEXT.html?ex=1025813651&ei=1&en=21f59dded2f9fad5).
39. Hammel J: Assistive technology and environmental intervention (AT-EI) impact on the activity and life roles of aging adults with developmental disabilities: Findings and implications for practice, *Phys Occup Ther Geriatr* **18**(1):37–58 (2000).
40. Hammel J, Lai J, Heller T: Impact of assistive technology and environmental interventions on function and living situation status with people who are ageing with developmental disabilities, *Disab Rehab* **24**(1–3):93–105 (2002).
41. Merritt R: Nerves of silicon: Neural chips eyed for brain repair, *EE Times*, March 19, 2003 (retrieved 11/21/04 from http://www.eetimes.com/story/OEG20030317S0013).

42. Davies DK, Stock SE, Wehmeyer ML: Enhancing independent task performance for individuals with mental retardation through use of a handheld self-directed visual and audio prompting system, *Educ Train Mental Retard Devel Disab* **37**(2):209–218 (2002).
43. Davies DK, Stock SE, Wehmeyer ML: Enhancing independent time-management skills of individuals with mental retardation using a Palmtop personal computer, *Mental Retard* **40**(5):358–365 (2002).
44. Furniss F, Lancioni G, Rocha N, Cunha B, Seedhouse P, Morato P, O'Reilly MF: VICAID: Development and evaluation of a palmtop-based job aid for workers with severe developmental disabilities, *Br J Educ Technol* **32**(3):277–287 (2001).
45. Lancioni GE, O'Reilly MF, Seedhouse P, Furniss F, Cunha B: Promoting independent task performance by persons with severe developmental disabilities through a new computer-aided system, *Behav Modif* **24**(5):698–716 (2000).
46. Lancioni GE, O'Reilly MF, Van den Hof E, Seedhouse P, Rocha N: Task instructions for persons with severe intellectual disability: Reducing the number of instruction occasions after the acquisition phase, *Behav Intervent* **14**(4):199–211 (1999).
47. Kautz H, Etzioni O, Borriello G, Fox D, Arnstein L, Ostendorf M, Logsdon R: Assisted cognition: Computer aids for people with Alzheimer's disease (unpublished manuscript, Seattle, WA, 2001).
48. O'Hara D, Seagriff-Curtin P, Davies D, Stock S: *Innovation in Health Education and Communication: A Research Project to Demonstrate the Effectiveness of Personal Support Technology for Improving the Oral Health of Adults with Mental Retardation*, poster presentation at Inaugural Conf Natl Center for Birth Defects and Developmental Disabilities, Atlanta, GA, Oct 2002.
49. World Health Organization: Prevention: Population and systems approaches, in *The Atlas of Heart Disease and Stroke*, WHO, Geneva, 2004.
50. Caro JJ, Huybrechts KF, Dúchense I: Management patterns and costs of acute ischemic stroke: An international study, *Stroke* **31**(3):582–590 (2000).
51. Dick MB, Hsieh S, Bricker J, Dick-Muehlke C: Facilitating acquisition and transfer of a continuous motor task in healthy older adults and patients with Alzheimer's disease, *Neuropsychology* **17**(2):202–212 (2003).
52. Festa P: W3C finalizes disability guidelines, ZDNet (online), Dec 17, 2002 (http://zdnet.com.com/2100-1104-978272.html).
53. Rizzolo MC, Braddock D, Bell R, Hewitt A, Brown C: Emerging technologies for persons with intellectual and developmental disabilities, in Lakin KC, Turnbull A, eds, *Goals of The Arc Research Conference*, American Association on Mental Retardation, Washington, DC, 2005.
54. Kaye HS: *Computer and Internet Use among People with Disabilities*, Disability Statistics Report 13, US Department of Education, National Institute on Disability and Rehabilitation Research, Washington, DC, 2000.
55. Abramson R: *Report: Digital Divide Widens. The Industry Standard*, Oct 16, 2000 (available at http://www.thestandard.com/article/display/0,1151,19429,00.html).
56. Braddock D: Emerging research frontiers and partnerships in developmental disabilities, Keynote Address at Annual Conf Association of University Centers on Disabilities, Bethesda, MD, Nov 1, 2001.
57. Wehmeyer ML: National survey of the use of assistive technology by adults with mental retardation, *Mental Retard* **36**(1):44–51 (1998).
58. Wehmeyer ML: Assistive technology and students with mental retardation, *J Spec Educ Techn* **14**:50–60 (1999).
59. National Down Syndrome Society: *Down Syndrome Research Survey—2001*, survey given to participants of 2001 National Down Syndrome Society, San Diego, CA, 2001.

60. Albrecht G: Rationing health care to disabled people, *Sociol Health Illness* **23**(5):654–677 (2001).
61. Cavuoto J: Neural engineering's image problem, *IEEE Spectrum* pp 32–37 (April 2004).
62. Braddock D, Hemp R, Rizzolo MC, Coulter D, Haffer L, Thompson M: *The State of the States in Developmental Disabilities: 2005*, Colorado, Coleman Inst Cognitive Disabilities, Dept Psychiatry and Univ Colorado, Boulder, 2005.

12

Assistive Devices for People with Cognitive Impairments

Hélène Pigot, Jérémy Bauchet, and Sylvain Giroux
University of Sherbrooke, Quebec, Canada

Cognitive orthotics are computer-based assistive devices designed for a particular individual for ADL-related tasks, entertainment, or work. In this chapter we first briefly sketch the occupational areas affected by the cognitive deficits. Then we review generic organizers used as ADL cognitive orthotics. Because of the limits of commercially available organizers, several adaptations are proposed to help in scheduling activities, show how to perform activities, and provide communication with caregivers. The second type of assistive technology examined focuses on helping individuals to perform specific ADLs: washing and medication. The third type of assistive devices addresses ADLs outside the home. Finally, we explore how social interactions of people with cognitive impairment may be encouraged through customized electronic mail and the use of multimedia.

12.1 INTRODUCTION

Alzheimer's disease and related dementia, whose incidences are on the rise as the elderly population grows, result in cognitive decline and impediments to patients remaining in the home under safe conditions. Adults suffering from schizophrenia, brain damage due to stroke or head injury, or developmental disabilities and mental retardation may face similar cognitive deficits and then similar situations. Therefore, individuals with cognitive impairment (CI) experience diminished independence. They all encounter difficulties in performing activities of daily living (ADLs), enjoying entertainment and social activities, and engaging in work. Hazardous situations may arise, requiring transfer to a care environment. More importantly, while such individuals prefer to continue living in

---

The Engineering Handbook of Smart Technology for Aging, Disability, and Independence,
Edited by A. Helal, M. Mokhtari and B. Abdulrazak
Copyright © 2008 John Wiley & Sons, Inc.

their communities, they need assistance from family or professional caregivers 24 h a day. They deserve to benefit from assistive devices to enhance their control and level of participation in their various areas of occupation. Most of the assistive technologies developed so far, however, have been designed to assist people with physical and perceptual impairments. With more recent improvements in computers and electronics, research into assistive technology now focuses on alleviating cognitive deficits.

In the late 1970s, computers were introduced in various rehabilitation centers for therapeutic purposes. Videogames, educational software, and home-customized software are widely used to train specific skills such as attention and visual memory. The remediation approach aims at restoring a damaged cognitive system or at least providing cognitive alternatives by making use of the remaining abilities. The use of computers for remediation falls outside the scope of this chapter; information about it can be found in review papers on cognitive rehabilitation [1]. Another rehabilitation approach focuses on ADL independence by providing compensatory techniques and devices. In the United States, assistive technology is defined in the *Technology-Related Assistance for Individuals with Disabilities Act* as "any item, piece of equipment, or product system, whether acquired commercially or off the shelf, modified, or customized, that is used to increase, maintain, or improve functional capabilities of individuals with disabilities" [2]. Commercially available products generally do not fit the specific needs of people with CI. Customization is required to take into account deficits in initiation, attention, memory, and planning as well as to ensure safety everywhere and at all times.

In this chapter, we explore cognitive orthotics that are computer-based assistive devices designed for a particular individual for ADL-related tasks, entertainment, or work. First, the occupational areas affected by the cognitive deficits are briefly sketched, fleshing out the outline of the assistive technologies presented herein. Then we review generic organizers used as ADL cognitive orthotics that assist people throughout the day and in all occupational areas. Such devices are widely provided to people with CI. Because of the limits of commercially available organizers, several adaptations are proposed to help in scheduling activities, show how to perform activities, and provide communication with caregivers. The second type of assistive technology (AT) reviewed focuses on helping individuals to perform basic specific ADLs: washing, the morning routine, and medication. The third type of assistive devices addresses ADLs outside the home. Finally, we explore how social interactions of people with CI may be encouraged through customized electronic mail and the use of multimedia.

12.2 INDEPENDENCE NEEDS

According to the Canadian Model of Occupational Performance (CMOP), occupational performance is the result of interactions between the person, the environment, and the occupation [3]. Physical, affective, and cognitive components characterize the person, with spirituality at the central core of being. Occupations are classified into three categories: self-care, productivity, and leisure. Productivity includes paid and unpaid work; leisure includes recreation (hobby, sport, etc.) and socialization. Katz defined self-care in 1963 as activities of daily living (ADLs), which means that all the activities that should be completed by individuals to take care of themselves, including personal hygiene, grooming, eating, and dressing. In 1969, Lawton gave the concept greater focus and introduced the idea of instrumental activities of daily living (IADLs) [4]. The IADLs relate to activities required to take care of the house and its inhabitants. They include preparing meals, shopping, housekeeping, using the phone, taking medication, and managing the budget. The IADLs are much more complex in terms of physical, perceptual, and cognitive abilities. Moreover, they generally call for good planning abilities in order to manage time and perform several activities concurrently. For instance, shopping involves drawing up the shopping list, leaving the house, remembering to refer to the list, and managing the budget.

Brain damage leads primarily to initiation, attention, memory, and planning deficits [5] (see Chapter 2 for an extensive discussion). While individuals with CI can be quite independent in performing personal care, their lack of initiative and difficulties in managing time necessitate continuous recall [6]. Individuals with CI evidence greater dependence with respect to IADLs. Their lack of initiative is also accompanied by problems such as focusing on an activity for too long, organizing time, and remembering how to proceed. Danger arises when they have to use electrical appliances. Caregivers are frequently requested to remember the activities that must be carried out and to guide people with CI. The family feels anxiety when leaving them alone. On the one hand, assistive devices aim at fostering the independence of people with CI; on the other hand, they provide information to caregivers and enable communication between all the caregivers involved.

12.3 GENERIC COGNITIVE ORTHOTICS FOR ADLS

Most cognitive orthotics offer individuals with CI nonspecific assistance in organizing their day and access to the information required. They do not address the specific characteristics associated with a particular activity. In that sense, they can be referred to as *generic cognitive orthotics*. Such devices are quite good at providing a reminder of when to carry out personal grooming or the time of a hair appointment as well as indicating the steps in making coffee or getting to church. The literature contains a number of reports on the state of the art, most notably two publications in 2004 [7,8]. In contrast to the approach indicated in these articles, we offer, in this section, a comparative analysis of cognitive orthotics and their functionalities centered on client needs. These needs are expressed in terms of support in capturing, storing, accessing, processing, and recalling mnemonic or executive information. Our approach is in line with the work of Maciuszek et al. [9], linking needs and functionalities. The functionalities offered must be adapted to clients and objectives. Yet the selection of a technological aid also depends, to a significant extent, on other criteria that we will discuss in this comparative study:

- Ease and effectiveness in managing information
- Integration and graphical accessibility of functionalities
- User's role in managing information
- Support for caregivers and potential for interacting with them
- System customization
- Related treatments offered to the user

Some generic cognitive orthotics are solely available on stationary computers, although most are offered on portable devices. Our analysis focuses only on portable devices providing cognitive assistance in the home and during movements. We begin by presenting mainstream systems. These meet a significant portion of client needs and are increasingly present in clinical settings. However, their complex, sometimes unsuitable method of use makes it necessary to design dedicated tools for individuals with cognitive impairments, which are presented later.

12.3.1 Mainstream Solutions

Many clinicians today foresee using portable technological devices as alternatives to paper memory books, which are basic tools used to compensate for mnemonic and organizational problems [10]. The most common of these devices is the personal digital assistant (PDA) and its equivalent, the smart phone, which is a cell phone equipped with PDA-like functionalities. There is a variety of PDAs on the market that differ primarily by their operating systems. The Operating system developed by Palm Inc and Microsoft Windows Mobile are comparable in terms of usability; they account for the major share of the market [11]. PDAs allow active information management (capture, storage, processing). They are like small computers with memory and a processing unit. Both Palms and Pocket PCs come bundled with software. The software bundle includes organization and management functionalities for all kinds of business: an appointment calendar, a task manager, and a note/contact manager. Appointments are activities that the user must carry out in the future with a specific time component (date, start time, and duration). The task manager deals with activities with a less precise timeframe, generally stated in terms of a deadline. Appointments and tasks relate to human prospective memory [12]. In contrast, notes and contacts are more general in nature and relate to long-term semantic memory [13].

PDA standard functionalities can be considered components of a cognitive orthotic because they help manage mnemonic, prospective, and semantic information. Moreover, this information is executive, since it is closely tied to undertaking and completing activities. The ability of PDAs to provide external cueing is the prime aspect featured in the literature [14]. It may appear excessive to use a PDA only as a prospective orthotic, such as a medication reminder; and, indeed, this essential function can be performed by a watch with an audible or vibrating alarm. However, the audible alarm does not specify the reason for the reminder. Individuals with dementia or cranial trauma are therefore taken unawares by such audible alarms and do not know how to respond [5]. A PDA, on the other hand, displays a text message describing the activity, which puts the reminder back into context.

The growing use of PDAs has led researchers to clinically assess their advantages for clients with mnemonic and executive impairments. A 1999 study [15] demonstrated how these tools can promote independence in daily life. The authors of most of these studies, however, express some reservations about using mainstream solutions for rehabilitation purposes. Several authors have criticized the complexity of use of such tools, particularly because of the many possibilities they offer [16–18]. These possibilities go beyond the needs of individuals with CI and hamper their learning. The complexity lies with the graphical interfaces that require too many steps to enter the information and do not offer direct retrieval of the information stored [19,20]. Consequently, users must have the initiative to check for the existence of information, which is beyond the cognitive capabilities of CI clients. For example, the lack of explicit prompts to information about an appointment, such as the address or means of transportation, means that users may not remember that such information exists. Similarly, certain typical problems with the graphical user interface pose a larger problem for the target group, for instance, when the user has to scroll down to view all the information [21]. As a result, part of the information may be lost to the user.

In addition to the software bundled with PDAs, some calendar and organizer applications feature commercial interfaces that are more appropriate for individuals with CI. First, applications to personalize the startup screen of Pocket PCs make it possible to easily display relevant information about the person's identity or tasks to do. Agenda Fusion, a software designed to manage time, tasks, notes, and contacts, features easy access to information (www.developerone.com/agendafusion/). The program uses a system of tabs instead of a complex menu to access the various tools. Icons and customizable colors can be used to specify and categorize time management, tasks, and notes. Finally, putting essential information in a single window means that the user does not have to use dropdown menus. Despite the work done on its interface, Agenda Fusion is not very well designed for people with mnemonic or executive disorders because too many tools are available. BugMe! is at the other end of the spectrum (www.electricpocket.com/bugme/). This highly simple software application is designed to manage notes. Notes can be grouped into categories, allowing the person to organize information. A sound based reminder can be used to recall information. BugMe!, however, lacks a structured means for entering information, making it poorly suited to the needs of individuals requiring a memory aid [22].

Mainstream solutions can be used by individuals with CI as memory orthotics to organize information and manage time. Moreover, they help minimize the marginalization of individuals with CI because such devices are also used by the people around them. At the same time, their complexity, the difficulty in accessing hidden information, the lack of structure for entering information, and the low level of personalization all contribute to make PDAs difficult to use for individuals with CI. As a result, a variety of dedicated solutions have appeared to respond to this specific clientele and set of issues.

12.3.2 Dedicated Solutions

Dedicated solutions vary according to the targeted clientele and objective. This section presents solutions grouped in ascending order of complexity of use for clients. First, pagers like NeuroPage are simple devices suitable for providing reminders about time use. Then multimedia procedure assistants—ISAAC, MAPS, and Visual Assistant—use pictures as prompts in reminding the individual of the steps involved in an activity. While in previous cases, information must be entered by a third party, organizers—ISAAC and OrientingTool—enable individuals with CI to easily organize their time and make notes. Dedicated tools such as MEMOS focus on communication between individuals and their caregivers. Finally artificial intelligence helps to improve tools adaptability and flexibility in managing time according to the activities to be performed.

12.3.2.1 Pagers

Providing reminders of activities is a basic-level intervention with people who have prospective or executive disorders, particularly in terms of initiation and organization. Unfortunately, as stated above, audible alarms do not specify the reason for the alarm and PDAs are often too complex. Although less powerful than PDAs, pagers are used in rehabilitation in response to this need. Pagers are limited to receiving and displaying alphanumeric information; complex processing must be carried out by a remote computer system. A number of companies have responded to the call by providing such services to the general public (www.neuropage.nhs.uk/, www.memotome.com and www.pageminderinc.com).

NeuroPage was the first service available on the market [23]. It sends a text message to the pager on a preprogrammed date at a specific time. The pager either sounds an alarm or vibrates to prompt the user to read the message, which indicates the activity to be performed. New activities can only be added by the service center, which must be notified 48 h in advance. Because of these complex procedures, NeuroPage is more appropriate in providing reminders about well-established, regular activities, such as taking medication or eating meals. NeuroPage has been the subject of a number of clinical assessments, most notably one conducted in 2001 with 143 individuals presenting primarily organizational problems [24]. The targeted activities corresponded to needs expressed by clients or their caregivers. The findings indicated that when the pager was used, the proportion of activities performed to activities targeted rose from less than 50% to about 76%. Removal of the device resulted in a reduction in the proportion of activities performed to 62%. As demonstrated in other clinical assessments, this tends to prove that cognitive orthotics also have a remedial effect on cognitive deficits. In addition, they find a high level of acceptance among individuals with CI.

The appearance of cell phones led a number of researchers to use this technology to deliver reminders [25]. Reminders for the target activities are sent by phone at a specific time in the form of prerecorded messages stored on a computer server. The advantage here is that the reminder is spoken, which eliminates the barrier of reading and requires no training. An individual with CI can use it like any other telephone to alert a caregiver or contact friends. A pilot study carried out with five participants demonstrated an improvement in the rate of activities performed as well as a reduction in planning and organizational challenges.

12.3.2.2 Multimedia Procedure Assistants

Memory and planning disorders often make it difficult for individuals to carry out complex activities independently. Individuals with CI require outside aid to remind them of the steps required by the activity. ISAAC [19], MAPS (memory aid prompting system) [26], and Visual Assistant, marketed by AbleLink Technologies, are tools that provide support in the procedures for carrying out the activity as well as with more general know-how. Procedural assistants use audio and visual messages to present information. The image provides nonverbal information, which is valuable for individuals who have difficulties communicating verbally, and allows for a considerable degree of personalization of information. For example, a photo of the user carrying out a step in his or her own environment delivers the information in a more meaningful and powerful way. Now that digital cameras are so widespread, such images are both easy to produce and affordable. Adding an audio message—in either the client's or caregiver's voice—can personalize the information still further.

MAPS and Visual Assistant display an image of each step of the activity that the individual with CI must carry out. While performing the activity, the individual inputs that the step has been completed and the assistant displays the following step right up until completion of the activity. In addition, MAPS provides for assigning a maximum amount of time in which to carry out each step. Once the time has expired, the assistant prompts the user to return to the current objective. Procedural assistants make use of two tools: (1) one that allows the client to work through the sequence of steps and (2) another that enables the caregiver to determine the pictorial description of the activity.

Thus MAPS designers have developed a simple utility that makes it easy to integrate images, verbal messages, and complementary information such as step duration when constructing a script.

Visual Assistant has been clinically assessed for use in performing simple activities, that is, those involving only a few steps [27,28]. The study, which involved a group of 10 individuals with intellectual disabilities, revealed a significant drop in requests for outside help when the task was carried out with the device. The authors of the study indicated that participants made fewer mistakes when using the device.

12.3.2.3 Information Organizer

Easy access to information for individuals with memory disabilities is the main goal of the two tools presented in this section. ISAAC's overriding objective is to improve the functional independence of individuals with traumatic or vascular brain injury (www.cosys.us/). It assists in managing procedures, remembering activities, and managing notes. The second device, called OrientingTool [22], aims to provide to people suffering from anterograde amnesia the necessary information to alleviate disorientation. Both of these tools present information in an effective, straightforward fashion, which is essential in fostering independence and above all does not exceed the cognitive capacities of the users.

On the observation that people with memory and executive disabilities are dependent on the people around them, ISAAC offers an appropriate graphical interface that highlights information to improve the user's independence. The emphasis is on knowhow with simplified, effective access to procedural information. Indeed, ISAAC is a full-fledged product, both software and machine, with a touch-screen roughly the size of a PDA screen. Unlike PDAs, however, which require a stylus, ISAAC has virtual buttons that are large enough to be finger-activated, making for easier use. Buttons can be personalized in terms of size, number, and labels. The information is hierarchical, with each button representing an information category containing subcategories. They provide an intuitive path to the last level of information, which consists of the steps the user needs to go through to carry out a task or activity. When users indicate that a step has been completed, the item is dimmed so that users can keep track of their places in the series. ISAAC also has a reminder functionality, which can be set at a specific time to help initiate the activity. It can also program itself while an activity is being carried out. To illustrate, the device can provide a reminder to turn off the oven 10 min after the last step in preparing a meal. This option, which can take the form of a text message on the screen or a spoken message, can be valuable in fostering user independence. Finally, it manages notes containing important information for the user, such as medical and personal information or people to contact, should the need arise. As is the case with many tools designed for individuals with CI and to facilitate handling the information, the content is authored by a third party. Dedicated authoring software for use on a PC is also provided. The caregiver can configure the interface, reminder times, categories of information, and procedural steps. ISAAC can also log user performance data, enabling caregivers to analyze the individual's reaction to reminders and adjust the content. ISAAC was tested with two individuals over a period of one year [19]. ISAAC had a positive impact on functional independence, and both individuals maintained their increased independence after the device was withdrawn.

OrientingTool focuses on a more specific objective of compensating for the disorientation experienced by individuals with anterograde amnesia. Individuals with this memory deficit have difficulties retaining current information, that is, information that is new to them [29]. On the other hand, they normally have good recall of memories prior to the condition and retain their procedural learning skills, which means that they can use a cognitive orthotic. The issue of disorientation arises when individuals find themselves in a new location and can no longer remember how or why. This can result in significant anxiety or even panic if no caregiver or landmarks memorized before the accident are present to provide a recognizable context. The purpose of OrientingTool is therefore to help them determine why they are at that particular location at that specific time. Unlike ISAAC, OrientingTool is a PDA software application. Thanks to the participatory design from future users, OrientingTool provides an effective response to the expressed needs. The graphical interface is based on a single window for entering responses to four questions to describe the current situation: when, where, why, and who. The first clinical studies indicated that the subjects experienced improved orientation in time and space [22]. The comments provided by participants point to wider use of OrientingTool, specifically in managing short-term activities in known settings.

12.3.2.4 Caregivers Put in the Loop

Improving the independence of the individuals assisted is a constant theme in cognitive orthotics. A related objective is reducing the burden on family and caregivers, which is often experienced as very heavy. The purpose of cognitive orthotics is not to eliminate third parties in the assistance process, but rather to lighten the load and foster their involvement. The patient gets the opportunity to receive operative instructions from the caregiver everywhere, and caregivers have the opportunity to intervene when the patient encounters a critical situation [30]. A variety of solutions integrate remote communication between the orthotic and a central computer system managed by caregivers. This is the case with NeuroPage; reminders are recorded on a remote computer and transmitted to the orthotic at the proper time. The systems presented in this section involve duplex (two-way) communication between the orthotic and the central computer system. This means that information about the degree of completion of the activity can be provided, in addition to the reminders being sent.

When there is no contextual information provided by sensors, the only way to determine whether the activity has been completed is user input. A wireless Internet connection transfer information from the PDA to the central computer that can relay it to a caregiver. Monitoring systems can inform caregivers only when a problem arise, as in MemoJog [21], or caregivers can remotely monitor to the full log of user actions, as in DOMUS software [31]. MemoJog is a simplified version of a PDA calendar function limited to consultation and dedicated for elderly clientele with memory deficits. It can also be used to record information such as contacts and birthdays. DOMUS software has many functions [32]. As a reminder system, it presents forthcoming activities. The graphical interface has been highly simplified to display a very limited number of activities indicating time use over only a few hours. It also enables the cargiver to gather ecological data related to medication side effects, having people suffering from schizophrenia in mind. Users can enter symptoms experienced. This contextual information provides medical staff with additional data to assess the proposed treatment between appointments with the physician. Clinical assessment is underway for young schizophrenic patients in Montreal, Canada.

MEMOS (mobile extensible memory aid system) has been designed as a memory aid for people with memory impairments [18,30]. As with the two tools presented above,

MEMOS is a client application connected to a remote central computer that sends and receives information about the scheduled activities. But MEMOS uses an ad hoc computer language for communication and an interpreter on the mobile device. This language allows MEMOS to provide a more complete description of the activity, including time constraints for completion. As a result, a reminder for an activity is only provided in advance when its performance is guaranteed. Confirmation is not accepted until the average time for performance has passed. Moreover, postponement of an activity will only be accepted if it can fit into subsequent time use. The language also provides a means for modeling the information to be presented to the user as a script. The interpreter on a smart phone dynamically converts the script into a user interface. More specifically, the language defines the text displayed, the associated buttons for user interaction, and the response when a button is selected. A clinical study of MEMOS is being assessed [33].

12.3.2.5 Toward Adaptive and Adapted Cognitive Assistance

The orthotics presented to this point have focused primarily on memory impairments, while executive deficits received more limited attention. MEMOS, however, uses an algorithm to process time constraints in order to confirm that an activity can be postponed on the basis of other scheduled activities. In general, artificial intelligence techniques can improve dramatically cognitive orthotics [34]. For instance, planning algorithms can be used to construct a sequence of actions to attain a goal [35].

PEAT (planning and execution assistant and trainer) is a cognitive orthotic with planner [36,37] (www.brainaid.com). It helps users with executive problems encountered in acquired or developmental cognitive impairments, more specifically, planning and initiation. From the standpoint of memory, PEAT manages prospective (activities and tasks) and semantic (notes and contacts) aspects. It uses recorded auditory messages or photographs as reminders. Overall, its graphical interface is fairly complex, particularly with respect to the use of menus. But PEAT views and functions can also be customized. Instead of presenting isolated activities, PEAT manages scripts, which are a set of activities aimed at achieving a common objective. Scripts guide users through hierarchical activities, each of which can in turn be a script. The level of assistance can therefore be adapted to user needs. While assistance provided at a higher level is more abstract, reminders are increasingly more specific down the hierarchy. Certain activities can be floating, which means that they do not require an exact start time. As in MEMOS, these activities can be postponed. PEAT, on the other hand, allows activities to be added during the day. It automatically manages time use by postponing floating activities based on their priorities and time constraints. Moreover, when two consecutive activities have to be carried out at different locations, the planner takes into account travel time. Finally, PEAT provides a certain degree of management over unexpected occurrences in performing activities as evidenced through interaction with the user. To illustrate, when the system reminds the user of the expected end time of an activity and the user disconfirms the reminder, PEAT assesses the impact that the delay will have on overall time use and alerts the user.

12.4 ASSISTIVE DEVICES DEDICATED TO SPECIFIC ADLS

The portable cognitive orthotics presented above respond to general needs related to memory and executive function. Moreover, they deal with prospective deficits related to future activities and their initiation, procedural deficits, and deficits in planning execution, while offering semantic data support (notes and contacts). These orthotics are not specific when viewed from the perspective of ADLs. In other words, they provide assistance for all activities related to the targeted deficit. In contrast, some research and commercial products provide responses to help performing specific ADLs. This may involve mobile or stationary solutions, depending on the targeted activity, as well as dedicated software or hardware. From the software standpoint, dedicated languages, such as COGORTH, can be used to implement specific strategies for monitoring a specific activity. For instance, COGORTH was tested with a 48-year-old man suffering from severe cognitive deficits [38,39]. After 3 days of task guidance, the man was able to remember to use a urinal periodically and solved his incontinence problem. He also received guidance in meal preparation and experienced improved independence with appropriate instructions. In this section, we first present COACH, an orthotic device dedicated to assisting in handwashing. Then solutions related to assistance with medication are discussed, given the importance of and consequences resulting from errors. Then movement, particularly using public transportation, is presented. The final topic on assistance for specific tasks addresses support to social interaction.

12.4.1 Assistance with Handwashing

Lack of initiative, planning deficits, and memory losses lead to difficulty in performing even the simplest ADL. The caregiver needs to stay close to the person and provide verbal prompts when the individual with CI is performing personal care. This encroaches on the person's privacy and may provoke aggressive behavior. COACH, an orthotic device, aims at fostering independence during washing tasks in order to limit caregiver intervention [40]. The handwashing task was selected because it entails limited risks of falling and is less intrusive, while being representative of the cognitive abilities required by personal care. The handwashing activity is divided into nine subtasks, including entering and leaving the bathroom. COACH uses several sensors and a single videocamera to monitor activity progress. The system detects whether the person is in front of the sink, the faucets are on, and the soap and the towel are used. Acoustic prompts are provided whenever a subtask is omitted or takes too long. Handwashing assistance was tested with a man suffering with dementia. The increased performance reduces the number of interactions with the caregiver. The context awareness of the device limits the cognitive load. The person does not need to inform the caregiver when a task is completed or to wear a mobile device. A second version of the prototype was developed to allow flexibility in the task sequence and provides more personalized prompts [41]. A 60-day study with 10 subjects with moderate to severe dementia showed an increase of the number of handwashing steps that the subjects were able to complete without caregiver assistance [42].

12.4.2 Medication

Medication compliance is one of the most difficult and important activities requiring monitoring. Indeed, it has been estimated that only a third of individuals comply with the dosage, whereas the other two-thirds evidence partial or zero compliance. Noncompliance can be harmful to the individual and impacts on healthcare costs. According to one study, in the United States alone, one-tenth of hospital admissions were associated with effects caused by noncompliance [43]. Individuals with CI fall within the majority of cases of concern with respect to medication management. No single solution is appropriate for every case. Needs and lifestyle must figure into determining the most appropriate choice. Solutions range from a simple pill organizer up to an automatic medication dispenser, which alerts caregivers when necessary.

Pharmacies market various models of pill organizers. The basic model resembles a plastic box with rows corresponding to daily doses. Pill organizers generally provide coverage for a week's medication, with three compartments per day. Although pill organizers, designed primarily for the elderly, help ensure that medication is taken regularly, they do not constitute an effective cognitive orthotic for individuals with CI. Such individuals need to be reminded when to take the medication, sometimes rather insistently. As well, the medication must not be accessible ahead of time to prevent the patient from taking the medication at the wrong time or mixing it up.

Devices with alarms remind users of when to take the medication, although they have the drawback of not specifying the reason for the alarm. In most cases, an individual with CI is unable to associate the watch sound or vibrations with taking his or her medication [5]. A number of pill organizers are equipped with an audible alarm, which clearly associates the sound with the need to take the medication. Such organizers, which are generally small and portable, allow the caregiver to prepare multiple doses that cover up to a week. The more sophisticated models dispense one dose at a time, which precludes overmedication. Yet automatic dispensing machines have several drawbacks. Some people may ignore the auditory prompts because they are impersonal and inappropriately timed. Furthermore, the dispenser cannot determine whether the medication has been taken and does not alert a caregiver when necessary [44].

MD.2 offers a monitored automatic medication dispenser, which alerts the caregiver by phone if medications are not dispensed (www.epill.com/md2.html). It stores up to 3 weeks of medication and provides three-way reminders: voice, text, and blinking light. Messages can be preprogrammed to guide users in taking their medication. On the other hand, since it is about the size of an electric coffeepot, all medication must be taken at the same location; and studies show that the elderly are used to taking pills in different rooms—kitchen, bathroom, or bedroom—depending on the time of the activity [44]. MedSignals, a portable device, partly meets this expectation (www.medsignals.com). Small enough to be worn at the waist, this device too provides three-way reminders. The medication is held in small compartments, and opening the compartment serves as confirmation that the dose was taken. However, MedSignals must be periodically docked on its base to transfer information related to the doses taken and download new instructions for the user remotely authored by a third party.

Medication management cannot be considered an isolated activity for which the user is solely responsible. An integrated approach involving all the parties concerned in medication management appears promising. An Internet-based care model is under study in Europe to facilitate interactions between all the stakeholders [43]. Patients are provided with a home unit (which holds a week's supply of medication), communication with the Internet-based portal, and a portable unit. The portable unit is equipped with alarms, sensors, and connections to the home unit to remind the patient to take medication and indicate whether the medication has not been taken. All stakeholders have access to the patient database, which contains the related medication information. The integrated approach was evaluated for 45 patients at four different sites. Patients seem to have greater independence and appreciated the delivery of service. Physicians and pharmacists indicated that less time was required in repeating and refilling prescriptions.

12.4.3 Movement out of the Home

Using mass transit is a major challenge for persons with disabilities. Those with physical handicaps tend to use paratransit. Individuals with cognitive deficits, however, are not faced with the same barriers; boarding a bus or navigating a narrow hallway represents no particular problem for them. It's the cognitive requirements of using public transportation that force them to depend on family and friends. In 2001, the national US Transportation Research Board (TRB) surveyed the major difficulties encountered by people with cognitive impairments in using mass transit:

- Reading and understanding directions
- Selecting the right vehicle
- Getting off at the right stop
- Understanding conductor/driver announcements

In an effort to optimize the independence of such people in using mass transit, MAPS [26] is an integrated system of assistive technologies that map out routes (strategic and microplanning), coupled with a supervisory system that enables the user to contact the caregiver at any time, in particular, when lost (tactical planning). Strategic planning requires cognitive capabilities that are usually beyond the capacities of the cognitively impaired. This planning, however, can be authored and stored in advance, which is what MAPS does. As described in the section on multimedia procedural assistants (Section 12.3.2.2), MAPS is a software application that has been specially designed for natural caregivers to enable them to easily author the movement script. Each step of the route is illustrated with a photograph representing a landmark that is meaningful for the client. Time and geographic positioning information are associated with each photograph. During the movement, the client refers to the script that had been transferred to his or her PDA. The photographs provide support for micro planning, serving as reminders about the action to be performed and as environmental cues that need to be taken into account. Challenges related to tactical planning are handled with GPS capabilities and a cell phone carried by the user. If clients miss their stop, the system uses GPS to detect the error and automatically messages the caregiver. Clients can call for assistance if they feel lost. Natural caregivers have expressed some reservations about the system's safety, since it hasn't been tested yet in an urban setting. Nevertheless, the picture prompts were tested with natural caregivers and young people [45].

The activity compass aims at assisting individuals suffering from Alzheimer's disease to reach their destination [46]. They wear a PDA equipped with a compass and a GPS. A server receives GPS data, learns familiar transportation routines, and predicts their most likely destination. The PDA is then used to guide them by using a very simple user interface displaying an arrow pointing in the right direction and an icon to remind the destination [47].

12.4.4 Social Interaction

Isolation characterizes the cognitively impaired, whether the impairment is acquired or developmental, or due to brain injury, dementia, CVA-related aphasia, mental illness, or intellectual impairment [48,49]. This isolation results from difficulty in initiating contact and following the thread of the conversation. Individuals with CI are highly reticent to communicate in either speech or writing out of fear of annoying the other person. In addition to cognitive and language deficits, they sometimes face physical challenges in writing or dialing phone numbers. Assistive technologies that compensate for physical and perceptual challenges are covered in Sections 12.3.1 and 12.3.2. Section 12.3.4 deals with assistive technologies for people with communication, speech, and language impairments. Certain technologies, however, are specifically designed to combat isolation and to encourage individuals with CI to communicate. As such, they are discussed in this chapter.

12.4.4.1 Communicating by Electronic Mail

Using a computer is difficult for individuals with attention or memory disorders. Indeed, computer interfaces are poorly designed for these people. Their attention is often drawn to secondary information, such as the bright colors or animation in advertising. Switching windows in a software application or Website requires good memory skills to stay focused on the objective and remember information that had already been seen. Several studies have highlighted certain of these problems with specific clienteles [50,51]. Computers provide significant possibilities for adaptive assistance, owing, on one hand, to their capacity for personalization, and, on the other hand, by opening a world of information and communication. Electronic mail and chatrooms make staying in touch easier, regardless of distance; email has the added advantage of enabling individuals with cognitive impairments to easily initiate contact because it is asynchronous in nature. In other words, clients can work at their own pace in writing and responding to messages. Commercial email applications, however, must be adapted to simplify sending and receiving for these clientele. In addition to problems associated with the use of standard word-processing commands, individuals with CI often face challenges in choosing a topic and developing ideas. In order to overcome these problems, researchers used four different writing prompt conditions for eight individuals who displayed a variety of cognitive–linguistic impairments [52]. The most flexible version bears the closest resemblance to standard email applications. The title at the top specifies the subject, and the SEND button is clearly identified. The user writes the message in the window with a standard text processor. The second version displays an outline under the title, which describes the usual structure of a message. When the message is sent, only the words written by the user are transmitted. In the third version, the user has to fill in blanks in prewritten sentences. The fourth version—the most highly structured of the four—presents multiple word choices instead of blanks for completing the sentences. The user selects a word among five on a menu. The four versions were tested with eight people with CI and their email partners. The versions were evaluated according to usability, message completeness, message clarity, and the correlation between user personality and the message. Testing revealed no clear participant preference between versions; rather, application personalization appeared to be most important. The experiment demonstrated how well email counters the isolation experienced by individuals with CI. The interest generated by communicating shows through in the lack of fatigue in all participants and their interest in communicating with others. Unfortunately, this exploratory study has not yet led to a commercial product that would certainly respond to the need for communication in the form of shared impressions as well as making appointments.

12.4.4.2 Communication and Reminiscence

Very early in the course of their disease, Alzheimer's patients withdraw from social interactions as a result of short-term memory loss. At the same time, older memories can stimulate and generate interaction with the people around them. The purpose of reminiscence groups is to improve self-esteem by stimulating interactions using pictures, music, or videos. Alongside traditional tools, the new generation of computer tools provide opportunities to support reminiscence therapy in an attractive, user-friendly, and intuitive way [53,54]. On one hand, multimedia supports diversified interactions because a single computer can host a variety of media such as text, images, music, speech, and video. On the other hand, a touchscreen on a wall can extend usage to a group, with each person having an opportunity to get involved. The CIRCA (computer interactive reminiscence and conversation aid) project uses interactive multimedia in reminiscence groups to enhance the quality of life in dementia-care environments [53]. This project, which takes a user-centered approach, was carefully designed from a multidisciplinary perspective based on psychology, computer science, and design. For example, the system was designed to provide a fail-safe experience. The themes dealt with in the reminiscence group reflect participant preferences: recreation, entertainment, and local life. They are presented on three different media supports, photographs, videos, and music. Since the purpose of a reminiscence group is to foster participation and exchanges between those taking part, lively musical sequences are kept to a minimum to prevent immersion and isolation. CIRCA was tested in a dementia care environment to assist reminiscence groups, including more than 30 people suffering from dementia and 40 formal and informal caregivers. CIRCA promoted a much more relaxed atmosphere, in which the elderly sang spontaneously, remembered memories never expressed before, were proactive, and shared their impressions and memories.

12.5 DISCUSSION

In this section, we propose a classification of assistive technology according to the sphere of activity, the assistive interaction and the advanced technology used (Table 12.1).

12.5.1 Classification According to Sphere of Activity

The assistive technologies herein have been presented according to the areas in which they apply, beginning with general aids centered on organizing activities, time, and memory. These portable devices are carried by individuals with cognitive impairments throughout the day, helping them in a variety of activity spheres, regardless of the specific nature of the activity. While commercial solutions have proved their effectiveness, they have also demonstrated their lack of adaptability to the needs of specific clients. As a result, many solutions have emerged to respond to the specific needs of clients, both to provide reminders of things to do and how to do them. Moreover, communication between the client and the caregiver has come to light as a requirement in increasing safety and confidence for everyone concerned. The designers of dedicated organizers have clearly demonstrated particular care in ensuring the usability of these assistive technologies by restricting or tailoring functionalities and simplifying interfaces.

Certain assistive technologies provide support for more specific activities. Many have been designed to help an individual perform certain basic activities of daily living, such

TABLE 12.1 A Classification of Technology for Cognitive Assistance

Assistive Technology	Category	Assitive Interaction	Advanced Technology
Commercial products	Organizer	Reminder	
Neuropage	Organizer	Reminder	Mobile computing
MAPS	Organizer	Guide	
Visual Assistant	Organizer	Guide	
ISAAC	Organizer	Reminder, Guide	
OrientingTool	Organizer	Reminder.	
DOMUS	Organizer	Reminder, Communicator, Informer	Mobile computing
MEMOS	Organizer	Reminder, Guide, Communicator, Informer	Reasoning.
PEAT	Organizer	Reminder, Communicator, Mediator	Artificial intelligence
COACH	ADL-specific	Guide	Machine learning. Context Awareness. Artificial intelligence
Alarm watch	Medication	Reminder	
Electronic pill dispensers	Medication	Reminder	
MD.2 and MedSignal	Medication	Reminder, Guide, Informer, Mediator	Internet
MAPS	Movement	Guide, Communicator, Informer	Mobile computing. Context Awareness.
Activity Compass	Movement	Mediator	Mobile Computing. Machine learning. Artificial Intelligence.
e-mail	Social interaction	Mediator	Internet. Artificial Intelligence.
Reminiscence group	Social interaction	Supplier	Advanced User interface

as handwashing, taking medication, and venturing outside the home. Finally, assistive technologies were presented to help individuals with CI combat isolation through social participation—one promotes contact using electronic means; the other, through expressing memories.

12.5.2 Classification According to Assistive Interaction

Many independence assessment tests use scales that take into account the type of assistance required to perform ADLs [55–57]. Similarly, assistive technologies can be classified according to the type of assistance provided: reminder, guide, communicator, informer, mediator, and supplier [9]. The reminder function is the pivotal feature of organizers and assistive technologies related to medication compliance. They remind the individual when to perform an activity, either with a simple alarm or by specifying what must be done. The guide function of assistive devices presented here uses pictorial sequences to show how to perform a task. The need for safety, felt by clients and caregivers alike, highlights the importance of the communicator function. When the client expresses the need to communicate with someone, the communicator identifies the speaker and establishes communication between them. This function is often available in assistive technologies when the client has to go outside. This assistance is often paired with the informer, which keeps the caregiver informed about the activities performed or certain important information, such as health status. The mediator makes the activity easier to carry out. It is the underlying principle of pill organizers, which deliver doses of medication prepared in advance. The activity compass facilitates spatial orientation using a screen that always indicates the direction to follow, while PEAT organizes the individual's activities according to the time allotted. The supplier of activities was exemplified with assistive devices involved in reminiscence groups.

12.5.3 Classification According to Advances in Technology

Technologic advances hold out hope for developing new assistive devices. The current dramatic rise in technology hints at how support is expected to broaden depending on the activities requiring assistance, the deficits to be compensated for, and the technologic means implemented. Jorge [58] identified the technology areas that would modify the assistance for individuals with cognitive impairments. The customizability of applications and interfaces takes on its full importance here, since such people are extremely sensitive to any change in their environments. Machine learning algorithms have already been implemented to adapt the technology to lifestyles and will be increasingly used as time goes on. The interactions between people and assistive technologies need to be customized according to means—whether audio, visual, or even tangible [59]. As a result of the widespread use of computers and context awareness, cognitive devices in the home will eventually be able to determine when people need assistance and how to provide it adequately. Yet, since cognitive orthotic devices are not actually aware of what is occurring in the environment, they may provide inappropriate advice, leading to hazardous situations. Furthermore, cognitive orthotics can also request CI patients to indicate when an activity has been accomplished, which may be beyond their cognitive abilities and should be addressed by a context-aware system. In the near future, RFID (radiofrequency identification) technology will bring solutions that specify information about activities performed in the environment by means of tags attached to various objects [60]. Several of the assistive technologies presented herein already use advanced techniques that enable them to locate the person outside, to automatically establish contact with their caregivers, or to determine what the user is actually doing.

12.6 CONCLUSION

Research on assistive technologies for individuals with CI is in its early stages. On one hand, commercial solutions fostering independence are often abandoned because they fail to respond to the specific needs of the consumers. On the other hand, few dedicated solutions have so far been marketed, although the fast-growing research sector promises a variety of solutions that will be available in the near future. Personalization will be a key issue in how successful assistive technologies are with the clientele. At this time, it is difficult to assess how individuals with cognitive impairments will react to the new technologies. The initiatives carried out so far, however, indicate that the consumers will adopt assistive technologies if they are well designed. Furthermore, the use of assistive technologies appears to depend primarily on caregiver comfort with new technologies [61,62]. Such findings hold promise for individuals with CI being very receptive of new technologies, especially since they have been modeled on devices available to the general public, which removes any handicap-related stigma. Should new assistive technologies fail to respond to the clientele's specific needs, however, they run the risk of being set aside by individuals with CI and their caregivers. Research findings have shown that around a third of all devices are completely abandoned, due partly to a lack of consideration of user opinion in device selection and a failure to adapt to user needs over the years [63]. Future users must take part in the design and development of new technologies. Finally, to be recommended, assistive technology must adequately mitigate cognitive deficits; however, it must also meet physical, psychological, social, and economic criteria.

REFERENCES

1. Lynch B: Historical review of computer-assisted cognitive retraining, *J Head Trauma Rehab* **17**(5):446–457 (2002).
2. Technology-Related Assistance for Individuals with Disabilities Act of 1988, PL 100-407, as it is referred in the website http://www.msprojectstart.org/techact.html, 1988.
3. Carswell A, McColl MA, Baptiste S, Law M, Polatajko H, Pollock N: The Canadian occupational performance measure: A research and clinical literature review, *Can J Occup Ther*, **71**(4) (2004).
4. Lawton MP, Brody EM: Assessment of older people: Self-maintaining and instrumental activities of daily living, *Gerontologist* **9**(3):179–186 (1969).
5. Muriel D. Lezak, Diana B. Howieson, David w. Loring, (eds.) (4th ed.). *Neuropsychological Assessment*, Oxford University Press, New York, 2004.
6. Pigot H, Savary JP, Metzger JL, Rochon A, Beaulieu M: Advanced technology guidelines to fulfill the needs of the cognitively impaired population, *Proc 3rd Int Conf Smart Homes and Health Telematic (ICOST)*, Magog, Canada, 2005, pp 25–32.
7. LoPresti E, Mihailidis A, Kirsch N: Assistive technology for cognitive rehabilitation: State of the art [electronic version], *Neuropsychol Rehab*, **14**(1/2):5–39 (2004).
8. Horgas A, Abowd G: The impact of technology on living environments for older adults, in Pew RW VanHemel SB, eds, *Technology for Adaptive Aging*, The National Academies Press, 2004, pp 230–252.
9. Maciuszek D, Aberg J, Shahmehri N: Whathelp do older people need? Constructing a functional design space of electronic assistive technology applications, *Proc 7th Int ACM SIGACCESS Confe Computers and Accessibility, Assets '05*, Baltimore, 2005, pp 4–11.
10. Sohlberg MM, Mateer CA: Training use of compensatory memory books: A three stage behavioral approach, *J Clin Experl Neuropsychol Official J Int Neuropsychol Soc* **11**(6):871–891 (1989).
11. Jeong SH, Lee K: The effects of experience with a PC on the usability of a mobile product, *Proc 6th Asian Design Int Confe*, 2003.
12. Einstein GO, McDaniel MA: Normal aging and prospective memory, *J Exper Psychol Learning Memory Cogn* **16**(4):717 (1990).
13. Tulving E: Multiple memory systems and consciousness, *Human Neurobiol* **6**(2):67–80 (1987).
14. Kapur N, Glisky EL, Wilson BA: Technological memory aids for people with memory deficits, *Neuropsychol Rehab*, **14**(1/2):41–60 (2004).
15. Kim HJ, Burke DT, Dowds MM, Georges J: Utility of a microcomputer as an external memory aid for a memory-impaired head injury patient during in-patient rehabilitation, *Brain Injury* **13**(2):147–150 (1999).

16. Cole E: Cognitive prosthetics; an overview to a method of treatment, *Neurorehabilitation* **12**:39–51 (1999).
17. Kim HJ, Burke DT, Dowds MM, Robinson Boone KA, Park GJ: Electronic memory aids for outpatient brain injury: Follow-up findings, *Brain Injury* **14**(2):187–196 (2000).
18. Schulze H: MEMOS: An interactive assistive system for prospective memory deficit compensation-architecture and functionality [electronic version], *SIGACCESS Access Comput* (77–78):79–85 (2003).
19. Gorman P, Dayle R, Hood C Rimrell L: Effectiveness of the ISAAC cognitive prosthetic system for improving rehabilitation outcomes with neurofunctional impairment, *Neurorehabilitation* **18**:57–67 (2003).
20. Thöne-Otto AIT, Walther K: How to design an electronic memory aid for brain-injured patients: Considerations on the basis of a model of prospective memory. *Int J Psychol* **34**(4):1–9 (2003).
21. Szymkowiak A, Morrison K, Gregor P, Shah P, Evans J, Wilson A: A memory aid with remote communication using distributed technology, *Personal Ubiq Comput* **9**(1):1–5 (2005).
22. Wu M, Baecker R, Richards B: Participatory design of an orientation aid for amnesics, *Proc SIGCHI Conference Human Factors in Computing Systems, CHI'05*, Portland, OR, 2005, pp 511–520.
23. Hersh N, Treadgold L: Neuropage: The rehabilitation of memory dysfunction by prosthetic memory and cueing, *Neurorehabilitation* **4**:465–486 (1994).
24. Wilson BA, Emslie HC, Quirk K, Evans JJ: Reducing everyday memory and planning problems by means of a paging system: A randomised control crossover study, *J Neurol Neurosurg Psychiatr* **70**(4):477–482 (2001).
25. Wade TK, Troy JC: Mobile phones as a new memory aid: A preliminary investigation using case studies, *Brain Injury* **15**(4):305–320 (2001).
26. Carmien S: End user programming and context responsiveness in handheld prompting systems for persons with cognitive disabilities and caregivers, *Proc Conf Human Factors in Computing Systems CHI'05*, 2005, pp 1252–1255.
27. Davies DK, Stock SE, Wehmeyer ML: Enhancing independent time-management skills od individuals with mental retardation using a palmtop personal computer, *Mental Retard*, **40**(5):358–365 (2002).
28. Davies DK, Wehmeyer ML: Enhancing independent task performance for individuals with mental retardation through use ot a handheld self-directed visual and audio prompting system, *Educ Train Mental Retard Devel Disab*, **37**(2):209–217 (2002).
29. Bachevalier J: Les troubles de mémoire et les système de mémoire, in T. Botez-Marquard T, Boller F, eds, *Neuropsychologie Clinique et Neurologie du Comportement* Presses Univ Montréal, 2005, pp. 391–413.
30. Voinikonis A, Irmscher K, Schulze H: Distributed processing of reminding tasks within the mobile memory aid system, MEMOS, *Personal Ubiq Comput*, **9**(5):284–290 (2005).
31. Moreau JF, Pigot H, Giroux S: Assistance to cognitively impaired people and distance monitoring by caregivers: A study on the use of electronic agendas, *Proc Int Conf Aging, Disability and Indenpendence (ICADI)*, St. Petersburg, FL, 2006, pp 29–30.
32. PigotH, Giroux S: Keeping in touch with cognitively impaired people: How mobile devices can improve medical and cognitive supervision, 2nd International Conference on Smart Homes & Health Telematics, ICOST. Sept. 15–17, 2004. Singapore in Zhang D, Mokhtari eds, Towards a Human-Friendly Assistive Environment, Volume 14, Assistive Technology Research Series, September 2004, 300p.
33. Schulze H: MEMOS: A mobile extensible memory aid system, *Telemed J e-Health* **10**(2): 233–242 (2004).

34. Pollack ME: Intelligent technology for an aging population: The use of AI to assist elders with cognitive impairment [electronic version], *AI Magazine* **26**(2):9–24 (2005).
35. Ghallab M, Nau D, Traverso P: *Automated Planning: Theory and Practice*, Morgan Kaufmann, 2004.
36. Levinson R: The planning and execution assistant and trainer (PEAT), *J Head Trauma Rehab* **12**(2):85–91 (1997).
37. Levinson R: A custom-fitting cognitive orthotic that provides automatic planning and cueing assistance, *Proc Technology and Persons with Disabilitites Conf,* California State University, Northridge Center on Disabilities, 2004.
38. Kirsch N, Levine SP, Lajiness-O'Neill R, Mossaro M, Schneider M, Donders J: Improving functional performance with computerized task guidance systems, *Proc Int Conf Association for the Advancement of Rehabilitation Technology* (*ICAART*), Arlington, VA, (1988).
39. Kirsch N, Levine SP, Lajiness-O'Neill R, Schneider M: Computer-assisted interactive task guidance: Faciltating the performance of a simulated vocational task. *J Head Trauma Rehab*, **7**(3):13–25 (1992).
40. Mihailidis A, Fernie GR, Cleghorn WL: The developpment of a computerized cueing device to help people with dementia to be more independent, *Technol Disab* **13**:23–40 (2000).
41. Mihailidis A, Fernie GR: Context-aware assistve devices for older adults with dementia, Gerontotechnology **2**(2):173–188 (2003).
42. Mihailidis A, Barbenel J, Fernie GR: The efficacy of an intelligent cognitive orthosis to facilitate handwashing by persons with moderate-to-severe dementia, *Neuropsychol Rehab*, **14**(1):135–172 (2004).
43. Nugent C, Finlay D, Davies R, Paggetti C, Tamburini E, Blac N: Can technology improve compliance with medication? *Proc 3rd Int Conf Smart Homes and Health Telematic* (*ICOST*), Magog, Canada, 2005, pp 65–72.
44. Dishman E: Inventing wellness systems for aging in place [electronic version], *Computer* **37**(5):34–41 (2004).
45. Carmien S, Dawe M, Fischer G, Gorman A, Kintsch A, Sullivan JF Jr: Socio-technical environments supporting people with cognitive disabilities using public transportation, *ACM Trans Comput Hum Interact* **12**:(2), 233–262 (2005).
46. Patterson D, Etzioni O, Fox D, Kautz H: The activity compass, *Proc 1st International Workshop on Ubiquitous Computing for Cognitive Aids, UbiCog '02*, Gothenberg, Sweden, 2002.
47. Patterson D, Liao L, Fox D, Kautz H: Inferring high-level behavior from low-level sensors, *Proc 5th Int Conf Ubiquitous Computing, UBICOMP 2003*, Oct 12–15, 2003.
48. Holmen K, Ericsson K, Winblad B: Social and emotional loneliness among non-demented and demented elderly people, *Arch Gerontol Geriatr*, **31**(3):177–192 (2000).
49. Lyon JG: Communication use and participation in life of adults with aphasia in natural settings: The scope of the problem, *Am J Speech-Lang Pathol* **1**:7–14 (1992).
50. Singh S: Designing intelligent interfaces for users with memory and language limitations, *Aphasiology* **14**:157–177 (2000).
51. Wehmeyer ML: Assistive technology and students with mental retardation: Utilization and barriers, *J Spec Educ Technol*, **14**:50–60 (1999).
52. Sohlberg MM, Ehlhardt LA, Fickas S, Sutcliffe A: A pilot study exploring electronic (or e-mail) mail in users with acquired cognitive-linguistic impairments, *Brain Injury* **17**(7):609–629 (2003).
53. Alm N, Ellis M, Astell A, Dye R, Gowans G, Campbell J: A cognitive prosthesis and communication support for people with dementia, *Neuropsychol Rehab* **14**(1/2):117–134 (2004).

54. Gowans G, Campbell J, Alm N, Dye R, Astell A, Ellis M: Designing a multimedia conversation aid for reminiscence therapy in dementia care environments, *Proc Conf Extended Abstracts on Human Factors in Computing Systems, CHI'04*, Vienna, Austria, 2004, pp 825–836.
55. Desrosiers J, Bravo G, Hebert R, Dubuc N: Reliability of the revised functional autonomy measurement system (SMAF) for epidemiological research, *Age Ageing* **24**(5):402–406 (1995).
56. Baum C, Edwards DF: Cognitive performance in senile dementia of the alzheimer's type: The kitchen task assessment, *Am J Occup Ther*, **47**(5):431–436 (1993).
57. Dutil E, Forget A, Vanier M, Gaudreault C: Development of the ADL profile: An evaluation for adults with severe head injury, *Occup Ther Health Care* **7**:7–22 (1990).
58. Jorge JA, Adaptive tools for the elderly: New devices to cope with age-induced cognitive disabilities, *Proc 2001 EC/NSF Workshop on Universal Accessibility of Ubiquitous computing, WUAUC'01*, 2001, pp 66–70.
59. Ullmer B, Ishii H: Emerging frameworks for tangible user interfaces, *IBM Syst J*, **39**(3–4) (2000).
60. Smith JR, Fishkin KP, Jiang B, Mamishev A, Philipose M, Rea AD et al: RFID: Tagging the world: RFID-based techniques for human-activity detection, *Commun ACM* **48**(9) (2005).
61. Gillette Y, DePompei R: The potential of electronic organizers as a tool in cognitive rehabilitation of young people, *Neurorehabilitation* **19**(3):233–243 (2004).
62. O'Neil-Pirozzi TM, Kendrick H, Goldstein R, Glenn M: Clinician influences on use of portable electronic memory devices in traumatic brain injury rehabilitation, *Brain Injury [BI]* **18**(2):179–189 (2004).
63. Phillips B, Zhao H: Predictors of assistive technology abandonment, *Assist Technol Official J RESNA* **5**(1):36–45 (1993).

PART III

Human–Machine Interaction and Alternative Communication

13

Computer Access in the Workplace

Karen Milchus and Carrie Bruce
Georgia Institute of Technology

Access to computer technology can mean access to the workplace for many people with disabilities. This chapter describes the range of functional limitations that an employee might face in the workplace with respect to computer access, and presents strategies to address these issues through assistive technology and universal design.

13.1 BACKGROUND

13.1.1 Computer Use in the Workplace

When people discuss accommodations to help a person with a disability gain and maintain productive employment, the issue of computer use is increasingly involved. We are living in an age when the majority of jobs require at least some computer use. In their survey of human resources professionals, Bruyere et al. [1] found that even in the industries with the lowest computer usage (e.g., transportation, utilities, manufacturing, retail/wholesale trade), over 40% of employees spent at least half the workday on computers. Among the insurance, high-tech, and finance sectors, the number jumped to 80%.

Clearly, access to computer technology can mean access to the workplace for many people with disabilities. For a person who has difficulty writing by hand, a computer can provide an alternative means to write reports, fill out forms, draw blueprints, or even solve equations. For a person with a visual impairment, electronic documents may be

---

The Engineering Handbook of Smart Technology for Aging, Disability, and Independence,
Edited by A. Helal, M. Mokhtari and B. Abdulrazak
Copyright © 2008 John Wiley & Sons, Inc.

easier to review and file. For a person who has a learning disability, the computer can assist with spelling, grammar, and organization. People who are deaf or hard of hearing can conduct communication in the workplace via email, rather than over the phone.

However, while computers can help reduce or remove access barriers to common work tasks, accessible technology is needed for that to be possible. In fact, Microsoft Corp. found that 22.6 million computer users are very likely to benefit from the use of accessible technology because they experience severe difficulties or impairments [2]. Unfortunately, most computer hardware and software has not been specifically designed for people with disabilities, and as a result, computer access is one of the accommodations most frequently required by an employee. For example, of the 30 studies of workplace accommodations reviewed by Butterfield and Ramseur [3], 19 included computer technologies.

13.1.2 Legislation and Technical Guidelines

When discussing computer access in the workplace, it is important to understand the influence of disability legislation and standards. There are several pieces of legislation that should be followed. The first is the Americans with Disabilities Act (ADA) of 1990, which is civil rights legislation that mandates that qualified employees be given an equal chance for employment, including "reasonable accommodations."[1] Reasonable accommodations are changes made to the way a job is typically performed or to the work environment that enable employees to perform work tasks that they would otherwise be unable to do. Reasonable accommodations range from restructuring a job, to changing the environment, to purchasing equipment. For example, a journalist who is able to research and write stories, but is having difficulty in typing them up because of a disability, might be provided with a system that allows the user to dictate articles into the computer. However, the ADA mandates only that either employees have access to equipment that they can use or that accommodations be provided—it does not specify *how* that should be done.

Some specifications are provided within the Web Content Accessibility Guidelines (WCAG) published by the Web Accessibility Initiative of the World Wide Web Consortium [4]. Although not specifically required by legislation, these guidelines provide technical specifications for Web accessibility that are lacking in the ADA. The guidelines include information about how to structure Websites, present graphical information such as images or charts, and include multimedia. Many of the principles outlined in the WCAG could also apply to the development of other software.

Finally, Section 508 of the Rehabilitation Act Amendments of 1998 was written to ensure that federal employees and members of the public with disabilities have access to the same information and data as people without disabilities.[2] It is perhaps the most significant legislation to specifically impact computer access in the workplace. This legislation requires that when federal departments and agencies procure, develop, maintain or use electronic and information technology (EIT), they must ensure that it complies with specific standards.[3] These standards cover EIT such as software applications and operating systems, Web-based intranet and Internet information and applications, multimedia products, and desktop and portable computers. The standards for Web-based information

---

[1] Americans with Disabilities Act of 1990, 42 USC §§ 12101 et seq.
[2] Section 508 of the Rehabilitation Act of 1973, as amended, 29 USC § 794(d).
[3] For a listing of these guidelines, see http://www.section508.gov.

and applications are based, in part, on WCAG's Priority 1 checkpoints. This legislation only applies to the development and procurement of EIT products by the federal government, but it has encouraged other companies to follow suit. Moreover, because the federal government is required to give priority to procuring products that meet the Section 508 standards, and as the government is a significant purchaser of EIT products, this legislation has created a new motivation for EIT product developers to make their products accessible.

13.2 APPROACHES TO COMPUTER ACCESS

13.2.1 Assistive Technology

Assistive technology (AT) is "any item, piece of equipment, or product system ... that is used to increase, maintain, or improve the functional capabilities of individuals with disabilities."[4] AT is typically used to help bridge the gap between a person's functional abilities and what is required to perform a task. For example, a wheelchair is technology that assists a person with a mobility limitation to move through the environment. A magnifier might be used to help someone read a book. AT for computer access includes alternative keyboards and cursor control devices, alternative ways of getting information out of the computer, and software to help individuals work faster and more efficiently.

13.2.2 Universal Design

Universal design is "the design of products and environments to be usable by all people, to the greatest extent possible, without the need for adaptation or specialized design" [5]. Whereas AT tends to involve retrofitting existing products and finding ways to bridge gaps between a user's abilities and the requirements of the product, the goal of universal design (UD) is to design products to be usable (and therefore accessible) from the start to meet the needs of people with disabilities or with less abilities than the general population.

There are seven principles of universal design [6]:

1. *Equitable Use.* The design is useful and marketable to people with diverse abilities. It provides the same means of use for all users: identical whenever possible; equivalent when not.
2. *Flexibility in Use.* The design accommodates a wide range of individual preferences and abilities, such as accommodating right- or left-handed access and use or facilitating the user's accuracy and precision.
3. *Simple and Intuitive Use.* Use of the design is easy to understand, regardless of the user's experience, knowledge, language skills, or current concentration level. The product interface provides consistency and feedback and eliminates unnecessary complexity.
4. *Perceptible Information.* The design communicates necessary information effectively to the user, regardless of ambient conditions or the user's sensory abilities. Information may be presented in different modes (pictorial, verbal, tactile) for redundant presentation of essential information.

---
[4]Technology-Related Assistance for Individuals with Disabilities Act of 1988, 29 USC Section 2202(2).

5. *Tolerance for Error.* The design minimizes hazards and the adverse consequences of accidental or unintended actions. It provides warnings of hazards and errors, provides fail-safe features, and discourages unconscious action in tasks that require vigilance.
6. *Low Physical Effort.* The design can be used efficiently and comfortably and with a minimum of fatigue. It allows the user to maintain a neutral body position, uses reasonable operating forces, and minimizes repetitive actions and sustained physical effort.
7. *Size and Space for Approach and Use.* Appropriate size and space is provided for approach, reach, manipulation, and use regardless of user's body size, posture, or mobility. For example, both seated and standing users can reach the components and have a clear line of sight to important elements.

In practice, computer access for people with disabilities uses a combination of AT and UD. The challenge is the human–computer interface—using the keyboard and mouse for input, reading from the monitor and printer for output, and interacting with the software applications. The specific problems faced depend on the functional limitations of the individual and the demands placed on the user in terms of the design. This chapter describes the range of functional limitations that an employee might face in the workplace with respect to computer access, and it presents strategies to address these issues through assistive technology and universal design.

13.3 COMPUTER ACCESS FOR PEOPLE WITH UPPER-EXTREMITY IMPAIRMENTS

13.3.1 Background

According to the US Census, 6.8 million people (3.2%) over the age of 15 have difficulty grasping objects [7]. Grasping difficulty is a functional limitation related to upper-extremity impairment, although it is not the only body function that can be affected by impairment. When people refer to *upper-extremity impairments*, they might be talking about functional limitations resulting from conditions such as arthritis, muscular dystrophy, spinal cord injury, cerebral palsy, stroke, or repetitive stress injury. Upper-extremity impairments include amputation, paralysis, paresis (muscle weakness), dyskinesia (coordination problems), and pain. Each condition and impairment will affect people in different ways and may be associated with one or several functional limitations that make performing work activities problematic.

13.3.2 Motor Abilities and Computer Access

Functional limitations related to dexterity or fine-motor movements can make computer input a challenge. In a recent survey, 46% of respondents with limitations related to "coordinating movements" reported difficulty with typing on a computer and/or using a computer mouse [8]. Access issues for individuals with upper-extremity impairments and associated functional limitations may include how an employee uses the keyboard or mouse—perhaps with only one hand, one finger, or hands-free. Additionally, employees with dexterity or fine-motor issues need to be concerned not only with completing a computer-based task, but completing it quickly and accurately, and being generally productive. In order to determine how to address access solutions, functional limitations in the upper extremity can be broken down into the following abilities or capacities: range of motion, strength, endurance, speed, and coordination. Many of these abilities impact each other, so design solutions may be shared among multiple issues. Furthermore, if hand and finger use is not an option, other body parts or functions may be used in the interface process.

13.3.3 Range-of-Motion Issues

Reduced range of motion in the arms, hands, and fingers results in an impaired ability to perform normal movements such as wrist flexion, finger extension and contraction, and bending the elbow. An employee who has reduced range of motion may have trouble reaching all the keys on a standard keyboard, moving a mouse, or pressing down on the keys or mouse buttons. Some individuals with range-of-motion issues might type and use the mouse with only one hand, while others might not be able to type on a keyboard, but can use a mouse. In fact, range-of-motion difficulties may be so severe as to prevent use of the fingers or hands whatsoever. People with reduced range of motion generally benefit from minimizing or eliminating the reach distance for typing or button pushing, and/or the travel distance required to move the cursor. Design characteristics that address these usability requirements include size, layout, and shape of the keyboard and the movement mechanism of the cursor control device.

13.3.3.1 Minimizing Travel: Keyboard Size, Layout, and Shape

Size, layout, and shape of the keyboard affect the distance an individual's hands and fingers have to travel to make selections. Shrinking the size of the keys and bringing them closer together creates a more compact and smaller keyboard overall. This smaller size is frequently easier to use for an individual with decreased range of motion. Alternate layouts, where the numbers, letters, and function keys are arranged in more ergonomic or efficient ways, can also be used to increase access and efficiency. The most commonly known alternate layout is the *Dvorak keyboard*, which was designed with frequently used letters on the home row and is available in left-handed and right-handed versions. Keyboards with articulating sections (the Comfort Keyboard—see Fig. 13.1), curved or domed (the Maltron keyboard—see Fig. 13.2) keyboards, and ergonomic keyboards can address distance through shape, which also affects typing speed, comfort, and accuracy for individuals with reduced range of motion.

13.3.3.2 Eliminating Travel: Keyboard Layout and Onscreen Keyboard

In same cases, travel must be eliminated entirely because of the severity of the functional limitation. This can be done by reducing the number of keys, requiring the user to select multiple keys at once to type. Chordic keyboards have fewer keys—only one for each finger and a couple operated by the thumb, as shown in Figure 13.3. Letters are typed by hitting a combination of keys, similar to playing a musical chord on a piano. Each letter has its own unique chord. This family of keyboards requires good finger coordination and memory. Note that chordic keyboards are also gaining popularity with wearable computing systems—the keyboard is small, and with some designs, the user can both hold the keyboard and type with the same hand.

If an individual is able to operate a mouse or mouse alternative, but does not have enough range of motion to reach all of the keys on even a compact keyboard, a virtual,

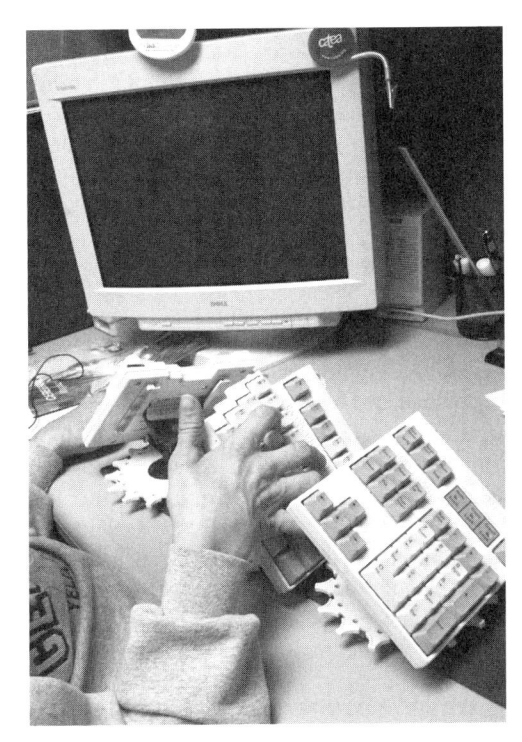

FIGURE 13.1 The Comfort Keyboard is an articulating keyboard that has several adjustments to enable the most comfortable hand position (Comfort Keyboard Company, Inc., http://www.comfortkeyboard.com/).

FIGURE 13.2 The Maltron keyboard is curved to minimize finger travel and facilitate one-handed typing [Applied Learning Corporation (Maltron Keyboard), http://www.maltron.com].

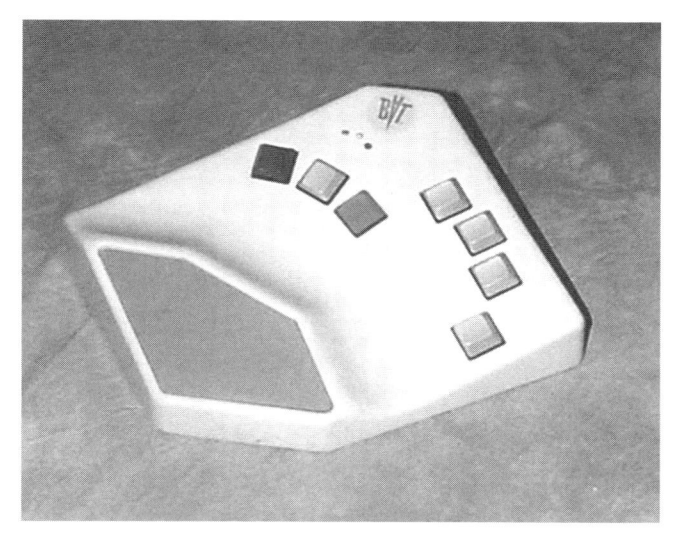

FIGURE 13.3 The BAT is a chordic keyboard that allows users to type by pressing down combinations of keys for each letter. Each finger operates one key; the thumb operates three keys (Infogrip, Inc., http://www.infogrip.com).

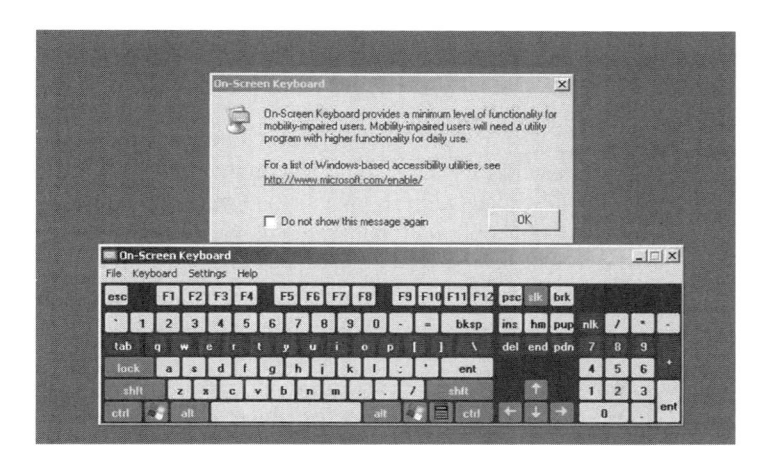

FIGURE 13.4 Onscreen keyboards allow a person to type by pointing to the desired letter with the mouse cursor.

onscreen keyboard may be considered. A picture of a keyboard is shown on the computer screen, and by pointing to a letter and clicking, the letter is typed (see Fig. 13.4). The keyboard that is shown may have a standard QWERTY layout, or it might have a different letter arrangement, show words rather than letters, or be customized for a particular application so that the most frequently used commands are shown.

13.3.3.3 Minimizing or Eliminating Travel: Movement Mechanism of Cursor Control Device

Cursor control settings can be adjusted to minimize or eliminate travel, but in some cases, other hardware is required. Movement mechanisms that minimize or eliminate travel are

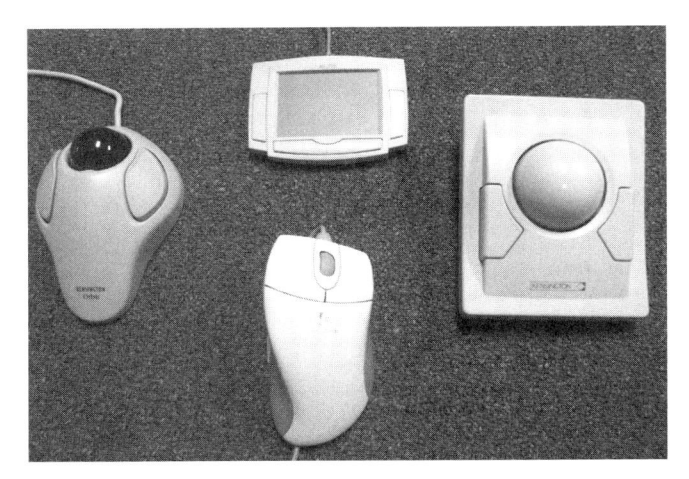

FIGURE 13.5 *A variety of mouse alternatives are available. Here are some examples of trackballs (left and right), a track pad (top), and a contoured mouse (bottom).*

designed to allow the hardware to maintain a fixed position while translating the user's interface actions into cursor movements. Trackballs and touchpads are devices that have this design characteristic (see Fig. 13.5). Trackballs work a bit like an upside-down mouse; instead of rolling the ball on the table by sliding the mouse around, the ball is moved directly by the user. Since the trackball does not need to be grasped, only nudged, an employee may choose to operate it by hand or a single finger, or with his/her chin, elbow, foot, or stick held in the mouth. To operate a touchpad, the employee moves his/her finger, or a stylus, around on a flat tablet. The cursor moves in a corresponding pattern on the screen. Most touchpads require only a small range of motion, and some are as small as 2×2 inches^2. Other options for individuals with range-of-motion issues in their fingers or hands include head tracking technology, joysticks, or scanning software.

13.3.4 Strength Issues

Strength is the amount of intensity, force, or power that an individual has to perform actions such as pressing, pulling, gripping, and squeezing. An employee who has reduced strength may have trouble pressing and holding down the keys and buttons on a keyboard or mouse. The Section 508 standards include an avoidance of tight grasping, pinching, or twisting of the wrist. This includes not just the keyboard and mouse, but also power switches and control buttons or dials on other devices (speakers, CD drive, printer, etc.) Design features that address this issue include using keyboards and cursor control devices that require minimal or no activation force, and using designs that eliminate the need to hold down buttons.

13.3.4.1 Minimizing or Eliminating Activation Force: Membrane Keyboards and Dwell Software

A maximum activation force of 5 lb (22.2 N) is set by Section 508 for all controls and keys. However, some individuals may find that a particular keyboard is still too stiff and requires too much force to operate. Since keyboards can vary in the force required, other keyboards should be tried. For extreme cases, sensitive membrane keyboards can reduce the amount of force needed to type letters. These types of keyboards may require the user to just brush up against each letter, rather than have to press it down.

Cursor control devices can also be chosen that require only minimal force for "clicking." For example, the touchpads described earlier typically will accept taps to the touchpad surface as another means of performing a "click." Another option for cursor control is to use a feature called "dwell click." Some mouse alternatives have a software feature where maintaining a steady position on the screen, or "dwelling," is interpreted as a mouse button click.

13.3.4.2 Eliminating Constant Pressure on Buttons: Drag/Click Lock

A prime example of a design that reduces the need to hold down buttons already exists on standard keyboards—the CAPS LOCK. However, cursor control has its own need for buttons to be held down, usually to perform a "drag" operation. Fortunately, some devices (particularly trackballs) and software have a DRAG or CLICK LOCK button. The user does not need to press a button for the entire time that a "drag" command is being carried out. Instead, text can be highlighted by positioning the cursor at one end of the text, hitting the DRAG button, moving the cursor to the end of the text, and hitting the button again.

13.3.5 Coordination Issues

Coordination is the manner in which muscles send and receive motor control information, and work together to perform actions. Employees who have coordination issues are not always able to control the initiation, accuracy, or termination of a movement. They might not be able to use both hands at the same time, may have spasticity or tremor that impacts precision, or, in severe instances, may not be able to move their hands or fingers at all. These individuals typically benefit from minimizing or eliminating bimanual actions, differentiating or enlarging targets, reducing sensitivity of controls, and increasing precision of controls.

13.3.5.1 Minimizing or Eliminating Bimanual Control: StickyKeys

Capitalization or keyboard commands that require the user to hold down two or more keys simultaneously can be a challenge. Fortunately, access features in the Macintosh and Windows operating systems offer a solution. StickyKeys allows the computer user to press a key (SHIFT, CTRL, or ALT) and subsequently press another letter (in the case of capitalization), rather than pressing both at the same time. StickyKeys works with most programs, but, software designers should consider this access issue, and avoid the use of unusual multikey commands.

13.3.5.2 Differentiating or Enlarging Targets: Keyboard Size and Keyguards

Employees who have trouble with accuracy and precision may need a system that reduces the selection of unwanted keys. Large keyboards can provide users with larger targets (see Fig. 13.6). However, larger targets result in a larger keyboard overall, requiring the user to travel farther to reach all of the keys. If the employee prefers to use a standard-sized keyboard, plastic overlays with finger holes (i.e., keyguards) can be attached to the keyboard. The user can steady his/her hand by resting it on the keyguard itself.

FIGURE 13.6 The Intellikeys is a membrane keyboard that provides large targets to assist users who have trouble with accuracy when typing (Intellitools, Inc., http://www.intellitools.com).

13.3.5.3 Reducing Sensitivity of Controls: FilterKeys and RepeatKeys

There is also software that can be used to adjust the sensitivity of the keyboard so that only intentional keystrokes are registered, and only the desired number of times. SlowKeys (Macintosh) and FilterKeys (Windows) will set the computer so that a key must be held down for a period of time before it registers as an intentional keystroke. This can reduce having extra letters input because they were accidentally bumped. Another access feature, RepeatKeys, prevents the computer from typing a string of letters simply because the person did not lift his/her finger from the key fast enough. In general, Section 508 specifies that the delay before key repeat must be adjustable to at least 2 s.

13.3.5.4 Increasing Precision of Controls: MouseKeys

Many applications require the user to position the cursor on very small targets. In this case, an ability to separate out the tasks of positioning the cursor and operating the mouse buttons may be beneficial. Trackballs with the DRAG button option, described earlier, are one solution. However, sometimes a cursor control method is needed that simply provides the user with very fine control. One method is MouseKeys, a utility included in both Windows and Macintosh operating systems, which enables the individual to use the number keypad for cursor control. For example, "8" moves the cursor up, "1" moves the cursor to the lower left, and so on. MouseKeys also provides a nice cursor control option for people who type with a mouthstick or pointing aid.

13.3.6 Speed and Endurance Issues

Many of the other functional limitations already discussed can impact how fast and how long a person can use the computer. An employee who uses significant physical effort to type or move the cursor may be able to work for only short periods of time, may take longer or become slower and less accurate over time. These individuals can improve speed and possibly work longer if keystrokes, movements, or timed responses are reduced or eliminated. Solutions or design characteristics that might address these usability requirements include software options and activation timing.

13.3.6.1 Reducing or Eliminating Keystrokes: Macros, Abbreviation Expansion, and Word Prediction

Three strategies that are used to reduce the number of keystrokes that a person must type, and thus increase speed, are the use of macros, abbreviation expansion, and word completion/prediction. The first two are similar, but are used for different tasks. *Macros* are shortcuts that will complete a set of commands in response to a set of keystrokes. For example, a macro could be created to open a file and type in the information to begin a letter. *Abbreviation expansion*, on the other hand, enables the user to type in an abbreviation for a word or phrase, and the software spells out the full text on the screen. For example, if an abbreviation could be set up to type "workplace accommodations" every time "wa-" is typed, the result would be a savings of typing 21 characters.

The third method, *word prediction*, involves software trying to guess what the person is typing. Following the last word typed and/or the first few letters of the current word, the computer generates a list of possible words that the person may be typing. The employee can choose the desired word from the list without typing all of the letters in the word. For each of these options, the keystroke savings may involve only a few characters, but for an individual who may have a typing speed of only 50 characters per minute, the increase in speed can be significant.

13.3.6.2 Reducing or Eliminating Timed Responses: Activation Timing

As mentioned earlier, some individuals may need a significant amount of time to respond to prompts. When possible, software and hardware should be designed with little or no set speed for completing tasks. When a timed response is required, however, designers should provide the option to request more time (a Section 508 standard).

13.3.7 Multiple-Access Issues

As mentioned previously, an employee may experience several of these difficulties in combination and possibly be unable to use her/his fingers and hands in any way for typing or cursor control. In these situations, a better solution may be to use other body parts or actions. People with severe motor impairments may use an onscreen keyboard and make their choices with switch-activated scanning or even activity in various parts of the brain. Morse code might also be used. Two of the more frequently used methods for eliminating hand use are the use of tracking systems (e.g., head pointers, eye gaze) and the use of voice input systems. Some of the techniques have already been referred to in previous sections; however, more information will be provided here.

13.3.7.1 Eliminating Hand Use: Tracking Systems

For people who cannot use their hands at all, a combination of hardware and software may be used to track movements of the head or eye to control the cursor head-tracking systems. An infrared or microgyroscope sensor, or perhaps a reflective dot, would be placed on the user's head. These systems measure signals from the sensors, or look at the way light reflects off the dot, to determine whether the user's head is moving up or down, right or left. Eye-tracking systems use the reflection from the retina or other point of reference to determine cursor movement. These systems rely on a camera that must be focused directly on the eye.

13.3.7.2 Eliminating Hand Use: Voice Input Systems

However, one hands-free approach—voice input—is attracting a user base that includes people with severe paralysis along with people with carpal tunnel syndrome. In a survey of people with dexterity limitations, 16% reported using voice input systems at work—more than any other computer access technology for dexterity issues [8]. Voice input computer systems (or speech recognition systems) learn how a particular user pronounces words and uses information about these speech patterns to guess what words are being spoken. Voice input systems usually allow a person to activate program menus via voice commands, and options for mouse control are also available. These systems require training, both of the user on how to use the software and correct recognition errors, and of the software, so that the user's speech profile will be optimized for better recognition. Is voice input the perfect solution for computer access? Input rate varies with the task being performed. Voice *macros*, which enter a whole phrase or paragraph, such as the standard closing on a letter, produce high entry rates, while tasks requiring the spelling of names and addresses result in lower entry rates. Additional time is also needed to check for and correct recognition errors. While some demonstrations produce input speeds that are close to 100 words per minute (wpm), one study found that, for people who had some use of their hands and could access a keyboard with single-finger typing, the time for nontext tasks was significantly slower with speech, and the average rate for entering text was no different with or without speech [9]. This suggests that in practice, voice input may not provide much benefit in terms of productivity for people if they are able to use another method to access the computer. Yet, it should be noted that 37% of the study participants still reported using speech recognition for more than half of their computer tasks, and they used it primarily to reduce upper-extremity pain and fatigue.

13.4 COMPUTER ACCESS FOR PEOPLE WITH VISUAL IMPAIRMENTS

13.4.1 Background

Most people will experience some changes in their ability to see over their lifetimes. Almost 8 million Americans (3.7%) over the age of 15 have difficulty seeing the words in ordinary newspaper print, even with glasses or contact lenses [7]. Over 60% of people with severe visual impairments are 65 years old or older. Vision includes the ability to perceive detail (acuity), color, and contrast, to distinguish objects, and adjust to glare. While most visual changes associated with age can be corrected, visual changes caused by disease, poor health, or injury can cause permanent vision loss. Vision loss can result in blindness (total loss) or low vision (partial loss) and can occur in one or both eyes. Individuals with low vision typically have reduced visual acuity and/or a significantly obstructed field of vision, but may still have some usable vision. Common eye conditions that affect visual abilities are cataracts (producing a visual field that is cloudy), glaucoma (loss of peripheral vision), and macular degeneration (loss of central vision). As a result of the wide variety of visual impairments, a unique set of problems related to computer access exists.

13.4.2 Visual Abilities and Computer Access

In 2001, 52.1% of employees who were blind or had a severe vision impairment reported using a computer at work [10]. Tasks that rely on visual skills include typing, cursor control, reviewing/editing documents, and using software applications. Typically, typing is not an issue for individuals with visual impairments if they are touch typists. However, not everyone can touch-type, and when an individual is not able to clearly see the keys (or see them at all), typing becomes a problem. Physical use of the mouse seldom presents a problem, but it does require that the user see the cursor on the screen to direct cursor movement and target a selection. Output access issues may include how well employees see the text on the monitor, how easily they can interact with vision-intensive, graphical user interfaces (GUIs), and how they review a printout. In a survey of workplace accommodations, 26% of the respondents with visual impairments reported difficulty in reading from a computer monitor—even higher than the responses for reading from paper (24%) [8].

Computer access for people with vision impairments can be significantly affected by acuity and visual field changes. To improve the communication of visual information to a person with acuity and visual field issues, design strategies such as enlargement, enhancement of targets, and alternative output can be helpful. Since the strategies for these difficulties are in many cases similar, they will be described here as solutions for both issues.

13.4.3 Acuity and Visual Field Deficits

Acuity refers to the sharpness of a person's vision, including the ability to read text. For employees who have low vision, legibility of text on the computer and information on the keyboard may be the primary concerns. Legibility will affect work activities such as composing emails, reviewing spreadsheets, and editing documents. *Visual field deficit* or *loss* is a restriction of the visual field. This restriction impairs the ability to vertically and/or horizontally scan, creating difficulty in seeing things as a whole. Visual field abilities will impact the arrangement and placement of text or graphics, and can make cursor control a demanding task.

13.4.3.1 Enhancing Objects and Text: Screen Color and Contrast

Boundaries can create visual separation, making it easier to visually scan and focus. Screen colors and the contrast provided by various combinations of colors can improve visibility. Light colors on dark backgrounds or dark colors on light backgrounds provide the highest contrast. White or yellow text on black or dark blue backgrounds are often preferred among people with low vision, since screens that are too bright can be uncomfortable to use [11]. But there is no one color scheme that works best for all users. Window's Accessibility Options allow users to adjust the computer monitor to their particular color scheme preference, including high-contrast colors.

However, these accessibility options work only for the standard operating systems and programs. Software designers must do their part by avoiding complicated backgrounds and keeping a high contrast between the color of text and the background. When designing a Website, programmers should keep in mind that users might want to view the page using their own color preferences. Web developers should use style sheets to set the look of their pages, but make sure that their pages still work when these style sheets are turned off (a Section 508 standard). This allows users to access the information, but with their own preferences for "look," which might include different colors or font sizes.

FIGURE 13.7 Stickers that make the letters larger and provide high contrast can be attached to a standard keyboard.

13.4.3.2 Enhancing or Enlarging Targets: Keyboard Size and Contrast

Visibility can also be an issue for finding letters on a keyboard. Sometimes, keyboards with larger keys may be used, but people will typically relabel their keyboards with large-print and/or high-contrast stickers over the existing letters, numbers, and function keys, as shown in Figure 13.7. In addition, if an individual requires or prefers tactile markers, Braille keyboards or labels are available.

13.4.3.3 Enlarging Objects and Text: Magnification

For some individuals, high contrast alone may not be enough. For them, screen magnification may provide improved access to a computer. Physical magnifiers that are mounted on a monitor or screen magnification programs can be used depending on the level of magnification required. For people with more significant vision loss, screen magnification is a preferred method for accessing a computer. In a survey of working-age people with visual impairments, 7% used screen magnification software [8]. Although some software, such as the standard Microsoft applications, allow a user to zoom in or out of a page to magnify text up to 500%, screen magnification programs enlarge not only the text in that application, but also icons and graphics. Since the entire image will not fit on the computer once it is magnified, requiring scrolling, programs will often have options to enlarge just the information at the cursor so that the overall layout is still presented (see Fig. 13.8), use a split screen with only part of the image magnified, or may use "tracking bars" to show what part of the screen is being magnified. People considering computer magnification should determine whether it enables them to read at a reasonable speed. If too much effort is needed to just identify each letter, it may be more practical to use other technology, such as screen-reading software.

13.4.3.4 Minimizing or Eliminating Visual-Only Information: Representing Screen Information as Text

The introduction of graphical user interface (GUI) operating systems in the early 1990s posed significant usage challenges for people with visual impairments [13]. Whereas character-oriented interface information did not require a conversion to text in order to

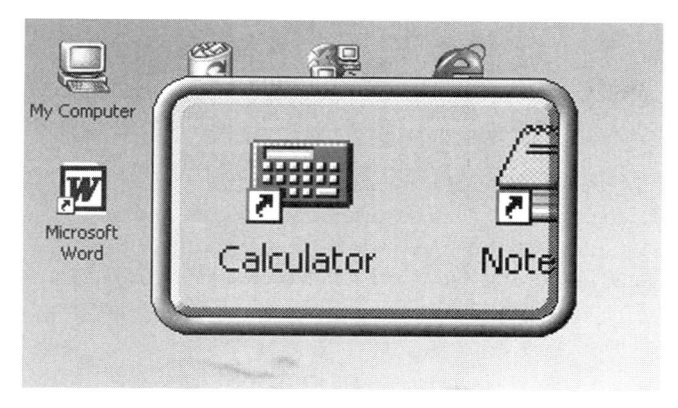

FIGURE 13.8 Screen magnification software can be used to enlarge the information on a computer screen.

be represented via another mode, graphical components consisted only of pixel values that could not be represented easily with text. Microsoft's Active Accessibility solution for this "convert to text" step was to develop tags that were assigned to screen information. For example, label tags can be associated with each icon and with the active window. Today, assistive technology for blind people is compatible with GUI operating systems and most major software applications.

However, software designers need to be aware that users need access to this textual information. Too many applications do not include the Microsoft Active Accessibility tags. Webpages, and even documents, can also pose challenges. For example, Adobe portable document format (PDF) files may not be accessible if they were created by scanning in a page and saving it as an image. Instead, the individual text elements must be stored. Similarly, the information on Webpages should be stored as text rather than images of text whenever possible. Section 508 specifies that every nontext element (e.g., graphics) should be associated with a text equivalent (e.g., ALT tag).

Another rule is to include descriptive labels on hyperlinks and buttons. A descriptive label such as "January Newsletter" in the text of a link is clearer than having a link that just says "click here." Similarly, buttons that are labeled STOP and GO are clearer than buttons that are only shaded red or green. Note that for this last example, having redundant text labels would also assist the 8% of males in the United States who have a color vision deficit, also known as "colorblindness" [13]. Finally, operating pulldown menus, clicking on an item within a folder, and clicking buttons in dialog boxes remain a challenge for employees who cannot see to accurately position the cursor. Screen reader users rely on keyboard commands for controlling both the screen reader and the business application. For example, in Windows, ALT-F followed by S will choose the File-Save menu command. The TAB key will advance a person through the links on a Webpage. Section 508 mandates that software include keyboard controls when appropriate.

13.4.3.5 Minimizing or Eliminating Visual-Only Information: Providing Redundant Audio Information

Once textual information has been provided, screen-reading features or programs can be used to perform audio output. These systems convert the information on the computer screen—including document information, icon labels, dialog boxes, and menu commands—into speech. Screen reading can be built in, but it is typically a third-party program that interprets the information presented on the computer and uses a speech synthesizer to speak the information. The voice may sound mechanical, but the speech needs to be understood only by the user, and speed and clarity are more important than how "human" it sounds.

One problem with screen-reading technology is that it requires training in order to make full use of the features, such as macro capabilities to read specific areas of the screen. Lack of training may be one reason why a recent survey of employees with visual impairments found that older individuals are less likely to use screen-reading technology—no respondents over the age of 65 used it, but it was used by 14% of the respondents who were under 55 [8].

13.4.3.6 Minimizing or Eliminating Visual-Only Information: Providing Redundant Tactile Information

Information may also be provided tactilely, typically by using Braille. Braille is a system of writing that is based on combinations of dots on a six-dot (standard) or eight-dot (technical) grid. Braille can allow users to review material in a character-by-character manner, which is useful when spelling is a concern or when reviewing material such as equations or programming code. Unfortunately, only a small percentage of people who are blind are "fluent" in Braille. In 1993, fewer than 9% of registered blind students could read braille [14], and these numbers are likely to be lower for adults who become blind later in life. Williams et al. [8] found that only 6% of employees with visual impairments used Braille documents, and 4% used Braille displays. Computer access products that employ Braille include keyboards (in which each key represents a dot and chordic input is used to type each letter), conversion programs that prepare text files to be printed in Braille, and various types of Braille printers.

Perhaps the most interesting of these technologies are refreshable Braille displays. These displays typically consist of a single row of eight-dot Braille cells, each of which contain a group of retractable pins. The pins extend to form a Braille letter. As the person continues to read though a document, the display is refreshed, and the pins extend in a different pattern to form a new letter. Displays can be created that represent a full page of text or even an image; however, the cost of the refreshable technology currently makes that prohibitive. Many of these systems provide screen reading along with Braille output.

13.5 COMPUTER ACCESS FOR PEOPLE WHO ARE DEAF OR HARD-OF-HEARING

13.5.1 Background

One in every ten (28 million) Americans has a hearing loss [15]. According to the US Census, almost 8 million Americans (3.8%) over the age of 15 have difficulty hearing conversation [7]. This number is expected to climb and nearly double by the year 2030 as baby boomers reach retirement age. Hearing loss may be conductive (outer ear and middle ear), sensorineural (inner ear), mixed (outer or middle and inner), or central (brain) and can be unilateral, bilateral, fluctuating, stable, progressive, sudden, symmetric, or assymetric. The severity of the loss is measured in decibels (dB) and affects how a person perceives and processes environmental sounds and speech. Hearing loss can be congenitally-related or be caused after birth by disease or infection, ototoxic drugs, exposure to noise, tumors, trauma, and the aging process. Individuals may benefit from assistive listening devices, hearing aids, or cochlear implants depending on the degree and type of hearing loss. Hearing ability varies according to the frequencies and loudness level a person can hear and understand. Keep in mind that more complex sound signals (e.g., speech) may be more difficult for a person with a hearing loss to perceive and understand than simpler sound signals (e.g., alert signals).

13.5.2 Hearing Abilities and Computer Access

Just over half of employees who are deaf or have a severe hearing impairment use a computer at work [10]. For people who are deaf or hard of hearing, the challenge posed with using a computer is related to computer output, specifically auditory output. Access issues may include not knowing when an auditory signal is provided as an alert (e.g., that email has arrived) or not knowing what is being said in audio/videostream multimedia (e.g., in a job training video). While some people who are hard of hearing may be able to hear auditory alerts or understand communication with the use of amplification or a hearing aid, that is not the case for all individuals. Therefore, computer access solutions usually involve presenting information in a method that does not involve hearing.

13.5.3 Perceiving and Understanding Simple and Complex Sounds

Employees who have difficulty perceiving and understanding may be assisted by providing redundant visual communication when auditory information is presented. It should be noted that providing an alternative to auditory information also helps users who may not have sound capability on their computers, are in a public setting, or have turned the volume off on their computers. Specific methods for presenting auditory information include using visual cues and providing text (e.g., captioning, transcript).

13.5.3.1 Minimizing or Eliminating Simple Audio-Only Information: Providing Alerts for Visual Cues

Sometimes, software applications use beeps or tones to indicate that something has happened on the computer. To be usable by a person with a hearing disability, such audio outputs should be accompanied by a video cue or a text equivalent. Windows does this by including an accessibility option called "SoundSentry," which will cause either the caption bar, active window, or desktop to flash when an audio cue is presented. Macintosh has a similar feature. However, this issue still must be addressed by people who are developing software applications or are creating Java applets on the Web.

13.5.3.2 Minimizing or Eliminating Complex Audio-Only Information: Providing Text or Interpretation for Spoken Information

Multimedia files that include speech, such as online movies, Webcasts, or Flash animations, should be captioned to provide a nonauditory means to access the information (a Section 508 standard). Captioning and/or sign language can be provided for users who are deaf or heard of hearing. There are two ways to provide captioning: closed captioning

(CC), which is text made visible only at the discretion of the viewer; and open captioning (OC), which always remains visible for all viewers. Sign language interpretation has become an option as video processing on computers has become quicker. However, not all individuals use the same form of sign language. It is difficult to provide captioning or sign language after the fact on the computer through assistive technology. Instead, the responsibility falls to software and multimedia developers to include captioning as part of their design. Various tools are available to include captioning within the design of multimedia. More recent versions of Flash have a feature to allow the insertion of open captions directly into an animation. Multimedia Access Generator (MAGpie)[5] software developed by the National Center for Accessible Media (NCAM) allows developers to add closed captions to most multimedia files that can be played by Apple QuickTime, Windows MediaPlayer, or RealPlayer.

13.6 COMPUTER ACCESS FOR PEOPLE WITH COGNITIVE IMPAIRMENTS

13.6.1 Background

Cognitive limitations may result from a range of conditions, including developmental disabilities, traumatic brain injury, or stroke. Within the workplace, learning disability is one of the more common conditions. It is estimated that there are almost 3.5 million Americans over the age of 15 with learning disabilities [7]. However, that number may be an underrepresentation, since many adults may have never been formally diagnosed. Among all students with disabilities enrolled at postsecondary education institutions, 46% report having learning disabilities [16]. In Williams' survey of working-age people with cognitive limitations, the functional limitations that they reported included problems with ignoring distractions (41%), sustaining focus (40%), and interpreting information (34%) [8]. In addition, other functional limitations may include deficits with short-term or long-term memory, following directions, organization and planning, literacy and numeracy, spatial relations, and problem solving.

13.6.2 Cognitive Abilities and Computer Access

For a person with a cognitive deficit, most challenges with using a computer are related to the software interface and the tasks of reading and writing. For example, an employee must to be able to choose menu commands from software applications, correctly position a mouse to make selections, write documents that are free of spelling errors, and review text documents. In this section, a sampling of functional abilities and ways of addressing them are discussed, including problem solving and ignoring distractions, spatial relations, literacy, and visual scanning and information processing.

13.6.3 Problem Solving and Ignoring Distractions

As software applications are released with an increasing number of features, the options that are found in control interfaces become more complicated. Employees may have trouble determining what options they want, and may be distracted by long lists of

---
[5]MAGpie—http://ncam.wgbh.org/webaccess/magpie.

choices. In addition, a lack of organization can make it challenging for individuals to find the selections that they want.

13.6.3.1 Simplifying Software Commands: Reducing Options

People with cognitive disabilities can benefit from simplified software commands. For example, a program may have basic, intermediate, and advanced menu settings, where the user can select whether only the most frequently used commands are visible (basic) or whether they all are (advanced). The common practice of "graying out" menu commands that do not fit the current application status is another way to simplify a user interface. An interesting variation of this approach is available with some onscreen keyboards—the software consults its dictionary as the person is typing, and displays only those letters that might follow next in the word. Such strategies can help a person with a cognitive deficit by presenting limited lists of options from which to choose.

13.6.3.2 Simplifying Interfaces: Organization

Simply organizing options can also help some individuals. Software commands and Web navigation should be grouped in a logical manner, and should be consistent throughout the program or Webpage. Another application of this strategy involves keyboards. A person who has trouble finding letters on a QWERTY keyboard may find that an alphabetical key arrangement is easier to use (see Fig. 13.9).

FIGURE 13.9 Several different layouts are available for keyboards. The top keyboard has an alphabetic layout; the lower one has a frequency-of-use layout.

13.6.4 Visuospatial Deficits

Individuals with visuospatial impairment have great difficulty localizing objects in two- and three-dimensional space. This means that they can have depth perception problems and may not be able to judge distances very well. Typically, cursor movement occurs through an indirect control method such as using a mouse or other device. However, indirect control can be challenging for a person with impaired visuospatial abilities. To overcome this barrier, it is important to provide direct control, which essentially simplifies the persons's task of making selections.

13.6.4.1 Minimizing or Eliminating Indirect Control: Direct-Control Interfaces

Direct controls can be provided through voice control and actual contact with graphics or words on the monitor. Voice control is not common as a cursor control interface, but does warrant mentioning. With voice control, a person can speak directional commands (e.g., left, right), recite keywords (e.g., "open email"), or select hotspots such as specific words or letters. Touchscreens are a form of direct control—a person makes selections by pointing to where an icon is displayed on the monitor. Some monitors have this feature built in (e.g., the screens on ATM machines), but clear, pressure-sensitive devices that fit over the face of a regular monitor also exist.

13.6.5 Literacy

Reading and writing are the main literacy components that affect use of the computer. Work tasks such as reading emails, word processing, and Internet searching can be arduous, time consuming, and frustrating at the very least for individuals with cognitive impairments. Software programs that provide literacy support, including cueing and auditory output, can be helpful for reading and writing difficulties.

13.6.5.1 Enhancing Literacy Support: Providing Spelling and Grammar Cues

People with cognitive disabilities can often benefit from supportive strategies, particularly those related to spelling and grammar. Spellcheck features, however, should have only a short list of options, and grammar check programs should present clear explanations for changes to avoid confusion [17]. Some people also use word prediction, described earlier as a technique for enhancing typing speed, as a means to provide spelling cues. If the user is better at reading than spelling, but can figure out the first few letters of a word, the computer can present a list of possible words, and the person can choose the one that they were trying to spell. The person may spend a fair amount of time, however, reviewing word lists. Voice input technology has also been used with learning-disabled people; however, the benefit provided from not having to spell words is sometimes lost due to the training required to use the system, and the need to focus on details such as misrecognized words.

13.6.5.2 Enhancing Literacy Support: Providing Redundant Multimodal Information

If an employee has difficulty reading or typing information because of literacy issues, providing that information in audio form may be beneficial. Voice output can be integrated into programs or can be accomplished through add-on programs such as text to speech and screen readers. Text to speech programs use speech synthesizers to speak the letters, numbers, words, and sentences that are typed. Screen readers can be used to speak words, sentences, and paragraphs in menus, dialog boxes, documents, emails, and Webpages for reading tasks. Voice output programs for individuals with literacy issues have several differences compared to those for people with visual impairments. The programs highlight words as the text is read so that the individual can follow along, and more "human-sounding" voices may be used. In addition, the software is typically controlled with a mouse and with simplified pulldown menus rather than entirely through keyboard controls that must be memorized.

13.6.6 Visual and Auditory Information Processing

Finally, people with cognitive disabilities may have trouble interpreting information, and they may find that it is easier to process and remember information that is presented by audio and/or visual modes. Strategies used by people with visual or hearing impairments may help make the information easier to understand.

13.6.6.1 Enhancing Visual Display: Using Color and Contrast to Improve Visibility

Many of the strategies used to provide access for people with sensory limitations are the same as those used by people who have trouble interpreting information. Some people find it easier to focus on text when it is presented in certain colors than in others. Larger font sizes and line spacing can also help some people keep their place while reading. Therefore, adjustments to screen colors, contrast, and object size may be useful, even if the employee does not have a specific vision limitation.

13.6.6.2 Minimizing Use of Visual-Only or Audio-Only Information: Providing Redundant MultiModal Information

Employees who have auditory or visual processing deficits may find that providing information in multiple modalities can be useful if they can more easily understand and remember information that is presented in one mode versus another. In these situations, some of the techniques described in previous sections such as screen reading, captioning, and audio and visual cues may be useful.

13.7 NEW OPPORTUNITIES

Advances in technology will lead to new options that hopefully incorporate universal design to better address the computer disabilities discussed in this chapter. It will be important for emerging and future computer interaction techniques to take into account the various abilities of the user population, the array of activities to be completed, and the diversity of environments in which the activities will be completed. Some research and development (R&D) efforts have already begun to focus on more flexible computer interfaces, such as projected keyboards, motion tracking, brain control, and haptic devices. First, keyboards that utilize red-light laser diodes for projection are already available for mobile phones,[6] and offer the possibility of keyboards that can not only be positioned

---
[6] VBK Keyboard—http://www.virtual-laser-keyboard.com.

anywhere but also be available in any size and layout. For people who need to operate a computer without their hands, motion tracking provides options. A computer camera may be used to capture images of a feature on the user's body and track movements by measuring changes in that image [18]. Brain control opens up computer access for people who have very little controlled movement. Electrodes are used to measure brain activity, and these signals can be used to control horizontal and vertical mouse movements. Finally, haptic technology has the potential for providing another way of presenting graphical information to people with visual impairments. The mouse or stylus of the haptic device is mounted on an arm that provides resistance or vibrates as the cursor is moved over various lines on the screen. As these technologies come to market, they will likely meet the needs of many different computer users, including those with disabilities. There is also a new movement toward universal design in software. Since the development of their GUI operating systems, Microsoft Corp. has used an accessibility model called *Microsoft Active Accessibility* (MSAA). At the time of writing this book, a new model, *User Interface Automation* (UI automation) was being introduced for Windows XP and Windows Vista [19]. The goal of this new accessibility model is to move toward a single accessibility standard that will be used across various operating systems. This move toward an industry standard will hopefully result in more applications being written to include accessibility features.

Finally, this chapter has reviewed computer access in the workplace, but many of the issues addressed apply to other forms of electronic and information technology (EIT), such as PDAs and cell phones. Already, assistive technology such as magnifying screens and word prediction for PDAs, and screen-reading features for specialized cell phones have been created. Fortunately, some universal design features have also been included in some products, including backlit displays for high contrast, text messaging as an alternate communication mode, and voice-activated dialing. Through the use of these assistive technology and universal design features, EIT in general is being made more accessible, and is providing access to the workplace for people with disabilities.

ACKNOWLEDGMENTS

This chapter was written by the Rehabilitation Engineering Research Center on Workplace Accommodations, which is supported by Grant H133E020720 from the National Institute on Disability and Rehabilitation Research, US Department of Education.

REFERENCES

1. Bruyere SM, Erickson W, VanLooy S: Information technology (IT) accessibility: Implications for employment of people with disabilities, *Work* **27**(4):397–406 (2006).
2. Forrester Research, Inc: Findings about computer users, in *The Wide Range of Abilities and Its Impact on Computer Technology*, Microsoft Corporation, 2003.
3. Butterfield TM, Ramseur JH: Research and case study findings in the area of workplace accommodations including provisions for assistive technology: A literature review, *Technol Disab*, **16**(4):201–210 (2004).
4. World Wide Web Consortium: *Web Accessibility Initiative: Web Content Accessibility Guidelines [WCAG] 1.0. W3C*, 1999 (retrieved 2/06 from www.w3.org/TR/WAI-WEBCONTENT/).

5. Mace R, Hardie G, Place J: Accessible environments: Toward universal design, in White ET, ed, *Innovation by Design*, Van Nostrand Reinhold, New York, 1991.
6. Center for Universal Design: *The Principles of Universal Design, Version 2.0*, North Carolina State University, Raleigh, 1997.
7. McNeil J: *Americans with Disabilities: Household Economic Studies*, US Census Bureau, Washington, DC, 2001.
8. Williams M, Sabata D, Zolna J: User needs evaluation of workplace accommodations, *Work* **27**(4):355–362 (2006).
9. Koester HH: Usage, performance, and satisfaction outcomes for experienced users of automatic speech recognition, *J Rehab Res Devel* **41**(5):739–754 (2004).
10. National Telecommunications and Information Administration. Computer and Internet use among people with disabilities, in *A National Online: How Americans Are Expanding Their Use of the Internet*, US Department of Commerce, Washington, DC, 2002.
11. Department for Education and Skills: *Adult Literacy Core Curriculum—Blind or Partially Sighted*, 2006 (retrieved 2/06 from www.dfes.gov.uk/curriculum_literacy/access/sight).
12. Ratanasit D, Moore MM: Representing graphical user interfaces with sound: a review of approaches, *J Visual Impair Blind* **99**(2):69–83 (2005).
13. National Federation of the Blind: *Color Vision Deficiency*, 2005. (retrieved 2/06 from www.preventblindness.org/resources/factsheets/ColorVision_FS56.PDF).
14. Jernigan K, ed: *If Blindness Comes*, National Federation of the Blind, 1994.
15. Self Help for Hard of Hearing People: *Facts on Hearing Loss*, 2004 (retrieved 2/06, from www.shhh.org/html/hearing_loss_fact_sheets.html).
16. National Center for Education Statistics: *An Institutional Perspective on Students with Disabilities in Postsecondary Education*, US Department of Education, Washington, DC, 1999.
17. Milchus KL: Computer applications for students with learning disabilities, *Proc RESNA '93 Natl Conf*, Las Vegas, NV, 1993.
18. Gips J, Betke M, Fleming P: The camera mouse: Preliminary investigation of automated visual tracking for computer access, *Proc RESNA 2000 Natl Conf*, Orlando, FL, 2000.
19. Taft DK: Microsoft changes its accessibility model, *eWeek* **22**(47):26 (2005).

14

Platforms and Operating System Accessibility

Barry Feigenbaum and Kip Harris
IBM Human Ability and Accessibility Center

14.1 INTRODUCTION

It is important for IT applications to be usable by all people, regardless of ability or disability. We say that an application is *accessible* to *persons with disabilities* (PwD) when the application is usable by people who may need the aid of one or more alternative input/output devices, which are called *assistive technologies* (AT). Accessibility can only be achieved if the platform that the application runs on is itself accessible and supplies services to the application and AT to help the total solution to be accessible.

In addition to the social imperative, support for PwDs can be a critical market success factor for IT products. A study in 2003 concluded that more than half of all working-age adults are likely to benefit from the use of assistive technologies [1]. Many accessibility features also improve the usability of systems both when they are used in nontraditional ways, such as outside of an office or home environment, and traditionally, where they can improve user productivity and user satisfaction.

Consider the possibility that anyone can be temporarily or situationally disabled. A person with an injured hand might be unable to activate multiple key combinations. A person in a noisy environment might be unable to hear the audio output of an application. Another major factor is the general aging of the population worldwide. With age, many cognitive, mobility, and perceptive issues become more significant and people will require ATs to help compensate. Support for this ever-increaing customer base looks like a good business investment.

The Engineering Handbook of Smart Technology for Aging, Disability, and Independence,
Edited by A. Helal, M. Mokhtari and B. Abdulrazak
Copyright © 2008 John Wiley & Sons, Inc.

14.1.1 Components of an Accessible Solution

Accessible IT solutions are dependent on the availability of more than one kind of input/output device through which a user can interact with an application. Consider, for example, the graphical user interface (GUI). The GUI approach depends on the end user's ability to view the screen. However, an end user who is blind will not be able to view the display or position the mouse. Ideally, a range of options should be available to the end user that permit access to the IT application through those modes of interaction that best suit that person's preferences. For example, a blind end user may need to have the contents of the display presented by a screen reader that operates a Braille or *text-to-speech* output device.

The ability to supply alternate input and output devices for the IT user interface is the key enabler for constructing accessible solutions. An accessible solution provides exactly this capability. Figure 14.1 shows the three interrelated elements that are required in any such solution:

1. The *platform*, which provides basic accessibility support and interfaces for applications to use.
2. The *application*, which uses the platform interfaces and good user interface design to enable accessibility.
3. *Assistive technologies*, which provide alternative user interfaces that meet the needs of PwDs. As part of delivering an alternate user interface, ATs frequently operate alternative input and output devices.

This chapter deals primarily with issues related to the platform and its support for accessibility.

14.1.2 Platforms

A *platform* is a software environment on which an application can run. A platform defines a unique set of *application programming interfaces* (APIs) and runtime protocols (such as the application's responsibilities for handling an event). An operating system

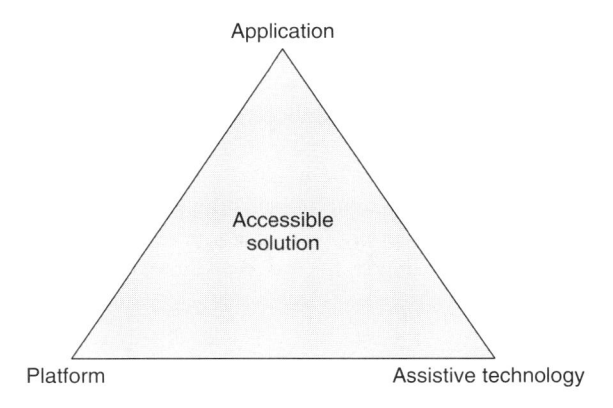

FIGURE 14.1   Three components of an accessible IT solution.

is perhaps the most straightforward example of a platform. So, for example, Microsoft Windows [2] XP [2] and its embedded set of runtime libraries is one platform, while the Fedora Core 4 [2] distribution of Linux [2] and runtimes is another.

Sometimes the platform is one or more software layers that run on top of an operating system. Examples of this latter scenario include the Java [2] platform, which runs on any of a large number of operating systems, and the Eclipse [2] platform, which itself happens to run on top of Java. Web browsers, such as Microsoft's Internet Explorer [2] and Mozilla's FireFox [2], also can be considered as application platforms. Figure 14.2 shows the layered relationship of some of these platform components.

Ideally, the platform would provide all the features that are needed to make an accessible solution, in which case the application could be developed without any special focus on accessibility concerns. However, this is not feasible with current technology. The platform cannot provide all the information needed by the AT to provide alternative interfaces. Also, the scope of hardware and software requirements that ATs need to satisfy is large and diverse, and most platforms cannot satisfy them all. Thus an accessible solution is achieved only when the platform and all applications running on the platform are participating in the accessibility framework, providing the end user with a broad range of ATs through which to access the applications.

14.2 GRAPHICAL USER INTERFACES

Many modern platforms and applications have GUIs. Modern operating systems support GUI libraries to enable applications to present these GUIs. In some cases these libraries are so integrated into the operating system they appear as an integrated subsystem. This is the case for the Microsoft *Windows* family of operating systems. In other cases the GUI libraries have been added over time and have separate identities (even if they come bundled with the operating system). Examples of this latter arrangement include the X-Windows [2] library for UNIX [2] and the libraries built on it such as Motif [2], GNOME [2], and KDE [2].

GUIs are created by composing user interface elements in a hierarchy. User interface elements are also known as widgets, controls, or components. A *widget* is a piece part; it has a state, a visual presentation of that state, a set of events that it generates, and a set of input events it responds to. Widgets are either base level (such as a label or text field) or composites (also called *containers*) that hold other widgets. In some GUI libraries, such

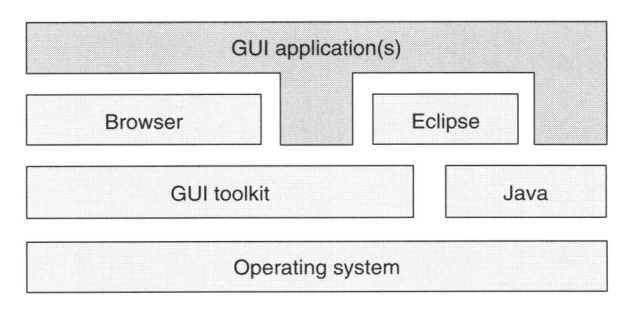

FIGURE 14.2 Platform component layers.

as Windows or Eclipse, widgets are supported by function in the host operating system, while in others, such as Java Swing [2], widgets are created (rendered) independently from the host operating system. These differences in implementation can significantly impact the accessibility of GUIs built with these different GUI libraries.

Current GUIs generally require fine-motor control to operate a pointing device (such as a mouse), good hearing to respond to auditory alerts, and good vision to see and perceive the information displayed on the computer's screen. To be accessible, GUI-based applications must support ATs that replace the mouse input, audio output and displayed output.

14.2.1 Application Enablement

Being "enabled for accessibility" means that the platform and application have done all that is needed to allow an AT to provide an appropriate alternate user interface. An application must have a well-formulated GUI design, and each widget in the GUI must provide, by default or through APIs, access to all of the widget's state, behavior, and any supplemental information provided to enhance an alternate presentation.

14.2.2 Assistive Technologies

Platforms need to provide support for, or enable, ATs that provide alternative user interfaces. These ATs can be supplied with the platform or be provided separately. Some operating systems platforms provide built-in ATs for keyboard access (such as an onscreen keyboard) and mouse access (such as mouse keys). Operating systems often also provide default enablement for standard GUI widgets, so that an application has some level of enablement by default. For example, some platforms automatically use any text associated with a button widget as the text to present to a user through any screen reader when the user interface has focus on the button.

Each platform should enable support for ATs for all the disabilities users may have. Modern operating systems platforms usually enable ATs for at least these disabilities:

- Hand and arm motor disabilities
- Differences in color perception
- Low or no vision
- Low or no hearing
- Certain cognitive disabilities

14.3 DEVICE SUPPORT

Most platforms provide settings to control the devices that are most important to accessible solutions. Microsoft Windows provides an accessibility control dialog (Fig. 14.3) for this purpose. Other platforms usually provide similar dialogs. The range and type of parameters is platform-dependent. End-user control over these parameters is critical to the usability of a platform, especially for PwDs. As we survey these devices, we will note the device settings that must be configurable through user and/or programmatic control.

FIGURE 14.3 Microsoft Windows accessibility control dialog box.

14.3.1 Keyboard Support

From an accessibility perspective the keyboard is one of the most important input devices. Keyboards, or keyboard alternatives, can be used by the widest class of PwDs. Keyboards can be used to emulate other input devices, such as mice. Also, much of the input to computers continues to be textual in nature. Thus it is critical that platforms provide support for keyboard and keyboard-like input. It is also critical that platforms allow alternates to keyboards to be used. Generally this is achieved for the platform by the alternative device emulating the keyboard's hardware interface.

The platform must provide user-configurable settings that provide these features:

- Keyboard repeat rate and repeat start delay
- Key debounce delay
- Suppression (or filtering) of frequently mistyped pairs of keys
- Converting combined keys into a key sequence
- Augmented feedback when changing state, such as SHIFT and CAPS LOCK
- Enablement and/or provision of onscreen keyboards
- Ability to replace of the keyboard with alternate devices

14.3.2 Pointing Device Support

Graphical user interfaces require the selection of small, visually displayed elements. This can be a challenge for a person with restricted hand mobility, hand tremors, or vision impairment. At least three techniques are used to overcome these problems:

1. Emulating a pointing device. The arrow keys on the keyboard can act as mouse motion. Other keys, such as ENTER, can act as mouse buttons. Other examples include mouth-operated joysticks and head-tracking devices.

2. Replacing pointing-device-based navigation with alternative navigation methods. For example, widgets can be selected through keyboard actions. This is best done when the widget is labeled by a keyboard *mnemonic*, which is a single-character shortcut that activates the control. Consider the "Save" button in Figure 14.4. The underlined "S" character indicates a mnemonic. The button can be triggered just by pressing "s" anywhere outside the "File name" text field. An *accelerator* is a mnemonic that can be triggered even if the containing environment is not active. This is especially helpful for actions in menus, as shown in the dropdown menu of Figure 14.5. The "Print" choice can be accessed directly (without showing the menu) by pressing "Ctrl + P" while not in the menu. If no mnemonic is supplied, the user must traverse some navigation path to reach the widget, often pressing "Tab" until the input focus reaches the widget, which is both a usability and productivity issue. If the widget is not part of any navigation path, it will be inaccessible.

3. Activating widgets without a pointing device. Once selected, many widgets can be manipulated. Any action that can be invoked with a pointing device also needs to be invokable with a keyboard action. For example, a "click" action on a button can be emulated by pressing the space bar. Also, selecting an item must be separate from activating any item. With a mouse this is often distinguished by a single vs. double mouse click. Key selections, such as by the arrows keys and activation by the ENTER key (on the keyboard) are typically supported equivalents.

For pointing devices, the platform must provide user configurable settings to

- Enable mouse movement and mouse button selection through the keyboard.
- Change the responsiveness of the mouse to movement
- Change the meaning of any mouse buttons

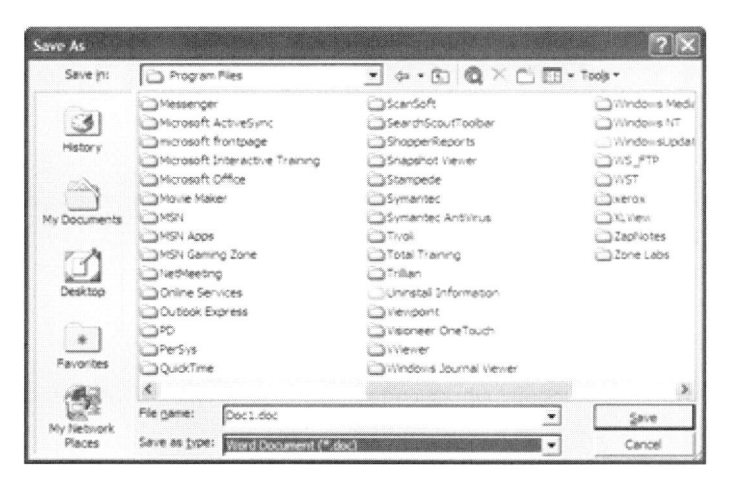

FIGURE 14.4 Example of mnemonic use in a dialog.

FIGURE 14.5 A drop-down menu accelerator assignments.

- Change the responsiveness of the mouse buttons
- Change the appearance and tracking history of the mouse
- Provide mouse location assistance
- Enable replacement of the mouse with alternate devices

14.3.3 Sound Support

Many platforms allow applications to present auditory information to users. This use of audio can span from simple alert tones to speech output to high-fidelity music. Most modern platforms provide rich user interaction, often employing multimedia techniques (such as combined audio/visualstreams). All of these uses of sound can be an issue for a person with reduced or no hearing. Platforms must provide alternative presentation of this audio information, especially if that information is critical to using the system.

Often platforms will use a short tone (or "beep") to alert the user of some need for action. Sometimes the system stops processing until the user responds. If the user cannot hear the beep, then this notification is a problem. Several solutions have been taken to address this issue. Examples include

- Provide a visual equivalent to the beep. A visual indicator, such as a flashing symbol, is used to indicate to the user that attention is required. The indicator is removed when the event is acknowledged.
- Provide a time-out to proceed. The system automatically proceeds with a default choice if the user does not respond in time. This can result in incorrect behavior.

If the system is providing speech output, alternate forms, such as a text transcript, should be provided. This allows the user to read the information instead of hearing it. This is similar to the *closed captioning* provided with many television programs.

If the system is providing combined audio/visual information, such as for help or as part of other application output, there needs to be an alternate presentation. Some content, such as music, may not have rich alternates, but all reasonable attempts should be made to provide useful alternatives.

14.3.4 Display Support

Graphical user interfaces utilize the very high rate of information transfer that is possible in still and animated images. They make many assumptions about the user's ability to perceive the entire GUI as a whole, and simultaneously interpret the GUI images as a collection of smaller logical groups, such as windows, controls, and text. This can result in many issues for persons with limited or no sight or persons with some cognitive disabilities. Platforms must provide ways for alternative presentations of this visually oriented information to be presented. There are many ways to do this; the most common methods are outlined here.

14.3.4.1 Configurable Display Characteristics

All platforms should provide features for user-selectable color palettes, display resolution, and color density. Users should also be able to control the shape, size, color, and blink rate of the cursor, as well as the system fonts. Assistive technologies such as screen magnifiers can provide even greater control over these parameters.

14.3.4.2 Additional Text Content for Alternate UI

In this approach, specific descriptive text and navigational metainformation is authored specifically for consumption by the alternate UI. An AT can present this information to the user in place of the image content. A typical example is the HTML <IMG> tag. An additional attribute, ALT, is added to hold this text, such as

```
<IMG SRC=....\myimage.gif
    ALT="A textural description of the image">
```

This approach is problematic for rapidly changing visual displays, such as movies and other real-time videostreams. Often it is difficult to provide enough alternative text to represent the changing images in the small window of time that is provided. Frequently the AT must present the information more slowly than in real time.

14.3.4.3 Accessing the Underlying Application Model

In this approach, the platform (or application) exposes the data model to the AT. With this much richer information, the AT can determine the best way to present the data in the model. For example, consider a pie chart image showing the results of five sales regions (see Fig. 14.6). This image might have an alternate description of "Sales results per region," which clearly does not convey nearly the full information content of the image. The pie chart was probably created from a simple table of regions and sales per region (see Table 14.1). If the AT had access to this table, it could provide a much more complete presentation of the information.

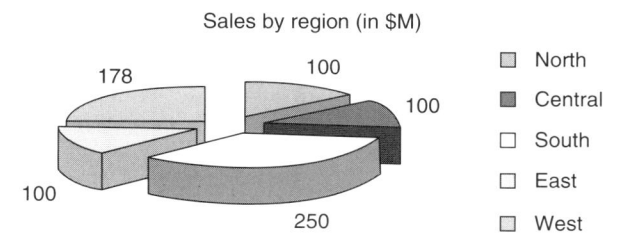

FIGURE 14.6 *Pie chart example of data presentation to AT.*

TABLE 14.1 Sales by Region

North	100
Central	100
South	250
East	100
West	178

14.3.4.4 Accessibility Architecture and APIS

Accessible platforms must provide a way for applications to export information about their user interfaces to AT products, and for ATs to observe state changes in the UI components. Additionally, they must provide for the AT device-independent access to applications. The programming interfaces and communication protocols associated with these facilities is called *platform accessibility architecture*. Platform architects carry the major responsibility for defining this architecture. It is critical that all platforms provide a public accessibility architecture and application programming interfaces (API).

Brunet et al. [3] present an analysis of the fundamental requirements that accessibility needs place on platform architecture. Highlights of that analysis are described in the following subsections.

14.3.5 Support for MVC Design Pattern

Good accessibility architectures implement the well-known and widely supported model–view–controller (MVC) design pattern. The MVC pattern creates a clear separation between the model, the view, and the control component of any GUI. A model reflects how the content and state of a GUI are maintained. Models can exist at many levels (see Fig. 14.7). At the lowest level each widget has its own model. At a middle level, models exist for a grouping of widgets, such as a whole dialog. At the highest levels, each application has one or more models of the data it maintains. Views are the actual presentation of the model. Any model can have zero or more views displayed at any time. Views often listen to models so that they can sense any change to the model and update themselves accordingly. The controller is the glue that unites the model and the view. It is responsible for making changes to the model on the basis of user inputs and updating any views that do not listen to the models directly.

The MVC pattern is so important because it allows ATs to provide either augmented or replacement views and/or controllers for all the models in a GUI. The ability to replace

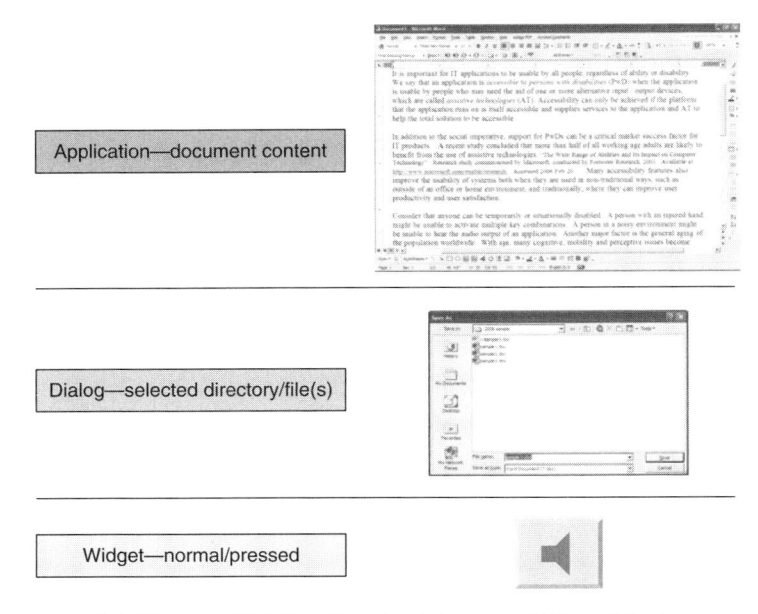

FIGURE 14.7 Models at three levels in accessibility architecture.

views makes ATs possible. Most accessible architectures are just the means by which ATs can add alternate implementations of views and/or controllers to existing user interfaces.

14.3.6 Access to Application Object Model

As noted in Brunet et al. [3], "The platform accessibility architecture must enable programmatic access to an object model for an application through a well-defined, public interface. Assistive technologies use this feature to access the semantic information in an application."

The simplest approach to providing an object model is to expose the normal widget APIs to ATs. While this might be attractive from a widget development cost perspective, it is a poor choice. As many ATs are not part of the application for which they are supplying an alternate user interface, it would be less than ideal (for design, development, and maintenance) if the AT would need to be so closely coupled with the application. Instead, abstraction and isolation interfaces are needed.

For this reason most platforms offer an accessibility API that provides an accessible object model that is often parallel to the normal widget hierarchy. Some examples of this are the technologies in Microsoft Active Accessibility [2] (MSAA) [4], Java Accessibility [5], GNOME Accessibility Project (GAP) [6], and Eclipse Standard Widget Toolkit (SWT) Accessibility APIs [7].

Accessible APIs can be either in-process or out-of-process. *In-process* APIs support ATs that run in the same process as the application. This mode is typically used for self-sufficient applications that provide their own ATs. These APIs tend to be easier to program to and require less overhead and thus result in more responsive ATs.

Out-of-process APIs support ATs that run in separate processes. These APIs tend to be more complex (they often resemble distributed APIs) and tend to be slower and less responsive. This mode is typically used when ATs are supplied by the platform or third parties and are shared across all applications.

14.3.7 Introspection/Discovery Capability

The platform accessibility architecture must provide some mechanism through which the AT can discover the complete set of invokable actions that a user interface element supports. Furthermore, all features of a user interface element should be invokable through a programmatic interface (vs. availability only through an invocation sequence that depends on a single device). Without this capability, the end user of an alternate user interface might not be able to determine, or to trigger, the full set of features that are available on a particular user control.

14.3.8 Relationships among User Interface Elements

An end user interprets a user interface by examining both the collection of widgets on the display and the relationships among those objects. A user interface depends not only on the widgets in the UI but also on the relationships among the widgets. For example, most of the information in a map is contained in the relationships among the locations depicted, that is, in the connections among the locations. Graphs and drawings are commonly employed user interface paradigms in the more knowledge-intensive applications. The platform architecture must support communication of the relationships that are depicted by such paradigms to assistive technologies.

14.3.9 Event Protocols and Event Semantics

The accessibility architecture must support a messaging framework (or event system) through which the AT is informed of state changes in the application. For example, buttons fire selection events and text widgets fire text changed events. ATs need to monitor these events to present them, as appropriate, in their alternate user interface.

The platform architecture must also permit the AT to monitor and modify user input events. The need to emulate both keyboard and mouse input has already been discussed, and the event system must support this by allowing the AT to intercept and modify the stream of events generated by both devices.

14.3.10 Roles and States: Key Attributes on Accessible UI Elements

Most accessible architectures include the notion of roles for user interface widgets. The role defines the basic function of the widget such that an AT can determine how to process the widget. Most platforms support dozens of roles, where each role identifies one of the widget types provided by that platform. In some platforms the roles are nearly one-to-one with the widget types. For example, some roles are Button, Menu, ComboBox, ListItem, Tree, TableColumn, and Text. As a real-world example, see the following list, which is a sample subset of the 56 roles supported by the Java Swing GUI toolkit:

CHECK_BOX	A choice that can be checked or unchecked and provides a separate indicator for the current state.
DIALOG	A top level window with title bar and a border.
ICON	A small fixed size picture, typically used to decorate components.
LABEL	An object used to present an icon or short string in an interface.
LIST	An object that presents a list of objects to the user and allows the user to select one or more of them.
LIST_ITEM	An object that presents an element in a list.
MENU	An object usually found inside a menu bar that contains a list of actions the user can choose from.
MENU_ITEM	An object usually contained in a menu that presents an action the user can choose.
PANEL	A generic container that is often used to group objects.
PUSH_BUTTON	An object the user can manipulate to tell the application to do something.

One major issue with roles is that they tend to be created by the platform authors who define the accessibility architecture and APIs. There is generally no mechanism for third-party widget developers to extend the set of roles. Thus, when there are new innovations in GUI widgets, often there is no standard way to identify them to ATs, frequently resulting in poor support for these new widget types. A new approach for handling this issue is reviewed later in this chapter.

Assistive technologies need to be able to present the state of widgets. For this to be possible, the AT must be able to query all the content and state of the widget. Consider, for example, a simple text field widget. The AT must be able to access, typically via an API, the current text that the user has entered into the field. If the text has any special attributes, such as multiple fonts, or actionable content, such as hyperlinks, they must be included in the information returned. Other states, such as the enabled state of the widget or selected ranges of text, must also be available via APIs. This is an area where many existing accessibility architectures are lacking. Few provide accessibility APIs that can access all of the state of the widgets they support.

14.3.11 User Interface Navigation

One significant challenge for AT is the support of navigation to widgets that do not accept focus. Absent any AT, focus is normally reserved for widgets that accept keyboard input; output-only controls tend to not accept focus. This can be a problem with labels (also called *static text*) that provide instructions on how to use the other widgets in the GUI. Another example is scrollbars. Sometimes they don't accept focus, so the GUI cannot be scrolled by the keyboard. Platform architectures need to enable ATs for support of these types of actions on nonfocusable widgets.

Efficient navigation is critical to productive use of a GUI. If the GUI has many widgets, shortcuts to critical widgets are needed. As mentioned earlier, keyboard mnemonics and accelerators can help reduce the number of tabs needed to move around the GUI. Most architectures create a tab order based on a top–down, left–right traversal of the widgets in a GUI based on the order the widgets are added to the GUI. This may have no relationship to the physical placement of the widgets or the logical order of the widgets.

Accessibility architectures should also offer a means to change the tab order via an API so that GUI designers can explicitly set the desired order.

14.4 PLATFORM ACCESSIBILITY ARCHITECTURES IN USE TODAY

We now explore several platform accessibility APIs in more detail. We chose these architectures because they are popular and illustrate a variety of in-process and out-of-process APIs.

14.4.1 Microsoft Active Accessibility (MSAA)

Microsoft Active Accessibility is the architecture that Microsoft features on all pre-Vista operating systems (i.e., Windows 95 through Windows XP and Windows Server 2003). It was the first widely adopted accessibility framework. Many of the features and design patterns in this framework were adopted later on other platforms.

MSAA is a COM-based technology that defines a generic object model for representing a user interface. As such, it is an out-of-process API. The *IAccessible* definition defines the key object type in this framework. Generally, every user interface element in an application is exposed to assistive technology through a unique instance of a parallel *IAccessible* object. An *IAccessible* instance includes

- Role and state information.
- Name of the object instance—for example, a pushbutton will expose the text on the button through the *name* attribute.
- Value—for example, the value of an editable text control would be the current text in the control.
- (x,y) location of the user interface element on the display.
- References to parent, child, and sibling *IAccessible* objects.

IAccessible provides methods for invoking the default behavior of the widget being exposed (this is usually the same behavior as a "click" on the user interface element would invoke), and to set selection and focus states.

In addition to the object model definition, MSAA defines an event system through which assistive technology can obtain notification of changes in the object model. Some events are fired by the intrinsic MSAA support that is built into Windows, whereas other events must be fired by the specific MSAA support for individual control instances.

The properties and behavior of an *IAccessible* implementation are unique for each class of control. The interface must be implemented for each class, and each implementation is referred to as an *MSAA server*. Microsoft distributes MSAA servers for the common controls that are distributed with the Windows operating system, but if a third-party vendor develops a custom control, they must also provide a corresponding MSAA server for the control to be accessible through MSAA. Such support has been implemented by many application programs, including IBM Lotus Notes [8,9], Adobe Acrobat [2,10], Macromedia Flash [2,11], and the Mozilla Firefox [2] browser [12].

MSAA is by far the most widely implemented architecture at the time of this writing. It is the basis for many solutions that deliver reasonable alternate user interfaces, particularly whe the original user interfaces use straightforward, common UI design paradigms.

MSAA (as well as other current accessibility architectures) becomes less satisfactory as a solution basis when stressed by the following factors.

- *Richness.* The *IAccessible* is generally the only interface available to expose a user interface element under MSAA. Consequently, every type of user interface element, from a progress indicator to the depiction of a node in a graph, must be represented within the vocabulary provided by *IAccessible*. This is very restrictive, even when considering only popular software in use today. AT implementations frequently must exploit other techniques, such as monitoring the contents of the display device, to build an adequate alternate user interface. Also, as UI designers invent new user interface paradigms, it becomes increasingly difficult to describe the innovation through the MSAA protocol.
- *Extensibility.* This is a complementary issue to the richness issue just described. There is no mechanism to accommodate a UI innovation that does not fit the object model or predefined event system.
- *Consistency of MSAA Server Implementations.* Various development teams implement MSAA servers for their unique implementations of custom controls. However, a few mechanisms verify whether a given MSAA server implementation is correct in its interpretation of attribute fields values or event-firing protocols. The end result is that two implementations of the same class of user interface element may appear quite different as viewed by an assistive technology through the MSAA interfaces. Interoperability problems result.

14.4.2 Microsoft UI Automation

Microsoft is introducing a new generation of accessibility architecture with its *UI automation* framework [13]. At the time of this writing, UI automation is not yet generally available, but Microsoft indicates that it will be available in the Windows Vista timeframe.

UI Automation seeks to provide better support for solving the richness and extensibility issues which were noted earlier. The richness issue is addressed by providing a mechanism for accessing the native object model for each application. An application can still be accessed using only the generic UI Automation object model, but an even greater level of descriptive ability can be obtained by interfacing with the object model that is specific to a particular application domain.

The extensibility issue is addressed by introducing *control patterns*. Control patterns are loosely analogous to class interface definitions; a control pattern defines the properties, methods, events, and structure of a given class of user interface elements. For example, UI Automation defines *Selection* and *ExpandCollapse* patterns. The combo box control and list control both implement the Selection pattern. Additionally, the combo box implements the ExpandCollapse pattern.

Ideally, a user interface element would no longer be identified by its role. Instead, the UI element would be viewed and manipulated by the collection of control patterns that the element supports. With this approach in place, the application developer need not be concerned with whether an innovative custom control fits into one of the existing "role" definitions. Instead, the custom control is described by the patterns it supports. This approach may further enable UI designers to describe innovative controls through the accessibility interfaces.

14.4.3 Java Swing Accessibility API

The Java Swing API implements a parallel hierarchy of accessible objects. Each GUI widget ("component" in Swing terminology) has an accessible counterpart. The desire is to create a platform neutral and portable accessibility API. ATs are able to access and manipulate the GUI entirely through the accessible hierarchy. Each Swing component implements the `getAccessibleContext` API, which provides access to the various accessible features of a component such as the accessible name, description, role, state, value, and relationships between components and any child components. This API is intended for use by in-process ATs but can also be used by out-of-process ATs through a bridge technology [14].

14.4.4 SWT Accessibility API

SWT is built on the host platform widgets; thus it exhibits the host platform look, feel, and other features, including accessibility support. If the host platform does not have adequate accessibility support, neither will SWT nor thus Eclipse. The SWT accessibility API is modeled after features common to both MSAA and the GNOME Accessibility Project. SWT repackages this API in a generally platform neutral way and adds some ease-of-use features.

MSAA and GNOME provide significant default accessibility for many of their own platform's widgets. Thus simple GUIs built using SWT are often highly accessible by default on these platforms. Still there are instances where extra application support is required to enhance this default implementation.

Many of the default accessibility features depend on careful construction of the GUI. For example, on Windows, each widget needs to be constructed in a logical order (often from top down, from left to right). MSAA will use the text of a label that precedes, in order of creation, certain widgets that themselves do not have accessible names, such as a text field, as the name of the text field. Some ATs also do automatic default accessible property setting, often by physical proximity, such as a label immediately to the left of a text field.

If the default accessibility is insufficient, then the SWT accessibility APIs can be used to augment it. Each SWT Control (a subclass of widget that has an identity in the host operating system), such as a button, can have an `Accessible` proxy to the host accessibility support for the control. The `Accessible` class, along with the `Accessible Listener` and `AccessibleControlListener` interfaces, provide a means, through APIs and application callbacks, for the application to specify accessible properties of the control.

14.5 CONCLUSION

In this chapter we introduce the three components of an accessible solution: (1) platform, (2) application, and (3) assistive technology. As the core of the system, platforms provide the foundation for an accessible solution in that they provide

- Access to input and output devices attached to the system. Platforms must provide support for standard and special input and output devices that can accommodate the

different needs of PwDs. They must allow for replacement of standard devices with alternates that are more accessible.
- Basic function of the system, including GUI toolkits. Platforms must provide a set of GUI toolkits and associated runtimes that are enabled for accessibility according to the platform accessibility architecture. In general, this means supplying a set of widgets that implement the necessary aspects of the accessibility architecture.
- An accessible architecture, including APIs, that applications and assistive technologies use to interact with the platform and each other. Platforms must provide an accessible architecture to allow the platform itself and applications running on the platform to enable accessibility and allow ATs to provide alternate user interfaces. Often this means providing APIs for the application to use along with techniques for developers to follow when developing GUIs using those APIs. We have discussed several approaches used by different platforms. ATs must exploit the accessibility services of the platform and any accessibility enablement provided by application to provide alternate user interfaces based on the needs of their target users. These alternate user interfaces should coexist and cooperate with standard platform user interfaces.

Providing an accessible solution does not come for free; there is additional cost in additional development time and possibly in information content authoring. We describe how providing accessible solutions increases the usability of any system for all users, thus increasing the popularity of both the platform and its supported applications, and thus creating a positive return on investment for the enablement effort.

REFERENCES AND NOTES

1. Microsoft: *The Wide Range of Abilities and Its Impact on Computer Technology*, research study commissioned by Microsoft, conducted by Forrester Research, 2003 (available at http://www.microsoft.com/enable/research/; accessed 2/20/06).
2. Trademark, service mark, or registered trademark of Adobe Systems Incorporated, Eclipse Foundation, GNOME Foundation, KDE e. V., Linus Torvalds, Microsoft Corporation, Mozilla Foundation, Netscape Communications Corporation, Red Hat, Incorporated, Sun Microsystems Incorporated, or The Open Group.
3. Brunet P et al: Accessibility requirements for systems design to accommodate users with vision impairments, *IBM Syst J*, **44** (3):445–466 (2005).
4. *Microsoft Active Accessibility* Webpage, Microsoft Inc. (available at http://www.microsoft.com/enable/developer.aspx (accessed 2/20/06).
5. *Java Accessibility* Webpage, Sun Microsystems, Inc. (available at http://java.sun.com/j2se/1.5.0/docs/guide/access/index.html; accessed 2/20/06).
6. *Disability Access to GNOME* Webpage (available at http://developer.gnome.org/projects/gap/; accessed 2/20/06).
7. *Eclipse* Webpage. (availabile at http://www.eclipse.org/; accessed 2/20/06).
8. Trademark, service mark, or registered trademark of International Business Machines Corporation.
9. *Lotus Software* Webpage (available at http://www.ibm.com/software/lotus/; accessed 2/20/06).
10. *Accessibility* Webpage, Adobe Systems Inc. (available at http://www.adobe.com/enterprise/accessibility/main.html; accessed 2/20/06).

11. *Accessibility Resource Center* Webpage, Adobe Systems Inc. (formerly Macromedia Inc.) (available at http://www.macromedia.com/resources/accessibility/; accessed 2/20/06).
12. Leventhal A: *Access Mozilla* Webpage (available at http://www.mozilla.org/access/; accessed 2/20/06).
13. Haverty R: *New Accessibility Model for Microsoft Windows and Cross Platform Development*, MSDN Library, Sept 2005 (available at http://msdn.microsoft.com/library/default.asp?url=/library/en-us/dnanchor/html/accessibility.asp; accessed 2/20/06).
14. *Java Access Bridge for Windows Operating System* Webpage; (available at http://java.sun.com/products/accessbridge/; accessed 2/20/06).

15

Voice Interactive Systems

Rudzionis Algimantas and Kastytis Ratkevicius
Kaunas University of Technology, Kaunas, Lithuania

Vytautas Rudzionis
Vilnius University, Kaunas, Lithuania

15.1 INTRODUCTION

People with disabilities meet barriers of all types accessing information. These barriers can be grouped into three functional categories: barriers to providing computer input, interpreting output, and reading supporting textual data. Using voice-processing technology tasks such as reading and writing documents, communicating with others, and searching information on the Internet could be handled by people with disabilities more easily. This chapter describes the benefits that voice technology establish for people with various kinds of disabilities or impairments, to show the possibilities and limitations of modern state-of-the-art technologies and to present some examples of successful implementation of voice technologies for the benefits of disabled people.

One major advance of the human–machine interfaces has been the advent of the graphical user interface (GUI). It has popularized icons and the mouse, which are extremely comfortable tools used to communicate with the computer for the majority of people. But GUI left behind the blind and the vision-impaired. It is noted that prior to the GUI era [1], it was easier for impaired people to work with the computer using a braille reader to assist them. System navigation was done with menus, tabbing, and function keys—all of which could be learned on a keyboard by a blind user. A similar scenario was observed in Internet development. The Internet existed in a text format for many years, but it was difficult to use and navigate. Then the World Wide Web (WWW) became popular. Early Web browsers brought GUI to the Internet, and opened up access to information on the

---

The Engineering Handbook of Smart Technology for Aging, Disability, and Independence,
Edited by A. Helal, M. Mokhtari and B. Abdulrazak
Copyright © 2008 John Wiley & Sons, Inc.

Net for millions of people. But the vision-impaired were left out in an even more difficult situation than during the prebrowser era.

If the situation for hearing-impaired or the motor-handicapped people might now seem better, in fact it is not. Everyone can see the obvious reason for that—impaired or disabled people cannot use one or more of the modalities that conform to the foundation of modern human–machine interfaces—monitor, keyboard, or mouse. Other modalities are necessary in such situations. Also, it is well known that speech is the preferable modality for the majority of disabled people. If impaired people cannot use their hands to move a mouse or type, issuing a voice command is the logical solution. If people can't see, then applying the text-to-speech technique to read the content is the most convenient solution. Voice technologies are the key element in the devices that are developed to satisfy the needs of many impaired people.

The success of the development of specialized tools for impaired people mainly relies on two factors: development of the voice technology being used and knowledge of the special requirements of disabled people. We will briefly describe the basics of the major voice-processing technologies: speech recognition and text-to-speech synthesis. Those who are interested in more details should refer to the vast amount of existing technical and research literature. But one point must be noted—despite decades of significant research efforts and large amounts of money spent to develop speech technologies, there still are no machines that have speech-processing capabilities similar to those of humans. But today speech technologies provide a lot of useful and economically viable solutions. Disabled people are often ready to use the same limited and imperfectly developed voice technologies that normal people often refuse to use.

15.2 VOICE TECHNOLOGY BASICS

Three major groups of voice technologies are discussed here: text-to-speech synthesis, speech recognition, and speaker recognition. Text-to-speech synthesis and speech recognition are particularly important in applications intended for disabled people. Below we briefly describe the basics of these technologies prior before giving the specific details of applications designed for impaired people.

15.2.1 Text-to-Speech Synthesis

The main purpose of the text-to-speech (TTS) synthesizer is to generate speech signals from text or other sources of information. In a very simplified view, one might imagine TTS as a conversion of each word or command into sound and concatenation of the result into a single utterance. However, things are more complicated than this simplistic view suggests. Pronouncing words correctly is only part of the problem. In order to achieve natural-sounding speech, a good TTS system must, for example (1) appropriately emphasize (accent) certain words, (2) control certain aspects of voice quality, and (3) know that a word should be pronounced longer if it appears in certain parts of the sentence. Difficulties also arise when writing systems fail to specify many kinds of important information in speech. The orthographic systems used in some languages such as Chinese or Japanese fail to give information on the location of word boundaries. Humans are able to perform these tasks largely because they understand the semantic content of the text.

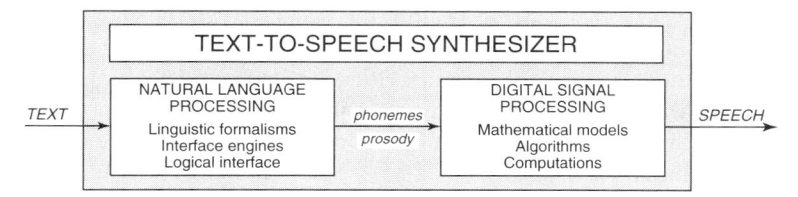

FIGURE 15.1 Text-to-speech synthesizer block diagram.

Often the TTS problem is subdivided into two broad tasks (see Fig. 15.1). The first task involves the conversion of text into some form of appropriate linguistic representation. This representation must include information on the phonemes to be produced and their duration, the locations of pauses, and the pitch contour to be used. The second task involves the actual speech synthesis—taking linguistic information generated as the output of first task and converting it into a speech waveform.

The first part may be broken down into several subtasks: text preprocessing (including expansion of abbreviations and numerals, end-of-sentence detection, and part-of-speech assignment), accent assignment, word pronunciation, intonational phrasing, segmental durations, and pitch contour determination.

The speech synthesis stage is often broken down into two parts: (1) the selection and concatenation of appropriate units given the phoneme string and (2) the synthesis of speech waveform given the units and a model of glottal source.

15.2.1.1 Text and Linguistic Analysis

One of the first tasks for TTS is to divide text into reasonable chunks; the most natural chunk is the sentence. In most cases some delimiter is used to mark the end of a sentence. Unfortunately, in English and in some other languages the same symbols can be used to mark the end of an abbreviation (e.g., Mr., Dr.), and the TTS system must be able to recognize and expand such symbols. Many abbreviations are ambiguous, and expansion must rely on the context. The next task in text processing is *word tokenization*. In languages like English, tokenization could be based largely on a white space mark. In contrast, in many Asian languages the situation is much more complex since spaces are never used to delimit words and an online dictionary that enumerates wordforms is necessary.

In many languages various words in the sentence are associated with accents, which usually are related with upward or downward movements of pitch. A good first step in assigning accents is to make accentual determination on the broad basis of lexical categories or parts of speech. The next stage of analysis involves computing pronunciations for the words, given the orthographic representation of those words. The solution of this task depends very strongly on the language. The simplest approach is to have a set of "letter-to-sound rules". This approach is best suited for languages with relatively strict connection between orthography and phonology (e.g., Spanish). English language at the same time requires a much more accurate pronunciation model.

15.2.1.2 Speech Synthesis

Once the text has been transformed into phonemes and their associated parameters have been computed, the system is ready to compute the speech parameters for synthesis. There are two independent parameters in the TTS system: (1) the choice between a rule-based scheme and a concatenative scheme and (2) the actual parameter chosen (articulatory parameters, formants, in concatenative scheme—control of loudness, pitch, voicing, timing, etc.). Rule-based systems are memory-efficient, facilitating the implementation of new speaker characteristics for different voices and phone inventories for new languages and dialects. But they are also more restrictive since they rely on both an understanding of the relation between parameters and signals and the ability to compute the dynamics of parameters.

The concatenative scheme is able to store the dynamics of the speech and produce high-quality synthetic sound given the right choice of units. In this approach, short segments of natural speech are connected to form a synthetic utterance. The majority of speech segments are transitions between pairs of phonemes. However, some segments consisting of three or more phoneme elements are often necessary. The concatenative approach requires that speech samples be stored in some parametric representation that will be suitable for connecting the segments and changing the loudness, pitch, and spectrum. More detailed description of speech synthesis techniques can be found in various sources, such as those by Dutoit [2] and Holmes and Holmes [3].

15.2.2 Speech Recognition

Speech recognition refers to the ability of a machine to convert a speech signal to a symbolic form of information (usually textual), providing a transcription of what was stated by a human. Speech recognition by machine is difficult because of variability in the signal. Sources of variability include within-speaker (intraspeaker) variability in maintaining consistent pronunciation and use of words, across-speaker (interspeaker) variability due to the physiologic differences, and transducer variability while speaking over different microphones or telephone handsets.

Historically, several approaches to speech recognition have been proposed: acoustic–phonetic, pattern-matching, or artificial intelligence approaches. The most widely used *pattern-matching approach* involves two steps: pattern training and pattern comparison. A speech pattern can represent a phoneme (smaller than a word unit), a word, or a whole phrase. Also, a speech pattern can be in the form of a speech template or a statistical model.

The pattern-matching scheme is depicted in the Figure 15.2. The speech signal is analyzed first, and a feature representation is obtained. This representation will be used to compare with either reference templates or statistical models. A decision part of the recognition system determines the word or phoneme of the incoming speech according to the matching scores. Two reference patterns can be used: (1) the *nonparametric pattern*, which is created from one or more spoken tokens of the signal associated with the pattern,

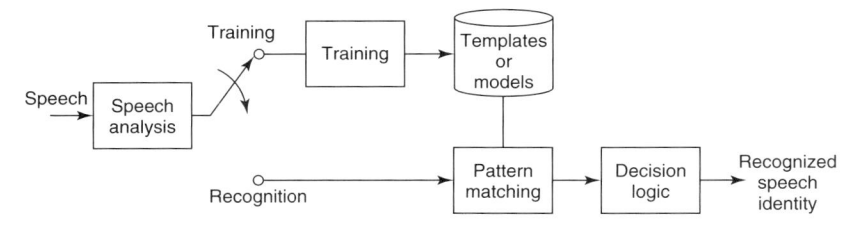

FIGURE 15.2 *Pattern-matching scheme in automatic speech recognition system.*

and (2) the *statistical model*, which is created as a statistical description of the tokens' parameters.

The first part in any speech recognition system is signal analysis. This analysis is typically done on successive and possibly overlapped speech signal segments, due to the time-varying nature of speech. The duration of such segments is 10–30 ms in most systems. The representation could be in various forms: spectral parameters, linear predictive coding, or temporal parameters such as zero crossings. However, the most popular type of representation is with cepstral parameters (MFCC), due to their relative efficiency. The cepstral parameters are often augmented with delta and acceleration parameters that characterize the dynamic aspects of the speech process.

The pattern-training stage specifies the method of creating reference patterns from representative sound patterns for the speech unit being trained. These patterns are used by the pattern-matching algorithm. Pattern training in the majority of speech recognition systems today is performed using the hidden Markov model (HMM) approach.

The HMM is a statistical characterization of the dynamics and statistics of speech during pronunciation. The states in the Markov chain are not observable with full certainty, and that's why the model is called "hidden". The model shown in Figure 15.3 has three states (corresponding to three distinct "sounds" within the speech), each of which proceeds from left to right in time. Within each state the features of the speech signal are characterized by a mixture of the Gaussian density of features (called *observation density*), energy distribution, and a state duration probability. The states represent the changing nature of speech in time. The training in HMM consists of estimating the parameters of statistical distributions within each state (for Gaussian distribution, these are the mean, the variance, and the mixture weight) along with the state transition probabilities. Efficient training techniques (e.g., the Baum–Welch method) have been developed for this task. In-depth description of HMM-based speech recognition can be found in the literature [4,5].

Pattern matching refers to the process of evaluating the similarity between two speech patterns. One pattern represents unknown speech and the other, the reference pattern. A major problem in comparing speech patterns arises from speaking rate variations. HMM provides implicit time normalization as part of the likelihood measurement process called *Viterbi search*. For template approaches, explicit time normalization is required. This can

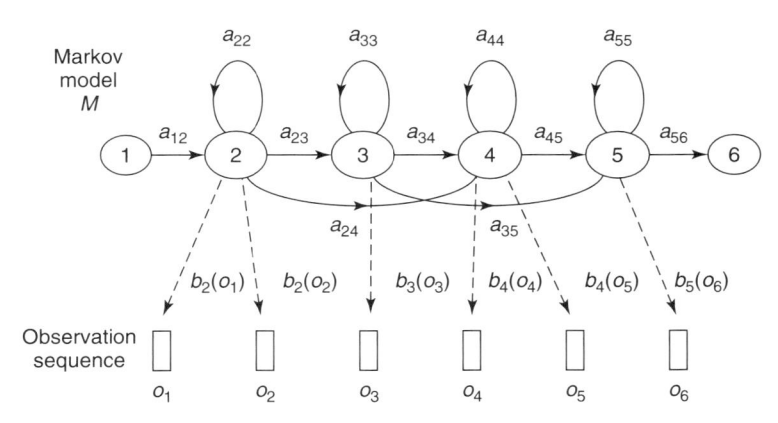

FIGURE 15.3 Three-state left–right hidden markov model structure.

be accomplished using a dynamic programming procedure called dynamic time warping (DTW) (described in further detail by Furui [6]). The decision module of the automatic speech recognition system (ASR) takes all the matching scores, finds the "closest" one, and decides whether the quality of the match is good enough to support a recognition decision. If not, the user normally is asked to provide another token of speech for another recognition attempt.

Isolated word recognition systems deal with words pronounced in isolation. System designers can construct a separate model for each word. Continuous speech recognition is the most challenging task. As the size of the vocabulary grows, it becomes impractical to train each word separately. Hence, continuous speech recognition systems use subword speech units as the basic elements to be trained, and use the lexicon to define the structure of the word patterns. For the basic subword unit, the most common choice is to select phonemes. The English language contains about 40–50 phonemes. This approach is usually called *context-independent* (CI) *phoneme-based recognition*. Unfortunately, phonemes are highly variable according to different contexts, and CI recognition does not provide high accuracy. A straightforward way to improve it is to augment the CI set with phoneme models that are context-dependent (CD), which leads to the improved recognition accuracy.

Once the basic set of subword units is chosen and trained, one can use lexical modeling to represent words. The lexicon used in most recognizers is extracted from pronouncing dictionaries. Most speech recognizers implement language modeling as well. In order to find the best match for the sentence system, one has to evaluate not only the acoustic match but also the language match score (corresponding to the match of the words to the grammar and syntax). Language match scores are computed according to a production model of the syntax and the semantics. Language models include N-gram word probabilities, word pair models, and finite-state models.

15.3 VOICE TECHNOLOGY APPLICATIONS FOR PEOPLE WITH DISABILITIE

Voice technology is potentially of enormous benefit to people with physical disabilities. The tremendous richness of human speech communication gives the user many degrees of freedom for control and input [7]. Applications of speech technology can be grouped in the areas of access, control, communication, and rehabilitation/therapy. For people with different types of impairment, different types of speech technologies are more important. For people with visual impairments, speech synthesis is essential as a way to access information; for people with hearing impairments, perceptual speech processing and amplification are crucial; for people with other disabilities, other areas of speech technology can be more important; overall, it is really difficult to find people with some sort of impairment who cannot benefit from voice technology. To be successful, applications implementing voice processing should effectively account for the specific needs of user groups and have the ability to adapt to the needs of the individual.

Typical computer input modes used in modern control and communication devices—keyboard input and visual output—are not suitable for disabled people because of the physical disorder. Voice technology is often the preferable method for such people—to use speech recognition for recognizing commands as a substitute for keyboard or mouse-based control and to use speech synthesis to read the content of the computer screen as a substitute for typical screen reading by the human eye. The ability to control the home is an essential aspect of independence and e-inclusion. Interfaces for home environmental control with speech recognition have been introduced more recently, and a number of such systems are available on the market.

15.3.1 Voice Technologies for Visually Impaired People

Visually impaired people suffer much inconvenience in everyday life in comparison to the general population. Various assistive devices and technologies have been developed to help blind people. The more recent advent and widespread use of computers and the Internet have provided new challenges for these people and the developers of assistive technologies.

The major obstacle to computer access for visually impaired people is the inability to use a monitor. One way to avoid this obstacle is to use a screen reader—software that can read information from the computer screen using text-to-speech technology. Modern software uses a pixel (picture element)-based system to present information, requiring greater sophistication to determine information about the screen's content without visual interpretation.

The main information input mode for visually impaired people is the keyboard. The keyboard activity of users can be filtered by specific "keyboard hooks." In most cases the filtering is used to speak the words typed, or to speak about keyboard operations, such as "cursor up." One difficulty with Windows and other GUI system applications is that the screen is presented in pixel format on the user's screen with no textual representation available via the operating system. The traditional way to address this problem is to hook screen updates via system messages and to transfer decoded message to the text-to-speech engine. The architecture of a typical screen reader is shown in Figure 15.4.

Many screen readers employ synthesizers as a separate independent engine. This means that a user can select many of the available speech synthesizers. Of particular value in separation of the screen reader from the synthesis engine is the possibility

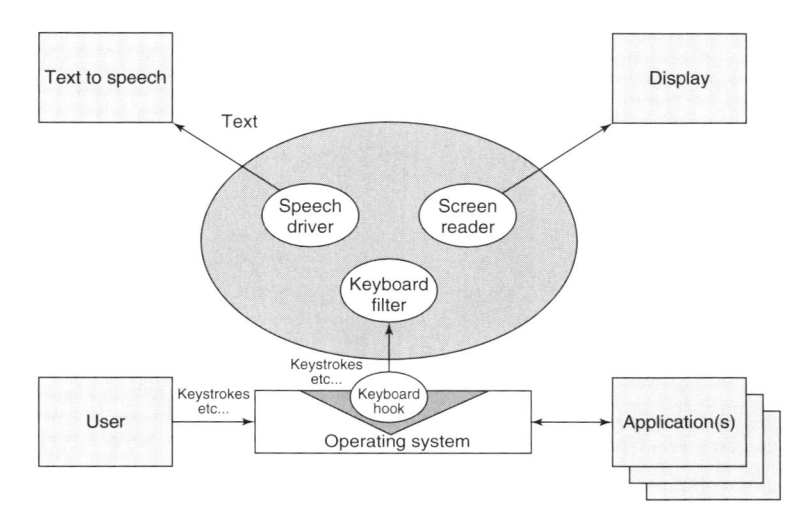

FIGURE 15.4 Screen reader's block diagram.

of employing multilingual reading systems. Often users need to obtain information in several languages. This is especially true for speakers of smaller-area languages, such as Lithuanian. In practice, this means that the user can select several preinstalled speech synthesizers to read the selected text (screen content). Any synthesis tool can be used in applications for visually impaired people, but speech synthesizers that particularly target blind people should satisfy the following requirements: variable speed [including the ability to speak very quickly, faster than 500 words per minute (wpm)], quick response, understandablility (this should not necessarily be construed as a requirement to "sound very natural"), flexibility to work under either Windows or Linux for compatibility with other software, and support indexing (a screen reader should be able to determine which word is currently spoken).

Variable speed is a particularly important practical feature for blind people. Visually impaired people usually feel uncomfortable when listening to or reading information from the screen up to a certain point of interest. Many of users prefer to read faster, even at the cost of loosing speech quality (not too significantly!).

Various screen readers models are available on the market. We briefly describe several popular screen readers and their characteristics here:

- *JAWS for Windows.* This software provides speech technology that works with your computer operating system to provide access to popular software applications and the Internet. JAWS software is the most popular screen reader within the visually impaired community who work with personal computers.
- *JawBone.* Many users reported problems with the simultaneous use of JAWS screen-reading software and Dragon Systems continuous speech voice recognition software, which can also lead to difficulties in the areas of training and maintenance of voice files. JawBone is a specialized interface program that enables the coordinated use of Dragon NaturallySpeaking Professional and JAWS for Windows. The product includes a lexicon of new commands that make operating the PC by voice—whether to exercise commands or generate text—easier for the visually impaired or dyslexic user.
- *OutSpoken for MAC.* This software is designed especially for Mac computer users. It has a talking interface announcing virtually everything on the screen using the Apple's PlainTalk Text-to-Speech.
- *Window-Eyes.* This software has Windows compatibility and the ability to read more screens than its nearest competitor. It also gives total control over what you hear and how you hear it, and with the new Braille support, it extends that control to what you feel. It also offers lightning-fast access to the Internet.

Information presented on Webpages has one important property—there is always someone who in fact participated in the design of assistive technology but is not directly involved in it and may not consider adaptability for the people with special needs as a priority. This is the Webpage designer. Despite all the efforts of speech synthesizer and screen reader developers, inappropriate of Webpage design (graphic files with nonsense names, etc.) can ruin these efforts. Good design of World Wide Web (WWW) resources must include consideration of how this resource would suit disabled people. Several agencies offer training materials and testing to assist in implementing assistive technologies. The Information Technology Council (www.itic.org) offers a Voluntarily Product

Accessibility Template for evaluating any system against US government information accessibility requirements. The Web Accessibility Initiative (www.w3.org/WAI) offers training materials for developers at three levels of accessibility. The Center for Applied Technology (CAST) offers an analysis program, called "Bobby" (www.cast.org/bobby), which could be used to check any Website for WAI compliance.

Access to Webpage information is not the only source of information that blind people might need to access. Other sources could be books, articles, or any long text files. Text-to-speech interfaces present text in sequence. Long text files might be difficult to listen to in one single session, and it could be necessary to return to the same location and continue listening later. This could also be interesting for Webpage browsing since informative texts are seldom read from beginning to end. The selective reading method requires an interface that permits efficient random access to the relevant text regions. Various text-processing techniques have been proposed (telegraphic text compression, linear text segmentation, discourse structure methods, etc.), but thorough analysis of these methods is beyond the scope of this chapter. The software tools used for long text reading purposes are called *book readers*. Several examples of commercial book readers are listed here:

- VERA (a *v*ery *e*asy *r*eading *a*ppliance) allows one to read books, magazines, personal correspondence, and other matieral. It will read aloud, or the user can view the optional VERA display screen, or TV set.
- OPENBook is designed for blind and visually impaired people, enabling them to read, edit, and manage printed media, by scanning the material and converting it to digital information. This information is then read by the internal voice synthesizer or through a customizable screen display. Essentially it turns the computer into a scanning and reading machine.

15.3.2 Voice Technologies for Hearing-Impaired People

One of the uses of voice technology for hearing-impaired people is related with the hearing tools. Rehabilitative intervention to assist people with hearing impairment typically occurs through the provision of amplification. The principal role of amplification is to increase sounds to levels that hearing-impaired people can detect and to enable them to make use of the auditory signal.

Amplification in the form of hearing instrument is considered the primary option for many individuals who are hearing-impaired. The rapid development of hearing instrument technology more recently has made it possible to produce higher-fidelity and more portable instruments. *Portability* means that smaller hearing instruments are being produced and the amplification device could be worn even within the ear canal.

Existing options include such hearing-aid styles as body style (BS), behind-the-ear (BTE), in-the-ear (ITE), in-the-canal (ITC), and completely in the canal (CITC) instruments. BS instruments are used primarily in the most severe hearing loss cases when the other type of instruments cannot provide a strong enough signal level for the patient. BS instruments consist of a receiver that is connected to the hearing aid with a cord. The receiver is usually worn in a shirt pocket or is clipped to the clothing. Today these instruments are rarely used. BTE-style instruments consist of a hearing instrument held in a casing positioned behind the ear. The sound signal travels through the hearing instrument into an earmold and into the ear canal. BTE instruments are often preferable for children because of growth changes. The biggest advantage of the BTE-style instrument is its compatibility with the telecoil and its direct audio input. The telecoil picks up electromagnetic signals (e.g., from a telephone) and converts them to the electrical signal that is amplified by the hearing device. BTE instrument with direct audio input can be attached to a hardwired or wireless audio connector, which links the hearing instrument to a personal or sound-field amplification system. ITE-type instruments fit within the concha and outer-ear cavity. ITE-style devices can provide stronger amplification than ear canal hearing-aid instruments, and many people use this style comfortably. Because it is worn within the ear canal, it is more visually appealing than larger devices. One disadvantage of ITE-style instruments is the necessity to change its tiny batteries from time to time. ITC-style hearing instruments are worn within the ear canal but are unable to provide as much amplification as the larger hearing aids. ITC-style instruments are controlled digitally and use digital signal processing. Digital programmable tools use frequency-selective amplification that complies with the perceptual characteristics of the human ear.

Another group of voice technology applications for people with hearing impairment is related to information access. Hearing-impaired people have significant problems in using communication tools such as phones and other devices that use speech as the major means of transferring information. It is well known that visual information obtained by speechreading and interpretation of body gestures improves speech perception. This has led to the idea to try to develop tools for telephone communication aids for hard-of-hearing people by exploiting simulation of facial gestures of a speaker. An example of such a tool is the teleface project [8] at the Swedish KTH Institute. The device generates a synthetic face that articulates in synchrony with telephone speech. Control parameters for the face are determined by analysis of the telephone speech signal. A visual hearing aid is implemented as software running on a PC, or as a special standalone unit called *teleface*. This complex technology, combining achievements of voice technology and visual processing, was successfully implemented to assist hearing-impaired people.

15.3.3 Voice Technologies for Motor-Handicapped People

Motor-handicapped people are generally keen to use voice technology. This is especially true for people with problems that limit manual dexterity and/or use of the upper body, including people with arthritis and carpal tunnel syndrome. The major requirements for software tools designed to enable information access for motor-handicapped people are described as follows: (1) user input is conveyed by spoken commands and (2) output is conveyed by an unaltered visual rendering using "saycons" (which tell the user how to activate the various links by voice) and is optionally combined with speech synthesis for eyes-free browsing when necessary.

Examples of such Webbrowsers are the Converse voice surfer, the hands-free browser by EduMedia, the Indtal browser [9], and also add-ons shipped with some versions of IBM's ViaVoice and Dragon natural-speaking commercial speech recognition software. All such browsers are developed with an advisory for motor-handicapped end users and should underlie a number of a priori defined design criteria. The design criteria include the independence of Website language, support for different Web standards, and minimal maintenance after release since such browsers are often developed through targeted projects.

Modern houses are equipped with a set of household appliances ranging from simple lights to hi-fi (high-fidelity) systems, DVD players, and TV sets. Usually these devices are controlled by buttons found directly on the unit, or on remote controls. People with special needs often suffer significant difficulties in operating many home appliances. Voice technology can substantially facilitate the use of household devices for these people. It is important to note that such devices do not need continuous speech recognition and could successfully use the limited vocabulary of isolated word recognition. Various appliances are now equipped with voice control features. Unfortunately, there are serious challenges in matching different device interfaces and avoiding conflicting commands. Various efforts to develop speech-activated smart-home control systems focusing on people with special needs by providing a unified speech-controlled interface have been reported [10]. The ultimate goal of the home environment is to achieve a level where users can express their desires and the system will orchestrate the home appliances in order to fulfill their specific wishes.

High recognition accuracy is the most important requirement applied to the speech-oriented interface. Although recognition rates have improved since the early systems were introduced and continue to improve, clinical experience indicates that a significant proportion of switched-scanning users still reject speech recognition as a control method for two reasons [7]: (1) speech control is less accurate than switched-scanning—the threshold of acceptance appears to be of the order of 80% accuracy, which is seldom achieved in the home environment; and (2) false activation by environmental noise is a frequent occurrence and a source of significant frustration.

Other requirements for well-designed smart-home voice interface include the potential for providing commands without the need to remember a specific list of commands, audio feedback should be provided to enhance usability for the blind users, all dialogs should be as unrestricted as possible, and the system must operate in real time and respond within a time that would be unnoticed by the user. To achieve uninterrupted performance, the voice activity detector (VAD) must be integrated. The VAD is a module designed to detect when someone is speaking. Most VADs are based on some energy-based measure [11], trying to detect timeslots when the energy of the acoustic signal achieves a level higher than the predefined threshold. Other VAD algorithms have been proposed, such as methods based on spectral change rate detection [12].

Voice technology could be successfully used to assist disabled people when navigating with in the environment. One possible solution would be provision of relevant information for these people. An example of such a system might be the *mobility support geographic information system* used in Japan to provide barrier and barrier-free information on maps. This system, when used directly, is inconvenient for elderly and disabled people. A proposed solution was to develop a speech input interface based on speech recognition technology [13]. But to achieve better performance, users still needs to obey restrictions of the interface. GIS speech input interface can use only a limited number of commands.

There have also been attempts to integrate communication technologies, including voice processing into traditional assistive tools for disabled people such as wheelchairs. The *e-wheelchair* [14] is an electronic wheelchair with integrated communication equipment based on IPv6 protocol. This approach provides many benefits for disabled people and their caregivers.

15.3.4 Voice Technology for Rehabilitation and Therapy

Voice technology could be used for rehabilitation and therapy purposes of people with speech disorders. Improving motor performance requires repeated practice, with accurate and consistent feedback. Much of the skill of a speech and language therapist is devoted to several tasks:

Where is the patient going wrong?
How does the patient's performance compare to average normal speech production, and is the next attempt better or worse than the previous attempt?

Providing meaningful feedback is a very labor-consuming process. The auditory perception system of human beings naturally adopts to a speaker's utterances, and the therapist's feedback might not accurately reflect the patient's intended meaning. This motivates attempts to develop software tools that can play the role of speech therapist using some objective measures. Speech recognition systems have been successfully used to help speech therapists evaluate their perceptions by providing additional measures.

Speech is a highly integrated system, and therefore it is not surprising that one area of dysfunction can have an effect on other areas; thus, although one's speech might not be impaired, it might not be able to function normally as because of the secondary effects of other types of impairment. Many patients with severe dysarthria demonstrate inconsistent attempts to articulate the same sound combinations. Reducing this inconsistency helps improve the functional consequences for access to e-technology but can also impact on overall vocal effectiveness and general personal feeling. So voice technology, particularly speech recognition, could be used as a training tool to improve speech production efficiency. Many people with speech disorders are eager to use training speech recognition software as a tool not only to achieve better accuracy rates and obtain better access to technical devices and information but also as a means to improve speech quality. Rather than basing feedback on recognition decisions, the OPTACIA method [15] provides visual feedback related to the instantaneous acoustics.

People suffering from chronic illnesses such as Parkinson's disease, aphasia, and autism could benefit from voice technology today. Computer programs and animations containing speech recognition software interact with patients to provide the intense and repetitive instruction and practice needed to help them. While many teachers face time and resource constraints, the speech recognition tool will repeat the information as many times as needed. Aphasia patients look at a picture on a computer monitor and receive feedback about the sentences that they have used to describe the picture. Parkinson's disease patients can use programs that interact through speech and its corresponding facial expressions to help patients improve and control their own speech. So, voice technology is also seen as a tool to improve the actual impairment forming the barrier.

15.4 VOICE SERVER AS THE ASSISTIVE ENVIRONMENT BASIS

More recent advances in speech technologies have introduced the need to establish some speech technology standards. These standards, although not directly intended to develop tools for disabled people, have enormous potential impact for assistive technology as well. Standardization based on the complex technologies described in this chapter should apply for a broad class of developers. Today new groups of standards are being used in voice applications with a Web application infrastructure using standards-based interface languages such as Voice Extensible Markup Language (VoiceXML) (www.voicexml.org) and Speech Application Language Tags (SALT) (www.saltforum.org). These technologies allow developers to leverage their skills to create converged voice and data applications as easily as they create applications for the PC and Internet. Speech technologies used in voice servers have the potential to dramatically reduce the number of routine inquiries and transactions handled by agents and boost customer satisfaction by offering easy-to-use, always-available access from any phone. The wider implementation of voice technologies in many computer and telephony applications has obvious benefits for the disabled people discussed above.

The main benefit of voice servers for disabled people—individuals with physical or perceptual disabilities—might be greater access to Internet-based services; for example, visually impaired and handicapped people can search for information from the Internet by voice using speech recognition and can obtain responses using text-to-speech technology. There are two main alternatives for the developing and deploying speech-enabled Web applications: the Microsoft Speech Server (MSS) and the IBM WebSphere Voice Server.

15.4.1 Microsoft Speech Server

In 2004 Microsoft released Speech Server as part of an effort to make speech more mainstream. Microsoft Speech Server 2004 is a server-based system that uses Web technologies, speech-processing services, and telephony capabilities to extend existing or new Web applications for speech-enabled access from telephones, mobile phones, and Pocket PCs.

The Microsoft Speech Server has three main components (Fig. 15.5): speech application (SDK), speech engine services (SES), and telephony application services (TAS). SES provides speech recognition and speech output for voice-only applications and also for Pocket PC and smartphone devices using multimodal speech applications. SES includes subcomponents such as enterprise-grade automatic speech recognition, a world-class text-to-speech (TTS) engine, and a prompt database engine, which manages recorded and TTS prompts. TAS provides the communication link between the telephone system,

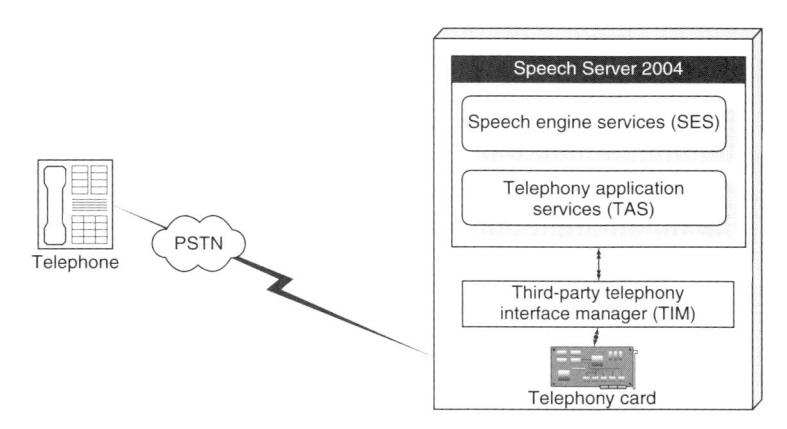

FIGURE 15.5 *The main components involved when telephony applications are received.*

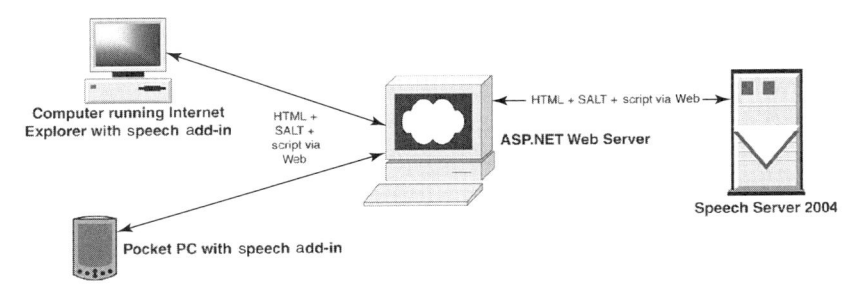

FIGURE 15.6 Multimodal applications communications with Speech Server process.

speech engine services, and the Web server; SALT interpreters interpret SALT tags in standard Webpages that define the telephony application.

MSS also includes an open interface for connection to popular phone switches and PBXs. Through this interface, MSS works with third-party telephony cards and call management software. The user's telephone communicates directly with the server's telephony card across the public telephone network. Depending on the speech server version, TAS can handle up to 96 telephone ports per node, with the ability to add an unlimited number of additional nodes.

Telephony applications can be either voice-only, DTMF (dual-tone multifrequency) only, or mixed. Multimodal applications allow the user to choose the appropriate input method, whether speech or traditional Web controls. The application can be used by a larger customer base because it allows the user to choose. Since not all customers will have access to microphones, the multimodal application is the ideal way to offer speech functionality. Multimodal applications are accessed via Microsoft Internet Explorer (IE) on the user's PC or with IE for the Pocket PC (see Fig. 15.6).

15.4.2 IBM WebSphere Voice Server

The IBM WebSphere voice server provides the automatic speech recognition and text-to-speech resources required to enable speech-based applications. It compiles grammars and uses them to perform automatic speech recognition on a stream of audio data. In this context, a *grammar* is a set of syntax rules that specify what utterances constitute a valid word or phrase. The voice server synthesizes spoken voice from the supplied text and streams the audio back to the VoiceXML browser. The WebSphere voice server uses the WebSphere application server as its architectural foundation. This allows the WebSphere voice server to harness the advanced features of the WebSphere application server, providing extensive administrative and performance benefits to the users. A basic IBM WebSphere voice server solution consists of several components to answer and manage calls such as a telephonic environment that has an IVR to accept, process, and direct calls; a voice browser that runs VoiceXML applications that interact with the user on the telephone; and a voice server that offers ASR and TTS services. These two services are invoked at different times by the running VoiceXML application. Developer could also add a *voice toolkit* for WebSphere Studio machine to develop grammars and lexicons as well as utilize the *voice toolkit voice trace analyzer*. The voice toolkit has the ability to use local WebSphere voice server ASR and TTS engines or point to a remote WebSphere voice server machine.

15.4.3 Comparison of Microsoft Speech Server 2004 and IBM WebSphere Voice Server

The differences are as follows:

Speech Markup Language. The IBM WebSphere voice server is a VoiceXML 2.0-enabled speech environment. Because it is different from IBM, MS uses SALT 1.0. The VoiceXML focuses on telephony application development, whereas SALT is focused on multimodal speech applications.

Telephony Interface Hardware. Currently, the Intel Call Manager support telephony hardware ranging from 4 ports to 96 ports working with Speech Server. The IBM WebSphere voice server is scalable, starting from basic analog telephony boards to high-density digital solutions with a T1/E1 interface.

Call Controls. Both the IBM WebSphere voice server and the MS speech server can provide simple call controls such as transfering, making (initiating), and answering calls. In some cases, to implement complex call controls, one must use the Call Control eXtensible Markup Language editor in the WebSphere voice server and the computer-supported telephony application data extension controls in the speech server.

OS Platform and Speech Recognition Language Support. The IBM WebSphere Voice Server V4.2 is able to be run on AIX, Windows, and Linux platforms. On different OS platforms, it supports different, multiple languages. So far, the MS speech server works only on the Windows 2000/XP/2003 platform and supports US English, US Spanish, and Canadian (Quebec) French for speech recognition and TTS.

15.4.4 SALT and VXML Standards for Voice Technology Applications

In the same way that the growth of the Web was catalyzed by the creation of the HTML scripting language, the acceptance of standards for speech services is propelling the adoption of this technology in both traditional and Web-based applications. Two emerging language standards—VoiceXML and SALT—enable developers to write platform-independent applications that handle synthesized speech, to record and recognize spoken input, and to control telephony.

VoiceXML markup tags are specifically intended for defining speech user interfaces, while SALT markup tags can define "multimodal" user interfaces involving both speech and a range of devices such as a graphic display, mouse, keyboard, or pen. VoiceXML defines a complete standalone language with markup elements for defining a speech interface along with data and control flow. SALT defines a small set of tags for creating a speech interface within various markup environments. VoiceXML and SALT represent two different approaches to a speech markup language. Each provides open specifications and supports the industry preference for known tools and programming models.

15.4.5 Standards in Perspective

There will always be new and competing ideas on standards, and while either SALT or VXML may one day emerge as the dominant player, they may coexist equally for a significant period of time. In fact, there's even talk that the two standards may one day merge into one. We can also be certain that standards such as VXML and SALT will continue to evolve, and that new standards will be created to address new functionality in the future.

REFERENCES

1. Rogoff, R: Making electronic information accessible to everyone, *Proc IPCC'01*, Oct 2001.
2. Dutoit T: *An introduction to Text-to-Speech Synthesis*, Kluwer, 1997.
3. Holmes J, Holmes W: *Speech Synthesis and Recognition*, Francis & Taylor, 2001.
4. Rabiner L: A tutorial on hidden markov models and selected applications in speech recognition, *Proc IEEE* **77**(2) (1989).
5. Huang H, Acero A, Hon H: *Spoken Language Processing—a Guide to Theory, Algorithm, and System Development*, Prentice-Hall, 2001.
6. Furui S: *Digital Speech Processing, Recognition, and Synthesis*, Marcel Dekker, 2000.
7. Hawley M, Green P, Enderby P, Cunnigham S, Moore R: Speech technology for e-inclusion of people with physical disabilities and disordered speech, *Proc Interspeech'05*, Lisbon, Portugal, 2005.
8. Beskow J, Dahlquist M, Granström B, Lundeberg M, Spens K-E, Öhman T: The Teleface project—disability, feasibility and intelligibility, *Proc Fonetik -97, Swedish Phonetics Conf*, Umeå, Sweden, 1997.
9. Brondsted T, Aaskoven E: Voice-controlled internet browsing for motor-handicapped users. Design and implementation issues, *Proc Interspeech'05*, Lisbon, Portugal, 2005.
10. Vovos A, Kladis B, Fakotakis N: Speech operated smart-home control system for users with special needs, *Proc Interspeech'05'* Lisbon, Portugal, 2005, pp 193–196.
11. Srinavasan K, Gersho A: Voice activity detection for the cellular networks, *Proc IEEE Speech Coding Workshop*, Oct 1993.
12. Rudzionis A, Rudzionis V: Noisy speech detection and endpointing, *Proc Workshop "Voice Operated Telecom Services. Do They Have a Bright Future?*, Ghent, Belgium, 2000.
13. Jitsuhiro T, Matsuda S, Ashikari Y, Nakamura S, Yairi I, Igi S: Spoken dialog system and its evaluation of geographic information system for elderly persons' mobility support, *Proc Interspeech'05*, Lisbon, Portugal.
14. Ernst T: E-Wheelchair: A communication system based on IPv6 and NEMO, *Proc ICOST'04*, Singapore, 2004.
15. Hatzis A, Green P: A two dimensional kinematic mapping between speech and acoustics and vocal tract configurations, *Workshop on Innovation in Speech Processing WISP'01*, Stratford-upon-Avon, UK, 2001.

16

The Communication Assistant (Alternative Communication)

Leanne L. West
Georgia Institute of Technology

When augmentative–alternative communication (AAC) devices are discussed, the often subjects are people who cannot express themselves verbally. More often than not, these expressive communication disabilities are in reference to people with conditions such as cerebral palsy, stroke, head injury, multiple sclerosis, a specific speech or language disorder, autism, and deafness [1], but not to those who are hard of hearing. This chapter gives a brief overview of traditional AAC devices, and then specifically looks at a project that attempts to make these systems compatible with today's wireless mobile technologies. In addition, this chapter redefines AAC devices to include systems that assist people who are heard of hearing, in addition to new technologies related to sign language. Finally, this chapter discusses the design considerations of a wireless personal captioning system developed by the author.[1]

16.1 AUGMENTATIVE AND ALTERNATIVE COMMUNICATION

Augmentative–alternative communication (AAC) represents any supplement to written or verbal communication in order to compensate for impaired functionality with one or both

---

[1] Many of the research projects discussed in this chapter were conducted in the Rehabilitation Engineering Research Center on Mobile Wireless Technologies for Persons with Disabilities (Wireless RERC) in Atlanta, Georgia under National Institute for Disability and Rehabilitation Research grant number H133E010804.

The Engineering Handbook of Smart Technology for Aging, Disability, and Independence,
Edited by A. Helal, M. Mokhtari and B. Abdulrazak
Copyright © 2008 John Wiley & Sons, Inc.

of these processes. At times, everyone uses some form of alternative communication, such as nodding your head to answer "yes" or pointing to a place on a map to get directions in a foreign country. The game of Charades is based on alternative communication where you act out or gesture a song or book title so that your teammates can guess the correct response. Some people must use alternative forms of communication all the time, which can include gesturing, but for others, gesturing can be too difficult or impossible.

AAC can be used for communication, both to help people convey information and help them understand what is being said to them. The act of communicating has several purposes, ranging from a transfer of information, to an expression of wants or needs, to social interactions. When communication increases, so do personal achievements such as school performance and opportunities for employment, as well as feelings of self-worth and social inclusion [2].

There are several traditional forms of AAC that exist to help people who need assistance with communication, and these forms can be unaided, aided, low-tech, or high-tech. Depending on the situation, most AAC users employ several different forms of AAC, which are often a mixture of unaided and aided as well as low-tech and high-tech [1]. But these specialized systems seldom keep up with the latest advancements in modern communication technology. While most people's lives are being made easier with technologies such as cell phones and pagers, many people who could really benefit from the independence and safety offered by these systems are being left behind. Fortunately, some advancements have created greater accommodation for individuals with disabilities, and much research is being conducted to utilize new technologies to create new forms of access or to enhance old ones.

16.1.1 Target Population

While probably less than 1% of the worldwide population has severe communication impairments [1], millions of people are represented by this number. According to Beukelman and Ansel, there are approximately 2.5 million Americans who could benefit from the use of traditional AAC systems, which translates into 8–12 individuals for every 1000. This number refers to all communication impairments, including deafness, but these numbers do not represent all people using AAC, only those who are candidates for it [3,4]. Nor do these numbers represent the demographic of people who are hard of hearing.

Even though the definition of AAC includes helping people understand what is being said to them, people who are hard of hearing, as well as the systems that give them access, are ignored in the discussions of traditional AAC. A large portion of the population suffers from communication impairment because they are hard of hearing, and this number is growing as the population ages. While some levels of hearing impairment can be compensated for by the use of hearing aids, many people still need assistive devices in certain situations as an alternative or augmentation to spoken language.

According to Kochkin [6], there are over 31 million people in the United States with hearing loss, with baby boomers and the 75+ age brackets seeing the largest increase between 1989 and 2004. This number is expected to grow by another third to 41 million people by 2025 [5,6]. Of the 31 million who have hearing loss currently, approximately 1 million are functionally deaf [7], while the remainder are hard of hearing.

16.1.2 Traditional Forms of AAC

Some people will use traditional AAC throughout their lives as a result of a permanent impairment from cerebral palsy or a learning disability, while others might use it for only a short time because of temporary impairment after an injury or accident. Still others might develop the need to use AAC because of a stroke or brain injury or other acquired conditions such as motor neuron disease (MND) or Lou Gehrig's disease [amyotrophic lateral sclerosis (ALS)] [8].

Unaided communication makes use of a person's own body without any additional materials or equipment. Included in unaided communication are gestures, signing, eye blinks, and other facial and body movements. An advantage of unaided systems is that you cannot forget to bring them; they are always with you and ready for use.

Sign language is an example of an unaided "system" and an alternative form of communication, where spoken language is replaced by hand gestures and signs, as well as facial expressions and body postures. It is a complete language with its own rules for punctuation and grammar, and it is grammatically very different from written and spoken language. American Sign Language (ASL) is the first language of North Americans who are deaf, and the fourth most common language in the United States. But not all people who are deaf use sign, nor do hardly any people who are hard of hearing [9]. Sign languages are not universal, just as no one oral language is universal. For example, ASL is very different from British Sign Language. It is actually closer to French Sign Language, sharing considerable vocabulary [10].

Aided communication makes use of additional materials or equipment that are not a part of a person's body. There are a wide array of aided communication tools, and these may be low-tech or high-tech. Traditional AAC tools consist of pointing devices, letter or picture boards/charts, books, bracelets, voice output communication aids (VOCAs), and electronic devices that perform functions similar to those of the nonelectronic aids [11,12]. These aids often give the user a customized representational system for communication, as well as a means of accessing the communication medium when necessary [11].

Low-tech forms of aided communication are nonelectronic devices that do not operate on electricity or battery power. Depending on the needs of the individual, a variety of representational sets or a combination thereof can be used as the basis for communication. These sets can be made of letters or words, graphic symbols, enhanced symbols, or three-dimensional objects. Other factors such as the display, the layout, and the scanning method are important to consider for meeting the needs of the individual.

High-tech aids serve the same purpose as do low-tech aids, but they are electronic and provide amenities such as computer access and voice output, which can be synthesized speech or recorded speech [12]. In addition, most high-tech aids allow various types of user input to accommodate a wide range of physical limitations and disabilities. These inputs include a touchscreen, a joystick, a pushbutton, a "sip and puff," an eyebrow switch, or eyetracking [11,13]. Because of "technical difficulties," such as dead batteries or loose cables, which can be encountered with high-tech systems, low-tech aids are often recommended as a backup to high-tech aids [11].

This chapter does not discuss further details of AAC devices or specific products available on the market today. Instead, this chapter highlights some examples of research being conducted at the Rehabilitation Engineering Research Center on Mobile Wireless Technologies for Persons with Disabilities (Wireless RERC) to integrate traditional high-tech AAC technologies with the latest mobile wireless technologies. The following section describes two studies that were performed to give users of AAC access to mobile wireless communication [14].

16.2 INTEGRATION OF AAC AND MOBILE WIRELESS TECHNOLOGIES

The convenience, independence, and communication options offered by mobile wireless communication technology are significant, but the use of current mobile wireless communication technology is virtually impossible for many users of AAC. In addition to speech impairments, the small buttons and controls, which are common on mobile wireless technology, pose a challenge for people with limited mobility or physical function. Adapting traditional AAC devices to be compatible with current mobile communication technologies will give the user new freedom and independence. To meet this challenge, two studies were conducted at the Wireless RERC [15].

The first study intended to make the Pathfinder by Prentke Romich Company compatible with the RIM 950 two-way pager. The RIM 950 is supplied with a docking station for use with a personal computer to load new programs onto the pager and to synchronize calendars and address books with the computer. The pager is always on and employs *push technology*, meaning that no user action is required to receive email; the user is notified of new email by a vibration or adjustable tone. Messages sent from the RIM 950 to telephones use a synthesized text-to-speech voice.

To make the RIM 950 compatible with an augmentative communication device, special software had to be written. The participant chosen to test the software with her ACC system was a young lady whose fine-motor control of her hands and fingers and ability to speak were affected by cerebral palsy, shown in Figure 16.1 with the principal investigator of the project. She used a Pathfinder to generate speech, which can be activated by pressing only one button. The software generated for the project allowed her to completely operate the RIM 950 two-way pager through her Pathfinder, therefore none of the buttons on the pager needed to be used to communicate. With this solution, the user was able to schedule public transportation and to send messages to her friends at any time and from nearly anywhere.

FIGURE 16.1 Principal investigator John Anschutz sending a message from RIM 950 with a Pathfinder.

There were problems, however. In particular, operation at night was not practical. The RIM 950 has a hardware function for operation of the backlight, and no means of controlling the backlight through software could be found. Low battery life was also a problem. The typical 1–2 week battery life for the pager was shortened to 1–2 days because full-time operation of the display when mounted with the Pathfinder. Additionally, breaks in the connection between the pager and the docking system would occur while driving over bumpy terrain, again affecting reliability of the system. Consideration in future models of similar two-way pagers could alleviate these problems. Moreover, integrating the mobile wireless technology into the AAC device or allowing for a direct connection with Bluetooth could solve some or all of these issues as well.

The second study included a man with advanced ALS. He used a ventilator and had no voice of his own. He was an avid technology user through the use of a single fiberoptic switch mounted to the frame of his eyeglasses. The switch was activated by eyebrow movement and allowed for full use of his computer and AAC system.

To give this participant wireless capabilities, a Sierra Wireless Aircard PC card was coupled to his Words + EzKeys, which works with a personal computer to serve as the AAC system. The EzKeys system uses dual-word prediction and abbreviation expansion. Instant phrases are also available, as well as rapid text-to-speech voice output. The system is designed so that alternative inputs provide complete mouse emulation. The Sierra Wireless Aircard plugs into laptop computers to provide wireless broadband access to the Internet, text messaging, email using Outlook Express, and cell phone operation. Because of his own declining function, the participant had been unable to use a telephone for quite some time. But with the added wireless capabilities, the participant was able to independently answer his phone and talk to his 15-year-old daughter, all through the use of a single fiberoptic eyebrow switch and his AAC system.

16.3 NEW AND EMERGING FORMS OF AAC

Recall that part of the definition of AAC is to help people understand what is being said to them. For example, hearing aids are not traditionally regarded as AAC, but they are a technology that enables people to better understand what is being said to them. With the emergence of new wireless and computer technologies, these and other standard technologies and methods of communication are being updated. Sign language is possible from remote locations; virtual translators are using the latest techniques in speech recognition technology and computer animation to generate sign language; and text generation and presentation technologies are becoming more ubiquitous and discreet as technology advances.

16.3.1 Technologies Related to Sign Language

Videophones and video relay services are making it possible to have telephone conversations in sign language. With multimedia features such as streaming video making their way to cell phones, video relay services are now available on a mobile platform [16]. Current limitations include image quality and limited bandwidth availability [17].

Products such as SigningAvatar and the iCommunicator are examples of virtual translators. These products generate ASL from speech input in the form of three-dimensional characters, making sign language translation possible without an interpreter. These systems are designed only for one-way interpretation, however; human sign is unable to be translated into text. Different virtual translators exist that translate from sign to speech and speech to sign. While still under development, Telesign [18,19] is a wearable ASL-to-English translator that allows face-to-face communication between a deaf person and a hearing person when an interpreter is not available. The system uses gesture recognition technology to identify the signed phrase and speak it aloud. A current prototype adds an intermediate step to the system, where the software actually matches what it sees with a preprogrammed list of phrases from which the user must select the desired phrase. As the technology develops, the final version should offer communication options when an interpreter is not available.

16.3.2 Text Messaging

Short Messaging Service (SMS) text messaging is a part of the new wave of alternative communication for people who are deaf. For this community, smartphones like the T-Mobile Sidekick or RIM Blackberry provide a mainstream communication technology that does not call attention to a person's disability. Using these types of devices, people who are deaf and hard of hearing are now able to participate in distance communication with the rest of the population.

As revolutionary as SMS is, it could potentially be better. Current text input methods for mobile phones are slow, because the 12-button keypad was designed for numerical input, not text, and the small keys of the mini-QWERTY keypad are sometimes difficult to access (note that smaller is not always better). For these reasons, several groups and companies are investigating alternative keypads and text entry methods for cell phones and smartphones.

Both multitap and T9 are text entry methods that utilize the standard 12-button keypad of a cell phone. To type the letter "a" with the multitap method, the number 2 must be hit once; to type the letter "b," the number 2 must be hit twice, and so on. Each letter requires 1–4 taps of the numerical digit to which it corresponds. The T9 predictive text entry on cell phones replaces the multitap method by reducing the number of keystrokes to only one stroke per letter by comparing the typed combination of numbers to a word database. The user has the option to choose a word from a list that is different from the predicted word. With traditional multitap and T9, users average 8–20 words per minute (wpm). For comparison, mini-QWERTY keyboard users are able to achieve 30–60 wmp [20,21].

An example of an alternative input technology is the Twiddler, made by HandyKey Corporation, shown in Figure 16.2. The Twiddler utilizes a 3×4-button layout that is similar to that on a standard mobile phone, but the keyboard is meant for single-handed use and employs a chording technique for text entry. During a comparative study at the Georgia Institute of Technology, novice users achieved rates of 20 wpm with multitap, 47 wpm with the Twiddler, and 60 wpm with a mini-QWERTY. One experienced Twiddler user was able to achieve rates of 120 wpm. In a "blind" comparative study where the user was not allowed to visually access the keyboard while typing, mini-QWERTY typing rates dropped to 45 wpm with error rates much higher than those encountered with the Twiddler. In addition, the research group has created a prototype mobile phone with Twiddler-style keypad [20,22–24].

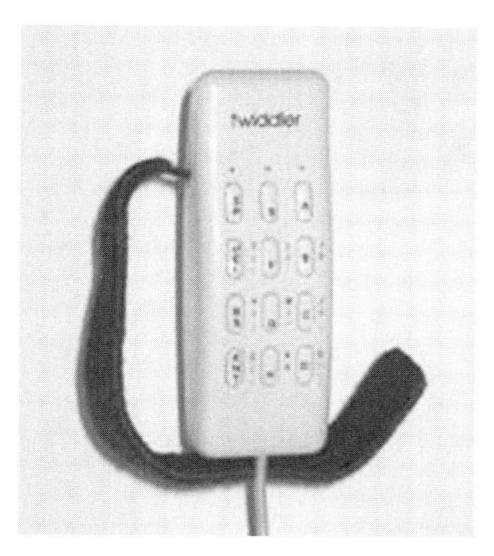

FIGURE 16.2 Twiddler keypad by HandyKey Corporation (picture courtesy Kent Lyons, Georgia Institute of Technology).

16.3.3 The Communication Assistant

The *Communication Assistant* is a new form of augmented communication developed in a project as a part of the Wireless RERC. The system is a wearable captioning presentation system intended for use in a wide variety of public venues, including movie theaters, live theaters, schools, sports arenas, places of worship, and museums. This assistive technology system enables users to easily receive information that is being presented audibly to all patrons. Previous forms of text presentation have been large communal screens or systems that are specific to only one venue, such as movie theaters.

The research team developed this technology to fill the void of accessibility in public places for people who are deaf or hard of hearing. The lack of captioning in community venues prevents equal access to information for individuals with hearing impairments and prohibits their full involvement in the community. Additional uses for the system include the transmission of multiple languages and the transmission of other information that might be desired, such as statistics at a sporting event or stockmarket information at work.

16.3.3.1 System Overview

The Communication Assistant relies on mobile wireless technology and consists of three components: a transmitter, a receiver, and a liquid crystal display. Design considerations for system components are discussed further in the next section. Multiple system configurations are available. The venue and user preference determine the best configuration for any given situation. The venue management owns and operates the transmitter and is responsible for providing the captions. Users may borrow the receiver and display from the venue, or provide their own. A diagram of the system components is shown in Figure 16.3.

The Communication Assistant uses the 802.11b wireless protocol. Wireless-enabled smartphones, personal digital assistants (PDAs), and laptops can be used as both receivers and displays. For some applications, though, users may require a display that is smaller,

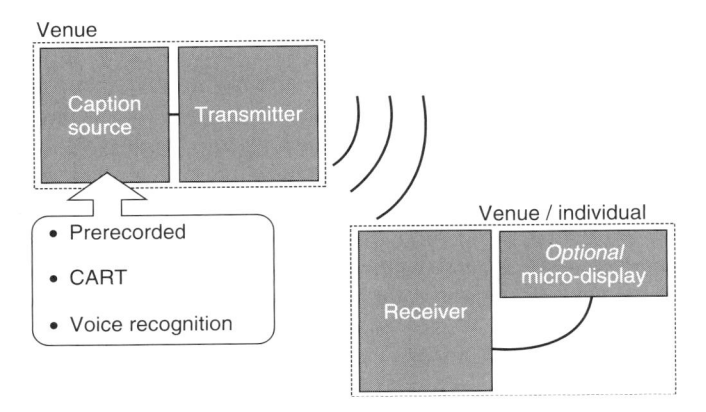

FIGURE 16.3 Diagram of Communication Assistant components.

more private, and hands-free. For those instances, a miniature VGA display is worn in front of one or both eyes. This display is plugged into a PDA or smartphone. The smartphone functions as the wireless receiver and controls the microdisplay, as well as provides power. The microdisplay can be attached to the user's glasses or worn on a headband. Although positioned close to the eye, the display uses optics that make its screen appear to float several feet away, giving users relaxed viewing of both the captions and of the world around them. The display creates the illusion of captioned text overlaid on the user's visual field; the wearer's real-world view is augmented by the captions.

Input for the transmitter can be prerecorded, typed in realtime, or generated by speech recognition. In cases where captions can be created ahead of time, they will be stored digitally and then transferred to the transmitter. A movie theater is an example of this situation. In most other cases, the captions are generated in real time. One method of creating real-time captions is by using a CART (communication access real-time translation or computer-assisted real-time translation) provider. A CART provider transcribes a speaker's comments verbatim using a stenograph keyboard and specialized software. The output from the stenograph station is delivered directly into the Communication Assistant transmitter. The system can be made compatible with other forms of real-time text generation as well, such as C-Print, developed at the National Technical Institute for the Deaf. C-Print provides a real-time summary of the information being presented, as opposed to a verbatim transcript. Real-time text generation can be used at sporting events, business meetings, lectures, places of worship, and other events.

The third source for captions is automatic speech recognition (ASR) technology. In cases where the speaker will be interacting repeatedly with individuals who are deaf or hard of hearing, such as in a classroom or place of worship, the speaker can pretrain speech recognition software to his or her voice. However, speech recognition technology in its current state has several problems. A 2004 analysis of performance trends in computer speech recognition systems estimated that human-like speech recognition performance cannot be achieved until somewhere around 2040 or 2050 [25]. Even before ASR reaches human-like performance, though, it will prove to be a beneficial tool for providing captions. Further discussion of ASR technology appears later in this chapter in Section 16.3.3.2.4.

In complex environments such as movie theaters where there is a need for multiple simultaneous datastreams, the wireless system will utilize multiple transmission "channels." "Channel" options offer the advantage of using the same hardware to access multiple streams of information in a single facility. Currently, when the software is started, a "list of available captions" automatically appears on the smartphone screen. The smartphone software knows what is being transmitted in the area and presents the user with a list of titles to choose from. Once the person chooses a title, the captions automatically begin and continue until the person chooses to disconnect. This simultaneous presentation of different text streams also accommodates of people who do not speak English or who use English as a second language by providing the possibility of sending multiple languages at the same time.

Channel options are just one form of system control provided to users. The user interface also provides options for text size; text and background colors, popup or scrolling captions, monocular or binocular versions of the microdisplay, quick inversion of text/background color, a text-saving option,[2] focus adjustment, and center or left justification of text. Additionally, the Smartphone and microdisplay can be formatted independently from each other. The formatting options stemmed from the results of user testing, which is described in the section on user input and testing (Section 16.3.3.3) of this chapter.

An additional component of the system for the classroom is a built-in chat feature. The system will be available with three modes of operation. (1) "lecture" for one-way transmission from a lecturer to a member of the audience or classroom, (2) "question" to enable a student to send a question directly to the teacher by typing the question on the laptop, and (3) "chat" to enable students in a classroom to engage in a group discussion with one another. The student has the option to save a transcript of the discussion session, just as she does to save the lecture. Using of a chat feature as a means of discussion in the classroom when there are both students who are hearing and deaf has been tested at the National Technical Institute for the Deaf [26]. The benefit of having the chat feature built into the system means that no external connection to the Internet is necessary to log on to a chat room, and again, the transcript can be saved.

Proof-of-concept prototypes of the Communication Assistant have been built and tested within the deaf and hard of hearing communities. Feedback on the system has been extremely positive, and a commercial product is currently being finalized with an industry partner.

16.3.3.2 Design Considerations

Many considerations go into the design of any system. Sometimes it is difficult to balance the desired features of the end user with what is feasible with today's technology. Tradeoffs always exist between size, weight, cost, functionality, and practicality. In the end, it is important to consider the options and weigh the benefits and disadvantages that each component brings to the system, while keeping in mind that the most important person to consider is the end user. It is also important to be flexible with the system design to keep abreast of the rapidly changing pace of technology. Building systems that can move forward with technology as it changes will prevent the system from becoming

---

[2]The venue is allowed to give the user the "text save" option. For copyrighted material, the venue can turn off this option at the transmitter. For a lecture or classroom for example, the user can chose to save the text to a .txt file for later review.

dated before it reaches the market. Also, multipurpose systems have advantages to those that only fulfill one need for one group of people. Modular design and off-the-shelf components can help the system stay current.

16.3.3.2.1 Wireless Transmission System

When the development project that led to the Communication Assistant first began, there were several choices for the wireless medium. At the time, cell phone screens were too small to be used to read captions; therefore cell phones were discounted almost immediately. Today, however, screens on cell phones have become larger and have better resolution, making them a more viable option than they were at any point during the project. The remaining choices were radio FM frequencies, proprietary wireless systems, 802.11b local-area networks, and Bluetooth. Bluetooth was very new at the time, and not as widely available as it is today. It was appealing for both the cost and size of its components and the promise that it held for future technologies. However, the range of communication (designed for 10 m, with specialty products able to reach 100 m) was very limited when considering outfitting an entire sports arena, for example.

Just like Bluetooth, FM radio transmissions were very appealing for the cost and size of the components, as well as the availability when compared to 802.11. The components for FM transmission and reception were widely available, whereas 802.11 hotspots were in their infancy, and the FM components were at least a factor of 10 cheaper than 802.11 components. Also, FM transmission is a one-way link and, as a passive receiver, requires much less power than does an 802.11 two-way receiver. Less power translates to smaller batteries and a smaller, lighterweight package for the end user.

Frequency-modulated transmission was appealing for text transmission because the audio signal of the FM frequency can be accompanied by digital data over a very large broadcast area. On a car radio, for example, the name of the radio station, the artist, or a song title might be displayed. The radio data system (RDS) is the method of transmitting this additional digital data. RDS-capable radios can display the text that is being transmitted. There are three features of the RDS standard: the program identification code (PIC), the program service name (PSN), and radio text (RT). The PIC feature allows a radio station to transmit its call letters. The PSN feature allows a radio station to transmit short messages, such as the station's name, that contain a maximum of 8 alphanumeric characters. The RT feature allows a radio station to transmit more complex messages such as advertisements or traffic data.

The RT feature of RDS was tested as the means of transmission for the captioning system. While RDS is great for limited text, or text that is repeated over and over, it is not able to keep up with the text rate necessary for a captioning system. Only messages lasting ≥ 3 s were displayed without error. Messages received every 1 or 2 s would have text characters misplaced or completely missing. This behavior was also observed with some of the local commercial stations that make use of RDS.

With FM frequencies ruled out because of the inability to transmit data accurately and completely [in addition to issues with Federal Communications Commission (FCC) licenses for operation], the choice was between proprietary wireless systems and standard 802.11b. There was one proprietary system available that operated in the 2.4-GHz band. While this system had the advantage of being a broadcast technology, the disadvantage was that it would allow a maximum of only four simultaneous captioning streams in one location. Using the 802.11 system provided the option of a multitude of different captioning streams, numbering in the hundreds or even thousands. The prototype captioning system was actually tested with a proprietary wireless system similar to 802.11, but during the development cycle, the cost of 802.11 components dropped significantly and the form factor of the personal digital assistants (for use as a receiver/display unit) improved greatly.

Choosing the standard 802.11 system versus a proprietary system allowed the use of off-the-shelf components as opposed to having to develop our own receiver/display unit, driving down the price and providing wider availability. The system offers other uses to the venue as well. Wireless networks allow users to check email and browse the Web at places like airports and Starbucks Coffee locations. A captioning service could be added to these locations inexpensively or to any location expanding into an 802.11 hotspot. Also, 802.11 systems can be equipped with high-gain antennas to make it easier to cover larger areas with less infrastructure, especially in cases where a low population density makes it more cost-effective.

In the end, off-the-shelf components will be cheaper and more prolific, and will have the ability to better adapt as the state-of-the-art of technology changes in the future.

16.3.3.2.2 Display Options
There are several options for the display component of the Communication Assistant system. In general, captions are often presented in an open-caption format in public venues, meaning that everyone in the audience can see the captions. But a communal screen at the front of a venue can be limiting. Patrons must sit where they have a good view of the display to be able to read the captions. Also, placement of the screen can be problematic for a venue. For example, it can be difficult to place the captioning display screen where it does not interfere with the aesthetics of a play. Therefore, the Communication Assistant offers multiple personal display options.

Currently, the end user is able to watch captions on the screen of the smartphone, on a laptop screen, or on a microdisplay screen. Different situations or venues warrant the use of the different displays, which is why flexibility was built into the system. In some venues, such as a place of worship or a conference meeting, the smartphone screen might offer the best viewing option. The display is easily portable and discreet, and the audio may not be accompanied by other visual content that would require attention.

In a classroom setting, where computers can be a common feature, the computer monitor may provide the best option for caption display. The computer provides a means of additional access for the classroom, such as the chat feature to allow discussions among students. The keyboard also allows the student to send a question directly to the teacher.

In this age of multimedia presentations, some classroom lectures could also benefit from a head-mounted display or microdisplay. Microdisplays are also necessary in venues such as movie theaters, live theater, and sports arenas where a large focus of the event is on visual action. Microdisplays can be mounted to a pair of glasses or a headband. The microdisplay "floats" the words in front of the wearer, superimposing them on the wearer's visual field; thus, the wearer's visual field is augmented by the text, as demonstrated in Figure 16.4. A person's binocular vision allows this overlay of text on the visual field. One eye views the unaltered world, while the other eye views the text on the microdisplay. The brain combines the image from each eye to give the augmented view.

There are several different types and styles of microdisplays. Each different microdisplay has various features and characteristics that were considered when choosing a microdisplay for this system. Many head-mounted displays are not "micro" at all; rather,

308 THE COMMUNICATION ASSISTANT (ALTERNATIVE COMMUNICATION)

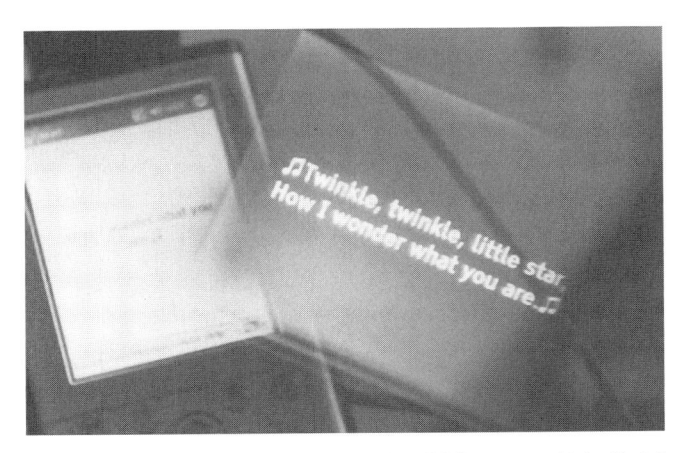

FIGURE 16.4 Microdisplay text "floating" in front of a PDA screen. Note that to be completely accurate, the double musical note (♫) in this image should be a single musical note (♪).

they are very large with almost a "helmet-like" appearance. These systems are not discreet or lightweight, and are therefore not the choice for a system that will be utilized for multiple hours in a row by a group of people who would rather not have it known that they need a special system for assistance.

The research team originally tested the prototype with a low-resolution, black-and-white ASCII (American Standard Code for Information Interchange) text viewer that was worn mounted to a pair of glasses. There were only three text size options, and the display connected to the PDA with an RS232 serial connector. The battery pack and display control were located in the middle of a long, fragile cord. No focus adjustment was available. The form factor of the display itself was excellent; it was very discreet, as shown in Figure 16.5 of this chapter and Figure 17.8 of Chapter 17.

While the form factor of the display is the same, Figure 16.5 actually shows a later version of the display where the serial connector and the battery/control pack have been removed and replaced by a compact flash card. The display system draws power from

FIGURE 16.5 Inventor Leanne West with PDA receiver and microdisplay.

the PDA and can be fully controlled by it. This intermediate display uses a 640 × 480, full-color VGA display. A two-hand focus adjustment is available as well.

As technology has advanced, there are now several microdisplays on the market today—both monocular and binocular versions. The current system microdisplay has features that make it more user-friendly than previous versions. While the form factor of the display is slightly larger and less discreet, the overall design is much more rugged for daily use. The cord is much less fragile, as is the positioning mechanism. In addition, the focus adjustment has been designed for use with one hand as opposed to two, with a much finer scale of adjustment. A headband mount is available for the monocular version for people who do not wear glasses, and a binocular version that slips on like a pair of glasses is also available.

Other wearable display systems utilize retinal writing to produce the image that is overlaid on the user's visual field. These systems are typically large and relatively heavy. But aside from these characteristics, these systems were not considered for the captioning device for two reasons. First, in retinal writing, a laser is employed to draw the image directly on the retina. The laser renders the display monochromatic; in other words, there is only one color available for the text[3] [27], and it is the color of the laser used in the system (usually red). This characteristic limits the customizability of the system, and studies have shown [28] that white text is preferred to colored text for captions. The second reason has to do with marketability of the commercial product. During our testing, we learned that many people who have a hearing impairment are very protective of their eyesight. While these retinal writing displays are not dangerous, the concept of shining a laser in a person's eye to directly stimulate the retina can be an unsettling thought for the consumer.

When designing a system that will utilize a head-mounted display, the characteristics and desired features of the system being designed should be considered carefully. While one display may be best for a certain use or target population, this does not mean that it is appropriate for all uses and users. There are always tradeoffs that must be taken into account.

16.3.3.2.3 Font Options
Some portions of the system development effort can be more difficult than originally anticipated. A choice of font style was requested in our testing of the prototype, but providing this option proved to be difficult. At the time, Windows-based PDAs came with two font choices—Arial and Times New Roman. Research has shown that for captions, sanserif fonts are preferred to "fancier" fonts [29]. Therefore, Arial is the more ideal font for providing captions because it is a sanserif font, whereas Times New Roman is not. However, it is also imperative to use a font that has a musical note symbol (♪). According to the *Captioning Key*, produced by the Captioned Media Program, song lyrics must contain a music icon "at the beginning and end of each caption within a song, but use two music icons at the end of the last line of a song" [30]. Unfortunately, the version of Arial included on the Pocket PC platform does not have a music icon, but the Times New Roman does. The research team found another option. The Royal National Institute for the Blind allowed the researchers to use Tiresias[4] font, which they had specially developed to be easy to read by persons with low vision.

---
[3]Microvision developed a full-color display prototype named Spectrum™ in April 2001; however, the full-color version was not available in their product line as of February 2006.
[4]Tiresias Fonts ©2000 Royal National Institute of the Blind. All rights reserved.

16.3.3.2.4 Automatic Speech Recognition

In planning for future improvements to ASR technology, the Communication Assistant was designed to handle ASR as an input to the system. There are currently several limitations that outweigh the benefits of ASR when compared to real-time captioning services. However, in looking to the future, ASR will surpass real-time services as the input method of choice.

The Liberated Learning Project (LLP) conducted by St. Mary's University in Nova Scotia, Canada, completed a 3-year classroom study of ASR based on subjective evaluations by students with a variety of disabilities [31]. The LLP created class transcripts in real time with a specialized version of IBM's ViaVoice (circa 2000) and projected the transcript on the wall behind the lecturer. Through focus groups and interviews with students, the LLP showed that ASR technology has potential as an effective and accepted tool for improving the educational experience of university students both with and without disabilities. The greatest obstacle identified was the accuracy of the ViaVoice ASR software. It is important to note, however, that newer ASR systems are significantly improved.

The Communication Assistant research team performed tests with ASR during its development process. At the time, IBM's ViaVoice and Dragon NaturallySpeaking® were the two leading ASR products on the market, and Dragon NaturallySpeaking® Preferred version 7 was chosen for tests. Currently, Dragon NaturallySpeaking version 8 is considered the best available ASR software for Windows-based platforms [32] and has been chosen for commercially available systems such as the iCommunicator™ [33]. IBM's ViaVoice is still the next-closest competitor, but IBM ceded all sales and distribution activities to the makers of Dragon, and the product has not been upgraded since 2001 [34]. Dragon, on the other hand, has had four major updates since 2001, including version 9, released in July 2006.

During the tests, there proved to be several problems with ASR software [35]. The chosen text was 357 words in length and was read in a conversational manner in a quiet environment. Dragon was able to achieve accuracy rates of 95–98% with basic recommended training (≤ 10 min from start to finish) and utilizing the file-reading option to learn specialized vocabularies and user syntax. However, when it was incorrect, it completely changed the meaning or made nonsense of the speaker's comments. Additionally, punctuation is not automatically entered into the transcript, and it is unreasonable to expect a speaker to say "period" at the end of every sentence. Finally, to increase accuracy, speech recognition technology buffers the transcript to evaluate the sentence before printing the transcript. Buffering time depends on several factors, but the main one is computer speed. While this buffering takes anywhere from 5 to 30 s (usually around 8 s), even the 5-s delay is too distracting or confusing for people who have limited hearing or who are lip reading. Note, however, that CART and C-Print also involve presentation delays because the typist must hear the text and then type it. Note also that CART and C-Print are not 100% accurate, either. Much of the accuracy depends on the preparation of the provider.

Dragon NaturallySpeaking® version 9 has made advancements to address some of the problems encountered during the tests. The Nuance (formerly Scansoft) Website claims 99% accuracy for Dragon 9 and a 20% improvement over Dragon 8 (which had a 25% improvement over Dragon 7) [36]. The newest verisons have also made progress toward automatic punctuation by including commas and periods in a limited capacity. The tests with Dragon 7 showed that punctuation was not always inserted correctly, if at all. The research team has not performed any tests with Dragon 8 or 9 to verify improvement in this area. Version 9 also comes with a noise-canceling headset because historically, a third concern for ASR is accuracy in noisy environments [37,38]. The use of noise-canceling headsets and directional speakers has been shown to significantly reduce the barrier of a noisy environments.

There are several benefits to using ASR when compared to real-time text generation methods, assuming that accuracy has reached acceptable standards and punctuation can automatically be inserted. First, ASR technology is readily available for laptop and desktop computers; therefore scheduling and deployment is much simpler than dependence on the availability of a captionist. ASR software is also cost-effective when compared to captioning services. Nuance offers Dragon NaturallySpeaking Preferred 9 for a one-time fee of $199.99, while CART average costs are $120–$200 per hour.

It should also be noted that ASR systems do not need rest breaks. Rest breaks are necessary for CART and C-Print providers to keep up accuracy performance and to reduce fatigue and the risk of repetitive strain injury. While no federal or state regulations currently restrict the time captionists can be required to perform without a break, the National Institute for Occupational Safety and Health (NIOSH) recommends a minimum of 10 min rest per hour when typing constantly on a computer [39].

16.3.3.3 User Input and Testing

The project began by approaching a local advocacy group for people who are deaf and hard of hearing. The idea for the project was posed to the Georgia Council for the Hearing Impaired (GaCHI) to make sure that the system we envisioned would be of interest to the population we intended to serve. The author cannot stress enough the importance of this first step in assistive technology development and research. It is imperative to involve members of the community from the very beginning when creating an assistive technology. The end user (and caregivers, where appropriate) will know what their needs are. They will know whether they are likely to use what is being proposed for development, and they will have insight as to what features are important for them.

During the course of the Communication Assistant project, two formal rounds of testing occurred to elicit feedback and comments from the deaf and hard of hearing community. GaCHI played a vital role in recruiting volunteers for the initial round of testing. The device was further tested at the Self Help for the Hard of Hearing (now called the Hearing Loss Association of America) annual conference. The tests were conducted in a simulated movie theater setting with one to four volunteers at a time. After a brief introduction to the device, volunteers were asked to watch anywhere from 15 min of a movie to a full-length feature (up to 1.5 h), while using the microdisplay system to receive the captioning of the movie. The following information and quotes come directly from the questionnaires that the volunteers filled out after using the device to watch the movie.

Including both rounds of testing, 80 participants were recruited to test the device, representing a variety of age groups ranging from 15 to over 75 years old. Volunteers included people who were hearing (usually an ASL interpreter or an interested family member), deaf from birth, late-onset deaf, and hard of hearing (the majority of testers were hard of hearing). Almost all of the adult volunteers had a college degree or higher.

Most volunteers thought that the display "took some getting used to," but it normally took less than 10 min to get the display in comfortable reading position. Most volunteers also thought that the text was easy to read, but desired a choice of fonts. The most frequently noted suggestions to improve the readability were to include a text-size option and a display focus adjustment, both of which were not part of the original prototypes but were included in the final product. The focus adjustment allows the wearer to focus the text at a desired distance, for example, in the plane of the movie screen. This adjustment relieves any strain caused by a difference in depth perception of the words and the object or scene being viewed. From the researchers' own experiences, wearing a microdisplay of any type seems unfamiliar at first and requires some adaptation. However, after several uses of the device, the wearer becomes accustomed to the microdisplay and adaptation is almost instantaneous. The researchers have found that adaptation is even easier when wearing the binocular system.

The desire for custom formatting of text was strongly indicated during testing. Many of the younger testers wanted to have multiple options for background and text color, while more experienced readers of captions preferred a black background with white text. The more experienced caption readers also preferred popup-style captions in two lines of text because this is the format in which they are used to receiving captions. However, slower readers preferred to keep a full screen of text in case they fell behind or wanted to look back at what had been said. The ability to customize the captions to suit the individual is not met by text presentation systems such as the Rear Window®[5] system available in some movie theaters or where words are displayed on a communal screen available in some live theaters, classrooms, and places of worship.

Almost none of the volunteers thought that wearing the microdisplay would make them feel self-conscious. The few who said it would gave comments such as "wouldn't mind in theater, but in lighted situation would be hesitant unless with others wearing it, too"; "I am only self-conscious a little. I would use it in a movie theater no problem. I might be more self conscious when lights are on"; "Only if I'm the only one using it"; or "If it helps enough for me to get what is going on in the movie, then I don't care what others think." Since this testing occurred, an increasing number of mobile wireless technologies have come on the market such as the Microsoft Zune and Apple Video iPOD, making head-mounted electronics even more common and ubiquitous.

Access and independence are the key benefits that the system offers. While the system is not intended to replace interpreters, one user commented that "Even in lip reading I miss some words, therefore it's good to have a back-up. For the back-up, I would prefer to have the Communication Assistant than an interpreter—I feel more independent."

The system has also been demonstrated with a member of the deaf community at the Georgia Tech baseball stadium. A CART reporter provided the transcription of the announcer and color commentary of the game. During the demonstration, the first question asked by the deaf volunteer was, "Where do I have to sit?" When he was told that he could sit anywhere, he was very excited and chose to sit at the far end of the stadium near the left fielder. Overall, he was happy with the system and felt that it provided him with a more complete experience at the ballgame.

16.3.3.4 Caption Format Standard

One of the main difficulties with creating a captioning presentation technology intended for use in a variety of venues is the lack of a captioning standard. As discussed, several systems can generate text, such as CART and C-Print. Each of these systems creates text with different formatting codes. Therefore, when the text enters the Communication

---

[5]Rear Window® Captioning was provided by the Media Access Group at WGBH.

Assistant, the Communication Assistant software must have prior knowledge of these codes to present the text properly. The same is true for the captions generated for first-run movies. The format of the captions depends on the company that generates the captions for the studio that creates the film, although this problem is being dealt with as the movie industry moves to digital cinema. A captioning standard is being developed for digital cinema, although the standard will not apply to captions created for 35-mm film.

While the providers of CART and C-Print are willing to share their formatting standards to better provide access, some companies are unwilling to do so. Creating these limits on the means of accommodation limits the effectiveness of the accommodation. To make all movies and venues more accessible, captions should be created in an open standard format that is available for use in any captioning presentation system. The more products for captioning there are on the market, the greater the demand will be for captions. For example, movie studios will be ensured that if they provide captions for a first-run movie, it will be seen by the largest number of people possible. The captions they provide will not be limited to theaters that own certain captioning presentation equipment; a theater that owns any captioning presentation equipment will be able to provide access to their patrons—and the benefit will be self-perpetuating. The more options that a venue is given regarding captioning presentation technology, the more likely they are to install a system. The more theaters that provide a means of access, the more willing movie studios will be to provide captions for their movies. More first-run movies that are captioned will lead to more theater owners who will be willing to install captioning presentation systems, and so on. Standardizing the format of captions will allow captions to reach more patrons with current or future technologies.

16.3.4 Technology Transfer

There is a critical step in the development process that should be started as soon as possible. This step is *technology transfer*, which is turning the system from a laboratory prototype into a real-world commercially available technology. Beginning technology transfer early is especially important when developing wireless or other cutting-edge technology. Because of the rapid changes and advancements that occur in this field, a technology can become obsolete before it reaches the market if there are lengthy delays in licensing the technology or finalizing a research prototype for commercialization.

16.4 CHAPTER SUMMARY

Access to alternative and augmentative communication is vital to allow personal advancement and social inclusion. Redefining traditional AAC to include the new and emerging forms of technology that enable individuals who are hard of hearing understand what is being said to them is important. As stated previously, there are over 30 million people who are hard of hearing, and this number is growing every day as the population ages.

In this rapidly changing face of technology, smaller and faster can be beneficial to most wireless designs. As technology advances, system components, such as microdisplays, will become more discreet and less expensive. Batteries will last longer and weigh less. ASR technology will become more accurate and reach "human-like" performance. Modular designs that can change as technology advances, off-the-shelf components that can meet multiple needs, and systems that allow customization for the end user are all design factors that should be considered when developing a new system.

Mobile wireless technologies are important to future communication. Access to these devices is necessary to ensure that all people will be able to receive pertinent information and communicate to the best of their ability, giving people further freedom and independence.

ACKNOWLEDGMENTS

Funding for the Communication Assistant was provided by the National Institute on Disability and Rehabilitation Research of the US Department of Education under grant number H133E010804 and the Georgia Tech Research Institute. The opinions contained in this publication are those of the grantee and do not necessarily reflect those of the US Department of Education or the Georgia Tech Research Institute.

The author would also like to thank the project development team of Jack Wood, John Stewart, Jay Sexton, and Ethan Adler for their expertise and hard work in making the vision become a reality; Thad Starner and John Anschutz for descriptions of their projects; and Jack Wood and Jay Sexton for their review and editing assistance.

REFERENCES

1. Millar S, Scott J: What is augmentative and alternative communication? An introduction, in *Augmentative Communication in Practice: An Introduction*, CALL Centre & Scottish Executive Education Dept., 1998, pp. 3–12 available at http://callcentre.education.ed.ac.uk/downloads/acpsbook/introbook.pdf#1; accessed 2/29/05).
2. American Speech-Hearing-Language Association: *Augmentative Communication: A Glossary* (available at: http://www.asha.org/public/speech/disorders/acc_primer.htm; accessed 2/29/05).
3. Beukelman D, Ansel B: Research priorities in augmentative and alternative communication, *Augment Altern Commun* **11**(2):131–134 (June 1995).
4. Matas J, Mathy-Laikko P, Beukelman D, Legresley K: Identifying the non-speaking population: A demographic study, *Augment Altern Commun* **1**:17–31 (1985).
5. Kochkin S. MarkeTrak VI: The VA and direct mail sales spark growth in hearing aid market, *Hearing Rev* **8**(12):16–24, 63–65 (Dec 2001).
6. Kochkin S: *World Age Demography Data-base*, Better Hearing Institute, Aug 2004.
7. Mitchell R: How many deaf people are there in the United States? Estimates from the survey of income and program participation, *J Deaf Stud Deaf Educ* **11**(1):112–119 (2006).
8. Hill K, Romich B: *A Rate Index for Augmentative and Alternative Communication* (available at http://www.aacinstitute.org/Resources/MethodsandTools/2002rateindex/paper.html; accessed 12/29/05).
9. Burgstahler S: *Creating Video and Multimedia Products that Are Accessible to People with Sensory Impairments* (available at http://www.washington.edu/doit/Brochures/Technology/vid_sensory.html; accessed 2/31/06).
10. National Institute on Deafness and other Communication Disorders Website (available at http://www.nidcd.nih.gov/health/hearing/asl.asp; 2/13/06).
11. International Society for Augmentative and Alternative Communication (available at http://www.isaac-online.org/en/aac/what_is.html; accessed 2/29/05).
12. Augmentative and Alternative Communication: *Washington Assistive Technology Alliance* (available at http://wata.org/resource/communication/index.htm; accessed 12/30/05).

13. Jans D, Clark S: Alternative access to communication aids, in *Augmentative Communication in Practice: An Introduction*, CALL Centre & Scottish Executive Education Dept, 1998, pp. 46–50 (available at: http://callcentre.education.ed.ac.uk/downloads/acpsbook/introbook.pdf#1; accessed 12/29/05).
14. Anschutz J: *Mobile Wireless Communication Access* (available at http://www.wirelessrerc.gatech.edu/projects/development/d3.html; accessed 2/23/06).
15. Anschutz J, Shepherd Spinal Center, Atlanta, GA: Personal communication, unpublished work, Feb 16, 2006.
16. Sprint Video Relay Service Website: http://www.sprint.com/business/products/products/videoRelayServices_tabA.html; accessed 4/27/06.
17. Reardon M: Tight squeeze for mobile TV, CNET News.com (article online posting date 10/3/05; available at http://news.com.com/Tight+squeeze+for+mobile+TV/2100-1039_3-5886537.html; accessed 2/18/06).
18. Brashear H, Starner T, Lukowicz P, Junker H: Using multiple sensors for mobile sign language recognition, *Proc 7th IEEE Int Symp Wearable Computers*, Oct 2003.
19. McGuire R, Hernandez-Rebollar J, Starner T, Henderson V, Brashear H, Ross D: Towards a One-way American sign language translator, *Proc 6th IEEE Int Conf Automatic Face and Gesture Recognition*. Seoul, Korea, May 2004.
20. Starner T: Homepage (available at http://www-static.cc.gatech.edu/~thad/030_research.htm; accessed 1/31/06).
21. *A Better Smartphone Keypad* (available at http://www.chicagologic.com; accessed 2/17/06).
22. Lyons K, Starner T, Plaisted D, Fusia J, Lyons A, Drew A, Looney E: Twiddler typing: One-handed chording text entry for mobile phones, *Proc CHI 2004*, Vienna, Austria, April 2004.
23. Lyons K, Plaisted D, Starner T: Expert chording text entry on the twiddler one-handed keyboard, *Proc Int Symp Wearable Computers*, Arlington, VA, Nov 2004, pp 94–101.
24. Lyons K, Gane B, Starner T, Catrambone R: Improving novice performance on the twiddler one-handed chording keyboard, *Proc Int Forum on Applied Wearable Computing*, Zurich, Switzerland, March 2005.
25. Arrowood J: State of the art in speech synthesis, recognition, and understanding, *Proc Wireless RERC State of Technology Conf*, May 2004.
26. Schull J: MultiChat: A multi-person, browser-based, real time text-as-you-type chat system designed to facilitate face-to-face and in-class interaction between deaf and hearing students, *Proc Int Symp Instructional Technology and Education of the Deaf*, Rochester, NY, June 2005.
27. Spectrum™ Prototype Delivered to the Cleveland Clinic Foundation for Evaluation in Surgical Applications: *PRNewswire* (online posting date 4/10/01; available at http://www.prnewswire.com/cgi-bin/stories.pl?ACCT=104&STORY=/www/story/04-10-2001/0001466146&EDATE=; accessed 2/22/06).
28. National Center for Accessible Media: *Advanced Television Closed Captioning Research Report* (online posting date 1998; available at http://www.cfv.org/caai/nadh128.pdf; accessed 2/14/06).
29. *ATV Closed Captioning Findings* (available at http://ncam.wgbh.org/projects/atv/atvccfindings.html; accessed 2/15/06).
30. *Captioning Key: Guidelines and Preferred Techniques*, Captioned Media Program, National Association of the Deaf, 2006.
31. Leitch D, MacMillan T: *How Students with Disabilities Respond to Speech Recognition Technology in the University Classroom* (available at http://www.liberatedlearning.com/research/FINAL%20YEAR%20III%20LLP%20REPORT.pdf; accessed 11/20/04).

32. Breeden J: Recognition apps help users find their voice, *Govt Comput News* (online posting date 5/00; available at http://www.gcn.com/state/vol6_no5/reviews/700-1.html; accessed 2/22/06).
33. iCommunicator Website. http://www.myicommunicator.com; accessed 1/30/06.
34. Moore C: *Road Warrior Mailbag* (online posting date 5/24/04; available at http://www.macopinion.com/columns/roadwarrior/04/05/24/; accessed 11/20/04).
35. West L, Wood J, Stewart J, Sexton J, Adler E: The Communication Assistant, captioning and community venues. *Proc Australian Rehabilitation & Assistive Technology Association Conf*, Melbourne, Australia, June 2–4, 2004.
36. Nuance sales literature (available at http://www.nuance.com/naturallyspeaking/professional/; accessed 2/23/06).
37. Stinson M, Stuckless E, Henderson J, Millser L: Perceptions of hearing impaired college students towards real-time speech to print: RTGD and other educational support services, *Volta Rev* **90**(7):339–348 (Dec 1988).
38. Steinfeld A: The benefits of real-time captioning in a mainstream classroom as measured by working memory, *Volta Rev* **100**(1):29–44 (1998).
39. Hastings D, Breklein K, Cermak S, Reynolds R, Rosen H, Wilson J: *Notetaking for Deaf and Heard of Hearing Students*, Northeast Technical Assistance Center (available at http://www.netac.rit.edu/downloads/TFR_Notetaking.pdf; accessed 2/23/06).

17

Wearable Systems Design Issues for Aging or Disabled Users

Maribeth Gandy, Tracy Westeyn, Helene Brashear and Thad Starner

TSRB-IMTC

17.1 INTRODUCTION

For Americans without disabilities, technology makes things easier. For Americans with disabilities, technology makes things possible.
— Mary Pat Radabaugh, Director, IBM National Support Center for Persons with Disabilities, 1988

What is "wearable computing?" Wearable computers often conjure images of their early adopters—individuals with a display covering one eye, a hand-crafted computer concealed on the body, and small keyboards to provide input. However, the definition of wearable computing is broader. Wearable computers are any device worn or carried on the body capable of receiving input, processing information, and providing output to a user. Modern mobile phones and music players, for example, are considered to be wearable computers. Typical wearable computer input methods are one-handed keyboards, speech recognition, knobs, and sliders. Output can be provided by head-up displays (HUDs—displays mounted on glasses or headbands), audio feedback, tactile feedback, and embedded screens. The first commercially available wearable computers had mainly industrial applications. They made use of HUDs for onsite machine repair, airline maintenance, and poultry inspection. Prior to these industrial applications, wearable computers were (and still are) used in academic research.

In the past, wearable computing research applications explored spontaneous notetaking, on-demand/just-in-time information retrieval, augment reality [using head-

---

The Engineering Handbook of Smart Technology for Aging, Disability, and Independence,
Edited by A. Helal, M. Mokhtari and B. Abdulrazak
Copyright © 2008 John Wiley & Sons, Inc.

mounted displays (HMDs) to overlay computer graphics onto reality], using physiologic sensors to assess the user's affective state, and sensing the context of the user in the environment. Today, wearable computing has become commonplace (e.g., mobile phones, MP3 players, insulin pumps, and deep-brain stimulators, to name just a few). More recent increases in on-body computing power coupled with continuous processing abilities can allow wearable computers to be used as communication aids (such as translators), memory aids (helping people to remember where they left things), physiological monitoring systems (continually monitoring heart rate, blood pressure, and other vital statistics), and for the sensing/perception of the surrounding environment.

Assistive technologies can benefit from a wearable computer's sensing ability by continuously monitoring an individual. For example, a mobile phone augmented with motion sensors could be used to monitor how often an elderly woman moves around her house, or how her gait has changed as the result of a chronic illness. Likewise, a combination of sensors on the body and in the environment could determine what someone is doing (eating, taking medication, etc.) and whether that person is doing them correctly.

In addition to continuous monitoring abilities, wearable computers have the potential to augment a person's natural abilities, especially with respect to communication. These augmentative capabilities make wearable computers an attractive platform for assistive technologies. For example, a study by Henderson shows how teenagers in the deaf community use mobile phones and other wireless mobile devices (such as the T-Mobil SideKick) to communicate with both hearing and deaf individuals [1]. In some cases, these wireless mobile devices allow deaf teenagers, who natively communicate with American Sign Language, to converse with hearing teenagers without requiring the presence of an interpreter.

While wearable computers, in theory, might assist the disabled populations in living more independent lives, it is only important whether if wearable computers will be used in practice. Studies aimed at identifying and prioritizing ergonomic needs of users with disabilities for mobile wireless technologies indicate that people with disabilities want mobile computing devices [2]. According to the study, 72% of the participants own mobile wireless devices while 84% who did not own a wireless device planned to buy one in the next year. Individuals who do not have mobile wireless devices want them and those who have them state that the use of mobile, wireless technologies is important to their daily life. Participants who did not own wireless devices indicated two prohibitive factors: the cost of the device with wireless service and the lack of design accommodating the participants' specific impairment. In fact, 90% of all participants were interested in evaluating new designs. This study shows that while the disabled population wants mobile, wireless devices, the usability of current devices remains an obstacle.

Usability of current wearable computers can be challenging, if not impossible, for people with vision, dexterity, and hearing impairments. In part, this lack of usability is due to the newness of the devices in general markets. Typically, the design criteria for wearable computers concentrate on four areas: networking, power consumption/heat dissipation, privacy of data, and device interface. A device's networking capabilities depend on its intended use. Is it a real-time communication device or a device that can connect to a network occasionally for updates? Minimizing the device's power consumption reduces its operating temperature and its weight (due to batteries). Additionally, heat produced by the device must be dissipated to prevent the device from overheating and malfunctioning. Minimizing the user's discomfort due to this heat dissipation influences how the device can be worn or carried on the body. Placement of the device on the body is also influenced by the interfaces for the device and the sensitivity of data generated or received by the device. For example, if the data displayed by the device are sensitive, a HMD may be used to prevent others from observing the output. Depending on the sensitivity of the data, they can be stored either locally on the device or transmitted wirelessly to be stored elsewhere. Users of wearable computers are often experts, highly motivated to use the device. Less importance has been stressed on the creation of an accessible interface between the device and a nonexpert or disabled user.

While the four design requirements mentioned above are important to all wearable computers, designing wearable computing devices for the purposes of assistive technologies requires additional consideration:

1. First and foremost is to address the users' needs. Specifically, what problem of the special population is being addressed?
2. What demands are placed on the interface due to the impairments of the population?
3. What sort of technology is required to solve the problem?
4. What is the social impact of the device?

This chapter discusses a wearable application design process. A survey of assistive applications is presented to highlight the steps of the process as well as the decision and tradeoffs that their designers were forced to make. As each application is described, the assistive technology (AT) design issues are addressed and their solutions (successful or unsuccessful) are highlighted.

17.2 DESIGN ISSUES AND DISABILITY

When developing an on-body system for use by a disabled or elderly population, unique issues may arise. The previously discussed design tradeoffs and challenges that are present in any wearable system still exist but are often magnified or skewed when the goal is to specifically address the needs of users with disabilities. This section presents a set of design needs that can be applied to all wearable projects but are of particular interest for assistive technology. Others have explored the set of unique needs that exist for wearable medical or disability applications. For example, Martin presents a set of requirements for wearable medical monitoring systems [3]. These requirements include small device size with little user input required; a greater emphasis on privacy; sensors that are robust, comfortable to wear, and unobtrusive; and finally, an awareness on the part of the developer of the responsibility the system has to the user when the user is relying on it to provide services such as diagnosis and emergency response.

Figure 17.1 illustrates the components of a wearable computing system: the user, the community that the user is part of, the application that will be providing services to the user, and the physical device (computing platform, input/output devices, etc.) that the user will be wearing and interacting with. While the user's needs lie within the user, the remaining physical, data, technical, and social needs that must be addressed by the design exist at the connections between these components. The *physical needs* are those requirements related to the physical nature of the system and how it affects the user, such as placement of equipment on the body and the user interface. The *data needs* concern

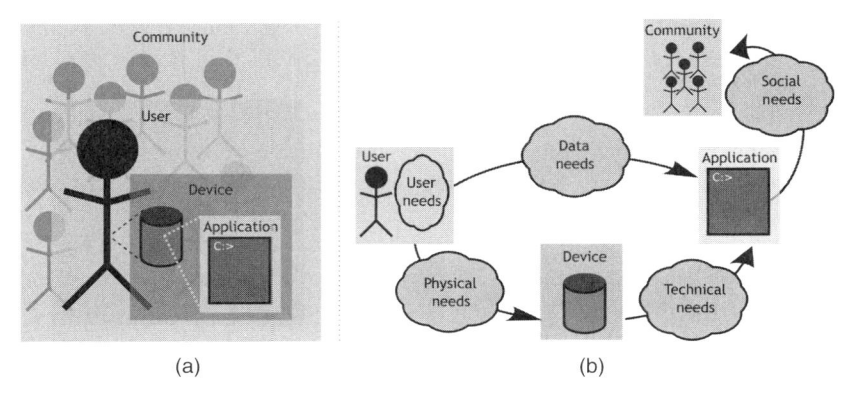

FIGURE 17.1 (a) Components of a wearable computing system and their relationship to each other; (b) Flowchart illustrating how the different needs that the designer must satisfy exist at the connection points between the system components.

the communication of data between the user and the application and how the application will acquire the contextual information it needs about the user and the environment. This need addresses issues such as what values should be measured and which sensors will be used. The *technical needs* encompass the hardware and software in the device that will be required to make the application a reality. This need will include issues such as battery life and processing power. Finally, the *social needs* are those requirements that relate to the application's interactions with the community in which it is used, such as privacy and obtrusiveness.

Figure 17.2 illustrates the iterative process through which a designer will address each of the requirements starting with the gathering and analysis of user needs. Following that

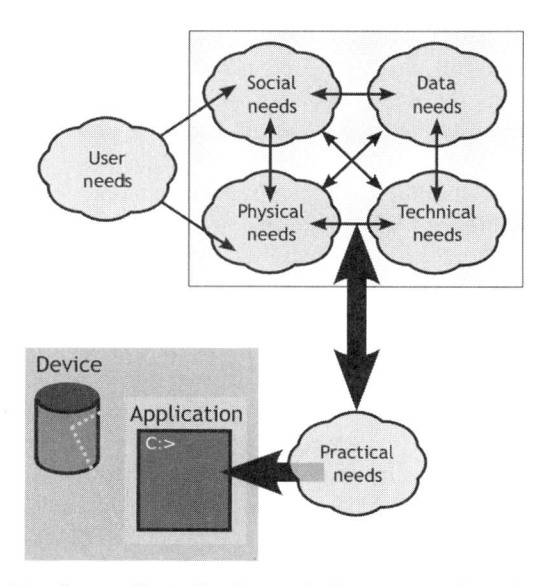

FIGURE 17.2 A state diagram illustrating how a designer moves through the design process.

step the designer progresses to the task of prioritizing and tackling each of the remaining needs. While the traditional wearable computing design process is often viewed as linear, these design needs must be addressed in an iterative fashion as the various requirements and tradeoffs must be visited and revisited to maximize usability and usefulness for each particular application. Once the design process has met each need to the level that is required, the design will enter the "practical" stage where the designer must consider issues such as cost of the device, government policies, industry or international standards, community acceptance, and existing infrastructure. All of the practical issues might require a return to the "needs" states where various parts of the design are adjusted to accommodate these concerns.

17.2.1 User Needs

The first step in the design process is to determine who the target users are. One approach to defining your users' capabilities, called *universal design* aims to provide a system that the widest range of people will be able to use. When we as developers and designers create a system that requires user interaction—whether it is computer software, a kitchen appliance, or a doorknob—we often fall victim to a common mistake: we use ourselves as the model for our system's potential users. Even developing for an "average user" is a pitfall that results in numerous users whose needs are overlooked. The average user might account for the largest spike under a bell curve, but nonaverage users account for a much larger percentage of the general population. Additionally, the number of people possessing all of the average attributes being considered in a design is very small. The designers' goal should be to broaden the section of the bell curve that their system targets [4].

The practice of universal design has resulted in many products originally intended for the disabled population that benefit everyone—closed captioning, books on tape, and even the telephone, for example. Conversely, sometimes a product's designers don't anticipate the large market that their device will have among the disabled community. The RIM Blackberry, a wireless handheld device that can send and receive email and text messages, has become hugely popular in the deaf community because it lets people who might not be able to speak on a cell phone have mobile communication access.

However, universal design is not always the correct approach. In some cases it is more appropriate to employ a user-centered design process where just the needs of the particular target population are considered [5]. This can be necessary for systems aimed at those users with uncommon needs or disabilities. Using universal design in these cases would result in a system that, while satisfying a wider range of possible users, would not meet the unique needs of the target population.

Once the target population has been determined, the process continues with gathering and understanding the user needs. While this step is required in the development of any usable system it is even more critical in the development of an application for a disabled user population because the researchers are often further removed personally from the target user. When user needs and user abilities are not properly understood by the researchers, resources will be wasted in creating systems that the target user neither needs nor wants. This pitfall is the most common for wearable computing researchers looking to develop systems to aid the disabled; they fail to include their target population in every step of the process (especially the initial idea stage) and make assumptions about what types of support and augmentation would improve their users' lives. For example, many systems utilize Braille as an output for users with low vision. However, these systems are often of little use to actual users since only a small percentage of that community can actually read Braille. If the researchers did information gathering and needs assessment before starting the project they would realize that other types of auditory or tactile feedback would be more appropriate.

The user needs assessment includes getting to know the target users, exploring their existing problems of daily living, isolating problems that might be solved via wearable/mobile technology and determining the types of interface approaches that would be usable by this population, and considering issues such as what level of responsibility this device will incur on the basis of the services it will provide. Often there is more than one stakeholder in the system—people other than the target user that will either be interacting with a component of the system themselves (e.g., a monitoring system where data are gathered from the user and sent to a caregiver), will be helping the disabled user operate the system, or are responsible for the health and well-being of the user. When developing a system for a disabled user, it is even more likely that there will be other peoples' needs that must be considered beyond that of the target user. Even when the additional stakeholders will not be using the system directly, their buyin can be critical to the successful adoption or use of the device. The users may interact with other people on a daily basis who will be impacted by design choices. These individuals can help designers understand the context in which the technology will be used, as well as provide valuable support for device adoption. This group of people may include professionals such as educators, therapists, and physicians, as well as family and friends who participate in daily routines [6]. For example, in designing a system to teach deaf children about language, it is necessary to include the needs and concerns of the parents and teachers into the design process.

17.2.2 The Design Process

Once the designer completes the user needs assessment, the process will enter any one of the four remaining states and will continue to iterate through them until a satisfactory design has been reached. In each application some of the needs will be more important than others. It is important for the designer to determine via the user needs assessment what states require the most attention. For example, when designing a device to aid children with disabilities, social needs might be paramount (e.g., the user could be self-conscious about classmates seeing the device), whereas a system designed to provide advanced warning of an epileptic seizure might require a focus on data needs since it would not initially be clear to the researchers what types of physiologic measurements could be used to detect these events.

- *Social Needs.* When addressing the social needs of a design the developer must ask questions about the privacy, security, and obtrusiveness requirements for the system.

  Will this system collect sensitive medical data that must be protected or encrypted to protect privacy?

  Should use of the device be restricted to one or a group of authorized users?

  Is it important that others not be aware that the user is wearing a device (e.g., a user might not wish for her employer to know that she has a heart condition)?

Will the user feel embarrassed or isolated by wearing the device?

Will others feel that their privacy is infringed by the user's device (e.g., the device is recording conversations the user has)?

- *Physical Needs.* The physical needs of the system involve issues of wearability and comfort. Also, how users perceive the comfort of wearable devices can be influenced by the device functionality [7]. In the Bodine–Gemperle study participants were given two different devices to wear and were provided with one of three descriptions of device functionality (e.g., police monitor, medical monitor, or party wearable). Significant differences in desirability and comfort ratings were found between these functional conditions. To address the physical needs, a designer must ask questions regarding the potential look and feel, the physical capabilities/disabilities of the target user, and the interface to the system:

Where can the device(s) and/or sensors be physically placed on the body?

What type of movement will the user be doing while wearing this device, and does the placement impede that?

What factors of the user's disability might affect physical placement of the device?

What type of body placement will accommodate the input and output modalities best (e.g., the device uses audio output so a transducer needs to be near the ears, or a keypad must be placed in a way that the user can comfortably type)?

What features other than size affect comfort and body placement choices (e.g., heat of the device, noise that it makes)?

How can the input and output devices be designed and placed to ensure ergonomic efficiency?

What does the device and interface look like?

- *Data Needs.* The data needs for the system address the requirements for data collection on the device. At a high level you must determine what it is you are trying to detect or measure (a person's current activity, that the user wants to turn on the television, whether this user may be developing Parkinson's disease etc.). Then the designer must think about the lower layer and decide what kind of data is required to provide that high-level information. For example, the designer might determine that different activities could be detected according to the person's body movements. The designer then determines what sensing approaches will provide that data. In the case of the activity recognition, the designer might initially consider a camera placed on the user and watching body movements. However, the designer might then determine that placing a set of accelerometers on the user's body would also provide the level of detail required for this application while requiring less technical resources and causing less privacy concerns.

What event(s) needs to be measured or recognized?

What data will adequately represent these events?

- *Technical Needs.* The technical needs for the wearable system encapsulate the decisions the designer must make about the actual implementation of the system such as computing platform, algorithms for processing data, the input and output devices, and power consumption or heat dissipation requirements. In this state the designer must determine whether the design they wish to develop is technically feasible and what parts will be put together to create a working system. Often this effort will require several iterations, with initial prototypes ignoring issues such as power consumption so that evaluations can be performed. The results will help the designer work toward meeting the requirements associated with the other needs. However, the technical needs will also dictate how closely the designer can satisfy all of the other requirements. Often a perfect system will not be possible because of limitations such as computing power, display technology, battery life, or the lack of good algorithms.

17.2.3 Design Process Examples

To illustrate how this set of needs can be addressed in a wearable computing design process; the following sections provide several examples of our own work and that of our colleagues that highlight the challenges inherent to creating useful devices for persons with disabilities. The goal is to provide examples of the design issues that will arise in these types of projects and to inform the process for future projects in this domain.

17.2.3.1 A Cognitive Prosthetic for Car Location

In this first example, we present a case study of a wearable system for finding a user's car. The system was designed specifically for users with traumatic brain injury (TBI) [8]. This example details the process of assessing the user needs, how these user needs informed the overall direction of the project, and then how the design team prioritized and approached the physical, social, hardware, and data needs. In the initial idea stage of the project, the researchers decided to a wayfinding device focused on users with TBI (see Table 17.1). First they identified two willing participants with TBI rehabilitating at the Shepherd Center, an Atlanta-based catastrophic care hospital. The researchers began the process by interviewing Shepherd Center clinicians about the problems of daily living that exist for these participants. The effects of TBI depend on the location of the damage to the brain. In these participants' cases the TBI had resulted in loss of working memory; thus making new memories was very difficult for them. TBI has a different demographic than many disabilities—80% are men. TBI patients also tend to be young as these injuries often result from sports, car, hunting, or job accidents. Since TBI often occurs in people who are otherwise young and healthy, they are ideal candidates for wearable technology. They suffer from a very specific lack of ability that can be compensated by using the unaffected abilities. Other cognitive disabilities related to Alzheimer's disease or stroke result in disparate and wide-ranging problems that may not be easily accommodated via wearable devices.

TABLE 17.1 Needs Analysis for Car Location Cognitive Prosthetic

Needs	Description
User	A device to locate car. Must work with "first time" user. A simple system for a simple task versus a powerful yet complex device.
Physical	Must be with the user at all times (integrated into a standard accessory). Design can not be "childish", but simple interface required.
Data	System uses location of user and car. GPS provides data. In the future it might be necessary to know who is holding the device for security.
Technology	Undetermined computing platform (system not implemented), with possible future need for biometric hardware.
Social	Device must not announce its presence without user input. Security features required to protect user from car theft.

During the first step of assessing the user needs, the interviews revealed a seemingly simple problem that was significantly impacting the quality of life for the participants: locating their cars in parking lots. While the injury did not preclude the subjects from working and living relatively independently, only working memory was affected; the participants retained both their same level of intelligence and their long-term memories. However, from the interviews the researchers learned that the participants were having significant problems finding their cars to the extent that it was affecting their ability to hold jobs. This problem might seem trivial, but the interviews revealed that in some cases a participant had spent hours looking for the car and, finally in the middle of the night, called friends or relatives to help. This problem not only results in safety issues but also was embarrassing for the participants and limited their independence. As an initial solution, the clinicians at the Shepherd Center had used the combination of a consumer GPS device coupled with a detailed instruction booklet to help the participants record the location of their cars and then navigate to them later. The GPS device was complex to operate, especially for a user who retained little knowledge about its controls from use to use. Therefore the clinicians created a booklet of instructions containing 57 steps. The goal was to lead the users step by step through recording a position when they left theirs car and then navigating back to that location later. These steps contained complex and confusing instructions such as "Press WHITE WHITE WHITE (the page button) 3 times to get to the menu screen."

Clearly, this approach to the car location problem was not appropriate for these users. Therefore the researchers decided to proceed with the needs assessment, ignoring the technical needs and limitations. This needs assessment highlighted some of the unique usability barriers that existed for this population of users. For example, owing to their difficulty forming new memories, the participants may not remember that they have a problem finding their cars, nor do they remember that they have a device to help them. Thus, solutions such as having them remember to write down where they are in the parking lot will not work. Even if they have a device to help them, they may not remember to bring it with them or use it. The participants were able to absorb some new information; however, the process of storing a new piece of information permanently was lengthy and somewhat unreliable. Therefore, the researchers realized that the resulting device would have to be of a form factor such that the participants would naturally carry it with them. The design of the device would need to communicate its function and interface to the user as if he/she were seeing it "for the first time" every time. The researchers also learned that a current strategy used by the participants to locate their cars was to use their keyless-entry fobs to make the car horn honk.

Continuing to gather information on user needs, the team focused on what functionality the device would have and what services it could provide to the user. Initially the team encountered a common mistake made by those developing cognitive prosthetics. They assumed that since they were already making a system to help users find their cars, then the device could also offer other memory support services, such as medication reminders and day planning. They imagined that the device could consist of a PDA with customized software. While the approach of creating a specialized PDA to serve as a cognitive prosthetic has been successful in other circumstances [9], the researchers soon realized, from their interviews and user needs assessment, that this approach of putting several memory aids into one complex device would not work for these users or this problem domain. As discussed above, both TBI participants were capable of acquiring new information and skills, but the process was lengthy and sometimes unreliable. It was very unlikely that either subject would be able to learn how to use the many functions of the device that the researchers originally envisioned. The team learned from the clinicians that the participants would be much more likely to remember that they had a device for finding their cars and how to use it if there were a one-to-one mapping—a single, simple function associated with a single, simple device.

Once the team had decided to restrict the device to the function of car location, the next design step was to determine physical and data needs such as the form factor and interface of the device. The needs assessment had revealed that the participants would have trouble remembering to carry a device. Therefore, they decided that the device should be incorporated into something they would normally carry or wear, such as a wristwatch, belt buckle, or keychain. In the interviews the researchers had learned that the participants never forgot to lock their cars (since this was a habit learned before they were injured). Therefore, it seemed appropriate to incorporate the car location device into the keychain. This design also leveraged the fact that one of the original strategies that the participants employed to find their cars was to honk the horn via their keychain fobs. It would also be necessary for the device to have information on the location of the car and the user. GPS was the obvious technology to provide this functionality.

The interface must be simple and transparent, and the physical interface should mirror the device's function. However, it was also important that the device not appear childish or condescending to the users, who would be unlikely to use a device that they found embarrassing or insulting to their intelligence. The design used for evaluation consisted of a single button labeled FIND CAR (see Fig. 17.3). The small display shows an arrow pointing the user in the direction of the vehicle and its distance away. The device retains the original keyless entry capability and thus has the LOCK and UNLOCK buttons. The researchers also experimented with adding a voice memo feature to the device. When exiting the car the user could press the RECORD/PLAY button to record a memo about where the car was parked. Once a memo was available, the same button would light. The hypothesis was that the confused user would see the blinking light on the device and press the button, thus hearing the description of where the car was parked. Of course, this strategy was contingent on the user remembering to record a memo in the first place.

To evaluate this design, the researchers first performed a cognitive walkthrough with the Shepherd Center clinicians and caregivers, followed by a cooperative evaluation with

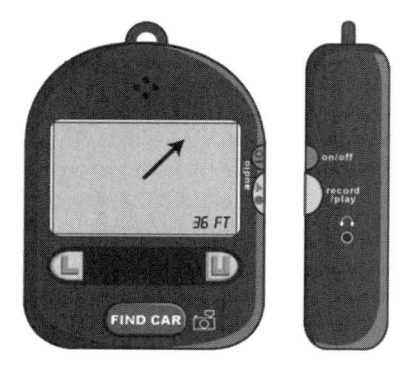

FIGURE 17.3 Mock-up of device used for evaluation.

the participants. Because of the technical challenges of creating a working prototype, the team used a Web prototype for the evaluations. The experiments revealed several issues with the design, and simply turning on the device was problematic. As discussed above, a common issue with creating memory aids is that users might not remember having taken the a device with them, and this proved to be the case with the car location system as well. The researchers were relying on the participants taking the key fob out of their pocket in order to honk the horn and thus noticing or remembering its purpose as a car locater. However, with no means of alerting the user to its presence, the device might be ignored while he/she searches the parking lot. A possible addition to the device could be an audio alert that triggers at the time when the user would typically be leaving work, or approaching the car from a certain distance.

As anticipated, the audio recording feature was not particularly useful as it was unlikely that the participant would remember to record a memo and play it back later. Other problems were due to the simple arrow display. The arrow would not help with navigation if there was only a nonlinear path to the car (e.g., the car was on the other side of a wall). Similarly, the researchers envisioned the actual implementation using GPS technology to record the location of the car and the user. However, this approach would fail in covered areas (where the device could not receive satellite signals) or in cases where the car could be on multiple levels (e.g., the device could not tell the user on which parking deck level the car was parked).

During the evaluation process, the researchers encountered unique challenges in working with TBI participants. The participants had to follow very rigid daily schedules. These schedules allowed them to learn their routines over time, but it also meant that it was often difficult for the team to schedule times to interview or run evaluation studies with them. The loss of working memory meant that it was sometimes difficult for the participants to follow the study protocol; sometimes forgetting comments during the evaluation that they had planned to share with the researchers.

The car location device was also evaluated informally with non-TBI users. The results showed that this device would be useful to all types of users, even those without loss of working memory. However, in such a case the universal design techniques would not have been appropriate. Many of the comments from the non-TBI users negated findings from the previous evaluation. Some of the non-TBI users felt that certain features were unnecessary, while the researchers knew from the previous evaluation that these approaches were necessary for disabled users. In this situation, a traditional user-centered design approach was warranted. Although the resulting device could be useful to many people, the design focused on the particular user group for whom the functionality was most needed.

In this initial design the researchers did not prioritize the social needs for this system, but the evaluation results highlighted the issues of privacy and security that can arise when creating devices for users with disabilities. For example, an approach to the problem of turning on the device could be to use a timed audio to alert the user to the presence of the car locator fob. However, this feature could result in loss of privacy for the user. What if the user stayed late at work one day and the device were to suddenly emit an audio alert? The user might be embarrassed by either having to explain to coworkers the purpose of the device or by obvious confusion as to the device's function.

There are also security concerns related to this device. The fact that it can unlock the car doors as well as lead someone to the car means that it could be a target for thieves. Security features could be added to the device to ensure that it could be used only by the owner. However, with this user population it would be difficult to find a workable solution. The TBI user might not be capable of remembering a password or ID number, and the hardware to allow for this feature could make the device larger and more expensive. Likewise, the use of biometrics such as fingerprint scanning would make the device more complex to both manufacture and use.

Technical needs were of a low priority for this project since the goal was to explore possible designs for a cognitive prosthetic rather than to build a finished system. However, by focusing on the user needs the researchers designed a device that would be difficult to implement fully. To produce an effective device, both technical needs and practical concerns, such as cost, would have to be addressed in the design. These issues might result in a need for further iterations of the design.

17.2.3.2 Wireless Sensor for Diagnosing Children with Autism

Autism is a developmental disorder affecting a child's social development and ability to communicate. Children with autism display differing levels of these interaction abilities, referred to as their *level of functioning*. While not all children will communicate, almost all autistic children exhibit abnormal behavior such as vocal stuttering and brief bouts of vigorous activity (e.g., violently striking the back of the hands), to cope with everyday life. Depending on the child's level of functioning, these highly individualized, self–stimulatory ("stimming") behaviors can be disruptive and socially awkward. Caregivers and researchers would like to explore the correlation between a child's stimming behaviors and environmental factors, behavioral treatments, mood, or physiologic markers.

Some researchers attempt to automate the recording and analysis of these behaviors because of the impracticality of continuous monitoring of a child for episodes of stimming. Westeyn et al. have published the development of a wireless on-body sensor system and applied algorithms for recognizing autistic self-stimulatory behaviors [10]. This work was a pilot study for a larger exploratory research project using wireless body worn sensors to assist in the treatment and diagnosis of children with autism (see Table 17.2). The goal of the pilot study was to provide a proof-of-concept system capable of collecting data from a child with autism and providing automatic indices into that data (i.e., quickly highlighting stimming events) to aid therapists' analysis of autism (see Fig. 17.4).

TABLE 17.2 Needs Analysis of Wireless Sensors for Diagnosing Children with Autism

Needs	Description
User	system to automate the recording and analysis of these self-stimulatory ("stimming") behaviors in children with autism. Must address needs of the teachers and parents that will be using the system.
Physical	Body placement designed for minimal invasiveness and robustness. Placement and fit such that the sensors cannot be incorporated into stimming activities. Childproofing required.
Data	Information on when children are stimming. What types of data to gather is still being researched, but researchers chose to measure body movements, specifically the movement of the thigh, waist, and wrist via accelerometer. Designed to minimize number of sensors.
Technology	Mobile computing device to receive data (laptop, cell phone, PDA). Battery life of a day.
Social	Minimal.

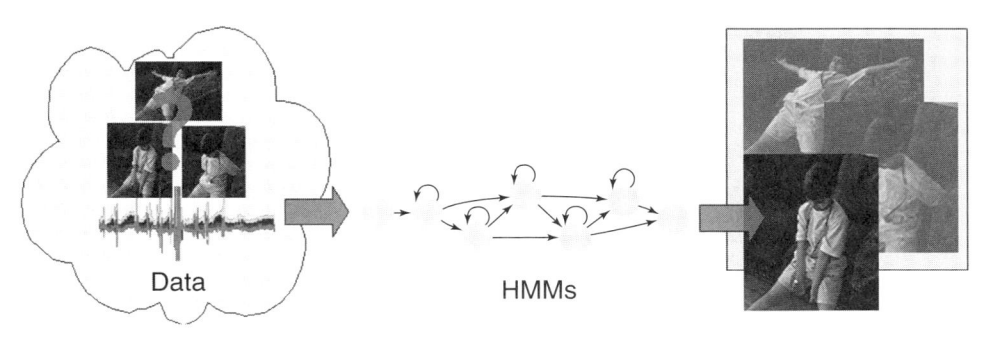

FIGURE 17.4 *The data are gathered from the user and passed through hidden Markov models for classification. The output distinguishes stimming activities from other activities.*

These episodes could then be analyzed or even replayed alongside other captured information such as video. An automated data collection system may provide insight into a given child's mental and physiologic state and also provide detailed, quantitative data for researchers in the field.

The pilot study revealed several technical challenges in systems engineering related to data needs. The first challenge was that stimming behaviors can manifest in many types of actions and that little is known about their causes. As a result, it was not clear even what type of collected data to would be meaningful for later analysis. The second challenge was to determine the type of wireless sensors to use for the on-body sensor system. The choice of sensors was directly influenced by the type of data that needed to be collected from the target population. Autistic self-stimulatory behaviors can involve all five senses but typically involve extreme repetitive body motions and/or repetitive vocal stutters. To simplify the system design, the researchers decided to focus on recording data from repetitive movements using wireless accelerometers. These sensors use the Bluetooth protocol and can transmit data to any device supporting Bluetooth. Therefore, data can be collected by desktop or laptop computers, cell phones, and other mobile devices.

Because researchers were interested in monitoring the everyday lives of autistic children, the physical needs required the monitoring system to be mobile and noninvasive. The location of the sensors on the body was crucial. The positioning of the accelerometers greatly influenced the quality of data that could be recorded. For example, an accelerometer positioned at the wrist of a child exhibiting a repetitive hand-flapping behavior would provide better data than one positioned at the ankle. The goal of the sensor system was to minimize the number of sensors needed to collect data from as many stimming events as possible. In this pilot study, an adult would mimic seven typical autistic self-stimulatory behaviors interspersed with random daily activities. To help determine the best sensor placement on the body, researchers conducted an extensive literature search of activity recognition using accelerometers. Research in this field suggested that activities could be recognized with two accelerometers positioned at the waist and thigh. They decided to use three accelerometers: a sensor on the thigh, a sensor on the waist, and a sensor on the wrist using soft, Velcro straps (see Fig. 17.5).

As this project continues forward, the researchers are currently exploring further solutions to the physical needs of this system. Since it will be used by young active users it must be "childproofed." Also, unique characteristics of children with autism require that

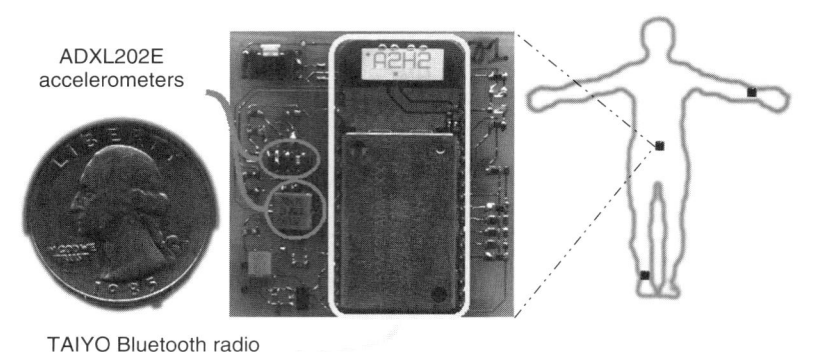

FIGURE 17.5 *Accelerometers and their placement on the body.*

any equipment or sensors placed on the body fit in such a way that the child would be unlikely to incorporate them into his/her stimming activities (banging them on surfaces, spinning them on the wrist, etc.).

This project is still in its early stages, and the work thus far has focused on exploring the design issues for such a device and developing algorithms for detecting stimming behavior on the basis of movement input. The researchers plan to develop a fully deployable version of this design for use in a formal user study involving autistic children and their therapists, teachers, and parents.

17.2.3.3 Mobile Wireless Activity Monitoring to Prevent Pressure Sores in Wheelchair Users (Similar to Decubitus)

For people who use wheelchairs, pressure ulcers are a major public health problem. The ulcers occur in approximately one-third of persons with spinal cord injuries. The sores are painful, life-threatening, and expensive medical complications. Wheelchair users can avoid pressure ulcers by performing formal weight shift exercises. To learn how to perform the exercises, users can visit a seating clinic where special pressure monitoring pads are placed in the chair; an expert evaluates each user's individual body type and explains how to perform the shifts accordingly. However, when not at the clinic, it is difficult for the user and the clinician to know whether these movements are being performed properly and with enough regularity. Therefore, a system was needed that could provide real-time information about the amount and type of weight shifts (both as formal exercises and as natural movement) that a user performs on a daily basis. To address this need, a mobile wireless activity monitoring system (MAM) was designed to track weight shifts performed by wheelchair users [11]. The system was intended to help in analyzing and preventing the development of pressure sores and to perform continuous activity measurements (see Table 17.3).

The goal of this system was to encourage the user to perform regular weight shifts and to allow caregivers to intervene when high-risk periods of inactivity were detected. The MAM system could be used by consumers at home or while moving about the community. This system is different from the accurate but expensive pressure mapping that is done at wheelchair seating clinics as well as from the low-cost, on off monitoring of some current products sold for home use. Some researchers believe that intentional weight shift exercises are not as effective as the natural shifting movements that some

TABLE 17.3 Needs Analysis of Wheelchair Pressure Monitoring

Needs	Description
User	A way for wheelchair users and their physicians to keep track of the users' weight shift activities in order to maintain skin health.
Physical	Device(s) must not change fit and geometry of wheelchair cushion (which could cause sores to develop). Device must not change weight balance of wheelchair or add more than two pounds of weight.
Data	Knowing when and how a user shifts his/her weight in the wheelchair during the day. Data gathered via FSR sensors placed under cushion.
Technology	A network device to gather and process sensor data before uploading to website in approximately real-time. Power consumption that allows for continuous use throughout the user's day (current design does not meet this need).
Social	Minimal.

active wheelchair users perform unintentionally throughout the day. Therefore, another goal of this system was to record all types of shifting activity not only to provide feedback for individual users but also to produce data that could be used by researchers to determine what types of shifts are most effective for pressure sore avoidance.

The physical needs were paramount in the design of this system since any modification of the wheelchair seat could cause pressure sores to develop. The cushion on a wheelchair is very carefully chosen and fitted according to the individual's body type. Therefore it would have been dangerous for the researchers to modify the seat of the chair. The wheelchair users were justifiably concerned about changes to their seating cushions and were often reticent to even try modified pads for any length of time. This reluctance meant that the sensors for measuring activity had to be placed under the cushions, and researchers could not change the structure of the pad in any way. As a result, the researchers chose to use an array of small flat force-sensing resistors (FSRs) to measure shifts.

Another physical need that was revealed during the design process was that of weight, not just the amount of the added weight but also its placement on the chair. Weight is always a concern when developing wearable systems, but in this case the team incorrectly assumed that weight was not of great importance since the system would not be carried by a user but would be integrated into a wheelchair. When testing prototypes with users, the researchers soon learned that even a small amount of weight (~2 lb) affected the balance of the chair, making it difficult for users to perform common maneuvers such as tipping the chair onto a curb. Therefore, the researchers were forced to focus on both decreasing the weight of the system and mounting the equipment in such a way so as to not disturb the center of balance. The practical considerations for this project require that the system be relatively inexpensive. As a result, the researchers designed their activity detection algorithm to minimize the number of required sensors.

The main technology hurdle was data upload. The system requires approximate real-time upload of data along with extensive network coverage. A Blackberry two-way pager was chosen to process the data from the sensors in the chair and to transfer the electronic records to a central database. These data are accessible via a Web interface tailored for both the wheelchair user and skin care specialists (see Fig. 17.6). A technology problem that still exists with the current design is power consumption. The power management of the device is not sufficient for continuous use of the system in the field. Future iterations of the design will focus on maximizing battery life.

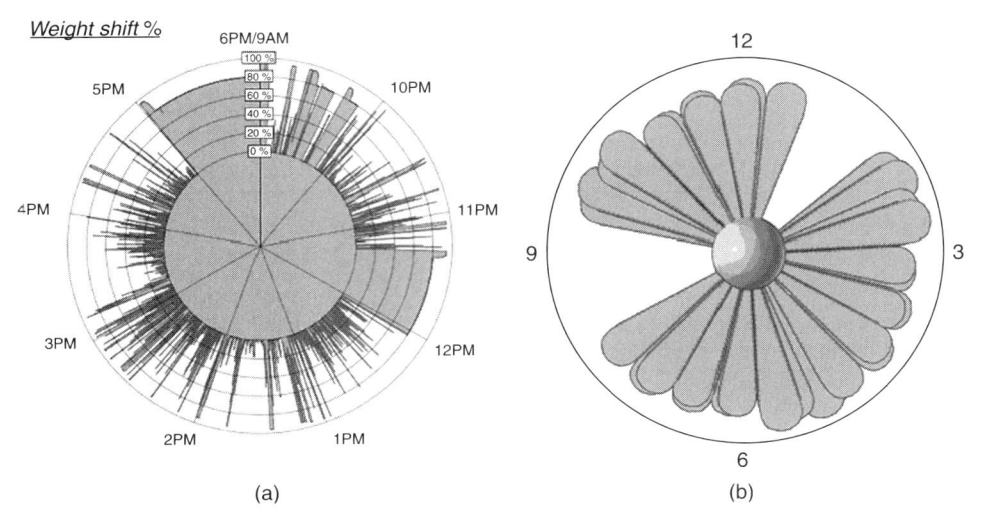

FIGURE 17.6 (a) A polar plot graph from the Web interface database query tool. In the radial dimension, graph values depict shift percentage from 0% to 100%. Angular position around the circular graph represents time. (b) An alternative visualization for the user presenting the same data using a flower petal metaphor.

The results of the first round of tests shows that the MAM system's findings agree with a standard pressure mapping system used in seating clinics. Additionally, the testing has shown that a wheelchair user's activity can be detected beneath the seat cushion nearly as well as above it. Future research is necessary to determine whether the MAM system will allow users and caregivers the ability to more easily detect and correct patterns of inactivity that lead to skin problems.

17.2.3.4 Telesign

American Sign Language is often the first language for the deaf in the United States. Since ASL and English are significantly different languages, English skills often lag behind ASL skills. Although interpreters are commonly hired by the deaf for special occasions, they are expensive and require scheduling. Thus, daily interactions between deaf and hearing people often rely on paper-and-pencil communication in written English. Depending on the skill level of the participants, communication can be slow and error-prone. The situation is analogous to an English speaker who has had only one or two courses in high school Spanish trying to communicate in written Spanish. However, a native Spanish speaker understands intuitively that a native English speaker may have difficulty communicating in this manner. In the case of a native ASL signer conversing with a hearing person, the English speaker often assumes that the deaf person is fluent in English (i.e., incorrectly assumes that ASL is simply a gestural version of English as opposed to an actual language). Consequently, the English speaker may become frustrated with the speed of correspondence during the written conversation or assume that the deaf person is "stupid" because his/her grammar and spelling are incorrect.

Meetings with our native deaf consultants revealed a need for informal communication where an interpreter is infeasible yet paper and pencil is unsatisfactory. Telesign provides an option that is similar to using a tourist phrase book for communicating in a different

TABLE 17.4 Needs Analysis of Telesign

Needs	Description
User	Communication between a deaf user and a person who does not know ASL. Focusing on specific scenarios such as searching for an apartment to rent. Scenario constrained so that the deaf user asks questions and the hearing person responds non-verbally.
Physical	Must be mobile and wearable. Must be comfortable and relatively inconspicuous.
Data	Recognition of ASL gestures. Problem made easier by constraining vocabulary and using a "push to talk" system. Hand movements are gathered via camera and accelerometer on wrist.
Technology	Device must be small enough to be worn for long periods of time and while mobile.
Social	User should be both physically and socially comfortable with the system. It should support useful conversational exchanges.
Practical Issues	Current prototype is cost prohibitive for large scale deployment. Device must be refined before attempting to gain acceptance by deaf users.

language (see Table 17.4). Telesign would not replace interpreters, since the interactions would be limited, but could expand communication options for many activities. One activity suggested by our consultants was searching for an apartment. During an apartment search, one must visit many different apartments and collect information about them. Instead of transporting an interpreter to many different appointments with landlords in an area, the most common questions and interactions could be entered into a phrase book. The signer then references these questions when interacting with the hearing landlord. Telesign allows the deaf person to select these phrases with sign.

The Telesign system consists of a wearable computer, a head-up display for the user interface, a hat-mounted camera to observe the signing, wrist-mounted accelerometers, and a speaker to vocalize the English phrases. The system is designed as a limited one-way phrase level translator for American Sign Language (ASL) [12]. Figure 17.7 shows an example interaction from the apartment hunting scenario. The deaf user wears the system and signs. User's can observe their signing and the system status in the head-up display. The system classifies the signing and displays possible matches from a library of English phrases. Next, the user can select the best match, and the system uses speakers to vocalize the phrase in English. The system can be loaded with phrases for specific tasks such as apartment hunting, navigating an airport, and consulting a physician in much the same way that tourist phrase books are organized by task.

The system has evolved from consultant feedback from the ASL recognition project at Georgia Tech. The design criteria have been through several iterations and continue to evolve. There is a balance between designing prototypes for functionality and for aesthetics. Using off-the-shelf components can result in a system that appears odd or unusual and may draw unwanted attention. Although many of the functional prototype systems provide a chance to study the capabilities of the system, research continues on embedding the technology in inconspicuous ways. It is easy to imagine designing the system into a hat and integrating sensors and interface devices into a watch or bracelet.

Development continues on this project. Further user studies will focus on current modes of face-to-face interactions between deaf and hearing people, as well as "Wizard of Oz" studies to evaluate the quality of interactions using the Telesign system. Aesthetic prototypes will be tested for both physical and social comfort, as well as usability.

FIGURE 17.7 Diagram showing how the Telesign system is used.

The group also focuses on improving ASL recognition rates and increasing the robustness of the mobile sensing.

17.2.3.5 Augmenting a pH Medical Study with Wearable Video

Gastroesophageal reflux disease (GERD), a medical condition that affects 2% of the adult population of the United States, involves the reflux of stomach acid into the esophagus and can lead to complications such as esophageal cancer and lung damage. The most common symptom of GERD is heartburn. Typical treatments for GERD include diet modification and medication. However, for some patients these treatments may prove ineffective, and the patient may be evaluated for more drastic measures such as surgery.

If surgery to correct GERD is considered an option, the patient usually undergoes a 24- or 48-h pH study to measure the percentage of time that the patient is in reflux during normal daily activities. In the 24-h study, a pH probe is inserted into the subject's nose and lowered through the esophagus to a position above the stomach. Since the probe is attached to a line that is retained in the patient's nose and throat, several pH sensors can be placed at varying locations along the patient's esophagus. The probe is attached to a wearable computer that records the patient's pH levels. The patient typically uses the wearable computer to record times of meals, periods spent in a supine position (e.g., sleeping), and occurrences of symptoms. In 2004, in order to investigate the recurrence of GERD symptoms after a previous surgery, a 24-h pH study was performed on one of the authors. Two pH sensors were placed in the esophagus, and readings were recorded by a Medtronic Function Diagnostics Polygram 98 (version 2.01) wearable computer.

The purpose of the study was to determine what types of activities resulted in GERD symptoms (see Table 17.5) [13]. Therefore, the design of this system revolved around the

TABLE 17.5 Needs Analysis of Wearable Video for a pH Medical Study

Needs	Description
User	Method of correlating interesophagal pH readings with the user's activities for 24 hours.
Physical	Must be mobile and wearable so that user can pursue normal activities during test.
Data	Categorization of activities and movements/posture. Captured via camera mounted at chest height looking out. Human reviews data to classify activities.
Technology	Wearable computer to capture pH and video data.
Social	Maintain privacy of people in view of the outward facing camera.

data needs. What types of data would appropriately characterize the author's activity? What was the best way to capture "activity" data for a day?

Because of the relatively small amount of data (<24 h) to be analyzed, there was no need for sophisticated algorithms for recognizing and labeling activities. Instead, the author attached a camera at chest height to the strap of the wearable computer. The camera viewed the area in front of the user. After the data were collected (pH and video), the author and his physician reviewed the synchronized video and data to look for correlations between reflux episodes and his activities.

While the physical needs were minimal for this system because of its short one-time use, there were significant social needs. Because of the camera, inadvertent recording of bystanders was a concern. In future incarnations of this system the video could be obfuscated so as to preserve the privacy of those people interacting with the user. For example, a hyperfisheye lens could be added to a wearable camera that caused individual faces to be unrecognizable in the image due to lack of resolution and detail, while still allowing the wearer to recognize activities in the recorded video.

After conclusion of the, the study an examination of the captured video and pH record revealed unexpected results. In most subjects, reflux occurs during sleep when the body is horizontal. However, the author's reflux occurred during eating and during mechanical strains to the stomach, such as bending at the waist. These correlations would not have been observed by either of the two current pH study methods without the video augmentation. Informed by the study, the author made minor changes to his lifestyle and avoided repeat surgery.

17.2.3.6 Wearable Captioning

When an individual who is deaf or hard of hearing is in a public venue where sound is a primary mode of communication (e.g., movie theater, baseball stadium, airport), she/he is severely limited by isolation from important and, in the case of emergencies, life-saving information. Therefore a system is needed to provide these individuals with such information in an accessible form. The researchers envisioned a captioning system, not unlike the closed captioning required for television, which would make speech-based information available in visual form.

The wearable captioning device (discussed more thoroughly in Chapter 16 of this book) was developed to provide text captioning for individuals who are deaf or hard of hearing (see Table 17.6) [14]. Since the main requirement of the system was the communication of text to the user, the researchers first decided that a small head mounted display (HMD) would show the captions in a discreet manner (shown in Fig. 17.8).

TABLE 17.6 Needs Analysis of Wearable Captioning

Needs	Description
User	System to provide captioning of audio information broadcast in public venues such as movie theater, airports, sports stadiums etc. Must also consider how other users (e.g. venue staff) will create text captioning stream.
Physical	Must be small lightweight system. Display must not harm user's vision.
Data	Text captioning of audio stream. Can be generated manually at venue or automatically from audio stream using speech to text software.
Technology	Wearable device to receive text and drive head mounted display.
Social	Display must not be too obtrusive or it must be widely used so that users do not feel conspicuous.
Practical Issues	Building infrastructure, getting venues to use system, public policy work to require captioning systems in public venues, getting companies to build devices.

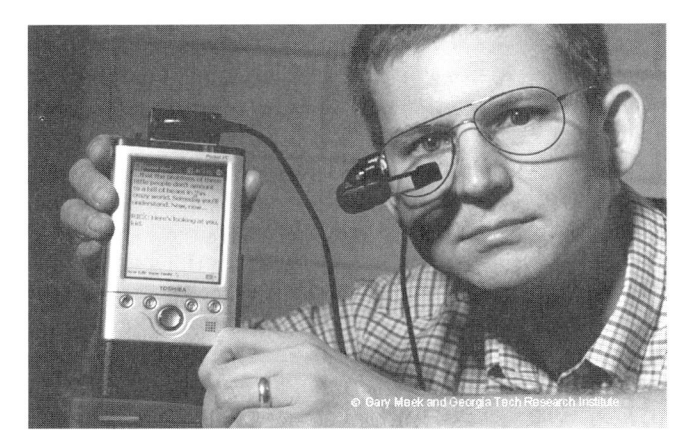

FIGURE 17.8 A person wearing the captioning device.

In the course of developing the captioning system, the researchers discovered that the potential users were concerned that the HMD would affect their sight. This concern was due to the fact that the target users rely on their sense of sight even more than do non-hearing-impaired people. Therefore, it was necessary to both ensure that the display chosen for the device would not harm the users' vision and to reassure the participants in the project that their sight would not be affected.

The other need that was of high priority during the design process was social. The researchers were concerned that potential users would be reluctant to wear this system in public venues as the HMD is somewhat obtrusive and might cause the wearer to feel conspicuous. Therefore, in the course of their experiments the researchers questioned users as to whether they would wear the system in public. Most of them replied that they would wear the device if there were other people at the location wearing similar devices or if they would be in a darkened venue such as a movie theater where they would not be easily seen. Also, as the system becomes widely used, it will no longer seem unusual—just as portable headphones and, more recently, hands-free mobile phone headsets are no longer unusual in our culture.

This device is another example of where much of the work comes after the system itself is designed. Since the system uses wireless technology to receive text streams from transmitting stations in community venues such as theaters, schools, businesses, and government facilities, infrastructure and commitment is required at these locations. The research team is currently managing the practical aspects of deploying this system: interesting venues in the system, developing the appropriate business models (e.g., whether the users own these captioning devices or whether they available for rent at the venues), and forming licensing deals with companies to manufacture the devices and build the required infrastructure at the venues. There is also a public policy component as the team works to secure government support for requiring captioning systems in public locations.

17.3 CONCLUSION

In this chapter we have presented a framework for a wearable computing design process that is of particular use when developing applications for older adults or for persons with disabilities. It is important for the researcher to first determine who the target population is and then involve members of that group (along with caregivers, therapists, teachers, and advocacy groups when applicable) early in the design process. A common mistake is to not fully understand the user needs for these populations; the result can be wasted time and resources as well as a system that is not useful for the target population. Once the user needs are well defined, the researcher moves into the iterative process of prioritizing and addressing the technical, physical, social, and data needs for the application. A perfect system will typically not be achievable. Therefore, it is important for the researcher to understand which needs are critical and which can be modified within the limitations or the restrictions imposed on the design by technology, society, and the resources for the project. In some cases, the researchers must use an annealing process, where various parameters of the system are modified in one dimension in order to achieve a more maximal outcome for another need (e.g., exploring a different type of sensor for data collection that would be less accurate but is an order of magnitude smaller in physical size).

Unfortunately, producing a compelling and viable wearable system is not the final step in the process. A large gulf exists between the world of research, where exciting new applications are developed to address the needs of users with disabilities, and the "real world," where the target users can actually acquire such systems. Many useful systems have been developed but have never left the laboratory. While not every research project should be pushed into full deployment, in some cases it is important to take this last step in order for the users to actually benefit from the research. Practical issues include convincing national and international advocacy groups, companies, and/or government agencies to accept a study's findings and to facilitate the transfer of research into real-world products.

REFERENCES

1. Henderson V, Grinter R, Starner T: *Electronic Communication by Deaf Teenagers*, Technical Report GIT-GVU-05-34, Georgia Institute of Technology, College of Computing, GVU Center, Oct 2005.

2. Mueller J, Jones M, Broderick L, Haberman V: Assessment of user needs in wireless technologies, *Assist Technol*, **17** (1), (Spring 2005).
3. Martin T, Jovanov E, Raskovic D: Issues in wearable computing for medical monitoring applications: A case study of a wearable ECG monitoring device, *Proc 4th Int Symp Wearable Computers* (*ISWC'00*), Oct 18– 21, 2000, Atlanta, GA, 2000, p 43.
4. Gandy M, Ross D, Starner T: Universal design: Lessons for wearable computing, *Pervasive Comput IEEE* **2**(3):19–23 (July– Sept 2003).
5. Newell A: Clarkson J, Coleman R, Keats S, Lebbon C, eds: Inclusive design or assistive technology, in *Inclusive Design: Design for the Whole Population*, Springer, 2003.
6. Bryant B, Bryant DP: *Assistive Technology for People with Disabilities*, Pearson Education, 2003.
7. Bodine K, Gemperle F: Effects of functionality on perceived comfort of wearables, 2003. *Proc 7th IEEE Int Symp Wearable Computers*, Oct 21– 23 2003, pp 57–60.
8. Bilotta J, Strong A, Shi Y, Nichols T: *Cognitive Prosthetics: Mobile Way-finding Devices for Persons with Traumatic Brain Injury* (available at http://swiki.cc.gatech.edu:8080/cs6750a/18, accessed 2/17/06).
9. Haberman V, Jones M, Mueller J: Wireless technology for individuals with cognitive impairments, *Proc RESNA*, 2005.
10. Westeyn T, Vadas K, Bian X, Starner T, Abowd G: Recognizing mimicked autistic self-stimulatory behaviors using HMMs, *Proc 9th Int IEEE Symp wearable computing* (*ISWC 2005*), Oct 18– 21 2005, Osaka, Japan.
11. Wilson J, Peifer J: Mobile wireless activity monitoring to prevent pressure sores in wheelchair users, *Proc RESNA 2004 Annual Conf*, Orlando, FL, 2004.
12. McGuire RM, Hernandez-Rebollar J, Starner T, Henderson V, Brashear H, Ross DS: Towards a one-way American sign language translator, *Proc 6th Int IEEE Conf Automatic Face and Gesture Recognition*, Seoul, Korea, May 2004.
13. Starner T, Ashbrook T: Augmenting a pH medical study with wearable Video for treatment of GERD, *Proc IEEE Symp Wearable Computing* (*ISWC 2004*), Arlington, VA, Nov 2004.
14. West L, Sexton, J: The Communications Assistant, *Proc Int Conf Aging, Disability, and Independence* (*ICADI*), Washington, DC, 2003.

18

Tactile Displays

Stephen A. Brewster, Steven A. Wall, Lorna M. Brown, and Eve E. Hoggan

University of Glasgow, Glasgow, UK

18.1 INTRODUCTION

The work presented in this chapter focuses on potential uses of tactile displays for visually impaired and older adults. According to the Royal National Institute for the Blind, UK (www.rnib.org) there are two million people in the UK with sight problems (with 378,000 registered blind), and 85% of these are over 65 years of age. The aging population in Western countries means that this group will form an increasing proportion of the whole population. According to estimates from the US Census Bureau's International Database (in 2004), the proportion of those in the UK who are over 60 is expected to increase from 20% in the year 2000 to 27% by 2025. Gregor et al. [1] note that older people are a very diverse group, with a diverse range of abilities, and it is difficult to draw a simple profile or stereotype. The individual variability of physical, sensory, and cognitive functions increases with age, with many people facing multiple smaller declines. These factors mean that careful consideration is required to design effective user interfaces for these important and diverse groups.

Tactile displays can offer an alternative channel through which to present information if other senses are impaired. The traditional use of encodings such as Braille is effective at presenting textual information nonvisually, but touch can also be used to present or enhance iconic and pictorial data for those whose sight is beginning to fade. Alternatively, for someone with hearing problems, touch can be used to present alarms or other messages that might otherwise be given in sound. One major benefit with the tactile modality is that it is private, unlike audio, which can be overheard by others. Another powerful aspect is the multimodal combination of touch, hearing, and sight, which allows information to be presented to the sense that is most appropriate (see Chapter 17 for more discussion of multimodal interactions).

The Engineering Handbook of Smart Technology for Aging, Disability, and Independence,
Edited by A. Helal, M. Mokhtari and B. Abdulrazak
Copyright © 2008 John Wiley & Sons, Inc.

Because of their compact size and power requirements, tactile displays offer a discrete, affordable means of providing access to data via the sense of touch. Displays are often small enough to be mounted on other interaction devices such as a mouse, keyboard, or games controller, or portable devices such as mobile telephones and personal digital assistants (PDAs). Mobile telephones use simple vibrations to provide nonaudio indications of incoming calls or messages. Tactile information has also found widespread acceptance within the videogaming community as an inexpensive means of providing touch feedback in handheld game controllers. Tactile sensations are crucial to success in object manipulation, edge detection, palpation, and texture perception [2]. They are also implicated in more expressive and qualitative contexts such as nonvisual communication (e.g., a firm handshake or a caress on the hand), and perceptions of product quality.

This chapter provides some background on the use of touch for human–computer interaction (HCI), focusing on cutaneous perception and reviewing the main research in sensory substitution, in particular Braille/raised paper, pin arrays, and vibrotactile displays. It concludes with some discussion of what tactile output may offer older adults and disabled people in the future.

18.2 DESIGN IMPLICATIONS OF CUTANEOUS PERCEPTION

The human sense of touch can be divided into two separate channels. *Kinaesthetic* perception refers to the sensations of positions, velocities, forces, and constraints that arise from the muscles and tendons. *Force-feedback* devices appeal to the kinaesthetic senses by presenting computer-controlled forces to create the illusion of contact with a rigid surface [3]. The *cutaneous* class of sensations arise through direct contact with the skin surface. Cutaneous stimulation can be further separated into the sensations of pressure, stretch, vibration, and temperature. Pain is sometimes also referred to as a separate sensation, although excessive stimulation of the other parameters will lead to a feeling of pain. Tactile devices generally appeal to the cutaneous senses by skin indentation, vibration, skin stretch, and electrical stimulation.

It is important to know the capabilities and limits of the sense of touch when designing tactile user interfaces. This section gives a practical overview of the most important aspects of cutaneous perception from an interface designer's perspective, with a discussion of the effects of ageing on perception. There is a great deal of work in the area of cutaneous perception and psychophysics. For a detailed review, see Klatzky and Lederman [23].

18.2.1 Amplitude

The fingertip is the most sensitive region for the detection of indentation, estimated by psychophysical studies to be in the region of 10 μm for step indentations [4]. The highest thresholds for detection occur at low frequencies of stimulation [5], and the minimum thresholds occur in the region of 250 Hz. Discrimination capacity for amplitude of indentation is dependent largely on the location of stimulation; it is finer at those points of the body with lower detection thresholds [6]. As with the vision and audition, discrimination capacity is not constant throughout the stimulation amplitude range. Indentation amplitude discrimination is lower-resolution at low intensities but becomes more sensitive in the range 200–700 μm, progressively degrading with increasing stimulus amplitude [7]. Craig (as reported in Schiff and Foulke [8]) found a difference limen (threshold) of 0.2

for amplitude when 160 Hz vibrations were presented to the index finger, indicating that an increase or decrease of 20% is necessary for a change in amplitude to be perceived. Discrimination capacity for amplitudes is reported to be roughly independent of frequency of stimulation [9].

18.2.2 Frequency

While humans can hear sounds in the range 20–20,000 Hz, the practical frequency range of the skin is much smaller, ranging from 10 to 400 Hz, with maximum sensitivity [10] and finer spatial discrimination [11] at ~250 Hz. The resolution of temporal frequency discrimination is finer at lower frequencies. Investigations by Goff involving the stimulation of the subject's finger with a single probe showed that for lower frequencies (<25 Hz), the discrimination threshold was less than 5 Hz and for higher frequencies (>320 Hz), discrimination capacities were degraded [12]. Measures for discrimination thresholds of frequency are problematic, as perception of vibratory pitch is dependent not only on frequency but also on amplitude of stimulation. Geldard [6] found that subjects reported a change in pitch when frequency was fixed, but stimulation amplitude was changed. This is similar to the effect of volume on pitch perception in audio, but the effect is more pronounced for vibratory stimuli on the skin. Sherrick [13] found that combining frequency and amplitude redundantly allowed a greater number of identifiable levels to be created. He found that people could distinguish three to five different levels of frequency, but that this range could be increased to eight by adding amplitude as a redundant parameter. The perceptual interaction between frequency and amplitude should be considered when designing tactile user interfaces.

18.2.3 Waveform

Different waveforms can be generated and used to create different tactile sensations. Brown et al. [14] have looked at the effects of amplitude modulation to create stimuli of different "roughness." A study showed that participants perceived the modulations as varying levels of roughness, and that roughness increased as modulation frequency decreased (with the exception of a pure sinusoid that was perceived as smooth). They suggest that up to three roughness levels can be used, with a study showing that participants could recognize them with 80% accuracy.

18.2.4 Duration

Geldard [6] reports that the temporal duration just noticeable difference (JND) increased from 50 to 150 ms with increasing stimulus duration from 0.1 to 2.0 s. Gescheider (as reported in Ref. 9) measured the time difference between the onset of two tactile "clicks" on the fingertip, necessary for them to perceived as two separate sensations. The minimum threshold reported was 10 ms, although this estimate could have been limited by the experimental apparatus. When using duration in tactile interface design it is important to ensure that stimuli are detectable, but not so long as to make information transfer too slow. Interactions between duration and perceived amplitude should be considered when using duration, as it has been shown that short, intense signals can be confused with longer, lower-intensity signals. Gunther et al. [15] suggest that stimuli lasting less than 0.1 s may be perceived as taps or jabs, whereas longer stimuli may be perceived as smoothly flowing tactile phrases. Craig and Sherrick [11] warn that durations that are too short may result in sensations such as pokes or jabs, which might be undesirable.

18.2.5 Rhythm

Building on single-pulse durations, more complex stimuli can be formed. Rhythms are created by grouping together pulses to create temporal patterns that are similar to rhythms in music. Summers [16] encoded speech information by modulating vibration frequency and amplitude, and by presenting the temporal pattern of the speech. Users obtained most information from the temporal pattern and very little from the frequency/amplitude modulation. This result suggests that rhythm could be an effective parameter in tactile displays.

18.2.6 Body Location

Different body locations have different levels of sensitivity and spatial acuity. The most sensitive part of the human body is the fingertip. The two-point difference threshold of contact discrimination is 0.9 mm when the stimuli are placed against the subject's fingertip in the absence of any movement lateral to the skin's surface. Two points of contact closer than this threshold cannot be resolved into distinct stimuli. Experimental evidence suggests that active exploration marginally increases sensitivity, decreasing the threshold to 0.7 mm [17].

The fingers are often used for tactile displays because of their high sensitivity. However, they are often required for interaction and manipulation tasks. Other body locations may be more suitable, or several sites may be needed for a complex display. An important factor to consider is whether stimuli are presented to glabrous (nonhairy) or hairy skin, as sensitivity differs greatly between them [10] and might require more discriminable stimuli. Certain body locations are less suitable for use; for example, transducers should not be placed on or near the head, as this can cause leakage of vibrations into the ears, resulting in unwanted sounds [15].

Craig and Sherrick [11] suggest the back, thigh, and abdomen as suitable body locations. They report that, once subjects have been trained in vibrotactile pattern recognition on the back, they can almost immediately recognize the same patterns when they are presented to the thigh or abdomen. This transfer also occurs to some extent when patterns are presented to different fingers after training on one finger, but is not so immediate. Cholewiak and Collins [18] investigated tactile localization on the forearm using seven actuators. They found that when a stimulus was close to an anatomic reference point, in particular a point of mobility such as the wrist or elbow, performance was greatest. Cholewiak et al. [19] conducted a study on the abdomen, where the main anatomic references are the spine and navel, and again found that localization was most precise when the stimuli occurred at these reference points. They also found that people were unlikely to mistake stimulation at another point for stimulation at one of the reference points.

18.2.7 Effects of Aging

Sensitivity to tactile stimulation is reduced with age (in line with the other senses). There are many reasons for this, including diabetes, skin trauma, and physiological changes in the skin itself. Stuart et al. [20] investigated the reductions in sensitivity to sinusoidal vibrations on different areas of the body, comparing people up to the age of 27 to a group between 55 and 90 years old. They compared detection thresholds at the fingertip, forearm, shoulder, and cheek. The older group showed significantly increased detection thresholds in all areas, except for the fingertip. The oldest participants showed the greatest declines in sensitivity. Similar research by Goble et al. [21] studying the palm and fingertip found differences between older and younger people's detection thresholds. One reason for the varying results is the different methods used to stimulate the skin in both studies. The results of both studies do suggest that the intensity of stimulation would need to be increased to ensure that older users could detect the stimuli being presented. Tactile user interface should include an intensity control, much like a volume control in an audio interface.

18.3 SENSORY SUBSTITUTION

The previous section has shown the main parameters of cutaneous perception and some guidance for tactile display. This section presents a review of the work on the applications of tactile displays and, in particular, the key topic of sensory substitution. The process of sensory substitution involves the sensing of stimuli by electronic means, transformation of the stimulus via signal processing, and presentation of the transformed stimulus in another sensory modality. The main application of these systems is increasing accessibility for those with sensory impairments. As early as the 1920s, researchers were interested in using vibration as a means of information transfer (e.g., Gault in 1926, cited by Craig and Sherrick [11]). The earliest sensory substitution devices converted visual stimuli to tactile representations for blind and visually impaired people.

Traditionally, information was presented to the skin via printed Braille or raised-paper diagrams. These can be very effective but are nondynamic and slow to produce. Dynamic, refreshable displays offer greater flexibility and independence. The most commonly used tactile displays evoke sensations using mechanical perturbation of the skin. This is commonly done by vibrating a small plate pressed against the skin, or via a pin or an array of pins on the fingertip. Other types of actuator technology are available, including pneumatic and electrotactile, but these tend to be of lower resolution and more difficult to control, with few commercial products an interface designer can use. For a full review, see Kaczmarek et al. [4].

This section outlines some of the key ways in which information is displayed to the skin and outlines the main technologies used and their applications. It is structured around the three main methods of presenting information: Braille/raised paper, pin arrays, and vibrotactile displays. Each method is described with examples of its use.

18.3.1 Braille and Raised-Paper Diagrams

Braille is the most common tactile presentation method used by visually impaired people. Each Braille character consists of a three-row × two-column "cell" with combinations of raised dots allowing 64 individual patterns. The patterns represent the letters of the alphabet, punctuation, and various contractions that stand for frequently recurring letter groups. Inspired by the work of William Wait in the late nineteenth century (cited by Schiff and Foulke [8]), experimental evidence gradually built up that demonstrated the superiority of Braille codes over embossed letters in terms of reading speed and comprehension of text. The main drawback of Braille is that reading speeds are much slower than for vision, at around 104 words per minute (wpm) for experienced adult users [8] (in comparison, the average reading speed for sighted high school students is 250–300 wpm, with some adults reaching 2 or 3 times that speed).

Raised-paper diagrams are most commonly used to present pictorial information. They are produced via embossing or heat raised paper and have been employed for presentation of pictorial information, including illustrations, photographs, graphs, and maps. The nomad tool [22] allowed the use of traditional tactile diagrams augmented with audio information. This overcomes the traditional drawbacks inherent in the static nature of tactile diagrams, and allows information to be presented in speech that would otherwise clutter the diagram with Braille. Embossed diagrams still possess many advantages over more technological solutions—they are cheap to produce, have no moving parts, and can be quickly and easily explored with the whole of both hands to provide a good overview of the information being displayed. They are, however, limited in size, can become easily cluttered with information, are subject to wear and tear, and are inherently nondynamic in nature, plus the fact that they often require sighted assistance to produce.

18.3.2 Pin Arrays

This type of display uses a pin or array of small pins to stimulate the fingertip (see Fig. 18.1 or the displays produced by Summers and Chanter [23]). One of the most common uses for this type of display is for presenting Braille. Dynamic Braille displays are made up of a line of cells (often 40 or 80), each with 6 or 8 pins that move up and down to represent the dots of a Braille cell. The user can read a line of Braille cells by touching the pins of each cell as they pop up (for more information, see www.tiresias.org). Summers and colleagues have developed a much higher-resolution array with a 10×10 matrix of pins over an area of 1 cm^2 [23]. Such devices can present fine cues for surface texture, edges, and lines for pictorial information.

Tactile–vision substitution systems were the earliest to be developed, in order to present visual information to blind people. In a typical system, a camera receives visual information that is converted to a tactile representation on a two-dimensional pin array. The Optacon (Fig. 18.2) was one of the first devices to employ a matrix of pins for tactile–vision substitution and was the first device of this kind to be developed as a commercial product. It converted printed letters into a spatially distributed vibrotactile

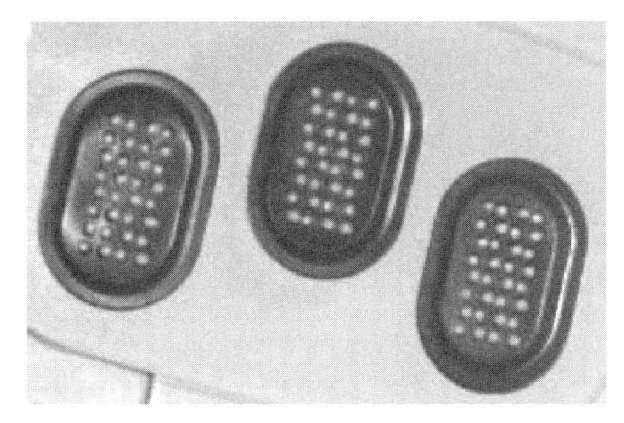

FIGURE 18.1 *A tactile pin array for fingertip display, consisting of three 4×8 arrays of pins.*

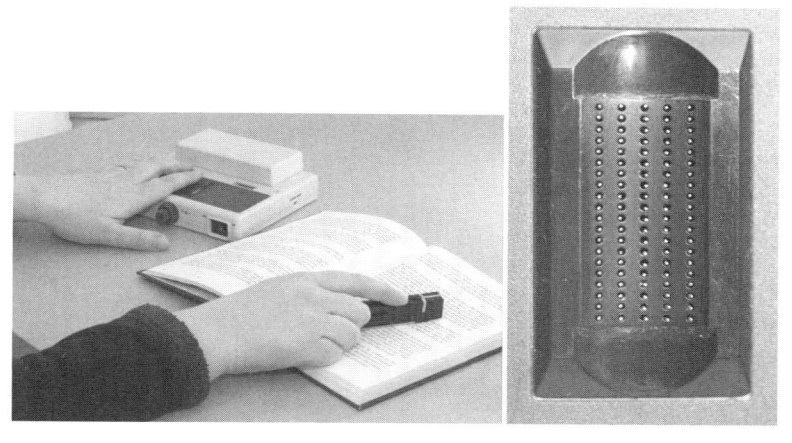

FIGURE 18.2 *Using the Optacon device to read text. The image on the right is a close-up view of the pin array.*

representation on the fingertip using a miniature handheld camera [11]. The input to the device is a 6 × 24 array of photosensitive cells, which detects patterns of light and dark as material is moved underneath. The display part of the device is a 6 × 24 array of pins on which users place their fingertip. The output of the camera is represented by vibrating pins on the tactile display. The pins vibrate at a frequency of 230 Hz, which is close to the maximum sensitivity of the skin. Reading speeds with the Optacon are around 10–12 wpm after the initial 9-day training period, reaching 30–50 wpm after further training and experience [11].

Early pioneering work in tactile–visual substitution (TVSS) was also performed by Bach-y-Rita and colleagues in the late 1960s. Early systems displayed visual information captured by a tripod-mounted TV camera to a vibrotactile display on the user's back. Owing to limited spatial resolution, tactile masking effects, and a low dynamic range, the system was not suitable for day-to-day navigation. However, subjects could easily recognize simple shapes and discriminate orientation of lines. It was also reported that experienced users could perform more complex tasks, such as recognition of faces, or electronic assembly using the system [24].

To allow exploration of a larger tactile image with a device limited to the size of one or two fingertips, several researchers have adopted a strategy of mounting a tactile display on a computer input device, such as a mouse (see Fig. 18.3) or graphics tablet stylus. This allows the motion of the user's fingertips to be tracked within the limits of a certain workspace and the tactile display to be updated accordingly, depending on where the user is on a "virtual image." They can be distinguished from devices such as the Optacon in that they are most commonly employed to represent information that is stored digitally on a computer, rather than present in the user's distal environment. Active exploration is necessary to perceive the entirety of the image being displayed.

Researchers are currently investigating how best to employ tactile displays like these to present pictorial information. Potential applications include making graphs and maps more accessible to visually impaired users. Wall and Brewster [25] investigated the identification of positive and negative gradients relative to a horizontal line using a VTPlayer mouse (see Fig. 18.3). They found that blindfolded participants were correctly able to

FIGURE 18.3 The VTPlayer tactile mouse: a commercially available virtual tactile display with two 4 × 4-pin arrays from VirTouch (www.virtouch2.com).

identify positive and negative gradients within ±4.7° of the horizontal, compared to ±3.25° for a forced-feedback mouse, and ±2.42° for raised paper representations. Using the raised-paper diagram provides the richest combination of tactile cues. Improving the size, resolution, and bandwidth of tactile displays could potentially move discrimination closer to that observed for raised paper.

Jansson and Pedersen [26] studied performance in a map-browsing task using the VTPlayer. They noted that the tactile feedback had no beneficial effects over the performance that could be achieved with audio feedback. This was due to the difficulty that the visually impaired people had using a mouse. The information available through the pin arrays is very limited compared to the rich, distributed cues of vision, or those available with a raised-paper map [26].

Wall and Brewster [27] also conducted a more qualitative experiment using the VTPlayer to represent bar charts. Many of the blind users consulted were also uncomfortable with mouse use, so the tactile cues were presented to the nondominant hand to supplement navigation with a graphics tablet used in the other hand. The graphics tablet provided an absolute position reference that allowed users to plan their exploration better. A tangible overlay was used to disambiguate resources such as the graph's axes, so that they could be quickly apprehended by the user. The pins of the display were raised if the user was on a bar, and lowered if not, thus supporting navigational information (e.g., "Am I on a bar?" or "How many bars have I crossed") and indirect access to information ("How high is the bar?"). Supplementary audio cues were used for contextual information as to position on the graph, and provided details on the titles and values of bars.

This research shows that the needs of users can still outstrip the capabilities of current tactile displays for some applications. Improving the pin spacing and amplitude of pin movement would allow more complex information to be displayed. Performance in feature identification has been shown to increase with decreasing pin separation, and would also allow more pins on the display [28]. Improving the range and resolution of pin movement would allow height to be used as a filtering mechanism to disambiguate different picture elements, such as edges and texturing [29]. Wall and Brewster suggest presenting information through other modalities to avoid cluttering the tactile representation, and using a tangible relief to provide persistent, unambiguous guidance using static interface elements such as axes and gridlines [27].

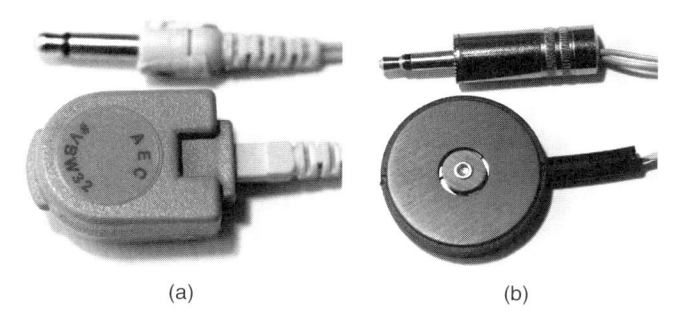

FIGURE 18.4 (a) A TACTAID VBW32 transducer; (b) an EAI C2 Tactor.

18.3.3 Vibrotactile Displays

Most vibrotactile actuators use electromagnetic actuation to drive a mass in either a linear or rotational fashion to provide vibrotactile stimulation to the skin. Two typical vibrotactile devices, the TACTAID VBW32 (www.tactaid.com) and the EAI C2 Tactor (www.eai.com), are shown in Figure 18.4. Both of these devices are resonant at 250 Hz with significantly reduced response at other frequencies (which reduces the usefulness of frequency as a parameter for vibrotactile interfaces). Vibrotactile cues are much lower-resolution than pin arrays but can exert more force (so can be felt through clothing); they can also be distributed over the body to give spatial cues (often mounted in a vest on the user's back or in a belt around the waist). For a more detailed review of vibrotactile devices, see Summers [10].

Poupyrev et al. [30] have designed sophisticated tactile displays for handheld computers. Lee et al. [31] have also developed a vibrotactile stylus for use on touchscreens and handheld computers. There is commercial interest in this area, as most mobile telephones include tactile feedback to accompany ringtones. For example, Immersion's VibeTonz (www.immersion.com/vibetonz) attempts to extend this simple feedback to enhance games and ringtones. Vibrotactile displays have been incorporated into canes used by visually impaired people. The UltraCane (www.soundforesight.co.uk) uses ultrasound to detect objects in a user's environment and displays the location and distance to targets by vibrating pads on the handle of the cane.

Work on vibrotactile displays was motivated by tactile–audio substitution for profoundly deaf people, which did not develop much until the late 1970s and early 1980s. One of the earliest devices was the Tacticon, a commercial device that adjusted the perceived intensity of 16 electrodes, each of which corresponded to a range of frequencies in the auditory spectrum, in order to improve speech comprehension, auditory discrimination, and the clarity of the users speech [24]. Another early device, the *tactile acoustic monitor* (TAM), was developed by Summers [16]. The TAM employed a single vibrotactile stimulator to provide unencoded information about the loudness of the user's speech and other sounds in the environment. Sound is picked up by a microphone, which is then compared to a threshold level. If the microphone signal is above the threshold, the vibrotactile actuator is turned on at a constant amplitude and frequency, whereas if the sound level falls below the threshold, the actuator is turned off. Evaluation showed that the TAM was useful for lip reading applications, prompting a variety of experiments investigating speech perception via a single vibratory transducer [16]. For a full review of work in this area, see Summers [10].

Significant early work in tactile displays for desktop human–computer interaction was carried out by Akamatsu and colleagues, who investigated the addition of an electromagnetically controlled pin to a standard mouse. This allowed users to feel vibrations through a fingertip. Akamatsu et al. [32] investigated the impact of their tactile feedback on target acquisition in a Fitts law pointing study. They examined whether targeting was aided when sound, tactile, and color feedback were used to indicate target acquisition in a desktop-type pointing interaction. Tactile feedback had a greater effect in reducing the time a user spent over a target than either sound or color. In a second study, Akamatsu and MacKenzie [33] examined the contribution of tactile and forced-feedback on targeting. Tactile alone and forced-feedback + tactile reduced targeting times by 5.6% and 7.6%, respectively. Forced-feedback alone resulted in slightly higher targeting times.

Cockburn and Brewster [34] looked at combinations of different feedback modalities, including vibration feedback from a Logitech iFeel vibrotactile mouse (www.logitech.com), for selecting small targets on a computer desktop. They found that, in simple Fitts law–type tasks (where discrete targets are used, so there are no distracters), tactile and audio feedback both reduced targeting time (confirming Akamatsu's results described above), but the combination of audio plus tactile was not as good as when each was used alone. However, in a more realistic task (choosing items from dropdown menus), the tactile feedback caused problems and actually increased targeting time over a standard graphical display. The reason for this was the close proximity of many tactile targets (each menu item gave tactile feedback) causing feedback "overload."

Jacko and colleagues have looked at how tactile displays (and more generally multimodal ones) can help older adults with age-related macular degeneration (AMD) (which is a leading cause of visual impairment in individuals of 65 years and over). Their evaluations use drag-and-drop-type interactions with the Logitech Wingman force-feedback mouse (www.logitech.com), which is vibrated to produce tactile feedback. When different combinations of audio, tactile, and visual feedback were added to drag-and-drop, there was little benefit to the tactile feedback over a standard visual display, except when it was in combination with audio [35]. A second study showed that AMD had a major effect on the drag-and-drop task, with AMD sufferers performing significantly worse than fully sighted people of the same age. Again tactile showed little effect on its own, improving performance by a small amount. However, when it was combined with audio it had a much greater effect. AMD sufferers got more benefit from the addition of extra feedback than the fully sighted [36].

Results from this work appear to conflict with those of Cockburn and Brewster [34] as they showed that audio and tactile feedback were more beneficial when used on their own. It is difficult to compare the two studies as they used different users, devices, and stimuli. These results do show that the use of tactile displays is an active research area with many questions still to be answered. Designers must be careful to test their applications with the devices they will actually use to ensure that usability is improved.

Brewster and Brown [37] have investigated an alternative encoded form of tactile presentation: the Tacton, or tactile icon. Tactons are structured, abstract messages that can be used to communicate messages non-visually. Visual icons and their auditory equivalent Earcons [38] are very powerful ways of displaying information, but there is no tactile equivalent. In the visual domain there is text and its counterpart, the icon;

the same is true in sound with synthetic speech and the Earcon. In the tactile domain there is Braille, but it has no "iconic" counterpart. Visual icons can convey complex information in a very small amount of screen space, much smaller than for a textual description. Earcons transmit information in a small amount of time as compared to synthetic speech. Tactons can convey information in a smaller amount of space and time than can Braille. The shared temporal property between audio and tactile means that certain audio characteristics such as rhythm, tempo, and duration could be transformed into tactile stimuli (and vice versa). Therefore, the same information may be presented interchangeably via the two different modalities. This is a bidirectional form of sensory substitution where the information could be presented to one sense or other depending on the user's particular disabilities or current situation.

Tactons are created by manipulating the parameters of cutaneous perception (detailed previously) to encode information. For example, Brown et al. [14] encoded two pieces of information into a Tacton to create messages for mobile telephones. The type of call or message (voice call, text message, or multimedia message) was encoded in the rhythm, while the priority (low, medium, or high) of a call or message was encoded in the roughness (via amplitude modulation). Using this mapping, the same rhythm would represent a high/low-priority voice call, but they would each be presented using a different waveform, whereas a high-priority voice call and a high-priority text message would share the same waveform, but have different rhythms. An initial study [14] on these nine Tactons showed that participants could identify them with over 70% accuracy, with rhythms identified correctly 93% of the time. These results show that Tactons can be a powerful, nonvisual way of communicating information, and useful to users who cannot see.

18.4 CONCLUSIONS

This chapter has reviewed the contribution of tactile displays for sensory substitution and supplementation for sensory impaired users. Tactile feedback offers an alternative channel through which information can be communicated when other channels are impaired or overloaded. This might be in addition to graphical or audio displays, or as an alternative depending on the user's preferences and any disabilities.

The human sense of touch is very powerful, but abilities change with age. There is some detailed research into the effects of these changes at the physiological level, but this has not yet fed into much of the applied research on tactile displays for sensory substitution. There is much to be done on determining what changes might need to be made to ensure that tactile displays are useful to users with a wide range of abilities. Basic things such as the ability to control the amplitude of stimulation are important. Devices such as the Optacon allowed this so that the user could set a comfortable, perceivable level. This is not possible with many other available devices, which may make them difficult for someone with less sensitivity to use, or painful for someone with heightened sensitivity.

Other important issues for designers were raised in the review of perception. The interaction between frequency and amplitude means that care must be taken if one parameter is varied as it may change the way the other is experienced. The duration of stimulation is important, too. If it is too short, then stimuli may go unnoticed, too long and information transfer will be too slow. Rhythm has also been shown to be a good parameter for information display, mapping well to auditory stimuli if crossmodal presentation is required. Finally, location on the body must be considered. The fingertip is very sensitive but may not be usable if a user needs to type or hold a mouse. Other body locations are possible, but sensitivity will be lower and the effects of age may affect different sites in different ways. When multiple stimulation sites are required, each actuator should be positioned near an anatomical reference point for accurate localization. All of these issues are important to tactile HCI, and further research will help designers deal with them to avoid problems of cues being missed or misinterpreted.

There are no standard tactile devices; they are evolving at the same time as the applications that use them. This can make it difficult to generalize results from one device to another. As the area generates more attention and more studies are undertaken, this problem will be resolved. However, at the present time it is important for designers to test out their applications with the specific devices that they intend to use to be sure of the usability benefits.

Before the full potential of touch can be realized in computer systems, further technology developments are required. From an interaction perspective, there are important requirements for new devices. For vibrotactile devices we need to be able to present a wider range of frequencies to the skin. Presently the frequency range is limited to ~250 Hz on most devices. If this could be widened, it would allow greater use of the skin's ability to detect vibration. Much of the work on pin arrays presented above used devices with small numbers of widely spaced pins that can be raised or lowered only with no resolution in between. To simulate textures accurately or represent detailed images, much higher-resolution displays are needed. The two-point difference threshold has been estimated at 0.7 mm, which is the necessary spacing of pins to fuse stimuli into a continuous image. To enable height to be used as a filtering mechanism to give information on relative importance of items in a scene, the amplitude of the pins needs to be controllable. Summers' work is going in this direction with arrays of much higher density [23].

There are many new application areas that could benefit from tactile displays. The use of mobile devices has grown very rapidly since 2003 or so. Mobile telephones, handheld computers, and handheld computer games are now very common, with new devices and applications appearing on the market all the time. There is a strong research focus in computing science on how better interfaces might be designed for this new type of device, but many are currently difficult or impossible for disabled people to use. Small screens make it difficult to display information at a size that people with poor eyesight can see. Tactile displays have an important role to play in making these devices usable by older or visually impaired people. Information could be presented using sophisticated tactile displays that could give people access to the user interface in a form that is suitable for them.

More sophisticated tactile cues could be used to provide much more information to help users navigate without using vision. Vibrations could be presented to the left or right side of the body to indicate changes in direction or assist in more complex obstacle avoidance. In a context-aware mobile device a tactile display could give information about the environment surrounding the user who is mobile, for example, encoding information about the type of building the person is next to, where the door is and the number of steps to get inside. This has advantages as information delivered through sound can often be problematic if the environment is noisy or the information is confidential. A tactile display is private to the user and less affected by the environment.

The work reviewed here shows that the sense of touch has great potential as a channel for communication. A range of different applications for disabled people has been developed over the years. It is now becoming possible to use tactile displays creatively in mainstream HCI research to design a new generation of accessible user interfaces.

ACKNOWLEDGMENTS

This work was funded by EPSRC Advanced Research Fellowship GR/S53244, grant GR/S53251, and PhD Studentship GR/S53244.

REFERENCES

1. Gregor P, Newell AF, Zajicek M: Designing for dynamic diversity—interfaces for older people, in Jacko JA, ed, *Proc ASSETS 2002*, Edinburgh, UK, ACM Press, 2002.
2. Klatzky R, Lederman S: Touch, in Proctor R, ed, *Handbook of Psychology*, Vol 4, *Experimental Psychology*, Wiley, Hoboken, NJ, 2003, Chapter 6.
3. Burdea G: *Force and Touch Feedback for Virtual Reality*, Wiley-Interscience, New York, 1996.
4. Kaczmarek K, Webster J, Bach-y-Rita P, Tompkins W: Electrotactile and vibrotactile displays for sensory substitution systems, *IEEE Trans Biomed Eng* **38**:1–16 (1991).
5. Lofvenberg J, Johansson RS: Regional differences in sensitivity to vibration in the glabrous skin of the human hand, *Brain Res* **301**:65–72 (1984).
6. Geldard FA: Adventures in tactile literacy, *Am Psychol* **12**:115–124 (1957).
7. Werner G, Mountcastle VB: Quantitative relations between mechanical stimuli to the skin and neural responses evoked by them, in Kenshalo D, ed, *The Skin Senses*, Charles C Thomas, Springfield, IL, 1968.
8. Schiff W, Foulke E, eds, *Tactual Perception: A Sourcebook*, Cambridge Univ Press, 1982.
9. Tan HZ: Information transmission with a multi-finger tactual display, in *Electrical Engineering*, MIT Press, Cambridge, MA, 1996.
10. Summers IR, ed, *Tactile Aids for the Hearing Impaired*, Whurr Publishers, London, 1992.
11. Craig JC, Sherrick CE: Dynamic tactile displays in Schiff W, Foulke E, eds, *Tactual Perception: A Sourcebook*, Cambridge Univ Press, 1982.
12. Goff GD: Differential discrimination of frequency of cutaneous mechanical vibration, *J Exper Psychol* **74**:294–299 (1967).
13. Sherrick C: A scale for rate of tactual vibration, *J Acoust Soc Am* **78**:78–83 (1985).
14. Brown LM, Brewster SA, Purchase HC: A first investigation into the effectiveness of tactons, in Bergamasco M, Bicchi A, eds, *Proc Worldhaptics 2005*, Pisa, Italy, IEEE Press.
15. Gunther E, Davenport G, O'Modhrain S: Cutaneous grooves: Composing for the sense of touch, in *New Instruments for Musical Expression*, University of Limorick, Dublin, 2002.
16. Summers IR: Single-channel information transfer through the skin: Limitations and possibilities, in Summers IR, Whybrow J, eds, *International Sensory Aids Conf*, Exeter, UK, 2000.
17. Phillips JR, Johnson KO: Neural mechanisms of scanned and stationary touch, *J Acoust Soc Am* **77**:220–224 (1985).
18. Cholewiak RW, Collins AA: Vibrotactile localization on the arm: Effects of place, space and age, *Percept Psychophys* **65**:1058–1077 (2003).
19. Cholewiak RW, Brill CJ, Schwab A: Vibrotactile localization on the abdomen: Effects of place and space, *Percept Psychophys* **66**:970–987 (2004).

20. Stuart M, Turman AB, Shaw J, Walsh N, Nguyen V: Effects of aging on vibration detection thresholds at various body regions, *BMC Geriatri* **3**(1):20 (2003). http://www.biomedcentral.com/1471-2318/3/1.
21. Goble A, Collins A, Cholewiak R: Vibrotactile threshold in young and old observers: The effects of spatial summation and the presence of a rigid surround, *J Acoust Soc Am* **99**:2256-2269 (1996).
22. Parkes D: "Nomad": An audio-tactile tool for the acquisition, use and management of spatially distributed information by visually impaired people, *Proc 2nd Int Symp Maps and Graphics for Visually Impaired People*, London, 1988.
23. Summers IR, Chanter CM: A broadband tactile array on the fingertip, *J Acoust Soc Am* **112**:2118-2126 (2002).
24. Kaczmarek KA, Bach-y-Rita P: Tactile displays, in Barfield WAFTA, ed, *Virtual Environments and Advanced Interface Design*, Oxford Univ Press, New York, 1995.
25. Wall SA, Brewster SA: Sensory substitution using tactile pin arrays: Human factors, technology and applications, *Signal Process* **86** (2006).
26. Jansson G, Pedersen P: Obtaining geographical information from a virtual map with a haptic mouse, *Proc 22nd Int Cartographic Conf (ICC2005)*, a Coruna, Spain, ICA, 2005.
27. Wall SA, Brewster SA: Feeling what you hear: Tactile feedback for navigation of audio graphs, *Proc ACM CHI 2006*, Montreal, Canada, ACM Press/Addison-Wesley, 2006.
28. Kammermeier P, Schmidt G: Application-specific evaluation of tactile array displays for the human fingertip, *Proc IEEE/RSJ Int Conf Intelligent Robots and Systems (IROS)*. Lausanne, Switzerland, IEEE, 2002.
29. Challis B, Edwards ADN: Design principles for tactile interaction, in Brewster SA, Murray-Smith R, eds, *Haptic Human-Computer Interaction*, Springer LNCS, Berlin, 2001.
30. Poupyrev I, Maruyama S: Tactile interfaces for small touch screens, *Proc UIST 2003*, Vancouver, Canada, ACM Press, 2003.
31. Lee JC, Dietz P, Leigh D, Yerazunis W, Hudson SE: Haptic pen: A tactile feedback stylus for touch screens, *Proc UIST 2004*, Santa Fe, NM, ACM Press/Addison-Wesley, 2004.
32. Akamatsu M, MacKenzie IS, Hasbrouq T: A comparison of tactile, auditory, and visual feedback in a pointing task using a mouse-type device, *Ergonomics* **38**:816-827 (1995).
33. Akamatsu M, MacKenzie IS: Movement characteristics using a mouse with tactile and force feedback, *Int J Human-Comput Stud* **45**:483-493 (1996).
34. Cockburn A, Brewster SA: Multimodal feedback for the acquisition of small targets, *Ergonomics* **48**:1129-1150 (2005).
35. Jacko J, Scott I, Sainfort F, Barnard L, Edwards P, Emery VK, Kongnakorn T, Moloney K, Zorich B: Older adults and visual impairment: What do exposure times and accuracy tell us about performance gains associated with multimodal feedback? *Proc ACM CHI 2003*, Fort Lauderdale, FL, ACM Press/Addison-Wesley, 2003.
36. Jacko J, Barnard L, Kongnakorn T, Moloney K, Edwards P, Emery VK, Sainfort F: Isolating the effects of visual impairment: Exploring the effect of AMD on the utility of multimodal feedback, *Proc ACM CHI 2004*, Vienna, Austria, ACM Press/Addison-Wesley, 2004.
37. Brewster SA, Brown LM: Tactons: Structured tactile messages for non-visual information display, in Cockburn A, ed, *Proc Australasian User Interface Conf 2004*, Dunedin, New Zealand, Australian Computer Society.
38. Blattner M, Sumikawa D, Greenberg R: Earcons and icons: Their structure and common design principles, *Human Comput Interact* **4**:11-44 (1989).

PART IV
Assistive Robotics

19

Assistive Robotics for Independent Living

Bessam Abdulrazak
Université de Sherbrooke, Quebec, Canada

Mounir Mokhtari
Institut National des Télécommunications, Évry, France

The technologic advances in mechatronics, electronics, and computer sciences have allowed building diverse categories of assistive technologies that enhance the well-being of people with special needs (PwSN). Assistive robotics (AR) is one of the more recent technologies that have grown significantly, providing PwSN with systems that compensate for movement limitation (object manipulation with arm robot) or increase mobility (smart electric wheelchairs). Some systems, such as mobile robots in living environment, adopt a different approach in enhancing PwSN mobility by causing objects to move to the user's location (e.g., a robot can bring a glass of water from the kitchen).

This chapter focuses mainly on ARs that allow PwSN to manipulate objects. It is an attempt to provide a summary of the AR systems as well as the history of the AR, with a special interest in issues that the community of AR is facing. Various categories of AR are detailed in this chapter, from pioneer systems to the most popular, most advanced, or even most commercially available AR systems.

19.1 INTRODUCTION

Assistive robotics, also defined as *service robotics* or even *welfare robotics*, is one of the most complex technologies more recently considered as important in the lives of people

---

The Engineering Handbook of Smart Technology for Aging, Disability, and Independence,
Edited by A. Helal, M. Mokhtari and B. Abdulrazak
Copyright © 2008 John Wiley & Sons, Inc.

with special needs (PwSN). It deals with advanced robotics technology to provide people with physical disabilities with systems that enhance well-being, and improve quality of life and work productivity. AR also assists PwSN to live independently, maintain good health, and remain socially active. AR could also contribute in providing relatives, friends, and caregivers means when interacting with PwSN.

Assistive robotics is a technology that *serves* PwSN *using* robotics tools combining mechatronics, electronic, and software engineering. In particular, it focuses on two main field of research: the field of assistive technology (AT), which covers all technologies for the use of PwSN (e.g., electric wheelchairs, environmental control systems, communication systems), and the field of robotics, which focuses on mechatronics (completely self-contained electronic, electric, and mechanical devices) to develop reprogrammable and multifunctional systems. Robotics systems can be programmed to perform several tasks (e.g., gripping objects and transporting them from one place to another) without human intervention.

The first applications of robotics were (and still remain) mainly industrial (e.g., the automobile industry, manufacturing). Meanwhile, the improvement of robotics combined with technologic progress in other fields (computer science, networking, etc.), has allowed developing human-friendly communicating systems for different types of applications, including space exploration, marine exploration, and in hostile environments (such as nuclear applications), for security and safety (military and police), and even for entertainment (e.g., sensing robotic toys). Nonetheless, many technologic and acceptability issues have somewhat impeded the research and development of robotics in the assistive, rehabilitation,[1] and health areas. The most important factors are

Reliability, Security, and Safety. When we focus on robots in close interaction with a human in daily environment, the most important factors include reliability, security, and safety. For example, we could tolerate or even consider identified errors in the industrial field. However, when a robot is used by a person, these errors are not allowed because it could result in injuries (e.g., the gripper might open slightly when the user is moving a cup of hot tea).

User Interface. This is an important issue, since it provides the means to control a robot; the nonadaptation of the user interface in the user's requirement could result in a nonacceptability of the robot. Because of the physical and even cognitive limitations of PwSN, noncomplex, accessible, and personalized user interfaces are required. For example, a person with muscular dystrophy, having limited force at the fingers level, may need a small keypad, whereas a person with spinal cord injury, having no movement at finger level, may need a joystick to control the system.

Mechanical and Ergonomic Infrastructure. Most of the earliest robotic structures were complex, heavy, and bulky, imposing many restrictions in the displacement and the installation of the system. For example, installation of a robotic system in the user's environment requires an expert to configure the system with sometimes heavy cabling issues. Any installation necessitates a thorough investigation on the structure of the user's home or office. In addition, moving these systems from one place to another and mounting them on bases or wheelchairs were also obviously impossible.

---

[1] *Rehabilitation technology* is defined as technology that enables disabled people to reach or maintain their best mental, physical, and/or social functional level.

Hardware and Software. The hardware and software issues are very important components that need continuous improvement in order to build assistive robots. The robotic systems require better computation power to handle the event or data related to the sensors, the communication, and control of the mechanical structure. Real-time operating systems, algorithms, and software architectures also should be enhanced to perform a suitable control of the mechanical structure. Miniaturization of processors and electronic boards was necessary to embed them inside the existing mechanical structure (e.g., arm mounted on wheelchair or mobile base).

Since the mid-1970s, technology has reached a level where most of the issues that have limited the impact of AR may be overcome, allowing the development of more acceptable and durable materials; numerous more accessible user interfaces have appeared on the market, the systems are becoming more reliable, and so on. As direct results of these advances in technology, we have seen an increase in the number of research laboratories working in this field; numerous systems have been developed, and various scientific activities have emerged (as observed through conferences, exhibitions, publications, etc.). We could mention several main conferences focusing specifically on assistive robotics for therapy and well-being, such as the International Conference on Rehabilitation Robotics (ICORR), the International Conference on Smart Homes and Health Telematics (ICOST), the conference organized by the Association for the Advancement of Assistive Technology in Europe (AAATE), and the conference organized by the Rehabilitation Engineering Society of North America (RESNA). In addition, the most promising aspect is the expanding use of assistive robots by PwSN. The list of these robots includes numerous types: an arm manipulator mounted on a wheelchair or mobile base, a feeding robot, a humanoid companion, and robotic workstations.

This chapter is an attempt to provide a state of the art of the worldwide research work in AR, focusing on systems that compensate a physical handicap, providing users, even those with four-limb impairment, the ability to manipulate objects. Section 19.2 presents a brief historical background of AR describing the complexity and tremendous efforts needed to obtain the current results; Section 19.3 addresses the diverse categories of assistive robots. In order to better clarify the different categories, we detail briefly some systems, mainly those that are well known by the scientific community, and those commercially available. In order to provide some idea about the future, we conclude this chapter by discussing some issues that are actually addressed by the research community of AR.

19.2 HISTORY: FROM ROBOTICS TO ASSISTIVE ROBOTICS

Even with the intense research activity on robotics in the 1990s, teams working on assistive and rehabilitation robotics remain limited and based primarily in North America and Europe. More recently, several teams have appeared in Asia, particularly in South Korea and Japan. The expertise acquired in designing robotic systems has enabled researchers to design usable, reliable, and safe robotic systems, which subsequently has enabled researchers to build assistive robots. The initial research work in the area of AR was in the early 1960s [1,2] and at approximately the same time in North America and Europe. Most early attempts began with a motorized prosthetic arm, followed by the addition of a user interface to control the arm robot. Most of the user interfaces consisted of either a simple switch with scanning inputs or a complicated voice recognition operated system.

In the United States, early attempts at developing rehabilitation robots was the "golden" arm developed in 1969 at Rancho Los Amigos Hospital in Downey, California. It is a powered orthosis with 7 degrees of freedom (DOF) that uses seven tongue switches in a sequential mode to successfully move the arm in space [3]. Similar work was also done at Case Institute of Technology. They developed a 4-DOF manipulator controlled directly via myoelectric signals and a head-mounted light source to trigger light sensors in the environment [4]. Also, an early system developed in the 1970s was "Mason" from the VA (Veterans Affairs) Prosthetics Center in New York. The system was a 4-DOF robotic arm mounted on a wheelchair (in fact, this was the first wheelchair-mounted robotic arm [5,6]). The Seamone–Schmeisser workstation at Johns Hopkins University (1974) was another early attempt at robotics in the United States [7,8].

Currently, two of the best-known rehabilitation robotics researchers in the United States are M. Van Der Loos at the Palo Alto VA Hospital and L. Leifer at Stanford University, both in northern California. Their work has resulted in numerous systems based on an industrial PUMA robot: the DEVAR *d*esktop *v*ocational *a*ssistant *r*obot system, the PROVAR (*p*rofesional *v*ocational *a*ssistant *r*obot) system (an improved version of DEVAR) [9], and the MIME system [10], which is a robot designed for upper-limb therapy for stroke patients. Another team at MIT (Massachusetts Institute of Technology) developed a similar therapy robot, the MIT-MANUS system, which is now commercially available in the United States and also in Europe [11].

In Europe, an early attempt at developing rehabilitation robots was the Roesler workstation in Heidelberg, Germany in the 1970s [12,13]; it was also the earliest example of a robotic system designed for the workstation. In France, robotics for people with disabilities appeared in 1985 with the Spartacus project, in an attempt to study the feasibility of the use of the robotics manipulators by people with high spinal cord injuries [14,15]. One of the most important results of the project was to mount a manipulator arm on a wheelchair, to increase the effectiveness of manipulation rehabilitation [15]. Later, the Spartacus work evolved into many systems, including the Dutch MANUS telemanipulator [16], the UK RTX robot [17], and the French AFMASTERworkstation [18,19]. In 1987, in the UK, Dr. M. Topping at Keele University began working on a robotics system to help a 12-year-old boy with spastic paraplegia to feed himself. The work marked the launching of the REHAB company, which has sold more rehabilitation robots than any other with their Handy 1 robot [20]. Most of the R&D projects in Europe have been supported by the European Commission. The TIDE (*t*echnology *i*nitiative for *d*isabled and *e*lderly people) initiative was one of the main programs in Europe that supported Manus manipulator and RAID–MASTER workstation development.

In 2001, Korea launched a vast research program on human-friendly welfare robotics for 9 years. Professor Zeungnam Zenn Bien has led this ongoing program at KAIST (Korean Advanced Institute of Sciences and Technology) (KAIST), which resulted in the KARES (KAIST rehabilitation engineering system) I and KARES II systems [21,22].

During the mid-1970s, numerous research projects have been ongoing in the area of AR around the world. Most of these projects were quite similar to those described above. Some of these projects have yielded significant results due to the devoted efforts extended in by the researchers, while other projects are still in ongoing. These activities have resulted in a considerable number of robotic systems; however, only a few have resulted in marketable products. In the next section, we categorize these robotic systems and describe some of the more widely known ones.

19.3 ASSISTIVE ROBOT CATEGORIES

Support within the AR the scientific community has been divided between two approaches: (1) the fully automated control of the robot and (2) manual or semimanual control of the robot. In approach 1, the robot is controlled via automatic modes, allowing the user to perform complex tasks autonomously. The user is not in the control loop of the robot and must only initiate the task and wait for the robot to perform it. The development that has been ongoing within approach 1 has focused mainly on robotic workstations, with a very structured environment and very precise tasks. In approach 2, which supports manual or semimanual control of the robot, the user is in the command loop of the robot and must always devise strategies to perform tasks. For example, to move an object from point A to B, the user has to plan the path and order the robot to follow that path. The US, research investigation has focused on the development of robotic arms that can be mounted on a wheelchair or a mobile base.

Adopting approaches 1 and 2 described above, a variety of projects and research activity have been ongoing. In order to illustrate this variety, we classified AR into five main categories: workstation robots, unifunction robots, manipulators on a base, wheelchair-mounted telemanipulators, and mobile autonomous manipulators. In the following sections, we describe each category and take a closer look at one or two of the better-known systems.

19.3.1 Workstation Robots

Robotics workstations are composed of robotic arms, generally an existing industrial robot, and of a structured environment where the objects to be manipulated are identified and accessible within the workspace of the robot. The tasks and movements of the robot are fully automated; the user has only to select the desired task and initiate it, for example, picking up a videotape, inserting it into the VCR (videocassette recorder), then push the "PLAY" button of the VCR. The user interface generally offers different types of input devices such as speech recognition or graphical interface controlled with a standard mouse or with an adapted input such as a single switch. These stations have the advantage of performing tasks in optimized trajectory and adequate time. This category of robotic system is very practical for assisting users in the specific environment such as the office, and for specific applications such as manipulating books, flipping book pages, and drinking beverages. These systems have the advantage of possessing excellent mechanical stability. However, the robot operates only in structured and fixed environments (it is difficult to move the system from one place to another).

The earliest system in this family of workstation robots for people with disabilities was the Heidelberg manipulator [12]. Since that time, several workstations have been developed with approximately comparable ideas, such as the Canadian system RAA (robotic assistive appliance) (1983) [23], the REGENESIS workstation of the *Neil Squire Society* in Canada [24,25], the work of HADAR in Sweden (1990) [26,27], and the Wolfson desktop-mounted workstation system at BIME (Bath Institute of Medical Engineering) in the UK [28,29]. In the following text we present the most-known workstations: the AFMASTER and the DeVAR/ProVAR.

FIGURE 19.1 The workstation MASTER.

19.3.1.1 AFMASTER

AFMASTER (Fig. 19.1) workstation is the result of many successive projects: MASTER, RAID, and RAID2/MASTER2.

19.3.1.1.1 MASTER1
CEA (Commissariat à l'Energie Atomique) began development of the MASTER1 (Manipulator Autonomous at Service of Tetraplegics for Environment and Eehabilitation) workstation in 1985 [30–32]. Following the recommendations of those involved in the Spartacus project [33], this workstation was composed of an RTX (Fig. 19.2) industrial robotic arm [17] that moves on rails. It was equipped with an end-effector, a structured environment with several storage spaces, multiple communication peripherals (telephone, telecopy, and printer), and a PC to manage different input physical interfaces (devices). The arm was programmed using a teach pendant, and direct manipulation modes are also available. To control the system, the user had an LCD display with different menus of actions, which can be selected by various physical input devices such as keypad, switch, mouse or joystick, or voice recognition.

Many improvements came afterward, during the EPI European project, which gave rise to MASTER2 station [34].

19.3.1.1.2 RAID
The RAID (*robot to assist in the integration of the disabled*) robotics workstation was developed in 1991–1993 by different research groups of CEA in France, the PAPWORTH group in the UK and CERTEC, and Lund University in the EPI-RAID European project of the TIDE program [35]. The workstation was designed primarily for users with upper-limb disabilities working in office environments. This system enabled the user to open racks, pick up objects and documents, and bring the selected item into the direction of the user.

The RAID station was equipped with an RT100 arm modified and assembled on a rail. The workspace of the robot was a desk with two racks and several storage areas. The workstation had two interchangeable grippers: one to turn pages and to serve as a tool for picking up objects, and another specially designed to pick up books. Control of the system was mainly via a joystick and a visual interface, allowing users to choose, by clicking on the mouse, which gripper to use and which objects to be pick up [36,37].

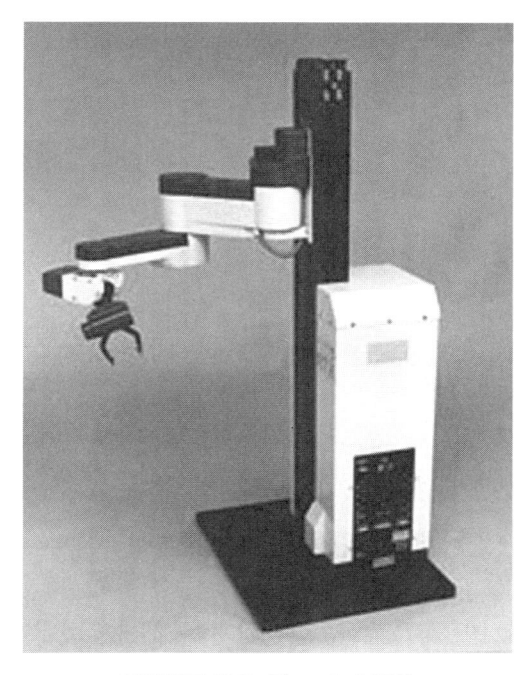

FIGURE 19.2 The robot RTX.

19.3.1.1.3 RAID2 and MASTER2 The two systems are similar. They are also known by the name of RAID-MASTER (Fig. 19.3). They emerged from the European project EPI-RAID (evaluation of prototype and improvements of the RAID workstation) (1993–1996), which was part of the TIDE program. In the RAID-MASTER project, the size of the space that the station occupied was reduced, the robot arm was modified by the RT200, and there have been other improvements of the arm extremity organs, while the human–machine interface was that developed for MASTER1. Evaluation of the RAID-MASTER station was carried out at three European sites (Rehabcentrum Lun-Orup in Sweden; Kerpape in France, and Papworth in the UK) [32].

FIGURE 19.3 The workstation RAID.

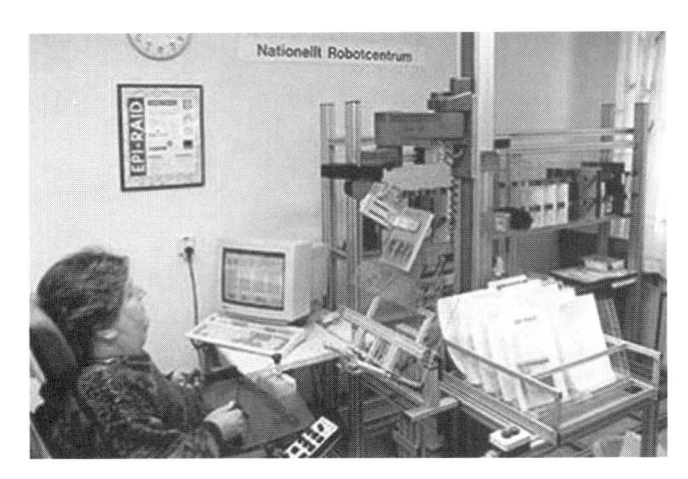

362 ASSISTIVE ROBOTICS FOR INDEPENDENT LIVING

FIGURE 19.4 RAIDII, MASTERII workstation.

Later, in 1998, APPROCHE (Association pour la Promotion des Plates-formes Robotisées Concernant les Personnes HandicapéEs) with AFMA Robots (a French manufacturer of industrial robots) began to develop and commercialize the AFMASTER workstation [9] (Fig. 19.4). This workstation was based on principles that had been developed experimentally by CEA on MASTER, RAID, and EPI-RAID workstations, which were constructed by applying the methods and quality control of an industrial manufacturer [18,19].

19.3.1.1.4 DeVAR and ProVAR The $d$esktop $v$ocational $a$ssistant $r$obot (DeVAR) is the result of a research work at Palo Alto VA Hospital and Stanford University in the United States. The system was developed for office activities such as printing and other computer-related tasks. It was designed mainly for people with quadriplegic disabilities.

The system consists of a PUMA-260 6-DOF robotic arm and an Otto-Bock Greifer gripper with a maximum payload of 2.3 kg. The arm moves on a rail hooked to the ceiling (Fig. 19.5), which allows expansion of the robot workspace and reduces obstructions. As in the RAID-MASTER station, the DeVAR station permits the execution of tasks in an

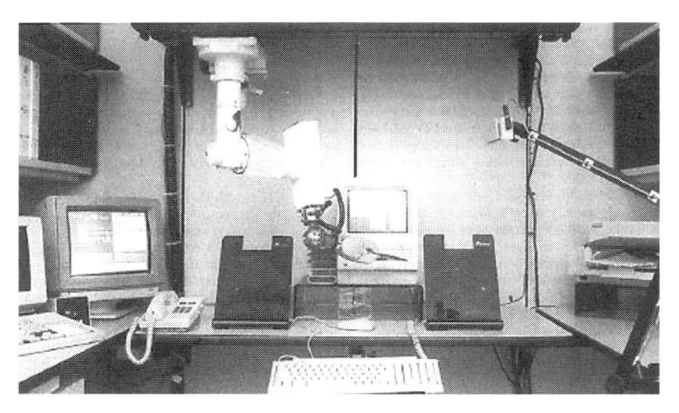

FIGURE 19.5 DEVAR system.

FIGURE 19.6 *ProVAR workstation.*

automatic mode in a structured environment. It uses a vocal recognition system such as the input interface [9,38,39].

The *p*rofessional *v*ocational *a*ssistant *r*obot (ProVAR) (Fig. 19.6) project was a continuation of the DeVAR project (1996–1999). It was designed to provide easier control, better functionality, and greater economic feasibility. During the project the system had been equipped with a new human–machine interface, allowing plug-in of a variety of input devices adapted to the end user and available on the market; the workstation also had an Internet connection, allowing remote control. One of the most innovative aspects of this project is the telediagnostic and the telemaintenance of the robotics stations via Internet networks [40].

19.3.2 Unifunction Robots: Robots with Specific Tasks

The unifunction robots are simple systems intended to help the end user carry out elementary daily tasks such as eating. These AR systems are compact, lightweight, consist of a small telemanipulator, and are easy to move from one place to another. Several users in the same location can easily utilize and share one system. Nevertheless, the telemanipulator remains dependent on the workspace where it operates. These systems also have the advantage of being less expensive than other assistive robots.

In this category of robotic systems, we can find only a small number of robots; the best known are the Winsford feeder from North Coast Medical Inc. in the United States [2,41], the Neater Eater from Neater Solutions Ltd. in the United Kingdom [42], and MySpoon, which we describe in the next subsection.

19.3.2.1 MySpoon

MySpoon (Fig. 19.7) is a robot with 5 DOF designed mainly to assist users with reduced mobility to eat. The research and development on MySpoon began in 1991 at the laboratory of Intelligent Systems (IS) in Japan [43]. MySpoon has been commercially available since 2002 from the SECOM Company in Japan [44].

The food is positioned in a tray with compartments. The user controls the spoon/fork, which is fixed in the extremity of the arm, via a standard joystick or a simple switch.

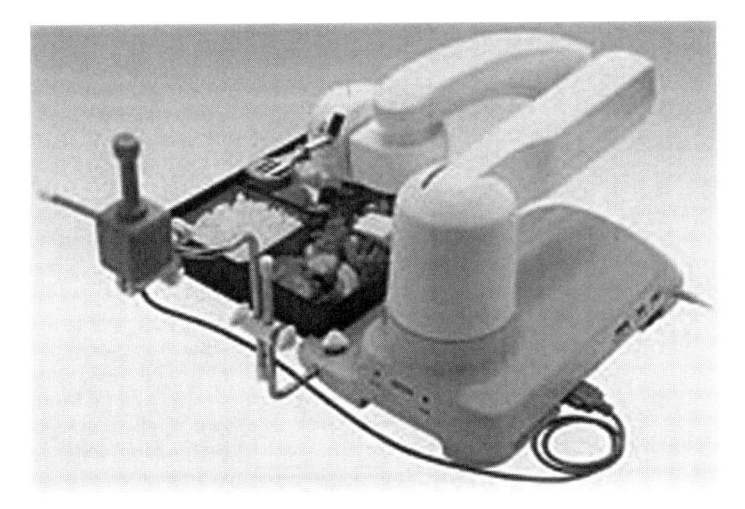

FIGURE 19.7 *MySpoon system.*

These input devices can be placed close to the user's chin or fingers. The user can control the system in three modes: manual, semiautomatic, and automatic. In the *manual mode*, employing the joystick, the user guides the robot to go to the compartment that contains the desired food, adjusts the position of the spoon near the item, commands the spoon to grasp the food, and instructs the robot to approach the mouth automatically. The spoon moves back when the mouth comes in contact with it automatically also. In the *semiautomatic mode*, the user selects compartment that contains the desired food and gives the order, using the joystick. The system will automatically complete the task; it adjusts the position of the spoon, picks up the item, and approaches the mouth and moves back when the task is completed. In the *automatic mode*, the user simply presses a button to perform the task [45].

19.3.3 Manipulator on Bases

These systems are composed of arm manipulators assembled on a simple mobile or fixed platform, for use in various places of the user's habitat. The arms of these system are more sophisticated than those described in Section 19.3.2 (unifunction robots), as they can execute more complex tasks. Similar to unifunction robots, these systems are intended to carry out domestic tasks in direct relation with the user. In addition, they have the advantage of being easy to move, and more easily sharable by numerous users. Nevertheless, these systems have an important limitation—their bases occupy floor space, limiting maneuverability and dexterity. For example, moving them from one place to another is often difficult.

Many projects have been ongoing in this category of assistive robotics (AR) such as WESSEX at BIME in the United Kingdom [46], TOU at the Technical University of Catalonia in Spain [47], and ISAC (*i*ntelligent *s*oft-*a*rm *c*ontrol) at the Center for Intelligent Systems, Vanderbilt University, in the United States [48]. However, only a small number of significant results have been achieved. The exception to that was the Handy system, which was also successful on the market. The Handy system is described in the next section.

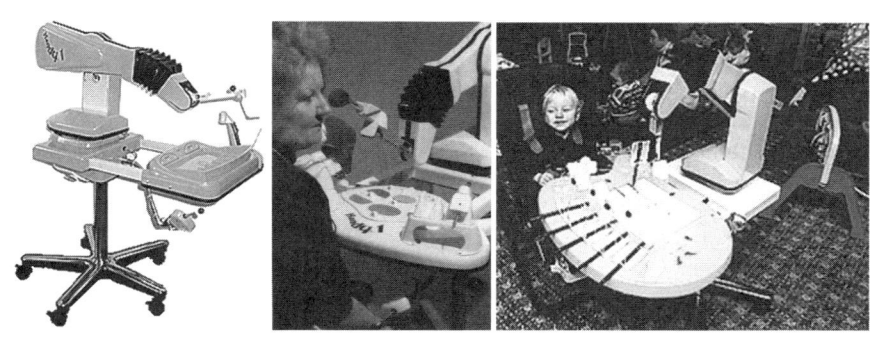

FIGURE 19.8 Handy robots.

19.3.3.1 Handy

The Handy robot (Fig. 19.8) is a simple model developed originally in 1988 at Keele University to give certain autonomy to disabled people. The system was dedicated mainly to allow these people to eat or to drink without the assistance of another person. It consists of a robotic arm with 5 DOF and a food tray mounted on a wheeled base unit, while it carries out tasks in automatic mode. The preprogrammed feeding tasks can be activated by a single switch, which is an input form that people with motor disabilities can often manage. On a small board facing the users, a number of LEDs illuminate in sequence, allowing the user to choose the desired function. The LED scanner enables the user to select the food to be picked up from the dish [35].

Different projects, including BIOMED2-RAIL, have allowed improvements in the user's ability to control the robotics arm and an increased number of preprogrammed tasks. The usage of the system has been extended to assist users in other daily activities, such as hygiene, applying make up, drawing, painting, and playing games (Fig. 19.8). Actually, the makeup module was widely appreciated, principally by women, who wanted to apply makeup by themselves. The Handy system has been commercially available since 1992 from the REHAB Company. This company has sold more assistive robots than has any other company in the world [20,49].

19.3.4 Wheelchair-Mounted Robots

The wheelchair-mounted robot system is one of the best solutions that fits the needs of people with motor disabilities. Indeed, the assistive system resulting from this assembly would increase the user's mobility and ability to handle objects. Unlike the workstations with a restricted workspace, this wheelchair-mounted robot solution approaches the reality of the daily living activities of people with disabilities, where users have to move from one place to another and have to handle various tasks. The tasks performed by the robot are not restricted to any limited space such as the office. The workspace of the robot becomes more important (anywhere) and the tasks to be realized become more diverse.

Because of their mobility-enhancing potential and proximity to the user, these systems must have intrinsic and extrinsic characteristics that enable them to interact with users and their environment. In addition, any design of a system of this AR category must factor in aspects related to safety, security, and ergonomic design. In addition, because of the robot's weight, wheelchair stability should be studied and controlled carefully.

Most of the initially developed wheelchair-mounted robotic systems are controlled manually. To achieve a given goal (such as picking up a cup), the user has to develop a strategy using several orders at the interface level and/or the arm extremity level. That compels the user to undergo a great deal of training and have good manual dexterity, which are often lacking. Therefore, the wheelchair-mounted systems have had to integrate or combined the control modes: manual, automatic, and/or semiautomatic.

A mentioned earlier in this chapter, the first wheelchair-mounted robot was Mason at the VA Prosthetics Center in New York [5,6]. This system was followed by numerous other systems in the world, such as the pneumatically driven INVENTAID from the INVENTAID Company in the United Kingdom [50,51]; the WESTON system from BIME in Britain [28,46,52], which was designed to extend the functionality of the Wessex system [46] and that uses vertical sliders and then a horizontal swing arm to provide functionality; the KARES system from KAIST in Korea [53], and *WMRA* from the United States [54]. In 2000, RTD-ARC (Rehabilitation Technologies Division of Applied Resources Corporation) began work on the RAPTOR system [55], which has been commercially available through Applied Resources Corp in the United States. The other wheelchair-mounted robot that has been commercially successful is MANUS.

19.3.4.1 MANUS

MANUS is the most popular wheelchair-mounted robotic system. It is designed to at support the independence of severely handicapped people, mainly those who have lost the ability to use their arms, by increasing their activity potential and compensating for their inability to grip objects. The system helps users perform a variety of tasks such as drinking, eating, and picking up objects. The MANUS manipulator resulted from a Dutch collaborative project launched in 1984. The project was conducted in The Netherlands at the Organization of Research for Applied Physics (TNO) and the Institute for Rehabilitation Research (IRV). While the project was developed in response to a request made by a Dutch association for muscular dystrophy, it was based on the specifications retained at the end of the Spartacus project [56].

MANUS is a 6-DOF robot, with an arm scale of 80 cm and a two-fingered gripper on its extremity (Fig. 19.9). This gripper enables the user to pick up and move objects in all directions. The arm can be mounted at either the right or left side of an electric wheelchair. The entire system (arm + gripper) is controlled by a 4×4 keypad or a joystick and can be controlled by pointing devices such as a mouse or a trackball [16,57]. A display unit gives information on the state of the MANUS system and displays certain

FIGURE 19.9 MANUS telemanipulator.

functional modes. Arm joint motorization is ensured via belts connecting the joint axes to the engines located in the base of the arm. This principle of transmission allows the arm to have a natural compliance and an acceptable degree of obstruction, but with a weak payload (around 2 kg on the most recent model). A control system enables the user to operate MANUS through Cartesian and joint modes [58].

In the COMMANUS and AMOR projects in Europe,[2] various improvements have been made, changing the software/hardware design to enhance the mechanics of the arm. The improvements include incorporation of new input interfaces adapted to end users and integration of various new modes, such as the pilot mode, which allows the user to control the arm in the direction of the gripper. Automatic and semiautomatic modes also have been integrated, enabling the user to give only one order to activate a task or a series of tasks, such as opening a door, picking up an object, eating, or and enjoying leisure activities.

Since 1990, MANUS robot has been produced and marketed by the Exact-Dynamics Company in The Netherlands. Manus has been sold in many countries, including The Netherlands, France, Germany, Sweden, Italy, South Korea, the United States, and Japan. The customers are research institutes and people with disabilities. To date, more than 500 units have been in use, and the sales of the MANUS robot continue to increase, especially with the acceptance of many European social security systems (similar to the US Social Security), for inclusion in the list of financed assistive technologies.

19.3.5 Mobiles — Autonomous Manipulators: Companion Following the User

The mobile autonomous robot is an assemblage of an autonomous mobile base and a robotic manipulator. These robots usually follow the user (or the user's wheelchair) in the environment. Moreover, they have the ability to move independently from the user's wheelchair. Similar to the wheelchair-mounted robots, these systems have the advantage of carrying out tasks in an open environment, and nondependence on their the wheelchair enhances their mobility and potential to be shared between several users.

Control of the robotic arm is not automatic for most of the existing mobile systems; it is either semiautomatic or manual. In both cases, the user has to initiate the command or control the system remotely. In general, the user controls the system via diverse input devices and a screen on which a robot camera image is viewed.

Four functions characterize the autonomy of these systems: locomotion, perception–decisionmaking, localization, and handling. To ensure these functionalities, mobile autonomous robot systems are required to include (1) accurate and sophisticated sensors such as laser, cameras, or belts with ultrasound and (2) very complex algorithms for control.

Numerous robots were developed within the framework of a feasibility study, without any serious evaluation on a large scale. The possible improvements and evaluations were stopped because of a lack of finding. Most of the results obtained were transferred to space or military research laboratories such as the MoVAR (*m*obile *v*ocational *a*ssistant *r*obot), which was initiated in 1983 at the Palo Alto VA and Stanford University [39,59,60]. Other mobile autonomous robots have been developed, such as WALKY from CERTEC, University of Lund in Sweden [61,62]; URMAD (*u*nita' *r*obotica *m*obile per *a*usilio ai *d*isabili) from SSSA (Scuola Superiore Sant'Anna) in Italy [63]; MOVAID also from

---

[2]The authors of this chapter directly participated in these projects.

SSSA [64,65], which has been supported by the TIDE program; the ARPH (*a*ssistance *r*obotisée aux *p*ersonnes *h*andicapées) system from CEMIF in France [66–68]; TAURO from AACHEN University in Germany [69]; KARES II from KAIST in Korea (more details are available in Chapter 20) [70,71]; and the ISAAC/Helpmate system developed by TransAxis company, which was the work of Joe Engelberger, the "father" of US robotics [72]. Among the most important works in this field, we can quote the Care-o-bot II system [73].

19.3.5.1 Care-O-Bot II

Care-O-bot II was designed at the Fraunhofer Institute for Manufacturing Engineering and Automatio (Germany) to assist elderly people in their daily living. This system is unique in terms of including diverse assistive robotic systems in one. Care-O-bot II provides support to users during walking (more information about walker systems is available in Chapter 26), performs simple household services such cleaning and delivers and disposes of objects (meals, snacks, drinks, etc.). The system also provides other services such as videotelephon, interactive communication, and incoming call notification, which are very important for the social integration of the senior user [73].

The Care-O-bot II system (Fig. 19.10) was built on the top of the Care-O-bot I mobile platform base. It is equipped with a manipulator arm, adjustable walking supporters, vision system, and a tilting sensor head. The vision system is designed for the navigation functions, facilitating the recognition/detection of objects in the user's environment, and enabling the user to supervise the execution of a task via a videostreaming to the user screen [74].

The system is controlled via a touchscreen handheld control panel or speech input. When it operates in semiautomatic mode, memory of the structure and objects of the user's environment is stored in a database. The database can be updated manually by adding or deleting objects in specific locations. The user has only to select the object to be manipulated or the task that the robot should perform and order this action, and can change or stop the action at any time.

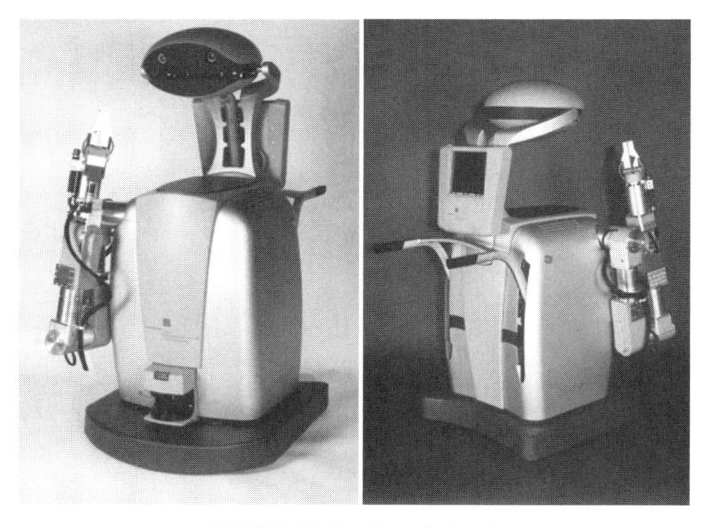

FIGURE 19.10 Care-O-bot II.

19.4 DISCUSSION: THE MATS ROBOT

The assistive robotic systems that have been discussed in this chapter are usually tied to a specific location (office, home, etc.) or attached to a mobile base such as a powered wheelchair, which defines the robot's workspace. The tasks usually performed are also limited by the characteristics of the extremity (usually a simple symmetric gripper), which are not changeable because of the mechanical complexity involved in plugging in a gripper.

A new generation of robots is under development to provide improved functionalities in any workspace. The MATS robot (Fig. 19.11) is an example of this generation. It is a flexible system for use in diverse environments, it is not tied to a specific location or a base; it can change places and environments and can climb or even move from or to walls, ceilings, tables, wheelchairs, and any bases by attachment of it tips to these objects. The system also has the ability to attach various accessory tools as effectors such as simple grippers, or specific tools for eating, shaving, and applying cosmetics, and other routine tasks.

The MATS robot is a lightweight (11-kg), 5-DOF manipulator arm, with 1.3 m of reach. The arm is flexible and symmetric and includes all the control systems onboard. It does not need wiring from an electric outlet; it needs only powering. The robot is controlled remotely via wireless communication and using a friendly human–machine interface (HMI) [75,76].

The MATS robot was developed by the European Consortium (MATS project), which includes the University of Staffordshire (UK), the Scuola Superiore Sant'Ana in Pisa (Italy), the University of Lund (Sweden), and the University Carlos III of Madrid (Spain).

19.5 CONCLUSION

The types of robots that we covered in this chapter are unlike the ordinary industrial systems. The industrial robots have structured and deterministic environments, performing specific pre-programmed tasks, and the human interaction with these systems is usually remotely controlled and limited. This may not be the case in AR. The robot is considered as an extension to human body, and the user is permanently included in the robot control process and in the task context. In this case, the robot may be considered as a partial

FIGURE 19.11 *MATS robot.*

substitution to the human physical limitation, which implies that robots must operate in a nondeterministic environment.

Various previous attempts to develop assistive robots have failed because of the limited implication of the end user during the design process neglecting user interface and accessibility issues. Therefore, special attention has to be paid to the user's profile, including the individual's limitations, needs, living environment constraints, and social requirements. Also, targeting potential users in the development process, such as in the evaluation and validation of the system in the actual living environment, is highly recommended. The user-centric approach allows better design of mechanical structure (including mobility, arms and end-effectors), accurate robot control, and more ergonomic and accessible human–machine interfaces. As a practical result, the integration of these features, with the user-centric approach, allows AR developed to build useful, usable, accessible, and acceptable robotic systems.

Although an accessible flexible assistive robot for general use is required for PwSN, we must remember that the environments of these people include other assistive devices such as mobility systems, environmental controls, computers, and communication systems for interaction with the external world, including alarm systems, and other features. The main objective of assistive devices is to serve the end user, and the main point of assistive robots is to execute physical tasks in the environment of this end user. Therefore, it is important to integrate the assistive robots in this environment into an assistive environment; a complete system where robots are compatible with other environmental devices, capable of communicating with them, and that allows the user to control the entire system via an accessible generic interface. Actually enabling this concept of assistive environment is possible through the convergence of two communities: (1) the pervasive computing/smart spaces community and (2) the robotics community. Smart spaces have limitations in pervasive computing, mainly in manipulating objects, while robotics has a limited interaction with the environment. However, combining these two communities should complete the spectrum of the user's daily interaction with the external environment.

Finally, the most important aspect is that a large number of PwSN should be able to acquire these systems and use them, which means that these systems should be commercially available and affordable. This aspect has been perhaps the most difficult to reach by the AR community. The assistive robot are primarily customer base people with disabilities and not the general population, which means that (1) the size of the market is small, so it is difficult to mainstream the products; (2) most disabled people have low or no income (purchasing power), so they cannot purchase this kind of high-tech assistive technology by themselves; and (3) except in certain cases, this kind of high-tech assistive technology is not reimbursed or financed by the different agencies, including governmental agencies, Social Security systems, and insuranc companies, so we (the developers) have limited funding for this assistive technology. Several possibilities can be investigated to overcome these market limitations, such as (1) targeting markets in more countries, to form multinational and regional partnerships, thereby expanding the population target; (2) moving the assistive robotics, as much as possible, into the grand public market, by integrating the robot with daily household appliances such as vacuum cleaners; and (3) encouraging different agencies to include assistive robots in their list of Reimbursed or Repyed products. One way to do this is to demonstrate the usefulness of these systems and to prove to these agencies that the use of AR technology actually reduces the cost of healthcare on a global scale. A very encouraging experience, which we want to publicize globally, is that of the robot Manus, which was funded by the Dutch by a Government Agency (equivalent to US Social Security system). This funding has proved invaluable in increasing the number of Manus robots produced and thus enhancing the lives of people with disabilities.

REFERENCES

1. Webster JG, Cook AM, Tompkinsa WJ, Vanderheiden GC: *Electronic Devices for Rehabilitation*, J Wiley, New York, 1985.
2. Harwin WS, Rahman T, Foulds RA: A review of design issues in rehabilitation robotics with reference to North American research, *IEEE Trans Rehab Eng*, **3**(1) (1995).
3. Allen JR, Karchak A, Bontrager EL: *Design and Fabrication of a Pair of Rancho Anthropomorphic Arms*, Attending Staff Assoc., Rancho Los Amigos Hospital, Inc., Technical Report, 1972.
4. Reswick JB: The moon over Dubrovnik—a tale of worldwide impact on persons with disabilities, in *Advances in External Control of Human Extremities*, Dubrovnik, Croatia, 1990.
5. Mason CP, Peiser E: Medical Manipulator for Quadriplegic, *Proc Int. Conf. Telemanipulators for the Physically Handicapped*, IRIA.
6. Mason CP, Peiser E: A seven degree of freedom telemanipulator for tetraplegics, *Int Conf Telemanipulators for the physically Handicapped*, 1979, pp 309–318.
7. Seamone W, Schmeisser G: Early clinical evaluation of a robot arm/worktable system for spinalcord-injured persons, *J Rehab Res Devel* 38–57 (1985).
8. Seamone W, Schmeisser G: Evaluation of the JHU/APL robot arm workstation, in Foulds R, ed, *Interactive Robotic Aids*, World Rehabilitation Fund Monograph, New York, 1986.
9. Van der Loos M: VA/Stanford rehabilitation robotics research and development program: Lessons learned in the application of robotics technology to the field of rehabilitation, *IEEE Trans Rehab Eng* **3**(1):46–55 (1995).
10. Shor PC, Lum PS, Burgar CG, Van der Loos M, Majmundar M, Yap R: The effect of robotic-aided therapy on upper extremity joint passive range of motion and pain, *Proc 7th Int Conf Rehabilitation Robotics (ICORR)*, INT-Evry, France, IOS Press, 2001, pp 79–83.
11. Krebs HI, Volpe BT, Palazzolo J, Rohrer B: Robot-aided neuro-rehabilitation in stroke, *Proc Int Conf Rehabilitation Robotics (ICORR)*, INT-Evry, France, IOS Press, 2001, pp 45–59.
12. Roesler H, Küppers HJ, Schmalenbach E: The medical manipulator and its adapted environment: A system for the rehabilitation of severely handicapped, *Proc Int IRIA Conf Telemanipulators for the Physically Handicapped*, 1978, pp 73–77.
13. Verburg G, Kwee H, Wisaksana A, Cheetham A, van Woerden J: Manus: The evolution of an assistive technology, *Technol Disab* 217–228. (1996).
14. Guittet J, Kwee H, Quetin N, Yclon J: The Spartacus telethesis: Manipulator control and experimentation, *Proc Int IRIA Conf Telemanipulators for the Physically Handicapped*, 1978, pp 79–100.
15. Kwee H: Spartacus and Manus: Telethesis developments in France and the Netherlands, in *Interactive Robotic Aids—One Option for Independent Living*, World Rehabilitation Fund, 1986, pp 7–17.
16. Abdulrazak B, Mokhtari M, Grandjean B: Toward a new high level controller for Manus robot: The Commanus project, *Proc 7th Int Conf Rehabilitation Robotics (ICORR)*, INT-Evry, France, IOS Press, 2001, pp 221–226.
17. Walker N: RTX robot arm, *Personal Comput World* 176–181 (Dec 1986).

18. Rodolphe G, Françoise C, Bernard L, Jean-Marc L, Michel B: AFMASTER: An industrial rehabilitation workstation, *Proc 6th Int Conf Rehabilitation Robotics (ICORR)*, Stanford, CA, 1999, pp 149–155.
19. Gelin R, Lesigne B, Busnel M, Michel JP: The first moves of the AFMASTER workstation, in *Advan Robot* **14**(7):639–649 (2001).
20. Toppong M: Handy 1, A robotic aid to independence for severely disabled people, *Proc 7th Int Conf Rehabilitation Robotics (ICORR)*, INT-Evry, France, 2001, pp 142–147. IOS Press.
21. Jung JW, Song WK, Lee H, Kim JS, Bien Z: A study on the enhancement of manipulation performance of wheelchair-mounted rehabilitation service robot, *Proc 6th Int Conf Rehabilitation Robotics (ICORR)*, Stanford, CA, 2003, pp 42–49.
22. Bien Z, Song WK, Kimm DJ, Han JS: Vision-based control with emergency stop through EMG of the wheelchair-based rehabilitation robotic arm, KARES II, *Proc 7th Int Conf Rehabilitation Robotics (ICORR)*, INT-Evry, France, 2001, IOS Press, pp 177–185.
23. Stranger CA, Anglin C, Harwin WS, Romilly DP: Devices for assisting manipulation: A summary of user task priorities, *IEEE Trans Rehab Eng* **2**(4):256–265 (1994).
24. Birch GE, Cameron W, Fengler M, Young J, Carpenter A, Apkarian J: Regenesis robotic manipulator for persons with severe disabilities, *Eur Rev Biomed Technol* **12**(5):320–323 (1990).
25. Birch E, Fengler M, Gosine RG: Regenesis robotic appliance evaluation progess report, *Proc 18th Annual Conf Rehabilitaion Engineering and Assistive Technology Society of North America (RESNA)*, 1993, pp 501–503.
26. Holmberg L: The installation of a robotized workstation at Samhall-HADAR, *Proc 2nd European Conf Advancement of Rehabilitation Technology (ECART)*, Stockholm, may 1993.
27. Trulsson BG, Persson EM: Coordinated work-oriented rehabilitation and workplace adaptation at HADAR, *Proc 2nd European Conf Advancement of Rehabilitation Technology (ECART)*. Stockholm, May 1993.
28. Hillman M, Hagan K, Hagan S, Jepson J, Orpwood R: A wheelchair mounted assistive robot, *Proc 6th Int Conf Rehabilitation Robotics (ICORR)*, Stanford, CA, 1999, pp 86–91.
29. Hillman M, Jepson J: Evaluation of a trolley mounted robot—a case study, *Proc 5th Int Conf Rehabilitation Robotics (ICORR)*, Bath-IT, UK, 1997, pp 86–91.
30. Pédelucq JP, Brélivet L, André JM, De Bamon H, Ganis V, Colbeau J, Busnel P, Le Guigo J: Résultats des l'évaluation en centre spécialisés du système robotisé MASTER I, *Acte de 6émes Entretiens de l'Institut Garches*, Garcehs, France, 1993.
31. Cammoun R, Detriche JM, Lauture F, Lesigne B: Robotised workstations for handicapped people, *Proc 1st European Conf Medical Robotics (ROBOMED)*, Barcelona, Spain, 1994, pp 131–135.
32. Dallaway JL: Human-computer interaction within robotic workstation, *Proc 21st Annual Conf Rehabilitaion Engineering and Assistive Technology Society of North America (RESNA)*, (1996).
33. Gelin R, Lesigne B, Détriché JM: Contribution of the French Atomic Energy Commission in rehabilitation robotics, *Proc 5th Int Conf Rehabilitation Robotics (ICORR)*, Bath-IT, UK, 1997, pp 18–22.
34. Lesigne B, Detriche JM: MASTER, un robot d'assistance aux personnes totalement dépendantes, *Réadaptation* **387**:24–27 (1992).
35. Hawkins P, Topping M: The design and development process for the Handy 1 robotic aid to eating and drinking, *Proc 5th Int Conf on Rehabilitation Robotics (ICORR)*, Bath-IT, UK, 1997.
36. Dallaway JL: RAID—A vocational robotic workstation, *Proc 3rd Int Conf Rehabilitation Robotics (ICORR)*, Keele Univ, UK, 1992.

37. Busnel M, Pédelucq JP, Brélivet L, André JM, De Barmon H, Ganis V, Colbeau-Justin P, Le Guigo J: Résultats de l'évaluation en centre spécialisés du système robotisé MASTER I, *Actes des 6èmes Entretiens de l'Institut Garches*, Garches, France, 1993, pp 57–66.
38. Hammel JM: The role of assessment and evaluation in rehabilitation robotics research and development moving from concept to clinic to context, *IEEE Trans Rehab Eng* **3**(1) (1995).
39. Leifer LJ, Van der Loos M, Michalowski SJ: Design issues in the development of a robotic aid for human services, *Proc 2nd Annual Int Robot Conf*, Long Beach, CA, 1984, pp 116–121.
40. Van der Loos M, Wagner JJ, Smaby N, Chang K, Madrigal O, Leifer LJ, Khatib O: Provar assistive robot system architecture, *Proc Int IEEE Conf Robotics and Automation (ICRA)*, Detroit, MI, 1999, pp 741–746.
41. Mahoney R, Phalangas A: Consumer evaluation of powered feeding devices, *Proc 21st Annual Conf Rehabilitaion Engineering and Assistive Technology Society of North America (RESNA)*, 1996.
42. www.neater.co.uk.
43. Ishii S, Tanaka S, Hiramatsu F: Meal assistance robot for severely handicapped people, *Proc IEEE Int Conf Robotics and Automation (ICRA)*, 1995, Vol 2, pp 1308–1313.
44. www.secom.co.jp/myspoon/index_e.html.
45. Soyama R, Ishii S, Fukase A: The development of meal-assistance robot "MySpoon"— selectable operating interfaces, *Proc 8th Int Conf Rehabilitation Robotics (ICORR)*, Daejeon, Korea, 2003, pp 88–91.
46. Hillman M, Hagan K, Hagan S, Jepson J, Orpwood R: The Weston wheelchair mounted assistive robot—the design story, *Robotica*, **20**:125–132 (2002).
47. Casals A, Villá R, Casals D: A soft assistant arm for tetraplegics, *Proc 1st TIDE Congress*, Brussels, 1993, pp 103–107.
48. Kawamura K, Peters RA, Wilkes DM, Alford WA, Rogers TE: ISAC: Foundations in human-humanoid interaction, *IEEE Intelligent Syst Appl* **15**(4):38–45 (2000).
49. Topping M: Handy 1, a robotic aid to independence for severely disabled people, *Proc 7th Int Conf Rehabilitation Robotics (ICORR)*, INT-Evry, France, 2001, pp 142–147.
50. Hennequin J, Hennequin Y: Inventaid, wheelchair mounted manipulator, *Proc 2nd Cambridge Workshop on Rehabilitation Robotics*, Cambridge, UK, 1991.
51. Jackson RD: Robotics and its role in helping disabled people, *Eng Sci Educ J* 267–272 (1993).
52. Hillman M: A feasibility study of a robot manipulator for the disabled, *J Med Eng Technol* **11** (1987).
53. Jung JW, Song WK, Lee H, Kim JS, Bien Z: A study on the enhancement of manipulation performance of wheelchair-mounted rehabilitation service robot, *Proc 6th Int Conf Rehabilitation Robotics (ICORR)*, Stanford, CA, 1999, pp 42–49.
54. Alqasemi RM, McCaffrey EJ, Edwards KD, Dubey RV: Wheelchair-mounted robotic arms: Analysis, evaluation and development, *Proc Int Conf Advanced Intelligent Mechatronics (ASME)*, Monterey, CA, 2005, pp 1164–1169.
55. Mahony RM: Raptor wheelchair robot system, *Proc 7th Int Conf Rehabilitation Robotics (ICORR)*, INT-Evry, France, IOS Press, 2001, pp 135–141.
56. Kwee H, Dulmel J, Smith JJ, Tuinhof JJ, Moed A, Van Woerden JA, Kolk VD, Rosier JC: The Manus wheelchair-borne manipulator: System review and first results, *Proc 2nd IARP Workshop on Medical and Healthcare Robotics*, Newcastle-upon-Tyne, UK, 1989.
57. Abdulrazak B, Mokhtari M, Grandjean B, Dumas C: La robotique d'aide Aux personnes Handicapées, le projet Commanus, *Proc Handicap 2002, 2nd Conf Institut Fédératif de Recherche (IFRATH)*, Pour l'Essor des Technologies d'Assistance, Porte de Versailles, Paris, 2002, pp 89–94.

58. Evers HG, Beugels E, Peters G: MANUS: Towards a new decade, *Proc 7th Int Conf Rehabilitation Robotics (ICORR)*, INT-Evry, France, 2001, IOS Press, pp 155–159.
59. Dario P: Wheels and legs in rehabilitation, *Proc 1st European Conf Medical Robotics (ROBOT-MED)*, Barcelona, Spain, 1994, pp 75–82.
60. Guglielmelli E: Mobile robots in residential care, *Proc 1st European Conf Medical Robotics (ROBOT-MED)*, Barcelona, Spain, 1994, pp 89–103.
61. Neveryd H, Bolmsjö G: WALKY, an ultrasonic navigating mobile robot for the disabled, in *Proc 2nd TIDE Congress, The European Context for Assistive Technology*, Paris, April 26–28, 1995, pp 366–370.
62. Neveryd H, Bolmsjo G: WALKY, a mobile robot system for the disabled, *Proc 4th Int Conf Rehabilitation Robotics (ICORR)*, 1994, pp 137–141.
63. Dario P, Guglielmelli E, Mulé C, Di Natale M: URMAD: An Autonomous Mobile Robot System for the Assistance to the Disabled, *Proc Int Conf Advanced Robotics (ICAR)*, Tokyo, 1993, pp 341–346.
64. Dario P, Guglielmelli E, Laschi C, Teti G: MOVAID: A personal robot in everyday life of disabled and elderly people, *Technol Disab J* **10**:77–93 (1999).
65. Bonifazi M, Favi F, Leo T, Longhi S, Zulli R: A developing environment for the solution of the navigation problem of mobile robots with non-holonomic constraints, *Proc 4th IEEE Mediterranean Symp New Directions in Control and Automation*, Maleme, Krete, Greece, 1996, pp 107–112.
66. Ait Aider O, Hoppenot P, Colle E: Localisation by camera of a rehabilitation robot, *Proc 7th Int Conf Rehabilitation Robotics (ICORR)*, INT-Evry, France, IOS Press, 2001, pp 168–176.
67. Hoppenot P, Colle E: Location and control of a rehabilitation mobile robot by close human-machine cooperation, *IEEE Trans Neural Syst Rehab Eng* **9**(2) (2001).
68. Rybarczyk Y, Ait Aider O, Hoppenot P, Colle E: Commande à distance d'un système d'assistance robotique aux personnes handicapées, *Proc. Handicap 2002, 2nd Conf Institut Fédératif de Recherche (IFRATH), Pour l'Essor des Technologies d'Assistance*, Porte de Versailles, Paris, 2002, pp 81–87.
69. Pauly M, Kraiss K-F: A Concept for symbolic interaction with semi-autonomous mobile systems, *Proc 6th IFAC/IFIP/IFORS/IEA Symp Analysis, Design and Evaluation of Man-Machine Systems*, Boston, 1995, pp 121–126.
70. Bien Z, Song WK, Kim DJ, Han JS, Choi JY, Lee HE, Kim JS: Vision-based control with emergency stop through EMG of the wheelchair-based rehabilitation robotic arm, KARES II, *Proc 7th Int Conf Rehabilitation Robotics (ICORR)*, INT-Evry, France, IOS Press, 2001, pp 177–185.
71. Kim DJ, Han JS, Lee HE, Kim JS, Bien Z: User's servoing and EMS signal classification for rehabilitation robotic system, KARES II: Realisation and clinical evaluation, *Proc 8th Int Conf Rehabilitation Robotics (ICORR)*, Daejeon, Korea, 2003, pp 155–158.
72. Engelberger J: A day in the life of Isaac, *Industr Robot Int J* **27**(3):176–180 (2000).
73. Graf B, Hans M, Schraft RD: Mobile robot assistants—issues for dependable operation in direct cooperation with humans, *IEEE Robot Autom Mag* 11, No. 2, (special issue on human centered robotics and dependability) **11**(2):67–77 (2004).
74. Hans M, Graf B, Schraft RD: Robotic home assistant Care-O-Bot: Past-present-future, *Proc 11th Int IEEE Workshop on Robot and Human Interactive Communication*, 2002, pp 380–385.
75. Balaguer C, Gimenez A, Jardon A, Cabas R, Correal R: Live experimentation of the service robot applications for elderly people care in home environments, *Proc IEEE Intelligent Robots and Systems Conf (IROS)*, Alberta, Canada, 2005, pp 2345–2350.
76. Balaguer C, Gimenez A, Huete AJ, Sabatini AM, Topping M, Bolmsjo G: The MATS robot: Service climbing robot for personal assistance, *IEEE Robot Autom Mag* **13**(1):51–58 (2006).

20

Mobile Platform-Based Assistive Robot Systems

Zeungnam Bien, Kwang-Hyun Park and Myung Jin Chung
Department of Electrical Engineering and Computer Science, KAIST, South Korea

Dae-Jin Kim and Jin-Woo Jung
Human-friendly Welfare Robot System Engineering Research Center, KAIST, Republic of Korea

Pyung-Hun Chang
Department of Mechanical Engineering, KAIST, South Korea

Jin-Oh Kim
Kwangwoon University, Seoul, Republic of Korea

This chapter presents three different types of mobile platform-based assistive robotic systems: (1) a wheelchair-based robotic arm system, KARES II (KAIST Rehabilitation Engineering Service System II), which was developed for people with disabilities (specifically, quadriplegias); (2) a robotic hoist, which assists people with lower-limb paralysis to move in indoor environments; and (3) a vocational assistive robot with an omnidirectional wheel mechanism and a forklift system to help disabled workers in the manufacturing industry. We have conducted various user trials of the prototypes in real environments. On the basis of user feedback, we have modified these robotic systems and have improved the performance and user-friendliness.

20.1 INTRODUCTION

Among many forms of assistive robotic systems, rehabilitation robots are particularly typical. Rehabilitation robotics is concerned mostly with the application of the robotic technology for rehabilitation of disabled and elderly people [1]. Rehabilitation robotic systems aim to solve daily living problems in individual activities. One may claim that

---

The Engineering Handbook of Smart Technology for Aging, Disability, and Independence,
Edited by A. Helal, M. Mokhtari and B. Abdulrazak
Copyright © 2008 John Wiley & Sons, Inc.

the primary role of rehabilitation robotic systems is to endow as much independence as possible for the elderly and/or disabled people to improve their quality of life.

Rehabilitation robotics is a specific category in service robotics, and such robotic systems are considered as some form of assistive devices in rehabilitation engineering. There are two major functions of rehabilitation robotic systems: the restoration (or rehabilitation therapy) of disabled functions [2–4], and assistance in mobility and manipulability of people with disabilities. Here, we concentrate on developing the second type of robotic system.

In assistive robotic systems, human–robot interaction has become a critical concern as user's convenience and safety should be ensured in addition to the assistance provided by the robot. In this chapter, we report some important design features of KARES II, the assistive robot developed at KAIST (Korea Advanced Institute of Science and Technology), and present its various human-friendly interfaces and adaptability to the user. We also present two kinds of interesting assistive robotic systems: (1) a robotic hoist to help lower-limb-paralyzed people to transfer from place to place, and (2) work assistant robotic system for disabled workers in the manufacturing industry. (These assistive robotic systems are also discussed in Section 19.2 of Chapter 19.)

Assistive robotic systems are categorized into three types, based on the form of implementation: (1) workstation-based system, (2) mobile-robot-based system, and (3) wheelchair-based system. Some of the workstation-based systems assist the user through voice commands. DeVAR (*d*esktop *v*ocational *a*ssistant *r*obot) [5], TIDE-RAID (*r*obot for *a*ssisting in the *i*ntegration of the *d*isabled) [6], ISAC (*i*ntelligent *s*oft-*a*rm *c*ontrol) [7], IST-MATS (mechatronic assistive technology system) [8], and AFMASTER [9] are well-known examples. Basically, a workstation-based system performs various delicate tasks in a stable mode; however, its operation is confined to a predefined limited workspace. The mobile robot-based system consists of robotic arm and a mobile platform. This system is used for various asks such as transportation of small baggage, guidance of the user, and so on. WALKY [10], MoVAR (*mo*bile *v*ocational *a*ssistant *r*obot) [11], TIDE-MOVAID (*mo*bility and activity *a*ssistance system for the *d*isabled) [12], Care-O-bot I/II [13], and Helpmate [14] are good examples of this category. The wheelchair-based system assists elderly and physically disabled people in their individual daily activities. This type of assistive robotic system adopts various user interfaces. MANUS [15], FRIEND [16], and RAPTOR [17] are well-known examples of this category. Our research group at KAIST has also been developing a series of wheelchair-based assistive robotic systems named KARES (KAIST rehabilitation engineering system) I (1996–1997) and KARES II (1998–2003). KARES II in particular differs from other wheelchair-based robotic systems such as FRIEND because its manipulator is decoupled from the wheelchair. Thus, in this chapter, we shall describe KARES II with its design philosophy, implementation, and human–robot interfaces.

The Human-friendly Welfare Robot System Engineering Research Center (HWRS-ERC) at KAIST has been developing the Intelligent Sweet Home (ISH) system since 1999. During the development of ISH, many subjects asked about the possibility of developing a robotic hoist for their transfer task. In particular, transfer between a bed and a wheelchair is most important in their daily living activities. Many health equipment manufacturers offer devices to help disabled people transfer between wheelchair and bed. Most of these devices are suitable for institutional use and require a caregiver to assist in the transfer procedure (multilift and "easy base" systems [18]; AryCare patient support system [19]). In addition, some other systems (e.g., ceiling track lift system [20]) require complicated home modification for its installation. Considering these drawbacks, we have designed and tested a compact robotic system for automatic transfer of disabled people between bed, wheelchair, bathtub, stool, and other locations.

We have also found that mobile platform-based assistive robotic systems are critically important in the manufacturing environment. Although a variety of assistive robotic systems have been developed and used at present, these systems are often restricted to indoor living environments, and provide disabled people with only limited assistance in daily activities. On the contrary, the objective of assistive robotic systems is to make disabled people independent in performing daily activities, which then turns them into productive citizens, not burdens to society. In this view, design and implementation of vocational assistive robotic systems are essential. However, most existing vocational assistive robots are limited to office environments. The robot RAID [21], which was developed at the Rehabilitation Engineering Research Center in Sweden, assists the disabled in picking up books from a bookshelf, bringing documents, and serving drinks at office environment. The robot ProVAR (*pro*fessional *v*ocational *a*ssistant *r*obot) [22] is capable of speech recognition and helps disabled people in performing office work such as serving beverages and preparing or retrieving documents, diskettes, videotapes, and so on. Moreover, it displays the current status of the robot on a display. The robot WALKY [10] can avoid obstacles while it maneuvers to transport items in a laboratory environment. Amid the existence of these robotic systems, vocational robotic systems in real manufacturing environments has not yet been well demonstrated, although most employers would prefer it if there were such systems to help disabled workers. The objective of our research is to develop such a mobile robotic system to assist disabled people working in a real manufacturing environment. The proposed assistive robotic (AR) systems are expected to assist disabled people to deliver their capabilities to the manufacturing industry, and thereby become productive members of society. Consequently, the AR system that we propose should help increase the working population of the society.

This chapter is organized as follows. In Section 20.2, a wheelchair-based assistive robotic system, KARES II, is introduced with a brief description. In Section 20.3 we describe a robotic hoist system in the livingroom environment; and in Section 20.4, the work assistant mobile robot. A detailed feedback through our user trials is presented in Section 20.5. Concluding remarks are given in Section 20.6.

20.2 WHEELCHAIR-BASED ROBOTIC SYSTEM: KARES II [23]

It was 1996 when we first had developed a *wheelchair-based rehabilitation robot* system called KARES I (KAIST rehabilitation engineering service system type I) [24,25]. It was designed to perform four basic tasks to help a severely physically disabled people (1) pickup a cup from the table, (2) pickup an object from the floor, (3) bring a cup to the user, and (4) turn on/off electricity on the wall switch. KARES I consists of a 6-DOF (degree of freedom) robotic arm with a monovision system for visual servoing, a voice recognizer, a six-dimensional (6D) force–torque sensor, and a three-dimensional (3D) input device (SpaceBall^{TM}). All the subsystems are integrated into a powered wheelchair platform. KARES I can provide various useful functions mentioned in the relevant literature [10,26], but we found that the system needed improvement in the aspects of human-friendliness and adaptability to the levels of disability. Furthermore, due to elasticity of the rubber tires of the powered wheelchair, vibration of the robotic base was unavoidable when the robot arm was in operation, which caused very unstable operation during the task.

From our experiences of operating KARES I and a survey study on existing rehabilitation robots, we had reached the following conclusions:

1. A new kind of rehabilitation robot system, which could provide both user comfort and robust operation, is required. Although KARES I is a compact version of various sensors and technologies, exact operation is difficult to achieve because of vibration of the robotic base caused by the rubber tires of the powered wheelchair. One may claim that a workstation-based system (e.g., ISAC of Vanderbilt University [7]) is one solution for resolving vibration problems since such a system enables the robot to operate in stable mode. However, the workstation-based system cannot provide enough workspace because of its limited mobility capability. Thus, an innovative combination of wheelchair-based systems and workstation-based systems would lead us to the future development of rehabilitation robotic systems. A major concern is the ability of the mobile base to maintain stable operation during stoppage and to have a "free to move" capability.

2. In order to cope with a variety of disabilities, the human–machine interaction/interface should be realized in a modular form. Contrary to conventional rehabilitation robot systems, futuristic rehabilitation robot systems will have to provide a wide range of services in view of a variety of disabilities. The modularized approach to accommodate various degrees of disability will give the user the selection choice of minimally redundant components and subsystems. In this way, disabled people can pay only for the effective components and subsystems depending on their particular disabilities.

Thus we had launched a project of developing a better system that is capable of reflecting these two issues, and in the year 1999, we had realized a new system: KARES II, which implements various interactions and interfaces to enable users to choose according to the degree of their disabilities.

KARES II system is implemented according to the principle of task-oriented design (TOD) [27], which confirms realization of the predefined tasks, and as a byproduct, it may further attain additional tasks owing to the flexible nature of robotic systems. To determine the fundamental tasks for the system, we surveyed, as a first step, the basic activities of end users (i.e., people with spinal cord injuries and the other physically disabilities) and their caregivers for a period of 6 months (see Table 20.1).

The information collected in the survey was thoroughly evaluated, and about 150 items were identified as possible tasks. These items were then categorized according to their usability, feasibility, and suitability for developing assistive robotic devices. Finally, 12 basic tasks were determined as described in Table 20.2. These tasks were the ultimate target for TOD that guided us to develop subsystems such as the robotic arm, user interfaces, and other hardware modules.

TABLE 20.1 Information of Survey Sample

Parameter	Period: January–June 1999
Locations	Hospital (1), industrial workplace (3), asylum (6)
Type (numbers)	Quadriplegia (21), poliomyelitis (9), mental disorder (6), others (4)
Living situations	Inpatient (24), outpatient (or dwelling at home) (16)

TABLE 20.2 Tasks for KARES II

Task Number	Task Name	Distance between User and Robot Hand
1	Serving a meal	Near
2	Serving a beverage	Near
3	Wiping/scratching face	Near
4	Shaving	Near
5	Picking up objects	Far
6	Turning switches on/off	Far
7	Opening/closing doors	Far
8	Making tea	Far
9	Pulling a drawer	Far
10	Playing games	Near/far
11	Changing CD/tapes	Near/far
12	Removing papers from printer/fax machine	Near/far

Along with the notion of TOD, we have considered the concept of *user-friendliness* in our design philosophy. Since the robotic arm is designed to interact with human users, safety should be guaranteed when the robotic arm makes contact with the user. For the user interfaces, easier accessibility to the system is required since few disabled people are familiar with robotic systems. To enhance the user-friendliness of the robotic arm, we have adopted active compliance control for user safety while in contact with the robotic arm. For easier accessibility to the system, all user interfaces are capable of rapid execution of each task. We have also paid particular attention to the appearance of every subsystem of KARES II, and made them look user-friendly.

The third important design philosophy considered in KARES II is *modularization* of subsystems. Considering the variety of disabilities, accessible interfaces should differ from person to person for cost-effectiveness and simplicity. In modularized subsystems, the assistive robot is optimized for a particular disability.

KARES II system consists of a wheelchair platform onto which various user interfaces (Fig. 20.1a, items 3–6) are attached. The robotic arm on the mobile platform is compliant and is capable of visual servoing (Fig. 20.1a, items 1,2). The mobile platform is essential for the robot arm to perform tasks at a distance from the user.

The mobile platform of KARES II provides better mobility, and extends its workspace. Among the 12 tasks listed in Table 20.2, we have found that the mobile platform is very effective in performing those tasks that were to be carried out at a distance away from the user: picking up objects, turning switches on/off, and opening/closing doors. We have also concluded that the mobile base has to be autonomous, but not necessarily omnidirectional. For robotic arm manipulation, a 6-DOF robotic arm with all revolute joints was developed to perform the 12 predefined tasks. It has the PUMA-type Denavit–Hartenberg parameters [28], and the lengths of links were optimized for each predefined task. Through the design procedure using task points of the predefined 12 tasks, the optimized arm was obtained [27]. The determined DH parameters are $d_1 = 70$ cm, $l_2 = 43$ cm, $l_3 = 37$ cm, $d_6 = 10$ cm, and $l_1 = l_4 = l_5 = l_6 = d_2 = d_3 = d_4 = d_5 = 0$ cm, based on the configuration of the PUMA-type arm. The maximum torques for each joint were determined to be 9.8 N·m for joint 1, 42 N·m for joint 2, 15 N·m for joint 3, 1.9 N·m for joint 4, 0.8 N·m for joint 5, and 0.8 N·m for joint 6.

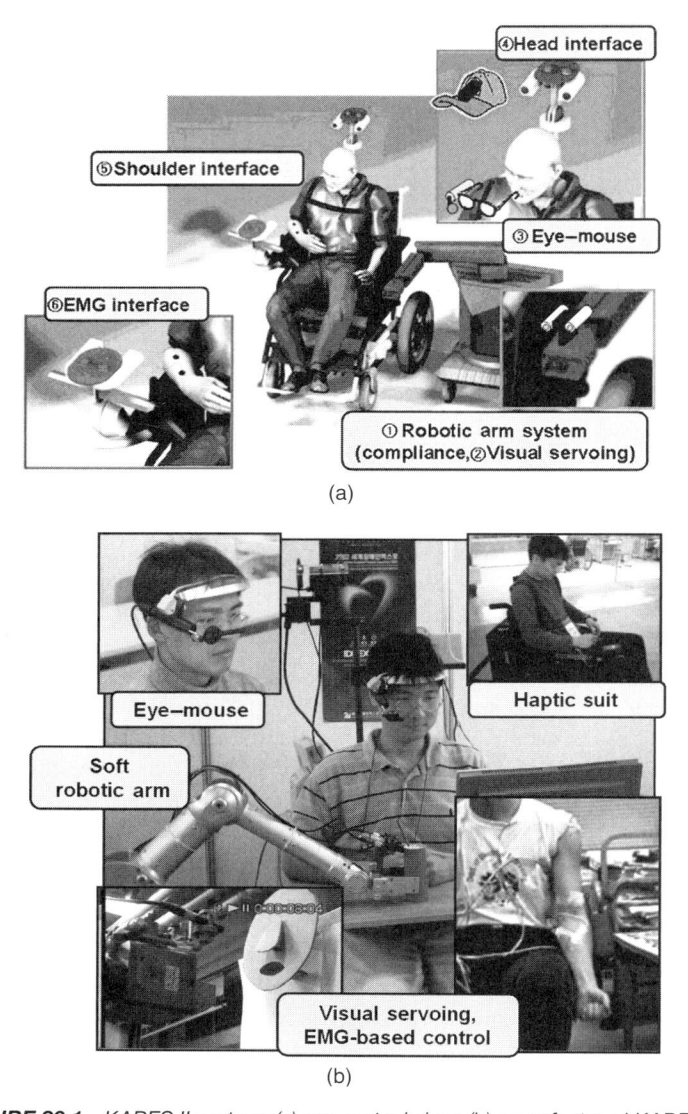

FIGURE 20.1 *KARES II system: (a) conceptual view; (b) manufactured KARES II.*

A powered wheelchair with programmable capability was adopted [1] as the platform for human–robot interfaces to enable the interfaces developed thus far to control the wheelchair. Figure 20.2 shows the interactions between subsystems of KARES II. As we can see in this figure, the KARES II system includes various human–robot interfaces for smooth communication and comfortable interaction between the user (the elderly and people with spinal cord injuries) and the robotic arm (Fig. 20.2, item 1). Each interface commands velocity and position in response to the inputs from the user. The user can control the robotic arm and wheelchair using various interfaces such as the electromyogram (EMG), eye–mouse, head, and shoulder interfaces (Fig. 20.2, items 6, 3, 4, and 5, respectively). The choice of which interface to use is dictated

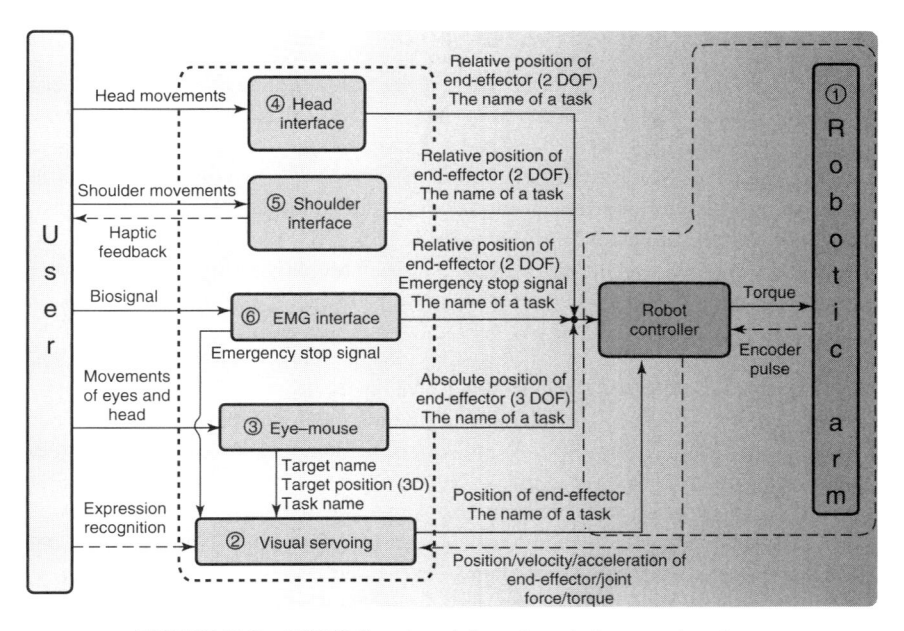

FIGURE 20.2 KARES II system: interactions between subsystems.

by the level and nature of the disability. The shoulder interface allows the user to acquire status information of the system through a haptic feedback function. The visual servoing subsystem (Fig. 20.2, item 2) provides two kinds of service: (1) autonomous service, in which the user's intervention is not necessary; and (2) user-friendly service, in which the user's intention can be acquired through the user's facial expressions.

Realization of the KARES II system as a whole hinges on the development of an efficient control architecture. If the user selects a certain task through the GUI, an overall task sequencer has to decide the necessary interfaces and the task sequence. According to the arrangement of the overall task sequencer, a submodule of the task sequencer determines the corresponding module's actions, such as requesting information to be transmitted to that submodule, commands to the actuators, notification of the result (if any), and so forth. The sequencer acts as the central coordinator in the control architecture [29].

We have confirmed that the integrated system based on the control architecture described above works reasonably well; however, there is room for improvement. One of our key findings was to that top−down architecture is more appropriate for the evolutionary design approach in terms of the following factors [29]:

- Development and reusability of software
- Modularity of subsystems to facilitate flexible exchange of components
- Implementation of the distributed system concept in order to achieve scalable computing performance

In the following subsections, we describe the soft robotic arm and the human−robot interfaces in further detail.

20.2.1 Soft Robotic Arm with Visual Servoing

Two human–robot interaction technologies are incorporated in the KARES II robotic arm: compliant motion and visual servoing. The KARES II robotic arm is designed to be compliant. As shown in Table 20.2, tasks 3 and 4 require compliant motion of the arm in task execution. The compliant motion of the robot arm ensures safety when it comes in contact with the user. In addition, compliant motion makes the service of the robot arm more comfortable for the user. The KARES II robotic arm is also equipped with visual servoing functionality, which is required for detecting and locating objects autonomously, as well as for basic intention reading by analyzing facial expressions of the user.

20.2.1.1 Active Compliance Control of the Robotic Arm [27,30,31]

The KARES II robotic arm is capable of adjusting the level of compliance required by the 12 tasks listed in Table 20.2. We have implemented active compliance control (ACC) on the robotic arm without using force or torque sensors. The conventional active compliance control requires both position and forced feedback; however, we developed a sensorless forced-feedback mechanism that lead us to a simple and low-cost design. The sensorless forced-feedback mechanism is explained below.

When a contact is at static equilibrium, the output torque of a motor (τ_{motor}) is equal to the external torque (τ_{ext}) at the contact; thus knowledge of the motor torque can be used to infer the external torque at the contact. However, this simple technique works only if backlash and friction effects are negligible, which are seldom satisfied because of the presence of speed-reducing gears in the arm. Most gears, by nature, have a considerable amount of friction and backlash. To remedy this problem, the KARES II robotic arm uses a cable-driven mechanism for speed reduction. The cable-driven mechanism has a negligible friction and backlash [32], ensuring accuracy of the sensorless torque-sensing technique described above.

To realize the desired compliance, we have proposed a method known as *time-delay control-based compliance control* [30], which realizes efficient control performance. This method is easy to implement and increases the level of safety against unexpected collisions. Furthermore, it makes the user feel comfortable when performing contact-type tasks such as shaving and wiping of his/her face.

20.2.1.2 Visual Servoing [25,33]

Visual servoing is often used for autonomous functions of robotic arms [34,35]. In the KARES II robotic arm, the visual servoing (Fig. 20.1, item 2) module provides vision-based control for the autonomous functionality of the robotic arm. It also helps implement a user-friendly interface for face recognition and intention reading.

In KARES I [36], the first version of our wheelchair-based rehabilitation robotic systems, we found difficulties in implementing visual servoing due to the requirements of real-time control and robustness to varying illuminations. In particular, the performance showed deteriorations due to the sustained vibrations of the robotic base caused by the elastic rubber tires of the wheelchair. Therefore, in KARES II, we have separated the robotic arm from the wheelchair, and adapted to it a new vision technique called *space-variant vision*, which helped realize real-time control and robustness to varying illuminations.

For effective execution of the predefined tasks, we have used a novel stereocamera head in the eye-in-hand configuration [25]. The small, lightweight stereocamera head is

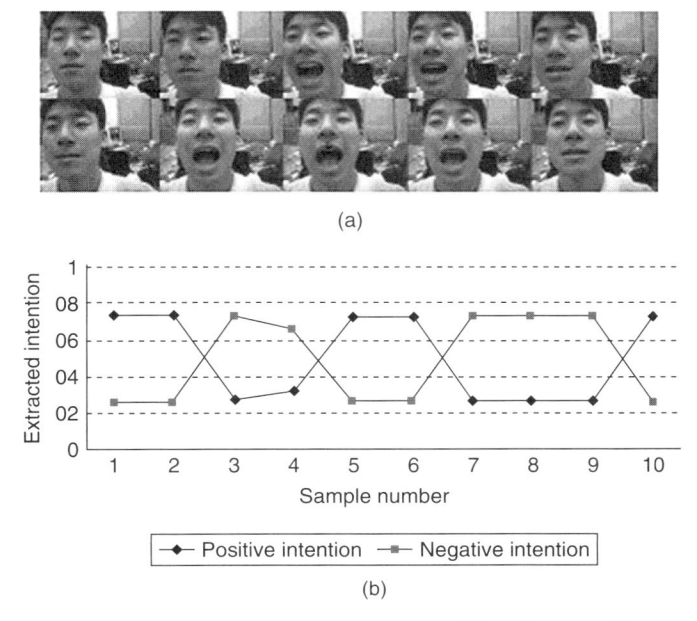

FIGURE 20.3 Intention reading from an images sequence: (a) face images; (b) extracted intention.

installed on the robotic arm in the eye-in-hand configuration [37]. For fast image processing, the log–polar mapping (LPM) method, which is a space-variant vision technique [38], was used. Since the LPM image shows invariance to scaling and rotation, in addition to its high image reduction ratio (22:1 in our system), it is well suited for visual servoing with the eye-in-hand camera configuration [39].

We have also performed an "intention reading" experiment by utilizing the visual images obtained through visual servoing. Assuming that one can show his/her intention to drink or not to drink a beverage by opening or closing his/her mouth, we have implemented an intention-reading skill based on the image information of the user's mouth [33]. Figure 20.3 shows an image sequence of the user's face with different degrees of mouth openness, together with the results of the intention-reading module. According to the features extracted regarding the user's mouth, we can easily estimate the positive/negative level of the user's desire for a drink. With 110 images, this method resulted in a reasonable classification rate (92.7 %) [33].

20.2.2 Intelligent Human–Robot Interfaces

In KARES II, there are four types of human–robot interface, and it is left for the user to decide and choose a proper combination of these interfaces according to his/her level of disability. This method allows users to select the most appropriate assistive robotic system for them. Table 20.3 presents guidelines for selecting appropriate interfaces according to the level of disability. Here, C4 means that nerves below the fourth cervical nerve in Figure 20.4 cannot function if there is an injury in the fourth cervical nerve [40]. In fact, interface selection is determined not only by the level of disability but also by the residual motor functionality of the user.

TABLE 20.3 Appropriate Human–Robot Interfaces According to Disability Level and Residual Motor Functionality

	C4		C5	
Interface	Head/Neck	Shoulder (Partial)	Shoulder	Arms (Partial)
Eye–mouse	O	O	O	O
Head interface	O	O	O	O
Shoulder interface	×	△	O	O
EMG interface	O	O	O	O

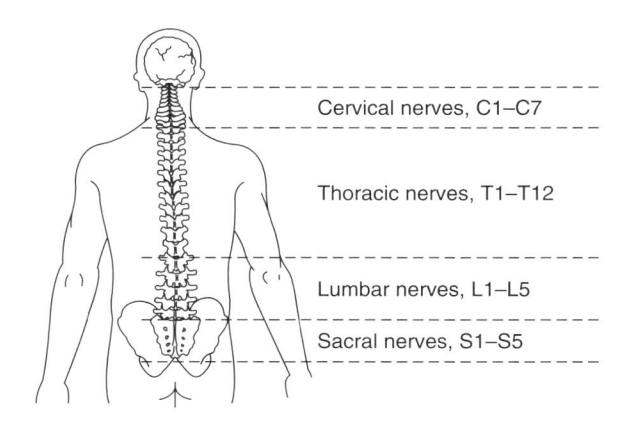

FIGURE 20.4 Types of spinal cord injury.

20.2.2.1 Eye–Mouse System [41,42]

To enable people with severe motor disability such as C4 lesion to use the KARES II system, we recommend use of the *eye–mouse* system as the input device. The eye–mouse mounted on the wheelchair allows the user to indicate the position of the object that he/she wants to grab and then to command the robot arm to execute the task.

So far, many techniques to obtain eye-gaze direction have been reported [43]. Those methods can be divided into two types: the contact method and the noncontact method. In the noncontact method, no device is attached onto the user's head, whereas the sensor located around the user estimates the user's eye-gaze direction (line of sight). Charge-coupled device (CCD) cameras [44,45] have widely been used since they do not require attachment of accessory devices that may cause inconvenience for the user. However, CCD cameras have a lower accuracy compared with contact methods, and also require a head-pursuing system. In contact methods, head position and eye movements are obtained by attaching sensors onto the user's head [46,47]. Contact methods are more accurate than the noncontact methods, and they require no head-pursuing systems. However, contact methods cause inconvenience to the user because of the attached device on the head. Nevertheless, we adopt the contact method in KARES II because the interface for disabled people should be accurate and reliable to allow free head movement. Other commercial systems that have used contact methods are also available [46,47].

We have developed a user-friendly eye–mouse system based on the opinions of disabled people. As shown in Figure 20.5, the "magnetic sensor receiver" on the cap

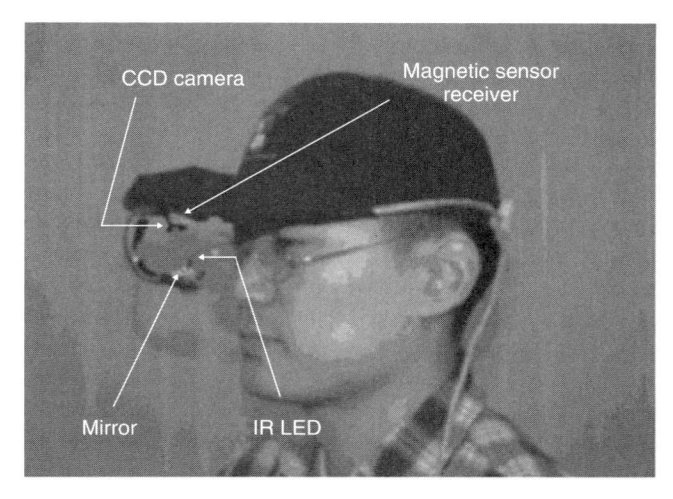

FIGURE 20.5 *Proposed eye–mouse system.*

measures the head position. Eye-gaze direction is acquired by an image-based method, which uses a CCD camera, IR LED, and a mirror [45,48,49].

20.2.2.2 Biosignal-Based Interface [50]

An *electromyogram* (EMG) signal is a form of electric manifestation of neuromuscular activation associated with contracting muscle. KARES II provides an *EMG interface*, which can be used by severely disabled people, yet retains some limited motor functionality in the shoulder or head for controlling a robotic arm or a powered wheelchair. We have developed a small, LNA (low-noise-amplification)-type EMG AMP with differential amplifiers, and effectively used to remove common mode noise. A two-biquad (second-order) notch filter was developed to reduce the hum [51] and a bandpass filter, to remove the high-frequency band.

To extract the user's intentions from muscle movement of the shoulders, we identified eight basic motions. The EMG signals show subject-dependent characteristics [50]. Therefore, we proposed a classification algorithm using a fuzzy C-means algorithm and a rough set-based technique. This algorithm selects necessary and sufficient set of features out of all extracted feature combinations, and is capable of classifying the biosignals (biologic signals) obtained from different subjects into predefined classes.

The overall signal-processing procedure is briefly explained as follows. EMG signals of the predefined motions are measured from four predetermined muscles (channels) with electrodes attached to each subject. A second-order highpass Butterworth filter with 30 Hz cutoff frequency is used to reduce low-frequency noise such as motion artifacts. Well-known features such as integral absolute value (IAV), variance (VAR), zero crossing (ZC), and frequency ratio (FR) are extracted to classify the predefined motions from noiseless EMG signals.

By applying a well-established feature extraction algorithm [50] to these numerous extracted features, we can obtain the minimized feature combination sets that contain enough information for complete classification. The minimized feature combination sets extracted by the proposed algorithm are used as training data for the fuzzy min-max neural networks (FMMNNs) to ascertain the motions. After the motions are ascertained

FMMNN gives the classified results and activates the robotic arm in accordance with the user's movement. In the experiment,[1] the basic motions are recognized with success rates of approximately 90% for four untrained users.

20.2.2.3 Head–Shoulder Interface [52,53]

The *head interface* is a 2-DOF interface designed for people with C4 lesions. It is used for body-operated control of a wheelchair and a robotic arm. The force-sensitive resistor (FSR) is cheap, easy to use, of arbitrary shape, and thin; thus, it is an appropriate sensor for developing a human–robot interface. Human head motion was analyzed in order to determine the dynamic range of the head interface. Average maximum tilt angles were measured as 41° (front), 73° (rear), and 60° (right and left). A head interface valid in the analyzed range (73°) has been developed.

The *shoulder interface* is a wearable sensor suit that senses human body motion [52,53]. Human shoulder motion was also analyzed in the same way described earlier. The average maximum ranges of shoulder motions were determined as 7.5 cm (front), 7 cm (rear), 10.1 cm (up), and 2.5 cm (down). We have also found the lift motion of the shoulder to be useful for human–robot interaction. A tension sensor that senses the lift motion of the shoulder has also been developed.

20.3 ROBOTIC HOIST: ROBOTIC TRANSFER SYSTEM IN LIVINGROOM ENVIRONMENT [54]

The robotic hoist shown in Figure 20.6 was developed to automatically transfer the user to a place of her/his interest such as a bed, wheelchair, bathtub, or stool. We used a simple mechanical hoist system as the base for our robotic hoist. In addition, we developed a mobile base and installed the hoist on it. A sling system was attached to the horizontal bar of the hoist to hold the user safely and comfortably. The height of the hoist and

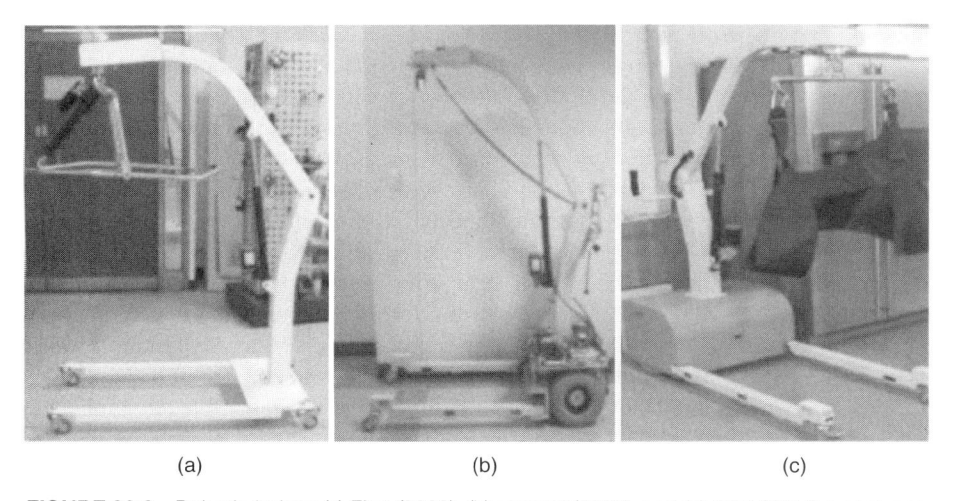

FIGURE 20.6 Robotic hoists: (a) First (2002), (b) second (2003), and (c) third (2004) prototypes.

---

[1]Each user underwent 10 trials of each motion for validation.

orientation of the horizontal bar can be controlled manually or automatically, to lift or lower the user. A simple pendant was developed for manual operation of the system. To control the mobile base and the lifting mechanism, we have designed a controller on a NOVA-7896F PC running the Pentium III (700 MHz) CPU and WOW 7.3 Paran R3 operating system. Two 200-W brushless DC motors were used to drive the wheels through a 80:1 speed reduction gear to obtain a maximum speed of 0.4 m/s.

The robotic hoist can be controlled in two modes. In *manual* control mode, the user on the bed or wheelchair sends commands to the mobile base and navigates it using the pendant-type interface device. After achieving the appropriate position and orientation, the hoist transfers the user. In *automatic* control mode, the computer control system automatically navigates the mobile base until it reaches the desired position and orientation.

To simplify the navigation task and achieve precise positioning of the mobile base, many systems use immobile fixed references, such as the ceiling in an indoor environment. The Minerva robot at the Carnegie-Mellon University compares the current image data and the mosaics of a ceiling generated as the robot drives [55]. This approach requires a complex and sophisticated algorithm and may result in an incorrect location depending on lighting and illumination. To reduce this limitation, the NorthStar, Evolution Robotics Co. Ltd, uses an infrared (IR) light projector to create bright spots on the ceiling, which are observed by a NorthStar detector mounted on the mobile robot [56]. The position and orientation of the robot are calculated from the location of the IR lights in the image data. However, the benefit of this approach is obtained at higher cost and complexity, due to the involvement of the IR projector. To overcome the disadvantages of the existing systems, we propose a simple and low-cost landmark navigation system, called *Artificial Stars*, which consists of two parts: ceiling-mounted active landmarks and a PC camera to detect these landmarks. The PC camera is attached to the mobile

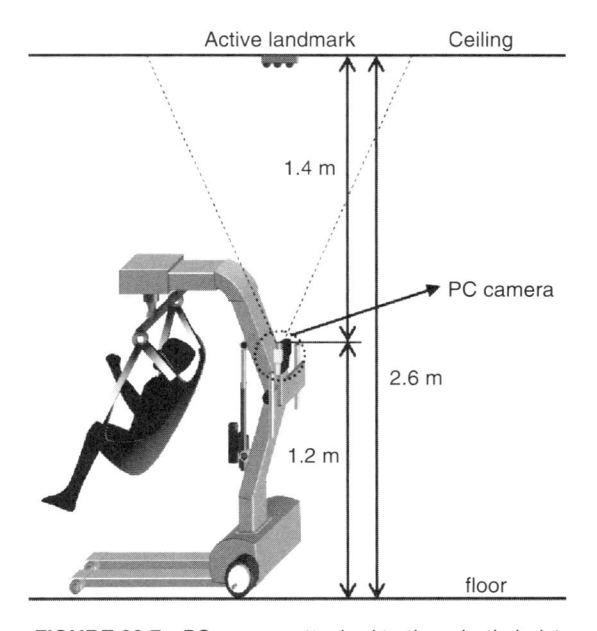

FIGURE 20.7 *PC camera attached to the robotic hoist.*

robotic base as shown in Figure 20.7. Each landmark consists of three IR light-emitting diodes (LEDs; Model EL-8L with maximum wavelength 940 nm and viewing angle 34°) arranged on a 4 × 4-cm printed circuit board (PCB). To make the camera insensitive to ambient light, we covered the camera lenses with an IR pass filter.

To recognize the information from each landmark in a proper way, we choose configurations in such a way that the LEDs are positioned at different distances from each other (see Fig. 20.8). To obtain the position and orientation information, we first detect landmarks in the camera image using the preliminary knowledge that the landmark consists of three LEDs arranged in a predefined range, and then compare the distances between each pair of LEDs. The shortest distance is considered to be the first coordinate axis; for example, line AB in Figure 20.8 indicates the first coordinate axis. The positions of the LED labeled C in Figure 20.8 with respect to the coordinate axis AB are used to determine the north or south direction and identify each landmark.

Because the position of each landmark is known a priori in the global coordinates, information from detected landmarks (landmark IDs) is used to determine the position of the mobile base. Orientation of the mobile base with respect to the landmark is determined by calculating the angle θ between the x axis in the camera coordinate and the line that connects points A and B (Fig. 20.9). Because the camera is fixed to the mobile base, camera coordinates (x and y axes in Fig. 20.9) correspond to the orientation of the mobile base.

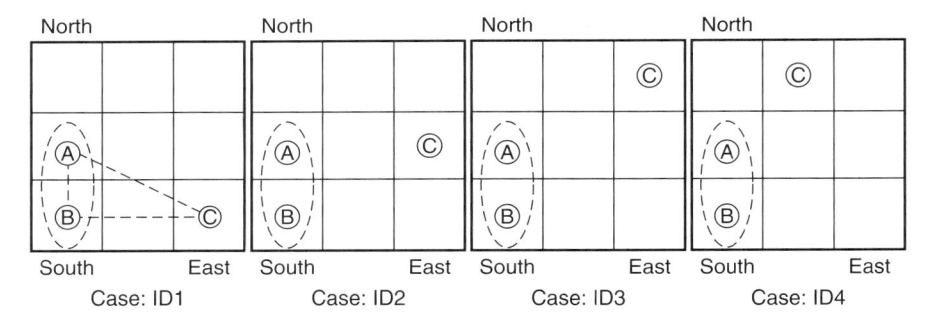

FIGURE 20.8 Possible configurations for different landmarks with three IR LEDs.

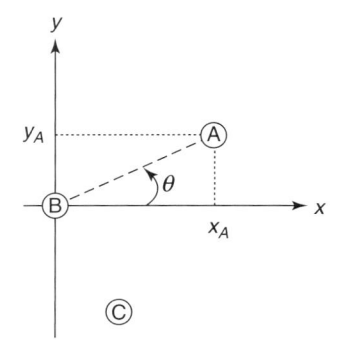

FIGURE 20.9 Calculation of the orientation angle in the image.

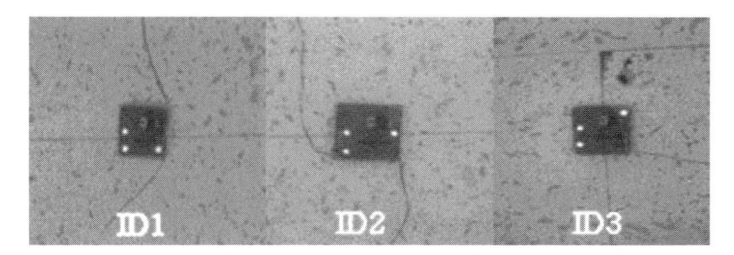

FIGURE 20.10 Active landmarks implemented with three IR LEDs.

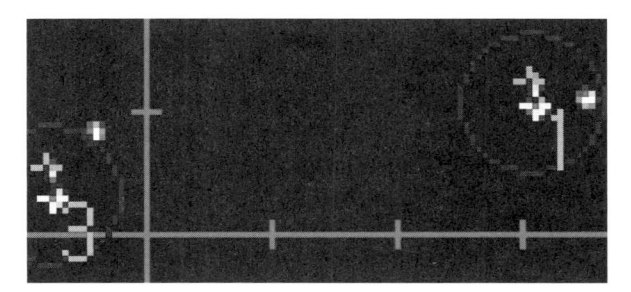

FIGURE 20.11 Recognized landmarks (ID1 and ID3).

Figure 20.10 shows landmark prototypes attached to the ceiling, and Figure 20.11 shows the recognized IR LEDs in the camera image. The circles in Figure 20.11 denote the identified LED groups (landmarks), and the numbers correspond to the IDs of the recognized landmark. Figure 20.11 illustrates the case when the camera system recognizes two landmarks and identifies them as ID1 and ID3. Since the positions and the orientations of these landmarks are predetermined, the position and the orientation of the mobile base in the global coordinate can be easily obtained. We assume that at least one landmark module is always seen by the camera. For cases where some of the landmarks in the area are not functioning or a landmark cannot be seen by the camera, "dead reckoning" is applied to complete navigation information. In our tests, the system has shown that the localization is very robust under various illumination conditions, including ceiling lamp illumination, direct sunlight, and darkness. We have also obtained position accuracy better than 20 mm and orientation accuracy better than $1°$ when the viewing area was 1.15×0.88 m.

20.4 WORK ASSISTANT MOBILE ROBOT FOR PEOPLE WITH DISABILITIES IN A REAL MANUFACTURING ENVIRONMENT [57]

This robotic system was developed to assist disabled workers in the manufacturing industry. To achieve this goal, we should consider the real working environment and conditions, and critical requirements for disabled people to deliver their contribution to the workplace [58].

We focused on workers who suffer lower/upper-arm disabilities, and developed a robotic system to convert them into productive and competent employees in the manufacturing industry.

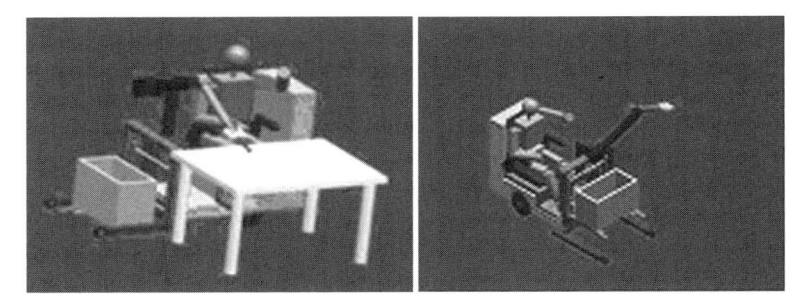

FIGURE 20.12 *Scenario of work assistant mobile robot — type I.*

20.4.1 Work Assistant Mobile Robot — Type I

The work assistant mobile robot provides mobility for users who suffer lower-limb disability, helping them move boxes between a warehouse and a worktable using the forklift attached to the mobile platform, and also helping to perform requiring tasks manual dexterity (soldering, assembling, etc.) using a robot arm. The mobile robot is small enough to move through an aisle between tables and between a table and a warehouse. The robot has collision avoidance functionality in order to enhance the safety of the disabled user, and an emergency button is installed. A rear monitoring camera and a display screen provide the disabled user with the rear-viewing functionality while in a convenient pose, without having to twist his/her body.

Figure 20.12 illustrates how the work assistant robot helps the disabled user to accomplish the work at the worktable and for moving boxes inside the warehouse. To support table tasks, the mobile robot is parked parallel to the table, and the robot's chair is rotated toward the table. This setting helps the user position the robot arm and the forklift in the best configuration.

The forklift of the work assistant mobile robot is designed to lift heavy boxes; thus, its driving mechanism is a major design concern. We considered two driving mechanisms: forward wheel steering/backward wheel driving and forward wheel driving/backward wheel steering. The former design is widely used in three/four-wheel scooters. However, this mechanism is not appropriate for the work assistant robot because of the presence of the forklift in front. The later mechanism is widely used in commercial forklifts, and is more appropriate for the work assistant robot.

The work assistant robot has one driving motor, one steering motor, 10 ultrasonic sensors for collision avoidance, four limit switches for the emergency stop, a digital signal-processing (DSP) circuit for motor controls, rear-mounted camera and display, and one onboard computer to manage the system. Figure 20.14 shows the work assistant robot type I, and Figure 20.13 shows its functional block diagram.

20.4.2 Work Assistant Mobile Robot — Type II

The feedback from the users regarding work assistant mobile robot type I lead to the modifications required, and the advanced version type II was developed. In type II, the robot arm is installed on the table because it is used almost always for manual-dexterity-requiring tasks on the table, and is seldom used while the robot is moving. The foldable forklift was considered to make the robot smaller. The wheel

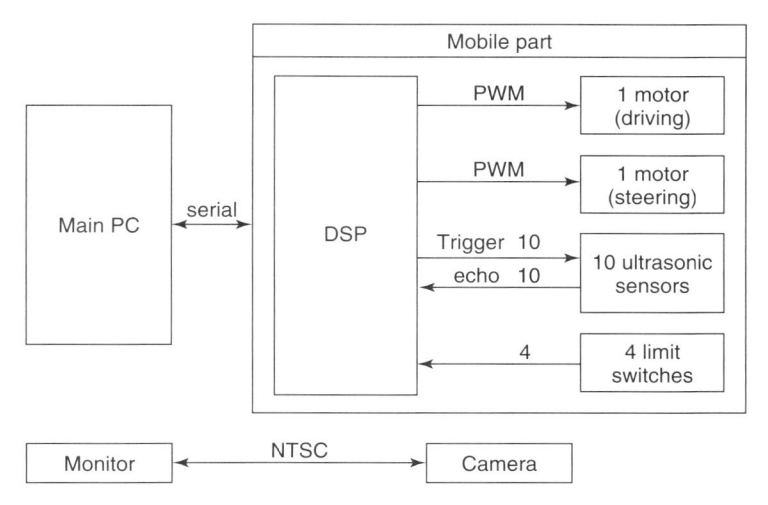

FIGURE 20.13 Block diagram of work assistant mobile robot — type I (showing only the mobile platform, with forklift and robot arm connected to PC).

FIGURE 20.14 Work assistant mobile robot — type I.

orientation of the driving mechanism was also changed to omnidirectional to make positioning tasks more convenient for upper-limb-disabled people.

The work assistant mobile robot type II is equipped with four omnidirectional wheels, a forklift, two sonar sensors, and a rotating chair, and all these components are controlled by a joystick and switches. Figure 20.15 illustrates the task of moving boxes from the warehouse to the worktable. The omnidirectional wheel-driving mechanism makes positioning much easier, as the steering radius is nearly zero. When the user is working at the table, the chair rotates toward the table as shown in Figures 20.15d and 20.15e.

Figure 20.16 shows the block diagram of the work assistant mobile robot type II. Figure 20.17 shows the developed work assistant mobile robot type II. This robot

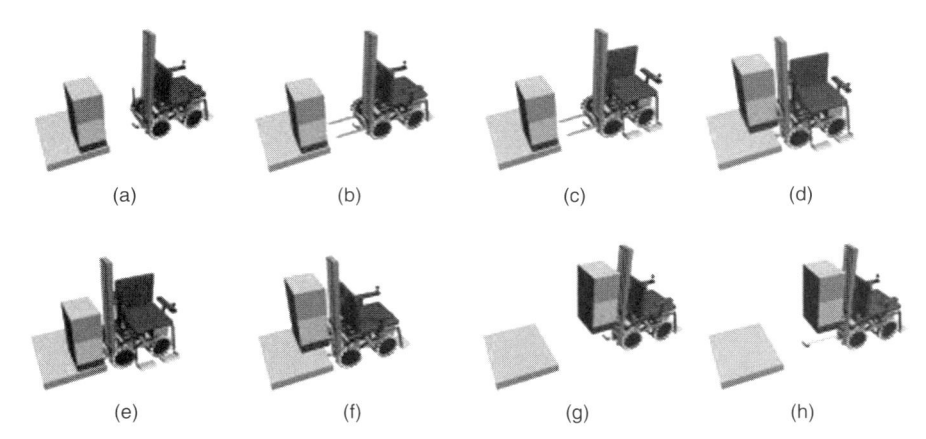

392 MOBILE PLATFORM-BASED ASSISTIVE ROBOT SYSTEMS

FIGURE 20.15 Work assistant mobile robot – type II: (a) robot moves to warehouse and faces rear of box on pallet; (b) user unfolds fork; (c) user rotates chair and gets ready to pick up box: (d) robot moves toward box and picks up pallet; (e) user makes robot lift the fork; (f) user rotates chair to forward direction; (g) robot moves toward table; (h) when moving boxes, two sonar sensors are stretched out to avoid receiving false echoes from the forklift.

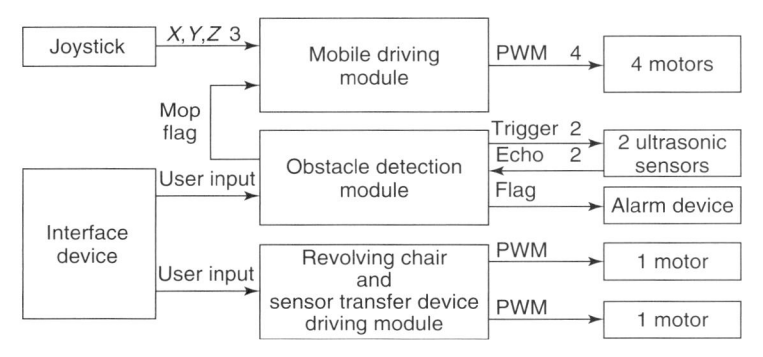

FIGURE 20.16 Block diagram of the work assistant mobile robot - type II (This shows only the mobile part)

facilitates table tasks better because of its small size, particularly because it is parked parallel to the table. The effectiveness of type II is further proved by the rotating chair and foldable forklift, which can be used for box feeding as well.

20.5 USER TRIALS

20.5.1 User Trials with KARES II [23]

Six people with spinal cord injuries participated in trials of various functions of the KARES II system. These subjects underwent rehabilitation at Korean NRC (National Rehabilitation Center) in Seoul (see Table 20.4).

The trials were conducted as follows. First, we showed the subjects how to perform task 2 in Table 20.2 using KARES II system. The subjects were briefed on the history

FIGURE 20.17 Work assistant mobile robot — type II (dimensions in mm).

TABLE 20.4 Information on Subjects Involved in KARES II Trials

| | | | | Residual Motor Ability | | | |
Subject ID	Sex	Age	Lesion Level	Head–neck	Shoulder	Arms	Technical Aids
A	M	33	C4	O	△	×	None
B	M	36	C5	O	O	×	None
C	M	35	C4	O	△	×	None
D	M	51	C5	O	O	O	Powered wheelchair
E	M	21	C4	O	△	×	None
F	M	31	C5	O	O	△	Powered wheelchair

and purpose of the KARES II and then were allowed to operate, observe, and experience various interface subsystem/modules of the KARES II system. At every step of the way, short questionnaires were used to obtain feedback from the subjects on subsystems and modules. On the basis of their qualitative answers and quantitative measurements for each subsystem, we determined the degree of satisfaction (0–100%) according to the predefined evaluation aspects of each subsystem.[2]

20.5.1.1 Robotic Arm

Routine tasks such as shaving and washing one's hands and face involve physical contact between the robot arm and the subject. For such a task, the robot must have some level of compliance to ensure the safety of the user. In these cases, the magnitude of compliance may depend on each individual and on the nature of the task. We investigated a preferred compliance level for each task by performing task trials and receiving feedback from the subjects in the form of a questionnaire.

Compliant motion was realized for the first three joints of the robot arm with respect to link length. Level 1 is the lowest compliance level (or the highest stiffness case), and level 3 is the highest compliance level (or the lowest stiffness case). On the basis of

---

[2]Each user underwent 10 trials of each motion for validation.

the investigation of human arm compliance reported by Gomi and Kawato [59] we have designed three compliance levels; the first one is smaller than that of the human arm, the second one is nearly the same as that of human arm, and the third one is larger than that of the human arm.

For the shaving task, we applied the three compliance levels in the trials. According to the observed performance level and responses from the subjects, we ascertained that levels 2 and 3 provide safety and comfort for the user. In addition, we found that the subjects prefer level 2 compliance for the shaving task. Level 2 corresponds to the compliance motion of a weak nurse's arm [56].

For the face-cleaning task, we have found that all three levels of compliance fail to render a satisfactory result; the degree of satisfaction was very low. The subjects preferred a compliance level still lower than what was presented, which means that the face-cleaning task requires a stronger contact force with greater stiffness to perform the task satisfactorily. The subjects also preferred placement of the towel at a convenient location to facilitate their face-cleaning tasks.

20.5.1.2 Visual Servoing

The visual servoing subsystem consists of a stereocamera in the eye-in-hand configuration. The functionalities of object recognition, face recognition, and intention reading from facial expressions are incorporated. In the user trials, the subjects were asked for their opinions about physical appearance of the visual servoing mechanism. In addition, it was known that the stereocamera head needed a redesign to make it seem more user-friendly. Many users also claimed that they had difficulties with the language of our graphical user interface (GUI) because of its small font size and English-only expressions. In fact, the GUIs of assistive robotic systems designed for disabled people and the elderly should be able to interact with the user's language, and the characters should be large enough for convenient reading. In the object recognition subsystem, the objects to be recognized should be predefined by the user. More objects can be defined and introduced to enable the robot to cope with various objects. All users were satisfied with the intention-reading functionality. For more general usage of intention reading, recognition of multiple areas of the face in addition to the mouth is recommended.

20.5.1.3 Eye–Mouse System

We carried out user trials with the proposed eye–mouse system. The accuracy of the eye-gaze direction was obtained for a 500 mm distance between the user and the monitor. With these errors, the appropriate size of the interface button was determined. It is noted that the result is worse than the resolution (14 × 12) obtained in laboratory tests [49], and the results are different for different users. The possible reasons for these results are as follows:

- To determine eye-gaze direction using the eye–mouse system, the center coordinate of the eye should be obtained anatomically with respect to the receiver of the magnetic sensor.
- Since the motions of eyes include saccadic motion, concentration is needed for users to fix their gaze on one point
- Because the proposed pupil-tracking method is a vision-based method, it can be affected by the surrounding illumination:

From the survey results, we may claim that most of the users were satisfied with the structure of the interface. The convenience of the additional OK button for click operation was particularly commended. The users also said that it was easy to control the pan/tilt unit because of the "automatic pushing" function when the mouse pointer moves into the button on the monitor. The degree of satisfaction regarding the design and comfort of (wearing) the system turned out to be acceptable. The users wanted the system to be light and not tight-fitting. They also pointed out the problem of perspiration on the surface of contact. Since the proposed method is a "contact" method, user fatigue is also a critical problem when the device is used for a long period of time; thus, the fatigue level of tiredness needs to be observed by increasing the duration of trials.

20.5.1.4 Head–Shoulder Interface

Two experiments were performed to evaluate the performance of the shoulder and head interfaces that produce 2-DOF signals. The experimental process was as follows:

1. Becoming familiar with the interface. This step involves wearing the interface and attempting to make four directional signals: forward, backward, right, and left.
2. Operating the wheelchair through the interface.
3. Driving the wheelchair along a predefined path, while recording the elapsed time from start to finish, number of collisions, and recognition rate of the interface.
4. Evaluating the performance of the interface.

We conducted another experiment using this same procedure with healthy (control) subjects using a joystick in which an elapsed time of 21 s, and a average number of 0.5 collisions were recorded. The corresponding results for disabled users were 42 s (half the speed of healthy users) and five collisions (10 times more frequent than in healthy subjects). On the other hand, those who suffer spinal cord injuries did not spend much time adapting to the interface to control the wheelchair. They controlled the wheelchair along the path recording two collisions on average. This result revealed the potential of using the head/shoulder interfaces even for severely disabled people to control a wheelchair. It should also be mentioned that the head/shoulder interfaces may not work perfectly with different disabled people. For example, in the trials with the shoulder interface, the first and the fifth subjects could not use either shoulder, and therefore the experiment was not carried out. Also, in the trials with the head interface, the first subject had difficulties in roll motion of the head, and hence could not turn in the appropriate direction.

According to the survey results, we may claim that the subjects were satisfied with the overall impression of the two interfaces. Most subjects who used the shoulder interface placed inside their overcoats appreciated the device because it did not attract other people's attention.

20.5.1.5 EMG Interface

The EMG interface can also be used to control the wheelchair. The performance of the EMG interface was assessed by similar trials as mentioned in the previous section in that elapsed time and number of collisions were recorded while each subject was driving along a predefined path. After the trials, users' feedbacks about the EGM interface were received in an appropriately designed questionnaire.

There are two driving modes for the wheelchair: modes 1 and 2. In mode 1, the wheelchair moves as long as the user keeps the command on, such as both shoulders up for forward driving. On the contrary, mode 2 employs toggle switches to command the wheelchair forward, stop, and so on. In this mode, the wheelchair drives itself according to the most recently switched command, and the user does not have to keep the command on while driving. We used four electrodes (two channels, bipolar type) for measuring EMG signals in both trapezius muscles of the user.

The subjects who underwent the trials claimed that they felt tired by mode 1 as they had to keep the motion command on during entire motion of the wheelchair. On the contrary, subjects effectively used mode 2; in fact, they caused the wheelchair to move forward quite conveniently, simply by momentarily raising both shoulders. One drawback of mode 2, however, is its response delay, which confuses the untrained user as to whether the controller had accepted the command correctly. After using this controller for a while, however, the user adapted to this delay time, and felt more comfortable than with the forward command in mode 1.

The users also commented about electrode attachment and its appearance. Some users did not like this attachment and the procedure that it entailed (including the skin preparation). The results of these trials have ascertained that the EMG interface based on head or shoulder movement could be applied to control a wheelchair for users with spinal cord injuries with lesion level C4 or C5.

20.5.2 User Trials with Robotic Hoist: User Transfer between Bed and Wheelchair [54]

This task involves the synchronous actions of the intelligent bed, intelligent wheelchair, and robotic hoist. It is assumed that the user has lower-limb paralysis, yet still retains sufficient motion range and muscle strength in the upper limbs. The transfer task can be performed easily as illustrated in Figure 20.18. The task execution sequence is illustrated in Figure 20.19, and involves the following execution procedure:

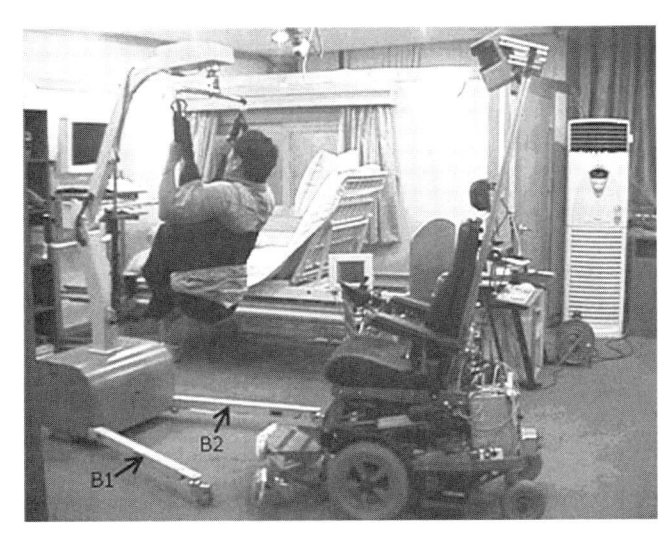

FIGURE 20.18 Transferring user from bed to wheelchair.

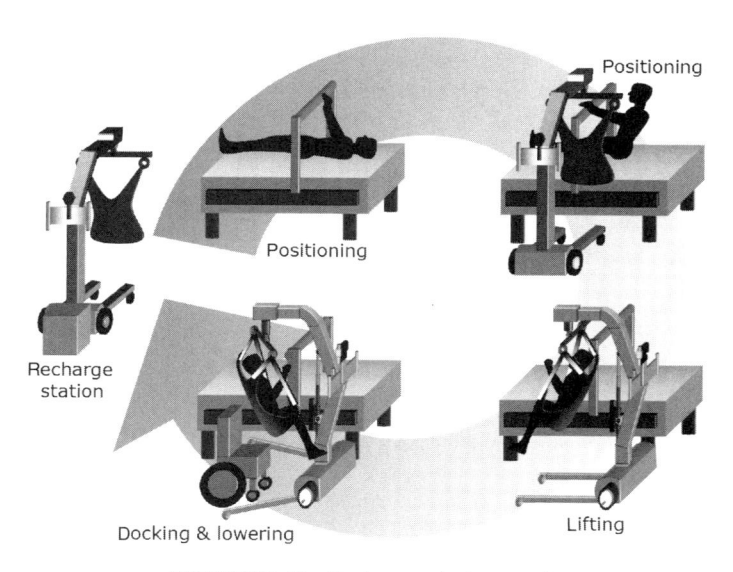

FIGURE 20.19 *Task scenario for transfer.*

Step 1. The user initiates the transfer task using a vocal command and/or a hand gesture. The command is interpreted by the management system, which generates the action strategy and distributes the subtasks to the intelligent bed, intelligent wheelchair, and robotic hoist.

Step 2. The pressure sensor system outputs information on the user's position and posture. The horizontal bar of the intelligent bed moves close to the user and assists the user in changing body posture on the bed.

Step 3. The position and posture information of the user is analyzed by the management system. The robotic hoist moves to the intelligent bed and lifts the user.

Step 4. The intelligent wheelchair moves to the bed and docks with the robotic hoist.

Step 5. The robotic hoist lowers the user onto the intelligent wheelchair when the wheelchair sends a signal that docking has been completed.

Step 6. The intelligent wheelchair autonomously navigates to the destination.

Step 7. The robotic hoist returns to the recharge station.

In step 4, the laser range finder (LRF) is used for autonomous navigation of the wheelchair to dock with the robotic hoist based on a priori shape information of the robotic hoist. The wheelchair detects two long bars in the lower part of the robotic hoist from the LRF scan data as it approaches the robotic hoist. In our experiments, we have achieved a ± 100 mm position accuracy for the center position and $\pm 4°$ angular accuracy for the orientation with a processing time of 0.46 ms.

20.5.3 User Trials with Vocational Assistive Mobile Robot System [57]

20.5.3.1 *Vocational Assistive Mobile Robot System — Type I*
The vocational assistive mobile robot type I was tested in actual manufacturing factories. We conducted a series of user trials of the developed vocational assistive mobile robot

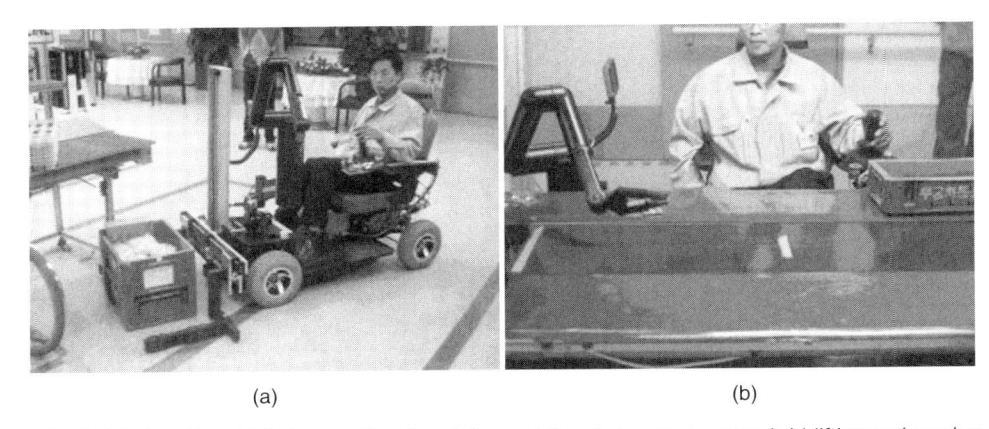

FIGURE 20.20 User trials for vocational assistive mobile robot system — type I: (a) lifting and moving items; (b) working at desk.

system with the participation of disabled workers at BoramDongsan and Mugungwha Electronics in Korea. We also received these subjects' feedback about the vocational assistive mobile robot. The subjects were randomly selected among factory workers suffering from lower/upper-limb impairments. Figure 20.20 shows the trials in which these disabled workers participated.

After the trials with the vocational assistive mobile robot system type I, we interviewed the subjects about driving and steering speeds, the convenience of a joystick interface, the comfort of riding, whether driving was risky, and whether the rear-view display was helpful. The speeds of forward and reverse motions were confirmed by the subjects as appropriate, while claiming slow steering. This problem was caused by the speed reduction gear used to generate high torque. This problem was resolved by using a lower speed reduction gearbox and at the same time replacing the motor with a high-torque one. The subjects also claimed that the joystick interface was very convenient. While moving around, they said that they felt safe. This is due to the intuitive joystick control method and the ultrasonic sensor system that enables the user to avoid collision with obstacles. However, these subjects habitually did not use the rear monitoring system.

In addition to the outcome of the trials, we found other required modifications as follows: (1) the robot arm system is difficult to control, and needed to be designed smaller or installed on a workdesk; (2) the mobile base and the turning radius of the robot needed to be designed smaller, and the chair needed to be rotated electrically and at a lower height; (3) the fork of the forklift system needed to be designed smaller or to be foldable electrically. These modifications were implemented in the vocational assistive mobile robot system type II.

20.5.3.2 Vocational Assistive Mobile Robot System — Type II

The vocational assistive mobile robot—type II was tested in an actual manufacturing factory as shown in Figure 20.21. The subjects mentioned that it was very nice to be able to move boxes around, and that the robot was small enough, similar to the size of a powered wheelchair. They further commented that, because of the small size of the system and omnidirectional wheel-driving mechanism, tablework was possible without transferring to another chair at the table. They appreciated the controllability and collision

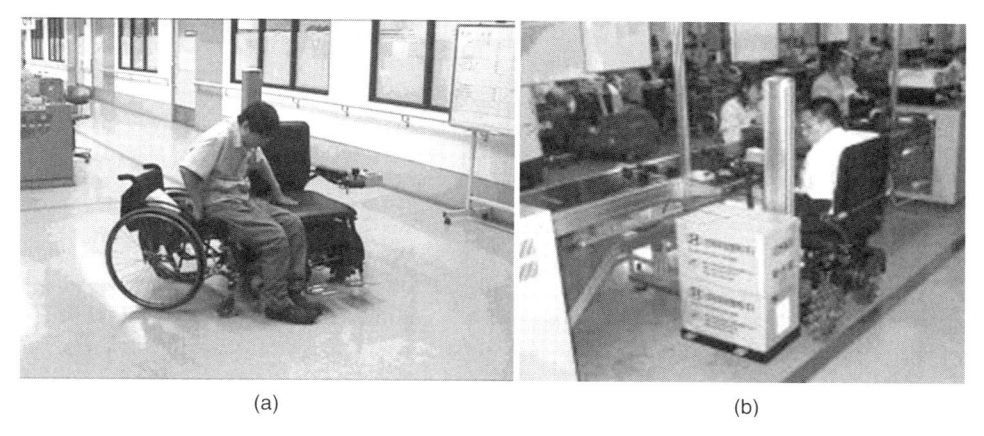

FIGURE 20.21 User trials for vocational assistive mobile robot system — type II: (a) transferring; (b) working at desk.

avoidance capability of the mobile robot. The vocational assistive mobile robot type II did not have a rear-viewing device, however, and some subjects claimed that it should be incorporated to avoid collisions in the rear of the robot.

20.6 CONCLUDING REMARKS

As summarized by Dallaway et al. [10] and Iwata et al. [26], the following issues should be seriously considered in R&D of future assistive robotic systems:

- Adaptable intelligent interaction/interface to the levels of disability
- User-friendly design that assumes user comfort
- Development of the technology for user safety
- Improved system autonomy to relieve the user from laborious direct control

With these issues in mind, we have been studying and developing various types of mobile assistive robotic systems. Specifically, we have suggested and implemented several subsystems for mobile platform-based assistive robotic systems to assist disabled people who suffer from quadriplegia, poliomyelitis, and hemiplegia. These subsystems were further modified on the basis of trial results and feedback from disabled subjects who underwent the trials. The existence of many different subsystems helped us develop versatile assistive robotic systems that are capable of providing various services to the disabled user. The following conclusions can be drawn from our observations of the AR systems that we developed:

1. Proper hybridization of workstation-based design and wheelchair-based design leads to a novel type of rehabilitation robotic system, which has improved features of both designs. The modularized human–machine interface/interaction helps users cope with a variety of disabilities. In realizing the user's input commands and interaction mechanism, various human–robot interfaces including the eye–mouse

system, head/shoulder interfaces, and EMG signal interfaces were developed to help users cope with these diverse disabilities.

2. A novel robotic hoist was developed and tested in a smart home environment. Our robotic hoist consists of a user-friendly designed sling, an easy-to-use interface, autonomous navigation function, and a voice-interactive command system. Through several user trials, the functionality of the robotic hoist has been improved.

3. Vocational assistive mobile robots, types I and II, were developed for vocational use in actual manufacturing factories. The robots that we developed were tested with the participation of disabled people performing tasks such as moving boxes between worktable and warehouse and assembling. It was verified by user trials and feedbacks that the proposed vocational assistive robot is capable of assisting disabled workers to effectively perform their work.

ACKNOWLEDGEMENT

This research was supported by the Human-friendly Welfare Robot System Engineering Research Center (sponsored by the SRC/ERC Program of MOST/KOSEF, Grant R11-1999-008) of KAIST, and the Ministry of Science and Technology of Korea, as a part of Critical Technology 21 Program on "Development of Intelligent Human–Robot Interaction Technology."

We would like to acknowledge various forms of support from Professors Ju-Jang Lee, Byung Kook Kim, Jong-Tae Lim, and Heyoung Lee and their students in developing Intelligent Sweet Home. We extend our sincere thanks to Dr. Dimitar Stefanov for his helpful comments.

We also acknowledge the consistent support from Professor Dong-Soo Kwon and his students in developing the KARES II system. Finally, sincere gratitude is due to Dr. Byung-Sik Kim and his staff at the National Rehabilitation Center, Korea for his support in conducting user trials.

REFERENCES

1. Hillman M, Hagan K, Hagan S, Jepson J, Orpwood R: The Weston wheelchair mounted assistive robot—the design story, *Robotica* **20**:125–132 (2002).
2. Krebs HI, Hogan N, Volpe BT, Aisen ML, Edelstein L, Diels C: Robot-aided neuro–rehabilitation in stroke: Three-year follow–up, *Proc ICORR1999*, 1999, pp 34–41.
3. Lum PS, Burgar CG, Shor PC, Majmundar M, Van der Loos HFM: Robot-assisted movement training compared with conventional therapy techniques for the rehabilitation of upper limb motor function after stroke, *Arch Phys Med Rehab* **83**:952–959 (2002).
4. Rao R, Agrawal SK, Scholz JP: A robot test-bed for assistance and assessment in physical therapy, *Advan Robot* **14**(7):565–578 (2000).
5. Erlandson RF: Applications of robotic/mechatronic systems in special education, rehabilitation therapy, and vocational training: A paradigm shift, *IEEE Trans Rehab Eng* **3**:22–32 (1995).
6. Harwin WS, Rahman T, Foulds RA: A review of design issues in rehabilitation robotics with reference to North American research, *IEEE Trans Rehab Eng* **3**:3–13 (1995).

7. Kawamura K, Isakarous M: Trends in service robots for the disabled and the elderly, *Proc IROS'94*, 1994, pp 1647–1654.
8. IST-MATS: http://www.bcdi.be/en/projects/data.html.
9. Afma-robots: AFMASTER, 2003, http://www.afma-robots.com.
10. Dallaway JL, Jackson RD, Timmers PHA: Rehabilitation robotics in Europe, *IEEE Trans Rehab Eng* **3**:35–45 (1995).
11. Van der Loos HFM: VA/Stanford rehabilitation robotics research and development program: Lessons learned in the application of robotics technology to the field of rehabilitation, *IEEE Trans Rehab Eng* **3**:46–55 (1995).
12. Conte G, Longhi S, Zulli R: Motion planning for unicycle and car-like robots, *Int J Syst Sci* **27**(8):791–798 (1996).
13. Care-O-bot, 2003, http://www.care-o-bot.de/english/Care-O-bot_2.php.
14. ISRA: *The Service Robot Market, an In-depth Study from the International Service Association*, ISRA, 1995.
15. Kwee HH: Integrated control of MANUS manipulator and wheelchair enhanced by environmental docking, *Robotica* **16**(5):491–498 (1998).
16. Martens C, Ivlev O, Graser A, Lang O, Ruchel N: A FRIEND for assisting handicapped people, *IEEE Robot Autom Mag* **8**(1):57–65 (2001).
17. Colello MS, Mahoney RM: Commercializing assistive and therapy robotics, in Keates S et al, eds, *Universal Access and Assistive Technology*, Springer-Verlag 2002, pp 223–234.
18. Access Unlimited: http://www.accessunlimited.com/html/home_lifts.html.
19. AryCare: http://arycare.tripod.com.
20. Aluminum Extrusion: http://www.aec.org/assets/pdf/ShowcaseCeilingTrack.pdf.
21. Eftring H, Bolmsjö G: RAID—a robotic workstation for the disabled, *Proc 2nd European Conf Advancement of Rehabilitation Technology*, Stockholm, 1993, p 24.3.
22. Van der Loos HFM, Wagner JJ, Smaby N, Chang K, Madrigal O, Leifer LJ, Khatib O: ProVAR assistive robot system architecture, *Proc Int 1999 IEEE Conf Robotics and Automation*, Detroit, MI, 1999, Vol 1, pp 741–746.
23. Bien Z, Chung MJ, Chang PH, Kwon DS, Kim DJ, Han JS, Kim JH, Kim DH, Park HS, Kang SH et al: Integration of a rehabilitation robotic system (KARES II) with human-friendly man-machine interaction units, *Auton Robots* **16**(2):165–191 (2004).
24. Jung JW, Song WK, Lee H, Kim JS, Bien Z: A study on the enhancement of manipulation performance of wheelchair-mounted rehabilitation service robot, *Proc 6th Int Conf Rehabilitation Robotics*, Stanford, CA, 1999, pp 42–49.
25. Song WK, Bien Z: Blend of soft computing techniques for effective human-machine interaction in service robotic systems, *Fuzzy Sets Syst* **134**:5–25 (2003).
26. Iwata H, Hoshino H, Morita T, Sugeno S: A physical interference adapting hardware system using MIA arm and humanoid surface covers, *Proc Int IEEE/RSJ Conf Intelligent Robots and Systems*, 1999, pp 1216–1221
27. Chang PH, Park HS: Development of a robotic arm for handicapped people: A task-oriented design approach, *Auton Robots* **15**(1):81–92 (2003).
28. Craig JJ: *Introduction to Robotics: Mechanics and Control*, Addison-Wesley, 1989.
29. Martens C, Kim DJ, Han JS, Graeser A, Bien Z: Concept for a modified hybrid multi-layer control architecture for rehabilitation robots, *Proc 3rd Int Workshop on Human-friendly Welfare Robotic Systems*, Daejeon, Korea, 2002, pp 49–54.
30. Chang PH, Kang SH, Park HS, Kim ST, Kim JH: Active compliance control for the disabled with cable transmission, *Proc 8th Int Conf Rehabilitation Robotics (ICORR2003)*, Daejeon, Korea, 2003 pp 84–87.

31. Chang PH, Park HS, Park J, Jung JH, Jeon BK: Development of a robotic arm for handicapped people: A target-oriented design approach, *Proc 7th Int Conf Rehabilitation Robotics (ICORR2001)*, 2001, pp 84–92.
32. Townsend WT: *The Effect of Transmission Design on Force-Controlled Manipulator Performance*, PhD thesis, MIT, Cambridge, MA, 1988.
33. Kim DJ, Song WK, Han JS, Bien Z: Soft computing based intention reading techniques as a means of human-robot interaction for human centered system, *J Soft Comput* **7**:160–166 (2003).
34. Chen N, Parker GA: Inverse kinematic solution to a calibrated puma 560 industrial robot, *Control Eng Pract* **2**:239–245 (1994).
35. Peters II RA, Bishay M, Cambron ME, Negishi K: Visual servoing for service robot, *Robot Auton Syst* **18**:213–224 (1996).
36. Song WK, Lee H, Bien Z: KARES: Intelligent wheelchair-mounted robotic arm system using vision and force sensor, *Robot Auton Syst* **28**(1):83–94 (1999).
37. Choi J: *Design of a Behavior-Based Controller Using a Novel Camera Head and Its Application to Service Robots (in Korean)*, MS thesis, KAIST, Korea, 2001.
38. Bolduc M Levine MD: A review of biologically motivated space-variant data reduction models for robotic vision, *Comput Vision Image Understand* **69**(2):170–184 (1998).
39. Jruger V: *Optical Flow Computation in the Complex Logarithmic Plane*, diploma-thesis, Univ Kiel, Germany, 1995.
40. *The MERCK Manual of Medical Information*, 2nd Home ed, (online version: http://www.merck.com/mmhe/sec06/ch093/ch093a.html).
41. Kim DH, Kim JH, Chung MJ: A computer interface for the disabled using eye-gaze information, *Int J Human-friendly Welfare Robot Syst* **2**(3):22–27 (2002).
42. Yoo DH, Chung MJ: Vision-based eye gaze estimation system using robust pupil detection and corneal reflections, *Int J Human-friendly Welfare Robot Syst* **3**(4):2–8 (2002).
43. Glenstrup AJ, Engell-Nielsen T: *Eye Controlled Media: Present and Future State*, BS dissertation, Copenhagen Univ, 1995.
44. ASL504: Model 504, 2003, http://www.a-s-l.com/504_home.htm.
45. Ebisawa Y: Improved video-based eye-gaze detection method, *IEEE Trans Instrum Meas* **47**(4):948–955 (1998).
46. ASL501: Model 501, 2003, http://www.a-s-l.com/501_home.htm.
47. 3D VOG Video-oculography. http://www.smi.de/3d/index.htm.
48. Kim JH, Lee BR, Kim DH, Chung MJ: Eye-mouse system for people with motor disabilities, *Proc 8th Int Conf Rehabilitation Robotics (ICORR2003)*, Daejeon, Korea, 2003, pp 159–163.
49. Lee BR: *A Real-Time Eye-Gaze Tracking System Using Infrared Rays and Vision Sensor* (in Korean), MS dissertation, Korea Advanced Institute of Science and Technology, 2002.
50. Han JS, Bang WC, Bien ZZ: Feature set extraction algorithm based on soft computing techniques and its application to EMG pattern classification, *J Fuzzy Optim Decision Making* **1**:269–286 (2002).
51. Johnson DE: *Rapid Practical Designs of Active Filters*, Wiley, New York, 1975.
52. Lee K, Kwon DS: Sensors and actuators of wearable haptic master device for the disabled, *Proc Int 2000 IEEE/RSJ Conf Intelligent Robots and Systems (IROS)*, 2000, pp 371–376.
53. Lee K, Kwon DS: Wearable master device for spinal injured persons as a control device of motorized wheelchairs, *J Artif Life Robot* **4**(4):182–187 (2001).
54. Bien ZZ, Lee JJ, Kim BK, Lim JT, Kim JO, Lee H, Park KH, Jung JW, Kim DJ, Do JH et al: Robotic smart house to assist people with movement disabilities, *Auton Robots* Park KH, Bien Z, Lee JJ, Kim BK, Lim JT, Kim JO, Lee H, Stefanov DH, Kim DJ, Jung JW, Do JH, Seo KH,

Kim CH, Song WG, Lee WJ: Robotic smart house to assist people with movement disabilities, Autonomous Robots, **22**(2):183–198 (2007).

55. Thrun S, Bennewitz M, Burgard W, Cremers AB, Dellaert F, Fox D, Hähnel D, Rosenberg C, Roy N, Schulte J et al: MINERVA: A second-generation museum tour-guide robot, *Proc Int IEEE Conf Robotics and Automation*, 1999, pp 1999–2005.
56. NorthStar: http://www.evolution.com/products/northstar, Evolution Robotics, Inc.
57. Hong HS, Kang JW, Chung MJ: Work assistant mobile robot Type I and II for the handicapped in a real manufacturing environment, *Proc 6th Int Workshop Human-friendly Welfare Robotic Systems*, Daejeon, Korea, 2006, pp 309–314.
58. Hong HS, Jung SY, Jung JH, Lee BG, Kang JW, Park DJ, Chung MJ: Development of work assistant mobile robot system for the handicapped in a real manufacturing environment, *Proc 9th IEEE Int Conf Rehabilitation Robotics*, Chicago, 2005 pp 1001–1004.
59. Gomi H, Kawato M: Human arm stiffness and equilibrium-point trajectory during multi-joint movement, *Biol Cyber* **76**:163–171 (1997).

21

Robot Therapy at Elder Care Institutions: Effects of Long-term Interaction with Seal Robots

Takanori Shibata
Ministry of Economy, Trade and Industry, Tsukuba, Japan

Kazuyoshi Wada
Tokyo Metropolitan University, Tokyo, Japan

21.1 INTRODUCTION

Mental care of elderly people is an important issue for caregivers at elder care institutions. For that purpose, several types of recreation, such as singing songs, coloring, drawing pictures, and paper crafts are conducted, while caregivers try to communicate with elderly people as much as possible. However, some people are too embarrassed to sing songs, and others have difficulty moving their fingers when they try to draw pictures because of their illness or impairment. In addition, caregivers often have difficulty in communicating with the elderly because of a lack of common interests.

Interaction with animals has long been known to be emotionally beneficial to people. The effects of animals on humans have been applied to medical treatment. Especially in the United States, animal-assisted therapy and activities are now widely used in hospitals and nursing homes [1,2]. *Animal-assisted therapy* (AAT) has clear goals set out in therapy programs designed by physicians, nurses, or social workers, in cooperation with volunteers. In contrast, *Animal-assisted activities* (AAA) refers to patients interacting with animals without particular therapeutic goals, and depends on volunteers. AAT and AAA are expected to have three effects:

The Engineering Handbook of Smart Technology for Aging, Disability, and Independence,
Edited by A. Helal, M. Mokhtari and B. Abdulrazak
Copyright © 2008 John Wiley & Sons, Inc.

- Psychological effect (e.g., relaxation, motivation)
- Physiologic effect (e.g., improvement of vital signs)
- Social effect (e.g., stimulation of communication among inpatients and caregivers)

However, most hospitals and nursing homes, especially in Japan, do not accept animals, even though they acknowledge the positive effects of AAT and AAA. They are afraid of negative effects of animals on human beings, such as allergy, infection, bites, and scratches.

We have proposed robot therapy [3–20], using robots as a substitute for live animals in AAT and AAA. The major goals of this research are follows:

- Investigation of psychophysiologic influences of human–robot interaction, including long-term interaction
- Development of design theory for therapeutic robots
- Development of methodology of robot therapy suitable for the subjects

Here, *robot therapy* includes two cases: (1) *robot-assisted therapy*, which includes therapy programs designed by physicians, nurses, or social workers; and (2) *robot-assisted activity*, where patients interacting with robots without particular therapeutic goals. This activity does not depend on the help volunteers, so the facility staff usually monitor the activity.

A robot named Paro, designed to resemble a seal, has been developed for robot therapy (Fig. 21.1). We conducted an experiment of robot therapy in the pediatric ward of a university hospital [10]. The children's ages ranged from 2 to 15 years, and some of them had immunity problems (were immunocompromised). During *11 days* of observation, the children's moods improved on interaction with Paro, who encouraged the children to communicate with each other and caregivers. In one striking instance, a young autistic patient recovered his appetite and speech abilities during the weeks when Paro was at the hospital. In another case, a long-term inpatient experienced pain when she moved her body, arms, and legs, and could not move from her bed. However, when Paro was given to her, she smiled and was willing to stroke this seal robot. A nurse said that Paro had a rehabilitative function, both physically and mentally.

We have also used Paro for robot therapy among the elderly at a day service center for *5 weeks* and at a health service facility for the aged for *3 weeks* [11–15]. Interaction with Paro improved their moods, making them more active and communicative with each other and caregivers. Results of urinary tests showed that interaction with Paro reduced stress among the elderly. In one interesting instance, at the day service center, an elderly woman who rarely talked with others began communicating after interacting with Paro. In another example, at the health service facility, an elderly man who was a cantankerous, difficult person and with whom caregivers could hardly communicate, liked Paro very much. He often laughed and sang to it, and made the people around him-laugh as well. The caregivers were surprised by the change.

In addition, the neuropsychological effects of Paro on patients with dementia were assessed by analyzing their EEG tracings. The results showed their cortical neurons activity to be improved by interaction with Paro, especially for those patients who liked the robot [16].

Meanwhile, other studies have been conducted using questionnaires distributed at exhibitions held in six countries; Japan, the United Kingdom, Sweden, Italy, Korea, and

Brunei, in order to investigate how people evaluate the robot. The results showed that the seal robot was widely accepted on a subjective level [17–19].

As for other research groups, Dautenhahn has used mobile robots and robotic dolls for therapy of autistic children [21]. Additionally, other animal robots (e.g., as the imaginary animal robot Furby, the dog robot AIBO [22], the cat robot NeCoRo.) have been released by several companies. Robot therapy using these robots has also been attempted [23–27]. For example, Yokoyama used AIBO in a pediatric ward, and observed the interaction between children and AIBO [23]. He pointed out that when people meet AIBO for the first time, they are interested in it for a while. However, relaxation effects such as those obtained from petting a real dog are never evoked from AIBO. Kanamori et al. examined effects of AIBO on elderly residents in a nursing home [26]. They found that the stress levels of these subjects decreased after one hour of interaction with AIBO by measuring hormone content in the saliva, and that their feelings of loneliness or isolation improved after 20 sessions during a 7-week period. Tamura et al. also used AIBO with dementia patients in a 5-min occupational therapy session and compared the AIBO effects with those of a motor-driven stuffed toy dog [27]. They found that AIBO encouraged interaction to a lesser extent and required more intervention from the occupational therapist.

The commercially produced robots described above are easily mishandled and broken by interaction with people because they were not originally designed for therapy. Therefore, it is difficult to use those robots in robot therapy on a long-term basis.

In this chapter, we discuss the application of the seal robots for psychological enrichment of elderly people at a health service facility for the aged, by observing their psychological and social effects for *one year*.

21.2 SEAL ROBOT: PARO

The seal robot, Paro, is shown in Figure 21.1. Its appearance is modeled from a baby harp seal, and its surface is covered with pure white fur. Ubiquitous surface tactile sensors are inserted between the hard inner skeleton and the fur to create a soft, natural feel and to measure strength and position of human contact with Paro [20]. Paro is equipped with

FIGURE 21.1 Seal robot, Paro.

the four primary senses: sight (light sensor), audition (determination of sound source direction and speech recognition), balance, and the tactility, described above. Its moving parts are as follows: vertical and horizontal neck movements, front and rear paddle movements, and independent movement of each eyelid, which is important for creating facial expressions. Its weight is about 2.7 kg. Its operating time with the installed battery (NiHM, 9.6V, 1500mAh) is about 1.5 h. However, Paro can continue operating during use by employing a charger that mimics a human infant's pacifier.

Paro has a behavior generation system (Fig. 21.2) consisting of two hierarchical layers of processes: proactive and reactive. These two layers generate three types of behaviors: proactive, reactive, and physiological.

21.2.1 Proactive Behavior

Paro has two layers to generate its proactive behavior: a behavior-planning layer and a behavior-generating layer. By addressing its internal states of stimuli, desires, and a rhythm, Paro generates proactive behavior.

21.2.1.1 Behavior-Planning Layer

This laser consists of a state transition network based on the internal states of Paro and Paro's desire produced by its internal rhythm. Paro has internal states that can be represented by terms indicating emotions. Each state has a numerical level that is changed by stimulation. The state also decays in time. Interaction changes the internal states and creates the character of Paro. The behavior-planning layer sends basic behavioral patterns to the behavior-generating layer. The basic behavioral patterns include several poses and movements. Here, although the term *proactive* is used, Paro's proactive behavior is very primitive compared with that of human beings. We implemented a behavior in Paro similar to that of a live seal.

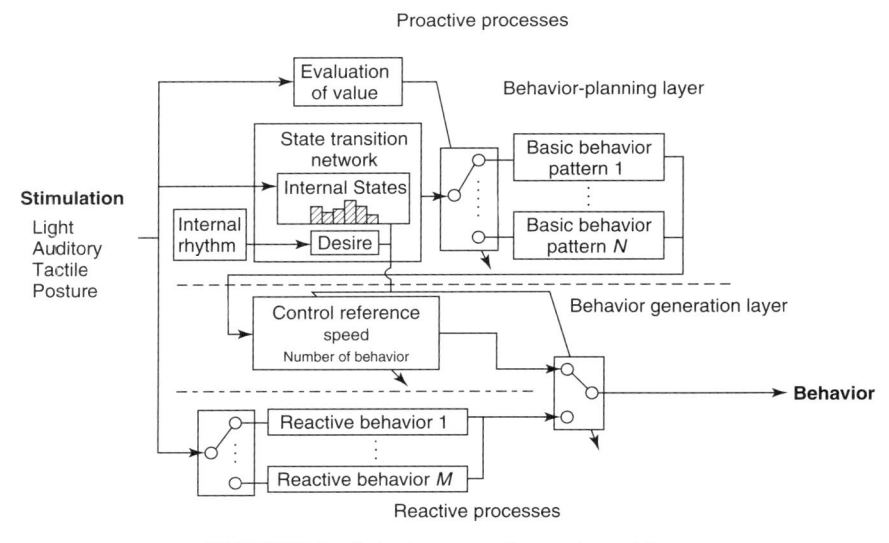

FIGURE 21.2 Behavior generation system of Paro.

21.2.1.2 Behavior-Generating Layer

This layer generates control references for each actuator to perform the determined behavior. The control reference depends on magnitude of the internal states and their variation. For example, parameters can change the speed of movement and the number of instances of the same behavior. Therefore, although the number of basic patterns is finite, the number of emerging behaviors is infinite because of the varying number of parameters. This creates the life-like behavior of Paro. In addition, to gain attention, the behavior generation layer adjusts parameters of priority of reactive behaviors and proactive behaviors according to the magnitude of the internal states. This function contributes to the behavioral situation of Paro, and makes it difficult for a subject to predict Paro's action.

21.2.1.3 Long-Term Memory

Paro has a function of reinforcement learning, which has a positive value on preferred stimulation such as stroking. It also has a negative value on undesired stimulation such as beating. Paro assigns values in terms of the relationship between stimulation and behavior. The users are prevented from changing its behavior program manually; however, Paro can be gradually shaped to the preferred behavior by its owner. In addition, Paro can memorize a frequently articulated word as its new name. The users can give their preferred name through natural interaction.

21.2.2 Reactive Behavior

Paro reacts to stimulation. For example, when it hears a loud sound, Paro pays attention to it and looks in the direction of the sound. There are several patterns in which stimulation and reaction are combined. These patterns are assumed as conditioned and unconscious behavior.

21.2.3 Physiologic Behavior

Paro has a diurnal rhythm. It has several spontaneous needs, such as sleep, that are based on this rhythm.

21.3 ROBOT THERAPY FOR THE ELDERLY

We have applied Paro as to robot therapy for elderly people at a health service facility for the aged in order to investigate its long-term effects on the elderly. The facility provides services such as institutional residence, daily care, and rehabilitation for elderly people whose condition of impairment or disease are stable, not necessitating hospitalization. People who stay there receive daily care and instruction on how to live independently.

Figure 21.3 shows activities of these people durig their free time. They communicated little, and the atmosphere was gloomy. In addition, caregivers had difficulty in communicating with them because of a lack of common topics or interests.

Before starting robot therapy, we explained the purpose and procedure to the elderly people and received their consent. Symptoms varied or were unclear, so we questioned the nursing staff to determine who would participate. Final subjects numbered 14, all of whom were women, aged 77–98. Thirteen subjects presented dementia, in which case, the nursing staff judged the dementia level of each subject in terms of the revised

FIGURE 21.3 Scene of usual activity of elderly people at a health service facility for the aged.

Hasegawa dementia scale (HDS-R). Their dementia levels were as follows: nondementia, 1 person; slight degree, 4 people; moderate degree, 5 people; and somewhat high degree, 4 people.

21.3.1 Method of Interaction

Two seal robots were given to the elderly people at the facility twice per week. They interacted with the robots for about one hour at a time. We prepared a desk for the robots in the center of the table, and people assembled around it. Since not all subjects could interact with the robots at the same time, we had them take turns for equal periods of time. In addition, once every 2 weeks, we asked them to groom Paro using a special spray cleaner. They helped clean up Paro during their activity sessions with this robot.

21.3.2 Methods of Evaluation

In order to investigate the effects on the elderly people before and after interaction with Paro, the following two types of data and additional information were collected:

- Face scale (Fig. 21.4) [28]
- Geriatric depression scale (GDS) [29]
- Comments of nursing staff

The original face scale contains 20 drawings of a single face, arranged in serial order by rows, with each face depicting a slightly different mood state. A graphic artist was consulted so that the faces would be portrayed as genderless and ethnicity-neutral. Subtle changes in the eyes, eyebrows, and mouth were used to represent slightly different levels of mood. The faces were arranged in decreasing order of mood and numbered from 1 to 20, with 1 representing the most positive mood and 20 representing the most negative mood. However, sometimes the subjects were confused by the original face scale because it contained too many similar images. Thus, the scale was simplified by using seven

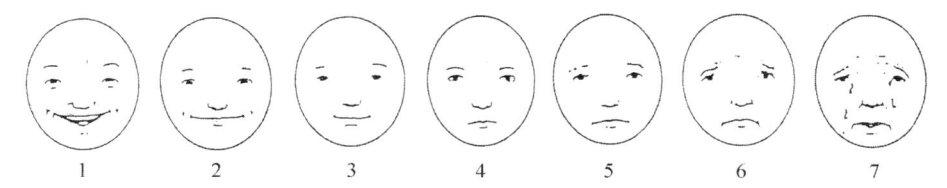

FIGURE 21.4 Face scale, ranging from very happy (1) to very sad (7). Each subject was asked to select the facial expression (by number) that most closely reflected her mood.

images, numbered 1, 4, 7, 10, 13, 16, and 19 from the original set. As the examiner pointed at the faces, the following instructions were given to each subject: "The faces above range from very happy at the left to very sad at the right. Check the face that best shows the way you feel right now."

The original GDS consists of 30 items developed from 100 popular questions commonly used to diagnose depression. A 15-item short version has also been validated. In this research, we used the short version that was translated into Japanese by Muraoka, et al. [30] The scale is in a Yes/No format. Each answer counts 1 point; scores greater than 5 indicate probable depression.

The face scale and GDS were applied at 4 weeks and 1 week before Paro was introduced, and then every 2 weeks thereafter. In particular the face scale was applied before and after interaction with Paro. As a statistics analysis, Wilcoxon's sign rank sum test was applied to the scores before and after interaction with Paro for each week by using SPSS 12.0 for Windows.

21.3.3 Results of Robot Therapy

"Hello, hello," "Come on Paro," "You are so cute"—the elderly interacted with Paro joyfully from the first day, speaking to, stroking, and hugging it. Sometimes, they kissed it with a smile (Fig. 21.5). Paro became a common topic among the elderly people and their caregivers (Fig. 21.6). They talked about its appearance, different kinds of animals, moods, and so on. Comments included "Its eyes are so big," "It looks sleepy," and so on. The elderly people came to love the Paro very much and gave them new names: "Maru" and "Maro." Even while cleaning Paro, they enjoyed and talked to it, with remarks such as "You are more beautiful, Maru." Later, 3 months after the initial introduction, we added one more seal robot to the facility because many other elderly people at the facility had voluntarily joined in the activity. The "new Paro" was given the name "Hana-chan" by the elderly. Moreover, as the original Paro was so widely accepted by caregivers that they made a permanent home for it in the facility (Fig. 21.7). These heartwarming interactions with Paro were observed for over one year. In addition, thanks to their thoughtful grooming, Paro remained as clean as a brand-new robot.

Face-scale and GDS data were obtained from eight subjects for 5 months. Table 21.1 lists their basic attributes. The average face scale scores before interaction varied from 3.3 to 2.0 over a 5-month period (Fig. 21.8). However, scores after interaction were almost always lower than those before interaction for each week (except on November 29). In particular, a statistically significant difference was noted on November 15 (Wilcoxon's test: $p < 0.05$). Therefore, Paro improved their moods over 4 months.

FIGURE 21.5 An elderly person kissing the seal robot.

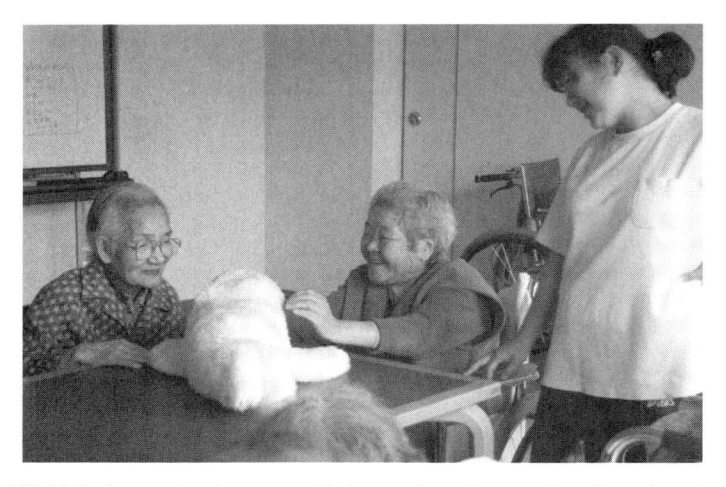

FIGURE 21.6 Interaction between elderly people and a caregiver through seal robot.

Figure 21.9 shows the GDS results for the same period. Scores after October were improved, compared with those before the introduction of Paro. We concluded that when Paro took root in the facility, with the participation of most of the elderly people at the facility (including those not asked to participate in the study), Paro was effective in improving or eliminating depression among those people.

After November, many subjects couldn't participate in the robot therapy because of hospitalization, poor health, or departure from the facility. It then became difficult to analyze the data statistically. Therefore, we introduce several case studies.

Figures 21.10 and 21.11 show the face scale and GDS scores of an 89-year-old-woman who exhibited symptoms of dementia (slight degree of HDS-R) but was sociable and

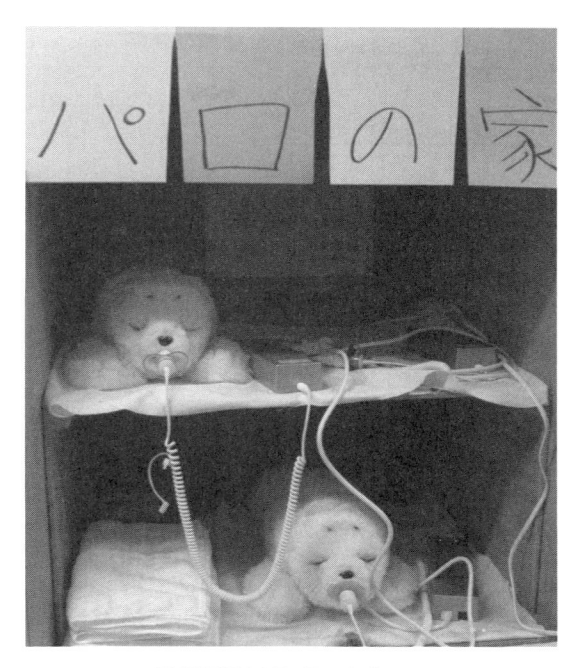

FIGURE 21.7 Paro's home.

TABLE 21.1 Basic Attributes of Eight Elderly People

Sex		All women
Age (average ± standard deviation)		90.3 ± 4.5
Level of dementia (HDS-R)	Slight degree	4
	Somewhat high degree	4

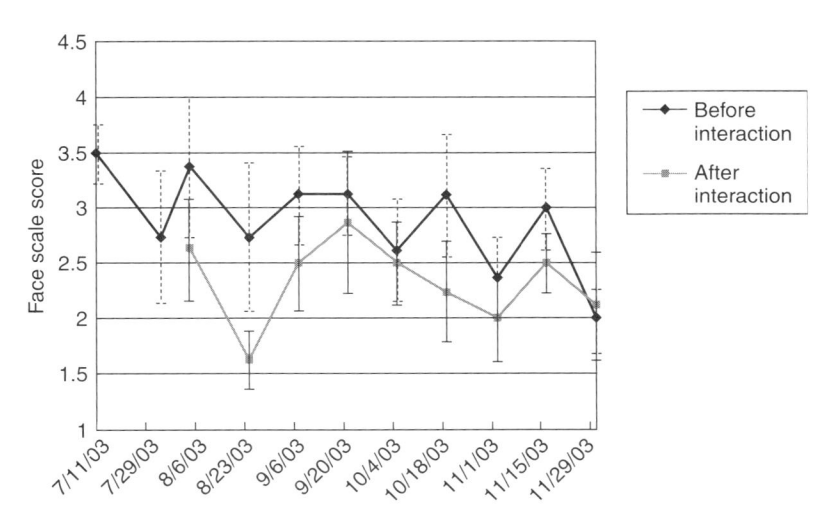

FIGURE 21.8 Variation in average face scale scores of eight elderly people over 5 months. (Score: 1 = best mood, 7 = worst mood.)

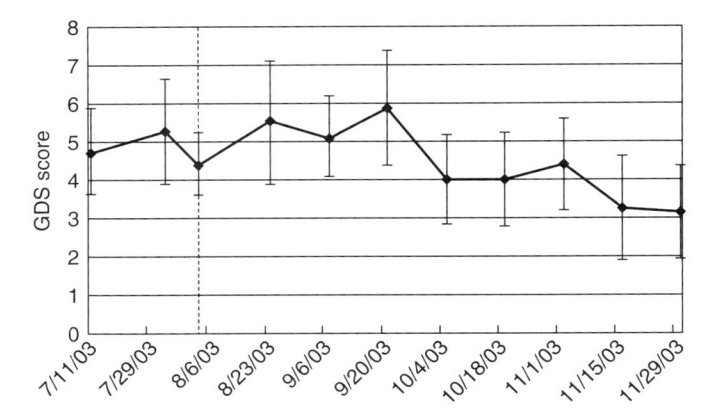

FIGURE 21.9 Variation in average GDS scores of eight subjects over 5 months. (Score: healthy condition ⇐ 5 < probable depression.)

comparatively independent. On the first day of the interaction with Paro, she was slightly nervous about the experiment. However, she soon came to like Paro. She treated it like her child or grandchild. Her face scale scores after interaction were always lower than before interaction after the first day (Fig. 21.10). Unfortunately, she was hospitalized during December 10–26. The day after her discharge from the hospital, she could participate in the activity with Paro, and told it: "I was lonely, Paro. I wanted to see you again." She was stroking and whispering to Paro for long time. Paro became an indispensable presence for her. Her GDS score then improved (Fig. 21.11). To the present, she has continued to join in the activity and willingly interacted with Paro.

Caregivers commented that interaction with Paro made the elderly people laugh and become more active. For example, their facial expressions changed, softening, and

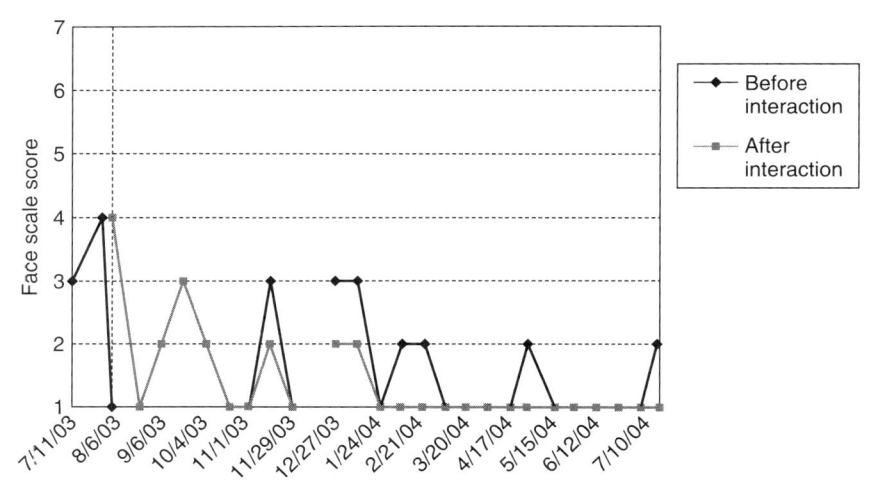

FIGURE 21.10 Variation in face scale scores of one subject over one year. (Score: 1 = best mood, 7 = worst mood.)

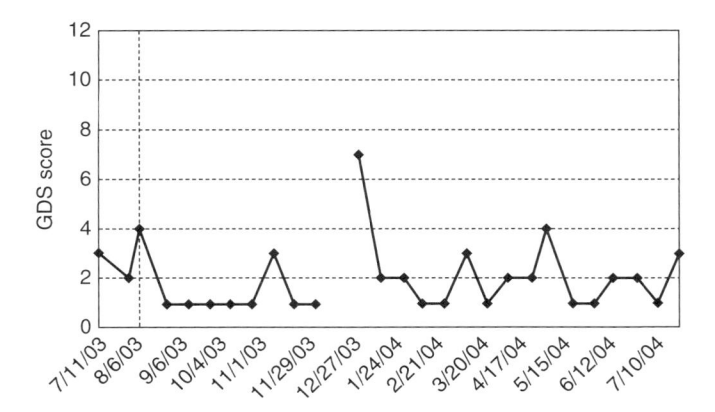

FIGURE 21.11 Variation in GDS scores of a subject for one year. (Score: healthy condition ⇐ 5 < probable depression.)

brightening. On the day of activity (robot therapy), they looked forward to Paro, sitting down in their seats before beginning the interaction. Some people who usually stayed in their rooms came out and willingly joined in the activity. In addition, Paro encouraged the people to communicate, both with each other and with caregivers, by becoming their common topic of conversation. Thus, the general atmosphere became brighter.

21.4 DISCUSSION

Before the experiment, most residents spent their free time on their beds, or sitting in a chair only in the diningroom. They rarely communicated with each other. Against this, caregivers tried to speak to the residents actively and provided recreation such as painting, origami, and singing. In addition, volunteers visited the facility at odd intervals. However, the caregivers felt difficulty in communicating with the residents because of a lack of common topics or interests. Furthermore, many residents could not participate in the recreation because of their physical disabilities (e.g., paralysis and shaking of fingers/hands). In addition, some people felt awkward or embarrassed at these recreational sessions. As for the comfort activities provided by volunteers, most activities (e.g., musical performances, conjuring tricks) constituted passive activity for the residents. The activities in which the residents actively participated were very few. Under these conditions, the people were exposed to high risk of depression and progress of dementia. The results of this research showed that animal robot therapy has a high potential for preventing these problems.

Yokoyama referred to the studies by Reeves and Nass [30] and said that if people unconsciously treat computers or computerized objects as live creatures, such as human beings, they would confuse animal robots with real animals, and the psychological effects of real animals would be similar to those that might emerge through interaction with robots [23]. In addition, regarding the differences between AIBO and real animals, they [31] pointed out that AIBO could evoke transitory stimuli, but that it is difficult to build up a comfortable and stable relationship that is obtained through owning animals for long time.

Furthermore, he said that a cat robot named NeCoRo covered with soft fur elicited responses that were more steady than exciting in comparison with AIBO. However, more common, familiar animal robots, such as those resembling a dog or cat, are easily compared with real ones. In these cases people evaluate the robots more strictly; besides, there may be preconceptions such as fear or dislike of dogs or cats.

In contrast, Paro's appearance is designed using a baby harp seal, a relatively unfamiliar animal, as a model. The seal is widely accepted beyond barriers such as cultural differences and borders between countries [17–19]. We consider that a bond similar to that between animals and human beings were constructed between the elderly and Paro because they had enjoyed playing with Paro and its psychological effects had been shown for one year. Long-term interaction is important for that bond. No breakdown or accident occurred during the observation period. Paro fulfills the durability and safety requirements of a robot, which are very important when it interacts with human beings on a long-term basis.

21.5 CONCLUSION

We have used seal robots, Paro in RAA for elderly people at a health service facility for the aged since August 2003. The results showed that interaction with Paro improved their moods and depression, and then the effects showed up through one year. Urinary tests were conducted to establish the physiologic effects. The details will be described in future studies.

This experiment is still on-going. We will report more long-term influences on the elderly in the future. Moreover, we plan further experiments and research on different conditions and situations and the relationship between function of a mentally committed robot and its effects on the elderly in robot therapy.

ACKNOWLEDGMENT

We would like to thank the staff members of the health service facility for the aged, Toyoura, for their cooperation to this experiment.

REFERENCES

1. Baum MM, Bergstrom N, Langston NF, Thoma L: Physiological effects of human/companion animal bonding, *Nurs Res* **33**(3):126–129 (1984).
2. Gammonley J, Yates J: Pet projects animal assisted therapy in nursing homes, *J Gerontol Nurs* **17**(1):12–15, (1991).
3. Shibata T et al: Emotional robot for intelligent system—artificial emotional creature project, *Proc 5th IEEE Int Workshop on ROMAN*, 1996, pp 466–471.
4. Shibata T, Irie R: Artificial emotional creature for human-robot interaction—a new direction for intelligent system, *Proc IEEE/ASME Int Conf AIM'97*, Paper 47, June 1997.
5. Shibata T et al: Artificial emotional creature for human-machine interaction, *Proc IEEE Int Conf SMC*, 1997, pp 2269–2274.

6. Tashima T, Saito S, Osumi M, Kudo T, Shibata T: Interactive pet robot with emotion model, *Proc 16th Annual Conf RSJ*, 1998, Vol 1, pp 11, 12.
7. Shibata T, Tashima T, Tanie K: Emergence of emotional behavior through physical interaction between human and robot, *Proc IEEE Int Conf Robotics and Automation*, 1999.
8. Shibata T, Tashima T, Tanie K: Subjective interpretation of emotional behavior through physical interaction between human and robot, *Proc Systems, Man, and Cybernetics*, 1999, pp 1024–1029.
9. Shibata T, Tanie K: Influence of a-priori knowledge in subjective interpretation and evaluation by short-term interaction with mental commit robot, *Proc IEEE Int Conf Intelligent Robot and Systems*, 2000.
10. Shibata T et al: Mental commit robot and its application to therapy of children, *Proc IEEE/ASME Int Conf AIM'01*, Paper 182, July 2001.
11. Wada K, Shibata T, Saito T, Tanie K: Effects of robot assisted activity for elderly people and nurses at a day service center, *Proc IEEE* **92**(11):1780–1788 (2004).
12. Wada K, Shibata T, Saito T, Tanie K: Analysis of factors that bring mental effects to elderly people in robot assisted activity, *Proc IEEE Int Conf Intelligent Robot and Systems*, 2002.
13. Saito T, Shibata T, Wada K, Tanie K: Examination of change of stress reaction by urinary tests of elderly before and after introduction of mental commit robot to an elderly institution, *Proc 7th Int Symp Artificial Life and Robotics*, 2002, Vol 1, pp 316–319.
14. Wada K, Shibata T, Saito T, Tanie K: Psychological and social effects to elderly people by robot assisted activity at a health services facility for the aged, *Proc 1st Joint Int Conf Soft Computing and Intelligent Systems and 3rd Int Symp Advanced Intelligent Systems*, Paper 23Q1-3, 2002.
15. Saito T, Shibata T, Wada K, Tanie K: Change of stress reaction by introduction of mental commit robot to a health services facility for the aged, *Proc 1st Joint Int Conf Soft Computing and Intelligent Systems and 3rd Int Symp Advanced Intelligent Systems*, Paper 23Q1-5, 2002.
16. Wada K, Shibata T, Musha T, Kimura S: Effects of robot therapy for demented patients evaluated by EEG, *Proc IEEE/RSJ Int Conf Intelligent Robot and Systems*, 2005, pp 2205–2210.
17. Shibata T, Mitsui T, Wada K, Tanie K: Subjective evaluation of seal robot: Paro—tabulation and analysis of questionnaire results, *J Robot Mechatron* **14**(1):13–19 (2002).
18. Shibata T, Wada K, Tanie K: Tabulation and analysis of questionnaire results of subjective evaluation of seal robot in Japan, U.K., Sweden, and Italy, *Proc IEEE Int Conf Robotics and Automation*, 2004, pp 1387–1392.
19. Shibata T: An overview of human interactive robots for psychological enrichment, *Proc IEEE* **92**(11):1749–1758 (2004).
20. Shibata T: Ubiquitous surface tactile sensor, *Proc 1st IEEE Technical Exhibition Based Conf Robotics and Automation*, 2004, pp 5, 6.
21. Werry I, Dautenhahn K: Applying mobile robot technology to the rehabilitation of autistic children, *Proc 7th Int Symp Intelligent Robotic Systems*, 1999, pp 265–272.
22. Fujita M, Kitano H: A development of an autonomous quadruped robot for robot entertainment, *Auton Robots* **5**:7–18 (1998).
23. Yokoyama A: The possibility of the psychiatric treatment with a robot as an intervention—from the viewpoint of animal therapy, *Proc 1st Joint Int Conf Soft Computing and Intelligent Systems and 3rd Int Symp Advanced Intelligent Systems*, Paper 23Q1-1, 2002.
24. Libin E, Libin A: Robotherapy: Definition, assessment, and case study, *Proc 8th Int Conf Virtual Systems and Multimedia*, 2002, pp 906–915.

25. Ohkubo E et al: Studies on necessary condition of companion robot in the RAA application, *Proc IEEE Int Symp Computational Intelligence in Robots and Automation*, 2003, pp 101–106.
26. Kanamori M et al: Maintenance and improvement of quality of life among elderly patients using a pet-type robot, *Nippon Ronen Igakkai Zasshi* **39**(2):214–218 (2002) (in Japanese).
27. Tamura T et al: Is an entertainment robot useful in the care of elderly people with severe dementia? *J Gerontol Med Sci* **59A**(1):83–85 (2004).
28. Lorish CD, Maisiak R: The face scale: A brief, nonverbal method for assessing patient mood, *Arthritis Rheum* **29**(7):906–909 (1986).
29. Yesavage JA: Geriatric depression scale, *J Psychopharmacol Bull* **24**(4), (1988).
30. Muraoka Y et al: The physical and psychological and social background factor of elderly depression in the community, *Japanese Journal of Geriatric Psychiatry* **7**(4):397–407 (1996) (in Japanese)
31. Reeves B, Nass C: *The Media Equation: How People Treat Computers, Television, and New Media Like Real People and Places*, Stanford Univ Center for the Study, 1996.

22

Prostheses: Human Limbs and Their Artificial Replacements

Richard F. ff. Weir
Northwestern University

An artificial or prosthetic limb is fitted to restore some of the function and appearance lost as a result of amputation. There have been many attempts to design fully articulated arms and hands in an effort to recreate the full function of the hand. While the ultimate goal of upper-extremity prosthetics research is the meaningful, subconscious control of a multi-functional prosthetic arm and/or hand—a true replacement for the lost limb—the current state-of-the-art electric prosthetic hands are generally single-degree-of-freedom (opening and closing) devices usually implemented with myoelectric control (electric signals generated as a byproduct of normal muscle contraction). Current prosthetic arms requiring multidegree-of-freedom control most often use sequential control. Locking mechanisms and/or special switch signals are used to change control from one degree of freedom (DOF) to another. As currently implemented, sequential control of multiple motions is slow; consequently transradial prostheses are generally limited to just opening and closing of the hand, greatly limiting the function of these devices (Fig. 22.1). Persons with recent hand amputations expect modern hand prostheses to be like actual human hands. Because these devices fail to meet some user's expectations, they are frequently rejected [1]. The area of upper-limb prosthetics is dominated by considerations of prosthesis control, weight and power, while the area of lower-limb prosthetics is dominated by considerations of passive mechanisms, material properties, weight, and limb–prosthesis fit.

The Engineering Handbook of Smart Technology for Aging, Disability, and Independence, Edited by A. Helal, M. Mokhtari and B. Abdulrazak
Copyright © 2008 John Wiley & Sons, Inc.

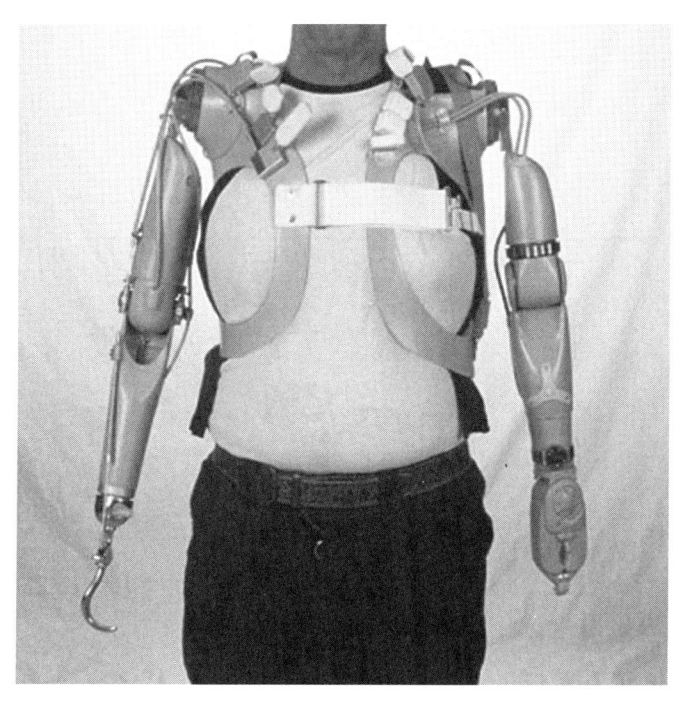

FIGURE 22.1 Current state-of-the-art prosthesis for a man with bilateral shoulder disarticulation amputations.

22.1 UPPER-LIMB PROSTHESES

The task of replacing a lost hand or arm is a daunting one. There are 50 muscles acting on the forearm and hand: 5 controlling forearm pronation–supination; 7 controlling wrist motion; 18 controlling digital flexion–extension; and 20 small muscles within the hand controlling small, precision movements [2]. The human hand has 27 major bones, and at least 18 joint articulations with ≥ 27 DOF. The arm contributes another 7 DOF. Even if the hand is replaced with a simple 1-DOF gripper, as is usually the case, this still remains an extremely challenging problem. The primary role of the human arm is to position the hand in space. The control of the arm is directed at controlling the position of the hand. Even though humans control their arms with what appears to be great simplicity, this is a highly complex and demanding task. Consider the example of the backhoe operator. The backhoe is essentially a mechanical arm that is under the control of the operator. When working this mechanical arm, the operator uses both arms to pull levers, both feet to press pedals to operate the arm, and both eyes to monitor the task being performed by the digger. All this attention is needed, just to control a single mechanical arm! Now consider the plight of a person who has lost both arms at a high level (e.g., above the elbow), and you begin to have some appreciation of the task that a limbless person faces in controlling an artificial (prosthetic) arm or arms. The problem of providing persons with artificial arms that are anywhere near as functional as the arms that were lost has been called one of the most challenging problems of medical engineering.

22.1.1 Design Constraints

Robotics concepts have had little impact on commercial prosthetics because of the severe physical constraints required for a prosthetic device to be successful. In any prosthetic device, size, weight, and power are all at a premium, far more so than in the related fields of robot or manipulator design. Limb replacements, it is thought, should be anthropomorphic in general shape, size, and outline. *Anthropomorphic* does not necessarily imply that the artificial limb look exactly like its human counterpart, but it does mean that any replacement should have similar kinematics and kinetics; that is, there should be a joint that operates like an elbow joint where one would expect to see an elbow joint, and the various limb segments should be of a size consistent with that of a normal human being.

Contrary to what one might think, an artificial limb should be lighter than the limb that it replaces. To be effective, artificial arms should be worn by the user for periods in excess of 12 h per day. The lack of an intimate connection between amputee and limb replacement means that the prosthesis will be perceived as an external load and therefore as something that must be carried.

Power must be constrained in prostheses. If the power source is the amputee, namely, the bodypower, then the prosthesis should not require excessive effort so as not to tire the user over the course of the day (frictional losses need to be minimized). If the artificial limb is externally powered (i.e., uses a power source other than the body, usually electric storage) the limb should be able to run all day from the same power source without needing to be recharged. In addition, it is desirable for the power source to be contained within the prosthesis. Electric batteries are the main source of energy for modern prosthetic arms, although pneumatic gas cylinders have been used. Both are heavy and occupy space. The problem of portable prosthesis power is analogous to the power issues in the laptop computer industry, where a major contributor to the weight of a portable computer is the battery.

The relative importance of function versus appearance is another issue that faces the amputee, surgeon, and prosthetist when deciding on a particular type of prosthesis, if any. Often there is a tradeoff to be made between function and appearance. Some amputees may be solely concerned with the visual presentation and reject a body-powered prosthesis because of the unsightly appearance of the control harness or of a hook-shaped terminal device. Others might find the function provided by these devices to outweigh poor appearance. Choice of prosthesis is ultimately based on many psychological and practical factors. Other factors affecting choice are age, sex, occupation, and degree of physical activity of the amputee; the amputee's attitude toward training; the type of amputation involved; and whether it is unilateral or bilateral limb loss.

The level of amputation is an important element in the restoration of functional control over a prosthesis. The higher the level of amputation, the fewer the available control sources, but the greater the amount of function that must be replaced. A *control source* is the means used by the amputee to control a specific function or degree of freedom of the prosthesis, such as the opening and closing of an artificial hand. Childress [3] presented the following attributes of prosthesis control as desirable. While some of these attributes may be difficult, if not impossible to achieve in practice, they are seen as desirable goals:

1. *Low Mental Loading or Subconscious Control.* The prosthesis should be such that the user can employ it without undue mental involvement. The prosthesis should serve the user; the user should not be the servant of the prosthesis.

2. *User-Friendly or Simple to Learn to Use.* Any device should be intuitive and natural. An amputee should be able to learn to use the prosthesis quickly and easily.
3. *Independence in Multifunctional Control.* Control of any function or degree of freedom should be executable without interfering with the other control functions of a multifunctional prosthesis.
4. *Simultaneous, Coordinated Control of Multiple Functions (Parallel Control).* The ability to coordinate multiple functions simultaneously in effective and meaningful ways without violating the first and third attributes.
5. *Direct Access and Instantaneous Response (Speed of Response).* All functions, if possible, should be directly accessible to the user and should respond immediately to input commands.
6. *No Sacrifice of Human Functional Ability.* The prosthesis should be used to supplement, not subtract from, available function. The control system should not encumber any natural movement that an amputee can apply to useful proposes.
7. *Natural Appearance.* Movements that appear mechanical in nature attract unwanted attention in social situations and may not be pleasing to the eye.

Ultimately it is the control constraints (shortage of independent control sources) rather than the physical constraints that impede the development of today's prosthetic systems. It is for this reason that upper-limb prosthetics is often dominated by considerations of control.

The presently available terminal devices have a single degree of freedom (opening and closing). Prosthetic arms requiring multi-DOF control use sequential control with locking mechanisms to switch control from one degree of freedom to the next. Generally, since vision is the primary source of feedback, the greatest number of functions that are controlled in parallel is two; otherwise the mental loading becomes excessive. In spite of these limitations, many amputees become skilled users of these devices and show surprising adaptability and inventiveness in overcoming functional challenges faced by them in everyday life.

22.1.2 Prehension or Grasp

The reduction of the hand to a single-degree-of-freedom (1-DOF) terminal device in most artificial limbs was done to reduce the number of control sites required to control prehension.

Numerous different classifications of hand prehension have been defined; some of the literature is listed in the REFERENCES section at the end of this chapter [4–7]. But the six patterns as defined by Keller et al. [7] have endured the test of time and are the most widely accepted in the field of prosthetics:

1. Tip prehension
2. Lateral prehension
3. Palmar prehension
4. Cylindrical prehension
5. Spherical prehension
6. Hook prehension

Tip prehension, lateral prehension, and palmar prehension are primarily the function of the thumb working in opposition with the index and middle fingers. Tip prehension, or fingernail pinch, is used mainly to grasp small objects. In lateral prehension the thumb holds an object against the side of the index finger, as is the case when using a key. In palmar prehension (sometimes referred to as *tridigital pinch* or "three-jaw chuck") the thumb opposes either a single finger or two or more fingers. This is the grip most commonly used in daily activities. Cylindrical and spherical prehension are examples of power grasps as described by Napier [6]. Power grasps use all the fingers of the hand to provide an encompassing grasp that firmly stabilizes the object being held. Hook prehension is achieved by flexing the fingers into a hook; the thumb is either alongside the index finger or used to lock the object held. Carrying a briefcase is a good illustration of this kind of prehension.

The grip of the hand is further improved by the ability of the hand to passively adapt to the shape of an object grasped. A grasped object depresses, or indents, the skin and underlying soft tissues of the hand, at first meeting with little reaction. Consequently, the soft tissue adapts easily to the shape of the object grasped. However, the mechanical properties of the soft tissue are quite nonlinear, and the conforming tissue becomes turgid as pressure is increased. This is demonstrated by blanching on the sides of the pads of the fingertips if sufficient force is applied. The rise in tissue stiffness after conformation to shape enables objects to be grasped with great security. This feature of the human hand would seem to be useful for robotic and prosthetic systems.

22.1.3 Prehension with Prostheses

The finding by Keller et al. [5], that palmar prehension was the most frequently used pattern has meant that most prosthetic terminal devices incorporate this pattern as the dominant pattern. The persistence of this configuration in prosthetic hand designs and its general acceptance over the years tends to support this finding. The passive adaptability, afforded by the soft tissue of the hand, is mimicked, to some extent, by lining the device with a soft plastic and covering it with a cosmetic glove. To adequately reproduce all six prehension patterns in an artificial hand-like prehensor requires 3 or 4 DOF: 2 DOF for the thumb, 1 DOF for the index finger, and 1 DOF for the remaining three fingers. This DOF number cannot at present be controlled in a meaningful way owing to the lack of suitable control sites.

22.1.3.1 Hand-Like Prehensors

As was mentioned previously, the prosthetic hand or prehensor of today is a 1-DOF device that opens and closes. Commercially available hand-like prehensors are predominantly externally powered. The de facto standard hand-like prosthesis is a mechanism manufactured by Otto Bock Orthopaedic, Inc. Hugh Steeper (Roehampton, England), Ltd., also manufacture devices for the adult. Child-size hands are also available, and there is a trend today to fit young children with congenital or traumatic below-elbow deficiencies as early as possible. A number of child-size hands are manufactured by Variety Village, Otto Bock Orthopaedic Inc., and Hugh Steeper Ltd., among others. For reviews, see Michael [8] and Heckathorne [9].

Palmar prehension in these hand-like prehensors is achieved by using monocoque (single-joint) fingers that are fixed in slight flexion at a position approximating the interphalangeal joint. The resulting finger shape also creates a concave inner prehension surface that can be used to provide cylindrical prehension [9].

Body-powered, hand-like prehensors are available but few are used effectively as active terminal devices. Problems of frictional loss and poor mechanical advantage in the hand mechanism limit pinch force. In addition, restriction of motion by the glove and the bulkiness of the hand's shape, which blocks vision, all serve to diminish the effectiveness of these devices [10].

22.1.3.2 Body-Powered, Non-Hand-Like Prehensors

Non-hand-like prehensors have the advantage of being able to incorporate many of the previously mentioned prehension patterns into a 1-DOF device. The split hook is an example of such a prehensor. It can perform tip, palmar, lateral, cylindrical, and hook prehension. This in large part accounts for the popularity of split-hook prosthesis despite its less-than-aesthetic appearance. Supplied by the Hosmer-Dorrance Corp. and Otto Bock Orthopaedic, Inc., split hooks are available in many variations on the basic theme. For a review, see Fryer and Michael [10].

22.1.3.3 Externally Powered, Non-Hand-Like Prehensors

The Hosmer-Dorrance NU-VA Synergetic prehensor and the Motion Control work prosthesis both try to capitalize on the success of the split hook. They use a split hook in an externally powered configuration. Other commercially available, externally powered, non-hand-like prehensors include the Otto Bock "Greifer". The NU-VA Synergetic Prehensor, the Otto Bock Greifer, and the Steeper Powered Gripper incorporate many of the previously mentioned prehension patterns. They can perform the equivalent of the tip, palmar, lateral, and cylindrical patterns. For a review, see Heckathorne, [9].

22.1.3.4 Passive Prostheses

There is a final class of terminal devices that do not offer prehensile function. Devices in this class, usually hands, are regarded as passive or passively functional prostheses. They have no moving parts and require no cables or batteries for operation. They are typically lightweight and reliable. Generic (standard) passive hand prostheses may consist of a cosmetic outer glove over a soft plastic hand with wire reinforcements in the fingers. Traditionally, cosmetic gloves have been made of poly(vinyl chloride) (PVC), although silicone is becoming the material of choice. Individualized hands, when expertly done, have a preferable appearance to generic hand replacements. Highly realistic hands, fingers, and finger parts can be custom-sculpted and painted to an individual's size and skin coloring. Such prostheses confer to persons what Beasley has called the highly important function of "social presentation."

Passive work prostheses may be a simple post to provide opposition, or they may incorporate specialized features to aid in certain occupations. A custom-designed system that serves only one function may aid the wearer more than one that is supposed to be multifunctional. In such cases the prosthetic device is worn only on those occasions when it is needed. These devices range from tool adapters to sports mitts.

22.1.4 Artificial Arms

The field of prosthetics has moved away from designing complete arm prostheses systems to specific or modular components, such as externally or body-powered elbow joints;

powered or passive wrist rotators; passive humeral rotators; and whole ranges of different hooks, hands, and prehensors. For reviews, see Michael [8], Fryer and Michael [10], and Heckathorne [9]. The current trend is to use a "mix and match" approach to optimize the function available. This modular approach has the advantage of providing great flexibility and practicality for system design and also the possibility of maximizing the available components for the small size of the market. However, it will probably never be able to attain the high functional goals that may be possible from a more integrated standpoint.

Prosthetic components for the upper limb fall into one of two categories: body-powered or externally powered. *Body-powered devices* are functional prostheses that use some motion of the body to provide both the excursion and force necessary to power and control the prosthetic component. *Externally powered devices*, as their name suggests, receive their power from a source external to the body, usually electric.

22.1.4.1 Body-Powered Prosthesis

Modern body-powered prostheses were greatly influenced by techniques used in aircraft flight surface control. Of particular note was the adaptation by the Northrop Aircraft Co. of the Bowden cable for use in the prosthetics field. These cables, named for their inventor and the founder of the Raleigh bicycle company, are as useful in prosthetics as they are in bicycle brakes.

The basic principles of the prosthetic design for body-powered devices are the same today as they were in the 1950s. These devices require a harness to be worn about the shoulders to which one or more Bowden cables are attached. The conventional below-elbow body-powered prosthesis has a single control cable that runs from the harness to a terminal device. Terminal device opening and closing is then controlled by biscapular abduction and/or glenohumeral flexion.

Body-powered prostheses of many kinds are available, and they are the most common kind of prosthesis used in the United States. Body-powered prostheses have been so successful presumably because of the way the input and output are so intimately related through the cable. For a review of the many implementations of body power in limb prostheses, see Fryer and Michael [10]. Although generally successful, body-powered prostheses have a number of shortcomings. The major issues are the uncomfortable harness mechanism; the somewhat ungainly control motions, particularly in the case of above-elbow prostheses; restricted range of motion; and limited load-lifting capacity. For a review of harnessing techniques, see Fryer [11].

22.1.4.2 Externally Powered Systems

Externally powered prostheses are a relatively new addition to the armamentarium of prosthetic devices. The electrically powered, myoelectrically controlled prosthesis did not become commercially available until the late 1960s and did not gain widespread clinical acceptance until the early 1980s. These electrically powered hands are the most widely used powered systems in limb prosthetics. Heckathorne [9] has carefully reviewed the specifications of available electrically powered systems for prostheses.

22.1.4.3 Hybrid Systems

When body-powered and externally powered systems are linked together, they are called *hybrid* systems. Hybrid systems are used most frequently with persons who have amputations above the elbow or who have bilateral arm amputations. Such systems can provide the user with the high-gripping and/or high-lifting capacities of powered systems and with the fine control of body power. An example of hybrid control is illustrated in prosthetic limbs for persons with bilateral limb loss at the shoulder level. By providing the person with a body-powered limb on one side and with an electrically powered limb on the other side, the wearer is able to use the limb that is most appropriate a specific task. This method also decouples the limbs so that body motion to operate the body-powered side does not influence the state of the powered limb and vice versa.

22.1.5 Control

A major factor limiting the development of more sophisticated hand/arm prostheses is the difficulty in finding sufficient control sources to control the many degrees of freedom required to replace a physiologic hand and/or arm. In addition most multi-DOF prosthetic hands are doomed by practicality, even before the control interface becomes an issue. Most mechanisms fail because of poor durability, lack of performance, and complicated control. No device will be clinically successful if it breaks down frequently. A multifunctional design is inherently more complex than a 1-DOF counterpart. However, some of the robustness and simplicity must be traded if the increase in performance possible with a multi-DOF hand is ever to be realized.

Numerous methods of control have been explored. Chief among these were the harness and Bowden cable and/or mechanical switches for body-powered devices and electromechanical switches and myoelectric control for externally powered devices. Childress and Weir [12] classify the available control options into biomechanical and bioelectric/acoustic. A partial list of current and potential control options follows:

1. Biomechanical
    a. Movement/force from a body joint or multiple joints (position, force/pressure)
        (1) Chin and head force/movement
        (2) Glenohumeral flexion/extension abduction/adduction
        (3) Biscapular and scapular abduction
        (4) Shoulder elevation and depression
        (5) Chest expansion
        (6) Elbow or wrist movement
    b. Direct force/motion from muscle(s)
        (1) Force/motion from a muscle tunnel cineplasty
        (2) Force/motion from skin that is adherent to underlying muscle
        (3) Krukenberg surgical procedure (long transradial amputation)
2. Bioelectric/bioacoustic
    a. Myoelectric potentials (muscle electricity)
    b. Myoacoustic (muscle sounds)
    c. Neuroelectric potentials (neuron and nerve signals)

Biomechanical inputs have been extensively used for control of body-powered prosthetic components and have been mentioned in passing throughout the text. These same motions can be used to control externally powered components through the use of the appropriate electromechanical switch or force transducer. In general, either on/off or proportional velocity control is used with externally powered devices.

Proportional control is a form of control where the amount or intensity of the controlled output variable is directly related (proportional) to the amount of the input signal. The output speed of a variable-speed power drill is proportional to the amount that the trigger is pressed. This is an example of velocity (speed) control; that is, output speed is proportional to the amount of input signal (in this case how far the drill trigger is pressed in). Proportional control is used where a graded response to a graded input is sought.

Position control is similar to velocity control only when the controlled variable is in output position; that is, the output position of a prosthetic joint is proportional to the amount of the input. The *amount of input* refers to the method of actuation of a particular form of control. It is possible to use the position of another joint to control the output position of the prosthetic joint. This would be an example of position actuated, position control. An example is the power steering of a car. Here the position of the steering wheel is related directly (proportional) to the position of the front wheels. Such a system is an example of a position follower or a position servomechanism. If, as is the case in the power steering example, the input and output are physically linked, then the system becomes an "unbeatable" position servomechanism or an extended physiologic proprioception (EPP) system.

Position control of upper-extremity function relates prosthesis position directly to the input control signal; the amputee's ability to perceive and control prosthesis position is directly determined by his or her ability to perceive and control the input signal. Position control, unlike velocity control, must maintain the input signal to hold an output level other than zero. Although the merit of this control scheme for hand prehension remains to be seen, it has been shown that position control for positioning of the terminal device in space is superior to velocity control [13,14]. Equally well, it has been observed that velocity control may be better suited to the control of prehension [15,16].

22.1.5.1 Myoelectric Control

While most of the currently available externally powered prosthetic systems use some form of velocity control, the merits of velocity control are being reevaluated, particularly in the context of position control, which in some in cases appears preferable. Myoelectric control has received considerable attention since it first came on the scene during the 1940s. It was advanced as a natural approach for the control of prostheses since it enabled amputees to use the same mental processes to control prosthesis function as had previously been used in controlling their physiological limb. Myoelectric control uses the remaining neuromuscular systems in the amputation stump.

The term *myoelectric control* is derived from the term *electromyogram* (EMG), which it uses as a control input. When a muscle contracts, it produces electric potentials (the electromyogram or EMG), as a byproduct of that contraction. The intensity of the EMG produces increases as muscle tension increases. If surface electrodes are placed on the skin near a muscle, they can detect this signal. The signal can then be electronically amplified and processed and used to control a prosthesis. For a review, see Parker and Scott [17].

22.1.5.2 Neuroelectric Control

Neuroelectric control, in its broadest context (i.e., where a descending neural command is readily interpreted and an ascending command is returned), holds the allure of being able to provide multiple-channel control and multiple-channel sensing. There has been much research into interfacing prosthesis connections directly to nerves and neurons

[18–21], but the practicality of human–machine interconnections of this kind is still problematic. Nervous tissue is sensitive to mechanical stresses, and amputated nerves are more sensitive still, in addition to which, this form of control also requires the use of implanted systems. Edell [18] attempted to use nerve cuffs to generate motor control signals. Kovacs et al. [19] tried to encourage nerve fibers to grow through arrays of holes in silicon integrated circuits that had been coated with nerve growth factor. Andrews et al. [20] reported on their progress in developing a multipoint microelectrode peripheral nerve implant. Horch [21] has more recently demonstrated the control of prosthetic arm with sensory feedback using needle electrodes in the peripheral nerves, but these are short-term experiments, where the electrodes are removed after 3 weeks.

The development of BIONs® [22] for functional electrical stimulation (FES) is a promising new implant technology that may have a far more immediate effect on prosthesis control. These devices are hermetically encapsulated, leadless electric devices that are small enough to be injected percutaneously into muscles (2 mm in diameter by 15 mm long). They receive their power, digital addressing, and command signals from an external transmitter coil worn by the patient. The hermetically sealed capsule and electrodes necessary for long-term survival in the body have already been approved for experimental (Investigational Device Exemption (IDE) approval) use in people by the FDA in functional electrical stimulation systems. As such, these BIONs represent an enabling technology for a prosthesis control system based on implanted myoelectric sensors.

Weir et al. [23] are involved in an effort to revisit [24] the idea of implantable myoelectric sensors. *Implantable myoelectric sensors* (IMESs) have been designed that will be implanted into the muscles of the forearm and will transcutaneously couple through a magnetic link to an external exciter/data telemetry reader. Each IMES will be packaged in a BION II [25] hermetic ceramic capsule (see Fig. 22.2). The external exciter/data telemetry reader consists of an antenna coil laminated into a prosthetic interface so that the coil encircles the IMES. No percutaneous wires will cross the skin. The prosthesis controller will take the output of a exciter/data telemetry reader and use this output to decipher user intent. While it is possible to locate three, possibly four, independent (free of crosstalk) surface electromyographic (EMG) sites on the residual limb, it will be feasible to create many more independent EMG sites in the same residual limb using implanted sensors. There are 18 muscles in forearm that are involved in control of the hand and wrist. Using

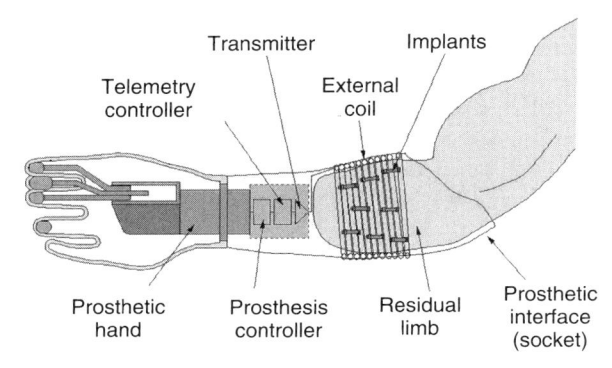

FIGURE 22.2 Schematic of how implantable myoelectric sensors will be located within forearm and encircled by the telemetry coil when prosthesis is donned.

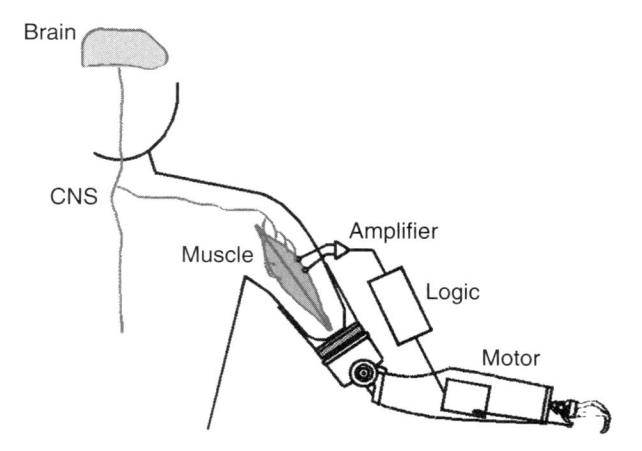

FIGURE 22.3 A muscle as a biologic amplifier of the descending neural command.

intramuscular signals in this manner means that the muscles are effectively acting as biologic amplifiers for the descending neural commands (see Fig. 22.3). Neural signals are on the order of microvolts, while muscle or EMG signals are on the order of millivolts. Intramuscular EMG signals from multiple residual muscles offer a means of providing simultaneous control of multiple degrees of freedom in a multifunction prosthetic hand.

At levels of amputation above the elbow, the work of Kuiken [26] offers a promising new surgical technique to create physiologically appropriate control sites. He advocates the use of *targeted muscle reinnervation* to improve the control of artificial arms. Kuiken observed that although the limb is lost in an amputation, the control signals to the limb remain in the residual peripheral nerves of the amputated limb. The potential exists to tap into these lost control signals using nerve–muscle grafts. As first suggested by Hoffer and Loeb [27], it may be possible to denervate expendable regions of muscle in or near an amputated limb and graft the residual peripheral nerve stumps to these muscles. The peripheral nerves would then reinnervate the muscles and these nerve–muscle grafts would provide additional EMG control sites for an externally powered prosthesis. Furthermore, these signals relate directly to the original function of the limb.

In the case of the high-level amputee, the median (M), ulnar (U), radial (R), and musclocutaneous (MC) nerves are usually still present (Fig. 22.4). The musclocutaneous nerve controls elbow flexion, while the radial nerve controls extension. Pronation of the forearm is directed by the median nerve and supination by the radial and musclocutaneous nerves. Extension of the hand is governed by the radial nerve and flexion, by the median and ulnar nerves. Since these nerves all innervate muscles that control the motion about different degrees of freedom, they should theoretically supply at least four independent control signals. The nerves are controlling functions in the prosthesis that are directly related to their normal anatomic function.

Implantable myoelectric sensors (IMESs) located at the time of initial surgery would complement this procedure nicely by providing focal recording of sites that may be located physically close together. This approach has been successfully applied with one bilateral, high-level subject to control a shoulder disarticulation prosthesis and two transhumeral amputees. In the shoulder disarticulation case, each of the residual brachial plexus nerves was grafted to different regions of deinervated pectoralis muscle and in

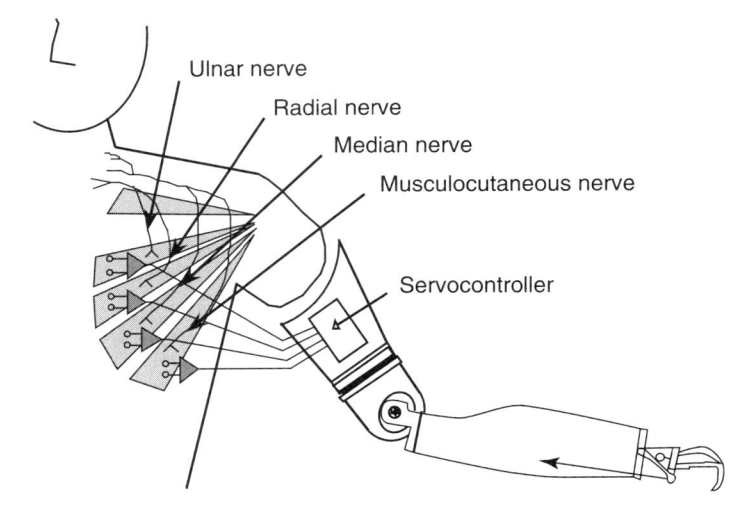

FIGURE 22.4 Schematic of "neuromuscular reinnervation" showing how pectoralis muscle is split into 4 separate sections and reinvervated with the foru main arm nerve bundles.

the transhumeral cases the nerves were grafted to different regions of deinervated biceps brachii.

Kuiken's [26] targeted reinnervation technique is available and is being performed experimentally in people; IMES sensors are should be available for human testing in a few years (from the time of this writing). However, the problem is not solved. Now that multiple control signals are available for control, we need to figure out how to use information they provide to control a multifunction prosthesis in a meaningful way.

22.1.5.3 The Issue of Feedback

Myoelectrically controlled systems are open-loop feedforward in nature. A control signal is sent from the user to the device, but nothing in the way of feedback is returned except visual information. This lack of proprioceptive feedback is perhaps the greatest problem associated with either myoelectric or switch-controlled externally powered systems. Without proprioceptive feedback, subconscious multifunctional control of a prosthesis is probably impossible.

With velocity control the user must integrate velocity in order to control position. Constant visual monitoring, because of the essentially open-loop nature of myoelectric control, is therefore required for effective operation. For the control of multiple degrees of freedom, this places excessive mental load on the user, greatly diminishing any benefits that a prosthesis of this complexity might offer. Visual and auditory feedback are slower, less automated, and less programmed than normal proprioceptive feedback and therefore place a greater mental burden on the operator [28].

Upper-limb prostheses are currently controlled primarily through *visual feedback* with some assistance from feedback that is incidental rather than by design. Examples of *incidental feedback* include motor whine, prosthesis vibration, and socket forces (see Fig. 22.4). Deliberate attempts have been made to provide feedback by means of mechanical vibration or electrical stimulation of the skin. These forms of feedback have been called *supplementary sensory feedback* (SSF) [29], because they are supplementary to the normal sensory feedback paths of the body. *Artificial reflexes*, which bypass the human operator altogether, is another method employed to reduce mental loading. Artificial reflexes seek to remove the operator from the control loop and automatically respond to some external sensor input. They are essentially closed loops within the mechanism or prosthesis itself. A slip detector, for example, detects slippage of an object grasped by a prehensor and automatically increases prehension force until it detects that the slippage has ceased. From the operator's perspective, artificial reflex approaches to improving prehension are feedforward; no attempt is made to provide the amputee with any feedback other than visual.

Feedback information can be received through the control interface, as in power steering for an automobile. *Control interface feedback* [30] provides feedback to the operator concerning the state of the prosthesis through the same channel through which the prosthesis is controlled. Information concerning prosthetic joint position, velocity, and the forces acting on it, is available to the operator through the proprioceptors of the controlling joint. Feedback through the control interface is usually in forms that are easily interpreted by the user and can be interpreted at a subconscious level. Consider the example of power steering for a car. The driver eventually learns to subconsciously equate vehicle heading with steering wheel position. Central to the implementation of feedback through the control interface is the design of the controller. Few prosthesis controllers, however, provide control interface feedback, and it is for this reason, it could be argued, that externally powered limb replacements have not gained the widespread acceptance expected of them.

22.1.5.4 Surgery for Improved Control

The role of surgery is vital to the success of a prosthetic fitting. History has shown that the greatest success in prosthetic fitting is achieved when the surgeon, amputee, prosthetist, physical therapist, and engineer work together as a team. Muscle tunnel cineplasty is a good example of where this interdisciplinary approach was needed to ensure success. In muscle tunnel cineplasty surgical intervention is used to provide direct mechanical connection between a muscle and prostheses. The procedure involves the construction of a skin-lined tunnel, by way of skin grafts, through a muscle belly. It was developed in its modern form by the German surgeon Ferdinand Sauerbruch [31]. Sauerbruch attributed much of the success of the procedure to the fact that he collaborated with engineers and therapists at the same facility.

The more recent trend in the fitting of high-level, upper-limb amputees is to use a hybrid system that incorporates both body-powered and externally powered components. The use of surgical techniques to create pectoral or other tunnel cineplasties offers a means of creating more badly needed control sites at these higher levels of amputation. Marquardt [32] described a unilateral forequarter amputee who controlled an electromechanical hand and wrist rotator with a pectoral cineplasty in conjunction with sequential switch control. Lucke et al. [33] discussed the indications for use of a pectoral cineplasty in amputations in the region of the shoulder girdle and described how four functions could be obtained from one muscle using a four-stage switch.

The use of miniature tunnel cineplasties in muscle that has undergone targeted reinnervation offers the possibility of creating control inputs to externally powered prosthetic components that would retain some sensory information similar to that provided in a cable-operated system. If the controller embodies the concept of extended physiologic proprioception (EPP), then feedback information about prosthesis state can be given to the amputee through the cineplastized muscles' own proprioceptive receptors. Weir [34] has shown the efficacy of tunnel cineplasty control when compared to the control of a conventional above-elbow, body-powered prosthesis.

In Sweden, pioneering work in the area of direct skeletal attachment of prostheses to humans has been performed by Dr. Per-Ingvar Branemark and his team [35]. These surgeons and orthopedic engineers have created infection-free interfaces for direct skeletal attachment systems for upper- and lower-limb amputations. Dr. Branemark began work in this area in the 1960s with titanium sockets in the jaw bone for holding artificial teeth, then progressed to the placement of titanium sockets in the skull to retain maxillofacial prostheses and for the attachment of highly efficient bone conduction hearing aids. Branemark seems to have solved the infection problem that have dogged previous efforts [36,37] with innovative surgical techniques and postoperative procedures. While this work has been demonstrated only over long periods of time for high loads in the mouth and for low loads with skull attachments, the early results with amputees are very encouraging. Should direct skeletal attachment prove itself viable, it could revolutionize the prosthetic fitting of amputees.

22.2 LOWER-LIMB PROSTHESES AND WALKING ROBOTS

Humans can ambulate reasonably well on artificial legs, particularly if the amputations are below the knee. Persons with one limb missing below the knee can walk almost normally if they are reasonably healthy, if they have good gait training, and it they have a well-fitted functional prosthesis. Walking on two artificial below-knee prostheses is something akin to walking on stilts, and many people can also walk quite naturally with two limbs missing below the knee. Today's below-knee prostheses use modern materials to achieve combinations of shape and compliance that are appropriate for walking and running. These prostheses, products of Flex-Foot Inc., are made of composite carbon fiber material. The foot is shaped in the form of a flexible cantilever beam that bends during walking. In addition, the pylon to which the cantilever is attached is piston-like and will shorten under load through the readily visible leaf spring. Control of the limbs comes through the close-fitting sockets, which provide extended physiologic proprioception (EPP). Foot function is achieved through shape and through bending (compliance), which provides both shock absorption and shape modification under load.

Humans require good balance to stay upright during walking. *Static balance*, in which the center of mass of the body projects on the base of support, is achieved in quiet standing (walking with zero velocity). *Dynamic balance*, in which the center of mass often projects outside the base of support, is required for bipedal walking. In other words, walking can be regarded as a process of falling and catching oneself. Perry and associates [38] have described walking as a continuous event of falling from one foot to the other to move the body forward. Balance is key to bipedal walking, and the lack of good artificial balancing ability is one of the primary reasons why it is difficult to build bipedal walking machines (walking robots) that can walk at a range of speeds over various kinds of terrain, and on sloping surfaces. Besides balance, a walking person must be able to transfer weight from one limb to the other (which is partially a balance issue), and be able to advance the location of one limb with respect to the other (again, balance is involved). Although balance dominates, the main issues of walking can be summarized as (1) balance, (2) weight transference, and (3) foot advance and clearance. Children begin to learn walking skills at about one year of age. Ultimately walking becomes second-nature. Human bipedal gait is an existence proof for the reasonable possibility of constructing agile bipedal walking machines, just as birds were existence proofs for the possibility of building heavier-than-air flying machines.

Humans can walk bipedally on two above-knee artificial limbs; that is, they can walk on passive artificial knee and ankle mechanisms in both limb replacements. Although their speed of ambulation is reduced from that of typical human gait, the ambulation ability they achieve is a tribute to their excellent balance system and to their control of muscles around the hip joint and pelvis. A person amputated at the hip level on one side can also walk reasonably well on a hip disarticulation prosthesis. Walking ability of this nature testifies also to the capacity of a remaining limb to compensate for one that is missing.

Legged locomotion is an interesting area of robotics, prosthetics, and animal studies. Raibert [39,40] points out that legged locomotion has potential practical applications for vehicles that could travel with mobility over rough terrain. He also points out that technical development of walking machines may assist with the understanding of animal movement, including human bipedal ambulation. Likewise, he notes that animal studies may facilitate the design of walking machines. It might be added that study of walking on prostheses may help us understand normal human walking and/or robotic walking and that knowledge about robotic walking and human walking may influence artificial limb designs. This kind of interplay between disciplines is, of course, not closed. It is worth noting, for example, that the photographic studies of animal locomotion (originally studies of horses) by Edweard Muybridge in the United States and by E. J. Marey in France played important roles in the development of cinematography.

Comprehensive introductions to locomotion and walking machines may be gained through Todd [41] and Raibert [42] and through two special issues on legged locomotion published by the *International Journal of Robotics Research* [39,40]. Suggested introductions to human walking are Perry [43] and Rose and Gamble [44] Perry's book examines human pathological ambulation as well as normal walking. The Rose–Gamble book [44] contains a chapter by C. W. Radcliffe concerned with walking on prostheses. McMahon [45] provides readers with a general overview of locomotion issues, particularly as related to humans and other animals.

22.3 CONCLUSION

Presently, the field of limb prosthetics finds itself in a stage of development similar to that of the aircraft industry back in the 1930s, when the DC-3 airplane was introduced. In the aircraft industry this plane represented a watershed between seat-of-the-pants empirical design and scientific design using theoretical constructs of aerodynamics. The field of prosthetics seems to be at a similar point in its development. Significant advances have been made, to a great extent, by empirical means. Now, at the dawn of a new century, it is anticipated that even greater gains will be made through the enhancement of empiricism by theoretical and computational science.

REFERENCES

1. Weir RF ff: Design of artificial arms and hands for prosthetic applications, in Kutz M, ed, *Standard Handbook of Biomedical Engineering & Design*, McGraw-Hill, New York, 2003, pp 32.1–32.61.
2. White WL: Restoration of function and balance of the hand and wrist by tendon transfers, *Surg Clin N Am* **40**:427 (1960).
3. Childress DS: Control of limb prostheses, in Bowker JH, Michael JW, eds, *Atlas of Limb Prosthetics*, Surgical, Prosthetic, and Rehabilitation Principles, 2nd Edition, Mosby-Year Book, St. Louis, 1992, Chapter 6D, pp. 175–199.
4. Schlesinger G, DuBois-Reymond R, Radike R, Volk S: Der mechanische Aufbau der künstlichen Glieder. I.: Der Eratzrarm, in Borchardt M, Hartmann K, Leymann H, Radike R, Schlesinger G, eds, *Ersatzglieder und Arbeitshilfen für Kriegsbeschädigte und Unfallverletzte*, Julius Springer-Verlag, Berlin, 1919, pp 321–573.
5. Keller AD, Taylor CL, Zahn V: *Studies to Determine the Functional Requirements for Hand and Arm Prostheses*, Dept Engineering, Univ California at Los Angeles, 1947.
6. Napier JA: Prehensile movements of the human hand, *J Bone Joint Surg* **38**(4) (Nov 1956).
7. Kamakura N, Matsuo M, Ishii H, Mitsukoshi F, Miusa Y: Patterns of static prehension in normal hands, *Am J Occup Ther* **34**(7):437–445 (1980).
8. Michael JW: Upper-limb powered components and controls: Current concepts, *Clin Prosth Orth* **10**(2):66–77 (1986).
9. Heckathorne CW: in Smith DG, Michael JW, Bowker JH, eds, *Atlas of Amputations and Limb Deficiencies—Surgical, Prosthetic and Rehabilitation Principles*, 3rd ed, American Academy of Orthopaedic Surgeons (AAOS), Rosemont, IL, 2004.
10. Fryer CM, Michael JW: Body-powered components, Smith DG, Michael JW, Bowker JH, eds, *Atlas of Amputations and Limb Deficiencies—Surgical, Prosthetic and Rehabilitation Principles*, 3rd ed, American Academy of Orthopaedic Surgeons (AAOS), Rosemont, IL, 2004.
11. Fryer CM: Harnessing and controls for body-powered devices, in Smith DG, Michael JW, Bowker JH, eds, *Atlas of Amputations and Limb Deficiencies—Surgical, Prosthetic and Rehabilitation Principles*, 3rd ed, American Academy of Orthopaedic Surgeons (AAOS), Rosemont, IL, 2004.
12. Childress DS, Weir RF FF: Control of limb prostheses, in Smith DG, Michael JW, Bowker JH, eds, in *Atlas of Amputations and Limb Deficiencies—Surgical, Prosthetic and Rehabilitation Principles*, (3rd ed, American Academy of Orthopaedic Surgeons (AAOS), Rosemont, IL, 2004, Chapter 12.
13. Doubler JA, Childress DS:, An analysis of extended physiological proprioception as a control technique *J Rehab Res Devel* **21**(1):5–18 (1984).
14. Doubler JA, Childress DS: Design and evaluation of a prosthesis control system based on the concept of extended physiological proprioception, *J Rehab Res Devel* **21**(1):19–31 (1984).
15. Carlson LE, Primmer KR:, Extended physiological proprioception for electric prostheses, in *Advances in External Control of Human Extremities*, Proc 6th Int Symp External Control of Human Extremities, Dubrovnik, Yugoslavia, Yugoslav Committee for Electronics and Automation (ETAN), Belgrade, Yugoslavia, Aug 28–Sept 1, 1978.
16. McKenzie DS: Functional replacement of the upper-extremity today, in Murdoch G, ed, *Prosthetic and Orthotic Practice*, Edward Arnold, London, 1970, pp 363–376.
17. Parker PA, Scott RN: Myoelectric control of prosthesis, *CRC Crit Rev Biomed Eng* **13**(4):283–310 (1985).

18. Edell DJ: A peripheral nerve information transducer for amputees: Long-term multichannel recordings from rabbit peripheral nerves, *IEEE Trans Biomed Eng.* **BME-33**(2):203–214 (Feb 1986).
19. Kovacs GT, Storment CW, James B, Hentz VR, Rosen JM: Design and implementation of two-dimensional neural interfaces, *Proc 10th Annual Conf*, *IEEE Engineering in Medicine and Biology Society,* New Orleans, 1988, pp 1649–1650.
20. Andrews B, Warwick K, Jamous A, Gasson M, Harwin W, Kyberd P: Development of an implanted neural control interface for artificial limbs, *Proc 10th World Congress of Int Society for Prosthetics and Orthotics (ISPO),* Glasgow, Scotland, July 1–6, 2001, ISPO Publications, Copenhagen, Denmark, p TO8.6.
21. Horch K: Neural control Speech to Advisory Panel, DARPA Advanced Prosthesis Workshop, Maryland, Jan 10–11, 2005.
22. Loeb GE, Richmond FJR, Olney S, Cameron T, Dupont AC, Hood K, Peck RA, Troyk PR, Schulman JH: Bionic neurons for functional and therapeutic electrical stimulation, *Proc IEEE-EMBS* **20**:2305–2309 (1998).
23. Weir RF ff, Troyk PR, DeMichele G., Kuiken T: Implantable myoelectric sensors (IMES) for upper-extremity prosthesis control—preliminary work, *Proc 25th Silver Anniversary Int Conf IEEE Engineering in Medicine and Biology Society (EMBS), Cancun, Mexico*, Sept 17–21, 2003, pp 1562–1565; see also Weir RF ff, Troyk PR, DeMichele G., Kerns D: Technical details of the implantable myoelectric sensor (IMES) system for multifunction prosthesis control, *Proc 27th Annual Int Conf IEEE Engineering in Medicine Society (EMBS)—Innovation from Biomolecules to Biosystems*, Shanghai, China, Sept 1–4, 2005.
24. Reilly RE: Implantable devices for myoelectric control, in Herberts P, Kadefors R, Magnusson RI, Petersén I, eds, *Proc Conf Control of Upper-Extremity Prostheses and Orthoses,* Göteborg, Sweden, Charles C Thomas, Springfield, IL, Oct 6–8, 1971, pp 23–33.
25. Arcos I, David R, Fey K, Mishler D, Sanderson D, Tanacs C, Vogel MJ, Zilberman Y, Schulman JH: Second-generation microstimulator, *Artif Organs* **26**(3):228–231 (March 2002).
26. Kuiken TA: Consideration of nerve-muscle grafts to improve the control of artificial arms, *Technol Disab* **15**(2):105–111 (2003).
27. Hoffer JA, Loeb GE: Implantable electrical and mechanical interfaces with nerve and muscle, *Ann Biomed Eng* **8**(4–6):351–360 (1980).
28. Soede M: Mental control load and acceptance of arm prostheses, *Automedica* 4:183–191 (1982).
29. Prior R, Case P, Scott C, Lyman J: Supplemental sensory feedback for the VA/NU myoelectric hand: Background and feasibility *Bull Prosth Res* **10**(26):170–190 (1976).
30. Childress DS: Closed-loop control in prosthetic systems: Historical perspective, *Ann Biomed Eng* **8**:293–303 (1980).
31. Sauerbruch F: *Die Willkürlich Bewegbare Künstliche Hand. Eine Anleitung für Chirurgen und Techniker*, Julius Springer-Verlag, Berlin, 1916.
32. Marquardt E: Come-back of the pectoral cineplasty, *J Assoc Children's Prosth Orth Clin* **22**(2):32 (1987).
33. Lucke R, Marquardt E, Carstens C: Kineplasty according to Sauerbruch—the fresh indication for the pectoralis canal in amputations in the region of the shoulder girdle, *Proc 6th World Congress Int Society for Prosthetics and Orthotics (ISPO)*, Kobe, Japan, Nov 12–17, 1989.
34. Weir RF ff: *Direct Muscle Attachment as a Control Input for a Position Servo Prosthesis Controller*. PhD dissertation, Dept Biomedical Engineering, Northwestern Univ, Evanston, IL, 1995.

35. Blomberg E: [Titanium gives sure hold for prosthesis], *Allt om Hjälpmedel, Handikappinstitut*, (Vällingby, Sweden) **48**(1) (May 13, 1993).
36. Hall CW, Eppright RH, Engen T, Liotta DA: Permanently attached artificial limbs, *Trans Am Soc Artif Internal Organs* **13**:329–331 (1967).
37. Hall CW, Rostoker W: Permanently attached artificial limbs, *Bull Prosth Res* **10**(34):98–100 (1980).
38. Perry and Associates: *Normal and Pathological Gait Syllabus*, Pathokinesiology Service and Physical Therapy Dept, Rancho Los Amigos Hospital, Downey, CA, 1981.
39. Raibert M: Introduction" to the special issue on legged locomotion, *Int J Robo Res* **3**(2) (1984).
40. Raibert M: Introduction, *Int J Robot Res* **9**(2) (1990).
41. Todd DJ: *Walking Machines: An Introduction to Legged Robots*, Chapman & Hall, New York, 1985.
42. Raibert M: *Legged Robots that Balance*, MIT Press, Cambridge, MA, 1986.
43. Perry J: *Gait Analysis: Normal and Pathological Function*, SLACK Inc., 1992.
44. Rose J, Gamble J: *Human Walking*, Williams & Wilkins, Baltimore, 1994.
45. McMahon TA: *Muscles, Reflexes, and Locomotion*, Princeton Univ Press, Princeton, NJ, 1984.

PART V

User Mobility

23

Wheelchairs within the Context of Smart House Design

Dimitar Stefanov
University of Coventry, Coventry, UK

23.1 INTRODUCTION

The structure of smart houses for people with lower-limb disabilities should include an efficient system for indoor and outdoor transportation that allows the user to access independently the main living areas (kitchen, diningroom, bathroom, garden, etc.). Independent mobility is not only a matter of the user's comfort but also an issue that is directly linked to the user's safety since the smart house design needs to allow the user a way to leave the house easily in case of emergency (fire, gas leakage, flooding, etc.). The home architecture should offer barrier-free access of the human transporter to all house areas and enough space for maneuvering and docking of the transportation system.

Some smart house solutions for indoor transportation are based on a ceiling-mounted rail and motorized electromechanical hoist that moves on it. The solution combines lifting and transportation. The user can be lifted from the bed and transferred to the wheelchair or chair. The approach is particularly convenient for patients with very limited self-movement [1] and has a certain advantage in the case of narrow indoor spaces. A serious disadvantage of the same solution is the requirement for considerable house modification for the installation of the rail on the ceiling. Additionally, the user's access is limited to a few preliminary defined locations.

Most existing smart house designs for people with severe paralysis are based on a powered wheelchair that can transport the user to various locations within or outside

---

The Engineering Handbook of Smart Technology for Aging, Disability, and Independence,
Edited by A. Helal, M. Mokhtari and B. Abdulrazak
Copyright © 2008 John Wiley & Sons, Inc.

the house. This way, the user can access various objects (opening the fridge and taking objects from there, taking books from the book shelf, checking the mailbox, etc.). Some other smart house concepts [2,3] consider special mobile agents (mobile robots) that can deliver various objects to the user who is sitting in the wheelchair or lying on the bed (see also section 19.3.5). In this way, the mobile robot can bring for example, some food or drink from the fridge located in the kitchen while the user is watching an interesting TV movie or talks on phone, circumventing the necessity of driving the wheelchair there. The mobile robot is navigated either automatically or by the user via special remote controller.

23.2 WHEELCHAIR BASICS

Wheelchair design has been improved dramatically since the mid-1950s, and currently, a variety of wheelchairs are available on the market to meet the needs of different user groups.

Depending on the method of their powering, wheelchairs can be grouped into two large classes:

- Manual wheelchairs (hand-propelled)
- Powered wheelchairs

23.2.1 Manual Wheelchairs

Manual wheelchairs suit users with enough muscle power in at least one limb for its propulsion [4]. For many years, most wheelchairs have been based on the folding cross-brace frame proposed by Ernest and Jennings in the 1930s. The standard design includes two large wheels and two casters attached to a folding frame where the seat is mounted. Depending on the manual power that the user apples to each drive wheel, the wheelchair can change its trajectory or turn. Some earlier models have a single caster. Such a solution gives some advantages on certain uneven terrains but affects the wheelchair stability.

Depending on the method of powering, the manual wheelchair can be classified into the following groups:

- Two-arm drive wheelchairs
- One-arm drive (hemiplegic) wheelchairs
- Foot-drive wheelchairs
- Attendant-propelled wheelchairs

Most manually operated wheelchairs are two-arm-propelled, where the user applies manual power to special pushrims linked to each drive wheel. The pushrims are mounted on the outside of the large wheels, and their diameter is slightly less than that of the wheels.

One-arm wheelchairs can facilitate people who have enough muscle strength in one arm only. The design is based on a special drive mechanism that consists of two pushrims located on the side of the active user's arm. One of these pushrims is fixed to the first rear wheel, while the second pushrim is connected to the second drive wheel via special linkage mechanism. The user pushes one of the pushrims to make a turn or drives both pushrims simultaneously to move the wheelchair forward or backward.

Patients who have weakness of their arms but have preserved muscle power of at least one foot can benefit from the foot-driven wheelchairs. There are two types of such wheelchairs designed for patients who have better performance when pushing or pulling their legs, respectively. In some solutions, the user pushes or pulls not directly to the ground but on a special intermediate ball [5]. This solution allows better posture and greater performance of some patients.

Attendant-propelled wheelchairs are designed for people who do not have sufficient muscle strength in their upper and lower extremities. Such wheelchairs are propelled not by the person sitting in the chair but by an external attendant who pushes on special handles located on the wheelchair back. Usually, these wheelchairs have small-diameter wheels. The design of such wheelchair should allow the attendant to maneuver it easily with minimal stress on hands and arms.

Brakes are an important component of the wheelchair design. They immobilize the wheelchair when the user needs to stop on a slope and help the attendant to slow the wheelchair when pushing it on inclined terrain.

Depending on their application, the manual wheelchairs can be classified as

- Standard wheelchairs used both indoors and outdoors
- Sports wheelchairs
- Beach wheelchairs
- Bath wheelchairs (shower wheelchair)
- Wheelchairs for institutional use (depot wheelchairs)

Sports wheelchairs are designed especially for active users to allow them to practice certain sports (basketball, tennis, badminton, athletics, Rugby, cricket, wheelchair dance, football, etc.). The design depends on the sport that will be practiced with it. Such wheelchairs have a lightweight frame with improved rigidity, antitippers, and special brakes that improve stability and allow easy turning. More recent technologies have enabled the manufacture of new lightweight models with improved performance.

Beach wheelchairs are designed to transport people with disabilities over sand and into the water. Usually, these chairs are not self-propelled and need a second person to push them, but the large (often pastic) wheels allow them to be pushed easily on sand, gravel, grass, and unpaved roads.

Bath wheelchairs focus on the personal hygienic needs of people with disabilities. Such a chair is usually built of rust-free materials such as PVC, aluminum, or stainless steel. The chair allows the caregiver to transfer the patient in and out of the tub or shower with less effort.

Depot wheelchairs are designed to be used temporarily by a number of people in hospitals, airports, and other facilities. They have large seats, footplates, solid tires, removable armrests, and handles for the attendant who will push the chair. The seat design should allow easy cleaning or decontamination. The CEA in France has developed a completely nonmagnetic wheelchair called PASS'PORT that has no metal components, allowing persons with reduced mobility to pass through airport control points without triggering detection [6].

Wheelchair design should consider carefully user's anthropometrics (height, size, weight, strength, body segment sizes). The wheelchairs design should respond the needs from all user's groups. Many companies offer a range of heavy-duty wheelchairs and extrawide wheelchairs that can be used by large individuals [7]. For example, the Benton "Super Extra Wide Wheelchair" has a 26 inch seat and weight capacity 550 lb [8]. Children's wheelchairs are often offered in a variety of sizes, colors, and pattern options. Redundant footplates are usually removed for people with lower-limb amputations, and the position of the seat with respect to the wheels is slightly shifted to allow better stability.

23.2.1.1 Caster Flutter and Camber

Caster assembly allows the front wheels to swivel in the direction in which the user pushes the wheelchair. The caster module includes a wheel fork unit that houses the caster wheel and ends with a swivel post that can rotate freely into an upright caster barrel welded to the wheelchair frame. Bearings are used for easy rotation and fixation of the upright swivel post within the fixed cylindrical barrel.

One major problem that may occur when a wheelchair with a front caster is moving at a fast walking pace, is "shimmy" (uncontrolled vibrations) of the caster wheels; this effect is also known as "flutter." When caster wheels flutter, the wheelchair resistance increases. The user needs to apply increased manual efforts to drive it. Oscillatory flutter creates serious potential danger of sudden forward tips, particularly in situations when the user coasts down a slope or accelerates the wheelchair stridently. If oscillatory flutters occur in such moments, the caster resistance increases at a lip that is quite similar to the case when a fast-moving wheelchair is stopped with a jerk by braking on the front wheels only.

Caster flutter is linked to the caster *trail*, which is the distance measured on the ground between the steering axis (the axis of the swivel post) and the wheel-to-ground contact patch. Caster oscillations can be avoided if the trail is large enough. The greater the trail, the greater the caster stability at high speed. However, the large trail will cause a significant increase in steering effort of the user in case of fine maneuvers. The caster module will become larger because more space will be needed for the caster fork to swivel.

Some wheelchair designs apply cambering of the rear drive wheels. The angle of the wheel relative to vertical, as viewed from the front or the rear of the wheelchair, is known as *camber angle*. The approach has several positive effects:

- It reduces the stiffness between the wheelchair frame and the rolling surface. Thus, the camber improves the wheelchair suspension and increases the traveling comfort.
- When a positive camber angle is applied, the distance between the wheel-to-ground contact patches of both drive wheels increases. That increases the lateral roll stability of the wheelchair.
- Turning becomes quicker. In some cases, a more efficient propulsion strategy can also be achieved. That is why the camber is applied to most sport wheelchairs.
- In case of nonprecise steering when the wheelchair is driven near walls, doorways, or furniture, the obstacles will make contact with the bottom of the wheel. This will keep the upper part of the pushrim far enough from the obstacle to protect the user from serious hand injuries.

A detailed review of wheelchair and their design can be found in Cooper [4].

23.2.2 Powered Wheelchairs

Powered wheelchairs are suitable for people who cannot use manual wheelchairs because of serious arm or leg muscle weakness but who can produce voluntary fine motions of some parts of the body or brain activity to be used as control commands for wheelchair steering.

A basic block diagram of a powered wheelchair is shown in Figure 23.1.

23.2.2.1 Control Interface

The *control interface* is the method of transferring user's commands to the wheelchair. Wheelchair manufacturers usually offer a range of input devices that fit to any particular wheelchair model to enable patients with various movement disabilities to use it. Additional third-party interfaces with standard parameters can also be adapted to the same wheelchair. In Figure 23.1, the interface and the controller are linked with a two-way line, illustrating that the information flow has two directions: (1) the user's instructions are transferred to the controller and (2) information about the wheelchair state is transferred to the control panel, to be presented there as lights signals, text, sounds, speech messages, and other forms.

Because of the rapid progression of some neuromuscular conditions in some patients, the initially implemented interface system needs frequent adjustment or change. Joysticks are the most common wheelchair interface. They can be classified into two main groups:

- Displacement joysticks that produce continuous output signals when their control handle is inclined.

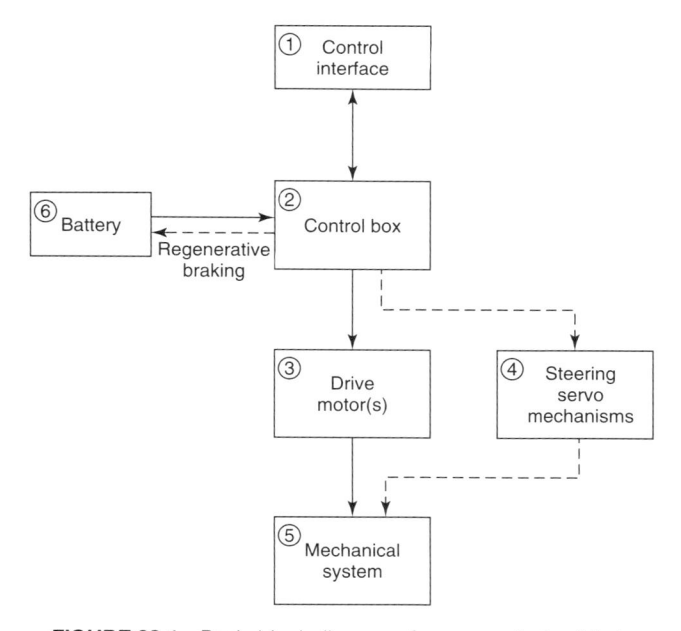

FIGURE 23.1 Basic block diagram of a powered wheelchair.

- Isometric joysticks where control handles are fixed in a certain position and built-in force sensors transform the force applied to the lever into electrical signals. Isometric joysticks give better results to some tremor-affected patients.

Standard wheelchairs can be controlled by a two-dimensional joystick that produces signals for the wheelchair heading (on left or right and on forward or backward). The control signals result either from the handle inclination (displacement joysticks) or from the force applied to the handle (isometric joysticks). Omnidirectional wheelchairs need control instructions for moving on forward or backward, sideways, or turning on the left or right. Such control is usually achieved by three-dimensional joysticks. As a departure from the two-dimensional joysticks, the three-dimensional joysticks are design to respond to twisting the stick to the left (counterclockwise) or right (clockwise). Depending on the signals they produce, joysticks are classified as proportional or switch-based. Displacement and isometric joysticks usually produce proportional signals. Proportional joysticks allow fine control of the wheelchair speed and direction. Greater deflection (or greater force) of the joystick results in greater output signal and, accordingly, in greater wheelchair speed. Switch-based joysticks have four built-in switches. Inclination of the stick leads to closure of one or two switches. When the wheelchair control is based on a switch joystick, the user cannot change the direction and the speed simultaneously. However, to change the speed, the user can turn the controller in a special speed selection mode (usually two or three different speeds can be selected). Instead of the speed selection mode, some simple wheelchairs controllers have a special potentiometer for speed adjustment. When a switch joystick is used, the movement trajectory is usually very coarse, but in return the switch joystick gives better results to some patients with tremor or lack of fine motion.

Important for the proper functioning of the wheelchair is the setting of a "neutral" zone. If the handle is not inclined or its inclination is below a certain threshold, the output signals of the interface device are zero. Respectively, the isometric joystick should keep its output signals to zero if the forces applied to it handle are less than a certain value. The neutral zone is a simple approach for neutralizing the effects of electronic component drift, sensor imbalance, and nonintentional small motions of the user's fingers. Joysticks are often integrated with the wheelchair control box.

Some wheelchairs are equipped with two joysticks: one for the user and another for the attendant. The attendant uses the joystick to control the wheelchair in order to save the user control efforts when tired, in cases where the wheelchair must be operated for easy uploading on a van, or in situations when the user is unable to take control because of a learning incapacity or hand weakness. In the latter case, the wheelchair has only one joystick for the attendant.

Usually, joysticks are activated by hand (standard use). In some cases, joysticks are additionally adapted to be driven by foot, chin, intentional shoulder motions, head via special lever system (head-activated joystick), or other means.

Single switches are used when the user does not have enough manual dexterity to operate with a standard joystick but possesses other preserved motions that make it possible to activate an array of switches. For example, such switches can be activated by hand, knees, feet, or head. The switch array can be mounted on a breastplate and activated by the chin or other means. The assembly should contain enough switches for selection of direction, reverse, on off state, and so on. In most cases of single-switch control, the wheelchair is used for indoor transportation or short-distance movement only and the wheelchair speed is set in advance to low level. When a switch is activated, the wheelchair moves slowly at a constant speed in that direction. The external switches are usually connected in parallel to the internal switches of the joystick. In some custom adaptations, "sip and puff" switches can be used instead of standard single switches.

Head motion is also often used for wheelchair control. Some solutions are based on an array of large-diameter switches, embedded in the headrest and activated by the head. There are also proportional head interfaces based on ultrasonic transducers [9], capacitive sensors, and a special linkage system connected to a joystick. The head-tracking devices are widely used because of their ability to produce up to three independent proportional signals that correspond to the forward–backward head tilt, left-right head rotation, and lateral head tilt.

Finger joystick suits users who have very limited strength in their fingers [10]. If the user's finger is in the center of the control hole, the wheelchair will be stationary. The wheelchair will then drive in the direction that the finger moves.

The "Touch-Drive" interface of Switch-It Inc. [11] consists of a force-sensitive surface that detects the position of the tip of the finger. The user can set the heading and the speed by moving his/her finger within the sensitive area. The device produces proportional control signals. The operation is quite similar to the operation of a joystick.

The scanning interface can help users who cannot operate with joystick but can activate a single switch. The scanning interface consists of a panel where the main wheelchair movement directions are represented schematically by arrows [10]. These include forward, forward-right, rotation on the right, backward turn, backward, backward-left, rotation on the left, and left-forward. These directions become active sequentially at a certain pace. An LED indicates the active movement direction. When the intended direction becomes active, the user presses the switch and the wheelchair starts moving on that direction as long as the switch is pressed. Before starting to steer the wheelchair, the user can choose the speed from special speed selection menu. In some settings for persons with high-level paralysis, a "puff and suck" switch can be fitted for selection of movement direction. Compared with the proportional joystick, scanning systems have increased access time, which slows the control and increases the cognitive load of the operator.

Tongue motions remain well preserved even in cases of severe movement paralysis. That powered the idea for development of tongue-activated interface devices that can be beneficial, for example, to patients with spinal cord injury, muscular dystrophy, spina bifida, cerebral palsy, multiple sclerosis, and other neuromuscular diseases. The "Tongue Touch Keypad" system of the newAbilities Systems Inc. [12] consists of a special mouthpiece device with nine pressure-sensitive keys. A tiny radio transmitter and a small watch-type battery are components of the same module. The switches are activated by tongue movement inside the mouth. The radio signals of the mouthpiece are detected by a receiver that is mounted on the headrest and electrically connected to the wheelchair controller. The mouthpiece device is attached to the back molars via special clasps. The battery can last about 6 months. The system allows the user to drive a wheelchair and additionally, to control a computer, make and receive phone calls, to call an attendant, turn on a light, and select a TV channel.

The InnerPilot's interface system [13–15] is based on the fact that tongue movements, speech, and even thoughts create minute air pressure changes in the ear canal. The Think-A-Move's InnerPilot™ technology allows a user to control a device by making small tongue movements inside his/her mouth. The InnerPilot earpiece sensor monitors ear pressure changes and transmits digital signals to a digital signal processor, designed as a small-sized board. The signals from the earpiece can be transmitted to the processing module via a thin cable or wirelessly.

The application of the EMG and EOG signals for wheelchair controls has also been researched. The EagleEyes interface system is based on measurement and processing of the EOG (electrooculographic) potentials that correspond to the eye movements [16]. EagleEyes works through five electrodes placed on the person's head. The soft computing technique offers new perspectives on application of the EMG signals in wheelchair control, allowing effective extraction of informative signal features in case of strong interference between useful EMG signals and strong noise signals resulting from motion artifacts [17].

Some head-tracking techniques involving detection of the facial direction have been tested by the design of wheelchairs that respond to the rotation of user's head. The WATSON wheelchair control system developed at the Robotics Laboratory of the Nara Institute of Science and Technology [18,19] uses one or two cameras directed at the user. After processing the image signals and calculation of the directions of the face and eyes, the signals are used to control a wheelchair. The user can stop the wheelchair by repetitive rapid head motions.

The brain–computer interface (BCI) has become a hot topic of many research projects. The development of communication system that enables the user to control a wheelchair by mental only means is an attractive perspective for patients with severe movement paralysis. The feasibility of the brain–computer interfaces for wheelchair control has been explored by several research groups [20–23]. The method is based on sampling and preprocessing of EEG signals associated with movement intentions of the user, followed by signal pattern recognition. The voluntarily modulated EEG signals are then used as a motor control. The cerebral cortex is a particularly suitable site for capturing signals related more directly to limb motion. Both invasive and noninvasive techniques have been explored. The *noninvasive approach* is based on the recording of the cerebral electric activity via electrodes attached to the scalp. The device usually consists of a cap wired with electrodes. As an alternative, *invasive methods* consist in an implantable array of microelectrodes that allow faster and much precise detection of details of motion.

23.2.2.2 Controller

The wheelchair controller (position 2 of Fig. 23.1) processes the signals coming from the HMI (human–machine interface) and sensors and produces appropriate controls for the wheelchair motors. The schematics of the wheelchair controllers vary from simple analog solutions to powerful microcontrollers. The microprocessor-based hardware not only reduces the size of the wheelchair controller and improves its reliability but also adds abilities for easy preprogramming and customising the wheelchair response on a way that suits the particular user. This is important predominantly for users whose movement abilities tend to change quickly (children, patients with progressing disease and deteriorating movement abilities, etc.). The wheelchair controller can be tuned by using a handheld programmer that can be connected to it temporarily to allow setting of parameters such as maximal forward speed, reverse speed, forward acceleration and deceleration, reverse acceleration and deceleration, and neutral zone parameters. The microprocessor modules have many advanced safety and protection features, including automatic cancelation of inappropriate commands and generation of warning messages to the operator when the battery becomes low or some of the wheelchair cables are disconnected. The wheelchair failure can be diagnosed very easily, and in many cases the problem can be fixed quickly by the attendant. Most of the wheelchair controllers apply closed-loop control algorithm when the actual speed of each drive wheel is compared with the calculated speed value and additional controls are generated to eliminate the error. In this way, the wheelchair speed does not change when the wheelchair climbs on slopes, overcomes curbs, moves slowly, or travels on rough terrain, which greatly facilitates wheelchair steering for the user.

The microprocessor output signals are linked to the drive motors via power drivers [usually full-bridge drivers built on metal oxide semiconductor field-effect transistor (MOSFET) transistors]. Depending on the control signals, the drivers change the current flow from the battery to each motor. The full-bridge scheme allows easy reversal of motor direction. The drivers usually operate in switching mode, allowing an efficient usage of the energy from the battery. Recuperative braking is often used in case of DC motor control to allow the recycled energy to go back to the vehicles' battery.

23.2.2.3 Motors and Gears

Several types of electric motors (position 3 of Fig. 23.1) are used in wheelchair design. Most of the models are based on permanent magnet DC motors that are armature-controlled. Gearless and brushless electric wheelchair motors are a fairly recent innovation. Often the electric wheelchair motor and gearbox are formed as a single module.

Gears are used with a drive motor to provide additional speed reduction and torque multiplication. The relationship of input speed divided by the output speed forms the speed ratio. Some designs use belt gears. These gears operate silently, but their efficiency is not high. The tooth gears (mostly helical and spur gears) possess higher efficiency but are usually quite noisy. Worm gears have a simple and cheap design and allow high gear ratio. Combined gears (worm gear connected to the drive wheel and linked to the motor via a belt) are another wheelchair gear solution. The belt component gives some elasticity of the gear train and reduces the noise. Drive wheels with embedded motor and gear are a relatively new solution with many advantages. In some models, the control circuit is also integrated with the same wheel.

23.2.2.4 Mechanical System

The mechanical system (position 5 of Fig. 23.1) usually comprises a frame, wheels with tires, footrests, seat, armrests, and headrest. Many wheelchairs utilize the traditional cross-brace frame that is used in the design of manual wheelchairs. However, the frame is made strong enough to support the extra weight of the battery and motors. The cross-brace system allows the wheelchair to be collapsed and folded for storage or transport once the batteries have been removed. Another design solution is the rigid frame. Such frame can accept high static and dynamic loads coming from the heavy motors and batteries when the wheelchair moves on uneven terrain. Most wheelchairs for farm and mountain use are based on rigid frames. In some models, the wheel modules are designed in a way that allows wheels to be removed easily when the wheelchair needs to be transported by car or stored. The rigid frame offers more space and better arrangement for life support equipment such as respirators and oxygen containers. When a four-wheeled wheelchair moves on uneven terrain, at some moment one of its wheels looses contact with the ground, which affects the wheelchair stability and steering. This problem can be solved by designing a three-wheeled chassis, but such constructions are usually less stable.

The traditional cross-brace frame possesses some flexibility that allows some adaptation of the caster wheels when the terrain becomes bumpy. In case of a rigid frame, better adaptation can be achieved when the barrels of each caster module are welded not directly to the wheelchair frame but to the upright segments of an additional parallelogram-shaped linkage mechanism. The chassis is then connected to the parallelogram mechanism via a single rotating joint (Fig. 23.2).

The platform-based concept includes a power base and a seat attached on the top of it. The power base usually includes all motors, gears, controller, and battery. In some cases, the base also embraces a built-in lifting mechanism to allow the user to raise and lower the seating platform. The platform-based solution offers some important advantages:

- The seat can be dismounted from the power base for easy transportation. The seat and its back can be further folded.
- All motors, gears, and the controller can be integrated as a very compact module.
- One and the same power base can be used with different seating. That allows easy assembly of various wheelchairs and better fit to the user's needs and preferences.

Wheelchair frames are made usually by lightweight materials that can provide the required strength. Stainless steel, chrome, aircraft aluminum, titanium, and chrome alloys are among the most widely used frame materials.

Powered wheelchairs usually have pneumatic tires that are much wider than those of the standard wheelchairs to accommodate the external weight of the battery and motors. The diameter of the drive wheels can differ from those of the freely rotating wheels. Depending on the wheel size, the design concepts can be classified into several groups:

- Wheelchairs with four small wheels. In some cases, the rear wheels can be slightly larger; this design is more suitable for wheelchairs for indoor usage and smooth surfaces.
- Wheelchairs with large rear wheels and small caster wheels. Larger wheels necessitate a small gear ratio that can be achieved by simple and cheap belt gear.
- Wheelchairs with wide front wheels with a wide diameter and small rear wheels. This design facilitates the climbing of curbs.

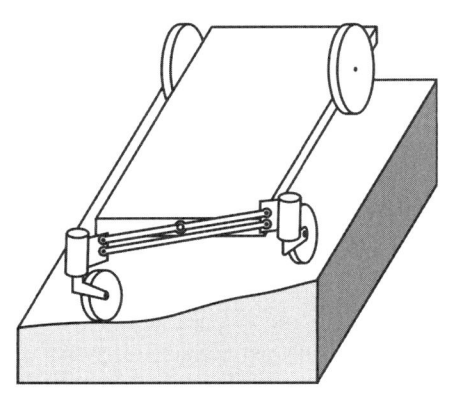

FIGURE 23.2 *The parallelogram-shaped linkage mechanism improves the casters' contact with the ground.*

Several drive concepts are commonly used in wheelchair design. Most frequently used is the drive scheme with two drive wheels and two front caster wheels. Each drive wheel has its own motor. The idea is similar to those of the manual wheelchairs. The speed and the heading (forward, backward, left, and right) are achieved by controlling the speed of each motor. The next concept is based on a single-drive motor connected to both rear wheels. Similar to the car-steering mechanism, both front wheels are joined via special linkage mechanism that is driven by a special steering motor (position 4 of Fig. 23.1). The advantage of this design is that it works stably on uneven terrain. The linkage mechanism prevents flitter at high speeds. Most outdoor wheelchairs follow this design.

Some wheelchairs apply a special occupant-controlled mechanism that allows a person to move from a seated to standing position with power assistance [24–26]. Standup function is usually realized by gas springs or an electromotor. The mechanism allows the user to access high objects (e.g., high shelves), to look through the window or enjoy the scenery from standing position, or to interact with others at the same level. On the other hand, the standup action may alleviate pressure areas, improve blood circulation, aid digestion, and relieve the user in cases of spasm.

A number of wheelchairs are fitted with a user-controlled mechanism to adjust the user's posture. Such wheelchairs include motorized mechanisms for repositioning the seatback and footplates, to enhance user comfort and prevent pressure sores. The position change can also help some people inhale and exhale more easily.

Wheelchair cushions with automatic alternating pressure provide the user with additional pressure relief and prevent development of pressure sores. The system changes cyclically the pressure contact points. It contains a pneumatic cushion, valves, and a microprocessor controller. The user can set the level of pressure alteration and the timing of pressure cycle. For example, the Aquila Corporation produces a line of dynamic alternating pressure relief wheelchair cushions [27].

23.3 INNOVATIONS AND CHALLENGES IN ELECTRICALLY POWERED WHEELCHAIRS

New industrial design and research on mobility devices is consolidated by the intensive progress of new materials, technologies, and electronics. The more recently developed products and concepts for transportation are directed at improved comfort, abilities for traveling over various types of terrain, and easy control that demands less user involvement in the navigation task of planning and steering.

Pushrim-activated power-assisted wheelchairs (PAPAW) are driven by a combination of human power and electric power [28–30]. The wheelchair has two electric motors that provide power assistance to each drive wheel. Special sensors monitor the torque that the user applies to each pushrim. In this way, the wheelchair controller recognizes the user's intention regarding the speed and direction of movement. The level of motor assistance can be tuned for providing an optimal physical load to the user. The motors, for example, support the additional load when the wheelchair climbs or coasts down slopes. The PAPAW may fit users who have insufficient arm strength to propel a wheelchair.

The INDEPENDENCE IBOT 3000 Transporter (IBOT), invented and developed by Dean Kamen [31–35], was introduced on the market in the late 1990s. In 2005, the newer "Independence Technology IBOT 4000 Transporter" superseded the initial model. As a departure from the standard wheelchair design, this highly effective transporter is capable of climbing stairs and travelling over rough ground in the presence of sand, rocks, and curbs. The IBOT mobility system has two pairs of large drive wheels and a pair of caster wheels. Depending on the terrain and transport task, the user can choose among four modes of movement: balancing, stair climbing, four-wheel drive, and standard transportation. In balancing mode, the front drive wheels rotate on top of the back wheels and the wheelchair balances on two wheels. The wheelchair design includes gyroscopes and sensors to monitor the user's center of gravity and perform automatic balancing and stabilization. The electronic balance system is individually adjusted to the user. That mode allows the user to easily access high shelves, shop independently, and communicate with others by being elevated to standing eye-level position. While the machine is in stair-climbing mode, the user can climb up and down stairs or steps, and the system keeps the seat in horizontal position. The four-wheel mode enables the user to travel across a wide range of variable surfaces, including grass, gravel, sand, and other forms of uneven terrain. The transporter's seat remains flat, which increases the user's comfort. The standard mode enables the user to operate the personal mobility system in the same manner as if in a traditional power chair.

Apart from the movements inherent to standard wheelchairs, the omnidirectional powered wheelchairs can move sideways, allowing them to change movement direction instantly. Such wheelchairs can be driven forward, backward, sideways, and diagonally, and also turned around 360° on the spot. Their high manoeuvrability can greatly facilitate indoor mobility [36–40]. Omnidirectional movement is particularly essential for tasks where the wheelchair needs to be positioned precisely toward other household objects such as a table, a bed, and walls. The user can move easily within the indoor space, performing complex manoeuvring by giving a small number of instructions. Many omnidirectional wheelchair constructions are based on synchronously driven wheels [41,42], free rollers ("The Vuton II") [43], "The Vuton II" with an "omnid is" mechanism [44], or "mechanum" (Ilon) wheels [36–39]. The MIT omnidirectional wheelchair has four balls instead of wheels [45].

Walking chairs are another innovation in wheelchair design. The WL-16 walking robot [46] was created at Takanishi Lab of Waseda University in Tokyo and the Japanese robotics company Tmsuk. It uses 12 actuators and can move forward, backward, and sideways while carrying an adult weighing up to 60 kg. The prototype is radio-controlled.

Krovi et al. [47] proposed a wheelchair system that consists of a chair equipped with wheels and legs. The legs swing down to push the wheelchair up onto a curb or other uneven surface.

Ishimatsu and colleagues (at Nagasaki University, Japan) [48–51] propose a concept for a "barrier free" stair-climbing wheelchair mechanism with high single-step capability. The novel design allows the wheelchair to be boarded directly to and from a van.

23.4 WHEELCHAIRS IN SMART HOUSE DESIGN

The structure of the wheelchairs used in smart houses is usually expanded with several additional modules that allow the wheelchair control system to communicate with other home-installed devices, to receive instructions and to send information about its position,

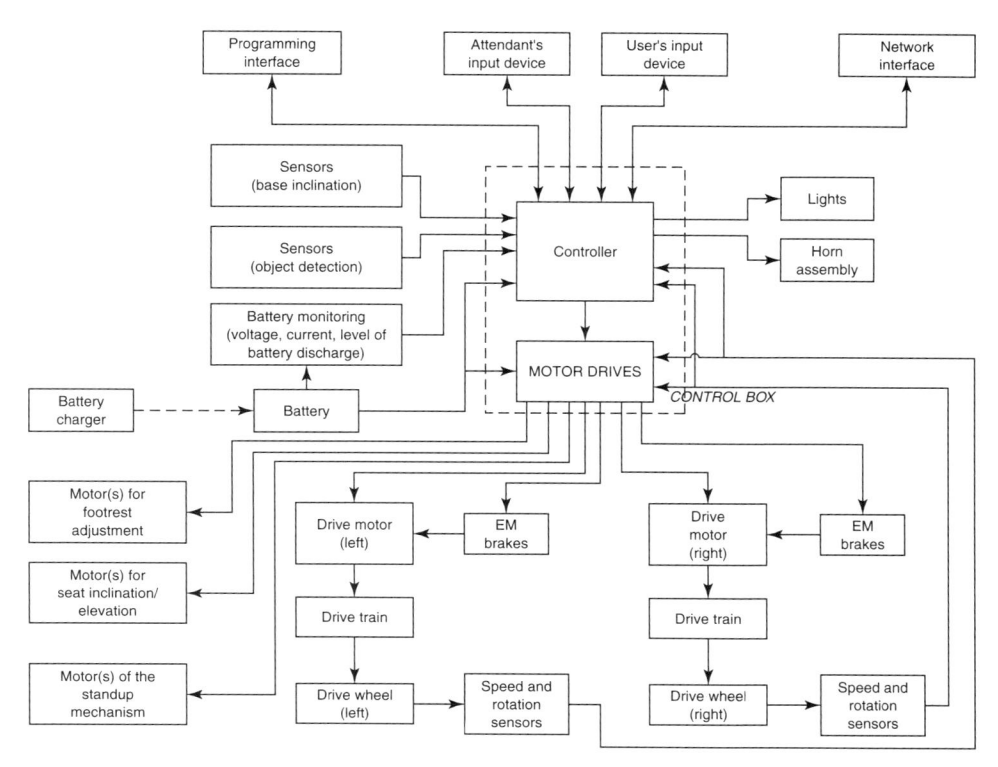

FIGURE 23.3 A general block diagram of a wheelchair used in smart house design.

speed, and status, and the health status of its user. The wheelchair is linked to the home-installed LAN via a wireless connection. The user's commands regarding control of other home-installed system are also transferred through the same link.

A general block diagram of the intelligent wheelchair is presented in Figure 23.3. The scheme is an extended version of Figure 23.1.

23.5 AUTONOMOUSLY GUIDED WHEELCHAIRS

Autonomously guided wheelchairs (AGWs) can be a promising solution for indoor transportation of older persons and people with severe dexterity limitations. Utilization of such wheelchairs offers the user an easy and independent access to different home positions. After receiving the user's instruction about the intended destination, the navigation system autonomously steers the wheelchair to that destination. In order to respond much better to the user's needs, most of the more recent R&D focuses on designing wheelchairs that cannot only follow the path to the users's intended destination but also compose the routine toward the end position and automatically modify the initially generated path during task execution if obstacles appear on the originally intended route. The AGW dramatically reduces the number of user commands and significantly decreases the cognitive load of the user.

23.5.1 Methods for Navigation

Most developments within that area concern wheelchairs that operate in structured or semistructured home environments. Regarding navigation algorithm, AGWs can be classified into two large groups: beacon-based AGWs and AGWs, with natural landmark navigation. Beacon-based navigation systems determine current wheelchair position by detection of beacons that are strategically placed at predefined locations within the home environment, measurement of the distances to these beacons, and calculation of the angles of the beacon directions. Some more recent wheelchair projects apply navigation by natural landmarks from the structured environment such as furniture edges and doorframe edges. The procedures for landmark identification are usually based on processing of the visual information from one or two cameras. The procedure includes identification of the reference edges, calculation of the length of each landmark and orientation regarding the floor plane, and estimation of landmark elevation from the floor. Beacon-based systems can be further grouped into systems that refer to active beacons (light-emitting, sound-emitting, or radiowave-emitting beacons, installed on the walls or furniture) and systems that refer to passive beacons. The latter usually utilizes specific images whose patterns, dimensions, reflection characteristics, and colors are unique for the environment. Such markers, usually of low cost, can be easily attached to the walls and simply rearranged within the house, but the techniques for their detection typically involve CCD visual sensors and very complicated computing procedures. As an example for wheelchair navigation based on passive markers, we may mention the wheelchair systems developed at the University of Notre Dame [54,55]. The wheelchair is navigated through special markers attached to the walls and to the furniture. The reference paths are physically "taught" to the system during the setup procedure. In "run" mode, the error between the current estimated position and the reference path are calculated and used to control the wheelchair steering in order to follow the reference path. The user selects the destination, and then the wheelchair system controls the chair to the desired location. In run mode the navigation system not only follows the precomposed path to the goal but also automatically modifies the routine if obstacles on the initial path are detected. After the obstacle overcome, the wheelchair returns on the original trajectory. The navigation systems with active beacons are usually highly resistant to ambient-light artifacts and apply simpler hardware for detection of the current position than do those with passive markers, but the rearrangement of the active beacons can be a problem since each active beacon should be separately powered and controlled.

The guidepath navigation systems can be considered as a special class of beacon-based systems where the beacons are embedded in the floor. The guidetrack can be designed as a reflective or colored tape attached to the floor, as a cable that emits a high-frequency electromagnetic field, as a permanent-magnet array embedded in the floor, or as a magnetic tape with prerecorded information tracks on it. Although the approach is widely used in many materials-handling applications, its utilization in the design of home-operated wheelchairs is limited by the complexity of the wheelchair movement routines and the requirements for easy reconfiguration of the path. An additional limitation arises from the necessity for embedment of the guidepath in the floor. A wheelchair navigated via a magnetic tape guidepath was reported in 1992 [56]. The solution includes a strip of flexible magnetic material attached to the floor surface and a magnetic stripe follower based on an array of fluxgate or Hall-effect sensors, mounted on the board of the vehicle.

The natural landmark navigation schemes vary from detection of ceiling-mounted lamps and calculation of their positions [57] to detection of doorframes and furniture edges [56,57]. In the VAHM project, the vertically located edges of home furniture are used as natural landmarks for navigation [60,61]. Each natural landmark is identified by the metrics of its edges and distance to the ground. The TAO-1 wheelchair, developed at the Applied AI Systems Inc., uses two CCD color cameras for landmark-based navigation and infrared sensors for obstacle detection and collision avoidance [58]. Mobile robot localization by representation of a path of sequential color strings has been proposed [62]. The code of each string includes information about the color and geometric characteristics of the vertical edges of the furniture. In general, the navigation systems based on passive bacons possess more flexibility than do those with active beacons. Since the natural landmark navigation does not require installation of any special beacons, the user can easily modify the existing travel routines and add new travel paths without assistance from specialized technical staff. On the other hand, the solutions based on natural landmarks require highly sophisticated sensors, involve complex algorithms for analysis of the visual scene, and require very powerful hardware.

Similar to the strategies adopted in the design of mobile robots, most algorithms for autonomous wheelchair guidance usually run two procedures simultaneously for estimation of the current wheelchair position: the landmark navigation procedure and the dead-reckoning navigation procedure, which allow calculation of the current wheelchair position by memorizing the coordinates of previously determined position(s) and applying to it the direction and distance traveled since that point. Calculations are usually based on measurement of the rotation angles of the driving wheels, which is typically realized by wheel-embedded encoders. Despite the sensitivity of the dead-reckoning method to errors resulting from wheel slippage and tire deformation, this combined approach significantly improves the wheelchair performance in situations when one or more beacons/landmarks are missing, malfunctioning or temporarily hidden from the navigation sensors by other objects that lie between them.

The odometry information plays a dominant role in the positioning of some autonomous wheelchairs [63,64]. The wheelchair path can be described as the sequence of the angular positions that the driving wheels have in each point. Such path representation is quite simple, and computation does not require heavy hardware resources. During the task execution, the odometry module provides only rough position information, and the exact wheelchair position is calculated on the information from ultrasonic range sensors or eye-safe infrared scanners.

When the wheelchair operates in semiautonomous navigation mode, the wheelchair control is shared between the user and the automatic controller [36]. In that mode the user sets the general direction of the wheelchair and the controller modifies the user's commands in order to prevent possible collisions with obstacles. That mode essentially facilitates successful doorway passage and can be particularly helpful to users who are unable to issue precise commands because of tremor, vision problems, or other disabilities. The algorithm is based on processing the information from wheelchair-mounted proximity sensors. Since the AGW design usually includes sensors for obstacle detection and applies an algorithm for automatic avoidance, in most cases, the AGW controller can operate in both full autonomous and semiautonomous modes. As an example, we may refer to the "NavChair"—a wheelchair developed at the Mobile Robotics Lab of the University of Michigan [65,66]. The user sets the general direction of travel and the NavChair follows it. It automatically avoids obstacles, trying to maintain user-specified direction as closely as possible. Twelve Polaroid ultrasonic sensors are used for both obstacle detection and wall following. The TinMan supplementary wheelchair controller, developed at the KISS Institute for Practical Robotics (KIPR), is a special control module that sits between the joystick and the existing wheelchair controller and modifies joystick signals in order to avoid obstacles detected by its proximity sensors [67,68]. The navigation system of the "Wheelesley" wheelchair employs infrared-, sonar-, and Hall-effect sensors [69]. The user sets the desired movement direction, and the controller generates commands for collision avoidance and centering the chair in the hallway. The Drive assistant system, developed at the VTT Machine Automation, Finland, uses ultrasonic sensors for environmental perception and modifies the user's commands in case of obstacle avoidance [70].

REFERENCES

1. *Horcher Lifting Systems*, UNILIFT Ceiling Hoist Series (http://www.barrierfreelifts.com/uk/ceiling_hoists.php).
2. Bien Z, Do J-H, Kim D-J, Jung J-W, Stefanov DH: Smart high-tech house as a large-scale care robot for the elderly and disabled people, *Int J Human-Friendly Welfare Robot Syst* **6**(1):15–26 (March 2005).
3. Bien Z, Kim D-J, Stefanov DH, Han J-S HS, Chang PH: Development of a novel type of rehabilitation robotic system KARES II, in *Universal Access and Assistive Technology*, Springer-Verlag, London, 2002, Chapter 20, pp. 201–212.
4. Cooper R.: *Rehabilitation Engineering Applied to Mobility and Manipulation*, Medical Sciences Series, 1995.
5. *BALLER™—Novel Foot-Powered Wheelchair Locomotion System*, Perpetuum Mobile Ltd., Gerontech-the Israel Center for Assistive Technology and Ageing (http://jointnet.org.il/gerontech/textversion/030.html).
6. *CEA, Non-magnetic Wheelchair Called PASS'PORT* (http://www.cea.fr/; http://www.azom.com/details.asp?newsID=4043).
7. Invacare (http://www.invacare.com/cgi-bin/imhqprd/index.jsp?s=0).
8. Benton Medical Equipment Inc. (http://www.bentonmedical.com/extrawide.html).
9. Jaffe DL: Ultrasonic head controlled wheelchair/interface—a case study in development and technology transfer, *Proc 13th Annual RESNA Conf*, Washington, DC, June 1990.
10. Dynamic Controls Inc. (http://www.dynamicmobility.co.nz/).
11. Switch-It Inc., 5829 W. Sam Houston Pkwy North, Suite 808 Houston, TX 77041 Touch Drive (http://www.switchit-inc.com/touch_drive.htm).
12. newAbilities Systems Inc. (http://www.newabilities.com/).
13. Think-A-Move Ltd. (http://www.think-a-move.com/).
14. Vaidyanathan R, Huynh TV, Gupta L, Chung B, Allen TJ, Quinn RQ, Tabib-Azar M, Zarycki J, Levin J: Human-machine interface for tele-robotic operation: Mapping of tongue movements based on aural flow monitoring, *IEEE Int Conf Intelligent Robots and Systems (IROS)*, Sendai, Japan, 2004.
15. Vaidyanathan R, Kook H, Gupta L, West J: Parametric and non-parametric signal analysis for mapping air flow in the ear-canalto tongue movement: A new strategy for hands-free human-machine interface, *Int Conf Acoustics*, *Speech, and Signal Processing (ICASSP 2004)*.
16. Yanco HA, Gips J: Preliminary investigation of a semi-autonomous robotic wheelchair directed through electrodes, *Proc Rehabilitation Engineering Society of North America Annual Conf*, Pittsburgh, PA, June 20–24, 1997, RESNA Press, 1997, pp 414–416.

17. Han J-S, Stefanov DH, Park K-H, Lee H-B, Kim D-J, Song W-K, Kim J-S, Bien Z: Development of an EMG-based powered wheelchair controller for users with high-level spinal cord injury, *Proc Int Conf Control, Automation and System*, Jeju Island, Korea, 2001, pp 503–506.
18. Matsumoto Y, Ino T, Ogasawara T: Development of intelligent wheelchair system with face and gaze based interface, *Proc 10th IEEE Int Workshop on Robot and Human Communication (ROMAN 2001)*, 2001, pp 262–267.
19. Nara Institute of Science and Technology, Graduate School of Information Science, Robotics Lab. (http://robotics.naist.jp/research/watson/index_e.html; http://robotics.naist.jp/en/).
20. Millan J del R, Renkens F, Mourino J, Gerstner W:. Brain actuated interaction, *Artif Intell*, **159**:241–259 (2004).
21. Millan J del R, Renkens F, Mourino J, Gerstner W: Non-invasive brain actuated control of a mobile robot by human EEG, *IEEE Trans Biomed Eng*, **51**:1026–1033 (2004).
22. Serruya MD, Donoghue JP: Design principles of a neuromotor prosthetic device, in Horch KW, Dhillon GS, eds., *Neuroprosthetics: Theory and Practice*, Imperial College Press, 2003, Section 7.9, pp 1158–1196.
23. Donoghue JP, Nurmikko A, Friehs G, Black MJ: Development of a neuromotor prosthesis for humans, in Hallett M, Phillips II LH, Schomer DL, Massey JM, eds, *Advances in Clinical Neurophysiology* (Suppl to *Clin Neurophysiol* **57**) (*Proc 27th Int Congress of Clinical Neurophysiology*, AAEM 50th Anniversary and the 57th Annual Meeting of the ACNS Joint Meeting, San Francisco, Sept 15–20, 2003), Chapter 63, pp 588–602.
24. LEVO AG (http://www.levo.ch/2_Englisch/Start-E.htm).
25. Mankowski JP: *Stand-Up Wheelchair*, US Patent 5,096,008, 1990.
26. Wier JP, Garrett RA: Integrated Wheelchair and Ambulator, US Patent 4,390,076, 1983.
27. Aquila Corporation (http://www.aquilacorp.com/).
28. Arva J, Cooper RA, Spaeth DA, Corfman TA, Fitzgerald SG, Boninger ML: User power reduction in Yamaha JWII pushrim activated power assisted wheelchair, *Proc Annual RESNA Conf*, Orlando, FL, June 28–July 2, 2000, pp 399–401.
29. Cooper RA, Corfman TA, Fitzgerald SG, Boninger ML, Spaeth DM, Ammer W, Arva J: Performance assessment of a pushrim-activated power-assisted wheelchair control system, *IEEE Trans Control Syst Technol* **10**(1): 121–126 (Jan 2002).
30. Simpson R, LoPresti E, Hayashi S, Guo S, Frisch R, Martin A, Ammer W, Ding D, Cooper R: The smart power assistance module for manual wheelchairs, in Keates S, Clarkson PJ, Langdon P, Robinson P, eds, *Designing a More Inclusive World (Proc CWUAAT '04)*, Springer-Verlag, 2004, pp 51–54.
31. Kamen D, Ambrogi R, Heinzmann R, Key B, Skoskiewicz A, Kristal P: *Human Transporter*, US Patent 5,701,965, Dec 30, 1997.
32. Kamen D, Ambrogi R: Heinzmann R, *Transportation Vehicles with Stability Enhancement Using CG Modification*, US Patent 5,975,225, Nov 2, 1999.
33. Kamen D, Ambrogi R, Duggan R, Heinzmann R, Key B, Dastous S: *Control Loop for Transportation Vehicles*, US Patent 5,791,425, Aug 11, 1998.
34. Kamen D, Ambrogi R, Duggan R, Field D, Heinzmann R, Amsbury B, Langenfeld C: *Personal Mobility Vehicles and Methods*, World Patent WO 00/75 001 A1, Dec 14, 2000.
35. Independence Technologies (http://www.independencenow.com/).
36. Borgolte U, Hoyer H, Bühler C, Heck H, Hölper R: Architectural concepts of a semi-autonomous wheelchair, *J Intell Robot Syst* **22**(3): 233–253 (1998).
37. Bühler C, Heck H, Jochheim A, Borgolte U: OMNI: A sensor-assisted omni-directional wheelchair for vocational Rehabilitation, *Proc 6th European Congress on Research in Rehabilitation*, Berlin, 1998, pp 535–536.

38. Borgolte U, Hoyer H: OMNI—results and outlook: Conclusions from a successful project, *Proc 1st MobiNet Symp*, Athens, Greece, 1997, pp. 101–114.
39. Borgolte U, Hoelper R, Hoyer H: An omnidirectional wheelchair with enhanced comfort features, *Proc 5th Int Conf Rehabilitation Robotics*, Bath, UK, 1997, pp. 31–34.
40. Kamata M, Ishii Y: Development of powered wheelchair with omnidirectional drive system, Marinček C, Bühler C, Knops H, Andrich R, eds, *Assistive Technology—Added Value to the Quality of Life*, IOS Press, Amsterdam, 2001, pp 232–237.
41. Everett HR: *Sensors for Mobile Robots, Theory and Application*, AK Peters, Wellesley, MA, 1995.
42. Jung M-J, Kim J-H: Mobility augmentation of conventional wheeled bases for omnidirectional motion, *IEEE Trans Robot Automat* 18:81–87 (Feb 2002).
43. Hirose S, Amano S: The VUTON: High payload high efficiency holonomic omni-directional vehicle, *Proc 6th Int Symp Robotics Research*, Hidden Valley, PA, 1993, pp. 253–260.
44. Damoto R, Cheng W, Hirose S: Holonomic omni-directional vehicle with new omni-wheel mechanism, *Proc IEEE Int Conf Robotics and Automation*, Seoul, Korea, 2001, pp 773–778.
45. Mascaro S, Asada H: Docking control of holonomic omnidirectional vehicles with applications to a hybrid wheelchair/bed system, *Proc IEEE Int Conf Robotics and Automation*, Leuven, Belgium, 1998, pp 399–405.
46. Sugahara Y, Hosobata T, Mikuriya Y, Sunazuka H, Lim H, Takanishi A: Realization of dynamic human-carrying walking by a biped locomotor, *Proc IEEE Int Conf Robotics and Automation, (ICRA 04)*, April 26–May 1, 2004, vol. 3, pp 3055–3060.
47. Wellman P, Krovi V, Kumar V, Harwin W: Design of a wheelchair with legs for people with motor disabilities, *IEEE Trans Rehab Eng*, 3(4): 343–349 (Dec 1995).
48. Ishimatsu T, Sugiyama K, Kurihara M: Development of a stairclimbing machine in Nagasaki, *Proc 3rd Int Workshop of Advanced Mechatronics*, Kanwon, Korea, 1999, pp 214–217.
49. Lawn M: A robotic hybrid wheelchair for operation in the real world, *Shoho J* 8 (Computer Science Center, Nagasaki Institute of Applied Science) 65–97 (Dec 1997).
50. Lawn M, Takeda T: Design of a robotic-hybrid wheelchair for operation in barrier present environments, *Proc 20th Int Conf IEEE Engineering in Medicine and Biology Society*, Hong Kong, Oct 29–Nov 1, 1998, pp. 2678–2681.
51. Lawn MJ, Ishimatsu T: Modeling of a stair-climbing wheelchair mechanism with high single-step capability, *IEEE Trans Neural Syst Rehab Eng*, 11(3): 323–332 (2003).
52. Simpson RC., Smart wheelchairs: A literature review, *J Rehab Res Devel*, 42(4): 423–438 (July/Aug 2005).
53. Simpson R, LoPresti E, Hayashi S, Nourbakhsh I, Miller D: The smart wheelchair component system, *J Rehab Res Devel*, 41,(3B): 429–442 (May/June 2004).
54. Baumgartner E, Skaar S: An autonomous vision-based mobile robot, *IEEE Trans Autom Control* 39(3): 493–502 (1994).
55. Yoder JD, Baumgartner E, Skaar S: Initial results in the development of a guidance system for a powered wheelchair, *IEEE Trans Rehab Eng* 4(3): 143–302 (1996).
56. Wakuami H, Nakamura K, Matsumara T: Development of an automated wheelchair guided by a magnetic ferrite marker lane, *J Rehab Res Devel* 29(1): 27–34 (1992).
57. Wang H, Kang CU, Ishimatsu T, Ochiai T: Auto navigation on a wheelchair, *Proc 1st Int Symp Artificial Life and Robotics*, Beppu, Oita, Japan, (1996).
58. Gomi T, Griffith A: Developing intelligent wheelchairs for the handicapped, *Proc Evolutionary Robotics Symp*, Tokyo, (1998) pp 461–478.

59. Kreutner M, Horn O: Contribution to rehabilitation mobile robotics: Localization of an autonomous wheelchair, *Proc 7th Int Conf Rehabilitation Robotics*, Evry, Paris, (2001), pp 207–214.
60. Bourhis G, Horn O, Habert O, Pruski A: An autonomous vehicle for people with motor disabilities, *IEEE Robot Autom Mag*, **7**(1): 20–28 (2001).
61. Pruski A, Habert O: Obstacle avoidance module for the VAHM-2 Wheelchair, *5th Conf Advancement of Assistive Technology (AAATE'99)*, Düsseldorf, Germany, (1999).
62. Lamon P, Nourbakhsh I, Jensen B, Siegwart R: Deriving and matching image fingerprint sequences for mobile robot localization, *Proc ICRA 2001*, Seoul, Korea, (2001)
63. Beattie PD, Bishop JM: Self-localisation in the "Senario" autonomous wheelchair, *J Intell Robot Syst*, **22**:255–267 (1998).
64. Katevas NI, Sgouros NM, Tzafestas SG, Papakonstantinou G, Beattie P, Bishop JM, Tsanakas P, Koutsouris D: The autonomous mobile robot SENARIO: A sensor-aided intelligent navigation system for powered wheelchairs, *IEEE Robot Autom Mag* **4**:60–70 (1997).
65. Simpson RC, Levine SP: Automatic adaptation in the NavChair assistive wheelchair navigation system, *IEEE Trans Rehab Engi* **7**(4): 452–463 (1999).
66. Simpson RC, Levine SP, Bell DA, Jaros LA, Koren Y, Borenstein J: NavChair: An assistive wheelchair navigation system with automatic adaptation, in Mittal V, Yanco H, Aronis J, Simpson R, eds, *Lecture Notes in Artificial Intelligence: Assistive Technology and Artificial Intelligence—Application in Robotics, User Interfaces and Natural Language Processing*, Springer-Verlag, (1998), Vol **1458**, pp 235–255.
67. Miller DP, Slack MG: Design and testing of a low-cost robotic wheelchair prototype, *J Auton Robots* **2**:77–88 (1995).
68. Miller DP: Assistive robotics: Semi-autonomous movement towards independence, in Mittal V, Yanco H, Aronis J, Simpson R, eds: *Lecture Notes in Artificial Intelligence: Assistive Technology and Artificial Intelligence—Application in Robotics, User Interfaces and Natural Language Processing*, (1998), Springer-Verlag, Vol **1458**, pp 126–137.
69. Yanco H: Wheelesley: A robotic wheelchair system: Indoor navigation and user interface, in Mittal V, Yanco H, Aronis J, Simpson R, eds, *Lecture Notes in Artificial Intelligence: Assistive Technology and Artificial Intelligence—Application in Robotics, User Interfaces and Natural Language Processing* (1998) Springer-Verlag, Vol **1458**, pp 256–286.
70. Peussa P, Virtanen A, Johansson T: Improving the mobility of severely disabled, *Proc 2nd European Conf Disability, Virtual Reality and Associated Technologies*, Skövde, Sweden, Sept 10–11, 1998, pp 169–176.

24

People with Special Needs and Traffic Safety

Nahid Shahmehri, Ioan Chisalita, and Johan Åberg

Linköping University, Linköping, Sweden

24.1 TRAFFIC SAFETY

The automobile is arguably one of the most important inventions of the twentieth century [1]. The development of society has been profoundly influenced by the expansion of the road system and the resulting increase in freedom of movement. However, it has always been the case that wherever there are cars, there are traffic accidents. This is not a minor issue; with more than one million people worldwide dying on the roads every year, and billions of US$ in accident-related property losses, traffic safety continues to be a serious and difficult problem [2,3].

The statistics underscore the seriousness of the situation. For example, although traffic fatalities in the European Union (EU) have consistently decreased since the mid-1990s (see Fig. 24.1), there were still more than 42,000 fatalities in the enlarged EU (including 25 countries) alone in 2004. In addition to loss of life and limb, the financial impact of traffic accidents is enormous; for example, in 2003 the total of accident-related losses reported in the United States was more than $230 billion USD [4].

24.2 OLDER DRIVERS AND ACCIDENTS

Due to societal improvements in healthcare, living standards, and socioeconomic status, an increasing number of people are living to an advanced age [5]. It is not an uncommon desire among the elderly to sustain mobility and continue with their daily activities, such

---

The Engineering Handbook of Smart Technology for Aging, Disability, and Independence,
Edited by A. Helal, M. Mokhtari and B. Abdulrazak
Copyright © 2008 John Wiley & Sons, Inc.

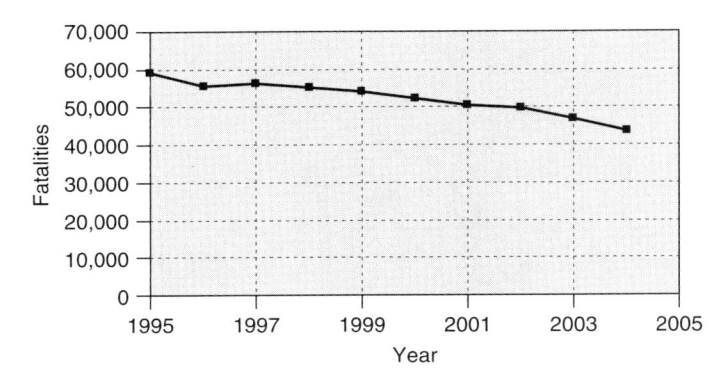

FIGURE 24.1 *Fatalities in EU25 (enlarged) between 1995 and 2005.*

as driving, and thus remain independent [6]. However, older drivers are more likely than other drivers to sustain serious injuries that lead to disability or death [7]. This presents an opportunity for technology to play a role in improving traffic safety while preserving the mobility of older people.

In an effort to improve traffic safety, extensive investigations into the causes of accidents and crash countermeasures have been conducted since the mid-1990s [8,9]. Many (90%) of these studies identified driver error as the major cause of crashes. Consequently, a great deal of effort has been directed toward helping drivers and reducing operator error. Work has been done both on improvement of the road infrastructure (e.g., using roundabouts at crossroads) and integration of support systems into vehicles. However, accidents vary tremendously in the way they occur, and developing a system that is efficient in any traffic situation is challenging. The following is an overview of different types of accidents and their rate of occurrence; four types of accidents are most predominant:

- *Intersection accidents*, including angle crashes at crossroads caused by vehicles that run "stop" or "give way" signs
- *Rear-end accidents*, including crashes in which a vehicle strikes the rear end of another vehicle, implying an inattentive or distracted driver
- *Lane change accidents*, such as crashes that occur when a vehicle unexpectedly enters a lane already occupied by another vehicle
- *Road departure accidents*, such as crashes due to a temporary loss of control of the vehicle

Figure 24.2 presents an example of the distribution of these types of accidents over the total number of accidents in United States in 2003.

It is generally believed that accident risks change according to the age of the drivers [2]. Two types of risk are thus considered to be age-related:

- Risks that drivers pose to other traffic participants
- Risks that drivers face in traffic

A large body of work has been done on quantifying the correlation between age and accident distribution. In statistical studies, driver age is generally plotted against other

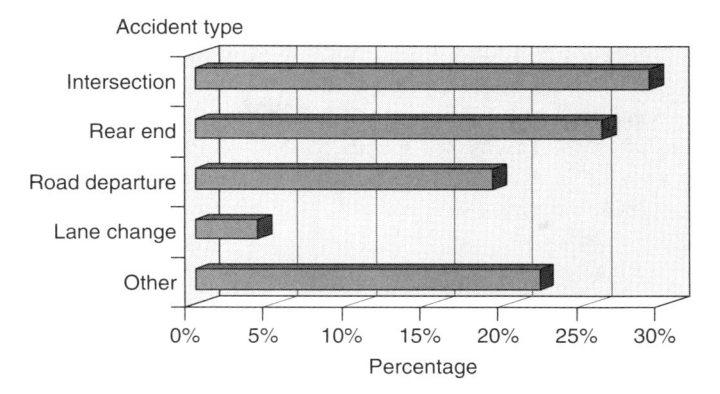

FIGURE 24.2 Distribution of accident types.

variables such as fatalities per year or fatalities per kilometer traveled. An example is presented in Figure 24.3, which illustrates the number of fatalities as a function of age groups in the initial 15 countries of the European Union in 2003.

However, care must be taken when interpreting the statistics. On one side, in many cases older drivers were categorized as dangerous to others, because the accident statistics showed that they were the responsible parties in a large number of crashes [10]. Furthermore, the accident risk for older drivers was indicated to be generally higher than for other age groups [11]. On the other side, older drivers, who were strong, defensive drivers, were involved in fewer accidents in which other drivers were responsible [2]. This is due to the specific driving behavior exhibited by older drivers. These drivers tend to drive slowly and cautiously, and usually adopt a defensive driving style. Therefore, they may achieve a high percentage in avoiding accidents that are due to errors produced by other drivers. Additionally, older drivers travel a significantly lower distance per year than do younger drivers, which reduces the risk of accidents. For instance, by analyzing road departure accidents where pedestrians were injured, it was determined that renewing

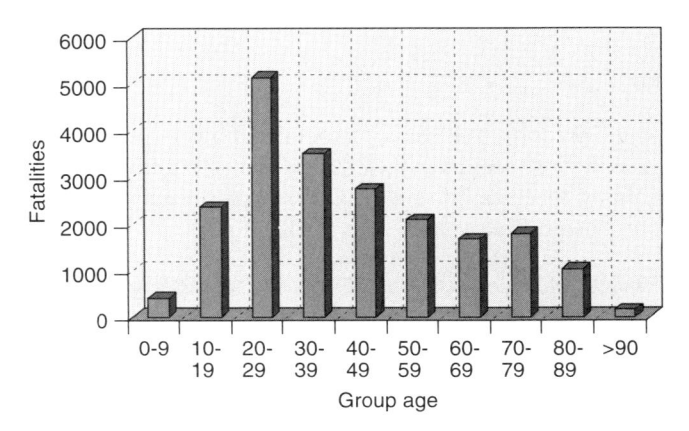

FIGURE 24.3 Fatalities classified by age group in EU15 in 2003.

the driver license for one year for an 80-year-old person would result in more than 30% lower risks than renewing the driver license of a 45-year-old person [2].

Nevertheless, the various risks faced by drivers in traffic increase with age. For instance, older people are several times more likely to be killed than middle-aged people in the same kind of crash. This is due mainly to the fragility of older drivers. In addition, as drivers advance in age, the types of accidents they are involved in change. For instance, road departure accidents with rollover, which are common for younger drivers, seldom occur with older drivers. Typical accidents that involve older drivers are intersection crashes and lane change crashes. In general, older drivers seem to face problems when exposed to more complex driving situations such as at crossroads [11].

In view of the aspects discussed above, it is essential to consider both the weaknesses and the strengths of older drivers, in order to perform a correct assessment of the risks they pose to other traffic participants.

Whereas older people may not really be more dangerous in traffic than are other age groups, they may experience a number of issues that are less common for other drivers. Some of these problems can interfere with the activity of driving and can induce difficulties in safely performing certain driving tasks. We consider below these aspects in detail. Although elderly people are a highly heterogeneous group, there is general agreement that several functions that are important for driving tend to degenerate with increased age. These functions are related mainly to cognitive and motor capabilities [12].

Cognitive functions affect a person's intellectual abilities, including perception, memory, problem-solving ability, spatial orientation, information management, and attention. Research on driving-related problems has focused on perception, which has been shown to have a strong relationship to accident occurrences [12,13]. In addition, older drivers are slower at handling information when it comes to making difficult decisions. They also have difficulty maintaining all of the necessary information for making decisions, due to deterioration in attention and memory. When older drivers act on the information they have gathered, they may be slower than what the situation may demand. The decay of motor capabilities for older people implies a decrease in movement range and reaction time [13]. Examples of motor impairments are

- Head movement, such as looking to the side
- Body coordination, such as simultaneously operating the pedals, the steering wheel, and the blinkers
- Slow reflexes

With respect to visual perception, it has been found that older people may have increased difficulties in perceiving impulses from their surroundings. For traffic situations, they have difficulties determining speed and distances. Other impairments related to vision that are more likely to affect older drivers are

- Decreased visual field, including failure to see approaching traffic
- Blurred vision, such as difficulty in reading traffic signs
- Impaired night vision, including difficult night driving

Specific health problems must also be considered when investigating the risks for older drivers. Examples of such issues are

- Sudden change in health condition
- Disease-related impairments
- Physical frailty

Certainly, some older drivers are less affected by the abovementioned problems. Additionally, these problems can be experienced in one way or another by other drivers as well. For instance, a large number of people suffer from myopia, which can cause impaired night vision. Still, it is highly important to acknowledge the difficulties that may induce risks for older drivers in traffic. Developing solutions that help them overcome these risks will also benefit other drivers.

24.3 CRASH COUNTERMEASURES

Crash statistics clearly indicate that traffic safety is in need of radical improvements. Four main areas have been identified as major contributors for crash countermeasures:

- Driver education
- Road infrastructure
- Vehicle safety design
- In-vehicle safety systems

Driver education is a continuous process, and addresses both new and experienced drivers. As advances in technology drive integration of new systems into vehicles, drivers must constantly be familiarized with the vehicles' new functionalities. Furthermore, the capabilities of new vehicles far exceed those of old vehicles, which may cause drivers to modify their driving behavior and perform driving maneuvers in a different way. A classic example is the use of the brakes using the antilock braking system (ABS), where the driver can brake heavily even when driving on slippery surfaces and still manage to control the vehicle. This is seldom the case when the vehicle is equipped only with a simple servo brake, since the wheels lock up under heavy braking, which results in a loss of steering control. Also related to driver education is the promulgation of laws and regulations that prevent drivers from harming other traffic participants. An example from Swedish traffic legislation is the regulation that vehicles must stop and give way to pedestrians when they wait to cross the road, not only when the pedestrians actually start to cross.

The safety design of the road infrastructure is intended to protect drivers from dangers in traffic. It is also intended to help drivers in avoiding maneuvers that can lead to accidents. A typical case is the deployment of roundabouts at crossroads, which significantly reduce the risks of lateral crashes. Road structure, road geometry, and traffic sign positioning are other areas of improvements within the safety design of the roads.

Vehicle safety design is intended to provide maximum protection to drivers and passengers in the event of a crash. Significant improvements have been achieved since the mid-1980s in making vehicles safer. In addition, vehicles are currently designed to protect not only the occupants in case of a crash but also other traffic participants such as pedestrians. Vehicle safety features are now important considerations when buying a car.

In-vehicle safety systems are intended not only for driver protection in accidents but also to help the driver avoid accidents. In the following section we discuss these systems in detail.

Deploying safety systems in vehicles is essential to obtain a high level of improvement in traffic safety. Two main lines of development for safety systems that can be installed in vehicles have been undertaken. The first line deals with the development of *passive safety systems*, which react when dangerous situations happen and try to reduce the consequences of inevitable accidents. An example of a system that has already proved its efficiency is the smart airbag. The second line addresses the development of *active safety systems*, which are intended to prevent vehicles from colliding with each other. If this is not possible because of the specifics of the traffic situation, these systems should at least reduce the consequences of accidents. For instance, in the case of rear-end collisions, active systems should at least ensure a reduction in the velocity of the vehicle at the back at the moment of impact. The two most common representative examples of active systems are collision warning and collision avoidance. These systems notify the driver of potential dangers in traffic, and may employ automatic actions such as emergency braking or steering on behalf of the driver. The major difference between passive and active systems lies in the level of support they can provide to drivers. Thus, passive safety systems are designed to protect the driver when a dangerous situation is already underway. They are certainly essential for making traffic safer, but because of their reactive mode of operation, they cannot provide a high level of improvement for traffic safety on their own [1]. Active safety systems actively participate in preventing traffic situations from developing into accidents. They have the ability to predict the possibility for a hazard to occur, and thus are able to act well in advance of potentially hazardous conditions.

24.3.1 Active Safety Systems Background

Two approaches have been considered for developing active safety systems. The first approach addresses the development of *autonomous systems* that collect and analyze information from the local environment of a vehicle [15]. These systems usually employ technologies such as radar (e.g., millimeter-wave or light-based), and machine vision (e.g., videocameras and image processing) for acquiring information about obstacles situated in front of, laterally to, and behind a vehicle. The second approach is the development of *collaborative systems* that employ the wireless exchange of information among vehicles and possibly between vehicles and servers located on the roadside [16]. These systems require the development of *vehicular communication networks*. Collaborative systems function similarly to autonomous systems, but they use both data collected by sensors and data received via wireless communication from other vehicles when assessing dangers in traffic.

Active safety systems can also be connected with passive safety systems. Examples are systems that offer support to passive systems by anticipating an imminent collision using radar technology. On the basis of these data, the passive systems (e.g., seatbelt, airbag) can be activated in advance, which can lead to a reduction in the severity of injuries that the vehicle occupants may suffer. An example of such passive-active systems is the Toyota "Pre-crash Safety System."

The proposals for active safety systems can be categorized further according to the type of support they provide to drivers:

- *Information delivery systems*—control the content and the presentation of warnings. These systems present the driver with information that can increase his/her situation awareness and let the driver take the appropriate measures.
- *Automatic control systems*—delegate certain driving tasks to the vehicle. These systems aim at providing more support to the driver by automating certain aspects of driving.

24.3.2 Technologies for Developing Active Safety Systems

The operation modes of active safety systems impose specific requirements on the functionality of the support technology. The following is a set of generic requirements for active safety systems:

- Active safety systems must be reliable and must be efficient in determining dangers in traffic and performing actions accordingly.
- Active safety systems must be accurate and must provide effective support to the driver.
- Active safety systems should not lead to the mental overload of the driver.
- Active safety systems need to operate in a wide variety of traffic situations.
- Active safety systems need to be economically feasible.
- Active safety systems need to consider diverse regulations.

Many research areas such as sensors, kinematics, positioning, information systems, and communication networks can contribute to the development of efficient active safety systems. In this section we discuss three technologies that are considered most promising for implementing active safety systems: radar and laser sensor systems, computer vision, and communication systems [1].

Since the ultimate goal of active safety systems is to keep vehicles from colliding with each other and with other objects, vehicles can be equipped with devices that can identify the presence of obstacles. Such devices are usually radar sensors or lidar sensors (i.e., sensors based on laser) that can detect obstacles that exist around a vehicle and may interfere with its traveling path [1,9]. Standard radar systems use sensors that send narrow microwave beams that are reflected by objects and received back by the radar system. From this information, the relative position and speed of other objects can be determined. Lidar systems use lightbeams for the same purposes.

The major limitation associated with sensor systems is their local perception. This is due to the fact that sensor systems usually require a line of sight (LOS) for object detection [17]. Thus, they cannot detect more distant or hidden objects (i.e., objects that are not in the LOS), and therefore may not be able to provide information about more complex traffic situations.

Several other problems arise with the utilization of sensor systems with regard to both the operation modes and the current state of the art technology. For example, lidar sensors are considered less appropriate because rain and snow affect their functionality. Even worse, the accumulation of dust and mud may make them unusable [1]. Issues such as cost, sensor integration within vehicles (which may require modification of the car body), and regulatory aspects addressing the frequency spectrum also need to be considered when developing sensors for vehicles. For instance, radar systems operating at 76–77 GHz, which were initially used in adaptive cruise control systems, are currently considered less appropriate because of their high cost. Consequently, new 24-GHz radar systems have been proposed. However, because of their narrower operation range, 24-GHz radar systems may not be so effective in cases when detection of more distant obstacles is needed.

Another technology that has been considered for improving traffic safety is computer vision. One important safety application addresses collision avoidance where vehicles use vision for detecting obstacles such as pedestrians and other vehicles that can interfere with the traveling path of a vehicle. Another important type of application using computer vision addresses the monitoring of the vehicle movement based on elements characteristic to roads, such as lane markers. In these applications, stereocameras are used to monitor the environment around a vehicle, and image processing is employed to determine the occurrence of dangerous situations, such as when a vehicle dangerously approaches the lateral side of a road. These systems then alert the driver to such situations. However, as with the utilization of sensor systems, limitations related to the local perception of the vehicles (e.g., LOS object detection and monitoring) apply for active safety systems based on computer vision.

We note that computer vision can also be used for monitoring driver condition. In such applications, videocameras analyze the driver by monitoring behavior-related aspects such as eye movement. This gives indications about the driver's capacity for paying attention to the road conditions and successfully fulfilling the driving tasks. An application that received much attention is the determination of the driver's state of drowsiness.

Relying on data from local sensors is an inherent weakness of active safety systems based on sensors and computer vision. This limits their utility to detect objects that are not in the line of sight, such as vehicles entering an intersection. One solution to these limitations is to equip vehicles with communication capabilities, allowing the exchange of safety traffic information. Using communication, a vehicle can then obtain data about vehicles that are not detected by sensors (e.g., radar) or by computer vision systems. Consequently, the perception of a vehicle is extended. Considering this advantage, vehicular communication was predicted to have a major impact on the development of effective active safety systems that can help reduce the number and severity of crashes [1,16]. Furthermore, it was envisioned that a large variety of safety services, such as collision warning, collision avoidance, or traffic jam notifications, could be provided to the driver when vehicles have communication capabilities.

We note that communication networks for vehicles can be formed only by vehicles, or by vehicles and servers located on the roadside. Thus, two types of vehicular communication were defined:

- *Vehicle-to-Road Communication (VRC).* Exchange of data between vehicles and communication servers located on the roadside. Even if data must be exchanged between two vehicles, this is performed via a roadside server (Fig. 24.4).
- *InterVehicle Communication (IVC).* Direct exchange of data between vehicles (Fig. 24.5).

24.3.3 Collaborative Active Safety Systems

The concept of collaborative safety communication is illustrated in Figure 24.6. We use an example with two vehicles, a concept similar to that in which more vehicles

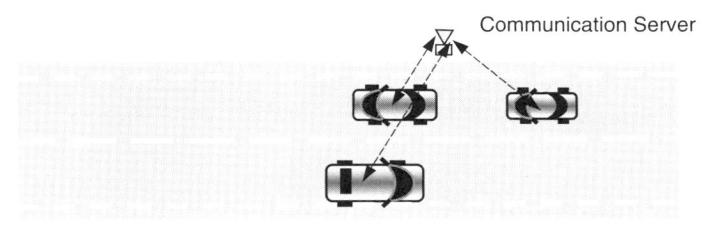

FIGURE 24.4 Vehicle-to-road communication example.

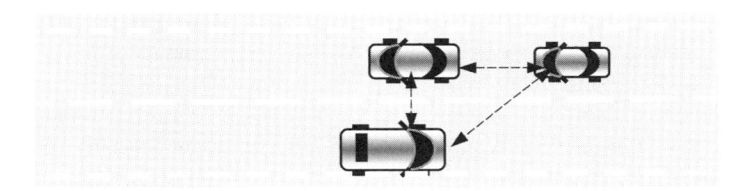

FIGURE 24.5 Intervehicle communication example.

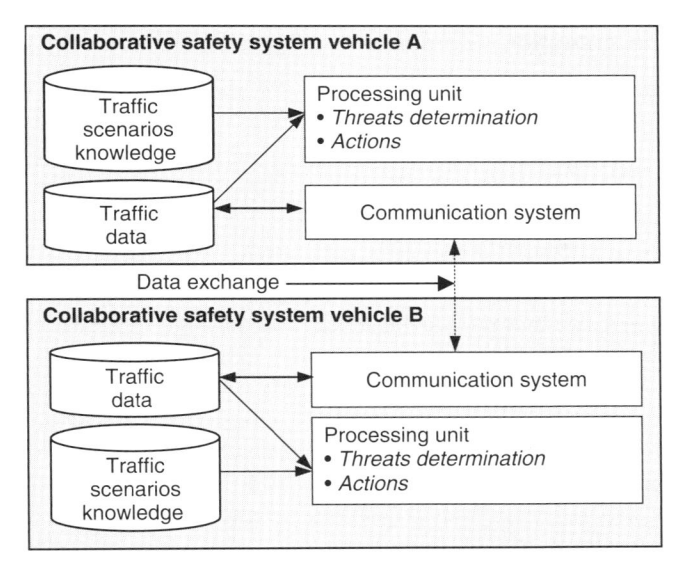

FIGURE 24.6 Collaborative communication concept.

interact with each other. The collaborative active safety systems contain a communication system for data exchange between vehicles, a traffic database (i.e., the *traffic data* component), a knowledge base for traffic scenarios patterns (i.e., the *traffic scenarios knowledge* component), and a processing unit.

The communication system is used to exchange safety-related information such as front-end data characterizing vehicles (e.g., velocity, position, heading), and data describing the road (e.g., slipperiness coefficient). This information is registered in the traffic database.

The knowledge base for traffic scenarios contains patterns of potential accidents, which are used to detect the occurrence of dangerous situations in traffic. This information is quasistatic and may need to be updated. This can be done statically (e.g., during regular vehicle tuneups) or dynamically (e.g., using a vehicular communication system).

24.4 INVESTIGATING COUNTERMEASURES

We focus on one of the most common accidents among the elderly: the road intersection accident [2]. We analyze in depth to what extent collaborative safety systems can help to avoid intersection accidents involving elderly drivers. A temporal reasoning system (ECAM) previously developed by us was used to analyze the impact of information transfer properties (transmission delay of warning messages), driver characteristics (reaction time), and accident scenario characteristics (e.g., speed), on collision avoidance [18]. We further assess the feasibility of a solution based on communication by simulating the operation of the safety system within a realistic simulator. The results indicate the strong potential of safety systems based on vehicular communication for helping older drivers maintain safe driving in road intersections.

24.4.1 Road Intersection Accidents

Studies have indicated that a significant majority of accidents involving elderly drivers take place at intersections. The main difficulties elderly drivers face at intersections are [12,19]:

- Estimation of a safe gap and the estimation of velocity of other vehicles.
- Fast execution of driving maneuvers (e.g., turning)
- Failure to sense and comprehend traffic signals and signs
- Inability to perceive and process information about high traffic volume

Figure 24.7 illustrates an accident involving elderly drivers that occurs when two cars traveling on perpendicular paths enter an intersection at the same time. This type of accident accounts for more than 30% of the total number of accidents that occur each year at intersections [13]. It is also considered to be of high risk for elderly drivers [11].

The scenario depicted in Figure 24.7 shows several vehicles that approach or have passed through an intersection. Of interest are vehicles V1 and V2, marked in white in the figure. The driver in vehicle V2 is elderly (e.g., over 65) and the driver in V1 is middle-aged (e.g., 40–49). Vehicle V1 is traveling on the priority road. Vehicle V2 is initially stopped at the "stop" sign and plans to cross the intersection. When V2 starts to cross, it is accelerating slowly, as the elderly driver tends to drive carefully. Let us assume that V2's driver does not notice the presence of V1, perhaps because the driver fails to make a correct estimate of V1's distance and velocity. The driver in V1 is misled by the maneuver of V2 and assumes that V2 will not pass through the intersection or will pass through it in time. At some later time, V1's driver realizes that these assumptions are not valid and intends to brake in order to stop. However, because of a small separation distance between vehicles, V1 crashes into V2.

Now, the question is how to avoid this type of accident.

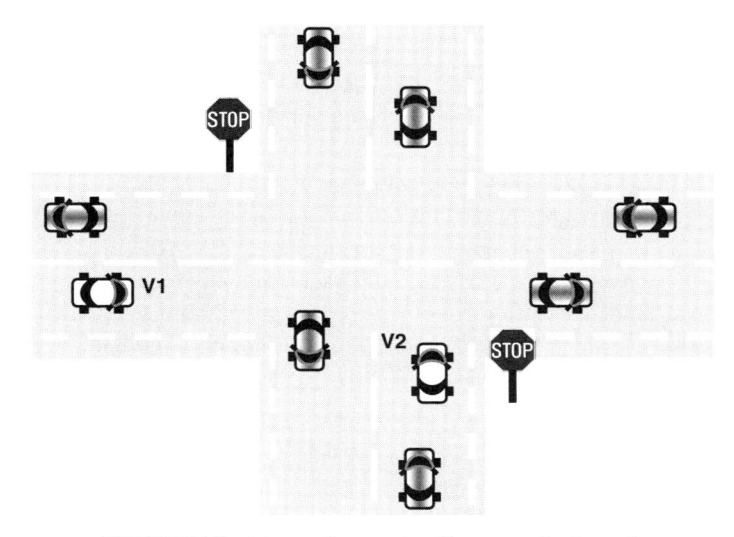

FIGURE 24.7 *Intersection crash with perpendicular path.*

24.4.2 Accident Avoidance Experiments

The specific issues that were addressed are presented below:

- Information transfer requirements that the vehicular communications systems must fulfill
- Impact of the accident scenario conditions and the properties of the information transfer on accident avoidance

To perform the analyses we primarily used ECAM, a temporal reasoning system for modeling and analyzing accident scenarios [20]. ECAM is a formal framework that provides a reasoning engine for studying the time evolution of traffic accidents. It is based on a well-known logical formalism, the *event calculus*, and it is implemented using logic programming (i.e., Prolog). This system makes it possible to investigate the relationship between events that occur in traffic and their possible consequences. It is thus able to model changes that take place when different actions occur in a traffic situation. To conduct analyses, the system can be questioned to determine whether, and at what point, certain traffic conditions related to vehicles involved in a scenario become valid. For instance, it can be determined whether, and at what point, a collision between two vehicles has occurred within a traffic scenario. Furthermore, by modifying different parameters in the scenario (e.g., initial speed of vehicles) or introducing new actions that modify the development of the scenario (e.g., heavy braking), changes in the scenario behavior can be examined. For instance, the possibility of avoiding a collision can be identified by performing such analyses.

We started with the assumption that each vehicle was equipped with a collaborative active safety system. This system operated by presenting the driver with notifications about dangers in traffic, and could also employ automatic actions if it were set in an automatic mode. The assumptions that were made in the course of the investigations were as follows:

- When vehicle V2 starts to cross the intersection, a warning message is sent to vehicle V1.
- The safety system in V1 receives the warning message and reacts to it, either by notifying the driver that V2 has started to cross the intersection, or by braking automatically.
- The driver in V1 reacts to the notification and starts to brake heavily after a driver reaction time has passed (a reaction time of 0 indicates automatic braking).
- The acceleration of V2 when entering the intersection is fixed, and fairly low (e.g., 1.5 m/s^2). This assumption is based on the fact that many older drivers drive slowly, as a compensatory measure for their limited cognitive abilities [10].
- The distance of vehicle V2 from the entry point into the intersection is fixed and is set to 4 ms.
- Vehicle V2 starts crossing the intersection at 1 s after the beginning of the scenario.
- A maximum deceleration of 9 m/s^2 is considered for V1.
- The width of a road lane is set to 4 m.

The avoidance of the accident between V1 and V2 can be achieved as the result of the heavy braking maneuver performed by V1 when it receives the warning message sent by V2. Therefore, we investigated the maximum delay for the warning message sent by V2 that would still ensure avoidance of the accident. The experiments were performed by varying the scenario conditions and dynamics, represented by the variation of the reaction times of the driver and of the initial speed of vehicle V1. These independent variables are detailed below:

- Delay of V2's warning message: 0–2.3 s
- Speed of V1: 10–25 m/s or equivalently 36–90 km/h
- Driver reaction time (DRT): 0–3 s

The variation of the driver reaction time was based on research in collision avoidance. We note that a driver reaction time of 0 s corresponds to an automatic active safety system. For the overall population, a DRT of 1.5 s is an upper limit for simple reactions [21]. However, this value has been adopted as a normal value, since it is known that older people tend to have longer reaction times. A DRT of 3 s is an extreme upper bound that rarely occurs in real cases.

The dependent variable used in the experiments was the *cutoff distance* for V1. This parameter is defined as the minimum distance from the entry point into the intersection at which V1 needs to be positioned when V2 issues the warning message, for the collision between V1 and V2 to be avoided.

Figure 24.8 presents the results obtained by modifying the initial speed of vehicle V1 (i.e., the speed until V1 performs the braking due to the warning message), when we employed a 1.5 s driver reaction time. The accentuated black dotted lines in the figure mark the *accident range*, which is the distance range where the initial collision between V1 and V2 occurs (i.e., when no active safety system is used). Thus, if V1 is initially situated at distances either below or above these dotted lines, the accident will not occur. (Note that the accident range increases in size with increased speed of V1.) Furthermore, by representing the cutoff distance for V1 as a function of V2's warning message delay,

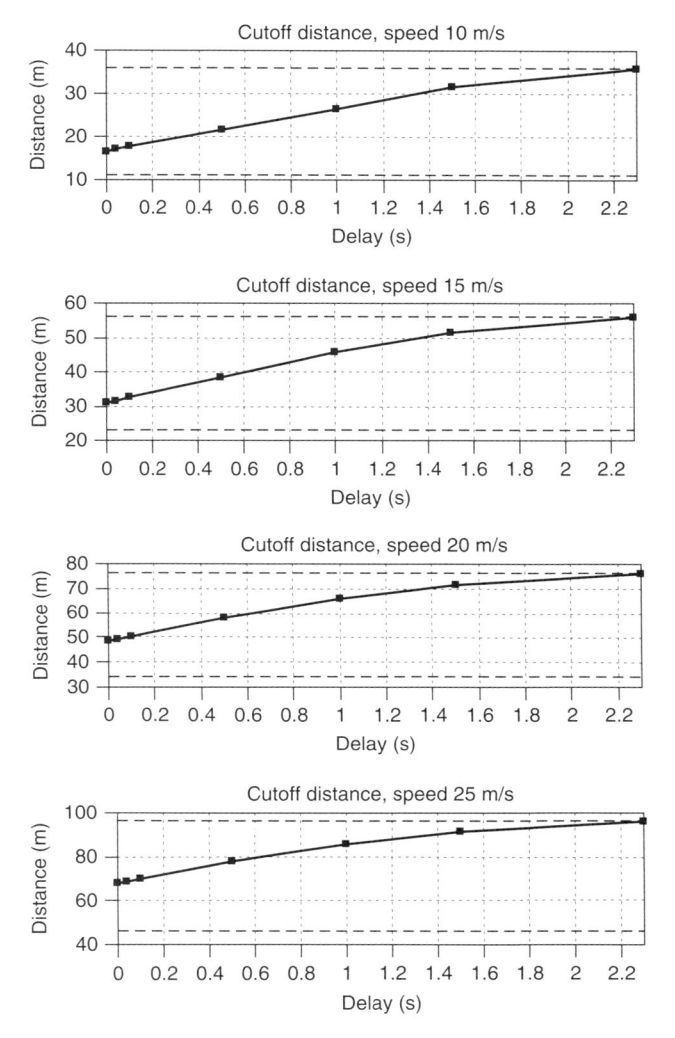

FIGURE 24.8 *Cutoff distance as a function of communication delay (DRT 1.5 s; velocity $10 \div 25$ m/s).*

the representational space was divided into accident and nonaccident areas. Thus, the area above the separating (continuous) curve represents the cases where a collision was avoided, while the area below the curve represents the situations where, in spite of an emergency braking, a collision still occurs.

Figure 24.9 presents the results obtained for using the other two representative values for the driver reaction times (DRT):

- DRT = 0 s. This corresponds to the active safety system in V1 set to the automatic mode and performing a heavy braking without any delay when the warning message from V2 is received.
- DRT = 3 s. This is an extreme upper bound that rarely occurs in real cases.

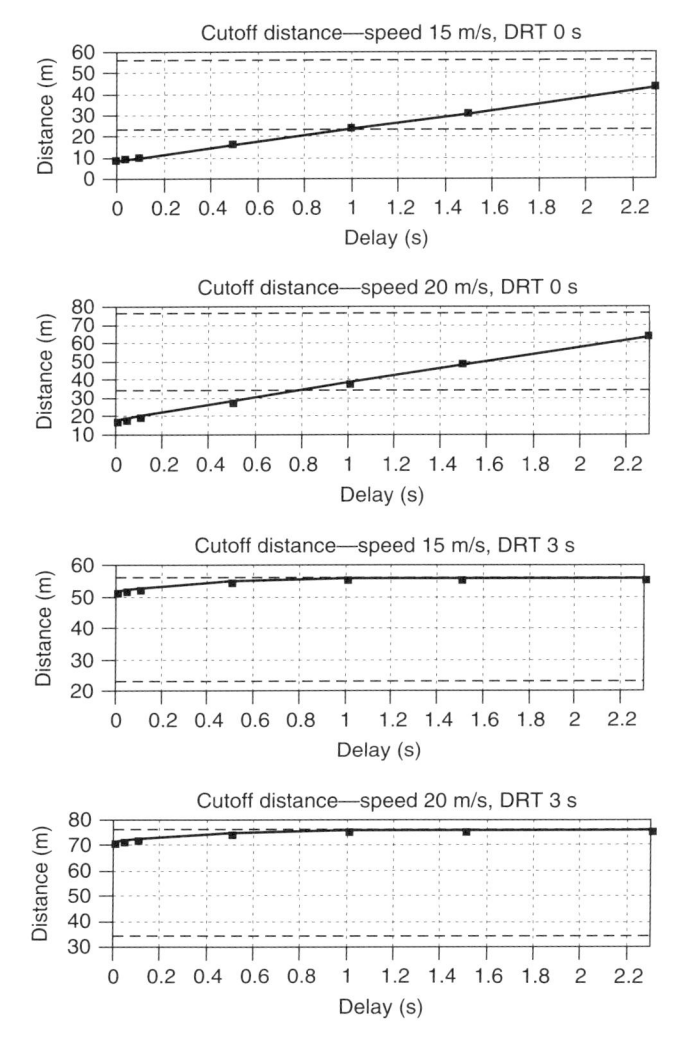

FIGURE 24.9 Cutoff distance as a function of communication delay (DRT 0, 3 s; velocity 15, 20 m/s).

The graphs in Figure 24.9 illustrate the results for initial speeds of V1 of 15 and 20 m/s respectively. Observe that a considerable portion of the accidents in the accident range for DRT of 0 s would be avoided with vehicular communication. On the other hand, with a DRT of 3 s, very few accidents would be avoided.

A peculiarity with the cutoff distance curves for DRT of 0 s is that the curve continues below the lower part of the accident range (where accidents are not supposed to happen). The explanation for this is that the automatic braking performed when the warning message arrives can actually lead to accidents if the message is received when V1 is too close to the intersection. If V1 had not started to brake, and continued at normal speed, V1 would have cleared the intersection before V2 had entered, and thus the accident would have been avoided.

From the graphs in Figure 24.9 we note that delays above approximately 2.3 s mean that no accidents can be avoided. With a DRT of 3 s, the corresponding maximum delay is around 1 s. The maximum delay for a DRT of 0 s cannot be determined directly from Figure 24.9, but in further experiments we have determined the maximum delay to be around 3.8 s.

24.4.3 Communication Performance Experiments

The experiments illustrated in the previous section indicate that accident avoidance by making specific information available to the driver is possible. For supplying this information, we have considered the use of a driving assistant system that analyzes safety data that are wirelessly exchanged between vehicles. However, such collaborative safety systems can operate efficiently only when the supporting intervehicular communication can provide the data in a timely and reliable manner. For instance, for the intersection scenario introduced in the previous section, the latency provided by the communication system for delivering the warning message should ensure a high possibility of avoiding the accident. In addition, we assumed that the vehicles in question always receive the notification. However, we need to investigate whether this is possible, that is, whether communication problems such as packet collision and shadowing did not prevent the successful reception of the notification. We investigate these aspects below.

In previous work, we proposed solutions for networking and communication in mobile networks for vehicles [22–24]. Our proposals exploit the particularities of the vehicular environment for creating a communication system that is adaptable to the traffic conditions. Thus, we propose techniques that use contextual information to organize the vehicles into manageable clusters, and for disseminating safety data among vehicles. The protocol that we proposed is both proactive and reactive. The *proactive operation* implies the regular sending of information used by the safety systems for detecting hazards in traffic and reacting to them. The *reactive operation* implies the sending (transmittal) of explicit notifications for warning upcoming vehicles of hazards in traffic. This happens when certain events take place in traffic, and the safety system in the (sender) vehicle decides that other vehicles need to be informed about these events. The proactive approach can be more effective than the reactive one, because it is directed toward trying to avoid the occurrence of dangerous situations. Thus, using a proactive exchange of data, in-vehicle safety systems can perform early detection of possible hazards in traffic and can efficiently act toward eliminating them. In comparison, the reactive approach is directed only toward limiting the consequences of dangerous situations that have already occurred. However, in certain cases, providing an explicit announcement about the traffic situation is important for increasing the probability of avoiding collisions. This is also the case with the intersection accident presented above. In the followings text, we make use of this particular accident for investigating the performance of safety vehicular communication.

Thus, for the provision of the warning message issued by vehicle V2, we investigated whether the proposed communication system could deliver it safely and in time. To perform this investigation, we developed a simulation environment where the vehicular communication system was integrated within an established mobile network simulator, namely, GloMoSim, developed at the University of California at Los Angeles (UCLA). The movement traces corresponding to the vehicles in the scenario were then generated and inputted into the simulation environment. Additionally, we increased the number

TABLE 24.1 Warning Message Delay and Dissemination Success

Metric	Value
Maximum warning message delay (s)	0.000647128
Average warning message delay (s)	0.000647069
Warning message delay at V1 (s)	0.000647059
Information dissemination success (%)	100

of the vehicles traveling on the streets that form the crossroad to further stress the communication network. The simulations were performed with both operation modes of the protocol active. Thus, the vehicles also exchange messages every 0.1 s containing traffic information such as vehicle heading and position. We note that V2's warning message was subject to retransmission when received by the vehicles in the simulation. We measured the maximum delay of the warning message and its dissemination success, specifically, the ratio between the number of vehicles that correctly received the messages and the number of vehicles that should have received them. As we addressed an intersection accident that can propagate and involve other vehicles, we considered that all the vehicles in the simulation were interested in receiving the warning.

The results of the test are summarized in Table 24.1. Very low values were obtained for the dissemination of V2's warning message. Additionally, the message reached all vehicles in the simulation. These results indicate that the vehicular communication system can effectively support an onboard active safety system.

24.4.4 Conclusion

We have performed investigations similar to those presented in this section for various types of accidents where specific features related to the driving behavior of elderly drivers were considered. From these experiments we determined that the transmission delay has a fairly large influence on collision avoidance, but appropriate values can be provided by new vehicular communication systems. However, even very small delays may not be of much help for people with very long reaction times. We also note that besides the delay in transferring safety data between vehicles, there are additional delays in processing the information and presenting it to the driver. Taking all of this into account, an automatic system can still be a feasible solution. In addition, note that even though an accident may not be entirely avoided, its consequences can be limited as a result of braking in response to a warning message (e.g., by reducing the speed at collision time). In many cases, a significant reduction of the vehicle speed at the moment of impact (e.g., by 40–80%), can be achieved.

24.5 APPLYING COUNTERMEASURES

Research in driving behavior indicates that drivers are able to successfully cope with secondary tasks such as the use of safety systems that issue warnings. However, the presentation of warnings should not distract or overload the driver. The content of the notifications and the method of presenting them are important. Therefore, a wide variety of interfaces such as audio (e.g., chimes, voice), video (head-up display, car computer display, rear/side mirror display), or tactile (e.g., seat vibration, brake pulse) are currently under investigation. In certain cases, there is the possibility of producing successive notifications for indicating the development of a dangerous traffic situation. Using different levels of emergency is a convenient method for avoiding mental overload of the driver. Furthermore, the safety system needs to issue notifications early enough to enable the driver to employ maneuvers that help in avoiding or mitigating collisions. The safety system also needs to ensure a small number of false and nuisance alarms. If a large number of warnings are presented to the driver or if they are presented too early, the driver's confidence in the system degrades significantly.

In addition, drivers differ a great deal both as a group and as individuals. For instance, elderly drivers might need special features to be provided by safety systems in order to overcome problems related to depreciated cognitive and motor capabilities. For example, a driving assistant system that frequently presents successive warnings may be useful to elderly drivers who experience problems with short-term memory. These features may not be needed by young drivers. Young drivers, however, may require a different type of functionality of the safety system. Therefore, since drivers react differently when facing the same type of traffic situation, the provision of a customizable system would be a great advantage.

It is possible that safety systems will not be able to help in avoiding all types of accidents. Attention needs to be given to the development of systems that address at least the most predominant accidents such as rear-end, intersection, and lane change. Furthermore, accidents are very different one from another and safety systems using only one of the enabling technologies would most probably not be very effective in avoiding all possible accidents. For example, collaborative systems or autonomous systems using radar or lidar may be less efficient in avoiding road departure accidents. This is not the case for systems using vision, which monitor the markers at the side of the road. Similarly, systems using vision or radar may not be so effective for avoiding crashes in complex situations such as crowded intersections. Also, collisions with single objects on the road can be best supported by systems using radar. Consequently, active safety systems that can integrate multiple enabling technologies will perform best in avoiding collisions.

The successful deployment of active safety systems requires the development of systems with reasonable costs. Moreover, it may be possible that safety systems would need to be integrated with systems providing nonsafety services in order to ensure their commercial success. Examples of such systems are traveler information, mobile office and entertainment, or smart card services such as toll collection, automatic docking, or automatic payment at gas stations and parking places.

24.6 FINAL REMARKS

Because of the large number of casualties and extensive property damages, traffic safety is currently a major problem for society. Consequently, research is being conducted in developing systems that will help reduce the severity of crashes, or even completely avoid collisions between vehicles. However, even if important improvements in traffic safety have been obtained, the number of collisions with severe consequences is still unacceptably high. Therefore, safety systems that can provide a better service to the driver need to be developed.

The careful investigation of traffic safety statistics addressing older drivers and the analyses of possible problems they can face in traffic reveal that advanced age is certainly not a determinant cause of crashes. However, it is obvious that older drivers have special needs in traffic, and consequently crash countermeasures need to be developed considering the specific characteristics of the drivers. Therefore, in-vehicle safety systems should be adaptable to the needs of the driver.

Traffic safety systems that take automatic action show the best potential for accident avoidance. But such systems need to be more complex than information delivery systems that leave the driver in control. As we saw in the example of investigating countermeasures, automatic braking in response to a warning may actually introduce an accident. This indicates that further analysis is needed for the eventual realization of fully dependable automatic active safety systems. Such automatic systems cannot just react to warnings, but must be deliberative and reason about potential consequences of their actions.

Current supporting technologies for developing safety systems are maturing rapidly. New solutions have been proposed, and early prototypes of systems have begun to appear on the market. An example is *adaptive cruise control* (ACC), which uses radar sensors to help drivers maintain a safe distance between vehicles. However, a problem with safety systems that will delay their development and successful deployment is the lack of standardization and well-defined provision of services. For example, for systems using communication, standards are still under development and products are not available. Furthermore, there is no agreement regarding who will provide the service, even if car manufacturers are generally believed to be willing to be the service providers. Another issue is that not only the data exchange but also the applications running on vehicles may need to cooperate, and they may need to operate in similar modes in order to avoid the introduction of collisions due to automatic actions performed by safety systems. It is also possible that legislative initiatives would be needed to regulate this situation and to speed up the deployment of systems that can improve traffic safety. Precedents exist in this respect, an example being the compulsory use of automatic collision notification (ACN) systems on commercial vehicles.

Even with all these difficulties, the road ahead looks bright and in-vehicle safety systems are considered to be the key to a future with safer traffic, where elderly drivers can maintain mobility.

REFERENCES

1. Jones WD: Keeping cars from crashing, *IEEE Spectrum* **38**:40–45 (Sept 2001).
2. Evans L: *Traffic Safety,* Bloomfields Hills, MI, Science Serving Society, 2004.
3. Community Road Accident Database, European Commission, March 2006.
4. National Center for Statistics and Analysis: *Traffic Safety Facts 2003*, Report DOT HS 809767, National Highway Traffic Safety Administration, Washington, DC, 2004.
5. US Bureau of the Census: *World Population Profile: 1998*, Technical Report WP/98, US Government Printing Office, Washington, DC, 1998.
6. Owsley C: Driving mobility, older adults, and quality of life, *Gerontechnol J* **1**(4):220–230 (2002).
7. McCoy GF, Johnson RA, Duthie RB: Injury to the elderly in road traffic accidents, *J Trauma* **29**:494–497 (1989).

8. US Department of Transportation: *Motor Vehicle Crashes—Data Analysis and IVI Program Emphasis*, ITS Joint Program Office, Nov 1999.

9. Bretz EA: Transportation 2000, *IEEE Spectrum* 91–96 (Jan 2000).

10. Hakamies-Blomqvist L: *Aging Europe: The Challenges and Opportunities for Transport Safety*, European Transport Safety Council, Brussels, Jan 2003.

11. Preusser D, Williams A, Ferguson S, Ulmer R, Weinstein H: Fatal crash risk for older drivers at intersections, *J Accident Anal Prevent* **30**:151–160 (March 1998).

12. Caird R, Creaser V, Edwards H, Horrey B: *Contributing Factors to Accidents by Older Drivers: R&D Plan and Empirical Studies*, Cognitive Ergonomics Research Laboratory, Univ Calgary, Canada, 2002.

13. Pierowicz J, Jocoy E, Lloyd M, Bittner A, Pirson B: Intersection Collision Avoidance Using ITS Countermeasures, US Department of Transportation, National Highway Traffic Safety Administration, Office of Advanced Safety Research, Sept 2000.

14. McDowd P, Shaw R: Attention and aging: A functional perspective, *The Handbook of Aging and Cognition*, Lawrence Erlbaum Publishers, 2000.

15. Andrisano O, Verdone R, Nakagawa M: Intelligent transportation systems: The role of third generation mobile radio networks, *IEEE Commun Mag* 144–151 (Sept 2000).

16. Aoki M, Fujii H: Inter-vehicle communication: Technical issues on vehicle control application, *IEEE Commun Mag* **34**:90–93 (Oct 1996).

17. Miller R, Huang Q: An adaptive peer-to-peer collision warning system, *IEEE Vehicular Technology Conf*, Birmingham, AL, May 2002, pp 317–321.

18. Shahmehri N, Chisalita I, Aberg J, Maciuszek D, Hellqvist M: Using vehicular communication to support older drivers at road intersections: A feasibility study, *Int Conf Smart Homes and Health Telematic (ICOST)*, Singapore, Sept 2004, pp 33–41.

19. Corben F, Fildes H, Oxley R: *Older Driver Highway Design: The Development of a Handbook and Training Workshop to Design Safe Road Environments for Older Drivers*, Accident Research Centre, Monash Univ, Melbourne, Australia, 2002.

20. Chisalita I, Shahmehri N, Lambrix P:, Traffic accident modeling and analysis using temporal reasoning, *7th IEEE Conf Intelligent Transportation Systems*, Washington, DC, Oct 2004, pp 378–383.

21. Gartner N, Messer C, Rathi A, eds: *Traffic Flow Theory*, US Federal Highway Administration, Turner-Fairbank Highway Research Center, 2002.

22. Chisalita I, Shahmehri N: A peer-to-peer approach to vehicular communication for the support of traffic safety applications, *5th IEEE Conf Intelligent Transportation Systems*, Singapore, Sept 2002, pp 336–341.

23. Chisalita I, Shahmehri N: A context-based vehicular communication protocol, *IEEE Personal, Indoor and Mobile Radio Communication Symp*, Barcelona, Spain, Sept 2004, pp 2820–2824.

24. Chisalita I, Shahmehri N: Traffic safety: The role of vehicular communication, *IEEE Int Conf Systems, Man and Cybernetics*, The Hague, The Netherlands, Oct 2004, pp 3903–3908.

25

Blind Navigation and the Role of Technology

Nicholas A. Giudice
University of California, Santa Barbara

Gordon E. Legge
University of Minnesota

25.1 INTRODUCTION

The ability to navigate from place to place is an integral part of daily life. Most people would acknowledge that vision plays a critical role, but would have great difficulty in identifying the visual information they use, or when they use it. Although it is easy to imagine getting around without vision in well-known environments, such as walking from the bedroom to the bathroom in the middle of the night, few people have experienced navigating large-scale, unfamiliar environments nonvisually. Imagine, for example, being blindfolded and finding your train in New York's Grand Central Station. Yet, blind people travel independently on a daily basis. To facilitate safe and efficient navigation, blind individuals must acquire travel skills and use sources of nonvisual environmental information that are rarely considered by their sighted peers. How do you avoid running into the low-hanging branch over the sidewalk, or falling into the open manhole? When you are walking down the street, how do you know when you have reached the post office, the bakery, or your friend's house?

The purpose of this chapter is to highlight some of the navigational technologies available to blind individuals to support independent travel. Our focus here is on blind navigation in large-scale, unfamiliar environments, but the technology discussed can also be used in well-known spaces and may be useful to those with low vision.

The Engineering Handbook of Smart Technology for Aging, Disability, and Independence,
Edited by A. Helal, M. Mokhtari and B. Abdulrazak
Copyright © 2008 John Wiley & Sons, Inc.

In Section 25.2 we look at some perceptual and cognitive aspects of navigating with and without vision that help explain why most people cannot imagine getting around in its absence. Section 25.3 presents four often ignored factors, from engineering blunders to aesthetic bloopers, which should be considered when developing and assessing the functional utility of navigational technologies. In Section 25.4, we summarize several of these technologies, ranging from sonar glasses to talking lights, giving the strengths and limitations of each. Section 25.5 concludes, the chapter by reviewing key features of these products and highlighting the best trajectory for continued development of future technology.

25.2 FACTORS INFLUENCING BLIND NAVIGATION

Two of the biggest challenges to independence for blind individuals are difficulties in accessing printed material [1] and the stressors associated with safe and efficient navigation [2]. Access to printed documents has been greatly improved by the development and proliferation of adaptive technologies such as screen-reading programs, optical character recognition software, text-to-speech engines, and electronic Braille displays. By contrast, difficulty accessing room numbers, street signs, store names, bus numbers, maps, and other printed information related to navigation remains a major challenge for blind travel. Imagine trying to find room n257 in a large university building without being able to read the room numbers or access the "you are here" map at the building's entrance. Braille signage certainly helps in identifying a room, but it is difficult for blind people to find Braille signs. In addition, only a modest fraction of the more than 3 million visually impaired people in the United States read Braille. Estimates put the number of Braille readers between 15,000 and 85,000 [3].

Braille signs indicating room numbers are installed by law in all newly constructed, or renovated, commercial buildings [4]. However, many older buildings do not have accessible signage, and even if they do, room numbers represent only a small portion of useful printed information in the environment. For instance, a blind navigator walking into a mall is unable to access the directory of stores or in an airport the electronic displays of departure and arrival times. When traveling without vision in an unfamiliar outdoor setting, accessing the names of the shops being passed, the name of the street being crossed, or the state of the traffic signal at a busy intersection can also be challenging. Although speech-enabled GPS-based systems can be used to obtain access to street names and nearby stores and audible traffic signals can provide cues about when it is safe to cross the street, these technologies are not widely available to blind navigators. Where an environment can be made accessible for somebody in a wheelchair by removing physical barriers, such as installing a ramp, there is no simple solution for providing access to environmental information for a blind traveler [5]. As our interest is in blind navigation and environmental access, most of the navigational technologies discussed in this chapter collect and display environmental information rather than require structural modifications. For a review of the benefits of some physical modifications that can aid blind navigation, such as the installation of accessible pedestrian signals, see the article by Barlow and Franck [6].

Compared to the advances in accessing printed material in documents, there has been far less development and penetration of technologies to access print-based information in the environment or to aid navigation. The reason for this limited adoption inevitably stems from several factors. Most navigational technologies cost hundreds or thousands of dollars. This makes it prohibitively expensive for most blind people to buy these devices on their own budgets. Rehabilitation agencies for the blind will often assist in the purchase of adaptive technology for print access but rarely provide their clients with technologies for navigation. In addition to cost constraints, broad adoption of navigational technologies will likely not occur until greater emphasis is given to perceptual factors and end-user needs. In other words, there needs to be more research investigating whether these devices are providing a solution to something that is in fact a significant problem for blind navigators (see Sections 25.3 and 25.5 for more detail). Until then, safe and efficient travel will continue to be a stressful endeavor for many blind wayfinders.

Another factor to be addressed is the population of potential users of navigational technologies. The vast majority of impaired vision is aged-related with late onset [7], such as from macular degeneration, glaucoma, or diabetic retinopathy. Those with age-related vision loss may have more difficulty than younger people in learning to use high-tech devices. Compounding the problem, older people often have coexisting physical or cognitive deficits that could render the adoption of some technology impractical. Given these concerns, more research is needed to address how to best develop devices to aid navigation for people with late-onset vision loss.

While the goal of navigating with or without vision is the same, that is, safely locomoting from an origin to a destination, the environmental information available to sighted and blind people is quite different. Understanding the challenges to blind navigation requires appreciation of the amount of spatial information available from vision. Think of walking from your front door to the mailbox at the end of your driveway. If you are sighted, your movement is guided entirely by visual perception. You simultaneously observe the distant mailbox and intervening environment from your door, and navigate a route that gets you there as directly as possible while circumventing the bicycle on the front path and the car in the driveway. You likely pay little attention to what you hear from the environment as you avoid the obstacles along the way. With vision, it is trivial to see the spatial configuration of objects in the environment around you and how the relation between yourself and these objects changes as you move. This example represents what is called *position-based navigation* or *piloting*. Piloting involves use of external information to specify the navigator's position and orientation in the environment [8]. Although vision is typically used to estimate distance and direction to landmarks and guide one's trajectory, a navigator can also use tactile, auditory, or olfactory information, as well as signals from electronic aids, such as GPS-based devices for piloting [9]. Navigation can also be done without reference to fixed landmarks, such as through velocity-based techniques that use instantaneous speed and direction of travel, determined through optic or acoustic flow, to keep track of translational and rotational displacements. Inertial techniques may also be used that utilize internal acceleration cues from the vestibular system to update these displacements (see Refs. 8 and 10 for general discussions of these navigational techniques).

Since both position- and velocity-based navigation are best served by visual cues, navigation using other sensory modalities is typically less accurate. For instance, auditory, olfactory, or tactile input conveys much less information than vision about self-motion, layout geometry, and distance or direction cues about landmark locations [11,12]. Given that this information is important for efficient spatial learning and navigation, lack of access puts blind people at a disadvantage compared to their sighted peers. As we will see in Section 25.4, navigational technologies attempt to close this gap by providing blind wayfinders access to the same critical environmental information available to sighted navigators.

Another major difference in navigating without vision is the added demand of learning to interpret nonvisual sensory signals. Blind navigators need to learn how to safely traverse their environment. They must learn how to detect obstructions to their path of travel, find curbs and stairs, interpret traffic patterns so as to know when the light is red or green, not veer when crossing the street, find the bus stop, and myriad other navigational tasks. They must also keep track of where they are in the environment and how their current position and orientation relates to where they want to go. These tasks are cognitively demanding and often require conscious moment-to-moment problem solving. By comparison, sighted people solve these problems visually in a more automatic, less cognitively demanding way. In other words, vision-based navigation is more of a perceptual process, whereas blind navigation is more of an effortful endeavor requiring the use of cognitive and attentional resources [13–15]. Vision also affords access to many orienting cues in the environment. For instance, use of local landmarks such as street signs or colorful murals and global landmarks such as tall buildings or mountain ranges can aid spatial updating and determination of location. Since access to this type of environmental information is difficult from nonvisual modalities, blind wayfinders must rely on other cues for orientation which are often ambiguous and unreliable (see Ref. 12 for a review). Most sighted people have never considered how they avoid obstacles, walk a straight line, or recognize landmarks. It is not something they consciously learned; it's just something they do. By contrast, the majority of blind people who are competent, independent travelers have had specific training to acquire these skills. This is called *orientation and mobility* (O&M) *training*.

The navigational components of orientation and mobility are sometimes ambiguously defined in the literature, but in general, *orientation* refers to the process of keeping track of position and heading in the environment when navigating from point A to point B, and *mobility* involves detecting and avoiding obstacles or drop-offs in the path of travel. Thus, good mobility relates to efficient locomotion and orientation to accurate wayfinding behavior. Effective navigation involves both mobility and orientation skills. As we will see, the aids that are available to augment blind navigation generally provide information that falls within one of these categories.

25.3 TECHNOLOGY TO AUGMENT BLIND NAVIGATION

Many navigational technologies have been developed throughout the years, but few are still in existence. Part of the reason may be due to a disconnect between engineering factors and a device's perceptual and functional utility; that is, a device may work well in theory but be too difficult or cumbersome in practice to be adopted by the intended user. Four important factors should be considered when discussing the design and implementation of technology for blind navigation.

25.3.1 Sensory Translation Rules

Most of the navigational technology discussed in this chapter conveys information about a visually rich world through auditory or tactile displays. These channels have a much lower bandwidth than does vision and are sensitive to different stimulus properties. For instance, where cues about linear perspective are salient to vision, this information is not well specified through touch. By contrast, thermal cues are salient to touch but not vision. Thus, any mapping between the input and output modality, especially if it is cross-modal (e.g., visual input and auditory output), must be well specified. Rather than assuming that any arbitrary mapping will work, we need more insight from perception (auditory and tactile) and a clearer understanding of the cognitive demands associated with interpreting this information to guide the design principles of more effective mappings. The ideal device would employ a mapping that is intuitive and requires little or no training. How much training will be required, and the ultimate performance level that can be obtained, are empirical issues. As these prerequisite issues are often ignored, improved performance measures for evaluating such mappings are necessary.

It is tempting but probably misleading to assume that people can easily interpret arbitrary mappings of two-dimensional (2D) image data, such as video images, into auditory or tactile codes. The history of print-to-sound technology is instructive in this regard. The first efforts to build reading machines for the blind involved mapping the black-and-white patterns of print on a page to arbitrary auditory codes based on frequency and intensity. These efforts were largely unsuccessful; the resulting reading machines required too many hours of training, and reading speeds were very slow [16]. Print-to-sound succeeded only when two things happened: (1) optical character recognition algorithms became robust and (2) synthetic speech became available. In other words, arbitrary mappings from print to sound did not work, but the specific mapping from print to synthetic speech has been very effective. A related point is that the translation from print to synthetic speech requires more than analog transformation of optical input to acoustic output. There is an intervening stage of image interpretation in the form of optical character recognition. It is likely that the future of successful high-tech navigation devices will rely more and more on computer-based interpretation of image data prior to auditory or tactile display to the blind user.

25.3.2 Selection of Information

To be effective, the product must focus on conveying specific environmental information. To facilitate training with any navigational technology, it is important to understand exactly what information it provides. The complexity of the display is directly proportional to the amount of information that the developer wishes to present. It may be tempting to design a device that strives to convey as much information as possible, acting as a true visual substitute. However, more is not always better. For instance, the best tactile maps are simple, uncluttered displays that do not try to reproduce all that exists on a visual map [17]. An inventor should be cognizant of the basic research addressing such perceptual issues and carry out empirical studies to ensure that the display is interpretable and usable to the target population. Most of the technology discussed employs auditory or tactile output (see Ref. 18 for a review of echo location and auditory perception in the blind and Refs. 19 and 20 for excellent reviews of touch and haptic perception).

25.3.3 Device Operation

The optimal operating conditions depend largely on the characteristics of the sensor used by the device. For instance, sonar-based devices can operate in the dark, rain, and snow. This versatility provides a functional advantage of these devices for outdoor usage.

However, they are not ideal for use in crowded or confined places as the sonar echoes become distorted, rendering the information received by the user unreliable. By contrast, camera-based technology can work well under a wide range of operating conditions both inside and outside, but these systems may have difficulty with image stabilization when used by moving pedestrians, and wide variations in ambient luminance within and between scenes. GPS-based devices are fairly accurate across a range of atmospheric conditions, but the signal is line of sight and can thus be disrupted or completely occluded when under dense foliage or traveling among tall buildings. Also, GPS does not work indoors. The bottom line is that each technology has its own strengths and weaknesses, and successful navigation over a wide range of environmental conditions will probably require the integration of multiple technologies.

25.3.4 Form and Function

Another often neglected consideration is the aesthetic impact on the user; that is, a device should be minimally intrusive. A survey carried out by Golledge and colleagues found wide variability in the "cosmetic acceptability" of navigational technology [21]. The finding that some people felt strongly enough to rate this issue as more important than having a device that improved navigation shows that aesthetic impact cannot be ignored.

25.4 REVIEW OF SELECTED NAVIGATIONAL TECHNOLOGIES

Tools used in blind navigation are often called *mobility aids* or *electronic travel aids* (ETAs). While they generally provide information useful for mobility or orientation, they can be further divided into two categories depending on the information displayed. The most common devices are used as a mobility aid and serve as obstacle detectors. Such aids are generally limited to providing low-resolution information about the nearby environment (see Ref. 22 for a review). Another class of devices attempts to convey more detailed environmental information over a wider range of distances. These ETAs are called *environmental imagers* as they serve as vision substitution devices (see Ref. 23 for a review of vision substitution). The following discussion highlights some key technologies from these categories and provides some strengths and weaknesses of each. This review is not meant as an exhaustive list, but focuses instead on providing a brief historical context of each technology while emphasizing those devices that are commercially available or part of an active research program. For a more thorough discussion of blind navigation and some of the technologies discussed below, see the classic book on orientation and mobility by Blasch and Welsh [24].

The long cane and guide dog are the most common tools for mobility. The cane is a simple mechanical device that is traditionally used for detecting and identifying obstacles, finding steps or drop-offs in the path of travel, or as a symbolic indicator to others that a person is blind. Although direct contact with the cane is limited to proximal space, its effective range for detecting large obstacles is increased with the use of echo location cues created as a result of tapping [25].

The guide dog performs many of the same functions as the cane, although navigation is often more efficient because the dog can help take direct routes between objects, instead of following edges, or shorelining, which is a standard technique with a cane.

The dog also helps reduce veering, which is often a challenge when crossing streets or traversing large open places. The cane and guide dog have similar limitations. They are most effective for detection of proximal cues, are limited in detecting overhanging or non-ground-level obstructions and do not provide much in the way of orientation information about the user's position and heading in the environment.

It is important to note that most of the electronic travel aids discussed here are meant to complement, not replace, use of the long cane or guide dog.

An ETA can be regarded in terms of its sensor, the component receiving information about the environment and the display, where the information is conveyed to the user. Some devices, such as GPS-based navigation systems, also incorporate a user interface where specific information can be entered or queried from the system. In the following discussion, the navigational technologies are classified according to their sensor characteristics: sonar-based (using sonic sensors), vision-based (using cameras or lasers), infrared (IR), or GPS devices. All of these technologies provide auditory and/or tactile output to the user (devices based on visual enhancement or magnification are not included in the following discussion).

25.4.1 Sonar-Based Devices

The first sonar-based mobility aid was the handheld sonic torch, using a special ultrasonic sensor developed by Leslie Kay in the early 1960s. Kay's company, Bay Advanced Technologies (BAT), has developed many sonar-based devices since then; the latest is the BAT 'K' Sonar-Cane. This cell-phone-sized device costs around $700 and can be affixed to the handle of a long cane, increasing its effective range to detection of a 40 mm diameter object out to 5 m [26]. With the BAT 'K' Sonar-Cane, a user is able to hear echoes from multiple sources, facilitating simultaneous tracking of more than one object in the environment. The auditory output, delivered threw earphones, modulates pitch proportionally to distance. Low-pitched sounds are heard for close objects, and high-pitched sounds relate to far objects. This is Kay's latest product, and no empirical studies have yet been carried out with the device. It employs a simpler display than do several other of his devices (see text below) indicating that the complexity of the earlier ETAs may have limited their acceptance by blind users.

Kay's sonic glasses (or Sonicguide) and Trisensor (also called KASPA) were designed to provide a sonic image, albeit coarse, of the environment. The Sonicguide was a head-mounted binaural device, commercially available through the mid-1990s, utilizing ultrasonic echo location. KASPA, which became commercially available in 1994, costing around $2500, used a triad of high-resolution ultrasonic spatial sensors on a head-mounted device. The three sensors covered a $50°$ forward field of view, and the auditory "image" was heard through stereo headphones. The auditory information provided by the three sensors, one centrally mounted and two peripherally, was meant to model the visual information that would be available from the central and peripheral visual field of view. KASPA afforded access to detection and location of multiple objects in 3D stereo space up to 5 m ahead of the user. The frequency of the tones provided information about distance, direction was indicated through delivery of the sounds in the binaural headphones, and the timbre from the multiple reflections provided information about the object's unique surface properties. By learning the invariant sound signatures reflected from different objects, navigators could, in theory, learn to recognize specific objects and build up a 3D representation of the space they are navigating. Much work has gone into merging the technology with our understanding of the perceptual aspects of visual and auditory processing and the associated neural correlates of 3D auditory perception [27,28]. The results from behavioral studies carried out using these more complex ETAs are mixed (see Ref. 29 and Kay's Website [26] for several theses and technical reports).

In contrast to Kay's high-resolution sensors, several sonar-based mobility aids have been developed that use a relatively simple display. These ETAs provide extended information about object detection but do not attempt to convey complex sound signatures about multiple objects in the environment. The Sonic PathFinder, developed by Tony Heyes and his company Perceptual Alternatives, is an outdoor device meant to complement other obstacle avoidance techniques, such as the long cane or guide dog [30]. The Sonic PathFinder costs around $1600 and is a head-mounted system employing five ultrasonic transducers that are controlled by a microcomputer. The system uses the notes of a musical scale to give a navigator advanced warning of obstructions to their path of travel. As the person approaches an object, the musical scale descends with each note representing a distance of ~0.3 m. Objects picked up from the left or right of the user are heard in the left and right ears respectively. Those straight ahead are heard in both ears simultaneously. Rather than adopting a fixed distance, the range of the device is determined by the walking speed of the user. Thus information is provided about objects that would be encountered during the next 2 s of travel. Behavioral studies with the device yielded mixed results, demonstrating that it did not improve travel time but did reduce contact of the cane with obstacles in the environment [31,32].

Two other devices using ultrasonic echo location are the Miniguide and UltraCane. The Miniguide is a handheld device, produced by GDP Research and costing approximately $600 [33]. In addition to auditory output, the Miniguide uses vibration to indicate object distance. The faster the rate of vibration, the closer the object. It is used to detect single objects at a range of 0.5–8 m (with the optimal size, accuracy tradeoff for object detection at 4 ms). Since this device cannot detect drop-offs, it must be used in conjunction with a cane or guide dog.

The UltraCane, developed by Sound Foresight and costing approximately $800, works in a similar fashion out to 4 m but has front- and upward-facing ultrasonic sensors that are part of the long cane's handle. This design makes it possible to easily detect drop-offs, via the cane and overhangs, via the sensors. Detection of overhangs by this and other devices is particularly useful, as canes and guide dogs provide poor access to this information. In addition to indicating distance through vibration, the arrangement of the UltraCane's vibrators provide coarse spatial information about where the object is located; for instance, a head-level obstruction is felt on the forward vibrator, and ground-to-chest-level obstacles are indicated by the rear vibrator [34].

The final sonar-based device discussed here is the GuideCane, developed in the Advanced Technologies Lab at the University of Michigan. Although research and development of this product have been discontinued, it is included here because of its interesting approach to information presentation.

The focus of the GuideCane was to apply mobile robotic technology to create a product that reduced conscious effort from the person by acting autonomously in obstacle avoidance decisions. As accurate mobility can be cognitively taxing, the philosophy of the GuideCane was to reduce the effort associated with determining a safe path of travel. The device resembled an upright vacuum cleaner on wheels and employed 10 ultrasonic sensors to detect obstacles in a 120° forward field of view. To operate, the user pushed the GuideCane and when the ultrasonic sensors detected an obstacle, an embedded computer determined a suitable direction of motion to avoid the obstruction. The GuideCane then steered the user, via force feedback in the handle, around the obstacle and returned to the original path of travel. The system determined and maintained position information by combining odometry, compass, and gyroscope data as it moved. (For technical details on the system and how it dealt with accumulated error from the sensors and determination of the best path of travel, see Ref. 35.)

In an attempt to reduce complexity, the GuideCane analyzes the environment, computes the optimal direction of travel, and initiates the action automatically. This transparent automaticity, while lauded as a benefit by the developers, is also a limitation as the user is simply FOLLOWING the device. The reduction of information to this single FOLLOW action by a fully autonomous device during navigation is potentially dangerous as it removes all navigational decisions from the operator's control. Although the problems of detection and avoidance of obstacles are often tedious to a blind person, being actively engaged in this process is important for spatial learning. For instance, contacting an object with the long cane allows the user to know that it is there and encode this location in memory. Simply being led around the object does not allow one to know what is in one's surrounds. Even with the guide dog, the first tenant of the handler is that they are always supposed to be in control. While you let the dog alert you to obstructions or suggest a path of travel, you must always be the one to make the final decision and give the commands.

Several clear benefits to the various sonar devices are discussed in this section. Both the mobility aids and more complex vision substitution systems extend the perceptual reach of a blind navigator from single to multiple meters. Not only do they alert user's to obstacles in the immediate path of travel; most devices also provide access to off-course objects or head-height obstructions, elements that are difficult to find using the long cane or guide dog. The availability of this information may benefit safe and efficient travel as well as the opportunity for blind individuals to learn about their surroundings. Finally, regarding expense, since all necessary hardware is carried by the user, no installation or maintenance costs are incurred by third parties. This provides an up-front benefit to mass penetration of sonar devices, as there is no need for retrofitting of the environment in order for the device to work.

Sonar-based devices have limitations. They are not very effective in crowded environments because the signal is prone to reflection errors. The technology is also expensive, as the ultrasonic sensors are not built on off-the-shelf hardware and software, such as commercially available sonar range-finding devices. With the exception of the vibrating interfaces, these devices provide a continuous stream of audio information. Since blind people rely heavily on listening to their environment, the presence of auditory output could be distracting, or could interfere with other ambient cues from the environment. Given the importance of acoustic cues, such as hearing traffic, the reflected echoes from cane tapping, or distinctive auditory landmarks, masking this information could have deleterious effects on safe and efficient navigation.

Another major limitation is the time and effort needed to become proficient using these devices. The learning curve will be especially steep for ETAs like KASPA or the Sonicguide, which afford access to a much higher-resolution display than the basic obstacle detection devices. In addition, while the cane-mounted devices are integrated into the aid that they are designed to augment, the head-mounted systems are less aesthetically discreet, which may be undesirable to some people.

25.4.2 Optical Technologies (Camera or Laser-Based Devices)

The first incarnation of a laser-based navigational technology was the Nurion laser cane, developed in the late 1970s and now updated and commercially available for around $3000. This device is similar to the cane-mounted sonar ETAs but uses diode lasers rather than ultrasonic sensors. Three laser transmitters and receivers, directed up, ahead, and down, provide the user with three levels of extended obstacle detection, including drop-offs and overhead obstructions, out to 4 m [36]. The output is signaled by the rate of auditory tones or vibration felt in the cane's handle.

The talking laser cane is another cane-mounted ETA using a laser sensor. This device, developed by Sten Lofving of Sweden, is no longer being produced because of to funding limitations but is discussed here because of its novel design. In addition to providing auditory feedback about the presence of objects in the forward path of travel with a 20° spread angle, the receiver could also be used to pick up reflections from special retroReflective signs out to 10 m. Each sign consisted of a different barcode (thick or thin strips of retroreflective tape). When the laser detected a sign, a distinctive beep was sounded and a microprocessor in the unit tried to identify the bar codes. If recognized, the navigator heard a spoken message from a small built-in loudspeaker. Personal communication with the developer clarified that sign recognition occurred significantly closer (≤ 3 m) than its original detection, but empirical tests have not been conducted. Each sign conveyed 4 bits of information, allowing 16 specific labels to be predefined with a verbal message. The 16 spoken messages consisted of the numerals 0–9 and words like door, elevator, or bathroom. The device worked both indoors and outside, and the signs could be attached to any landmark that might help facilitate navigation. Thus, this device served as both a mobility aid and an orientation tool, as it could be used to detect obstructions and also provide position and direction information about specific landmarks in the environment. For ongoing research using recognition of passive signs to provide orientation information, see the DSS project discussed in Section 25.4.5.

As with the sonar devices, laser-based ETAs require a line-of-sight (LOS) measurement and the reflections can be easily blocked or distorted, such as by a person walking in the hall or from a door being opened.

Another approach to optical sensing uses cameras to capture environmental information. The vOICe Learning Edition video sonification software, developed by Dutch physicist Peter Meijer, is designed to render video images into auditory soundscapes. This is called "seeing with sound." It is the most advanced image to sound product available and according to the developer's listserv, is actively being used by blind people on a daily basis. For a detailed explanation of the software and demos, hints on training, user experiences, and preliminary neuroscientific research using vOICe, see the developer's expansive Website [37]. The vOICe software works by converting images captured by a PC or cell phone camera, through a computer, into corresponding sounds heard from a 3D auditory display. The output, called a soundscape, is heard via stereo headphones. This is a vision substitution device that uses a basic set of image-to-sound translation rules for mapping visual input to auditory output. For instance, the horizontal axis of an image is represented by time; for example, the user hears the image scan from left to right at a default rate of one image snapshot per second. The vertical axis is represented by pitch, with higher pitch indicating higher elevation in the visual image. Finally, brightness is represented by loudness. Something heard to be louder is brighter; black is silent and white is heard as loudest. For instance, a straight white line, running from the top left to the bottom right, on a black background, would be heard as a tone steadily decreasing in pitch over time. The complexity of each soundscape is dependent on the amount of information conveyed in the image being sonified (for details, see Ref. 38).

The vOICe software also allows the user to reverse the polarity of the image, slow down or speed up the scan, and manipulate many other parameters of how the image is heard. The power of this experimental software is that it can be used from a desktop computer to learn about graphs and pictures or used in a mobile context. In this latter capacity, the software is loaded on a laptop, wearable computer or PDA-based cell phone, coupled with a head-mounted camera, and used to sonify the environment during navigation. The continuous stream of soundscapes heard by the user represents the images picked up by the camera as they move in real time.

In theory, the system could enhance mobility, by detecting potential obstacles and orientation, as the information provided could be used to locate and recognize distal landmarks in the environment. As of yet, there is no performance data with the vOICe software demonstrating that it can support these spatial operations. In deed, beyond individual case studies [39], it is not clear whether people can easily learn the mapping of visual images to soundscapes. If the information can be used in a meaningful way, it will require a steep learning curve. In addition, processing of the continuous, complex signals inevitably imposes stiff cognitive demands, something that could negatively impact safe navigation by blind wayfinders, which also requires significant cognitive effort.

An advantage of the vOICe experimental software over other devices that we have discussed is that it is free of charge and runs on all modern Windows-based computers, works with off-the-shelf cameras and headphones and requires no installation of specialized equipment in the environment. These factors make the vOICe accessible to a broad base of people. However, to be adopted, more behavioral research is needed demonstrating that the vision-to-sound mappings are interpretable and that the utility of the information provided is commensurate with the learning curve required to achieve competence.

Finally, another camera-based device that may be used for object detection and navigation is the tactile tongue display. This technology converts images from a camera into patterns of vibrations delivered through an array of vibrotactile stimulators on the tongue. Stemming from the pioneering work in the early 1970s by Paul Bach-y-Rita, the original research demonstrated that vibrotactile displays on the back or abdomen can be used as a vision substitution device [40]. Although the empirical studies with the system focused on detecting or recognizing simple objects, it was hoped that it could also work as a navigational technology. The modern incarnation of the system uses vibrotactile stimulators on the tongue, which has a much higher receptor density than does the back or stomach. In theory, this could sufficiently improve resolution such that the camera images could convey information about the distance or direction of objects, which could then be represented as a 2D image via the tongue display. The efficacy of this system as a navigational technology has not been shown, but research with the device by Bach-y-Rita and his colleagues is ongoing [41].

25.4.3 Infrared Signage

The most notable remote infrared audible signage (RIAS) is a system called "Talking Signs." This technology, pioneered and developed at the Smith-Kettlewell Eye Research Institute in San Francisco, consists of infrared transmitters and a handheld IR receiver

[42]. The cost of the receiver is approximately $250, and the transmitter and its installation total $2000. The Talking Signs system works by installing the transmitters in strategic locations in the environment. Each sign sends short audio messages, via a constantly emitted IR beam, which can be decoded and spoken when picked up by the receiver. A person carrying the Talking Signs receiver uses hand scanning to search the environment for a signal. The signal can be picked up from up to 20 m away, and when detected, the navigator hears a message from the onboard speaker (or attached headphone) indicating that he/she is in the proximity of a particular location. For example, when scanning, one might hear "information desk," "entrance to main lobby," or "stairs to the second floor." Users can navigate to the landmark by following the IR beam, such as walking in the direction of the message they are receiving. If they go off course, they will lose the signal and will need to rescan until they once again hear the message. The signals sent out by the transmitter are directional, and for maximum flexibility, parameters such as beamwidth and throw distance are adjustable. Talking Signs work effectively in both interior and exterior environments and can be used anywhere landmark identification and wayfinding assistance are needed. In contrast to most of the technology previously discussed, Talking signs are an orientation device as they convey positional and directional information. If more than one transmitter is installed (e.g., multiple signs to indicate the location of several doors in a transit station), a person may detect several messages from a single location. This can aid in learning the spatial relations between multiple landmarks [43]. As transmission of the infrared messages are frequency-modulated, there is no cross-interference between nearby transmitters; only information from the strongest signal detected is spoken at a time [44]. Several studies have shown that Talking Signs can be used to identify bus stops and information about approaching buses [45], to describe orientation information as a navigator reaches an intersection [42], and to improve efficient route navigation of large environments, such as San Francisco transit stations (see Refs. 44 and 46 for discussions). These studies also demonstrated that access to Talking Signs increased user confidence and reduced navigation-related anxiety.

The main limitation of Talking Signs is that they require access to a permanent source of electrical power, which can require expensive retrofitting of a building or city. At $2000 per sign, an installation base of sufficient density to cover the major landmarks or decision points in a city or every room number in a building would cost many millions of dollars. Thus, the more practical solution is to have Talking Signs provide information about only key landmarks in the environment, but this means that many potentially important features remain inaccessible to the blind navigator. It should be noted that while the up-front cost of installing the signs is significant, they have little subsequent costs. By contrast, other orientation technologies, such as GPS-based devices, may have a minimal initial cost but incur significant back-end expense in order to stay up to date with changing maps and other databases of location-based information.

In contrast to IR technology, radiofrequency (RF)-based signage systems are omnidirectional. Thus, messages are accessible from all directions and can be received without the need for environmental scanning. In addition, RF signals are not LOS and so are not blocked by transient obstructions. However, because of their omnidirectionality, RF signals generally have a smaller range and provide no information about the direction of a landmark with respect to the user. A study comparing navigational performance using Talking Signs Versus Verbal Landmarks, a RF-based audible signage system, found that access to Talking Signs resulted in significantly better performance than the RF alternative

[47]. This result demonstrates the importance of providing directional information to aid orientation in navigational technology.

25.4.4 GPS-Based Devices

The global positioning system (GPS) is a network of 24 satellites, maintained by the US military forces, that provides information about a person's location almost anywhere in the world when navigating outdoors. GPS-based navigation systems are a true orientation aid, as the satellites provide constantly updated position information whether or not the pedestrian is moving. When in motion, the software uses the sequence of GPS signals to also provide heading information. Because of the relatively low precision of the GPS signal, providing positional information on the order of one to 10 m accuracy, these devices are meant to be used in conjunction with a mobility aid such as a white cane or a guide dog.

The first accessible GPS-based navigation system developed by Jack Loomis and his colleagues at the University of California, Santa Barbara, was initially envisaged in 1985 and became operational by 1993 [48]. This personal guidance system (PGS) employs GPS tracking and a GIS database and has been investigated using several output modalities, including a haptic interface using a handheld vibratory device, synthetic speech descriptions using spatial language, and a virtual acoustic display using spatialized sound (see the PGS Website for more information [49]). The use of spatialized sound is especially novel, as it allows a user to hear the distance and direction of object locations in 3D space. Thus, the names of objects are heard as if coming from their physical location in the environment. Use of this system has proved effective in guiding people along routes and finding landmarks in campus and neighborhood environments [50–52].

Although there are many commercially available GPS-based devices employing visual displays (and some that even provide coarse speech output for in-car route navigation), these are not fully accessible to blind navigators. The first commercially available accessible GPS-based system was GPS-Talk, developed by Mike May and Sendero Group in 2000. This system ran on a laptop computer and incorporated a GPS receiver and a GIS database that included maps of most US addresses and street names. It was designed with a talking user interface that constantly updated the wayfinder's position and gave real-time verbal descriptions of the streets, landmarks, or route information at their current location. A strength of this system was that it was highly customizable; for instance, verbal directions could be presented in terms of right left, front back, clock face, compass, or 360° headings. A person could get information about the length of each block, the heading and distance to a defined waypoint or destination, predefined and programmable points of interest, or a description of each intersection. There was also a route-planning facility that allowed creation of routes from a current position to any other known position on the map. Another advantage of this system was that it could be used in virtual mode, such as using the keyboard to simulate navigation of the digital map. This allowed a person to learn and explore an environment prior to physically going there. Research on a similar European GPS initiative, MoBIC, demonstrated the benefits of this pre-journey planning for blind wayfinders [53].

Sendero's most current version, the BrailleNote GPS, works on the popular BrailleNote accessible PDA and is now one of three commercially available GPS-based navigation systems for the blind (see Ref. 54 for a review). Many of the core features between the three systems are similar but while Sendero's BrailleNote GPS and Freedom Scientific's

PAC Mate GPS work on specialized hardware, Trekker, distributed by Humanware, runs on a modified mass-market PDA. Trekker is a Braille input and speech output device, where the other two systems have configurations for Braille or QWERTY keyboard input and speech or Braille output.

Whether this GPS technology is used as a pre-journey tool to explore a route or during physical navigation, the information provided is expected to greatly improve blind orientation performance and increase user confidence in promoting safe and independent travel. No other technology can provide the range of orientation information that GPS-based systems make available. As we discussed in Section 25.2, effective orientation can be particularly difficult for blind navigators. Thus, these devices have great potential to resolve the orientation problem that has been largely unmet by other navigational technologies.

There are several notable limitations to GPS-based navigation systems. First, although the accessible software may not be very expensive, the underlying adaptive hardware on which it runs can be quite costly (e.g., up to $6000). The user must also periodically buy new maps and databases of commercial points of interest, as these change with some regularity.

In addition, GPS accuracy is not currently sufficient for precise localization unless the user has additional differential correction hardware, which is expensive and bulky. GPS technology is also unable to tell a user about the presence of drop-offs, obstacles, or moving objects in the environment, such as cars or other pedestrians. Thus, these systems are not a substitute for good mobility training. The base maps are also often incorrect, such that a street name may be wrong or the system may try to route the navigator down a nonexistent road or even worse, along a freeway or thoroughfare that is dangerous to pedestrian travel. As GPS signals are LOS, the signals are often disrupted when the user is navigating under dense foliage or between tall buildings and indoor usage is not possible. As orientation information is as important inside as it is out, this lack of coverage can be a significant challenge to blind wayfinders (see text below).

25.4.5 Technology for Indoor Navigation

While the advent of GPS technology has driven tremendous innovation in the development of accessible navigation systems for use in outdoor environments, much less is known about methods for tracking position and orientation indoors. Besides Talking Signs, which have a small installation base and provide information about specific landmarks only, there are no commercially available products to aid indoor wayfinding. This can pose a problem as it is often challenging for blind or visually impaired people to find their way in unfamiliar, complex indoor spaces such as schools or office buildings.

While several technologies may share in solving the problem of indoor wayfinding without vision, they all have a major limitation, namely, they are restricted to providing fixed messages about the immediate local environment. Braille, infrared or RF-based signage, "Talking Lights," fluorescent lights that are temporally modulated to encode a message [55] and use of wi-fi (wireless-fidelity) signals from known 802.11 wireless access points to locate a pedestrian within a building [56] are all based on static information. A more flexible system would couple an inexpensive method for determining a pedestrian's location and heading indoors with readily accessible information about the building environment. This system should be capable of guiding pedestrians along routes, supporting free exploration, and describing points of interest to the pedestrian.

The authors of this chapter are currently part of a team addressing the indoor navigation problem through research on a digital sign system (DSS) (see Ref. 57 for a preliminary report). The DSS consists of a handheld device that emits an infrared beam. The user pans the beam until a reflection is returned from a retroreflective barcoded sign. The image of the sign is "read" by computer software, and its identification code is fed to a building database. This database is part of a software application called "Building Navigator" that provides information to users, via synthetic speech about the content of the sign, the layout of nearby points of interest, and routing information to goal locations in the building. The codevelopment of indoor positioning technology and relevant indoor navigation software sets this project apart from most other methods of location determination, which are unable to provide context-sensitive and user-queriable information about the surrounding environment.

Critical to the success of this project is a clear method of describing the environment being navigated. To this end, several studies were conducted that investigated the efficacy of a verbal interface to support accurate spatial learning and wayfinding. These studies employed dynamically updated verbal descriptions, messages that are contingent on the user's position and orientation in the environment, as the basis of accessing layout information during navigation. The results from these studies demonstrated that both blind and sighted people could effectively use context-sensitive verbal information to freely explore real and virtual environments and find hidden target locations [58,59]. These findings provide strong initial support for the success of an integrated indoor navigation system incorporating the Building Navigator and DSS.

25.5 CONCLUSIONS

Many factors are involved in developing an electronic travel aid, but there is little consensus about the information that should be provided. On the one hand, we have vision substitution devices that attempt to convey a rich image of the environment, such as Leslie Kay's KASPA or Peter Meijer's vOICe. Although the resolution of these devices varies, they represent a school of thought predicated on the view that navigational technologies should provide blind people with as much information about the world as is possible. On the other hand, there is the notion that the most useful technology is based on a simple display, such as Tony Heyes's Sonic PathFinder or GDP Research's Miniguide. From this perspective, conveying detailed surface property information about multiple objects in the environment leads to undue complexity. Rather, a device should focus on providing only the most critical information for safe and efficient navigation, such as detection of objects in the immediate path of travel. These divergent perspectives bring up two important issues.

1. More impartial behavioral studies are needed to demonstrate the efficacy of ETA's. Most of the limited research in this area has been based on extremely small sample sizes or was carried out by the developer of the device. Given the extant literature, it is not possible to determine whether high-resolution displays are, indeed, providing useful information or if they are overloading the user with an uninterpretable barrage of tones, buzzes, and vibrations. In addition to perceptual issues, the functional utility of the device must also be considered. Ideas on the "problem to be solved" and best feature set of a device may differ between an O&M (orientation–mobility) instructor and the

engineer developing the product. The disconnect between what a product does and what the user wishes it would do is compounded as there is often inadequate communication between engineers and rehabilitation professionals or potential blind users. This lack of communication about user needs, coupled with the dearth of empirical research and limited funding opportunities for purchasing ETAs, are major reasons why navigational technologies have not gained broader acceptance in the blind community.

2. In addition, where the long cane and guide dog are tried and true mobility aids, it is not clear whether blind navigators want (or require) additional electronic devices that provide extended access to mobility information in the environment. This is not to say that such ETAs can't serve as effective mobility aids; it simply raises the question whether people find the cost–benefit tradeoff of learning and using the device worth the information provided. It is possible that the success of accessible GPS-based devices, demonstrated by the more recent emergence of three commercially available systems and the results of rigorous scientific studies, stems from the fact that this technology provides information that does not overlap with what is provided by the cane or guide dog. Since GPS-based navigation systems convey updated orientation information, incorporate huge commercial databases about the locations of streets and addresses, and often allow for route planning and virtual exploration of an environment, they provide access to a wide range of information that is otherwise difficult for a blind navigator to acquire. Given that no other technology directly supports wayfinding behavior, the growing success of GPS-based devices makes sense from the standpoint of addressing an unmet need for blind navigators.

Table 25.1 provides an overview of some of the navigational technologies discussed in Section 25.4.

As can be seen in the table, there are multiple approaches for conveying environmental information to a blind navigator. We believe that the future of navigational technology depends on consolidating some of these approaches into an integrated, easy-to-use device. Since there is no single, universal technology that aids in providing both orientation and mobility information in all environments, an integrated system will necessarily incorporate several technologies. The goal of such a system is to complement the existing capabilities of the user by providing important information about her/his surroundings in the simplest, most direct manner possible. The notion of an integrated platform for supporting blind navigation is not new. Work by a European consortium on a project called MoBIC represented the first attempt at such a system [53]. Although now defunct, the MoBIC initiative incorporated talking and tactile maps for pre-journey route planning, audible signage and GPS tracking for outdoor navigation. Another system being developed in Japan uses GPS tracking, RFID (radiofrequency identification) tags, and transmission of camera images to a central server via cell phone for processing of unknown environmental features [60]. An integrated Talking Signs–GPS receiver has also been shown to facilitate route guidance and on-course information about landmarks [52]. Finally, a consortium of five US institutions and Sendero Group LLC have been working on a integrated hardware and software platform to provide a blind user with accessible wayfinding information during indoor and outdoor navigation. This project brings together several of the technologies discussed in this chapter but is still in the R&D stage (see Ref. 61 for more information about the Wayfinding Group).

TABLE 25.1 Overview of Navigational Technology

Device	Input Transducer	Output Display	Information Conveyed	Mode of Operation	Requires Special Infra-Structure	Operating Environment	Approximate Cost	Developer
BAT 'K' Sonar Cane	Sonar	Acoustic	Presence of multiple targets, out to 5 m distance, including drop-offs and over-hangs	Cane-mounted	No	Indoors or outdoors	$700	Bay Advanced Technologies, http://www.batforblind.co.nz
Kaspa	Sonar	Acoustic, stereo sound	Acoustic image of multiple objects in 3-D space (out to 5 m), including over-hangs	Head-mounted	No	Mainly outdoors	$2,500	Bay Advanced Technologies, http://www.batforblind.co.nz
Sonic Path-finder	Sonar	Acoustic, stereo sound	objects contacted by a pedestrian in the next 2 seconds (including over-hangs)	Head-mounted	No	Mainly outdoors	$1,600	Perceptual Alternatives, http://www.sonicpathfinder.org
Mini-guide	Sonar	Acoustic and vibro-tactile	Object distance (0.5 to 8 m) including over-hangs	Hand-held	No	Mainly outdoors	$600	GDP Research, http://www.gdp-research.com.au
UltraCane	Sonar	Acoustic and vibro-tactile	Object distance (1 to 4 m) including drop-offs and over-hangs	Cane-mounted	No	Indoors or outdoors	$800	Sound Foresight, http://www.soundforesight.co.uk

TABLE 25.1 (Continued)

Device	Input Transducer	Output Display	Information Conveyed	Mode of Operation	Requires Special Infra-Structure	Operating Environment	Approximate Cost	Developer
Nurion Laser cane	Laser	Acoustic and vibro-tactile	Object distance (out to 4 m) including drop-offs and over-hangs	Cane-mounted	No	Indoors or outdoors	$3,000	Nurion-Raycal, http://www.nurion.net/LC.html
vOICe Learning Edition	Camera	Auditory sound-scapes	Sonic image of multiple objects in 3-D space	Head-mounted or hand-held	No	Indoors or outdoors	Free	Peter Meijer, http://www.seeingwithsound.com/
Braille-Note GPS	Global Positioning System Receiver	Speech and Braille	Direction and distance to local points of interest, route planning, active and virtual navigation modes	GPS receiver and accessible PDA worn over shoulder	Presence of GPS signal	Outdoors	$2,199 (including software, GPS receiver and all U.S. maps).	SenderoGroup, http://www.senderogroup.com/
Personal Guidance System (PGS)	Global Positioning System Receiver	Spatialized sound, haptic interface	Direction and distance to object locations in 3-D space, route navigation.	GPS receiver, compass, and laptop worn in backpack	Presence of GPS signal	Outdoors	Not comercially available	UCSB Personal Guidance System, http://www.geog.ucsb.edu/pgs/main.htm
Talking Signs	Infrared	Speech	Message about direction and location of landmarks in local environment	Hand-held	Talking sign transmitter (requires power)	Indoors or outdoors	$2000 per sign	Talking signs, http://www.talkingsigns.com/tksinfo.shtml
Digital Sign System (DSS)	Infrared	Acoustic, and speech	Indoor location and nearby points of interest	Hand-held	Passive bar-coded signs	Indoors	Not comercially available	Tjan et al. (2005) [57]

FIGURE 25.1 *A blind pedestrian is using a guide dog and five technologies for navigation. This figure illustrates the need for an integrated navigational system. The guide dog aids with mobility and obstacle avoidance. The compass provides the user with heading information when stationary. The GPS receiver integrates with a GIS database (digital map) to provide position and heading information during outdoor navigation. The talking signs receiver gives orientation cues by identifying the direction and location of important landmarks in the environment. The digital sign system (DSS) receiver picks up barcodes from signs and sends them to a database to facilitate indoor navigation. The BrailleNote accessible computer represents the "brain" of the system, allowing Braille input and speech and Braille output. In theory this device could serve as the hub to which all other technologies interface.*

As of yet, there is no commercial product that seamlessly integrates multiple technologies into a single system, but one can readily imagine such a product. Figure 25.1 shows components from several technologies, a Talking Signs receiver, a DSS receiver, a GPS receiver, a compass, an accessible PDA, and a guide dog.

Now imagine that the electronics for the compass, Talking Signs, DSS, and GPS receivers are merged into one housing. The maps needed for outdoor environments and indoor databases are consolidated onto one large compact flash storage card, and the accessible PDA serves as a common input/output device, providing speech and Braille access for all subsystems. With this configuration, a blind navigator receives traditional mobility information from the guide dog and uses the integrated PDA for all other orientation information in both indoor and outdoor environments. This system would be minimally intrusive, utilize a clear and customizable user interface, work under a wide range of environmental conditions, and guarantee compatibility and interoperability between the various technologies. Although training would inevitably be a critical factor in effective use of such a system, a major advantage is that all environmental sensors would utilize a common output modality. People would need to learn only one set of rules and could choose the information from the sensors that most benefited their needs.

If an ETA could be designed that could provide much of the information that many of the above mentioned devices did, in a package that seamlessly integrated mobility and orientation information, both indoors and out, it would probably experience a much higher level of acceptance than many of the existing technologies in isolation.

ACKNOWLEDGMENTS

Preparation of this chapter was supported by NRSA grant 1F32EY01596301 and NIDRR grant H133A011903

REFERENCES

1. National Research Council: *Visual Impairments: Determining Eligibility for Social Security Benefits*, National Academy Press, 2002.
2. Golledge RG: Geography and the disabled: A survey with special reference to vision impaired and blind populations, *Trans Inst Br Geographers* **18**:63–85 (1993).
3. Legge GE, Madison C, Mansfield JS: Measuring Braille reading speed with the MNREAD test, *Visual Impair Res* **1**:131–145 (1999).
4. Americans with Disabilities Act (ADA), 2006 (http://www.ada.gov/).
5. Arditi A, Brabyn J: Signage and wayfinding, in Silverstone B, Lange MA, Rosenthal B, Faye E, eds: *The Lighthouse Handbook on Vision Impairment and Rehabilitation,* Oxford Univ Press, New York, 2000, Vol 1, pp 637–650.
6. Barlow JM, Franck L: Crossroads: Modern interactive intersections and accessible pedestrian signals, *J Visual Impair Blindness* **99**(10):599–610 (2005).
7. Lighthouse International: *The Lighthouse Handbook on Vision Impairment and Vision Rehabilitation*, Oxford Univ Press, New York, 2000.
8. Loomis JM, Klatzky RL, Golledge RG, Cincinelli JG, Pellegrino JW, Fry PA: Nonvisual navigation by blind and sighted: Assessment of path integration ability, *J Exper Psychol General* **122**(1):73–91 (1993).
9. Loomis JM, Golledge RG, Klatzky RL, Speigle JM, Tietz J: Personal guidance system for the visually impaired, *Proc 1st Annual ACM/SIGGAPH Conf Assistive Technologies*, Marina Del Rey, CA, 1994.
10. Gallistel CR: Insect navigation: Brains as symbol-processors, in *Conceptual and Methodological Foundations,* MIT Press, Cambridge, MA, 1990, Vol 4.
11. Strelow ER: What is needed for a theory of mobility: Direct perception and cognitive maps—lessons from the blind, *Psychol Rev* **97**(2):226–248 (1985).
12. Thinus-Blanc C, Gaunet F: Representation of space in blind persons: Vision as a spatial sense? *Psychol Bull* **121**(1):20–42 (1997).
13. Rieser JJ, Guth DA, Hill EW: Mental processes mediating independent travel: Implications for orientation and mobility, *Visual Impair Blindness* **76**:213–218 (June 1982).
14. Rieser JJ, Guth DA, Hill EW: Sensitivity to perspective structure while walking without vision, *Perception* **15**:173–188 (1986).
15. Bigelow A: Spatial mapping of familiar locations in blind children, *J Visual Impair Blindness* **85**:113–117 (March 1991).
16. Cooper F, Gaitenby J, Nye P: Evolution of reading machines for the blind: Haskins Laboratories' research as a case history, *J Rehab Res Devel* **21**:51–87 (1984).

17. Golledge RG: Tactual strip maps as navigational aids, *J Visual Impair Blind* **85**(7):296–301 (1991).
18. Kish D: Echolocation: How humans can "see" without sight, 2006 (http://www.worldaccessfortheblind.org/echolocationreview.rtf).
19. Loomis JM, Lederman SJ: Tactual perception, in Boff K, Kaufman L, Thomas J, eds, *Handbook of Perception and Human Performance,* Wiley, New York, 1986, Vol 2, Chapter 31.
20. Klatzky R, Lederman S: Touch, in Weiner IB, Healy AF, Proctor R, eds, *Experimental Psychology, and Comprehensive Handbook of Psychology,* Wiley, New York, 2002, Vol 4, Chapter 6.
21. Golledge RG, Marston JR, Loomis JM, Klatzky RL: Stated preferences for components of a personal guidance system for non-visual navigation, *J Visual Impair Blind* **98**(3):135–147 (2004).
22. Brabyn J: *A Review of Mobility Aids and Means of Assessment*, Martinus Nijhoff, Boston, 1985.
23. Loomis JM: Sensory replacement and sensory substitution: Overview and prospects for the future, in Roco MC, Bainbridge WS, eds, *Converging Technologies for Improving Human Performance: Nanotechnology, Biotechnology, Information Technology and Cognitive Science*, Kluwer Academic Publishers, Boston, 2003.
24. Blasch BB, Welsh RL, Wiener WR: *Foundations of Orientation and Mobility*, 2nd ed, AFB Press, 1997.
25. Schenkman BN, Jansson G: The detection and localization of objects by the blind with the aid of long-cane tapping sounds, *Human Factors* **28**(5):607–618 (1986).
26. Bay Advanced Technologies Ltd. (http://www.batforblind.co.nz/; accessed 2006).
27. Kay L: Auditory perception of objects by blind persons using bioacoustic high resolution air sonar, *J Acoust Soc Am* **107**(6):3266–3275 (2000).
28. Kay L: Bioacoustic spatial perception by humans: A controlled laboratory measurement of spatial resolution without distal cues, *J Acoust Soc Am* **109**(2):803–808 (2001).
29. Farmer LW: Mobility devices, in Welsh LW, Blasch BB, eds, *Foundations of Orientation and Mobility*, American Foundation for the Blind, New York, 1980.
30. Perceptual alternatives, 2006 (http://www.sonicpathfinder.org/).
31. Dodds AG, Clark-Carter Dd, Howarth CI: The Sonic PathFinder: An evaluation, *J Visual Impair Blind* **78**(5):306–310 (1984).
32. LaGrow S: The use of the Sonic PathFinder as a secondary mobility aid for travel in business environments: A single-subject design, *J Rehab Res Devel* **36**(4) (1999).
33. GDP Research, 2006 (http://www.gdp-research.com.au/).
34. Sound Foresight, 2006 (http://www.soundforesight.co.uk/).
35. Borenstein J, Ulrich I: The GuideCane: A computerized travel aid for the active guidance of blind pedestrians, *Proc IEEE Int Conf Robotics and Automation*, Albuquerque, NM, 1997.
36. Nurion-Raycal, 2006 (http://www.nurion.net/LC.html).
37. vOICe Learning Edition, 2006 (http://www.seeingwithsound.com/).
38. Meijer PB: An experimental system for auditory image representations, *IEEE Trans Biomed Eng* **39**(2):112–121 (1992).
39. Fletcher JE: Seeing with sound: A journey into sight, *Tucson 2002 Conf "Toward a Science of Consciousness,"* Tucson, AZ, 2002.
40. Bach-Y-Rita P: *Brain Mechanisms in Sensory Substitutions*, Academic Press, New York, 1972.
41. Bach-y-Rita P, Tyler ME, Kaczmarek KA: Seeing with the brain, *Int J Human-Comput INTERACTION* **15**(2):285–295 (2003).

42. Crandall W, Brabyn J, Bentzen BL, Myers L: Remote infrared signage evaluation for transit stations and intersections, *J Rehab Res Devel* **36**(4):341–355 (1999).
43. Marston J: Spatial knowledge acquisition and the blind: The effect of environmental auditory cues on spatial awareness, *Conf Workshop on Assistive Technologies for Vision and Hearing Impairment*, Granada, Spain, 2004.
44. Crandall W, Bentzen BL, Myers L, Brabyn J: New orientation and accessibility option for persons with visual impairments: Transportation applications for remote infrared audible signage, *Clin Exper Optometry* **84**(3):120–131 (2001).
45. Golledge RG, Marston JR: *Towards an Accessible City: Removing Functional Barriers to Independent Travel for Blind and Vision Impaired Residents and Visitors*, California PATH Program, Inst Transportation Studies, Univ California, Berkeley, 1999 (UCB-ITS-PPR-99-33 for PATH project MOU 343).
46. Marston JR: *Towards an Accessible City: Empirical Measurement and Modeling of Access to Urban Opportunities for those with Vision Impairments, Using Remote Infrared Audible Signage*, unpublished doctoral dissertation, Dept Geography, Univ California, Santa Barbara, 2002.
47. Bentzen BL, Mitchell PA: Audible signage as a wayfinding aid: Comparison of "Verbal landMarks" with "Talking Signs," *Rehab Res Devel* **36**(4) (1999).
48. Loomis JM, Golledge RG, Klatzky RL: Personal guidance system for the visually impaired using GPS, GIS, and VR technologies, *Conf Virtual Reality and Persons with Disabilities*, Millbrae, CA, 1993.
49. UCSB Personal Guidance System, 2006 (http://www.geog.ucsb.edu/pgs/main.htm).
50. Loomis JM, Golledge RG, Klatzky RL: Navigation system for the blind: Auditory display modes and guidance, *Presence Teleoperators Virtual Environ* **7**:193–203 (1998).
51. Loomis JM, Marston JR, Golledge RG, Klatzky RL: Personal guidance system for people with visual impairment: A comparison of spatial displays for route guidance, *J Visual Impair Blind* **99**:219–232 (2005).
52. Marston JR, Loomis JM, Klatzky RL, Golledge RG, Smith EL: Evaluation of spatial displays for navigation without sight, *ACM Trans Appl Percep* **3**(2):110–124 (2006).
53. Petrie H, Johnson V, Strothotte T, Raab A, Fritz S, Michel R: MoBIC: Designing a travel aid for blind and elderly people, *J Nav* **49**:45–52 (1996).
54. NFB Access Technology Staff: GPS technology for the blind, a product evaluation, *Braille Monitor* **49**:101–108 (2006).
55. Talking Lights LLC, 2006 (http://www.talking-lights.com/).
56. Commercial software EPE 2.1 available from Ekahau, 2006 (http://www.ekahau.com/).
57. Tjan BS, Beckmann Pj, Roy R, Giudice NA, Legge GE: Digital sign system for indoor wayfinding for the visually impaired, *Proc 1st IEEE Workshop on Computer Vision Applications for the Visually Impaired*, in conjunction with CVPR 2005, San Diego, 2005.
58. Giudice NA: *Navigating Novel Environments: A Comparison Of Verbal and Visual Learning*, dissertation, Dept Psychology, Univ-Minnesota, Twin Cities, 2004.
59. Giudice NA, Bakdash JZ, Legge GE: Wayfinding with words: Spatial learning and navigation using dynamically-updated verbal descriptions, *Psychol Res* **71**(3):347–358 (2007).
60. Ohkugo H, Kamakura K, Kitakaze S, Fujishima Y, Watanabe N, Kamata M: Integrated wayfinding/guidance system using GPS/IR/RF/RFID with mobile device, *20th Annual CSUN Int Conf Technology and Persons with Disabilities*, Los Angeles, 2005.
61. The wayfinding group, 2006 (http://www.wayfinding.org).

26

Walker Systems

Andrew Rentschler
CED Accident Analysis

26.1 INTRODUCTION

Technological advances in medicine and living have resulted in a continuous increase in expected lifespan [1]. As the members of the generation of baby boomers from the 1940s and 1950s continue to age, the number of people age 65 and above will be higher than ever before [2]. The population growth rate for this age group is more than double that of the general population [3]. There will be 65 million people over the age of 65 in the year 2030, and 15 million people over the age of 85 by 2050 [4]. The current cost of healthcare for the elderly is predicted to rise to over $4.0 trillion from the current cost of $1.3 trillion [5]. There were approximately 1.5 million people age 65 and above who lived in nursing homes in 1997, and this number could rise to as high as 3 million by the year 2030 [6,7].

The increase in elderly population will be mirrored by an increasing need for effective and interactive assistive mobility devices. Fuller G.F., White House Medical Clinic, reported that one-third of community-dwelling elderly persons and 60% of nursing home residents fall each year [8]. The costs of such falls amounted to $20.2 billion in 1994 and are predicted to reach approximately $32.4 billion by the year 2020 [9]. Eakman found that approximately one-third of accidental deaths in the 65+ age group result from falls and complications from falls [10]. A significant increase in mortality and morbidity is also associated with even minor slips and falls in the 80+ age group [11].

One of the most important factors in the quality of life for the elderly is the ability to move about freely and independently [12]. Many factors involving both physical and mental health are dependent on mobility. This includes the ability to perform activities of daily living as well as maintaining fitness and a sense of independence. Mobility,

The Engineering Handbook of Smart Technology for Aging, Disability, and Independence,
Edited by A. Helal, M. Mokhtari and B. Abdulrazak
Copyright © 2008 John Wiley & Sons, Inc.

wayfinding, and independence can all be affected by gait disturbances and spatial disorientation brought on by dementia in older adults [13–15]. Memory loss can also complicate simple day-to-day navigation in both familiar and unfamiliar environments [16]. Nursing home residents are at an even greater risk for the dangers associated with mobility issues, as they tend to be older, have more cognitive impairments, and experience more serious falls [17]. Rubenstein et al. reported that as many as 75% of nursing home residents fall annually [18].

The primary goal of robotic walkers currently being designed and tested is to assist frail elderly users with mobility and navigational assistance. Elderly individuals with visual, cognitive, and mental deficiencies can often have difficulties negotiating obstacles and navigating in their environments. The use of regular walkers therefore becomes ineffective and even hazardous. A mobility device that can help users avoid obstacles and even guide them to predetermined locations while reducing the need for supervision could reduce the cost of care and increase the independence and well-being of thousands of individuals.

The interaction between a human–machine system can be very complex and must be made reliable and intuitive in order to appeal to and ultimately benefit the frail elderly population. Both parts feed information into the system, which produces an output greater than any single part could provide. Robotic walkers need to avoid obstacles in a smooth and predictable manner to guarantee the safety of the users, whose population consists of individuals with reduced mobility and visual or cognitive impairments. This requirement complicates the development of an effective obstacle avoidance algorithm that disallows sharp and potentially hazardous turns [19]. Any actions taken by the device to avoid obstacles must also be balanced with the user's need to feel in control of the device.

Most robotic walkers are currently being designed to operate in single-level indoor environments such as nursing homes and retirement centers. For safety reasons, many walkers depend on the user to provide the propulsion force. This allows the users to maintain a sense of control and prevents any sudden movements or accelerations. Some walkers are self-propelled, which is effective for extremely frail individuals who may not have enough strength to push the device. The goal of these devices is to provide the basic support of a traditional walker coupled with the ability to perform obstacle avoidance and path navigation. Ideally, these devices would function like a normal walker most of the time, but provide navigational and avoidance assistance whenever necessary.

Many of the current devices employ a shared control algorithm. Under normal circumstances without the presence of obstacles or hazards, the operator has full control over the direction of the walker. Once an obstacle is detected, the devices can alter the path of travel, usually by changing the angle of the front wheels. Several different systems currently under development utilize an array of different algorithms, sensors, and feedback systems.

The navigational programs designed for robotic walkers consist of two different approaches. The first approach is a predetermined path following mode. In this mode, after selecting a destination, the user will be guided by the walker to it utilizing the shortest obstacle-free path. If obstacles are encountered along the way, the walker will avoid them and recalculate its path to the intended destination. This method requires the walker to be able to reliably determine its current position in a global environment and identify hazards and make instantaneous adjustments.

The other type of navigational assistance currently being investigated involves estimating user intent. The idea behind this method is to evaluate the forces and movements of the user and incorporate them with the current position and state of the walker to determine the user's intended path of travel. Robotic walkers with force sensors in the handlebars can measure the forces and moments applied by the user and then use this information to determine the intended direction of travel of the user. User intent algorithms involve quantitative estimates that are both deterministic and probabilistic [20]. Several of the robotic walkers currently under development are described in the following section.

26.2 CURRENT ROBOTIC WALKERS

26.2.1 Guido

The leading causes of visual impairments among older adults include macular degeneration, cataracts, glaucoma, and diabetic retinopathy. According to the American Federation for the Blind, the number of individuals age 65+ who have severe functional limitations in vision will increase to 284 % from the year 2000 to the year 2050. A report by the US Census Bureau on Americans with disabilities states that 7.6 million of the 267.7 million noninstitutionalized individuals surveyed have some sort of visual impairment [21]. A total of 1.7 million are unable to see, and the other 5.9 million have difficulties seeing words and letters. Elderly individuals over the age of 65 accounted for over half of this group. The American Foundation for the Blind reported that approximately 26 % of all nursing home residents had some level of visual impairment [22]. A study performed by Goodrich projected that by the year 2010 there would be over 147,000 legally blind veterans and 880,000 veterans with severe visual impairments [23]. Studies have also shown that visual impairment increases the risk of falls and fractures and therefore also increases the likelihood that an older person will be admitted to a hospital or nursing home [24]. Current mobility devices for the elderly and visually impaired require certain levels of function and dexterity that few users possess. These statistics underline the need for the research and development of new assistive mobility devices that will reduce limitations and enhance the function of these individuals.

Guido, also known as the Veterans Affairs Personal Adaptive Mobility Aid (VA-PAMAID), is designed to provide physical support and navigational assistance to visually impaired individuals [25]. The walker was designed by Dr. Gerard Lacey and Dr. MacNamara while at Trinity University in Dublin, Ireland and has been marketed by Haptica Incorporated [26]. Guido is built on the design of a basic walker. A computer controls motors that guide the front wheels of the walker. Laser and ultrasonic sensors are mounted on the front and sides of the walker. These sensors can help to identify obstacles and landmark features such as junctions and corridors. The user controls the walker through a set of spring-loaded handlebars that are equipped with an encoder that senses the direction in which the user wants to travel. A second set of optical encoders is mounted to the rear wheels and measures the total distance traveled by the device. Figure 26.1 shows a front view of Guido.

Guido has three control modes: manual, automatic, and park. In manual mode, the user has total control of the walker. Information detected by the sensors is issued as voice messages describing landmarks and obstacles. In automatic mode, the user and the computer share control of the walker. The computer uses motors connected to the front wheels to steer the device away from obstacles. The controller will override user input when attempting to negotiate obstacles. Voice messages are still given as well. In park mode, the front wheels are oriented to prevent movement of the device.

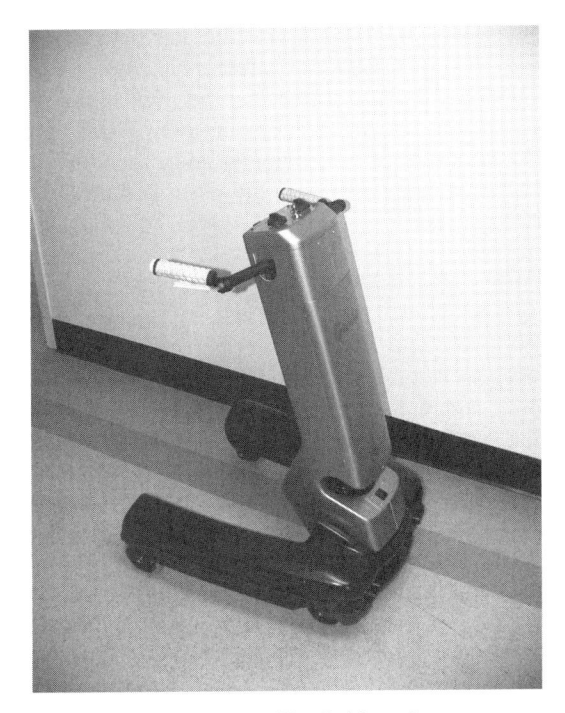

FIGURE 26.1 The Guido walker.

The current version of Guido utilizes what is known as the "clean-sweep algorithm" [19]. This algorithm has two parts: (1) generation of a map of the local environment and (2) using this map in the main obstacle avoidance method. The clean-sweep system runs on an embedded PC running Linux. Task control architecture was used as a framework for the software design. The mapping program receives information from the laser and sonar sensors, as well as the wheel encoders. The map that is generated is then sent to the navigation program, which factors in the position of the walker and the intended direction of travel of the user. The clean sweep algorithm was designed to help the walker navigate through cluttered environments. The system is also intended to react quickly to the user input so that it will go in the direction intended by the user.

Guido has four different types of sensors. The SICK LMS scanning laser (accurate to ± 1 cm over 30 m) is the main sensor used for obstacle and landmark detection. The laser gives an accurate 180 horizontal view of the environment in front of the walker. The laser scan returns a ray's length measurement for every degree, so there are 181 measurements in each scan. Since the laser produces only a 2D plane view, nothing above or below the height of the plane is visible to the laser. Polaroid ultrasound sensors are positioned around the front and sides of the walker to help detect the objects out of view from the laser. They also detect glass and other transparent materials that the laser might not detect. Two optical encoders are also positioned on the rear wheels of the walker. These encoders calculate the walker position and orientation in absolute values. The fourth sensor is a potentiometer on the steering wheel that receives user input. The signal is converted to an angle, $-60°$ to $60°$, from left to right and used to determine the direction of the front wheels.

The map module keeps a local view of the environment (4 × 4 m), but not a global map [19]. The map receives information from the laser sensor, the sonar sensors, and the wheel encoders. The map structure is a list of points stored as absolute coordinate points. There are two separate lists of points in the map: the current laser view and a history of points from the previous positions of the walker no longer visible to the laser. The system maintains a list of all of the walker positions and laser ranges for a number of iterations. The points that are in front of the current laser baseline are placed into the current sensor points array. All of the points that are behind the laser baseline are placed in the historical data points array. The resulting window of points is a 4 × 4-m grid (1 m behind the walker, 2 m to each side, and 3 m in front of the walker).

The clean-sweep program is a geometry-based obstacle avoidance method where the space in front of the walker is searched in a geometric pattern for clear paths [19]. These paths checked by the system consist of circular paths corresponding to a given steering angle. A virtual wheel angle corresponds to a given turn radius of the device. Two separate circles are defined by the system that represents the sweep area that the outermost edges of the device would occupy for a specific turn radius. This method ensures that the outermost edge of the device will not contact obstacles during turning. The parameters for the area checked for a clear path include the search area circle, the left and right search limits, the baseline, and the maximum and minimum sweep edges. The system first checks between the minimum and maximum sweep edges. The second check detects points in front of the baseline. The next check tests inside the search area circle. The last check uses the left- and right-side limits.

Clinical studies with Guido have shown promising results. The ability of the walker to accurately detect obstacles and safely negotiate around them is of utmost importance since the target population of the device includes the severely visually impaired elderly.

26.2.2 PAMM

Dr. Steven Dubowsky and colleagues at Massachusetts Institute of Technology's Field and Space Robotics Laboratory have developed a prototype walking aid system to assist the elderly who are either living independently or in senior assisted-living facilities [27]. The walker-based PAMM (personal aid for mobility and monitoring) has omnidirectional drives, locates itself by reading signposts, detects and avoids obstacles, and measures the forces and torques on the handle to estimate the user's intent. The device utilizes both user input and obstacle detection to prevent collisions; however, the user has control over which obstacle free path he or she wishes to traverse. The PAMM control system is designed to allow admittance-based user interaction control. A dynamic model is created, and the system is then made to behave like the dynamic system specified by the model. Information from force–torque sensors mounted on the handles that determine user intent is integrated with instruction from the schedule-based planner, facility map information, and signals from the obstacle avoidance sensors in order to control the system. Figure 26.2 shows a front view of the PAMM.

The device has four different control modes. The first mode gives full control of the walker to the user. The controller performs path planning and obstacle avoidance in mode 2 and the user responds to and directs the device. In mode 3, the walker performs path planning, navigation, and localization. The user supplies the desired destination. Mode 4 involves task planning and communication by the walker. Currently, a cane-based system is being evaluated. The walker-based device is still in development. The goal of this

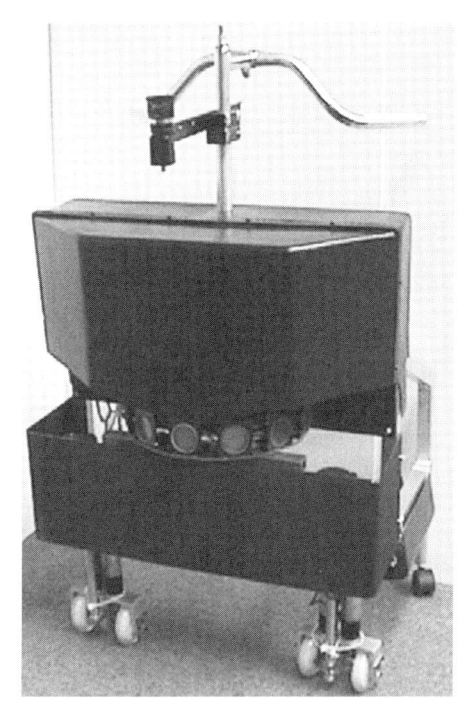

FIGURE 26.2 The PAMM walking aid system.

research is to prevent individuals from having to move from assisted-living facilities, or their own homes, to skilled nursing facilities. The target population of the PAMM project is elderly individuals with cognitive and physical impairments.

26.2.3 COOL AIDE

Researchers with the Medical Automation Research Center at the University of Virginia have investigated several different types of walker control systems, including a warning-only system, a safety braking system, a safety braking–steering system, and a path-following system [12,20,28–33]. All four control systems are based on the following design principles: diverge from user input slowly, keep walker turns in direction indicated by user, and make walker compliant to user. The project is investigating what can be accomplished with passive devices in home environments. The most current version of the walker is known as COOL AIDE (*coo*perative *l*ocomotion *aide*). A front view of COOL AIDE is shown in Figure 26.3.

The warning-only system can neither steer nor brake the walker [28]. Small motors in the walker's handles vibrate when the system detects a nearby obstacle. The safety braking system is the next progression in control systems. Braking is initiated by the system when either the walker comes to a stop or a possible collision is detected. The braking process occurs gradually so that the user can feel the resistance increase and is not disrupted by a sudden stop.

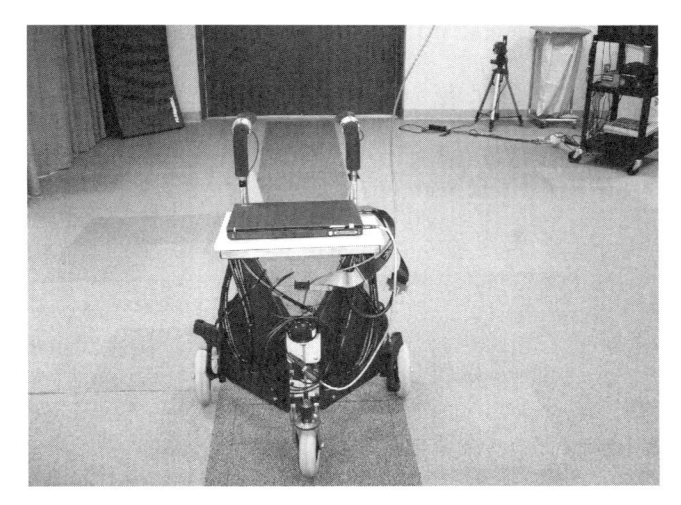

FIGURE 26.3 The COOL AIDE walker.

The safety braking–steering system attempts to make decisions on the basis of an estimate of the user's goals and takes corrective action only if an immediate environmental danger is detected [12]. The walker consists of a Sprint three-wheel rollator from Invacare, two 6-DOF load cells US120-160 from ATI Industrial Automation, an infrared sensor, an automated braking system, and a front-wheel motor. The load sensors are mounted inline between the handles and the frame in order to measure the load transfer between the walker and the user. A radial depth map of the environment is produced by the infrared sensor, and a histogram in motion mapping is utilized for the map-building process [29,34,35]. Development of this walker was a collaboration of a multidisciplinary team from the University led by Dr. Glenn Wasson of the Computer Science Department, Dr. Majd Alwan of the Medical Automation Research Center, and Dr. Pradip Sheth of the Mechanical and Aerospace Engineering Departments.

The walker is a shared control device in that the user has control over the navigation of the walker and the system activates only when necessary [32]. The walker cannot move without a physical input from the user and therefore moves at the user's pace. The control system also detects user behavior and intent by using a physics-based math model. As the user continually attempts to achieve his or her goals, the device does likewise in order to be able to assist the user. The control system attempts to determine the user intent from the following three factors: the forces and moments exerted on the handles by the user, the current state of the environment as measured by the sensors, and the state of the control system. The walker uses the environment and state data to detect any hazards along the paths that are suggested by the force data. A control signal that attempts to balance the user's intent with a safe path is then sent to the wheel motor to direct the walker.

According to the developers, the walker is passive, cooperative, and submissive [12,30]. The device is passive because it can only brake and adjust the direction of its front wheels [35,36]. The walker is cooperative because it attempts to infer the user's path and then uses this information to decide how best to avoid obstacles in the path. The walker is submissive because it continually monitors the user for signs of resistance through braking and steering and then adjusts its movements until the user agrees with the decision or manually overrides the controller.

The walker attempts to infer the intended path of the user by utilizing a combination of sensory data, user input, history, and position and orientation data [30]. A probabilistic representation is created using the data from the sonar and infrared sensors [38,39]. With each step that the user takes, the path inference algorithm used by the walker estimates the probability that the user is traveling on each possible arc from its current position by assigning a weight to each path. The paths are first weighted by the orientation of the walker. Any path that includes a translation component in the same direction as the walker's sensors indicate it is facing is given more weight than the others. Paths are next weighted by length, with longer paths weighted more. The paths are also weighted according to a history of the user's steering input. Additional weight is added to paths that are similar to the arc followed in the last timestep. Weight can also be subtracted depending on steering input. When a user exerts more force on one handle, the walker will turn in the opposite direction. A larger force equates to more rotation and less translation. If the user exerts an equal force on both the left and right handles, then the walker will move straight forward or backward. The relative weights added for length and history are approximately the same, while the weight added for correct translation direction is an order of magnitude greater.

The walker will only take action to avoid collisions or falls in the presence of danger. The action taken will depend on the path that the walker believes the user is on [30]. At a given distance of d_1 from an obstacle, the walker will take evasive steering action. If the walker is within a distance of d_2 ($< d_1$), then it will proportionately engage the brakes in order to slow without causing the user to lose balance. If the obstacle is very close to the walker, a distance of d_3 ($< d_2$) or less, then the automatic brakes will fully engage. The values of d_1-d_3 are dependent on both the width of the path that the user is believed to be following and the user's resistance to the walker's decisions. With respect to the width of the path, the walker will change the value of the tolerances according to the distance between the obstacles on either side of the path. If the user wishes to get closer to an object for the purpose of docking by resisting the steering motion of the walker, then the walker will reduce the tolerance to a minimum level to allow the user to get as close as possible. Researchers are also developing a path-following control system that will guide the user along a specific path and can adjust to the capabilities of the user to actively provide more or less guidance.

Investigators at the University of Virginia have more recently developed a navigational control system known as COOL AIDE (*coo*perative *l*ocomotion *aide*) [31]. COOL AIDE utilizes a dynamic model of the walker system to detect walker sliding and loss of stability. Sensor information, consisting of the forces and moments that the user exerts on the handles, as well as current location and walker state, is used to predict the user's short-term path. The control system can then assist the user in navigating to the intended goal. In addition to the sensors mounted on the handles, the walker is equipped with encoders on the front and rear wheels to estimate velocity, location, and heading, and an infrared obstacle detection sensor (PBS-03JN Hokuyo Automatic Co.) creates a 180° radial depth map of the environment.

The infrared scanner collects 121 data points, each 1.8° apart [31]. COOL AIDE then processes a 180° arc between 200 and 3000 mm. A 40 × 80-grid map with a size of 100 mm is created. The most current and previous maps are combined in order to develop a local map for navigation. The forces and moments of the user, along with the map of the environment, are then used to determine the most likely goal of the user and the system decides what control mode, if any, should be implemented.

The COOL AIDE system manipulates the walker's direction of travel by steering the front wheel [31]. This is achieved through the use of a belt–pulley system driven by a stepper motor. Huang et al. used the following five requirements to regulate control of the walker: (1) the virtual moment is effective only within a certain distance from the obstacle, (2) the walker will not make any sharp corrections that could compromise the stability of the user, (3) the infrared sensor only detects obstacles in the half-plane in front of the walker, (4) an obstacle in front of the walker has a greater influence than an obstacle to the side, and (5) the influence of the relative velocity between the walker and the obstacle is considered when processing possible movements.

COOL AIDE implements obstacle avoidance when any obstacles are detected on or near the path of the walker [31]. Once the repulsive virtual moment exceeds a specific threshold, COOL AIDE takes over control of the steering. Control of the walker is transferred back to the user when either the moment drops below the threshold or the user stops walking. If the user fights the guidance provided by the walker, control will be ceded back to the user.

COOL AIDE attempts to determine the user's short-term intent by applying the Dempster–Shafer theory to extract the user's navigational intent from historical observations [31]. This is accomplished through a three-step process: (1) assigning belief mass to valid passages on the map by analyzing the predicted path, (2) tracking the valid passages in subsequent maps, and (3) applying Dempster–Shafer's evidence combining rule to determine the possibilities that the valid passages are the user's navigational goal. Results from testing have shown that COOL AIDE can successfully determine users' navigational intents and implement the proper control actions that will help them safely achieve their goals while avoiding hazards. Future testing is planned with elderly walker users.

26.2.4 IMP

Researchers at Carnegie Mellon University and the University of Pittsburgh have developed a robotic walker designed to develop a hierarchical model of users' daily walking routines that can be used to provide guidance [40,42]. The walker is also capable of parking itself and returning to the user when signaled with a remote control device. The walker is currently known as the *intelligent mobility platform* (IMP).

A four-wheeled walker was implemented with a drive system that consists of a clutch that comes into contact with the wheels when the walker is lowered [40]. A drive assembly was added to each of the rear main wheels so that the walker had a relatively small turning radius. The walker is equipped with two types of sensors; one gathers environmental information, and the other gathers feedback from user actions. The environmental sensor is a SICK LMS laser range finder that gathers a 180° horizontal planar slice of the distances between it and any obstacles or obstructions. The control system uses this information in conjunction with a precomputed map of the environment to know where it is positioned at all times. The feedback system consists of six buttons positioned around a laptop display. A BasicXmicrocontroller monitors the state of each button and transmits the information to the laptop at 20 Hz.

The software components of the walker allow for navigation, localization, map building and editing, motor control, and sensory interface. [40] CARMEN (Carnegie Mellon's

Navigation Toolkit) was used as the basis for allowing the walker to autonomously park and return to the user when signaled [41]. The navigational capabilities of the walker are dependent on a room-based planner. The topology of the environment is graphed with weighted edges, where the nodes represent doors or borders, the edges represent rooms or areas, and the weights on the edges represent the distances between borders. When the graph is created, the user location is then added as a new node with edges connecting it to the doors in the room. A* Room-based planning is then used to find a sequence of doors that represent a path for the user to take to the desired room.

The user interface for the walker was designed with the following goals in mind: enable the user to park and retrieve the walker, allow the user to select a destination from a list, keep the user informed of their current location, dynamically guide users to their chosen destinations, provide feedback on distance traveled, and minimize distraction [40]. A map of the residence showing the current location of the walker is shown on a graphical display on the screen of a laptop attached to the walker's seat/platform. Four possible destinations are shown in a large, high-contrast font, and the user can scroll through additional destinations or select one by pressing a button. As the user ambulates through the environment, the map dynamically rotates and translates the walker's position so that the current location and heading of the walker is centered and facing upward. Additionally, a large arrow on the screen continuously points the user toward the next sequential room on the shortest path to the selected destination. A distance-traveled indicator is also displayed on the screen in order to provide feedback to the user about her/his current level of mobility.

The most recent prototype developed by Glover et al. is designed to learn models of people's motion behaviors [42]. The model is composed of three different levels, including an activity level with subdivided categories of walking activities, a topologic motion level that uses topologic regions as its basic element, and a metric motion level at which location is described by metric coordinates. A hierarchical hybrid semi-Markov model is used to combine the three different levels into a single coherent mathematical framework.

The metric motion level consists of the $x-y$ location and heading direction θ of the user [42]. The location vector at time t, (i.e., α_t) is obtained by running the CARMEN software program. The topologic location of the user is found using an environmental map that is manually partitioned into topologic regions corresponding to areas such as rooms and corridors. The topologic location at time t (i.e., β_t) is a function of the metric location. The activity level is divided into two different categories: activities carried out in a single location and activities the involve motion between multiple locations. Each activity is given a unique identifier and is denoted at time t by γ_t. While changes at the metric level occur continuously, the changes at the topologic level are less frequent, and the changes at the activity level are even more infrequent. Therefore, different time indices, k and s, are used for the topologic and activity levels, respectively.

The hierarchical probabilistic semi Markov model is defined through the following four conditional probability distributions that characterize the evolution of state over time [42]:

1. $p(\beta'|\beta, \gamma)$ represents the transition probability between topologic locations, conditioned on the activity γ and defines state transitions at the topologic level.
2. $p(\delta|\beta, \gamma)$ represents the distribution over durations spent in topologic regions β, conditioned on the activity γ.

3. $p(\gamma'|\gamma)$ measures the transition probability for activities.
4. $p(f(t[s])|\gamma)$ (where [s] denotes time in seconds) measures the time of day at which activity γ may be initiated.

The probability of the data sequences B (topologic events) and C (activities) are then given as follows:

$$P(B,C) = \prod p(\beta k|\beta k-1, \gamma k-1)p(\delta k|\beta k, \gamma k) \cdot \prod p(\gamma s|\gamma s-1)p(f(t[s])|\gamma s)$$

Glover et al. used a Bayes filter to calculate, for any time t, the probability that the person's activity is γ_t given the present and past data.

Glover et al. then conducted experiments where they collected more than 60,000 position data over 4 days and derived 213 topologic state transitions. The map was subdivided into 86 locations spanning three different buildings with three floors each. Glover found that their model predicted people's activity with 100 % accuracy, for a total of 61 activities and topological location changes.

26.2.5 Pearl

The Nursebot project was established in 1998 by a multidisciplinary team of healthcare and computer science researchers from the University of Michigan, the University of Pittsburgh, and Carnegie Mellon University. One of the current goals of the project was to develop mobile robotic assistants for elderly people living at home and in assisted-living and nursing homes. Pearl is a robotic assistant that can remind people about routine activities, as well as guide them through their environments [43,44]. Pearl's software architecture utilizes probabilistic artificial intelligence techniques at all levels of perception and decisionmaking. The most recent version of Pearl is shown in Figure 26.4.

The inception of the project involved a team of researchers from Carnegie Mellon University and the University of Pittsburgh [45]. The device was built on top of a Nomad XR4000 mobile robot platform equipped with an omnidirectional drive. The sensor system consists of two circular arrays of Nomadics infrared near-range sensors, three large touch-sensitive doors, and a SICK LMS laser range finder. The visual display consists of a LCD monitor that informs the user of the walker's position with respect to the room [46]. A large rotating arrow points the user to the direction of the next waypoint. The haptic interface of the walker consists of two handlebars equipped with constrained prismatic handgrips. There are force-sensing resistors embedded in the handlebars that are used to convert the pressure readings into translation and rotational movement. If the user pushes forward on the handlebars, then the walker moves forward. If the user pushes on one handlebar and pulls on the other, the walker will rotate.

The navigation system is based on CARMEN. CARMEN is a probabilistic software system in which information is represented by probability distributions [47–49]. A metric map of the environment, with a resolution of 10 cm, is first created by manually driving the walker through the environment [50,51]. Potential target locations are then manually marked in the maps. A Monte Carlo localization is used to produce an accurate estimate of the walker's location with respect to its environment. A conditional particle filter algorithm is also used to track people by detecting the differences between actual measurements and the map [52].

FIGURE 26.4 The Pearl robotic walking assistant.

CARMEN also provides navigation modules that integrate real-time fast collision avoidance with the ability to plan and modify goal paths to target locations within a map [45]. A sequence of viapoints is calculated in 2D space that minimizes the pathlength while providing clearance for nearby obstacles. The sequence of points is dynamically calculated on the basis of the map, target location, and the walker's current position. New viapoints are calculated if the walker deviates from the chosen path, and the viapoints are converted into actual commands by a fast local controller [53]. All of the sensor measurements are dynamically processed at the control level in order to provide collision avoidance. The result, according to Morris et al. [45], is a walker that is capable of moving smoothly from any location to any other location in the environment while avoiding collisions with both active and stationary obstacles.

The key elements of the control software include both the user-intended and robot-intended trajectories [45]. In order to determine the user-intended trajectory, data from the handlebar force sensors are input into the user motion model to ascertain user-desired translational and rotational velocities. The robot-intended trajectory is determined by localizing the position of the walker in the world map and setting the target location. The navigation system then generates a path from the walker to the target location taking into account obstacles and obstructions.

The shared control system of the walker involves three different modes of operation: passive mode, active mode, and forced mode [45]. In passive mode, the robot-intended trajectory is ignored and the user has control of the walker. The control system primarily prevents collisions and monitors user position. In active mode, the robot-intended trajectory is given preference. If the estimated trajectory of the user deviates by more than a given angle, the walker will begin to slow and eventually stop unless the user realigns the walker with the desired path. Only the robot-intended trajectory is used in the forced mode. The user has no control over the direction of the walker and can only start and stop the device.

The most current version of Pearl has SICK laser range finders, sonar sensors, speech recognition microphones, speech synthesis speakers, stereocamera systems, a differential drive system, two onboard Pentium PCs, and a wireless Ethernet [43,44]. Three new modules concerned with people interaction were added to the navigation systems described by Burgard and coworkers [54,55].

Identifying and safely navigating with people is one of the most vital factors that a robotic walker must focus on in a community setting [43,44]. Pearl utilizes map differencing to detect people instead of the more traditional method of analyzing sensor measurements to detect features. Map differencing involves having the robot learn a map and then using it to detect people through significant deviations from the map. The problem of people tracking is a combined posterior estimation problem and model selection problem. The posterior estimated by Pearl is factored into $N+1$ conditionally independent estimates: $p(x^t|z^t, u^t, m)\Pi p(y_{n,t}|z^t, u^t, m)$. The robot path x^t, is then estimated using a particle filter. Every particle is associated with a set of N particle filters, each representing one of the people position estimates $p(y_{n,t}|z^t, u^t, m)$. The conditional particle filters represent people position estimates conditioned on robot path estimates. Montemerlo et al. [49] found that the data association between measurements and people were correct in the vast majority of actual situations.

In order to provide safer navigation in the presence of elderly people, Pearl's operation area was restricted to avoid densely populated regions by using a manually augmented environment map [43,44]. Because probabilistic techniques cannot guarantee that Pearl will obey a safety constraint, the researchers augmented the robot localization particle filter with a sampling strategy that is sensitive to the increased risk of high-traffic areas. Doing so minimizes the likelihood of being mislocalized in such areas or entering prohibited regions undetected. Testing has shown that Pearl was well localized in high-risk areas.

A hierarchical variant of a partially observable Markov decision process (POMDP) is used for Pearl's high-level control architecture [43,56]. Control decision is based on the full probability distribution generated by the state estimator, $p(y_{1,t}, \ldots, y_{N,t}, x^t|z^t, u^t, m)$. The distribution includes several multivalued probabilistic state and goal variables that encode information such as the robot's and client's locations and observed input from the interaction sensors. Pearl selects 19 actions that fall into three broad categories: communication actions, movement actions, and miscellaneous actions. Every action invokes a sequence of operations on the part of the robot. Pearl's hierarchical version of POMDPs break down the exceedingly large decisionmaking problem into a collection of smaller problems that are more easily solved. The cornerstone of the hierarchical algorithm is an action hierarchy to achieve a collection of POMDPs that are individually smaller than the original POMDP, but collectively define a complete policy. Once the action hierarchy has been defined, an independent policy for each subtask is optimized in order to create a collection of corresponding local policies. During operation, the controller then monitors the state of the system and looks up the appropriate control in the local policy set [57].

The other main function of Pearl is to serve as a cognitive orthotic that can provide elderly people with reminders about daily activities [43]. The software component of Pearl that provides these functions is called *Autominder* and consists of three main components: the *plan manager*, which stores and updates daily activities as well as resolves scheduling conflicts; the *client modeler*, which observes user activities and tracks the execution of the activities plan; and the *personal cognitive orthotic*, which analyzes differences between what the plan calls for and what the user is actually doing and determines when to issue reminders [43]. Testing has been performed with Pearl at a retirement community in Pennsylvania. All of the guidance tasks were successfully completed and postexperimental debriefings demonstrated a sense of excitement among the elderly users.

26.2.6 Care-O-bot II

The Care-O-bot II consists of two autonomous systems; the bottom is a mobile platform with walking supporters, and the top consists of a manipulator arm and sensor head [58,59]. The top platform of the Care-O-bot II consists of a tilting sensor head containing a 3D laser scanner and two cameras. The laser scanner is used to detect obstacles and prevent collisions. The two independent control systems are both based on an industrial PC and connected by an Ethernet link. The mobile platform PC controls the autonomous movement of the walker and can also adjust the handlebars. Both control systems are run by software based on the "Robotics Toolbox," developed by Fraunhofer IPA, which controls all of the walker functions, such as autonomous navigation and obstacle avoidance. A flexible path planning method for nonholonomic mobile robots is used to navigate the walker. A static map of the environment is used to generate a path that is smoothed and modified in response to any active obstacles or external forces.

The user controls the walker through either speech input or by utilizing the integrated touch screen. Feedback is provided to the user through the same channels. The display is part of a handheld control panel that attaches to the back of the walker. The panel is connected to the walker PC through radiofrequency and allows users to control their walkers even when they are not following behind them. The user can modify the behavior of the walker at any time and even bring up the current camera view of the walker on the display screen. The walker has two different modes of operation: direct-control mode and target mode. The direct-control mode allows the user to propel the walker to any location while the control system detects and avoids obstacles in the pathway. In target mode, the user is guided by the walker to a preplanned location along an optimal pathway.

26.3 FUTURE DEVELOPMENT

The future development of robotic walkers will be coupled to the technologic advancement of system hardware, including sensors and processors, as well as the improvement to software algorithms that will provide faster and more accurate obstacle avoidance and navigational programs. Experimental studies that examine the actions and movements of walker users will also be beneficial in allowing programs to more accurately predict user intent.

As the technology behind robotic walkers progresses, so, too, will the applications evolve. Alwan et al. are already performing experiments to determine the stability of steering-controlled walkers [12]. Robotic walkers will soon be able to react to not only the environment but also the user, by providing counteractive measures if the user loses balance or falls. Gait analysis of users and corrective strategies may also arise from the development of robotic walkers. User monitoring functions will also likely become more readily available. Walkers that can not only navigate through the environment but also monitor a user's physical condition, such as heart rate and blood pressure, can lead to dynamic customizable mobility or exercise plans.

The effective working environment of robotic walkers is also expected to change. Walkers that can function in the outdoor environment will provide even more independence and therapeutic value to the elderly. Devices that can detect and adapt to level changes, accurately detect and identify common objects, and safely navigate users through the community would be invaluable. The challenge for researchers and developers in this area is to design a lightweight portable robotic walker dedicated to elderly people and usable as a manual walker in any type of environment.

REFERENCES

1. Freid VM, Prager K, MacKay AP, Xia H: *Chartbook on Trends in the Health of Americans. Health United States, 2003*, National Center for Health Statistics, Hyattsville, MD, 2003.
2. Biomedical innovations, baby boomers, and aging, *Pfizer J* (Impact Communications, Inc, NY), **3**(1) (Spring 1999).
3. Kinsella K, Velkoff V: *An Aging World: 2001*, report of the United States Census Bureau, 2001 available at http://www.census.gov/Press Release/www/2001/cb01-198.html).
4. MacRitchie RF: *Reducing the Incidence of Falls among Elderly Nursing Home Residents: An Evaluation of an Ameliorative Pilot Program*, Southern Connecticut State Univ, May 2001, p 4.
5. Ciole R, Trusko B: HealthCare 2020: Challenges for the millennium, *Health Manage Technol* 34–38 (Aug 1999).
6. Kramarow E, Lentzner H, Rooks R, Weeks J, Saydah S: *Health and Aging Chartbook. Health United States, 1999*. National Center for Health Statistics, Hyattsville, MD, 1999.
7. Sayhoun NR, Pratt LA, Lentzner H, Dey A, Robinson KN: The changing profile of nursing home residents: 1985–1997 National Center for Health Statistics, Hyattsville, MD, 2001 (Aging Trends **4**).
8. Fuller GF: Falls in the elderly, *Am Fam Phys* **61**(7):2159–2168, 2173–2174 (2000) Review. PMID: 10779256.
9. Englander F, Hodson T, Terregrossa R: Economic dimensions of slip and full injuries, *J Forens Sci* **41**(5):733–746 (1996).
10. Eakman, A, Haven M, Ager S, Buchanan R, Fee N, Gollick S, Michels M, Olson L, Satterfield K, Stevenson K: Fall prevention in long-term care: an inhouse interdisciplinary team approach, *Top Geriatr Rehab* **17**:29–39 (1998).
11. Rubenstein L, Powers C, MacLean C: Quality indicators for the management and prevention of falls and mobility problems in vulnerable elders, *Ann Intern Med* **135**(8):686–693 (2001).
12. Alwan M, Rajendran PJ, Ledoux A, Huang C, Wasson G, Sheth P: Stability margin monitoring in steering-controlled intelligent walkers for the elderly, *AAAI Symp (EMBC)*, Nov 2005.
13. Kirasic KC, Allen GL, Haggerty D: Age-related differences in adults' macrospatial cognitive processes, *Exper Aging Res* **18**(1–2):33–39 (1992).
14. Nolan B, Mathews RM, Truesdell-Todd G, and VanDorp A: Evaluation of the effect of orientation cues on wayfinding in persons with dementia, *Alzheimer's Care Q* **3**(1):46–49 (2002).
15. Graafmans WC, Lips P, Wijlhuizen GJ, Pluijm SM, Bouter LM: Daily physical activity and the use of a walking aid in relation to falls in elderly people in a residential care setting, *Z Gerontol Geriatr* **36**:23–28 (2003).
16. Passini R, Rainville C, Marchand N, Joanette Y: Wayfinding in dementia of the Alzheimer's type: planning abilities, *J Clin Exper Neuropsycholo* **17**(6):820–832 (1995).

17. Bedsine RW, Rubenstein LZ, Snyder L, eds: *Medical Care of the Nursing Home Resident*, American College of Physicians, Philadelphia, 1996.
18. Rubenstein LZ, Josephson KR, Robbins AS: Falls in the nursing home, *Ann Intern Med* **121**:442–451 (1994).
19. Cassidy D: *Improved Obstacle Avoidance for a Human-Machine System*, Univ Dublin, Trinity College, Sept 2002.
20. Wasson G, Sheth P, Huang C, Ledoux A, Alwan M: A physics-based model for predicting user intent in shared-control pedestrian mobility aids, *Proc 2004 IEEE/RSJ Int Conf* Intelligent Robots and Systems, Sendai, Japan, Sept 28–Oct 2, 2004.
21. US Census Bureau: *Americans with Disabilities—Household Economic Studies*, 1997.
22. National Center for Health Statistics: *National Nursing Home Survey*, 1997.
23. Goodrich GL: *Growth in a Shrinking Population: Visual Impairment in the Veteran*, Palo Alto Health Care System, Palo Alto, CA, 1997 (1995–2010).
24. Ivers RQ, Cumming RG, Mitchell P, Attebo K: Visual impairment and falls in older adults: The Blue Mountain eyes study, *J Am Geriatr Soc* **46**:58–64 (1998).
25. Rentschler AJ: *Engineering and Clinical Evaluation of the VA-PAMAID Robotic Walker*, Univ Pittsburgh, PA, 2004.
26. Lacey G, MacNamara S: User involvement in the design and evaluation of a smart mobility aid, *J Rehab Res Devel* **37**(6):709–723 (2000).
27. Dubowsky S, Genot F, Godding S, Kozono S, Skwersky A, Yu LS, Yu H: PAMM—a robotic aid to the elderly for mobility assistance and monitoring: A "helpful-hand" for the elderly, *IEEE Int Conf Robotics and Automation*, San Francisco, April 2000, IEEE Press, Piscataway, NJ, 2000, pp 570–576.
28. Wasson G, Gunderson J, Graves S, Felder R: Effective shared control in cooperative mobility aids, *Proc 14th Int Florida Artificial Intelligence Research Society Conf*, May 2001, pp 509–518.
29. Alwan M, Wagner MB, Wasson G, Sheth P: Characterization of infrared range-finder PBS-03JN for 2-D mapping, *Proc 2005 IEEE Int Conf Robotics and Automation (ICRA '05)*, Barcelona, Spain, 2005.
30. Wasson G, Gunderson J, Graves S, Felder R: An assistive robotic agent for pedestrian mobility, *Int Conf Autonomous Agents*, 2001, pp 169–173.
31. Huang C, Wasson G, Alwan M, Sheth P, Ledoux A: Shared navigational control and user intent detection in an intelligent walker, *AAAI Fall 2005 Symp (EMBC)*, Sept 2005.
32. Wasson, G, Sheth, P, Alwan, M, Granata, K, Ledoux, A, Huang C: User intent in a shared control framework for pedestrian mobility aids, *Proc Conf Intelligent Robots and Systems*, Lausanne, Switzerland, (IROS), 2003.
33. Alwan M, Wasson G, Sheth P, Ledoux A, Huang C: Passive derivation of basic walker-assisted gait characteristics from measured forces and moments, *IEEE Trans Eng Med Biol*; (Sept 2004).
34. Borenstein J, Koren Y: Histogramic In-motion mapping for mobile robot obstacle avoidance, *IEEE Trans Robot Autom*; **7**(4):535–539 (1991).
35. Murphy R: *An Introduction to AI Robotics*, MIT Press, Cambridge, MA, 2000.
36. Colgate J, Wannasuphoprasit W, Peshkin M: Cobots: Robots for collaboration with human operators, *Proc Int Mech Eng Conf Exhib*; **58**:433–439 (1996).

37. Schneider O, Troccaz J, Chavanon O, Blin D: Synergistic robotic assistance to cardiac procedures, *Proc 13th International Congress and Exhibition (CARS'99) Comput Assist Radiol Surg* 23–26 (1999).
38. Moravec H: Sensor fusion in evidence grids for mobile robots, *AI Mag* **9**(2):61–74 (1998).
39. Thrun S, Fox D, Burgard W: A probabilistic approach to concurrent mapping and localization for mobile robots, *Autono Robots*; **5**:253–271 (1998).
40. Glover J, Holstius D, Manojlovich M, Montgomery K, Powers A, Wu J, Kiesler S, Matthews J, Thrun S: *A Robotically Augmented Walker for Older Adults*, Technical Report CMU-CS-03-170, Carnegie Mellon University, Computer Science Dept, Pittsburgh, PA, 2003.
41. Montemerlo M, Roy N, Thrun S: *Perspectives on Standardization in Mobile Robot Programming: The Carnegie Mellon Navigation (CARMEN) Toolkit*, Carnegie Mellon Univ, Pittsburgh, PA, March 2003 (available at http://www.cs.cmu.edu/~carmen).
42. Glover J, Thrun S, Matthews JT: Learning user models of mobility-related activities through instrumented walking aids, *Proc IEEE Int Conf Robotics and Automation (ICRA)*, 2004.
43. Pollack ME, Engberg S, Matthews JT, Thrun S, Brown L, Colbry D, Orosz C, Peintner C, Ramakrishnan S, Dunbar-Jacob J et al: A mobile robotic assistant for the elderly, *AAAI Workshop on Automation as Eldercare*, Aug, 2002.
44. Montemerlo M, Pineau J, Roy N, Thrun S, Verma V: Experiences with a mobile robotic guide for the elderly, Proce *AAAI National Conf Artificial Intelligence*, 2002.
45. Morris A, Donamukkala R, Kapuria A, Steinfeld A, Matthews JT, Dunbar J, Thrun J: A robotic walker that provides guidance, *Proc. ICRA '03*, IEEE Int Conf Publication **1**:25–30 (2003).
46. Steinfeld A, Tan H, Bougler B: Naturalistic findings for assisted snowplow operations, *Proc Human Factors and Ergonomics Soc 45th Annual Meeting*, Santa Monica, CA, 2001.
47. Thrun S, Beetz M, Bennewitz M, Burgard W, Cremers AB, Dellaert F, Fox D, Hähnel D, Rosenberg C, Roy N, et al: Probabilistic algorithms and the interactive museum tour-guide robot Minerva, *Int J Robot Res*; **19**(11):972–999 (2000).
48. Thrun S, Fox D, Burgard W, Dellaert F: Robust monte carlo localization for mobile robots, *Artif Intell* **128**(1–2):99–141 (2000).
49. Montemerlo M, Whittaker W, Thrun S: Conditional particle filters for simultaneous mobile robot localization and people-tracking, *IEEE Int Conf Robotics and Automation (ICRA)*, Washington, DC, 2002.
50. Moravec HP: Sensor fusion in certainty grids for mobile robots, *AI Mag* **9**(2):61–74 (1988).
51. Thrun S: A probabilistic online mapping algorithm for teams of mobile robots, *Int J Robot Res* **20**(5):335–363 (2001).
52. Doucet A, de Freitas JFG, Gordon NJ: *Sequential Monte Carlo Methods in Practice*, Springer-Verlag, New York, 2001.
53. Roy N, Thrun S: Motion planning through policy search, *Proc Conf Intelligent Robots and Systems (IROS)*, Lausanne, Switzerland, 2002.
54. Burgard W, Cremers AB, Fox D, Hähnel D, Lakemeyer G, Schulz D, Steiner W, Thrun S: The interactive museum tour-guide robot, *Proc AAAI-98 Conf*, 1998.
55. Thrun S, Beetz M, Bennewitz M, Burgard W, Cremers AB, Dellaert F, Fox D, Hähnel D, Rosenberg C, Roy N et al. Probabilistic algorithms and the interactive museum tour-guide robot Minerva, *Int J Robot Res* **19**(11) (2000).

56. Kaebling L, Littman M, Cassandra A: Planning and acting in partially observable stochastic domains, *Artif Intell* **101**(1–2):99–134 (1998).
57. Pineau J, Thrun S: High-level robot behavior control using pomdps, *AAAI-02 Workshop on Cognitive Robotics*, 2002.
58. Hans M, Graf B, Schraft R: Robotic home assistant care-o-bot: past-present-future, *Proc 11th IEEE Int Workshop on Robot Human Interactive Communication*, 2000, pp 380–385.
59. Graf B, Hans M, Schraft RD: Care-O-bot II development of a next generation robotic home assistant, *Auton Robots* **16**(2):193–205 (2004).

27

Accessible Public Transportation Services in America

Katharine M. Hunter-Zaworski

National Center for Accessible Transportation, Oregon State University

27.1 INTRODUCTION

Accessible transportation is essential for people with disabilities to access education and employment, and to live independently. Accessible transportation is a fundamental human right and this is embodied in US Federal Civil Rights Legislation. The spectrum of human abilities is very large, and this is the fundamental challenge in the planning, design, and operation of accessible transportation services. This chapter presents a high-level overview of accessible transportation services in America, and discusses many of the challenges that exist for both the providers and consumers of accessible transportation.

It is important to understand who are the users and beneficiaries of accessible transportation services. The short answer is all of us; young, old and in between. The amenities associated with accessible transportation benefit all travelers. The National Center for Accessible Transportation (NCAT) is working on a number of research and development projects that will change the current thinking in accessible transportation. First, instead of considering the stakeholders as people with disabilities, NCAT approaches problems from the perspective of *abilities*. In design solutions, NCAT does not look at the most common approach to design by merely satisfying the "customer requirements," but rather NCAT looks at Design for Experience. This chapter reflects the holistic and broad approach to accessible transportation that is central to the mission of NCAT.

The Engineering Handbook of Smart Technology for Aging, Disability, and Independence, Edited by A. Helal, M. Mokhtari and B. Abdulrazak
Copyright © 2008 John Wiley & Sons, Inc.

Accessible transportation service has traditionally been most concerned with providing transportation to individuals with obvious disabilities such as people who use crutches, canes, and wheeled mobility aids such as wheelchairs and scooters. However, many people who have hidden disabilities are more dependent on public transportation than are those with obvious disabilities. Some of these disabilities include epilepsy, traumatic brain injury, or chronic fatigue syndrome. People with sensory impairments such as low vision or blindness cannot drive their own vehicles, and individuals who are hard of hearing or deaf, require travel information in visual rather than audible formats. In addition, many people with disabilities travel with service animals that are essential travel partners and make a significant contribution to independent travel. Service animal accommodation is a key element of accessible transportation. All people are beneficiaries of accessible transportation. Anyone who has traveled with a child in a stroller or rolling luggage appreciates curb cuts, level boarding, and elevators. Absent minded or distracted travelers benefit when essential travel information is presented in both audible and visual formats.

27.2 FEATURES OF ACCESSIBLE TRANSPORTATION SYSTEMS

A trip is accessible only if all the links on the trip chain are accessible. If any of the links are missing or broken, then it is unlikely that a trip can be successfully completed. Figure 27.1 shows the elements of the trip chain.

All accessible transportation systems have certain features that characterize the service and make it accessible. These features will be discussed in terms of, infrastructure, systems, and information.

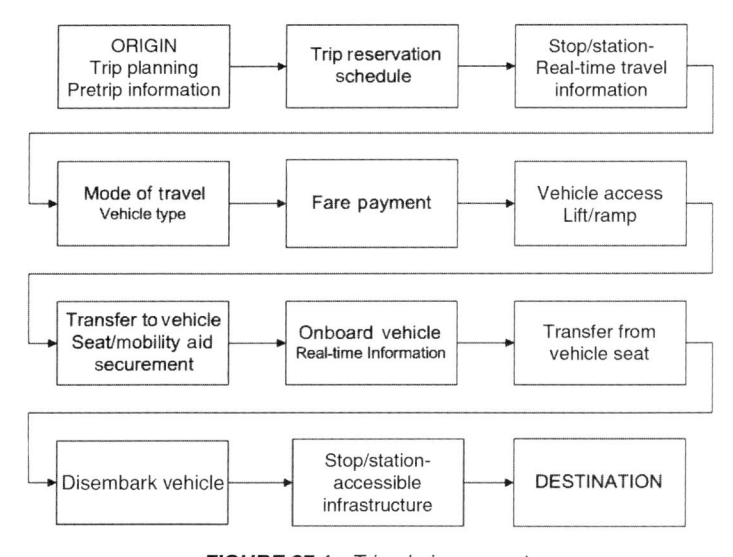

FIGURE 27.1 Trip chain concept.

27.3 INFRASTRUCTURE

The basic element of the accessible transportation system is that all the civil and mechanical infrastructure is free of barriers. The accessibility of civil infrastructure is often beyond the scope of the public transportation provider because it is controlled by different agencies such as the public works department, airport authority, or operating railroad. The infrastructure includes interfaces such as terminals, stops, stations, and the local area around these facilities. On the other hand, public transportation agencies are responsible for the design, procurement, and operation of the accessible vehicles that must interface with the civil infrastructure and facilities. One of the challenges in the provision of accessible transportation is the transition between the civil infrastructure and the vehicles. The transition is also the interface between the vehicle and terminal. This transition is often the broken "link" on the trip chain. An additional challenge in accessible transportation is that the terminal designs must meet the requirements of *The Americans with Disabilities Act (ADA) Requirements for Buildings and Facilities Vehicles* [1], and many of the vehicles must meet similar guidelines for vehicles. The interface or "gap" between the vehicle and terminal is often the problem. The gaps are bridged by lifts, ramps, bridging plates, kneeling vehicles, gangways, or devices specifically designed to "bridge the gap." *The Americans with Disabilities Act (ADA) Accessibility Guidelines* (ADAAG) *for Transportation Vehicles* [2] provide a number of specifications for this equipment. Despite the guidelines and regulations, the operating environment of public transportation is very harsh, and these devices require regular and ongoing maintenance. Public transportation systems that have large numbers of people with disabilities using the system in general have regular and intensive maintenance programs for this equipment. As a result, many of these transit agencies also have excellent maintenance and reliability records.

27.4 TYPES OF ACCESSIBLE TRANSPORTATION SYSTEMS

There are two basic categories of public transportation systems and these are surface transport and air transport. Each of these systems may consist of a number of modes. The surface transportation modes include urban public transportation that is provided by rubber-tired, steel-tired, or passenger ferry vehicles. There are also intercity public transportation modes that include over-the-road buses (ORTBs), passenger rail (Amtrak), and passenger ferry. Air transportation is often categorized by the size of aircraft, the route or segment length, domestic or international services, or the size of airport. The categories of service are discussed in the following sections.

27.4.1 Urban Public Transportation Modes

Urban public transportation is defined by two basic types of service: fixed-route–fixed-schedule and demand-responsive. Fixed-route service can be provided by rubber-tired vehicles, such as buses or steel-tired vehicles, such as metrorail, light rail, or commuter rail. Demand responsive service is almost always provided by rubber-tired vehicles that range in size from personal automobiles, and accessible taxis, vans, to small and large buses. There are also several cities in the world that have passenger ferry service integrated into the urban public transportation system as well. Typically these vessels do not carry vehicles. In many regions it is difficult to draw the line between urban public transportation and intercity public transportation, due to long-distance commutes. In many parts of the United States, urban public transportation modes provide service on route segments and trip lengths that are provided by intercity public transportation modes in other parts of the world.

27.4.2 Vehicle Accommodations

Vehicle accommodations include design elements on the vehicle itself that ensure the safety of all passengers. These elements include safe stair geometry and contrasting stair nosing (rounded front edge of a stair) as well as strategically placed stanchions, handrails, and grab bars. Good illumination at stairways is also very important.

For vehicles with level boarding, design elements include wide aisles that permit transportable mobility aids to easily enter the vehicle and navigate the aisle to the securement location. There are many details in vehicle design that may increase the risks for semi-ambulatory passengers. For example, on transit buses, the side-facing priority seats near the driver are dangerous for many elderly passengers because there are no stanchions for each person to hold onto. Often seats are upholstered in vinyl that is easy to maintain, but in some circumstances can be very slippery. Seat orientation is also important for accessibility. Forward-facing or rear-facing seats provide more secure seating for older passengers, but these seats may not be available near the operator, and passengers who are older or have a disability may feel less secure. On rubber-tired vehicles, the interior must be configured with handholds and stanchions so that all passengers have something to grab onto in case of sudden accelerations or decelerations. The floor surface and texture can also impact the ease of access to the vehicle. Slip-resistant hard surfaces are recommended, and the use of carpet is strongly discouraged.

The safe securement of mobility aids is a complex topic. The type and level of securement is dependent on the size or mass of the transport vehicle and the vehicle's operating environment. Smaller vehicles require securement systems that are more robust than those on large massive vehicles. This is a result of the acceleration forces transmitted to and experienced by the passengers. Large urban rail systems operating on an isolated guideway do not require any securement. Mobility aid securement systems need to be designed to accommodate a vast range of mobility aids, and also to meet the needs of the particular vehicle and its operating environment. Passenger restraint systems for mobility aid occupants should also be provided on smaller vehicles and in particular any vehicle with a gross vehicle weight of less than 15,000 lb. It should be noted that although personal restraints are strongly recommended for use, certain physical conditions prevent the use of a personal restraint system. There are also certain mobility aids that cannot be safely secured by any of the commonly available securement systems. Most of these mobility aids can, however, be accommodated by "docking type" securement systems that require the use of additional interface hardware that is permanently attached to the frame of the mobility aid. These docking systems are commonly used by mobility aid users who drive a vehicle while seated in their mobility aids. Anchorage, Alaska is the only public transit system in the United States that uses docking-type securement systems in regular fixed-route operations. Anchorage has been using this system since the mid-1990s.

27.4.3 Rubber-Tired Vehicles

Rubber-tired vehicles used in public transportation range in size from small sedans providing demand-responsive service up to double decked buses or articulated buses that can carry almost a hundred passengers! *Articulated buses* are long buses that bend in the middle. There are several key characteristics of rubber-tired vehicles that pertain to accessible transportation. The mass of the vehicle has a direct impact on the type and level of mobility aid securement and occupant restraint. In general, the smaller and lighter the vehicle, the more robust the securement and restraints systems need to be to provide an adequate level of occupant protection. Large massive transit buses, by virtue of their mass and power transmission systems, experience low acceleration forces. The type of operating environment also influences the level of mobility aid securement and occupant restraint. Vehicles that operate on isolated guideways or in exclusive bus lanes have a more controlled operating environment than do vehicles operating on congested urban streets. Urban topography can also have an influence on the options for mobility aid securement.

Rubber tire vehicles are either high floor or low floor. Typically an accessible rubber-tired vehicle is equipped with a lift or a ramp. There are advantages and disadvantages to both high- and low-floor vehicles. In recent years there has been a trend toward the procurement of low-floor vehicles since these are easier for all passengers. The disadvantage of a low-floor vehicle is that in areas where there are no sidewalks, the ramp deploys directly to the ground and is often at too steep an angle for a mobility aid user to access the vehicle independently. Some low-floor vehicles also have difficulty on nonpaved road surfaces, but this is rare for most urban operating environments. Low-floor vehicles do not have any steps so the boarding and deboarding times are much lower than with high-floor vehicles, and these vehicles are much easier for all passengers to board. Also, the ramps on low-floor vehicles usually accommodate larger mobility aids than many lifts, but this can cause problems. Many of the larger mobility aids are wide as well as longer than the footprint of a "common wheelchair."[1] Even if these mobility aids can get up the ramp, many cannot get past the fare machine or maneuver to the securement station. In urban environments where the fleet of vehicles includes both high- and low-floor vehicles, passengers with large mobility aids are often stranded because not all trip segments are served by the same type of accessible vehicle.

The disadvantages of accessible high-floor vehicles are the stairs at boarding and the lift. Many vehicles have the lift at the front of the bus and negate the use of the stairs when the lift is deployed. The cycling of the lift and the time for securement and restraint add to the vehicle dwell time and detract from the on-time performance. Most lifts also limit the size of mobility aid that can access the transit vehicle. Many high-floor vehicles are also kneeling buses, which reduces the height of the first step at boarding, but for many older passengers the stairs are still a barrier.

The transit vehicle lift environment is very harsh, and regular maintenance is mandatory. The high-floor vehicles are better equipped to operate in rural and unimproved areas where the lift may need to descend to the ground.

The type of operating environment also direct influences the type of access to vehicles. In many parts of Canada and Sweden, where snow is common, the access to

---

[1] A common wheelchair is defined as fitting within a 30-inch-wide × 48-inch-long footprint. On some low-floor vehicles the width of the "common wheelchair" is too wide for the wheelchair to move past the fare box. Some transit agencies (not US ones) recommend a maximum width of 24 inches.

demand-responsive vehicles is at the back of the vehicle. There are several drawbacks to this approach particularly in the United States. Mobility aid passengers are usually relegated to the "back of the bus," where they ride behind the rear axle. The ride quality, particularly in smaller vehicles, is much better just over or behind the front axel. In addition, mobility aid users are further from the driver.

Demand-responsive public transportation can serve the general public or only eligible individuals. There are federal regulations that pertain to complementary paratransit service, but almost every agency has its own procedures for determining who is eligible. In many suburban and rural areas, the demand-responsive service is available to all, and in a few rural regions, it is integrated with the school bus service. Typically, demand-responsive public transportation requires the user to plan ahead and reserve a trip. Many agencies still prioritize trips according to trip purpose, this is not permitted under the Americans with Disabilities Act. However, since many systems have major supply and demand problems, trip purpose is often used as a method to prioritize trips.

Vanpools and carpools provide an option for many commuters. In Washington and Oregon, accessible vehicles are provided by the vanpool organizations when requested. Accessible taxis are very popular for providing more spontaneous service, particularly after hours or for visitors and tourists. In Portland, Oregon, accessible taxi service is regulated to make sure that service is available and affordable. In London, England, there are purpose-built vehicles that are low-floor and have ramps and securement systems. In the United States, many large cities do not have any accessible taxi service.

At the other end of the vehicle size and operating spectrum is bus rapid transit (BRT). Bus rapid transit systems include rubber-tired vehicles, enhanced stations, limited-use guideways, or exclusive bus lanes, and provide service with the amenities of light-rail transit. A number of new vehicles are being designed for BRT service and accommodate a variety of wheeled mobility aids, including segways, bikes, and strollers. Most of these new vehicles are articulated and low-floor and can accommodate three or more mobility aids. Rear-facing securement systems are being designed and procured for many of these vehicles. Rear-facing securement includes a compartment that permits mobility aid users to travel facing the rear of the bus without being secured with belts or other devices. Rear-facing securement lets people travel independently and does not involve the vehicle operator. Many of the new BRT vehicles include "café"-type seating, so other passengers also travel in rear-facing seats.

Several types of transit vehicles are shown in Figure 27.2

27.4.4 Steel-Tired Vehicles

Steel-tired vehicles include streetcars, light rail, heavy rail, and commuter rail. Typically a streetcar is electric with power from on overhead wire or catenary and runs on rails in the street. Streetcars are usually a single car, although sometimes they can be hitched together in a "married" pair. Light-rail transit (LRT) vehicles are usually larger than street cars, have electric power from overhead wires, and run on rails. However, one of the differences between streetcars and light rail is that LRT systems almost always run two-, four-, or six-car train sets. Many of the newer LRT systems include low-floor vehicles, and many older systems run a mix of high- and low-floor vehicles. Both LRT and streetcars have stations that are part of the sidewalk area. The floor level of the vehicles influences the design of these stations. Some stations include mini-high platforms or wayside lifts to accommodate high-floor vehicles. The national trend is

FIGURE 27.2 Transit vehicles: (a) paratransit vehicles Eugene Oregon; (b) double-decker and low-floor buses with "common wheelchairs" (BC Transit); (c) high-floor transit bus (Lane Transit District, Eugene, OR); (d) rear-facing securement compartment in an urban low-floor bus (BC Transit); (e) accessible bus stop (Translink).

toward level boarding with low-floor vehicles. Also, LRT systems run a mix of isolated guideways and on-street service. In general, LRT stations provide more amenities than do streetcars and nearly always include off-vehicle fare payment mechanisms.

There is no clear distinction between light rail and heavy rail. Skytrain, which operates in Vancouver, Canada, uses light-rail vehicles, but the system has all the features of a heavy-rail system. The power is provided by a powered third rail, the guideway is completely isolated, and vehicular propulsion is provided by linear traction motors that permit the system to operate on steeper slopes than traditional propulsion systems, where the friction between the tire and the rail is the limiting factor. Linear traction motors "pull" the train along. Skytrain is like many systems in the world that are completely computer-controlled. There are no drivers on the vehicle. This type of control is possible only on systems that run on completely separated guideways. Computer-controlled systems have the potential to operate with shorter headways and with more energy efficiency than do operator controlled systems. There are always tradeoffs. Isolated guideways are more expensive to construct than in street systems, but they are more flexible and have fewer capacity constraints. There are tradeoffs between the initial construction costs and the long-term operational efficiencies. The heavy-rail urban systems run independently of the street system. In cities with large underground networks, these systems also can run in adverse weather or congested traffic conditions.

Both LRT and heavy-rail fixed-guideway systems also have an impact on urban growth and development. Real estate values tend to increase within a quarter mile of stations, and decrease as the distance from the station increases. There are also a number of cities where the transit station has become the catalyst for urban development and renewal.

Commuter rail systems operate with either electric or diesel engines and in general provide longer distance service than do urban rail systems. Typically commuter rail systems operate multiple car trains with stations spaced miles apart. In the United States many of these systems share the rails with freight operations as well. Some of the vehicles are bilevel and provide "business"-class level of service with many onboard amenities. Many of the features of commuter rail are similar to those of intercity rail and are discussed in more detail in Section 27.4.6.

A key element of both urban rail and commuter rail service are stations that provide "park and ride" options for passengers. It is important that park-and-ride lots provide accessible parking, and an accessible route from the parking facility to the station. The station itself needs to be accessible, and the transition between the platform and the vehicles needs to be bridged by a ramp, lift, or bridging plate.

In addition to fixed infrastructure for accessible transportation, the public information system, fare machines, and safety and security features need to be designed to accommodate passengers with a spectrum of physical, sensory, and cognitive abilities.

Several types of rail systems are shown in Figure 27.3.

27.4.5 Passenger Ferry Service

Passenger ferry service (see example in Fig. 27.4) is an integral part of many urban transportation systems, and this is not surprising considering that many of the world's oldest and largest cities are major ports, harbors, or other facilities located on waterways. For most commuter systems the ferry vessel only serves pedestrian traffic. Many of the ferry vessels and docks were designed and built years before there was any consideration for accessibility for passengers who use wheeled mobility aids, and as a result they are not particularly accessible. Newer systems are more accessible, and most of the old systems that have undergone major overhauls and retrofits are becoming more accessible. The forces of nature, such as tides and weather, often affect the slope of gangways and can make even the most accessible systems a challenge at certain times. In general, most passenger vessels accommodate mobility aids; however, on older vessels with raised doorsills, many of the restrooms are not accessible.

TYPES OF ACCESSIBLE TRANSPORTATION SYSTEMS   **527**

FIGURE 27.3 Rail: (a) commuter rail bilevel cars; (b) entrance gangway; (c) Seabus gangway; (d) wayside lift—intercity passenger rail; (e) "adaptive engineering" wayside lift, used on high-level railcar.

FIGURE 27.4 Vancouver BC "Seabus."

27.4.5.1 Intercity Public Transportation Modes

Intercity public transportation modes include over-the-road buses, passenger rail service, ferry service, and air transportation. Typically the vehicles and vessels are larger than those that provide urban public transportation, there are infrequent stops, and the trip segments and trip lengths are much longer than those of urban public transportation. Intercity public transportation includes amenities such as food service and onboard lavatories. Because there are significant differences between the air transport and surface modes, they are discussed separately.

27.4.5.2 Surface Modes

The surface modes include passenger rail, over-the-road buses, and passenger ferry. The major issues for accessibility on these modes include boarding the vehicle, onboard circulation, accessible onboard lavatories, access to amenities such as food service, onboard information and communication systems, and safety and security procedures.

27.4.6 Passenger Rail

In the United States the accessibility of passenger rail is highly dependent on the rail vehicle or rolling stock, and these in turn are regional. The passenger rail vehicles that operate up and down the west coast are very different from those that operate in the northeast corridor. The higher-speed rail vehicles on the US west coast and the stations are comparatively new, and most stations have low level platforms. The "Cascadia" service that operates between Eugene, Oregon and Bellingham, Washington uses the "talgo" train technology developed in Spain. The train interiors were designed to be accessible. The ramp is mounted to the interior of the train vehicle. The restroom is quite spacious, and for many people with disabilities, it meets their needs. Wayside lifts are used on the west coast Amtrak stations to access the West Coast Starlight. This is a bilevel train that runs from southern California to Seattle, Washington. Accessible accommodation is available only on the lower level, and many of the amenities such as the dining car are not available to passengers who use mobility aids.

On the east coast the high-speed train "Acela" was derived from French technology. This train was also designed to be accessible. Despite improvements in vehicles, some stations still are not accessible. There are also many challenges in North America for passenger rail accessibility, but one of the major ones is shared track. In western Europe and Japan, passenger rail generally operates on its own rail or track. In North America many passenger rail systems operate on shared track with freight operations. This creates problems for schedule adherence and platform integrity. Morlock [3] states that

> This conflict emerges where high level platforms are used (at stations) on tracks that are also used by freight trains, because such platforms intrude into the normal clearance envelope of freight trains. High level platforms are now most commonly used in the Northeastern U.S., but more extensive use elsewhere is contemplated because of various benefits for passenger service.

Long-distance train service that includes accessible overnight accommodation depends on the style of vehicle. The accommodation must be booked in advance. In general, people who use wheeled mobility aids have limited access to the train's amenities.

27.4.7 Over-the-Road Buses

Over-the-road buses (OTRBs) transport include intercity buses (Fig. 27.5). For discussion purposes, the public transportation aspect of this industry includes only the regular scheduled service. The discussion does not include the large charter coach industry. There is Amtrak Thruway Bus service across the county; some of the service is provided under contract to Amtrak. In Oregon and Washington, Amtrak operates a fleet of accessible coaches or thruway buses that provide feeder service that interfaces directly with the mainline rail operations. The OTRB industry has been slower in adopting accessibility than many other modes. An accessible vehicle provides a lift at the front, middle, or rear of the bus. Mobility aid securement is also provided, although many passengers prefer to transfer from their mobility aid to regular seats if they are so able. The mobility aid is then secured. Passengers also may choose to travel in their

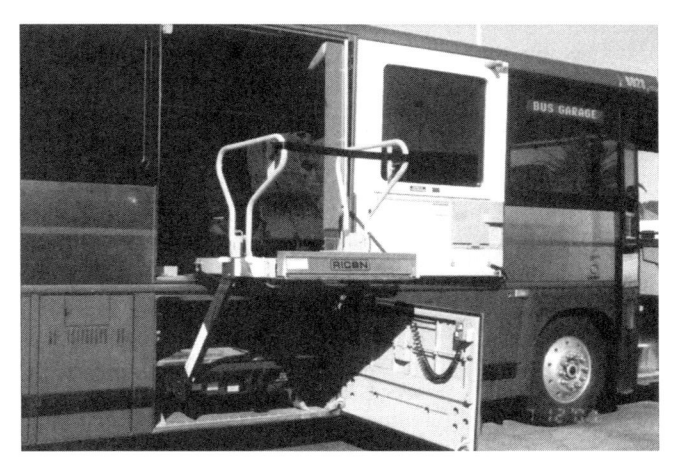

FIGURE 27.5 Accessible intercity or over-the-road bus.

own mobility aids. A key issue with OTRB is the provisions for accessible lavatories onboard the vehicle. The dynamics of an OTRB moving on a roadway are significantly different from those of a passenger rail system. Moving about on a moving vehicle is much more of a challenge for all passengers, and using the onboard lavatory is a challenge for all. Many passengers prefer to have the option of using accessible restrooms at bus stations or stops. The OTRB industry has been slow to purchase vehicles with an onboard accessible restroom; however, there is an increase in the number of lift-equipped vehicles.

27.4.8 Passenger Ferry

Intercity passenger ferries may or may not carry motor vehicles. It really depends on the size of the vessel, the trip length, and the destination. Passenger ferries are essential for accessing coastal communities. For vessels that carry motor vehicles, occupants are encouraged to leave their vehicles for the duration of the trip, and it is important that provisions be made for drivers and passengers who use wheeled mobility aids. In general, this implies accessible parking spaces that permit egress on either side of the vehicle and an accessible path to the passenger amenities. Many older vessels have retrofitted elevators, and many newer vessels have accessibility features designed and built in. Many ships have raised door sills not only between the exterior doors and interior space but also throughout the vessel. The raised door sills are being removed to make the interior circulation space more accessible to all. Stairs and raised door sills are barriers for all, not just people who use wheeled mobility aids. Passenger vessels are also being retrofitted or designed with accessible lavatories. New vessels often include accessible unisex lavatories that meet the needs of families as well as individuals. Regulations for accessible accommodations for cruise ships and passenger ferries are still under development, and so many vessels do not have ADA-compliant sleeping accommodation. Individual agencies will try to accommodate passengers with special needs, as long as adequate advance notice is provided.

27.4.9 Air Transport

Travel by air (Fig. 27.6) for many people is essential for employment and education as well as for family gatherings. In the United States the Air Carrier Access Act has provisions for improving access to aircraft; however, a lack of enforcement together with significant challenges in the commercial air travel industry have made air travel for people with disabilities very inconsistent. The inconsistency in levels of accessibility is one of the most frustrating aspects of travel by people with disabilities. The National Center for Accessible Transportation completed a survey of all commercial service airports in the continental United States and the major airports in Alaska and Hawaii. The survey was completed by airport management and not by passengers. The general trend was that most airports are making significant improvements to meet the needs of travelers with physical disabilities. However, many of the survey respondents had never considered any modifications for travelers with sensory or cognitive disabilities. The survey results indicated that most airports had at least one individual who had job responsibilities related to accessibility. Almost universally, all respondents indicated the need for additional technical and financial assistance and training to make improvements for travelers with disabilities. Questions were not asked directly about boarding of smaller aircraft, but this

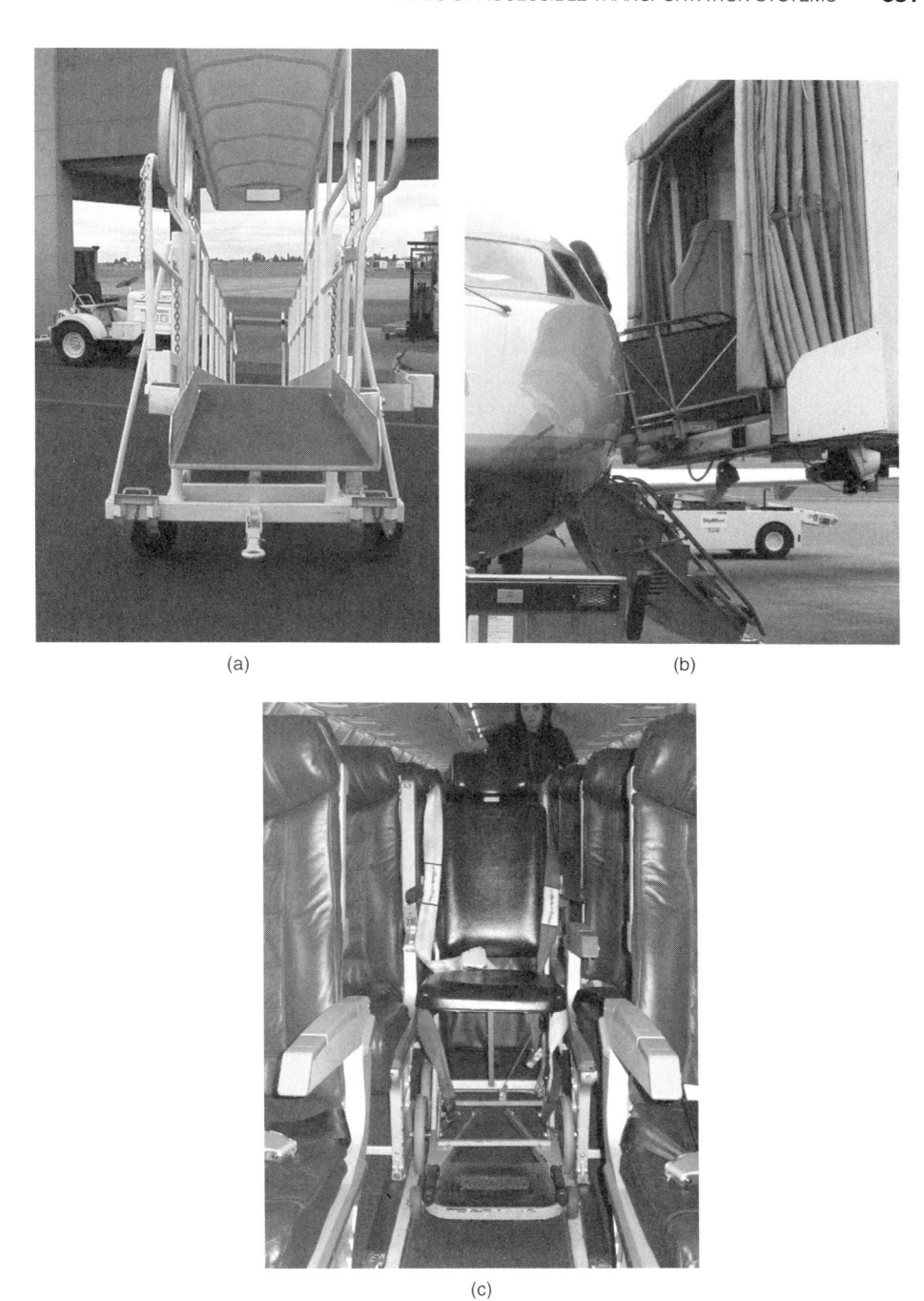

TYPES OF ACCESSIBLE TRANSPORTATION SYSTEMS **531**

FIGURE 27.6 Air transport (a) ramp for a small regional aircraft; (b) miniramp to adapt a jetway to regional jets (United Airlines); (c) an aisle chair in an aircraft aisle.

emerged as a significant problem in the open comment section and by phone calls that were received [4].

The building accessibility requirements of the airport terminal are covered by the ADAAG. Several aspects of air travel are a challenge for travelers with disabilities, and these include security, aircraft boarding, onboard lavatories, and real-time passenger information. The Transportation Security Administration has regulations for screening passengers with disabilities; however, these regulations are not always followed consistently by frontline staff. Passengers who use supplemental oxygen or ventilators often encounter problems when traveling by air. These problems often include security screening of the equipment, and the procurement of supplemental oxygen canisters during transfers between aircraft and at final destination. Passengers who use wheeled mobility aids encounter many challenges, including the safe transport of their personal wheelchair, transfers to and from the boarding area to the aircraft, and use of onboard chairs and lavatories. Passengers with sensory and cognitive impairments often encounter difficulties at checkin, security screening, and departure gates and onboard the aircraft.

Air travel is becoming more of a challenge for all travelers, but these challenges are increased for travelers with special needs, such as those who are obese or frail or have disabilities. Airport terminals and their operators are increasing the level of accessibility of the infrastructure. The world's major aircraft manufacturers are actively developing new aircraft interiors that are more accommodating and accessible. Most airlines are operating under very challenging economic conditions, and simply trying to stay in business. One of the major challenges for improving the accessibility of aircraft is the high value of aircraft real estate. Every seat has the ability to produce significant annual revenue for the airline, and high load factors contribute to the airline's prosperity. Increases in the size of seat pitch, aisle widths, seat widths, and lavatories all come with a huge price. The improvements for passengers with special needs will benefit all passengers and will contribute to passenger satisfaction; however, the costs are very high. There are airlines that have high regard for the customer, and many of these airlines are the most progressive in making accommodations for travelers with disabilities. Some of these accommodations include specialized training and position descriptions of frontline staff who work directly with travelers with disabilities. Often these people are the friendly and helpful customer service representatives at the end of the phone, or the specialized staff assisting with transfers from personal wheelchairs to boarding chairs and aircraft seats. At other levels there are corporate staff making decisions to outfit aircraft with interiors that are more accommodating of the special needs of travelers with disabilities.

In the United States, air travel is an essential mode for travel because of the vast size of the country. A number of advances in accessible air travel are occurring, and the next decade will see the implementation of new technologies that make air travel more accessible and easier for all. Some of these advances include onboard accessible lavatories, more dignified boarding equipment, and in-flight entertainment systems that can be used by passengers with sensory and agility challenges. The aging society will travel and will demand that all modes provide safe and dignified travel experience.

27.5 PASSENGER INFORMATION SYSTEMS

Accessible public transportation systems must also include accessible real-time passenger information and communication systems. Well-designed information and communication systems benefit all users of the systems, not just people with visible disabilities. Tourists or infrequent users can be intimidated by the complexity of public transportation route and fare structure. All systems users require basic information on how to use public transportation. Pretrip information that is available on accessible Websites can permit tourists, people with disabilities, or the infrequent user an opportunity to become familiar with a transit system. Many large transit systems are investing in sophisticated trip-planning systems that allow users to plan multimodal trip itineraries ahead of time. Trip planning gives all travelers an added sense of confidence and increased likelihood of a successful trip. Once en route, travelers like to know where they are, and if they are on time. En route and real-time information are particularly important if there are detours, emergencies, or unforeseen events that disrupt a trip. For people with sensory and/or cognitive disabilities, it is very important that real-time information and communication systems provide the same information in multiple sensory modalities. All people benefit from the use of open captioning, and visual and oral paging. All public transportation providers should ensure that there are technologies available to provide real-time emergency information in both oral and visual formats. The ADA has required that major bus stops be announced. In many US cities this is being automated with the application of intelligent transport system technologies. Many of the automated systems are available in both audio and visual formats.

The use of wireless personal communication devices is revolutionizing the dissemination of real-time information. For example, in Japan, many blind pedestrians use cell phones equipped with GPS and cameras for orientation and mobility. A person who is lost or disoriented takes a picture and transmits the picture and GPS coordinates and then receives specific wayfinding and guidance information.

27.5.1 Fare Payment

In Europe, Asia, and part of the North America, new methods of fare payment are simplifying travel for all. In many regions a single "smart card" can be used to pay for parking, transit, and other consumer purchases. Off-vehicle fare collection speeds up the boarding process, decreases dwell time, and improves overall system operations. Prepaid fares and monthly pass programs make public transportation easier for all. Unfortunately, there are very few ticket machines, ATMs, or travel kiosks that are accessible to people with physical and or sensory impairments. Even some "accessible" machines are installed on pedestals that make them too high for use by a person in a wheelchair, and render them "inaccessible."

27.5.2 Illumination

Illumination is a key aspect of an accessible public transportation system that is often overlooked. Lights are very important at all transition points, at fare machines, and in waiting areas. Good lighting on stairs and ramps can minimize tripping and falls. Lighting is an essential element for safety and security.

27.5.3 Travel Training

In most public transportation entities, the highest priority is the removal of visible barriers, and for many individuals there is a fear of the unknown. Progressive public transportation agencies have recognized this and established a number of programs that provide travel training, orientation, and practice opportunities for people transitioning and using public transportation for the first time. "Travel buddy" programs include opportunities for people with disabilities to act as ambassadors and escorts for other travelers with disabilities. Many new friendships have resulted from these opportunities.

27.5.4 Service Animals

All modes of travel have developed procedures for accommodating service animals. For many individuals with disabilities, service animals are essential for an independent lifestyle. Under the various regulations there are provisions to ensure that legitimate service animals are treated with respect and transported in as safe and dignified manner as their handlers.

REFERENCES

1. *The Americans with Disabilities Act (ADA) Accessibility Guidelines for Buildings and Facilities Vehicles*, Part 1191, US Access-Board, April 13, 1998.
2. *The Americans with Disabilities Act (ADA) Accessibility Guidelines for Transportation Vehicles*, Part 1182, US Access-Board, 1998.
3. Morlock E: Resolving the conflict between mobility impaired passenger requirements and freight Service on mixed high and low platform U.S. railroad lines, *Transportation Research Record 1848*, Transportation Research Board, National Research Council, Washington, DC, 2003, pp 70–78.
4. Hunter-Zaworski KM, Zaworski J, Lesser V: Survey of airport features for persons with disabilities, Paper 06-0384, *Proc Transportation Research Board Annual Meeting*, Washington, DC, Jan 2006.

28

Transportation Services in Europe

Isabelle Dussutour
Conseil Général des Côtes d'Armor, Saint Brieuc, France

Is mobility a basic human right? When reading the latest documents related to the future of the European Union, treaties, and the constitutional treaty currently discussed through adoption processes, the new interpretation of the Lisbon agenda, strong emphasis is placed on economic development and the benefit of competition and liberalization of markets, which in our perspective means that the economic activities will settle where the social, administrative, and employment situations are the best to be found, and not where people live, shop, and socialize. If in the 1980s some tentative urban policies tried to concentrate activities close to housing for better quality of life and mobility purposes, this trend is no longer current, and implementation of economic activities is not planned in a "societal" way.

This means that people have to follow economy in many cases (although efforts exist in reimplementing shops and services in city centers), and not the other way around, making mobility one of the scarce resources in the very near future; this is already the case in big cities such as London, where some people have to commute 1.5 h to and from work using public transportation. Within this context of increasing mobility needs, it is increasingly unacceptable that a large part of the population is—although at a different level—excluded from the mobility accommodations provided by transport systems, public or private, and therefore depend on others in the best-case scenario.

This study aims at summarizing the situation on accessibility in transport in European countries and to gather examples in legislation and examples of implementation

---

The Engineering Handbook of Smart Technology for Aging, Disability, and Independence,
Edited by A. Helal, M. Mokhtari and B. Abdulrazak
Copyright © 2008 John Wiley & Sons, Inc.

to illustrate the complementarity between all levels of European government, national, regional, and local—or maybe their lack of complementarity! What strikes the user of public (and private) transport is that very few persons with reduced mobility (PRM) who are to be seen using transport systems: some in buses, almost none in the underground, and few in cars, compared to the overall amount of travelers. It is an understatement to say that PMR mobility should be increased by all means: pretrip and on-trip information, infrastructure, type of vehicle, use of the road, and respect of specific infrastructures (bus stops, parking), and general services. However, for EU cities, it appears that the situation varies from city to city, even in the same country. This means that there is no unified framework, thus the policy depends on the local budget, policy vision, lobbying power of disabled people associations, number of PMR, and other factors.

On the technology front, progress has been made in vehicle technologies, but implementation of the necessary measures to ensure a globally accessible transport system is very slow, and there does not appear to be an adequate overall urban policy for making not only transport but the city itself fully accessible to PMR—why spend money on transport systems if there are no requirements regarding accessibility of buildings and administrative services or cultural and health services in the city? However, even if integrating new technologies in new infrastructures were relatively easy, retrofitting old infrastructures would be extremely costly and difficult to achieve.

Significant improvements have been seen since the mid-1990s in legislation and its implementation, but there are still many obstacles in developing a real transport policy based on accessibility for all. A key factor seems to be the consultation of all relevant stakeholders in defining accessible transport policies, including the PMR themselves; vehicle manufacturers; local, national, and EU government representatives; representatives of the elderly, who will constitute an important part of the PMR in the future; and nondisabled citizens, as the accessible transport system should benefit all citizens by making their trips more comfortable in all circumstances.

28.1 BACKGROUND OF ACCESSIBILITY POLICIES IN EUROPE

Around the mid-1980s, and especially during the year honoring disabled people in 1981, decisionmakers in several countries in Europe and the United States realized that the accessibility of transport services was problematic in most of cases and that not only severely disabled people but more broadly "PMR" were disadvantaged in their access to mobility both in cities and rural areas. Several national governments took action following this new awareness, as very few policies existed nationally (except in Sweden). The framework for developing legislation was therefore set up, as well as a movement to better account for accessibility in transport policies. At the same time new trends in demography showed that the population was aging rapidly, and thus in the near future that many persons would become PMR, not necessarily because of accidents or disease, but because of aging. The PRM issue in the field of transport was therefore expected to become everybody's problem one day or another, and the decisionmakers in public authorities realized that the elderly part of the population was increasing instead of decreasing as projected, and needed special attention. Accessibility became an integral part of transport issues, although with fewer legislative actions than studies or reports.

This trend is part of an overall societal trend promoting equal opportunities for all in all sectors of society. It underlines the fact that accessibility to public transport is not an isolated issue and should be factored in broader legislative processes, including land use planning, health, education, employment, and economic policies.

However, the retrofitting of transport equipment and infrastructure, especially public transport, is a costly and difficult process; therefore legislation is required with measures to accommodate the following needs:

- A significant amount of technology is involved in building new systems or retrofitting older ones; therefore, research and development (R&D), experimentation, and programs are necessary for supporting this innovation in infrastructure, vehicle manufacture, and information systems.
- Disabled people are often less wealthy than their fellow citizens and need financial support for accessing public transport systems and specialized and tailor-made transport, including private cars, which are more costly.
- A change in behavior from decisionmakers and the general population is needed, and PMR issues must become part of the daily management of the city.
- Access to employment must be facilitated and equal for all citizens.
- Personnel in transport services and any other public services should be properly trained to support and welcome PMR.[1]

A report from ECMT [1] presented the status of the legislation in 1986 and stated that at that time, European countries were split into two categories:

- Those that did not have a structured policy such as Denmark, Finland, Ireland.
- Those having a well-structured and a detailed legislation in the field of PMR such as Germany, France, Sweden.

However, the policies were more social/societal in nature and less related to transport and mobility, as they should have been. Only Sweden had a specific legislation, and in France and Germany, legislation existed for economic and social overall issues (education, training, and employment).

When negotiating the Disability Discrimination Act in 1995, the UK government and stakeholders raised the issue of the impact of legislation compared to the impact of other measures. There were several reasons for legislation:

- Although the majority of transport providers and manufacturers agreed to apply guidelines, some of them did not, preventing the achievement of an integrated system.
- A timeline and deadlines for implementation of accessible transport systems and vehicles were needed; otherwise the cost would delay the process indefinitely.
- Norms or standards were needed for integration and interoperability at both national and Europe-wide levels.

Since the mid-1980s, the issue of mobility and access to public transport has emerged in legislative processes. This issue has been adequately accounted for relatively recently, however, and still needs further development.

---

[1] In April 2005, a bus driver in Brussels refused to allow a passenger in a wheelchair to board his bus, arguing an issue with insurance in case of accident in his bus, an issue that is nonexistent as STIB insurance covers passengers with special needs. The issue of training is therefore not an anecdotal one.

28.2 CURRENT ACCESSIBILITY LEGISLATION IN EUROPE

Nowadays transport accessibility legislation and regulations exist, and they are accompanied by guidelines that are not binding but are sometimes followed more thoroughly than legislation, as they are the result of a consensus-building process involving all levels of government and the population as well as the industry. These guidelines and other measures include economic incentives (fiscal and financing of new systems) and voluntary initiatives (as in Grenoble, France, where such initiatives served as the basis for the legislative process), which often precede legislation at the national level.

During the expert group discussion, it was agreed that legislation is necessary at it sets up a framework and some mandatory measures and basis for norms and interoperability; however, information on and awareness of the issues are essential for the commitment of all stakeholders in the process. In many countries there are no committees for accessibility in the transport ministries and the information does not reach the industry properly.

Accessibility remains at the margin of the legislative mainstream, which needs to be corrected by a long-tem planning process, enabling the preparation of financial investments and retrofitting.

28.3 EUROPEAN CITIZENS WITH REDUCED MOBILITY: STATUS, EVOLUTION, AND MEASURES

At the same time as legislative processes and guidelines emerged, the definition of "handicapped" people changed to a broader perspective of PRM or "mobility impaired," covering very different situations, ages, and categories of people. Five main categories of impairment can be differentiated:

1. Difficulty in walking and balance impairment
2. Difficulty in standing or sitting
3. Difficulty in gripping or holding rails and other supportive objects
4. Vision and hearing problems
5. Orientation and memory problems [2]

It is therefore clear why an integrated transport policy or legislation for accessibility for all citizens is very difficult; it needs to accommodate not only passengers in wheelchairs but also many other aspects, especially those related to the elderly, with aging of the population. It is also interesting to notice that the most difficult aspects to treat in the field of transport might well become the most developed (memory, standing, seeing, etc.) and cover a broader range of population than do handicapped people in the sense of physical mobility (walking, etc.) (Table 28.1). In 2000 some 380 million inhabitants lived in the EU, 62 million were over 65 years old, and 38 million had severe or moderate disabilities [3]. A total of 100 million people are therefore of concern in accessibility policies. Table 28.1 lists different categories of people with reduced mobility and therefore hints on how broad the legislative framework should be to achieve maximum efficiency [2].

Demographic studies indicate that the number of elderly is steadily increasing and that by 2010 some 70 million people will be over 65 years old (a 15% increase from 2000), and 43 million people with disabilities are foreseen (Eurostat [3] data) according to extrapolated data on population trends since the mid-1990s.

TABLE 28.1 Types of Mobility Impairment

Permanent mobility impairment
    People with physical, sensory, or psychological disabilities
        Physical disability (wheelchair users, balance problems, etc.)
        Sensory disability (deafness, blindness, etc.)
        Speech impairment, illiteracy
        Orientation difficulties
        Size-related difficulties (obesity, very small stature, etc.)
        Mental or psychological disability
    People with age-related disabilities
        Elderly people
Temporary mobility restrictions
    People with temporary age-related disabilities (small children, etc.)
    People with temporary mobility restrictions
        Illness or injuries
        Pregnant women
        Passengers carrying heavy loads (luggage, etc.)

In 2003, as indicated in the BVG report [2], the most popular measures where special dedicated services based on demand-responsive transport services. However, those services allow only restricted mobility, not full freedom of movement.

Taxis also constitute an alternative to nonadapted transport systems; a wide range of vehicles are equipped for PRM, but cost is a barrier in the absence of specific financial support from public authorities.

Private automobiles with built-in accessibility-specific equipment are also available, but this alternative should be considered on a case-by-case basis and not substitute the legal obligations for adapting measures in the public transport system, especially in large metropolitan areas. For trips by public transport, no specific data can be collected and therefore an estimation of the number of trips and users is difficult to estimate.

28.3.1 Review of the Legislation

In 1993 the European Commission produced an action plan for accessible public transport; in 2001 the white paper on transport policy also underlined accessibility as a priority and set up guidelines. On legislation, in 2001 the European Union adopted a directive for vehicles carrying passengers occupying eight or more seats (directive 2001/85/EC), focusing mainly on safety but also including provisions for accessibility through technical solutions and combined with infrastructure adaptation. Within this framework the member states are free to achieve improved mobility through the most appropriate solutions (under 22 seats) vehicles with ≥ 22 seats must comply with requirements concerning:

- Steps
- Seats and space for PRM
- Pictograms for fitted vehicles
- Nonslip surface for floors
- Wheelchair accommodation
- Restraining systems for wheelchairs
- Door control

- Lighting
- Boarding aids, lifts, and ramps

The directive for high-speed rail interoperability (1996/48/EC) makes reference to requirements detailed in the technical specifications for interoperability adopted by the EU in May 2002. In the third railways package published by the European Commission, measures are planned for interoperability and accessibility, pushed forward (advanced) by disabled people community representatives' organizations at the EU level. In the "passenger rights" regulation, measures are proposed for access to rail services, the adoption process is ongoing.

It is difficult to make comparisons between the different member states as the legislative framework differs considerably from one country to the other, and as legislation dedicated to accessibility in transport is often embedded in broader legal context and acts. Moreover, regions sometimes have their own legislative powers and manage legal aspects of accessibility locally.

The issues are different from one country to the other according to the level of decentralization and the repartition of responsibilities between local and central governments. This brings in the necessity of indicators and benchmarking processes for ensuring that the requirements are implemented consistently by the responsible parties at the appropriate levels. For example, the local government in northern Italy implements accessibility measures and decide makes decisions regarding the financial support for these measures for transport operators as they control them. In southern Italy, the transport services are provided by private operators and the legislation is poorly implemented because of a lack of control and clauses in tendering processes. For taxis, the law says that all mandates vehicles should provide services to all citizens without giving more precision on measures and support tools. Moreover, the law does not stipulate the percentage of the public transport fleet that needs to be accessible, thus introducing uncertainty in the implementation process of the law.

The examples discussed below describe the different methods adopted by national governments for improving accessibility, relying on national law or guidelines:

1. Framework legislation includes provisions for mobility; for instance, the *Italian* legislation of February 1992 provides provisions for the integration of the handicapped people and their right for assistance, social integration, and mobility. Specific articles related to transport list the modalities to be followed by cities and regions for public and individual transport, This framework is completed by provisions for buildings (June 1989), public transport, and infrastructure (July 1996), The EU directive is implemented through legislation passed in June 2003 related to passenger transport (buses, taxis, and car rental are covered by a law from 1992).

2. *Sweden* was a pioneer in developing legislation for transport, with the adoption in 1979 of a law related to public transport accessibility for disabled people. Its implementation was entrusted to the Transport Council, which monitored the compliance to the national road, rail, and civil aviation administration regulations. However, reports show that the implementation is not as efficient as it was supposed to be, especially in terms of infrastructure.

3. In *The Netherlands* a transportation act in 2000 requires that authorities, when contracting out public transport service, have to make sure that the system will

be accessible. Standards have been developed for accessible buses but are not mandatory.

4. In the *United Kingdom*, the disability discrimination act (DDA) applies to public transport services but not to rail vehicles. The DDA sets a timeframe for adaptation of vehicles and infrastructure (October 2004 for service providers to alter their premises, including transport-related buildings) to make the service accessible, leaving the accessibility criteria to their judgment. The rail operators produced a code of conduct for complying with the DDA of 1995.

5. In *France*, a national charter on transport and accessibility was signed in December 2003 by national government, representatives from local government, and public transport authorities. The charter commits the signatories to work with disabled people for improving accessibility of the whole of the transport chain. No subsidies will be granted if the transport systems do not comply with the principles of the charter. Related legislation was passed in June 2004.

6. In *Germany* the federal ministry of transport published a comprehensive manual on evaluation and computer-aided recording of barriers to accessibility of buildings and transport facilities. The manual covers the buildings, stations, stops, and pedestrian areas; information and guidance systems are also covered. This was completed in April 2003 by a guide on legal and financial framework and services such as ticketing.

However, specific legislation applied to public transport (especially low-floor buses) should be accompanied by legislation on the building environment and street design; cooperation between local government, transport operators, and road operators is thus the cornerstone of a successful implementation of legislation. An overview of legislation suggests the conclusions described below.[2]

28.3.1.1 Public Transportation

Belgium, Greece, Ireland, Luxembourg, and The Netherlands do not have national-level legislation on the accessibility of transport for PRM.[3] In Belgium requirements concern public buildings. In Greece there is one national law on improvement of accessibility of buildings; there is a similar law in Ireland with provisions for accessibility of transport terminal facilities for PRM. In The Netherlands legislation containing accessibility requirements is under development, as a Dutch version of the US Disabilities Act.

Most of the EU countries have legislation on access to buildings, including transport terminals and interchanges, but regulation directly applicable to transport systems themselves are more limited. France, Germany, Italy, Portugal, Sweden, and Britain have more detailed regulations and guidelines for interpretation of law. In this respect, enforcement is a major issue, as legislation in this field initiates huge costs as they relate to development of infrastructure (new or retrofitting) and vehicles.

28.3.1.2 Vehicles (Public and Private)

In Britain the DDA provides provision for public service vehicles (2000) and taxis and rail vehicles (1998). These regulations contain requirements and specifications and cover the areas mentioned in Section 28.3.3.1 of the present chapter. Furthermore, local transport

---

[2] See ECMT report [1] on legislation for tables on each country—CEMT/CS/TPH (2000).
[3] See BVG study [2] for DG TREN, where most of these data come from.

plans made by local government under the control and guidelines of central government make provisions for accessibility. In Sweden, the PRM accessibility is taken into account in the transport planning process. In 2000 an act was adopted by the government for creating an accessible society for people with disabilities; within this context provisions are made for access to public transport, requiring it to be fully accessible by 2010. In Germany, the federal government shares competencies with the Lander on transport and accessibility issues, and provisions are made for accessibility of new vehicles. In Italy, national-level legislation mandates wheelchair access to public transit vehicles, and nearly all regions have adopted regulations for accessibility of transport, delegating the implementation to local governments. France and Spain have regulations for adaptation of public transport; in Portugal it is restricted to taxis. A specific issue arises for coaches, as the room necessary to accommodate wheelchairs implies loosing 4 or 5 seats out of an average total of 45 seats per vehicle, thus indicating a financial loss for the bus company; the lift system enabling wheelchair-bound passengers to board the coach is also costly and heavy, and increases fuel consumption and taxes on motorways. Coordination with taxes and financial incentives is therefore necessary.

28.3.1.3 Infrastructure

National legislation on infrastructure is weak; most countries have regulations on buildings and architectural barriers, or more broadly on equal rights for all, which do not mandate adaptation of infrastructure. The United Kingdom and Germany have DDA stipulating that no one should be hampered from using public space, services, and resources, and therefore that all public infrastructure be barrier-free. France, Italy, and Portugal have regulations for lifts and ramps that apply mostly to underground stations.

28.3.1.4 Transport Services

Finland, France, Italy, Denmark, and Sweden have regulations on special services for disabled people. National legislation sets the framework for bus stops, travel itineraries, and timetables, and the responsibility falls under local government umbrellas.

In Finland, the act on services and assistance for disabled people provides that people with severe disabilities can make at least 18 trips a month for daily life purposes (medical appointments, etc.), in addition to trips linked to work and studies. The implementation of the act is the responsibility of municipalities.

In France, the internal transport orientation legislation states that special measures are to be taken for the mobility of impaired people in the framework of the right to mobility.

In Denmark, the county have to provide mobility for the severely disabled people for therapy, treatment, and other health-related trips. In Sweden, transport operators have to ensure that transport services are adapted for passengers with reduced mobility.

28.3.1.5 Information Systems

Although good information systems would help PRM to organize, prepare for, and obtain information on their travel; these services are not the most developed, despite some legislation on signs in the vehicles and audio signals for opening and closing doors.

Only the United Kingdom has national legislation on audio signals for routes, stops, and destination as well as for the use of ramps and lifts to the vehicle. In Sweden the requirements are similar, with audio signals and help for visually impaired people. However, these systems, which are simple and not very costly, are still underused in transport, adding difficulties for PRM and the elderly, as well as, for example, regular users who are unfamiliar with the bus lines and transit systems.

28.3.2 Role of the Member States and Application of Legislation, Financing, and Enforcement

Legislation is one of the prerequisite factors for progress in accessibility at all, as it sets up a framework for action at other levels of government and for private companies. Alongside legislation, member states have to develop support measures in order to accelerate implementation of national or Europe-wide EU) legislation. Among the most important accompanying process are the financing system for improving systems, vehicles, and infrastructure and the enforcement and the consultation of PRM representatives and organizations. One important issue is the "equal treatment" of all kinds of disabilities; it is felt that walking impairment is subject to more measures than is visual or hearing impairment. The high cost of infrastructure, vehicles, and equipment usually requires public funding for allowing rapid progress in transport systems. Support for bearing the cost of the special services is also granted in several countries (see Table 28.1). In Germany, support for measures for equipment or retrofitting is subject to a regulation for subsidizing processes through grants. People with severe disabilities can access public transport for free. In Italy, grants from the Ministry of Transport are available for adaptation of transport systems. In France, measures related to safety, accessibility, and special services are subsidized by the state. People under a fixed threshold of income can benefit of a reduction of at least 50% of the price of public transport tickets. In Austria, the federal law adopted in 2000 applies to financing adaptation of systems through accessibility measures to compensate for physical impairment.

In some cases federal (national) funds can be specifically linked to the improvement of accessibility. In Ireland, the national development plan of 2000–2006 states that all stations (rail and buses) built or equipped within the framework or according to the specifications of the plan must be accessible for PRM, all rail vehicles should be accessible to PRM, and all buses purchased since 2000 should be low-floor vehicles. In The Netherlands, part of the state funding for transport is earmarked for adaptation for better accessibility (vehicles and infrastructure). In Britain, all new infrastructure planned in transport plans should be accessible. In Belgium, the newly adopted plan for railways stipulates accessibility of stations and vehicles as first priority for investment. In the Czech Republic, disabled people are grouped under three categories from light to severe disability, and benefits range from seat allocation to free transport. Special fares are seen by ECMT as a powerful tool for support mobility of the PRM[4] and ECMT recommends that national framework set up guidelines for fares even though they are decided mostly at the local level. In Britain, the 2000 Transport Act stipulates the categories of disabilities, citing the benefit of a 50% reduction of fares. Some studies prove that accessible buses are safer (with fewer accidents due to the low-floor design, i.e., absence of steps), so these buses are more cost-effective. In Italy the commercial speed was improved by 4–5% on average for buses and by 10% for trams, which present a nonnegligible return on investment. The return on investment for an accessible vehicle is estimated at 5 years.

For the citizens themselves, support is also needed as PRM with severe disabilities have to use door-to-door services that are expensive (5–6 euros per trip) or taxis and cannot afford it generally, or at least not on a regular basis. In the suburbs the problem is even bigger as the taxi is often the only alternative for mobility.

---

[4]ECMT report [1], May 6, 2004, *Improving Accessibility of Public Transportation*.

Consultation with the population and with disabled people representative associations helps in clarifying and accounting for their needs in both variety and evolution. However, consultation is not institutionalized in many countries, depending on national cultures.

In the United Kingdom, where consultation is integrated to the development of many legislation documents, and where lobbying of NGOs (nongovernmental organizations) is established, a consultative committee for transport and disabled people (DPTAC) was been created in 1985 and offers advice on issues related to PRM to the Ministry of Transport. The DDA further develops this process and states that the committee should be systematically consulted for all legislation related to accessibility of buses, coaches, trains, trams, and taxis. The committee is consulted for giving guidance to local government for fare reduction. In Ireland, a similar committee was established in 2000 for advising the Ministry of Transport. In France, the liaison committee for the transport of handicapped people advises the government. In Austria, such a committee was created in 2004, and in Sweden the transport legislation was developed together with the federation of disabled people. As underlined by ECMT,[4] these committees can also play a role in the training of personnel having to deal with PRM in transport; this awareness is a major factor for the success in implementation of the legislation. The involvement of end-user organizations proves to be a central part of the process. In Torino, Italy, a structured end-users organization exists and caused the city to move forward rapidly, in contrast to other cities where such organizations do not exist. In France the movement created by the initiative taken in Grenoble led to the publication of guidebooks and recommendations to governments. However, consultation needs some preparation and the training of the partners so that the attitudes, culture, and requirements of each others are understood by all. Transparency of decisions is also a requirement, as reaching a consensus often means downsizing demands of individual partners.

In France, companies and service providers that do not comply with legislation can be sued; this applies with respect to all legislation on accessibility, not only the transport aspects of this legislation. In Italy, the government also, implemented the EU directive, and in February 2006 it started to be mandatory for all new fleet to comply with it. The issue is now to "convince" the operators to substitute the old fleet with accessible ones. More generally, penalties can include withholding of an operating license, legal action, and possible criminal penalties, but vary greatly between countries.

Very few national-level studies exist for monitoring progress and publicizing results. A national survey realized by the Swedish government, mentioned by ECMT (see footnote 4, above), is an example of what should be developed at the EU level. A similar study was been launched in 2002 by the Irish government, assessing both quantitative and qualitative measures implemented by transport operators and giving recommendations for future developments. In England, a study is undertaken for air and maritime sectors, recommending that the road transport sector should also be covered after 2004, conclusions with as to whether legislation is needed for pushing companies and manufacturers to develop innovations. Also in England, the assessment of local transport plans allows assessment of measures and implementation of commitments.

Besides national governments, the European Commission has a central role in ensuring a framework, guidelines for legislation, awareness-raising campaigns, and financial support for R & D of innovation and local measures.

The European Commission sets up framework conditions through legislation as exposed in Part 1, with each member state translating the directives into national legislation and measures.

Beyond these legislative processes, the EU adopted in the Lisbon process the concept of *national action plans* (NAPs) for social inclusion. England, Ireland, The Netherlands, Portugal, and Spain have included provisions for PRM transport in their plans. The Irish plan is, however, the only one providing recommendations and guidelines concerning vehicles and infrastructures; the NAP includes guidance for policies for the introduction of low-floor vehicles in urban areas and adaptation of taxis as well as provisions for making new and upgraded bus stations accessible for PRM. Germany has guidelines on transport services, but no reference is made in NAPs on services and information systems apart from this, despite their importance in improving mobility of PRM.

The European Commission (EC) organized the European year for Disabled people, which brought this issue high on the agenda, but for one year only. Nonetheless, awareness raising is necessary for having PRM interests and needs perceived, understood, and integrated by all the stakeholders, both public and private. The EC should also develop systems for obtaining reliable and comparable statistical data, which are needed for more accurately defining the overall needs in legislation and support measures.

28.3.3 Local Experiences and Measures

In order to complete the review of the national-level legislation and accompanying measures, Polls gathered information on local initiatives that also have a strong impact on improving transport accessibility for PRM. These measures apply to several transport modes and are implemented by local governments, transport operators, and authorities organising transport. Two trends appear when reviewing the policy implemented by cities: (1) the lack of reliable data on the number of mobility-impaired people using transport systems and (2) the overall commitment of local governments to improve citizen mobility through better public transport and dedicated services. Cities have sufficiently broad overview of the main obstacles to mobility, but rarely have any realized systematic analysis of the needs of PRM or a reflection of the types of disabilities as described above in this chapter. The main obstacles mentioned are

- Difficulties in boarding vehicles (public transport)
- Stops and stations not handicap-adapted
- Stations not easily approach and access too difficult
- Illegal parking at bus stops (thus rendering low-floor vehicles virtually useless)
- Barriers to access by wheelchairs-bound and blind people
- Lack of information and guidance on transport services and trip preparation
- Boarding in rail vehicles
- Absence of wheelchair lifts and ramps
- Vehicle design (steps in double-decker buses)
- Pavement design
- Architectural barriers
- Absence of support staff and personnel
- Door-opening systems
- Lack of space in crowded vehicles

According to these barriers, the preferred modes are taxi, bus, special bus services, trams, and underground trains, ranging from the best to the least accessible. The bus fleet seems the most accessible to PRM when using public transport, with almost 55% of buses in low-floor design in cities in 2003. Improvements in bus fleets include low-floor technologies, design of doors providing boarding facilities such as wheelchair lifts, design of bus stops, and providing facilities for wheelchair securement inside the bus. Safety is seen as an important aspect as PRM are less safe and balanced than other users, and restraining systems for wheelchairs as well as comfortable systems for holding in crowded vehicles and beside seats must be investigated. Beyond these measures, improvement is sought for visually and hearing-impaired people with audio signals and information as well as Braille guidance.

28.3.3.1 Specific Measures for Buses, Trams, Underground Trains, Information Systems, and Flanking Measures

One key measure, besides providing low-floor buses, is the new design of bus stops, with low pavement, new pavement surfaces, and prohibiting cars and other privately owned vehicles from parking at bus stops. Bus corridors represent in this context a major step forward, especially for safety, boarding, and waiting. Buses are integrated to broader measures on urban design and access to streets for PRM. Trams are less frequently used by disabled people than buses, although they are a growing mode of transport in cities that heavily invest in tram systems. Trams recently designed are low-floor and present internal design adapted to PRM, but old trams are mostly inaccessible because of steep, high steps and doors systems that are too narrow. The new tram systems currently developed in cities like Bordeaux, Paris, and Clermont-Ferrand in France are fully accessible and provide all the necessary technology for most of the disabilities found in passengers. Underground trains (e.g., the Paris Metro) are traditionally the less accessible mode for PRM, as transporting heavy luggage makes the trip uncomfortable and uneasy for any user, not to mention wheelchairs and other mobility devices. Built mostly in the early or mid twentieth century, the underground is not regarded as PRM-friendly, and upgrading it would be a very costly process. Vehicles are the easiest part, as the corridors, stairs, and access to the platform where steps are omnipresent is a bigger barrier. However, the number of stations equipped has steadily grown since the mid-1990s, and new systems are also fully accessible. The BVG survey [2] shows that from 16% of stations accessible in a sample of 35 cities in Europe, this rate increased to 49% in 2000. Some measures like timetables, guidance in stations, and in-station or onboard information are being developed. However, as mentioned earlier, pretrip information is very poor despite available technologies.

The following case studies illustrate what can be achieved by complying with legislation and combining it with local specificity and initiatives. The first example shows how accessibility is included in a transport planning process monitored by the central government (Lancashire); the second one, how a city develops its initiatives and guidelines (London); and the third one, how local measures are developed prior to any legislative process (Grenoble).

1. The "Lancashire Transport Plan, provisions for accessibility" shows how local government defines its own policy, targets, and assessment of accessibility in a transport plan. Achieving social inclusion is a key objective of the central government, which has issued guidance on how accessibility to services can be improved to promote social inclusion and so enhance economic regeneration, reduce health inequalities, and improve education attendance. Transport has a crucial role to play in supporting these wider social objectives by making opportunities more accessible. *Accessibility* can be characterized

as the opportunity for people to be able to get to key services at reasonable cost, in reasonable time and with reasonable ease. The County Council supports the national objective through its own objective to make Lancashire a good place to live and work, now and in the future, a place where everybody matters, and a place where people can feel safe, lead healthy lives, learn and develop, work and prosper, get help if they need it, enjoy a high-quality environment, and travel easily and safely. Lancashire is preparing its Accessibility Strategy to accompany the Local Transport Plan, and both will be submitted to the government at the end of March 2006. The Accessibility Strategy will make a valuable contribution toward the County Council's commitment to ensure accessible, high-quality, value-for-money services that meet people's needs. We will give particular consideration to bringing forward measures that will assist those people who suffer disadvantage through poor accessibility. Mechanisms must be put in place to ensure that users' needs can influence these partnerships. In their report *Making the Connections*, the Social Exclusion Unit recognized that different people have different accessibility and transport needs. In the delivery of the Accessibility Strategy, the County Council will consider the requirements of different groups including disabled people, women, older people, younger people, career people, people from ethnic communities, and people on low incomes. An effective accessibility strategy can be delivered only through a partnership approach. This is crucial as accessibility is a system approach that relates transport, location, service delivery, and design to peoples' needs. There are many and varied bodies from the public, private, and voluntary sectors involved in this service delivery system.

2. The Mayor of London set up a global transport strategy in which accessibility has a large part. This plan is to be completed by local plans in the boroughs. The mayor works with the stakeholders in order to improve accessibility, especially with transport for London, the transport operator. It was noticed that despite the introduction of low-floor buses, the accessibility of public transport was not the best, that the ramps can only embark one wheelchair and that the new powered wheelchairs do not fit within the current norms for doors and ramps, and that they also require large storage place and recharging points. Only 29 out of 253 underground stations are step-free, and even the stations with lifts are not always easy to use (in one case the user needs to be accompanied by an underground staff member). The plan for "unlocking London for all" plans to have 100 step-free stations by 2020. All new stations should be accessible, and road schemes should also be accessible to all, and traffic management should also make the use of cars easier for disabled people. The Town and Country Planning Act of 1990 stipulates that planning authorities draw the attention of developers, when granting permission, to the provisions of the Chronically Sick and Disabled People Act of 1970, the British Standards 1979 Code, and to the design note on access to education buildings. The building regulation 2000 makes provision for access of disabled people to buildings and the use of their facilities as well as sanitary conveniences. The government announced a review in 2004 for strengthening the regulations by the introduction of the lifetime home standards. Disability Discrimination Act (DDA) 1995; in 2004 the final stage of the goods, facilities and services provisions of Part III of the Act came into force. The new features will apply to business and other providers of services to the public where physical features make access impossible or unreasonably difficult for PRM.

3. The Grenoble "syndicat mixte des transports en commun" (SMTC = operator) planned the future system of public transport with a strong emphasis on mobility of PRM before the French legislation made it compulsory. While planning the new system,

the SMTC and the subcontractors had regular meetings for developing the project and including accessible services for trams (in 1987) and buses (in 1994). A study defining the concept of accessibility has been realized in order to define the specifications of vehicles and stops. Then a prototype vehicle has been built and operated to validate the specifications. Research centers such as INRETS has been involved in this process as well as representative organizations for disabled people. After validation, the system has been built. The vehicles (trams and buses) are all equipped with powered ramps, and the stops have been designed for full accessibility, after extensive research work. A brochure entitled "accessibility for all" has been published and disseminated for encouraging the use of the systems; this brochure also presents future development of the transport system. Grenoble was far ahead of any other French (and European) city by then, and its plan provides for 50% of stops accessibility by 2005 and implementation of an accessible trolley.

REFERENCES

1. European Conference of Transport Ministers (ECMT): *Améliorer l'Accès aux Transports Publics* [Improving accessibility of public transportation] (752004082P), Nov 2004;, *Transport et Vieillissement de la Population* [Transport of the elderly in the population], Feb 2002; *Aspects Économiques de l'Accessibilité des Taxis* [Economic aspects of accessibility in taxis] (752001152P), Nov 2001 (http://www.cemt.org/index.htm).
2. BVG Berliner Verkehrsbetriebe for the European Commission DG Tren: *Accessibility of Urban Transport of PRM*, Berlin, 2003.
3. European Commission: Eurostat (http://ec.europa.eu/eurostat)

FURTHER READING

1. Certu: *Guide Accessibilité*, 2001 (available at www.certu.fr).
2. Certu: *Les Bus et Leurs Points d'Arrêt Accessibles à Tous* [Accessibility of buses and bus stops for everyone], study report, May–June 2000, Certu, directive on transportation (available at www.certu.fr; accessed 12/00).
3. City of de Grenoble: *Plan des Cheminements Praticables et Accessibles* [Plans for making roadway travel practical and accessible], directive on travel and accessibility, Oct 2000 (http://www.grenoble.fr/jsp/site/Portal.jsp?page_id=16).
4. Department of Transport (London): *Accessibility Planning* (http://www.dft.gov.uk/stellent/groups/dft_localtrans/documents/divisionhomepage/032400.hcsp).
5. Disability Portal: *Accessibility in Singapore* (http://www.disability.org.sg/services/accessibility.asp).
6. French Ministry of Transportation and Housing Equipment: *Accessibilité*, Information Letter 2 (article on Grenoble) (http://www.transports.equipement.gouv.fr/frontoffice/index.jsp#).
7. International Union for Public transport (UITP), *Improving Access to Public Transport* (in partnership with ECMT [1]), Jan 2004 (http://www.uitp.com/publications/index2.cfm?id=6).

29

Transportation Services in Asia

Joseph Kwan
Rehabilitation International, (Asia Pacific), Hong Kong

Eric Tam
Hong Kong Polytechnic University, Hong Kong

The early years of the current decade are witnessing rapid change in Asia and the Pacific. Japan and Australia have taken a lead in national legislation mandating inclusive transport systems. Hong Kong has become a model for the rest of Asia with its "family of accessible services" ranging from accessible rail and low-floor bus lines to service routes and door-to-door service. Access to commuter rail and subway systems is found in most Japanese cities and at some key stations in some cities in China, Korea, Thailand, Singapore, and India. An initial deployment of low-floor buses is planned in India. Initial deployments of service routes as well as door-to-door services are found in Tokyo, while a small door-to-door service was more recently started in Kuala Lumpur. Advocacy is moving ahead, with "access audits" reported in India, Malaysia, Cambodia, Laos, and Thailand. An *Access Exchange International* (AEI) guide has been published in Chinese and Japanese, with other versions planned by nongovernment organizations (NGOs) in Malaysia, Indonesia, and India. A Department for International Development (DFID)-sponsored key bus corridor has become more accessible in Pune (Poona), India. In this chapter, the development, advocacy, and present implementation of accessible transportation of some Asia countries are reviewed.

The Engineering Handbook of Smart Technology for Aging, Disability, and Independence,
Edited by A. Helal, M. Mokhtari and B. Abdulrazak
Copyright © 2008 John Wiley & Sons, Inc.

29.1 PEOPLE WITH DISABILITIES IN ASIA

At present, the exact total number of people with disabilities in Asia is unknown. Figures vary widely between countries, due to the lack of comparability and disability definitions in each country. When comparing the figures from the World Health Organization (WHO)—which estimates 1 out of every 10 people having a disability in developing countries—there is a vast difference. It is highly probable that the figures presented below grossly underestimate the true scenario for a variety of reasons endemic to each country; for example, 80% of all the disabled in India are found in remote rural areas. The 1000 or so islands in the Philippines make it geographically difficult to obtain an accurate survey and also complicate the survey methodology and definitions used. It is broadly recognized that disability rates tend to correlate with poverty and aging rates. Poverty, misinformation, ignorance, and superstition reinforce all the ill effects of disability and exasperate accessibility awareness—denying those who are most in need. Rural-to-urban migration compounds the problem and overburdens already densely populated urban areas and its transportation. Such movements result in stressful conditions, a breakdown of family ties that eventually force some individuals with disabilities to resort to begging on the streets. In some Asian countries, special circumstances such as civil strife may create larger-than-expected disability rates across the board.

According to India's NSSO (National Sample Survey Organisation) survey of 1991, it was estimated that 1.9% (19.9 million) are disabled (with sensory and physical impairments), with a prevalence of physical disabilities of 20 and 16 per 1000 in rural and urban areas, respectively. For Malaysia, from its 1980 population census, it was estimated that 0.8% of the population (106,000) are disabled people. Of this total, 12.8% are visually handicapped, 28.9% are hearing-impaired, and 58.3% are mentally impaired or are otherwise disabled. In the Philippines, the 2000 census estimated disability at a rate of 1.11% (942,000), including 50.2% visually impaired, 18.3% auditory or speech-impaired, 14.4% physically disabled, 14.1% with cognitive disabilities, and 2.9% with multiple disabilities. For Japan, the disabled population was estimated to be over 3,000,000, the majority suffering from limb and spinal impairments. In Korea, individuals with disabilities accounted for 3.03% (1.45 million) of the total population. In Hong Kong, according to the Social Welfare Department of the government in 2002, 6.19% (430,000) were individuals with disabilities, including 32% with mental handicaps, 2.6% with autism, 21.9% with mental illness, 17.8% with visual impairment, 9.4% with hearing impairment, and 16.9% physically handicapped. In China, the estimated population for individual with disabilities was about 60 million in 1990.

In many Asian cities, we seldom see many persons with disabilities (PwDs) using the streets or public transportation. Reports of the PwDs being disadvantaged and sidelined in education, recreation, employment, and commerce, particularly in some Asian countries, has been highlighted before. The issue of unaccessibility often originates from discrepancies and disregard for accessible planning, design, and construction of the structurally accessible environment, which only adds to their frustrations of day-to-day living. It is widely recognized that the transportation services and interface facilities are crucial to the quality of life for PwDs, especially in the area of mobility.

The lack of accessible transportation results in a denial of much needed services as well as inefficient use of public funds to provide these services (retrofitting is more expensive than initially securing accessible design). Those most in need, in the poverty-stricken, remote rural areas with a higher percentage of disabilities, are denied accessible public transport, which exacerbates the vicious poverty–disability cycle, denying them access to opportunities.

Although advocacy for accessibility exists at national and municipal levels, actual implementation may be slow as a result of a variety of factors depending on the country—lack of funds, huge foreign debts, problems of poverty, disease, education, political instability, harsh climatic conditions, difficult terrain, and civil strife—to name only a few. The implementation of accessible transport lags behind that of accessible buildings and public open space because this usually requires more complex and extensive research and design, modifications, funds, changes in procedures, public awareness, driving habits, and traffic systems. In addition, it must also be highlighted that accessible transport cannot exist without accessible supporting pedestrian infrastructure—the entire trip chain must be accessible for it to qualify as such. Despite some progress in accessible transportation facilities seen in a few Asian countries and cities, including Japan, Singapore, and Hong Kong, accessible public transport in Asia is still in its early infancy and has begun to emerge only relatively recently. Examples include the New Delhi Metro Rail (launched in 2002) and Putra-LRT Kuala Lumpur, Malaysia, which will nevertheless begin the gradual cycle of change throughout the region.

29.2 AN OVERVIEW OF TRANSPORT ACCESS IN MAJOR ASIAN CITIES

In the mid-1990s, accessible public transport did not exist in Asia. There was virtually no public transportation for PwDs in the region apart from very limited specialized services for clients of social service agencies; for instance, a small door-to-door service has started in Kuala Lumpur 1993, Malaysia, and there is now a "Dial-A-Ride" service in Bangalore 1998, India. Nevertheless, the implementation of accessible public transportation is beginning slowly.

Accessible transportation requires suitable pedestrian infrastructure as well as barrier-free public transport facilities. For pedestrian infrastructure, dropped curbs (curb ramps) are developed to allow all users to transit from the street grade to the raised sidewalk without the need to negotiate steps. These features can now be found in many street corners of major Asian cities, including Shanghai, Tokyo, Hong Kong, and Singapore. In the Philippines, crossings are now regulated with dropped-curb cutouts and tactile warning strips. In Korea, special projects have been conducted to establish barrier-free pedestrian environments for PwDs, including building accessible streets, parks, stations, and buildings. These establishments benefit not only PwDs but also the growing elderly population of many Asian countries.

In terms of barrier-free public transport facilities, accessible commuter rail stations are essential. Unfortunately, many of these facilities were built long before realization of the needs of PwDs, and retrofitting them was very expensive, if not impossible. Generally, transportation for PwDs was provided using low-floor buses, lift-equipped buses, small buses and vans, private cars, and specially designed taxis. The following reviews are limited to surface transport and related infrastructure. There may be many instances of fresh implementation of access features unknown to the authors at this point, and conversely, there is always the possibility of loss of accessibility, as occurred in the case of the Philippines' unsuccessful implementation of a low-floor bus.

29.2.1 India

Section 44–46 of the Persons with Disabilities Act 1995, provides for nondiscrimination for PwDs, including structurally accessible environment and transportation, depending on the economic capacity of the state. The issue of accessible transportation did not receive any attention prior to its enactment. The 1995 Act makes it mandatory to provide accessibility in the transportation system. Although the idea has yet to be fully realized, because of the vast requirement of resources, there has at least been perceptible change in awareness and sensitivity among the concerned stakeholders.

29.2.1.1 Rail

Currently, there are reportedly ~150 railway stations with disabled parking, ramps, lowered ticket windows, resting areas, and toilets. Mumbai's (Bombay's) local train service has one compartment that is barrier-free. The best example of the accessible local transport has been provided by the Delhi Metro Rail Corporation (DMRC), which in its policy and planning included access needs of people with diverse disabilities. The DMRC proposes to cover 110 km by the year 2010 and almost 90 stations. The first stretch of 8.3 km, with four coaches and six stations, was inaugurated in 2002. The station provides for exterior parking for PwDs, ramps with handrails, guiding and warning blocks, bright color contrast, large-lettering-information displays and signage, lifts with low-level control panels with Braille and raised control buttons, auditory signals, and designated PwD space within coaches.

Although the government provides subsidies (50–75%) to PwDs and their escorts, many with locomotive disabilities find it difficult or impossible to use the majority of the remaining railways stations for the following reasons:

- *Stations*—overhead bridges with no ramps, hazardous and tedious luggage collection system, and unavoidable crossing over railway tracks.
- *Nonaccessible coaches*—RDSO's (Research Design and Standards Organization) previous attempt at developing 50 prototypes of accessible coaches were unfortunately not successful. New efforts are underway to develop accessible coaches–this time in consultation with the agency Samarthya Centre for Promotion of Barrier Free Environment for People with Disabilities [1].

29.2.1.2 Buses

Some semi-low-floor buses in Chandigarh are plying. The government of Delhi is planning to introduce high-capacity bus system (HCBS) low-floor buses with audiovideo information. A total of seven corridors have been identified, five of which are designated for HCBS and two for electric trolley buses (ETBs) with dedicated lanes. Groundwork on the (DFID (Department for International Development)-sponsored) pilot corridor has already begun with the initial deployment of low-floor buses along the Pune bus corridor. It will also provide accessible features, including approaches to the bus shelters, bus shelters, and the bus system itself. Delhi's previous semi-low-floor diesel bus (Volvo) plied for 6 months in 2001, but was eliminated with introduction of the Clean Air Act [2].

Currently, many truck-chassis buses are still running, and obviously, owing to financial constraints, modifications are not always feasible. Bus stations and terminals are being encouraged to provide ramps.

Accessible transport requires accessible supporting infrastructure—the entire trip chain must be completely accessible. The major challenge for an accessible bus system is that the actual bus shelters, road conditions, and pavement and traffic situation—as well as public awareness, and bus driver sensitivity and driving skills—must be conducive to its success.

29.2.1.3 Minibuses and Vans

Kolkata's National Institute for the Orthopaedically Handicapped provides a minibus equipped with a ramp under its false floor. Bangalore's "Dial-A-Ride" service offers a van with a hydraulically operated lift. In Delhi, a NGO working in the disability field provides a van equipped with a tail-end lift (funded by the Government of Japan), which is basically used for school transportation.

29.2.1.4 Conclusions

India, with its vast magnitude and diverse terrain, may not be able to provide accessible transportation to the entire length and breadth of the country. Its government has many other priorities, including poverty, education, and unemployment. Even though its efforts are rather scattered and lacking concerted cocoordinated efforts, it has embarked on providing accessible transport. As a result, there is an increased sensitivity and awareness among government agencies, the private sector, NGOs, and other stakeholders. It may not be easy to modify the existing fleets of buses or rail coaches, but with its future research and development projects along with proper planning, accessible transportation may not be a distant dream but a reality.

29.2.2 Malaysia

The lack of accessibility, usability, and safety of public transportation in Malaysian cities creates more barriers for PwDs. Visual observations and more recent surveys conducted in Kuala Lumpur of pedestrian movement, public transportation, and building access have shown few PWDs or elderly users, owing to

- Little consideration given to them in the overall pedestrian planning
- Evident lack of facilities for PwDs within the city, to permit easy mobility
- Inconsistent design standards in the construction of walkway facilities with obstructing signage, lamp-posts, garbage bins, and so on
- Many buildings and malls lacking adequate universal access
- Public transport facilities—light-rail transit (LRT), taxis, and buses not designed to cater to PwDs and the elderly [3].

Malaysia's plan of action for the promotion of accessible transport deals with the issues discribed in Sections 29.2.2.1–29.2.2.4.

29.2.2.1 Advocacy for Access to Transport

In 1993 the Malaysian Minister of Transport assigned to Kuala Lumpur City Hall the task of investigating the low commuter usage of the light-rail transit (LRT) system (between STAR (Sistem Transit Aliran Ringan) and Putra LRT) via studies, surveys, forums, and other projects.

Despite the existing bylaws pertaining to accessibility to all new public buildings, it was the 1994 demonstrations that finally rendered the second station (LRT) at Putra accessible (lifts, assistance service, ramps, Braille lift buttons and guide tiles), but changes to the First station are still awaited. This indicates the serious lack of application by some sectors regarding the provision of accessible features. This is a widespread phenomenon, where, at the regional level, ESCAP (Economic and Social Commission for Asia and the Pacific) reports had stated that "even where guidelines and legislative measure exists, poor implementation and enforcement remain serious issues" [4].

29.2.2.2 Access to Streets, Pathways, Shelters, Waiting Areas, and Bus Stops

Various surveys, observations, and interviews [1] revealed the majority of streets and open spaces to be generally unsafe, uncomfortable, and inaccessible:

- 71% felt that dropped curbs were impractical and unsafe for visually impaired people and wheelchair users.
- 63% felt that the traffic signals at pedestrian crossings were unsafe for the visually impaired.
- 81% felt that the pavement was unsuitable and difficult to use.
- 84% said that the path did not have sufficient safety requirements.

If street environments were not accessible, public transportation systems would not work. The following is a comment made by a blind woman who had no choice but to take public transport [5]:

> Most blind persons prefer to take taxis rather than buses. Generally, we are fearful to go out, and had faced lots of problems by taking public transport system such as buses. Often, when there is traffic jam, the bus stops away from the stand, so we do not know where to find the bus. Missing a bus is normal. We also encounter a lot of problems with bus drivers that seem to be uncooperative and sometimes abusive.

29.2.2.3 Access to Transit Vehicles

Even though the feeder buses for the Putra LRT routes are advertised as accessible, the ramps cannot be implemented because of the existing traffic systems and procedures. The problem is that the overall traffic system should provide for well-planned dedicated bus lanes for smooth traffic flow and efficiency. The overall planning and design of streets needs to account for the mobility of PwDs from vehicles to curbs and vice versa. Awareness programs for all road users and bus drivers catering to the needs of PwDs and the elderly will provide a long-term investment toward a "caring society".

29.2.2.4 Rail

The purpose of one of the studies [6] by the Accessibility and Safety Research Centre (ACCESS), Faculty of Built Environment, University of Malaya, was to investigate and identify accessible design (focusing on wheelchair users) on selected light-rail transit (LRT) stations in Kuala Lumpur. The objectives were to

- Ensure that the design of accessibility complied with the law, regulations, standard requirements, and guidelines

- Understand the current situation and what was required to ensure equal rights and opportunities for PwDs.

The research was drawn from reliable literature, targeted-user questionnaires, and checklists of building audits ensuring accessible design. Building access surveys were carried out on selected stations and covered three main stages indicative of passenger paths and patterns:

Stage 1 —from the road curb to the ticket counter
Stage 2 —from the ticket counter to the platform
Stage 3 —from the platform to reaching the LRT train

Results of these findings have been analysed to assist the LRT management and station in upgrading their facilities to a comfortable, accessible, and safe environment benefiting and encouraging more users, including PwDs. A lesson learned was that all possible users in its main customer policies should have been addressed from the very beginning. Advocacy groups could play crucial watchdog roles by reporting to the relevant authorities as to whether the building, facility, or public transportation provides adequate access. Disabled representatives liaising with the government would be crucial in bringing about change and action.

29.2.2.5 Conclusion and Future Prospects

In Malaysia, and in many countries in the Asia–Pacific region, legislative means are often not enough to do the work necessary in implementing policies and projects that promote a barrier-free environment. Legislation provides for the necessary mechanism in facilitating the implementation and function. However, there is an evident lack of urgency and slow progress where this matter is yet to be seen as a priority by the public administration sector, including technical government personnel agencies, and the construction industry, where the related professions are concerned [7].

Despite establishment of the National Coordinating Council on Disability in 1997, after the midpoint review on the Asian and Pacific Decade of Disabled Persons for 1993–2002, there had been a disappointing lack of progress regarding legislation. Part of the solution lies in the disability awareness training of public administrative and technical personnel, in Penang, 1991 (ESCAP) and the *Regional Training of Trainers for the Promotion of Non-handicapping Environment in Bangkok* (ESCAP, JICA (Japan International cooperation Agency), Royal Thai Government, 2000). These courses dealt with (1) recognizing barriers, (2) disability simulation, and (3) access surveys. One of the government participants commented that the vision of a barrier-free environment would have been arguably more difficult had these courses not been introduced [8].

Malaysia, one of Asia's newly industrialized economies, has progressed rapidly, and its status as a developing country is rapidly shifting to that of a developed country. However, the cultural and socioeconomic opportunities for PwDs are greatly lagging behind the rapid Malaysian economic growth. There are still many bridges to be crossed before this disadvantaged group can enjoy the benefits of a more equitable social system. Universal design in public transportation and related architecture [9] is not just more accessibility in the traditional sense; it is a redefinition of goals—of careful planning and crucial design. Everyone—not only PwDs—stands to benefit from universal design.

29.2.3 Philippines

Metro Manila is served mainly by privately owned buses, jeepneys, tricycles, and taxis, contributing to serious traffic congestion and different levels of service, even at the expense of general passenger safety and environmental degradation [10]. Buses are limited to the major wider corridors, and jeepneys cover the majority of the primary and secondary roads, also functioning as a feeder transport for bus, LRT, and MRT3 operations. Vehicle maintenance and repair is not regulated. The Urban Rail service was introduced as the backbone of mass transportation, with the objectives of alleviating existing traffic/transport problems and providing accessible public transport. There is currently no accessible public transport, with PwDs having to rely mainly on taxis.

The Philippines Accessibility Law, when first enacted, showed a general lack of understanding of PwDs' accessibility problems. Subsequent updates and revisions have resulted after a review, with the research and information collected from interviews of PwD representatives of various disability groups [11,12]. Problems of misinterpretation, ambiguity, lack of funds, resources, and enforcement hamper its implementation.

- All public transportation (land, air, and sea) is required to have designated seating and signage.
- Strategic LRT stations are to be accessible.
- A certain percentage of buses are to be accessible.
- No franchise or permit to operate public transportation units shall be granted, issued, or renewed unless they are constructed or renovated in accordance with the requirements pertaining to accessibility.
- If feasible, all existing public transport utilities shall modify or renovate in accordance with specifications and regulations to accommodate PwDs.
- All street crossings must cater to people with a wide range of disabilities.
- Parking areas must be accessible to PwDs.

Because the Philippines has so many islands, difficulties in the necessary water transport between the islands are common; however, there are currently no standards for maritime vessels, and this issue lies outside the scope of this chapter. However, under the Accessibility Law, assistance, designated seating, and accessible safety measures and procedures are required for all domestic maritime vessels.

To date, legislation under the Philippine Plan of Action for Older Persons (OPs), parallel to the promotion of the welfare of PwDs, has resulted in new buildings or renovations of public transport utilities mandated to comply with specifications/designs for universal access, MRT (mass rapid transit) stations to be accessible, and designated seating for buses and trains.

29.2.3.1 Rail
Thirteen MRT stations in Manila are now equipped with elevators, ramps, and signage. All LRT and MRT trains have designated seating, and all PNR (Philippine National Railways) commuter-line stations have ramps except for the Paco station.

29.2.3.2 Buses
There are presently no PwD-accessible public buses; the only existing one was not maintained long enough to continue operation and unfortunately had to be shelved by

the Department of Transportation and Communications (DOTC) because of its high purchase and maintenance costs; instead, the DOTC is now preoccupied with designing the standards for accessible buses to be used as guidelines for local manufacturers. Buses have mandatory designated seating.

29.2.3.3 Small Utility Vehicles
Public utility vehicles such as taxis and jeepneys are currently mandated to stop when flagged down by PwDs, but compliance is poor and enforcement lax.

Throughout the Philippines, PwDs encounter various problems when dealing with different types of transportation; these problems are seldom recognized by the transport sector, nor are considered in the planning/designing stages of related infrastructure and transport. Only a few individuals are actually working toward equal opportunities and better provisions for this sector, and very little support is received for funding or resources, thereby making progress rather slow and difficult.

29.2.4 Korea

In Korea, efforts to establish more accessible transportation were undertaken via contributions from the central government, the local governments, and nongovernmental organizations (NGOs). The population for PwDs in Korea is 3.03% (1.45 million).

The Korean government first initiated the Welfare of Disabled Persons Act in 1981. To promote a barrier-free society, the government enacted the Convenience Facilities for the Disabled Act in 1997, and in 2004, the Act on Mobility Facilities Promotion for the Less Mobile Persons was established. The main objectives of the 2004 Act are to transfer the jurisdiction to the Ministry of Construction and Transportation, standardize barrier-free design and oblige for implementation, to introduce low-floor buses, build the regional special transportation service system, support the disabled driver, and designate the pedestrian priority zone.

29.2.4.1 Buses
In 2004 Seoul and six other major cities in Korea planned to provide 10% of the total city buses as low-floor accessible buses by 2013. According to the plan, by 2006, a total of 1180 and 867 low-floor buses should be made available in Seoul and six other major Korea cities, respectively.

29.2.4.2 Taxis
In addition to bus services, PwDs can also use Call-Taxi Service as a transportation means in Seoul. In 2003 there were 100 vehicles serving 67,000 severally disabled individuals, with fares representing are only 40% of the general taxi fare.

29.2.5 Vietnam

Since the lifting of economic sanctions in the mid–late 1990s, Vietnam is now reaching a stage of development to address issues such as accessibility. Concerted efforts have been undertaken to draft accessibility laws and standards regulating the construction of barrier-free buildings. More recently, delegations including transport and social welfare officials and PwD representatives have been sent to Hong Kong and Singapore to study accessible public transportation in these cities. Plans are now underway in Vietnam to implement accessible low-floor buses in the cities, to be followed by a system of accessible rail linking the major centers of Vietnam from north to south.

29.2.6 Thailand

29.2.6.1 Rail

Intercity rail systems in Thailand are currently outdated, with train cars and stations totally inaccessible. The rolling stocks have narrow doors and several high steps that prohibit easy access by most passengers with or without baggage. The train compartments are not equipped with accessible toilets, and the aisle between seats is too narrow for the passage of wheelchairs. Cross-border trains to neighbouring Laos, Cambodia, and Vietnam are equally antiquated and inaccessible. Terminals and mainline stations are not provided with accessible washrooms and toilets, ticket counters, public telephones, service counters, or induction loops for the hearing-impaired. There are even fewer facilities for passengers who are low-vision or blind.

29.2.6.2 Skytrains and Underground Trains

When the Bangkok Skytrain system was constructed in the mid–late 1990s, the accessibility needs of PwDs were not considered. Built above busy carriageways and some 20 m high above ground, the Skytrain was designed without lifts or elevators to bring passengers up to the elevated station platforms. The local disability groups became aware of the inaccessibility of the system and lobbied the municipal government, but without success. It was only after a mass demonstration in the streets of Bangkok by PwDs that the government finally conceded to their request and set aside funding to install lifts and elevators to these stations. Today, only about one-third of the Skytrain stations are equipped with lifts.

Since 2002 or so, Bangkok has begun to build its third and fourth lines for a new underground mass transit railway. Unlike the previous Skytrain system, these new underground MRT stations are provided with ramps, and lifts that bring the passengers from street level down to the concourse and platform levels. Accessible toilets, wide entry gates, and internal lifts are now part of the standards at these stations.

29.2.6.3 Buses

In Bangkok, the majority of the population commutes daily by bus, operated mostly by privately hired. As there are currently no regulations governing the provision of accessible transportation, the majority of the bus fleets are not accessible. Most buses have high floors with several steps, and narrow doorways that impede easy access. More recently, some buses have been equipped with wheelchair lifts (Fig. 29.1) to facilitate transportation for PwDs.

29.2.7 Taiwan

The underground mass transit rail system in Taipei was constructed shortly after the MTR system in Hong Kong by consultants who originally worked on the Hong Kong projects. Therefore, similar design and details were adopted, which unfortunately meant the replication of the same inaccessible MTR system that existed at the time. Figure 29.2 shows a pedestrian walkway with dropped curb, but the subway entrance

FIGURE 29.1 Bus equipped with wheelchair lift.

FIGURE 29.2 Pedestrian walkway with dropped curb and nonaccessible subway entrance with a few steps in Taipei.

is not wheelchair-accessible. Taipei, like Hong Kong, therefore had to undergo major retrofitting programs to remove the barriers or to construct ramps or lifts to transport elderly and disabled passengers down to its underground stations. Today, only a few stations are fully accessible to PwDs.

29.2.8 Japan

Japan, currently has a population of 125 million, 2.3% of whom are individuals with disabilities and 16.5% of whom are elderly. Concerns about accessible transportation first surfaced in the early 1980s, when the Ministry of Land, Infrastructure and Transport prepared a guidebook on public transport for PWDs. In 2000 the Japanese government implemented the Transportation Accessibility Improvement Law, with the objective of enhancing mobility and safety for the elderly and PwDs.

29.2.8.1 Rail

Railway is a major public transportation for the Japanese. The railway network is very complex, high-density, and involves many railway companies. Negotiating level changes in terminals is a key aspect of mobility. The train platform of many railway stations in Japan were not built at street level, and passengers need to use escalators, lifts, or stairs to get to the train. In 2003 it was reported that only 52% of the stations were installed with lifts and 67% had escalators. For wheelchair users, accessing these stations could be particularly difficult, if not impossible.

To solve the problem, Japanese train stations sometimes use specially designed stair lifts (Fig. 29.3) to carry the wheelchair up and down. Alternatively, some stations use a special escalator design to transport wheelchair (Fig. 29.4) between levels. This special escalator can extend three consecutive steps horizontally to form a platform, allowing wheelchairs to be carried safety.

To facilitate visually impaired passengers, many train stations were equipped with tactile maps showing the layout of the station and tactile guidepaths for navigations. More

FIGURE 29.3 Stair lift at railway station in Japan.

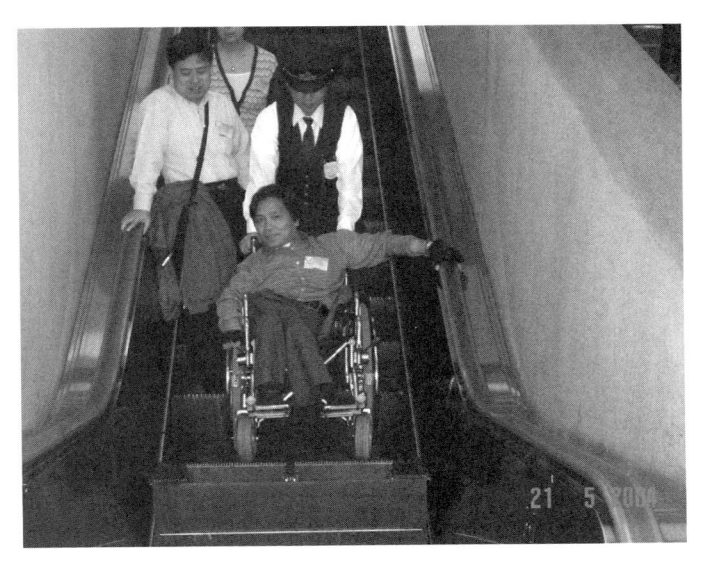

FIGURE 29.4 Specially designed escalator allowing wheelchair access.

recently, the Railway Technical Research Institute developed a personalized interactive guidance system for individuals with visual impairment. The system consists of a cane, a portable information terminal, and a number of radio tag-installed Braille blocks. Within the tag-installed Braille block, IC chips programmed with location information were embedded. During usage, the user needs to first indicate his/her destination within the station environment. Then, while walking, he/she will use the cane to pick up location information from the tag-installed Braille blocks. These signals will be transmitted via an antenna to the portable information terminal, where a verbal guidance device will be provided to guide the user to the right platform to board the desired train.

29.2.8.2 Buses
In 2001 there were 1496 stepless (low-floor) buses, 3254 one-step buses with step height of 550 mm, and only 326 buses that were equipped with wheelchair lifts. In Tokyo, some stepless buses are equipped with manually operated retractable wheelchair ramps (Fig. 29.5).

29.2.8.3 Taxi and Special Transport Services
When PwDs and the elderly cannot use or have difficulties in utilizing public transportation, taxi services became an alternative means of mobility. In Japan, there are over 260,000 taxis; some of these are involved in one of the six different modes of accessible transportation for limited-mobility persons. These included taxis operating welfare transport services; private ambulances providing transport for patients requiring stretchers or gurneys between hospitals; universal-design taxis that can be used by any passengers, including wheelchair users; and "caretaking" (healthcare-providing) taxis, operated by trained drivers who have healthcare-providing qualification. Qualify caretaking taxi passengers enjoy financially subsidized fares; they often pay for only 10% of their traveling expenses. Other modes, including special transport services, are operated by volunteer groups and the social welfare councils of different cities and towns.

FIGURE 29.5 *Bus with retractable wheelchair ramp.*

The type of vehicles used for accessible taxi feature low-floor or microclass vehicles equipped with a wheelchair ramp at the rear and a sedan-type vehicle with swivel seat installed at the either front or back to facilitate seat transfer and standing up. In the future, a side entrance design will be used. The wheelchair user can access the vehicle with a ramp and be secured inside with a four-point wheelchair tiedown and a three-point occupant restraint, all of which comply with ISO (International Standard Organization) standards.

29.2.9 Mainland China

In most cities of mainland China, public transport services were not designed to be barrier-free. Railway transport systems generally do not have specific facilitates for PWDs. Transports for individual with disabilities were dependent on lightweight buses equipped with wheelchair lifts operated by nongovernment agencies. In larger cities like Beijing, Shanghai, and Shenzhen, barrier-free access gained higher priority. On pedestrian walkways, dropped curbs were incorporated, and newly build subway stations were wheelchair-accessible. With the upcoming Olympics in 2008, the Chinese government at all levels has attached high importance to barrier-free construction, and looks forward to seeing more and better accessibility on public transportations by 2010.

29.2.10 Hong Kong

Over the years, the Hong Kong Government has been working with transport operators to improve transport facilities so that individuals with disabilities can enjoy a barrier-free environment. In general, most public transport facilities, including trains, trams, buses, ferries, taxis, and lightweight buses, have certain arrangements to facilitate PwDs in using their services. For wheelchair users, trams were not accessible, and alternative means of transport must to be sought.

29.2.10.1 Mass Transit Railway

The Mass Transit Railway (MTR), consisting of 6 lines and 50 stations, is the major transport operator in Hong Kong. To facilitate PwDs, particularly wheelchair users, who ride on the subway, MTR provides lifts or stair-climbers at their stations to provide access between street, concourse, and platform levels. Tactile guidepaths are also installed to lead visually impaired passengers to use the station facilities, and audible devices are installed to inform visually impaired passengers of escalator locations. To facilitate wheelchair passengers, MTR has wheelchair pictogram clearly located on the platform to direct wheelchair passengers to the train compartment where designated wheelchair parking is available. In addition, large panel displays were also available in trains and on platforms to provide essential train information for passengers, including those with hearing impairment.

29.2.10.2 Rail

Like the MTR stations, railway stations in Hong Kong has been made wheelchair-assessible by creating ramps and lifts. Braille maps, high-contrast signs tactile guide-paths, voice-assisted vending machines, and other audible devices have been installed to facilitate visually impaired passengers. Induction loops are provided at ticket offices and customer services centers for hearing-impaired passengers. Although the MTR and railway operators have made their facilities as barrier-free as possible, there remains one major obstacle that has prohibited streamlining of their services—the platform gap problem.

29.2.10.3 Platform Gap

In Hong Kong, because of the geographic constraint, the concept of having straight aligned platforms to minimize the platform gap was not incorporated in the original designs of many train stations. Wide platform gaps in some stations has posed potential dangers to all passengers, not to mention PwDs. In fact, there have been reports of incidents where passengers have fallen into these gaps and suffered injuries. There were also height discrepancies between the platform and the train entrance, which made access even more difficult. In view of this situation, a new gangplank was developed to bridge the platform gap.

The design objective of this new gangplank (Fig. 29.6) is to enable a single operator to seamlessly bridge the platform gap for wheelchair access within a 20-s limit, based on the stopping time of the train at each station. Other passengers with limited mobility can also benefit from this new device. The overall dimension of the gangplank is 1700 × 1200 mm ($L \times W$), the weight is 120 kg, and the maneuvering radius is 1220 mm. The gangplank can bridge a maximum gap of 500 mm and handle a height difference of 190 mm. The maximum carrying capacity is 250 kg. An audiovisual warning system was incorporated to warn other passengers when the gangplank is operating on the platform.

29.2.10.4 Buses

Public bus services in Hong Kong are provided by five franchised bus companies. Of all the vehicles, over 41% are currently wheelchair-accessible. To facilitate passengers with

FIGURE 29.6 Specially design gangplank in Hong Kong.

visual impairment, these buses also provide high-color-contrast and textured handrail systems inside the compartment, as well as audio announcement to inform passengers of the next bus stop. Large display screens have also been incorporated on buses to benefit both visually and hearing-impaired passengers.

29.2.10.5 Special Transport Services

In addition to the public transport services, PwDs in Hong Kong can also use a door-to-door transport services (Rehabus Service; Fig. 29.7) subvented by the government and operated by a nongovernment agency. The Rehabus Service has a fleet of 87 vehicles, including 12-seat and 30-seat buses. It service covers the travel needs of PwDs mainly for work and school. Currently, 54 scheduled fixed-route services are

FIGURE 29.7 Accessible bus (Rehabus) for door-to-door transportation of PwDs in Hong Kong.

provided. During off-peak hours, PwDs can also use the service for social participations and leisure activities. All Rehabuses are equipped with wheelchair lift platforms and proper wheelchair tiedown and passenger restraint systems meeting ISO standards to ensure a safe ride.

29.3 CONCLUSIONS

While some Asian countries are progressing toward providing barrier-free transportation, many others still have developing-nation status and face many more immediate problems such as poverty, education, unemployment, malnutrition, and huge foreign debts in varying degrees. Economies in countries such as Indonesia, Vietnam, Cambodia, and Laos are examples.

In most of Asia, it is mandatory to provide accessibility in the built (accessibility-structured) environment/infrastructure and transportation systems in varying degrees. But the idea has yet to be fully realized because of the vast requirement of resources and administrative procedures to deal with the implementation. There is, however, a perceptible change in awareness and sensitivity among the stakeholders concerned. The spread of "first steps" in major cities throughout the region has been remarkable since the early 1990s or so. Barrier-free design is still in its early infancy in Asia, but—given time—accessible public transportation may not be a distant dream but a reality.

Although legislature for accessibility exists, it is not always sufficient in implementing policies and projects that promote a barrier-free environment. In addition to the insufficient resources and administrative procedures, there seems to be lack of urgency and slow progress. It must also be highlighted that accessibility laws need continual periodic reviews—updating, revising, and fine-tuning—to make them relevant and responsive to the growing and changing needs of PwDs.

Taking advocacy a step further, the disability awareness training of government personnel and "training of trainers" (TOT) courses introduced since the mid-1990s by UN-ESCAP (United Nations—Economic and Social Commission for Asia and the Pacific) seem to have "breathed" new life into the accessibility challenge.

Accessible public transportation requires accessible supporting pedestrian infrastructure, and with increasing changes being made in the latter, it will be only a matter of time before the transportation sector catches up. The trend has been to start with access to pedestrian infrastructure and move on to access to transport modes. Specifications and legal frameworks for infrastructure are uniformly more developed than they are for transportation in Asia, but this may begin to change as more models of accessible transport systems are put into place.

There seems to be a tendency to focus on high-profile large-vehicle systems for the initiation of accessibility improvements, while overlooking the large fleets of small buses, vans, jeepneys, and taxis that tend to dominate much of the public transport picture in many parts of Asia. But this could be seen as changes beginning in the larger overall picture that are slowly making their way down to the smaller details.

Only relatively recently have disability NGOs, transport officials, public works officials, and others begun to collaborate to plan access in an incremental but integrated manner. Universal design or inclusive design is rapidly becoming more the norm, with planners, architects, and designers incorporating these concepts in newly built environments. Public transportation is now not just about more accessibility in the traditional sense; it is a redefinition of goals—of careful planning and crucial design. Everyone, including PwDs, stands to benefit from universally designed infrastructures, built environments, transportation modes, equipment, and products. Besides, in today's global economy, a convenient, safe, and efficient mass public transportation system is an essential feature of any city and community—and is meant to serve and benefit all people, including the elderly and persons with varying abilities.

REFERENCES

1. Agarwal A, Sachdeva S: Samarthya Centre for Promotion of Barrier Free Environment for People with Disabilities.
2. Ministry of Information and Broadcasting: *India*, 2003, Government of India Annual Report, 2001–2002, Ministry of Social Justice and Empowerment.
3. PAG Consult SB/Japan International Co-operation Agency/Dewan Bandaraya, Kuala Lumpur: *The Study on Pedestrian Friendly City in Kuala Lumpur*, Interim Report, June 1999.
4. UN ESCAP report: *Asian and Pacific Decade of Disabled Persons: Mid-point—Regional Perspectives on Multisector Collaboration and National Coordination*, United Nations, New York, 1999.
5. Naziaty NM and Access Initiative Group: Group discussion report on the elderly, mothers with young children and disabled persons, *Accessible Transportation Seminar*, Kuala Lumpur, Oct 12, 2000.
6. International Special Seminar, Proc *10th Int Conf Mobility and Transport for Elderly and Disabled People (TRANSED 2004)*, Hamamatsu, Japan, May 23, 2004.
7. Yaacob NM: Disability awareness training for local government technical personnel: Experience from Malaysia, *UIA/ARCASIA Seminar Proc "Design for All—an Inclusive Approach."*
8. Report from the Department of Transportation and Communications, Philippines.
9. Hussein H: *Faculty of Built Environment*, Dept Architecture, Univ of Malaya.
10. Eustaquio A: Updating the accessibility law—towards a truly barrier free environment, *UIA/ARCASIA Seminar Proc "Design for All—an Inclusive Approach."*
11. Silva J: Architect, FUAP, Visually Disabled and Representative/Member for Committee on Accessibility, United Architects of the Philippines, Subcommittee on Accessibility/Telecommunication, (NCWDP) and Consultative Advisory Group (NCWDP).
12. Eustaquio A, Chairman, Technical Support Group, IACA (Inter-Agency Committee on Accessibility) Department of Transport and Communications/Road-Transport Report, Memorandum Brief 3: *Philippine Plan of Action for Older Persons*, Japson CR, Road Transportation Planning Division, May 2003.

PART VI

Technologies for Smart Environments

30

Modeling the Well-Being of Older People

Andrew Sixsmith

University of Liverpool, Liverpool, UK

30.1 INTRODUCTION

The potential of new technology for enhancing the quality of life and support the independent living of older people has become increasingly recognized [1]. A key aspect of this is use of information and communication technologies (ICTs) to monitor at-risk elders. This paper focuses on the development of pervasive computing applications and draws on conceptual work carried out within the Care in the Community Virtual Centre (CIC) [2], which is developing technology to monitor long-term activity trends that may indicate changes in the "well-being" of an older person living at home. The aim is to provide information that could be useful to formal and informal caregivers and the clients themselves in helping them to live independently. The CIC Centre comprises a number of related projects to specify, develop, and demonstrate a prototype well-being monitoring system. The chapter has several objectives; it

- Discusses the potential of pervasive computing in monitoring the well-being of older people
- Examines different approaches to research and development (R&D) and suggests the need for a more theory–based approach
- Presents a general model of "well-being" as a framework for guiding R&D in this area
- Presents a specific model or "facet model" that relates the general dimensions of well-being to observable phenomena and activities amenable to monitoring

---

The Engineering Handbook of Smart Technology for Aging, Disability, and Independence,
Edited by A. Helal, M. Mokhtari and B. Abdulrazak
Copyright © 2008 John Wiley & Sons, Inc.

- Provides an example of monitoring depressive symptoms to illustrate the potential benefits of the approach

30.2 PERVASIVE COMPUTING AND MONITORING

The development and widespread use of community alarms [3] was a result of concerns about the safety and security of older people living alone in their homes. These allow older people to raise an alarm if they are unwell or have fallen, simply by pressing a button on their telephone or on a device (e.g., a pendant) that they wear. Benefits include reduced levels of stress and anxiety, reduced hospital admissions and earlier discharge, delay of entry into nursing homes, and reduced need for homecare [3]. However, a significant weakness is that a person who is incapacitated, or is not wearing the alarm device, will be unable to raise the alarm. Developments within ICTs provide the basis for a second generation of home monitoring systems [4]. These use sensors to monitor the person and software to interpret the data generated by the sensors in order to automatically detect emergency situations [5] and generate an alert in a call center or nurse station. A system may include a range of sensors to monitor activity, such as infrared motion detectors, door contact sensors, and pressure mats, similar to those found in home security systems. These devices monitor levels of activity as an indicator of possible illness or incapacity. Sensors in bathrooms and kitchens can be used for hazard detection, such as low temperatures, bath overflow, and unlit gas. A number of systems are now commercially available in the United States and Europe and offer considerable potential for helping older people live independently. However, there are indications that monitoring systems will develop even further, exploiting the potential of "pervasive computing" [6]:

> A concept ... beyond the current "keyboard and screen" interfaces to enable ALL citizens to access IST (Information Society Technology) services wherever they are, whenever they want, and in the form that is most natural for them. It involves new technologies and applications both for the access to, and for the provision of applications and services. It calls for the development of multi-sensorial interfaces that are supported by computing and networking technologies present everywhere and embedded in everyday objects. It also requires new tools and business models for service development and provision and for content creation and delivery.

Research and development in this field includes an intelligent inactivity/fall detector developed within the SIMBAD project [7], based on a low-cost, array-based passive IR sensor. The process is also moving person monitoring away from dedicated tasks, such as hazard detection, to more system-level solutions to support independent living, involving the integration of sensors and computer systems to create "smart spaces." The potential for using sensors in voice recognition and face and gesture recognition also promises a shift to a different level of person–machine interactivity based on natural communication and intuitive system usability. A number of demonstration projects have been set up worldwide to explore the potential of pervasive computing to support older people living at home [8].

Devices and systems for monitoring older people have primarily focused on ensuring safety and security rather than on enhancing quality of life in a more general sense [8]. For instance, most attention has been given to fall detection and automatic shutoff devices. Clearly these are important, but the developments in pervasive computing offer opportunities for more positive uses of technology [8]. The basic idea here is to use pervasive technologies that are able to respond to the activity patterns of the dweller to provide a more supportive and life-enhancing intelligent living environment. This was the stimulus for CIC to develop and implement a system for monitoring the well-being of older people living at home. *Well-being* can be defined in terms of an individual's physical, mental, social, and environmental status with each aspect interacting with the other. A change in the different aspects of well-being may be reflected in an alteration in behavior or the performance of a task or activity. The underlying assumption is that a person's well-being can be determined, at least to some extent, from some observable indicators, such as that person's activity and/or environmental phenomena. Monitoring these may help informal and professional carers to understand the person's needs better and provide more timely and appropriate interventions. A working prototype of the CIC well-being monitoring system has been developed and tested in the United Kingdom.

30.3 THEORY-DRIVEN RESEARCH AND DEVELOPMENT

The potential offered by pervasive computing presents problems as well as opportunities to technology developers. The "pervasive" and "ubiquitous" nature of emerging technology means that it can be embedded in most aspects of everyday life, demanding new approaches to R&D. It is possible to identify a range of different approaches:

30.3.1 Technology-Led

Much of the early R&D was driven by agendas formulated within the engineering and IT communities and within the commercial sector. For example, there may be a vested interest in exploiting a particular piece of technology. Technology developers may have only a limited perspective on the requirements of the user and may impose their own ideas and value judgments about these [9]. The weakness of this approach is that it may fail to address the real needs of users, leading to systems and equipment that are of limited practical use.

30.3.2 Needs-Led

Much of the more recent work has tried to address the problems of the technology driven approach by basing R&D on a "user-centric" analysis of the needs within particular user groups. Approaches and methodologies have been developed to support the kinds of user research required to develop system specifications such as those described by Poulson et al. [10] and Lunn et al. [11]. However, there are certain weaknesses evident in this approach. The concept of "need" is difficult to pin down, while the user requirements research may focus on a specific need and ignore other relevant contextual factors. Moreover, the idea of a "needs-led" approach has arguably become equated to a "problem-led" approach, focusing on the so-called problems experienced by older people. For example, Sixsmith [8] suggests that technology for people with dementia has focused on issues of safety and security at the expense of exploiting opportunities for more positive, life-enhancing interventions. Arguably, these "problems" are problems for the care providers as much as they are for the older persons themselves, leading to a focus on devices and systems that aim to monitor, control, and protect. While the problems of old age should not be underestimated, they are not the only worthwhile avenues for technology development.

30.3.3 Theory-Driven

While the needs-led approach has certainly made more recent R&D more relevant and useful, a third approach is emerging that is based on a wider theoretical understanding of the everyday lives of older people. This simultaneously considers both the perspective of the person (their preferences, desires, experiences, functional limitations, etc.) and the objective circumstances within which they live (support, physical environment, social network, etc.). The benefit is that the approach attempts to consider all relevant factors and to incorporate them within a systematic framework that can be used to scope the problem domain. It is particularly important if the technologic development is to meet the diverse and complex needs of users, particularly if the aim is to improve quality of life. The problem here is that the appropriate theoretical frameworks and relevant empirical knowledge lie within social science, and are not easily accessible to the IT and engineering communities. It is with this in mind that CIC developed a collaborative way of working based on a simple yet robust theoretical model of quality of life that guided the developmental work.

30.4 AN "ECOLOGICAL" MODEL OF QUALITY OF LIFE

While terms such as *well-being* and *quality of life* are commonly used, they are concepts that are not readily defined. The academic literature distinguishes between objective circumstances and subjective factors contributing to quality of life, but beyond this there is no agreed-on definition, and the research reflects a wide range of perspectives, ideas, theories, and methods. Various researchers, including Hughes [12] and Tester et al. [13], have outlined a number of factors relevant to frail older people, such as characteristics of the person [e.g., functional abilities, physical and mental health; social factors (family and social networks); environment (household status, housing conditions, neighborhood; subjective factors such as life satisfaction, psychological well-being, morale, and happiness].

The conceptual modeling of well-being was thus the initial challenge facing CIC. Gerritsen et al. [14] suggest that these models can help to ensure that all the relevant aspects of a problem area are defined and provide ideas about interrelationships between these different aspects. The specific objective in CIC was to develop a model that would be of practical use within the specific problem domain:

- *Be semantically efficient*—the well-being model should be clear and straightforward for use within a multidisciplinary R&D project group, but still represent the key components of well-being.
- *Be robust*—the model should stand up to practical and academic scrutiny and provide a strong justification for the direction of the R&D.
- *Be relevant*—the model should provide information that is directly applicable to the development of intelligent monitoring.

The perspective taken in CIC was to develop what can be called an "ecological" model, based on a comprehensive review of the area, that attempts to combine the objective and subjective aspects of quality of life, but pays particular attention to how these could

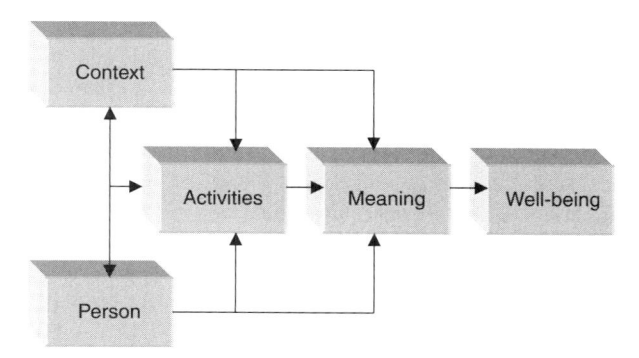

FIGURE 30.1 Ecological model of well-being.

potentially be monitored by the CIC system (Fig. 30.1). The ecological model was particularly appropriate because it focused on the practical aspects of everyday activities (doing), highlighting opportunities for intelligent monitoring. The model is based on the work of researchers such as L. Powell Lawton [15] and Tom Kitwood [16], where activities are influenced by person factors and attributes of the context ("being" factors). How a people derive meaning from their everyday activities and environment is central to their well-being. Positive well-being is where all these factors work together, while conversely apparently minor obstacles in any of them can prevent a positive outcome. The ecological model can be divided into three main domains of well-being: being, doing and experiencing.

30.4.1 "Being" Factors

The term "being" factors refers to the attributes of the older people along with the context within which they live. Person factors include the attributes that have a direct bearing on well-being, such as physical and cognitive functional capacities, general level of health and fitness, and psychological attributes that may help them to adapt to life changes that may occur in later life. Physical illness and mental health, such as depression, are also relevant. Context factors also have an important bearing on well-being by either facilitating or constraining the person's everyday activities. These include the home environment, social network and social support, neighborhood, services available, and financial situation. It is also essential to see person and context as a functional relationship, where features of the home environment emerge as barriers to independence as a person's functional capacities change. For example, stairs and conventional doorways may restrict mobility of wheelchair users, while cookers and heaters may become hazardous for people who are forgetful. Much of the R&D in technology for older people has focused on hazard detection and providing environmental control. Some attention has been given to monitoring the individual, but this remains an important area for research and development; if changes in functional capacities can be identified early, then intervention can be put in place to prevent the breakdown of independent living.

30.4.2 "Doing" Factors

These refer to the activities of a person that can be seen as an outcome of the personal and situational "being" factors. Activities of daily living (ADLs) include the everyday tasks and activities a person needs to do in order to live independently, such as washing, dressing, eating, preparing food, and cleaning. Also important are those activities that represent the person's self-identity, such as personal appearance and grooming. Social interaction is an important aspect, and the particular focus of well-being monitoring is on people who live alone and includes social interaction in the home (e.g., visitors) and the person's engagement with the outside world. Enjoyable activities are of particular importance to the individual, such as hobbies and leisure activities. For some people this may be reading and watching TV, or it may be something more creative, such as artistic and craft activities. There are also other activities that may undermine well-being, including so-called risky and negative activities. "Risky" activities are where the person engages in an activity that may be dangerous in some way, such as using domestic appliances in an incorrect or inappropriate way. "Negative" activities are those where the person consciously engages in activities that may have significant negative outcomes, such as self-harm and neglect. Health-related activities are those that contribute to positively enhancing physical or mental health, such as exercise.

30.4.3 "Experiencing" Factors

These refer to the subjective aspects of well-being, or the subjective meanings, associated with a person's everyday situation and activities and subjective well-being outcomes, such as happiness and life satisfaction. "Meaning" refers to the person's own interpretation of situations or activities through which activities become significant and meaningful. For example, a low level of social contact may be a common situation, but for one person may mean "loneliness," while for another it may mean "peace and quiet." It is clearly impossible to monitor these personal meanings directly. However, they have implications for well-being monitoring, in that the significance of situations and activities can be understood only in the context of the person's subjective perspective. The semantics of an activity are likely to be complex, and it is unlikely that meanings can be determined solely from oberving the activity. The semantics may also depend on a range of factors, such as tacit knowledge about the activity and the personal aims and goals of the person. Some broad generalizations are possible. For example, overall level of activity could be taken as a measure of engaged activity (assertion of desire or will). However, the variation between individuals is likely to be considerable, making judgments about underlying mental states difficult. This places limitations on the idea of well-being monitoring. Any system can be concerned only with observable or instrumentable phenomena, such as a person's activities. It is possible to identify "being" and "doing" factors that may suggest that a person is "at-risk," but these judgments need to be made through consultation with the person or with someone who knows them intimately on either a personal or professional level.

30.5 A FACET MODEL OF WELL-BEING MONITORING

While the ecological model maps out the key domains of well-being, it is still of only limited value for the development of intelligent monitoring, as it does not provide the level of detail in terms of the phenomena and activities for monitoring. In this section a "facet model" of well-being monitoring is presented as a way of linking the general model of well-being to the more specific behavioral phenomena that are amenable to sensing within a pervasive computing environment (Fig. 30.2.). Facet theory [17] is a

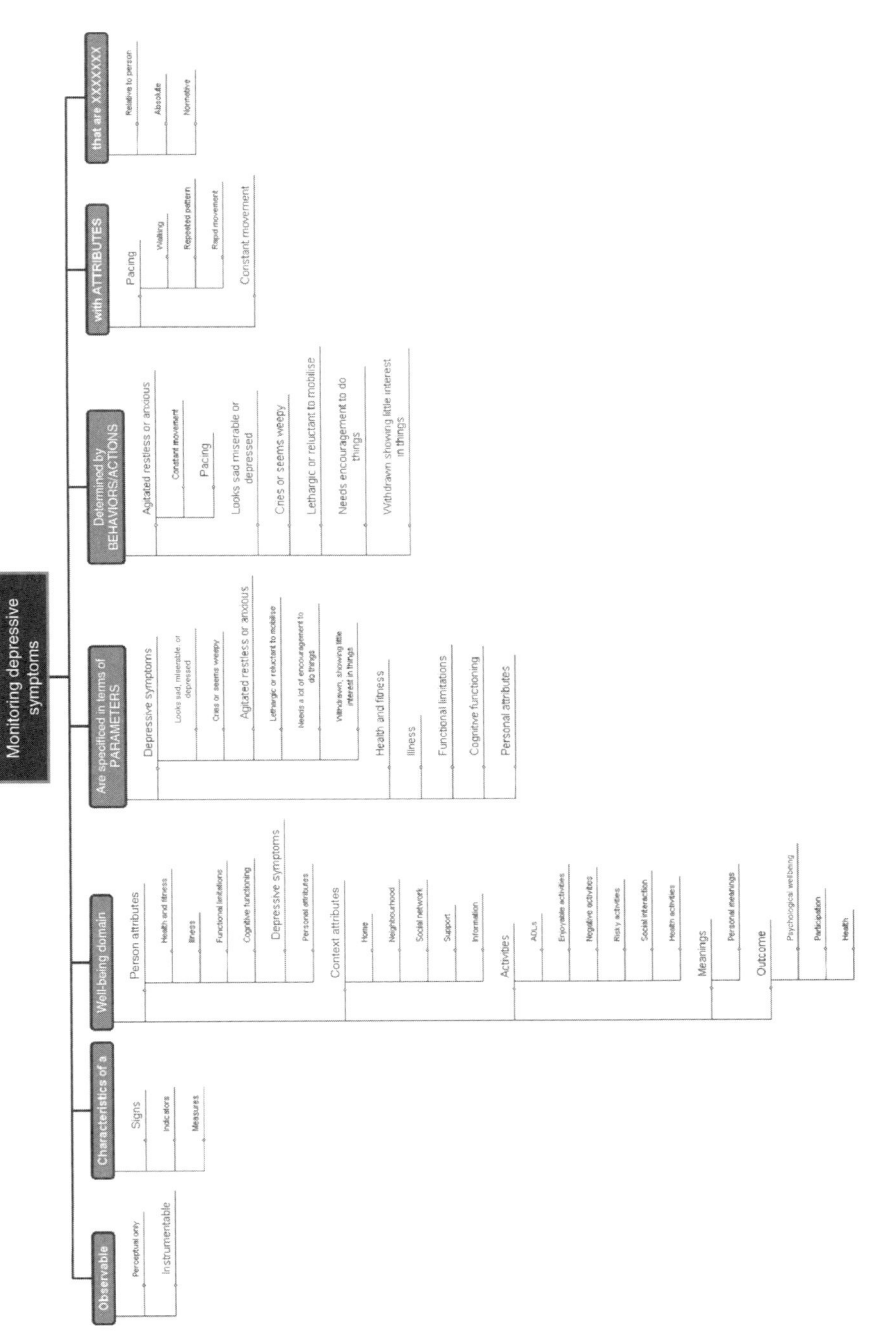

FIGURE 30.2 *Mapping sentence of depressive symptoms.*

research strategy in which theory building and data analysis are viewed as an integral whole, based on a strict definition of items (or facets). The approach is useful because it emphasizes a strict formal definition of behavioral phenomena based on the "necessity of defining the universe of observations to be researched implies that the definitional system should be in a form that facilitates perceiving correspondences with aspects of the empirical data" [18, p. 117].

This has certain requirements: a formal definition of the variables being studied, hypotheses of some specified relationship between the definition and an aspect of the empirical observation, and a rationale for the correspondence between a and b. The definition is given by the facets from which the variables derive. In turn, facets represent the categories within which the "universe of content" (i.e., everything that is relevant to the system that is being considered) can be meaningfully organized as a conceptually coherent system. The value of this approach is that it provides a metatheoretic framework for empirical research that provides clear "rules" for making the transition between conceptual scheme and empirical observation. Theory building and empirical observation and research are thus seen as an integral whole, where the whole process is confirmatory, where hypotheses, data selection, and data observation are coherent and complementary. A key aspect to this is that all relevant phenomena need to be incorporated within the content universe and that the relationships. Guttman [19] summarizes facet theory as an "effective approach for the fruitful design of content, leading to appropriate data analysis techniques and producing laws of human behaviour in a cumulative fashion. One by-product is the establishment of more solid bases for policy decisions."

This "byproduct" is itself a major consideration when undertaking applied research. If it is the task of the researcher to supply decisionmakers (e.g., people who are responsible for the care and support of older people) with coherent and usable information about some area of concern, then it is important that all relevant issues are incorporated within the content universe. There is a tendency to simplify phenomena for various reasons. For example, the need for scientific "rigor" may actually mean that many important issues are excluded from user research, because they are not amenable to measurement. There is also a tendency to conceive phenomena as "problems" to facilitate practical intervention (e.g., technologies or services) in the way that reinforces conventional practice and received wisdom. This harks back to the earlier discussion of "needs," where the conceptualization of the problem may be based more on the requirements of the service provider than on the user. While this may be helpful in improving the operations of existing systems and services, it fails to address alternative approaches and new ideas about the help and support provided to older people. However, there is an equal problem of making something too complex and all-embracing, where the complexity ultimately undermines any practical action. The "trick," therefore, is to define any theoretical framework in a way that preserves the integrity of the phenomena in question, while at the same time presenting these ideas so that they are understandable and accessible. Canter [20] suggests that facet theory is useful in this sense because it facilitates "the exploration of applied problems and generates results which are potentially more open to application: more open in the sense that they have a form and structure which is more synomorphic with the form and structure of decision-making than are results of conventional approaches to research."

One way of summarizing the facet structure of a system or phenomenon is in the "mapping sentence." This is a ordinary-language statement of the range of a problem-area, including the connections between its component facets [17]. A "facet" is any category or domain of a system, as long as the different elements within the facet are mutually exclusive. In effect, it provides a rigorous framework for formally defining and describing the variables being examined within a problem-area. The facet model shown in Figure 30.2 is effectively a "mapping sentence" for well-being monitoring. It is worthwhile to examine each of the facets within the mapping sentence in turn.

30.5.1 Observable ...

This refers to whether it is possible to instrument the activities or phenomena in question. As discussed above, the "experiential" domain of the well-being model refers to inner states of mind that cannot be directly monitored, although there may be behavioral characteristics that reflect these inner states. There may be technical limitations as to whether it is possible to develop and implement sensors to monitor some specific activity. Also there may be practical limitations placed on the monitoring system, such as cost restrictions, power consumption, and installation and maintenance requirements.

30.5.2 Characteristics ...

The development of intelligent monitoring systems highlights a crucial divergence between disciplinary domains; the information required by ICT engineers cannot easily be extracted from the knowledge base within behavioral science. Indeed, the nature and level of the available data may be inadequate, particularly with respect to precise definitions of behavioral phenomena. Much of this knowledge is tacit, based on professional expertise or basic human understanding; for example, does the person "look sad" or "seem weepy"? The interaction between engineering and behavioral science is therefore opening up whole new avenues of research; monitoring technologies have the potential to provide huge amounts of data on people's everyday activities, while behavioral researchers need to meet the challenge of developing new approaches to describing and measuring phenomena. In the mapping sentence, a range of different ways of determining phenomena are relevant to sensing:

- *Signifiers.* These are "clues" that we can make judgments about an activity. However, these may be unsubstantiated and based on expertise or "best guesses." These may also be based on common sense and general human experience. The key thing here is that they signify the performance of some activity, but have no basis in scientific evidence.
- *Indicators.* These are validated procedures for inferring something indirectly from observable phenomena, where there is some level of statistical confidence about the conclusions that are drawn. There are well-established protocols for validating indicators within social and behavioral science, covering criteria such as reliability or sensitivity. Equivalent protocols are required for the inferences made by intelligent monitoring systems. An example of this is the reliability of a fall detector reported by Sixsmith and Johnson [7], which gives probabilities of false positives and false negatives within the system.
- *Measures.* These are direct measurements of something that has a precise and definite outcome. An example is a biometric measure, such as heart rate or blood pressure monitoring.

Presently, the majority of the phenomena and activities within the ecological model could be monitored only at the level of "signifiers." For example, social participation may be signified by the number of visitors into a person's home or the amount of time a person spends out of the home. However, these may not give a wholly reliable picture of a person's interaction with others. Moreover, the phenomena covered by the ecological model are often inherently qualitative in nature and involve the domain of "meanings" and are not measurable. Again, the example of social participation is illustrative; a person may have numerous interactions but may perceived them as being superficial and of only limited personal value.

30.5.3 Well-being Domain . . .

This refers to the key quality of life domains outlined in the ecological model. However, in the facet model, these have been populated to include a range of relevant components for each of the facets of well-being, based on reviews of relevant literature. For example, the facet of person factors includes health and fitness, illness, functional limitations, cognitive functioning, depressive symptoms, and personal attributes. It would also be possible to populate these through carrying out surveys or interviews with users, which would be particularly useful if specific population groups were being targeted, for example, people with specific illnesses or conditions. However, the model does provide a flexible framework for including any relevant factors.

30.5.4 Parameters

These refer to the specific activities to be monitored by the well-being system. The assessment of human states and activities is generally done through self-report, such as interviews, or through observation by human experts who have been trained within the different clinical and social care disciplines, for example occupational therapists. The key issue here is that the well-being system will have to be based on observable phenomena. Some aspects of well-being can be relatively easily monitored through direct observation of behaviors. Others are less amenable, referring to inner states or where behavioral outcomes are unclear or ambiguous. Depressive symptoms are an example of the latter and are discussed in more detail below.

30.5.5 Behavior and Actions

Once the key observable phenomena have been identified, then the specific behaviors or actions that signify these need to be defined in more detail. Considerable knowledge exists within the clinical and social care professions in the assessment of a person's needs, functional limitations, and so on. In other areas, considerably less knowledge exists on the behavioral outcomes associated with the various well-being facets. The key here is the need to develop sets of observable activities that can reliably map back on to the various well-being facets described above.

30.5.6 Attributes . . .

It is at this point where current knowledge within social and clinical science is less able to provide the necessary information. As will be discussed in Section 30.6, relatively little observational research has been carried out that provides clear information about the specific behavioral attributes of an activity. However, it is also this point where specific information is required so that sensor data analysis algorithms can be developed that are capable of identifying these behaviors. This represents a key challenge to well-being monitoring that will involve behavioral and clinical scientists working closely with IT and engineering personnel to generate the appropriate information. At the current time, R&D may have to concentrate on what is relatively easily achievable in the short term, based on any current knowledge that is available.

30.5.7 Relative or Absolute Values

This last point leads to another issue in the monitoring of activities. It may be possible to measure something, but what would this actually signify? For example, the number of interactions with others may be an indicator of social participation, but it would be difficult to conceive an actual value that could discriminate between what might be a "good" or "inadequate" level. In the mapping sentence this is covered in item "relative/absolute." Absolute values are those where we could actually say "good" or "bad", perhaps in the area of biometrics. However, few judgments are likely to be amenable to this sort of treatment. Another approach could be described as "normative," where typical or average patterns are used as benchmarks. People with levels of social interaction significantly lower than the general norm could be seen as "socially isolated" and at risk of experiencing loneliness. However, the complexity of human experience and the huge variation between individuals may make this a dubious approach. Ultimately, the use of individualized parameters may be the only logical route. This last approach that has been adopted within intelligent monitoring has been to determine "typical" patterns of activities for a specific person, based on data collected over a period of time. If the system then detects patterns of activity that are outside these typical patterns, then the system flags this up as an "alert." The huge capacity of these systems to routinely log activities over extended periods of time makes this possible, compared to previous times when such an undertaking would rely on human observation. However, it is still not possible to say definitively whether any activity level is "good" or "bad," and inevitably any "alert" will require reference back to the person concerned or to someone with close knowledge of that person's needs. This suggests that any system monitoring human activity will have to be embedded within any wider knowledge system about the person. In the case of older people, the clinical and/or social care assessment and case management process would provide this larger framework. The intimate knowledge held by family caregivers is also relevant. In both cases, this knowledge and understanding is essential to the interpretation of activity data. The CIC Virtual Centre has devoted considerable effort to developing graphical user interfaces that will provide activity data to care assessors and caregivers and an easily digestible form that can be used to enhance the care and support that is provided to the older person [21].

30.6 EXAMPLE: MODELING OF DEPRESSIVE SYMPTOMS

The aim of the facet model was to represent the universe of content in a systematic and efficient way, that is, to make sure that all the components were included in the simplest way possible. This task is, in fact, very ambitious; the idea of quality of life is all-encompassing, touching on all aspects of person and context, objective and subjective factors. Certainly, there may be oversimplifications, and the ecological model is open for further development. However, the facet model presents a huge challenge if all the different facets were to be populated. The CIC Centre has made a start by addressing a few key activities that are representative of well-being.

In this section, the example of modeling depressive symptoms is used to illustrate the relationship between the general well-being domains and the specific attributes that contribute to a person's well-being as summarized in the mapping sentence. The presence of depressive symptoms is very closely associated with a poor overall quality of life. Indeed, depression may be an overriding factor determining the well-being of a person, irrespective of any of the other factors. In the ecological model, depression is identified as a person factor (although it is also possible to see it as an outcome). Prevalence of depression within the older (65%) population is about 15%, although there are variations associated with age, sex, and other demographic variables [22]. However, there are considerable problems associated with the diagnosis and treatment of depression among older people. The fact that depression is "hidden" means that it is often unrecognized and remains untreated.

Various scales, such as the geriatric depression scale [23] and the geriatric mental state (GMS) exam [24] have been devised for screening purposes. These involve respondents answering a series of questions on symptoms such as feelings of guilt, irritability, and concentration. However, these kinds of approaches have inherent weaknesses. For example, respondents may not be telling the truth, or their perspectives on life may be affected by having to fill in the questionnaire. Often assessments are done in unfamiliar environments and also represent the situation only at the specific time of administration of the test. In this context, there may be considerable potential in monitoring observable behavior patterns as indicators of depression among elderly people living in their own homes in the community, as this might provide a more accurate view of the person, or at least provide additional information on which clinical judgments can be made. One should also consider the potential benefits of the real-time monitoring of depressive symptoms. For example, it may be possible to identify behaviors that are associated with self-harm, self-neglect, or even suicide (in the general model, these are defined as "negative activities"). Real-time monitoring may also provide useful information about the etiology of depression, by aiding the identification of possible contributory factors within the person's everyday life. This parallels interesting work using experience sampling methodology, where patients are asked to log their activities, thoughts, and feelings at random points in the day in order to provide clues to environmental factors that may affect their experience of depression.

Of particular relevance to well-being modeling is a depression screening protocol devised by Hammond and associates [25], which asks third-party informants (such as a nurse or family caregiver) to answer "yes" or "no" to the following questions:

- Does the person look sad miserable or depressed?
- Does the person ever cry or seem weepy?
- Does person seem agitated, restless, or anxious?
- Is the person lethargic or reluctant to mobilize?
- Does the person need a lot of encouragement to do things for him/her-self?
- Does the person seem withdrawn, showing little interest in things?

It may be possible to model and instrument some of these. For example, a facial recognition system could be trained to determine whether the person looked "sad," although this would present considerable challenges at the current time. Some of the other behaviors may be more amenable to monitoring; it may be possible to determine when a person might be crying. However, answering the questionnaire depends largely on the informant's subjective evaluation of each item. Within intelligent monitoring, a more precise definition of what should be observed is required. While an intelligent monitoring system would be essentially making similar judgments, based on observing the person over a period of time (e.g., whether the person seems lethargic or withdrawn), the system would require some clear criteria for making these judgments on the basis of instrumentable phenomena.

While there are no well-tested observable indicators of depressive symptoms, a potentially useful signifier may be agitation or restlessness. The modeling of this requires us to drill further down to identify specific behaviors with particular observable attributes. In the mapping sentence, agitation is characterized by a number of possible behaviors, including pacing and constant movement. Deconstructing this further, the behavior "pacing" can be characterized by particular attributes. First, pacing involves the person walking around. However, a monitoring system would have to be able to discriminate walking associated with "pacing" from nonpathologic walking activities. Pacing can be further characterized by a more rapid gait associated with agitation, while the pattern of movement may be repeated several times. Pacing may occur in particular locations within the house, or at particular times of day. It may be characterized as a very specific activity, with no other ancillary activities associated with it. However, a clear definition of "pacing" would require more detailed observational research to identify all the associated behavioral attributes required by the monitoring system. Despite this, there is considerable potential for monitoring agitation-related activities such as pacing as signifiers of possible depressive symptoms.

30.7 CONCLUSION

This chapter has examined the potential of pervasive computing for the monitoring of well-being among older people, with a view to providing information that will be useful in the provision of care and support to enhance quality of life and independence. While the potential of this kind of technology has been widely recognized, the whole area presents considerable conceptual and technical challenges, especially if these systems are to meet the real needs of users. This chapter has presented two models that are potentially useful in guiding research and development in this area: (1) an *ecological model* of well-being, which was presented to define the key domains of "well-being"—the value of this approach is that it focuses on practical aspects of everyday activities of the person, highlighting opportunities for technology interventions to support these activities; and (2) a *mapping sentence*, which was developed to provide the detail required to move from the general level provided by the ecological model to the specific level of the observable phenomena and behaviors associated with well-being. The all-embracing scope of the ecological model, the behavioral detail, and the problems associated with instrumentation, data analysis, and interpretation present huge challenges to the idea of "well-being monitoring." However, the selection of a few powerful signifiers may be a valuable first step in this area. Current work being carried out in the CIC Virtual Centre

[2] has involved the deployment of a demonstrator system, based on the monitoring of six key signifiers of well-being:

- Leaving and returning home (category: social interaction)
- Visitors (category: social interaction)
- Preparing food and eating (category: ADLs)
- Sleeping patterns (category: ADLs)
- Personal appearance (category: personal goals)
- Leisure activities (category: personal goals)

The preliminary results of some user trials has provided enough evidence about the value of the approach to suggest that it is an avenue for further development and more extensive user trials, prior to practical implementation in a social care setting. The specific example of monitoring depressive symptoms (in Section 30.6) also illustrates the considerable potential that intelligent monitoring might have with respect to both (1) the general monitoring of "well-being" and (2) clinical and social care assessment and intervention. The chapter did point to some key weaknesses in the approach, notably the lack of statistical validity of the so-called signifiers. However, the weaknesses of existing assessment procedures outlined earlier are noteworthy. In this context, intelligent monitoring could provide an additional or complementary dataset on which assessments and diagnoses could be made. Also noteworthy are the strengths of the approach:

- *Naturalistic Settings.* The data are collected from the person's own living place, rather than in a clinical setting. This makes it more difficult for symptoms to be "hidden."
- *Data collected over Time.* The capacity to routinely collect data means that activity patterns can be observed over time, rather than at a specific moment.
- *High Volume of Data.* Routine data collection using sensor-based systems is able to build up a much more extensive database compared with human observation.
- *Triangulation of Measures.* A range of signifiers or indicators can be used, providing confirmatory evidence.
- *Exogenous Interpretation.* The activity data can be fed back and assessed by an informant, such as the person her/him-self, a family caregivers, or a professional.

Taken together, these can provide strong evidence about depression. While these may be only "signifiers," the value as a data source for both clinical assessment and research should not be underestimated, and analogies can be made with alternative models of validity within qualitative research [26] such as "thick data" and "extended engagement." The point here is that well-being monitoring can provide additional complementary information from sources that are currently not accessible. However, the limitations of well-being monitoring have to be considered, especially the tenuous link between observable actions and the subjective meaning of those actions. Thus, any information from the well-being monitoring system has to feed into some kind of client-centered decisionmaking process. For example, an individual client will have a care plan that specifies that person's individual needs and goals, providing criteria for judging the possible significance of an activity. Users of the well-being data (care organizers, family caregivers) would also be able to use their knowledge to interpret the situation. Of course, consulting the elderly persons themselves can provide the best interpretation, but this may not be possible for people with cognitive impairments.

The key issue underlying this chapter lies in the need to bridge the gap between the knowledge systems of social scientists and clinicians (who have knowledge—theories and empirical information) and ICT engineers who need to be able to use this knowledge to create useful systems and devices to improve the quality of life of users. This chapter has illustrated the value of conceptual modeling in providing a theoretical base for user requirements research and the need for a systematic approach to transforming higher-level theoretical and conceptual frameworks into clear definitions of empirical phenomena.

REFERENCES

1. US Department of Commerce: *Technology and Innovation in an Emerging Senior/Boomer Marketplace*, US Department of Commerce, Technology Administration, Washington DC, 2005.
2. Brown S, Hine N, Sixsmith A, Garner P: Care in the community, *BT Technol J* **22**(3):56–64 (2004).
3. Fisk M: *Social Alarms to Telecare*, Policy Press, Bristol, UK, (2003).
4. Doughty K, Cameron K, Garner P: Three generations of telecare for the elderly, *J Telemed Telecare* **2**(2):71–80 (1996).
5. Sixsmith A: An evaluation of an intelligent home monitoring system, *J Telemed Telecare* **6**:63–72 (2000).
6. European Commission: *Information Society Technologies: Workplan 2003–2004*, 2003 (ftp://ftp.cordis.lu/pub/ist/docs/wp2003-04_final.pdf Accessed 12/4/05).
7. Sixsmith A, Johnson N: A smart sensor to detect falls of the elderly, *IEEE Pervas Comput* **3**(2):42–47 April–June, (2004).
8. Sixsmith A: New technologies to support independent living and quality of life for people with dementia, *Alzheimer's Care Q*, **7**(3):194–202 (2006).
9. Sixsmith A, Sixsmith J: Smart home technologies: Meeting whose needs? *J Telemed and Telecare* **6**(Suppl 1):190–192 (2000).
10. Poulson D, Ashby M, Robinson S: *USERfit: A Practical Handbook on User-Centered Design for Assistive Technology*, European Commission, Brussels, (1996).
11. Lunn K, Sixsmith A, Lindsay A, Vaarama V: Traceability in requirements through process modeling, applied to social care applications, *Inform Software Technol* **45**(15):1045–1052 (2003).
12. Hughes B: Quality of life, in Peace S, ed *Researching Social Gerontology*, Sage, London, (1990).
13. Tester S, Hubbard G, Downs M, MacDonald C, Murphy J: Exploring perceptions of quality of life of frail older people during and after their transition to institutional care, *Research Findings 24, Growing Older Project*, (available at www.shef.ac.uk/uni/projects/gop/GOFindings24.pdf; accessed 12/4/06).
14. Gerritsen D, Steverink N, Ooms M, Ribbe M: Finding a useful conceptual basis for enhancing the quality of life of nursing home residents, *Qual Life Res*, **13**:611–624 (2004).
15. Lawton MP: A multidimensional view of quality of life in frail elders, in Birren J, Lubben J, Rowe J, Deutchman D, eds, *The Concept of Measurement of Quality of Life in Frail Elders*, Academic Press, San Diego, (1991), pp 3–27.
16. Kitwood T: *Dementia Reconsidered: The Person Comes First*, Open Univ Press, Buckingham, UK, (1997).

17. Shye S: *Theory Construction and Data Analysis in the Behavioral Sciences*, Josey-Bass, San Francisco, (1978).
18. Levy S: Use of the mapping sentence for co-ordinating theory and research, *Qual Quant* **10**:117–125 (1976).
19. Guttman L: New developments in integrating test design and analysis, 40th *Int Conf Testing Problems*, New York, (1979).
20. Canter D: The potential of facet theory for applied social psychology, *Qual Quant* **17**:35–67 (1983).
21. Brown S, Sixsmith A, Garner P: Care in the community—well-being demonstrator, in *NWTM Perspectives Pervasive Computing*, IEE, London; 2005, pp 157–162.
22. Forum: *Older Americans 2004–Key Indicators of Well-being*, Federal Interagency on Aging Related Statistics, Washington, DC, (2004).
23. Hoyle MT, Alessi CA, Harker JO: Development and testing of a five-item version of the Geriatric Depression Scale, *J Am Geriatr Soc* **47**:873–878 (1999).
24. Copeland J, Kelleher M: Kellet J A semi-structured clinical interview for the assessment of diagnosis and mental state in the elderly: The geriatric mental state schedule, *Psychol Med* **6**:439–449 (1976).
25. Hammond M, O'Keeffe S, Barer D: Development and validation of a brief observer-rated screening scale for depression in elderly medical patients, Age Aging **29**:511–515 (2000).
26. Lincoln Y, Guba E: But is it rigorous? Trustworthiness and authenticity in naturalistic evaluation, in Williams D, ed, *Naturalistic Evaluation*, Jossey-Bass, San Francisco, 1986, pp 73–84.

31

Context Awareness

Jadwiga Indulska and Karen Henricksen
University of Queensland, Australia

31.1 INTRODUCTION

As shown in the previous chapters, the range of pervasive computing technology available to support the aging and disabled population continues to evolve, allowing for an increasing variety of wireless sensors, devices, and actuators to be deployed to produce assistive "smart spaces." Software applications embedded in smart spaces can intelligently assist elderly or disabled people in a variety of tasks. They can support an individual's healthcare needs and activities of daily living, while extending social interaction, environment control, and information flow to family and caregivers. This needs to be achieved without compromising an individual's medical care, privacy, or security, and should allow an individual to maintain maximal independence. Variations in cognitive and physical capability also need to be considered.

Software applications for smart spaces require a degree of autonomous behavior in order to adapt to changes in operating conditions (e.g., to changes in sensed data such as data about the user's current location, differences in user profiles, or changes in user priorities). Such adaptive applications are called context-aware applications, as they are able to monitor and evaluate the context in which they operate and adapt if the context changes. Due to the variety of user activities and capabilities that should be intelligently supported, and the heterogeneity of sensors, computing devices, communication technologies, and interaction protocols between devices, these applications require a rich set of context information.

In this chapter, we explore the use of context information to enable a wide variety of context-aware applications, including applications supporting independent living

---

The Engineering Handbook of Smart Technology for Aging, Disability, and Independence,
Edited by A. Helal, M. Mokhtari and B. Abdulrazak
Copyright © 2008 John Wiley & Sons, Inc.

of elderly or disabled people. First, we explore definitions of context information and discuss its role in context-aware applications, both in general and in smart technologies for aging/disability. We also discuss the importance of formal context models and the requirements that such models should meet, and provide an overview of various approaches for modeling context information. Finally, we discuss the use of software infrastructure to support context-aware applications by assisting with tasks such as gathering and evaluating context information.

31.2 CONTEXT DEFINITIONS AND EXAMPLES

The term *context* is loaded with a wide variety of meanings. Various areas of computer science differ in their understandings of context, but even in the research community working on context-aware adaptive applications there is no consensus. Dey [1] presents a survey of alternative views of context, which are largely imprecise and indirect, typically defining context by synonym or example. Common examples of context are location, time, temperature, noise level, user activity, and a plethora of information related to the computing environment, including computing devices and their characteristics, network connectivity, communication bandwidth, and so on.

Dey also offers the following definition, which is now widely (but not universally) accepted in the field:

> Context is any information that can be used to characterize the situation of an entity. An entity is a person, place, or object that is considered relevant to the interaction between a user and an application, including the user and applications themselves.

The meaning of "the situation of an entity" is never precisely defined by Dey, but instead is illustrated through simple examples (e.g., presence of other people near the user in the case of a mobile tour guide application). Situations can be either simple (e.g., determined from a single context fact that describes where a particular person is located) or complex (constructed from many context facts, as in the case of a situation involving a person lying motionless in the middle of a room, which is inferred from the readings of several sensors).

One reason for the lack of consensus and precision in context definitions is the lack of clear separation between the concepts of context, context modeling and context information. While *context* is difficult to define, *context models* and *information* are well defined and understood. The latter two are of primary interest when constructing context-aware systems. We use the following definitions:

- The *context* of a computing application (such as a patient-monitoring application) is the set of circumstances surrounding it that are potentially relevant to its execution.
- A *context model* identifies a concrete subset of the context that is realistically attainable from sensors, applications, and users, and able to be exploited in the execution of the application. The context model that is employed by a given context-aware application can be specified by the application developer (although it need not be fixed at design time, but can instead evolve as required).
- *Context information* is a set of data, gathered from sensors and users, that conforms, to a context model. This provides a snapshot that approximates the state, at a given

point in time, of the subset of the context encompassed by the model. Context information often takes the form of a set of context facts.

Context information can be gathered from a variety of sources. These include

- *Sensors*, including sensors embedded in the home or carried by occupants. Examples of the former are wall-mounted microphones or cameras, while the latter category includes positioning devices such as location badges. Sensors may also be logical rather than physical, as in the case of a software sensor that monitors activity on a computer according to the frequency of keystrokes.
- *Profiles* describing capabilities of hardware devices or preferences of users.
- *Applications* that report their current state, such as whether they are actively being used and for what task, for use in adaptation decisions by other applications.
- *Data fusion/interpretation services*, which combine or reason about context information to derive higher-level information, including situations of the kind described earlier.

Context sources of these types produce information of varying degrees of quality, with varying update/refresh rates. Issues related to the quality of information provided by context sources will be discussed later in Section 31.5.1.

We define a *context-aware application* as a computing application that uses context information in order to automatically adapt its behavior to match the situation. In the same fashion, a *context-aware system* is a computing system (e.g., one or more context-aware applications and supporting hardware and software) that exhibits similar adaptive capabilities. Context-aware applications are reactive applications—that is, they invoke adaptation actions in response to context changes. However, as well as being reactive, they should be pro-active in anticipation of user needs.

31.3 ROLE OF CONTEXT IN SMART TECHNOLOGIES FOR AGING, DISABILITY, AND INDEPENDENCE

Context-aware applications can intelligently support users in a variety of tasks, including tasks that promote independent living of elderly or disabled people. Context-aware applications can create smart home environments, provide healthcare, services, and also support user tasks. Their functionality may range from hiding heterogeneity of devices and communication technologies (e.g., by supporting seamless behavior regardless of device or network changes) to more complex support for independent living of the elderly/disabled. The latter may include seamless control of sensors and appliances, support for daily activities (e.g., by facilitating remote help from family or local community members), health monitoring, and social interactions. Below we describe some common classes of application for independent living.

Flexible Communication. Such applications provide instant communication with a family member, friend, or healthworker, achieved using context-aware choice of communication channel (telephone, SMS, etc.) according to the current activity, available communication devices, and preferences of the communicating people.

Support for Social Interactions and Virtual Communities. Such applications have diverse goals, but are concerned primarily with providing support for independent living in communities of elderly people and may include

- Assistance with everyday tasks by remote family or community members
- Dynamic formation of groups of people who are interested in activities such as shopping or playing chess based on their preferences and availability
- Awareness of the activities of others in nearby homes using abstract visual representations, helping to minimize isolation, and providing assurances of others' well-being.

Smart Spaces. Such spaces can provide automatic configuration and reconfiguration of assistive devices and home appliances in order to adapt their functionality/behavior to user needs and preferences.

Multimodal Assistive Technologies and Home Appliances. Context-sensitive adaptive interfaces can assist individuals by providing alternate modes of interaction with common devices such as phones, microwaves, and television sets.

Healthcare Applications. These applications can provide health monitoring, accident monitoring, behavioral trend monitoring, and cognitive health monitoring. Other healthcare applications provide reminders for eating, taking medications, and a variety of other tasks and activities.

31.4 DEVELOPING CONTEXT-AWARE APPLICATIONS AND SYSTEMS

Although context-aware applications have the potential to support independent living in innovative ways, as shown by the example applications just discussed, current deployments are limited. One of the challenges inhibiting the development and deployment of context-aware applications is their complexity. Context-aware systems involve a variety of cooperating hardware and software components, including sensors, additional devices such as actuators and user input/output devices, and various pieces of application software, all communicating via wired or wireless networks.

In early context-aware systems, each application was directly responsible for communicating with sensors, interpreting the sensor outputs to determine the context, and adapting itself (or the environment, via actuators). An example application that follows this approach is shown in Figure 31.1. The application provides monitoring of activity in the home, and generates alerts when abnormal circumstances arise. The application can accept explicit input from the user via a 'panic button', which forces an alert to be produced. However, the application also continuously tracks the user's activity via sensors embedded in the home or carried by the user. These include

- A location badge (i.e., an "active bat" [2] or similar device), which can estimate the user's position in the home
- "Smart" light switches, which can report their current status (i.e., on or off)

As the application has been developed in a naive way, without using an explicit context model or supporting software infrastructure (both of which are discussed further later in this section), it communicates directly with the sensors and processes the raw sensor outputs to determine when alerts are required. This entails remote communication using

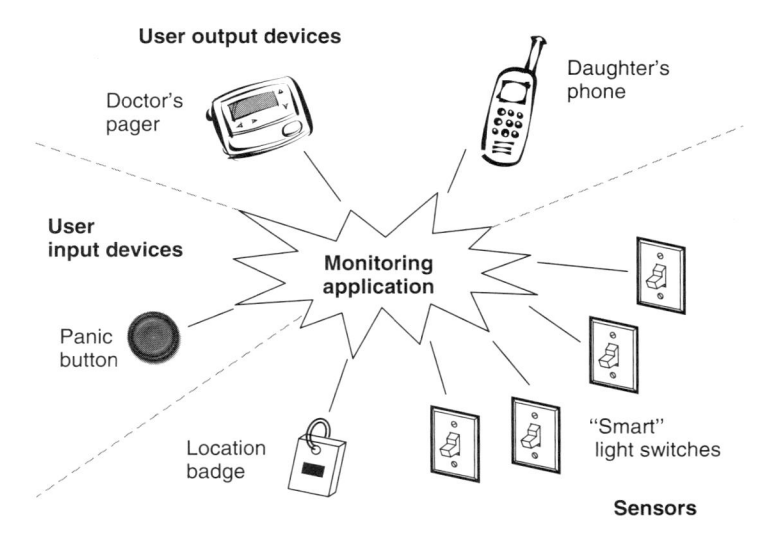

FIGURE 31.1 Architecture of a monitoring application for independent living.

a variety of networking protocols, polling sensors at regular intervals, handling sensor errors, and interpreting sensor outputs (e.g., mapping positioning information to symbolic locations, such as names of rooms in the house). In addition, the application incorporates algorithms that learn patterns of "normal" versus "abnormal" behavior. When abnormal behavior is detected, such as the user remaining motionless for a long time or not switching lights off at the usual time, the application sends alerts to appropriate output devices, such as a family member's mobile phone or (in serious cases) a physician's paging device.

In this example system, the software used to interface with the sensors and the algorithms used to interpret the sensor outputs are directly incorporated into the application software, making these components difficult to modify, extend, share or reuse. For example, adding new hardware, such as embedded microphones for enhanced activity tracking, involves substantially extending the application software, while developing a second "smart home" application, such as an appliance controller that switches devices on or off according to the user's location and activity, involves duplicating part of the monitoring functionality. Moreover, applying this software engineering approach to applications that involve many types of sensors or sophisticated interpretation algorithms can easily yield large and complex pieces of software.

For these reasons, context-aware applications are today developed using a variety of abstractions and supporting pieces of software infrastructure that can be shared between applications. Typically, these include explicit, high-level context models, which provide a uniform and integrated description of context information gathered from various sources, as well as software components that populate the context models by gathering and interpreting information on behalf of applications. Figure 31.2 shows how these components modify the architecture of the monitoring system described earlier. In the new architecture, the application queries a high-level context model, stored in a context repository, to determine the user's symbolic location and the status of all light switches in the house, rather than obtaining separate low-level information from each sensor. The interpretation

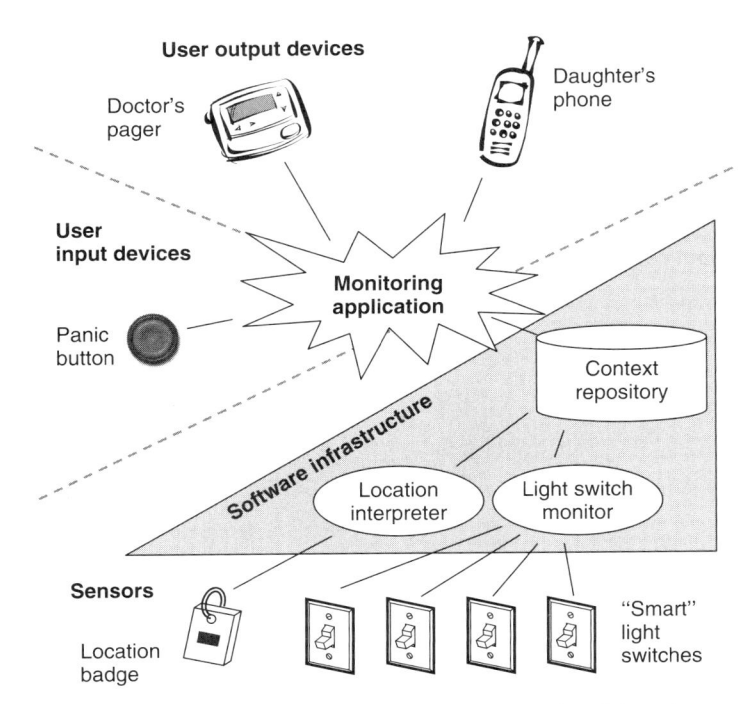

FIGURE 31.2 Architecture of a monitoring application for independent living when a context model and basic software infrastructure are incorporated.

of the sensor outputs occurs in separate software components that feed information into the context repository. These components, together with the context repository, make up the software infrastructure that supports the application. This architecture eliminates the need for the application software to handle sensor errors or implement multiple networking protocols for communicating with sensors. In addition, the context model can be extended when new sensors are added to the home, and can be shared by any number of context-aware applications. Note that, in this case, the software infrastructure is quite simple. More sophisticated forms of infrastructure are described later in this chapter.

The following sections review the current state of the art in context modeling (Section 31.5) and software infrastructure for context-aware systems (Section 31.6).

31.5 CONTEXT MODELING

Context modeling aims to produce a formal or semiformal description of the context information present in a context-aware system. As discussed in Section 31.2, this context information can include information derived from sensors as well as a variety of other sources, such as context-aware applications and user profiles. By providing a uniform description of types of context information, as well as runtime instantiations of the types (context facts), context information from various sources can be easily combined, queried, and reasoned about. This promotes sharing and exchange of information between applications, and provides information representations that are straightforward for applications to process compared to other formats such as streams of raw sensor output.

A variety of context modeling approaches have been proposed. These vary according to the prior technologies or standards with which they are aligned and the aspects of the software engineering process they address. For example, some modeling approaches are aligned with World Wide Web Consortium (W3C) standards such as the Web Ontology Language (OWL) [3], while others are based on database modeling techniques. Similarly, some aim to support requirements analysis (i.e., identification of the kinds of context information needed for a particular context-aware application, and with what level of quality), while others are intended for run-time representation and reasoning. This section discusses some general requirements for context-modeling approaches, followed by a survey of some of the approaches that have been proposed.

31.5.1 Requirements

In order to be broadly applicable to a variety of context-aware applications and to serve as useful abstractions for software engineering as discussed in Section 31.4, context-modeling approaches should meet the following requirements.

31.5.1.1 Support for Imperfect Context Information

A common problem in context-aware systems is the presence of imperfect context information. For example, problems with sensor-derived information can arise as a result of sensor failures, power shortage, noise in the environment, faulty sensor installation, or inaccuracy in the algorithms used to abstract context information from sensor outputs. Similarly, user- or application-supplied information can be subject to problems such as staleness.

Consequently, when modeling context, it is necessary to be able to represent

- Information that is incomplete.
- Information that is imprecise.
- Information that is ambiguous (e.g., conflicting location reports provided by different location sensors).
- Quality indicators (information source, timeliness, granularity, sensor accuracy, etc.) for information that may be imprecise or erroneous. These can be used by context-aware applications to determine when to trust the available context information, and can also be used to trace faulty context information back to malfunctioning sensors, which can then be repaired or replaced.

Applications should be able to effectively query and reason about the available context information, so as to continue operating satisfactorily even when that information is incomplete, imprecise, ambiguous, or otherwise imperfect.

31.5.1.2 Support for Context Histories

Context-aware applications often require not only information about the current context but also past or future contexts. Therefore, context-modeling techniques must provide natural ways for modeling histories of information, and applications should be capable of querying and reasoning over these histories. Histories can be used to detect patterns in user behavior and predict future requirements, as seen in the monitoring application described in Section 31.4.

31.5.1.3 Support for Software Engineering

A key role of context models is to simplify and introduce greater structure into the task of developing context-aware applications. The greatest benefit is often derived when a formal or semiformal context model is introduced early in the software engineering lifecycle and refined incrementally over the lifecycle. Early in the lifecycle, a context model should be produced that sets out the types of context information required by the application, as well as constraints on the data, such as information quality and privacy requirements. This model can be used to evaluate the suitability of any context sensing infrastructure that is already in place and to identify any additional hardware or software requirements. In addition, it can be used to inform the design and implementation of the application.

The model can also be refined to produce a runtime context model that can be populated by various sources of context information and queried by applications. This is the model that resides in the context repository shown in Figure 31.2. Additionally, context models can be used as the basis for generating test cases to allow systematic testing of context-aware functionality [4].

There are currently no context-modeling approaches that address all of these software engineering issues, although some address one or more of them. The majority of the approaches, however, are concerned with runtime context representation, querying, and reasoning, not on requirements analysis, design, or testing.

31.5.1.4 Support for Runtime Querying and Reasoning

One of the most important forms of context model is the runtime model. This model is typically stored in one or more context repositories and queried by context-aware applications. Unlike context models used for analysis and design purposes, runtime models must address representational issues—that is, how to represent information at runtime so that it can be efficiently stored in a repository, queried, and reasoned over to support decisionmaking by context-aware applications about how to react to context changes. For example, the runtime context model for the monitoring application described earlier must be capable of representing histories of location information and light switch "on/off" events that can be used for learning patterns and reasoning about which sequences of location changes and switch events are abnormal.

The runtime model should incorporate information about the known *types* of context and their characteristics (metadata), as well as concrete pieces of context information gathered from various sources (context instances or facts). Querying and reasoning over both kinds of information should be possible. The runtime model should also be easily extensible to new types of context information. The ability for context-aware applications to query and reason about the currently known context types (the model metadata) helps them tolerate evolving context models and exploit newly available information.

Although the example context-aware system presented in Section 31.4 (Fig. 31.2) involves only a single context repository, more complex systems may contain context information that is distributed among a large number of context repositories. The context representation used by the runtime context model (as well as the query and reasoning mechanisms) must therefore be able to support this type of distribution.

31.5.1.5 Support for Interoperability

Context-aware applications may be required to cooperate at runtime with components that were not known to the application designer, such as new applications or sensing hardware. They should be able to exchange context information with these components, which requires a form of interoperability. This can entail one of the following:

1. Supporting transformations between alternative representations of the same information, using a shared context modeling approach (e.g., mapping between different units of measurement, or mapping one term to another equivalent term)
2. Supporting transformations between different modeling approaches (e.g., mapping from an ontology-based approach to an approach based on database modeling techniques)

Problem 1 is reasonably straightforward, provided that the modeling approach provides a way to define the required mapping rules. Problem 2 is more challenging. If a given pair of modeling approaches differ in terms of their expressive power, complete transfer of information between them may not be possible.

An important way to address interoperability is through standardization. By introducing standard ways to represent context information (i.e., common modeling approaches), as well as standard vocabularies and concepts for describing instances of context information, it is possible to avoid the problem of mapping between different context representations. Unfortunately, there are currently no widely accepted standards for context modeling, although some standardization work has been carried out for particular application domains. Indulska et al. [5] carried out some early work on the development of a common context model to support independent living applications for the elderly.

31.5.2 Markup Scheme Approaches

The remainder of Section 31.5 provides a survey and analysis of a variety of context-modeling techniques that are in use today. One of the earliest modeling approaches built on the popularity of markup schemes such as XML [6]. A well-known example that typifies this approach is composite capability/preference profiles (CC/PP) [7], which was standardized as a W3C recommendation during 1998–2004. CC/PP aims to support the transfer of simple context information and preferences (e.g., device characteristics and user language preferences) from Web browsers to servers, in order to support dynamic adaptation of the Webpages returned by the servers to browsers. For example, information about the screen size of the user's device can be used to resize or remove images to fit.

CC/PP is based on RDF [8], a framework for representing information in a common graph-based format capable of representing resources and their properties. CC/PP is intended to be used as a runtime model (i.e., it does not address software engineering tasks such as requirements analysis). It principally addresses the transfer of information between software components (typically, between Web servers and clients); however, storage and querying of CC/PP information is also supported by a variety of tools (both RDF and special-purpose CC/PP tools). CC/PP supports little in the way of reasoning, as it is traditionally used only for representing simple types of information about which reasoning is not necessary.

An example snippet of an XML-encoded CC/PP profile is shown in Figure 31.3. This example shows a description of device hardware (specifically, the display capabilities) and software (operating system name, vendor and version).

```
<ccpp:component>
  <rdf:Description rdf:about="http://mydomain.com/TerminalHardware">
    <rdf:type rdf:resource="http://www.wapforum.org/profiles/UAPROF/
                            ccppschema-20010430#HardwarePlatform"/>
    <prf:ScreenSize>320x200</prf:ScreenSize>
    <prf:ColorCapable>No</prf:ColorCapable>
    <prf:ImageCapable>Yes</prf:ImageCapable>
  </rdf:Description>
</ccpp:component>
<ccpp:component>
  <rdf:Description rdf:about="http://mydomain.com/TerminalSoftware">
    <rdf:type rdf:resource="http://www.wapforum.org/profiles/UAPROF/
                            ccppschema-20010430#SoftwarePlatform"/>
    <prf:OSName>EPOC</prf:OSName>
    <prf:OSVendor>Symbian</prf:OSVendor>
    <prf:OSVersion>1.0</prf:OSVersion>
  </rdf:Description>
</ccpp:component>
```

FIGURE 31.3 *An excerpt from an example CC/PP profile, describing device hardware and software.*

Since CC/PP was initially proposed, various extensions have appeared, including CC/PP vocabularies such as the Open Mobile Alliance's User Agent Profile (UAProf) [9] and other independent extensions for describing relatively advanced types of context, such as location, network characteristics, application requirements, sessions, and constraints on properties [10]. In addition, a similar RDF-based proposal called *comprehensive structured context profiles* (CSCPs) [11] was developed to provide greater expressive power than CC/PP. CSCP lifts some of the limitations imposed by CC/PP on the structure of the profiles, bringing the expressiveness closer to the original expressive power of RDF. However, with the growing popularity of ontology standards that are capable of describing more sophisticated concepts than the markup schemes described here, such as equivalence and cardinality constraints—and thereby supporting reasoning over these concepts for purposes like consistency checking—the popularity of simple modeling approaches along the lines of CC/PP and CSCP is waning.

31.5.3 Ontology-Based Approaches

The distinction between the markup scheme approaches covered in the previous section and the approaches discussed in this section, which are classfied as *ontology-based*, is useful but somewhat artificial. An ontology may be viewed as a comprehensive and rigorous description of a given domain, defining important terms or concepts, as well as relationships between these. However, confusion arises because this definition encompasses most of the context modeling approaches discussed here, yet they are not all classed as ontology-based. In addition, ontology standards are often encoded using markup languages such as XML, in a manner similar to those for CC/PP and CSCP.

To clarify, therefore, this section addresses context-modeling approaches that are aligned with recent work in ontology language standardization—specifically, OWL [3] and closely related precursors such as DAML + OIL [12]. These modeling approaches are more sophisticated than the markup scheme approaches described in the previous section, in that they support additional concepts, such as set operators for defining classes (union, intersection, etc.), cardinality constraints on properties, and equivalence between pairs of classes or properties. Importantly, they are also based on logical formalisms that support reasoning (although the same may actually be said of RDF, on which both CC/PP and CSCP are based). Like the markup scheme approaches, the ontology-based approaches focus on runtime context modeling, not software engineering issues like analysis of required context types, their quality, and other similar characteristics.

One of the earliest ontology-based proposals, by Strang et al. [13], was the *context ontology language* (CoOL). CoOL structures context information according to an *aspect—scale–context* (ASC) model. *Aspects* are kinds of context, such as position or temperature. Each aspect has one or more *scales*, corresponding to units of measurement. Mappings between pairs of scales within a given aspect must be defined. Each piece of context information belongs to a given scale within an aspect, and characterizes a particular *entity*. Context information may also have associated *quality information*, which is itself context information with its own scale and aspect.

Strang et al. provide mappings of the ASC model into the OWL, DAML + OIL and F-logic languages, and use the OntoBroker tool for reasoning about context. The types of reasoning that can be performed using this approach include reasoning to validate the consistency of a context model, map information between context models using interontology relationships, and "complete" an ontology by computing implicit relationships, such as subclass relationships.

The main strengths of CoOL are that it provides one form of support for interoperability (through defined mappings between different units/scales) and supports reasoning using widely available tools. However, this reasoning does not take into account imperfect context information (e.g., quality indicators or ambiguity).

CoOL differs from other work in ontology-based context modeling in that it introduces core context modeling constructs (aspects, scales, etc.) that are separate to the underlying ontology languages used (OWL and DAML + OIL). Wang et al. [14] and Chen et al. [15] take a different approach. They use the standard OWL constructs, but focus instead on creating extensible domain ontologies that define standard concepts and vocabularies that can be used for describing context.

Wang et al. propose the use of two levels of ontology to capture general concepts and domain-specific concepts, respectively. General concepts, which include entities such as locations, people, activities, and computing applications and services, are defined via a common upper ontology. The upper ontology can be extended by various domain ontologies, which define concepts relevant to specific environments such as homes or offices.

Wang et al. [14] show that it is possible to use reasoning to derive high-level context (e.g., the current activity of the user) from lower-level context (e.g., location information derived from sensors). This requires the definition of appropriate axiomatic rules. However, OWL does not support such rules, so they are instead represented in a separate (non-standard) format. Further, Wang et al.'s original proposal does not address quality of context information. Their later work [16] introduces extensions for modeling the derivation of context information (sensed, derived, aggregated, or deduced) and relevant quality indicators. However, this work requires nonstandard extensions to OWL, and therefore is not supported by OWL tools.

The work of Chen et al. [15] is similar to that of Wang et al. in its aims, but broader in scope. Chen et al. propose a set of OWL ontologies, collectively referred to as *SOUPA*, that address numerous modeling issues related to context-aware applications, including context modeling, modeling of concepts from the field of intelligent agents, such as roles, beliefs, and intentions, and modeling of privacy policies for controlling access to sensitive information. SOUPA builds on a variety of well-known ontologies, such as "friend-of-a-friend" [17] and DAML-time [18]. SOUPA also incorporates an earlier set of ontologies called COBRA-ONT, which were developed by Chen et al. [19] for modeling context information in smart meeting rooms.

The principal aim of SOUPA is to provide a broad coverage of common context concepts, so that application developers rarely need to define their own. This promotes interoperability. As in Wang et al.'s work [14], a distinction is made between core concepts (defined by the SOUPA core ontologies) and additional domain-specific concepts (defined by the SOUPA extension ontologies).

The SOUPA ontologies support basic types of reasoning. For example, the ontologies that deal with location and time define relationships that allow reasoning to derive information such as the current occupants of a building, or the precedence/ordering of a given set of events. However, the ontologies provide minimal support for imperfect context information. Conflicting context information can be detected via reasoning and resolved manually by users; however, the ontologies do not provide any mechanisms for representing ambiguous information or quality of information.

Ranganathan and Campbell [20] propose a very different approach that is based primarily on first-order logic, but also makes use of simple ontologies expressed using DAML + OIL. They represent context information in terms of predicates, such as "Temperature(room 3231, "=", 98F)" and "Location(chris, entering, room 3231)" [20]. The role of the DAML + OIL ontologies is to define the structure of the predicates and the types of argument. The ontology definitions can be used to check the validity of predicates, and also as a basis for defining mappings between different predicates, in order to support interoperability.

Context predicates can be combined to form complex logical expressions using the operators AND, OR and NOT, and the universal and existential quantifiers. As there are decidability and safety problems associated with reasoning over unconstrained first order logic expressions, Ranganathan and Campbell [14] adopt a many-sorted logic. This means that quantified expressions, such as "chris is in some location" (written $\exists_{Location} x$ Location(chris, in, x)) are evaluated only over a finite set of objects known to the system. In the example expression, this implies that only a fixed set of locations are considered as possible values for x. This ensures that evaluations always terminate, but can still introduce serious performance problems when the sets of known objects are large. For this reason, this approach for context modeling and reasoning is most appropriate for use in small smart spaces, such as meeting rooms.

Although Ranganathan and Campbell [14] show that it is possible to store histories of predicates and corresponding timestamps in a database, their many-sorted predicate logic does not provide any special support for querying historical information. Additionally, this modeling approach does not address modeling of, or reasoning over, imperfect context information. However, as Ranganathan and Campbell point out, it is possible to layer various reasoning mechanisms, such as temporal or fuzzy logics, on top of their predicate-based representation of context. Another context-modeling approach that incorporates a somewhat similar logic-based reasoning approach, but handles certain types of imperfect context information using a three-valued logic, is discussed in Section 31.5.5.

31.5.4 A Requirements Analysis Model for Sensed Context

The context-modeling approaches discussed so far address the runtime representation of context information, and, to varying degrees, runtime context querying and reasoning. In contrast, the final two approaches that are covered are predominantly concerned with software engineering issues, focusing on structured or semistructured techniques to support the analysis and design of context-aware applications.

Gray and Salber's proposed model for analyzing sensed context information [21] is considerably less formal than the modeling approaches covered thus far. It aims to support a systematic evaluation of the types of context information needed by a context-aware application and the required or anticipated characteristics of this information. Its focus is not on the constructs/concepts used to represent and reason about context information, but rather on properties of the information that are relevant from the application development perspective, such as the data representations, the information quality, the source of the information, and the set of transformations required between the source (sensor) and the high-level data representation. Gray and Salber refer to these properties of the context information as *meta-attributes*. They argue that the software engineering process (and its end result) can be improved by rigorously analyzing the possible design choices for these meta-attributes.

Gray and Salber [21] provide a checklist of information quality aspects that should be considered - namely, coverage of sensors, resolution of sensor output, accuracy, repeatability/stability, frequency, and timeliness. They also describe a set of related issues that must be considered in relation to particular sensing technologies—reliability, intrusiveness, security/privacy, and cost. Finally, Gray and Salber relate their identified set of context meta-attributes to the software engineering process by recommending a simple design approach consisting of the following activities (from Ref. 21):

- Identifying sensed context possibilities
- Eliciting and assessing information quality requirements
- Eliciting and assessing requirements of the acquisition process
- Consideration of issues of
  Intrusiveness, security, privacy
  Transformations of the data from source to "consumer"
  Transmission and storage
- Eliciting and assessing sensor requirements

Gray and Salber's model provides a good basis for analyzing the context requirements of a context-aware application and helping to ensure that potential problems, such as information quality or privacy problems, are identified as early as possible in the application development process. However, it lacks the formality to support a straightforward mapping of the context types identified at the analysis/design stage to a context model that can be stored, queried, and reasoned over at runtime. The following section describes a more formal context-modeling approach that supports elements of analysis and design, as well as mapping to a run-time context model.

31.5.5 The Context Modeling Language

Henricksen et al. propose a context-modeling approach that supports incremental development of context models, beginning during the requirements analysis and design phases of the software engineering process, and continuing through to application deployment, execution, and beyond [4,22]. This approach builds on the *object–role-modeling* (ORM) technique [23], which is traditionally used for database modeling. ORM uses a graphical notation for creating a diagrammatic representation of relevant concepts and relationships between the concepts. In the terminology of ORM, concepts are known as entities and relationships as fact types. Concrete instances of relationships (e.g., "Fred is located in Room 633") are known as facts.

As ORM is designed for database modeling, not context modeling, it lacks powerful ways to describe relevant meta-attributes of context, such as sources of information and quality attributes. For this reason, Henricksen et al. extended ORM with a number of special-purpose context modeling constructs [22], originally introduced in an earlier context-modeling notation [24]. This extended variant of ORM is known as the *context-modeling language* (CML).

A simple example model specified using the CML notation is shown in Figure 31.4. This model captures types of context relevant to the monitoring application that was discussed in Section 31.4. It incorporates various types of user-supplied information (so-called profiled fact types), including information about the occupants of a home, the rooms in the home, the light switches in each room, and assignments of location badges to particular people. In addition, the model contains two types of sensor-derived information (sensed fact types): estimated positions of location badges in the home to the nearest room, and status information for light switches. Both sensed fact types are

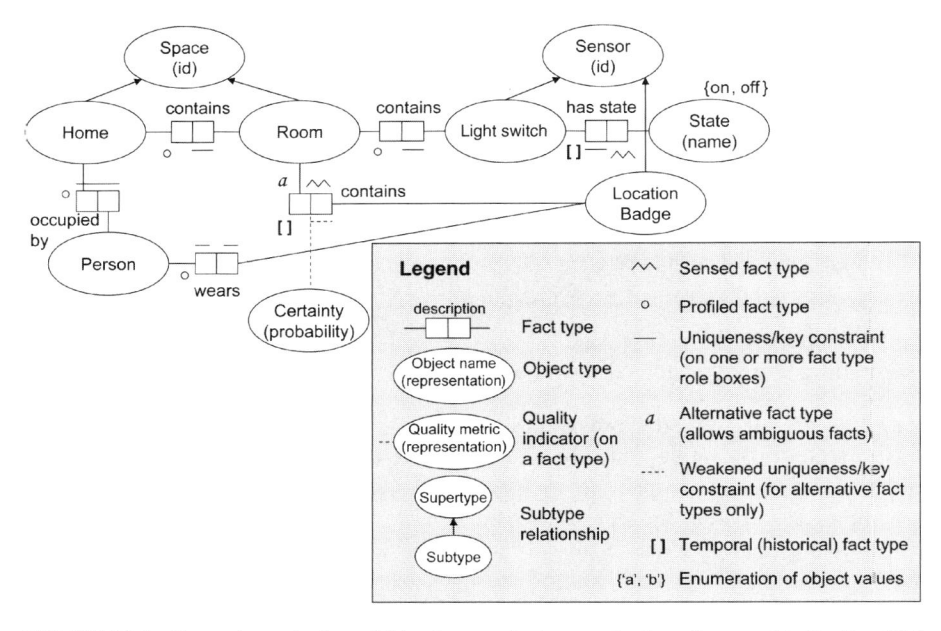

FIGURE 31.4 *Example context model for the monitoring application discussed in Section 31.4.*

marked as "temporal" fact types, implying that histories of facts, marked with timestamps, should be retained in the context repository at runtime. For the former information type (badge location), uncertainty is allowed by marking this as an "alternative" fact type. This allows two or more contradictory facts, such as "bedroom 1 contains badge 343" OR "hallway 1 contains badge 343," to be represented whenever the positioning system is unable to more accurately resolve the location of a badge. In addition, each location fact is associated with a probability.

ORM, the database modeling approach on which CML is based, is well established as a requirements analysis technique, and therefore much has been written about the process of constructing ORM models in cooperation with experts in the domain that is being modeled and/or intended database/application users. This process can be adapted to provide guidelines for analyzing context requirements and constructing a context model using CML. In addition, there is a straightforward mapping of ORM models to relational databases. This mapping procedure can be extended to allow mapping of CML models to runtime context models stored in context repositories that take the form of enhanced relational databases supporting specialized context meta-attributes and constraints. The run-time models can be queried using either standard relational database query languages, or by evaluating predefined "situations" expressed using a form of predicate logic. Situations provide basic support for evaluating ambiguous context (such as the conflicting location facts discussed above) using a three-valued logic (where situation expressions can be "true," "false" or "possibly true"); in addition, situations can incorporate special forms of existential and universal quantification, in which variables are constrained by binding them according to a fact template, thereby ensuring efficient and safe evaluation.

31.5.6 Analysis

This survey of context modeling approaches is intended to be illustrative rather than exhaustive; however, it covers most of the well-known work in the area. Owing to the immaturity of the field of context-awareness, none of the modeling approaches has been widely adopted. CC/PP has the advantage of being standardized as a W3C Recommendation, but it is unsuitable for representing many types of information [10], and its support for reasoning is limited. OWL-based modeling approaches are better able to support reasoning and are currently enjoying favor. However, these address predominantly runtime issues (representation of context information, reasoning, and interoperability), not software engineering tasks such as requirements analysis and design. Therefore, models of the sort presented in the latter part of the survey also play an important role. CML, discussed in the very last section of the survey, offers the particular advantage that it supports the mapping of a requirements model to a runtime model.

Table 31.1 summarizes the strengths of the various approaches. As none of the approaches is comprehensive in the sense that it addresses all of the requirements introduced in Section 31.5.1, hybrid modeling approaches are being considered—for instance, approaches that take elements from mature database modeling techniques, which support requirements analysis as well as efficient run-time representation and querying, and augment them with descriptions written in ontology languages, so as to enable interoperability through constructs such as equivalence definitions and concept mappings [25,26].

TABLE 31.1 Analysis of Context-Modeling Approaches[a,b]

Requirement	Markup Schemes	Ontology-Based Approaches	Sensed Context (Analysis) Model	CML
Support for imperfect context information	√[c]	√[c]	√	√
Support for context histories	√[d]	√[d]	×	√
Support for software engineering	×	×	√	√
Support for runtime querying and reasoning	√	√	×	√
Support for interoperability	√[e]	√[f]	×	×

[a] These context-modeling approaches are discussed in Sections 31.5.2–31.5.4 with respect to the requirements introduced in Section 31.5.1.
[b] (Symbols Key: √ = comprehensive support, √ = partial support, × = no support.
[c] Imperfect information can usually be represented in some form (although rarely in a very natural way), but reasoning over imperfect information is not supported by conventional tools.
[d] Can be represented, but the majority of the approaches do not define natural concepts/vocabularies for doing so.
[e] Based on the use of standard vocabularies.
[f] Based on the use of standard vocabularies and defined mappings between concepts.

31.6 SOFTWARE INFRASTRUCTURE FOR CONTEXT-AWARE SYSTEMS

Creating models of context requirements, as well as runtime context models, are important steps in developing context-aware applications. An equally important requirement is gathering the context information specified by the model from various sources at runtime. This task is usually delegated to a software infrastructure shared by a number of context-aware applications; however, the infrastructure may also handle other related tasks. This section discusses the components and functionality that may be found in a software infrastructure for context-aware systems, and then introduces some representative examples of infrastructure.

31.6.1 Reference Architecture for Context-Aware Systems

When discussing software infrastructure for context-aware systems, it is instructive to have a typical—or reference—architecture in mind, with which various solutions can be compared. Figure 31.5 shows such a reference architecture. This architecture incorporates various components that may be present in current context-aware systems—however, it is important to note that some of the components will be absent in many systems. This is either because the systems are sufficiently simple that the components are not required (e.g., the monitoring application discussed in Section 31.4 does not require actuators), or because the functionality of some components is incorporated directly into the applications (as in the initial design of the monitoring system that was shown in Fig. 31.1). In addition to the application components, sensors, and actuators, shown at the two extremities in Figure 31.5, the reference architecture contains the following infrastructural components:

1. Components that (a) assist with discovering suitable context sources (most commonly, sensors) and processing the data produced by these sources to populate

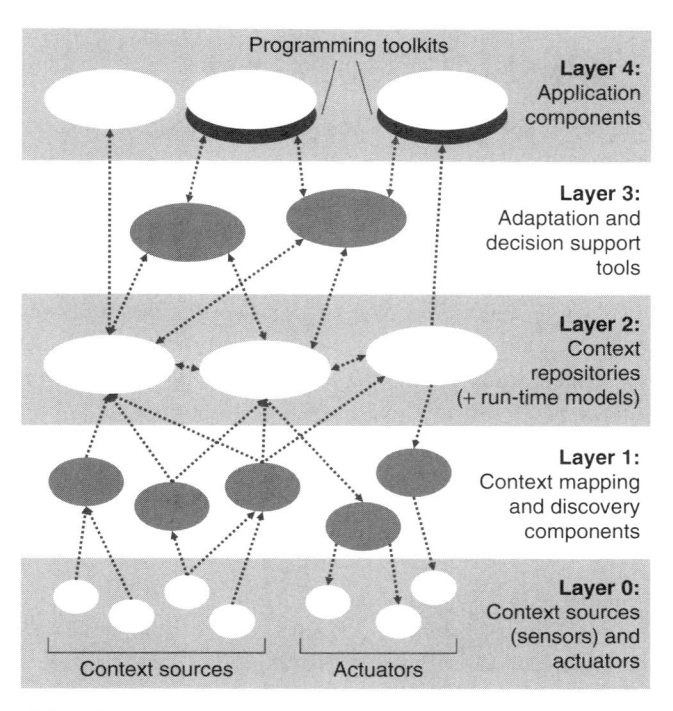

FIGURE 31.5 Reference architecture for context-aware systems.

applications' runtime context models[1] and (b) map update operations on the models back down to actions on actuators when required (layer 1)
2. Context repositories that provide persistent storage of runtime context models, query and update facilities, and optional support for reasoning over context (layer 2)
3. Decision support tools that help applications select appropriate actions and adaptations based on the information in the runtime context models (layer 3).

Programming toolkits are often also incorporated at the application layer (layer 4) to support the interactions of the application components with the infrastructural components. One responsibility of these toolkits is to handle tasks such as discovery of, and remote communication with, context repositories and decision support tools.

The following sections describe examples of infrastructure proposed by the research community, positioning their functionality with respect to layers of the reference architecture.

31.6.2 The Context Toolkit

One of the pioneering software infrastructures for context-aware systems was Dey et al.'s "context toolkit" [27]. The toolkit addresses primarily layer 1 issues (i.e., interpretation and discovery of context information derived from sensors). It also handles some layer 2 issues; however, it does not support explicit runtime context models of the type discussed

---
[1] Note that other context information may be directly inserted by users or applications.

in Section 31.5. This means that applications must directly query the software components responsible for acquiring and/or interpreting context information, rather than querying a single high-level context model.

The toolkit defines a set of abstract component types that can be instantiated and composed to gather context information from sensors. The component types include

- *Widgets*, which acquire information directly from sensors (effectively acting as software wrappers for sensors)
- *Interpreters*, which raise the level of abstraction of context information to better match application requirements (e.g., transforming the raw location coordinates reported by a positioning device to a building and room number)
- *Aggregators*, which group related context information together in a single component to facilitate querying
- *Services*, which are used to invoke actions on actuators (effectively acting as software wrappers for actuators)
- *Discoverers*, which can be used by applications to locate suitable widgets, interpreters, aggregators, and services

The toolkit is implemented as a set of abstract Java objects representing the component types described above. These objects implement a simple communication protocol based on HTTP and XML to support transparent distribution of the components over multiple devices. Libraries of reusable components of each type can be created to support standard sensor and context types.

A variety of applications have been developed using the toolkit, including a home intercom built using speakers, microphones, and location sensors, and an in/out board for the office that provides basic presence awareness, also using location sensors.

31.6.3 Solar

A more recent solution by Chen et al. [28] addresses issues similar to the Dey et al. [27] context toolkit, but adds an operator graph abstraction for selecting/composing context sources and data fusion methods using high-level descriptions. It also adds tolerance for sensor mobility and failures. In the operator graph model, context acquisition and processing is specified by application developers in terms of sources, sinks, and channels. Here, sensors are represented by sources and applications by sinks. Operators, which are responsible for data processing/fusion, act as both sources and sinks. Similarly to the context toolkit, no explicit runtime context model is present.

Chen et al. have implemented support for the operator graph model in the form of *Solar*, a peer-to-peer platform that instantiates the operator graphs at runtime on behalf of applications. The Solar hosts support application and sensor mobility by buffering events during periods of network disconnection, and also address component failures by providing monitoring, recovery, and preservation of component states.

31.6.4 The PACE Middleware

The two software infrastructures just described address layer 1 issues and a small subset of layer 2. The PACE middleware developed by Henricksen et al. [29] focuses on layers 2 and 3, but also provides some support for layer 4. It consists of

- A context management system (layer 2) that manages run-time context models, including

  Model metadata (i.e., model definitions)

  Context facts from layer 0 and 1 sources, user profiles, and applications
- A preference management system that provides user-customizable decision support for context-aware applications (layer 3)
- A programming toolkit that facilitates discovery and use of context and preference repositories by context-aware applications (layer 4)
- Tools that generate components that can be used by all layers, including a flexible messaging framework for transparently transmitting context information over a variety of communication protocols (RPC-based and message-based) using custom-generated stubs produced from context model descriptions

The context and preference management systems are the key parts of the middleware. The former provides run-time support for Henricksen et al.'s context-modelling language (CML) and situation-based query mechanism, both of which were described in Section 31.5.5. The preference management system provides preference-based decision support for applications, using a novel solution for specifying context-dependent user preferences. The preferences use a scoring mechanism to indicate the suitability of application actions for particular contexts. The actions are application-specific—for example, an action for a document retrieval application might correspond to selecting a given document or search term. In addition to numerical scores that capture relative preference, users can describe policies such as obligation (actions that must be taken) and prohibition (actions that must not be taken).

A benefit of this preference-based decision support is that most of the evaluation of context information is done as a side effect of preference evaluation, rather than directly by context-aware applications. This reduces the coupling between the application and the context model, allowing the application to better tolerate changes in the model. For instance, new kinds of context information can be used simply by adding preferences that reference this information, without modifying the application.

Like the Dey et al. [27] context toolkit, the PACE middleware has been used to implement various context-aware applications, including context-based routing of phone calls [30] and automatic profile switching for the Nokia 6600 mobile phone.

31.6.5 Discussion

The examples of software infrastructure that have been described here are experimental solutions developed by the research community. None of them was developed particularly with independent living of the elderly or disabled in mind; however, all could be adapted for this purpose. Mature commercial implementations do not yet exist, but will be required before context-aware applications can be widely developed and deployed. In addition to mature solutions, there is still also a need for comprehensive solutions that provide strong support for all layers of the reference architecture, plus support for other important concerns that cross-cut the architectural layers, such as privacy, security, fault tolerance, and scalability. Further analysis of the current state of the art in this area is provided by Henricksen et al. [29].

31.7 CONCLUSIONS

In this chapter we addressed the use of context-awareness to intelligently assist elderly and disabled people. Context-aware applications can address healthcare needs and support activities of daily living, and can also be used to extend social interaction, environment control, and information flow to family and caregivers.

To facilitate a discussion of issues related to designing and implementing context-aware applications, we introduced definitions of context and context information and highlighted their roles in context-aware applications. We described several examples of context-aware applications designed to assist elderly or disabled people, in order to illustrate both the possible functionality of such applications and the rich types of context information that many of these applications require. We also emphasized the importance of formal context models in the design and development of context-aware applications, in order to facilitate sharing of context information between applications, as well as to simplify the development and maintenance of context-aware software. We showed the requirements that such models should meet and provided a survey of current context modeling techniques. Finally, we discussed the support that software infrastructure/middleware can provide for context-aware applications in tasks such as gathering, processing and evaluating context information, and supporting context-based adaptation decisions.

REFERENCES

1. Dey AK: Understanding and using context, *Personal Ubiq Comput* **5**(1):4–7 (2001).
2. Harter A, Hopper A, Steggles P, Ward A, Webster P: The anatomy of a context-aware application, *Wireless Networks* **8**(2–3):187–197 (2002).
3. McGuinness DL, van Harmelen F: *OWL Web Ontology Language Overview*, W3C Recommendation, Feb 10, 2004.
4. Henricksen K, Indulska J: Developing context-aware pervasive computing applications: Models and approach, *J Pervasive Mobile Comput*, **2**(1):37–64 (2006).
5. Indulska J, Henricksen K, McFadden T, Mascaro P: Towards a common context model for virtual community applications, *2nd Int Conf Smart Homes and Health Telematics*, Vol 14 of *Assistive Technology Research Series*, IOS Press, pp 154–161.
6. Bray T, Paoli J, Sperberg-McQueen C.M, Maler E, Yergeau F: *Extensible Markup Language (XML 1.0)*, (3rd ed,) W3C Recommendation, Feb 4, 2004.
7. Klyne G, Reynolds F, Woodrow C, Ohto H, Hjelm J, Butler MH, Tran L: *Composite Capability/Preference Profiles (CC/PP): Structure and Vocabularies 1.0*, W3C Recommendation, Jan 15, 2004.
8. Manola F, Miller E: *RDF primer*, W3C Recommendation, Feb 10, 2004.
9. Open Mobile Alliance *User Agent Profile Version 20*, May 2003, OMA document OMA-UAProf-v2_0-20030520-C.
10. Indulska J, Robinson R, Rakotonirainy A, Henricksen K: Experiences in using CC/PP in context-aware systems, *4th Int Conf Mobile Data Management*, Vol 2574 of *Lecture Notes in Computer Science*, Springer, 2003, pp 247–261.
11. Buchholz S, Hamann T, Hubsch G: Comprehensive structured context profiles (CSCP): Design and experiences, *Proc 1st Workshop on Context Modeling and Reasoning (PerCom'04)*, IEEE Computer Society, 2004, pp 43–47.

12. Horrocks I: DAML + OIL: A description logic for the semantic web, *IEEE Data Eng Bull* **25**(1):4–9 (2002).
13. Strang T, Linnhoff-Popien C, Frank K: CoOL: A context ontology language to enable contextual interoperability. *4th Int Conf Distributed Applications and Interoperable Systems*, Vol 2893 of *Lecture Notes in Computer Science*, Springer, 2003, pp 236–247.
14. Wang Z, Zhang D, Gu T, Dong J, Pung HK: Ontology based context modeling and reasoning using OWL, *Proc Workshop on Context Modeling and Reasoning (PerCom'04)* Orlando, FL, IEEE Computer Society, 2004, pp 18–22.
15. Chen H, Finin T, Joshi A: *The SOUPA Ontology for Pervasive Computing*, Ontologies for Agents: Theory and Experiences. (Series), Springer, 2005.
16. Gu T, Wang XH, Pung KK, Zhang DQ: An ontology-based context model in intelligent environments, *Communication Networks and Distributed Systems Modeling and Simulation Conf*, San Diego, 2004.
17. Brickley D, Miller L: *FOAF Vocabulary Specification*, Names-pace document, July 27, 2005.
18. Hobbs JR, et al: *A DAML Ontology of Time*, Nov 2002 (http://www.cs.rochester.edu/ferguson/daml/daml-time-nov2002.txt).
19. Chen H, Finin T, Joshi A: An ontology for context-aware pervasive computing environments, *Knowledge Eng Rev*, **18**(3):197–207 (2004).
20. Ranganathan A, Campbell RH: An infrastructure for context-awareness based on first-order logic, *Personal Ubiq Comput*, **7**(6):353–364 (2003).
21. Gray P, Salber D: Modelling and using sensed context information in the design of interactive applications, *8th IFIP Int Conf on Engineering for Human-Computer Interaction*, Vol 2254 of *Lecture Notes in Computer Science*, Springer, 2001, pp 317–336.
22. Henricksen K, Indulska J, McFadden T: Modeling context information with ORM, *OTM Federated Conf Workshop on Object-Role Modeling*, Vol 3762 of *Lecture Notes in Computer Science*, Springer, 2005, pp 626–635.
23. Halpin TA: *Information Modeling and Relational Databases: From Conceptual Analysis to Logical Design*, Morgan Kaufman, San Francisco, 2001.
24. Henricksen K, Indulska J, Rakotonirainy A: Modeling context information in pervasive computing systems, *1st Int Conf Pervasive Computing*, Volume 2414 of *Lecture Notes in Computer Science*, Springer, 2002, pp 167–180.
25. Henricksen K, Livingstone S, Indulska J: Towards a hybrid approach to context modelling, reasoning and interoperation, *UbiComp 1st Int Workshop on Advanced Context Modelling, Reasoning and Management*, Nottingham, UK, 2004, pp 54–61.
26. Becker C, Nicklas D: Where do spatial context models end and where do ontologies start? A proposal of a combined approach, *UbiComp 1st Int Workshop on Advanced Context Modelling, Reasoning and Management*, Nottingham, UK, 2004, pp 48–53.
27. Dey AK, Salber D, Abowd GD: A conceptual framework and a toolkit for supporting the rapid prototyping of context-aware applications, *Human-Comput Interact*, **16**(2–4):97–166 (2001).
28. Chen G, Li M, Kotz D: Design and implementation of a large-scale context fusion network, *Proc 1st Annual Int Conf Mobile and Ubiquitous Systems*, IEEE Computer Society, 2004, pp 246–255.
29. Henricksen K, Indulska J, McFadden T, Balasubramaniam S: Middleware for distributed context-aware systems, *Int Symp Distributed Objects and Applications*, Volume 3760 of *Lecture Notes in Computer Science*, Springer, 2005, pp 846–863.
30. McFadden T, Henricksen K, Indulska J, Mascaro P: Applying a disciplined approach to the development of a context-aware communication application, *3rd IEEE Int Conf Pervasive Computing and Communications*, IEEE Computer Society, 2005, pp 300–306.

32

Middleware for Smart Spaces

Daqing Zhang, Tao Gu, and Manli Zhu
Institute for Infocomm Research, Heng Mui King Terrace, Singapore

32.1 INTRODUCTION

Ubiquitous computing envisions the future physical spaces such as homes, cars, and hospitals augmented with stationary and mobile devices, sensors, and actuators. Those physical spaces that can provide us with a wealth of environmental information and thus empower the occupants to intelligently interact with the environment are often called "smart spaces". An example of smart space with great research potential is smart homes for elderly and disabled, where the aim is to assist them for independent living and to improve their quality of life. The applications built in smart spaces are required to not only interact with massive heterogeneous devices such as embedded sensors, augmented appliances, stationary computers, mobile handheld devices but also consider the contextual information from the human being and environment in order to deliver the right services to the right person. The complication in building applications in a smart space necessitates the presence of such software, which can free the application developers from handling low-level and common components. In addition, it is desirable for the software to provide services to facilitate rapid development, ease of integration, improved reliability, and increased scalability [1]. Middleware for smart environments provides a solution to such software, and this chapter describes the challenges and technologies in building middleware for smart environments.

In traditional computing paradigm, middleware is the connectivity software that consists of a set of enabling services that allow multiple processes running on one or more machines to interact across a network [2]. It lies between the applications it supports and the platform it is based on, creating transparency, scalability, and interoperability through communication mechanisms. Middleware is defined by the application programming

---

The Engineering Handbook of Smart Technology for Aging, Disability, and Independence,
Edited by A. Helal, M. Mokhtari and B. Abdulrazak
Copyright © 2008 John Wiley & Sons, Inc.

interface (API) that it provides to applications that utilize it and the protocol(s) that it supports. The employment of middleware should reduce the complexities of the network, the host operating systems, and any available resource servers creating value in simplifying these for the applications using it and the developers who write them [3].

In smart environments, however, the middleware should be designed to cater for the emerging challenges specific to the system designs:

- The first challenge is how to enable the heterogeneous devices to interact with each other, for both static and mobile devices in smart spaces.
- The second challenge is how to acquire and understand the context information; typical context information is about the who, what, when, and where of the entities in smart spaces [4].
- The third challenge is how to represent different entities in smart spaces such as the people, devices, things, and software functions on which a unified programming model can be based.
- The fourth challenge is how to ensure the scalability of smart space solutions and another challenge is about security/privacy/trust guarantee among the interaction of entities.

The goals of this chapter are to study the challenges uniquely posed by the smart environments and illustrate how our proposed middleware has addressed those challenges. To offer a comprehensive understanding toward middleware technology, we also introduce some of the prevailing standards in current use and present a brief survey of middleware solutions and projects in the world. Our hope is to provide an understanding of the link between middleware technology and characteristics of smart environments that can inspire some insights, ideas, and options for other smart environments projects.

32.2 CHALLENGES IN BUILDING SMART SPACES

In this section, we examine several technical challenges that we feel must be overcome before the vision of smart spaces becomes a reality. Those challenges are by no means an exhausted list of issues posed; however, they do represent some of the key issues for building smart spaces. Those challenges include

- Device interaction and integration
- Context processing and management
- Interoperability of heterogeneous entities
- Security, privacy, and trust
- Scalability in terms of device, service, and space

32.2.1 Device Interaction and Integration

Smart spaces are expected to contain large number of devices that interact with one another to achieve different goals. The interactions are characterized by a number of challenges: device interaction can be ad hoc and spontaneous; devices and environments are heterogeneous; and context of user, device, and environment is dynamic. Currently, the developers must preprogram devices to recognize the specific protocols, standards, data formats, and operations of all the peer device type that they expect to encounter in order to talk to each other. With the rapid increase in numbers, types, and operating domains of the devices and the services they may provide, it is unreasonable to expect that every device will have prior knowledge of every other type of device. Consider, for example, a Bluetooth adapter purchased by a user for a laptop computer. It may be reasonable for the user to expect the laptop to work with Bluetooth printers that she discovers around her. But, while the presence of Bluetooth in both devices allows the laptop to discover the presence of such a printer, the laptop is unable to use it without the specified device driver installed.

There are two approaches to achieve spontaneous interaction between devices: centralized control and peer-to-peer collaboration. The centralized approach utilizes servers to aggregate information for all the devices registered in a local environment that will facilitate the communication and interaction between the client devices and the environment. The key challenge for the centralized approach is developing an open service architecture that allows the heterogeneous client devices to control the devices in a new environment [5], and yet makes minimal assumption about standard interfaces and control protocols. A data-centric scheme provides the solution to the challenge. It utilizes an interface definition language enabling exported object interfaces to be mapped to the client device control interface. The control messages are thus generated as the RPC command sent from the client user interface to the corresponding service demon. The centralized approach is preferable in a relatively static environment; however, for the scenarios where most devices tend to join or exit the environment freely, frequent registering of the devices and updates of the information bring excessive burden to the system. Therefore peer-to-peer collaboration, that directly enables the interaction between two peer devices, is more desirable in dynamic environment [6].

With peer-to-peer collaboration ability, a device can connect to another device, provide metadata about itself, be controlled, and provide references to other devices. In order to accommodate enormous heterogeneous types of devices in the world, the infrastructure must provide a generic approach for the interactions between devices. Instead of specifying a detailed, continuously evolving communication protocol, it defines a simple, fixed set of interfaces that allow the two devices exchange capabilities, communicate with each other, and use whatever communication protocols are appropriate for the information transferring. In other words, the approach establishes the minimal set of development–time agreements to defer all other agreements required until runtime. It then delivers these agreements in the form of mobile code, which can extend a recipient's behavior to make it compatible with a new peer.

32.2.2 Context Processing and Management

Context information plays an important role in making the physical spaces "smart". Users and applications in smart spaces often need to be aware of their surrounding context and adapt their behaviors to context changes. We believe that an appropriate context management framework requires the following support:

1. *A Common Context Model Shared by All Devices, Services, and Spaces.* Understanding context information is the basis for context sharing among devices and services in one smart space or across different spaces. An appropriate model should address

different characteristics of context information such as dependence and uncertainty. In our earlier work, we proposed an ontology-based context model [7] to describe context information in a semantic way, which exhibits features such as expressiveness, extensibility, ease of sharing and reuse, and logic reasoning support.

2. *Context Acquisition, Context Lookup, and Context Interpretation.* These services are essential for building applications with context-awareness in smart spaces. Context acquisition is closely coupled with sensors to acquire context data from physical or virtual sensors. Context lookup provides users and applications both synchronous context query service and asynchronous context event notification service. Considering that context information is widely spread over wide-area networks across multiple smart spaces, a robust lookup service can be challenging. Such challenges can be, for example, building an underlying lookup mechanism to allow context lookup from anywhere in the system considering the temporal characteristics of context information. Context interpretation provides the support of deriving high-level context from low-level context. Different interpretation techniques can be applied such as logical reasoning and machine learning. Our earlier work such as that concerned with semantic space [8] and SOCAM [9] provided the set of such services to build our middleware for smart spaces.

32.2.3 Interoperability of Heterogeneous Entities

Within a smart space environment, entities can range from sensors, objects, and devices to software functions. Those heterogeneous entities interact and service one another to complete different tasks. This sounds fine, except that these entities are likely to originate from different sources and therefore use different ways to present their capabilities and connectivity requirements. As a result, entities within a smart space will not be able to interoperate with one another. This interoperability problem can be addressed by using service-oriented architecture.

Service-oriented architecture (SOA) is a *software architectural* concept that defines the use of services to support the *requirements* of entities. In a SOA framework, entities in the environment are represented in form of services and made available to other entities in a standardized way. As the functions of every entity are described using common convention, entities can thus understand each other and collaborate to achieve a certain goal. The problem of interoperability between entities is solved through SOA, even though the functions and resources of each entity may differ significantly.

Once the descriptions of entities are defined in format understandable to entities, other mechanisms such as service announcement, service registration, service discovery, and composition are needed for advanced service management.

32.2.4 Security, Privacy, and Trust

In smart spaces, the interaction and information exchange between entities and services must be secure, private, and trustworthy [10]. *Security* includes the three main properties of confidentiality, integrity, and availability. *Confidentially* is concerned with protecting the information/service from unauthorized access, *integrity* is concerned with protecting the information/service from unauthorized changes, and *availability* is concerned with ensuring that the information/service remains accessible.

Privacy is the claim of individuals, groups, or institutions to determine for themselves when, how, and to what extent information is communicated to others. Privacy is about protecting users' personal information. *Privacy control* relates not only to the process of setting rules and enforcing them but also to the way privacy is managed or controlled adaptively according to changes in the degree of disclosure of personal information or user mobility from one smart space to another.

A new enabling component of smart space is trust management, developed as a trust specification that can be analyzed and evaluated before appropriate interactions or transactions really starts. As entities and services in smart spaces often interact and collaborate with each other in an ad hoc manner, those entities and services may come from unfamiliar administrative domains and therefore be completely unknown to each other. To safely take advantage of all the possibilities, it is essential to assess the confidence level of the involved parties, estimate the likely behavior of entities, and recommend a certain level for interactions, which is the so-called trust management. Trust management involves the trust model, the trust and recommendation specifications for different entities from different certified authorities, and risk threshold. In smart spaces, the trust management service uses the trust model to compute the trust value for each interaction. The trust value indicates the degree of confidence and is used as a parameter to determine the access level of services or degree of information exchange or interaction.

32.2.5 Scalability in Terms of Device, Service, and Space

Scalability is a critical requirement in designing middleware solutions for smart spaces with thousands or millions of pervasive devices and services. A robust design not only enables the middleware scale up to a large number of devices and services in a single smart space but also provides the supports across multiple smart spaces. Many existing systems deploy a centralized approach. With the scalability requirement, this approach may not be suitable because of its single processing bottleneck and single point of failure. Here, as in our earlier attempt, we have built a semantic peer-to-peer (P2P) overlay network [11,12] to facilitate efficient lookup for context information in multiple smart spaces. The basic idea is to cluster peers on the basis of their data semantics and organize them in a semantic P2P overlay network for efficient lookup. Context data that are semantically similar are "tied" together in the system so that they can be retrieved by a query that has the same semantics. While the system is designed for context lookup, the similar approach can be applied to device and service lookup across multiple smart spaces.

32.3 STANDARDS AND TECHNOLOGY FOR MIDDLEWARE

32.3.1 Jini

Jini is a distributed service-oriented architecture developed by Sun Microsystems [13]. It aims to turn the network into a flexible, easily administered tool on which human and computational clients can find services in a flexible and robust fashion. Jini services can represent hardware devices, software programs, or a combination of the two. A collection of Jini services form a Jini federation. Jini services coordinate with each other within the federation. One key component of Jini is the Jini Lookup Service (JLS), which maintains dynamic information about the available services in a Jini federation. Every service must discover one or more JLSs before it can enter a federation. When a Jini service wants to join a Jini federation, it first discovers one or many JLSs from the local or remote networks. The service then uploads its service proxy (i.e., a set of Java classes) to the JLS. The service clients can use this proxy to contact the original service and invoke methods on the service.

Jini has a low footprint on the network and does not incur a large amount of traffic overhead. The use of leasing in Jini ensures that knowledge of the services and the state of the system are very up-to-date. Jini is flexible from the service's perspective. The service can be implemented to run locally, provide an RMI stub, or communicate through some other protocol. However, Jini is Java-specific, and JVMs can be too slow for very limited hardware, so Jini may not be ideal for embedded devices. Jini also has limitations on service matching. It implements exact or wildcard matching, but not range matching.

32.3.2 UPnP

Universal Plug and Play (UPnP) (www.upnp.org) is an evolving architecture designed to extend the original Microsoft Plug-and-Play peripheral model to a highly dynamic world of many network devices. UPnP works primarily at lower-layer network protocol suites (i.e., TCP/IP). It attempts to ensure that all device manufacturers can quickly adhere to the proposed standard without major hassles.

UPnP uses the Simple Service Discovery Protocol (SSDP) to discover services. When entering a network, devices broadcast an advertisement containing its type, unique identifier, and an URL. These advertisements are stored by control points. Searching for a device is done by broadcasting a request for the desired type of device. This request is intercepted by all control points, and matching advertisements are sent back to the requester. Next, the service requester retrieves device descriptions and service descriptions of the devices found, using URLs embedded in the advertisements.

Services are described in XML, and the XML can be a complete abstract description of the type of service, the interface to a specific instance of the service. XML is extremely flexible, so it can deliver almost any kind of information.

UPnP has no specific security features. It depends on the network and Web infrastructure for its security. UPnP can work with no central directory of addresses, but clearly the full XML capability requires a Web server somewhere.

32.3.3 OSGi

The OSGi Service Platform (www.osgi.org) is a Java-based framework, originally designed specifically for residential gateways, but now (release 3) supporting a much broader range of service platforms. The OSGi service platform makes it easy to develop applications (known as "bundles") for gateways, by giving a strong base of services, which applications can make use of. Furthermore, OSGi is responsible for lifecycle management, security, communication, and a number of other relevant services. Because it is Java-based, the OSGi framework runs on most hardware, making it easy to deploy gateways in a heterogeneous hardware environment.

32.3.4 Web Services

Web services are modular, self-describing, self-contained applications that are accessible over the Internet. They have been identified as the technology for business process execution and application integration. Given the dynamic environment in e-businesses, the power of being able to find Web services on the fly to create business processes is highly desirable. A key step in achieving this capability is the automated discovery of Web services. Currently, the standards for Web services are Simple Object Access Protocol (SOAP) (http://www.w3.org/TR/soap/), Web Services Description Language (WSDL) (http://www.w3.org/TR/wsdl), and Universal Description Discovery and Integration (UDDI) (http://www.oasis-open.org/committees/uddispec/doc) specifications. SOAP represents a standard for lightweight XML-based messaging protocol for Web services. It enables the exchange of information between two or more peers in a decentralized, distributed application environment. WSDL is used to describe Web services in a common XML grammar. The WSDL document associated with a Web service provides enough information to locate and access the methods of the Web service. With WSDL-aware tools, clients can automate this process, enabling the integration of Web services into existing applications with little effort. UDDI is a technical specification for describing, discovering, and integrating Web services. An UDDI registry implementation is a Web services-based registry that provides a mechanism to advertise and discover Web services. The registry contains information about businesses and the services that they offer, and it associates some of those services with the technical specifications of the Web service.

32.4 MIDDLEWARE FOR SMART ENVIRONMENTS

Since the mid-1990s, many middleware systems have been developed to support intelligent applications and enhance life for people in smart environments. These systems address the issues in smart spaces from different aspects such as resource management and discovery, interaction, programmability, context-awareness, scalability, user interface, security, and application support. The approaches used in these systems can be summarized as follows: agent-based, service-oriented, task-driven, Web-based, and activity-driven.

The Oxygen project (http://www.oxygen.lcs.mit.edu/Overview.html) aims at providing user interaction through speech and vision technologies, individualized knowledge access, and collaboration technologies. Oxygen is based on computational devices embedded in homes, offices, and cars that sense and affect a user's immediate environment. Additionally, it uses handheld devices that empower users to communicate and compute no matter where they are; dynamic, self-configuring networks help users locate the people, services, and resources that they want to reach.

Gaia (http://gaia.cs.uiuc.edu/) applies the resource management approach in the operating system for smart spaces, and it focuses mainly on programmability, context-awareness, and security. The system consists of a component management core for component creation, destruction, and upload, with currently seven services built on top of it.

Aura (http://www.cs.cmu.edu/~aura/) proposes a task-driven middleware for smart spaces. It addresses two problems:

1. It eliminates the problem of allowing a user to preserve continuity in his/her work when moving between different environments, and the framework has a key advantage over other approaches in that it allows the system to tailor the user's task to the resources in the environment.

2. It successfully solves the problem of adapting the ongoing computation of a particular environment in the presence of dynamic resource variability. As resources come and go, the computations can adapt appropriately. The key ingredients of this middleware are explicit representations of user tasks as collections of services, context observation that allows the task to be configured in a way that is appropriate to the environment, and environment management that assists with resource monitoring and adaptation.

The Ninja project deals with distributed Internet services. It presents an architecture for secure service discovery [14]. The SSDS is similar to other discovery protocols, with a number of specific improvements in reliability, scalability, and security. An important distinction of the SSDS provides extremely strong mandatory security: all parties are authenticated, and all message traffic is encrypted. Although SSDS is implemented in and relies on Java, it uses XML for service description and location. The Ninja project has explored the possibility of automatically mapping interfaces to each other using XML descriptions. This will be extremely important for "spontaneous" networking and interoperability of heterogeneous devices in smart spaces.

Context Fabric [15] proposes a context infrastructure that consists of three things to simplify the task of building applications: a context data store for modeling, storing, and distributing context data; a context specification language for declaratively stating and processing context needs; and protection mechanisms for safeguarding privacy needs.

Cooltown [16] proposes a Web-based system for smart spaces and enhances physical objects with Web content. Cooltown embeds information within a Web-based framework, associating each entity (a person, a place, and a thing) with a description retrievable via an URL. A simple location-based discovery mechanism is used for context lookup, which involves the use of beacons to transmit the URL of the local environment wirelessly.

Gator House [17] uses service-oriented framework to handle device self-integration, context-awareness, and knowledge management in the smart home. It focuses mainly on providing a scalable and cost-effective way to develop and deploy extensible sensors, actuators, devices, and software componenets.

SOCAM [11] proposes a service-oriented context-aware middleware architecture for the building and rapid prototyping of context-aware services. It provides efficient support for acquiring, discovering, interpreting, and accessing various contexts to build context-aware services. It also proposes a formal context model based on ontology using Web Ontology Language to address issues including semantic representation, context reasoning, and context classification and dependence.

MavHome [18] focuses on research involving the home as an intelligent agent that seeks to maximize the comfort of its inhabitants while minimizing resource consumption (e.g., power, water) and maintaining safety and data security. It also applies prediction algorithms to forecast future user actions, but parts of the prediction seem to rely on database support and batch training.

The Interactive Workspaces project (http://iwork.stanford.edu/) focuses on augmenting a dedicated meeting space with technology such as large displays, wireless/multimodal I/O devices, and seamless integration of mobile and wireless "appliances," including handheld PCs. It was built using high-resolution wall-mounted and tabletop displays, laptops, PDAs, wireless LAN, LCD tablets, laser pointer trackers, microphone arrays, and pan-and-tilt cameras. Their major research thrusts include a scalable distributed display architecture, architectures for the integration of multiple people and devices, interaction styles and associated toolkits, and a generalized interaction architecture.

While most of middleware systems target at generic smart environments, there are designated systems designed for a specific domain such as healthcare. Bardram et al. [19] propose a pervasive activity-driven computing infrastructure for healthcare. The system provides the support of mobility and nomadic work by keeping track of the user's activities and context, interruptions of a user's activity by making it easy to take turns in using a device, collaboration through sharing activities and contexts, and activity detection for proactive guidance for users. Rodríguez et al. [20] propose the SALSA middleware, which uses autonomous agents to implementation healthcare application in hospital settings. Bottazzi et al. [21] propose a group management middleware-level solution for supporting anytime and anywhere elder assistance. They focus on the creation and management of outdoor assistance teams and propose a group management system (AGAPE) that exploits visibility of location and group/user/device profile information as a key principle to trigger and control the team formation and team member interactions required to coordinate emergency activities.

Apparently, all the above mentioned middleware architectures focus on certain aspects of the system support to specific smart spaces but fail to address challenges such as context-awareness, spontaneous interaction, trust, and scalability at the same time. In the next section, we intend to propose a reference middleware for smart spaces, where spontaneous device interaction, context-awareness, system scalability, and interoperability, as well as trust, will be supported.

32.4.1 A Reference Service-Oriented Middleware for Smart Spaces

In order to address the challenges posed by smart spaces, we proposed a reference middleware architecture as shown in Figure 32.1. The proposed middleware takes the service-oriented system architecture, it contains a number of collaborating components, namely, physical and software entities, wrappers, service platform, context management services, and trust management services. As the middleware leverages on the device interaction mechanism and service-oriented architecture as detailed previously, it can accommodate the evolution of physical and software entities quite well. With the incorporation of interspace service/context discovery mechanism in middleware, it is scalable in terms of device, service, and across spaces.

As Figure 32.1 shows, the reference middleware contains the following logical layers:

1. *Physical and Software Entities.* *Physical entities* consist of various physical devices, objects, sensors, and actuators that are embedded or used in the environment. Typical physical entities include lamps, TV sets, clock radio, doorbell, chairs, beds, temperature sensors, motion sensors, stoves, and robots. *Software entities* are those functions and applications which can provide input or output to the environment. Logically, the physical and software entities lie in the bottom layer of the middleware architecture; they are the basic entities that we need to manage and build our services and applications on.

2. *Wrappers.* Wrappers are software agents or proxies that bridge the service platform with the physical and software entities. Wrappers transform the functions of those entities into the form of services and publish those services in the service platform for other services to access. Developers can thus compose any service for certain applications without having to understand how the physical and software entities work. Decoupling

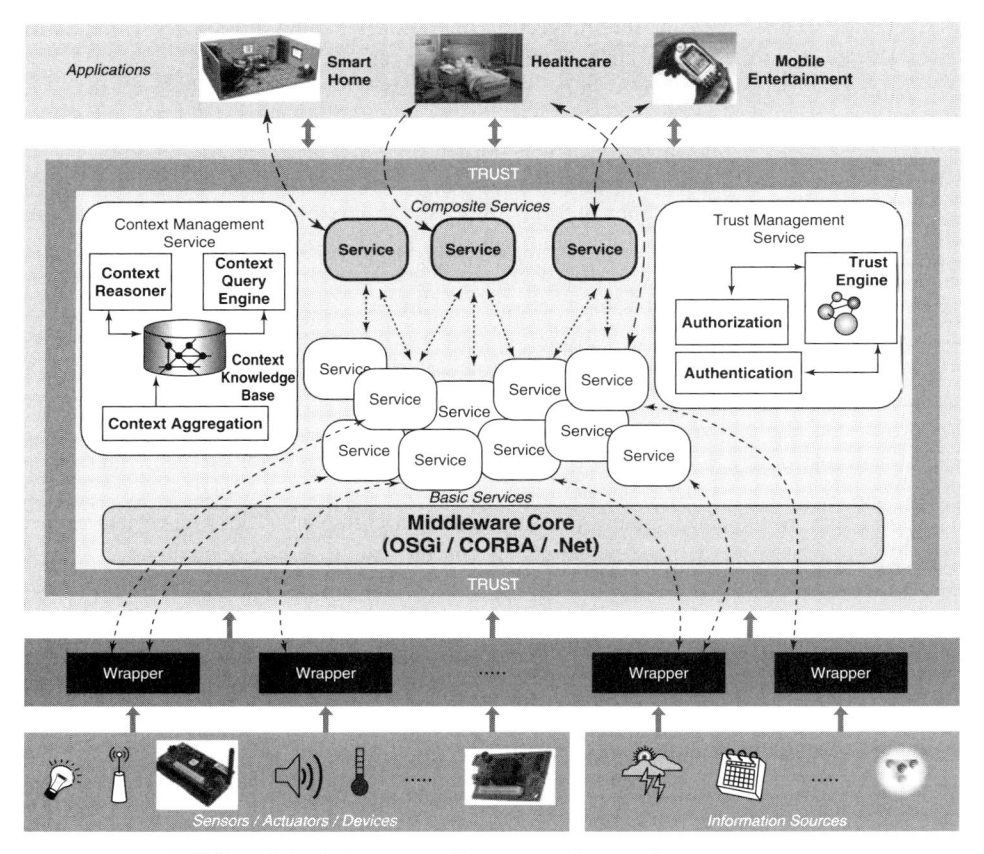

FIGURE 32.1 Reference middleware architecture for smart spaces.

entities from services provide great flexibility and openness to integrate new components into the smart spaces. Wrappers can turn entities into a form of services that is compliant with the service platform, such as UPnP service, OSGi service, Web service, and so on.

3. *Service Platform.* Service platform contains the service framework such as OSGi, CORBA (common object request broker architecture), or. NET, which manages the lifecycle of services. Basic services refer to functions provided either by physical or software entities, quite often the service framework also provides certain standard basic services such as communication service, registration service, and discovery service. Developers create composite services by combining more than one basic service, applications are essentially the composite services exposed to users in smart spaces.

4. *Context Management Services.* The context management services are essentially the context processing functions; all these functions are implemented in the form of context services. Context information is obtained from an array of diverse information sources and represented based on a shared context model. The context aggregation service merges the interrelated context and puts all the derived high-level context in the centralized knowledge base. With the context query service, applications can register and query their contexts of interest. The applications and composite services that depend on certain context information are called *context-aware services*. A context processing and

management engine called *Semantic Space* has been implemented to manage the context in a single space [11,17], it exploits Semantic Web technologies to support explicit representation, expressive querying, and flexible reasoning of contexts in smart spaces. The single-space solution has been extended using P2P overlay to accommodate the context/service lookup in multiple spaces [11,12].

5. *Trust Management Services.* The trust management services deal with the risk assessment and decision recommendation in the service framework. From the service providers' perspective, all the service consumers will be assessed before they are allowed to access or consume certain services, and their trust values will be adjusted according to their consuming behavior. From the application perspective, all the physical and software entities will be assessed before they are allowed to provide services; the trust values associated with the services are based on the reputation of the provider as well as the quality of the services, which also varies according to the service quality.

32.5 SUMMARY

Future smart spaces need middleware hiding the complexity of managing the sensors, devices, and actuators; extracting high-level user and environment context from various sources; providing appropriate abstractions for application design and development; and supporting system interoperability, scalability, security, reliability, efficiency, and other system properties.

In this chapter, we started with the introduction of the middleware concept and why it is an essential part of smart spaces. We then identified some key challenges in designing the middleware, such as device interaction and integration, context management, interoperability of entities, security/privacy/trust, and scalability. We then presented some popular industry standards and discussed the characteristics of the existing middleware solutions for smart spaces. Finally, we proposed a reference middleware architecture for smart spaces. The middleware uniquely supports the spontaneous device interaction, context-awareness, and system scalability and interoperability, as well as trust, which represent some of the key requirements for future smart spaces.

REFERENCES

1. Cook DJ, Das SK: *Smart Environments: Technology, Protocols and Applications*, Wiley, Hoboken, NJ 2005.
2. Bernstein PA: Middleware: A model for distributed services, *Commu the ACM* **39**(2):86–97 (Feb 1996).
3. Linthicum DS: *Next Generation Middleware*, July 1997. (www.dbmsmag.com/9709d14.html).
4. Dey A, Abowd G: Towards a better understanding of context and context-awareness, *Workshop on the What, Who, Where, When and How of Context-Awareness at CHI*, 2000.
5. Hodes TD, Katz RH, Servan-Schreiber E, Rowe LA: Composable ad-hoc mobile services for universal interaction. *Proc 3rd ACM/IEEE Int Conf Mobile Computing (Mobicom'97)*, Budapest, Hungary, 1–12 (Sept 1997).
6. Edwards WK, Newman MW, Sedivy JZ, Smith TF, Izadi S: Challenge: Recombinant computing and the speakeasy approach, *Proc 8th ACM Int Conf Mobile Computing and Networking (MobiCom 2002)*, Atlanta, Sept 23–28, 2002.

7. Gu T, Wang XH, Pung HK, Zhang DQ: An ontology-based context model in intelligent environments, *In Proc of Communication Networks and Distributed Systems Modeling and Simulation Conf (CNDS 2004)*, San Diego, 2004, 270–275.
8. Wang XH, Zhang DQ, Dong JS, Chin CY, Hettiarachchi SR: Semantic space: A semantic Web infrastructure for smart spaces, *IEEE Pervasive Comput*, **3**(2) 2004.
9. Gu T, Pung HK, Zhang DQ: Towards an OSGi-based infrastructure for context-aware applications in smart homes, *IEEE Pervasive Comput*, **3**(4) (2004).
10. Nixon PA, Wagealla W, English C, Terzis S: Security, privacy and trust issues in smart environments, in Cook DJ, Das SK, eds, *Smart Environments Technologies, Protocols and Application*, Wiley, Hoboken, NJ 2005.
11. Gu T, Tan E, Pung HK, Zhang DQ: A peer-to-peer architecture for context lookup, *Proc Int Conf Mobile and Ubiquitous Systems: Networking and Services (MobiQuitous 2005)*, San Diego, (2005).
12. Zhang DQ, Chin CY, Gurusamy M: Supporting context-aware mobile service adaptation with scalable context discovery platform, *Proc 61st IEEE Semiannual Vehicular Technology Conf (VTC2005)*, Sweden, May 30–June 1, 2005 Sweden.
13. Wollrath A et al: *The Jini Specification*, Addison-Wesley, Reading, MA, (1999).
14. Czerwinski S, Zhao BY, Hodes T, Joseph A, Katz R: *An Architecture for a Secure Service Discovery Service (MOBICOM'99)*, Seattle, 1999.
15. Hong JI, Landy JA: An infrastructure approach to context-aware computing, *Human-Comput Interact*, **16** (2001).
16. Barton JJ, Kindberg K: *The Cooltown User Experience*, Technical Report HPL-2001-22, 2001 (http://www.hpl.hp.com/techreports/2001/HPL-2001-22.pdf).
17. Helal S, Mann W, El-Zabadani H, King J, Kaddoura Y, Jansen E: The Gate Tech smart house: A programmable pervasive space, *IEEE Comput Mag* 50–60 (March 2005).
18. Cook DJ, Youngblood M, Heierman III EO, Gopalratnam K, Rao S, Litvin A, Khawaja F: MavHome: An agent-based smart home, *Proc 1st IEEE Int Conf Pervasive Computing and Communications (PerCom'03)*, IEEE Computer Society Press, March 2003, pp 521–524.
19. Bardram JE: Activity-based computing: Support for mobility and collaboration in ubiquitous computing, *Personal Ubiq Comput* **9**(5):312–322 (July 2005).
20. Rodríguez M, Favela J, Preciado A, Vizcaíno A: An agent middleware for supporting ambient intelligence for healthcare, *ECAI 2004 2nd Workshop on Agents Applied in Health Care*, Valencia, Spain, August 2004.
21. Bottazzi D, Corradi A, Montanari R: Context-aware middleware solutions for anytime and anywhere emergency assistance to elderly people, *IEEE Commun Mag* **44**(4): (April 2006).

33

Safety, Security, Privacy and Trust Issues

Abdallah M'hamed

Institut National des Télécommunications Évry France

33.1 INTRODUCTION

Owing to pervasive computing and advanced technology, assistive devices are deployed within smart environments to provide services dedicated to elderly and disabled users. Beside the significant help and usefulness provided by such environments for elderly and disabled users, there is still a high demand to make them both safe and secure.

The aim of this chapter is to first give an overview of security requirements for smart environments that have been studied more recently to better show the lack of security services for elderly and disabled users. These requirements must be fulfilled for elderly or disabled people among the various smart environments considered (homes, offices, schools, workplaces, hospitals, and cars). Considering this challenging task, the aim of our contribution will try to cover safety, security, privacy, and trust issues, in order to derive some guidelines for future research work dedicated to both elderly and disabled people. To better understand the meaning of the main issues addressed in this chapter, Section 33.2 defines relevant concepts that are discussed in the following sections. Section 33.3 is devoted to some of research work related to the four issues in smart environments and in which the authors have more or less made reference to the usefulness of their proposal for elderly or disabled people. In Section 33.4, we show some trends that can be taken from research work to highlight some interesting ways to be explored. In Section 33.5 we propose some key ideas that can be derived from the literature and seriously considered for future development.

The Engineering Handbook of Smart Technology for Aging, Disability, and Independence,
Edited by A. Helal, M. Mokhtari and B. Abdulrazak
Copyright © 2008 John Wiley & Sons, Inc.

33.2 BASIC CONCEPTS

Basically, the common goal of the four issues (safety, security, privacy, and trust) is to prevent threats that can affect any information—stored, used, or communicated—in smart environments. Since this information can be stored by both software and hardware components and can be associated with the user, computer devices, network protocols, or assistive devices, its protection techniques fall into one or several of these four issues. This is why it is usually difficult to consider each of these issues individually.

In Figure 33.1 we attempt to illustrate a comprehensive view for representing this information as a basic component to be protected for ensuring the four issues within smart environments. The bottom portion of this figure shows six different components derived from the contextual view of using this information that can be related to smart environment (SE) occupants (elderly and disabled users and their families, to the information and communication technology and caregivers), (ICT) system core or to the SE peripherals (home automation/assistive devices). The involvement of these components in the four issues is represented by the boldface lines.

The four components are defined here:

Safety describes all the techniques of assessing the risks associated with a given environment or situation, due to the occurrence of device failures in order to minimize their impact on the user's body, system, or environment. It aims to recover or restore the service when hardware, network connections, or system fail.

Security describes all the techniques used to secure both communications channels and required data. If we consider the protection of information storage and transport, security is based on three main proprieties: confidentiality, integrity, and availability.

Confidentiality is the ability to protect the information/service from any unauthorized access. It preserves the content secrecy of information.

Integrity is the ability to protect the information/service from any unauthorized changes or modification. It ensures the content accuracy and completeness of information.

Availability is concerned with ensuring that the information/service remains accessible, available when needed.

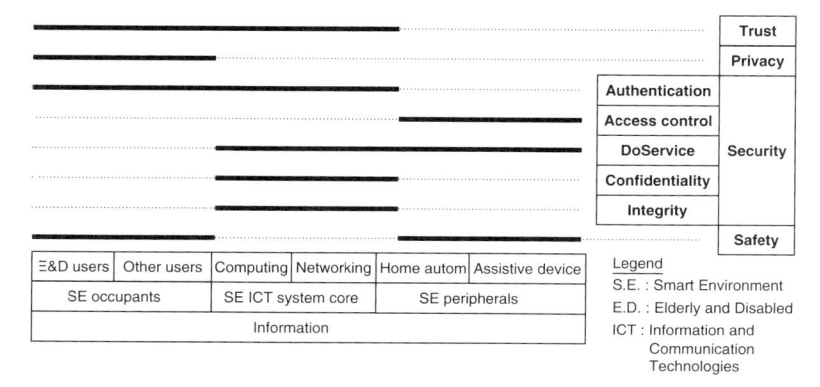

FIGURE 33.1 Involvement of smart environment components in Safety, Security, Privacy and Trust.

Considering the protection of user's personal information, there are growing concerns about privacy and trustworthiness of such environments and the data they hold.

Privacy is the ability to keep user's personal information and identities confidential.

Trust is the ability to determine the level of confidence related to users and the issued information.

Another concept, *dependability*, is defined as the reliance that can be placed on any delivered service. Dependability issues often include safety, security, reliability, and usability. A system is dependable to the extent to which its operation is free of failures. A system failure occurs when the delivered service deviates from fulfilling the system function.

33.3 SAFETY, SECURITY, PRIVACY, AND TRUST NEEDS IN SMART ENVIRONMENTS

In a more recent work partly supported by the SECURE[1] and GLOSS[2] projects, a perspective on the background and current status of security, privacy, and trust issues in smart environments has been shown [1]. After presenting the basic principles related to security, privacy and trust, Nixon et al. highlighted traditional and new approaches of dealing with these issues in smart environments [1]. Despite the vast literature reported, they have mentioned different areas not yet covered, including access control, identity management, legal and social issues, and biometric aspects.

33.3.1 Security Needs

Security requirements for smart environments can be summarized as follows: *security* of both communication and required data, *privacy* of user's personal information and identities, and *trust* or the level of confidence related to users and the issued information Through the research work, we can see that smart environments require proper and adequate security services to prevent unauthorized access and enforce security policies. The problem of securing applications that will access and control information resources in smart homes has been addressed by Covington et al. [2]. A new security system based on a generalized role-based access control (GRBAC) was introduced by incorporating the notion of object and environment roles with subject roles. GRBAC is compared to several existing access models in order to show its usefulness and effectiveness in aware home applications for elderly people.

In his thesis, Rattapoom Tuchinda has addressed the understanding of security and privacy issues in the intelligent room. He proposed a conceptual model that solves security and privacy problems through access control of multiple users in multiple locations by analyzing different scenarios [3].

The need to adapt a security requirement level to the smart spaces was integrated in the Gaïa project [4]. Context-awareness and automated reasoning were applied to the

---

[1] *Secure Environments for Collaboration among Ubiquitous roaming Entities*, IST-2001-32486.
[2] Global Smart Environments, IST-2000-26070.

identification process through authentication of users and access controls in ubiquitous computing environments.

A security management architecture (AETHER) that addresses specific requirements of access controls and trust establishment in ubiquitous environments has been proposed [5]. Security and profile management is also addressed by the UBISEC project, which follows a profile-based approach to manage any information in order to facilitate context-aware and highly adaptable applications [6]. A middleware is proposed for a secure management device and user profiles by integrating a profile database with a generic authentication scheme. User profiles are used to capture both preference information and basic abilities. Device profiles provide the main characteristics of the available devices, and context describes the current situation for each entity (user, device, application). Designed to be open and extensible, the system implements different security levels, each requiring an authentication threshold. Five different authenticators are available in that environment, each providing a different level of accuracy and security, depending on the authentication method used.

For access control to services, tickets—including all information needed by the profile manager or device manager—are granted to the user for the required service. The study by Markopoulos et al. [7] focuses on the profile maintenance in a personal-area network (PAN) through security properties such as authentication, availability, and confidentiality to unauthorized terminals and networks. This is achieved by implementing security mechanisms on two logical groups through

- *Certificates*, which provide the security in the transport–authentication layer
- *Profiles and roles*, which provide security in the application layer

In smart environments and active spaces, more and more devices become smaller and mobile. Because of mobility, there is a limit to the processing power, energy, and a memory that can be used by security mechanisms (cryptographic algorithms). There is still a great need for lightweight security components that can adapt to environments with scare resources.

A "smart home" is defined as an active environment populated with smart, dynamically configurable consumer devices able to interact with human and other smart devices. In such a dynamic and active environment, there is a great need for a flexible and lightweight distributed security mechanism.

Al-Muhtadi et al. discussed an approach to build a dynamic and secure smart home environment with the associated challenges [8]. To meet these challenges, the authors present "Tiny SESAME," which is a lightweight, component-based, Java implementation of a subset of SESAME and could be integrated with handheld and consumer devices. SESAME is an extension of Kerberos that supports public key technologies and provides additional services like digital signature, access control, key management, and delegation of access rights. A complete description of Tiny SESAME architecture and its integration within smart home environment is also given.

33.3.2 Privacy Needs

In ubiquitous computing environments, the increasing number of devices and technologies, like sensors and cameras, is intended to prevent other people from threatening the privacy of users. For preserving the user's privacy and keeping his/her communication anonymous, a new communication protocol called *Mist* was proposed in [9]. This protocol and its implementation are described in detail by Al-Muhtadi et al. [10]. Despite of the attracting service provided by Mist, some limitations in discovery and location detection protocols (e.g., cameras, voice recognition devices) are necessary if we want to really achieve full privacy.

After revealing the lack of the location and identity privacy [11], Al-Muhtadi et al. describe how, using the Mist protocol, we can provide an infrastructure for ubiquitous and private communication. An authentication framework has been introduced [12] showing how privacy was performed by Mist on the active space, through the use of wearable and embedded devices. These devices authenticate entities with varied levels of confidence, in a transparent, convenient, and private manner, allowing the framework to blend seamlessly into ubiquitous computing environments.

To increase the user acceptance of ambient intelligent techniques for well-being at home, the UBISEC (FP6) project is aiming for an advanced security infrastructure for context-aware and personalised authorization and authentication services in heterogeneous networks [13]. The implementation concept is directed mainly toward smart card technology to provide advanced personalization and localization features in order to establish privacy and to protect computing devices and personal user data. Among the key areas in the UBISEC project, the design of ubiquitous manager based on smart cards fulfills the following requirements: management of authentication (of users and devices), management of authorization, privilege delegation, and management of multicast-based security groups.

The profile management developed in UBISEC can be used to grant access rights to such security services only to trusted people (e.g., close family members or medical personnel) and also on a context-dependent basis.

To demonstrate the feasibility of the UBISEC approach, ongoing trials and validation are undertaken at the Pervasive Computing Environment Laboratory in Spain and the Ambient Computing Laboratory (AC-LAB) in Germany. The AC-LAB provides multimodal and multidevice user interfaces that adapt to specific situations. Different positioning and surveillance techniques based on W-LAN or on networked cameras provide means for increased personal security and context-based decisions, while contactless authentication with Java cards can be used for secure and easy access of rooms or services together within profile-based customization.

Another proposal shows how different contexts can influence the type and quality of data that may be transmitted in different situations, which can increase privacy [14].

33.3.3 Trust Needs

Trust-based security mechanisms are needed for making smart environment secure. Smart home middleware provides discovery services because it simplifies the installation of new smart appliances. By integrating a trust formation element into smart appliances access control mechanism, the SECURE project [15] aims to implement a formal trust model for security smart home environment with minimal user intervention.

To solve the security and trust problems within smart environments, a virtual-to-virtual (V2V) paradigm is proposed for virtualization of security services by applying the concepts of infospheres and security domains [16]. An *infosphere* deals with ownership of data, whereas a *security domain* deals with the protection and control of these data.

New ways of implementing security functions are proposed to provide both security and trust within personal [personal-area network (PAN), sensor networks], collective [local-, wide local-, and metropolitan-area network (LAN, WLAN, MAN)] and open [wide-area network (WAN)], and closed [Internet, general packet radio service (GPRS)] infospheres.

33.3.4 Safety Needs

The issue of dependability is critical to the development of appropriate technology solutions that are robust and satisfy user requirements. To meet the needs of older and disabled people effectively and efficiently within a home system of networked devices, system failures need to be minimised and controlled.

In smart environments, assistive technology greatly facilitates the lives of most disabled and elderly people. Nevertheless, the complexity of the necessary computer and network-based systems requires high dependability.

An ongoing project concerned with providing dependable ubiquitous computing in the home, an area that is currently being investigated, is described by Dewsbury et al. [17]. The authors attempt to outline some of the main issues relating to appropriate design of home technology to meet the needs of the occupants. This paper [17] proposes several areas of investigation that might form the basis for future and ongoing research toward an appropriate and dependable integration of assistive technologies.

Nowadays, safety may be achieved through networked cameras or sensor networks as described by Morris et al. in some cases studies, where several sensor-based scenarios for aiding people with different levels of cognitive impairments were proposed [18].

33.4 SECURITY FOR ELDERLY AND DISABLED PEOPLE

To improve the daily lives of the elderly or people with disabilities, smart environments are equipped with a large variety of connecting devices and advanced technology. However, their real-life deployment is still hindered by poor security, particularly the lack of proper authentication and access control techniques and privacy-preserving protocols. From this, it should be clear that we need to provide a more dynamic view of security for smart spaces, which will require development of new security models to handle a wider range of users.

Owing to the very high heterogeneity and complexity of involved devices in smart environments, there is still a major challenge for ensuring safety and security issues of elderly or disabled persons living in these spaces, to prevent unauthorized access and enforce security policies.

As we noted in Section 33.3, previous and ongoing research on the specific needs of elderly or disabled people has been relatively sparse. Some of proposed new security schemes developed for smart, pervasive, or ubiquitous environments must be extended to apply for elderly and disabled users.

Previous research has, however, suggested some interesting areas that might be explored, as described below.

33.4.1 Authentication and Access Control

Authentication and access control of users are crucial because, before enabling any security mechanism, we need to verify the identity of users and the resources to which they can access. As the security requirements of a smart space may vary according to the context of the space, context-awareness should be applied to the identification and authentication of users and access controls to resources and services. Authentication and access control must be able to adapt to the rapidly changing contexts of the spaces (context-awareness).

Most of the traditional *authentication* approaches in restricted environments are identity-based. They have focused on the user's identity and how they can authenticate this identity. *Access control* policies for smart space environments must reflect a user-set profile where users can be anonymous or undertake different levels of authentication. For *access controls*, the use of the environmental roles instead of organizational roles categorizes users according to relevant environmental context, such as location and time in conjunction with user information.

For elderly and disabled people, further specific requirements must be fulfilled according to user profile, user context, and environment. Among security services for elderly and disabled persons, authentication is more directly related to people. Since authentication can be performed using a large number and variety of devices and protocols, it is mandatory to design a new dynamic model that is able to find a more convenient, reliable, and secure device according to the user profile, environment, and platform.

For authentication of elderly and disabled persons in pervasive environments, we need a new dynamic adapted authentication model based on

- *User capabilities* (in terms of device manipulation and memorization)—providing an adapted device that allows users to communicate the necessary information to the system to confirm their own identities.
- *User location*—applying a suitable authentication techniques or devices according to the environment of the user (platform, language, operating system, and architecture)

Considering the user profile (preferences, driving capacity, visual capacity, hearing capacity, vocal capacity) will help us find a suitable device according to the user's specific impairment(s). To ensure an efficient authentication system in pervasive environments, we must consider not only the user profile and context but also the variety and heterogeneity of available authentication devices and protocols.

The authentication model proposed by the Handicom Laboratory [19,20] is designed to support a wide range of authentication devices that are handled by a single authentication protocol within a given smart environment. The aim of this model is to provide a common tool supporting a wide variety of authentication devices to enable the disabled or elderly user to find the most convenient and available device, according to her/his profile and preferences.

33.4.2 Nonobtrusiveness

Like assistive technologies, security or safety systems and devices must be nonintrusive, to be easily adopted by elderly and disabled persons. To provide these people with both security and safety without disturbing their lives, an intelligent house automation system based on sensors and artificial neural network (ANN) has been designed for monitoring these people to enable them to live independently [21].

Giuliani et al. studied the acceptance of technologic aids by elderly people and analyzed strategies to improve the performance of these people in their daily activities [22]. Although most older people do recognize the usefulness of these assistive devices, some of them are worry of the possible inherent risks in using these aids and are afraid that they will intrude on their privacy. Five adaptive strategies were considered: physical modification of the environment, formal help, informal help, change of behavior, and accommodation. The relationship between adopted strategies, successful aging, and satisfaction with life was investigated to identify which factors (personal, psychological, environmental, and/or situational) are related to the choice of adaptation strategies in different situations.

In situations related to safety (such as intrusion and home accident scenarios) or health and personal care (medicine and bathtub scenarios), people usually strive to find an alternative solution based mainly on modifying the environment.

A study by the IST Advisory Group (ISTAG) revealed the lack of trust to be one of the major obstacles to a broader proliferation of ambient and ubiquitous technology, suggesting the need for further research on security and privacy, specific for different domains such as healthcare and personal well-being. Well-being at home, especially with respect to healthcare and personal security, creates a conflict between fundamental privacy aspects and the personal monitoring devices or applications that ensure their safety. This conflict cannot be easily resolved, but a profiling approach that allows the establishment of personal security preferences may help to assure the user that her/his privacy will be respected.

Looking for an unobtrusive means to ensure ambient security, the UBISEC Consortium opted for smart card technology in conjunction with biometrics. This technology may be quite suitable for elderly persons as well, as it does not require learning complex technology and there is no need to memorize passwords.

33.4.3 User Profile Management

A modular and flexible information model such as the concept of the virtual home environment (VHE) can provide valuable help for security deployment within and across smart environments [23]. In the VHE, users are consistently presented with the same personalized features, user interface customization, and services in any network and any terminal, wherever the user may be located. The VHE can be characterized by

- Identification and authentication of the user.
- Terminal and access network characteristics: to ensure mobility between different access technologies and terminals. As the user moves, his/her environment may significantly change and would therefore influence the way his/her services can be delivered.
- Service adaptation to the user environment.
- User profile management: all information related to a single user can be retrieved from a single user profile that dynamically changes as a roaming user connects to different access networks with different terminals and invokes or manages her/his services.

Four architectures schemes are considered to implement the user profile and its associated VHE functions. Among the major advantages of the VHE, embedding data related to users and their environment into a generic, comprehensive, and flexible data model (user profile) provides easy access to the network functions, services, and applications.

33.5 CONCLUSION AND FUTURE DEVELOPMENT

In this chapter, we can guess the complexity of the challenging task of ensuring safety, security, privacy, or trust issues in smart environments for elderly and disabled people.

Most of proposed methods, models and tools are considering smart environments as a pervasive space but do not really deal with specific needs and features of dependent people. For making these living/working spaces safe and secure for disabled and elderly people, we must put the user as a main component by considering

- The specific requirements of the these people in terms of protection of their lives and regardless to their capabilities and preferences (people with movement disabilities, older persons, people with low vision, hearing-impaired people, cognitively impaired people)
- The strong vulnerability of some spaces such as medical care environments, where both reliability and security can affect timeliness and accuracy information for patient monitoring
- The wide range of evolved actors—physicians/nurses, pharmacies, emergency personnel, law enforcement agencies, government/community leaders among whom the shared information should be secure, private, reliable, consistent, correct, and anonymous
- The design or adaptation of security services to these users and their environment by enabling the deployment of security sensitive applications in the pervasive computing and communication environments.

As these spaces tend to be *ubiquitous*, which means "access to computing and communications everywhere and anytime," the main key of achieving our goal is to concentrate in the "who" word in the following security expression:

"*Who*" is doing "what" to "which" and "how much" critical information, "when" and from "where"

To meet these specific requirements, some crucial key ideas taken from the literature must be thoroughly investigated, as described below.

33.5.1 Nonintrusiveness

The use of assistive technologies by dependent (disabled and elderly) people is required to be safe and to provide a safe environment. Pervasive systems must include the relationship and sensitivity of user to any device or service in terms of safety and security. Security mechanisms must be both usable and nonintrusive, or many homeowners will simply avoid using them. Security and privacy are of major importance for user acceptance of well-being and health services as they employ a significant amount of monitoring and surveillance techniques to make the home environment a pleasant and safe place.

33.5.2 The User Profile

To fulfill security requirements for smart environments, authentication and access control of users are so crucial because, before enabling any security mechanism, we need to verify the identity of the users and the resources to which they can access. This raises questions regarding a smart space access to the user profile in order to gather enough information to perform a good authentication using suitable techniques (smart cards, biometrics, sensors, wearable devices).

New security devices, systems, and services must be user-behavior-aware and designed to consider specific user activities and preferences.

33.5.3 Context-Awareness

One of the main goals of smart environments is for the system to provide users with the same look and feel of their personalized services and user interfaces independent of their location (private or public).

Because of the dynamic behavior and the complexity of pervasive space, security policy must integrate the changing context for vulnerability models by providing different security levels according to the user's state and surroundings.

33.5.4 Privacy and Trust

In smart environments, a loss of privacy may discourage users from using a pervasive computing system. Privacy is strengthened by the fact that users within smart space are not theoretically limited by the environment in which they are temporarily located. Existing trust models need further development to include both dependent people and accompanying people (relatives, caregivers, etc...).

REFERENCES

1. Nixon PA, Wagealla W, English C, Terzis S: Security, privacy and trust issues in smart environments, in Cooke D, Das S, eds, *Smart Environments*, Pearson Press, 2004.
2. Covington MJ, Moyer MJ, Ahamad M: Generalized role-based access control for securing future applications, *Proc 23rd Natl Information Systems Security Conf*, Baltimore, MD, Oct 2000.
3. Tuchinda R: *Security and Privacy in the Intelligent Room*, thesis, EECS Dept, MIT, May 2002.
4. Al-Muhtadi J, Ranganathan A, Campbell R, Mickunas MD: Cerberus: A context-aware security scheme for smart spaces, Proc IEEE Int Conf Pervasive Computing and Communications (PerCom 2003), March 2003, pp 489–496.
5. Argyroudis PG, O'Mahony D: Securing communications in the smart home, *Proc Embedded and Ubiquitous Computing (EUC2004)*, Aizu-Wakamatsu City, Japan, 2004.
6. Ziegler M, Mueller W, Schaefer R, Loeser C: Secure profile management in smart home networks, *Proc 16th Int Workshop on Database and Expert Systems Applications*, Aug 2005, pp 209–213.
7. Markopoulos A, Arvanitis G, Psilakis P, Kyriazakos S, Stassinopoulos G: Security mechanisms maintaining user profile in a personal area network, *Proc 14th IEEE Personal, Indoor and Mobile Radio Communications (PIMRC 2003)*, 2003, Vol 3, pp 2770–2774.
8. Al-Muhtadi J, Anand M, Dennis Mickunas M, Campbell R: Secure smart homes using Jini and UIUC SESAME, *Proc 16th Annual Computer Security Applications Conf (ACSAC'2000)*, New Orleans, LA, Dec 2000.

9. Al-Muhtadi J, Campbell R, Kapadia A, Mickunas MD, Yi S: Routing through the mist: Privacy preserving communication in ubiquitous computing environments, *Proc 22nd Int Conf Distributed Computing Systems*, July 2002, pp 74–83.
10. Al-Muhtadi J, Campbell R, Kapadia A, Mickunas MD, Yi S: *Routing through the Mist: Design and Implementation*, Technical Report UIUCDCS-R-2002-2267, March 2002.
11. Al-Muhtadi J, Campbell R, Kapadia A, Mickunas MD, Naldurg P: *Socializing in the Mist: Privacy in Digital Communities*, Technical Report UIUCDCS-R-2002-2271, April 2002.
12. Al-Muhtadi J, Ranganathan A, Campbell R, Mickunas MD: A flexible privacy-preserving authentication framework for ubiquitous computing environments, *Proc 22nd Int Conf Distributed Computing Systems Workshops*, July 2002, pp 771–776.
13. Schaefer R, Eikerling HJ: Increasing the acceptance of ambient intelligence technologies for well-being at home through security contexts, *EUSAI Workshop on AmI Technologies for Well-being at Home*, Eindhoven, The Netherlands, Nov 2004.
14. Neustaeder C, Greenberg S: The design of a context-aware home media space for balancing privacy and awareness, *Proc 5th Int Conf Ubicomp*, Seattle, WA, 2003.
15. Seigneur JM, Jensen CD, Farrell S, Gray E, Chen Y: Towards security autoconfiguration for smart appliances, *Proc Smart Objects Conf*, Grenoble, France, 2003.
16. Naqvi S, Riguidel M: Security and trust assurances for smart environments, *IEEE Int Workshop on Resource Provisioning and Management in Sensors Network, 2005 (RPMSN05)*, Washington DC, Nov 7–10, 2005.
17. Dewsbury G, Rouncefield M, Clarke K, Sommerville I: Designing appropriate technology for home users: Developing dependable networks, *Proc CIB Working Group W084—Building Non-Handicapping Environments, "Inclusive Design and Mobility Response in Indoor/Outdoor Public Buildings and Facilities,"* Rome, Oct 2002,
18. Morris M et al: New perspectives on ubiquitous computing from ethnographic study of elders with cognitive decline, *Proc Ubicomp* 2003, pp 227–242.
19. M'hamed A, Mokhtari M: Providing a new authentication tool for dependent people in pervasive environments, *Proc IEEE Int Conf Information & Communication Technologies (ICTTA'04)*, Damascus, Syria, April 2006.
20. M'hamed A, Mokhtari M: Toward a new authentication model for smart homes dedicated to dependent people, *Proc Int Conf Aging, Disability and Independence (ICADI)*, St. Petersburg, FL, Feb 2006.
21. Chan M, Hariton C, Ringeard P, Campo E: Smart house automation system for the elderly and the disabled, *IEEE Int Conf Systems, Man and Cybernetics*, Vancouver, Canada, Oct 1995, Vol 2, pp 1586–1589.
22. Giuliani MV, Scopelliti M, Fornara F: Elderly people at home: Technological help in everyday activities, *Proc 14th IEEE Int Workshop on Robot and Human Interactive Communication*, Nashville, TN, Aug 2005, pp 365–370.
23. Bougant F, Delmond F, Pageot-Millet C: The user profile for the virtual home environment, *Commun Mag, IEEE*, **41**:93–98 (2003).

34

Automated Medication Management Devices

R. J. Davies, Christopher Nugent, D. D. Finlay, and N. D. Black
University of Ulster, Northern Ireland

D. Craig
Queens University Belfast, Northern Ireland

This chapter provides an overview of the needs, role, and trends in the area of medication management devices. The chapter begins with an overview of the problems associated with medication management, the reasons behind these problems, and the associated negative effects of medication noncompliance. Details of all stakeholders involved in the supply–intake chain of medication are then introduced along with the respective roles of these stakeholders in the medication management process. Following this, an overview of typical clinical approaches to noncompliance are introduced, followed by a description of automated medication management devices. The chapter concludes with a vision of how medication management and home-based remote healthcare will form the new care paradigms of the future.

34.1 INTRODUCTION

The term *compliance* has been widely used to indicate whether a patient is taking her/his prescribed medication in the right way. In general terms, *noncompliance* is not a simple issue to address. It is a complex, multifactorial problem that involves a large number of stakeholders and is related to the context within which the medication is prescribed, delivered, and ingested. From a research perspective, another term that has been widely

---
The Engineering Handbook of Smart Technology for Aging, Disability, and Independence,
Edited by A. Helal, M. Mokhtari and B. Abdulrazak
Copyright © 2008 John Wiley & Sons, Inc.

632 AUTOMATED MEDICATION MANAGEMENT DEVICES

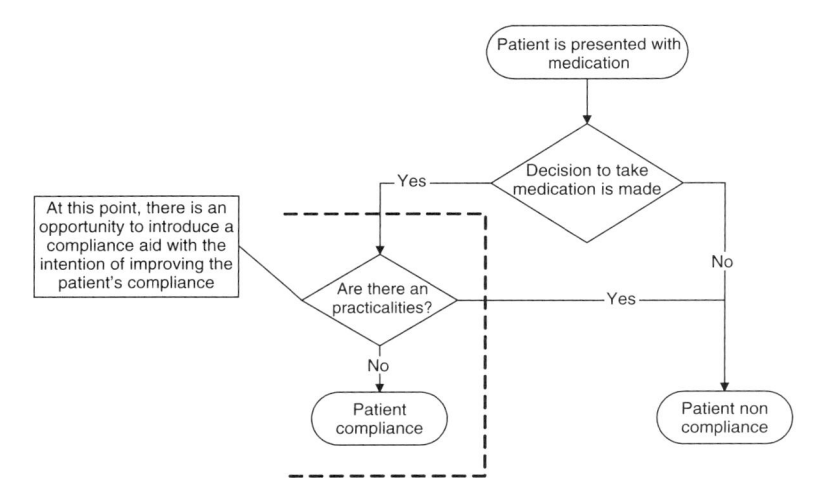

FIGURE 34.1 Representation of how a patient's perception to medication can affect compliance.

used as an alternative to compliance is *adherence*. This is felt to be a more favorable choice of terminology, implying that patients play active roles in their medication management and the recommendations of their physicians. For the remainder of this chapter, the terms *adherence* and *compliance* should be considered as synonymous.

Compliance can be categorized into two broad areas: primary and secondary non-compliance. *Primary noncompliance* generally refers to instances where for some reason the medicine is not dispensed to the patient. When we consider the scenario where the medication has been dispensed to the patient and not taken as intended, we refer to this as *secondary noncompliance*. If we consider the latter in further detail, it is possible to distinguish between instances of intentional and nonintentional noncompliance. In instances of intentional noncompliance, the patient has made a conscious decision not to take the medication as prescribed. With unintentional noncompliance the patient has not taken the medication as prescribed because of an inability to manage the medication regimen or other factors beyond his/her control. It should be stressed at this point that the introduction of any form of medication management device to those who can be categorized as intentionally noncomplying to the prescribed medication regimen will be of limited help unless the benefits delivered by the device lead to changes in the original underlying attitudes responsible for the person's conscious decision to avoid the medications; a person may deliberately not comply because the medication regimen is unduly complex, but if simplified through technologic support, improved compliance may result. For those belonging to the group of unintentional noncompliance, it is likely that benefits will follow if some form of aid is introduced. Figure 34.1 summarizes these two scenarios and indicates at which point compliance aids can be introduced to improve patient compliance in the unintentional categorisation.

34.2 UNDERSTANDING NONCOMPLIANCE

Research has tried to unravel the reasons behind patient noncompliance. Although the patient is at the center of this process and its associated problems, other areas such as the healthcare process and disease-related issues are also considered to contribute. From the patient specific perspective, some of the intrinsic factors that may contribute to non-compliance are

- Forgetfulness
- Physical difficulties in administering the medication
- Real or perceived experience of side effects
- Real or perceived assessment of patient's own disease or disorder (e.g., level of severity of disease, "silent" conditions such as high blood pressure)
- Large numbers of prescribed medications over prolonged periods
- Lack of understanding of terms used in the instructions for administration
- Unpleasant taste of medication, tablet size, or other complaint

Extrinsic factors relate to those relevant to the healthcare infrastructure, including

- Relationship between stakeholders and communication pathways
- Cost implications
- Appropriateness of the medication regimen to patient's diagnosis and/or lifestyle

As mentioned previously, noncompliance is an extremely complex problem; nevertheless, it is necessary to attempt to gain an understanding of how the problem arises and how it may be improved in order to improve compliance levels.

34.2.1 Impact of Noncompliance

Differences in healthcare systems throughout the world prevent an exact assessment of the compliance problem. Despite this, many statistics and figures have arisen that provide an estimation, although the collation of these figures and statistics is also a complex issue. Primarily, figures relating to the sheer volumes of medication that are prescribed and dispensed annually underline the potential for medication mismanagement issues. These are the most reliable statistics as pharmaceutical output in most countries is well governed and monitored. Secondary to this are figures that quantify the extent of adherence issues directly through projections based on estimations and scientific research. This is a more complex issue as it relies on accurate monitoring of compliance activity, which itself can affect the medication intake process. Finally, and probably most complex of all, is estimation of the adverse consequences of noncompliance and medication mismanagement. Such statistics can range from the number of deaths related to noncompliance to revenue lost through employee absenteeism. In the following paragraphs, some of the figures quoted are relevant to the aforementioned categories and are taken from reports that have been generated mainly from medication related activities in the United States (USA) and the United Kingdom (UK).

Considering the UK alone, it has been stated that medicines are the most common healthcare intervention made and account for over 15% of the national health service (NHS) budget [1]. It is estimated that approximately 20% of primary trust funds for the same region are spent on medication and related services each year [2]. In terms of how this translates to the actual population, it is estimated that at any one time 70% of the population in the UK are taking some form of prescribed medication [1].

As one would expect, the elderly population contribute significantly to this figure with 75% of people over the age of 75 taking at least one prescribed drug [3]. The issue of medication management in the elderly is particularly pertinent given the observation that almost 40% of the elderly take four or more medicines on a regular basis [3]. In terms of the actual levels of compliance, the most alarming figure of all is the observation that as many as 50% of patients do not comply with the terms of their prescriptions [4]. This is believed to relate not only to missed doses but also to irregular administration and incorrect quantities. The same studies [5,6], based in the USA, suggested that between 14% and 21% of patients never collect the medication as dedicated by the original prescription and 12–20% of patients take other people's medicines. In the UK, it is estimated that 10–20% of issued medications are never used [7] and each year approximately £100,000,000 worth of medications are returned to pharmacies unused [8]. It should be noted that this figure represents a direct cost of wasted medication and does not include downstream costs relevant to worsening disease states.

The effects of noncompliance are diverse and, as stated above, are difficult to establish. It has been suggested that in the USA around 125,000 people with treatable ailments die each year because they do not take their medications properly [5]. The nonfatal consequences are also accurately reported, with, in some regions, an estimated 23% of nursing home admissions and 10% of hospital admissions associated with noncompliance [9–11]. Particular patient cohorts have also been studied. For example, it has been reported that in a study of 2175 patients who had sustained a myocardial infarction, those who did not adhere well to the treatment regimen (defined as taking less than 75% of prescribed medication) were 2.5 times more likely to die within a year of follow-up [12]. Noncompliance with birth control medication has been associated with 10% of adolescent pregnancies [5,6].

34.3 STAKEHOLDERS IN THE PROCESS OF MEDICATION MANAGEMENT

A number of stakeholders exist in the supply–intake chain of medication. At a very broad level we have attempted to classify these stakeholders into two groups: internal stakeholders and external stakeholders. Those falling within the former category are likely to have direct contact with the patient and be involved in supporting and managing their medication management regimen. Examples of internal stakeholders include the physicians responsible for diagnosing the health problem and prescribing the medication as well as the pharmacists, undertaking the traditional role of dispensing the medication and a range of formal and informal caregivers, family, and friends who interact with the patient on a frequent basis to perhaps assist with the collection and delivery of the medication and monitoring of its administration. External stakeholders in the supply–intake chain are less likely to directly influence the patient and his/her medication regimen. This cohort of stakeholders includes drug manufacturers responsible for the actual preparation of the medication and pharmaceutical wholesalers who act as an intermediary and process the orders for the drug manufacturers as prepared by the pharmacists. This group of stakeholders also encompasses government health bodies and regulators who are responsible for the monitoring of adverse event profiles; enforcement of the policies and procedures surrounding laws of drug manufacture; and authorization for selling, pricing policies, and processes of reimbursement.

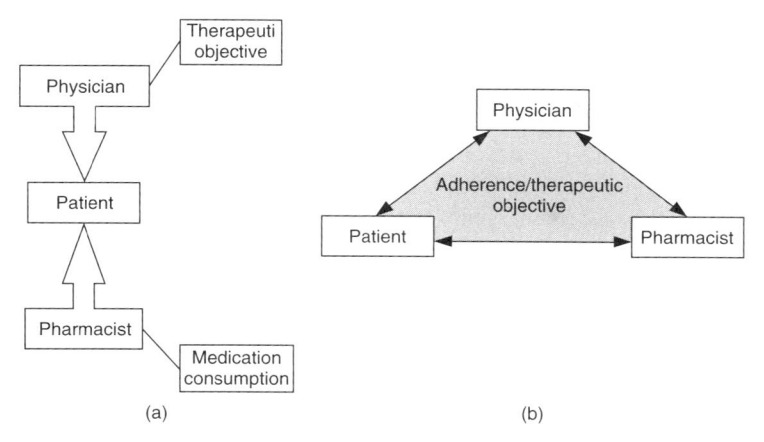

FIGURE 34.2 *Communication between professionals assisting with noncompliance: (a) classical approach — interaction between stakeholders; and (b) proposed triangular model — enhanced stakeholder interaction through "adherence" triangle.*

From an information flow perspective, it has generally been accepted that if the communication between the main internal stakeholders, especially those in close contact with the patient, can be enhanced, benefits will follow in relation to the effectiveness of the prescribed medication regimen. As depicted in Figure 34.2a, the classical form of communication has bilaterally involved the patient and physician and the patient and the pharmacist. This situation can be favorably enhanced by offering a means to introduce bidirectional interactions between all of these stakeholders. In such a sense, a "triangular" approach to medication management can be established (Fig. 34.2b), which subsequently offers an immediate improvement in the communication between the stakeholders. This model, applied within the context of specialist elderly care clinics in which the pharmacist and physician interact together "onsite" to target and improve those areas that may influence compliance, appears to attract an evidence base suggesting positive benefits in medication compliance potentially applicable to the wider patient community [13,14].

It has been the previous findings of the authors that potential widespread improvements in compliance rates can be expected if such a configuration is considered when designing new approaches to automated medication management devices and systems (Fig. 34.2).

34.4 USER REQUIREMENTS FOR MEDICATION MANAGEMENT DEVICES

Medication management and its noncompliance problem is a complex issue involving its many stakeholders and investors. In the current section an attempt is made to outline the requirements of each of the various stakeholders with respect to a compliance control device and associated supporting infrastructure or care model. In the first instance the desires of the patient are considered. Foremost in the patient wish list is the desire to have a device with high ergonomic integrity. This requirement encompasses a number of subrequirements, which include

Portability. The system should be portable or have a portable aspect. This should allow the patient to use the service both while moving around the home or when leaving the home for any period. This helps ensure that patients have a continuum of medication management services regardless of their location.

User-Friendliness. the system should meet the practical and technical competence of the complete range of users. The most prominent constraint for this requirement results from the elderly user who may not be comfortable with using technically complex solutions. A further consideration in "user-friendliness" is the facilitation of patients who may posses joint or neurologic disease limiting dexterity and who may have visual or cognitive limitations.

Complimentary Intervention. Also coming under the umbrella of ergonomics, any system must provide a set of alarms and interventions with which patients are comfortable and are willing to accept as part of their routine. Such a suite of alarms should be of a multimodal nature and allow the patient to choose, for example, at a very generic level, between audible or visual reminders.

Second in the list of patient's requirements are the very practical considerations that relate to medication management. The following are related to these specific considerations:

Capacity. Any system must be able to cater for an accurate supply of medication and medications other than those delivered through the oral route such as topical creams and eyedrops. Ideally, physician-led "rationalization" of medications should preempt the installation of any medication management technology allowing for the removal of unnecessary prescriptions with any potentially dangerous interactions that inevitably accumulate over time, particularly in elderly patients.

Reliability. The device must be reliable and not require intervention, whether it by the patient or by service staff; developers of proposed systems must consider the potential for downtime resulting from failure of complex components. The authors' experiences suggest that intricate mechanical components are most likely to cause problems.

A further category of consideration that is of the utmost importance is the issue of safety. This relates both directly to the patient and to any other individuals that may be at risk from misuse of the medication. Again, similar to the aforementioned requirements, a number of subrequirements exist:

Patient Identification. The system must avoid instances where the wrong person obtains the delivered medication. For this reason, where possible, some form of personal identification must be used to ensure that the intended patient is using the system. Depending on the user, this could be as simple as entering a personal identification number to release medication or incorporating some means of radiofrequency identification mechanism if a cognitive or physical handicap restricts manual interaction with the device itself.

Security. As well as ensuring that the wrong patients do not retrieve the incorrect medication, other persons within the same living environment should also be protected. In such instances the system should prevent, for example, children or cohabitants within the nursing home environment from gaining access to the supply of medication.

Medication Integrity. The system should ensure that no cross-contamination of medications occurs as a result of storage conditions inside any device.

Besides the several categories of need outlined above, several further miscellaneous requirements that must be considered, including

Aesthetics—the patient may be more likely to use the device if it is something that is more visually pleasing.

Cost—depending on the business model implemented by the healthcare provider, cost to the patient should be as low as possible.

Regarding the requirements of some of the other stakeholders in the supply–intake chain, the following section identifies requirements that are important to healthcare professionals, namely, GPs (general practitioners), pharmacists, and nursing staff as well as careworker staff who are not clinically trained but are entrusted with delivering medicines. These requirements also relate mainly to the provision of care and hence the supporting infrastructure that exists around the patient and his/her medication management routine. There is therefore much less emphasis on the physical compliance device.

The main requirement of all of these stakeholders is to have a mechanism to review the compliance activities of the patient for which they have some responsibilities—the extent to which this occurs is dependent on the stakeholder involved. *Extended profiling* refers to instances when, for example, the GP may wish to review a patient's compliance activity only when that patient is present for a scheduled appointment. This type of notification could be achieved on an "on request" basis, where the GP could, for example, consult an online report of the patient's compliance profile. A similar framework may be suitable for a pharmacist. At the more critical end of the spectrum, immediate profiling would be of benefit to a careworker or nurse who may need instant notification of a single noncompliance event, particularly if the patient is acutely unwell or suffers from a condition where noncompliance with even one or two doses may lead to direct clinical consequences (epilepsy, diabetic coma, etc.). For this purpose a request-based service is not suitable; instead, an alert or alarm must be sent directly to the relevant caregiver. Mobile messaging or an automated telephone recording may be most appropriate. A mechanism to access an extended profiling compliance record in these cases would have merit where medicines are regularly missed or authorities seek to monitor the quality of healthcare provision as it applies to the delivery of medicines through the provision of audit data that the extended profiling compliance record would contain.

This leads on to a second requirement of producing compliance statistics. Any system, whether it is based on a set of discrete electronic devices or an integrated care model framework, must be capable of providing compliance statistics to some degree. The scope of these statistics depends on the functionality of the compliance devices. Even in its most basic form, these statistics allow for patient profiling, which may be enhanced to provide a measure of health status evolution, signaling, for example, the onset of additional hitherto undiagnosed disease states such as dementia or arthritis, which may warrant clinical evaluation.

A final requirement for the healthcare professional-based stakeholders is the ease of integration with existing practices. This is a less obvious requirement but is important for successful uptake of any compliance device and its associated service.

A further group where needs must be considered in service development are those who are responsible for providing the technical aspects of the service. Their requirements are more straightforward and are based mostly on technical considerations. In particular, this cohort should be provided with a mechanism for maintaining the integrity of the service. Two-way communication with compliance devices is desirable as notifications of any faults can be received. This two-way communication also allows for remote provisioning and maintenance of any devices, particularly when faults occur.

34.4.1 Factors Facilitating the Decision to Assign Compliance Aids

In order to decide whether compliance support should or can be assigned to a patient, there are two main categories to consider. The first of these relates directly to the patient needs and relates primarily to the question of whether a particular patient needs a compliance aid. A number of issues must be considered in answering this question, the first of which relates to the patient's mental and physical capabilities and the possibility that these might affect the patient's ability to comply with a particular medication regimen. Secondary to this are constraints on the patient's personal circumstance in terms of her/his surrounding environment. This is the presence or absence of support from friends or family members to assist in meeting the medication regimen. If known, the patient's previous level of compliance may also assist in the decision. A factor that is indirectly linked to the patient is the actual medication regimen. The complexity, in terms of the frequency of the doses and the number of medications that are to be consumed, may influence the decision to assign an aid.

The second category of factors are those that are largely independent of the patient and related to the external healthcare environment. This relates entirely to the functionality provided in a healthcare system for filling and maintaining compliance aids. The roles of the pharmacists, nurses, and care workers are the most likely to affect this aspect.

34.5 MEDICATION MANAGEMENT DEVICES

From a clinical perspective, many approaches used to monitor adherence to medication have been reported. They may be categorized as being either direct or indirect methods of compliance monitoring. Direct methods may involve, for example, the observation of patients taking their medication or the measurement of drug levels in biological fluids such as urine or blood. On the other hand, indirect methods involve techniques such as questioning patients verbally about their compliance, the conducting of pill counts, assessment of compliance through family or nurse interview, and the use of electronic pill counters. Both direct and indirect approaches unfortunately have their drawbacks. The accuracy of measuring levels of medication within biologic fluids has been questioned because a wide range of variables can alter pharmacokinetic handling of a particular drug while the technique is more applicable to the context of pharmaceutical drug development as opposed to long-term medication management strategies. On the other hand, the accuracy associated with some of the indirect approaches can be considered similarly questionable. For example, with the approach of pill counting, patients may chose to remove some of the missed medications prior to the counting process. In addition, questioning patients in relation to their compliance has been demonstrated to be unreliable and subject to bias.

Alternative methods to the aforementioned techniques are automated medication management devices. These offer advantages of the ability to record and provide additional patient-related information and trends that can help physicians improve the long-term treatment process. The following sections examine these types of devices in further detail.

34.5.1 Automated Medication Management Devices

Medication management devices are available in several different forms and can be generally considered as devices or mechanisms that have been designed to store either solid or oral doses of medication for a prescribed period of time [15]. Depending on the level of support that the patient requires, the devices available range from very basic compartmentalized containers to more complex electronic devices incorporating the ability to communicate with remote healthcare-monitoring centers. These devices can be considered to fall within one of the following four categories of devices:

1. Pillholder [16–18]
2. Alarm-based device [19–24]
3. Automated dispensing device [25–27]
4. Monitoring device [24,25].

The following sections outline the functionalities that each of the aforementioned would be expected to offer.

34.5.1.1 Pillholders

The main functionality offered by this type of medication management device is to facilitate the storage of multiple types of medication across a wide range of intake times. The resulting device is typically a container containing a varying number of compartments, each representing a particular dosage interval. To accommodate different dosage intervals and the varying levels of medication, the size and shape may vary greatly between models. For example, some models provide a small number of compartments, typically three to six, to manage one day's worth of medication, while others incorporate enough compartments to deal with monthly medication regimens, for example, a set of seven containers with each container holding four medications. An additional feature offered by this type of device comes in the form of labels on the lids of each compartment that can be numbered, or labeled chronologically, such as day of the week or time of day. With this type of medication management device, the patient must remember to take the medication at the appropriate time. Loading of the device with the correct medication may be performed by any of the previously described internal stakeholders.

34.5.1.2 Alarm-Based

Alarm-based medication management devices operate a reminder system that ultimately activates an alarm to alert the patient at the correct time to take the medication. Essentially, these devices are available in the same variety of shapes and sizes as the pillholders, but with the ability to program the dosage time to suit the patient's needs. Containers of varying size are used in order to accommodate the varying needs of the patient in terms of differing numbers of medications and dosage intervals. The majority of these types of alarm-based medication management devices consist of a series of medication containers in conjunction with a small display module alongside some form of tactile button(s) to allow easy configuration of alarm times. When the medication time is imminent, an audible alarm sounds and the patient is prompted to open the compartments and retrieve the correct medication. Another popular alternative is to have an intelligent bottle cap on the medication container itself. On such a device a user would be able to program the alarm times for the medication stored in the container. Some bottle caps have the ability to record each time the bottle is opened and can display information such as the number of times the bottle has been opened and the time until the next medication dosage.

34.5.1.3 Automated Dispensing

Because of the inherent complexity of automated dispensing medication management devices, they tend to be less frequently deployed in common settings in comparison with the aforementioned pillholder and alarm-based devices. Their main advantage is the ability to deliver the correct medication to the patient in an automated fashion, eliminating any human error that might occur when retrieving the medication. This represents an appealing feature if manual dexterity problems are prevalent and is the feature that separates it from the aforementioned category of devices, which offer assistance in terms of organization of the medication and prompting as to when the medication should be taken. With an automated dispensing approach, the device not only prompts the patients to take their medication but also automatically dispenses the medication to them. As automated dispensing is highly complicated, the overall size of the device is generally quite large because of the electronic and mechanical components required. In addition, the cost of the device is reflected in this increased level of technically complexity.

34.5.1.4 Monitoring Devices

The primary feature of monitoring devices is their ability to examine the activities of patients in relation to their medication management regimen from outside the home environment. Usually, this involves recording all patient activity in relation to their medication regimen, with particular emphasis placed on instances of noncompliance. Any relevant information recorded can then be sent to a central repository from which alerts can be forwarded to relevant individuals such as the patient's GP or hospital consultant. Depending on the patient's needs, these types of devices can be monitored in real time or quasireal time, the former category permitting the immediate contacting of the patient in instances of noncompliance.

34.5.2 User Interfaces for Medication Management Devices

The previous sections have described the main categories of medication management devices. With the increasing uptake of the Internet, mobile phones, and information and communication technologies (ICTs) in general, the way in which users are likely to interact with their medication management devices is likely to evolve in the future as has been witnessed by more recently presented alternative medication management paradigms. An example of such an approach has been described by the MEDICATE system [28,29]. In the first instance this system has proposed to address the problem of noncompliance by incorporating all the internal stakeholders in the supply–intake chain of medication management. The entire system consists of software services and custom medication management devices that are connected together via a centralized

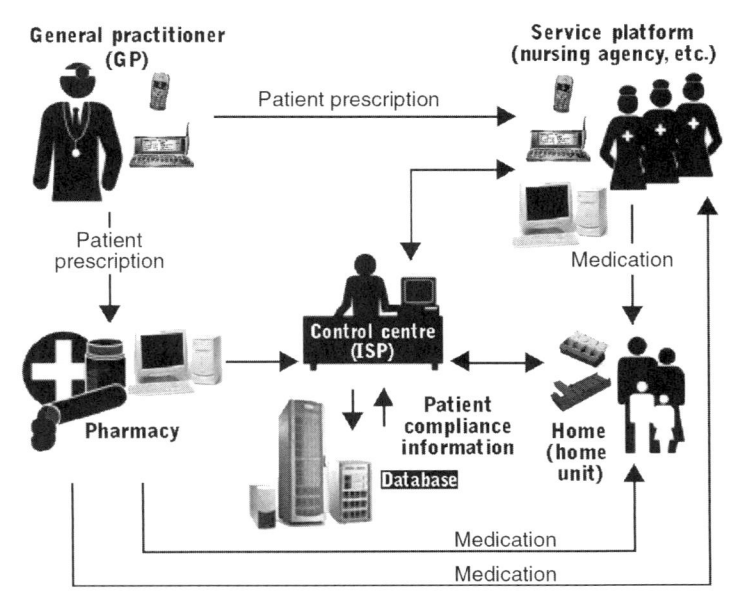

FIGURE 34.3 *MEDICATE Care Model and Internal Stakeholders.*

Internet-based portal. The provision of such services allows stakeholders to impart control within the supply–intake chain of medication, which ultimately results in a medication management care model (Fig. 34.3). The system essentially comprises the following components:

- A portable medication management device with alarm-based reminder facilities
- A home-based electromechanical system to act as a reservoir for the medication in addition to facilitating automated dispensing
- A suite of Internet-based services to support the prescribing of medication, the dispensing of medication, and monitoring patient compliance to the medication regimen within the home.

Although this system exhibits various features of the medication management devices as described in the previous sections, it also offers an extension in terms of its interacts with the users. Two examples of this are identified: delivery of a medication management service via a mobile phone and delivery of medication management services through digital television.

In the first instance a mobile medication management solution can be realized through the development of software applications that can be deployed on a mobile phone. In this example, the patient's medication regimen is entered via a simple Web-based interface at the point of medication prescribing. An application is deployed on a mobile phone that has the ability to automatically retrieve the medication regimen once the patient has been registered in the system. Once the entire prescription has been retrieved, the mobile device presents alerts to the patients and records any noncompliance information. On receiving an instance of noncompliance, the mobile application automatically updates a central resource. The noncompliance alerts can be viewed by a designated party via a Web interface, after which appropriate action can be taken. Although this facility offers the same principles of medication reminders as those described above, the application of the Internet- and mobile-phone-based technology can be seen as being a more suitable suite of services to certain cohorts requiring medication reminder services such as younger patients with complex medication regimens, such as those with HIV or psychiatric illness.

A further extension in terms of medication management services and their interaction with the user can be witnessed through the use of digital television services as the means of provision of the reminder. An example of such a system that offers this service has been reported [30]. This system provides the user with a medication management device that communicates with digital television services. In a fashion similar to those described above for other reminder systems, the patient's medication regimen can be entered via a suite of Web interfaces during the medication-prescribing process. The ultimate distinction with this service is the method in which the reminders are conveyed to the patient. In the first instance the ability of the medication management device to interact with a TV-set-top box in the patient's home allows medication reminders to be sent directly to the television where information can be displayed. This kind of reminder system is particularly suited to those patients who are quite capable of organizing their own medication and simply need to be reminded when to take it.

34.6 CONCLUSIONS

This chapter has presented details related to the issues of noncompliance, including how the problem arises, who is involved, the effects resulting from noncompliance, and how all of these issues can be addressed by the use of automated medication management devices. On the basis of these details, a key consideration when deploying an automated medication management device is the knowledge that some patients will make a conscious decision not to take their medication. This decision may often be insurmountable but should not be regarded as a fait accompli as some systems may in fact address the patient's underlying concerns that led to the conscious decision to withhold his/her medications in the first place.

For those who demonstrate practical difficulty in complying with their medication regimens, benefits can be accrued through the introduction of an automated medication management device. Nevertheless, it should still be remembered that the issue of noncompliance is a multifactorial problem involving a number of stakeholders and the way in which the medication is prescribed, delivered, and taken. Although a number of devices and services exist, the complexity of the problem suggests that a "one size fits all" approach cannot be adopted. In this sense, careful consideration must be given to the patient's needs, their diagnoses, and the model of healthcare delivery in place prior to the recommendation to use a medication management aid. If all of these issues can be addressed, then the chances of improving noncompliance are to be increased.

Future work in this area will continue to improve the process of introducing new and evolving technologic solutions to improve noncompliance into existing models of healthcare. It is becoming increasingly popular and acceptable to have home-based systems to support healthcare monitoring under the control of patients themselves within their own home environment. A challenge now exists to ensure that all of these systems have the ability to offer, from a technical perspective, a level of extensibility and interoperability to provide a holistic model of home-based healthcare delivery. Such a paradigm is moving a step closer toward a truly intelligent living environment where the activities and healthcare status of the patient are monitored and controlled by an adaptable environment containing a number of healthcare devices, sensors, and services. Such an environment will be mindful of the demographic changes challenging developed society in which large numbers of elderly patients, often with cognitive impairment and representing the typical recipients of polypharmacy, are appropriately served.

REFERENCES

1. Update on progress being made towards goals in "pharmacy in the future," Developing Future Pharmacy Conf, 2002.
2. *Natl Prescribing Centre MeReC Bull* **12**(6) (2006) (available at http://www.medicinescomplete.com/mc/merec/current/500046.htm; accessed 5/18/06).
3. *National Service Framework for Older People, Department of Health*, 2001, p1 (available at http://www.dh.gov.uk/assetRoot/04/07/12/83/04071283.pdf; accessed 5/18/06).
4. Marinker M, Blenkinsopp A, Bond C et al, eds: *From Compliance to Concordance: Achieving Shared Goals in Medicine Taking*, Royal Pharmaceutical Society of Great Britain, London, 1997.
5. *Just What the Doctor Ordered* (available at http://www.thehealthpages.com; accessed 1/01/03).
6. The Food and Drug Administration (available at http://fda.gov/) and Enhancing prescription medicine adherence: A national action plan, The National Council on Patient Information and Education, (available at http://www.talkaboutrx.org/documents/enhancing_prescription_medicine_adherence.pdf)
7. Bellingham C: How pharmacists can help to prevent wastage of prescribed medicines, *Pharm J* **267**(7175):741–742 (Nov 2001).
8. Pharmacy in the Future—Implementing the NHS Plan, London: Department of Health, London, 2000 (available at http://www.dh.gov.uk/assetRoot/04/06/82/04/04068204.pdf; accessed 5/18/06).
9. Standberg LR: Drugs as a reason for nursing home admissions, *Am Health Care Assoc J* **10**(4):20–23 (1984).
10. Robbins J, Schering Report IX: *The Forgetful Patient: The High Cost of Improper Patient Compliance*. Schering Labs, Kenilworth NJ. (1987)
11. Oregon Department of Human Resources: *A study of Long-Term Care in Oregon with Emphasis on the Elderly*, March 1981.
12. Horwitz RI, Viscoli CM et al: Treatment adherence and risk of death after a myocardial infarction, *Lancet* **336**:542–545 (1990).
13. Hanlon JT, Weinberger M, Samsa GP, Schmader E, Uttech KM, Lewis IK, Cowper PA, Landsman PB, Cohen HJ, Feussner JR et al: A randomized, controlled trial of a clinical pharmacist intervention to improve inappropriate prescribing in elderly outpatients with polypharmacy, *Am J Med* **100**:428–437 (1996).
14. Lim WS, Low HN, Chan SP, Chen HN, Ding YY, Tan T: Impact of a pharmacist consult clinic on a hospital-based geriatric outpatient in Singapore. *Ann Acad Med* **33**:220–227 (2004).
15. Walker R: Stability of medical products in compliance devices, *Pharm J* **248**:124–126 (1992).
16. *Modular Pill Dispenser* (available at http://www.bolton-bros.co.uk/d-commerce/healthcare.html; accessed 5/16/06).
17. *Medi-Dispenser for Pills* (available at http://www.bolton-bros.co.uk/d-commerce/healthcare.html; accessed 5/16/06).

18. *Dosett System* (available at http://www.dosett.com/enProd.htm; accessed 5/16/06).
19. *Pill Reminder* (available at http://www.vosca.com.tw/75tr400.html; accessed 5/16/06).
20. *MedGlider System. 1. Medication Reminder* (available at http://www.dynamic_living.com/medgliderl_pill_box.htm; accessed 5/16/06).
21. *Medication System. 7. Medication Reminder* (available at http://www.dynamic_living.com/medglider7_pill_box.htm; accessed 5/16/06).
22. *Kind Remind* (available at http://www.epill.com/kind.html; accessed 5/16/06).
23. *Talking Pharmaceutical Reminder* (available at http://www.epill.com/talkrx.html; accessed 5/16/06).
24. *Pillbox Diary* (available at http://www.informedix.com; accessed 5/16/06).
25. *MD.2 Personal Medication System Automated Medication Dispenser* (available at http://www.eyesonelders.com/md2/order.html; accessed 5/16/06).
26. *Pill Reminder and Dispenser* (available at http://www.epill.com/medtime.html; accessed 5/16/06).
27. *CompuMed Automatic Pill Dispenser* (available at http://www.epill.com/compumed.html; accessed 5/16/06).
28. Nugent CD, Finlay DD, Davies RJ, Paggetti C, Tamburini E, Black ND: Can technology improve compliance to medication? *Proce 3rd Int Conf Smart Homes and Health Telematics*, 2005, Vol **15**, pp 65–72.
29. Nugent CD, Fiorini P, Finlay DD, Davies RJ, Mulvenna MD, Black ND: From compliance to context: Advancing assistive technology capabilities for medication management, *Int J Human-Friendly Welfare Robot Syst* **6**(4):21–28 (2005).
30. Paggetti C, Tamburini E: Remote management of integrated home care services: The DGHome platform, *Proc 3rd Int Conf Smart Homes and Health Telematics*. 2005, Vol **15**, pp 298–301.

35

Virtual Companions

Nahid Shahmehri, Johan Åberg, and Dennis Maciuszek
Department of Computer and Information Science, Linköping University, Linköping, Sweden

35.1 INTRODUCTION

This chapter addresses the development of electronic assistive technology (EAT) for older adults. The research is directed mainly at "old–old" (75+) and "very old" (85+) people [1]—individuals who tend to have distinct special needs in comparison with younger citizens. For instance, in the aged population we find a higher prevalence of chronic conditions, greater numbers of functional limitations in daily activity, a higher incidence of cognitive impairment, and special psychosocial issues [1]. One or several of such problems can reduce an older adult's *quality of life* [2].

In order to maintain or improve quality of life, a frail older person is likely to *depend* on others [3] and will *work together* [4] or *collaborate* [5] with an assistant. Assistants may include *formal caregivers* (professionals, e.g., a nurse) and *informal caregivers* (the partner, relatives, friends). Assistance is given at a care institution or at the person's home. Often, elders desire to remain passably *independent*, and try to avoid having to move to an institution. This is the idea of *aging in place*.

There will not always be informal caregivers who can sacrifice larger amounts of free time to assist a person in need. In addition, formal care is limited by assigned hours and the elder's financial situation. To make things worse, it is often pointed out that in the decades to come, percentages of older people in most societies will rise dramatically, which will leave fewer and fewer young people to take care of the old [6]. Yet, visiting care institutions, and following stories in the media (Sweden—e.g., Ref. 7; Germany—e.g., Ref. 8) reveals: Today's care systems are already in a state of emergency!

The Engineering Handbook of Smart Technology for Aging, Disability, and Independence,
Edited by A. Helal, M. Mokhtari and B. Abdulrazak
Copyright © 2008 John Wiley & Sons, Inc.

How can, despite limited and decreasing resources, frail older people age with dignity? How can the job of caregivers become fun again? How do we enable aging in place? This is where recent technological breakthroughs in areas like pervasive computing (computer power made available anywhere) and artificial intelligence open up new possibilities for elders and caregivers. EAT, which goes beyond traditional assistive technology like a walker or a hearing aid, offers new possibilities for a comfortable and independent life, and can—as a supplement to human assistance—contribute to a better quality of life [Shahmehri in 9, 10].

The research presented in this chapter is a part of the *Virtual Companion* project at the Laboratory for Intelligent Information Systems (IISLAB) and the National Institute for the Study of Ageing and Later Life (NISAL) at Linköping University. It aims at making the vision of advanced EAT come true by developing an always-available collaborative and multifunctional electronic aid that assists with daily activities and considers the needs of its individual elderly user as well as the current environmental context [11].

One of this project's main developmental goals is *personalisation*, due to the high interindividual and intraindividual variance of frail older people's needs (*dynamic diversity* [12]). The long-term goal is to develop a *toolkit* that can automatically generate a package of interconnected personalized EAT applications from a repository of reusable software components, based on selections made by individual users, their caregivers, and experts in relevant domains.

This chapter presents a first foundation for this toolkit in the form of a *design framework* for user-led design and automated generation of virtual companions for later life. A framework is a "reusable design" of a system, a "skeleton [...] that can be customized by an application developer" [13]. In our case, *customization* means instantiation of the framework with personalized assistive applications for individual elderly users.

Development of such a framework demands the investigation of a number of research issues:

- In order to enable its user to be more independent without facing extra risks, EAT must be *dependable*. To attain this, what *requirements* must a design framework for virtual companions fulfill?
- How can a framework be developed that complies with these requirements, in both theory and practice? A suitable *software architecture* needs to be constructed and evaluated.
- The framework skeleton is to be filled with *applications*. What kind of applications should it support? What software components must it supply, and how should these work in order to provide realistic help? The *needs* of different elderly people must be studied, together with the *assistance* that can appropriately satisfy them.

This chapter provides tentative answers to these three research issues, organized as follows. In the next section we describe the metaphor of a virtual companion in more detail. We then proceed with an analysis of dependability requirements for virtual companions. After that we provide a framework design, tailored toward the dependability requirements. A prototype implementation of the framework is then evaluated by means of scenario-based tests, which lead to a refinement of the framework. We then describe a needs analysis and connect the results to the virtual companion framework. This is followed by a brief discussion of related work. Finally, we present our conclusions.

35.2 VIRTUAL COMPANIONS — A METAPHOR

A *virtual companion* for later life denotes a personal system of interconnected functions that aims at assisting an elderly user by imitating elder–caregiver interaction. Imagine a software program that "accompanies" its user to the kitchen. It might interactively explain preparation of the person's favorite meals, and at the same time monitor him/her to anticipate accidents.

Virtual companions can be contrasted with so-called smart homes. Virtual companions are different in the sense that a "human-like" presence is introduced, instead of making existing appliances smart. However, to function well, and make informed decisions, a virtual companion is dependent on information from the user's environment. Such information may include datastreams from sensors placed in strategic locations and connected to appliances. In some sense, smart appliances that make up a smart home may provide the virtual companion with such information. In other words, a virtual companion could very well be an addition to a smart home.

Note that although we talk about a virtual companion "accompanying" a user, we are deliberately not discussing the actual user interface of the virtual companion. In this chapter the functions come first and the user interface, second. This is not to say that the eventual user interface is of little importance, but rather that the "what" precedes the "how." However, when the time comes to design the user interface, it is important to make sure that there is a consistency to the design so that a user can make use of lessons learned from interacting with previous functions when starting interaction with a new function. This, of course, may represent a significant challenge for user interface designers, and is an interesting direction for future research on virtual companions.

35.3 DEPENDABILITY REQUIREMENTS

A good companion is somebody you can depend on. But what does this mean? Laprie's original definition of dependability calls it "the ability to deliver service that can justifiably be trusted" [14]. Vice versa, trust is often defined as a "willingness to depend" [15]. Hence, dependability and trustworthiness are basically equivalent [14]. Dewsbury et al. [16] consider Laprie's model too technical for domestic EAT. In their own model, they add attributes, and make it holistic in that it demands the whole interplay between user, technology, and environment be free of faults.

This section collects requirements to help designers define, design, and validate dependable virtual companions. Originally, our work was guided by the nonfunctional requirements multifunctionality, adaptivity, and realistic specification. These had been derived from literature and discussions with researchers in the area of aging, as well as a survey of EAT research. Subsequent design work, however, revealed a need for more differentiated, complete, and verifiable requirements. In search of accepted and suitable requirement types, we studied literature on dependability, extracted relevant attributes, and specified their meaning for the case of virtual companions. Table 35.1 presents the findings [3,14,16–27] with motivations. It lists the requirements as general objectives applicable to any companion software. For a concrete system, they still need to be made testable.

TABLE 35.1 Dependability Requirements

Attribute	Details	Motivation
Adaptability: design for interindividual variance; changeable configuration [16,17]	A virtual companion must be personalized for its individual user and his/her living environment; it must be possible to easily add, update, and remove services and personal data; updates should not lead to the inclusion of new errors	Applications made for "the elderly" may not work for a particular user; e.g., few older people are forgetful [8], or need reminders; they sometimes outperform younger people in everyday life prospective memory tasks; a user may become forgetful later, though, e.g., after the installation of the companion
Availability: readiness for correct service [14]	A companion must not only hold its services ready but also proactively offer them	Active user requests may not be possible in situations when help is needed most [17]; furthermore, patients trust human nurses to act in their interests without always spelling out what that means [19]
Relevance: support of the "right" tasks [20]	A virtual companion must be multifunctional, i.e., offer more than only a few solutions to a few problems	Assistive interaction in everyday life is complex; most frail older people receive help with two or more ADLs[a] or IADLs;[b] also, there is social, emotional, and other dependence; people regulate dependence by different strategies: selection, optimisation, compensation [3]
Acceptability: perceived as useful and easy to use [21]	Acceptability is threatened if a virtual companion cannot live up to its metaphor: (1) interaction with it must be pragmatic, so that independence increases, and quality of life is enhanced [17]; (2) the effort saved by using the system must significantly exceed the effort of using it [16] — interaction must be predictable and persistent, allowing the formation of mental models [22]	Acceptability is especially important because of a companion's expected pervasiveness in everyday life; it is conceived not as another tool, but an artificial "companion"; usefulness is important because of the ambitions of assistive technology; ease of use, because of a probable lack of computer skills on the part of many users
Competence: working properly by routine performance, technical facility, and expert knowledge [22]	A companion must be intelligent and deliver not only correct but also "good" service; this requires smart algorithms that process personal, care-related, and technical knowledge or rules in relation to the environment context; knowledge and rules must be obtained from the user, caregivers, and experts in relevant domains	Software engineers may implement routine competence, but technical facility and expert knowledge must come from people who know; having knowledge and rules constructed by trusted people should further increase initial trust in the system — e.g., initial trust in nurses is based on trust in the healthcare system — and preserve basic moral judgment — a quality beyond technical competence expected from caregivers [19]

TABLE 35.1 (*Continued*)

Attribute	Details	Motivation
Reliability: continuity of correct service [14]	A companion must be fault-tolerant; reliability is threatened if it does not anticipate, notice, or take care of errors; errors may be internal, on the user's part, or in the environment [23]	The user's quality of life may depend on correct service [16]; a human caregiver usually notices when he/she has done something wrong, and finds a way to compensate by doing the task differently; the technical equivalent would be concurrent error detection with rollforward [14]
Adaptivity: fitness for purpose; tailored to individual needs during use [16]	Services must automatically adapt their kind and degree of automation to changing user goals and preferences, as well as interests and motivation	Human caregivers provide needed assistance according to functioning in relation to ADL/IADL scales [24,25] and occupational therapy assessment [26]; however, too much help can cause an old person to give up learning [27]; functioning worsens or improves with time; interests and motivation should be considered, as a trustworthy nurse does not only care *for* a patient, but also *about* that person [19]
Safety: not causing harm [14,17]	Safety-threatening errors must be avoided; risks include inaccurate situation assessment and inaccurate response generation; a companion must therefore understand the environment context and consequences of actions; when uncertain, it should involve human judgment	Consequences of failure can be particularly severe for an already vulnerable user like a frail old person
Security: keeping information and services confidential [14]	Access to a companion must be restricted to authorized persons, especially with respect to network-based services	Unauthorized disclosure of information would have adverse effects, as this EAT relies heavily on personal information; unauthorized system state alterations would particularly threaten services for health and safety

[a] Activities of daily living: bathing, dressing, toileting, transferring, continence, eating [24].
[b] Instrumental activities of daily living: telephoning, shopping, food preparation, housekeeping, laundry, transportation, medication, finances [25].

35.4 DESIGN OF A DEPENDABLE FRAMEWORK

We are convinced that systems that meet the requirements listed in Table 35.1 can be realised. To aid the designer of virtual companions in accomplishing this, this section describes our own approach.

It would be inefficient if software engineers had to create a companion for each individual user from scratch. We therefore plan to give users, caregivers, and experts a generic toolkit that enables them to build and maintain individual companions on their own. It will come in the form of a simple tool or programming language that allows the formulation of specifications, validates these, and compiles them into an initial companion, or later adds, updates, and removes parts. The toolkit will be based on a well-defined

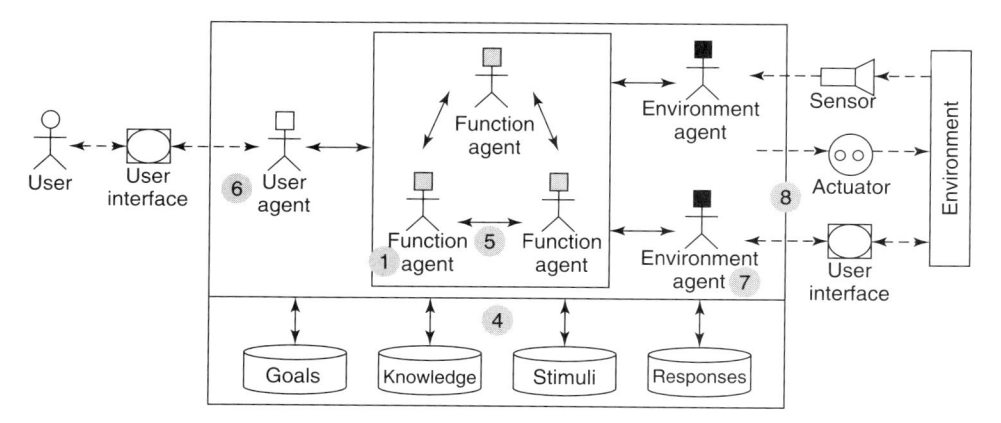

FIGURE 35.1 Generic framework architecture.

framework consisting of a generic multiagent *architecture* plus a *specification process* for selecting, combining, and instantiating preimplemented components.

A companion in terms of the architecture is a multiagent system (Fig. 35.1). An agent is understood as a software module capable of autonomous behavior, deliberation (i.e., reasoning on the basis of goals and knowledge), and/or reactivity (i.e., responding to outside stimuli), and for some agents, learning. In a multiagent architecture, multiple agents are active concurrently. They communicate and work together in order to realize the global behavior.

The specification process involves filling the architecture by specifying each desired agent, one at a time. These are high-level decisions that have pre-defined low-level effects. For instance, creating an agent as an *environment agent* (list item 7 below) automatically determines how it communicates. It will fit into the system like any environment agent, without bringing along new communication-related errors.

A description of the specification process and underlying architecture follows:

1. *Function Agents.* Each companion is initially configured with a set of services. A service is added by specifying a function agent. After configuration, every new function agent is activated. It will autonomously check for short-term user goals, and proactively help if it can. This implements *availability*.

2. *Combination.* Each function agent is specified as a pair of a *function* component ("the algorithms") determining autonomy, learning, and agent communication, and an *application area* component ("the data") determining goals, basic knowledge, and basic stimulus–response rules. By combining these two types of independent modules, many types of assistance in many possible situations can be defined, and *relevance* be achieved.

3. *Components.* An example of a function component would be a *trainer*. It stands for user–companion interaction in which a lesson is taught, and revised in an exercise. To attain usefulness, and thus *acceptability*, imitation of user–caregiver interaction must be pragmatic. Patterns of pragmatic elder–caregiver interaction can be derived from literature or, even better, through ethnographic studies. Our 10 basic functions (Fig. 35.2) will implement 10 patterns of assistive interaction

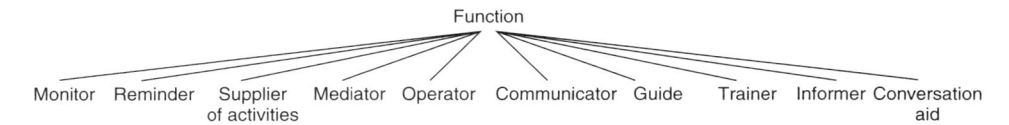

FIGURE 35.2 Functions.

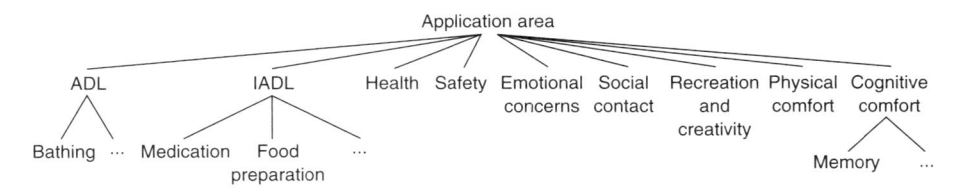

FIGURE 35.3 Application areas.

derived from analyzing literature on elder–caregiver communication. Application areas represent needs. We organized these in a hierarchy (Fig. 35.3).

4. *Databases.* Autonomous behavior and basic rules or knowledge that it works on come with a function agent's function and application area. Advanced technical facility and expert knowledge, however, will not be preimplemented, but obtained from users, caregivers, and experts through knowledge acquisition techniques. The toolkit will facilitate specification, so that a plumber can model safety risks without drawing transition systems, and an occupational therapist can enter an activity analysis without defining mathematical relations. This final function agent step lends *competence* to it.

5. *Multiple Function Agents.* Added function agents will communicate and work together. It is sensible to add redundant agents—different functions for the same application area—so that agents can choose which other agents to contact. Some agents will watch over others, notice errors, and learn their performance in certain situations. Redundancy and learning agents watching over each other should increase *reliability*.

6. *User Agent.* One user agent is added as an internal representation of the user. As a variant of traditional user modeling, it not only stores goals and preferences—which here are specified by user, caregivers, and experts—but also acts on the basis of this knowledge. It manages the user interface, and communicates with function agents, realizing two types of *adaptivity*—by matching its goals against function agent goals, it activates and deactivates function agents. By matching preferences against function agent knowledge, it attempts to provide assistance that helps enough, but not too much. Interests and motivation are also considered.

7. *Environment Agents.* Different environment agents are added as representations of people and things in the environment. For each agent, an *environment-type* component (e.g., *sensor world* or *vehicle*) is selected. It determines goals, basic stimulus–response rules, and, if needed, basic knowledge. Rules representing technical facility or expert knowledge are chosen and added by user, caregivers, and experts. Autonomous behavior and communication are the same for all environment agents. People and things are monitored through sensors, manipulated through

actuators, and interacted with through user interfaces. Function agents simulate environment agents' responses to stimuli before sending them to the real world. This adds *competence* and *safety*.

8. *Infrastructure.* User interfaces, sensor and actuator hardware, as well as a connected network are regarded as external to the framework and assumed as "given." We are, however, aware that mechanisms for authentication and control of data transfer are needed to restrict access from the outside. We refer to a paper by Herzog and Shahmehri [28], where possibilities and vulnerabilities of *residential gateways* as *secure* interfaces for remote access to connected homes are discussed.

35.5 FRAMEWORK EVALUATION

35.5.1 Method

A prototype of the virtual companion framework was implemented, and evaluated according to the dependability requirements. The emphasis was on having as many conceptual features of the design in the implementation as possible, even if that meant mixing advanced approaches with ad hoc solutions. On the other hand, we did not aspire to implement every function and application area. Instead, we made the implementation extendable by keeping concepts like a goal or a process generic, by making use of object orientation, and by making even parts of agent behavior reusable. For instance, the method to solve a problem is used by three function agent classes.

Implemented software components are the *monitor*, *reminder*, *guide*, *operator*, *communicator*, and *trainer* functions with the application areas *IADL* and *safety*. For the sake of the prototype, we regarded an IADL as a concurrent process, and chose the preparation of food recipes as an example (for clarity of what the agents do, this application area will from now on be called *food preparation*). For safety, we implemented the need for a safe environment. The implementation contains two types of environment agents: *sensor worlds* (that model and manipulate current states of the environment via sensors and actuators) and *persons* (who can be contacted for help).

The architecture was instantiated with agents for a particular user, Mr. Taylor. He has a mild dementia, but could remain independent during the day if helped with preparing lunch and the prevention of accidents. We restricted the supported environment to the kitchen where Mr. Taylor has a cooker, a sink, and a window and heating for regulating temperature. The appliances are equipped with different sensors and actuators. Because of our intention of evaluating core technical aspects before realistic applications, Mr. Taylor is a fictitious user, and the kitchen with sensors and actuators was simulated. Agents that were created by combining architecture components include a *food preparation trainer*, *food preparation guide*, *safety trainer*, *safety reminder*, *safety monitor*, *safety guide*, *safety operator*, *safety communicator*, three *sensor worlds*, two *persons* (Mr. Taylor's son and the fire brigade), as well as the *user agent* as a representation of Mr. Taylor. The case of Mr. Taylor was inspired by [1], yet the walking disability was exchanged by a dementia.

In order to evaluate framework design and prototype with respect to real-world requirements, we chose a method of scenario-based testing. Scenarios were extracted from personal interviews conducted in parallel to the implementation with eight elders at a retirement home and an assisted living facility (mean age 85 years) and six caregivers at the same retirement home. Additional data came from a focus group interview we did with four caregivers from different institutions. One group of scenarios concerns incidents from real life, and a second group describes hypothetical situations that were described in response to a presentation of our design of Mr. Taylor's virtual companion.

Extracted scenarios were filtered so that the chosen ones would guarantee a good coverage of the dependability requirements. From these, we generated technical test cases, performed the tests, documented the results, and then critically analysed them to yield framework refinements.

We were not able to achieve a good coverage for acceptability without considering real users and more sophisticated user interfaces. Like the UI, securing a network connection to the outside is regarded as external to the framework, and so far no special security mechanisms have been designed or implemented. Therefore, although we did generate a number of scenarios and tests for these requirements, we did in the end not perform them. Results would have been of limited significance.

35.5.2 Prototype Implementation

The prototype of the generic architecture was implemented in Java. Figure 35.4 depicts implemented Java classes as boxes, with white arrows where inheritance was used.

Each agent is a Java thread, that is, a process that runs concurrently with other processes. Agent behavior was implemented as infinite loops waiting for a reason to act. Such a reason can be the realization that an agent's goal is not fulfilled (e.g., a *safety monitor*, which continuously checks environment processes—through variables shared

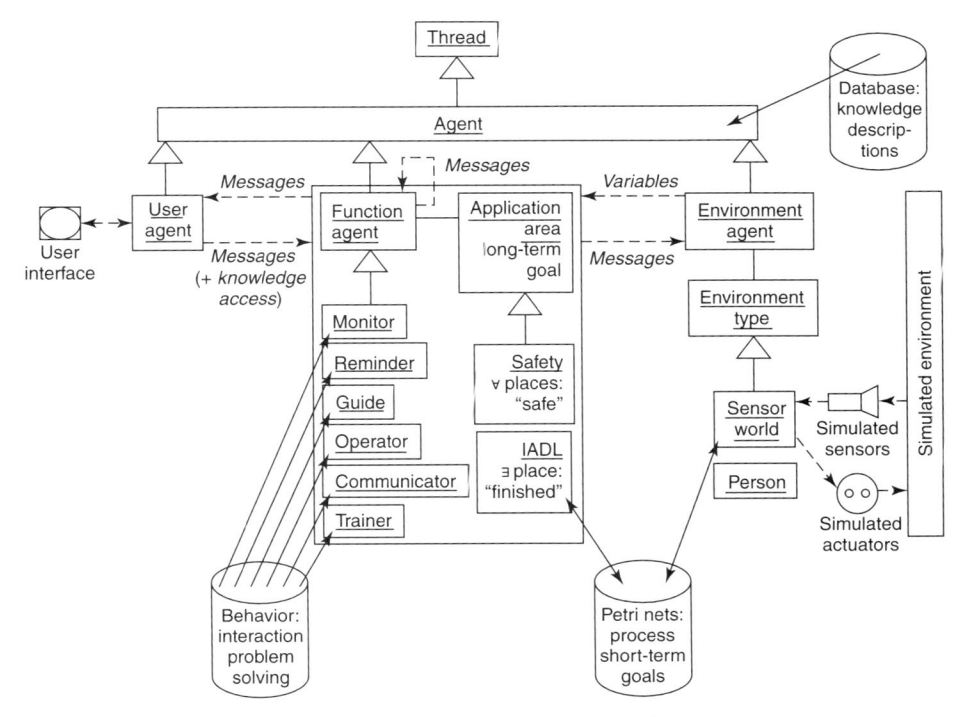

FIGURE 35.4 Prototype implementation.

with environment agents–notices that a cooker plate is too hot). It can then send a message to a *safety guide*, *operator*, or *communicator* in order to delegate the problem. Then the respective agent would itself have a reason to act, while the *safety monitor* concurrently continues monitoring. Agent behavior may further be invoked by the user agent, which handles all interaction with the user through a user interface. In the implementation, these are dialogue windows in which the user answers simple questions (e.g., shown on touchscreens throughout the home).

Agent behavior algorithms can be rather straightforward, such as when a *safety reminder* tries to fulfil a short-term goal, and reminds the user of a certain task to do in a certain situation. Then it just follows a specified rule in the dynamic data. Alternatively, a rather complex problem may need to be solved, for example, when a *safety operator* tries to attain its long-term goal (e.g., safety in relation to room temperature) by requesting the activation of actuators. To find out which actuators will correct the problem (e.g., it is cold), it will first reason on the basis of current context (the window is open, the heating is off) and a dynamic model of the respective *sensor world environment agent*. Dynamic data have been modeled with *Petri nets*, which are basically concurrent automata or transition systems. Problem solving is a search for all paths in Petri net reachability trees, specifically, paths including the transitions (the tasks to do) from a configuration in which the agent's goal is invalid to a configuration in which it is valid.

For handling Petri nets, we chose the publicly available *Petri Net Kernel* library and added own analysis algorithms. For static data, we created a *MySQL* database, which is accessed via Java's database interface *JDBC*. Except for monitoring processes where we employed shared variables, agents communicate with each other through a message-passing mechanism realized with Java *pipes*. Exchanged messages have the syntax of *FIPA XML*.

35.5.3 Scenario-Based Tests

We now turn to the results of the scenario-based tests. A selection has been made so that we discuss only those results that cover their respective requirements well, and which led to significant information for the goal of refining our framework.

35.5.3.1 Adaptability

It was already obvious from interviewing eight older people that every potential user will be a unique individual with unique, individual needs. We heard the complaints of a woman who moved to an assisted-living facility only to find that mostly leisure activities were offered when she would rather have safety monitoring, shopping possibilities, and help to get to the hairdresser. Yet, "It is not easy to find the right things for 71 residents," she said. However, this is our main concern in the vision of a companion-generating toolkit. Is a toolkit for composing very personalized assistive technology feasible?

Our case study with the fictitious Mr. Taylor indicates that reuse and recombination of generic software components can be an efficient tool in overcoming the variety-of-needs bottleneck. Mr. Taylor needs eight assistive technology applications. Traditional design would give him eight different devices for these needs. Each of them would require designing and implementing one set of data and one algorithm that works on the data from scratch. In our terms, these would be $8 \times 2 = 16$ components: *food preparation* + *trainer* + *food preparation* + *guide* + *safety* + *trainer* + *safety* + *reminder* +

safety + *monitor* + *safety* + *guide* + *safety* + *operator* + *safety* + *communicator*. In our design with software components, on the other hand, we were able to reuse the *food preparation* and *safety* components (data) and the *trainer* and *guide* components (algorithms). Thus, we needed only create 2 + 6 = 8 components: *food preparation* + *trainer* + *guide* + *safety* + *reminder* + *monitor* + *operator* + *communicator*.

35.5.3.2 Availability

According to the interviews, frail older people rarely actively request help. An alarm might not be reachable in the case of an accident, people might forget to request help, they might not want to bother caregivers, not notice when water is running, and so on. Here, our proactive agents that warn when the basin is full or offer food preparation assistance at the user's preferred meal times can be useful. Like human caregivers who often have to assist in different ways at the same time, being helped by one agent does not block another agent's concurrent behavior. If a *safety monitor* needs to deliver a warning or a *safety reminder* needs to remind during a *food preparation guide's* explanations, they do so. However, the tests showed us that in our framework the sequence of such interleaved behavior is arbitrary, and in fact the thread scheduling often prioritized a *guide* over a *reminder*, which from the user's perspective was questionable.

35.5.3.3 Relevance

Two interviewees found monitoring the actual *food preparation* activity more relevant in everyday life than a *safety monitor* for the cooker. In cooking, food may boil over or scorch. In section 35.5.3.1, we stated that it is technically easy to create new applications by just recombining available components. But does this result in relevant support? The idea with a *food preparation monitor* would be that a user has left the cooking area, and needs to be reminded that a cooking process is going on. We realized this function agent by adding two lines of code, and found its collaboration with the *food preparation guide* working technically correctly. However, far too many warnings were generated. This was because the goal of the respective application area was not formulated precisely enough. In addition, it was not considered whether a current cooking situation actually involved boiling or frying something, and whether the user actually was in the cooking area.

35.5.3.4 Reliability

Even though we were striving for a completely reliable system, we did compromise reliability with some design decisions—things that were not obvious to us in the first place. Like one interviewed caregiver, we were thinking the companion would be very *competent* if it reminded the user to turn off the cooker after finishing a cooking activity only when the cooker was actually on (context-awareness). That however made the *safety reminder* fail right away when we damaged the simulated sensor in the cooker that normally reports that the cooker is on.

Another decision was not to offer a *guide* but only an *operator* and a *communicator* in a situation of medium urgency, since guiding might take too long, thus compromising *safety*. We decided to offer neither *guide* nor *operator* but only a *communicator* in a situation of high urgency, since both might take too long or not work, again compromising *safety*. In the case of a fire, the fire brigade should be called right away. However, having a fire and a malfunctioning *communicator*, the user was left with no more working options.

35.5.3.5 Competence and Safety

When presented with the design of the virtual companion for Mr. Taylor, several of the interviewed caregivers were skeptical that complex activities such as food preparation could be understood by a computer. "You would need to develop a program that includes all potential options." "A lot of knowledge is necessary. Everything must be in it: Potatoes. vegetables, ... One would also need to describe where all the items are." "Cooking is a complex activity: deciding for a recipe, buying the corresponding ingredients, and so on."

With our technical prototype we could not test such realistic scenarios (but see, e.g., the meal planning system in Ref. 29). We saw however that it is reasonably easy—just a bit cumbersome—to manually add a new recipe taken from a Website. In the envisioned companion creation toolkit, input from the user, caregivers, and experts would be facilitated more by means of semiautomatic knowledge acquisition. Occupational therapists build advanced models of food preparation in order to assess user competence in relation to these [30]. Pigot et al. [31,32] incorporated such models into a cognitive assistance system. Our design is capable of storing and using realistic models; the only problem is that much of the information entered is syntactical (a Petri net graph) rather than semantic. This is easier to process (abstract path search in a reachability tree), yet it may no longer work with more advanced agent collaboration, which would be needed to realize the scenario description above.

It remains to be studied how electronic assistance can be so competent that it can realistically enable a frail older person to carry on with activities. When such empowerment succeeds, however, it is important that it does not negatively affect *safety*. It was a recurring theme in the interviews that people tend to give up activities such as food preparation or walking not because of a lack of user competence, but because they did not feel safe in doing them anymore.

35.5.3.6 Adaptivity

Adaptivity to the user's competence in performing certain tasks was tested successfully. When a *guide's* problem-solving method chooses one of several candidate solutions, it prefers those that the user be more likely to handle. On the contrary, a *trainer* practises tasks that are difficult. Although this does work for simple applications, our user modeling, which was inspired by occupational therapy and mathematical psychology models [26,30,33], still does not model, for example, a 30% user competence or the physical but not cognitive user competence to do a task. In addition, we have only sketched learning of changed user competence so far.

Adaptivity to the user's interests has been considered in specifying preferred mealtimes and a preferred bedtime. In a care institution, residents need to adapt to certain institutional schedules themselves, such as mealtimes that they are not used to. This can create unnecessary confusion. In our tests, the *food preparation guide* correctly offered its services at the times the user prefers, and he was also reminded to close the window at his usual time of going to bed. User habits can, of course, change just as user competence changes. but learning was not implemented yet.

35.5.4 Refinement

We present here a selection of some major improvements of the virtual companion design framework given the results of the scenario-based tests.

The new companion design framework makes comprehensive use of *semantic information*. Previously, semantic concepts like different levels of *risk* were used in the *safety* application area component. From these, *urgency* was computed. This is also needed for other application areas like IADLs in order to make these *relevant* and *competent* (and actually also more *acceptable*). We have already begun experimenting with semantic XML models of recipes that are semiautomatically extracted from Webpages. If these could be related to a recipe ontology, then the adding of new recipes (*adaptability*) would also be facilitated.

On the way to realizing realistic (*relevant* and *competent*) applications, *agent collaboration* must be refined. In order to be able to combine function agents for complex help behavior, there must be more than delegation of syntactical problems and indirect monitoring of agents' effects on process variables. A *shopping writing aid* will send shopping lists to *shopping operators* that order ingredients from which a *food preparation recommender* compiles recipes. Currently, functions represent single-agent design patterns realized as singular software components. Now there will be multiagent design patterns and formal connections of function components. One such connection is the attachment of a *safety monitor* to any *guide* in order to ensure that empowerment of a person does not result in a loss of *safety*. To attain *reliability*, *safety communicators* will be complemented by *guides* and *operators*.

User model knowledge becomes more refined with fuzzy values and prerequisite relationships. In order to be able to "turn off" something, one must be able to physically reach and to cognitively understand how it works. Changing user competence and user interests are learnt through interpretation of the user's actions. This will realize real *adaptivity*. In addition, the performance of agents in performing certain tasks is learned in order to improve *reliability*.

35.6 WHAT APPLICATIONS ARE NEEDED?[1]

In our proposed design of a framework for dependable virtual companions we suggested a set of 10 suitable patterns of interaction (Fig. 35.2), based on a literature survey. These patterns were complemented by a list of application areas corresponding to the expected needs of frail older people (Fig. 35.3). With these lists as a starting point we have conducted an empirical study trying to construct a functional design space for virtual companions for elders. In other words, we tried to shed more empirical light on the following interrelated questions:

1. What are the *needs* of frail older people?
2. Which of these are of high *importance*?
3. How can needs be supported, that is, what *patterns of assistive interaction* can be employed (by means of human help, traditional AT, and EAT)?
4. Which patterns support which needs, i.e. which pairs have a high positive *correlation*?

---

[1]This section is partly based on an earlier work: What help do older people need? Constructing a functional design space of electronic assistive technology applications, *Proc 7th Int ACM SIGACCESS Conf Computers and Accessibility (ASSETS'2005)*, Baltimore, MD, Oct 9–12, 2005, pp 4–11, © ACM, 2005 (http://doi.acm.org/10.1145/1090785.1090790).

5. Which patterns support many needs, that is, have a high degree of *reusability*?
6. Which patterns support needs together with other patterns, that is, have a high *interconnectivity*?

We were prepared to erase needs or patterns of interaction from the lists presented earlier as well as to add new needs or patterns, depending on the collected data. Owing to the complexity of everyday life and the dynamic diversity among older people, our expectation was that we would have to extend our lists rather than drastically cut them. This would be fine, since we were interested in obtaining and retaining a good design space from which to choose and produce artefacts for a variety of users (and not in finding the next "killer application").

35.6.1 Design Space

A number of formal approaches to the exploration of *design rationale* (Why is a design chosen?) and the construction of design spaces (What designs *can* be chosen?) have been proposed. We chose to follow an adapted version of the approach of Lane and Asada et al. (cited in Ref. 34). It allowed us to express design rationales that argue for an artefact or application of EAT because its way of assisting fits the supported user need. Here, we will not argue for a specific application, but instead assess the bigger picture: What applications are possible, and which of these have the potential of benefiting different older people?

Figure 35.5 introduces the general features of our design space notation. *Dimensions* relate to basic questions about a design. Here we have two dimensions. The *y* axis explores the question: What *need* of an elderly person does an application support? The *x* axis stands for the question: By what means, that is, by what *pattern of assistive interaction*, does it support a need? Supported needs can be chosen on the basis of their *importance* for older people. Patterns can be chosen on the basis of their *correlation*

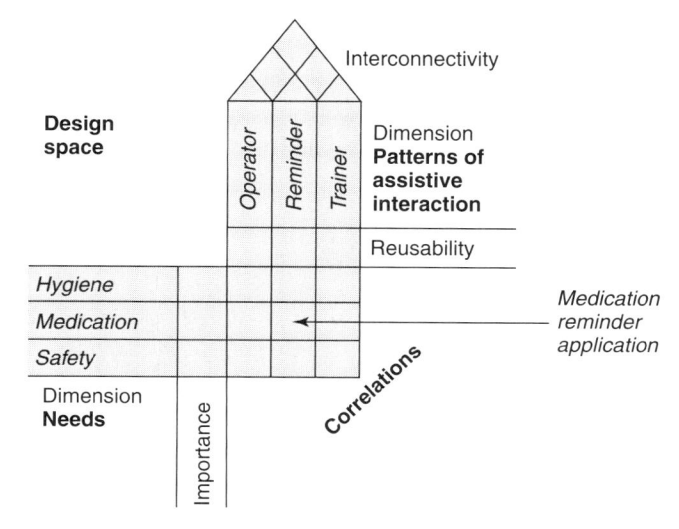

FIGURE 35.5 *Features of the design space.*

with the need to be supported (i.e., how well the pattern fits the need) and on the basis of their *reusability* (i.e., how many different needs it can support). A designer aiming for more complex applications may want to connect different patterns. *Interconnectivity* indicates how well two patterns fit together. Not considering such connections, a chosen application design is a pair of one chosen need and one chosen pattern.

35.6.1.1 Dimensions
We defined two dimensions for two basic questions that a designer ought to get straight before creating an EAT application:

1. What need does it support?
2. By what means does it assist?

These are very basic dimensions to result in a (relatively) small *functional* design space. They should allow for a first "reality check" when choosing or producing EAT: Are the products that I want available? Are chances good that my product will be of use? Inclusion of further dimensions (e.g., technical details or the user interface) was left for future work. It will require new decision-supporting features, such as dependability criteria or usability.

35.6.1.1.1 Needs
A need relates to a difficulty or an interest of the user, e.g. an ADL such as *hygiene*, an IADL such as handling *medication*, or a more general desire such as *safety*. These are *alternatives* in the needs dimension. They have been entered into Figure 35.5 as three examples. In creating an EAT application, the designer would choose (at least) one such alternative as the supported need.

35.6.1.1.2 Patterns of Assistive Interaction
A pattern of assistive interaction relates to the means by which an application assists. In Figure 35.5, three examples of patterns have been entered as alternatives: *operator*, *reminder*, and *trainer*. In creating an EAT application, the designer would choose a pattern to support the chosen need.

35.6.1.2 Choice of Application
A chosen application can be characterised by a pair consisting of a need and a pattern. Figure 35.5 holds nine empty cells for nine such pairs, namely, possible applications. When creating a *medication reminder*, a designer would go for the alternative to support the need *medication*, and for the alternative to do so by means of *reminding*.

What are 'good' choices of applications? The features importance, correlations, reusability, and interconnectivity are helpful decision criteria. For each of these, values based on empirical evidence can be entered. These values may represent qualitative or quantitative statements.

35.6.1.2.1 Importance
How important is a certain need for frail older people's quality of life? We can ask such general questions despite the *dynamic diversity* of older adults, since we assess the multitude of possible applications. Of course, for a certain user one would have to ask how important the need is for that particular person. As an example, the designer of the *medication reminder* may have known from evidence about the (supposedly) high importance of the need *medication* for older people's quality of life.

35.6.1.2.2 Correlations What is a good pattern of assistive interaction to support a certain need? Maybe the abovementioned designer also knew that a (supposedly) good strategy toward medication adherence is to *remind* the person. This would mean a high positive correlation between *medication* and *reminding*.

35.6.1.2.3 Reusability How many needs can a pattern support? Maybe the *reminder* pattern has a high reusability, and our designer can also use it to support *safety*.

35.6.1.2.4 Interconnectivity Which patterns can be interconnected to form a complex application? One might want to connect a *reminder* with an *operator*. Think of an electronic pillbox that emits an alarm signal *and* hands out pills automatically when it is time.

35.6.2 Patterns of Interaction

Before we start instantiating the design space, what are these patterns of interaction, and how do we use them in defining interactive virtual companions?

Patterns of interaction (e.g., see Ref. 35) are used to inform analyses of design spaces of human-centred systems with qualitative field study data. They are inspired by the pioneering work of Alexander [36] and related to *design patterns*. Patterns of interaction differ from design patterns in that they describe real-world social situations rather than prescribing technical solutions. Patterns of interaction can act as a *lingua franca* (common language) among actors in a design process [35].

Our design space is based on the assumptions that (1) needs of older people can successfully be supported by applying certain recurring interaction strategies—the patterns—and that (2) these patterns work in a comparable manner in the social situation of a human assisting and in the usage of an assistive technology device. We further assume that a pattern is generic in the sense that one pattern can support different needs. In addition, a particular pattern will be more suitable to support certain needs than other needs.

35.6.3 Method[2]

In order to answer the research questions and thus obtain a foundation for the design space to construct, we needed empirical data. This could have been a survey of existing EAT. However, our premise was that we were not certain whether the state of the art already provided the necessary applications. Thus, we opted for a field study that would take us to settings of older adults' everyday lives and to workplaces of caregivers. At homecare services, assisted-living facilities, and retirement and nursing homes, we expected to encounter needs and patterns in their natural context, independently of EAT usage. By looking at human assistance first and at human–machine interaction later, we prioritised a process-oriented view of the referent system (older adults' everyday lives) over a product-oriented view. This is a suitable approach when designing human-centred systems [35]. Resulting designs would be application-driven, rather than technology-driven.

---
[2] A more detailed account of our data collection and data analysis methods appears in a paper by Maciuszek et al. [37].

35.6.3.1 Data Collection

We were interested in the experiences of researchers, caregivers, and last but not least older people themselves. While caregivers were selected from a wide range of institutions to represent various kinds of assistance, we chose elders who received a moderate amount of assistance, but otherwise could actively take part in a conversation and give clear informed consent. (Participation and disclosure of information happened on a purely voluntary basis.) We thus opted for groups of healthier residents of retirement homes. These would also include people that might have been able to remain at their original homes had they been given "good enough" EAT. Since we had contacts in two countries (Sweden and Germany), we decided to use them, in order to not restrict results to a specific care system or culture.

The groups of informants were as follows: 19 researchers at two Swedish research institutions for the aged; 15 caregivers at a German homecare service; 4 German caregivers of a homecare service, 2 retirement homes, and a nursing home; 6 caregivers at a German retirement home; 7 elders at the same retirement home, and 1 at a German assisted-living facility; 14 elders and various caregivers at a Swedish retirement home.

35.6.3.2 Data Analysis

Since this initial study was not extensive enough to make confident and representative quantitative statements, we determined correlations and interconnectivity in qualitative terms. The symbol ● denotes a high positive correlation [34] or high interconnectivity. For a certain pattern, we looked through all coded need/pattern pairs, and considered the needs. If a need was among the more frequent needs (high quantity) or among the more comprehensively described needs (high quality) or had a medium quantity and quality for that pattern, the respective need/pattern correlation became ●. If neither of these was true, but the need had occurred at least once, the need/pattern correlation became ○—a low positive correlation. For needs not encountered with the pattern, no correlation was noted. An analogous procedure was applied to pattern–pattern combinations to find high and low interconnectivity. Reusability of a pattern became the number of top-level needs categories with which the pattern has some positive correlation. Both correlation and interconnectivity results were entered into the design space.

Each pattern found was further assigned a *validity ranking* [36]. For each of the different informant groups, we identified which patterns had the highest (1) positive correlations and (2) reusability (using intermediate results from the process described above). A high validity (two asterisks) was then assigned to the patterns that excelled in this way 8–10 times. A medium validity (one asterisk) was assigned to the patterns that excelled 3–5 times. A low validity (no asterisk) was assigned to those that excelled less often.

Finally, we conceived a simple pattern language that would make the results accessible to users and designers. It includes examples from the field study for human assistance (a quote), AT usage (all devices mentioned), as well as promising EAT (all designs and applications discussed that received positive comments). Note that the selection of EAT is biased, since the discussion of existing and potential EAT was based on ad hoc assessment of informant needs and the interviewer's knowledge of applications.

35.6.4 Results

As a whole, the design space is too large to be printed here. Figure 35.6 shows a subset for the three needs and three patterns of Figure 35.5.

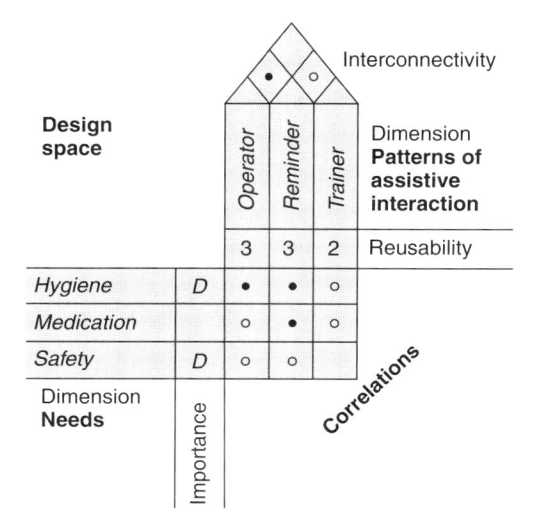

FIGURE 35.6 Instantiated design space.

The resulting needs dimension (y axis) is given in Table 35.2 in the form of a hierarchical taxonomy. The deeper in the hierarchy, the more specific a need category is. Classifying a certain need as a *medication times* need would mean to classify it as a *handling medication* need as well. Notice that *laundry* became a two-dimensional category, and *administrative tasks* became a three-dimensional category. The need "understanding the mail from the health insurance" can thus be specified as ⟨*cognitive, home-based, authorities*⟩. One could wonder whether further data would have resulted in dimensions such as physical/cognitive over all needs. In fact, the Canadian model of occupational performance [38] is a three-dimensional needs model with a physical/cognitive/affective dimension—however, not in relation to a concrete taxonomy.

The D in the importance cell of two needs in Figure 35.6 denotes an importance group. Considering the results from the focus group discussion and the needs that were mentioned the most by informants with certain backgrounds, we found strong relations between our data and Maslow's classic hierarchy of needs [39]. We thus grouped those high-level taxonomy needs indicated to us as most important accordingly; see the italicized pyramid contents in Figure 35.7 (headlines such as "meaningful activities" are labels for such groups that are frequently used in literature).

A main idea in Maslow's theory is that needs exist on different levels. In striving for quality of life, lower-level needs must be fulfilled before a higher-level need can be fulfilled. In particular, certain *deficit needs* (D) must be satisfied before one can strive for a *being need* (B). While this view can be criticised (e.g., all elders we met had an interest in recreation and creativity), an important realisation is that certain needs are more *immediate* (the lower ones), while others are more *meaningful* (the higher ones). Which needs should EAT support, then? It depends. Which needs can your user(s) still care for on their own? Which needs are sufficiently taken care of by human assistants? For instance, in one of the informant groups, (I)ADLs were well cared for, but elders desired more support for higher-level needs.

Our study was not meant to give the definite answer to the importance question. Figure 35.7 includes those high-level taxonomy elements described to us most often or

TABLE 35.2 Needs Taxonomy

Personal hygiene: washing/bathing; brushing teeth; hairdressing; shaving
Dressing
Using the toilet: physical toileting; cognitive toileting
Mobility:
   Physical: walking and walking aids; walking environment; transferring
   Cognitive: public transportation; navigation
Kitchenwork/eating and drinking
   Eating and drinking: physical eating; times; nutrition; menu
   Kitchenwork: food preparation — physical; doing dishes
   Kitchen environment: food storage and consumption; kitchen locations
Using technology:
   Telephone: number length; key size; physical telephoning; costs
   Other: computer; electronics; clock; assistive technology; kitchen appliances; bathroom appliances; credit cards
Shopping: grocery; pharmacy; clothes; gifts
Laundry: {physical; cognitive} × {washing machine; drying; tumble-drier; ironing; clothes management}
Housekeeping: cleaning; tidying; physical work outside; sewing; curtains; lightbulbs; bed; garbage
Handling medication: medication times; pillbox; procedures; effects
Administrative tasks: {physical; cognitive} × {home-based; offices; visits; general knowledge} × {bank; post; authorities; care services; finances}
Health
   Vital signs
   Diseases and well-being: diseases in general; own diseases
   Medical staff: medical contact; medical appointments; emergencies
Safety
   Safe environment: safe static environment; safe dynamic environment
   Falls
   Crime
Emotional concerns: encouragement; identity; comfort; feeling at home; deaths
Social contact: communication; visits; group activity; birthdays; friends
Recreation/creativity/education: walks; excursions; cemetery; nature; games; puzzles; sports; making music; dancing; painting; handicrafts; reading; creative writing; history; radio; TV; video; theater; religion; reminiscence; discussions; news; coursework
Physical difficulties:
   Sensory: seeing — near/far; hearing
   Motor: writing; reaching; bending; lifting; carrying; moving things; using ladder; opening/closing — containers, letters, doors, windows
   Exercise
Cognitive difficulties:
   Memory: prospective memory; remembering
   Talking; problem solving; declarative knowledge; orientation
   Routines: waking up; daily routine
   Deviating and dangerous behavior: "wandering"; other behaviors
   Living environment: static living environment; dynamic living environment
   Losing things: money; eyeglasses; handkerchiefs; alarm; tools

as most important. This need not mean that a need without a *D* or *B* in the importance column (Fig. 35.6) is of no importance. *Health* and *mobility* were almost included. Had we asked physicians, *health* would certainly have appeared in Figure 35.7. In fact, Haigh et al. [40] identified *health*, *mobility*, and *handling medication* as the top needs. Thus, no need was dropped; rather, the importance cell was simply left empty.

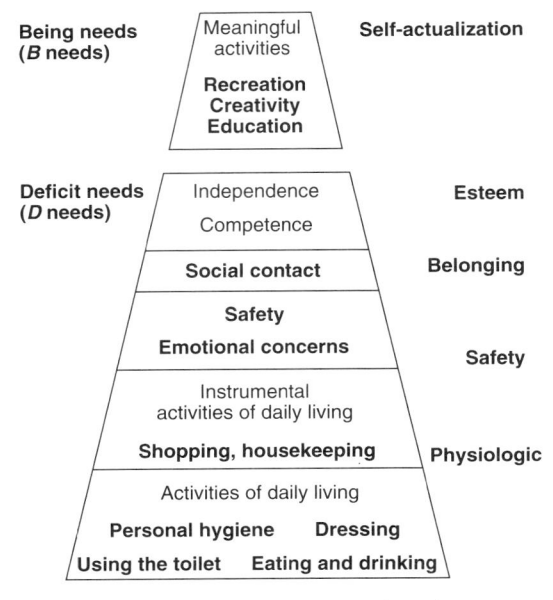

FIGURE 35.7 Importance of needs.

The resulting pattern alternatives (x axis in Fig. 35.6) are the 15 initially assumed ones plus 3 new patterns: *reinforcer* (praising a person), *participator in activities*, and *supplier of objects*.

In Table 35.3, we present those eight patterns of interaction that were most valid (they excelled in correlations or reusability in a group at least twice) in our simple pattern language. For each pattern, we included the highest correlation and interconnectivity values (i.e., normally all "•" values) as well as the reusability count (see section 35.6.3.2).

35.6.5 Discussion

It was obvious in our field study that there are shortcomings in care. Some of the worst stories we heard in interviews involved residents being drugged or immobilized simply because there were not enough staff to keep an eye on them. Then there are cases of elders who, due to a lack of time, are cared for (e.g., washed) while sitting on the toilet. On the other hand, we talked to an old woman who did not believe in aging in place (which EAT promises to enable). She moved to a home voluntarily for the social contact.

Promising EAT that might help overcome problems exists or is being developed. When discussing applications with elders and caregivers, certain trends in attitudes toward such technology became visible. *Operator* (having the carer do a task) is the dominating pattern in human care, often due to a lack of time—it is faster. Caregivers criticize this, and would rather allow elders to do more themselves. Interestingly though, in EAT (at least for *safety* needs) a majority prefer a high-automation *operator* application over a low-automation *guide*. Many carers imagined interactive guidance as too demanding for users. They would mostly want it for mentally fit people or in addition to human guidance. Several carers described a general *telecare* model where the user could contact a human assistant via video as a desirable alternative.

TABLE 35.3 Patterns of Assistive Interaction

(1) *OPERATOR***
Caregiver does a difficult task him/herself
Sample: "Shopping is done by my daughter, and by the institution on shopping day. I give them a list, and they go shopping."
Correlations: personal hygiene, transferring, kitchenwork/eating and drinking, shopping, laundry, housekeeping, administrative tasks, motor (all •, *reusability:* 15)
Interconnectivity: MONITOR, REMINDER (both •)
Used AT: microwave, dishwasher, person-lifter, automatic door
Promising EAT: home automation for safety (e.g., turning off tap or cooker, regulating temperature), washing/bathing robot

(2) *MEDIATOR* **
Caregiver makes a difficult task easier to do
Sample: "When I walk alone, I am insecure. I'm afraid I could fall. During winter, I only go out with my daughter. The carers take me to the hairdresser. If there were more staff, I would go out more."
Correlations: dressing, physical toileting, walking/walking aids, transferring, physical eating, telephone, housekeeping (all •, *reusability:* 12)
Interconnectivity: OPERATOR, RECOMMENDER (both ○) *Used AT:* cane, walker, wheelchair, lift, letter-opener, bookholder, stocking puller, forceps, handhold, trapeze bar, basic magnifying devices, "feeding cup"; automatic bed, chair; simplified toilet, scales, toothbrush, scissors, shoehorn, plate, telephone, games
Promising EAT: simple phone, magnifying devices (near and far)

(3) *SUPPLIER OF ACTIVITIES* *
Caregiver offers an activity; elder and caregiver engage in the activity
Sample: "We have bowling for the demented. It is not that difficult. We use soft balls (. . .) and — amazingly — people who otherwise can't move a finger (. . .) somehow they're all capable of bowling."
Correlations: Kitchenwork, shopping, group activities, recreation/creativity/education, exercise, memory (all •, *reusability:* 8)
Interconnectivity: RECOMMENDER (○)
Used AT: guitar, games, jigsaw puzzles, gymnastics apparatuses, books
Promising EAT: electronic crossword puzzles, mental exercise games, etc.

(4) *COMMUNICATOR* *
The elder needs to talk to somebody; caregiver identifies the person, and contacts him/her
Sample: "A blind and weak woman had two daughters in the States, with whom she talked regularly. Dialling was difficult, so we did this for her. We checked every 15 min if she was still telephoning."
Correlations: using technology, administrative tasks, medical staff, communication (all •, *reusability:* 11)
Interconnectivity: MONITOR (•)
Used AT: internal calling system, mobile phone, external alarm
Promising EAT: reachable alarms with quick response times, urgency indication for staff, and possibility of voice input; videophones and chat for social contact; telecare by video contact

(5) *LISTENER* *
The elder tells something about his/her life, and the caregiver listens
Sample: "They talk about their children, the garden, their husbands, war experiences, Christmas, . . . — so far I haven't experienced anyone who would not want to talk."
Correlations: emotional concerns, communication, reminiscence (all •, *reusability:* 5)
Interconnectivity: none (but helps caregiver in general)

(6) *MONITOR* *
Caregiver watches over elder or environment; when something unusual is noticed, caregiver reacts
Sample: "Since you know people's behavior, you look to see what Mr. X is doing; is he all right? But it cannot be preventive. You look into a room, 3 s later someone can fall. Or he's been lying there for 2 h."
Correlations: health, safety, deviating and dangerous behavior (all •, *reusability:* 11)
Interconnectivity: OPERATOR, COMMUNICATOR, GUIDE (•)

(continued overleaf)

TABLE 35.3 (Continued)

Used AT: institution newspaper *Promising EAT:* virtual community for sharing life stories and producing oral history	*Used AT:* blood pressure, smoke detector, external alarm *Promising EAT:* detector for food boiling over or scorching, monitoring of kitchen appliances with text/sound warnings to prevent accidents (divided opinion about relevance and cognitive demand), fall detector, warnings in traffic, warnings about intruders
(7) REMINDER Caregiver notices that a time has come or a situation has occurred, and reminds elder of something to be done *Sample:* "I leave a note 'Tomorrow you'll be showered' on the night table for 24 h. Otherwise they'd already be finished by then." *Correlations:* Personal hygiene, eating and drinking, medication times, administrative tasks, medical appointments, recreation/creativity/education, cognitive difficulties (all •, *reusability:* 12) *Interconnectivity:* OPERATOR (•) *Used AT:* calendar, notes, pillboxes *Promising EAT:* electronic cues that remind of safety precautions (e.g., "Turn off the cooker" after cooking food)	(8) GUIDE Caregiver explains how to do a difficult task. *Sample:* "And then, of course, the classic case of the remote control, which, even if it's for the hundredth time, is explained. Where to turn on and off the TV." *Correlations:* Mobility, kitchenwork, using technology, administrative tasks, cognitive difficulties (all •, *reusability:* 14) *Interconnectivity:* MONITOR (•) *Used AT:* written instructions, map, signpost *Promising EAT:* interactive assistance in food preparation (like a radio or TV cook) and maybe emergencies (but divided opinion about relevance and cognitive demand)

Key: ** = high validity; * = medium validity; (no asterisk) = low validity.

Our design space can help identify needed EAT. Yet, in its current form it contains 142 + applications (out of 18 high-level needs × 18 patterns = 324), and is not very convenient. Fortunately, a more compact form of this structure exists: the set of all needs and patterns alternatives together with their correlations. A set of 18 + 18 = 36 alternatives is more manageable. This is where the instrument becomes useful for choosing and (co)producing EAT.

35.7 RELATED WORK

Table 35.4 [40–52] is a collection of EAT systems that can be classified as virtual companions. These are projects that develop multifunctional, interactive assistance. Standalone devices have been excluded as well as pure *smart home* and *telecare* systems that emphasize home automation or remote human assistance, respectively, rather than advanced human–machine collaboration.

Many of these projects have in common that they started out with a certain *technology* that promises to benefit older people or people with special needs, and then designed a number of useful *applications* for it. This will work as long as users are pleased with the initial applications. Considering the dynamic diversity of elderly users, a previous user or a new one may express a completely new, not yet supported, need for assistance. If the EAT software in question then was not engineered for extensibility, adding or modifying

TABLE 35.4 Overview of Virtual Companion Projects

Project	Technology	Applications
Wakamaru [41]	Robots	Reminding, monitoring user and environment, informing
Nursebot/Pearl [42]	Robots	Reminding, mobility aid, monitoring user, communication with assistants, social interaction
Care-O-bot [43]	Robots	Transporting and operating objects, operating appliances, reminding, communication with assistants, monitoring user
RoboCare [44]	Robots, smart home	Initially reminding, entertainment, transporting objects, monitoring user and environment, locating, mobility aid
Intelligent sweet home [45]	Robots, smart home, interactive software	Mobility and other physical support, operating appliances, health monitoring, reminding
ILSA [40]	Interactive software (Web and telephone), smart home	Monitoring user, reminding, communication with assistants + more (open architecture)
DOMUS [46]	Interactive software, smart home	Locating objects, activity guidance, monitoring user
MoniC@re [47]	Interactive software (stationary touchscreen)	Monitoring user and environment, communication with assistants, informing, reminding, entertainment/memory training
SAID [48]	Interactive software (over digital TV)	Informing, reminding, recommending, planning visits
UTOPIA companions [49]	Interactive software	Usable interfaces
mPCA [50]	Mobile device, smart home	Reminding, training/guidance, locating, monitoring user
The Companion [51]	Mobile device	Hypothetical: communication with assistants, guidance, reminding, monitoring, locating
Isaac [52]	Mobile device	Picture communication, informing/reminding (clock/calendar); initially planned — communication with assistants, locating

applications would be cumbersome. This is why our own Virtual Companion project takes a systematic software engineering approach that does not favor predefined sets of applications, but instead aims for a toolkit generating variable functionality (Table 35.5. [11,53–56]).

Customization toolkits have been described for the less interactive paradigm of an assisting smart home, to support both the user's (CUSTODIAN) and the programmer's point of view (Olympus programming framework). These approaches center on customizing smart inventory of a house.

Toolkits that allow further specification of human–machine collaboration and thus come closer to our own visions can be found as well. One example is the Tentaculus system, in which users and designers can freely define event–condition–action rules for personalized interactive assistance in a home setting. Available actions during adaptation seem quite basic, though: "Turn on the lights, lock the door, ask the user a specific question," and so on [55]. More complicated interaction may need to be hardcoded for

TABLE 35.5 Overview of EAT Toolkits

Project	Technology	Applications
IISLAB Virtual Companion [11]	Interactive software (variable user interface) + toolkit	Variable
CUSTODIAN [53]	Smart home toolkit	Variable
Olympus framework [54]	Smart home toolkit	Variable
Tentaculus [55]	Interactive software, smart home + toolkit	Variable
Solo [56]	Interactive software (cognitive assistance) + toolkit	Reminding, guidance

each user. This is not necessary in our framework, as it comes with ready-made components. Interaction in the Solo system is more concrete than in Tentaculus. Solo allows the specification of interactive task guidance, facilitating task analysis by a graphical interface. Yet, compared to Tentaculus and our own multifunctional framework, it is restricted to reminding and guidance applications.

35.8 CONCLUDING REMARKS

In this chapter we have discussed electronic assistive technology (EAT) and virtual companions in particular. We have emphasized the need for virtual companions to be dependable, and have discussed corresponding dependability requirements in depth. We have also proposed a design for a framework for implementing dependable virtual companions, where a number of functions (corresponding to patterns of assistive interaction) can be connected to application areas (corresponding to user needs). This design facilitates reuse of already implemented components and is an important step toward truly multifunctional virtual companions. Further, we described a prototype implementation of the framework and described a scenario-based evaluation, and resulting refinement suggestions. Then, taking a step back, we dived into the needs of older people and investigated the functional design space of virtual companions through a fairly large empirical study. The resulting needs taxonomy, and patterns of assistive interaction should be taken into account when designing future virtual companions.

In concluding this chapter we would like to emphasise two key facts: (1) the needs of frail older people are highly individual, and (2) there are plenty of different kinds of needs. This means, first, that off-the-shelf products, or one-size-fits-all products are likely to fail, except when they target a very specific need—and even then, such a need may well change after a while, making the product less useful, or even useless. Moreover, given the large number of different needs, having one tool for each specific need does not seem feasible. Instead, a multifunctional virtual companion, where needs and patterns of assistive interaction can be combined to enable software reuse, and where the user can benefit from knowledge of one type of support when trying to use a different type of support, seems a better way to go.

ACKNOWLEDGMENTS

We thank our informers from the field studies and our partners at the national Institute for the study of Ageing and Later Life. This work has been partly supported by the Swedish Council for Working Life and Social Research.

REFERENCES

1. Glogoski C, Foti D: Special needs of the older adult, in Pedretti LW, Early MB, eds, *Occupational Therapy: Practice Skills for Physical Dysfunction*, 5th edn, Mosby, St. Lous, MO, 2001, Chapter 51, pp 991–1012.
2. WHOQOL Group: The World Health Organization Quality of Life Assessment (WHOQOL) (position paper from WHO), *Social Sci Med* **41**:1403–1409 (1995).
3. Baltes MM: *The Many Faces of Dependency in Old Age*, Cambridge Univ Press, Cambridge, UK, 1996.
4. Hellström I: Exploring *"Couplehood" in Dementia—A Constructivist Grounded Theory Study*, PhD thesis, Linköping Univ, 2005.
5. Strough J, Margrett J: Overview of the special section on collaborative cognition in later adulthood, *Int J Behav Devel* **26**(1):2–5 (2002).
6. US Bureau of the Census: *World Population Profile: 1998*, Technical Report WP/98, US Government Printing Office, Washington, DC, 1998.
7. Hellgren A: Elders in Mjölby may not have their evening meal, *Extra Östergötland* (May 16, 2005) (in Swedish).
8. Drieschner F: Care system in a state of emergency. End without mercy, *Die Zeit* (July 8, 2004) (in German).
9. Stålldal E, Erikson R, Caesar M, eds, *Ageing, Elderly Care and How It Can Be Used to Enhance the Quality of Life for the Elderly*, technical report from a Swedish Japanese seminar held in Stockholm, Sweden, 2001.
10. Maciuszek D, Shahmehri N: A framework for the specification of multifunctional, adaptive, and realistic virtual companions for later life, *Proc Int Conf Aging, Disability and Independence (ICADI)*, Washington, DC, 2003.
11. Shahmehri N, Aberg J, Maciuszek D, Chisalita I: Linköping University's Virtual Companion project, *IEEE Pervasive Comput* **3**(2):50 (2004).
12. Gregor P, Newell AF, Zajicek M: Designing for dynamic diversity—interfaces for older people, *Proc 5th Int ACM Conf Assistive Technologies (ASSETS 2002)*, Edinburgh, UK, 2002, pp 151–156.
13. Johnson RE: Frameworks = components + patterns, *Commun ACM* **40**(10) (Oct 1997).
14. Avizienis A, Laprie J-C, Randell B: *Fundamental Concepts of Dependability*, Technical Report UCLA CSD 010028, Computer Science Dept, Univ California, Los Angeles, 2001.
15. Gefen D, Karahanna E, Straub DW: Trust and TAM in online shopping: An integrated model, *MIS Q* **27**(1):51–90 (March 2003).
16. Dewsbury G, Sommerville I, Clarke K, Rouncefield M: A dependability model for domestic systems, *Proc 22nd Int Conf Computer Safety, Reliability, and Security*, Edinburgh, UK, 2003, Springer-Verlag, 2003, pp 103–115.
17. Miller CA, Haigh K, Dewing W: First, cause no harm: Issues in building safe, reliable and trustworthy elder care systems, *Proc AAAI 2002 Workshop on Automation as Caregiver: The Role of Intelligent Technology in Elder Care*, Edmonton, Alberta, Canada, 2002, pp 80–84.
18. Ferrini AF, Ferrini RL: *Health in the Later Years*, McGraw-Hill, Boston, 2000.
19. de Raeve L: Trust and trustworthiness in nurse-patient relationships, *Nursing Phil* **3**(2):152–162 (2002).
20. Carlshamre P: A Usability Perspective on Requirements Engineering, PhD thesis, Dept Computer and Information Science, Linköping Univ, 2001.
21. Davis FD: Perceived usefulness, perceived ease of use, and user acceptance of information technology, *MIS Q* **13**(3):318–340 (1989).

22. Muir BM: Trust in automation: Part I. Theoretical issues in the study of trust and human intervention in automated systems, *Ergonomics* **37**(11):1905–1922 (1994).
23. Schneider FB, ed: *Trust in Cyberspace*, National Academy Press, Washington, DC, 1999.
24. Katz S, Ford AB, Moskowitz RW, Jackson BA, Jaffe MW: Studies of illness in the aged. The index of activities of daily living, *JAMA* **185**:914–919 (1963).
25. Lawton MP, and Brody EM: Assessment of older people: Self-maintaining and instrumental activities of daily living, *Gerontologist* **9**:179–185 (1969).
26. Levine RE, Brayley CR: Occupation as a therapeutic medium. A contextual approach to performance intervention, in Christiansen CH, Baum CM, eds, *Occupational Therapy. Overcoming Human Performance Deficits*, Slack, Thorofare, NJ, 1991, Chapter 22, pp 590–631.
27. Intille SS: Designing a home for the future, *Pervasive Comput*, **1**(2):80–86 (2002).
28. Herzog A, Shahmehri N: Towards secure e-services: Risk analysis of a home automation service, *Proc 6th Nordic Workshop on Secure IT Systems (NordSec)*, Copenhagen, Denmark, 2001, pp 18–26.
29. Aberg: Dealing with malnutrition: A meal planning system for elderly, *Proc AAAI Spring Symp Argumentation for Consumers of Health Care*, 2006, pp 1–7.
30. Josman N, Birnboim S: Measuring kitchen performance: What assessment should we choose? *Scand J Occup Ther* **8**:193–202 (2001).
31. Pigot H, Lefebvre B, Meunier J-G, Kerherv B, Mayers A, Giroux S: The role of intelligent habitats in upholding elders in residence, *Proc 5th Int Conf Simulations in Biomedicine*, 2003, pp 497–506.
32. Pigot H, Mayers A, Giroux S: The intelligent habitat and everyday life activity support, *Proc 5th Int Conf Simulations in Biomedicine*, 2003, pp 507–516.
33. Albert D, Held T: Component based knowledge spaces in problem solving and inductive reasoning, in Albert D, Lukas J, eds, *Knowledge Spaces: Theories, Empirical Research, Applications*, Lawrence Erlbaum Associates, Mahwah, NJ, 1999, pp 15–40.
34. Shaw M, Garlan D: *Software Architecture: Perspectives on an Emerging Discipline*, Prentice-Hall, Upper Saddle River, NJ, 1996.
35. Crabtree A: *Designing Collaborative Systems. A Practical Guide to Ethnography*, Springer-Verlag, London, 2003.
36. Alexander C, Ishikawa S, Silverstein M, Jacobson M, Fiksdahl-King I, Angel S: *A Pattern Language: Towns, Buildings, Construction*, Oxford Univ Press, New York, 1977.
37. Maciuszek D, Aberg J, Shahmehri N: What help do older people need? Constructing a functional design space of electronic assistive technology applications, *Proc 7th Int ACM SIGACCESS Conf Computers and Accessibility (ASSETS'2005)*, Baltimore, MD, Oct 9–12, 2005, pp 4–11.
38. Townsend EA, ed: *Enabling Occupation*, Canadian Association of Occupational Therapists, Ottawa, 2002.
39. Maslow AH: *Motivation and Personality*, Harper & Row, New York, 1954.
40. Haigh KZ, Kiff LM, Myers J, Guralnik V, Krichbaum K, Phelps J, Plocher T, Toms D: *The Independent LifeStyle Assistant (ILSA): Lessons Learned*, Technical Report ACS-P03-023, Honeywell Laboratories, 2003.
41. Mitsubishi: *Wakamaru—Life with a Robot* (www.mhi.co.jp/kobe/wakamaru/english/).
42. Baltus G, Fox D, Gemperle F, Goetz J, Hirsch T, Magaritis D, Montemerlo M, Pineau J, Roy N, Schulte J et al: Towards personal service robots for the elderly, *Proc Workshop on Interactive Robotics and Entertainment (WIRE-2000)*, Pittsburgh, PA, April 30–May 1, 2000.

43. Hans M, Graf B: Robotic home assistant Care-O-bot II, in Prassler E, Lawitzky G, Stopp A, Grunwald G, Hägele M, Dillmann R, Iossifidis I, eds, *Advances in Human-Robot Interaction*, Springer, Berlin/Heidelberg, Germany, 2005, pp 371–384.
44. Cesta A, Bahadori S, Cortellessa G, Grisetti G, Giuliani V, Iocchi L, Leone R, Nardi D, Oddi A, Pecora F et al: The RoboCare project. Cognitive systems for the care of the elderly, *Proc Int Conf Aging, Disability and Independence (ICADI)*, Washington, DC, 2003.
45. Bien ZZ, Jung J-W, Lee H-E, Kim D-J, Park KH: Human-friendly assistive robotic system for independence of the handicapped/the elderly, *Proc 3rd Int Conf Smart Homes and Health Telematics*, Magog, Canada, July 4–6, 2005, pp 255–263.
46. Vergnes D, Giroux S, Chamberland-Tremblay D: Interactive assistant for activities of daily living, *Proc 3rd Int Conf Smart Homes and Health Telematics*, Magog, Canada, July 4–6, 2005, pp 229–236.
47. Prazak B, Fugger E, Mina S: The importance of user involvement in the design process of personal alerting systems—supported by a qualitative study, *Proc Conf and Workshop on Assistive Technologies for Vision and Hearing Impairment (CVHI 2004), State-of-the-art and New Challenges*, Granada, Spain, June 29–July 2, 2004.
48. Rodriguez T, Fischer K, Kingston J: Intelligent services for the elderly over the TV, *J Intell Inform Syst* **25**(2):159–180 (2005).
49. Cringean S, Benyon D, Leplatre G: Exploration of personality rich mobile companions, *Proc Human-Animated Characters Interaction Workshop, as part of HCI 2005: The Bigger Picture—The 19th British HCI Group Annual Conf*, Edinburgh, UK, Sept 6, 2005.
50. Giraldo C, Helal S, Mann W: mPCA—a mobile patient care-giving assistant for Alzheimer patients, *1st Int Workshop on Ubiquitous Computing for Cognitive Aids (UbiCog'02), in conjunction with 4th Int Conf Ubiquitous Computing (UbiComp'02)*, Göteborg, Sweden, Sept 29, 2002.
51. Vanderheiden G: A brief look at technology and mental retardation in the year 2000, in Rowitz L, ed, *Mental Retardation in the Year 2000*, Springer-Verlag, New York, 1992, pp 268–278.
52. Jönsson B, Philipson L, Svensk A: *What Isaac Taught Us*, Certec, Lund, Sweden, 1998.
53. Dewsbury GA, Taylor BJ, Edge HM: Designing dependable assistive technology for vulnerable people, *Health Inform J* **8**(2):104–110 (2002).
54. Ranganathan A, Campbell RH: Supporting tasks in a programmable smart home, *Proc 3rd Conf Smart Homes and Health Telematics*, Magog, Canada, July 4–6, 2005, pp 3–10.
55. *Tentaculus. Independent Living* (www.tentaculus.se).
56. LoPresti EF, Kirsch N, Simpson R, Schreckenghost D: Solo: Interactive task guidance, *Proc ASSETS 2005—7th Int ACM SIGACCESS Conf Computers and Accessibility*, Baltimore, MD, Oct 9–12, 2005, pp 190–191.

36

Textile Sensing and e-Textiles (Smart Textiles)

Rita Paradiso[†], Nicola Taccini[‡], and Giannicola Loriga[§]
Smartex, Italy

36.1 INTRODUCTION

The new generation of technologic tools, in particular in the field of telecommunication, has trained people to be continuously in "touch" with one another, never alone. This virtual link is revolutionary in the way of feeling, and when it is coupled with innovative sensing architectures, it could be revolutionary in the way of acting. On the other end, the improvement of early illness detection and medical intervention, with its associated costs for society, has raised growing attention and efforts on the implementation and enhancement of assistive technologies and services of various kinds, to help patients in compensating for their impairments, maintaining and increasing their independence, and thus their quality of life. In the meantime, demand for portable patient monitors has drastically increased pushing the need for research and development for user-oriented technologies.

These considerations, together with competitive pricing strategies and hospital network communications, encourage the setup of health systems based on a combination of telecommunication tools, data management, and personalized medical services. Renewed health managing systems, based on consciousness and interactivity concepts, have to be increasingly oriented to prevention more than cure, to guarantee continuity and personalized care and to offer customized delivery services.

[†]Presently on leave at Milior s.p.a., Prato, Italy, rita@smartex.it
[‡]Presently on leave at Smartex s.r.l.,Prato, Italy, taccini@smartex.it
[§]Presently on leave at Smartex s.r.l.,Prato, Italy, loriga@smartex.it

The Engineering Handbook of Smart Technology for Aging, Disability, and Independence,
Edited by A. Helal, M. Mokhtari and B. Abdulrazak
Copyright © 2008 John Wiley & Sons, Inc.

Naturally, this revolution has to be accepted by the final consumer. The monitoring interface has to be designed by considering motivation, user-friendliness, and personalization aspects, in order to allow, when necessary, continuous remote control, in a "natural" environment without any discomfort and without interfering with daily user activity.

Citizens of the incoming future will be more and more experts on telecommunication technology and information managing, and the idea of a surrounding virtual world will become a natural condition in life. New tools, capable of helping people to increase their health status awareness, will be used everywhere and anytime; these systems will train people to act at preventive level by addressing them toward an healthier lifestyle. The interaction between physician and patient will grow in quality and the contribution will come from both the parts.

Integration of monitoring capability into smart clothing seems to be one of the emerging technical solutions capable to match the potentiality of the most advanced technologies in the field of telecommunication and signal analysis. Sensing textile interfaces have shown to be compatible with the implementation of human-oriented monitoring systems able to address the needs of care of differentiated user groups, from healthy to chronically ill people [1].

Multifunctional fabrics, commonly referred as *electronic textiles* (*e-textiles*), enable the realization of easy-to-use, noninvasive, and fashionable wearable devices. Healthcare systems, exploiting these technologies, are conceived as innovative textile tools, integrating sensing, actuation, electronic, and power functions [2,3]. Owing to their multifunctional interactivity, e-textiles are considered relevant promoters of higher quality of life [4,5] and progress in biomedicine and in several health-focused disciplines, such as biomonitoring, rehabilitation, telemedicine, health-professional support, and sport medicine [6].

Biomonitoring, with both the meanings of health monitoring (including vital signs detection) and body-kinematics monitoring [7], would considerably benefit from the implementation of wearable sensory systems. In particular, garments with electrical and biosensing capabilities are able to ensure a daily health check and disease prevention through a continuous, personalized monitoring of vital signs and physiologic variables [8], while garments with strain-and-stress-sensing capabilities enable a tracking of posture and gesture of a subject by detecting kinematics variables of interest [9,10].

Finally, textile approach to the implementation of sensing interface allows the constraint of costs as well as to personalize the system through available industrial production processes.

36.2 E-TEXTILE FOR AMBULATORY MONITORING

A strong contribution to medical assistance is given by the possibility to monitor and assist patients through a remote medical advice service. The use of e-textile-based systems guarantees to physicians the data to timely detect and manage health risks, to early diagnose diseases, recommending treatments that would prevent further deterioration and finally to make confident professional decisions based on objective information possibly in a "safe" short time.

The common clinical approach for ambulatory monitoring is based on the use of devices capable to detect physiologic signals and parameters such as ECG, respiratory activity, blood pressure, blood oxygen saturation, activity index, posture, EOG, EMG, core body temperature, and skin temperature.

The list of signals detectable with noninvasive sensors can be enlarged or reduced according to specific application; more in general, among the possible combinations of signals, some of the most important information about the physiologic state of the user are given by the screening of cardiopulmonary activity. The monitoring of heart and respiratory functionality gives sufficient information to check patient health conditions.

The long period analysis of ECG signal performed with several electrodes allows a complete observation of heart functionality, which is of basic importance in the majority of cardiac pathologies, particularly in myocardial ischemia. The most common type of ambulatory monitoring for cardiac pathologies is a portable device for ECG acquisition (Holter); this instrument usually allows the acquisition of few channels, by means of small metal pads (electrodes) attached on the chest and connected to the recorder by wires. The electronic module is normally worn on a strap at the waist or over the shoulder. Such configuration is enough for a simple analysis of ECG frequency and the identification of arrhythmia but not for monitoring the rehabilitation process and for more complex investigations; besides, the electrodes have to be positioned on the body by trained personnel.

Holter monitoring provides a continuous 24–72-h record of the electrical signals from subject heart during daily activity. A diary of all the activities and symptoms completes the information about the patient. After the monitoring period, a health specialist compares the timing of patient activities and symptoms with the recorded heart pattern. Data analysis is performed offline, and only a delayed medical response can be provided when abnormalities are detected.

The use of textile material to realize clothes with integrated electrodes, distributed on the body surface according to the desired level of information, allows the acquisition of various ECG derivations; this approach leads to the mapping of the whole walls of the heart. Moreover, a shirt can be worn without any external help, and the use of a simplified system lets patients perform a daily health check without affecting their quality of life. A timely intervention in case of a serious situation is feasible when the system provides transmission of online data to a monitoring centre, by mobile network.

The opportunity to send continuously different physiologic signals, by means of an easy-to-wear monitoring system, allows carrying out the rehabilitation phase in domestic environment; during this phase the heart functionality can be continuously monitored, even for 24 h a day if the patient condition requires a strict control.

Another important physiological function is respiratory activity. Scientific publications [11–14] indicate that respiratory rate is the most sensitive respiratory parameter, but a nonspecific sign of respiratory dysfunction, while tidal volume estimate is useful for clinical decisionmaking in children and adults under resting, sleeping, and exercising conditions.

Starting from rate and volume indices, a number of respiratory parameters can be computed, such as ventilation, fractional aspiratory time and both aspiratory and expiratory flows.

The possibility of simultaneously recording different physiologic signals provides an integrated view of normal and abnormal pattern of activity, which could be otherwise impossible to detect by recording each signal in different time. For instance, ECG and respiration signal, simultaneously acquired, can be used to study the sympathovagal balance. The analysis of the heart rate variability (HRV) allows a good and reliable investigation of the autonomic nervous system controlling heart rate. In fact, an appropriate algorithm detect the QRS complex in ECG signal and provides the series of RR intervals (tachogram). The respiratory activity signal is sampled in correspondence with each cardiac beat. The tachogram and the respiration signal are analyzed in frequency domain by a spectral analysis (FFT). The power spectrum density (PSD) of beat-to-beat series presents two major oscillatory components. The first one, which represents the action of the respiration activity on the heart rate modulation mediated by the vagal activity, is described as HF (high-frequency, between 0.15 and 0.45 Hz), whereas the other one, corresponding to the slow waves of arterial pressure and related mainly to sympathetic activity, is described as LF (low-frequency, between 0.04 and 0.15 Hz). The LF/HF ratio can thus be calculated to provide an indication of the sympathovagal balance [15,16].

A further improvement is the in-context data interpretation, while a simple telemonitoring system would just transmit or record real-time physiologic signs, a textile-based system allows the integration of several sensors in a comfortable interface, this means that the system is able to process a set of physiologic parameters in context, so that appropriate feedback can be given in real time to the patient.

Finally it must be outlined that the possibility of recording physiologic variables in a more "natural" environment may help identify the influence of the psychoemotional state of the subject in the performance of a physic activity. This is not easily detectable when recording is done within a protected (medical) environment.

36.3 FROM PREVENTION TO CHRONIC DISEASES CARE

Among the categories of consumers who could benefit of textile-based healthcare system, it is possible to identify the following general list:

- Cardiac patients during rehabilitation phase.
- People with higher-than-average probability that health problems may occur, such as elderly people, people at risk for cardiovascular diseases, and convalescent and chronically ill patients
- Professional personnel at risk (working alone, working in a dangerous environment, etc.)

Starting from the technical requirements deriving from these users' needs, it is possible to extend to other consumer clusters the same technical solutions. As will be discussed later, the physiologic parameters that allow us to check the health status of a definite target group are compatible with the monitoring of larger categories, more in general the screening of cardiorespiratory activity leads to the evaluation of physical parameters that allow a model-based diagnosis.

36.3.1 Cardiac Patients

Heart disease is one of the leading causes of mortality and morbidity in western countries and, in the near future, probably will be even in developing countries. Patients with heart disease usually suffer a chronic condition, often requiring periodical hospitalizations and close follow-up. Efforts in the fields of homecare and preventive cardiac medicine are therefore of strategic importance from a public health perspective. Among patients with heart diseases it is possible to identify various categories that may benefit of customized textile-based systems, naturally people with high-risk profile have to be excluded, by considering that these systems cannot substitute the accuracy of tests done inside intensive care units (ICUs). A textile based healthcare system could help older and frailer patients recovering from an acute coronary syndrome to regain self-confidence in the convalescence phase, supervising their return to normal physical activities, helping in the reinforcement of risk factor control, and allowing a close follow-up for prevention of complications and a more precise treatment with cardiovascular drugs.

More in general for all the patients who need a rehabilitation program in dedicated hospitals or divisions, a wearable monitoring device could provide an effective supervision of home-based telerehabilitation programs [17]: monitoring patients during programmed general exercises, respiratory training, demanding daily activities, supporting risk factor control, and so on. Cardiac patients may provide a good model for the clinical use of wearable systems that could also be extended to other chronic diseases.

36.3.2 People with Higher-than-Average Risk for Health Problems

Extensive clinical and statistical studies have identified several factors that increase the risk of coronary heart disease and heart attack. Risk factors like age, sex, and heredity (including race) cannot be modified, while in other factors such as chronic pathology, or unhealthy lifestyle, modification is possible.

High blood cholesterol, hypertension, hyperglycemia, and obesity are pathologies that can be kept under control, and elimination or reduction of tobacco and alcohol consumption can increase life expectancy. Finally, stress factors, physical inactivity, and overweight are risk factors for coronary heart diseases; also, a more relaxed and active lifestyle helps to control blood cholesterol level, diabetes and obesity risk.

Monitoring systems based on e-textile provide a noninvasive and convenient tool for prevention support, the combination of functional clothes and integrated electronics to collect physiologic parameters and process them locally, and allow diagnosis and therapy recommendations based on clinical standards as well as immediate access to professional care in emergencies.

"On-body" processing consists of making diagnoses, detecting trends and prescribing drug treatments, together with appropriate external feedback devices, able to interact with the users as well as with professional services. These systems can help users fight major personal risk factors, avoid heart failure, sudden circulatory arrest (SCA), and other acute events by personalized guidelines; check results; give feedback; and provide the necessary motivation to change lifestyle.

36.3.3 Professional Personnel at Risk

Numerous professional positions are potentially end users of textile-based healthcare systems in both civilian and military fields. For civilians, these systems would be very useful in case of a required remote monitoring, such as someone working alone (effectively or potentially) with environmental and/or professional hazards. The most obvious example is represented by special corps such as fire fighters or police officers, but remote monitoring is also useful for in industry, airplane pilots, or long-haul truck drivers, where the textile-based remote monitoring device may be used as a "blackbox" in case of accident and also as a tool to avoid or reduce health risks. The interest of military people for remote monitoring is very high, soldiers in the field can be often alone or act in very small groups. They are individually and continuously in touch with their commanding/medical officer, and there is an increasing demand to integrate medical advices into this automated communication.

36.3.4 Signals to Be Monitored

In cardiac patients, and more in generally for people who require a remote monitoring to prevent health risks due to their habits or to the working environment, there is the need to control cardiorespiratory functionality. Complete information is given by recording at least 5 standard ECG leads, together with respiratory activity, posture, and skin temperature. In addition, it can be important to detect information about kinematic variables or an overall index of motion by means of suitably placed movement sensors. Moreover, the monitoring system may be combined with signals transmitted by blood pressure and pulse oximeter devices activated on demand. Information acquired through voice contact between clinician and user about critical symptoms (e.g., chest pain, shortness of breath) or general information useful for patient management (e.g., weight) can be integrated in the patients managing system through the portable device.

The following list of signals to be monitored can be used for all the categories described above, as the detection of cardiopulmonary functionality leads to a good identification of health risk factors.

- ECG: Einthoven leads and at least two precordial leads (V2, V5).
- Respiratory signal
- Motion index
- Posture (lying or standing)
- SpO_2 (peripheral oxygen saturation)
- Heart rate
- Skin temperature
- Blood pressure

The number, type, and location of sensors can be modified according to the specific context of use.

The integration of the information provided by this set of signals allows an accurate definition of cardiorespiratory function and its context (exercise, rest, etc.) and the identification of life-threatening situations (e.g., arrhythmias, myocardial ischemia, respiratory insufficiency). Moreover, the presence of multiple complementary parameters provides additional information in case of partial system failure.

36.4 TEXTILE SENSORS FOR BIOMONITORING

The intrinsic potentiality of textile technology has more recently been exploited for new high-tech applications. The innovation in terms of textile is related to the use of functional yarns integrated in the fabric structure for sensing and acquisition of signals such as the electrocardiogram or electromyogram, respiratory activity, skin conductivity, and index of motion.

Conductive yarns and fibers made of pure metals or by a combination of textile and metallic fibers have appeared on the textile market; their main applications have been for technical fabrics such as for shielding in the automotive industry or for bacteriostatic and antistatic purposes, for apparel and furnishings, and for purely fashion reasons, since the presence of metal changes the mechanical properties of fabric.

Such yarns and fibers fall into two main categories: (1) silver-coated polyamide fibers and (2) staple spun stainless-steel yarns and stainless-steel continuous filaments. Several companies have also developed textile-compatible metal threads.

Metal threads twisted around a standard textile yarn have been used in the past to give a wrinkled effect to fabric. Metals such as copper are usually coated to avoid oxidation problems, while stainless-steel wires are sufficiently stable and conductive to allow e-textile applications.

In terms of conductivity and ease of textile handling and draping, fibers containing silver would be considered the best option for the production of electrodes to be worn close to the body. Unfortunately, due to poor washability and sweat oxidization problems, they are less appropriate than fibers and yarns made of stainless steel. Several more stable new products based on silver have appeared on the market (Xstatic,[1] Shieldex[2]).

At present selected yarns that contain pure stainless steel fibres (Bekintex[3]) are more suitable for e-textile application; more specifically, such slivers can be blended with all spun fibers such as polyamide, polyester, and cotton at the spinning mill to obtain electrically conductive yarns in a wide range of yarn counts. The concentration of Bekinox® needed for blending depends on the nature of textile fiber and technical requirements of the application. Such yarns and fibers are easy to process, corrosion-resistant, inert, and stable in the presence of oxygen and can guarantee long lifetime.

It is important to emphasize that the fabric cannot be realized only with metal yarns; otherwise, this region of the garment will be too rigid and uncomfortable to wear, so the amount of metal in the fabric is a compromise between the required electrical properties and the necessity to keep mechanical behavior compatible with textile applications.

A piezoresistive yarn changes its electrical resistance according to strain; the variation of electrical properties is due to the different path of the electric current inside the fabric structure. Usually this properties can be observed in elastic conductive yarn where a mechanical solicitation affects the flow of carrier inside the structure. When the conductivity of the yarn is due to the presence of conductive particles like in nylon monofilaments with carbon shell, elongation of the yarn produces a different distribution of the conductive components in the structure leading to a modification of the charge transport mechanism. A yarn is a very complex structure in which several filaments or fibers are twisted together, the resulting fabric is a network where the contacts among the single filaments are random, as can be see in Figure 36.1.

Modeling of the charge transport mechanisms inside the textile structure is not easy; when the structure of the yarn and the resulting fabric is maintained planar as much as possible, the fabric sensor usually can be considered like a strain-gauge transducer for the selected interval of strain. The different architectures of the yarn and the resulting fabric confer a different response to the whole sensor.

---

[1] www.x-staticfiber.com.
[2] www.shieldextrading.com.
[3] www.bekintex.com.

FIGURE 36.1 Scanning electron micrographic image of a piezoresistive sensor.

The lithography technique is normally used to realize piezoresistive-coated sensors. During the process, a rubber or silicon solution containing conductive particles is applied to the fabric; then, after the removal of excessive materials, the conductive elements are immobilized in the structure by a treatment at high temperature. The mechanical properties of the final product are affected by the speed of coating process, the viscosity of solution, and the capability of the material used as substrate to adsorb it. The viscoelastic properties of fabric substrate affect the mechanical response of the textile sensor; hysteresis behavior can be reduced by acting at the level of textile structure, as well as by increasing the elastic properties of fabric. These fabrics behave as strain-gauge sensors and show piezoresistive properties comparable with knitted fabric sensors.

For textiles, there are two main fabric-manufacturing techniques: woven textiles and knitted textiles. Embellishments can be added to both of these fabrics by means of a printing, embroidery, coating, or finishing process.

A common textile process such as flat-knitting technology (Steiger SA,[4] Switzerland) allows the implementation of fabric where defined yarns are confined to insulated domains; at the same time it is possible to process different yarns together using the appropriate desired topology. Sensors, electrodes, and connections can be fully integrated in the fabric and produced in one single step, by combining conductive and nonconductive yarns.

The position of sensors can be implemented on the knitted fabric, and the final product can then be cut and sewn to get the sensors in the desired configuration and orientation. This means that the final position of sensors and connections on the garment are achieved mainly during the manufacturing phase. The importance of this last phase for the production of sensory garments is related to the fact that the electrical properties of the

---

[4] www.steiger-zamark.com.

knitted material are correlated with orientation of the yarn. Conductive connections realized along warp or weft directions behave very differently; the same effect has been observed for piezoresistive sensors. This is because the electrical properties of fabric are due to interactions between the fibers inside the yarn and between the individual loops inside the fabric. The whole textile structure must be considered as a complicated array of electrical impedances [18].

Using the knitting intarsia technique, it is possible to obtain a double-faced texture, with the external nonconductive part used to isolate the electrode from the external environment, while using another yarn in vanisè configuration allows one to obtain multilayered structures where the conductive surface is sandwiched between two insulated standard textile surfaces. The same conductive yarn can be used for the electrodes as well as for the realization of connections; an example a fabric obtained in this manner is shown in Figure 36.2.

Most sensors, used for detection of vital signs and user movement must be in close contact with the skin; for this reason, the garment has to be as close to the body as possible, like underwear or a "second skin." The use of seamless-knitting-dedicated machine (e.g., Santoni SpA[5]) can provide elastic, adherent, comfortable garments with these inherent properties. This technology consists in the fusion of two fields: the hosiery field, joined together with knitting machinery.

The seamless approach makes it possible to obtain elastic and closely fitting second-skin models, in a relatively short period of time, starting from the yarn and by passing cutting and sewing operations. This method is very effective for the augmentation of functional aspects as it is possible to implement different mesh areas with varying compression properties.

Flat-bed knitting technology permits a high degree of precision in the realization of patterns, domains, and positioning of secondary fibers in any part of the structure. Future exploitation of wearable e-textile products will be based on innovative techniques derived from both technologies in terms of combined technical solutions.

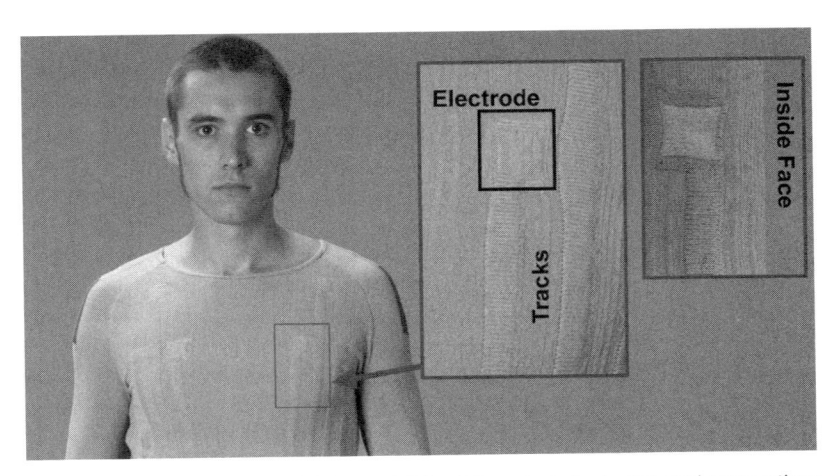

FIGURE 36.2 Example of a fabric containing integrated electrodes and connections.

---

[5] www.santoni.com.

36.5 NOVEL TEXTILE-BASED TRANSDUCER

A *transducer* is a device that converts one type of energy to another. A *sensor* is a transducer that responds to a physical stimulus (heat, light, sound, pressure, motion, flow, etc.) and generates a signal that can be measured or interpreted. The most common sensors produce an electrical signal.

Biopotentials are due to electrochemical activity of the cells. Electrical activity is caused by differences in ion concentrations within the body. A potential difference can be measured between two points with different ionic concentrations. There are several diagnostic application of biopotential: electrocardiography (ECG), electroencephalography (EEG), electromyography (EMG), and electrooculography (EOG). The electrical properties of biological tissues are even exploited for therapeutic and rehabilitation purposes such as pacemakers, defibrillators, muscle stimulation, and functional electrical stimulation (FES).

Biopotential electrodes transduce ionic conduction to electronic conduction and are used for measuring electric potential of biological origin, or to transmit electrical energy to and from a human subject.

Electrodes can be classified in two different categories: macroelectrodes and microelectrodes, differentiated with respect to the size of the transducer as well as the dimensions of the system investigated.

The electrodes can be classified according to conduction mechanism as

- "Perfectly" polarizable, characterized by a capacitive effect, with no charges flow between electrode and tissue (i.e., stainless-steel electrodes).
- "Perfectly" nonpolarizable, characterized by a resistive effect, with free charges flowing between electrode and tissue (i.e., Ag/AgCl).

In order to form a conductive bridge with the skin, an electrolyte medium is usually needed. Figure 36.3 shows an equivalent model of the electrode–electrolyte–skin system [19].

Macroelectrodes are applied directly on the body surface, and good skin contact is obtained through a thin layer of electrolyte. These electrodes can be realized using different kinds of material. The reusable ones are usually made of German silver, an alloy

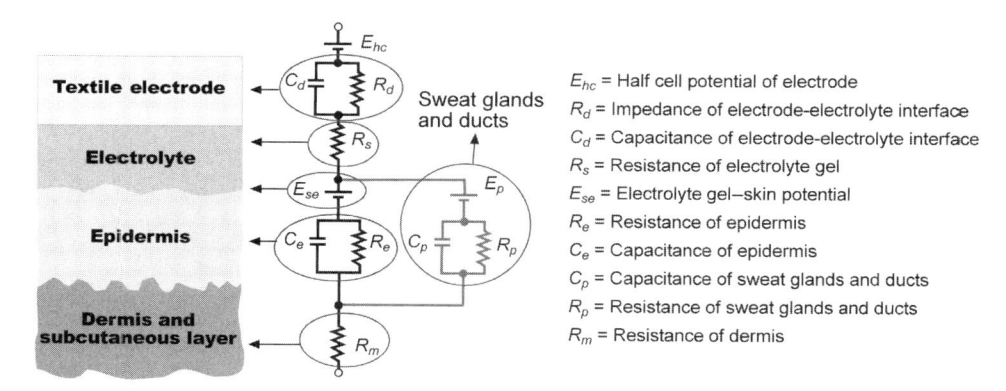

E_{hc} = Half cell potential of electrode
R_d = Impedance of electrode-electrolyte interface
C_d = Capacitance of electrode-electrolyte interface
R_s = Resistance of electrolyte gel
E_{se} = Electrolyte gel–skin potential
R_e = Resistance of epidermis
C_e = Capacitance of epidermis
C_p = Capacitance of sweat glands and ducts
R_p = Resistance of sweat glands and ducts
R_m = Resistance of dermis

FIGURE 36.3 *Schematic model of the electrode–electrolyte–skin interface.*

of zinc, copper, and nickel, and can last for several years. An example is the "Welch" bulb (suction) electrodes. Pregelled disposable electrodes (PDEs) are obtained mainly using Ag/AgCl and are employed for long-term ambulatory monitoring and when high stability is needed.

An alternative solution is obtained with stainless-steel polarizable electrodes, using an electrolyte containing salts of low corrosion potential.

Conductive fabric electrodes, obtained as described in Section 36.4, can be coupled with hydrogel membranes that act as electrolyte, by reducing the contact resistance between the skin and the electrode. In order to improve the stability of the contact, the hydrogel membrane is used in the form of a patch that is adhesive on both sides; this feature improves the signal quality by reducing motion artifact effects. The electrodes also play an important role in the therapeutic–rehabilitation field, as a conductive garment, such as socks, back braces, sleeves, and gloves, can be used in electrotherapy to produce electrodes. In this way the treatment area is entirely covered, allowing a better distribution of energy.

36.5.1 Fabric Electrode Performance

Scilingo et al. [20] have evaluated the performance of fabric electrodes in treatments using standard Ag/AgCl electrodes as reference. In their paper, a quantitative–qualitative approach is used to analyze physiologic signals acquired simultaneously with both types of electrodes. In particular, a qualitative approach allows a specific evaluation of the clinical interpretability and quality of the ECG recordings obtained with both systems.

Some of the most significant time parameters are extracted from the morphology waveform (P wave, QRS complex, ST segment, and T wave), and a spectral analysis (PSD) is performed on signals generated by both electrodes. The same approach is used to compare EMG signals gathered from the bicep brachii during isometric dynamic contractions simultaneously by textile and standard electrodes. The visual–PSD analysis underlines a substantial correspondence between the two systems.

Since stainless-steel electrodes have been reported in the literature [19] as being more polarizable than Ag/AgCl electrodes, appropriate tests on long-term acquisition have been conducted and have revealed no appreciable drift between the two signals.

36.5.2 Biomechanics Textile Sensors

Biomechanics is an interdisciplinary and multidisciplinary field of study that applies the laws of physics and engineering concepts to describe motion of body segments, and the forces that act on them during activity.

Textile sensors represent a suitable solution for monitoring biomechanics variables. The piezoresistive properties of these materials are used to measure breathing, limb and body movements, hand kinematics, and other functions.

A possible application of piezoresistive sensors is represented by monitoring flexoextension movement of the arms, detected by placing an appropriate fabric sensor near the elbow joints. Scilingo et al. [20], performed a validation experiment using a standard electrogoniometer and then compared signals acquired simultaneously with both systems. Two different tests have been carried out to measure slow and fast movements. In both cases the principal frequency components of the signals coming from the two different systems [20] are coincident. Piezoresistive fabric sensors can be used to monitor the respiratory activity by plethysmography (this technique is described in Sections 36.6.1.1 and 36.6.1.2).

36.6 WEARABLE TEXTILE-BASED MONITORING SYSTEM

Wearable monitoring systems, realized by integrating an appropriate setup of sensors and electrodes, allows a user-friendly acquisition of vital signs. For instance, the user shown in Figure 36.6 (in Section 36.7) wearing only a shirt, gives the green light for a complete checkup of his health status without any clinician support. Placement of the sensors in the garment ensures their correct location on the body. The patient does not need to be supervised by skilled personnel during system setup or during measurement; the clinician can analyze signals from a remote location (also in real time, if needed), assisted by an alert management system. Using a strategic layout of electrodes, it is possible to monitor all the needed ECG leads, standard or not, allowing the identification of many cardiac pathologies. Naturally the displacement and number of leads is the result of a mediation between clinician needs and the physical space on the garment for placement of all the required sensors.

Different configurations of electrodes are possible, such as the standard Einthoven and precordial leads or the EASI configuration [21]. Alternative nonstandard solutions are used in order to reduce movement artifacts, for instance, by placing two electrodes symmetrically on the chest below the pectoral muscles. In this case it is possible to integrate the electrodes in a band that can be worn more easily than a shirt.

36.6.1 Textile-Based Respiration Monitoring

Methods for monitoring respiration can be classified in two different categories: direct methods, using devices such as spirometers to directly measure airflow through the lungs, as well as indirect measurements that provide an estimate of body volume changes.

Direct spirometric measurement of breathing requires the use of a mask or mouthpiece, which may be intrusive in lengthy monitoring sessions. Respiratory parameters could provide interesting information about the clinical condition of patients, particularly if correlated with cardiac parameters.

Remarkable efforts have been carried out in order to equip wearable monitoring system with suitable tools of analysis of cardiopulmonary functions. Respiratory activity can be monitored using fabric sensors by different indirect techniques:

- Plethysmography by piezoresistive sensors
- Inductance plethysmography
- Impedance pneumography.

36.6.1.1 Plethysmography by Piezoresistive Sensors

In order to monitor breathing, two piezoresistive sensors can be used: the first one placed around the thorax and the other one around the abdomen. These sensors can be integrated either in elastic band or in a comfortable garment.

Scilingo et al. [20] studied the performance of a piezoresistive textile band (Lycra® fabric coated with carbon-loaded rubber) around the chest in comparison to that obtained

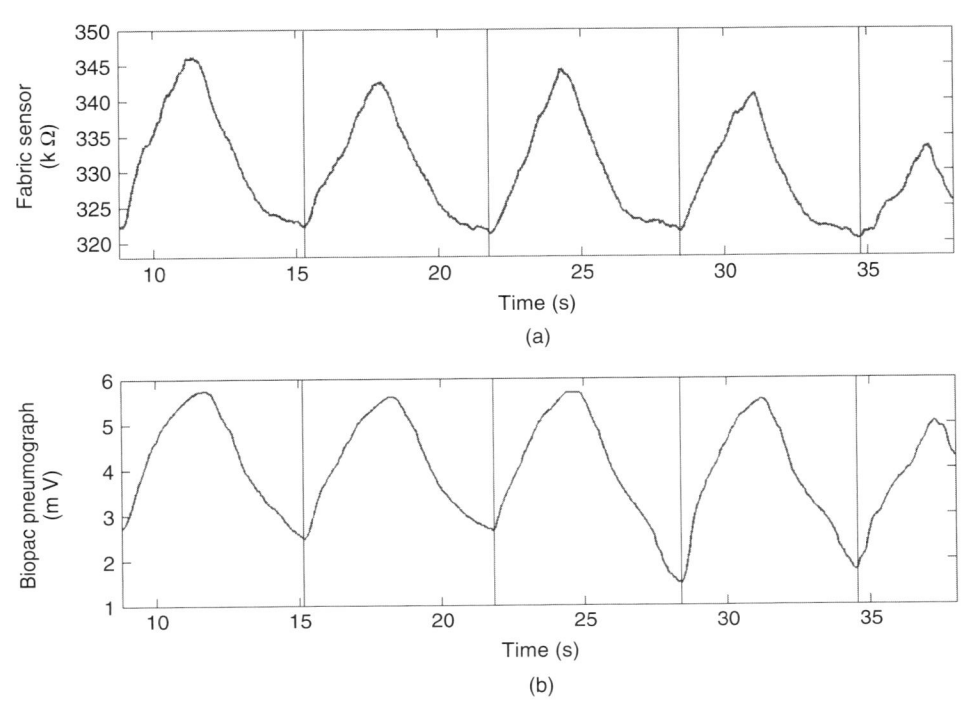

FIGURE 36.4 *Signals derived by piezoresistive fabric sensor (a) and pneumograph model SSL5B contained in the BIOPAC MP30 system (b) during normal respiration.*

using a piezoelectric sensor. The two signals presented the same morphology, and the respiratory rate extracted by an appropriate algorithm coincided.

Figure 36.4 shows signals gathered simultaneously by a piezoresistive fabric made with metal yarns, used as plethysmographic sensors, and a respiratory effort transducer. Perfect coherence between the two signals was demonstrated [22].

Piezoresistive sensors are intrinsically subjected to movement artifacts; even while the patient is resting, these sensors can provide information that is impossible to obtain using other methods (e.g., impedance pneumography), such as differentiating between abdominal function and thoracic respiration. The ability to discriminate between abdominal and thoracic movements using piezoresistive sensors makes it possible to distinguish these actions during paradoxical respiration, in which the chest and abdominal functions oppose each other; the patient exhales through the diaphragm while inhaling via the thoracic muscles, and vice versa. An example of a trial study of this form of simulated respiration is shown in Figure 36.5, where the upper and lower signals appear in opposite phases [22].

36.6.1.2 Inductance Plethysmography

Inductance plethysmography is a well-known method for monitoring respiratory activity [23]. Two conductive wires are placed around the ribcage and the abdomen in order to evaluate the volume in the thoracic and abdominal cavities. Each conductor can be considered as a coil. A magnetic field is generated by injecting a current into the two conductors, or coils. The process of respiration alters the cross-sectional area delimited

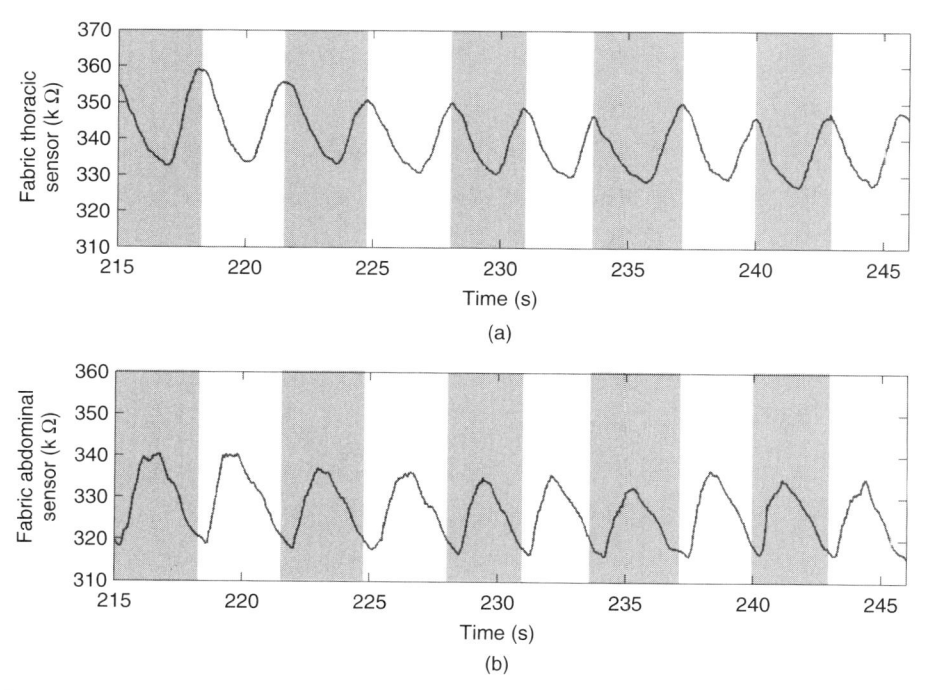

FIGURE 36.5 Thoracic (a) and abdominal (b) respiration signals obtained by fabric sensors during a trial of simulated paradoxical respiration.

by the coils, producing, in turn, an alteration in the magnetic field flowing through the coils. This change in flow causes variations in the self-inductance of the coil. It is possible to monitor the respiration activity by measuring the variation in the self-inductance value. This value is very small (the conductor presents an inductance value of only a microhenries few, so the changes detected are difficult to measure); therefore, an indirect method is used in order to evaluate this value. In fact, the coils can be used to modulate the resonant frequency of an appropriate LC (inductance–capacitance) oscillator. The breathing can be evaluated by monitoring variation in frequency of the sinewave produced by the oscillator due to the self-inductance changes. Using this method, the conductor has to present a high quality factor (Q), so a high-resistance conductor cannot be used. The technique described above is a suitable approach for monitoring respiratory activity by means of wearable systems. The method of volume calibration using this technique consists in breathing into a bag of known volume or into a spirometer. Then, the tidal volume is calculated by analyzing the information obtained from the two sensors.

Inductance plethysmography enables differentiation between abdominal and thoracic functions and detection of obstructive and typically a central apneas followed by an obstructive apneas.

This technology has been incorporated into continuous ambulatory monitoring systems, as in Lifeshirt® by Vivometrics.

36.6.1.3 Impedance Pneumography

Wearable electronic systems are also suitable for measuring body impedances. The ability to place the electrodes in the same position each time satisfies the requirement of bioimpedance measurement. Impedance measurement consists in evaluating the variation of body impedance after injecting a high-frequency low-intensity current through two electrodes and measuring the voltage drop caused by the current. Measured impedance depends on the body composition and the fluid flow within the body itself.

Impedance pneumography enables monitoring of the respiratory activity, relying on the thorax impedance variations determined by airflow through the lungs. Two different approaches are possible: the two-electrode measurement method and the four-electrodes technique. The two-electrodes method shows acceptable results only with resting subjects. To improve the performance of the system, it is necessary to use the four-wire measurement method, which utilizes four electrodes; the outer ones are exclusively used to inject a high-frequency low-intensity current, while the two inner ones allow measurement of voltage variations due to impedance variations caused by respiratory activity [24].

The frequency of this current can vary between 20 and 100 kHz, with a peak amplitude of a few milliamperes. Biologic tissues is not stimulated by currents with such characteristics.

The four-electrode measurement method, owing to the high input impedance of the measurement amplifier, makes it possible to neglect the contribution of the resistance of the cable wires and the contact resistance between the electrodes and the skin, which could significantly alter the impedance evaluation. Furthermore, the use of two electrodes to inject current, which are different from the electrodes used to measure the voltage, ensures that the spatial distribution of the current density between the measuring electrodes remains approximately constant.

This makes it possible to reduce the effect of impedance variations in the proximity of the "injection" electrodes, due to the higher current density in their proximity. Since measured impedance is a function of the air volume present in lungs, such a method can be calibrated with a spirometer. Using a wearable system comprising four integrated electrodes, the position of the electrodes is maintained almost constant for every single subject, and therefore the system needs to be calibrated only once. The relationship between impedance variation (ΔZ) and air volume change (ΔV) is approximately linear under most circumstances [25]. Coefficient $\Delta Z/\Delta V$ depends on physical dimensions of the subject and on the positioning of electrodes and lies between 0.3 and 1.2 Ω/L. Hence the impedance variation corresponding to each respiratory cycle is less than 1% of the basic impedance. Impedance pneumography presents fewer movement artifacts than do other indirect techniques for monitoring breathing. In order to obtain a meaningful signal, this method requires good contact between the skin and electrodes. This technology has been incorporated in the wearable monitoring system "WEALTHY," described in the next section.

36.7 WEALTHY SYSTEM

A wearable healthcare system based on e-textile [26] was developed in the European project named WEALTHY (IST-2001-37778) [27]. The system includes miniaturized electronics and modern telecommunication tools to collect, analyze (locally and in remote), and transmit in real-time vital signs, through a portable electronic, unit [portable patient unit (PPU)] with the dimensions of a modern mobile phone. Real-time analysis is possible by means of advanced signal processing able to extract the main parameters and generate alarms.

The system described above is designed to monitor user categories mentioned in the previous general description. The WEALTHY system acquires and analyzes the following signals:

- ECG: 3 Einthoven leads, V2 and V5 precordial leads
- Respiratory activity
- Core and surface temperature
- Motion activity of elbows and shoulders
- Posture (lying or standing)
- SpO_2 (partial oxygen saturation)

The Wealthy system is able to perform the majority of sensing functions that are usually obtained using standard physiologic sensors by means of textile-integrated sensors.

For this reason the WEALTHY textile interface presents nine electrodes used for ECG and respiratory activity monitoring and four piezoresistive sensors for motion activity of the shoulders and elbows. The six ECG electrodes are strategically placed in order to reduce movement artifacts, allowing the clinician to simultaneously obtain the clinical standard leads mentioned above. Information obtained from the V2 electrode is shared in impedance pneumography, where three additional electrodes are needed. Placement of the electrodes is shown in Figure 36.6.

Two nontextile microelectronic sensors (LM92 by National Semiconductor) are embedded in the garment to measure core and skin temperature of the users. The core temperature sensor is placed under the left armpit (axilla); the other one, on the external side of the left arm, at the middle of the humerus. A thermal insulation, obtained using a double layer of polyester polar fleece, allows measurement of the core temperature.

The portable patient unit (PPU) interfaces with the fabric sensors as well as the microcircuit sensors embedded in the garment. It contains the necessary modules for conditioning of physiologic signals and filtering and converting them to a digital format, using specific higher-level processing such as heart rate analysis and to communicate with a remotely located monitoring centre as well.

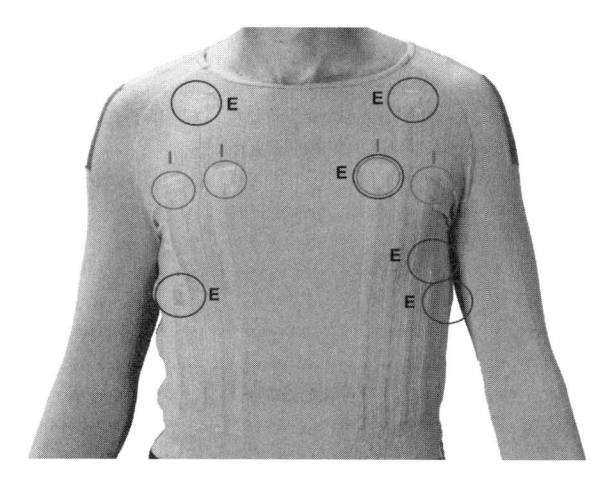

FIGURE 36.6 Textile interface: ECG electrodes (E), impedance pneumography electrodes (I).

In addition to the sensors described above, hard sensors are also used. They provide measurements of the peripheral oxygen saturation (SpO_2) and overall body acceleration. For this purpose a commercial oximeter (NONIN®) can be connected and a biaxial accelerometer is integrated in the PPU board.

ECG signals are sampled at 250 Hz by the PPU. Local processing is applied by appropriate algorithms to compute parameters such as heart rate (HR) and QRS duration with a significant number of samples.

In order to decrease the amount of data transmitted via GPRS, the ECG signal is decimated to obtain a sampling rate of 125 Hz, and only one lead is transmitted at a time (for GPRS bandwidth limitation reasons), selected remotely by the monitoring center.

An alternative solution, for short-range applications, provides a Bluetooth module that allows connection of the PPU to a local computer. The data obtained can be transmitted through any Internet connection (ADSL, LAN, WiFi, etc.) to the monitoring center, or directly visualized and recorded by appropriate software. This solution is useful when the user is located within a 100-m radius of the base unit, such as people at home or athletes in a gymnasium [28].

The WEALTHY central monitoring system (CMS) is a software module interpreting physical sensor data received from the portable patient unit (PPU) and representing them in simple graphical form. The CMS stores all data in a central database, accessible by physicians and other health professionals.

The smart alert subsystem provides emergency alerts, according to the medical values provided by the WEALTHY garment. Depending on the user, the alerts are customizable to each patient. In case of an alert, the monitoring system immediately informs the medical personnel of the central control module. Correlation of parameters to generation of the alerts are defined by a truth table.

36.7.1 Validation of WEALTHY System

The WEALTHY system has been tested on two different categories of users: cardiac patients and professional workers operating in extreme environmental conditions. A qualitative analysis of the signals and a comparison with the standard system for ECG and breath acquisition have been applied by two teams of clinicians.

In experiments conducted on cardiac patients, performance of the WEALTHY shirt compares well with that of standard ECG telemetry equipment.

Quantitative analysis shows near identity between the rest tracings obtained with the two systems in most patients; in some patients differences were related to major problems in the standard system, while in the remaining patients differences are not due to failure of WEALTHY system.

Qualitative analysis demonstrates that, for clinical purposes (i.e., to be interpretable by a physician), ECG quality appears to be very close between the systems. Both systems show degradation of ECG signals during physical activity, but WEALTHY does not seem to be significantly inferior compared to clinical telemetry in this setting. Although fine ECG analysis may be precluded during exercise, the QRS signal seems more robust.

In healthy subjects in extreme environmental conditions, Wealthy gave a signal as good as, or even better than, the reference system, in $82.6 \pm 4.1\%$ of the time for ECG and $88.4 \pm 1.5\%$ of the time for breathing signal [29].

This ratio increases significantly when the subject is sweating. After several minutes of heavy sweating, the signal from Wealthy is regularly better than the reference signal.

36.8 FUTURE APPLICATION

All the arguments presented in this chapter have focused mainly on physiologic measurements (body temperature, ECG, EMG, breathing rhythm, etc.), with a brief description of applications targeting a restricted categories of users. The new challenge is represented by the implementation of a biochemical transduction function onto textile-compatible material.

The use of textile-compatible biosensors could allow the monitoring of body fluids via sensors distributed on a textile substrate able to perform biochemical measurements.[6] The objective is to develop sensing patches, adapted to different targeted body fluids and biological species to be monitored, where the textile itself is the sensor. The extension of sensors to whole-body garments and integration with physiologic monitors would be a logical consequence of this research approach.

Textiles for applications in body fluid monitoring will benefit from distributed sensing with access to 90% of the body surface if sensors are integrated into clothing. This technology is expected to provide user comfort and accurate monitoring simultaneously, with a noninvasive approach and enabling multiparameter analysis.

Biochemical measurement of body fluids (blood, sweat, urine) should dramatically expand the field of applications. At the present time, biochemical analysis systems compatible with sensor integration into clothing are unfortunately lacking. This is a major drawback, for instance, in the case of sweat analysis, which is potentially very rich in health-related information. However, such analysis is rarely performed today because of the difficulty in sampling sweat in sufficient quantity. Only a real textile sensor embedded in a garment through textile techniques will allow direct collection of sweat on a large body surface; moreover, lower fabrication costs are expected. For blood analysis, the main interest will be to avoid invasive sampling and to allow continuous analysis.

Advanced research aims to develop basic technology modules and ad hoc electronic control and analysis modules for biochemical sensing compatible with integration into sensing textile. The goal is to demonstrate the feasibility of functional biochemical sensors and their integration in textile substrates. Key parameters to assess will be the sensitivity, accuracy, and dynamic range of measurement for each type of sensor. In particular, new research is addressing the possibility to monitor sweat composition (ions, pH), conductivity and rate; infection through blood and body liquid for burned people; and oxygen saturation of blood for medical, sport, and security applications

Possible detection methods include optics, electrochemistry, and electricity (impedance monitoring).

36.9 CONCLUSION

In this chapter has discussed the potentialities of novel textile transducers and their integration in healthcare devices. The main advantage ensured by these systems is the possibility of wearing them for long periods without discomfort, as the selection of sensory material is a compromise between comfort for the users and signal quality for the specialists. Moreover, the use of e-textile-based systems is a valid alternative to existing ambulatory monitoring instrumentation addressing several healthcare areas. Finally, the

---

[6]www.biotex-eu.com.

performance of textile transducers seems to promise successful commercialization in the near future.

REFERENCES

1. Billinghurst M, Starner T: Wearable devices: New ways to manage information, *IEEE Comput* **32**(1):57–64 (1999).
2. De Rossi D, Della Santa A, Mazzoldi A: Dressware: Wearable hardware, *Mate Sci Eng C* **7**:31–35 (1999).
3. Service RF: Electronic textiles charge ahead, *Science* **301**:909–911 (2003).
4. Park S, Jayaraman S: Enhancing the quality of life through wearable technology, *IEEE Eng Med Biol Mag* **22**(3):41–48 (2003).
5. Binkley, PF: Predicting the potential of wearable technology. *IEEE Eng Med Biol Mag* **22**(3):23–27, (2003).
6. Marculescu D, et al: Electronic textiles: A platform for pervasive computing, *Proc IEEE* **91**(12):1995–2018 (2003).
7. De Rossi D, Lorussi F, Mazzoldi A, Orsini P, Scilingo EP: Active dressware: Wearable kinesthetic systems, in Secombe J, ed, *Sensors and Sensing in Biology and Engineering*, Springer-Verlag, New York, 2003, pp 381–394.
8. Paradiso R, Loriga G, Taccini, N: Wearable system for vital signs monitoring, in Lymberis A, de Rossi D, eds, *Wearable eHealth Systems for Personalised Health Management*, IOS Press, 2004, pp 253–259.
9. De Rossi D, Carpi F, Lorussi F, Mazzoldi A, Paradiso R, Scilingo EP, Tognetti A: Electroactive fabrics and wearable biomonitoring devices, *AUTEX Res J* **3**(4):180–185 (2003).
10. De Rossi D, Carpi F, Lorussi F, Paradiso R, Scilingo EP, Tognetti A: Electroactive fabrics and wearable man-machine interfaces, in Tao X-M, ed, *Wearable Electronics and Photonics*, Woodhead Publishing, Cambridge, UK, 2004.
11. Rees JE: Early warning scores, *Update Anaesth* **17**(10) (2003).
12. Fieselmann J, Hendryx MS, Helms CM, Wakefield DS: Respiratory rate predicts cardiopulmonary arrest for internal medicine patients, *J Gen Internal Med* **8**:354–360 (1993).
13. Kenwood G, Hodgetts T, Castle N: Time to put the R back in TPR, *Nurs Times* **97**:32–33 (2001).
14. Stubbe CP, Davies RG, Williams E, Rutherford P, Gemmell L: Effects of introducing the modified Early Warning Score on clinical outcomes, cardio-pulmonary arrests and intensive car utilisation on acute medical admissions, *Anaesthesia*, **58**:775–803 (2003).
15. Bianchi AM, Paradiso R, Mendez MO, Loriga G, Scilingo EP, and Cerutti S: Analysis of heart rate and respiration variability signals obtained through a wearable system, *IFMB Proc. Medicon on Health Telematics. Health in the Information Society*, Ischia, Naples, Italy, July 31–Aug 5, 2004, Vol 6.
16. Task Force of the European Society of Cardiology and the North America Society of Pacing and Electrophysiology: Heart rate variability standards of measurement, physiological interpretation and clinical us, *Circulation* **93**(5):1043–1065 (1996).
17. Winters JM, Wang Y: Wearable sensors and telerehabilitation, *IEEE Eng Med Biol Mag* **22**(3):56–65 (2003).
18. Wijesiriwardana R, Dias T, Mukhopadhyay S: Resistive fibre-meshed transducers, *Proc 7th IEEE Int Symp Wearable Computers*, Piscataway, NJ, Oct, 21–23, 2003, pp 200–209.
19. Carim HM: Bioelectrodes, in Webster JG, ed, *Encyclopedia of Medical Devices and Instrumentation*, Wiley, New York, 1988 Vol 1, pp 195–226.

20. Scilingo EP, Gemignani A, Paradiso R, Taccini N, Ghelarducci B, De Rossi D: Performance evaluation of sensing fabric for monitoring physiological and biomechanical variables, *IEEE Trans Technol Biomed* **9**(3):345–352 (2005).
21. Liu X, Zhou H, Liu J, Qiu K, Warren JW, Fitz-Clarke JR, Horacek BM: Synthesis of 12-lead ecg from 3 easi leads: Investigation of population-specific transformation coefficients, *Adv Electrocardiol*, 675–678 (2004).
22. Loriga G, Taccini N, De Rossi D, Paradiso R: Textile sensing interfaces for cardiopulmonary signs monitoring, *Proc 2005 IEEE Engineering in Medicine and Biology 27th Annual Conf*, Shanghai, China, Sept 1–4, 2005.
23. Sackner MA, Inmann DM: Systems and Methods for Ambulatory Monitoring of Physiological Signs, US Patent Application 0,032,386, 2002.
24. Khandpur RS: *Handbook of Biomedical Instrumentation*, Tata McGraw-Hill, New Delhi, 1987.
25. Geddes LA, Baker LE: *Principles of Applied Biomedical Instrumentation*, Wiley, New York, 1989.
26. Paradiso R: *Knitted Textile for the Monitoring of Vital Signals*, WO2005053532, patent pending.
27. Paradiso R, Loriga G, Taccini N: A wearable health care system based on knitted integrated sensors, *IEEE Trans Technol Biomed* **9**(3):337–345 (2005).
28. Paradiso R, Loriga G, Taccini N, Gemignani A, Ghelarducci B: WEALTHY—a wearable health care system: New frontier on e-textile, *J Telecommun Inform Technol* **4**:105–113 (2005).
29. Bourdon L, Coli S, Loriga G, Taccini N, Gros B, Gemignani A, Cianflone D, Chapotot F, Dittmar A, Paradiso R: First results with the Wealthy garment ElectroCardiogram monitoring system, *Proc 32nd Annual Int Conf Computers in Cardiology*, Cinc Lyon, Sept 2005, pp 25–28.

PART VII

Smart Environments and Cyberinfrastructures

37

The Gator Tech Smart House: A Programmable Pervasive Space

Sumi Helal, Raja Bose, Steven Pickles, Hicham Elzabadani, Jeffrey King, and Youssef Kaddourah

University of Florida

Research groups in both academia and industry have developed prototype systems to demonstrate the benefits of pervasive computing in various application domains. These projects have typically focused on basic system integration—interconnecting sensors, actuators, computers, and other devices in the environment.

Unfortunately, many first-generation pervasive computing systems lack the ability to evolve as new technologies emerge or as an application domain matures. Integrating numerous heterogeneous elements is mostly a manual, ad hoc process. Inserting a new element requires researching its characteristics and operation, determining how to configure and integrate it, and tedious and repeated testing to avoid causing conflicts or indeterminate behavior in the overall system. The environments are also closed, limiting development or extension to the original implementers.

To address this limitation, the University of Florida's Mobile and Pervasive Computing Laboratory is developing programmable pervasive spaces in which a smart space exists as both a runtime environment and a software library [1]. Service discovery and gateway protocols automatically integrate system components using generic middleware that maintains a service definition for each sensor and actuator in the space. Programmers assemble services into composite applications, which third parties can easily implement or extend.

The use of service-oriented programmable spaces is broadening the traditional programmer model. Our approach enables domain experts (e.g., health professionals such

---

The Engineering Handbook of Smart Technology for Aging, Disability, and Independence,
Edited by A. Helal, M. Mokhtari and B. Abdulrazak
Copyright © 2008 John Wiley & Sons, Inc.

as psychiatrists or gastroenterologists) to develop and deploy powerful new applications for users.

In collaboration with the university's College of Public Health and Health Professions, and with federal funding from the National Institute on Disability and Rehabilitation Research (NIDRR), we are creating a programmable space specifically designed for the elderly and disabled. The Gator Tech smart house in Gainesville, Florida, is the culmination of more than 5 years of research in pervasive and mobile computing. The project's goal is to create assistive environments such as homes that can sense themselves and their residents and enact mappings between the physical world and remote monitoring and intervention services.

37.1 SMART HOUSE TECHNOLOGIES

Figure 37.1 shows most of the "hotspots" that are currently active or under development in the Gator Tech smart house. An interactive 3D model (available at www.icta.ufl.edu/gt.htm) provides a virtual tour of the house with up-to-date descriptions of the technologies arranged by name and location. The components of this smart house are listed here:

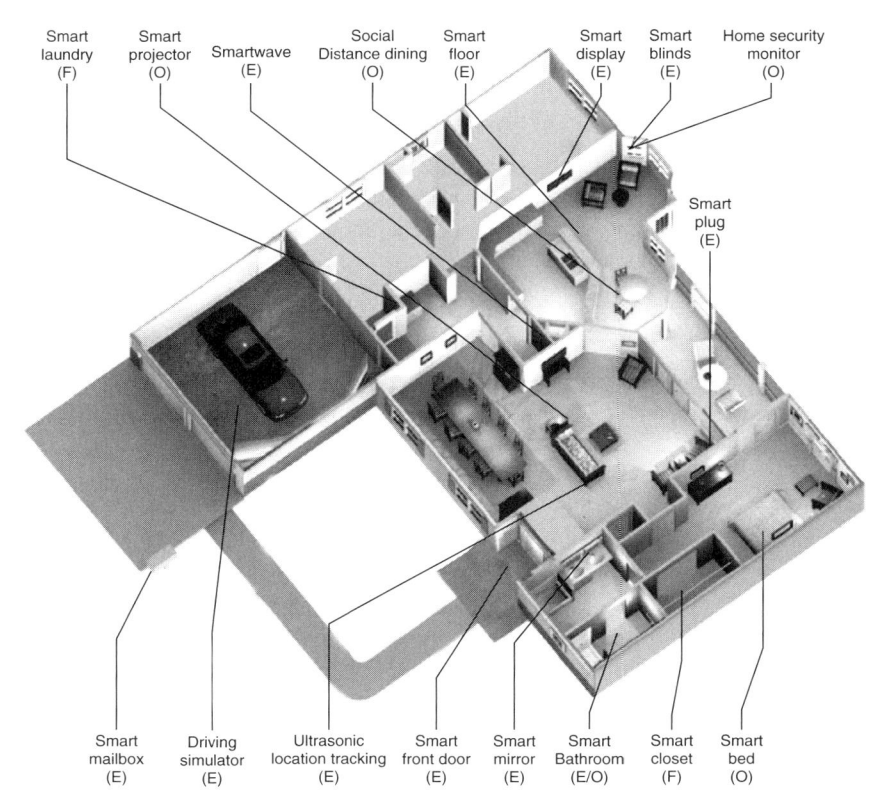

FIGURE 37.1 *Gator Tech smart house. The project features numerous existing (E), ongoing (O), or future (F) "hotspots" located throughout the premises.*

Smart mailbox—the mailbox senses mail arrival and notifies the occupant.

Smart front door—the front door includes a radiofrequency identification (RFID) tag for keyless entry by residents and authorized personnel. It also features a microphone, camera, text LCD, automatic door opener, electric latch, and speakers that occupants can use to communicate with and admit visitors.

Driving simulator—the garage has a driving simulator to evaluate elderly driving abilities and gather data for research purposes.

Smart blinds—all windows have automated blinds that can be preset or adjusted via a remote device to control ambient light and provide privacy.

Smart bed—the bed in the master bedroom has special equipment to monitor occupants' sleep patterns and keep track of sleepless nights.

Smart closet—the master bedroom closet will, in the future, make clothing suggestions according to outdoor weather conditions.

Smart laundry—in combination with the smart closet, future RFID-based technology will notify residents when to do laundry as well as help them sort it.

Smart mirror—the master bathroom mirror displays important messages or reminders (e.g., to take a prescribed medication) when needed. This technology could be expanded to other rooms.

Smart bathroom—the master bathroom includes a toilet paper sensor, a flush detector, a shower that regulates water temperature and prevents scalding, and a soap dispenser that monitors occupant cleanliness and notifies the service center when a refill is required. Other technologies under development measure occupant biometrics such as body weight and temperature.

Smart displays—with the display devices located throughout the house, entertainment media and information can follow occupants from room to room.

SmartWave—the kitchen's microwave oven automatically adjusts the time and power settings for any frozen food package and shows users how to properly prepare the food for cooking.

Smart refrigerator/pantry—a future refrigerator will monitor food availability and consumption, detect expired food items, create shopping lists, and provide advice on meal preparation according to the items stored in the refrigerator and pantry.

Social-distant dining—occupants will be able to use immersive video and audio technologies installed in the breakfast nook to share a meal with a distant relative or friend.

Smart cameras—image sensors monitor the front porch and patio for privacy and security.

Ultrasonic location tracking—sensors, currently installed only in the livingroom, detect occupants' movement, location, and orientation.

Smart floor—sensors in the floor, currently only in the kitchen and entertainment center area, identify and track the location of all house occupants. We are also developing technologies to detect when an occupant falls and to report it to emergency services.

Smart phone—this "magic wand for the home" integrates traditional telephone functions with remote control of all appliances and media players in the livingroom.

It also can convey reminders and important information to homeowners while they are away.

Smart plugs — sensors behind selected power outlets in the livingroom, kitchen, and master bedroom detect the presence of an electric appliance or lamp and link it to a remote monitoring and intervention application.

Smart thermostats — in the future, occupants will be able to personalize air conditioning and heat settings throughout the house according to daily tasks or context (e.g., they could slightly increase the temperature when taking a shower on a cold winter night).

Smart leak detector — sensors in the garage and kitchen can detect a water leak from the washing machine, dishwasher, or water heater.

Smart stove — this future device will monitor stove usage and alert the occupant, via the smart bed if the stove has been left on.

Smart projector — we are developing a projector that uses orientation information provided by ultrasonic location tracking and displays cues, reminders, and event notifications to the livingroom wall that the occupant is currently facing.

Home security monitor — a security system under development continually monitors all windows and doors and, on request, informs the resident whether any are open or unlocked.

Emergency call for help — a future system will track potential emergencies, query the resident if it suspects a problem, and issue a call for outside help when necessary.

Cognitive assistant — another system under development guides residents through various tasks and uses auditory and visual cues to provide reminders about medications, appointments, and so on.

37.2 MIDDLEWARE ARCHITECTURE

To create the Gator Tech smart house, we developed a generic reference architecture applicable to any pervasive computing space. As Figure 37.2 shows, the middleware contains separate physical, sensor platform, service, knowledge, context management, and application layers. We have implemented most of the reference architecture, although much work remains to be done at the knowledge layer.

37.2.1 Physical Layer

This layer consists of the various devices and appliances the occupants use. Many of these are found in a typical single-family home such as lamps, a TV, a set-top box, a clock radio, and a doorbell. Others are novel technologies such as the SmartWave and the keyless entry system adapted to the smart home's target population.

Sensors and actuators such as smoke detectors, air conditioning and heating thermostats, and security system motion detectors are part of the physical layer as well. In addition, this layer can include any object that fulfills an important role in a space, such as a chair or end table.

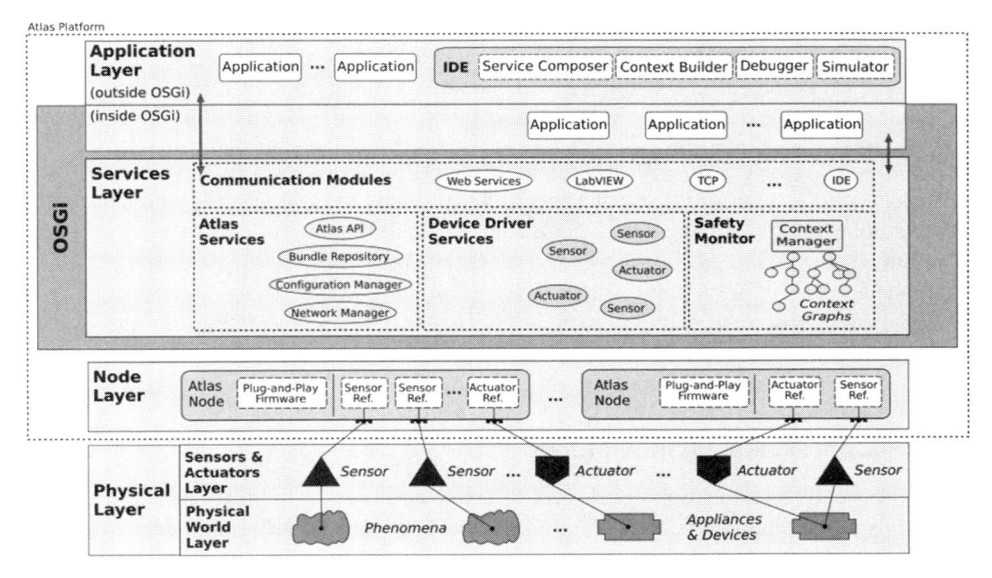

FIGURE 37.2 Atlas smart space middleware. This generic reference architecture is applicable to any pervasive computing environment.

37.2.2 Sensor Platform Layer

Not all objects in a given space can or should be accounted for. For example, it may be desirable to capture a toaster, which could cause a fire if inadvertently left on, but not a blender. Each sensor platform defines the boundary of a pervasive space within the smart house, "capturing" those objects attached to it. A sensor platform can communicate with a wide variety of devices, appliances, sensors, and actuators and represent them to the rest of the middleware in a uniform way.

A sensor platform effectively converts any sensor or actuator in the physical layer to a software service that can be programmed or composed into other services. Developers can thus define services without having to understand the physical world. Decoupling sensors and actuators from sensor platforms ensures openness and makes it possible to introduce new technology as it becomes available.

37.2.3 Service Layer

This layer contains the Open Services Gateway Initiative (OSGi) framework, which maintains leases of activated services.

Basic services represent the physical world through sensor platforms, which store service bundle definitions for any sensor or actuator represented in the OSGi framework. Once powered on, a sensor platform registers itself with the service layer by sending its OSGi service bundle definition.

Application developers create composite services by using a service discovery protocol to browse existing services and using other bundle services to compose new OSGi bundles. Composite services are essentially the applications available in the pervasive space.

A set of de facto standard services may also be available in this layer to increase application developers' productivity. Such services could include voice recognition, text-to-speech conversion, scheduling, and media streaming, among many others.

37.2.4 Knowledge Layer

This layer contains an ontology of the various services offered and the appliances and devices connected to the system. This makes it possible to reason about services—for example, that the system must convert output from a Celsius temperature sensor to Fahrenheit value before feeding it to another service.

Service advertisement and discovery protocols use both service definitions and semantics to register or discover a service. The reasoning engine determines whether certain composite services are available.

37.2.5 Context Management Layer

This layer enables application developers to create and register contexts of interest. Each context is a graph implemented as an OSGi service wire API linking various sensors together. A context can define or restrict service activation for various applications; it can also specify states that a pervasive space cannot enter.

The context engine is responsible for detecting, and possibly recovering from, such states. Our reference architecture has no fixed context-aware programming model.

37.2.6 Application Layer

This layer consists of an application manager to activate and deactivate services and a graphics-based integrated development environment with various tools to help create smart spaces. With the context builder, a developer can visually construct a graph that associates behavior with context; a programmer also can use it to define impermissible contexts and recovery services. In addition, developers can use the service composer to browse and discover services as well as compose and register new ones. Other tools include a debugger and a simulator.

37.3 CONTEXT-AWARENESS

Programming an intelligent space such as the Gator Tech smart house involves three distinct activities:

- *Context engineering*—interpreting sensory data and identifying high-level states of interest such as "hot" and "sunny"
- *Software engineering*—describing the various software components' behavior—for example, turning on the heater or generating a possible menu from a set of ingredients
- *Associating behavior with context*—defining which pieces of software can execute in a particular context and which pieces the system should invoke on a contextual change

Critical to this process is the observe–control interaction between sensors and actuators, as shown in Figure 37.3.

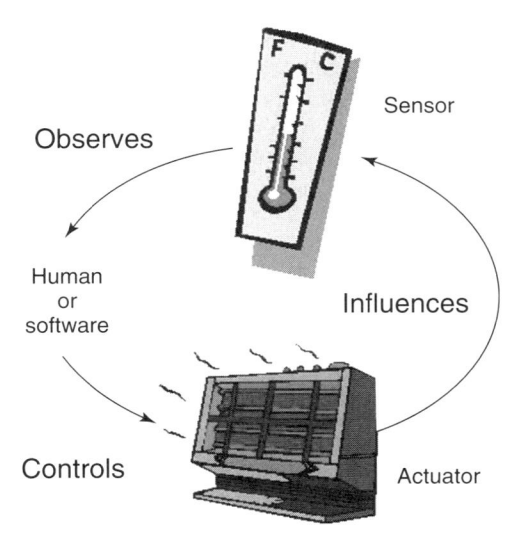

FIGURE 37.3 *Sensor–actuator interaction. Actuators influence sensors, which observe the state of the world and can in turn cause the system or a user to activate the actuator.*

37.3.1 Abstracting Sensory Data

The Gator Tech smart house obtains information about the world through various sensors and can use these data to undertake certain actions. The typical home likewise relies on sensors to effect changes—for example, if it gets too cold, the thermostat will activate the heater. However, what distinguishes a truly robust context-aware system such as this smart house is the ability to abstract state information and carry out actions that correspond to these high-level descriptions [2,3].

Most sensors are designed to detect a particular value in one domain. For example, a temperature sensor might determine that it is 95° Fahrenheit in the house, or a light sensor might record 10,000 lux of light coming through the window. However, hardcoding behavior for each possible combination of direct sensor values is difficult to implement, debug, and extend.

It is far easier to associate actions with abstractions such as "hot" and "sunny," which encompass a range of temperature and luminescence values. When it is hot, the system turns on the air conditioning; if it is sunny outside and the television is on, the system closes the blinds to reduce glare. This approach can easily be extended to various contexts—for example, if the resident is on a diet, the system could prevent the SmartWave from cooking a greasy pizza.

37.3.2 Context Management

In addition to sensors, the Gater Tech smart house consists of actuators—physical devices with which people can interact. An actuator can change the state of the world. Sensors can, in turn, observe an actuator's effect. For example, a light sensor might determine that the house or resident turned on a lamp. In response the observed state of the world, the house or resident might activate an actuator.

Every actuator in our smart house has a certain intentional effect on a domain, which a sensor that senses that particular domain can observe. For example, the intentional effect of turning on the heater is to increase the temperature.

Given a clear description of an actuator's intentional effect, it is possible to determine acceptable behaviors for a given context by examining all possible behaviors in the current state and identifying which intentional effects are mutually exclusive. This guarantees, for example, that the system will never invoke the air conditioning and heater simultaneously.

Context changes can occur as a result of an actuator's intentional effect—(e.g., after turning on the heater, the house temperature increases from "cold" to "warm") or a natural or otherwise uncontrollable force or event (e.g., the setting sun causes a change from "daytime" to "nighttime").

Ideally, a smart space that enters an impermissible context should try to get out of it without human monitoring. Toward this end, we are exploring ways that will enable the smart house to learn how to invoke a set of actuators on the basis of state information to automatically self-correct problems.

Given a standardized description of an actuator's intentional behavior in a certain domain and how a sensor value relates to a particular context, it should be possible to determine which actuator to invoke to escape from an impermissible context. If escape is impossible, the system can inform an external party that assistance is required. For example, if the pantry does not contain any food and no grocery delivery service is available, the system could inform an outside caregiver that it is time to restock.

37.4 SENSOR PLATFORM

Integration can become unwieldy and complex with the various types of sensors, software, and hardware interfaces involved. Consider, for example, climate control in a house. Normally, you would have to hardwire the sensors to each room, connect these sensors to a computer, and program which port on the computer correlates to which sensor. Further, you would need to specify which port contains which type of sensor—for example, humidity or temperature.

To systematically integrate the various devices, appliances, sensors, and actuators and to enable the observe-control loop shown in Figure 37.3, we created a sensor platform that we call Atlas that represents any attached object in a pervasive space simply as a Java program—more specifically, as an OSGi service bundle.

To control climate in a home, for example, you would install a wireless sensor platform node in each room, connect both a humidity sensor and temperature sensor to each node, and program the firmware for each node. In addition to the firmware, the sensor platform nodes would contain the sensor driver that decodes temperature and humidity data.

Simply powering up a sensor node causes it to transmit the driver wirelessly to a surrogate node, such as a home PC, where the sensors are immediately accessible via other applications. The PC would require no configuration or hardware interfacing. The sensor driver is surrogate software—Java bytecode that contains static information about the sensor and the services it provides—stored in an electrically erasable programmable read-only memory (EEPROM) on the sensor platform node. The platform itself does not understand or process the code; rather, it processes the firmware and other low-level C programs that send data between the sensor and platform.

FIGURE 37.4 *An Atlas sensor platform. The modular design provides for alternative and flexible configurations.*

The individual node architecture shown in Figure 37.4 is modular and provides for alternative and flexible configurations. We use a stackable design to connect alternative memory, processor, power, and communication modules.

The *memory module* provides a mechanism for easily modifying an EEPROM store used for read and write capabilities on the node. This storage contains bootstrap data that specify general sensor and actuator information.

The processing module currently uses an 8-bit Atmel ATmega 128 processor. The processor is housed on a board that is optimized for low power consumption and has two RS232 ports, a Joint Test Action Group (IEEE 1149) and ISP port, and more than 50 programmable input/output (I/O) pins. We are developing alternative modules with more powerful processing capability, including an onboard Java virtual machine.

The *communication* module currently uses RF wireless communication with a simple transmission protocol. We are also testing and debugging a 10baseT Ethernet module utilizing a simplified IPv4 stack. Future modules will support low-power Wi-Fi and powerline communication. The latter will also connect to an alternative power module.

When a sensor platform is powered up, its EEPROM data act as a bootstrap mechanism that provides the larger system (e.g., a network server or home PC) with the information and behavioral components required to interact with a specific device, appliance, sensor, or actuator. The data can be specified as either human-readable (XML, text with a URL, and so on) or machine-readable (e.g., Java bytecode) depending on the specific application. In addition to bytecode, stored data includes device-specific information such as the manufacturer's name, product serial number, and sensor type.

37.5 SMART PLUGS

Creating a scalable self-sensing space is impractical using existing pervasive computing technologies [4]. Few smart appliances available on the market today contain a controllable interface. In addition, numerous available protocols are incompatible. For example,

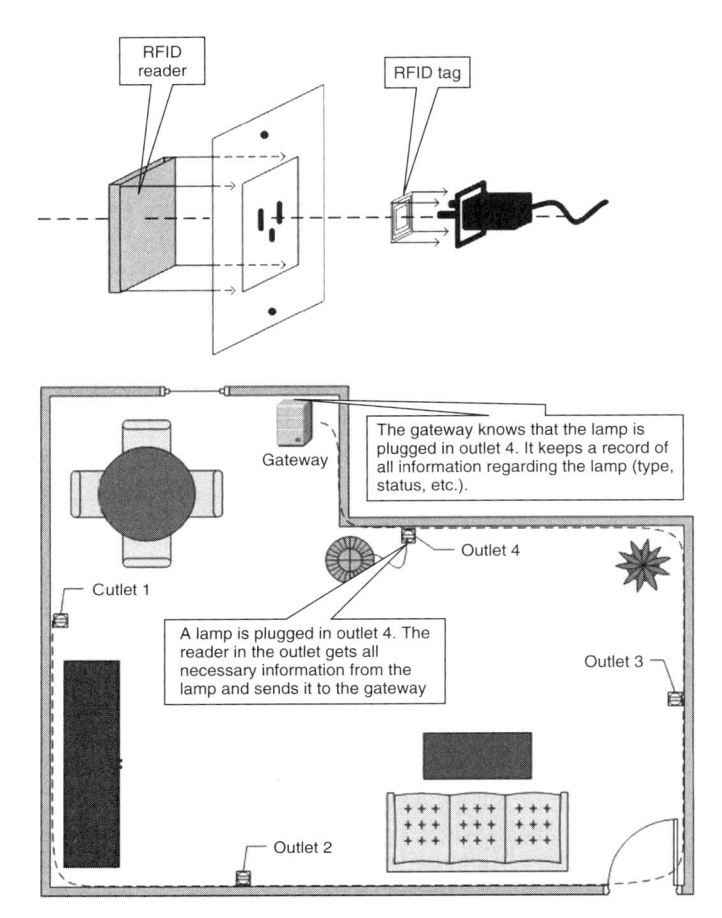

FIGURE 37.5 *Smart plugs. Each power outlet is equipped with a low-cost RFID reader connected to the main computer, while each electric device has an RFID tag attached to the plug's end with information about the device.*

the X10 protocol offers an easy, affordable way to turn a house into a smart one, but few smart devices are X10-enabled. Regardless of the technology used, a smart space should be able to communicate with any new smart device [5,6].

To address this problem, we have developed "smart plugs", which provide an intelligent way to sense electrical devices installed in an intelligent space. As Figure 37.5 shows, each power outlet in the Gator Tech smart house is equipped with a low-cost RFID reader connected to the main computer. Electric devices with power cords, such as lamps and clocks, each have an RFID tag attached to the of the plug end with information about the device. When a user plugs the device into an outlet, the reader reads the tag and forwards the data to the main computer.

OSGi bundles represent new devices to be installed in the smart space. A "bundle" is simply a Java archive file containing interfaces, implementations for those interfaces, and a special Activator class [7]. The jar file contains a manifest file that includes special OSGi-specific headers that control the bundle's use within the framework.

Each RFID tag has user-data-allocated memory that varies from 8 to 10,000 bytes. Depending on the size of its memory, the tag itself could contain the entire OSGi bundle representing the new device. If the bundle is too large, the tag could instead contain a referral URL for downloading the gateway software from a remote repository. The referral URL can use any protocol that the gateway server has access to, such as http and ftp. Using a Web server also makes upgrading the bundle as easy as replacing the software.

The gateway bundles installed in the framework perform all the required downloading and installation of the gateway software for the individual bundles. When a user installs a new device, the system downloads each bundle and registers it in the OSGi framework. On request, the framework can report a list of installed devices, all of which can be controlled via methods available in the bundle. In this way, the framework enacts a mapping between the smart space and the outside world.

Figure 37.6 shows a user—for example, a service technician at a monitoring center—controlling a lamp in the Gator Tech smart house via a remote application; a

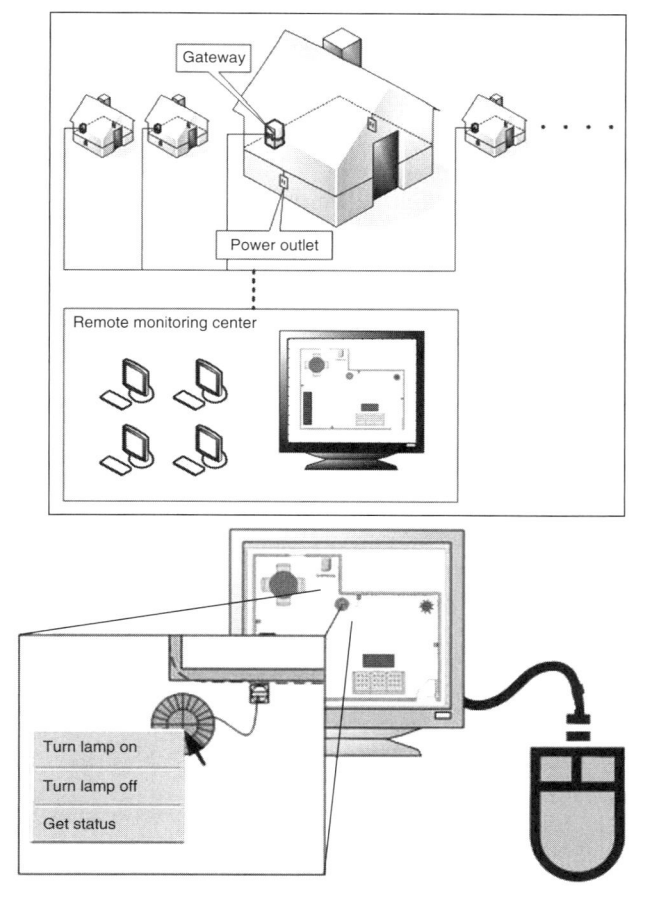

FIGURE 37.6 *Remote monitoring of electric appliances. Clicking on a method causes the remote application to send a request to the smart house gateway to execute the action.*

click on the lamp will download all available methods associated with this device. When the user clicks on a method, the remote application sends a request to the gateway to execute the action.

37.6 SMART FLOOR

In designing the Gator Tech smart house floor, we wanted to deploy a low-cost, accurate, unencumbered, position-only location system that could later serve as the foundation for a more powerful hybrid system. Drawing on extensive location-tracking and positioning research, we initially experimented with an acoustic-based location system. Using a set of ultrasonic transceiver pilots in the ceiling, the master device would regularly send chirps into the environment. Users wore vests in which transceiver tags attached to the shoulders would listen for the chirp and respond with their own.

While this technology provides precise user position and orientation measurements, it was inappropriate for our smart house. Each room would require a full set of expensive pilots, and residents would have to don special equipment, which is extremely intrusive and defeats the desired transparency of a pervasive computing environment [8,9].

Instead, we opted to embed sensors in the floor to determine user location. [10–12]. The benefit of not encumbering users outweighed the loss of orientation information, and the availability of an inexpensive sensor platform made this solution extremely cost-effective.

We had been using phidgets for various automation tasks around the smart house. The Phidgets Interface Kit 8/8/8 connects up to eight components and provides an API to control the devices over a universal serial bus (USB). Each platform also integrates a two-port USB hub, making it easy to deploy a large network of devices. We created a grid of 1.5-inch pressure sensors under the floor, as shown in Figure 37.7, and connected this to the existing phidgets network.

The smart house has a 2-inch residential-grade raised floor comprised of a set of blocks, each approximately one square foot. This raised surface simplified the process of running cables, wires, and devices throughout the house. In addition, the floor's slight springiness puts less strain on the knees and lower back, an ergonomic advantage of particular interest to seniors.

We discovered another, unexpected benefit of the raised surface—it allows us to greatly extend the pressure sensor's range. When a person steps onto a tile block, the force of that step is distributed throughout the block. A single sensor at the bottom center can detect a footstep anywhere on that block. In fact, we had to add resistors to the sensor cables to reduce sensitivity and eliminate fluctuations in the readings.

Table 37.1 details the costs of deploying the smart floor in the kitchen, nook, and family room, a total area of approximately 350 ft^2. We do not have to factor the price of the raised floor, which is comparable to other types of residential flooring, into our cost analysis because it is a fundamental part of the smart house and is used for various purposes.

The hardest part of deploying the smart floor involved mapping the sensors to a physical location. Installing the sensors, labeling the coordinates, and manually entering these data into our software took approximately 72 person-hours.

Figure 37.8 shows the mapping system we used for the kitchen, nook, and family room. Tiles with solid lines represent blocks with sensors underneath, while those with

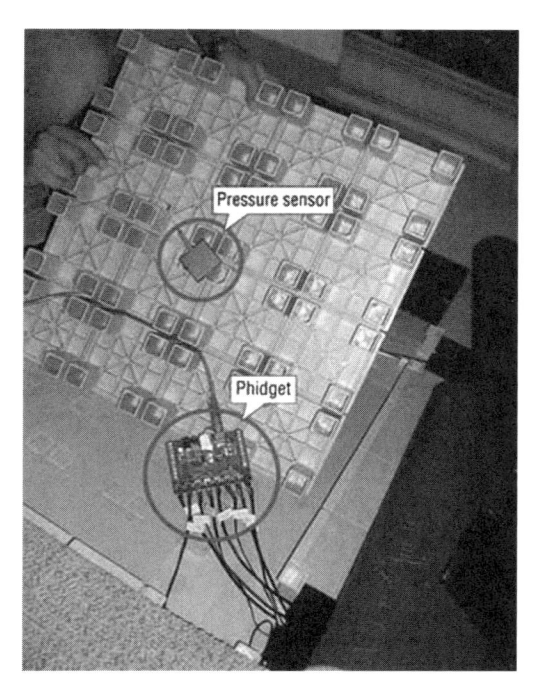

FIGURE 37.7 Smart floor tile block. The smart house floor consists of a grid of 1.5-inch pressure sensors connected to a network of phidgets.

TABLE 37.1 Smart Floor Deployment Costs in Kitchen, Nook, and Family Room

Number of Blocks	Sensors/Block	Sensor Platform/Block	Sensor Unit Price ($)	Sensor Platform Unit Price ($)	Total Cost ($)	Cost/ft^2
64	1	1/8	$10	$95	$1,400	$4

dotted lines indicate gaps in coverage due to appliances or room features such as cabinets or the center island.

In the future, we intend to redeploy the smart floor using our own sensor platform technology, which will include spatial awareness. This will greatly simplify the installation process and aid in determining the location of one tile relative to another. We will only need to manually specify the position of one tile, and then the system can automatically generate the mapping between sensors and physical locations.

Pervasive computing is rapidly evolving from a proven concept to a practical reality. After creating the Matilda smart house, a 900-ft^2 laboratory prototype designed to prove the feasibility and usefulness of assistive environments, we realized that hacking hardware and software together resulted in some impressive demonstrations but not something people could actually live in.

We designed the second-generation Gator Tech smart house to outlive existing technologies and be open for new applications that researchers might develop in the future. With nearly 80 million baby boomers in the United States just reaching their 60s, the

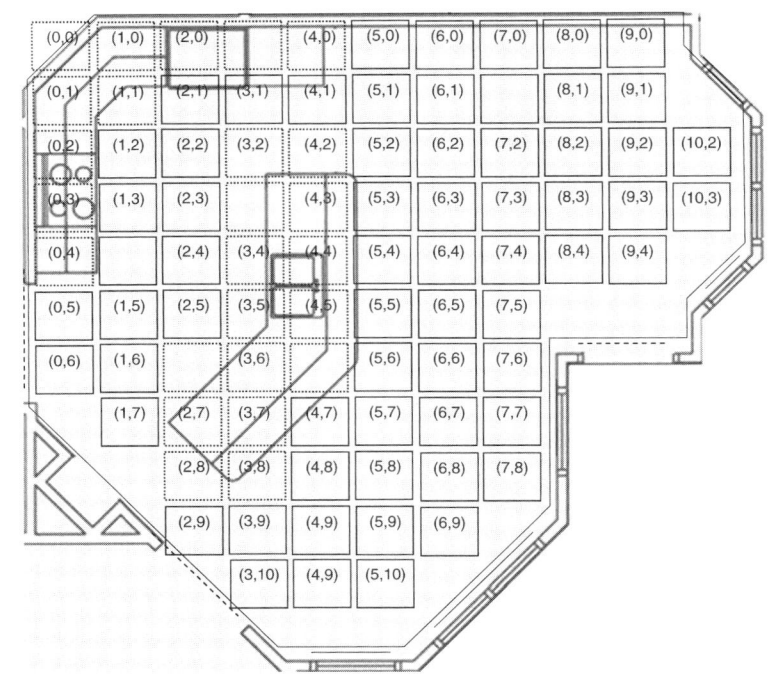

FIGURE 37.8 Smart floor mapping system. Tiles with solid lines represent blocks with sensors underneath, while those with dotted lines indicate gaps in coverage due to appliances or room features.

demand for senior-oriented devices and services will explode in the coming years. Ultimately, our goal is to create a "smart house in a box": off-the-shelf assistive technology for the home that the average user can buy, install, and monitor without the aid of engineers.

REFERENCES

1. Helal S: Programming pervasive spaces, *IEEE Pervasive Comput* **4**(1):84–87 (2005).
2. Dey AK: Understanding and using context, *Personal Ubiq Comput* **5**(1):4–7 (2001).
3. Chen G, Kotz D: *A Survey of Context-Aware Mobile Computing Research*, Technical Report TR2000-381, Dept Computer Science, Dartmouth College, 2001.
4. Harle RK, and Hopper A: Dynamic world models from ray-tracing, *Proc 2nd IEEE Int Conf Pervasive Computing and Communication*, IEEE CS Press, 2004, pp 55–66.
5. Gellerson HW, Schmidt A, Beigl M: Adding some smartness to devices and everyday things, *Proc 3rd IEEE Workshop Mobile Computing Systems and Applications*, IEEE CS Press, 2000, pp 3–10.
6. Gellersen H et al: Physical prototyping with smart-its, *IEEE Pervasive Comput* **3**(3):74–82 (2004).
7. Marples D, Kriens P: The open services gateway initiative: An introductory overview, *IEEE Commun. Mag*, **39**(12):110–114 (2001).

8. Hightower J, Borriello G: Location systems for ubiquitous computing, *Computer* 57–66 (Aug 2001).
9. Welch G, Foxlin E: Motion tracking: No silver bullet, but a respectable arsenal, *IEEE Comput Graph Appl* **22**(6):24–38 2002.
10. Addlesee MD et al: The ORL active floor, *IEEE Personal Commun* **4**(5):35–41 (1997).
11. Tan HZ, Slivovsky LA, Pentland A: A sensing chair using pressure distribution sensors, *IEEE/ASME Trans Mechatron* **6**(3):261–268 (2001).
12. Orr RJ, Abowd GD: The smart floor: A mechanism for natural user identification and tracking, *Proc Human Factors in Computing Systems (CHI 00)*, ACM Press, 2000, pp 275–276.

38

Health Application and Telecare

Mathijs Soede, Frank Vlaskamp, and Charles Willems
Institute for Rehabiliation Research, Hoensbroek, The Netherlands

38.1 INTRODUCTION

Health-related technology is entering the daily life of the general public. Many people adopt a healthy lifestyle, not only to prevent diseases, but also to feel physically fit. Technology contributes to an improvement of physical performance: bikes, treadmills, rowing machines, step counters, heart rate monitors, visits to the local fitness centre.

Technology is available for patients as well. Many technologies, once restricted to care environments (hospital, clinic) and operated by healthcare professionals, are also available for patients at home. This development is in line with efforts to keep hospital stays as short as possible, and to keep patients out of permanent institutional settings (nursing homes) and to provide homecare support instead.

Telecare can bridge the distance between a caregiver at a hospital or rehabilitation clinic and the patient at home. It requires a communication link between caregiver and patient (data, voice, possibly video), sensors to register medical or activity data, and a care arrangement that describes the rights and obligations, the service that will be given, and which response shall be given to questions and emergency calls.

This chapter gives an overview of the most important trends in care and technology and examples of telecare and telerehabilitation applications.

38.2 CARE TRENDS

38.2.1 The Aging Population and Availability of Healthcare Workers

In Western countries life expectancy has risen during the more recent decades. The size of the older population has increased, including the number of retired persons. At the

---

The Engineering Handbook of Smart Technology for Aging, Disability, and Independence,
Edited by A. Helal, M. Mokhtari and B. Abdulrazak
Copyright © 2008 John Wiley & Sons, Inc.

same time the birth rate has decreased, which creates tension in the labor market, because the working population is decreasing while the nonworking population is growing. It is expected that it will be difficult to allocate sufficient workers and financial resources to meet the care requirements of the aging population. Medical technology and care from remote locations may solve the problem of scarcity of resources. This might occur only if medical technology and remote care replace conventional methods by a new, more time-efficient, approach. It is also expected that medical technology will add quality to the life of patients at home. This may often be the case, but many chronically ill patients appreciate the personal contacts with caregivers when they visit a hospital or care center, or when they receive care at home. Telecare communication, such as by video, does not equal the direct interhuman communication, due to technical restrictions [1]. On the other hand, it is cheaper and easier to have more frequent telecare contacts compared to the conventional home visits and other patient–caregiver contacts. Not much research has been done in this area yet.

38.2.2 Cure versus Care; Care for Chronic Patients

Cure, obtained by solving acute health problems, with intervention by medical specialists, has a diagnosis-centered approach, following the medical model, with treatment at a hospital. *Care* is aimed at chronic patients, continuity of care, has a patient-centered approach, and is given in a home environment or long-time care facilities.

Hospital stay after a medical intervention (cure) has become shorter, due to improvement of medical interventions and surgical techniques. Early discharge makes care in the home environment more necessary.

Major gains of telecare can be expected with chronic patients because what they need is longlasting care at home, which imposes a very heavy load on the healthcare system.

38.2.3 Integrated Care; Continuity of Care

There is a shift from care in institutions (hospital, nursing home, rehabilitation centre) toward care in the community ("transmural care," "shared care," "hospital at home"). The drive for this comes from the need for cost reduction; a day in the hospital, where a complex care infrastructure is continuously available but seldom needed for the patient, is much more expensive then a day at home, even with additional care delivered at home. Moreover, people prefer to be in their own homes when possible and experience this as a higher quality of life. Even halfway solutions, such as care in a hotel-like facility near the hospital, are becoming common. It must be stated that the qualitative argument "being at your own home is always better" might be fading away. This shift toward "transmural care" is based on arrangements concerning cooperation among the local practitioner, medical specialists, hospital, rehabilitation center, pharmacy, and homecare staff. There are care arrangements for specific diagnoses and postoperative situations, specifying the roles and responsibilities of the different intramural and extramural caregivers involved in the care program. Information technology enables all caregivers to access the information they need regarding a specific patient.

38.2.4 Self-Care

Patients now take a more active role in the healthcare they receive and are more aware of prevention strategies. The current patient is more educated and has better access to information than previously. Medical instruments have become more available for patients (blood pressure measurement, blood glucose monitoring, oxygen saturation levels, heart rate measurement, etc.). These medical devices are operated by the patient or an informal caregiver (e.g., dialysis at home).

Patients are considered as partners in the treatment of their disease, and not as an "object" of treatment. Chronic patients gradually become experts in their own disease. Compliance is an important aspect in medicine. A patient well aware of her/his own problems may show a better compliance and be more motivated to accept a self-care solution. An interesting example is the night-time dialysis at home originating from Canada and now also applied successfully in The Netherlands [2,3]. All users of this system are very satisfied, but a few patients refuse it because they do not want "the hospital atmosphere [to enter] their own private home[s]" [4].

38.2.5 Ambulatory Care

People have become more mobile, they may require treatment at locations other than their homes. Chronic patients who do not want to be restricted to a home or institutional environment, may visit other places (for holidays or work related travel, etc.). Mobility requires easy access to patient information and availability of care services in the area where the patient stays. Progress is contingent on the availability of technical solutions regarding sensors and wearable systems (see Section 38.3). The availability of care services in other places is not an easily solved issue; there are solutions for emergency interventions, but the normal "consumption" of care elsewhere is difficult. Compared with mobile telephony, where networks, roaming, and billing infrastructures are accessible everywhere, healthcare is not currently very accessible for "roaming patients." International standards and agreements for medication, patient records, intervention protocols, and reimbursement are lacking in healthcare. Healthcare is still based on the assumption that a sick patient stays at home or in a nearby hospital.

38.2.6 Health and Lifestyle

The domains of health and lifestyle approach each other. There is much evidence of how health can be positively or negatively influenced by lifestyle. Physical exercise and low calorie intake are promoted for health reasons. A healthy lifestyle is adopted by many people, not because they are already ill or disabled, but to maintain and improve physical fitness. Healthy lifestyle activities, like walking, running, jogging, and sports, are also an attractive pastime. Many lifestyle activities include the use of technology, which is sometimes derived from medical applications. Examples are heart rate monitors, fitness equipment, and step counters.

38.3 TECHNOLOGY TRENDS

38.3.1 Sensor Development

In the near future implanted sensors will be used, allowing continuous measurement of body functions. Chronic patients sometimes require daily monitoring of body functions. In some cases body functions have to be checked to adjust medication, as is the case with diabetic patients, who have a delicate balance between blood sugar values, food intake, exercise, and medication. In other cases vital body functions are monitored, to take action if minimum or maximum values are exceeded, or to get a more general view in order to follow the course of a disease. Patient groups who may require monitoring are chronic obstructive pulmonary disease (COPD) patients, diabetics, or patients with a heart disease.

The sensors and devices for medical monitoring on the market have become smaller and more suitable for nonprofessional users outside the hospital environment.

Developers of medical technology often say that "we can measure almost everything." However, one does not realize that every new sensor system requires new research and adapted protocols (sensor characteristics, attachment of the sensor to the body, interpretation of sensor measurements, sensor maintenance, etc.). This is very true for invasive measurements as well; without a clear definition and full evaluation of the measurements protocol, a major intrusive intervention to implant a sensor will not be approved. Monitoring body functions is not only a technical problem: it is also an organizational problem. If measurements indicate that something is wrong with the patient, an adequate response should be available, in many cases 24 h per day.

38.3.2 Wireless Connectivity

If sensors are part of a system, there should be a communication protocol in place for information transmission. If sensors are mobile, or if sensors have to transmit to a moving object, the transmission medium should be wireless. The advantage of wireless connectivity is that no wiring is needed; the disadvantage is that the sensor has to be powered. Batteries have a limited lifetime and need to be replaced or recharged. In some cases the sensor can be powered by light, heat, movement, or induction. If wireless sensors have to be active for long periods of time (weeks or months), the available battery capacity and power consumption of the sensor and transmitter are serious considerations, especially when the sensors should provide a continuous datastream. Various transmission modes can be used: short-range transmission (e.g., Bluetooth, infrared, WiFi, Zigbee), or long-range transmission (e.g., GSM, GPRS, and UMTS). An ultrashort transmission range (<2 m) has the advantage that the required transmission power is extremely low. An example of an ultra-short-range transmission protocol is Medical Implant Communication Service (MICS).

The mobile telephone is a very useful medium for sending data from mobile patients to a care center. Mobile networks are available everywhere in populated areas. Many people own a mobile phones. Mobile phones do a lot more than merely send voice and data; the Internet can be accessed via many mobile phone models, emails and SMS messages can be sent and received, photographs can be sent, and so on. Furthermore, there is a billing infrastructure, allowing payment for services received.

Wireless systems for medical monitoring can be more comfortable for patients and less visible by others. Wireless systems also open up the possibility of continuous or more frequent measurements with minimal stress for the wearer. Ambulatory monitoring becomes possible in the patient's own environment and during normal daily activities.

38.3.3 Body-Area Network

If patients use several, implanted or unimplanted, sensors, those sensors can be part of a (wireless) body-area network (BAN). The data from the sensors can be collected by a data acquisition unit that preprocesses or analyzes them. The data may be stored locally, but can also be transmitted to a local network (LAN, WiFi) in a hospital, or to a care service via a GSM, GPRS, or UMTS telephone link. The choice of the right technology depends on several conflicting factors. Reaching a good compromise is not easy. The determining factors are at least:

- Battery consumption
- Bandwidth
- Available protocols for communication and connecting
- The choice of the place where data are processed [locally (peripherally) or centrally]
- Continuous measurement(s), or separated by time intervals
- Reach of operation
- Protection against intrusion
- Authorization, of access and authentication of the user
- Reliability
- Availability
- Billing systems for services

38.3.4 Ambient Intelligence

In the near future people will be surrounded by computer and networking technology, unobtrusively embedded in the environment [ambient intelligence (AmI)]. Multiple wireless and fixed sensors will be part of a network that supports human interaction, comfort, safety and security, and communication. The information gathered by many sensors in the environment can be analyzed by software, and, depending on the algorithms of this software, the information can be combined as part of an automatic decisionmaking process that initiates activity within the system. For instance, if a patient with dementia symptoms gets out of bed, starts walking around in the house, and opens the front door in the middle in the night, this may indicate risky wandering behavior, and help of a caregiver or warden will be necessary. The system initiates an alert procedure. An automatic speech message via a loudspeaker at the front door warns the patient that it is the middle of the night and not the time to go out. A care center will be reached, and a hands-free telephone connection will be opened. The caregiver talks with the patient (if possible) and organizes help from a professional homecare worker (when needed).

The same sensors that detect someone walking around can be used for a burglar alarm, for switching on an electric light at night, or be part of an activity-monitoring system that warns the caregiver if the patient shows unexpected inactivity.

Another aspect of AmI applications is security and the potential loss of privacy. In theory, the most optimal system in healthcare support is to use as much data as possible from various sources and to provide (hopefully) selectively these data to anyone who can be supportive to the client or patient. (e.g., entry codes in private homes). People are willing to share information (and allow a higher risk for privacy loss) if the service (i.e., care support) is delivering them a concrete advantage. The decision to share information should be based on full, transparent insight into the privacy aspects of the service (how the data are used, when and what and where the data are stored, and how to delete the data when the service ends, etc.).

38.3.5 Videophones and Camera Monitoring

The use of video technology in healthcare is increasing. It is, in principle, a "simple" solution to install cameras and monitors at the service desk of a care center. Usually video is bound to the environment where cameras can be installed. New developments in wireless technology make cameras mobile, carried by the client, or based on a robotic platform moving around in a living environment [5].

Plain continuous video is considered as intrusive and not acceptable in many cases. An acceptable case is the situation where a person's life is at risk. Therefore, a number of other techniques that enhance privacy can be added, such as

1. Techniques for automatic analysis of video by intelligent software; an example is the experimental TNO-UAS system called "unattended autonomous surveillance (UAS)" a video-based system with automatic processing of unusual activity. The only output of the system is an alert that is first transmitted to one person, who must decide what to do [6].
2. Automatic detection of particular emergency situations by other sensors (fall-detecting sensors, sensors in floormats close to a bed, movement detection devices, voice-activated alarms, etc.), which initiates a temporary videolink to a care center; instead of a videostream to be analyzed, enabling the clinician or caregiver to collect a variety of sensor data (movements, steps, temperature) and analyze them to detect specific patterns.
3. Use of infrared (IR) cameras, which can be more selective in recording the position of the human body, but are essentially the same as conventional video in terms of privacy issues.

In case of videotelephony privacy is not an issue because using a telephone is always the result of an intended action: making or receiving the call.

38.3.6 High-Speed Internet Linkage

The Internet is a powerful technology for telecare and other healthcare applications. The speed of data transmission is high and the physical connection to the Internet can be "always on." The connection can be wired or wireless. Wireless access points are supported by several protocols as mentioned above. They can be accessed by a PDA, a mobile telephone, a laptop, or any other appropriate ICT device. The "always-on" availability, such as that of GPRS and UMTS, where packages of data are transmitted only when made available, makes the Internet a fast and adequate link for most applications.

Internet and mobile communication devices are susceptible to viruses and security-breaching "hacker" attacks. The Internet is the focal point where datastreams can easily be connected to data from miscellaneous sources. Security and privacy concerns are realistic. Safety of data is now a major concern of developers and—as demonstrated in banking—it seems that solutions can be reasonably safe. But in case of serious attacks by hackers, a service can be temporarily interrupted. For critical applications, a backup system must be designed such that a minimum performance level can always be guaranteed. Internet-based feedback and central storage can be temporarily replaced by local analysis and local generation of feedback and instructions.

38.3.7 Availability of Information

An exceptionally large amount of medical data can be accessed via the Internet. However, it is not easy to get access to quality certified information about diseases, medication, and therapy. Moreover, it is a challenge to find the data that are relevant to a personal situation. Nevertheless, some companies, such as healthcare insurers, are investigating ways to develop personalized information by creating a personal profile that acts as a filter. It is not easy to solve the problem of accessibility, or to present information in one's native tongue, using understandable language adapted to the personal level of education. Personalization techniques are now being developed for commercial use on the Internet. These technologies could yield valuable results if they find evidence-based data for the "average and frequent" client and can apply these findings in searches on specific diseases, types of impairment, and individual clients.

As for illegal accessing of data and information on the Internet, even more concern is with handling of information. In general, it might seem that the use of data (viz., medical information) is safe and secure in the databases of care services (which, of course, are always subject to error). However, few people are aware that insurance companies have access to a lot of information about the client, from each client's payment history, medications, therapy, and so on, and that this information could adversely affect the insurer's decision to approve a new treatment or medication for that client [7,8]. The European SWAMI project has attempted to clarify these threats by developing an analysis of scenarios that handle these potentially dangerous situations [9]. The project uses scripts in which a potential risk is described in a situation and the qualitative analysis is to see how this risk can affect human integrity, privacy, and life in general.

38.3.8 Virtual Presence

Videotelephony has been around for a long time. More recent improvements in available bandwidth have made reasonable-quality streaming video possible. The price of airtime has gone decreased, making many new applications more affordable. Virtual reality (VR) applications may improve with screen and mirror technologies, enabling development of lines of sight that appear normal. Virtual presence has not yet been explored in many medical applications, but these applications surely differ from actual presence and conventional treatment and care modalities. In a field experiment we took a simple camera mounted on a telecontrolled movable base (a toy car that could move around the client). An actual sense of presence was felt even by simple technical means (see Fig. 38.1).

Good virtual presence does not merely entail providing a high-quality picture of the communicating party. "Presence" may also occur when simple but exact sensory feedback is given on a matter to be dealt with. Not much research has been done as yet on what actually determines the "feeling of presence."

38.3.9 Robotics

The domain of so-called rehabilitation robotics concerns technology that

1. Replaces or supports the functions of human limbs
2. Performs tasks by telecontrol
3. Is used for therapy and training

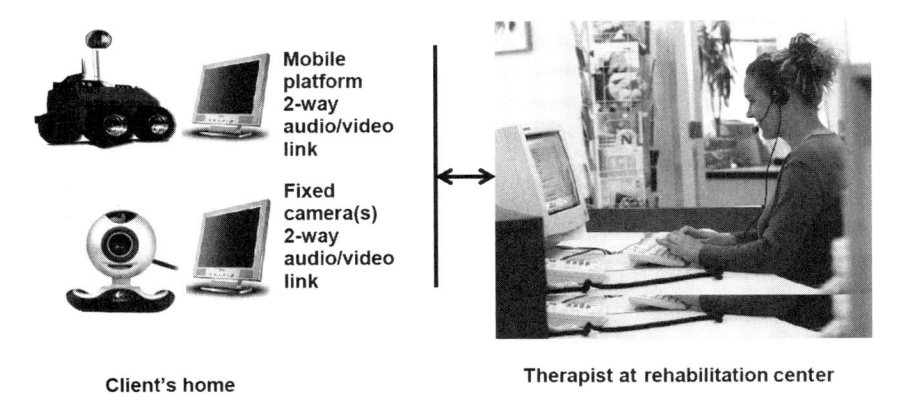

FIGURE 38.1 *A field experiment with fixed-base or toy-based camera for telesupport.*

An overview of all rehabilitation robotics, defined as all robotic applications supporting human functioning in case of an impairment or disease, is seen in the ICORR conferences [10].

In most cases replacement and support of human limbs concerns the arm and hand. The robot is an alternative for a prosthesis or an orthosis for the upper arm.

Present technology allows robotic devices to perform standalone functions, telecontrolled by the user. A robotic platform can execute tasks in another room, even at a worldwide distance. Some robots can perform household tasks, while others can be used as a camera platform, telecontrolled by caregivers.

A new application for the rehabilitation robot is assistance in therapy. A robot arm can move a limb without time restriction. Moreover, a robot can be programmed to exert resistance during active movement, or even anticipate a movement, with particular therapeutic goals in mind. A teletraining session can be arranged rather easily, because

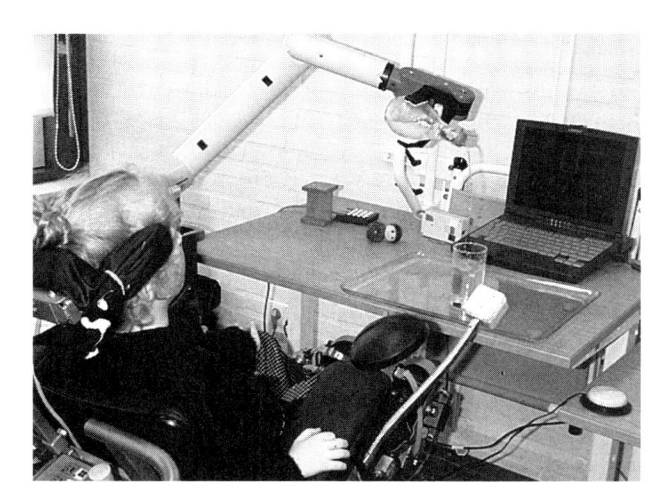

FIGURE 38.2 *A severely disabled young boy using the MANUS robotic manipulator as a self-help tool. Kwee HH et al, MANUS manipulator, Technology and Disability* **14**:*31–42, (2002).*

movement, resistance, and dynamics can be set from a distance. According to the same theory, the robot, with proper sensors, can be used as a telesensing device. Young, severely handicapped children who never experienced space and distance can push the robot arm against an object and get feedback on the skin about the pressure exerted by the object on the robot arm (see Fig. 38.2).

38.4 THE CARE AND TECHNOLOGY INNOVATION PROCESS

Technical solutions for telecare applications are abundantly available. Technology alone is not sufficient; it must fit within a concept of care. Innovation in telecare, however, is much slower then expected. Reasons are not easily found, but it is obvious that the process of care innovation is not well understood or treated. Care innovation is often intermingled with technology innovation, and new technology is not always sufficiently tested or adapted to users (clients, patients, and caregivers) (see Fig. 38.3).

Figure 38.3 illustrates the various aspects in care innovation. It is not just an issue of client and technology. In essence, care at a distance (i.e., from a remote location) differs from regular care, even if the actual given care (medications, etc.) is the same. Many more changes can be expected in telecare settings, where—because of the new technology—more body functions can be checked at the same time, or more frequent checks are possible because home visits can be partly replaced by remotely administered care, or care access to medical expertise can be obtained more quickly in a telesetting (the patient does not have to be transferred to another hospital, etc.).

Innovative care requires a change in the organization of care. A new process of care provision and quality assurance has to be designed, tested, and implemented (what are the changes in the cooperation between contributors, who is responsible for what, what is the influence of ICT, and how are logistics, billing, etc. done). The protocols of care are changed and need to be specified in greater detail (which activities follow each other). For the introduction of the new telecare support, a plan for information distribution has to be coupled with the processes mentioned above: who receives information on the measurements and activities and who gives input, who gives a response, and so on. Good communication on the implementation of the care innovation is needed to prevent unnecessary resistance from the people involved. Finally, conditions are to be met in applying existing regulations in care, safety, privacy, and the availability of financial support, which are to be authorized because the care innovation is offering better service and quality to people or is of lower cost for the insurance organizations.

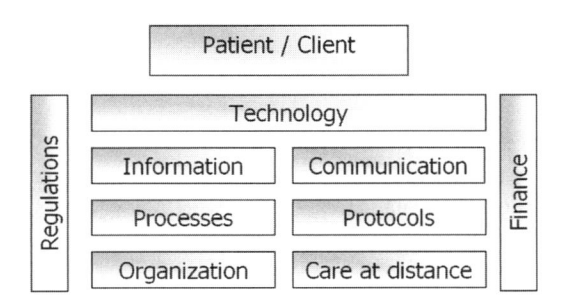

FIGURE 38.3 Components in the innovation of a telecare service.

38.5 HEALTHCARE INFORMATION

38.5.1 Medical Information on the Internet

The abundance of medical information on the Internet has undermined the professional monopoly on medical information. The caregiver is not the only information source for the patient, but can place the information in an individual perspective. Patients may be better informed when they consult a healthcare professional who takes the time to explain.

Medical information available on the Internet should be reliable. This is difficult to accomplish, because anyone can publish on the Internet. There are Websites that publish only information that is approved by a reviewing committee of health professionals [11]. Another example is the NHS Direct Online service [12].

38.5.2 Electronic Healthcare Record

During his or her lifetime, a patient builds up a history of contacts with health practitioners, therapies that have been followed, and medicines that have been prescribed. Information about the health status of a patient is important for medical decisionmaking. When a patient is treated by several caregivers, actual information about prescribed medicine is necessary to avoid unwanted interactions. Patients often complain that caregivers do not exchange necessary information, and that the same tests are done each time a caregiver is consulted.

For a long time the information exchange between caregivers was based on written messages, and was later on replaced by fax (facsimile) messages and emails. The disadvantage of this type of information exchange is that a caregiver does not have a complete record of the health status of a patient. Electronic healthcare records are the solution for this problem.

When more parties have access to an electronic healthcare record, the question about ownership of this record arises: Is it the patient, or is it the healthcare professional? Likewise, the access rights to patient information are an important issue.

38.5.3 Access to Electronic Healthcare Records

Electronic healthcare records can improve the availability—anywhere and at any time—of patient information. Most health practitioners use electronic healthcare records locally, but regional and national electronic healthcare records are still lacking. Huge problems in relation to standardization of electronic data exchange have to be solved: what to record and how to record information, safety and security, authorization of health practitioners, and identification of users.

38.5.3.1 Personal Electronic Healthcare Record

Electronic healthcare records are shared by professional caregivers. An active patient is an important partner in the management of his/her own disease or impairment. For instance, patients with a chronic disease sometimes become experts in their disease.

Patients can contribute important information to a personal electronic healthcare record. Some chronic diseases require regular measurements that can be performed by patients or informal caregivers. This information can be added to a personal electronic healthcare record that is maintained by the patient. Other information can be stored as well, such as remarks, observations, and questions to ask. The patient can authorize the caregiver to have access to (parts of) the personal electronic healthcare record.

38.5.4 Services for Traveling Persons

Healthy persons and patients are more mobile than ever before. If a traveler gets sick abroad, it can be difficult to get access to the electronic healthcare record maintained by the general practitioner and/or other medical professionals at home. To avoid this problem, services are available that store medical information in a Web database, which can be remotely accessed. These services are obligated to safeguard privacy, security, validity, and accuracy of medical information.

38.6 APPLICATION AREAS OF TELECARE

38.6.1 Personal Alarm Systems

38.6.1.1 Active Alarms

Older and handicapped persons use personal alarm systems at home. By pressing a (portable) alarm button, the user reaches a care center via a hands-free telephone link. Modern personal alarm systems have many interface options for inclusion of various sensors in the environment that monitor the well-being of the user and the safety of the living environment.

Access to the home of someone who has sent an alarm call to the care center is "a key problem." Care organizations often have a storage location for keys belonging to the subscribers of the personal alarm service. A caregiver has to pick up the key before the patient in need is visited. Sometimes a key is given to neighbors or friends of a subscriber; however, not everyone is prepared or willing to be a "key" person. Electronic key locks provide a solution, allowing safe remote control of the doorlock by a signal sent by the care center when the caregiver arrives.

An experiment in The Netherlands on the effects of technology for older (but still healthy) persons was conducted by providing an alarm service system as a preventive measure. Usually an alarm is installed after some type of incident (fall, sudden illness, etc.) occurred. In such a situation a decision is also often made to transfer the patient to an elderly home or a nursing home, and not to wait for another emergency situation. With a personal alarm system installed for preventive reasons, it has been proved that people stay longer in their own homes (on average at least 6 months). The system used in this study consisted of a standard personal alarm system with a modern distance-operated (remotely or GSM-operated doorlock system [13,14].

38.6.1.2 Passive Alarms

Several systems are currently under development that actively monitor activity patterns of persons at home. A variety of sensors are used, including infrared, on/off switches, and devices for data collection. On the basis of specific algorithms stored in the memory of these devices, threshold values are defined below or above the device sends an alarm to a caregiver. Depending on the nature of the aberration of the individually set pattern and possibly information on the specific cause of the alarm activation, a follow-up action is initiated [15].

38.6.2 Support for Chronic Patients at Home

The use of medical equipment is not restricted to professionals and institutional care environments. There is a range of small, user-friendly medical monitoring devices, which can be easily used by patients at home. The advancement of ICT and micromechanics has improved the user interfaces of medical devices, made onscreen instructions possible, and reduced the size of equipment.

There are also homecare versions of complex hospital equipment. An example is nighttime dialysis at home. Such applications require thorough user-training, self-monitoring checking equipment, with a 24/7 (24 h per day, 7 days per week) emergency response service from the hospital. The dialysis is done more frequently and thus a much better treatment result can be expected, and it will save time for the patient, who can be asleep during dialysis (while the monitoring takes place; the system could generate a warning were unsafe conditions to arise).

38.6.3 Contact with Caregivers: Health Buddy

Regular contacts with patients can be maintained by visits, phone calls, and emails. For some patients monitoring of health and well-being is necessary but does not require a daily voice contact between patient and caregiver. Not every patient needs daily contact. The "health buddy" [16] offers the possibility to monitor patients and to limit phone calls and home visits to occasions when help is actually needed. Via a small screen, patients receive a small interactive questionnaire daily. The questions can be answered by choosing one of the answer alternatives presented on screen, by pressing a button for each question presented. Questions address issues such as health, taking medicines, well-being, food intake, results of medical checks, and exercise. The results of the daily questionnaires are presented at the caregivers' office. The software analyzes the results and lists those patients who require special attention. The caregiver contacts these patients. There is special software for a number of chronic diseases.

38.6.4 Videoconferencing

Videotelephony is a mainstream technology that has a great potential for telecare. It is a very direct way of communicating, as partners see each others' facial expression. The conversation between client and caregiver can be directed toward the client's needs at that moment; it is spontaneous, as there is no strict protocol that structures the conversation. For example, in an "attention care" situation, persons with feelings of loneliness or inactive persons get remote support from a homecare professional.

Because of its flexibility, video can be used in a wide range of situations, including support for an informal caregiver, telehousecalls, videoconsultation, and monitoring the use of medicine.

38.6.5 Supporting the Informal Caregiver

Videocameras and sensors can be used for monitoring and surveillance of patients at home. This can be done continuously, or by appointment, on request or during emergency situations. Surveillance of behavior may interfere with the privacy of a patient.

For example, in "behavior-monitoring" situations, patients with dementia may be monitored by a caregiver at a care center during times when the healthy partner is away from home (for shopping, recreational activities, etc.).

38.6.6 Rehabilitation at Home

Rehabilitation—especially following a stroke—is labor-intensive and requires professional expertise. Many patients are rehabilitated in an institutional setting. Patients use training equipment and receive instructions from a physiotherapist. Training equipment can be provided with sensors that record the patient's movements. Patients who leave the institutional setting and return home would benefit from continuing training at home, guided by the therapist at the rehabilitation center, who evaluates progress and gives instructions via a datalink and/or a videolink to the patient at home.

Training and rehabilitation at home becomes a promising telecare service. It fits well within the current fitness trend, where people use training equipment in fitness centers, at home, or outdoors.

38.6.7 Mobile Support

Outdoor mobility is an aspect of participation in society. Mobility of people with disabilities is encouraged, and technology plays a role in solving their mobility problems. One issue is access to services wherever the person is located. Another problem has to be solved as well: Where is that person at the moment? Technology can solve these problems, and GPS-enabled phones can pinpoint the exact location of the caller. Much more difficult is creating a service that can send help anytime, anywhere. Services like the ambulance, the police, road services, and the fire brigade have that coverage, but there is no comparable service for sending a homecare worker to a mobile person in need.

People with dementia, for example, often experience problems with spatial orientation. Wandering behavior is very common among patients with dementia. Patients in the first stage of dementia can benefit from a device that supports orientation outdoors, or that transmits an alarm call and position information to a care center, if the patient crosses the boundaries of a predefined area. Important issues concern the privacy of the patient whose whereabouts are tracked, such as whether the patient should take the initiative to make an alarm call, and how to organize an adequate response whenever and wherever a patient becomes disoriented.

38.7 DISCUSSION

38.7.1 Privacy and Reliabilitation Information

The use of ICT in telecare poses questions about privacy of information, reliability of information, and who owns the information. Information can be exchanged quickly and easily via ICT, but can also be copied, changed, and multiplied. Electronic healthcare records need to be protected against misuse, and be made available only to caregivers who are authorized by the patient. But this is more easily said than done. If the level of protection is low, medical databases will be an easy target for hackers, and will lose credibility in a short time.

The use of sensors and videocameras allows caregivers to gather significant amounts of information about the health, well-being, and behavior of a patient. Moreover, information gathering can take place continuously. Data-mining techniques can combine and analyze information from several sources, depending on what the researcher wants to know. Even when misuse is nearly impossible, the question remains as to what extent a person wants to be monitored, even when caregivers say that it happens for his or her own good.

38.7.2 Who Is in Control: Caregiver or Patient?

Information and communication technology can link a patient and a caregiver close together. Medical information, emergency calls, messages, and questions are only a mouseclick away, at least when an infrastructure for healthcare records is accomplished. Caregivers are able to monitor health, well-being, even behavior of patients—and (sometimes well-informed) patients have immediate access to their own healthcare records.

38.8 SUMMARY

As described in the previous paragraphs, a wide range of technologies can be applied toward healthcare applications. For this technology to become effective, the users of the technology (professionals and clients) must be aware of the applications and the system's potential. They also have to invest in organizing the application. The development and implementation of healthcare applications using technology has become a very specific area in which technology developers must cooperate with application developers and application users. This is done best in an environment that is supportive and in which technology is ubiquitously present. The developments in communication and smart home technologies are very promising, suggesting that such an environment is indeed within reach. The European Union's 6th and 7th Framework Programs, Information Society and Technology Section, is aiming at such an environment.

As indicated in this chapter, other conditions must be established to stimulate the use of technology in healthcare:

1. Healthcare workers must be well grounded in the use of the technology as part of their professional approaches.
2. Clients have to appreciate the benefits of a different, more effective care provision process.
3. The healthcare system must be able to obtain and organize the financial means to apply the technology.
4. An appropriate solution has to be found for the standardization and integration of different technical approaches.
5. We will need to organize a common understanding on issues like data management and privacy
6. Health and telecare systems must be made accessible and affordable to everyone.

38.9 IN CONCLUSION

Health-related technology and telecare are developing very rapidly. As documented in this chapter, a broad area of technologies may be used to develop useful healthcare-related applications. This will be relevant not only in situations in which there exists a distance between care provider and care receiver; the process of healthcare provision in general will be enriched by the use of technology. This will result in a better quality of care and a healthcare system that will be more efficient (in delivering adequate services to an increased number of clients) and more effective as well (delivering a higher outcome as described in terms of better quality of care).

REFERENCES

1. Bouwhuis DG, Bondareva Y, Meesters LMJ: The applicability of behavioural measures in face-to virtual-face communication for elderly, *Proc 11th Int Conf Human Computer Interaction*, Las Vegas, NV, July 22–27, 2005.
2. Pierratos A, Ouwendyk M, Francoeur R, Wallace L, Sit W, Vas S, Uldall R: Slow nocturnal home hemodialysis, *dialysis transplant* 24(10):557–576 (1995).
3. Kooistra M: *Frequente Nachtelijke Thuishemodialyse in Nederland*, Project Nocturne (Frequent nightly hemodialysis at home in The Netherlands), Dianet Dialysecentra, Utrecht, 2004.
4. Blijerveld JFJ: *Innovating on the Innovation Process for Developing Health Care Technology*, ESST, The European Inter-University Association on Society, Science, and Technology. Thesis, Univ Maastricht/iRv, 2005.
5. Burzagli L, Emiliani PL, Graziani P: Ambient intelligence and disability: the technological perspective, *Proc Int Conf Human Computer Interaction*, Las Vegas, NV, July 22–27, 2005.
6. TNO, Defense and Safety Research, Soesterberg, The Netherlands: *Unattended Autonomous Surveillance System* (lmvanherten@tno.pg.nl).
7. Kempen M, Viezzer M, Bisson P, Nieuwenhuis CHM: The challenges of designing an intelligent companion, *Proc Int Conf Human Computer Interaction*, Las Vegas, NV, July 22–27, 2005.
8. Soede M: Ambient intelligence and disability: The user perspective, *Proc Int Conf Human Computer Interaction*, Las Vegas NV, July 22–27, 2005.
9. Friedewald M ed: *SWAMI Project, Safeguards in a World of Ambient Intelligence* (*SWAMI*), *Deliverable D1*: *The Brave New World of Ambient Intelligence: A State-of-the-Art Review*, Fraunhofer Inst Systems and Innovation Research, Karlsruhe, Germany.
10. Gelderblom GJ: *Rehabilitation Robotics Overview*, CD-ROM, iRv, 2004, Hoensbroek, The Netherlands.
11. Veterans Administration: *The Web-Site of the Veterans Admininstration Offers Americans a Personalized Service* (www.myhealth.va.gov).
12. NHS Direct Online service; service in the United Kingdom (www.nhsdirect.nhs.uk, 2006).
13. Willems C, de Vlieger S: The use of ICT in the delivery of unplannable care in assistive technology, in Pruski A, Knops H, eds, *From Virtuality to Reality*, 2005, pp 188–193.

14. Willems C, Vlaskamp F, de Vlieger S: Attention care and monitoring behaviour, in Mann WC, Helal A, eds, *Promoting Independence for Older Persons with Disabilities*, IOS Press, 2006, pp 99–105.
15. Glascock AP, Kutzik DM: The impact of behavioral monitoring technology on the provision of healthcare in the home, *J Comput Serv* **12**(1) (2006).
16. Health Hero Network: The Health Buddy® System (www.healthhero.com).

39

Immersive Telecare for Assisting People with Special Needs

Sumi Helal
University of Florida

Bessam Abdulrazak
Université de Sherbrooke, Québec, Canada

This chapter discusses a new concept of homecare delivery benefiting frail (elderly and disabled) people with special needs (PwSN). This new concept is an extension of the existing smart house (SH) concept, which is challenged when PwSN occupants need physical assistance. The telecare–robotics (TeCaRob) concept explores the use of robotics to remotely assist frail elders and other PwSN in diverse tasks of daily living.

39.1 INTRODUCTION

Home caregivers play a critical role in maintaining a decent quality of life for older adults and other PwSN. Simple manual assistance in handling daily living tasks such as moving from one place to another, performing hygiene, feeding, and administering medications makes a world of difference in the lives of PwSN. This problem is especially important given the sharp increase in the aging population around the world. In 2002, the elderly population was estimated to be about 13% in the United States and 20.0% in Europe. It was also estimated that the elderly population would double by 2030 [1,2]. This population will need more home nursing service as they age. As baby boomers will reach retirement age over the next 10–15 years (from the time of this writing),

---

The Engineering Handbook of Smart Technology for Aging, Disability, and Independence,
Edited by A. Helal, M. Mokhtari and B. Abdulrazak
Copyright © 2008 John Wiley & Sons, Inc.

the healthcare system in the United States will experience an overwhelming demand for homecare delivery. At the same time, the healthcare system is facing an increasing shortage of qualified caregivers [3,4]; For example, an epidemiologic study has shown that the current nursing shortage exceeds 10%. The shortage of skilled nurses is expected to reach 1 million by 2010 and 1.5 million by 2020. The American Hospital Association also reported in 2002 that 56% of hospitals face problems with nurse recruitment [3,4] (see also Website www.aha.org). The Bureau of Health Professions also reported that about 20% of the US population resides in areas where there are shortages of primary medical care health professionals. This supply–demand mismatch will have critical implications on the adequacy and quality of healthcare that can be delivered to the growing elderly population.

Several attempts have been made to use pervasive computing and ambient intelligence to develop "assistive environments" for the PwSN. These smart houses [5–13], utilize networks of sensors and actuators, devices, appliances, applications, and services. SHs assist PwSN in their daily living needs, allow them to live independently, and help them maintain a high quality of life and good health. They also help caregivers in their daily tasks. However, these SHs have limitations. They may be able to schedule reminders to take the medications, but they cannot physically assist in dispending and giving the medications; they may assist in preparing and cooking food, but they offer no help in hand-feeding it. In short, SHs, however smart they may be, are limited in that they do not offer close physical interaction with the enduser.

Assistive robototics (AR) is a technology that plays an increasingly important role in the life of PwSN. Indeed, numerous ARs have been developed since the mid-1970s, including smart wheelchairs for smooth navigation, walker assistance devices that aid users in their movement, AR telemanipulators that allow users to manipulate objects (see Chapter 19, this volume, and Refs. 14 and 15). These ARs are helping PwSN maintain a higher quality of life by improving work productivity and social activities. Meanwhile, AR systems also have limitations. For example, the structure of the existing ARs limits the number of tasks to be performed. The AR arm extremities, typically grippers, cannot be interchangeable and cannot be adapted for a variety of tasks, which means that ARs are not replaying to all PwSN needs.

More recent advances in telecommunication technology has stimulated research in telenursing. This practice allows caregivers to partially assist patients at remote sites using phone or videoconference technologies. Indeed, numerous healthcare systems employ the tele-nursing to reduce the cost of healthcare delivery [16,17]. However, nurses and other caregivers are still needed to travel to patients' residences to handle daily tasks that require physical interaction such as attending to their hygiene, medication, and transport needs. Such home visits are very costly in terms of caregiver time and resources. It is also a costly service for the elderly people or their family members and for subsidized healthcare. The existing telenursing/telecare is limited to verbal interventions, which restrains the practice of the telecare.

PwSN home healthcare needs have been increasing, the existing healthcare delivery faces a shortage of professionals, and the existing technology (including ARs and SHs) lack the ability to provide a complete solution for PwSN. This implies that there is an urgent need for a new, more effective solution. In this chapter the *telecare robot* (TeCaRob), we introduce a novel concept for telecare, which we call, which relies on a remotely guided robot that interacts with residents in their smart homes and that allows caregivers to "telepresence," to robotically or remotely deliver detailed care or assistance, which often requires close human–human, face-to-face interaction. Our system extends the definition of telecare to include the virtual and interactive physical presence aspect. TeCaRob explores research of robotics, pervasive computing, telepresence, and virtual and augmented reality. In Section 39.2, we discuss the TeCaRob in detail. In Section 39.3 we give scenarios of daily uses of TeCaRob. In the Section 39.4 we address the principal characteristics of the TeCaRob, and in Section 39.5 we conclude the chapter.

39.2 A NEWVISION OF TELECARE

The TeCaRob aims to provide customized, on-demand remote assistance. The idea is to create a system that allows caregivers to provide assistance and services remotely. TeCaRob is a generic platform that can be used by diverse caregivers, which enables various telecare practices, including telerehabilitation, telenursing, telemedication, telepsychotherapy, or even simple telepresence with a close family member. The system consists of two subsystems: (1) the end-user residence subsystem and (2) the caregiver's remote operation center subsystem.

39.2.1 The End-User Residence Subsystem

The TeCaRob subsystem at the end-user residences (Fig. 39.1) is composed of (1) a robotic platform, (2) an environment-sensing and actuation platform, (3) an interaction platform, and (4) a communication platform:

1. The robotic platform uses a toolbox to select the appropriate set of instruments to implement a remote action or gesture (by the caregiver remotely). The robotic platform consists of (a) a mobile base on a structural support (railing) that enables the robotic structure to move from one place to another, (b) robotic arms that allow the user to reach any point in the room, and (c) arm extremities (hand structures or diverse tools) that allow the user to exercise (for fitness).

2. The environment-sensing platform is composed of the latest monitoring technologies. It includes a simple system such as stereocameras, thermostats, and on/off sensors, and complex systems such as the location-tracking systems or security systems. The sensing platform creates a precise 3D rendering of the end user with respect to the remote caregiver. It is an important component necessary to enable the caregiver to respond accurately.

3. The interaction platform is composed of human–machine interaction (HMI) and multimedia technologies that allow positive, amicable interaction between caregivers and end users, such as the videoconferences. This interaction platform favors the acceptability of the system. It also enhances social activity.

4. The communication platform is based on a high-QoS broadband connection that supports telecontrol as well as the different interactions between the end-user residence and the healthcare center. This platform insures continuity of the connection between the center and the residence. It also insures security and privacy.

Using this TeCaRob system, caregivers are able to interact with end–user environment and perform most of the activities that a caregiver would normally perform at the PwSN residence. In other words, the robotic system is acting, behaving, and communicating as a "caregiver."

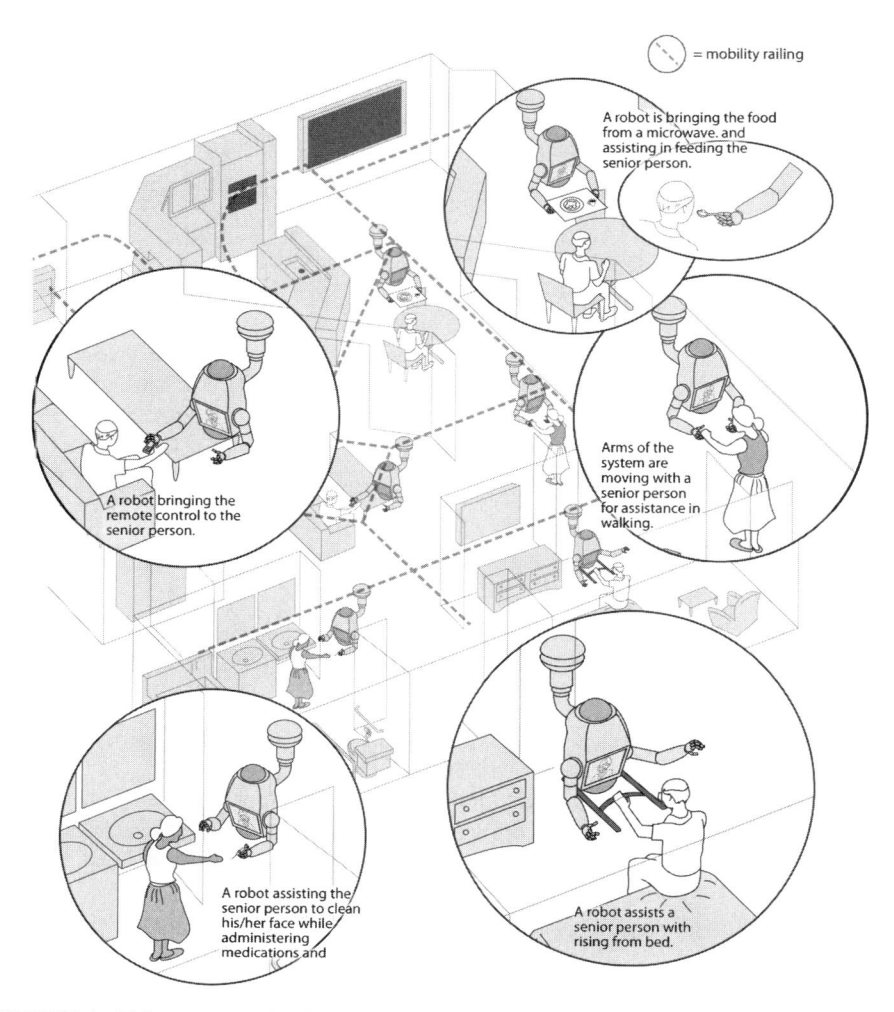

FIGURE 39.1 Telecare scenarios inside a house (end-user residence) (courtesy of the University of Florida).

39.2.2 The Remote Caregiver Operation Center Subsystem

The remote caregiver operation center consists of an array of telecare stations or cubicles (Fig. 39.2), with caregiver operators on standby, waiting for control signals from the users' smart homes. Each operator station (cubicle) (Fig. 39.2) has interfaces that carefully reproduce (model) the end-user environment, and that augment the operator's reality, immersing him/her into the end user's environment (the system accurately senses the end-user environment).

The station also has input interfaces that allow control of the robot and interaction with the entire TeCaRob system. We can imagine that the nurse projects his/her virtual presence via the robot, to be transferred into the end-user environment.

There is no doubt that both a good end-user–system and end-user–caregiver interactions are critical to the acceptability of the system. TeCaRob allows a virtual presence of

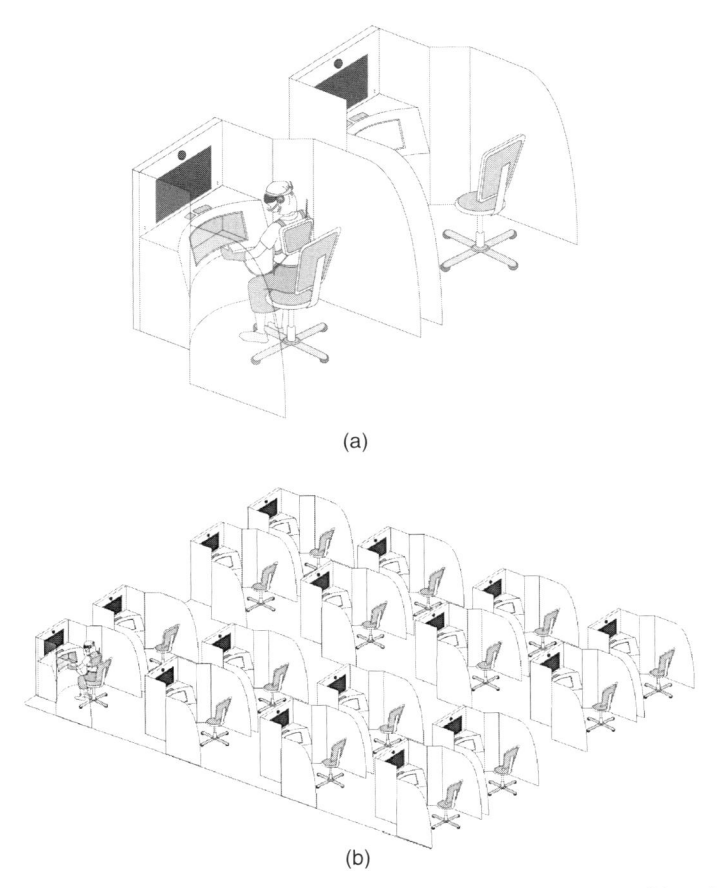

FIGURE 39.2 A remote healthcare center: (a) close-up view of two cubicles; (b) multiple cubicles (courtesy of the University of Florida).

the caregiver; it allows multicommunication modalities. The caregivers are able to express themselves through a speech system, robotic gestures, and screen displays (Fig. 39.1).

39.3 SCENARIOS

In order to understand the usage and effectiveness of our system within the senior end users everyday life, let us imagine an ordinary day of three elderly end users: Ms. Aseel, Ms. Muusa, and Ms. Sulaymaan. The situations of these women symbolize those of elder persons living independently in smart houses. It also illustrates diverse levels of disability associated with various ages.

Because of their ages and health conditions, these three women need varying levels of assistance. Ms. Aseel is fairly independent. Ms. Muusa needs assistance, and Ms. Sulaymaan needs extensive assistance. The situation of Ms. Sulaymaan is similar to that of a person with motor disability. The three women use home nursing care. Recently they switched from the traditional health system that requires physical presence of a nurse or other human caregiver to the TeCaRob system. Here are some scenarios of a day in the lives of these women before and after using TeCaRob.

39.3.1 Rising From Bed

The three women wake up in the morning ready to rise and start their daily activities.

- Ms. Aseel has relied on "fixed helms/bars" to rise from bed. *Now the TeCaRob robotic platform is moving with her to get off the bed smoothly (Figure 39.1).*
- Ms. Muusa needs more assistance then Ms. Aseel. When she wakes up, she calls for assistance. Previously, after a certain time, a human caregiver would come to help her rise from bed and get into a wheelchair. *Now, immediately after Ms. Muusa rings for assistance, a remotely located caregiver from the telecare center employs the robotic platform to remotely give her a hand, helping her get out of bed and into her wheelchair smoothly.*
- Ms. Sulaymaan needs the most assistance. She cannot get out of bed by herself. When she wakes up, she also calls for assistance. The caregiver previously operated an existing lift system to transfer Ms. Sulaymaan into a mobile base such as a wheelchair. For this task, the caregiver needs to start by helping Ms. Sulaymaan don the lift jacket. *Now the caregiver remotely operates the TeCaRob-adapted arms to raise Ms. Sulaymaan from the bed smoothly.*

39.3.2 Mobility

After rising, the first activity of these three women is to use the bathroom:

- Ms. Aseel previously used fixed bars or canes to move to the toilet. *Now the TeCaRob robot smoothly moves with Ms. Aseel and assists her in walking.*
- Ms. Muusa and Ms. Sulaymaan previously drove their wheelchairs to go from one place to another. Ms. Muusa occasionally asked the caregiver to drive her wheelchair, while Ms. Sulaymaan frequently asked for such assistance. *Now, whenever these two women request assistance in mobility, the caregiver remotely assists them, more quickly than previously.*

39.3.3 Hygiene

During the day, these three women need to use the bathroom and to wash themselves. Ms. Aseel and Ms. Muusa do not need much continuous assistance in this task; they usually can perform the hygiene tasks by themselves. However, human assistance is convenient for Ms. Sulaymaan. Frequently, Ms. Sulaymaan needs a human presence for the hygiene tasks.

- *Now the caregiver does not have to travel to Ms. Sulaymaan is residence but instead, remotely employs the TeCaRob, to provide the necessary assistance. The robotic system is equipped with many extensions, tools, and other accessories that enable caregivers to assist end users in performing hygiene tasks.*

39.3.4 Feeding

Ms. Aseel, Ms. Muusa, and Ms. Sulaymaan rarely cook. They eat prepared food delivered by a home food service. The kitchens in their smart houses are equipped with features allowing food preparation. Nonetheless, feeding tasks (eating and drinking) are not easy for them.

Ms. Aseel is able to serve food, eat, and drink slowly. Ms. Muusa is able to serve her food with difficulty, and eat and drink slowly. Ms. Sulaymaan can eat and drink with difficulty, but is unable to serve the food. She always needs human assistance. *Similar to the hygiene activities, now the TeCaRob enables the caregivers to assist these three women in feeding at any time, without traveling to their residences. Using adapted tools connected to the robotic system, caregivers remotely open boxes, and other contaimers; serve food on the dish; serve drinks in glasses, mugs, or cups; and spoon-feed the patient if necessary.*

39.3.5 Health Checks

The health condition of these three women needs continuous monitoring. Caregivers previously traveled to residences of these three women to perform diverse examinations. Generally, these checks are simple such as simply a looking to a patient. The most thorough checks such as a temperature or blood pressure monitoring, are less frequent.

Now the TeCaRob enables caregivers to handle complex thorough examinations remotely by using special tools connected to the robot. The simple checks are now a simple multimedia communication task.

39.3.6 Dressing

Ms. Aseel and Ms. Muusa are able to dress/undress and put on/remove shoes by themselves. Occasionally, caregivers help these three women with those tasks. Usually, human support consists of taking the clothes when these women dress/undress, helping them open/close buttonholes, put on/take off shoes and socks, and put on on/take off jewelry.

Similar to performing the other tasks, mentioned earlier in this section, caregivers are now able to help these three women to dress/undress easily without traveling to their residences. Caregivers have only to use the diverse tools associated with the TeCaRob, such as a buttonhole opening/closing mechanism and a device to put on/take off shoes.

39.3.7 Rescue

Many calls to emergency centers are from aging people who simply want to communicate with someone. The operator or dispatcher at the center may not be able to easily distinguish between an actual emergency call and a false alert. Usually when Ms. Aseel sends an alert, a group of caregivers (e.g., a nurse, a physician, or a paramedic) is sent to her location.

- If the call is a false alert, there is costly downtime: loss of the caregivers' time and the cost of travel to the patient's residence.
- If the call is for a simple intervention, deployment of a specialized group of care providers is not justified.

- If the call is a serious alert, to an actual emergency, time of travel is a very important factor. Depending on the traffic and the distance, the help might be too late.

Now the TeCaRob system prevents unnecessary intervention and expensive emergency service deployment. By a simple remote check, the telecare staff can determine whether the situation is in fact critical. If the robot resolves the problem, a caregiver intervenes quickly and remotely for follow-up. If the case is serious and requires urgent intervention, a caregiver starts to intervene remotely, while waiting for an ambulance to arrive at the patient is residence.

39.4 CHARACTERISTICS

The TeCaRob system has both functional and technical aspects.

39.4.1 Functional Characteristics

PwSN need special healthcare and daily living assistance. Under the complete control of the caregiver, the TeCaRob is able to assist in performing tasks in four interaction categories:

- Transferring and moving the end user (e.g., helping the person get out of bed and into a chair and assisting with end-user mobility to/from other locations)
- Performing tasks in the end-user environment (e.g., manipulating, lifting, or carrying objects such as mugs, bottles, plates, books, and medicines).
- Interacting closely with the end user (e.g., feeding, cleaning, and administering medications).
- Communicating with and monitoring the end user (e.g., chating with and monitoring the health of the end user)
- Performing these tasks according to schedule and in a timely manner in response to end-user demands)

39.4.2 Technical Characteristics

The TeCaRob system enables a continuous teleinteraction between end users and their caregivers and assists in accomplishing tasks that usually require close person-to-person interaction. The main characteristics of the system are (1) safety and security, (2) precision, (3) real-time operation, and (4) friendly and personalized interaction:

1. *Safety and Security.* The TeCaRob system is equipped with many safety and security services and features and can conduct many procedures. The robot path planner and obstacle avoidance system guarantee that the end user will not be injured, nor will any objects in the end user's environment be damaged at any time. The system is equipped with safety (foolproof) procedures. The system also provides other procedures as well to anticipate problems, such as power failure, interruption of communication, and failure of mechanical or electronic components.

2. *Precision.* The system is based on the latest robotic technologies that allow execution of the right action at the right time, with extreme accuracy.
3. *Real-Time Operation.* The system operates instantaneous. It has a real-time operating system and a real-time communication system.
4. *Friendly and Personalized Interaction.* The TeCaRob employs the most recent advances in ergonomics and human factor domains to enhance the end user's feelings of security and satisfaction, stimulate end-user motivation, increase collaboration in execution of tasks, and promote end-user acceptance of the system.

39.5 CONCLUSION

The TeCaRob system enhances independent living and improves the quality of life of people with special needs (PwSN) by providing customized and continuous remote physical assistance. TeCaRob is complementary to smart home technology, which is used in assisted-living environments (e.g., see Ref. 8). In case of critical situations, if assistance is needed or requested, the TeCaRob system allows caregivers to check the situation and intervene quickly if necessary. TeCaRob provides national and international healthcare systems with novel tools that promote the practices of telemedicine and telecare. TeCaRob decreases time and distance barriers, which optimize use of limited healthcare resources. The TeCaRob concept integrates the virtual physical presence, which eliminates both the time and cost of caregiver begin travel to the residence. This system also considerably reduces the time needed to begin interacting with the end user, thus saving valuable time needed for emergency care.

A multidisciplinary R&D team is essential for building such a system. The aim is to address problems in a multidimensional approach, beginning with the definition of user needs and prototype assessment. The process of building this system is organized in various groups of tasks: user needs, technical requirements, mechanical design, control design, communication design, telecontrol design, human–machine interaction, security and privacy aspects, and evaluation and validation.

REFERENCES

1. US Census: *Disability Status*, US Census Bureau, US Department of Commerce Economics and Statistics Administration, Washington, DC, March, 2003.
2. RNIB: Royal National Institute of the Blind, United Kingdom, 2002.
3. Aiken LH, Clarke SP, Sloane DM et al: Hospital nurse staffing and patient mortality, nurse burnout, and job dissatisfaction, *JAMA*: Vol. 288, 1987–1993 (2002).
4. Caron VF: *The Nursing Shortage in the United States: What Can Be Done to Solve the Crisis?* Schmidt Labor Research Center Seminar Paper Series, Univ Rhode Island, 2004.
5. Helal A, Mann W, Elzabadani H, King J, Kaddoura Y, Jansen E: Gator Tech smart house: A programmable pervasive space, *IEEE Comput Mag*: **38**(3): 64–74 (2005).
6. Cook DJ, Das S: *Smart Environments*, Wiley, Hoboken, NJ, 2005.
7. Abowd GD, Bobick GA, Essa I, Mynatt E, Rogers W: The aware home: Developing technologies for successful aging, *Proc AAAI Workshop on Automation as a Care Giver*, Alberta, Canada, July 2002.

8. Brumitt B, Meyers B, Krumm J, Kern A, Shafer S: EasyLiving: Technologies for intelligent environments, *Proceedings of the International Conference on Handheld and Ubiquitous Computing 2000,* Springer-Verlag, (2000), p. 12–29.
9. Stefanov D, Bien Z, Bang W: The smart house for older persons and persons with physical disabilities: Structure, technology arrangements, and perspectives, *IEEE Trans Neural Syst Rehab Eng* **12**(2): pp 228–250 (2004).
10. Mokhtari M, Abdulrazak B, Feki MA, Rodriguez R, Grandjean B: Integration of rehabilitation robotics in the context of smart homes: Application to assistive robotics, *Int J Human-Friendly Welfare Robot Syst* **4**(2):29–32 (2003).
11. Abdulrazak B, Mokhtari M, Feki MA, Ghorbel M: Integration of home networking in a smart environment dedicated to people with disabilities, *Proc IEEE Int Conf Information & Communication Technologies: From Theory to Application (IEEE-ICTTA)*, Damascus, Syria, April 2004.
12. Pigot H, Mayers A, Giroux S, Lefebvre B, Rialle V, Noury N: Smart house for frail and cognitive impaired elders, *1st Int Workshop on Ubiquitous Computing for Cognitive Aids (UbiCog)*, Göteborg, Sweden, Sept 29, 2002.
13. Noury N, Virone G, Creuzet T: The health integrated smart home information system (HIS2): Rules based system for the localization of a human, *Proc 2nd Annual Int IEEE-EMB Special Topic Conf Microtechnologies in Medicine & Biology*, Madison, WI, May 2–4, 2002, pp 318–321.
14. Hillman M: Rehabilitation robotics from past to present—a historical perspective, *Proc 8th Int Conf Rehabilitation Robotics (ICORR)*, South Korea, April 2003.
15. Van der Loos M: VA/Stanford rehabilitation robotics research and development program: Lessons learned in the application of robotics technology to the field of rehabilitation, *IEEE Trans Rehab Engi.* **3**(1):46–55 (1995).
16. Noel HC, Vogl DC, Erdos JJ Cornwall D, Levin F: Home telehealth reduces healthcare costs, *Telemed J e-Health* **10** (2):170–183 (2004).
17. Bynum AB, Irwin CA, Cranford CO, Denny GS: The impact of telemedicine on patients' cost savings: Some preliminary findings, *Telemed J e-Health 9*, **9**(4):361–367 (2003).

40

Smart Systems in Personal Transportation

Aaron Steinfeld
Robotics Institute, Carnegie Mellon University

40.1 INTRODUCTION

Intelligent transportation systems (ITS) have steadily evolved from research prototypes to successful commercial products. Certain trends in ITS provide key opportunities to (1) improve safety and access for drivers who are older and/or disabled and (2) reduce the cost of vehicle modification to end consumers and third-party payers and to increase availability of technicians and vehicles.

More recent advances in ITS have been most apparent in passenger vehicles. Automobile manufacturers (OEMs) have become more aware of technology as a means of branding and as an opportunity to offer more markup options for their vehicles. Telematics (wireless, in-vehicle voice and data), in-vehicle navigation systems, adaptive/intelligent cruise control, perception assistance systems, and automatic crash notification (ACN) systems are now all available in US showrooms. The added functionality of these systems has resulted in large shifts in the way vehicles are designed. The traditional practice of assigning one physical control per function is no longer an option. As such, the industry is moving toward new interaction models that, in many cases, directly affect accessibility.

There has been increased attention to applying universal design to automobiles. Specifically, there is a significant increased awareness of the aging of populations in developed countries and the impact that this demographic shift will have on use of automobiles [1]. While the use of the term "universal design" has not been particularly popular in the automotive industry, other related terms, such as "transparent enablers" have increasingly garnered attention in the press and industry [2]. The use of such indirect language reflects

---

The Engineering Handbook of Smart Technology for Aging, Disability, and Independence,
Edited by A. Helal, M. Mokhtari and B. Abdulrazak
Copyright © 2008 John Wiley & Sons, Inc.

an underlying ambivalence about addressing the needs of older people and people with disabilities directly. In the highly competitive automotive industry, marketing has a very high priority in making design decisions. Too close an association with aging and disability has been perceived as a marketing liability, particularly if such features conflict with styling goals.

Not only is the industry slowly changing their objectives to accommodate the aging population; they are also changing their design process to be more sensitive to the impact of aging and to experience design concepts as an older driver might [3,4]. The power of using "empathic models" [5] in design is demonstrated by the words of this quote from the manager of the Ford Human Factors and Ergonomics Division: "It's one thing to read customer feedback in a marketing study.... It's a whole different thing to feel what they are feeling while driving a car. This has been a real eye opener for our engineers" [2].

While most developments on this front have focused on interiors, there are clear opportunities to increase personal transportation safety and accessibility as a result of the current wave of intelligent vehicle functionality and systems.

40.2 ACTIVE VEHICLE CONTROL

40.2.1 Collision Warning Systems and Adaptive Cruise Control

Collision warning systems (CWSs) have been on the market for several years but have been installed mostly on commercial vehicles like tractor-trailers. Most are forward warning only, but there have been more recent attempts to integrate forward and side CWS [6]. Companies like Eaton-Vorad market systems use forward sensors to determine the presence and trajectories of potential obstacles. A user interface indicates to the driver when dangerous scenarios exist, thus prompting corrective action.

When CWS is tied to the automobile's cruise control, the vehicle can automatically respond to forward obstacles by releasing the accelerator, shifting to a lower gear, and/or activating the brakes. This system is referred to as *adaptive cruise control* (ACC). Currently, ACC is an option on some luxury cars and is available in some modern commercial trucks. While CWS and ACC will likely improve safety for the general public, there are certain design concerns regarding ease of use and legal liability. As such, most consumers in the United States will encounter ACC before CWS. In fact, most OEMs position ACC as a convenience system or "advanced technology" rather than a safety device.

40.2.2 Lane-Keeping Assistance

Tactile steering wheel displays and automated steering corrections are often recommended for lane departure crash-avoidance systems [7]. Vibrations in regions of the driver's seat are also a common suggestion. The major concern with this approach is confusion between a real event and a vehicle malfunction or change in road surface. In particular, research with transit operators suggests that steering wheel actions and seat vibrations are problematic for drivers who cover long distances and/or are very attuned to their vehicles [6]. However, there is still promise in the idea of a steering-wheel-based approach and several OEMs are pursing steering wheel torque and active control of steering wheel position for lane keeping assistance. Also worth noting is that systems using the visual mode only have been shown to be effective and adequate in low-visibility applications [8].

40.2.3 Opportunities for Leveraging Mainstream Systems

Adaptive cruise control, lane-keeping, and collision avoidance systems are already introducing a variety of vehicle-initiated actuation technologies. The removal of the physical linkage between the steering wheel and the front wheels (drive-by-wire) is also on the horizon. There are already vehicles on the market with no physical link between the accelerator and the engine. The automotive community has begun the process of developing communications protocols, functions standards, software interfaces, and specifications. This technology provides an opportunity to improve current vehicle control conversion methods and techniques (e.g., Fig. 40.1) by enabling a direct interface between alternative controls and the onboard vehicle control software. Furthermore, drive-by-wire offers the opportunity for OEMs to offer alternative modes for older drivers or those with limited dexterity by changing gains in the system.

40.3 PERCEPTION ASSISTANCE SYSTEMS

Aging, sensory disabilities, and in-vehicle factors such as loud car radios all can result in impaired perception of the surrounding environment. For example, when such distracting stimuli are present, older drivers can exhibit reduced performance with respect to visual field size, dynamic visual acuity, and velocity estimation, as well as other perceptual and cognitive characteristics [9].

The effects of multiple disabilities exaggerate limitations in performance. For example, drivers with restricted neck motion may also have hearing and vision problems. These drivers can have a reduced ability to detect horns, emergency vehicles, and other unusual events. Vehicle adaptations that accommodate these problems include parabolic rear-view mirrors and siren detectors. Unfortunately, the market for siren detectors has been very small, and such products are difficult to find. Ironically, the better sound insulation in modern vehicles exacerbates this problem.

40.3.1 Parking Aids

One technology that is particularly promising for drivers who have limited neck motion is the parking aid. Parking aids include rear proximity sensors and other parking collision

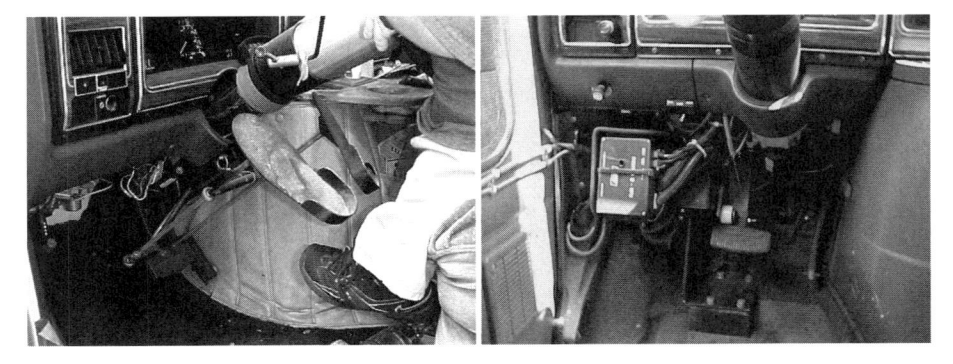

FIGURE 40.1 Vehicle modifications that could be better if supported by drive-by-wire and customizable multifunction displays.

avoidance systems [10]. These systems typically utilize audible alerts or iconic displays on the dashboard to indicate that the driver is about to back into an object. Audible alerts should work fine for drivers who have good hearing but may not be effective for drivers with hearing impairments; they should be designed with redundant visual displays on the dashboard and mirrors. There is also anecdotal evidence that such systems reduce the use of mirrors and direct visual inspection in the general public. If data bear this out, these systems could be making matters worse as they are not as accurate as users may believe.

Some OEMs are now introducing rear-view videocameras. For example, at one point the Infinity Q45 multifunction system in the rear parking camera view mode was the centerpiece of a heavily run advertisement (Fig. 40.2). Toyota has gone so far as to introduce an automated parking mode in vehicles. The driver uses the camera view to indicate where they want the car to park and then the car reverses into the spot [11].

40.3.2 Head-Up Displays

Head-up displays (HUDs) have been increasingly attractive to vehicle designers because they provide a means to superimpose visual information on the road scene. Theoretically, this will reduce the time that drivers take their eyes off the road to view instruments. HUDs in automobiles have been introduced to the market, yet few have been successful products. HUDs are mentioned specifically here because of the recurring enchantment that designers and marketers have with them. However, there are theoretical and practical reasons for choosing an instrument cluster, dashboard, and/or auditory option.

Experiments involving advanced technologies have shown that HUDs have promise for both older and younger drivers [12], but there are serious perceptual and cognitive issues that need to be addressed with additional research [13,14]. The first, and most worrisome, problem is that of cognitive capture [13]. Specifically, a driver who begins to ignore the real world in favor of a HUD may not notice "pop-up" forward obstacles. In

FIGURE 40.2 *Infiniti multifunction cluster showing rear-view parking camera.*

the most likely case this will be a pedestrian or someone exiting a parked vehicle. This is compounded by the fact that current CWS technology has difficulty sensing "soft" targets such as people, increasing the possibility that overdependence on a CWS could have a synergistic effect on cognitive capture. While head-down approaches remove the driver's attention from the forward road scene, they also carry an implicit feeling of uneasiness when looked at for too long. This uneasiness, coupled with low-complexity imagery, may lead to a lower likelihood that the driver will trust the display more than the real world.

The problem of cognitive capture is amplified when conformal imagery (also known as *contact analog*) is presented. For example, in a static study where subjects were asked whether HUD images of highlighted intersection road edges matched real-world backgrounds, there was one case in particular where high response times and error rates were recorded [15]. This case was for a mismatched scene where a cross intersection (conformal HUD imagery) was shown over a T-right scene with a driveway on the left. Even though the HUD imagery was for a different intersection, and therefore unaligned and incorrectly drawn, subjects repeatedly indicated that the HUD imagery matched the road scene. When recognized correctly, the response time was slower than other less confusing combinations.

Tufano [14] documented several problems related to automobile HUDs that deserve significant attention. A primary safety problem is the opportunity for misperception of distance in the real world. One can easily see how this poses a potentially significant problem in collision scenarios. Another safety problem presented by Tufano is poorer performance on responses to unexpected objects and obstacles (e.g., pop-up objects). While older drivers are often cautious of potential collisions and employ coping strategies as a mechanism toward increased safety, they will still encounter unusual events due to relatively unconstrained nature of the roadway system.

In short, HUDs will probably become more prevalent, but they will be introduced slowly since some key perceptual and cognitive problems have yet to be solved.

40.3.3 Nonvisual Warnings

Calls for standardized audible tones to reduce confusion—such as "Did that beep mean the ACC activated or did I get a new email?"—are becoming more common [16]. One interesting study was on the value of localized auditory warnings to assist drivers in identifying the location of hazards [17]. While the results suggested that such a feature is promising, the authors also found that such a system requires special care with respect to speaker location and sound choice. Regardless, using only an audible mode to convey safety related information does not provide sufficient information to drivers who are hearing-impaired.

Innovative new approaches have been attempted to transmit safety-critical messages to the driver without visual stimuli. Examples are accelerator pedals that push back, brake pulses [18], and torque or vibrations applied to the steering wheel [19,20]. The tactile modality is more direct and, like hearing, does not necessarily depend on selective attention to convey a message. Such systems would definitely be beneficial to people with hearing impairments and to the general population but would be less useful to drivers with limited tactile sensation or alternative vehicle controls. Thus, a combination of audible and tactile/haptic alerts may be ideal.

40.4 IN-VEHICLE INFORMATION

Vehicle safety can be compromised when many controls are available for adjustment while driving. One study documented a maximum duration of a single glance while using a car radio of 3.7 s [21], a highly unsafe scenario. Fortunately, auto companies have begun to express interest in multifunction interfaces that offer integration of many in-vehicle features through a limited set of buttons and selections using a "menu tree" [22].

40.4.1 In-Vehicle Navigation Systems

The notion of providing navigation information was initially thought to be the "killer-app" of in-vehicle information systems. To this day, it is frequently marketed as a major option in luxury vehicles. For some older drivers, the value of in-vehicle navigation may indeed be an important feature, due to reductions in confidence and/or ability to navigate in unfamiliar territory. If drivers acknowledge this difficulty, they drive only on very familiar routes. Thus, in-vehicle navigation systems are very attractive to drivers as a means to compensate for poor or impaired wayfinding abilities. This includes typical drivers in a new or confusing area who are "handicapped" by the unfamiliarity of the environment. These devices provide automated instructions on how to proceed from one address to another. Some offer points of interest such as libraries, hospitals, and supermarkets and a means to enter origin and destination selections.

The user interfaces of most navigation systems are small, flat-panel displays mounted on the dashboard. Audible directions are included in some systems and alternative visual are being examined as alternative display devices. Navigation directions are provided in the form of turn-by-turn instructions, overhead plan, or bird's-eye views (most high-end systems allow for several choices). Interaction problems can include difficult destination input methods [23], visual attention conflicts, and poor understanding of imagery. The most serious problem is misinterpretation of instructions. For example, in a real-world experiment of one system there were four critical incidents where subjects changed lanes on instruction from the system without checking for other cars [24].

Clearly, it is important that these new technologies do not distract drivers from scanning the road ahead or overload their mental capabilities. While systems that use speech output are clearly beneficial in reducing visual demand, they exclude use by people with hearing impairments unless visual information is also provided. Information has to be presented in a manner that has little or no significant impact on the safety of the driving task. The task of selecting choices and commands can also distract the driver. Voice recognition systems are often heralded as the safest input method, but, to benefit all users, they have to be usable for individuals with speech impediments or accents. Multiple language capabilities are also desirable.

40.4.2 Telematics

A late addition to the realm of in-vehicle information systems, and the undisputed killer-app for the general market, is telecommunication and information services, commonly referred to as *telematics*. The actual implementation of telematics is varied, but the clear leader in this market is OnStar. Ironically, the basic premise is rather low-tech compared to many other in-vehicle systems; at the push of a button a voice link will be established with live operator assistance—in short, a cell phone with speed dial. In reality, a bit more is happening behind the scenes. Vehicle and location data are also being transmitted to the operators for contextually guided assistance. Using their computers and information relayed from the vehicle through the system, operators can provide a variety of assistance to the driver.

OnStar has been the most successful telematics service provider in the United States, with more than 3 million subscribers since their initial deployment in the fall of 1996. The usage rates are impressive—1,000 airbag notifications, 11,400 emergency calls, 27,000 roadside assistance calls, and 353,000 route guidance calls. Product uptake and use has been dramatically benefited from inclusion of the system in standard option packages for a variety of automobile OEMs.

The OnStar interface consists of three, closely grouped, very small buttons in the car paired with a cellular connection to service centers. All information is presented to the driver via speech. Although OnStar could have great benefits to wheeled mobility users, the very small buttons restrict use by people who have manual dexterity limitations. Furthermore, users that cannot communicate via the voice cannel must request special TTY hardware from OnStar.

40.4.3 Multifunction Controls

The use of a few controls to manage a large assortment of functions is starting to become common in high-end vehicles (e.g., Fig. 40.2). Automobile manufacturers have a vested interest in promoting these new interfaces for branding and marketing purposes. As with antilock brakes, airbags, and CD changers, products now available only on high-end vehicles will soon trickle down to the general market. The impact of multifunction systems on vehicle accessibility is relatively unknown, especially for drivers who use hand controls or have upper-limb impairments.

Multifunction controls have promise, like drive-by-wire, that there will be opportunities to modify and configure vehicle dashboards for older drivers and those who need alternative control interfaces. The software-based approach allows designers to significantly reduce the number of buttons on a device and thus permit simpler interfaces, larger buttons, larger text, and more logical grouping of functions—all of which should be beneficial to older drivers and those with mobility impairments. However, the trade-off could be a longer selection period and additional glances to the dashboard. The need to switch visual attention several times between the road and the dashboard may be especially problematical for older drivers, given the necessity to refocus twice for each glance. Older eyes require more time to refocus as attention shifts from a distant object (road scene) to a close object (control panel). Of course, there is always the option of concealing vast portions of functionality from the driver when the vehicle is in motion. If this is done, it is advisable to provide an opportunity for the passenger to manipulate the system to reach the lower-priority functionality.

40.4.4 Vehicle Interfaces for Drivers with Hearing Impairments

The main problem with many in-vehicle information systems is that they are not accessible to people with hearing impairments. Some traffic safety experts may argue that this is good since there are fewer potential distractions for these drivers, but there are significant benefits for some of the features that these devices offer. For example, as any hearing person who lives in a large city can attest, receiving a warning about the location and reasons for traffic congestion over the car radio is immensely beneficial. Besides the time saved by being able to alter a route before getting mired in gridlock, there is a safety benefit because advanced warning of congestion leads to higher levels of alertness. Furthermore, the lack of entertainment beyond basic driving tasks during long trips can lead to increased boredom due to a lack of mental stimulation.

A classic example of a system falling just short for drivers with hearing impairments is the Toyota Prius. Owners who are hard of hearing (the first grade of hearing loss, followed by severely deaf, profoundly deaf, and totally deaf) have reported that the voice used by the information system is a pitch that is challenging to discern. Some have openly sought the ability to be offered a selection of voices so that one with a discernable pitch could be selected—much like a mirror can be adjusted for a driver's stature. In some extreme cases, drivers will equip their vehicles with a loop-based assistive listening system. It is rather ironic to think that drivers are resorting to technology developed in the first half of the twentieth century to gain greater access to their cutting-edge vehicles.

A more recent byproduct of Bluetooth-equipped vehicles, largely for hands-free phone use, is the introduction of a possible mode of access. Hearing aid and cochlear implant manufactures are beginning to introduce Bluetooth options for their users. Theoretically, such users could pair their hearing aids with their vehicles to achieve better sound transmission than that available with traditional acoustic approaches.

Bluetooth is also being explored as a mechanism for incorporating Internet use into automobiles. One positive characteristic of cars designed with Internet use in mind is that most email, chat, and Web information is in text form. For example, a potential application for drivers with hearing impairments is the ability to access traffic reports available on websites. However, the current trend for Internet-equipped vehicles is to use voice interaction, via speech recognition and digitized text-to-speech, rather than keyboards and screens.

An ideal solution would be to allow the use of keyboards and screens when the vehicle gearshift is in park so that drivers with hearing impairments can utilize the functionality of these systems. Passengers could safely use such systems while a vehicle is in motion, however. Systems could be designed to operate even when not in park as long as they were oriented only toward the passenger side of the vehicle, out of reach and view of the driver. This approach would allow passengers to access information without the driver being distracted. It should be noted that features such as text-based traffic alerts are useful to hearing-impaired drivers who have good eyesight, but the small text may lead to difficulty for older drivers. Of course, it is worth noting that a popular modification to in-vehicle television systems in Japan is to disable the "video in park only" mode so that drivers can watch television in dense, slow crawl traffic.

40.5 ERGONOMIC ISSUES FOR OLDER DRIVERS

While typically viewed as a rather mundane topic when compared to ITS, seating and positioning play major roles in supporting driving tasks and can directly affect the outcomes and use of smart systems.

The size of the "useful field of view," the "spatial area within which an individual can be rapidly alerted to visual stimuli," has been linked directly to accident frequency and driving performance in the older population [25,26]. Positioning the body for visibility is clearly constrained by the design of some automotive seating systems and the vehicles themselves. As such, consumers in focus groups reported that many of them use cushions to prop themselves up to get a better view of the road [27].

In focus groups conducted by Steinfeld et al. [27], older people with disabilities reported that they didn't use seatbelts or pulled the shoulder belt over their shoulders because doing so would make them uncomfortable and cause pain. Individuals who have had recent surgery or chronic health problems in the trunk of the body reported the most discomfort with seatbelts. The difficulty of buckling the belt and reaching shoulder belts and pulling them across the body was also a common complaint due to arthritis and limitations in range of motion. People who had paralysis or other limitations on one side of the body reported great difficulty using seatbelt buckles. Although some participants simply viewed seatbelts as a nuisance and unnecessary, stating that they had used cars successfully for a long time without them, others were positive about seatbelts and were explicit about their safety value.

40.5.1 Short-Range Wireless Access and Payment Systems

A good example of how in-vehicle ergonomics can be ameliorated by technology is support for interaction between drivers and roadside devices and tollbooths. Limitations in range of reach or grasp function can make it very difficult or impossible to use drive in banking, restaurants, or toll roads. One solution for tolls is electronic toll collection (ETC). This usually involves a component mounted in the vehicle's windshield that transfers information with a roadside counterpart to handle payment without driver interaction. Coming to a full stop is not needed, further reducing the risk of low-speed collisions while occupying a tollbooth queue. While these systems were originally designed to increase efficiency and reduce the potential for non-payment of tolls, they have significant benefit to people with mobility impairments. Drivers with limited reach no longer needs to hand money to a toll collector or pull close to roadside infrastructure and risk damage to their vehicles.

40.6 DISCUSSION

There are significant opportunities for leveraging mainstream efforts and enthusiasm for new technologies to provide greater access to all travelers. ITS applications have the potential to be powerful enablers, but, as demonstrated in the computer industry, barriers can be introduced inadvertently or result from inadequate effort in identifying accessible solutions. In order to provide truly effective opportunities for accessible and safe personal transportation, it will be important to ensure (1) consistent effort by policy and research entities to emphasize accessibility in the early stages of development and (2) greater support for customization and modification by OEMs, tiered suppliers, and the aftermarket sector.

REFERENCES

1. Waller P: The older driver, *Human Factors* **33**:499–505 (1991).
2. Ford R: Auto designs for the ages—marketers appeal to boomers, young drivers, *Boston Globe* A01 (March 5, 2000).

3. Block D: A well-suited approach to auto design for older drivers, *Pittsburgh Post-Gazette* (Jan 24, 1999).
   Cerrelli E: *Older Drivers: The Age Factor in Traffic Safety*, NHTSA, ... HS 807 402, Department of Transportation, Springfield, VA, 1989.
   James G: *Problems Experienced by Disabled and Elderly People Entering and Leaving Cars*, Transport and Road Research Laboratory Research Report, Institute for Consumer Ergonomics, Loughborough Univ, Loughborough, UK, Feb 1985.
4. Parker J: Innovative designs help aging baby boomers and motorists with disabilities drive with ease, *Detroit Free Press*, Dec 9, 1999.
5. Pastalan LA: Empathic model project, *Gerontological Society Annual Conf*, Houston, TX, 1971.
6. Steinfeld A, Duggins D, Gowdy J, Kozar J, MacLachlan R, Mertz C, Suppe A, Thorpe C, Wang C-C: Development of the side component of the transit integrated collision warning system, *IEEE Conf Intelligent Transportation Systems (ITSC 2004)*, 2004.
7. Dingus T, Jahns S, Horowitz A, Knipling R: Human factors design issues for crash avoidance systems, in Barfield W, Dingus T, eds, *Human Factors in Intelligent Transportation Systems*, Lawrence Erlbaum Associates, Mahwah, NJ, 1998, pp 55–93.
8. Steinfeld A, Tan H-S, Bougler B: Naturalistic findings for assisted snowplow operations, *Proc Human Factors and Ergonomics Society 45th Annual Meeting*, Human Factors and Ergonomics Society, Santa Monica, CA, 2001.
9. Hakamies-Blomqvist L: Research on older drivers: A review, *Int Assoc Traffic Safety Sci (IATSS) Res* **20**:91–101 (1996).
10. Ward NJ, Hirst S: An exploratory investigation of display information attributes of reverse/parking aids, *Int J Vehicle Design* **19**:41–49 (1998).
11. Associated Press, Jan 15, 2004: Look, no hands! New Toyota parks itself. (CNN.com. www.cnn.com/2004/TECH/ptech/01/15/car.selfpark.ap/index.html).
12. Steinfeld A, Green P: Driver responses to navigation information on full-windshield, head-up displays, *Int J Vehicle Design* **19**:135–149 (1998).
13. Weintraub D, Ensing M: *Human Factors Issues in Head-Up Display Design: The Book of HUD*, CSERIAC state-of-the-art report, Crew Systems Ergonomics Information Analysis Center, Wright-Patterson Air Force Base, OH, 1992.
14. Tufano D: Automotive HUDs: The overlooked safety issues, *Human Factors* **39**:303–311 (1997).
15. Steinfeld A, Green P: *Driver Response Times to Full-Windshield, Head-Up Displays for Navigation and Vision Enhancement*, Technical Report UMTRI 95-29, Univ Michigan Transportation Research Institute, Ann Arbor, 1995.
16. Kantowitz B, Moyer MJ: Integration of driver in-vehicle ITS information, *Proc Intelligent Transportation Society of America (ITSA) 9th Annual Meeting and Exposition* (CD-ROM), Intelligent Transportation Society of America, Washington DC, 1999.
17. Tan AK, Lerner N: *Acoustic Localization of In-Vehicle Crash Avoidance Warnings as a Cue to Hazard Direction*, DOT HS 808 534, National Highway Traffic Safety Administration, Washington, DC, 1996.
18. Lloyd M, Wilson G, Nowak C, Bittner A: Brake pulsing as a haptic warning for an intersection collision avoidance (ICA) countermeasure, *Proc Transportation Research Board 78th Annual Meeting* (preprint CD-ROM), Transportation Research Board, Washington, DC, 1999.
19. Schumann J, Lowenau J, Naab K: The active steering wheel as a continuous support for the driver's lateral control task, in Gale AG, Brown ID, Haslegrave CM, Taylor SP, eds, *Vision in Vehicles —V* Elsevier Science, Amsterdam, 1996, pp 229–236.

20. Hsu J-C, Chen W-L, Shien KH, Yeh EC: Cooperative copilot with active steering assistance for vehicle lane keeping, *Int J Vehicle Design* **19**:78–107 (1998).

    Cushman L, Good R, Annechiarico R, States J: Effect of safety belt usage on injury patterns of hospitalized and fatally injured drivers 55+, *Proc 34th Annual Association for the Advancement of Automotive Medicine*, Scottsdale, Az, 1990.

21. Ayres T, Donelson A, Brown S, Bjelajac V, Van Selow W: On-board truck computers and accident risk, *Safety Engineering and Risk Analysis* 1996, SERA, American Society of Mechanical Engineering, 1996, **6**, pp 1–6.

22. Sumie M, Li C, Green P: *Usability of Menu-Based Interfaces for Motor Vehicle Secondary Functions*, Technical Report UMTRI-97-19, Univ Michigan Transportation Research Institute, Ann Arbor, 1998.

23. Steinfeld A, Manes D, Green P, Hunter D: *Destination Entry and Retrieval with the Al-Scout Navigation System*, Technical Report UMTRI-96-30, Univ Michigan Transportation Research Institute, Ann Arbor, 1996.

24. Katz S, Fleming J, Green P, Hunter D, Damouth D: *On-the-Road Human Factors Evaluation of the Ali-Scout Navigation System*, Technical Report UMTRI-96-32, Univ Michigan Transportation Research Institute, Ann Arbor, MI, 1997.

25. Owsley C, Ball K: Assessing visual function in the older driver, *Clin Geriatr Med* **9**:389–401 (1993).

26. Ball K, Owsley C: Identifying correlates of accident involvement for the older driver, *Human Factors* **33**(5):583–596 (1991).

27. Steinfeld E, Tomita M, Mann W, DeGlopper W: Use of passenger vehicles by older people with disabilities, *Occup Ther J Res* **19**(3):155–186 (1999).

41

Tools for Studying Novel Proactive Healthcare Applications for Places of Living

Stephen Intille and Kent Larson
Massachusetts Institute of Technology

41.1 INTRODUCTION

With aging baby boomers, powerful demographic pressures will cause the US healthcare system to become increasing overburdened. Treatment of conditions such as obesity, type 2 diabetes, and congestive heart failure are particularly challenging because of their high personal and societal cost and the lack of effective strategies for their prevention. The disorders are best addressed by helping people live healthier lives through better diet, exercise, and medication adherence in the context of daily life, but medical professionals seldom have the time, tools, or financial incentives to focus on preventive care. Moreover, in the United States, the traditional medical establishment has little or no collective financial incentive to help people stay healthy *before* they get sick. Some industry followers have gone so far as to claim that the US medical system is primarily one of *sick* care, not *health*care, because the medical community reacts to short-term medical crises that go undetected as they develop.

There is a general agreement that a problem exists, but no consensus on how to maintain and improve quality of care while controlling spiraling costs. Our research group at MIT believes that solutions may be found by developing a new model for

---

The Engineering Handbook of Smart Technology for Aging, Disability, and Independence,
Edited by A. Helal, M. Mokhtari and B. Abdulrazak
Copyright © 2008 John Wiley & Sons, Inc.

healthcare that shifts the center of gravity of healthcare from crisis reaction to prevention; from the clinic to the home, from specialized devices to consumer electronics, from expensive procedures to proactively encouraging healthy behaviors, and from a reliance on reimbursement to consumer pay.

Prior to this century, the medical system was largely based in the home. Physicians lived in the communities they served, saw their future patients regularly, and traveled to homes to treat their patients when they got sick. As medicine modernized, the home was relegated to a place that was abruptly left when one got sick for the presumed safety of the hospital and other institutional medical environments. While this dramatically improved acute care and enabled a host of highly effective procedures, it also helped to disconnect healthcare from daily life and a focus on wellness and prevention.

Today, healthcare is beginning to migrate from the hospital back to the home, driven in large part by an effort by insurers to cut costs by minimizing expensive hospital stays. New technologies are helping to make this possible. Technologies may also play a role in reducing costs of traditional care by reducing the cost of expert care. Of most interest to our group, these new technologies may create entirely new ways of delivering tailored health services in the context of everyday life [1].

Our research group has been investigating how emerging sensing and user interface technologies could be used for preventive healthcare in the home. We have approached this problem with a multidisciplinary perspective, engaging researchers in medicine, engineering, human factors, user interface design, and architecture. Our goal has been to propose and pilot-test novel personalized health technologies that might improve the average quality of care of people when they are outside the traditional medical environments of hospitals and clinics. In particular, we have focused on exploiting emerging sensor technologies that may be capable of providing tailored and timely health information, reminders, and encouragement related to diet, exercise, and medication reminders. We hope to show how consumer-based technologies for the home might be used to help people stay healthy and happy as they age.

Research of this type is difficult to test and evaluate. We soon realized that while our laboratory prototypes seemed promising, they would remain little more than compelling "demos" unless we could demonstrate that they were effective in real homes with people going about their normal, complex, and varied activities. We realized that researchers did not have the sophisticated tools necessary to evaluate the viability of, for example, a context-aware medication reminder system. While we could instrument a laboratory to carefully study the technical aspects of a prototype, people do not behave naturally in a lab, and it was nearly impossible to study this use over an extended period of time. We also realized that our lab prototypes often relied on technology such as computer vision with controlled lighting, which would be extremely difficult to deploy in a real home. On the other hand, while we could install a prototype system in a volunteer's home over a longer period of time where behavior would be natural, it was extraordinarily difficult to collect the kind of interaction data that would have been possible in a lab. We often realized that both technical and user interface aspects of the system would have been designed differently if designed for testing in a real home. Moving from prototypes to valid studies was a conceptual and technical hurdle.

Health technology researchers face a related challenge: Funding agencies such as the National Science Foundation typically fund technology development but not evaluation of health systems, while the National Institutes of Health typically requires that larger studies be built on pilot data that demonstrate the viability of the technology behind an approach. Health technology researchers often fall in a gap between the two funding agencies. Tools are needed that can be used to efficiency test ideas and to generate credible pilot data.

To address this challenge, our group has developed two complementary tools that are optimized for the design and testing of novel, just-in-time health interventions and measurement systems in the home setting: the PlaceLab and a set of wireless sensors called MITes (MIT environmental sensors) that can be used as a portable research toolkit for research in nonlab environments. These two tools are now being used together to study topics such as medication adherence and motivating and measuring physical activity in the home setting. In this chapter we provide an overview of these tools and invite other researchers interested in studying home health technologies to contact us to learn more about how they might use them in their own work.

41.2 INTRODUCTION TO THE PLACELAB

The PlaceLab is a "living laboratory." Living laboratories (or live-in laboratories) are naturalistic environments instrumented with sensing and observational technologies used for experimental evaluation [2,3]. The PlaceLab was designed, in part, to conduct studies on proactive home-based technologies. The facility has the instrumentation of a sophisticated research lab while being a comfortable apartment in a residential building where people can live for weeks at a time. It is ideally suited for pilot studies that involve initial testing and evaluation and for iterative hypothesis generation and testing that involved the study of people and their interaction to new technologies and ideas about design (see Fig. 41.1).

The PlaceLab opened in July 2004 in an urban neighborhood in Cambridge, Massachusetts, developed as a joint initiative with TIAX, LLC. Volunteer research participants live in the PlaceLab for days or weeks as their temporary home. Great care has been taken to ensure the privacy of the participants. Data are collected locally and viewed by researchers only after approval by the participant at the end of the study. Sensing devices integrated into the architecture record a detailed description of human activities and environmental conditions. The PlaceLab was designed from the outset to support the collection of rich, multimodal sensor datasets of domestic activity.

We have used the PlaceLab to collect data to support health technology development, but we are also making PlaceLab datasets available to the research community,

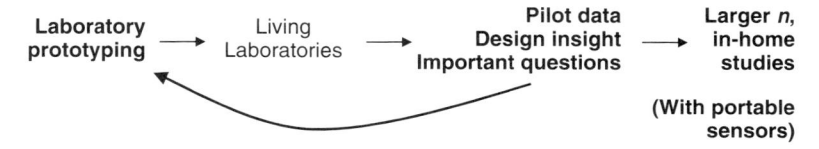

FIGURE 41.1 Living laboratories may help researchers bridge from laboratory testing to larger studies in real homes using portable ubiquitous computing technologies. This is particularly valuable when developing and testing home health technologies, where there may be complex (and unexpected) interaction between the technology and the end users.

including those working on sensor-driven health technologies [4]. Use of the PlaceLab also led directly to a new effort to create portable tools for doing long-term health technology research in any typical homes and generating shared datasets that can be used as a community resource for rapid prototyping of novel context-aware home health technologies.

41.3 PLACELAB OVERVIEW

The PlaceLab is a 1000-ft^2 apartment with a livingroom, dining area, kitchen, small office, bedroom, full bathroom, and half-bathroom (see Fig. 41.2). The interior of the PlaceLab consists of 15 prefabricated and reconfigurable cabinetry components. Each contains a microcontroller, an addressable speaker system, and a network of up to 30 sensors that capture a complete record of audiovisual activity, including information about objects manipulated, environmental conditions, and use of appliances. *All* wired sensors are discreetly integrated into the cabinetry, appliances, and furnishings and fixtures. The wireless sensors utilized are small (4.5 × 4.0 × 1.75 cm) and can be placed inconspicuously on any objects of interest.

New sensors can be easily added to this network as required. The exact list of portable sensors used varies slightly from study to study, depending on the principal goals at that time. As of March 2006, the sensors were as follows. Eighty small, wired switches detect on off and open closed incidents, such as opening of the refrigerator, shutting of the linen closet, or lighting of a stovetop burner. Interior conditions of the apartment are captured using distributed temperature (34), humidity (10), light (5), and barometric pressure (1) sensors. The PlaceLab also features electric current sensors (37), and waterflow (11) and gasflow (2) sensors. Wireless object movement sensors (described later) can be easily taped onto any nonwired objects. Currently about 125 such sensors are installed on objects such as chairs, tables, appliances, brooms, remote controls, large containers, and other objects that people may manipulate [5]. Ten infrared occupancy sensors [6] have also been added.

Participants in the PlaceLab can wear up to three wireless three-axis, 0+/−10-G accelerometers that measure limb motion. A wireless heart rate monitor (using a standard Polar chest strap) can also be worn. Five receivers spread throughout the

FIGURE 41.2 PlaceLab interior, showing interior millwork components, each containing a microcontroller, sensor bus, and a variety of state change sensors, environmental sensors, and communication devices.

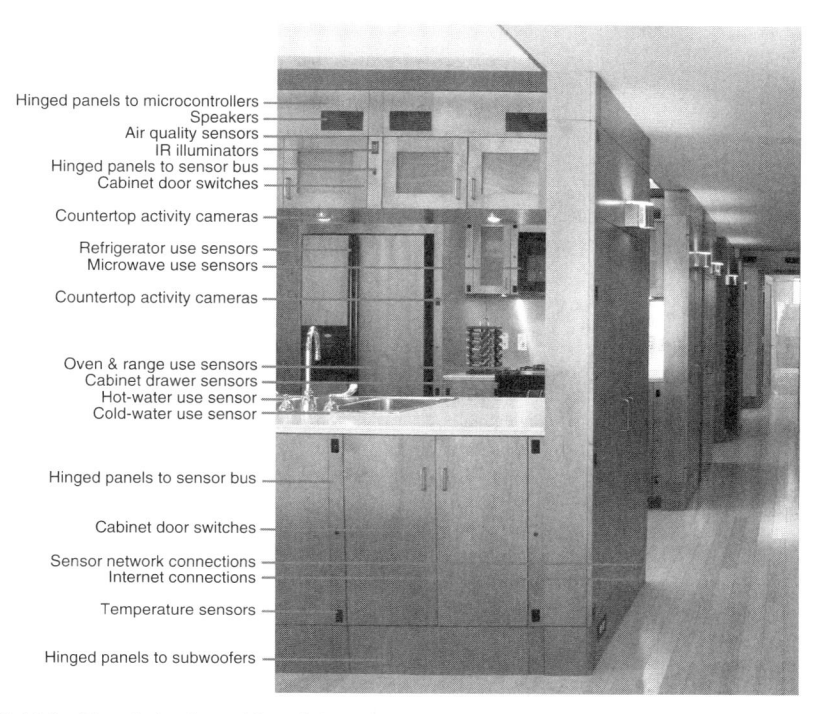

FIGURE 41.3 PlaceLab, viewed from livingroom into kitchen. All observational sensing components are built directly into the cabinetry. Although the sensors are ubiquitous, they become part of the design aesthetic (small black windows). Volunteers who have lived in the PlaceLab have commented that the sensors are easily overlooked.

apartment collect all wireless object motion, accelerometer, and heart rate data sent via the MITes wireless sensors [5]. Nine infrared cameras, 9 color cameras, and 18 microphones are distributed throughout the apartment in cabinet components and above working surfaces, such as the office desk and kitchen counters.

Eighteen computers use image-processing algorithms to select the four videostreams and one audiostream that may best capture an occupant's behavior, based on motion and the camera layout in the environment. Two other computers synchronize the audiovisual datastreams with the other sensor data and save all data to a single portable disk drive. Figure 41.3 shows the location of some of the sensors in cabinetry, and Figure 41.4 shows the location of some sensors on the floorplan. More technical details of the PlaceLab's sensor infrastructure are described elsewhere [4,7].

41.4 LIVING LABS: COMPLEMENTING EXISTING TOOLS AND METHODS FOR STUDYING PROACTIVE HEALTH APPLICATIONS

A key motivation for the creation of the PlaceLab arose from our prior work developing context detection algorithms in traditional laboratory settings. Controlled laboratory studies allowed dense sensor installation useful for the study of behavior and development of new context-aware algorithms, but simulated rooms or short stays severely constrained

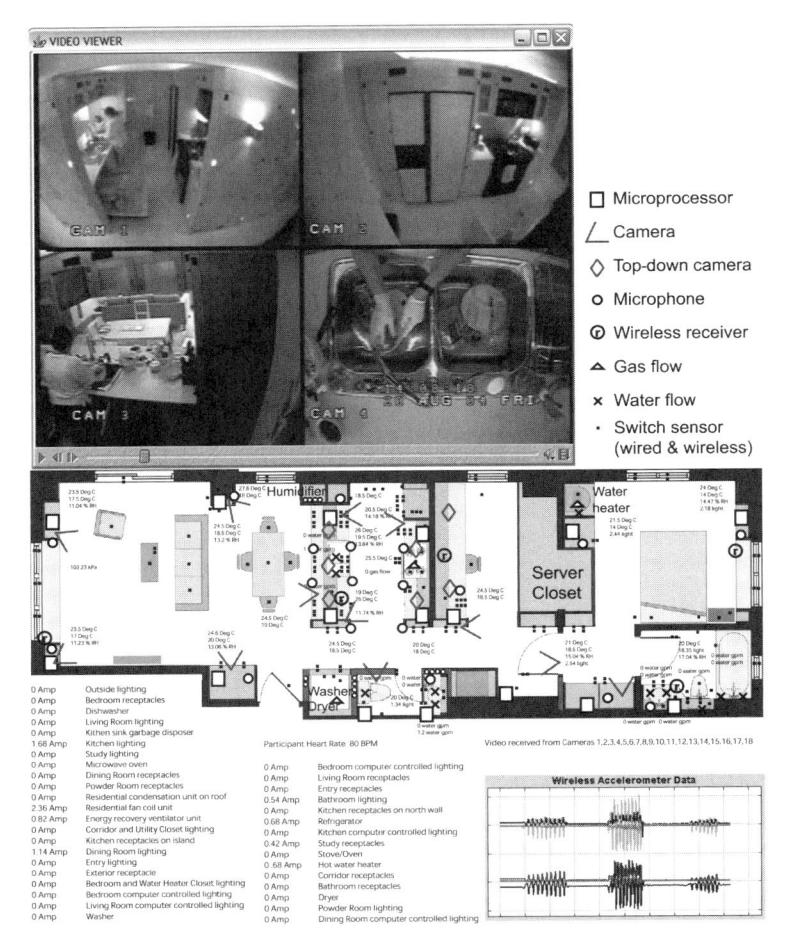

FIGURE 41.4 *A data visualization tool for the PlaceLab and a floorplan indicating the location of most sensors described in the text. Data from two wireless three-axis accelerometers outputting data at 67 Hz are also represented. The display shows the four views that were automatically selected from the 18 possible videostreams, using computer vision processing. An annotation tool allows researchers to click on a particular sensor and then see the rest of the data (including video and audio) at the time of that sensor's activation — this may simplify data analysis or searching for particular events of interest in multiple days of data.*

behavior variability. We thought that we needed a resource to bridge the (large) gap from studies in the lab to studies in real homes.

A common criticism of living laboratories such as the PlaceLab is that requiring people to move temporarily out of their own homes will reduce the complexity and variability of the home environment and may have a corresponding effect on the participant's behavior. We agree. However, just because behavior may be altered in some ways does not mean that we will not observe complex and important activity. Despite some limitations, a live-in lab still allows for more natural behavioral observation and data collection on everyday activities such as cooking, socializing, sleeping, cleaning, working from home, and relaxing than can be obtained from short laboratory visits. Our preliminary experiences using the PlaceLab to study novel health interventions suggest this to be true. Activities that present challenges for context detection algorithms—multitasking, interruption, task-switching, use of objects, context-dependent variation of behavior over time, and interaction with other people—have all been observed in the PlaceLab. These problems must be addressed by health monitoring and intervention technologies; otherwise the technologies will not work when deployed outside traditional laboratory settings.

The PlaceLab permits researchers to employ novel self-report strategies that can help the researcher understand not only easily visible behaviors of subjects who stay in the facility but also nonvisible states of mind expressed via self-report. One approach we are using extensively is context-triggered experience sampling [8]. Standard subject self-report with paper or electronic surveys can also be used.

As long as one is cognizant of the limitations of living laboratories, they can be used to complement other tools being used to study behavior in the home.

41.5 PLACELAB DESIGN GOALS

Most living labs built to date consist of relatively typical homes where ubiquitous computing technologies are included, but not in a truly ubiquitous way. Typically, a portion of the environment is wired with a few sensors of interest to the researchers who constructed the facility. Often different parts of the home have completely different technologies and each data type is not synchronized. In practice, individual researchers tend to tweak the highly specialized sensor subsystems as needed for specific projects (e.g., changing lighting and camera views for computer vision, installing directional microphones pointed at specific locations). The benefit of this type of approach is that specialized systems can be rapidly prototyped and tested for use on focused tasks (e.g., memory aids in the kitchen while cooking [9], testing gait recognition [10]).

We have deliberately chosen a different strategy. Each sensor subsystem of the PlaceLab is ubiquitous and consistent throughout the environment, and all data sources are synchronized and recorded in a common format. Our goal was to invest time up front to create a facility that would eventually allow researchers to spend less time custom-tuning sensor subsystems in specific locations and more time studying what might be called the "whole house" problem: how sensor fusion can be used to create useful ubiquitous computing systems, and how user interfaces that respond to multitasking, interruption, and so on can be created and evaluated.

Another key design decision was to focus on quantity and ubiquity of sensing rather than quality of any particular sensor. In part, this decision was justified based on our belief that many context detection tasks are simpler to solve with many distributed sensors and sensor fusion rather than a smaller number of more generalized sensors that require complex interpretation at the sensor itself. Distributed sensors may improve redundancy as well, allowing higher-level reasoning about activity–structure to be more easily encoded in useful representations. For example, promising results have been obtained for recognizing activities in the home using RFID (radio frequency identification) gloves and contact switches superseding the capabilities of most vision systems [11–14]. If deemed necessary, the PlaceLab allows any particular sensor to be easily replaced with a higher-quality version, supporting multiple strategies of investigation simultaneously. Our third key design decision was to create a system that would provide a single, unified, synchronized living laboratory dataset in a format that could be easily provided to other researchers and reused in multiple projects [7].

41.6 RUNNING A PLACELAB STUDY TO EVALUATE A NOVEL HEALTH INTERVENTION

During PlaceLab studies, its researchers and volunteers have no (or extremely limited) face-to-face interaction during the data collection period. Studies ranging from a few hours to 2.5 months have been run since opening in July 2004. The sensor infrastructure operates and saves some data types continuously, even when an official study is not ongoing, which is useful for monitoring system status and conducting environmental condition quality studies (e.g., our partner TIAX is studying topics such as changes in dust mite populations relative to indoor humidity and load balancing among power consuming devices during power outages).

41.6.1 Participants

The PlaceLab is optimized for studies that would benefit from multiday or multiweek observation of single individuals living alone or a couple. (In 2003, 26% of US households consisted of a person living alone [15]). Participants for the initial studies were recruited via electronic mailing lists, posters, and word of mouth. Advertisements contained lines such as "Teach researchers about your everyday life ... help us design better technologies and homes ...." Participants for studies were selected by questionnaires and interviews and ranged in age from 35 to 60 years. Each was compensated about $25 US per day for participation. The participants stated that the primary reason for their participation was a belief that this research could yield long-term social and scientific benefits. A database of interested volunteers has since been created to support future work, including not only individuals but also couples interested in participating together.

There is nothing inherent in the facility that prevents data collection and experimentation on multiple people. By default, the facility saves a single audiovideostream, but by simply adding an additional computer and disk space, one could save additional streams. Even with the current settings, studies that investigate activity recognition algorithms for detecting activity when the home is occupied by more than one individual could be done.

41.6.2 Participant Procedures

In each study, care is taken to ensure that participants maintain ultimate control over their data and that they recognize their right to withdraw from the study at any time for any reason. PlaceLab volunteers are informed of all the sensor locations in the apartment and how the recorded data will be used. Recordings from the PlaceLab are never observed in real-time, so the participants may choose to omit segments of audio, video, and/or sensor readings before releasing their data. Participants are asked to have visitors sign informed-consent forms.

In poststay interviews, participants commented that they quickly acclimated to the PlaceLab and that, despite the ubiquitous sensing, it is a pleasant, comfortable space. For example, one participant offered as evidence of her quick acclimation the fact that she fell asleep on the couch at night watching TV, an activity she thought she could do only in a familiar environment. At first, she was embarrassed to have this behavior captured on video, and she logged that the data from that time should be deleted. However, by the end of her stay, she decided the only data she needed to remove was some audio during personal phone calls. Furthermore, this participant made the PlaceLab more comfortable and personal during her stay by gradually bringing in items from home, including her bedspread, placemats, flower vases, coffee mug and coffeemaker, and, eventually, even her own coffee table. Nearly all PlaceLab subjects to date have expressed an interest in returning for another study; we believe this is a good sign that the facility and the experimental procedures in place establish a high level of comfort despite the ubiquitous sensing.

The behavior of our initial participants raises some issues that must be considered in future work. For example, when wireless object usage sensors [5] are used in the PlaceLab and participants bring new objects, procedures must be established whereby the participants or the researchers add sensors to the new objects. On the basis of the topics being studied at the time, procedures must be established to deal with visits from nonstudy participants and labeling the activities of multiple people.

41.7 MOVING STUDIES INTO MORE HOMES USING SENSOR KITS

Our group is interested not only in testing novel technologies in the PlaceLab but also in the actual homes of subjects. Exploratory studies conducted in the PlaceLab (or facilities like it) may help researchers develop, refine, and evaluate novel health technologies for the home, but at some point the systems must be deployed in more homes. The PlaceLab may help researchers understand which of a large set of possible sensors is the minimum set required when technologies are deployed in other home settings. On the basis of our experiences using the PlaceLab, our group is now creating a portable kit of sensors and observational equipment designed to be rapidly, easily, and robustly deployed in any home for research purposes.

Computing trends such as Moore's law suggest that at some time in the future it will be possible to deploy small and affordable sensors ubiquitously and inconspicuously throughout homes and on the body, perhaps enabling many novel and useful pervasive computing applications. Further, more recent work suggests that many sensors placed throughout a home environment [12,13,16–19] in combination with a few sensors worn on the body [20–22] may permit a system to automatically and unobtrusively recognize everyday activities and states as diverse as cooking, "making tea," ambulation, posture, "in conversation," and vacuuming. The same types of sensors can also be used to study behavior, providing designers and ethnographers with new data-gathering tools.

Despite the promise of pervasive sensing, most researchers today who wish to populate environments such as homes with multimodal sensors are likely to find this to be a difficult and costly (in time and money) endeavor. Past studies have generally been conducted either in homes that were specially (and laboriously) wired with sensors [23,24], in homes wired with a relatively small number of sensors [25], or in controlled laboratory home simulations.

To deploy experiments in a real home, we needed a portable kit of sensors. We were reluctant to invest time in preparing a new sensor kit given the number of systems that exist and the growing number of commercial sensor network products. Popular wireless sensor network platforms available to the research community include Motes in all their varieties (MicaDOT [26], Micaz [27], iMotes [28], tMotes [29], etc.), uParts [30] (previously Smart-Its [31]), ECOs [32], BTnodes [33], and Millennial nodes [34], among many others.

We considered each of the available options. While each of the systems has its strengths, none met our needs. In this section, we explain our goals:

- *Goal 1: Ease of Installation.* Many of the existing platforms were designed to permit multiple sensors to attach to the same wireless transmitter or transceiver. However, making each transmitter multifunctional and expandable adds size, weight, and complexity to the devices. Many use snap-in sensor boards, often with somewhat bulky battery boards (usually based on AA batteries). The iMote snap-in sensor board and battery board, for instance, more than doubles the original node's size and weight. Cumbersome antennas make some of the sensors more difficult to install and greatly increase likelihood of breakage or dislodgement.

- *Goal 2: Ease of Use.* Most wireless sensor network kits have been designed either to demonstrate novel wireless sensor network architectures [26,26,29] or for industrial applications [35]. In practice, some of the systems use generic but difficult to customize operating systems, as well as network and MAC protocols that require nontrivial configuration difficult to customize for researchers who are not experts in networked sensors. Quite often, the use of mesh network topologies that promise self-configuration and unlimited coverage area result in increased cost, complexity, points of failure (due to their research/prototype stage), and degraded battery life during research data collection. Also, existing systems are also not optimized for data collection from multimodal home sensors. Most available sensor network platforms are designed for either event detection from relatively low sampling rate sensors (e.g., Motes, µParts [30], and BTNodes [33]), or data collection from wearable sensors of relatively high sampling rate (e.g., ECOs [32], MIThril [36], iMotes [37]). There do exist some off-the-shelf sensor technologies that have been extensively tested in nonlaboratory settings by researchers in a diverse set of fields. Examples include actigraphs for aggregate measures of onbody acceleration [37,38], and power monitoring in electric devices (Watt's Up Pro [39]). These devices do not provide real-time data wirelessly since they were designed as data loggers. More importantly, there is no easy way to integrate data from these multiple devices without requiring a subject to wear an unacceptably cumbersome amount of gear. Acquiring real-time, synchronized multimodal data simultaneously from low- and high-sampling sensors is difficult with both wearable and in-home sensor systems that can be easily deployed in the field.

- *Goal 3: Adequate Performance in Natural Settings.* Performance parameters such as Tx/Rx (transmit/receive) ranges, battery life, and effects of environmental noise have not been reported in the literature for most of the existing sensor systems. Thus, it is difficult for a pervasive computing researcher to estimate resource needs and design a data collection study. Moreover, most sensor network platforms are either designed for laboratory settings with no robust packaging whatsoever or with bulky packaging for industrial applications.

- *Goal 4: Affordability.* A significant problem with most of the readily available sensor platforms is their high cost to the researcher. Assuming an installation of 200 sensors distributed throughout a home, the market price for a single system can be as high as >$15,000.

Of the existing wireless sensor solutions available as of 2006, the platforms that most closely met our usability and affordability design goals are the ECO system and μParts. ECOs are small (12×12×4.5 mm, no battery), relatively inexpensive (e.g., $57 production price each including a two-axis accelerometer) sensors designed for the particular task of monitoring motion in infants. However, their extremely small form factor results in a limited wireless range of 10.7 m (testing conditions not reported). Furthermore, ECOs do not allow multimodal data collection, just two-axis acceleration. μParts, on the other hand, are a system of small sensor nodes (10×10 mm) designed for settings requiring a high population of relatively low sampling rate sensors. The sensors were designed for low cost applications with a target market price of $36 (including a light, temperature, and a ball switch sensor for motion detection) in quantities of 100. μParts designers made design decisions explicitly to keep the cost of each device down, such as constraining components to a single side of the PCB and placing the battery on the opposite side. A similar strategy has been employed in the design of the MITes.

In summary, researchers who want to deploy large numbers of sensors simultaneously in settings such as homes have limited options for robust, affordable, and well-characterized sensor solutions optimized for longitudinal, nonlaboratory deployments. This observation led to the development of the MITes.

41.8 MITES: A PORTABLE KIT OF SENSORS FOR IN-HOME HEALTH RESEARCH

During prior work installing sensors in homes we identified a set of design goals for a portable sensing kit that could be easily retrofitted in existing homes and used in longitudinal pervasive computing experiments. We could not find an existing hardware platform that met these goals in 2006 and therefore designed and built a sensor system optimized for researcher and subject usability. MITes (MIT environmental sensors) are portable wireless sensors that can be used to collect data on people's activities in nonlaboratory settings such as homes. They were designed by House_n graduate student Emmanuel Munguia Tapia. MITes and the related pattern recognition and visualization tools comprise a subset of the PlaceLab tools. They create a portable toolkit that allows researchers to design longer-term studies with a larger sample size in normal environments. We have used the PlaceLab to test not only the performance characteristics of the MITes (e.g., see Ref. 40) but also health applications that would make use of the sensors and that could be deployed in other homes.

The MITes platform includes six environmental sensor types; five of them are among the most typically needed in ubiquitous and pervasive computing applications [41]: (1) movement using ball, mercury, and reed switches; (2) movement tuned for object usage detection (using acceleration); (3) light; (4) temperature; (5) proximity; and (6) current consumption. The MITes platform also includes five wearable sensors: (1) accelerometers to acquire body motion information, (2) heart rate, (3) ultraviolet radiation exposure, (4) an RFID reader in a wristband form factor, and (5) location beacons. In collaboration with MERL, an infrared occupancy version was also created [6]. All of these sensors can be used simultaneously, and a single receiver acquires the data, which is sent to a PC or mobile computing device for real-time processing. Some of the sensors are shown in Figure 41.5.

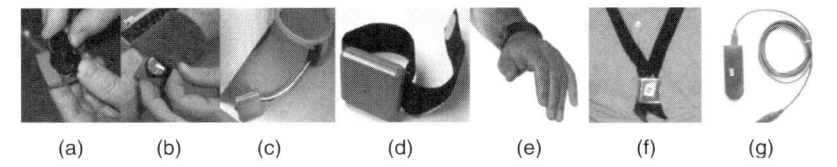

FIGURE 41.5 Images of MITes: (a,b) mobile; (c) current sensing; (d) UV; (e) RFID; (f) location; (g) USB receiver.

Usability criteria for researchers, particularly those interested in sensor-driven pervasive computing research, drove our design decisions. The MITes have been optimized to be easy for researchers and nontechnical home occupants to "install," wear, and use. Battery life has been optimized for conducting longitudinal experiments. A *single* power efficient receiver connected to a mobile device can gather data from a variety of sensor types. Device size has been optimized for comfort, flexibility, and ease of attachment to home objects. Finally, the entire system is designed so that components can be affordably manufactured and assembled by researchers, even in low quantities. The hardware and software specifications for MITes and technical performance criteria can be found in another publication [5].

More recent work by several groups has suggested that very simple and small sensors such as switches [12,13,42] and RFID tags or readers [16] nonobtrusively attached to many objects in an environment may enable a computer system to infer contextual information about the home occupant's movement and activities. Developing and testing such systems, however, requires laborious sensor installations and time-consuming maintenance of complex technical infrastructures. It is not surprising, therefore, that most prior work on home sensing was generally conducted with a single type of sensor tested in a single environment with a single user. Wearable sensor researchers interested in conducting nonlaboratory studies with comfortable, multimodal sensors placed on multiple parts of the body face similar challenges—sensor systems can be difficult to use and maintain in the field for longitudinal studies. Previous studies, even those where sensors have been installed in homes of subjects [12,13,18,19] have often relied on complex installation of switch sensors. A typical switch sensor that must be installed on a cabinet in a volunteer's home has a microprocessor, a reed switch, and a magnet. All three components must be placed on the cabinet in a way that properly activates the reed switch when the cabinet is operated but also in a way that will ensure that the sensor cannot be easily knocked off, cause damage to the cabinetry, or create aesthetic concerns that make the subject uncomfortable. Meeting all these concerns can be challenging, and we have found that a single such sensor takes 5–10 min to install and test. Installation of 200 sensors—a number that might be desired for some types of pervasive computing research in a moderately sized home—could require 16–32 person-hours of effort. This is a tremendous inconvenience to both the researchers and the subject in an experiment. Minimization of installation time, therefore, was a key MITes design goal. One way in which this was achieved was by minimizing points of contact for sensors using accelerometers instead of switch sensors. MITes based on accelerometers are self-contained and sufficiently small so that they can be placed on nearly any household object, and installation requires simply throwing a sensor in a drawer or sticking it with putty to a cabinet door. No multi-point alignment is required, and installation is reduced from 5–10 min to 5–60 s. Installing 200 single-point-of-contact sensors may take a little as 1–2.5 person-hours of effort, a tolerable amount of time for many subjects. When testing these object usage sensors in the PlaceLab, we discovered an additional piezo sensor was also required (see Ref. 40 for details).

Ease of use is just as important as ease of installation. Ease of use can be facilitated by having devices with robust communication protocols and good communication ranges so that additional complex devices that introduce failure points such as routers are not necessary. Sensors should require infrequent battery replacement, and when battery replacement is required, it should be possible for a nontechnical subject to perform this task. Further, it should be easy for a researcher or a subject to add and remove sensors with little or no postconfiguration. Finally, the system must perform well not only in the laboratory but also in natural settings. Devices should also be packaged robustly, since they can be bumped or jostled (especially the wearable ones), and sensors must perform predictably in realistic conditions, with environmental noise and EMI interference from electric household appliances such as vacuum cleaners, microwaves, cordless phones, WLAN, and Bluetooth devices.

The wireless and overall performance of the MITes are evaluated in various publications [5,6,40]. As each MITes type is used in ongoing work on health applications (see Section 41.9), researchers are validating their performance in use in natural environments.

41.9 USING THE PLACELAB AND MITES IN EXPLORATORY HEALTH RESEARCH

We have used the PlaceLab to test our portable sensor kit. One such study led to major revisions in the MITes object usage sensor design (see Ref. 40 for details). In short, the system worked perfectly in the laboratory, but some of our assumptions about the home environment were incorrect and negatively impacted MITes performance prior to a change to the design of the sensors. We have also used the PlaceLab to test the ability of portable sensors to be used for automatic detection of activities of daily living [43], and we have released the datasets used in this work to other researchers interested in automatic contect detection algorithms [4].

Although the PlaceLab has been valuable for testing portable sensor technology and pattern recognition algorithms, we have also used the facility to evaluate pilot systems designed to address two of the great behavior-related health challenges: encouraging physical activity and helping to ensure proper medication adherence.

Since the mid-1980s, substantial epidemiologic research has linked excessive television viewing with both obesity and type 2 diabetes. The average American watches over 4 h of TV per day, and about half want to reduce that time. In addition, millions of Americans wish to lose weight and become more active. Most fail in both of these endeavors. This has become an even greater problem as new forms of media technology entering the home often fundamentally transform the way that people spend their time. In the present day, daily "screen time" with televisions and other entertainment systems continues to rise. Within this climate of escalating media consumption, experts in the medical community have repeatedly voiced concerns about the public health crisis that looms over a largely sedentary US population. House_n researcher Jason Nawyn prototyped and tested "ViTo: a Persuasive Television Remote Control for the Promotion of Health and Well-Being." ViTo is a ubiquitous computing system intended to simultaneously decrease a user's television viewing while increasing that person's frequency and quantity of nonsedentary activities. It made use of the PlaceLab sensing infrastructure to recognize an individual's television viewing and used wearable accelerometers to detect physical movement. The primary user interface consisted of a handheld computing device that serves as a wireless remote control for a television–home theater system, as well as an interface for planning and reviewing daily activity (see Fig. 41.6). This device tracks daily activity patterns and uses theories of behavior modification to nonintrusively persuade users to decrease their daily television viewing while increasing physical activity. In particular, ViTo was designed to be fun, engaging, and positive so that its use could be sustained over time. It uses key points of decision such as turning on TV, channel surfing, and commercial breaks to suggest alternative activities.

Results from a 14-day PlaceLab study evaluation led to ideas for a set of design criteria for persuasive interfaces designed to influence user behavior without inducing a burden of annoyance [44].

House_n graduate student Pallavi Kaushik developed and tested a "Mobile Handheld Intervention for Providing Context-Sensitive Medication Reminders." Most commercial medication reminder/dispenser systems are timer-based, which requires the individual to predefine the time of activities such as waking in the morning, having lunch, and going to bed. These systems are only marginally effective, in part because life is typically more varied than this. Rather than being based on fixed times, this context-sensitive system determines a convenience score based on location and activity of the individual to deliver a carefully tailored reminder. The system consists of three major components: (1) a handheld computing interface for providing reminders, (2) a sensor subsystem integrated into the home environment, and (3) a central server that manages medical tasks and reasons over sensor data in real time. A volunteer participant adhering to a complex regimen of simulated medical tasks is closely observed in a residential research facility. The participant is presented with both context-sensitive reminders and reminders that are scheduled at fixed times during the day (see Fig. 41.7). The degree of adherence to the regimen, the delay after which reminders are acted on, and the participant's own assessment of the usefulness of each reminder (while blinded to the reminder strategy being used), were

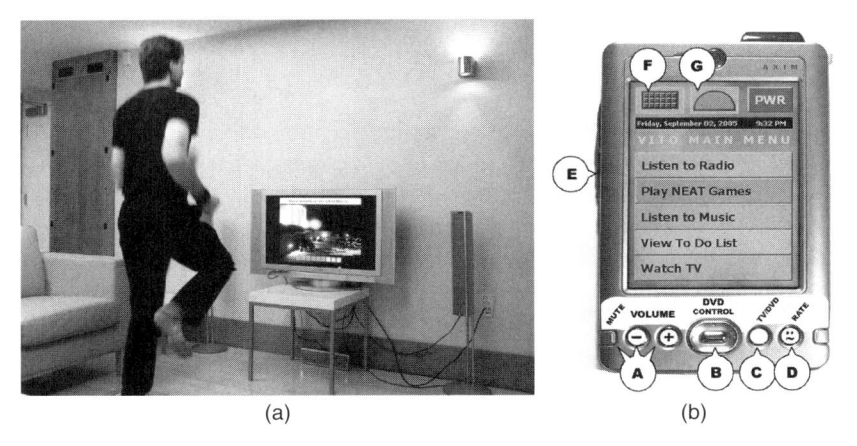

FIGURE 41.6 NEAT (Nonexercise activity thermogenesis) arcade in action. Physical movement, such as running in place, advances game play (a). ViTo main menu: callout markers indicate various buttons and displayed (described in Ref. 44), such as the NEAT physical activity meter and the TV usage meter (b).

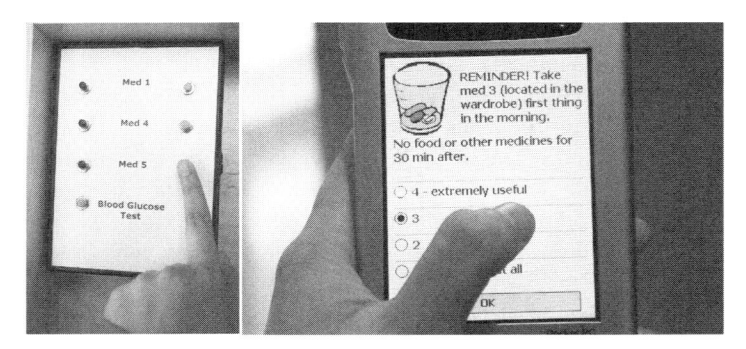

FIGURE 41.7 *Rather than taking actual medication, study participants held down medication buttons to simulate this task. Volunteers also rated the effectiveness of each reminder to allow an analysis of the perceived value.*

evaluated over the course of a 10-day study. This work also led to a set of recommendations about how one might design such a system that it will work in real homes [45].

The PlaceLab has been used primarily for early-stage exploratory pilot studies. MITes are designed for studies in "normal" environments. We have been able to deploy MITes in a variety of research projects by the authors and others. Of particular interest to medical researchers is that they allow the simultaneous measurement of two or more states. For example, medical researchers are using MITes to study the relationship between physical activity and other states, such as heart rate and use of objects in the home (e.g., television). The mobile MITes are being validated by researchers at Stanford Medical School who are reporting excellent performance relative to the state-of-the-art actigraphs used in that field, and they have been used in projects on detecting convenient times to interrupt, the correction of human balance, and feedback systems for rehabilitation, as well as context-awareness and activity recognition. They are being used in two external medical projects where the sensors are worn for days or weeks at a time to enable medical researchers to study the behavior of people in naturalistic settings, and in both cases the mobile MITes are being used in combination with other node types such as heart rate, current flow, and light. The UV MITes were developed for cancer researchers interested in the relationship between sun exposure and physical activity. The proximity MITes are being installed in an office to study behavior in office spaces and to develop real-time recognition of meeting, visiting, and chatting events and create new architecture design tools. Finally, object usage MITes have been used in several research studies in the PlaceLab.

A website with MITes hardware and software specifications provides more detail [32]. Researchers interested in using MITes in their own work should contact the authors. In practice, the greatest barrier to using MITes is ordering the MITes hardware, attaching the specialized sensors, and programming the EEPROM, since the devices are not commercial products.

41.10 CONCLUSION

The technical and administrative complexity of building and operating a residential living laboratory is great, and we therefore expect the number of living laboratories available to ubiquitous computing researchers to be small. However, our pilot testing has already created datasets that we could not have obtained in any other way. These datasets are a detailed record of home behavior synchronized with sensor data that simplifies the annotation of and searching for items of interest and can be used for context detection algorithm development and evaluation. We believe that living laboratories can provide valuable datasets for the ubiquitous computing research community, and in that spirit we are now applying our PlaceLab experience to create a portable system that is easy to copy and using it to acquire datasets from real homes that can be shared among researchers. We are making example data available to the community with the hope that researchers will report how they might use the data in their own work and what additional information would be beneficial. The PlaceLab and portable in-home sensors are not intended to replace other ethnographic research tools and sensor data collection methods, but rather to fill a gap. Living laboratories and portable sensors that can be easily deployed for research in homes may become increasingly important as researchers begin to migrate ubiquitous computing technologies from the traditional laboratory into actual homes.

ACKNOWLEDGMENTS

This work was supported, in part, by National Science Foundation ITR grant 0313065. The PlaceLab is a joint initiative between the MIT House_n Consortium and TIAX, LLC. The authors would like to thank Kenan Sahin, Tyson Lawrence, and other employees of TIAX for their support on PlaceLab development and operation and the PlaceLab participants for sharing their everyday life activities. The infrared occupancy MITes [6] were created by Mitsubishi Electric Research Labs (MERL).

REFERENCES

1. Intille SS: A new research challenge: persuasive technology to motivate healthy aging, *Trans Inform Technol Biomed* **8**:235–237 (2004).
2. Kidd CD, Orr RJ, Abowd GD, Atkeson CG, Essa IA, MacIntyre B, Mynatt E, Starner TE, Newstetter W: "The aware home: A living laboratory for ubiquitous computing research, *Proc 2nd Int Workshop on Cooperative Buildings—CoBuild'99*, 1999.
3. Matsouoka K: Smart house understanding human behaviors: Who did what, where, and when, *Proc 8th World Multi-Conf Systems, Cybernetics, and Informatics,* 2004, Vol. 3, pp 181–185.
4. MIT House_n, *PlaceLab Datasets* (http://architecture.mit.edu/house_n/data/PlaceLab/PlaceLab.htm; accessed 11/15/06).
5. Munguia Tapia E, Intille SS, Lopez L, Larson K: The design of a portable kit of wireless sensors for naturalistic data collection, in Fishkin KP, Schiele B, Nixon P, Quigley A, eds, *Proc PERVASIVE 2006*, Springer-Verlag, Berlin, 2006, Vol LNCS 3968, pp 117–134.
6. Wren C, Munguia-Tapia E: Toward scalable Activity recognition for sensor networks, in Hazas M, Krumm J, Strang T, eds, *Proc 2nd Int Workshop in Location and Context-Awareness (LoCA '06)*, Springer, Berlin, 2006, Vol 3987, pp 168–185.
7. Intille SS, Larson K, Munguia Tapia E, Beaudin J, Kaushik P, Nawyn J, Rockinson R: Using a live-in laboratory for ubiquitous computing research, in Fishkin KP, Schiele B, Nixon P, Quigley A, eds, *Proc PERVASIVE 2006*, Springer-Verlag, Berlin, 2006, Vol **3968**, pp 349–365.

8. Intille SS, Rondoni J, Kukla C, Anacona I, Bao L: A context-aware experience sampling tool, *Proc CHI '03 Extended Abstracts on Human Factors in Computing Systems*, ACM Press, New York, 2003, pp 972–973.
9. Tran Q, Calcaterra G, Mynatt E: Cook's Collage: Memory aid display for cooking, *Proc HOIT 2005*, 2005.
10. Dockstader SL, Berg MJ, Tekalp AM: Stochastic kinematic modeling and feature extraction for gait analysis, *IEEE Trans Image Process* **12**:962–976 (2003).
11. Philipose M, Fishkin KP, Perkowitz M, Patterson DJ, Fox D, Kautz H, Hähnel D: Inferring activities from interactions with objects, *IEEE Pervasive Comput* **3**:50–57 (2004).
12. Wilson D: Simultaneous tracking and activity recognition (STAR) using many anonymous, binary sensors, *Proc 3rd Int Conf Pervasive Computing (Pervasive '05)*, Springer-Verlag, Berlin, 2005, pp 62–83.
13. Munguia Tapia E, Intille SS, Larson K: Activity recognition in the home setting using simple and ubiquitous sensors, in Ferscha A, Mattern F, eds, *Proc PERVASIVE 2004*, Springer-Verlag, Berlin, 2004, vol. LNCS 3001, pp 158–175.
14. Wilson DH, Atkeson C: Simultaneous tracking & activity recognition (STAR) using many anonymous, binary sensors, *Proc PERVASIVE 2005*, Springer-Verlag, Berlin, 2005.
15. Fields J: *America's Families and Living Arrangements: 2003*, US Census Bureau, Current Population Reports, P20-553, Washington, DC, Nov 2004.
16. Philipose M, Fishkin KP, Perkowitz M, Patterson DJ, Hahnel D, Fox D, Kautz H: Inferring activities from interactions with objects, *IEEE Pervasive Comput Mag* **3** (2004).
17. Perkowitz M, Philipose M, Patterson DJ, and Fishkin K: Mining models of human activities from the web, *Proc 13th Int World Wide Web Conf* (*WWW '04*), New York, 2004.
18. Munguia-Tapia E, Intille SS, Larson K: Activity recognition in the home setting using simple and ubiquitous sensors, in Heidelberg B, ed, *Proc PERVASIVE 2004*, Springer-Verlag, Heidelberg, 2004, Vol LNCS 300, pp 158–175.
19. Wilson D: Simultaneous tracking & activity recognition (STAR) using many anonymous, binary sensors, *Proc 3rd Int Conf Pervasive Computing* (*Pervasive '05*), Munich, Germany, 2005.
20. Mantyjarvi JHJ, Seppanen T: Recognizing human motion with multiple acceleration sensors., *Proc IEEE Int Conf Systems, Man, and Cybernetics.*, 2001, pp 747–752.
21. Lee S-W, Mase K: Activity and location recognition using wearable sensors, *IEEE Pervasive Comput* **1**:24–32 (July–Sept 2002).
22. Bao L, Intille SS: Activity recognition from user-annotated acceleration data, in Ferscha A, Mattern F, eds, *Proc PERVASIVE 2004*, Springer-Verlag, Berlin, 2004, Vol LNCS 3001, pp 1–17.
23. Mozer M: The neural network house: An environment that adapts to its inhabitants, *Proc AAAI Spring Symp Intelligent Environments*, Menlo Park, CA, AAAI Press, 1998, pp 110–114.
24. Cook DJ, Youngblood M, Heierman E, Gopalratnam K, Rao S, Litvin A, Khawaja F: MavHome: An agent-based smart home, *Proc Conf Pervasive Computing*, 2003, pp 521–524.
25. Alwan M, Dalal S, Mack D, Kell S, Turner B, Leachtenauer J, Felder R: Impact of monitoring technology in assisted living: Outcome pilot, *IEEE Trans Inform Technol Biomed* **10**:192–198 (2006).
26. Crossbow Technology Inc: *MICA2DOT Wireless Microsensor Mote*, 2005 (http://www.xbow.com/Products/Product_pdf_files/Wireless_pdf/MICA2DOT_Datasheet.pdf; accessed 10/03/05).
27. Crossbow Technology Inc: *MICAz Wireless Measurement System*, 2005 (http://www.xbow.com/Products/Product_pdf_files/Wireless_pdf/MICAz_Datasheet.pdf; accessed 10/03/05).

28. Kling RM: Intel Mote: An enhanced sensor network node, *Proc Int Workshop on Advanced Sensors, Structural Health Monitoring and Smart Structures*, Keio Univ, Japan, 2003.
29. Moteiv: *tmote Sky: Ultra Low Power IEEE 802.15.4 Compliant Wireless Sensor Module*, 2005 (http://www.moteiv.com/products/docs/tmote-sky-datasheet.pdf; accessed 2005).
30. Beigl M, Decker C, Krohn A, Riedel T, Zimmer T: uParts: low cost sensor networks at scale, *Proc 7th Int Conf Ubiquitous Computing (UBICOMP '05)*, Springer-Verlag, Berlin, 2005.
31. Beigl M, Gellersen H: Smart-Its: An embedded platform for smart objects, *Proc Smart Objects Conf (sOc '03)*, Grenoble, France, 2003, pp 15–17.
32. Park C, Liu J, Chou PH: Eco: An ultra-compact low-power wireless sensor node for real-time motion monitoring, *Proc 4th Int Conf Information Processing in Sensor Networks (IPSN '05)*, Los Angeles, CA, 2005, pp 398–403.
33. Beutel J, Kasten O, Mattern F, Romer K, Siegemund F, Thiele L: Prototyping wireless sensor applications with BTnodes, *Proc 1st European Workshop on Sensor Networks (EWSN '04)*, Zurich, Switzerland, 2004, pp 323–338.
34. Net M: *MeshScape 2.4 GHz Modules and Assemblies*, 2005 (http://www.millennialnet.com/products/meshscape24.asp; accessed 10/03/05).
35. Crossbow Technology Inc: *MSP-SYS MSP Mote Developer's System*, 2005 (http://www.xbow.com/Products/Product_pdf_files/Wireless_pdf/MSP-Sys_Datasheet.pdf; accessed 10/03/05).
36. DeVaul R, Sung M, Gips J, Pentland A: MIThril 2003: Applications and architecture, *Proc 7th Int Symp Wearable Computers (ISWC '03)*, White Plains, NY, 2003.
37. Kling R, Adler R, Huang J, Hummel V, Nachman L: The Intel iMote: Using Bluetooth in sensor networks, *Proc 2nd Int Conf Embedded Networked Sensor Systems*, ACM, 2003. Baltimore, MD, ACM, 2003, p 318.
38. MTI Actigraph: *GT1M Actigraph*, 2005 (http://mtiactigraph.com/; accessed 10/03/05).
39. Electronic Educational Devices: *Watts Up? Pro KWH Meter Review*, 2005 (http://www.doubleed.com/powertear.pdf; accessed 10/03/05).
40. Tapia EM, Intille SS, Larson K: Portable wireless sensors for object usage sensing in the home: Challenges and practicalities, *Proc European Ambient Intelligence Conf 2007*, LNCS 4794 Heidelberg: Springer-Verlag, Berlin, 2007, Vol LNCS 4794, pp 19–37.
41. Beigl M, Krohn A, Zimmer T, Decker C: Typical sensors needed in ubiquitous and pervasive computing, in *Proc 1st Int Workshop on Networked Sensing Systems (INSS '04)*, 2004, pp 153–158.
42. Barger T, Brown D, Alwan M: Health status monitoring through analysis of behavioral patterns, *Proc 8th Congress of the Italian Association for Artificial Intelligence (AI*IA) on Ambient Intelligence*, Springer-Verlag, Berlin, 2003.
43. Logan B, Healey J, Matthai Philipose M, Munguia Tapia E, Intille S: A long-term evaluation of sensing modalities for activity recognition, *Proc Int Conf Ubiquitous Computing*, Springer-Verlag, Berlin, 2007, Vol LNCS 4717, pp 483–500.
44. Nawyn J, Intille SS, Larson K: Embedding behavior modification strategies into consumer electronic devices, in Dourish P, Friday A, eds, *Proc UbiComp 2006*, Springer-Verlag, Berlin, 2006, Vol LNCS 4206, pp 297–314.
45. Kaushik P, Intille SS, Larson K: User-adaptive reminders for home-based medical tasks. A case study, *Methods of Information in Medicine*, Vol **147**, pp 203–207, 2008.

42

Algorithms for Smart Spaces

Diane J. Cook
Washington State University, Pullman

G. Michael Youngblood and Gaurav Jain
University of Texas at Arlington

To many people, home is a sanctuary. For those people who need special medical care, they may need to be pulled out of their homes to meet their medical needs. As the population ages, the percentage of people in this group is increasing and the effects are expensive as well as unsatisfying. We hypothesize that many people with disabilities can lead independent lives in their own homes with the aid of at-home automated assistance and health monitoring. In order to accomplish this, robust methods must be developed to collect relevant data and process them dynamically and adaptively to detect and/or predict threatening long-term trends or immediate crises. The main objective of this chapter is to describe techniques for using agent-based smart home technologies to provide this at-home health monitoring and assistance. Inhabitant modeling and automation algorithms that are found in smart environments can also provide remote health monitoring for caregivers. Specifically, we address the following technological challenges: (1) identifying lifestyle trends, (2) detecting anomalies in current data, and (3) designing a reminder assistance system. We discuss one such smart environment implementation in the MavHome project and present results from testing these techniques in simulation and with volunteers in an apartment setting.

42.1 INTRODUCTION AND MOTIVATION

Since the beginning, people have lived in places that provide shelter and basic comfort and support, but as society and technology advance there is a growing interest in improving the intelligence of the environments in which we live and work. The MavHome (*m*anaging an *a*daptive *v*ersatile *home*) project is focused on providing such environments [1]. We take the viewpoint of treating an environment as an intelligent agent,

---

The Engineering Handbook of Smart Technology for Aging, Disability, and Independence,
Edited by A. Helal, M. Mokhtari and B. Abdulrazak
Copyright © 2008 John Wiley & Sons, Inc.

which perceives the state of the environment using sensors and acts on the environment using device controllers in a way that can optimize a number of different goals, including maximizing comfort of the inhabitants, minimizing the consumption of resources, and maintaining safety of the environment and its inhabitants. In this chapter we discuss methods by which we can adapt a smart home environment such as MavHome to perform health monitoring and assistance for persons with disabilities and for aging adults.

As Lanspery et al. [2] state, "For most of us, the word 'home' evokes powerful emotions [and is] a refuge." They note that older adults and people with disabilities want to remain in their homes even when their conditions worsen and the home cannot sustain their safety. In a national survey, researchers found that 71% of the respondents felt strongly that they wanted to remain in their current residence as long as possible, and another 12% were somewhat likely to remain there [3]. Nearly 25% of the respondents expected that they or a member of their household would have problems getting around their house in the next 5 years. Of these respondents, 86% stated that they had made at least one modification to their homes to make them easier to live in, and nearly 70% believed that the modifications would allow them to live in the current homes longer than would have otherwise been possible. A separate study supported these results and found that the most common modifications were an easy-to-use climate control system and a personal alert system.

Zola [4] maintains that the problems of aging and disability are converging. Improvements in medical care are resulting in increased survival into old age, thus problems of mobility, vision, hearing, and cognitive impairments will increase [5,6]. As the baby boomers enter old age, this trend will be magnified. By 2040, 23% will fall into the 65 + category [2]. An American Association of Retired Persons (AARP) report [3,7] strongly encourages increased funding for home modifications that can keep older adults with disabilities independent in their own homes.

While use of technology can be expensive, it may be more cost effective than the alternative [8]. Nursing home care is generally paid either out of pocket or by Medicaid. Typical nursing home costs are about $40,000 a year, and the $197 billion of free care offered by family members comes at the sacrifice of independence and job opportunities by the family caregivers.

Our goal is to assist the elderly and individuals with disabilities by providing smart space capabilities that will monitor health trends and assist in the inhabitant's day to day activities in their own homes. The result will save money for the individuals, their families, and the state.

42.2 OVERVIEW OF THE MAVHOME SMART HOME

Since the beginning, people have lived in places that provide shelter and basic comfort and support, but as society and technology advance, there is a growing interest in improving the intelligence of the environments in which we live and work. We define an *intelligent environment* as one that is "able to acquire and apply knowledge about its inhabitants and their surroundings in order to adapt to the inhabitants and meet the goals of comfort and efficiency" [9]. Smart space algorithms cover a broad spectrum of technologies, including prediction, decisionmaking, robotics, wireless and sensor networking, multimedia, mobile computing, and databases. With these capabilities, the space can adaptively control many aspects of the environment such as climate, water, lighting, maintenance, and multimedia entertainment. Intelligent automation of these activities can reduce the amount of interaction required by inhabitants, reduce energy consumption and other potential wastages, and provide a mechanism for ensuring the health and safety of the environment occupants [10].

As the need for automating these personal environments grows, so does the number of researchers investigating this topic. Researchers have designed interactive conference rooms, offices, kiosks, and furniture with seamless integration between heterogeneous devices and user applications in order to facilitate collaborative work environments [11–14]. Abowd and Mynatt's work [15] focuses on ease of interaction with a smart space, and work such as the Gator Tech smart house [16] focuses on development of devices to support elder care. Research on smart environments has become so popular that NIST has identified seamless integration of mobile components into smart spaces as a target area for identifying standardizations and performance measurements [17], although no performance metrics have yet been produced by the group.

Mozer's adaptive home [18] uses neural network and reinforcement learning to control lighting, heating–ventilation–air conditioning (HVAC), and water temperature to reduce operating cost. In contrast, the approach taken by the iDorm project [19] is to use a fuzzy expert system to learn rules that replicate inhabitant interactions with devices, but will not find an alternative control strategy that improves on manual control for considerations such as energy expenditure.

These projects have laid a foundation for the MavHome project. However, unlike related projects, we learn a decision policy to control an environment in a way that optimizes a variety of possible criteria, including minimizing manual interactions, improving operating efficiency, and ensuring inhabitant health and safety. We also ensure that our software need not be redesigned as new devices are registered, new spaces are tested, or new inhabitants move into the environment. To accomplish this goal, our intelligent environment must harness the features of multiple heterogeneous learning algorithms in order to identify repeatable behaviors, predict inhabitant activity, and learn a control strategy for a large, complex environment.

We take the viewpoint of treating an environment as an intelligent agent, which perceives the state of the environment using sensors and acts on the environment using device controllers in a way that can maximize the comfort of the inhabitants; minimize the consumption of resources; and maintain safety, security, and privacy of the environment and its inhabitants.

The MavHome architecture shown in Figure 42.1 consists of cooperating layers [9,20]. Perception is a bottom–up process. Sensors monitor the environment using physical components (e.g., sensors) and make information available through the interface layers. The database stores this information, while other information components process the raw information into more useful knowledge (e.g., patterns, predictions). New information is presented to the decisionmaking applications (top layer) on request or by prior arrangement. Action execution flows top–down. The decision action is communicated to the services layer, which records the action and communicates it to the physical components. The physical layer performs the action using powerline control, and other automated hardware, thus changing the state of the world and triggering a new perception.

All of the MavHome components are implemented and are being tested in two physical environments: the MavLab workplace environment and an on-campus apartment.

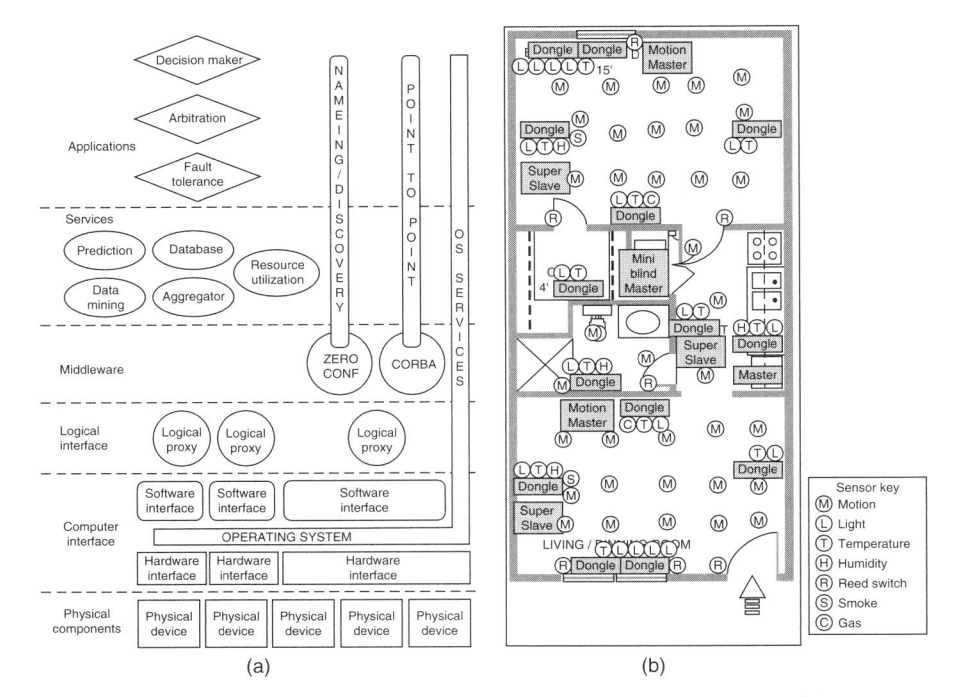

FIGURE 42.1 MavHome architecture (a) and MavPad sensor layout (b).

Powerline control automates all lights and appliances, as well as HVAC, fans, and miniblinds. Perception of light, humidity, temperature, smoke, gas, motion, and switch settings is performed through a sensor network developed inhouse. Inhabitant localization is performed using passive infrared sensors yielding a detection rate of 95% accuracy [21].

Communication between high-level components is performed using common object request broker architecture (CORBA), and each component registers its presence using zero configuration (ZeroConf) technologies. Implemented services include a PostgreSQL database that stores sensor readings, prediction components, data-mining components, and logical proxy aggregators. Resource utilization services monitor current utility consumption rates and provide usage estimates and consumption queries.

MavHome is designed to optimize a number of alternative functions, but for this evaluation we focus on minimization of manual interactions with devices. The MavHome components are fully implemented and are automating the environments shown in Figure 42.2 [22]. The MavLab environment contains work areas, cubicles, a break area, a lounge, and a conference room. MavLab is automated using 54 X-10 controllers, and the current state is determined using light, temperature, humidity, motion, and door/seat status sensors. The MavPad is an on-campus apartment hosting a full-time student occupant. MavPad is automated using 25 controllers and provides sensing for light, temperature, humidity, leak detection, vent position, smoke detection, carbon monoxide detection, motion, and door/window/seat status sensors. Figure 42.1 shows the MavPad sensor layout.

FIGURE 42.2 The MavLab (a) and MavPad (b) environments.

42.3 CORE TECHNOLOGIES

To automate our smart environment, we collect observations of manual inhabitant activities and interactions with the environment. We then mine sequential patterns from these data using a sequence mining algorithm. Next, we predict the inhabitant's upcoming actions using observed historical data. Finally, a hierarchical Markov model is created using low-level state information and high-level sequential patterns, and is used to learn an action policy for the environment. Figure 42.3 shows how these components work together to improve the overall performance of the smart environment. Here we describe the learning algorithms that play a role in this approach.

42.3.1 Mining Sequential Patterns Using ED

In order to minimize resource usage, maximize comfort, and adapt to inhabitants, we rely on machine learning techniques for automated discovery, prediction, and decisionmaking. A smart home inhabitant typically interacts with various devices as part of his/her routine activities. These interactions may be considered as a sequence of events, with some inherent pattern of recurrence. Agrawal and Srikant [23] pioneered work in mining

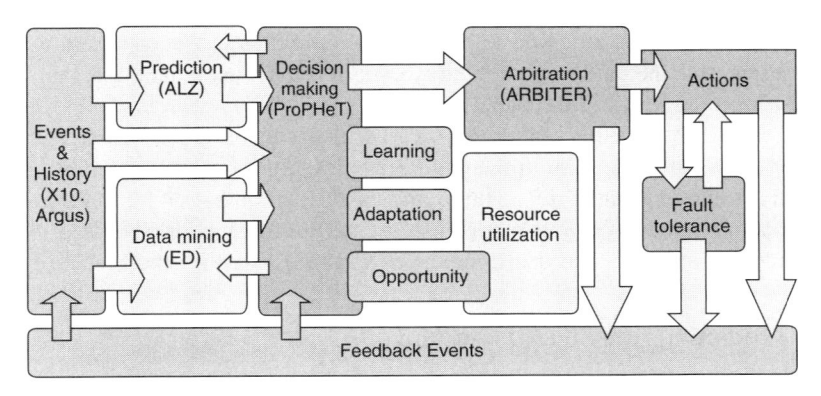

FIGURE 42.3 Integration of AI techniques into MavHome architecture.

sequential patterns from time-ordered transactions, and our work is loosely modeled on this approach.

Typically, each inhabitant–home interaction event is characterized as a triple consisting of the device manipulated, the resulting change that occurred in that device, and the time of interaction. We move a window in a single pass through the history of events or inhabitant actions, looking for episodes (sequences) within the window that merit attention. Candidate episodes are collected within the window together with frequency information for each candidate. Candidate episodes are evaluated, and the episodes with values above a minimum acceptable compression amount are reported. The window size can be selected automatically using the size that achieves the best compression performance over a sample of the input data.

When evaluating candidate episodes, the episode discovery (ED) algorithm [24] looks for patterns that minimize the description length of the input stream, O, using the minimum description length (MDL) principle [25]. The MDL principle targets patterns that can be used to minimize the description length of a database by replacing each instance of the pattern with a pointer to the pattern definition. The description length (DL) of the input sequence using the set of patterns Θ is thus defined as $DL(O, \Theta) = DL(O|\Theta) + DL(\Theta)$, or the description length of the input sequence compressed using Θ plus the description length of the patterns Θ. The compression of the corresponding encoding can be computed as $\Gamma(\Theta|O) = DL(O)/DL(O, \Theta)$. With this formula, it is easily seen that finding the model that yields the minimum description length of the data is equivalent to finding the patterns that provide the largest compression value, or $MDL(O) = \mathrm{argmax}_\Theta \{\Gamma(\Theta|O)\}$.

Our MDL-based evaluation measure thus identifies patterns that balance frequency and length. Periodicity (daily, alternate-day, weekly occurrence) of episodes is detected using autocorrelation and included in the episode description. If the instances of a pattern are highly periodic (occur at predictable intervals), the exact timings do not need to be encoded, (just the pattern definition with periodicity information) and the resulting pattern yields even greater compression. Although event sequences with minor deviations from the pattern definition can be included as pattern instances, the deviations need to be encoded, and the result thus increases the overall description length. ED reports the patterns and encodings that yield the greatest MDL value.

Deviations from the pattern definition in terms of missing events, extra events, or changes in the regularity of the occurrence add to the description length because extra bits must be used to encode the change, thus lowering the value of the pattern. The larger the potential amount of description length compression a pattern provides, the more representative the pattern is of the history as a whole, and thus the potential impact that results from automating the pattern is greater.

In this way, ED identifies patterns of events that can be used to better understand the nature of inhabitant activity in the environment. Once the data are compressed using discovered results, ED can be run again to find an abstraction hierarchy of patterns within the event data. As the following sections show, the results can also be used to enhance performance of predictors and decisionmakers that automate the environment.

42.3.2 Predicting Activities Using ALZ

To predict inhabitant activities, we borrow ideas from text compression, in this case the LZ78 compression algorithm [26]. By predicting inhabitant actions, the home can

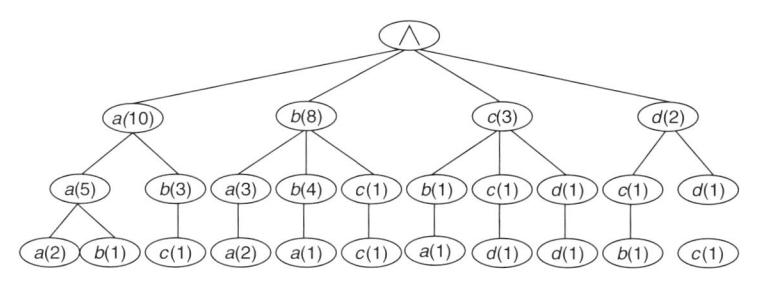

FIGURE 42.4 Trie formed by ALZ parsing.

automate or improve on anticipated events that inhabitants would normally perform in the home. Well-investigated text compression methods have established that good compression algorithms also make good predictors. According to information theory, a predictor with an order (size of history used) that grows at a rate approximating the entropy rate of the source is an optimal predictor. Other approaches to prediction or inferring activities often use a fixed context size to build the model or focus on one attribute such as motion [27,28].

LZ78 incrementally processes an input string of characters, which in our case is a string representing the history of device interactions, and stores them in a trie. The algorithm parses the string $x_1, x_2, \ldots, x_i$ into substrings $w_1, w_2, w_{c(i)}$ such that for all $j > 0$, the prefix of the substring w_j is equal to some w_i for $1 < i < j$. Thus, when parsing the sequence of symbols *aaababbbbbaabccddcbaaaa*, the substring *a* is created, followed by *aa*, *b*, *ab*, *bb*, *bba*, and so forth.

Our active-LeZi (ALZ) algorithm enhances the LZ78 algorithm by recapturing information lost across phrase boundaries. Frequency of symbols is stored along with phrase information in a trie, and data from multiple context sizes are combined to provide the probability for each potential symbol, or inhabitant action, as being the next one to occur. In effect, ALZ gradually changes the order of the corresponding model that is used to predict the next symbol in the sequence. As a result, we gain a better convergence rate to optimal predictability as well as achieve greater predictive accuracy. Figure 42.4 shows the trie formed by the active-LeZi parsing of the input sequence *aaababbbbbaabccddcbaaaa*.

To perform prediction, ALZ calculates the probability of each symbol (inhabitant action) occurring in the parsed sequence, and predicts the action with the highest probability. To achieve optimal predictability, we use a mixture of all possible higher-order models (phrase sizes) when determining the probability estimate. Specifically, we incorporate the *prediction by partial match* strategy of *exclusion* [29] to gather information from all available context sizes in assigning the next symbol its probability value.

We initially evaluated the ability of ALZ to perform inhabitant action prediction on synthetic data on the basis of six embedded tasks with 20% noise. In this case the predictive accuracy converges to 86%. Real data collected from six students in the MavLab for one month was much more chaotic, and on these data ALZ reached a predictive performance of 30% (although it outperformed other methods). However, when we combine ALZ and ED by performing predictions only when the current activity is part of a sequential pattern identified by ED, ALZ performance increases by 14% [30,31].

42.3.3 Decisionmaking Using ProPHeT

In our final learning step, we employ reinforcement learning to generate an automation strategy for the intelligent environment. To apply reinforcement learning, the underlying system (i.e., the house and its inhabitants) could be modeled as a *markov decision process* (MDP). This can be described by a four-tuple $<S, A, Pr, R>$, where S is a set of system states, A is the set of available actions, and $R : S \rightarrow R$ is the reward that the learning agent receives for being in a given state. The behavior of the MDP is described by the transition function, $Pr : S \times A \times S \rightarrow [0, 1]$, representing the probability with which action a_t executed in state s_t leads to state s_{t+1}.

With the increasing complexity of tasks being addressed, more recent work in decisionmaking under uncertainty has popularized the use of *partially observable markov decision processes* (POMDPs). Many published hierarchical extensions have allowed for the partitioning of large domains into a tree of manageable POMDPs [32,33]. Research has shown that strategies for new tasks can be learned faster if policies for subtasks are already available [34]. Although a hierarchical POMDP (HPOMDP) is appropriate for an intelligent environment domain, current approaches generally require a priori construction of the hierarchical model. Unlike other approaches to creating a hierarchical model, our decision learner, ProPHeT, actually automates model creation by using the ED-mined sequences to represent the nodes in the higher levels of the model hierarchy.

The lowest-level nodes in our model represent a single event observed by ED. Next, ED is run multiple iterations on these data until no more patterns can be identified, and the corresponding abstract patterns comprise the higher-level nodes in the Markov model. The higher-level *task* nodes point to the first event node for each permutation of the sequence that is found in the environment history. Vertical transition values are labeled with the fraction of occurrences for the corresponding pattern permutation, and horizontal transitions are seeded using the relative frequency of transitions from one event to the next in the observed history. As a result, the n-tiered hierarchical model is thus learned from collected data. An example hierarchical model constructed from MavHome test data is shown on the left in Figure 42.5a.

Given the current event state and recent history, ED supplies membership probabilities of the state in each patterns identified. Using this information along with the ALZ-predicted next action, ProPHeT maintains a belief state and selects the highest-utility action.

To learn an automation strategy, the agent explores the effects of its decisions over time and uses this experience within a temporal-difference reinforcement learning framework [35] to form control policies that optimize the expected future reward. Using the structure defined earlier, the utility value, $Q(s, a)$, is incrementally estimated for state–action pairs. This value represents the predicted future reward that will be achieved if the agent executes action a in state s. After each action, the utility is updated as $Q(s, a) \longleftarrow Q(s, a) + \alpha[r + \gamma Q(s', a') - Q(s, a)]$. This formula increments the value of $Q(s, a)$ by the reward r received for being in state s' plus a portion of the difference between the current value of Q and the discounted value of $Q(s', a')$, where a' is chosen according to the current Q policy. The current version of MavHome receives negative reinforcement (observes a negative reward) when the inhabitant immediately reverses an automation decision (e.g., turns the light back off) or an automation decision contradicts ARBITER-supplied safety and comfort constraints.

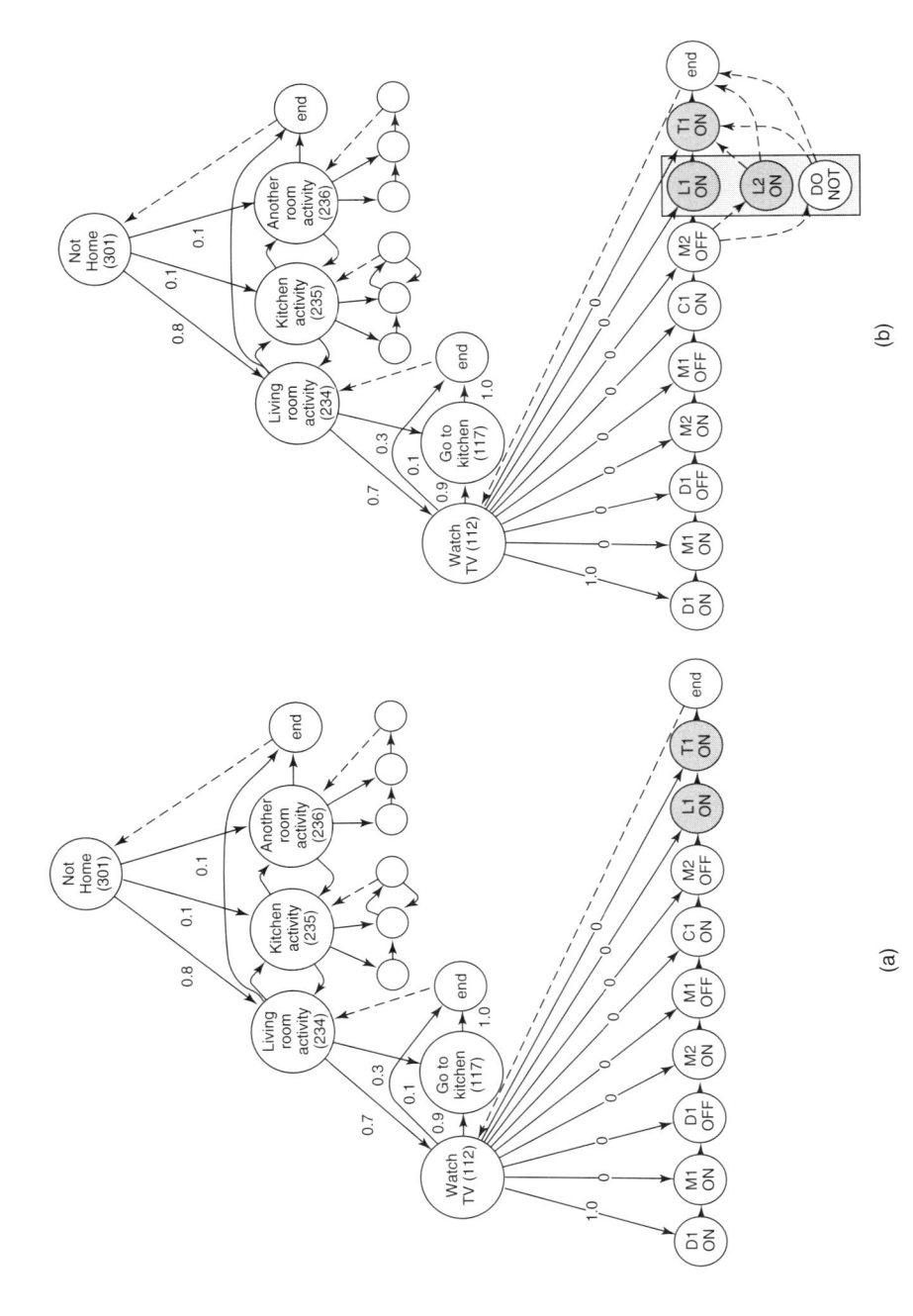

FIGURE 42.5 Hierarchical model constructed from static (a) and dynamic (b) smart home data.

Before an action is executed it is checked against the policies in the policy engine, ARBITER. These policies contain designed safety and security knowledge and inhabitant standing rules. Through the policy engine the system is prevented from engaging in erroneous actions that may perform actions such as turning the heater to 120°F or from violating the inhabitant's stated wishes (e.g., a standing rule to never turn off the inhabitant's night light).

42.4 INITIAL CASE STUDY

As an illustration of the techniques described above, we have evaluated a week in an inhabitant's life with the goal of reducing the manual interactions in the MavLab. The data were generated from a virtual inhabitant based on captured data from the MavLab and were restricted to motion and lighting interactions, which account for an average of 1400 events per day.

ALZ processed the data and converged to 99.99% accuracy after 10 iterations through the training data. When automation decisions were made using ALZ alone, interactions were reduced by 9.7% on average. Next, ED processed the data. Figure 42.6 shows the four-tier HPOMDP that is automatically constructed from the ED patterns. Because of space limitations, only the nodes at the higher levels of the model are shown. ED found eight interesting episodes with actions that could be automated, and further abstracted these to two metatasks. Livingroom patterns consisted of lab entry and exit patterns with light interactions, and the office also reflected entry and exit patterns. The other patterns occurred over the remaining eight areas and usually involved light interactions at desks and some equipment upkeep activity patterns. As a point of comparison, we automated the environment using a hierarchical Markov model with no abstract nodes. This flat model reduced interactions by 38.3%, and the combined learning system (the hierarchical ProPHeT-generated model bootstrapped using ED and ALZ) was able to reduce interactions by 76%, as shown in Figure 42.7a.

Experimentation in the MavPad using real inhabitant data has yielded similar results. In this case, ALZ alone reduced interactions from 18 to 17 events, the HPOMDP with

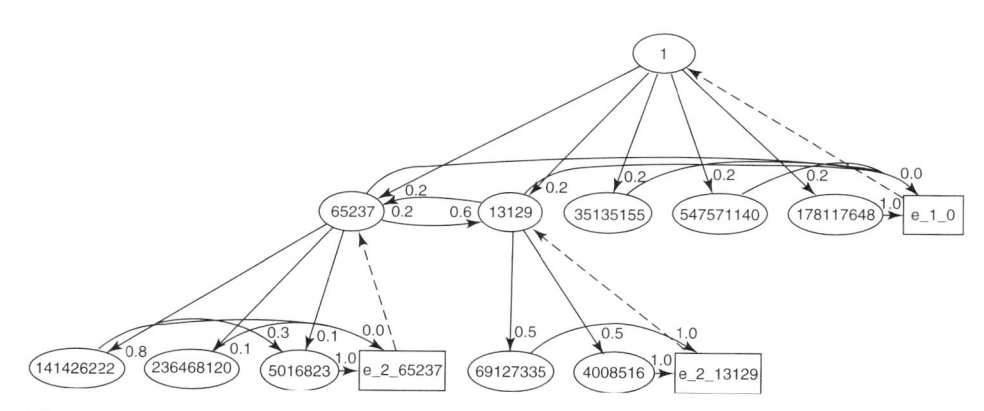

FIGURE 42.6 *ProPHeT-generated hierarchical POMDP (only the higher levels of the model are shown). There are eight abstract tasks found in the first iteration of ED and two metatasks (nodes 65237 and 13129) found in the second iteration. Boxes represent end nodes for each task sequence.*

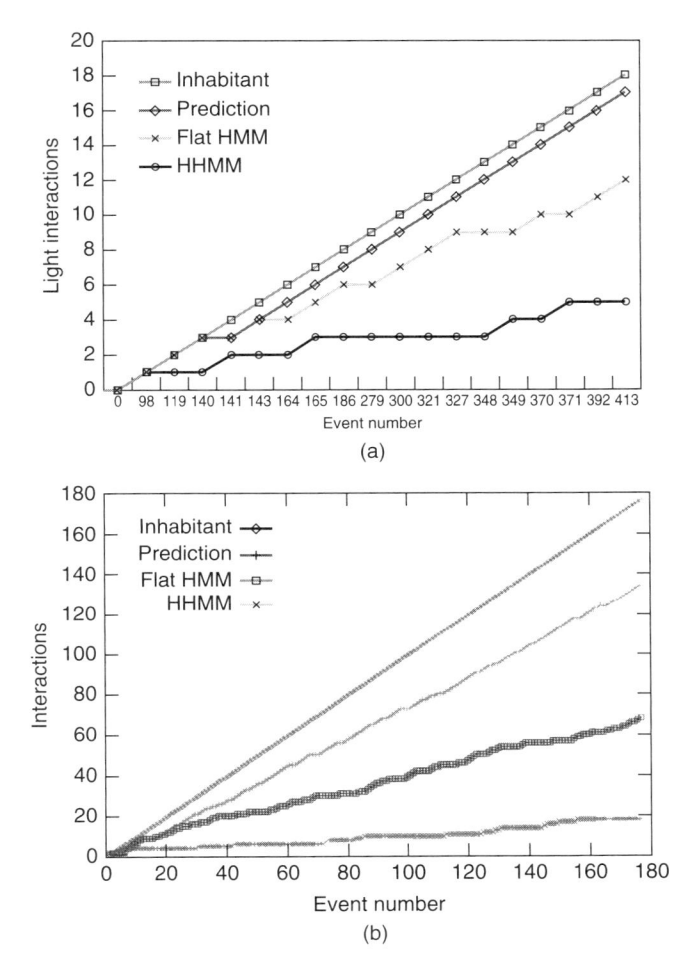

FIGURE 42.7 *Interaction reduction.*

no abstract nodes reduced interactions by 33.3% to 12 events, while the bootstrapped HPOMDP reduced interactions by 72.2% to 5 events. These results are graphed in Figure 42.7b.

42.5 USING A SMART HOME TO ASSIST THE ELDERLY AND PEOPLE WITH DISABILITIES

The data-mining, prediction, and multiagent technologies available in MavHome can be employed to provide healthcare assistance in living environments. Specifically, models can be constructed of inhabitant activities and used to learn activity trends, detect anomalies, intelligently predict possible problems and make healthcare decisions, and provide automation assistance for inhabitants with special needs.

A variety of approaches have been investigated to automate caregiver services. Many of the efforts offer supporting technologies in specialized areas, such as using computer vision techniques to track inhabitants through the environment and specialized sensors to detect falls or other crises. Some special-purpose prediction algorithms have been implemented using factors such as measurement of stand–sit and sit–stand transitions and medical history [36–38], but are limited in terms of what they predict and how they use the results. Remote monitoring systems have been designed with the common motivation that learning and predicting inhabitant activities is key for health monitoring, but very little work has combined the remote monitoring capabilities with prediction for the purpose of health monitoring. Some work has also progressed toward using typical behavior patterns to provide reminders, which is particularly useful for the elderly and patients suffering from various types of dementia [39,40].

Our smart environment can identify patterns indicating or predicting a change in health status and can provide inhabitants with needed automation assistance. Collected data include movement patterns of the individual, periodic vital signs (blood pressure, pulse, body temperature), water and device usage, use of food items in the kitchen, exercise regimen, medicine intake (prescribed and actual), and sleep patterns [10,41]. Given these data, models can be constructed of inhabitant activities and used to learn lifestyle trends, detect anomalies, and provide reminder and automation assistance.

42.5.1 Capability 1: Identify Lifestyle Trends

Many of the smart space algorithms can provide particular benefit to individuals with particular health needs who are living independently. The first such benefit is to process the captured data in order to identify lifestyle trends that may highlight a growing need for the individual.

As a motivating example, consider a scenario involving an elderly man recuperating at home alone after hospitalization. The patient's son lives several hundred miles away but wants to be informed of his father's state of health. If the patient is a smart space inhabitant, he can be regularly monitored for changes in health measurements, including heart rate, blood pressure, and body temperature. However, these data may not provide a complete picture of his health status. As such, the data need to be integrated with information on changes in other parameters such as the room temperature and humdity and the individual's movement around the house, eating patterns, medicine intake, and adherence to his daily routine. The smart environment algorithms learn the inhabitant behaviors and start reporting timely information about changes in his health. A few weeks later the son notices in a system report that his father has a sudden decrease in his movements around the house. He calls his father and finds out that in fact his father has not been feeling well the last few days.

A variety of approaches have been investigated to automate caregiver services. Many of the efforts offer supporting technologies in specialized areas, such as using computer vision techniques to track inhabitants through the environment and specialized sensors to detect falls or other crises. Some special-purpose prediction algorithms have been implemented using factors such as measurement of stand–sit and sit–stand transitions and medical history [36–38,42,43], but are limited in terms of what they predict and how they apply the results. Remote monitoring systems have been designed with the common motivation that learning and predicting inhabitant activities is key for health monitoring, but very little work has combined the remote monitoring capabilities with prediction for the purpose of health monitoring. Some work has also progressed toward using typical behavior patterns to provide emergency notifiers or inhabitant reminders, which is particularly useful for the elderly and patients suffering from various types of dementia [39,40,44–46].

In the MavHome project, collected data can be analyzed not only to provide automation but also to assess trends. In particular, our algorithms currently classify slow changes in collected data as one of a number of types of pattern *drifts*: cyclic, increasing, decreasing, chaotic, and stable. The size of sample windows is chosen in such a way that it is approximately 4 times to length of the longest detectable cycle and twice the length of other trend classes.

Tests for various classes of drifts are performed using temporal autocorrelation plots, which measure the correlation between timeshifted values in a time series. The test for a stable pattern is performed first. This describes data that are nearly constant (within a tolerance threshold) for the entire window of data. A cyclic trend, which is checked next, shows high upward peaks in the autocorrelation graph because correlation between cylic values is high. In Figure 42.8a, frequencies of an action are shown and the corresponding autocorrelation plot (Figure 42.8b shows upward-facing peaks at intervals of seven. This indicates that the length of the cycle is seven.

For increasing or decreasing trends, a high degree of autocorrelation is seen between adjacent and near-adjacent observations. For this type of drift, the autocorrelation plot will show a high correlation at lag 1 and will steadily decrease as the lag increases. The direction of the change can be determined by calculating the sum of the deviation in the adjacent data points. Any pattern in the sample window that is not classified as another type of drift is classified as chaotic. This type of drift may be caused by a large number of irregular changes, by a change in the type of drift, or by noise in the data.

Pattern drifts are reported by MavHome if their urgency is high. Urgency is calculated as a combination of the confidence in the drift and the criticality of the analyzed data (drifts involving blood pressure are more critical than those based on changes in television-watching schedules).

We analyzed seven weeks of MavPad inhabitant data for drifts and made the following observations. For most of the collected activity data, patterns were classified as stable or chaotic. Increasing and decreasing trends were detected at points based on motion detector data, which is due to the increased (or decreased) amount of time that the inhabitant is spending at home. An increased amount of time that the light was on was also observed, possibly because of longer night hours as the days grew shorter. Cyclic

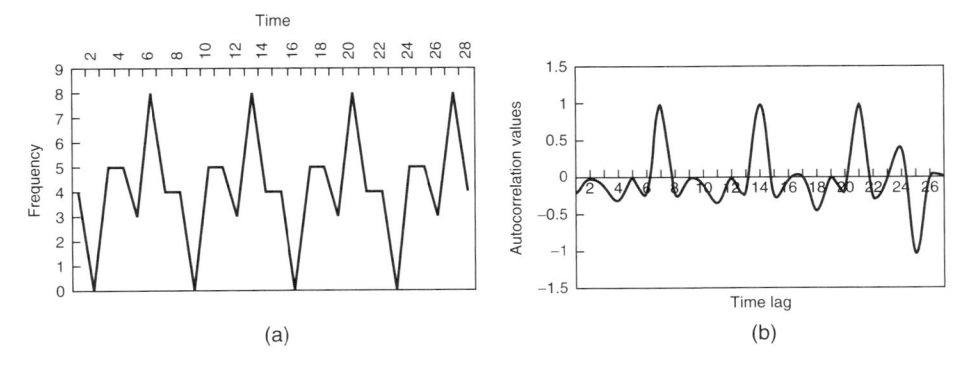

FIGURE 42.8 An example of cyclic data (a) and the corresponding autocorrelation plot (b).

drifts were the rarest. Although two cycles were detected, they only involved the use of lights and both were assigned a low confidence and a low criticality. In the case of health data, a decreasing trend was found throughout much of the collected time window. The inhabitant in this scenario is young and fairly healthy. We would expect different results when monitoring an elderly individual at home.

42.5.2 Capability 2: Detect Anomalies in Current Data

MavHome employs two techniques to detect outliers or anomalies in activity and health data. For the first method, we define an outlier as an extremely high or low value when compared to the rest of the data in the sample window. We use a z score, or standard score, to detect such outliers. This check is performed before looking for possible drifts.

The second approach makes use of the active-LeZi (ALZ) algorithm. ALZ predicts the expected next action of the inhabitant. As a side effect of the process, the algorithm generates a probability distribution over possible next events. If the probability of the observed event is greatly different from probabilities for alternative events, then the observed event (health data or observed data) is flagged as an anomaly.

In the case of the MavPad inhabitant, outliers were detected on day 31 for three different actions. As the graph in Figure 42.9 shows, the inhabitant's systolic value is zero in this day and the corresponding graph correlation is 1.5, which is identified as an outlier. We also see that the systolic values slowly decrease between days 10 and 23, which was identified as a decreasing drift of 11 days in length. The detected outlier is most likely due to an error in measurement, as the inhabitant was healthy on that day.

As with detected drifts, anomalies of a high criticality are identified for reporting. When a critical anomaly occurs, the home will first try to contact the inhabitant (through the interactive display for a lesser critical anomaly, or through the sound system for a more critical anomaly). If the inhabitant does not respond and the criticality of the anomaly is high, the caregiver will be made aware of the situation.

42.5.3 Capability 3: Design Reminder Assistance System

Reminders can be triggered by two situations: (1) if the inhabitant queries the home for her/his next routine activity, the activity with the highest probability will be given according to the ALZ prediction; and (2) if a critical anomaly is detected, the environment

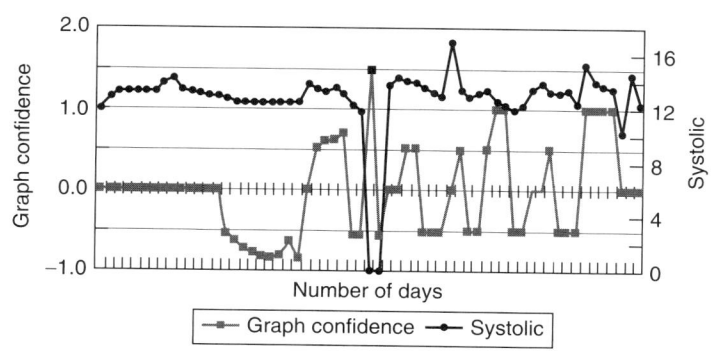

FIGURE 42.9 Plot of graph confidence and systolic values versus number of days for MavPad data.

will initiate contact with the inhabitant and remind her/him of the next typical activity. Such a reminder service will be particularly beneficial for individuals suffering from dementia.

As described in the initial MavHome design, automation assistance is always available for inhabitants, which is beneficial if some activities are difficult to perform. A useful feature of the architecture is that safety constraints are embedded in the ARBITER rule engine. If the inhabitant or the environment is about to conflict with these constraints, a preventative action is taken and the inhabitant notified. This can prevent accidents such as forgetting to turn off the water in the bathtub or leaving the house with doors unlocked.

42.6 CONCLUSION

We have demonstrated that the MavHome software architecture can successfully monitor and provide automation assistance for volunteers living in the MavPad site. However, there is much work to be done to enhance and test the benefits of the smart space algorithms for assisting the elderly and people with disabilities. We are currently collecting health-specific data in the MavHome sites and will be testing in the living environments of recruited residents at the C. C. Young Retirement Community in Dallas, Texas.

ACKNOWLEDGMENTS

This work is supported by US National Science Foundation under ITR grant IIS−0121297.

REFERENCES

1. Das SK, Cook DJ, Bhattacharya A, Heierman EO, Lin. T-Y: The role of prediction algorithms in the mavhome smart home architecture, *IEEE Wireless Commun*, **9**(6):77–84 (2002).
2. Lanspery S, Miller JR, Hyde J: Introduction: Staying put, in Lanspery S, Hyde J, eds, *Staying Put: Adapting the Places Instead of the People*, Baywood Publishing Company, 1997, pp 1–22.
3. AARP: *Fixing to Stay: A National Survey of Housing and Home Modification Issues*, 2000.
4. Zola IK: Living at home: The convergence of aging and disability, in Lanspery S, Hyde J, eds, *Staying Put: Adapting the places Instead of the People*, Baywood Publishing Company, 1997, pp 25–40.
5. Pynoos J: Neglected areas in gerontology: Housing adaptation, *Panel Presentation at the Annual Scientific Meeting of the Gerontological Society of America*, 2002.
6. Parr R, Russell S: Reinforcement learning with hierarchies of machines, in *Advances in Neural Information Processing Systems 10*, MIT Press, Denver, Dec 1997.
7. AARP: *These Four Walls ... Americans 45+ Talk about Home and Community*, 2003.
8. Grayons PJ: Technology and home adaptation, in Lanspery S, Hyde J, eds, *Staying Put: Adapting the Places Instead of the People*, Baywood Publishing Company, 1997, pp 55–74.
9. Cook DJ, Das. SK: MavHome: Work in progress, *IEEE Pervasive Comput* vol **3**, (2004).
10. Das SK, Cook DJ: Health monitoring in an agent-based smart home by activity predition, in Zhang D, Mokhari M, eds, *Toward a Human-Friendly Assistive Environment*, IOS Press, 2004, pp 3–14.

11. AIRE Group: *MIT Project AIRE—About Us*, Jan 2004 (http://www.ai.mit.edu/projects/aire).
12. Fox A, Johanson B, Hanrahan P, Winograd T: Integrating information appliances into an interactive space, *IEEE Comput Graph Appl* **20**(3):54–65 (2000).
13. Romn M, Hess CK, Cerqueira R, Ranganathan A, Campbell RH, Nahrstedt K: Gaia: A middleware infrastructure to enable active spaces, *IEEE Pervasive Comput* 74–83 (2002).
14. Streitz NA, Geiler J, Holmer T, Konomi S, Mller-Tomfelde C, Reischl W, Rexroth P, Seitz P, Steinmetz R: i-LAND: An interactive landscape for creativity and innovation, *CHI*, Proceedings of the Conference on Human Factors in Computing Systems, 120–127, Pittsburgh, PA, 1999.
15. Abowd GD, Mynatt ED: Designing for the human experience in smart environments, in Cook DJ, Das SK, eds, *Smart Environments: Technology, Protocols, and Applications*, Wiley, Hoboken, NJ, 2005, pp 153–174.
16. Helal A, Mann W, El-Zabadani H, King J, Kaddoura Y, Jansen E: The gator tech smart house: A programmable pervasive space, *IEEE Comput* **38**(3):50–60 (2005).
17. NIST: *Smart Space NIST Laboratory* (http://www.nist.gov/smartspace/).
18. Mozer MC: Lessons from an adaptive home, in Cook DJ, Das SK, eds, *Smart Environments: Technology, Protocols, and Applications*, Wiley, Hoboken, NJ, 2005, pp 273–298.
19. Hagras H, Callaghan V, Colley M, Clarke G, Pounds-Cornish A, Duman H: Creating an ambient-intelligence environment using embedded agents, *IEEE Intell Syst* **19**(6) (2004).
20. Das SK, Cook DJ: Smart home environments: A paradigm based on learning and prediction, in *Wireless Mobile and Sensor Networks*, Wiley, Hoboken, NJ, 2005.
21. Youngblood GM, Holder LB, Cook DJ: A learning architecture for automating the intelligent environment, *Proc Conf Innovative Applications of Artificial Intelligence*, 1576–1581, 2005.
22. Youngblood GM, Holder LB, Cook DJ: Managing adaptive versatile environments, *Proc International Conf Pervasive Computing*, 351–360, 2005.
23. Agrawal R, Srikant R: Mining sequential patterns, *Proc 11th Int Conf Data Engineering*, 1995, pp 3–14.
24. Heierman EO, Cook DJ: Improving home automation by discovering regularly occurring device usage patterns, *Proc Int Conf Data Mining*, 2003.
25. Rissanen J: *Stochastic Complexity in Statistical Inquiry*, World Scientific Publishing, Singapore, 1989.
26. Ziv J, Lempel A: Compression of individual sequences via variable rate coding, *IEEE Trans Inform Theory* **IT-24**:530–536 (1978).
27. Cielniak G, Bennewitz M, Burgard W: Where is . . . ? Learning and utilizing motion patterns of persons with mobile robots, *Proc 18th Int Joint Conf Artificial Intelligence*, 2003, pp 909–914.
28. Philipose M, Fishkin K, Perkowitz M, Patterson D, Fox D, Kautz H, Hahnel D: Inferring activities from interactions with objects, *Pervasive Comput* **3**(4):50–56 (2004).
29. Bell TC, Cleary JG, Witten IH: *Text Compression*, Prentice-Hall, Englewood Cliffs, NJ, 1990.
30. Gopalratnam K, Cook DJ: Active LeZi: An incremental parsing algorithm for sequential prediction, *Int J Artif Intell Tools* **14** (1–2):917–930, (2004).
31. Gopalratnam K, Cook DJ: Online sequential prediction via incremental parsing: The Active LeZi algorithm, *IEEE Intell Syst* **22**(1):52–58, (2005).
32. Pineau J, Roy N, Thrun S: A hierarchical approach to POMDP planning and execution, *Workshop on Hierarchy and Memory in Reinforcement Learning (ICML)*, 2001.
33. Theocharous G, Rohanimanesh K, Mahadevan S: Learning hierarchical partially observable markov decision processes for robot navigation, *IEEE Conf Robotics and Automation*, 2001.
34. Precup D, Sutton RS: Multi-time models for temporally abstract planning, *Adv Neural Inform Process Syst* **10**:1050–1056 (1997).

35. Sutton RS, Barto AG: *Reinforcement Learning: An Introduction*, MIT Press, Cambridge, MA, 1998.
36. Cameron K, Hughes K, Doughty K: Reducing fall incidence in community elders by telecare using predictive systems, *Proc Int IEEE-EMBS Conf*, 1997, pp 1036–1039.
37. Najafi B, Aminian K, Loew F, Blanc Y, Robert P: Measurement of stand-sit and sit-stand transitions using a miniature gyroscope and its application in fall risk evaluation in the elderly, *IEEE Trans Biomed Eng* **49**(8):843–851 (2002).
38. Najafi B, Aminian K, Paraschiv-Ionescu A, Loew F, Bula C, Robert P: Ambulatory system for human motion analysis using a kinematic sensor: Monitoring of daily physical activity in the elderly, *IEEE Trans Biomed Eng* **50**(6):711–723 (2003).
39. Kautz H, Arnstein L, Borriello G, Etzioni O, Fox D: An overview of the assisted cognition project, *Proc AAAI Workshop on Automation as Caregiver*, 2002.
40. Pollack ME, Brown L, Colbry D, McCarthy CE, Orosz C, Peintner B, Ramakrishnan S, Tsamardinos I: Autoreminder: An intelligent cognitive orthotic system for people with memory impairment, *Robot Auton Syst* **44**:273–282 (2003).
41. Das SK, Cook DJ: Health monitoring in an agent-based smart home, *Proc Int Conf Smart Homes and Health Telematics (ICOST)*, 2004.
42. Chen D, Wactlar H, Yang J: A study of detecting social interaction in a nursing home environment, *Proc Int Conf Computer Vision Workshop on Human-Computer Interaction*, 2005.
43. Glascock AP, Kutzik DM: Behavioral telemedicine: A new approach to the continuous nonintrusive monitoring of activities of daily living, *Telemed J* **6**(1):33–44 (2000).
44. Chan M, Hariton C, Ringeard P, Campo E: Smart house automation system for the elderly and the disabled, *Proc IEEE Int Conf Systems, Man and Cybernetics*, 1995, pp 1586–1589.
45. Inada H, Horio H, Sekita Y, Isikawa K, Yoshida K: A study on a home care support information system, *Proc 7th World Congress on Medical Informatics*, 1992, pp 349–353.
46. Lawton MP: Aging and performance of home tasks, *Human Factor* **32**:527–536 (1990).

PART VIII

Emerging Standards, Guidelines, and Design Methods

43

User-Sensitive Design for Older and Disabled People

Alan Newell
University of Dundee, Dundee, Scotland

Successful design requires designers to both achieve an empathy with their potential users and have access to sufficient relevant human factors knowledge about their needs, wants, and capabilities. A range of design techniques have been suggested to assist in this process. The need to be fully informed about the characteristics of users is particularly important when the user group is poorly represented in the design community—such as older and disabled people. This chapter considers designs techniques and methods appropriate in the field of development of products for older people and people with disabilities, and outlines how they differ from those used within traditional technologic research.

43.1 INTRODUCTION TO USER-CENTERED DESIGN

The design community has been aware of the importance of focussing on users' needs, wants, and capabilities for many years. *User-centered design*, a popular approach to this challenge, is a set of techniques and processes that enable developers to focus on the users within the design process [1–4]. The British Standard (ISO 1999) states that "[user-centered design] is characterised by the active involvement of end users and that the multidisciplinary team should include end users." Users should be "involved in" the process—the contribution of such users varies with their skills and experience and is also dependent on the particular phase of the research or development. Some parts of the process involve very intensive interaction with users (e.g., in evaluations

---

The Engineering Handbook of Smart Technology for Aging, Disability, and Independence,
Edited by A. Helal, M. Mokhtari and B. Abdulrazak
Copyright © 2008 John Wiley & Sons, Inc.

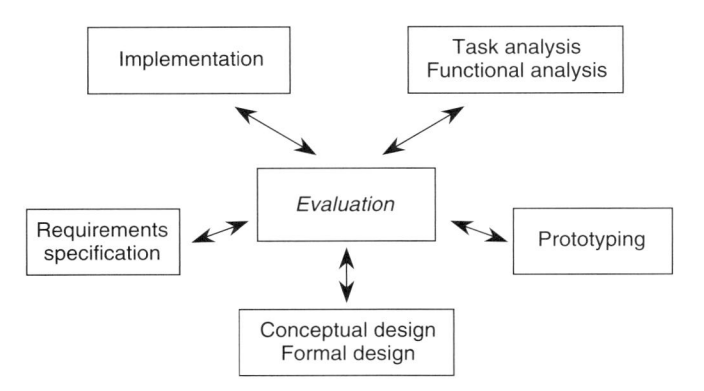

FIGURE 43.1 Model incorporating user-senistive design (adapted from Hartson and Hix [5]).

of prototypes); others, almost none (e.g., writing computer code, or designing electronic circuitry). Figure 43.1 [5] shows a model for user-centered design where the latest implementation or idea is evaluated with users both before and after each stage of the design process. Users, however, are not normally involved in the activities shown at the periphery of the diagram and need not always be involved in some of the evaluation procedures.

Participatory design [6,7] is also a design technique that proposes a focus on the users, and includes both the pragmatic approach of direct collaboration between designers and users and a more conceptual approach that incorporates complementary perspectives to help designers come up with better solutions.

Ethnography involves users within the design process [8], but, in this case, the ethnographer acts as an intermediary between the users (usually in their own environment) and the designers. The ethnographer's role is to present as full a picture as possible of the user, their culture, and their environment to the designers. These are often in the form of a written report, but other ways can also be used such as "experience models," "opportunity maps," profiles, scenarios, mockups, and prototypes,

The inclusion of older users and users with disabilities, however, can impose significant changes to these design philosophy and needs to be carefully considered [9–11]. Currently there tends to be (possibly artificial) distinctions between

- Mainstream design (which often seems to be exclusively for able-bodied people),
- The design of systems exclusively for people with disabilities (products of rehabilitation engineering—sometimes called "orphan" products) and, more recently
- "Inclusive" design

43.2 INCLUSIVE DESIGN

A number of initiatives have been launched to promote a consideration of people with disabilities within the user group of mainstream product development teams. These initiatives have had a number of titles, including "universal design," "design for all," "accessible design," and "inclusive design." Examples of such initiatives include the i-design project jointly with Cambridge, York, Dundee Universities and the Royal College of Art (http://www-edc.eng.cam.ac.uk/idesign/), the INCLUDE project within the European Union (http://www.stakes.fi/include), and, in the United States, the Center for Universal Design at North Carolina State University (http://www.design.ncsu.edu/cud/ud/ud.html), and work at the Trace Centre in Wisconsin—Madison (http://www.trace.wisc.edu).Newell and Gregor [9] also proposed the concept of "ordinary and extraordinary human–machine interaction," which is a different approach to including older and disabled people in the design process.

The i~design project seeks to provide tools to improve quality of life for the wider population. It focuses on enabling industry to design products that can be used effectively by the population as a whole, including those who are older and/or disabled. Clarkson and Keates [12] propose that, in order to maximize the usability for the largest number of possible users, the appropriate information on users should be available to designers. They suggest a structured design approach, including the concept of an "inclusive design cube." The axes of the cube represent motion, sensory, and cognitive capabilities of the users. The overall cube represents the whole population, but is subdivided in the "ideal" population of users for a particular product, and the population that can actually use the product. This cube can provide a way of assessing the proportion of the whole population that is excluded from using any particular device.

The INCLUDE project produced a methodology for "inclusive design" for telecommunication terminals [13], which was based on standard textbooks for user-centered design and usability engineering (such as those by Neilsen [14] and Ulrich and Eppinger [15]), and on an extension of the International Standards for human-centered design [16]. They underlined the importance of the design not being linear, but iterative, with constant reference back to evaluation with the users [17] (also indicated in Fig. 43.1, above). They suggested that one approach was "to compromise slightly on the product design so that, while the design retain the functionality required by people with disabilities, it still appeals to a wider audience." They also commented that "there were many different methods of choosing how to collect user needs and integrate them into product development, and that the suitability of this approach to accommodating a range of disabilities into the design process (in an effective and efficient manner) is unclear." They recommend "guidelines as a good cheap basis for integrating needs of people with varying abilities into design at an early phase." Examples of such guidelines can be found at their Website and within Hypponen [13], and other literature on "design for all."

The INCLUDE project recommendations are similar to general user-centered design principles. They include "flexibility in use," "simple and intuitive use," "perceptible information," "tolerance for error," "low physical effort," and "size and space be provided." They remind the reader to be aware of the needs of people with disabilities when following these guidelines. Their philosophy is based on the underlying premise of "equitable use"; that is: "the design should be useful and marketable to *any* group of users" (my emphasis). If taken literally, however, this imposes very substantial requirements on the designer, which may not always be appropriate. It should be remembered that—in its full sense, and, except for a very limited range of products—"design for all" is a very difficult, if not often impossible, task. The use of this term thus has some inherent dangers. Providing access to people with certain types of disability can make the product significantly more difficult to use by people without disabilities, and often impossible to use by people with a different type of disability. Also, the need for accessibility for certain groups of disabled people might not be required by the very nature of a product.

43.3 ORDINARY AND EXTRAORDINARY HUMAN–MACHINE INTERACTION

The concept of "ordinary and extraordinary human–machine interaction" was developed by Newell [10]. It addresses the relationship between the functionality of users and the environment in which they may operate. This draws the parallel between "ordinary" people operating in an "extraordinary" environment (e.g., high workload, adverse noise or lighting conditions), and an "extraordinary" (disabled) person operating in an ordinary environment. It made the point that the characteristics of both the environment and the users' functionality can change substantially from minute to minute, and from day to day, in addition to very long term changes due, for example, to aging and to changes in the physical environment and social situation [9]. They said that designers need to be explicitly aware of these concepts and understand how they can be used to the greatest benefit of everyone, including people who are either temporarily or permanently disabled. They gave a number of examples of designs that were specifically focused on older and/or disabled people, which led to very successful mainstream products. These include the cassette tape recorder (first developed by a company producing talking books for the blind), the predictive coding system available in mobile telephones (first developed to allow people with physical disabilities to use very large keys to input text), and the Ford Focus automobile, which was designed to cope with the mobility restrictions that occur in older people, and became the best-selling car in the UK Ford range. Newell and Gregor [9] recommend that there are significant advantages in first considering the challenges of older and disabled people and then extending the design to be appropriate for nondisabled people, rather than taking a main stream product and attempting to modify the design to make it more inclusive.

43.4 USER-CENTERED DESIGN FOR OLDER AND/OR DISABLED PEOPLE

There are some important distinctions between traditional user-centered design (UCD) with able-bodied users, and UCD when the user group either contains, either partially or exclusively, people with disabilities. These include

- Much greater variety of user characteristics and functionality
- The difficulty in finding and recruiting "representative users"
- Possible conflict of interest between accessibility for people with different types of disability
- Conflicts between accessibility, and ease of use for less disabled people ("temporary able-bodied") (e.g., floor texture can assist blind people but may cause problems for wheelchair users)
- Situations where "design for all" is certainly not appropriate (e.g. blind drivers of motor cars)
- The need to specify exactly the characteristics and functionality of the user group
- Provision for accessibility via the provision of additional components

If the design process is to be focused on older and/or disabled people, either for specialized products or as a way of developing inclusive products, the design process should include interaction with older and/or disabled users. Newell and Gregor [18] have pointed out the increased usability challenges of this group, and the difficulties in finding and recruiting "representative" users. They conclude that traditional methodologies do not cater well for these groups.

Older people can, very crudely, be divided into three groups:

- Fit older people, who do not appear—nor would consider themselves—disabled, but whose functionality, needs, and wants are different from those they had when they were younger
- Frail older people, who would be considered to have a "disability"—often a severe one—and in addition have a general reduction in many of their other functionalities
- Disabled people who grow older, whose long-term disabilities may have affected the aging process, and whose ability to function can be critically dependent on their other faculties, which will also be declining

This taxonomy serves to illustrate the fact that capability and disability are not opposites. Designers should recognize the whole range of capability levels, and understand that these are continua rather than binary (able-bodied—disabled). Other major characteristics of older people, when compared with their younger counterparts, include

- The individual variability of physical, sensory, and cognitive functionality of people increases with increasing age.
- The rate of decline in that functionality (which begins to occur at a surprisingly early age) can increase significantly as people move into the "older" category.
- Problems with cognition, such as dementia, memory dysfunction, and the ability to learn new techniques, appear more widely.
- Older people may have significantly different needs and wants due to the stage of their lives they have reached.
- The environments in which older people live and work can significantly change their usable functionality (e.g., the need to use a walking frame, to avoid long periods of standing, or the need to wear warm gloves).

As people grow older, their abilities change, with, in general, a decline over time in cognitive, physical, and sensory functions, each declining at different rates relative to one another for each individual. In addition, any given individual's capabilities vary in the short term [19].

Current technology, however, produces a static artefact with no, or very limited, means of adapting to the changing needs of users as their abilities change. Even the user-centered paradigm [1,2,14,16] assumes that the user has characteristics that are invariant with time. Thus the methodology of research and development must bring into focus not only the substantial variability that exists in user characteristics but also the changing nature of the functionality that they have, over both short and long timescales.

Many older users of computer systems can be affected by multiple disabilities, and such multiple minor (and sometimes major) impairments can interact, at a human–computer interface level, to produce a handicap that is greater than the effects of the individual impairments. Thus, for example, poor eyesight can be accommodated in computer systems by increasing font size, but this reduces the information on the screen at any one time and thus provides greater cognitive load on the user, and, if memory function is slightly impaired, this may mean that the swapping from screen to screen is impracticable. Blindness can be accommodated by using a speech synthesizer to read out the text, but many older people have reduced hearing, and many find that the additional cognitive load of interpreting synthesized speech, and remembering what has been said, offer substantial additional barriers to understanding. Thus research into accessibility that is focused on single impairments may not always provide appropriate solutions for older users.

There are additional specific challenges when older people and people with disabilities are part of the formal user group within a product development environment. For example, there can be serious ethical issues related to the use of these groups as "subjects." Some of these are medically related, and can also include the ability to obtain informed consent.

Research challenges when disabled people are part of the user group can include the following:

- It may be difficult to get informed consent from some users.
- The users may not be able to communicate their thoughts, or may even be "incompetent" in a legal sense.
- The user may not be the purchaser of the final product.
- Payments may conflict with benefit rules.
- Users with disabilities may have very specialized and little-known requirements.
- Different user groups may provide very conflicting requirements for a product.
- Conflicts of interest between user groups (including "temporarily able-bodied").
- The lack of a truly representative user group, and how to find and recruit an appropriate group of users.

Alm [20] and others have also considered the ethics of research with individuals with disabilities, including those with communication impairments. They conclude that it is not as straightforward to work with these users as it would be to work with disabled people who do not have communication dysfunction. Similar problems can occur when working with people with cognitive dysfunction.

In addition, the involvement of clinicians may also be needed when disabled users are involved. Their expertise is invaluable, but it is also vital that the clinicians be fully aware of the motivation and methodologies of the design process, which are very different from a normal clinical situation. Communication, between clinicians and engineers can be fraught with difficulties as they come from different backgrounds and have different jargon. A fully cooperative team of clinicians and engineers is a world-beating combination, but it needs to be developed and fostered—it does not happen by chance. Also, a reliance on expert opinion rather than observations of users could compromise the very process that user participation is supposed to serve.

In order to ensure that these differences are fully recognised by the field, Newell and Gregor [18] recommended that the technique be called "user-sensitive inclusive design." The term "inclusive" rather than "universal" reflects the view that "inclusivity" is a more achievable—and, in many situations, appropriate—goal than "universal design" or "design for all." "Sensitive" replaces "centered" to underline the extra levels of difficulty involved when the range of functionality and characteristics of the user groups can be so great that it is impossible, in any meaningful way, to produce a small representative sample of the user group, nor often to design a product that truly is accessible by all potential users.

43.5 AESTHETICS

Aesthetics is often seen to be less important in assistive technology (AT) than other equipment for domestic use [21]. There have been times when areas of fashion were particularly beneficial to older users. In Victorian times, the walking stick was a fashion accessory for many (and also could even serve as a repository for hard liquor or a weapon of defense or attack). In those days a wide variety of very beautiful walking sticks could be purchased, and a walking stick was a badge of honor rather than shame. This is still true for country-walking enthusiasts, but there seems little crosslinkage between design of walking sticks for outdoor pursuits and those intended for therapeutic purposes. The fact that the typical user of assistive technology is seldom the purchaser can have a major influence on equipment design. Assistive technology often has an institutional "air" about it—being more suited to a hospital ward than to a livingroom.

The difference between "need" and "want" has very important effects, particularly regarding the aesthetics of equipment. Those things that people want are usually beautiful—in the eyes of the purchaser, at least. In contrast, those products that others have determined that people "need" are seldom perceived to have the same requirement to be beautiful—their functionality is considered to be of primary, if not exclusive, importance. However, this need not be the case. There is no absolute reason why AT devices should be ugly, other than possibly a lack of motivation to produce beautiful products for the rehabilitation market, or a reluctance to employ designers with visual awareness, or to allow such designers to consider aesthetics as an important part of their remit. There are moves toward efficient artificial legs as a fashion statement, rather than a compromise of the design in an attempt to make them "cosmetic" (i.e., concealing that they are artificial), and "cool" wheelchairs for younger people, but most current AT is not considered to be a fashion accessory. Demographic changes, however, are likely to produce the need for incorporating aesthetic design within products. This will favor those AT designers who are fastest to respond to the true needs and wants of the users.

The questions that the assistive technology industry needs to address include the following:

1. Should assistive technology "delight" the user (and their friends and companions)?
2. Why can assistive technology not be a fashion statement?
3. Why should assistive technology for the home look as if it were designed for a hospital ward?
4. What is most appropriate way to do market research in this field?
5. What is the best way to market AT products to a wider group?
6. How can one best obtain accurate feedback from current users (including, but not exclusively, their professional carers)?

43.6 INVOLVEMENT OF DISABLED USERS

Users with disabilities and clinicians can make a tremendous contribution both to research and to the commercial products that have grown from research in this area.

Users can be involved in two major ways:

- As disabled consultants on the research team, where they act essentially as "test pilots" for prototype systems
- By the traditional user-centered design methodology of having
  User panels
  Formal case studies
  Many individual users who assess and evaluate prototypes

Within research in the School of Computing at Dundee University [22], disabled consultants are full members of the research team, and are chosen with great care, and make many very important contributions to the research [23–25]. The rewards for the disabled consultants on the research team have come from being internationally known in the field, attending international conferences and giving lecture tours [26]. From time to time, this group has employed researchers who happen to be disabled, but they are employed strictly on merit as researchers.

The panels of users at Dundee have enjoyed working with the group, and their reward has been to take part in a project, which may be useful to older and disabled people in the future. Some of them have been able to obtain the commercial products that have developed from our research, but it was made clear to them at the start of the research that the provision of such long-term support was not the responsibility of the project.

Dundee's School of Computing is one of the few computing departments that have employed speech therapists, nurses, special education teachers, linguists, and psychologists. By employing clinicians on research projects, rather than consulting service-orientated clinicians, we have ensured that the ethos of the whole team is a research ethos, which is vital for high-quality long-term research. In projects that do not have clinicians on the research team, we consult with clinical colleagues as appropriate.

43.7 INVOLVING OLDER AND DISABLED PEOPLE IN THE DEVELOPMENT PROCESS

Although most people agree on the importance of involving older people during the development of new technology, there are relatively few examples or guidelines for their successful involvement [27], and often traditional formats have to be adapted. Various researchers, however, report on the problems encountered when running focus groups with older people [28,29]. There are some case studies about design processes involving older people [30] that give valuable pointers as to how information can be elicited from this age group.

The cultural and experiential gap between designers and users is especially large when developing information technology (IT) products and other new technology for older users. Many older people have had little exposure to computers, while for younger people (especially those who develop new technology), much technology is an integrated part of their lives. They find it difficult to imagine life without it, and technical terms or metaphors, which may seem like normal words to younger people (*monitor* or *Windows*), can be difficult to avoid or to describe. Computing conventions such as visual language and interface metaphors used in computer systems can also cause confusion. A scrollbar is an example of a whole repertoire of "widgets," with which older people have limited or no experience. The approach of many older people is based on a fundamental lack of trust and a very limited understanding of the underlying concepts in the system, leading to a reluctance to experiment. Also, "time to complete the task" is rarely as important to older people as is "getting the job done" (see also Hardy and Baird [31]).

In addition, Eisma et al. [32] have found that older people, who can be reluctant to complain about or criticize products, can experience more computer anxiety and be more negative about the amount of effort required to learn to use them. This characteristic is often fueled by the assumption that they have no use for these products [33].

Challenges can be caused by decreasing abilities, for example, in sight, hearing, and short-term memory. In particular, traditionally structured focus groups have been found to be less than satisfactory when attempting to elicit information from groups of older people. Age-related cognitive deficits can also render self-reporting inaccurate (e.g., in a questionnaire), with more recent research showing that there are age differences in the ways in which people respond in self-reports [34]. In addition, challenges may arise because older people tend to tire more quickly [35], and this can severely limit the duration of sessions.

Some of the information that designers are trying to elicit can be particularly sensitive, and care needs to be taken to choose topics and appropriately introduce sensitive topics. For example, Russell [36] found that many older people may not want to talk about topics such as social isolation, "because such an acknowledgment challenged their identity as independent people."

In addition, motivations behind user participation should be considered: "If people are lonely, do they consent to be interviewed because of the social interaction it provides them?" [28, p. 25]. Sensitivity and an awareness of users' motivations for participating are important considerations in working successfully with older people. For example, the author and his colleagues, and Lines and Hone [28] have found that it is not easy to keep a focus group of older people focused on the subject being discussed. They suggest that a contributory factor to this is the motivation of the participants; many of our informants see these groups as vehicles for socializing as well as providing information to the researchers.

43.8 METHODOLOGY

43.8.1 Mutual Inspiration

Eisma et al. [37] proposed the concept of mutual inspiration to avoid the researcher–designer divide, which often threatens the effective communication of requirements to the design team. An essential part of this methodology is building a diverse user base, forming a longlasting partnership with older people, and developing approaches for effective interaction with this target user group. They propose that both the users and the designers should be involved in the initial requirement generation and prototype stages of the project, so that both sides are aware of the various criteria that shape the project, and both can influence early design choices. For this to be successful, however, a common ground must be established where both parties are willing and able to talk about their expertise in language comprehensible to the other party, and both have to be prepared to challenge suggestions, but always to respect the other's contribution and expertise. This is facilitated by making focus groups, or other activities, into pleasurable social events, by providing refreshments and, crucially, time for social interaction, both among the participants and between participants and researchers. Mival [38] report that the enjoyment that people get from learning about new products and technologies is an important motivation to participate, and to participate again. Hands-on sessions, where older people experience new technology, have proved more successful than verbal explanations or demonstrations, and these can often lead to spontaneous suggestions for improvements or for new products. This was also found by Inglis et al. [39], who, after passing PDAs around to older people as part of a user-centered design process for memory aids, commented on the responsiveness that the participants showed to the new technology. They also report that older people were less likely to ask for functionality than were younger, technically aware users. This underlines the need to spend time to transfer knowledge to the users involved in the design process to enable them to contribute. Mival [38] also reports that hands-on sessions allow researchers to observe the difference between what people report and what actually happens. For example, some users reported that they had no problems with using the systems despite the fact that observations had showed that this was not the case. Gheerawo and Lebbon [30] describe a similar process that they called "empathic bonding" to stimulate creative thinking and user-facilitated innovation.

43.8.2 Questionnaires

Questionnaires can be a very valuable way of gathering data, but research shows that there are age differences in the way older and younger people respond in self-reports Older respondents use the "don't know" response more than younger respondents do, and are also likely to use the "don't know" option to questions that have complex syntax or are semantically complex. Older respondents are generally also more "cautious" in their behavior, and need to "have higher threshold levels of certainty" before responding to questions [34], p. 238). Eisma et al. [32] specifically excluded a "don't know" response, but even this was thwarted by some respondents, a number of whom penciled in their own "don't know" column. These researchers found that the best way of addressing this reluctance was for a researcher to administer the questionnaire directly. This had the advantage of leading to spontaneous excursions into users' own experiences, and demonstrations of various personal devices were relatively common, and provided many useful insights.

43.8.3 Interviews

Older people, particularly those who are disabled or frail, are likely to spend more time in their homes. Care thus needs to be taken to avoid potential negative effects of inappropriate technologies, as this can dramatically alter the life of a vulnerable older person, especially if the installation of the equipment is time-consuming and disruptive [40]. Dickinson et al. [41] showed that in-home interviews produced many stories about how the equipment in the home was obtained, how people learned to use it, who supported them, and the reporting of a variety of both good and bad experiences. Monk and Baxter [42] have suggested the concept of examining "seriously bad outcomes" (SBOs), like loneliness, as part of in-home observations and interviews. These methods allow the researchers to see the users in context, to observe them using their current technology, and to note unexpected points, together with providing background information about the hardware and software used.

43.8.4 The Use of Theater

There are thus major challenges in interacting with older and disabled users. Newell and his colleagues therefore have investigated methods other than direct contact with users, and have examined the use of theater as a technique for transmitting important messages to an audience [43]. They studied the ideas of "forum theater" as described by Boal [44]. Boal's work was developed within his "theater of the oppressed" movement in Brazil. It was devised to ensure substantial interaction between the audience and the actors, and to enable the actors to portray the views of the audience about the particular issues that were being addressed by the theatrical presentation. In order to take full advantages of the theater, Newell and his colleagues explored the use of theatre professionals who were experienced in forum theater techniques—actors, script writers, and directors.

A script writer conducts detailed research on the subject area and produces a series of short plays that address the important issues to be discussed, but within a narrative style, with the emotional content and tension essential to good drama. In general, these scripts have a "beginning" and "middle" but no "end." In live forum theater, the play is performed and, when it reaches the end of the scripted section, the audience is encouraged by a trained facilitator to address the issues of the character's different motivations and emotions. The ideas that the audience—the "forum"—produce are then instantiated by the actors, who extemporize on the basis of suggestions from the audience. In this way, the audience essentially direct the rest of the play, and can see the effects of their suggestions acted out. Live theatre also allows replay of scenes—should the audience change their minds on the basis of what has occurred.

In collaboration with the Foxtrot Theatre Company, McKenna et al. [45] used a version of this technique within the requirements-gathering phase of a project developing a videocamera-based "fall" monitor and detector for older people in their homes. The script writer (2005/6 Leverhulme Artist in Residence in the School of Computing at Dundee University). produced four short scenarios, two involving an older person falling and two that addressed the issues of false alarms. The scenarios were written in a narrative rather than documentary style. They thus contained "human interest," humor, and dramatic tension as well as illustrating how the system may work, the errors that could occur in its use, and the effects of these errors on the participants. Each scenario lasted for approximately 5 min, which typically leads to about 20 min of discussion. Videos were produced of various scenarios using professional actors. In the style of forum theater, the videos contained "stopping points," where the video was stopped and discussion among the audience encouraged.

McKenna et al. [45] reports that that the dramatized scenarios provided an excellent way of setting a shared context for discussions between potential users and designers, focused discussion on specific scenarios of likely system usage, and were very effective in provoking discussion of relevant details because elderly users could imagine themselves within the scenarios shown in the video.

These results confirm the comments made by Sato and Salvador [46] that human-centered stories lead to a more detailed discussion, and that the drama provides a point of contact that makes their evaluative task much easier. Strom [47] also comments that human-centered stories, which explore problems via conflict, can lead to a more detailed discussion. He reports that he found it difficult to combine large or dramatic consequences with the exploration of an interface, but this was not an issue with the research by McKenna et al. [46]. Similar techniques were used as part of the UTOPIA (*u*sable *t*echnology for *o*lder *p*eople: *i*nclusive and *a*appropriate) project, whose primary aim was to develop techniques for changing the mindsets of designers concerning the needs of older people [48]. This project culminated in the production of the UTOPIA Trilogy, a series of videos addressing issues of older people's use of technology [49]. Overall, these videos were found to be a very useful method for provoking discussion and one that potential users find interesting and enjoyable. This ensured that user requirements were explored effectively early in the design cycle.

Newell et al. [50] believe that the success of these experiments was in large part due to the videos being narrative based—that is, they illustrated how the equipment would work within interesting story lines, with all the characteristics of a good narrative—and to the quality of the actors, who were all professions experienced in forum theater. This confirms the claims made by [51] that "(actors) build representations of fictional people whose responses one wishes to anticipate through immersion in realistic detail," that "theatre encourages discussion on a 'what if' basis," that "models of fictional people can be as engaging as models of real people," and that "fiction, based on research, can communicate useful knowledge."

Although these videos were very successful, Newell et al. [50] suggest that that live forum theater could be a very appropriate methodology for a wider range of tasks within user-centered design. Although video is reusable and thus a cost-effective way of communicating with a large number of people, Sato and Salvador [46] comment that video is neither quick nor inexpensive to produce, and that live theater involves a larger part of visual field of audience, and the audience themselves can become the authors. In addition, they comment that "Live performers cast a spell over the room; there was a heightened awareness and tension, and live actors can produce engaging and interactive experience." They reported that the audience answered questions more effectively and efficiently than if the session focussed on technical details. Dishman [52] and others have used actors in unscripted live drama to address design requirements for older adults. Dishman calls this "informance design."

Newell and his colleagues are thus experimenting with live performances and discuss [50] the pros of cons of this activity. Although the use of actors may not be wholly appropriate for very detailed evaluations of user interface, they describe the advantages both when a more holistic approach is required, and for very novel design briefs where an entirely new technology is being developed. They comment that script writers and actors are trained as professional observers of human behavior and their skill is presenting that behavior in a way which engages the viewer or audience. In addition, they suggest that actors could also be valuable in usability testing by encouraging dialog between the audience. Wixon [53] notes that "It is no accident that most usability testing involves encouraging entire design teams to watch the test, and it is well known that much of the effectiveness of the test comes from this active participation." In traditional usability laboratories, however, a two-way mirror provides a major barrier to any communication between users and designers. The use of actors also removes the ethical problems of "protecting the users," and it is possible to envisage a situation where the designers and the users can verbally attack one another as part of addressing the usability issues of a particular system—a situation that would be impossible, and probably unethical, in a traditional usability laboratory. Actors can also present a more generic picture of a user and can change their personas in response to requests from the designers (e.g., what would happen if you were older, if your sight/hearing were impaired, if you were under pressure).

Finally, theater encourages a creative approach to design, involving users as well as designers, rather than the traditional view of focus groups and usability testing being solely a method of eliciting users views and opinions and to determine their abilities to use specific interfaces and systems

43.9 CONCLUSIONS

It is essential that the voices of users are heard in the design process, but this provides significant challenges when the user population contains older and/or disabled users. Not only does this provide a much more diverse population than most traditional user groups; there are also communication challenges caused not only by sensory loss but also by culture, language, and attitudes to technology. In addition, there can be major ethical problems in dealing with such groups. All these effects can lead to the data from such interactions being flawed.

There are ways to minimized such effects, and it is recommended that the users be considered as part of the development team rather than subjects who are viewed as individuals without any real engagement in the development process, or are merely monitored as users of equipment. In addition, for older users in particular, it is important that the interactions between them and the designers are set within an enjoyable social experience.

The use of professional actors and live theater should also be considered as a way of facilitating discussions with users, or in those cases where it is too difficult or inappropriate to involve real users in experiments and dialogs. Although not an inexpensive option, the value that can be brought to the interaction by theater professions can be very significant.

ACKNOWLEDGMENTS

The work reported in this chapter was funded by the Scottish Higher Education Funding Council, the Engineering and Physical Sciences Research Council, and the Leverhulme Trust, who funded Ms. Morgan as Artist in Residence in Applied Computing.

REFERENCES

1. Preece J: *A Guide to Usability—Human Factors in Computing*, Addison-Wesley and Open University, 1994.
2. Shneiderman B: *Designing the User Interface: Strategies for Effective Human-Computer Interaction,* Addison-Wesley, Reading, MAs, 1992.
3. Newman WM, Lamming MG: *Interactive System Design*, Addison-Wesley, 1995.
4. Helander M, Landauer TK, Prabhu P, eds, *Handbook of Human-Computer Interaction,* Elsevier Science BV, 1997, pp 813–824.
5. Hartson HR, Hix D: Toward empirically derived methodologies and tools for human-computer interface development, *Int J Man-Machine Stud* **31**:477–494 (1989).
6. Muller MJ: Participatory design: The third space, in Jacko JA, Sears A, eds, *The Human-Computer Interaction Handbook,* Lawrence Erlbaum, Hillsdale, NJ, 2002, pp 1051–1068.

7. Kyng M, Mathiassen L, eds, *Computers and Design in Context*, MIT Press, Cambridge, MA. 1997.
8. Blomberg J, Burrell JM, Guest G: An ethnographic approach to design, in Jacko J, Sears A. eds, *The Human-Computer Interaction Handbook*, 2002, pp 964–986.
9. Newell AF, Gregor P: Human computer interfaces for people with disabilities, in Helander M. Landauer TK, and Prabhu P, eds, *Handbook of Human-Computer Interaction*, Elsevier Science BV, 1997, pp 813–824.
10. Newell AF: Extra-ordinary human computer operation, in Edwards ADN, ed, *Extra-ordinary Human-Computer Interactions*, Cambridge Univ Press, 1995.
11. Newell AF, Gregor P: Design for older and disabled people—where do we go from here? *Univ Access Inform Soc* **2**(1):3–7 (2002).
12. Clarkson PJ, Keates S: Inclusive design—a balance between product demands and user capabilities, *Proc DETC'03 ASME 2003*, *Design Engineering Technological Conf*, Chicago, Il Sept 2003.
13. Hypponen H: *The Handbook on Inclusive Design for Telematics Applications*, Helsinki, Finland, 1999.
14. Nielsen J: *Usability Engineering*, Academic Press, London, 1993.
15. Ulrich KT, Eppinger SD: *Product Design and Development*, McGraw-Hill, New York, 1995.
16. ISO 13407:1999(E): *Human-Centred Design Processes for Interactive Systems*, International Organisation for Standards, 1999.
17. Wood LE: *User Interface Design, Bridging the Gap from User Requirements to Design*, CRC Press, Boca Raton, FL, 1998.
18. Newell AF, Gregor P: User sensitive inclusive design—in search of a new paradigm, *Proc ACM Conf Universal Usability*, Washington, DC, Nov 2000, pp 39–44.
19. Gregor P, Newell AF: Designing for dynamic diversity making accessible interfaces for older people, in Jorge J, Heller R, Guedj R, eds, *Proc 2001 EC/NSF Workshop on Universal Accessibility of Ubiquitous Computing: Providing for the Elderly*, Alcacer do Sal, Portugal, May 22–25, 2001, ACM Press, 2001.
20. Alm N: Ethical issues in AAC research, In Brodin J, Ajessibm EB, eds, *Methodological Issues in Research in Augmentative and Alternative Communication, Proc 3rd ISAAC Research Symp*, Jonkoping, Universty Press, Sweden, 1994, pp 98–104.
21. Newell AF: Inclusive design or assistive technology, in Clarkson J, Coleman R, Keates S, Lebbon C, eds, *Inclusive Design for the Whole Population*, Springer, 2003, pp 172–181.
22. Gregor P, Newell AF: The application of computing technology to interpersonal communication at the University of Dundee's Department of Applied Computing, *Technol Disab*, **10**:107–113 (1999).
23. Waller A, Alm N, van der Merve K, Cunningham J, McDonald JS, McGregor A, Robertson J: Two documentaries about AAC, *Proc 7th Biennial Conf International Society for Augmentative and Alternative Communication*, Vancouver, Canada, Aug 7–10, 1996, pp 49–50.
24. Alm N, McGregor A, Arnott JL, Newell AF: Using prestored text in conversation by an AAC user, *6th Int Conf International Society for Augmentative and Alternative Communication*, Philadelphia, 1992 [abstract published in *Augment Altern Commun* (Aug 1992)].
25. McGregor A, Alm N: Thoughts of a non-speaking member of an AAC research team, *6th Int Conf International Society for Augmentative and Alternative Communication*, Philadelphia, 1992 [abstract published in *Augment Altern Commun* (Aug 1992).]
26. McGregor A: A voice for the future, *Proc European Conf Advancement of Rehabilitation Technology (ECART '95)*, National Secretariat of Rehabilitation, Lisbon, Portugal, Oct 10–13, 1995, pp 127–129.

27. Keates S, Clarkson PJ: Defining design exclusion, in Keates S, Langdon P, Clarkson PJ, Robinson P, eds, *Universal Access and Assistive Technology,* Springer-Verlag, London, 2002, pp 13–22.
28. Lines L, Hone KS: Research methods for older adults, in Brewster S, Zajicek M, eds, *A New Research Agenda for Older Adults*, Workshop at BCS HCI 2002, London, 2002.
29. Barrett J, Kirk S: Running focus groups with elderly and disabled elderly participants, *Appl Ergon* **31**:621–629 (2000).
30. Gheeraw RR, Lebbon CS: Inclusive design—developing theory through practice, in Keates S, Langdon P, Clarkson PJ, Robinson P, eds, *Universal Access and Assistive Technology*, Springer-Verlag, London, 2002, pp 43–52.
31. Hardy M, Baird C:Is it all about aging: Technology and aging in social context, in Charness N, Schaie W, eds, *Impact of Technology on Successful Aging*, Springer, New York, 2002.
32. Eisma R, Dickinson A, Goodman J, Syme A, Tiwari L, Newell A: Early user involvement in the development of information technology-related products for older people, *Univ Access Inform Soc*, **3**(2) (Dec 2003).
33. Marquie JC, Jourdan-Boddaert L, Huet N: Do older adults underestimate their actual computer knowledge? *Behav Inform Technol* **21**(4): 273–280 (2002).
34. Park D, Schwarz N, eds, *Cognitive Aging: A Primer*, Psychology Press, Taylor & Francis Group, Hove, UK, 2000.
35. Kayser-Jones J, Koenig BA: Ethical issues, in Gubrium JF, Sanker A, eds, *Qualitative Methods in Aging Research*, Sage, Thousands Oaks, CA, 1994, pp 15–32
36. Russell C: Interviewing vulnerable old people: Ethical and methodological implications of imagining our subjects, *J Aging Stud* **13**(4):403–417 (1999).
37. Eisma R, Dickinson A, Goodman J, Mival OJ, Syme A, Tiwari L: Mutual inspiration in the development of new technology for older people, *Proc Include 2003*, London, March 2003, Vol 7, pp 252–259.
38. Mival O: In search of the cybermuse: Supporting creative activity within product design, *Proc Creativity and Cognition Conf* 2002, Vol 4, p 20.
39. Inglis E, Szymkowiak A, Gregor P, Newell AF, Hine N, Wilson BA, Evans J: Issues surrounding the user-centred development of a new interactive memory aid, in Keates S, Langdon P, Clarkson PJ, Robinson P, eds, *Universal Access and Assistive Technology*, Springer-Verlag, London, 2002, pp 171–178.
40. Reed D: Towards dependability of technology assessment in the delivery of care to the elderly: A case study, in Brewster S, Zajicek M, eds, *A New Research Agenda for Older Adults*, Workshop at BCS HCI 2002, London, 2002.
41. Dickinson A, Goodman J, Syme A, Eisma R, Tiwari L, Mival O, Newell AF: Domesticating technology. In-home requirements gathering with frail older people, *Proc HCI Int*, Crete, June 2003.
42. Monk A, Baxter G: Would you trust a computer to run your home? Dependability issues in smart homes for older adults, in Brewster S, Zajicek M, eds, *A New Research Agenda for Older Adults*, Workshop at BCS HCI 2002, London, 2002.
43. Newell AF, Morgan ME, Gregor P, Carmicheal A: Theatre as an intermediary between users and CHI designers, *Proc CHI 2006*, Montreal, April 2006.
44. Boal A: *The Rainbow of Desire*, Routledge, London, 1995.
45. McKenna S, Marquis-Faulkes F, Newell AF, Gregor P: Scenario-based drama as a tool for investigating user requirements with application to home monitoring for elderly people, *Proc 10th Int Conf Human-Computer Interaction*, Crete, 2003.

46. Sato S, Salvador T: Playacting and focus troupes: Theatre techniques for creating quick, intensive, immersive and engaging focus group sessions, *Interactions* 35–41 (Sept–Oct 1999).
47. Strom G: Perception of human-centered stories and technical descriptions when analyzing and negotiating requirements, *Proc IFIP TC13 Interact 2003 Conf*, 2003.
48. Dickinson A, Eisma R, Syme A, Gregor P: UTOPIA: Usable Technology for Older People: Inclusive and Appropriate, in Brewster S, Zajicek M, eds, *A New Research Agenda for Older Adults*, *Proc BCS HCI*, London, 2002, pp 38–39.
49. Carmichael A, Newell AF, Dickinson A, Morgan M: Using theatre and film to represent user requirements, *Proc Include 2005*, Royal College of Art, London, April 5–8, 2005.
50. Newell AF, Carmichael A, Morgan M, Dickinson A, The use of theatre in requirements gathering and usability studies, *Interacting with Computers*, Elsevier, 2006, Vol **18**, pp 996–1011.
51. Grudin J: Why personas work—the psychological evidence, in Pruitt J, Adlin T, eds, *The Persona Lifecycle, Keeping People in Mind throughout Product Design*, Elsevier, 2006.
52. Dishman E: Designing for the new world, in Laurel B, ed, *Design Research*, MIT Press, pp 41–48.
53. Wixon D: Evaluating usability methods, Interactions, A.C.M., 29–34 (July–Aug 2003).

44

Universal Design/Design for All: Practice and Method

Edward Steinfeld
State University of New York at Buffalo

In this chapter, we examine how paradigms for design for aging and disability are merging through the concept of universal design. The basic elements of the universal design philosophy are described and key tools for practicing it are illustrated. Examples are used to demonstrate the application of universal design to issues of aging. The chapter concludes with a critical view of universal design and some thoughts on how the concept can evolve in the future.

44.1 INTRODUCTION

From the 1950s on, enlightened design for aging focused on the provision of specialized environments and products to accommodate the circumstances of late adulthood [1–3]. The primary goal is to provide supportive physical settings and devices to compensate for age-related changes in mobility, perception, and cognition. These specialized environments and products enhance safety and function for older people by ensuring that the demands of the environment are within their adaptive capacity [4]. Proponents of design for aging not only addressed support for independence in activities of daily living but also, on the basis of evidence from the field of environmental psychology that demonstrated how the physical environment mediated social relationships [5,6], developed interventions to support positive social relations as well as physical independence. Age-segregated settings were thus planned and designed to support increased friendship

---

The Engineering Handbook of Smart Technology for Aging, Disability, and Independence,
Edited by A. Helal, M. Mokhtari and B. Abdulrazak
Copyright © 2008 John Wiley & Sons, Inc.

formation and mutual assistance to offset the loss of friends and spouses, a common occurrence in older adulthood.

The concept of the environment as an accommodation to physical and social losses related to aging, or "prosthetic design," was a key paradigmatic shift. Prior to this conceptualization, the problems of aging, when addressed at all by designers, focused on basic shelter needs. Aging was associated with an inevitable decline in function and reduced participation in social life. People were expected to adapt to the environment rather than the other way around. The new paradigm shifted the blame for age-related declines from the individual to social and physical environments. Limitations in function and isolation were reconceptualized as a result of the interaction of individuals with environments that had not been designed with aging in mind, rather than just an inevitable result of the aging process itself. Design for aging demonstrated that people can indeed maintain independence and healthy social interaction in old age even when faced with significant physical and social losses, if provided with a supportive environment [7].

Assistive technology emerged in the field of rehabilitation. Rehabilitation specialists learned that they could improve function for people with disabilities through training and therapy, but new technologies were needed to help people become more mobile and independent. Barrier-free design expanded the reach of assistive technology by intervening in the community—schools, workplaces, homes, and eventually public buildings. It clearly incorporated the design-as-prosthesis paradigm. Interventions in the social sphere also emerged in design for disability as they did in design for aging. The concept of "normalization" focused on providing environments that did not stigmatize the individual or add to the stigma caused by disability [8]. However, rather than focusing on socializing with other people who had disabilities, normalization theory focused on the goal of community integration and was implemented in practice through policies of deinstitutionalization and the development of community-based programs of services to people with disabilities.

In the late 1970s, a new paradigm emerged for environmental interventions that address disability—universal design. This new idea had roots in both barrier-free design and normalization theory. The most commonly used definition of universal design is "The design of products and environments to be usable by all people, to the greatest extent possible, without the need for adaptation or specialized design" [9]. Often called "design for all" in Europe, universal design is based on the conception of the environment as a *field of opportunity*. It extends the idea of prosthetic design to the community and society as a whole. In universal design, the objective is not to design special "prosthetic" settings and devices for a protected class of people. Rather, the idea is to improve the general environment in order to reduce the need for such settings and devices. Everybody benefits from universal design, not just people with disabilities. The curb ramp is often used as an good example. When curb ramps were not universal, people who used wheeled mobility devices were trapped within a boundary of inaccessible sidewalks. When curb ramps became common, not only did people with disabilities gain more mobility in the community, but other citizens like parents with strollers, bicyclists, rollerbladers and skateboarders, soon realized that they benefited also. While not included in the definition itself, one important argument advanced to support adoption of universal design was to reduce the stigma caused by the association of special products and settings with disability. For example, although everyone can benefit from the added safety provided by grab bars in bathtubs and showers, few people without disabilities are willing to recognize their universal value because acknowledging a need for a grab bar is interpreted as perceiving oneself as disabled.

Universal design emerged as the disability rights and independent living movements were demonstrating that people with severe disabilities could function independently in integrated community settings, if the environment provided the opportunity for them to do so. This "ecologic" perspective on the relationship between the individual and the environment mirrors theory in design for aging. In fact, theorists in design for aging argue that poor "congruence" between abilities and environmental demands could occur when an older person lives in an environment that does not provide enough challenge or stimulation as well as when the demands of the environment are overwhelming [4,10]. Moreover, new theoretical perspectives view the environment as a field of resources and put more emphasis on how individual differences in motivation, skills, experience, and needs influence how an individual makes use of those resources over the latter part of the lifespan. More emphasis is placed on the perspective of the individual and how one interprets "congruence" and makes decisions such as whether to relocate, based on that personal interpretation [10]. This leads to a view of a successful environment to accommodate aging as one that provides as much of an opportunity as possible to exercise autonomy and choice. Universal design, if practiced in all domains of the environment, would, in fact, provide such a setting.

The appropriateness of the universal design paradigm has not been lost to advocates of older people, and thus, policy and practices for older people now reflect the universal design philosophy. Universal design has, in fact, blurred the boundaries between design for aging and design for disability. For example, the OXO Good Grips line of kitchen utensils, one of the first commercially successful examples of universal product design, were originally created by Sam Farber in response to the problems his wife had using conventional utensils when her arthritis became severe in old age [11]. New developments in housing for the older generation mirror earlier efforts at deinstitutionalization for young people with disabilities. The Olmstead decision by the Supreme Court is now being applied to reduce institutionalization for older people as well as younger individuals [12]. AARP's "livable communities" initiative also seeks to reshape American communities to support successful aging [13].

The evolution of universal design is paralleled by new conceptions of both disablement and aging. The World Health Organization, through its International Classification of Functioning, Disability and Health (ICF), defines the disablement process, interventions, and rehabilitation outcomes. The original version, called the *International Classification of Impairments, Disabilities and Handicaps* (ICIDH) [14], had a medical definition of disability that placed little emphasis on the role of the environment and individual differences in the disablement process. The new ICF [15], however, integrates environmental and personal factors and defines disablement in social as well as biological (medical) terms. Thus, the consensus paradigm for understanding disablement now reflects the same kind of thinking incorporated in the ecological model of aging [7].

Authors writing about design for aging have promoted many forms of the universal design paradigm. This is evident in terms like "lifespan design," "transgenerational design" [16], "design for aging in place" [17], and "livable communities" [13]. The ICF recognizes age as an important personal factor in the disablement process. This confluence of concepts and ideas is no coincidence because our conceptual model of aging has changed significantly over the years, as has our model of disablement. At one time, the older population was viewed as a monolithic block with similar needs that were defined by their chronologic age. Their age defined their "treatment." However, research in gerontology has demonstrated that chronologic age, biologic age, and social age are not always coincident [18]. As the older population increases, its diversity becomes more and more apparent. From a design perspective, the needs and desires of the older population cannot be pigeon holed as easily as they were in the mid-1970s–1980s. Thus, universal design increasingly makes sense as a response to the diversity of experiences among the aging.

Universal designs, intended for the broad consumer market, are likely to be more acceptable to the older population than assistive technology or accessible design because most older people do not self-identify as being "disabled." Disability plays an important role in the identity of someone who has had a functional impairment since birth. However, the vast majority of older people, while recognizing their age, find it difficult to define themselves as people with disabilities since they didn't have a disability in their formative years. Anything that signifies disability, therefore, can provoke a negative reaction. Thus, while a younger individual may see the great benefits of a wheeled mobility device, a cane, or a hearing aid, older people often resist using assistive technology until absolutely necessary, often with great risk, stress, and unhappiness.

In summary, universal design emerged from the fields of barrier-free design and assistive technology, but it shares a common conceptual foundation with design for aging. It represents a new paradigm and extends the idea of adapting the environment to the world at large. Rather than thinking about prosthetic support for special groups of people, universal design seeks to create a field of opportunities that supports choice and autonomy as well as function. Universal design emerged as our models of disablement and aging were changing. Today, the prevailing definitions of both are as much social definitions as they are biologic. So it is quite understandable that design for disability and design for aging are now merging through the universal design philosophy.

44.2 KEY TOOLS

The most important tool for the practice of universal design is a document titled *The Principles of Universal Design* [9,19]. This document was developed to clarify the scope of universal design and to provide some guidance in both design and evaluation activities. The developers were a multidisciplinary group of experts (including this author). The seven principles are

1. *Equitable use*—the design is useful and marketable to people with diverse abilities.
2. *Flexibility in use*—the design accommodates a wide range of individual preferences and abilities.
3. *Simple and intuitive*—use of the design is easy to understand, regardless of the user's experience, knowledge, language skills, or current concentration level.
4. *Perceptible information*—the design communicates necessary information effectively to the user, regardless of ambient conditions or the user's sensory abilities.
5. *Tolerance for error*—the design minimizes hazards and the adverse consequences of accidental or unintended actions.
6. *Low physical effort*—the design can be used efficiently and comfortably and with a minimum degree of fatigue.

7. *Size and space for approach and use*—appropriate size and space is provided for approach, reach, manipulation, and use regardless of user's body size, posture, or mobility.

Four or five guidelines give more specific criteria for meeting each principle. For example, one guideline for Principle 2 (Flexibility in Use) is "Accommodate right- or left-handed access and use." Many researchers and practitioners throughout the world have been using the definition and the Principles for almost 10 years. Translations have appeared in many languages [20]. In general, the definition and Principles have been widely accepted and have certainly helped to communicate and disseminate the idea of universal design. Researchers developed and tested a set of evaluative tools that can be used by both consumers and design professionals to compare and rate different designs using the principles and the guidelines [21].

44.3 UNIVERSAL DESIGN AND AGING

When applied to design for older people, universal design has many important implications. One way to understand them is to review current practices in different domains of design for aging.

At the community domain, universal design implies that community planning should seek to integrate older people into the community to the greatest extent possible and help them remain mobile as long as possible. Community planning and services can facilitate the development of social networks and participation in key social roles within one's peer group and also in the larger, multigenerational community. The traditional emphasis of planning for aging in American communities has been on developing "housing for the elderly" and "retirement communities"—both are prosthetic strategies. This emphasis may support peer group integration but not full community integration. Age segregated environments may, in fact, create an artificial type of socialization that is based on limited opportunity rather than mutual interests [22,23]. Neighborhoods with high concentrations of older people do not have to be totally age-segregated. In fact, early research on social contact and aging demonstrated that concentrations of seniors of 50% or more were sufficient to support increased social contact and other benefits [24]. The formative studies on age segregation were done before the advent of accessible public transportation, advanced information technology, and intelligent vehicular and highway systems. They were also completed at a time when practices in urban planning focused exclusively on the single-use, automobile-oriented land-use pattern, even in urban areas.

The vast majority of older people wish to remain living in their own neighborhoods and their existing housing [25–27]. Greater emphasis on design for pedestrian safety, security, and convenience; accessible forms of vehicular transportation; and communication and information technologies that enable aging in place and housing-remodeling technologies would support this clearly expressed preference. Moreover, planning for mixed use, walkable, high-density communities served by accessible public transportation or "traditional neighborhood development" would promote social integration across generations [13]. This type of development could include the size and types of dwelling units that older people would be attracted to and thus result in naturally occurring retirement communities (NORCs) out of choice rather than lack of choice.

At the scale of buildings and sites, facilities that are fully accessible according to laws such as the Americans with Disabilities Act certainly support independent use throughout the lifespan to a degree, but, the design standards used, do not address many of the functional limitations associated with aging. For example, access standards do not require acoustic environments that will support good legibility of speech by people with age-related hearing losses. Thus, restaurants, theaters, religious institutions, social halls, and classrooms and other social environments are often difficult and annoying to use by older patrons. Participating in events held in such places can be a trying and embarrassing experience for them.

Universal design, as opposed to simple code compliant accessible design, should address problems faced by older people that the codes do not cover. In addition to acoustics, other universal design applications not covered by access codes include glare-free illumination (artificial and natural), adjustable light levels, safe designs for stairways, nonslip walking surfaces, convenient places to rest, improved directional signs, easy-to-understand building layouts, and other facilities and features. While buildings designed for use primarily by the older generation clearly could benefit from universal design, it is less apparent but equally important that universal design be adopted in public accommodations such as civic buildings, health facilities, adult educational settings, and recreational facilities. Increasingly, the older generation, which has a much higher level of affluence than did previous elders and the highest disposable income of any age group in the population [28], will use these facilities more intensively than other age groups.

Inclusion of universal design in housing and long-term care settings intended to serve an older population seems obvious, but it is surprising how few universal design features are incorporated into such buildings. As in public buildings, the minimum requirements of accessibility codes are often viewed as sufficient to meet the needs of older residents, with the addition of some safety features such as emergency call systems. All multi-family housing and institutional facilities have to meet accessibility code requirements to ensure at least a minimum level of access. But the majority of Americans live in single-family housing that is not covered by accessibility codes at all except for very small numbers of units (5% in publicly funded projects). Condominium units in apartment buildings constructed since 1991 are covered by the Fair Housing Law and must comply with the Fair Housing Accessibility Guidelines. However, these guidelines apply only to units in elevator-equipped buildings and the first floor of walkups. They do not apply to single-family attached (townhouses) or detached units, even if they are sold in a condominium arrangement. All across the country, affluent retired people are moving into new housing that has stairs at all entrances and often stairs to reach bedrooms or a bathroom. In some cases, builders include sunken or raised sections of living areas, and, access to balconies and terraces often require negotiating steps. So-called retirement housing often has bathrooms and kitchens that are not large enough to use a wheelchair inside, doors that are too narrow for wheelchair passage, bathtubs and showers without grab bars, storage that is out of reach for someone who has a limited range of reach, kitchens that are unusable if one does not have the stamina or ability to stand up to work, and other barriers to aging in place. In addition, since children of older people generally live in inaccessible single-family homes, frail older people often have a difficult time visiting their closest relatives.

A new concept called "visitability" is gaining interest across the country. Visitable housing has basic access features that can be incorporated with very little cost. Although not fully accessible, visitable units can be used independently by most people with disabilities and can be adapted to accommodate more severe limitations much more easily than can housing that is not accessible at all. About 45 communities and states in the United States have adopted visitability ordinances or laws, with an additional 30 initiatives in process [29]. Most apply to all houses built with at least some public funding, but some apply to privately financed housing as well. Some visitability ordinances are not mandatory, and some provide incentives to incorporate the visitability features. The basic access features include at least one stepless entry, doors and passageways on the main floor that are wide enough to accommodate a wheelchair, and a bathroom that a person in a wheelchair can enter, close the door to, and exit. Some ordinances and laws also include reinforcement in bathroom walls for future installation of grab bars, and/or some include provisions for electrical controls to be located within reach of wheelchair users.

However, visitability does not provide a full complement of universally designed features. Other voluntary initiatives are promoting the idea of universal design in single-family housing as a means to "age in place." These initiatives include demonstration homes and commitment programs. The former are built in home shows or a "parade of homes" where the members of homebuilder associations show off their products. Universal design is viewed, by many builders, as helpful in marketing to the baby boomer generation because it does not carry a stigma of "design for disability." In a commitment program, a builder receives certification from a third-party organization if they meet certain requirements. The first program like this in the United States on a state level is Easy Living Homes in Georgia [30]. While the features of housing suitable for "aging in place" have not yet been codified in any way, they include stair-free entries, enhanced task lighting, higher electric outlets, kitchen countertops with multiple levels to accommodate sitting and standing work, major appliances that have easy-to-grip controls and high-contrast graphics, intercom systems, accessible full bathrooms, laundries and a sleeping area on the first floor, and smart home technologies.

The expanding older population is receiving attention from the consumer product industry. This is probably the means through which older people will first gain experience with universal design. Many universally designed products are already available on the market. Examples are utensils with larger nonslip handles that are easier to grip, large-format books, audiobooks, automated can and jar openers, lightweight garden tools, and laundry appliances with front-loading doors that are raised up on pedestals. However, the adoption of universal design varies significantly by product type. In the writing implement industry, for example, the adoption of universal design has been extensive. Most companies produce a line of pens with large grips. Extensive adoption has also occurred in the kitchen utensil industries. But, in some other industries, like small and major appliances and consumer electronics, adoption of universal design has been limited.

In some product industries, design trends have actually hindered usability by older people. For example, the mobile telephone industry continues to make more complex phones and reduce the size to the smallest possible package, which results in functions that are difficult for older people to understand, with very small keys and cramped interkey spacing. While voice activation features can reduce the need for using a keypad, they do not work well in noisy environments and require a greater understanding of the system to program properly. In Japan, older people were having so many problems with usability of mobile telephones that one company introduced a larger telephone with fewer features, designed specifically for the older consumer. However, Japanese experts in universal design report that this telephone was quickly labeled as an "old person's phone" and thus was not successful in the broader market place.

It should be noted that universal design can be used as a marketing ploy without much substance. For example, American and Japanese car manufacturers have devoted attention to adding design features for older buyers [31,32]. However, prevailing trends in the industry demonstrate that these efforts have focused on relatively minor concerns like easier to grasp controls or are relegated to high-price options or luxury cars. Two key features of automobile design that could dramatically improve use by older people are improving the usability and comfort of seatbelts and developing entry systems that make it easier to get in and out of the vehicle. Yet, there is practically no innovation in these two areas. Current fashions continue to emphasize the SUV (sport utility vehicle) and small sporty automobiles that have a low profile, basic platforms that are both difficult for older people to use. The former require climbing up into the vehicle, and, the latter require significant bending at the trunk and flexing at the hips and knees to get in and out [33].

In the public transportation sector, many good examples of universal design have been adopted in response to the ADA. Bus manufacturers, for example, have adopted low-floor designs that, combined with "kneeling" suspension systems and ramps, make entering a bus significantly easier for all users by eliminating stairs. Intercity transportation has been enhanced by accessible commuter trains, over-the-road buses with lifts, airplanes with accessible lavatories, and stair-free access to small commuter airplanes. Transit innovations include the provision of websites that help to identify the accessible routes and stations and even provide real-time information on elevator breakdowns at stations. Many cities are installing more bus shelters and including seating and other comfort and convenience features in them.

Universal design is making significant inroads in the communications and information technology industries. Information transaction machines [e.g., automatic teller machines (e.g. (ATMs)] are now required by law to meet accessibility requirements that include many universal design features, such as audible instructions and simplified and standardized protocols. Since the 2000 Florida punch card debacle, an effort has been underway to simplify the voting process, including the adoption of electronic voting machines that can adapt to the user's preferences and abilities [34]. The telecommunications industry has been gradually introducing additional accessibility features. The Americans with Disabilities Act required all states to establish a toll-free relay system for communicating with people who are deaf. More recent efforts have been focused on developing improved access to mobile phones by making them compatible with TTY's and hearing aids [35]. Computer operating systems like Windows and Mac DOS have accessibility features built into them to enable users to adjust the display to provide higher contrast, larger type, different type and background colors, and other options [36–38]. Accessibility to the Internet has addressed compatibility of websites with screen reading software used by people who are blind to convert screen text to spoken word. The Web Accessibility Initiative also has focused on developing guidelines that address improved visibility of websites for people with limitations of vision, simplification of navigation, and reduction in hand movements [39]. These developments, while focused on avoiding discrimination on the basis of disability, benefit the older population by making systems less burdensome, easier to perceive, and easier to understand. They also facilitate use of assistive technology such as screen readers. It should be noted that, although people with disabilities are aware of these accessibility advances, older people rarely know about them or utilize them effectively [40].

This short survey of progress in universal design as it applies to the older person demonstrates that the concept can be applied to any scale of the built environment as well as to communications and information system products. Some organizations are also now starting to explore how business practices can incorporate universal design. For example, a governor of Kumamoto Prefecture in Japan made universal design a key aspect of her campaign and, when elected, charged all the agencies in her government to develop at least one new application of universal design in their activities. This resulted in innovations such as public education programs that raise awareness in schoolchildren about how the environment can create barriers to independence and use. There are many possible applications of universal design in business practices that would benefit the older population. For example, universal design principles could be used to rethink the income tax filing system, voicemail systems, and even eligibility or means tests.

44.4 METHODS

One of the most interesting issues related to universal design is how it is implemented or "practiced." Rather than style or technology, the focus of universal design is on enabling the end user—human-centered design. Thus, it behooves practitioners to engage end users in the process to the maximum extent possible. Most designers are young or middle-aged adults who have little experience with functional limitations. Moreover, design professionals no longer design products for their own cultural context alone; design has become a global enterprise. This demands an even greater understanding of the end user's needs and perspectives.

With respect to design for aging, the differences between the designers and the end users are even larger. Not only do younger designers lack personal experience with the reality of late adulthood; there is also a gulf of understanding caused by different generational experiences. This creates a new kind of cultural difference, defined by time rather than geography or ethnicity. In a world of rapid and sometimes revolutionary change in technology, the values, attitudes, and expectations of the younger generation of designers are often vastly different from those of older people who use the products, environments, and systems that they create.

There are many ways to obtain greater awareness and understanding of the end user. The most obvious methods are second-hand—reading the research literature and hiring expert consultants. However, the literature is not very easy to access or interpret, and experts who can effectively translate the research literature for application to design are not always available or affordable for every project.

Consulting the end user directly during the design process is another effective approach. Focus groups bring small groups of people with specific backgrounds or a mixture of backgrounds together to give input at key stages of the design process. Focus groups are useful for "requirements gathering," identifying problems that end users have with existing products or systems, or to evaluate design guidelines and early prototypes. In universal design, focus groups should engage a broad range of people. Older participants may be just one of a number of end-user groups. An innovative method for implementing focus groups is the use of "theater," in which actors are used to videorecord scripted dramatizations of products and environments in use. These dramatizations are then presented to focus groups for comment [41].

A major limitation of focus groups is that only a small group of users can be engaged in the process. A concept called "reference users" is one way to overcome that limitation. Designers identify a set of hypothetical end users that the product, environment, or system needs to accommodate. These reference users may be identified by demographic criteria like age, ethnic background, education, and health status. They could also be identified by functional abilities or anthropometric variables like individuals with the 5th percentile range of arm motion or the 95th percentile in wheelchair size. Data must be available on the variables used to establish the reference users. The design process then seeks to satisfy the established needs and preferences of all the reference users selected as the target for design. Focus groups, selected on the same basis, could confirm the results.

The most intensive use of end users in the design process is as "expert user consultants" [42] in the creative phases of the design process, as well as in requirements gathering and evaluation activities. One approach to user participation in design is to develop a menu of potential options for different design features and engage representative users in selecting the features to be included. Scale modeling, in which end users can actually manipulate replicas of design elements to create architectural, landscape, or interior designs, is also an effective method, once components of the building are designed. Finally, full-scale modeling increases the reality of the simulation exercise by allowing end users to actually get inside and evaluate the anthropometric fit of an architectural space first-hand (see, e.g., Danford and Steinfeld [43]). Design participation projects are particularly effective if the participants are the actual clients. In the elder cohousing movement, for example, future residents of a project participate in the planning and design of their own homes and the overall community from the start [44]. In this process there is a close fit between the user's needs and the result, and, where the budget is not sufficient to provide everything that the residents need or desire, they are the ones who make the decisions about tradeoffs. In design participation activities, it is very important that the participants be well educated about universal design before the project begins.

Often, practitioners of universal design forget that producing a design that addresses the user needs and preferences of a wide range of people does not, in itself, guarantee successful completion of a development project. There are many other stakeholders in the process of design. The design has to be "sold" to decisionmakers, or "gatekeepers," in the producing organization. The more people who have to be persuaded to buy into a design, the more difficult it will be to gain adoption of a new design practice. The more change required to implement the new paradigm, the more resistance it is likely to engender [45]. Thus, universal design practitioners need to understand the process of innovation and ensure that the design is acceptable to the key people within the producing organization. Outside stakeholders may also have considerable decisionmaking authority. As an example, the incorporation of flexible plumbing connections in adjustable-height sinks requires acceptance by building code authorities. Developing national standards for a new technology application or submitting a product to a testing laboratory for review and evaluation can facilitate code acceptance. Much research has been completed on diffusion of innovations [45]. This literature is particularly useful in making decisions about the degree of innovation to include in any design cycle.

It is important to note that consumers also need to be persuaded to adopt innovations. While mass media are good at increasing awareness of new ideas, communication through existing social networks is the most effective strategy for persuading people to adopt an innovation [45]. The older population today may not use media in the same way as younger generations did. However, this will probably change drastically as the baby boomers enter maturity. Infomercials, cable television shopping channels, and telemarketing may be replaced by product placements in movies by Steven Spielberg and online blogs. Rather than using Lawrence Welk or Ed McMahon as pitchmen, it may be more effective to recruit celebrities from the new generation of elders like Martha Stewart and Bob Villa to become champions of universal design. Much needs to be learned, moreover, about how to use social networks to diffuse universal design. Should marketers focus on certain groups of baby boomers, for example, who may become opinion leaders and change agents? Should certain venues be targeted like resorts or the travel- and leisure-related industries? Could viral marketing techniques that are now being used to market new products to younger generations be effective with the next generation of older people?

To have an impact, a universal design ultimately needs to be commercially successful. Functional benefits alone are not sufficient to ensure this. Cagan and Vogel [46] studied the attributes of very successful, or "breakthrough," products. Their work led them to identify seven "value opportunities": emotion, ergonomics, aesthetics, identity, impact, core technology and quality [46]. The more value opportunities that a product addresses, the more likely that it will be successful in the marketplace. Cagan and Vogel demonstrate that the OXO Good Grips products became a "breakthrough product" because they addressed many of the value opportunities better than competitive products. While the good news is that OXO's emphasis on universal design helped them address many of the value opportunities, there were clearly additional reasons that led to its success besides universal design.

In summary, universal design can be characterized as user-centered design and thus requires methods to involve the end users in requirement setting, evaluation, and generations of design solutions. Also, as a process that most likely will result in innovation, universal design requires attention to how innovation is most effectively diffused to ensure that it actually will be implemented by the producing organization and accepted by consumers. Finally, it needs to address other issues besides universal design to be successful. Functional and social benefits by themselves will not necessarily mean success in the marketplace.

44.5 THE FUTURE OF UNIVERSAL DESIGN

To speculate on the future of universal design, it is helpful to start with a critical perspective on the concept as currently practiced. There has been criticism of both the definition of universal design and the "Principles." In fact, many variants have appeared in the literature, suggesting that they don't quite fit all stakeholders' needs.

Human factors experts argue that universal design is simply good human factors or ergonomic design. Universal design is indeed based on many human factors principles, but it includes an additional goal—a social justice agenda—that is not always addressed by ergonomic design. For example, design of a new mobile phone keyboard may accommodate a range of finger sizes; it may have voice activation; and, the volume control may provide options for different hearing abilities. But, can the keyboard be used by people who have deformed fingers, does it have voice activation that can be trained to the accent of a user with a speech impediment, and is it compatible with a TTY (teletype) machine used by many deaf people to send messages? Universal design should address all these issues. In general, it would include a search for new ways to increase the traditional user population served by mobile phones. Thus, universal design incorporates a philosophical commitment to rethinking problems and to discovering innovative solutions to increase inclusion. It is "ergonomic design with a social conscience."

Another criticism is that universal design is nothing more than assistive technology. In fact, assistive technology has historically been a source of ideas for innovative products. The telephone, email, and voice recognition all originated in assistive technology. Yet, universal design requires more than just functional benefits. It extends the concept of inclusion to aesthetics. Universal design would not be successful if only people with disabilities would use the product because its appearance was stigmatizing. Consider the built-up handles commonly used by occupational therapists to adapt silverware and utensils for people who have gripping limitations. It was not until the OXO, Friskars, and other companies adapted this concept to mass-marketed products that anyone else used built-up handles. Moreover, the availability of inexpensive, large, easy-to-grip handles on utensils and tools in the local hardware store and supermarket radically increased the availability and lowered the cost of this feature to people with disabilities. Eventually, the stigma associated with built-up handles was eliminated and they became an element of style on their own. This is an example of universal design as "assistive technology for the masses."

Another focus of criticism has been the language and form of the "Principles." The definition itself seems so general that it is criticized as being too obvious. Moreover, if taken literally, it seems utopian and unrealistic. Everyone knows, for example, that there will always be someone who will be unable to use a product or environment, but the definition does not explicitly convey that understanding. At least two of the Principles do not translate well into other languages, and some of the titles are not clear. For example, "tolerance for error" seems to imply that errors can actually be tolerated, whereas the intent of this principle is to reduce errors in the use of a product and environment. "Equitable in use" translates literally in at least one language to "equal opportunity," which is a legal term related to civil rights. Although it is a related concept, universal design in itself cannot guarantee civil rights, and it can be practiced without legal mandates. "Flexibility in use" seems to imply that all objects should bend during use.

The Principles also lack clarity in the goals that they embody. "Equitable in use" focuses on a social justice goal, "flexibility in use" seems to promote a design strategy, and the rest focus on performance goals. There has been criticism that the concept of social participation, as incorporated in the ICF, is missing in the definition and the principles. Some experts (even those in this group of authors) have also argued that, as worded and organized, the Principles are more suited to product design than other design activities.

Although universal design is generally associated with design based on functional abilities, some critics have argued that the concept can be used as a "big tent" to encompass many other aspects of design for social justice. For example, Leslie Kanes Weisman has described how conventional housing design practices discriminate against women, especially if they are single parents [47]. She argues that universal design should address these problems. Others suggest that it should also address affordability to ensure that the benefits of adopting universal design accrue to all income strata and societies with different levels of development. For example, although all the features that would be possible to include in a home for affluent retirees may not be affordable in public housing units for low-income seniors, some key features of universal design could be included in the latter without significantly affecting the affordability of the home. Obviously the result in terms of performance would be very different in the two economic contexts, so the relationship between resources and performance seems to be an important factor to consider. Finally, others have argued that universal design should address cultural differences that can affect usability and safety. Examples include the use of colors, whose meaning varies from culture to culture; differences in personal hygiene methods; or differences in norms for clothing that restrict movement and agility.

Another criticism of the definition and the Principles is that they do not provide any metric or standard against which to determine whether a product, environment, or system is indeed an effective universal design. This criticism is rooted in the lack of benchmarking. For example, how do we compare a universal design to one that isn't, and how do we establish best practices to be emulated? The lack of a body of evidence tied to the principles is a serious barrier to their use in practice. In fact, even the guidelines are not in a form that can be easily tied to the research and design literature. There is no information provided, for example, on what criteria one would use to determine whether a product did in fact accommodate both right- and left-handed individuals.

Efforts are underway to revisit the definition of universal design and the principles in order to address these criticisms. The Rehabilitation Engineering Center on Universal Design and the Built Environment, housed at the IDEA Center and codirected by the author, has started a long term project called "Evidence-Based Guidelines." The objective of this project is to assemble a body of evidence on universal design from existing documented research findings. This project will review the scientific literature to produce metrics for the guidelines and the design literature to gather best-practice examples to illustrate their implementation. To facilitate this work, we will propose changes to the definition and Principles and expand the guidelines to incorporate a full range of issues addressed in different domains of design. We will also propose ways to reconcile the definition and principles with the ICF. In particular, we will propose casting the definition of universal design in the context of available resources, incorporating a view of design as a continuous process of quality improvement and adding an explicit statement of social participation as a design goal. This work will provide a conduit to tie future research more directly to design practices and policy development. Another project, the "Effectiveness of Universal Design in Practice," will develop a method for setting benchmarks for universal design and establish benchmarks for selected high-priority environmental features.

44.6 CONCLUSIONS

Universal design should be viewed as a process rather than an end state. It may be more appropriate to use the term "universal designing." The most commonly used definition of the concept does not address this perspective and thus is often criticized as impractical. However, if one takes a long view and recognizes that the pace of innovation is often slow at first, small steps toward greater inclusion in design in any industry can be viewed as successful implementations. As we have seen in the computer technology field, experience with the initial incorporation of a few accessibility features in computer software that were easy for the developers to introduce resulted in full integration of many more features in later years. The initial cycle of innovations confirmed their value with little risk and set the stage for further cycles. This is likely to be a successful strategy in many industries for introducing universal design to the older consumer. But it is important that the early introduction of universal design actually address real needs effectively and also that it does not become associated as "design for disability" because then, the older consumer will think it is for "them" not for "us."

The "Principles of Universal Design" provided a way to communicate the essence of the concept widely, and they have been effective in reaching the disability and rehabilitation community. However, they have not been so effective in reaching mainstream consumers. While some design firms, manufacturers, and even entire industrial sectors have embraced universal design, it is far from an established practice. The definition and the principles need to be reconsidered so that they clarify the purpose and practice of universal design, avoid confusion, and provide more effective guidance to designers in implementation. Establishing a strong link between research and practice is particularly important as "evidence-based practice" becomes mainstream.

It is important that the dialog on universal design not lose sight of the fact that products, environments, and systems that improve functional independence and social participation for their users will not necessary be embraced by producers and related stakeholders or be successful in the marketplace simply for those reasons. Thus, more attention needs to be given to the process of diffusing new universal design ideas within the producer organization and related stakeholders in various industries. Likewise, effective methods to educate and communicate universal design to today's elders and the baby boomer generation are needed. One of the most promising ideas is the concept of endorsement and labeling. AARP and Home Depot launched a partnership to promote universal design using this approach. Studying this program could be very helpful in learning more about how to market the concept effectively.

Ultimately, there are many reasons why products, environments, and systems are successful. Thus, it is important that designers and producers not focus exclusively on the attributes of universal design as part of product development activities. While universal design is a good way to add value to products, other value opportunities need to be addressed to ensure success in the marketplace. The real goal is to produce really, really good products that incorporate universal design features.

ACKNOWLEDGMENT

This chapter was developed with funding from the US Department of Education, National Institute of Disability and Rehabilitation Research, Contract H133E050004. The contents of this report do not necessarily reflect the views of the US Department of Education.

REFERENCES

1. Koncelik JA: *Designing the Open Nursing Home*, Dowden, Hutchinson & Ross, Stroudsburg, PA, 1976.
2. Regnier V: *Design for Assisted Living: Guidelines for Housing the Physically and Mentally Frail*, Wiley, New York, 2002.
3. Perkins B, Hoglund JD, King D, Cohen E: *Building Type Basics for Senior Living*, Wiley, Hoboken, NJ, 2004.

4. Lawton MP, Nahemow L: Ecology and the aging process, in Eisdorfer C, Lawton MP, eds, *Psychology of Adult Development and Aging*, American Psychological Association, Washington, DC, 1973, pp 619–674.
5. Michelson W: *Man and His Urban Environment: A Sociological Approach (with Revisions)*, Addison-Wesley, Reading, MA, 1976.
6. Sommer R: *Personal Space: The Behavioral Basis of Design*, Prentice-Hall, Englewood Cliffs, NJ, 1969.
7. Lawton MP: *Environment and Aging*, Brooks/Cole, Monterey, CA, 1980.
8. Wolfensberger W: The normalization principle, and some major implications to architectural-environmental design, in Bednar MJ ed, *Barrier-Free Environments*, Dowden, Hutchinson & Ross, Stroudsburg, PA, 1977.
9. Connell B, Jones M, Mace R, Meuller J, Mullick, A et al: *The Principles of Universal Design*, 1997 (retrieved 6/20/05 from http://www.design.ncsu.edu/cud/univ_design/principles/udprinciples.htm).
10. Lawton MP: Environment and aging: Theory revisited, in Scheidt RJ, Windley PG, eds, *Environment and Aging Theory: A Focus on Housing*, Greenwood Press, Westport, CN, 1998.
11. Mueller J: *Case Studies on Universal Design*, Center for Universal Design, North Carolina, 1997.
12. *Olmstead v. LC* (98-536) 527 US 581. (US Supreme Court, 1999).
13. AARP: *Beyond 50.05. A Report to the Nation on Livable Communities: Creating Environments for Successful Aging*, AARP, Washington, DC, 2005.
14. World Health Organization: *International Classification of Impairments, Disabilities and Handicaps*, WHO, Geneva, Switzerland, 1980.
15. World Health Organization: *Introduction*, 2001 (retrieved 6/20/05 from http://www3.who.int/icf/intros/ICF-Eng-Intro.pdf).
16. Pirkl JJ: *Transgenerational Design: Products for an Aging Population*, Van Nostrand Reinhold, New York, 1994.
17. Pynoos J, Golant S: Housing and living arrangements for the elderly, in Binstock RH, George LK, eds, *Handbook of Aging and the Social Sciences*, 4th ed, Academic Press, San Diego, 1996, pp 303–324.
18. Birren JE, Schroots JJF: History, concepts, and theory in the psychology of aging, in Birren JE, Warner Schaie K, eds, *Handbook of the Psychology of Aging*, 4th ed, Academic Press, San Diego, 1996, pp 3–19.
19. Story MF: Maximizing usability: The principles of universal design, *Assist Technolo*, **10**:4–12 (1998).
20. Story MF: Is it universal? 7 defining criteria, *Innovation* **16**(1):29–32 (1997).
21. Story MF, Mueller JL, Montoya-Weiss M: Progress in the development of universal design performance measures, *Proc RESNA 2000 Annual Conf 2002*, pp 132–134.
22. Hochschild AR: *The Unexpected Community: Portrait of an Old Age Subculture*, Univ California Press, Berkeley, 1973.
23. Jacobs J: *Fun City: An Ethnographic Study of a Retirement Community*, Holt, Rinehart and Winston, New York, 1974.
24. Rosow I: Housing and local ties of the aged, *Conf Patterns of Living and Housing of Middle-Aged and Older People*, Washington, DC, 1965.
25. Mathew Greenwald & Associates, Inc: *These Four Walls...Americans 45 + Talk about Home and Community*, AARP Public Policy Institute, Washington, DC, 2003.
26. AARP: *Fixing to Stay: A National Survey on Housing and Home Modification Issues—Executive Summary*, AARP, Washington DC, 2000.

27. Commission on Affordable Housing and Health Facility Needs for Seniors in the 21st Century: *A Quiet Crisis in America: A Report to Congress by the Commission on Affordable Housing and Health Facility Needs for Seniors in the 21st Century*, Commission on Affordable Housing and Health Facility Needs for Seniors in the 21st Century, Washington, DC, 2002.
28. Administration on Aging: *A Profile of Older Americans: 2002*, 2002 (retrieved 9/11/02 from http://www.aoa.dhhs.gov/aoa/stats/profile/2001.html).
29. Maisel J: *Visitability as an Approach to Inclusive Housing Design and Community Development: A Look at Its Emergence, Growth, and Challenges*, IDEA Center, Buffalo, NY, 2005.
30. Smith E: *Easy Living Home Program*, 2002 (retrieved 2/23/06 from http://www.concretechange.org/ga_easy_living.htm).
31. Paukert C: *Aging Boomers Changing Face of Automobile Design*, 2005 (retrieved 2/23/06 from http://www.autoblog.com/2005/12/20/aging-boomers-changing-face-of-automobile-design/).
32. Thomas G: *Tokyo Motor Show*, 2005 (retrieved 2/23/06 from http://www.newmobility.com/review_article.cfm?id=977&action=browse).
33. Steinfeld E, Tomita M, Mann W, DeGlopper W: Use of passenger vehicles by older people with disabilities, *Occup Ther J Res*, **19**(3):155–186 (1999).
34. Vanderheiden GC: Using extended and enhanced usability (EEU) to provide access to mainstream electronic voting machines, *Inform Technol Disab*, **X**(2) (2004).
35. Federal Communications Commission: *FCC Acts to Promote Accessibility of Digital Wireless Phones to Individuals with Hearing Disabilities*, 2003 (retrieved 2/23/06 from http://hraunfoss.fcc.gov/edocs_public/attachmatch/DOC-236430A1.doc).
36. Trace Research Center: *Designing More Usable Computers and Software* (retrieved 2/23/06 from http://trace.wisc.edu/world/computer_access).
37. Microsoft: *Accessibility* (retrieved 2/23/06 from http://www.microsoft.com/enable).
38. Apple: *Accessibility* (retrieved 2/23/06 from http://www.apple.com/accessibility).
39. Web Accessibility Initiative: *Introduction to Web Content Accessibility Guidelines (WCAG) 2.0 Working Draft Documents*, 2005 (retrieved 2/23/06 from http://www.w3.org/WAI/intro/wcag20.php).
40. Mann W, Belchior P, Tomita M, Kemp B: Computer use by middle-aged and older adults with disabilities, *Technol Disab*, **17**(1):1–9 (2005).
41. Carmichael A, Newell AF, Dickinson A, Proc Morgan M: Using theatre and film to represent user requirements, *Include 2005*, Royal College of Art, London, April 5–8, 2002.
42. Ostroff E: The user as expert/mining our natural resources, *Innovation*, 33–35 (Spring 1997).
43. Danford GS, Steinfeld E: Measuring the influences of physical environments on the behaviors of people with impairments, in Steinfeld E, Danford GS, eds, *Enabling Environments: Measuring the Impact of Environment on Disability and Rehabilitation*, Kluwer Academic/Plenum Publishers, New York, 1999.
44. Durrett C: *Senior Cohousing: A Community Approach to Independent Living*, Ten Speed Press, Berkeley, CA, 2005.
45. Rogers EM: *The Diffusion of Innovations*, 5th ed, Free Press, New York, 2002.
46. Cagan J, Vogel C: *Creating Breakthrough Products: Innovation from Product Planning to Program Approval*, Prentice-Hall, Upper Saddle River, NJ, 2002.
47. Weisman LK: The home as metaphor for society, in *Discrimination by Design: A Feminist Critique of the Man-Made Environment*, Univ Illinois Press, Chicago, 1992.

45

Design for Well-Being

Andreas Larsson and Tobias Larsson
Luleå University of Technology, Sweden

This chapter introduces *design for well-being* (DfW) [1] as a guiding value system aimed at influencing product development organizations to routinely reconsider the ways in which they seek to understand customer needs and how they actually bring those needs into the design of innovative products for increased well-being. Although DfW is a complementary approach to several other "inclusive" design initiatives, it offers some unique qualities that go well beyond the conventional scope of assistive technology (AT) development. DfW is not about "fixing" people by diminishing disabilities through the design of assistive, inclusive, or universal technologies; it is about exploring completely new solutions to completely new problems. In this context, the word "new" could easily be substituted for the phrase "poorly understood," for that is essentially the key to the DfW framework; meeting previously unknown (or poorly understood) needs with previously unknown (or poorly understood) processes and products.

Consequently, DfW seeks to more closely orient product development organizations toward customer "well-being needs" for the plain reason that *really* understanding these needs could very well prove to be a hidden market potential of significant proportion. The initiative takes its stance in the observation that customers are not always aware of their needs, and even if they *do* have that awareness, they seldom have the possibility to directly influence the development of products and services that will ultimately fulfil their needs. Similarly, people that might be very aware of such needs, such as people working within healthcare (in the case of AT development), do not normally create new products. Ultimately, DfW is concerned with helping product developers care about well-being, assisting them in understanding what those well-being needs might be, and providing methods and resources to support exceptionally close collaboration between customers and developers in participatory product innovation processes.

The Engineering Handbook of Smart Technology for Aging, Disability, and Independence,
Edited by A. Helal, M. Mokhtari and B. Abdulrazak
Copyright © 2008 John Wiley & Sons, Inc.

45.1 INTRODUCTION

In this book's context of smart technologies for aging, disability, and independence, this chapter is specifically dedicated to just how such technologies are brought into being. The focus is not on singular devices or technologies that address specific needs within this context but rather on an overarching approach to product innovation where the key to success is to achieve an in-depth understanding of what aging, disability, and independence *actually means* to the people that are supposed to be the users of the resulting "smart technologies." The term "well-being" is used extensively throughout this chapter, and rather than defining specifically what kinds of qualities the term includes, we intend to emphasize the actual relevance of well-being from a user-centric perspective, specifically, what does well-being mean to the individual? This user-centric perspective is critical, because to develop technologies and products based on broad generalizations and assumptions about user behavior and user needs would be to completely miss the point.

DfW offers a perspective on life quality that goes beyond the traditional scope of assistive technology in that it aims to help people make a transformation from an *actual* state of being to a *desired* state of being—regardless of ability level. Here, "desired state of being" means that we do not necessarily focus on finding out what is "wrong," but also what could be different, and what life quality really means from the individual's perspective. This chapter argues that both needs and solutions are now part of the designer's responsibility, and that it is crucial to make a qualitative assessment of both the potential market impact and the "quality of life" improvements afforded by innovations. There is undoubtedly a growing need for engineering designers to engage in creative activities that result in innovative products and technologies for the benefit of society. However, from an engineering perspective, issues of "life quality" and "well-being" are currently heavily underprioritized, particularly with regard to people with disabilities, and DfW is a step toward creating a system where well-being aspects are considered in any product development project (albeit with particular relevance in assistive technology development).

DfW redirects the focus of product development from technology-based development to participatory product innovation. The initial objective of DfW has been to enable people with disabilities to influence their everyday living conditions through active participation in the design of the assistive devices they use daily, but it also goes on to focus energy on those people who are deviations off the "normal" or "average" consumer, along many different dimensions, not only physical ability. Consequently, the initiative uses the notion of "well-being design" to broaden both the scope and the potential user base of consumer product development. The aim is to highlight the concept of well-being as a true innovation opportunity that could provide significant benefits to both users and providers as well as for product development organizations in general. One part of the equation is to find and better understand the needs of customers (i.e., finding well-being opportunities) and another part is to link these needs to domains in which they can be met (i.e., designing well-being products). Here, the challenge is less about finding out how current state-of-the-art technologies can be applied in the context of aging, disability, and independence, and more about finding out how to better understand user needs and then design technologies (state-of-the-art or not) around those needs. The "smartness" of the technology is often not in its technical supremacy but in the impact it has on people's lives.

45.2 THE WELL-BEING AGENDA

The society of today is becoming increasingly aware and conscious of the challenges that people face, on both individual and societal levels. There are ongoing discussions on global issues such as the growing population, natural disasters, and poverty, while discussions about the aging population, healthcare, living conditions, and other issues are impacting both national and regional welfare policies. In the welfare society, great efforts have been put on making sure that help is available for people with disabilities of any kind. In the past, this help has largely been focused on "fixing" people by way of technologic aids. As discussed later in this chapter, this might not be the single best path since these people might not even have a desire to be "fixed." They might have a desire to take part of everyday life and explore the world as anyone else would, which does not always relate directly to a disability. The idea is to better understand *when, how*, and *why* a disability might impact a person's well-being, because these questions have serious implications on the ways in which products are designed to cater to the well-being needs of individuals. Clarkson et al. [2, p. 1] discuss how "disabled people have become increasingly assertive about their rights to access buildings and services, while for older people the emphasis is now on independence." This observation implies that these people want to be active participants in mainstream society, that they are starting to see themselves as consumers rather than "receivers" of healthcare, and that they are now demanding significantly better quality of service in the well-being domain.

The move toward increasing accessibility and inclusivity in mainstream design is an important one, and it also opens up for complementary design approaches that are genuinely sensitive to user needs and which address issues of how to successfully bring the awareness of such needs into new products and services for the benefit of people and society.

In a fairly recent report regarding future strategies for the engineering design area, published by the US National Science Foundation (NSF), engineering design is defined as a *"socially-mediated, technical activity that creates and realizes products, systems, and services that respond to human needs and social responsibilities"* [3].

Similarly, the UK Engineering and Physical Sciences Research Council (EPSRC) writes in a panel report that engineering is "the creative process of turning knowledge of science and technology into goods, services and infrastructure that benefit humankind" [4]. In the same report, they also note: "engineering improves our quality of life."

Within the European Commission 5th Framework Programme on "Quality of Life and Management of Living Resources," a key action was initiated to address issues with the aging population and disabilities. A priority was to come up with "technological products and systems contributing to greater mobility and less dependency, both inside and outside the home, including in the work-place" [5, p. 7].

The three reports quoted above clearly indicate the need for engineering designers to engage in creative activities that result in innovative products and technologies for the benefit of society. Addressing issues of "life quality" in engineering, however, should not be taken lightly. In fact, we argue that such qualities are heavily underprioritized, particularly with regard to people with disabilities. The assistive device area is currently characterized by high-cost low-volume development, and people with disabilities are normally excluded from the mainstream consumer market and forced through specialized channels in order to obtain their devices. This customization represents a significant cost to both the user and society, and that cost increases even further by the relatively high rate of device abandonment. In Phillips and Zhao's [6] study of 227 assistive device users, they noted that 29.3% of all devices were completely abandoned even though the need for the device (i.e., the disability) still existed. The authors related this abandonment to, for example, poor device performance and failure to take consumer opinions into account. Even when assistive devices actually *do* improve the user's physical, sensory, or cognitive abilities, this does not automatically lead to increased quality of life. As Scherer [7] notes on the impact of assistive technology, the larger questions are too often ignored. How does the individual define "well-being," "quality of life," or "rehabilitation success"? How does the device actually contribute to the fulfilment of that individual's needs?

With DfW, we firmly take the stand that there is more to assistive device development than the prospect of "fixing" people by diminishing disabilities. To reiterate:

> DfW is an attempt to go beyond the traditional scope of assistive technology by helping people make a transformation from an *actual state* of being to a *desired state* of being—regardless of ability level.

45.2.1 The Well-being Hypotheses

The underlying hypotheses behind DfW are

- In order to tap into the promising "well-being market," and to stay ahead of the competition, companies will have to establish an exceptionally close collaboration with future users—the needs base—thereby harnessing innovation opportunities that are not easily accessible to competitors.
- Until mass customization takes over, the only way people with physical, sensory, and cognitive impairments will get cost-effective products is through mainstream consumer product channels (e.g., one must avoid costly medical or custom channels), where designers with DfW competence are placed in corporate design teams with a mandate to extend each development cycle toward greater inclusiveness in the potential user base.
- The development of such competency requires changing designers and their formal education to include DfW thinking, needs focused, user-centered, and user-impairment-aware conceptualization.

The discussion in this chapter focuses primarily on the first point: getting designers closer to the users, since *users have the needs while designers may have solutions*. Hence, the DfW approach imposes the need for close interaction with users throughout the development of those solutions. This is also a way for engineering designers to become aware of the DfW view on design and to let DfW values influence their everyday design practice.

45.2.2 The Well-being Opportunity

Myerson [8] notes that "bringing people from the margins to the mainstream through inclusive design is important not just from the perspective of social equality but also for business growth through new products and services." This is specifically what we are targeting. DfW is an initiative that does more than react on what is wrong; it proactively builds on what is right. It could very well emphasize the already positive parts of individuals' lives rather than specifically "deleting" parts that might be perceived as less positive. It all depends on what people, *in fact*, need and value, rather than what designers and engineers "think" that people *ought to* need and value. This is in line with the notion of "complete health," which was defined (and has not been changed since) in 1946 by the World Health Organization (WHO) as "a state of complete physical, mental and social well-being and not merely the absence of disease or infirmity" [9]. It is notable that most of the efforts in the product development area, and society as a whole, are still focused on technical solutions to ill-health. [10, p. 13] The well-being opportunity is there for those willing to engage in more holistic approaches to "well-being design."

This also means that we might not only design products that address the needs of the "widest possible audience" [11]. We are really going deeply into what those needs could consist of. As such, this takes us well beyond mere ergonomic considerations and "assisting" or "fixing" people with motion, sensory, and cognitive disabilities (which was the initial goal of the Design for Well-being initiative). Instead, we lean toward what the Hasso Plattner Institute of Design at Stanford University (d.school) calls "making a difference," where the aim is to address inherently difficult and "messy" problems through a highly interdisciplinary approach [12]:

> We will use design thinking to tackle hard social problems: Stop drunk driving. Build better elementary schools. Develop environmentally sustainable offerings. And we aim to tackle hard industry problems that demand interdisciplinary solutions: Make commercial airplane travel less oppressive. Design enterprise software that actually helps people and organizations. Make waiting in line more fun.

45.2.3 Spotlight on Needs

Talking about a *desired state of being* makes "needfinding" [13] processes highly relevant since the actual user needs are considered to be more important than the "fix" of an objectively perceived problem. It also emphasizes the observation that needs last longer than solutions [14]. If the focus is *truly* aimed at people's needs, companies should be more concerned with adequately targeting those needs than with merely targeting the technical supremacy of their product offerings.

Furthermore, consumer products are primarily targeting a relatively large potential user base, and most companies have not yet seen the economic potential in well-being design. This is perhaps because they cannot separate this new domain from the traditional assistive technology domain, which is generally perceived as a low-profit, niche business. It can also be dependent on the access to user needs that might be harder to grasp in the health sector compared to the overall population, leading development firms to focus on special, well-defined application areas. Even if companies *do* realize the potential for profit, they still have to deal with the fact that well-being is a highly subjective concept, which is difficult both to capture and to generalize across a large user base. Fundamentally, companies need to improve their understanding of what well-being is about and how to incorporate such well-being "qualities" into mainstream consumer products. In terms of production systems, many companies currently seem to strive for ease of production rather than customization, since customization is difficult to achieve with large volumes. Mass customization [15] is here an area of interest that might add some degree of freedom in terms of design for well-being, since it will allow for low-cost development of high quality, individually customized products and services.

The NSF report [3] mentioned above implies that the focus of product development in the past may have been too much directed toward improving existing products and processes, while the greatest opportunity probably lies in the discovery of *completely new products and processes*. This introduces the need to successfully deal with a high uncertainty about what the end product will be, and also a high degree of uncertainty about what the process that leads us there looks like. Obviously, this kind of "wicked problem" [16] is nothing new within the area of engineering design; finding solutions to poorly understood problems is essentially what underlines the very idea of innovation.

45.3 DESIGNING EXPERIENCES

DfW is rooted in user-centred product development, but it would be wrong to assume that the viewpoint is also entirely product-centric. The technologies and products that are envisioned and created within the DfW framework are merely means to an end. It is becoming increasingly obvious that there is more to products than their functional value. For example, it is also important to consider the emotional qualities of products. While the manufacturing sector has had a focus on developing physical products (i.e., tangible assets), the service sector has largely focused on adding value to these products (i.e., intangible assets). The experience sector instead emphasizes the actual consumption of products and services (i.e., the feelings attached to the use of tangible and intangible assets) [17] So, while DfW builds primary on knowledge from the area of product design and development, it certainly is not "business as usual" with a well-being twist. To tap into the DfW opportunity, as described earlier, interdisciplinary approaches and solutions are required. "Well-being" is a value system that guides the development of future technologies, products, services, experiences, and what else is required to fulfil the well-being needs of individuals. Here, well-being could be considered a "core value," similar to, for example, Volvo Car Corporation's well-known commitment to safety. In the Volvo case, such a core value not only represents the technologies involved to accomplish protective safety (i.e., the functions activated in the unfortunate event of a collision), or the technologies involved to accomplish preventative safety (i.e., the functions that aid collision avoidance), but also the feelings and emotions that are associated with ownership of a "safe" car (e.g. caring for your family).

When IDEO worked together with health maintenance organisation Kaiser Permanente to develop a long-term growth plan, they discovered that what was needed was not necessarily investments in new and expensive medical facilities, it was rather a matter of redesigning the patient experience. [18] Their observation that health providers tend to focus on technologies, facilities, and medicines—while their patients are more concerned with service and information—resonates well with the DfW approach, much because it puts future users, rather than future technologies, at the center of attention.

Another example related to this is Prahalad and Ramaswamy's [19] observation that remote monitoring of cardiac pacemakers involves completely different priorities for the patient and for the provider. For example, the company view could emphasize the development costs of sensors and the identification and measurement of key parameters, while the customer could be more concerned with whether the company could be trusted, how the gathered information will be used and shared, and whether any risks are involved.

They further note that existing and emerging technologies must be seen not as enhancers of products, features, and functions, but as "facilitators of experiences" [19]: "a new technological capability is meaningful only when it is focused on improving the experiences desired by the customer" [19].

On a similar note, Gilmore [20] highlights the importance of "staging experiences" in the healthcare area, fundamentally meaning that the current focus on medical goods and healthcare services must be replaced by a "life-tending" focus: "Offerings in this sector must move beyond mere physiological treatment at the time of illness to the ongoing monitoring of wellness across multiple dimensions of self—as spouse, lover, parent, athlete, student, worker, caregiver, and so forth" [20].

45.3.1 Emotional Values in Design

The introduction of the "multiple dimensions of self", (discussed above) serves to link emotional aspects into the product innovation process. Donald Norman [21, p. 38] discusses three levels of emotions that affect the ways in which products are (or should be) designed; the *visceral*, the *behavioral*, and the *reflective* levels. Essentially, the visceral and behavioral levels concern "now" aspects of use—the feelings and experiences you get while actually seeing or using the product. These two levels are mainly about appearance and effectiveness of use (i.e., function, usability, and feel). Reflective design, however, is more about "long-term" aspects of use—the feelings and experiences you get from owning, displaying, and using a product over time. This third level has a lot to do with self-identity and pride, which from a product design perspective means that we need to *really* take into account what users need, want, and *feel*, because aside from a physical artefact, a product is also something that people attach meaning to [22], even if the product might, in fact, be ugly and even difficult to use.

Norman [21, p. 47] further notes that emotions "reflect our personal experiences, associations, and memories" and that the product itself is not always in focus: what matters to the users are often the stories and occasions recalled through the product. For example, that broken bicycle out in your garage might never be fixed, but it is almost impossible to throw it away because it was the first bike you bought with your self-earned money. As an example of reflective design, Norman [21, p. 91] highlights Motorola's headset for the National Football League coaching staff. The headsets obviously had to have visceral appeal and meet behavioral objectives, such as not breaking when thrown to the ground in acts of despair, but they also had to "satisfy the coaches, projecting the heroic, manly self-image of strong, disciplined leaders who managed the world's toughest players, and who were always in control."

In the context of well-being, this means that we need to move beyond behavioral issues of design and actually realize that there might be products, services, and experiences that represent an emotional value to a user, even if the "product" in itself does not completely satisfy the behavioral purpose. For example, this means that increasing the well-being of people with disabilities does not necessarily mean that we always need to specifically target (i.e., "fix") those disabilities. Again, we are really talking about a guiding value system for design. This value system includes design priorities that have to do with other things than functions and issues of usability. Since we are talking about emotions, feelings, pride, memories, well-being, and other arguably fuzzy issues, it is absolutely critical that designers become aware of why it is so important to involve users in a highly participatory innovation process.

When we look at the people whose well-being we are aiming to improve, we need to look at the "lives" of those people rather than at isolated "features" of their lives, such as a disability or a "problem." Norman points out that "tasks and activities are not well supported by isolated features. They require attention to the sequence of actions, to the eventual goal—that is, to the true needs." [21, p. 71] Once more, this stresses our point that designing for well-being moves away from "fixing people" towards "enhancing lives." However, enhancing does not necessarily mean a stepwise improvement to already existing solutions; it means that we are looking for innovations—completely new ways of improving people's well-being.

Keates and Clarkson [23, p. 15] note that much of the focus of existing "inclusive design" approaches has been on people with disabilities and elderly people, where special products for very specific needs have been developed, often from scratch, with long development times and high development costs. Furthermore, they state, usability issues were often overlooked and products were developed with "no thought of whether someone would actually want to use or be seen using them" [23, p. 15]—often resulting in "ugly, stigmatising, expensive and unusable products" [23, p. 15]. Certainly, this leads to situations in which people might need to use a particular product but do not want to use it for various reasons, some of which are emotional. Again, this leads us to reconsider what kinds of capabilities we are offering to customers. Are we simply offering capabilities that adhere to the norm, what people should expect, what any "normal" person would need? What kinds of innovation opportunities are we missing if we do not include the emotional values in the design process?

45.4 UNDERSTANDING CUSTOMER NEEDS

Traditionally, companies involved in industrial manufacturing gained their competitive edge by investing in physical assets to produce high-quality goods in high volume and at low costs, while the consumer preferences were assumed to be relatively constant. Today, customers are demanding a greater choice of products, services, and processes; even total care concepts. In the context of rapidly changing customer tastes and preferences, companies are realizing that they can no longer maintain their competitiveness by simply reducing the costs of development and production since this is not seen as a value-adding activity from the customer perspective. The way to add value to a product range now seems in reach by creating and exploiting *intellectual assets*—such as brand name, reputation, knowledge bases, product-related services, and innovative responses to customer needs [24]. DfW offers one such innovative response to customer needs through focusing on the desired state of being rather than on "fixing" isolated problems with a particular product. There are also different roles of the customer, since there are *business-to-business* as well as *business-to-consumer* situations. Thus, the "customer" is not always the end user, and in the healthcare sector, for example, an assistive aid might be sold to a clinic or a hospital (i.e., the customer), but used by a patient (i.e., the user).

According to Mello [25, p. 3], the key to product success is simple but paradoxical: "delight the customer by creating a product that fills specific needs in the marketplace better than competing solutions." However, Mello argues, the perceived simplicity of this idea belies the complexity of actually carrying it out. The general idea to listen to what the customer says and then respond with a product that exceeds that expectation has been the longstanding norm for customer-focused product development, and a vast amount of research and literature exists on how to capture and retain the customer's perspective, using, for example, the *quality function deployment* (QFD) [26] methods. However, it is a question of not only listening to customers and their outspoken needs and preferences; but also understanding unspoken needs and including customers and users in the actual work of designing the products.

In industry and academia, phrases like *customer orientation, customer-driven, voice of the customer*, and *customer-centric* are commonly used to emphasize that the customers and the market drive the development. In reality, however, there is a gap between how well industries *think* they address customer needs and how well they manage to do so.

Largely, this gap could have to do with a limited understanding of the "fuzzy front end" [27] of innovation, meaning the very earliest phase, or even prephase, of product development. While companies often put a lot of effort into structuring the development phases, it is not uncommon to just take for granted that the predevelopment phases are "unstructured," "chaotic," or "fuzzy." Once the product requirements have been set, the development work usually progresses in reasonably well-structured ways, but the high degree of uncertainty in the front end of innovation is seldom seriously addressed. This means that although the end product might very well meet the specifications, there are still doubts as to whether it really meets customer needs. If the customer needs are allowed to stay "fuzzy," the downstream development activities will inevitably suffer from this "fuzziness" as well. Koen et al. [28] have decided not to use the word "fuzzy" in their definition of the front end of innovation, just because they do not agree that the front end cannot be better managed. DfW is perhaps not an approach to "manage" the fuzzy front end, but surely an approach toward a more detailed *understanding* of the customer needs on which all subsequent development activities rely so heavily.

DfW deals with the dual observation that product development companies do not always know what the customer needs and that the customers, in turn, are not always right. Companies might very well know how to develop certain products according to specifications, but that does not necessarily mean that they know the relative customer value of features incorporated in their products. Lutz' [29, p. 13] first law of business postulates that customers are not always right and that customers do not always know what they want. Product definitions seem to be too focused on *known* product features, causing companies to miss *real* customer needs that might not be expressed in today's features. Related to this, Norman [21, p. 81] observes that engineers and designers often assume that they know what people need, because they are people themselves, and that engineers and designers simultaneously know too much (about technology) and too little (about other people's lives and activities) to develop truly useful and usable products.

45.4.1 What Customers Really Do

People are not always required to articulate the knowledge they bring to a particular situation, and they may even occasionally lack the vocabulary to talk about these situations [35]. The distinction between *ideal* and *manifest behavior* basically points out that what people say and what they do are not always the same. Ideal behavior is what every "good" member of the community *should* do, while manifest behavior is what people *actually* do [35]. It has been shown that when asked to describe their own behavior, people tend to give an account that is closer to the ideal than to the manifest. It is not a case of being dishonest, but rather a way of telling people what they want to hear, or living up to cultural expectations. In relation to this, Norman [21, p. 82] notes that "We humans like to think that we know why we act as we do, but we don't, however much we like to explain our actions."

In terms of design and engineering, this is an important observation, because if we are talking about designing "well-being" products and services, we cannot rely solely on peoples' ability to tell us what their well-being needs are. Fulton Suri [30, p. 164] draws attention to "thoughtless acts," stating that the actions we are not even conscious of (i.e., our intuitive interpretations in daily life) might be a significant source of insight for designers. Furthermore, she makes the very important distinction between a focus on "actions" and a focus on "things," emphasizing that designers might be better tuned to user needs if focusing more closely on people's behavior: "Observation forces us to focus on the actions that we are trying to support, rather than on the things we will ultimately produce" [30, p. 168]

DfW is focused on the practical actions of people partaking in society, which means that we are interested in the moment-by-moment activities where our sense of "what is going on" might, and is likely to, change as events unfold [31]. When targeting user needs, we really need to target user behavior. DfW is interested in understanding just *how* such behavior takes place. We want to observe people to "sharpen our awareness of how people respond to particular arrangements and elements ... and that helps us make better predictions about how people will perceive and interpret the things we design so we can better elicit the kind of response we intend" [30, p. 171]

These thoughtless acts could be exemplified with the way we position ourselves in a line, how we find our way in an unknown building, or how we seek shade on a hot summer day. This kind of manifest, and often unconscious, behavior are just adding to the bulk of reasons why product development organisations should seek to better understand the needs that currently drift around in the "fuzzy front end."

45.4.2 Designers ≠ Users: Users ≠ Designers

Since we increasingly deal with "wicked," "fuzzy," or "messy" problems, we need to accept the possibility that a company, or a design team, will have major difficulties figuring out what the users need and how to address these needs: (1) it is very difficult to find objective and general indicators of what well-being is, and (2) there really is no such thing as an "ordinary user" when discussing radically innovative solutions. Traditional market research falls short of this objective, and even some user-centered approaches lack the kind of user involvement that is needed to successfully address highly ambiguous problems. We need to empower users so that they can inform the development process more actively. According to von Hippel [32], it is critical to identify and involve "lead users" in the development processes, mainly because they have the following important characteristics (paraphrased):

- Lead users face needs that will become general in a marketplace, but they encounter them months or years before the rest of the marketplace.
- Lead users are positioned to benefit significantly by a solution to those needs.

As such, these users have a high motivation to solve problems, and since they are taking part in the development of solutions to their "own" needs, they are likely to appreciate involvement in the innovation process. It is important to notice that lead users are not the same as the early adopters or pioneering customers that are commonly used for early testing. Lead users are ahead of market trends and have needs that existing products do not meet [33]. In terms of "well-being," we believe that there currently exists a vast range and variety of unmet needs, which leads to a real DfW innovation opportunity.

"Empowering the users" also means that we need to take an increased interest in real-world observations of future consumers. As noted earlier, users may not always be able to verbalize what they need, and their experience probably does not allow them to imagine possible innovations, which is why Leonard and Rayport's concept of "empathic design" [34] resonates well with DfW. We are aiming at addressing people's needs, but we further aim to facilitate this needfinding process so that also the unarticulated needs are brought forward. With its references to the ethnographic tradition [35], this technique is well known to the design research community, but observations in the user's own environment are still too rare in industry.

The increasing importance of bringing a user-centric approach into design education has also been described by Dym et al. [36]:

> While creativity is important, and may even be teachable, design is not invention as caricatured by the shouting of "Eureka" and the flashing of a light bulb. Design problems reflect the fact that the designer has a client (or customer) who, in turn, has in mind a set of users (or customers) for whose benefit the designed artifact is being developed.

We have already noted that both needs and solutions are now part of the designer's responsibility, and that it is very important to make a qualitative assessment of both the potential market impact and the "quality of life" improvements afforded by innovations [37]. One problem with such an increased responsibility is, again, that those that should know the most about people's quality of life (i.e., the people themselves or people working in the healthcare sector) do not normally develop products; designers do. In practice, this means that designers have the responsibility to not only ask people about the well-being needs they have experienced or observed but now also make these discoveries themselves; both through observation and practical experience. If not taking this responsibility seriously, there is a risk that we end up in a situation of "design exclusion," where designers fail to take real user needs into account, since they instinctively seek to provide the functionalities needed for someone with physical and skill capabilities similar to their own [23,38].

45.5 CONCLUSIONS

Several initiatives, such as *inclusive design* [2], *design for all* [39], and *universal design* [40], consider the possibilities for people with disabilities to participate in society on equal terms. It is important to note that DfW does not seek to replace these other initiatives, because they are indeed highly complementary. Fundamentally, what makes DfW different is that it is not so interested in optimizing products and technologies to be more "inclusive"; it is interested more in coming up with completely new solutions to completely new problems. In a sense, the DfW innovation opportunity can be summarized as meeting previously unknown (or poorly understood) needs with previously unknown (or poorly understood) processes.

The DfW framework thus offers an extension to those initiatives by moving beyond the idea of "fixing" people by diminishing disabilities through the design of assistive, inclusive, or universal technologies. DfW also introduces a complementary approach to help companies expand their potential user base by mainstreaming their technologies to also embrace the "outsiders"—the people whose needs are neither well understood nor well addressed today.

DfW is a perspective on life quality that goes beyond the traditional scope of assistive technology in the sense that it aims to help people make a transformation from an actual state of being to a desired state of being—regardless of ability level.

ACKNOWLEDGMENTS

Support for this research has been provided by VINNOVA, through the Polhem Laboratory at Luleå University of Technology, the Kempe Foundations, the Center for Design Research at Stanford University, and the Stanford Learning Lab. We like to specifically thank Professor Larry Leifer, Dr. Machiel Van der Loos, and Dr. John Feland for their contributions to this chapter and to the Design for Well-being initiative as a whole.

REFERENCES

1. *Design for Well-being*, Luleå Univ Technology (http://www.designforwell-being.org; accessed 2/28/06).
2. Clarkson J, Coleman R, Keates S, Lebbon C: *Inclusive Design: Design for the Whole Population*, Springer-Verlag, London, 2003.
3. NSF: *ED2030: Strategic Plan for Engineering Design*, National Science Foundation (NSF), Workshop Report, Janu 2005.
4. *The Wealth of a Nation: An Evaluation of Engineering Research in the United Kingdom*, Engineering and Physical Sciences Research Council (EPSRC), Panel Report, Feb 2005.
5. European Commission, Key Action 6, Directorate-General for Research—RTD-F-3:—*Quality of Life and Management of Living Resources: The Ageing Population and Disabilities*, 2002 (europa.eu.int/comm/research/quality-of-life/pdf/ka6-ageingpopulation.pdf; accessed 2/28/06).
6. Phillips B, Zhao H: Predictors of assistive technology abandonment, *Assist Technol* 5(1):36–45 (1993).
7. Scherer MJ: *Living in the State of Stuck: How Assistive Technology Impacts the Lives of People with Disabilities*, Brookline Books, Cambridge, MA, 2000.
8. Myerson J: *Design DK: Inclusive Design*, Danish Design Centre, Denmark, 2001, p 3.
9. Preamble to the Constitution of the World Health Organization as adopted by the International Health Conference, New York, June 19–22, 1946; signed on July 22, 1946 by the representatives of 61 States (Official Records of the World Health Organization, nr. 2, p 100) and entered into force on April 7, 1948 (http://www.who.int/about/definition/en/; accessed 2/28/06).
10. Shah H, Marks N: *A Well-being Manifesto for a Flourishing Society*, New Economics Foundation, 2004 (http://www.neweconomics.org/gen/z_sys_PublicationDetail.aspx?PID=193; accessed 2/28/06).
11. DTI Foresight: *Making the Future Work for You*, UK Department of Trade & Industry, London, 2000.
12. Hasso Plattner Institute of Design at Stanford, Stanford University, (http://www.stanford.edu/group/dschool/projects/making_a_difference.html; accessed 2/28/06).
13. Faste R: Perceiving needs, *SAE Future Transportation Technology Conf Exposition*, Society of Automotive Engineers, Inc, Seattle, WA, 1987, pp 419–423.

14. Patnaik D, Becker R: Needfinding: The why and how of uncovering people's needs, *Design Manage J* **10**(2):37–43 (1999).
15. Pine BJ: *Mass Customization— The New Frontier in Business Competition*, Harvard Business School Press, Boston, 1993.
16. Rittel H, Webber M: *Dilemmas in a General Theory of Planning*, Policy Sciences (series), Elsevier Amsterdam, 1973, Vol **4**, pp 155–169.
17. Pine BJ, Gilmore JH: *The Experience Economy, Work is Theatre and every Business a Stage*, Harvard Business School Press, Boston, 1999.
18. Nussbaum B: The power of design, *Business Week* (May 17, 2004) (http://www.businessweek.com/magazine/content/04_20/b3883001_mz001.htm; accessed 2/28/06).
19. Prahalad CK, Ramaswamy V: The new frontier of experience innovation, *Sloan Manage Rev*, **4**(81):12–18 (2003).
20. Gilmore JH: *Frontiers of the Experience Economy*, Batten Briefings, Darden Business Publishing, Charlottesville, VA, Aug 2003, (http://www.darden.virginia.edu/batten/pdf/bf_gilmore.pdf; accessed 2/28/06).
21. Norman D: *Emotional Design: Why We Love (or Hate) Everyday Things*, Basic Books, New York, 2004.
22. Csikszentmihalyi M, Rochberg-Halton E: *The Meaning of Things: Domestic Symbols and the Self*, Cambridge Univ Press, UK, 1981.
23. Keates S, Clarkson PJ: Defining design exclusion, in: Keatess et al, eds, *Universal Access and Assistive Technology*, Springer-Verlag, London, 2002, pp 13–22.
24. Teece DJ: *Managing Intellectual Capital: Organizational, Strategic and Policy Dimensions*, Oxford Univ Press, Oxford, UK, 2000.
25. Mello S: *Customer-Centric Product Definition: The Key to Great Product Development*, American Management Association, New York, 2002.
26. Hauser JR, Clausing D: The house of quality, *Harvard Business Rev* **88**:68–72 (1988).
27. Reinertsen DG: Taking the fuzziness out of the fuzzy front end, *Res Technol Manage* **42**(6):25–31 (Nov–Dec 1999).
28. Koen P et al: Providing clarity and a common language to the "fuzzy front end," *Res Technol Manage* **44**(2):46–55 (March–April 2001).
29. Lutz R: *Guts: The Seven Laws of Business that Made Chrysler the World's Hottest Car Company*, Wiley, New York, 1998.
30. Fulton Suri J: *Thoughtless Acts?* Chronicle Books, San Francisco, 2005.
31. Randall D, Harper R, Rouncefield M: *Fieldwork for Design: Theory and Practice*, Kluwer Academic Press, Amsterdam, 2007.
32. von Hippel E: Lead users: A source of novel product concepts, *Manage Sci*, **32**(7):791–805 (1986).
33. Lead User Concepts, Inc. (www.leaduser.com/what_is_lead_user_research.html; accessed 2/28/06).
34. Leonard D, Rayport JF: Spark innovation through empathic design, *Harvard Business Revi* 102–113 (Nov–Dec 1997).
35. Blomberg J, Giacomi J, Mosher A, Swenton-Wall P: Ethnographic field methods and their relation to design, in Schuler D, Namioka A, eds, *Participatory Design: Principles and Practices*, Lawrence Erlbaum, Hillsdale, NJ, 1993, pp 123–155.
36. Dym CL, Agogino AM, Eris O, Frey DD, Leifer LJ: Engineering design thinking, teaching, and learning, *J Eng Educ* 103–120 (Jan 2005).
37. Feland JM, Cockayne WR, Leifer LJ: Comprehensive design engineering: A new path to innovation, *Int Conf Engineering Design (ICED'03)*, Stockholm, Sweden, 2003.

38. Cooper A: *The Inmates are Running the Asylum: Why High-tech Products Drive Us Crazy and How to Restore the Sanity*, SAMS, Indianapolis, IN, 1999.
39. *Design for All Foundation* (http://www.designforall.org/en/downloads/dossier-DfA-Fd-ang.pdf; accessed 2/28/06).
40. Vanderheiden G, Tobias J: *Universal Design of Consumer Products: Current Industry Practice and Perceptions* (http://trace.wisc.edu/docs/ud_consumer_products_hfes2000/; accessed 2/28/06).

46

Technology Evaluation within Healthcare and Social Care

Suzanne Martin, George Kernohan, Bernadette McCreight, and Christopher Nugent

University of Ulster, Northern Ireland

46.1 INTRODUCTION

The rationale for utilizing assistive technologies and electronic assistive technologies to support both aging-in-place and disabled people is multifactorial. Globally, changes in the demographic profile of the world population pose serious concerns relating to future financial funding of sustainable services. Challenges also surround workforce availability to contribute to the healthcare system. In tandem, the forecast prevalence of chronic illness and increased age of mortality suggests an increased demand on service utilization [1]. Because of this dual impact, effective evaluation has become an essential tool in planning implementation of health technology policy and practice.

In 2001 the World Health Organization (WHO), within the International Classification of Functioning Disability and Health (ICF), proposed the *biopsychosocial model* of disability [2]. This consolidates the medical model of disability [3] and the social model of disability [4]. The experience and presentation of disability is acknowledged as being complex, at levels of both human physiology and social interaction between the individual and the environment. Within this framework, technology can be integrated into the life experience of the individual, impacting on personal autonomy by influencing the interaction between the individual's health condition and the contextual factors that the individual experiences, that is, environmental factors (architectural design) and internal personal factors (age, gender); technology can impact on both. In terms of technology evaluation, it then becomes critical to consider and understand the impact of provision at an individual level, at the service level, and within the wider social context.

The Engineering Handbook of Smart Technology for Aging, Disability, and Independence,
Edited by A. Helal, M. Mokhtari and B. Abdulrazak
Copyright © 2008 John Wiley & Sons, Inc.

When considering technology in healthcare, classification and description are both important. Cook and Hussey classify assistive technology as "a broad range of devices, services, strategies and practices that are conceived and applied to ameliorate the problems faced by individuals who have disabilities" [5]. A crucial feature that differentiates *electronic assistive technology* from *assistive technology* is the utilization of information and communication technologies in some form. Technology state of the art at the outset of this millennium is diverse and multifaceted. Within assistive technologies the range, composition, and potential of devices has expanded. Often innovate materials and concepts from other disciplines (e.g., engineering) are used to create technologies with the potential to make a meaningful difference in the lives of disabled people. Within the domain of electronic assistive technologies, new devices onto the market tend to be smaller in size than the predecessor, with greater operational potential. Networking, connectivity, and interoperability of technologies using either wired or mobile communication platforms is attainable. Emerging information and communication technologies has enabled advances in the functionality, capability, and reliability of electronic assistive technologies, at decreased financial cost. The effect has increased the potential for integration into healthcare and social care. This has spawned the emergence of innovative service models impacting on service model composition, how staff deliver services, and the experience of the individual service user [6].

Jenkins [7] states that

> Many therapies have a tradition of authority-based dogma. Whereas this may have been adequate in the past, changes in the expectations of consumers, professional colleagues and funding organizations now require a more vigorous validation of clinical practices ... high quality research to provide substantial and convincing evidence to support the claims of optimal patient management has been lacking and is thus urgently required.

To provide this evidence, clear, investigative methodologies are required. This will enhance the understanding and knowledge of clinicians and provide robust evidence to inform clinical practice. This chapter presents an overview of the issues to be considered when developing and investigation evaluating the impact of technology when integrated into healthcare and social care [8].

46.2 EVALUATIONS; ARE THEY RESEARCH OR AUDIT?

An evaluation aims to "determine the value" of a particular item [9]; in this case of a technology used within healthcare. There are two ways to do this: audit current practice using the technology or research the impact of the intervention (i.e., technology within a service). When designing work to evaluate technology in healthcare, it is important to determine at the outset whether it is research or audit. Both are relevant; however, they differ in design and methodology. There is no general consensus as to the definition of either [10]. Audit has been defined by Sale [11] as "the systematic critical analysis of the quality of medical care, including the procedures used in diagnosis and treatment, the use of resources and the resulting outcome and quality of life for the patient." Bailey [12] provides this definition of research as the "systematic process of gathering and synthesizing empirical data so as to generate knowledge about a given population for a selected topic." There are many similarities and differences between research and audit

[12]. Wade [13] identifies that both start with a research question, and the expectation that clinical practice will be changed and/or influenced in some manner as an outcome of the investigation. Both require formal data collection on participants, using appropriate methodology and rigorous design to produce robust conclusions. Both are systematic in approach.

Differences exist, however, in that *audit* consists of assessing practice, using existing practice to improve intervention, while *research* aims to generate new knowledge to improve or refine interventions on the basis of the acquisition of empirical data [14]. The impact of research outcomes may have global impact on populations whereas audit may only impact on a particular setting. Wade [13] also identifies that while research requires evidence of ethical approval as a prerequisite to funding or publication, audit does not, and yet the responsibility for classification lies primarily with the investigator.

This issue is particularly relevant to technology used within healthcare and social care. The opportunity of audit may appear to be more readily accessible than that of research, as clinicians can investigate emerging services. However, the value of research in this area to provide both qualitative and quantitative data should not be lost. It is proposed here to introduce at a high level issues for consideration when developing research proposals to explore technology within healthcare and social care.

46.3 A MODEL OF THE RESEARCH PROCESS

Each evaluation can be regarded as a small circle spinning off a continuum of knowledge. This is depicted in Figure 46.1. The project begins with knowledge and understanding of current thinking about the subject, and on completion adds to the growing knowledge base. The project cycle has three distinct phases; planning for the research, performing the research, and communicating the findings. Without any one of these phases, the cycle is not complete.

Within each phase there are a range of activities to be completed, although the exact nature of these may differ depending on the project.

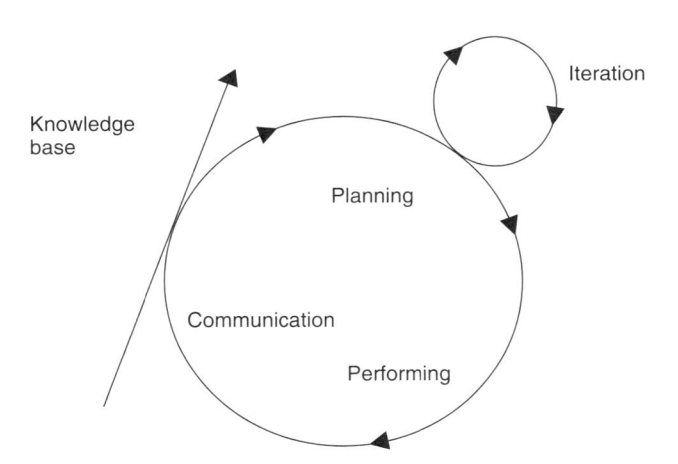

FIGURE 46.1 Representation of the three stages of a research project. (Source: Jenkins [7].)

46.4 DESIGNING RESEARCH

Research design is the subject of many textbooks, which should be consulted for a full exposition. Here we give a brief overview of how the methodologies may be applied to health technology. A systematic and logical approach to designing research is essential to ensure clarity of procedural methodologies for the investigators and offer the potential to facilitate replication. The first part of the process is to develop a research proposal should state (1) what you are planning to investigate; (2) the purpose of the study; (3) population under investigating; (4) intervention to be administered; what data will be collected, and in what way; and (5) proposed method for data to be analyzed. Designing a research proposal requires a substantial amount of time and effort to create the simplicity of format that adequately communicates the investigators intentions to interested stakeholders (i.e., supervisors, funding agencies, and ethical committees).

When designing a research proposal with a focus on technology integrated into healthcare and social care, clarity is essential to avoid the ambiguity that could pertain with such a complex interventions. As researchers, you must make initial decisions about the work focus; are you interested in the impact of the device on service providers, how they deliver and experience caring and working in a service model that is dependent on technology, or are you interested in the service user's experience. Dependent on perspective and purpose, there will be occasions when both service providers and people being supported by the services user are in effect users of the technology integrated into service models, and as a researcher, interest may pertain in both components.

46.4.1 Writing a Research Proposal

The research proposal is a written plan that states the question and the protocol or method that will be used to investigate the topic. In developing the proposal the main researcher is generally referred to as the *principal investigator*.

Formulating a structured *research question* and generating a proposal detailing investigative methodologies must be an iterative process. Developing a well-structured, appropriate research question is an extremely important part of the total process. The research question is critical to the development of research methodologies. From identification of the particular topic of interest the question is both developed and then refined. Often, new researchers start with a problem that is very complex and broad and therefore unlikely to be answered by one investigation. The process of refining should lead to a narrower question that defines the scope of the investigation, and possibly generate other research questions to be dealt with via different investigations at another time. Primary research will investigate a specific intervention in relation to a particular group of participants [15]. Secondary research will attempt to answer a question, not by conducting a trial, but by reviewing published evidence already made available by completed trials. The Cochrane collaboration is a major contributor to the publication of secondary research. Supported by a global network of affiliated collaborators, information is made available to enhance evidence based healthcare [16].

Having an idea of the type of research helps establish the boundry of the intended study; narrowing the possibilities for study design and assist with concise description of the study to colleagues. A logical systematic approach to development and implementation will contribute toward success. The principal investigator should have a clearly defined reason for doing the research, with explicit goals that map to the research purpose. These statements of purpose should assist in indicating the focus of the work. When considering technology within healthcare and social care, is the research focus on the structure of the delivery system, the process of delivery, or outcomes of provision? The International Classification of Functioning Disability and Health can be applied as a framework to establish the level the research will focus for example; society or the individual.

A well-referenced *background/introduction* about the research topic should form the initial section stating the significance and relevance of the issue under investigation. Previous studies, including work of other researchers, should be reviewed within a separate section of a *literature review*. This will help ascertain the "added value" the proposal in hand will bring. The research topic should be relevant to existing knowledge within the subject. The literature review of published evidence is required to put the research and proposal in context. Comment should be made on the value of the reported work. The literature review will also help to identify the intellectual origins of the work, show familiarity with existing ideas, and justify choice of topic and approach to the investigation, and it will assist the principal investigator in refining the research question and objectives [17].

A *methods* section follows on from the literature review; generally this is the longest section of the proposal. It is descriptive and provides detailed information on the following categories [7]:

1. Study design
2. Study objectives
3. Hypothesis/guiding questions
4. Subjects/participants
5. Variables
6. Materials
7. Procedures for data collection
8. Methods for data analysis
9. Ethical considerations
10. Timetable for proposed work
11. Resources and costs

The *study design* is a descriptive statement of the general approach that will be adopted by the researchers working on the investigation. Functioning as an overarching framework, this conveys relevant information about the work at a high level to interested parties. Batavia [18] identifies two basic types of study design; nonexperimental (descriptive, correlational) and experimental (experimental, quasiexperimental) [18]. Nonexperimental designs tend to be *qualitative* in nature and are constructed in a way that answers questions by descriptive means. The researcher functions as an observer and does not, in the pure sense, intervene. Correlational designs, although not truly experimental, are used frequently within healthcare research and make a significant contribution in advancing knowledge. With this approach the researcher is both attempting to describe something while also attempting to analyze whether a relationship or pattern exists among the characteristics being described. Correlational designs offer less control over variables within the research; however, they offer greater control, and less threat to internal validity than do purely descriptive studies. It is reasonable that a correlation design is used to establish whether a relationship between characteristics is present, although not confirming cause and effect, and subsequently test this with an experimental study design. A variety of approaches to correlational design exists including cross-sectional studies, validity and reliability studies, cohort studies, and case–control studies.

Experimental studies attempt to answer questions about causality; for example, "Does a bed lever reduce the risk of falling?" In this scenario the researcher manipulates variables on the participants to establish if causality exists. Experimental designs are *quantitative* in approach. The researcher actively intervenes in the study by manipulating an independent variable that is administered to one group and withheld from another. At least two groups of participants are involved in experimental design, with randomization used to allocate participants to either an intervention group (that receives an independent variable) or a control group that does not. In quasiexperimental design either the control group or randomization is absent. Combined or mixed methods approach to research design has also emerged, combining both quantitative and qualitative methodologies; each is discussed in the following section. The type of design should be dictated by the research question to be answered.

46.4.2 Quantitative Study Design

Quantitative research methods are preeminent within physical sciences, enabling outcomes to be measured to a high degree of precision and facilitating replication of findings. When the information collected on participants is numerical in nature the research is defined as quantitative. Within quantitative studies the experimental design approach of the randomized control trial (RCT) is cited as the 'gold standard' study design for evaluation of health care interventions [19]. However debate exists around the quality of design within some report RCT trials. Moher [20] expresses the view that "despite several decades of educational efforts, the reporting of RCT's needs improvement ... inadequate reporting makes the interpretation ... difficult ... borders on unethical practice when biased results receive false credibility" [20].

The Consolidated Standards of Reporting Trials (CONSORT) statement was originally developed and subsequently revised by an international collaboration of clinical trialists, statisticians, epidemiologists and biomedical editors, to improve the quality of RCT reporting. It consists of a 22-item checklist and flow diagram that for convenience are referred to as CONSORT. The authors suggest that CONSORT is used in the development of simple two-group parallel RCTs, and also that the underlying philosophy of the statement can be applied to any design. The tools of CONSORT are also useful to assist reviewers in the scrutiny of projects and academic literature. Table 46.1 provides information on the key features of both randomized and non-randomized experimental study designs.

Within RCTs there are various types of study design that can be exploited dependent on the needs of the investigation, for example, parallel group trials, crossover trials, cluster randomized trials, N-of-one trials, and patient preference trials.

46.4.3 Qualitative Study Design

Qualitative study designs enhance understanding of the participant's thoughts and feelings on a particular intervention or theme. The type of information gathered tends to be verbal

TABLE 46.1 Typology of Randomized and Nonrandomized Experimental Designs

Design	Key Features	Advantages	Disadvantages
Randomized controlled trial	Participants are randomly assigned to intervention or control group	Groups are balanced in everything except treatment if received; if randomization concealed, bias can be prevented	Time and effort to design and administer
Cluster randomized controlled trial	Groups of participants (e.g., occupational therapists, students) are randomized to the intervention or control group	May be logistically easier than individual randomization. More suitable for some interventions than others	Need large sample of participants; analysis of data is more complex
Controlled trial	Participants nonrandomly assigned to interventions or control group	Easier to carryout, no need to prepare and conceal randomization	Selection bias may occur
Before/after comparison	Data are collected before and after the intervention on a group of participants and a paired comparison is made	Paired data reduces variability	Other factors to intervention may have an impact
Randomized crossover trial	As above, but each participant receives control and intervention treatment in random order; paired comparison is then made	Paired data reduce variability	Unsuitable for conditions with long term effects or conditions that change over time
Historical controlled study	Data collected after an intervention and compared to data collected on some other group that did not experience the intervention; unpaired comparison is then made	Requires minimal data collection	Differences may exist between the intervention arm and the historical arm other than the experimental intervention

Source: Tilling et al. [19].

or pictorial enabling the researcher to gain insights into the participant's views, opinions, feelings and beliefs within their own natural setting [21].

In approaching qualitative research, various frameworks exist which help the researcher develop the research proposal [22]. It is important to acknowledge that each approach has specific distinctive features that relate to the type of questions they are suited to answer, the kinds of data collection that are consistent with this, and also the type of analysis and dissemination format that fit with the approach. *Phenomenology* originates within philosophy and psychology. A phenomenologic approach aims to describe, interpret and understand the meanings of the experiences at both a general and unique level. It will focus on the quality and depth of experience of the participant, using interviews and narratives as data-gathering tools. Generally analysis is using a *thematic* approach generating common themes that present throughout. *Grounded theory* is another qualitative approach, originating within sociology and social psychology. Grounded theory aims to develop a theory in relation to how individual and groups make meaning together and interact with it other. A variety of methods are suitable for data gathering within grounded theory, particularly open-end questions. The data analysis is used to stimulate the generation of new social models and theories. Within an *ethnographic approach* the aim is to describe interpret and understand the characteristics of a particular social setting, acknowledging all its cultural diversity and multiplicity. Generally, intensive fieldwork is required within this approach using participant observation, interviews and visual data. Other approaches are ethnomethodology, symbolic interactionism, feminism, Marxism, and structuralism/poststructuralism [23].

Within qualitative research there are numerous forms of data collection, all underpinned by a variety of different methodological and theoretical approaches. Most research of this type would aim toward adopting an emic perspective; trying to establish the participants subjective view of his/her world, without the researcher making any value judgments on this. The ultimate aim of this type of work is to connect social theory to the core of living in the everyday world. Qualitative research, in seeking explanation of social phenomenon relies on the interpretation participants place on the reasons behind their actions. It assumes numerous interpretations of reality, with the researcher seeking to understand how the participant produces their own reality within their social world. This naturalist paradigm allows for multiple perspectives. The process of how social worlds are constructed in also important in relation to participant personal biographies, lifecycles, and social change. For example, how do people view assistive technology and whether specific instructions must be followed for successful utilization will people adhere to this [24]? A variety of nonexperimental qualitative study designs are outlined in Table 46.2.

46.4.4 Combined Qualitative–Quantitative Study Design

Combined qualitative–quantitative studies are sometimes referred to as "mixed-method research": using techniques from each area either sequentially or in parallel within the

TABLE 46.2 Types of Nonexperimental Qualitative Study Design

Study Design	Key Features
Case report/case study	Reports on an unusual case, it is low in cost and has minimal ethical considerations, although it may often be factual based on the observations of the reporting author rather than reporting on the experience of the participant
Case series	Used to describe the characteristics of several persons; evidence for the presence of a particular characteristic is strengthened; however, as case reports it tends to be factual reporting rather than adding to existing theories on a particular subject
Longitudinal study	Enable information to be gathered on how a particular characteristic may change over time
Cross-sectional studies	These are developmental studies that enable you to describe a particular characteristic within a population, over time, for example, speech production in children, young people, and adults.

research [25]. They ways in which research methods are combined include *triangulation* and *complementarity*. *Triangulation* is the method of checking the findings from one study against the findings of another, therefore enhancing validity. In some instances this could result in the findings of a quantitative study being compared with the findings of a qualitative study. It has been suggested that this comparison is in fact not valid, even when exploring the same topic as the same elements may not be exposed [26]. *Complementarity* is the method of using the strengths of one method to in some way enhance the performance of another method. Cresswell [27] suggests four questions to consider during determination of a mixed methods strategy;

1. What is the sequence of qualitative and quantitative data collection?
2. What priority will be give to qualitative and quantitative data collection and analysis?
3. At what stage will the data and findings be integrated?
4. Will an overall theoretical perspective be used?

It has been suggested that up to 40 types of topologies exist for mixed method designs often reflecting the way in which qualitative and quantitative designs have been brought together during research. Cresswell [27], however, proposes six major mixed method approaches; these are outlined in Table 46.3.

Within mixed methods research intra-method mixing refers to concurrent or sequential use of one single method that includes both qualitative and quantitative components.

TABLE 46.3 Typology of Mixed-Method Strategies

Strategy	Key Features
Sequential explanatory strategy	Generally priority would be given to the quantitative data and the two methods are integrated during the interpretation phase of the study; generally the findings from the qualitative work would assist in explaining and interpreting the findings from the quantitative study
Sequential exploratory strategy	An initial phase of qualitative data collection is followed by quantitative data collection and analysis; the findings are integrated in the interpretation phase
Sequential transformative strategy	Two distinct phases of data collection are employed; either method may be used first, and the findings integrated at the interpretation phase; generally this type of study would have a strong theoretical framework guiding the investigation
Concurrent triangulation strategy	Within a single study the researcher will attempt to confirm or cross-validate finding from qualitative and quantitative methods; integration usually happens during the interpretation phase
Concurrent nested strategy	Quantitative and qualitative data are collected concurrently but there is a dominant method to the study; the less dominant method is nested within the main method but may serve to answer a different question or seek information form a different level; the two data types are mixed in the analysis phase of the project, which involves the data being changed to a format that facilitates integration
Concurrent transformative strategy	This is guided by a theoretical perspective and may take the form of triangulation or nested strategies with the integration most likely to occur in the interpretation phase

Source: Cresswell [27].

In contrast, intermethod mixing is the concurrent or sequential mixing of two or more methods. It is important in utilizing a mixed-method approach to avoid ad hoc mixing of strategies, which would in effect nullify the validity of each method. Creswell [27] provides a checklist to assist in designing a mixed methods procedure, which considers the type of information to include and how mixing of methods might be achieved.

Qualitative research is about the emergence of new social theory or the development of existing social theory. It can be complementary to quantitative research in two ways: before carrying out quantitative research the use of qualitative research can suggest theories that can then be used to generate hypotheses to be tested; and after quantitative surveys qualitative research can provide a deeper exploration of the mechanisms that may link variables [23].

46.4.5 Subjects and Participants

Generally the term '*subject* is applied during experimental or quasiexperimental investigations, while *participant* is used in qualitative research to describe the people who take part in the research. Detail must be provided on the number participants, source of recruitment, participant characteristics, for example, age and gender or other data relevant to the study. If the subject is to be allocated to a particular group within the study the method of allocation must also be explicitly stated.

It is advantageous if the findings from research can be *generalized* to a wider population rather than only pertaining to the participants of the study. Short of carrying out a whole population study, applying *sampling* techniques can assist, helping to ensure that the sample size is of a sufficient size to reflect the characteristics of the larger population. In the latter scenario *inferential statistics* can then be administered; seeking the advice of a statistician for sample size determination at an early stage is a good idea! A rule of thumb is that the larger the sample size, the more likely it is to be representative of the population. Sampling enables the researcher to investigate a subset of the population of interest. For the sample to be useful, however, it must be representative of the population from which they are drawn. Failure to achieve this will mean that generalization cannot be achieved and could lead to invalid assumptions about the population in question [28].

46.4.6 Types of Sampling

There are two types of sampling: (1) *probability sampling*, which is based on the idea that a probability exists that the people chosen to participate in the study will be a cross-sectional representative of the total population (see Table 46.4 types of probability sampling); and (2) *non-probability* sampling is presented in (Table 46.5), which is the preferred method, when the researcher cannot conclusively state that without this approach the chosen sample would represent the wider population. The researcher may not have sufficient information about the population to undertake probability sampling, or it may be extremely difficult to contact a sample of the population. Consider, for example, working with the homeless or itinerants. With nonprobability sampling each member of the population does not stand an equal chance of selection to participate in the research.

The decision about whether to use sampling within qualitative research will depend on a range of factors, including the aims of the study, specific question to be addressed, and what is practical within time and resources. The strategies in relation to sampling, although not based on recognized formulas, should be explicit and systematic. The selection of participants within an investigation may be based on any of the established techniques described in Tables 46.4 and 46.5.

Within the research proposal the *sampling frame* should be defined. This is an objective list of the population from which selections for sample composition were taken. Schools register or telephone directories are both examples of a sampling frame. Some professional organizations will also provide access to mailing lists, for a fee. Denscombe [21] identifies that whilst "There is no absolute reason why qualitative research cannot use principles of randomness, or operate with large numbers. There are, however, some sound theoretical reasons why most qualitative research uses non-probability sampling techniques and good practical reasons why qualitative research deals with small numbers of instances to be researched."

Following confirmation of the sample, within experimental/scientific designs it may also be desirable to allocate participants to a particular group within the study. It may be that as part of the study some people will be subject to a particular intervention, for example, the provision of a particular assistive technology and others not. Random group allocation is used in an attempt to minimize bias in this situation. Randomization is used to ensure that the groups of participants do not differ systematically with respect to known and unknown variables. As the total number of participants increases within the investigation, that balance of characteristics between the groups is more likely to improve. Randomization has been discussed earlier in this chapter as a higher-level descriptor of overall research design. It can also be used within a number of research methodologies. The type of scheme adopted should always be concealed from researchers on the study.

TABLE 46.4 Types of Probability Sampling

Sampling Method	Key Features
Random sampling	Every member of the target population should have an equal chance of being selected for the study; by default, it is therefore an essential pre-requisite that the researcher has knowledge of the total population of interest (!); once this is established, a raffle type draw or random number tables can be used to identify the sample for the study
Stratified random sampling;	The researcher defines all relevant subgroups of the population and uses either "raffle" or random-number tables to draw a random sample from each subgroup; every member has an equal chance of being selected in relation to their proportion within the total population
Systematic sampling	The researcher is required to determine in what systematic way, generally numeric, participants will be chosen for inclusion in the sample; e.g., it may be decided to seek participation from every third person or every seventh person from those available. [28]
Cluster sampling	The researcher focuses on naturally occurring clusters of populations from which the sample will be derived, for example a university
Multistage sampling	Each sample is drawn form previously selected samples; any number of levels can be used, but each must be drawn from the previous level of samples

TABLE 46.5 Types of Nonprobability Sampling

Sampling Method	Key Features
Purposive sampling	The sample is handpicked; the researcher may already know something about the population and deliberately selects those who are more likely to produce the most valuable data—the researcher may choose to focus on extreme cases to illuminate the research question
Snowball sampling	The sample emerges through the process of reference from one person to the next; each participant of a small initial sample may be asked to nominate two or more people for the researcher to contact; participation of the nominees is hoped for, and if achieved, these participants are also asked to nominate, and so the process continues; snowballing works well with purposive sampling
Theoretical sampling	The selection into the sample follows a route of discovery based on the development of theory that is "grounded" in evidence; at each stage new evidence is used to modify or confirm a theory, which then assists in developing a further stage of research
Incidental sampling/convenience sampling	The most easily accessible people from the population of interest are selected to be part of the sample; it may, however, produce a sample that is not truly representative of all the characteristics of the wider population (e.g., if you are interested in the use of mobility aids but only a sample people referred for provision of walking aids following a fall are considered, you may have a limited sample)
Quota sampling	It is crucial that population characteristics, likely to be important to the study, be known in advance; once this is established, the sample gathered must have a percentage quota of the characteristic represented within the sample of participants that is proportional to their existence within the total population; this is often used with incidental/convenience sampling

46.4.7 Types of Randomization

There are four types of randomization:

- Simple randomization
- Block randomization
- Stratified randomization
- Minimization

Information should be provided on the characteristics that will enable participants to progress within the study is cited as the *inclusion criteria*. When the existence of a characteristic requires the exclusion of a recruited participant from the study, this is cited as *exclusion criteria*. For example, you might want to include adults below the age of 50 years, but exclude people who cannot read. The proposal should state under which conditions participants may be withdrawn from the study, for example, if consent to participate has been withheld. It the norm that only those people who meet the inclusion criteria would then be eligible to avail of the *withdrawal criteria*.

The proposal should state the *variables of interest*, and any *extraneous variables*, such as medication that the participant may be taking. Any means of controlling the extraneous variable must be stated.

46.4.8 Material and Procedures

A detailed description of all commercially available material to be used during the study must be provided. If instrumentation requires calibration detail an overview should be provided here with more detail in an appendix section.

46.4.8.1 Quantitative Data Collection

Quantitative data collection methods include questionnaires, standardized measuring instruments, ad hoc rating scales, or observation schedules [29]. Numerous quantitative measurement tools offer the opportunity to collect meaningful and useful data that, if chosen carefully, will relate to specific aspects of the research question under investigation. However, many are limited in their scope as they tend to have been developed for a particular population, are developed for a particular healthcare setting, or often focus on a particular functional component (e.g., hand function). However, some tools do exist that are worth considering as having potential to make a positive contribution to research data gathering. For examples:

- *The Quebec User Evaluation of Satisfaction 2.0 (QUEST 2.0) with Assistive Technology* [30] proposes that user satisfaction should be used as the main indicator of usability. Demers et al. [30] suggest that satisfaction can be monitored by service providers to help clinicians, researchers and managers to improve what they do, while creating a positive attitude among users. QUEST can be used to evaluate user satisfaction against a broad range of technologies in a structured and standardized way. The tool is composed of a 12-item scale; 8 items consider device characteristics; 4 items consider the assistive technology service.
- *The Psychosocial Impact of Assistive Device Scale* (*PIADS*) is a 27-item self-report paper-and-pencil measure of the impact of rehabilitation devices and assistive technologies on the quality of life of their users. By application of three subscales, the concepts of competence, adaptability, and self-esteem are explored, and considered to be fundamental dimensions of quality of life. The competence subscale is composed of 12 items related to perceived functional capability, independence, and performance (adequacy, efficiency, and skillfulness). The adaptability subscale is composed of 6 items reflecting inclination or motivation to participate socially or take risks. The third subscale is that of self-esteem, within which 8 items reflect self-confidence, self esteem and emotional well-being [31,32].
- *The Matching Person and Technology* (*MPT*) is both a model and an assessment tool; it is multidimensional considering three domains: *milieu*, which assesses the characteristics of the environment and psychosocial setting in which the technology will be used; *personality dimensions*, which focus on the individuals personality, temperament, and preferences; and the *technology dimension*, which considers the characteristics of the technology itself [33].

Some researchers explore quality-of-life measures; however, this can be problematic, as the term *quality of life* is in itself often misunderstood and misused. While the concept is interesting, it is difficult to define exactly what it means; it generally means different things to different people. *Health-related quality of life* (HRQL) refers to the impact of health services on the overall quality of life of individuals, the functional effect of both illness and therapeutic intervention on the individual. Assistive technologies address the long-term effects of disease and injury and therefore affect the HRQL as experienced at an individual level.

46.4.8.2 Qualitative Data Collection

Variety exists in the methods open to the researcher for utilization during qualitative data collection. It is the theoretical approach adopted by the researcher and applied during data analysis and generation of findings that impact on interpretation of data and how the outputs of the research are presented within dissemination activities. This section presents information on some of the qualitative data collection methods available; however, the contribution is by no means definitive.

46.4.9 Interviews

In defining interviewing, Oakley [34] describes it "rather like a marriage: everybody knows what it is, an awful lot of people do it, and yet behind each closed front door there is a world of secrets." Yet, interviews are probably the most common tool used to gather information on users within healthcare. Interviews provide data on the thoughts, feelings, and behavior of people and their inner perspectives in an accessible way. Interview formats range from face-to-face, or over the phone. It is generally a two-way informal process between the researcher and the individual participant, exploring the topic of interest. Interviews may be categorized as structured or unstructured, depending on the detailed preparation and guidance that the researcher uses during the time with the participant, to frame the interview. However, in both situations the researcher should approach the interview with an open mind to gather as much information as possible from the perspective of the participant.

46.4.10 Focus Groups

A *focus group* is a generic term for a group discussion organized to explore a particular set of issues. The focus is on the collective activity, such as debating a particular set of questions or reflecting on a similar experience. The interaction between the group participants is used to both generate data and influence how the data are analyzed. This method enables the researcher to witness the many types of communication that people use, for example, jokes and anecdotes; the variety potentially produces useful insights [35].

46.4.11 Observational Studies

Observational studies draw on the direct evidence available to the eye of the principal investigator. It is based on the premise that for certain purposes to observe what actually happens is best. It facilitates direct data collection, recording what people do rather than what they say they do. Using an observation schedule enables a systematic and rigorous approach to data collection. It can, however, focus on the overt behavior rather than participant intentions.

Within qualitative studies the researcher should practice *reflexivity*, an active and constant reflection on all aspects of the research process. The response to the participant's contribution should always be skeptical. The overall goal is not to produce a neutral, impersonal, and objective report that any other researcher in the same situation would produce. Rather to provide and enlightening perspective of a particular situation based on detailed study.

The *data collection procedure*, which refers to the actual process of data collection, to include the detail of instrument administration should be clearly stated. For example, are quantitative tests self-administered? Are qualitative interviews face to face or carried out over the telephone.

Following on from this *data analysis* methodologies should be outlined. If computer software packages are being used, these should be specified. For quantitative research, the application of statistical concepts may be required. Data can be coded and grouped to assist with analysis and assist presentation in a graphical format. With qualitative data, numerous approaches to interpretation are available. The range of techniques available is too wide and detailed for realistic representation within this one chapter; however, it does warrant substantial consideration by the principal investigator (PI) prior to investigation initiation,

46.5 ETHICAL CONSIDERATIONS

By embarking on an evaluation of technology, we open up an ethical debate that asks many questions of the investigator. Perhaps the starting point is to ask

Does this technology ever cause any harm and, if so, what is the nature and extent of the harm?
What is the risk of injury, distress or discomfort?
Can this risk be balanced by a potential benefit?

That the benefits outweigh the risk, is the essential ethical consideration.

A statement of ethical considerations of the study should be included and a copy of consent documentation placed within the appendix. If the overall integrity, quality, and worthiness of the research are conveyed by the proposal itself, then the main recurrent ethical issues to be considered are

- *Informed consent*—do the participants, whom the PI wants to include have full information about the research, including why and how they have been chosen? Is consent freely given?
- *Privacy*—in what ways will the research intrude into people's privacy?
- *Confidentiality and anonymity*—how will the information be safeguarded and the identity of people or places be protected? How can anonymity be preserved?
- *Ownership of data and conclusions*—who will own the data after the analysis and dissemination of results?
- *Use and misuse of results*—does the PI have a responsibility to ensure, as much as possible, that the results are not misused?

Other less frequent, but equally important, ethical issues involve honesty and trust, reciprocity (what participants gain from the research), intervention/advocacy (what do I see or hear that is harmful), harm, and risk to the participants.

Within the United Kingdom the Research Governance Framework [36] has been developed and implemented as a core standard for healthcare organizations. Within this there is an explicit statement of the systems that should be in place to ensure that research undertaken by and supported within the Health and Personal Social Services is done so properly and sensitively; respecting the rights, dignity, safety, and well-being of patients and clients. The responsibilities of funders, researchers, employing organizations, care organizations, and participants are all identified. *Good clinical practice guidelines* are embedded within this framework and state that the researcher must demonstrate that by training, education, and experience that they are qualified to undertake the research. *Good clinical practice* is an international ethical and scientific quality standard for designing, conducting, recording, and reporting trials that involve human participants. Origins of the guidelines link back to the International Conference in Harmonization [37] and the Declaration of Helsinki [38] produced by the World Medical Association of America in 1964. The Declaration of Helsinki guides the work of research ethics committees within United States, Canada, United Kingdom, and Australia. All international guidelines relating to health research suggest the presence of ethical committees at the organizational level, and support an ethical review process.

A major challenge of any investigation is *adhering to schedule*. It is essential that the PI establish a realistic timescale within which all the tasks and activity required to ensure successful completion of the research can be completed. It is common practice now for research proposals, submitted to funding organizations to contain either a Gantt chart or timeline, generated using computer software and visually plotting activity against time for the duration of the project. All research requires stringent project management, which can be challenging, especially if individual members of a project team are responsible for different tasks within the research proposal (e.g., data gathering or analysis).

A key role of the PI is identification of *resources* required to successfully complete the research. This requires detailed consideration of the personnel, consumables, travel, and technologic hardware needed throughout the duration of the research project. During costing it is important to understand the financial formulae of your institution and apply this, for example, to allow for annual increments in research staff salaries. If successful in acquiring funding from an outside agency to undertake the research, then stringent budgetary controls must be applied to ensure that the project doesn't overspend.

46.6 DISCUSSION

The development of research methodologies to investigate the integration of technology into healthcare is complex. Cook and Hussey [52] propose the *human activity assistive technology* (HATT) *model* as an acceptable way to consider the use of technology. Application of this model is also proposed to reduce the probability of device abandonment or rejection if applied systematically, and as an overarching framework to guide the development of research methodologies. In doing so, each element of the HATT can be related to particular outcome measures. This would certainly prove useful within the holistic paradigm of occupational therapy. The measurement of outcomes achievable by the provision of technology is not an easy task. One school of thought supports gathering a wide range of outcome data, and then deciding which data will be used, how much information is are needed, and how focused the measures need to be.

Exploiting ICT within healthcare is influenced by the professional paradigm of those involved and can be considered at two levels. Emerging service models reflect macroorganizational-level developments, as total services integrate a range of complex

ICT systems into an interagency care provision collaborating, for example, with housing associations to support disabled people at home. Conversely, it may be simple, with standalone commercially available ICT devices integrated into services at an individual client level to sustain people within communities. As an example, providing a pressure pad/alarm to alert a community-based family about the nocturnal mobility of an older person with dementia living in the same dwelling may provide a solution to a difficult problem.

Research has as a core value "striving for accuracy," and so producing valid data using reliable methods. This standard should be applied to all evaluations. It requires the developers of research proposals to devote a considerable amount of attention to the design and implementation of investigations. For the social science researcher, two broad questions are relevant: whether the data are valid; and whether the methods applied are reliable. The complexity within healthcare systems, diversity of environmental context, and unpredictability of both human behaviors and subjective experience limit the value and applicability of solely applying classical quantitative methodologies [39]. For this reason qualitative methodologies have a strong and positive contribution to make.

In clinical practice the question to be answered seldom can be totally resolved by quantitative methodologies. In healthcare and social care, utilizing qualitative components acknowledges the emotions, perceptions, and subjective experience of the participants. It also enables data to be gathered by the professionals and healthcare staff who deliver services, enhancing knowledge and understanding on how they perceive technology integration within services, impact on service users, and impact on the caring role.

Within the domain of technology in healthcare and social care, *device abandonment* is a recognized phenomenon, evidenced by the fact that a service user stops using a device, even when the need for the device still exists. Philips and Zhao identified four key factors related to this; failure of providers to take consumers' opinions into account; easy device procurement; poor device performance and changes in consumer needs or priorities [40]. This work highlights the need to consider technology provision as more than a part, or single entity but rather as a component of a larger system.

When considering the impact of technology within healthcare and social care, it would be remiss to omit economic evaluation. Given that resources are scarce, whether it is financial, staff time, or equipment, and that different technologies or services may vie for resource allocation, then it is reasonable that economic evaluation should complement clinical evaluation. That said, however, an economic evaluation is complex and requires the input and expertise from personnel with knowledge and understanding of the techniques available within this paradigm.

Legislation and policy within the developed world supports governments in fostering strategic direction that will encourage the exploitation of technology to facilitate healthcare and social care. Local service responses have been both planned and sporadic. At an operational level service commissioners and planners have funded innovative service approaches to traditional provision. Evidence is also present of innovation by enthusiastic clinicians who integrate technology into practice, and mainstream services that emerge from pilot projects. The use of technology within healthcare and social care is not new. Cook and Hussey [5] cite examples of assistive technology from the Stone Age! Historically, records show occupational therapists utilizing electronic assistive technology in the form of environmental control systems (ECSs) within the community setting from as early as 1953.

There is huge potential for diversity of health and social applications based on the integration of technology, which has stimulated a high level of societal interest in this area. This is reflected within the media, clinical practice, and academic publications. Traditionally within healthcare the provision of technology was the role of the occupational therapist; however, evidence is emerging of other interested healthcare contributors [37] who recognize its potential to support aging in place and sustain disabled people within communities.

There is a wide range of published literature available on healthcare technology, located within a variety of sources. For example, computing, mathematics, and engineering literature considers the detail of the information and communication technology (ICT) specification, technical capability, and reliability, citing research that is advancing technologic innovation. The health, telecare, and telemedicine literature considers the application of various devices to a variety of client groupings ranging from disabled people with mental health problems to those with physical disabilities; all age groups are investigated [42]. However, much of the research to date has focused on device efficiency. Studies tend to investigate the feasibility of using a particular device with a particular classification of disabled population, rather than investigating the outcomes of a particular intervention in relation to generally accepted interventions for the particular client group. This "proof of concept" testing to validate the efficacy of a particular device is important, but once established, further work should be encouraged to provide the evidence required to support mainstream service developments.

Effective practice in healthcare and social care is dependent on a partnership approach [43]. Within this the integration of technology into services generally requires intraagency partnerships and interagency collaboration with commercial sector providers. Technology may be used directly by service users and/or by service providers to supplement, enhance, enable, and/or inform the care process [44]. As an example, a bath hoist may be recommended to enable a caregiver (formal or informal) to bathe a disabled person in a way that is safe and comfortable for both. In a similar vein, a networked home may enable a disabled person but also provide information to the care provider and so inform the overall care process. The complexity within deployment can introduce ambiguity relating to the purpose and impact and to utilizing technology as an intervention during contact with service providers.

46.7 CONCLUSION

It is recognized that the evaluation of technology within healthcare and social care is complex [45]. Ultimately it is the research question that should drive the design of the evaluation. It is only by systematic and logical development of research methodologies, that coherent robust research will be produced. The World Health Organization suggests the ICF, which has been accepted by all member states, as a conceptual basis for the definition, measurement, and policy formulation of health and disability. As such, it offers potential to frame evaluations. In reality, technology is transient, yet the requirement for service provision is a constant. A challenge is to provide evidence to underpin the use of current state of the art technologies within services that are flexible enough to adapt to integrate emerging technologies. And so the process of evaluation continues!

REFERENCES

1. World Health Organization, Europe: *The European Health Report 2002*, WHO Regional Publications European Series, nr 97 (available at http://www.euro.who.int/europeanhealthreport; accessed 12/18/06).
2. World Health Organization, Geneva: *Towards a Common Language for Functioning Disability and Health (ICF)* (available at http://www3.who.int/icf/intros/ICF-Eng-Intro.pdf; accessed 12/18/06).
3. Schwartz Barker K: History and practice trends in the treatment of physical dysfunction, in Pedretti LW, Early MB, eds, *Occupational Therapy Practice Skills for Physical Dysfunction*, 5th ed, Mosby, St. Louis, 2001, pp 15–17.
4. Clarke A: *The Sociology of Healthcare*, Pearson Educational Limited, UK, 2001
5. Cook AM, Hussey SM: *Assistive Technologies Principles and Practice*, Mosby, St. Louis, 2002.
6. Curry RG, Tincom MT, Wardle R: *Telecare; Using Information and Communication Technology to Support Independent Living by Older, Disabled and Vulnerable People*, Department of Health, July 2003.
7. Jenkins S, Price CJ, Straker L: *The Researching Therapist; a Practical Guide to Planning, Performing and Communicating Research*, Churchill Livingstone, New York, 1998.
8. Taylor MC, ed: *Evidence-Based Practice for Occupational Therapists*, Blackwell Publishing, Oxford, 2000.
9. *The Chambers Dictionary*, Chambers Harrap Publishers, UK, 1998.
10. New Zealand Research Development Office: *Distinguishing Research and Audit* (available at www.adhb.govt.nz/rdo/distinguishing_research_and_audit; accessed 8/12/05).
11. Sale D: Defining the terms, in Taylor MC, ed, *Evidence-Based Practice for Occupational Therapists*, Blackwell Publishing, Oxford, 2000, p 4.
12. Bailey DM: Defining the terms, in Taylor MC, ed, *Evidence-Based Practice for Occupational Therapists*, Blackwell Publishing, Oxford, 2000, p 4.
13. Wade DT: Ethics audit and research: All shades of grey, *Br Med J* (Int ed) **330**(7489):468 (Feb 26, 2005).
14. Punch KF: *Developing Effective Research Proposals*, Sage Publications, London, 2000.
15. Denscombe M: *Ground Rules for Good Research a 10 Point Guide for Social Researchers*, Open Univ Press, Maidenhead, UK, 2002.
16. *Health Technology Assessment, Methodology Descriptors* (available from http://www.hta.ac.uk/consumers/methodology.htm; accessed 07/01/06).
17. *Cochrane Collaboration* (available at http://www.cochrane.org/index1.htm; accessed 07/01/06).
18. Batavia M: *Clinical Research for Health Professionals; A User-Friendly Guide*, Butterworth and Heinemann, Boston, 2001.
19. Tilling K, Jonathan S, Brookes S, Peters T: Features and designs of randomized controlled trials and non-randomized experimental designs, in Bowling S, Ebrahim S, eds, *Handbook of Health Research Methods; Investigation Measurement and Analysis*, Open Univ Press, Maidenhead, UK, 2005.
20. Moher D, Schultz KF, Altman D: The CONSORT statement: Revised recommendations for improving the quality of reports of parallel-group randomized trials, *Lancet* **357**:1170–1171 (2001).

21. Denscombe M: *The Good Research Guide for Small Scale Social Research Projects*, Open Univ Press, Maidenhead, UK, 1998.
22. Holloway I, ed: *Qualitative Research in Health Care*, Open Univ Press, New York, 2005.
23. Carter S, Henderson L: Approaches to qualitative data collection in social science, in Bowling S, Ebrahim S, eds, *Handbook of Health Research Methods; Investigation Measurement and Analysis*, Open Univ Press, Maidenhead, UK, 2005.
24. *Qualitative Research Methods in Health Technology Assessment; a Review of the Literature* (available at http://www.hta.ac.uk/project.asp?PjtId=929).
25. Adamson J: Combined qualitative and quantitative designs, in Bowling S, Ebrahim S, eds, *Handbook of Health Research Methods; Investigation Measurement and Analysis*, Open Univ Press, Maidenhead, UK, 2005.
26. Bryman A: Quantitative and qualitative research; further reflections on their integration, in Bowling S, Ebrahim S, eds, *Handbook of Health Research Methods; Investigation Measurement and Analysis*, Open Univ Press, Maidenhead, UK, 2005.
27. Cresswell JW: Research design: Qualitative, quantitative and mixed methods approaches, in Bowling S, Ebrahim S, eds, *Handbook of Health Research Methods; Investigation Measurement and Analysis*, Open University Press, Maidenhead, UK, 2005.
28. Hicks C: *Research Methods for Clinical Therapists; Applied Project Design and Analysis*, 3rd ed, Churchill Livingstone, New York, 1999.
29. Finch E, Brooks D, Stratford P, Mayo N: *Physical Rehabilitation Outcome Measures; A Guide to Enhanced Clinical Decision Making*, 2nd ed, Lippincott, Williams & Wilkins, Ontario, Canada, 2002.
30. Demers L, Monette ML et al: Reliability, validity and applicability of the Quebec user evaluation of satisfaction with assistive technology (QUEST 2.0) for adults with multiple scelerosis, *Disab Rehab* **24**(1/2/3):21–30 (2002).
31. Day H, Jutai J: Development of a scale to measure the psychosocial impact of assistive devices: Lessons learned and the road ahead, *Disab Rehab* **24**(1/2/3):31–37 (2002).
32. Jutai J, Rigby P, Ryan S, Stickel S: Psychosocial impact of electronic aids to daily living, *Assis Technol* **12**(2):123–131 (2000).
33. Galvin JC, Scherer MJ: Evaluating, selecting and using appropriate assistive technology, in Cook AM, Hussey SM, eds, *Assistive Technologies Principles and Practice*, Mosby, St. Louis, 2002.
34. Oakley A: Interviewing women a contradiction in terms, in Holloway I, ed, *Qualitative Research in Health Care*, Open Univ Press, New York, 2005.
35. Kitzinger J: Focus group research: Using group dynamics to explore perceptions, experiences and understandings, in Holloway I, ed, *Qualitative Research in Health Care*, Open Univ Press, New York, 2005.
36. *Research Governance Framework* (available from http://www.dh.gov.uk/PolicyAndGuidance/ResearchAndDevelopment/ResearchAndDevelopmentAZ/ResearchGovernance/fs/en; accessed on 1/23/06).
37. *International Conference on Harmonization* (available from http://www.ich.org/LOB/media/MEDIA482.pdf; accessed 1/23/06).
38. *Declaration of Helsinki* (available from http://www.wma.net/e/policy/b3.htm; accessed 1/23/06).
39. Dieppe P: Research on health and care, in Bowling S, Ebrahim S, eds, *Handbook of Health Research Methods; Investigation Measurement and Analysis*, Open Univ Press, Maidenhead, UK, 2005.

40. Philips B, Zhao H: Predictors of assistive technology abandonment, *Assist Technol* **5**(1):36–45 (1993).
41. Roelands M, Van Oost P, Stevens V, Depoorter A, Buysse A: Clinical practice guidelines to improve shared decision-making about assistive device use in home care: A pilot intervention study, *Patient Educ Counse* **55**(2):252–264 (Nov 2004).
42. *J Telemed Telecare* (available from http://www.rsmpress.co.uk/jtt.htm; accessed 1/26/06).
43. Carnwell R, Buchanan J: *Effective Practice in Health and Social Care; a Partnership Approach*, Open Univ Press, Maidenhead, UK, 2005.
44. Harlow E, Webb S: *Information and Communication Technologies in the Welfare Services*, Jessica Kingsley, London, 2003.
45. Medical Research Council. A framework for development and evaluation of RCT's for complex interventions to improve health 2000 (available at http://www.mrc.ac.uk/utilities/Documentrecord/index.htm?d=MRC003372; accessed 24/01/06).

47

Usability in Designing Assistive Technologies

Jean-Claude Sperandio and Marion Wolff
Ergonomics Unit, Paris Descartes University, Paris, France

Usability is a simple and intuitive concept; in the context here, it refers to the quality that makes an assistive device easy to use by an elderly or disabled person. According to the definition given by the International Standardization Organization (ISO 9241-11), "a system can be said to be usable when specified users, in specified circumstances, with specified goals, can use it with effectiveness (including completeness and accuracy), efficiency (resources expended) and satisfaction of users."

To reach a high degree of usability of a given product, designers need not only to account for all factors that make any user's normal use easier (or at least a given group of well-defined users, e.g., a given category of handicapped people) but also to use suitable methods in order to evaluate the usability degree with precise criteria, suitable for a given goal (of use) and a specific (target) population. According to the product, the population of potential users can be very large or strictly limited. Consequently, identifying precisely the users as well as the necessary characteristics of the product is essential.

The usability of a product first relies on the handling of various components, particularly controls and displays. Controls have to be compatible (i.e., congruent) with the user's hands, arms, or legs, and displays have to be compatible with the state of the user's sensory organs. For some assistive devices, the user's cognitive capacities or mental level are also relevant data.

The usability of a well-designed device also concerns the first installation and then each use. A good design should facilitate the familiarization with and memorization of the operating instructions. It should also allow users to transfer the knowledge or training that they have acquired from similar devices. The aesthetic quality and safety

---

The Engineering Handbook of Smart Technology for Aging, Disability, and Independence,
Edited by A. Helal, M. Mokhtari and B. Abdulrazak
Copyright © 2008 John Wiley & Sons, Inc.

aspect of an assistive device (particularly an individual aid usable outside the home) are also important criteria for handicapped people; some refuse any aid if the device is ugly, or visible to others, or unsafe to operate. Obviously, the product should be unobtrusive-looking, useful, and safe not only for the user but also for others.

Therefore, the concept of usability is now very important and includes usefulness, efficiency, safety, accuracy, and user satisfaction, although semantically those qualities are distinct from usability in the strict sense. It is possible indeed to design an efficient but difficult-to-use product or conversely, an easy-to-use but defective one, and so on. A good *ergonomic* product (a term now used in a quality labeling) must combine all these qualities whose expected consequences increase user satisfaction.

Such definitions are generic. They are not specific to the field of assistive devices or products usable by the handicapped or the elderly, but in this chapter we consider products designed for these populations, and differentiate between products usable by the general public with or without disabilities, and products specially designed for the impaired.

47.1 USABILITY: A CONCEPT LINKED TO DEVELOPMENT OF HUMAN–COMPUTER INTERFACES

The term *usability* is a neologism coined during the 1970s, at the beginning of technologic research and development (R&D) in the human–computer interface. Until then, computers worked without interfaces in the current sense of the word, and without any real-time interaction with users. Brian Shackel [1], at HUSAT Research Institute (Human Sciences and Advances Technology, Loughborough University, UK), was a major pioneer in stressing benefits to be expected from systems (hardware and software) specially adapted to users. *Usability* criteria gradually expanded in such a way that now the term has become almost synonymous with the term *ergonomic* although *usability* is an important part of the *ergonomic* criterion, it is still only a part).

The literature on usability, particularly concerning computers, interfaces, and Websites is very important. However, usability does not concern only computer systems, or even high technology. The concept can be applied to any object, simple or complex, intended for human used, including a door handle, home appliances, professional tools, or an aircraft cockpit, as well as a multioperator workplace. It must be noted that ergonomics, long before the term was used, has always focused on improving technical objects, tools, or complex systems, in order to make them easily usable by human operators (or users)—that is to say, more compatible with human characteristics. Objects must be compatible with human physical and mental characteristics, as well as with their activities and environment.

(*Note*: In practice, in terms of usability, the terms *user* and *operator* are almost synonymous. *User* is "object-oriented" while *operator* is "work-oriented.")

47.2 USABILITY AT THE CROSSROADS OF THREE PHILOSOPHIES

In terms of design, *usability* is situated at the convergence of three complementary philosophies: (1) a user-centered design (described in more detail in Chapter 44), instead of a technology-driven design; (2) an ecologic approach, that is, a design that factors in the use of the product integrated with other products and devices, in a given physical and social environment; and (3) a design-for-all approach (described in more detail in Chapter 45), given that the handicapped and the elderly are part and parcel of the general population.

The principle of "user-centered design" is simple; it means that product developments should be driven from user requirements rather than from technologic characteristics or capabilities [2]. The ISO 13407 standard (*Human Centered Design Processes for Interactive Systems*) provides guidance for achieving quality in use by incorporating user-centered design activities throughout the lifecycle of interactive computer-based systems, from the earliest stages of a project. Five user-centered design activities are noted:

1. Planning the human centered design process
2. Understanding and specifying the context of use
3. Understanding and specifying user and organizational requirements
4. Producing adapted design solutions
5. Evaluating designs against user requirements

Activity 5 (evaluation) is a cycle that crosses all other activities of a design process.

Even if the ISO 13407 norm relates to computer-based systems, the philosophy is not limited to such products. It should apply to any technology, including assistive technology. For the latter, user requirements include particular needs related to particular impairments, for a given category of handicaps or for a single person. Data required include not only the classical characteristics (height, weight, sensorial capacities, mental level, etc.) and evidently all the data related to the impairment, but also data concerning the physical and social environment of the user.

A system (human–machine couple)-oriented design takes that context into account in addition to the aspects that strictly concern the technology itself. A device well adapted to one impaired person may not fit another, even if they both suffer from the same kind of impairment. Consequently, an analysis of everyone's needs is required. To do so, designers cannot play the role of impaired users. Yet, involving handicapped users in the design process is a good thing, and some of them turn out to be good codesigners!

The third underlying philosophy is the "design for all" one; any object should be usable for as many persons as possible, including people with disabilities [3]. Many assistive devices could not exist if designers of all common objects had taken into account disabled people in the population of potential users. Small flaws may not be noticed or may be of minor importance for young, unimpaired people, but the handicapped and the elderly have a more limited capacity to overcome the consequences of bad design. The major benefits to be expected from good design are a significant reduction of the need of assistive devices for many moderately impaired people and enhanced comfort for everyone, even for the young and unimpaired.

The design-for-all philosophy is not limited to the usability of common objects. It extends to efforts to make society (home, built environment, transports, services, information, etc.) more accessible (i.e., usable) for anyone. Good social integration for an assistive device also means that the aid designed for an impaired person does not impede other persons (e.g., a voice synthesizer for the blind could disturb other persons all around, particularly in an office). But to be or not to be tolerant of the handicapped and of the elderly (using assistive devices or not) is a question of society, not a question of ergonomics.

However, even if we strongly support the design-for-all philosophy, some impaired people need specific assistive devices. Such devices require particular attention to usability, focused on individual characteristics. The same system cannot satisfy several persons with different disabilities, since they may have contradictory requirements (e.g., an interface adapted to the blind is not suitable for the deaf). In the same way, there are important differences between persons with the same kind of impairment. The elderly also have special individual needs, since even in the same age range degrees and types of deficiency are very heterogeneous. Therefore, products for the handicapped and for the elderly need to be particularly adjustable.

47.3 NORMS AND STANDARDS OF USABILITY

Norms and standards, as well as guidelines, are important for designers (this issue is discussed further in Part II of this volume). Some standards directly concern usability (but not all aspects of usability). Standards only partially express the knowledge of specialists. They are not exhaustive and generally not very innovative in terms of technology, because they are not always abreast of the latest technologies. In the International Standardization Organization, Technical Committee 159 ("Ergonomics") works on standardization in the field of ergonomics, including terminology, methodology, and human factor data, mainly with respect to employment (workplaces, tools, dangerous professions, etc.). The main concern is the safety of operators rather than usability of common products. Technical Committee 173 focuses on "technical systems and aids for disabled or handicapped persons." There are also several organizations in various countries, for example, the European Committee for Standardization (CEN), which is doing a good job in the standardization of assistive systems.

Myriad more recent norms concern computer-based systems (e.g., ISO 9241), but the principles can apply to other products as well. For Web accessibility, guidelines have been developed by an international consortium (W3C). Here is an abstract of the program:

> Web Content Accessibility Guidelines 2.0 covers a wide range of issues and recommendations for making Web content more accessible. This document contains principles, guidelines, success criteria, benefits, and examples that define and explain the requirements for making Web-based information and applications accessible. "Accessible" means usable to a wide range of people with disabilities, including blindness and low vision, deafness and hearing loss, learning difficulties, cognitive limitations, limited movement, speech difficulties, and others. Following these guidelines will also make the Web content more accessible to the vast majority of users, including older users. It will also enable people to access Web content using many different devices, including a wide variety of assistive technologies.[1]

From one country to another, there are different policies and regulations, generally advanced, regarding accessibility and usability (two closely related concepts, indeed). A good example in the United States, is Section 508 of the Rehabilitation Act:

> In 1998, Congress amended the Rehabilitation Act to require Federal agencies to make their electronic and information technology accessible to people with disabilities. Inaccessible technology interferes with an individual's ability to obtain and use information quickly and easily. Section 508 was enacted to eliminate barriers in information technology, to make

---

[1] Available at http://www.w3.org/TR/2005/WD-WCAG20-20051123/.

available new opportunities for people with disabilities, and to encourage development of technologies that will help achieve these goals. The law applies to all Federal agencies when they develop, procure, maintain, or use electronic and information technology. Under Section 508, agencies must give disabled employees and members of the public access to information that is comparable to the access available to others.

Although this law is limited to the field of information technologies, it could pave the way for other products.

47.4 CLASSICAL USABILITY CRITERIA

For reasons already explained, it is not possible to provide a final, permanent list of criteria that would be suitable for product and any user. A battery of criteria are required for each user group and for different tasks and contexts to be considered. However, the main items related to usability are classically:

- Adjustability
- Learnability
- Memorability
- Accuracy
- Productivity
- Usefulness
- User satisfaction

Several classical criteria are exhibited for computer-based devices, particularly for interfaces and the Web, but they can also be applied to other products:

- *Compatibility*—degree to which operations fit in with a user's expectations, based on his/her real-world experiences
- *Explicitness*—degree of clarity regarding how the device should be used
- *Effectiveness*—extent to which the user's goal or task can be achieved
- *Efficiency*—amount of time and/or effort (number of operations) to achieve the user's goal or task
- *Consistency*—degree to which similar tasks are performed in similar ways
- *Learnability*—degree to which interface helps the novice user learn about a device's capabilities
- *Feedback*—degree to which user actions are acknowledged with some meaningful response
- *Error prevention*—degree to which possibilities for error are minimized
- *Error recovery*—degree to which a user can recover quickly and easily from errors
- *Legibility*—ease with which text and other elements can be discerned and comprehended
- *Visual clarity*—degree to which information is displayed so that it can be read quickly, easily, and without causing confusion
- *Prioritization of functionality and information*—degree to which the most important functionality and information are easily accessible to users

47.5 METHODS FOR COLLECTING DATA RELATED TO USABILITY

There are two major opposite processes when designing products for the handicapped or the elderly; you either (1) start from the observed needs you look for the best possible solution, or (2) try to find an application for a given technology. In case 1 (need-oriented), the needs are generally well identified, but the risk is to rely on an obsolete or inadequate technology. In case 2 (technology-oriented), the main aim is often to apply a particular technology instead of finding the best possible solution to a precise problem, with the risk of giving a good response to imaginary or minor needs. In both cases, an appropriate methodology is needed to define the real needs and evaluate the degree of usability.

The literature on methods is vast. Of course, it deals mostly with computer-based devices (but...it can be applied to other products!). The contributors are many (e.g., see Refs. 4–7). The book by Nielsen [8], *Usability Engineering*, gives a wide panorama of methods (and other points of interest). dealing with usability, but does not focus on assistive devices or handicapped users. Some institution, university or research program Websites provide detailed and interesting guides on evaluation methods. For example, the USERfit Website presents a methodology focused on the generation of usability specifications for the assistive technology field, developed within the USER European Project TIDE-1062 [9–11] (see also. http://www.sc.ehu.es/acwusfit). Another rich Website about methodology (and other points of interest) is provided by INCLUDE (*INCLU*sion of *D*isabled and *E*lderly people in telematics, Project 1109, Finland).

The methods concerning the design process itself, already discussed (see Chapter 46), are not covered in the present chapter, which deals only with how to obtain data about users, activities, and contexts of use. A first and main principle must be kept in mind—neither designers nor experts are the final users; conversely users (handicapped or not) are not designers and are not always right when they demand a particular assistive system or particular fittings. Handicapped users generally know their own needs, but do not express them very well in terms of technology. With very few exceptions, handicapped users are unfamiliar with recent technologies and consequently can yearn even for an inadequate device. Therefore designers need a methodology focused on precise data about users' needs, on their actual behaviors and performances levels, not someone's subjective opinion.

There are different methods and many different techniques for each method. Usually, methods are divided into subjective and objective ones. Subjective methods are based on users' or experts' opinions (or testimonies or personal experiences), and data are obtained verbally. Objective methods are based only on behaviors and performances (of final users or experts). In practice, the two methods are combined and carried out together.

47.5.1 Subjective Methods

47.5.1.1 Interviews
A usual subjective method consists in interviewing the users directly, either a single user (e.g., for a specific assistive device) or a sample of current or potential users. Interviews are usually carried out as semidialogs centered on users' needs, difficulties of use, particularities of the context, and so on. This method allows for collecting a large amount of useful data, but that depends on many factors, such as interviewers' skill, choice and size of the sample, users' knowledge, and their abilities to verbalize.

Choosing a good sample of representative subjects is difficult because the number of persons dealing with a given category of handicap or device can be small and also because we don't know a priori the relevant variables to be factored in to set up a significant sample.

47.5.1.2 Discussion Groups

Another method consists in gathering a group of users, as heterogeneous as possible. Each one can express his/her opinion, personal needs, difficulties or experience, or suggestions for improvement, and so forth. The main advantage of this method is that each person can react to other participants' statements. A disadvantage is that statements can be contradictory. Moreover, a particular association may impose their view points, even if suchview point do not provide the best criteria for selecting a technology! Involving final users in the design process is certainly a good thing [12,13], however, and involving associations of handicapped users is also a good thing, politically necessary, but it is also carries a risk of bias, because associations can be established on obsolete ideas or can militate in favor of only a few of the people concerned.

47.5.1.3 Questionnaires

The method of questionnaires is widely used. It provides large inquiries and statistical analysis, if the number of responding subjects is sufficient (that is rarely the case with handicapped people). A questionnaire, oral or written, is a fixed list of questions. The main advantage of a questionnaire is that questions are asked in the same order for all subjects. A disadvantage with written questionnaires is that some subjects may not understand the questions exactly. In the case of verbal questionnaires, however, the investigator can complete or correct them if inadequate understanding is detected. But this also carries a risk of bias!

47.5.1.4 Inspection

A typical method for evaluating products, particularly new products, consists in systematically inspecting all the features of a given product. This method can be used in order to verify whether norms, standards, or recommendations are respected. That does not warrant that the product is good and very usable, only that it is conform to existing standards, for example, ISO standards. Thus, standard ISO 9241 provides methodological points to be respected in order to assess the conformity of a product to international standards.

The general method includes various techniques. A simple technique is the "formal usability inspection" carried out by one expert or a group of experts. According to Nielsen [14], four or five experts are enough to achieve a good gathering of significant bugs, flaws, or qualities. However, this group of experts must include experts of both the technology and the disabilities concerned. Each expert examines the product following a list of items according to a set of criteria and evaluates each item. The value of the data obtained depends on the experts' proficiency and chosen criteria. Such criteria are typically taken from guidelines of usability designing, or from a list of special criteria (e.g., for a new technology or a particular assistive device), or also from experts' experience.

Inspection methods can also include scenarios. A *scenario* in this context is a set of tasks linked together in order to achieve a set of particular goals. For example, experts play the role of final users and "walk through" a reasonable number of tasks. It is a method particularly suitable for inspecting devices with many functions, such as interfaces with many menus. Inspection methods can be carried out for existing or potential products, or also for products in the making. For example, with the "cognitive walkthrough," experts play the role of users working with that product and act through the tasks as if the product were actually built.

(*Note:* Scenarios can also be used for observations, experiments, or testing; in the field; in laboratory; or in any simulated environment.)

47.5.2 Objective Methods

47.5.2.1 Observations
Observing users directly in the appropriate environment is a good way to see how products are used [15,16]. According to the USERfit Website, "observing users in the field is often the best way to determine their usability requirements." Data can be collected by various techniques, according to the problem and the field (site or area) studied (home, public transport, workplace, medical building, etc.), with different recording equipment and techniques. All observation techniques need an observation plan, quite similar to an experimental plan as used in the laboratory, for studying functions and other factors. Observations are usually completed by interviews.

Observations are typically carried out directly in the field, but for some particular purposes, such as using special recording tools, observations can also be carried out in the laboratory, where the user's normal environment can be simulated. However, the behaviors observed should be those that the users usually manifest, with as little change as possible. This is the main difference between an observation and an experiment; *observations* avoid any change or disturbance of usual activities, while in *experiments*, the task, which may or may not be "realistic," is organized by the investigator and performed by subjects according to precise instructions.

47.5.2.2 Scenarios for Observations
In order to control different factors and standardize the protocols of observations, scenarios can be used. Tasks and scenarios must be realistic and chosen from among the users' normal activities. A high degree of realism is required especially for observations in the field and also for experiments. Generally, subjects are the final users, but this method can also be used if subjects are experts at "playing the role" of final users. However, in both cases (real users or experts), measurements concern behaviors and not opinions or judgments, contrary to inspection methods.

47.5.2.3 User-Based Testing
Usability testing consists in experiments carried out in measuring performances of subjects using a given system, in order to obtain precise responses to precise questions about the role of implied factors. It is the precise impact of factors that is studied rather than a global evaluation of a given product. The various methods of testing have in common a significant sample of representative users, experimental tasks, standardized measures, and an experimental design. A usability testing includes several parts: identifying the relevant factors to be tested, identifying the relevant users, choosing the tasks and scenarios, designing an experimental plan, recruiting the representative subjects, running the tests, and analyzing data [17–19].

Typically, tests are carried out in the laboratory, but also in the field if sufficient control of factors is possible. In the laboratory, compared to the field, what is gained in rigor and precision may be lost in realism. Subjects are typically final users, but can also be experts in a given domain (handicapped field or technology). Tasks must be realistic.

47.6 Specific Methodology Difficulties with Handicapped and Elderly People

The ISO 9241 standard recommends that subjective or objective methods include a large number of participants, allowing for statistical analysis of users' performances, and it is a wise recommendation. However, in practice, gathering a large representative sample of handicapped people is difficult. Even a simple observation in the field can be more difficult with the handicapped or the elderly.

First, recruiting a sufficient number of subjects, as required by any methodology (not only by experiments), can be a major obstacle, particularly for rare disabilities. Entering a laboratory for testing a new device, for example, can be laborious for these people, and conversely to go to their homes for interviews, observations, or tests can also be difficult for practical reasons (e.g., the place may be inappropriate or too far away) or because these persons may be timorous or nervous.

For testing, the control of interesting factors is done by way of an experimental design. The choice of subjects is particularly important, depending on the objectives of the tests. Since final users are generally heterogeneous, significant samples normally include various kinds of subjects (novice/experienced, male/female, young/old, etc.), balanced according to an experimental plan. Now, in practice, recruiting a sufficient number of representative handicapped subjects from a referred population is generally difficult. It is recommended that the number of factors, not be multiplied, because the number of necessary subjects depends on the number of factors. That is a problem common to other methods, but it is particularly difficult in the case of experimental testing, which requires a fixed, sufficient number of subjects in each cell induced by the intersection of different levels of factors.

More generally, rules for sampling require that subjects be randomized from a large population, but that may be impossible for practical reasons. In practice, recruiting is made from lists of subjects given by associations or institutions of care or from friends and relations. It must be pointed out that persons who agree to be subjects of interviews, observations, or experiments are the most dynamic and motivated ones, which is not a negligible bias.

47.7 RECOMMENDATIONS FOR THE ELDERLY

Given that the effects of aging differ between persons in the same range of age and evolve irregularly in time, products for the elderly and particularly all assistive devices must be adjustable. It is, in this case, the first quality of usability. The INCLUDE program, for example, asserts that

> Many of the problems that elderly and disabled people face in using interfaces (also with other devices) can be solved by developing interfaces with an underlying philosophy that they be adjustable to individual users' needs. It is recommended that the maximum degree of adjustability be built into interfaces, and where possible this should also include the

capability of connecting specialized control switches so that a standard product can be easily adapted for a severely disabled person to use.

The INCLUDE Website provides also general recommendations for designing devices for the elderly:

- Keeping tasks simple
- Providing consistency of operation
- Providing cues for operation
- Providing feedback of operation
- Providing error correction
- Reducing the complexity of all operations
- Providing adjustable user interfaces
- Designing for slow user response
- Avoiding cluttered displays

Some principles of usability can be associated with frequent features of aging:

- Decrease in sensorial capacities—display characters must be magnified (adjustable), contrasts must be optimal, sound must be increased (adjustable), and so on.
- Movements are limited and reactions are slower—do not force the elderly to behave quickly.
- Decrease in physical strength—to be taken into account for materials requiring a certain muscular force (e.g., wheelchairs).
- Memory is diminished—avoid passwords or numerical codes, for example.
- Little motivation for new technologies—the elderly are usually interested in new products or releases only if a real benefit is obvious.
- Fear of dramatic mistakes and irreversible errors—an adapted training and continuous help are to be provided, as well as "undo" controls and other corrective features.

47.8 FITTING WORKPLACES TO HANDICAPPED OPERATORS

Improving the usability of products and assistive devices also means fitting workplaces to handicapped operators, for example, decreasing or increasing the height of worktables, in order to enable work someone to from a wheelchair, or installing a special software with a Braille terminal or a voice synthesizer for blind users. Ergonomics provides methods for analyzing tasks and users and for evaluating new devices directly in the field. A good design of systems for any handicapped operator requires a precise analysis of special needs linked to the characteristics of the work, activities, tools, workplace, social environment, and so on. Under these circumstances, for the handicapped operator, the usability of a product, tool, or workplace is not the only quality, nor even the primary one to be reached. Efficiency, rapidity, safety, and nondisturbance for other operators are to be taken into account first, and these concerns often prevail.

Generally, the usual tools or physical environment at work (including architecture, despite some laws or norms in favor of accessibility for all handicapped people) were not designed for handicapped operators and consequently have to be specially adapted. Sometimes, a special fitting of the workplace is required, but usually the needed reengineering is neither very heavy nor or very expensive. This provides many handicapped people with normal workloads, and allows them to be autonomous and take their place in society.

REFERENCES

1. Shackel B: Usability-context, framework, definition, design and evaluation, in Shackel B, Richardson, S: *Human Factors for Informatics Usability*, Cambridge Univ Press, 1991.
2. Norman DA, Draper SW, eds, *User Centered System Design: New Perspectives on Human-Computer Interaction*, Lawrence Erlbaum, Hillsdale, NJ, 1986.
3. Vanderheiden GC: Design for people with functional limitations resulting from disability, aging, and circumstance, in Salvendy G, ed, *Handbook of Human Factors and Ergonomics*, 2nd ed, Wiley, New York 1997, pp 2010–2052.
4. Galer M: *Methodology for the Evaluation of Aids for the Disabled*, 2nd ed, Institute for Consumer Ergonomics (ICE), University of Technology, Loughborough, July 1983.
5. Batavia AI, Hammer GS: Toward the development of consumer-based criteria for the evaluation of assistive devices, *J Reha Res Devel*, **27**(4): pp 425–436 (1990).
6. Barnicle K: Evaluating assistive devices: what you need to know, *Proc 6th Annual Conf Technology and Persons with Disabilities*, Los Angeles, March 20–23, 1991, pp 43–52.
7. Arnold AK, Wallersteiner U, Ingelman JP: Human factors evaluation of information systems on board public transportation vehicles: Implications for travelers with sensory and cognitive disabilities. *Ergonomics and design*, *Proc IEA 94*, 12th Triennial Congress of the International Ergonomics Association, Toronto, Aug 15–19, 1994, vol **4**, pp 230–232.
8. Nielsen J: *Usability Engineering*, Morgan Kaufman, San Diego, 1994.
9. Poulson D, Ashby M, Richardson S: *USERFIT: A Practical Handbook on User Centred Design for Assistive Technology*, ECSC-EC-EAEC, Brussels–Luxembourg, 1996. (http://www.stakes.fi/include/1-4.htm).
10. Abascal J, Nicolle C: The application of USERfit methodology to teach usability guidelines, in Farec C. Vanderdonckt J. eds, *Tools for Working with Guidelines*, Springer-Verlag, Berlin, 2000, pp 209–216.
11. Abascal J, Arrue M, Garay N, Tomás J Velasco C: Accessibility- and usability-oriented design through USERfit tool, *Upgrade* **4**(1) (Feb 2003) (http://www.upgrade-cepis.org).
12. Buhler C, Schmidt M: User involvement in evaluation and assessment of assistive technology. ECART 2, *Proc European Conf Advancement of Rehabilitation Technology*, The Swedish Handicap Institute, Stockholm, May, 26–28, 1993, Section 30.1.
13. Gjoderum J: User involvement in assessment and user influence in standardisation of consumer products and assistive technology. Tuning in to the 21st century through assistive technology. Listen to the music, *Proc RESNA'04 Annual Conference*, Nashville, TN, June 17–22, 1994, TN, pp 240–242.
14. Nielsen J, Mack RL, eds: *Usability Inspection Methods*, Wiley, New York, 1994.
15. Drury CG: Methods for direct observation of performance, in Wilson JR, Corlett EN, eds, *Evaluation of Human Work*, Taylor & Francis, London; 1992.
16. Bevan, N, MacLeod M: Usability measurement in context, *Behav Informa Technol*, **13**(1/2): 132–145(Jan/April 1994).

17. Dumas JS, Redish JC: *A Practical Guide to Usability Testing*, Norwood, Ablex, NJ, 1993.
18. Lindgaard G: *Usability Testing and System Evaluation: A Guide for Designing Useful Computer Systems*, Chapman & Hall, London, 1994.
19. Rubin J: *Handbook of Usability Testing: How to Plan, Design, and Conduct Effective Tests*, Wiley, New York, 1994.

48

Smart Home and Health Telematics: Standards for and with Users

Milan Erbes
Home & Cenelec SmartHouse RG, Bourg la Reine, France

To be able to understand the new home networking and the residential gateway concept, we have to look into today's residential access environment with different network access technologies coming to the home via the existing telephone network (xDSL), the coaxial (coax) (and fiberoptic) cable TV networks, the emerging electrical grid network access, both middle-voltage (MV) and low-voltage (LV), and different wireless access. Coupled with this, today we also have direct broadcast satellite networks, switched digital video networks, PCS networks, and probably others. These are probably not all at the same place and same time and are not competing networks, but are incompatible at various levels of the OSI model. The incompatibility and competition among those networks are in functions, price, and availability, which means that residential customers will have to work with a complicated connection and switching problems. So, the solution is to design a technology-based architecture that will handle all these functions and hide the complexity from the consumer.

48.1 HOME NETWORKING TRENDS

Innovations in the telecom (telecommunication) industry have reshaped the way we communicate, with more connectivity, more bandwidth, more services, and more scalability, and we want that all, not just certain elements. If we have a high-speed Internet access at work, than we want it also at home. The demand goes not only for a high-speed access, but also other applications such as linking telecommuters with corporate offices, controlling a home alarm system from the other side of the country, turning the dishwasher on from the office, or downloading a movie from one computer to another within our homes.

Reliable broadband services delivered to the home will enable a variety of applications that will enrich our quality of life with new multimedia services for voice, video, videoconferencing, interactive gaming, high-speed Internet access, telecommuting; services for white goods, metering, healthcare for the ill, elderly, and disabled; and security, monitoring, and intelligence.

While aiming for more functionality from high-speed connections, the challenges that service providers are facing are in finding a way to uniformly serve customers with different demands. Many providers are turning to broadband gateways as a solution that could bring together multiple technologies without compromising end-user service. This new "digital home" is the converging point of Internet, multimedia, computing, and telecomm.

48.1.1 The Architecture of the Residential Gateway

The term "architecture" is used to describe the open framework around which all components and other entities operate in an intelligent and connected manner. There are potential interactions between security systems, heating and cooling systems (lowering the temperature and raising the air conditioning settings when the home is unoccupied) and lighting (turning off unused lighting but simulating occupancy when the home is unoccupied). In reality, the list of possible interactions is effectively endless and increases as new devices are invented or become network-enabled. A *home residential gateway* (HRG) is a complete, full-featured, performance-optimized solution for "to the home" and "within the home" connection. It supports access devices like cable modem, DSL modem, powerline access, broadband wireless access, and satellite access. HRG has a modular architecture and futureproof design and is based on Open Standards. Up to 80% of the solution is to be prebuilt and preintegrated on silicon chips. This translates to a substantial cost savings and time to market advantage to the product OEMs in the residential broadband, small businesses, home/SOHO networking, and CPE market segments.

The HRG is the device that interfaces various LAN connections in the home and connections to the outside world. The HRG acts as the primary access point for a number of different in-home networks (Ethernet, PLC, MOCA, 802.11a/b, 1394, USB, Bluetooth, etc.), providing a secure handover of encrypted content to an authorized domain. As users demand a single store for all their digital content from various digital devices throughout the home, the HRG will also become a primary storage device. There is a single, logical, residential gateway and a single logical architecture that will support any subsystem architecture. The term *logical* is important because the residential gateway has to function as a single entity routing in and out of the house in the most efficient and secure manner. Voice calls may be routed externally over the traditional copper PSTN, over GSM, GPRS, and 3GPP cellular wireless telephony or over Voice over IP (VoIP) depending on time of day, tariff, and availability. Data may be routed over cable modem, telephone line, or wirelessly by WiMax, WiFi, 3GPP, or GPRS. The logical architecture of the gateway does not imply that this must always be a single physical unit, as it could be physically distributed to allow for the expansion as further media or networks are added either inside or outside the house.

The four categories of the HRG market are as follows:

- *Home residential gateway*—addresses entertainment (video and audio), communications (telephony), high-speed data access, and control and monitoring (HVAC, security, lighting, etc.) functions.
- *Internet residential gateway*—connects multiple computers, multiple high-speed access problems in the home.
- *Set-top box gateway*—the CATV digital solutions. They are new-generation boxes that originated from the analog TV set-top box with more capabilities and features. They are IP-based new-generation boxes that evolved from the analog TV set-top box and provide digital media content to a TV in the livingroom. They have PVR (personal videorecorder) features and enable IPTV subscribers to view video, photos, and listen to music. The IP-STB box (DVB-T ETSI EN 300 744) [1] includes easier customization, remote management capabilities, different voice and video codecs and DRM and uses OpenCable standards and IP networks The STBs evolve to include DOCSIS set-top gateways (DSGs) [2], with dual tuners to enable concurrent video access for multiple television sets or PVR functions.
- *Utilities and security services gateways*—physical security systems and energy utilities are providing de facto gateways. These have low bandwidth with specific needs of data integrity and assured communication.

The HRG has a control function between external networks and in-home networks and devices. It serves as a traffic control and routing device and has the following key functions:

- The location to terminate all external access networks to the home, with multiple residential services delivered over any type of access network
- The location to terminate all home networks, such as telephone, television, computing, alarm, telemetry, and data
- To seamlessly interconnect public and private networks

The network interface units are selected to match the appropriate external network. The customer's premises interfaces are selected to match internal home networks or specific home appliances. The processor serves to operate the backplane as a switching point to allow for highly flexible translations and interconnections while hiding the complexity from the customer.

By connecting the electronic devices, consumers can perform tasks such as adjust heating or air conditioning via a home computer. The home networking products appeared on the market a while ago, but what we are missing is the home residential gateway to tie everything together. Using the home residential gateway, users can share a single broadband connection for all PCs in their home and share that connection, by setting up home LANs, sharing files, and playing interactive games.

48.1.2 The Intelligent Home

The term *intelligent home* refers to the convergence of intelligent devices and entertainment systems in the home. An increasing number of devices contain processors, and are therefore becoming intelligent, capable of communicating with other systems, and they are increasingly populating the home. The introduction and deployment of those intelligent devices, networks, applications, and services in the home are a direct result of manufacturers providing new technologies and of consumers becoming aware and demanding new services, applications, and equipment.

48.1.3 Home-Area Networks

The home-area network is a short-range communications system designed for the residential environment and is independent of the home network physical (PHY) layer medium (Fig. 48.1), where this may include, but is not limited to

- Coaxial cable
- CAT5 and CAT6 cable (twisted pairs—balanced)
- Telephone wire (unbalanced)
- Powerline communications
- Optical fiber
- Radiofrequency (RF) wireless
- Infrared (IR) wireless

The home network physical layer protocol and data link protocol may include, but are not limited to:

- Bluetooth™ (see Section 48.2.4.2, below)
- Ethernet or IEEE 802.3
- HomePlug™ (Home Powerline Alliance)
- HomePNA™ (Home Phoneline Networking Alliance)
- HomeRF™ (HomeRF Working Group)
- IEEE 802.11a/802.11b

As can be seen from this list, there are many network technologies, so it may not be possible to deliver all home services over the network technologies listed above.

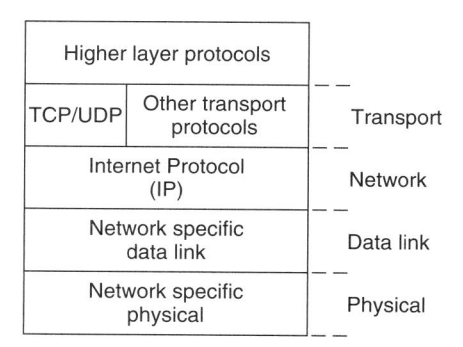

FIGURE 48.1 Home network protocol stack.

Typically, devices within a home network communicate with each other using a peer-to-peer architecture as opposed to the client/server model that is used in corporate networks. In peer-to-peer networks, devices can connect to each other directly without a server as an intermediary. In client/server architecture, all devices connect to a central server, which provides services like Internet access, applications, and file sharing. Many more devices can connect in a client/server network than in a peer-to-peer network.

48.2 EXISTING COMMUNICATIONS: CABLED INFRASTRUCTURE OF "NO NEW WIRES" NETWORKS

48.2.1 Phoneline Networks

This technology uses a home's internal phone wiring to connect devices together. Most phoneline networks require that all devices be connected to the same phoneline (i.e., the same pair of wires). A phoneline can carry multiple signals at different frequencies, which is why one can talk on the phone and still use a DSL modem for Internet access. Network traffic over phonelines uses frequencies higher than DSL or voice bands. The mission is to offer a mass deployment of a single-phoneline networking standard that is consumer-friendly, with "no new wires," and low-cost: under $100 per node. The latest R & D offers very high-speed [V2.0 up to 32 Mbs (Mbits/s), V3.0 > 200 Mbs] solution for in-home, phoneline-based networking.

This de facto industry standard is set by the Home Phoneline Networking Alliance (HomePNA)[1] offering a quality of service (QoS), which enables real-time audiovideo precedence over other data. The HomePNA announced the approval by the International Telecommunication Union (ITU) of a critical technical specification for a single, worldwide standard for high-performance multimedia home phoneline networking Recommendation G.9954 [3] (phoneline networking transceivers—enhanced physical, media access, and link layer specifications) that covers extensions and enhancements to the networking technology defined by existing Recommendations G.989.1, G.989.2, and G.989.3 [4], which are required to address the evolving needs of the industry for reliable transport of multiple high-speed multimedia streams over existing home wiring. The new standard provides for data rates of up to 240 Mbps with guaranteed quality of service (QoS) targeting the requirements of "triple play" service for providers wishing to deploy standard and high-definition TV along with toll-quality VoIP and high-speed Internet data.

48.2.2 Powerline Networks

Powerline communication (PLC) uses the existing power distribution cabling and inside wire running from 120 to 240 V, depending on the electric grid standards in place (Fig. 48.2). In Europe, for example, the standard calls for communications over the 240-V grid at frequencies from 30 to 150 kHz. In the United States, the standards for the 120-V grid allow the use of frequencies above 150 kHz as well. Power utilities use the frequencies below 490 kHz for their own telemetry and equipment control purposes. The powerline environment is challenging for the communications, as they were not designed for communications applications. Electric distribution cables and inside wires are highly susceptible to EMI electromagnetic interference (EMI) and radiofrequency interference

---

[1] http://www.homepna.org/.

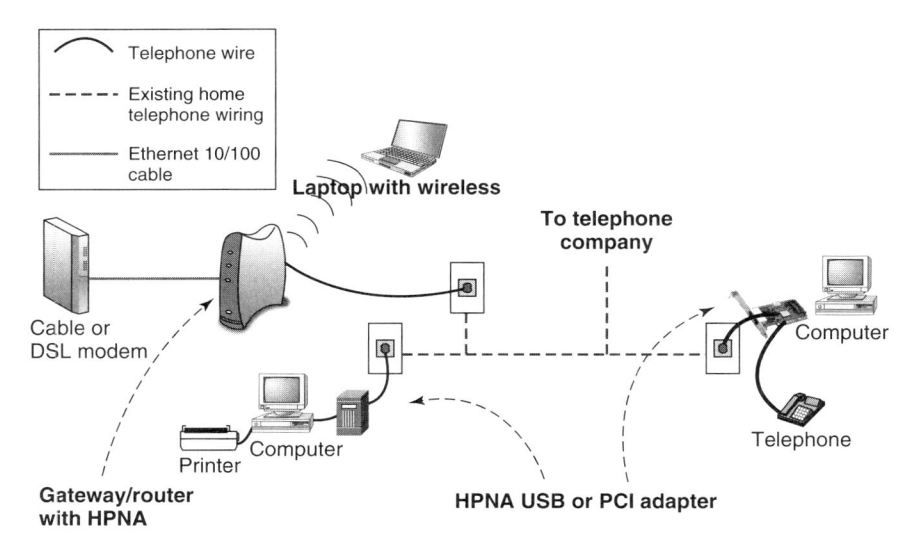

FIGURE 48.2 Powerline-based home network.

(RFI) [5]. Signals from radio stations, CB radios, wireless intercom systems, and other radio systems can cause crosstalk and other problems. Vacuum cleaners, electric drills, electric sanders, and other devices that employ universal series-wound motors generate considerable impulse noise. Also, TV sets create distortion, and light dimmers (i.e., rheostats) cause spurious noise.

Powerline communications is a wireline technology that is able to use the current electricity networks for data and voice retransmission. It includes *broadband over powerlines* (BPL) [6] / with data rates reaching > 200 Mbps and *narrowband over powerlines* with much lower data rates. The carrier can communicate voice and data by superimposing an analog signal over the standard 50- or 60-Hz alternating current (AC). Traditionally, electric utilities used low-speed powerline carrier circuits for control of substations, voice communication, and protection of high-voltage transmission lines. More recently, high-speed data transmission has been developed using the lower-voltage transmission lines used for power distribution. A short-range form of powerline carrier is used for home automation and intercoms.

There are three "promoters' groups" focused on specific standards initiatives and key technology areas within the Alliance:

- HomePlug 1.0 + AV (in-home connectivity, including digital home and consumer electronics applications)
- HomePlug BPL (to-the-home, broadband-over-powerline applications)
- HomePlug Home Automation (command-and-control applications)

With multiple outlets in almost every room, residential powerlines are already the most pervasive network in the world. As Internet use explodes, broadband access expands, and consumers plug a new generation of electronic devices into the Web, powerlines present a cost-effective, easy-to-adopt home networking solution for consumers around the globe. Powerline networks send data signals through existing AC powerlines. The HomePlug set of specifications offers a high-speed connectivity at Ethernet-class data rates and allows consumers to connect PCs and other devices conveniently at any power outlet. It coexists with already-popular devices that use residential power lines to communicate like X-10,[2] CEBus [7] and LonWorks a networking platform created by Echelon.[3]

Powerline networking challenges are in-home powerline wiring that was not designed for communicating data signals, and only recently has the market demanded a way to use them for high-speed data networking in the home. The physical properties and topology of the home wiring, the appliances connected, and the behavioral characteristics of the electric current, all combined create technical obstacles to the use of powerline as a networking medium.

48.2.2.1 HomePlug 1.0

HomePlug 1.0 [8] is the specification for a technology that connects devices to each other through the powerlines in a home. HomePlug-certified products connect PCs and other devices that use Ethernet, USB, and 802.11 "WiFi" technologies to the power line via a HomePlug "bridge" or "adapter." Some products—such as connected audio players—even have HomePlug technology built in.

48.2.2.2 HomePlug

HomePlug AV [9] was designed to support the high-bandwidth and low-latency demands of several simultaneous streams of HDTV and VoIP, made concurrently available in over 90% of power outlets in a home. The target applications are in-home distribution of audiovideo in home theater and data-networking environments. For this reason, in the given frequency range, HomePlug AV has pushed Shannon's law to its limit and provides a 200-Mbps class service at the PHY (physical) layer. After overhead considerations, the MAC layer will support >100 Mbps. HomePlug AV use frequencies in the range of 2–28 MHz. There is currently no plan to use frequencies above 30 MHz, but there is a possibility for expanding this range to higher frequencies depending on governmental regulations in the future. HomePlug AV provides a convenient and cost-effective method of distributing HDTV in the home without new wires, with secure connectivity and built-in quality-of-service (QoS) functions and features geared toward meeting the latency and jitter requirements of all emerging AV and IP applications.

HomePlug AV has a mechanism to detect the existence of neighboring networks. This mechanism is required to ensure that HomePlug AV systems in homes and apartments that are sharing the same physical wire do not interfere with each other. In other words, the need for bandwidth sharing exists inherently within HomePlug AV itself, and the bandwidth management solutions needed for in-home HomePlug AV applications can easily be extended to HomePlug BPL.

48.2.2.3 BPL Access

Broadband powerline (BPL)[4] refers to a to-the-home broadband access technology. The HomePlug Alliance formed the HomePlug Access BPL Working Group, whose first charter was to develop the Market Requirements Document (MRD) for a HomePlug Access BPL specification. The Alliance extended an open invitation to the BPL industry

---

[2] http://www.x10pro.com.
[3] http://www.echelon.com.
[4] http://www.powerlinecommunications.net/blog/2005/04/broadband-powerline-commun_111276370096974093.html.

to participate in the development of or provide input for consideration in the MRD. After several months of collaboration between utilities, ISPs, and other BPL industry groups, the MRD was completed in June 2005.

Access BPL is a form of PLC that uses certain elements of the existing electric power grid as a sort of local loop for delivery of broadband services. The typical power grid comprises generators, high voltage (HV) lines, substations, medium-voltage (MV) lines, transformers, and low-voltage (LV) lines. At the utility substation where the high-voltage lines are stepped down to medium voltage for the distribution network, a fiber network connection is terminated in a device that accomplishes the optical-to-electric conversion process. Inductive couplers wrapped around the powerlines, without touching them, serve as injectors, injecting the communications signals onto the distribution lines.

The RF carrier supporting the communications signals can share the same line with the electrical signals as they operate at different frequencies, a method know as *frequency-division multiplexing* (FDM) of telecom and electrical power, with the BPL signal using frequencies between 2 and 80 MHz. Repeaters, which must be spaced every 300 m or so, serve to reamplify, retime, and regenerate the signal as it travels from the utility substation toward the customer premises. The signals are removed from the powerlines by extractors placed just ahead of the transformers, which typically serve a number of households.

Interest for the Access BPL is in deploying of broadband in sparsely populated rural areas where DSL, PON, and cable modem options are unlikely to exist and where the business case cannot be made for *wireless local loop* (WLL) [10] technologies, including systems conforming to the emerging WiMax (IEEE 802.16) standard. There is also concern with potential interference issues. As high- and medium-voltage power transmission lines are largely unshielded and aerial in nature, they emit considerable electromagnetic fields that potentially can interfere with shortwave (e.g., ham) and other radio signals. There are certain excluded frequency bands to avoid interference with amateur and aircraft radio in the zones in proximity to sensitive operations such as the US Coast Guard, US Navy, and radio astronomy stations.

In-house PLC technologies may be more recent than Access BPL, but they aren't exactly new, either. Some key telephone systems and intercom systems have used it for decades. Standards for in-house BPL, a home networking technology, however, are a relatively recent development. HomePlug uses the Ethernet framing format, with some modifications. HomePlug-compatible devices include PCs, routers, bridges, and other devices that use Ethernet, USB, and WiFi (IEEE 802.11) technologies. Any such device can plug into standard electric sockets via a bridge or adapter about the size of a typical power adapter and, thereby, connect directly with the low-voltage electric lines (110/220 V at 50–60 Hz) in a home or office. So every electric outlet effectively becomes a port into a high-speed LAN.

- *Attenuation*, or loss of signal strength, is a fact of life. As an electromagnetic signal travels through a medium (electric signals through copper conductors) and across various components (fuse boxes, splices, surge suppressors, and circuit breakers), the signal loses some of its strength. Within the limits of the loss budget, which considers the strength of the transmitter, the sensitivity of the receiver, and the various attenuating factors between the two, the system will perform adequately. HomePlug currently offers a range of as much as 300 m without repeaters, which is well over the 100 m supported by 10/100baseT—and without the need for running CAT5 data-grade cable.

- *UPS* (uninterruptible power supplies) contain transformers, which stop the data communications signal in its tracks. UPS also typically condition the electric current by running it through a trickle-charge battery pack to smooth the AC waveform in order to filter out power spikes and dips and to compensate for short power.
- *Interference* issues can be significant. EMI (electromagnetic interference) sources include brush motors, switching power supplies, fluorescent lights, and halogen lamps, all of which produce impulse noise that can affect communications signal integrity over the shared electrical bus. HomePlug deals with these challenges through a combination of forward error correction (FEC) and automatic repeat request (ARQ).
- *RFI* (*radiofrequency interference*) from amateur radio can impact certain frequencies; therefore HomePlug employs spectral density notches around the ham radiofrequency bands, thereby reducing the number of OFDM carriers that can be used. As noise on the powerline can be highly local to the receiver, and as the quality of the channel between any between any two links connecting transmitter and receiver over the common electric bus will vary, HomePlug 1.0 uses a channel adaptation technique to turn off heavily impaired subcarriers.
- *Security* is always an issue, particularly so with technologies using a shared bus topology. As multiple premises typically are served from a common electrical transformer, the physical reach of an in-house BPL network can extend well beyond the walls of an individual home or business. HomePlug 1.0 standards include several security options, including 56-bit DES (Data Encryption Standard). In order to secure a given logical network (i.e., in-house), all transmissions between stations are encrypted with a unique, shared network encryption key.

48.2.3 Data over Cable Service Interface Specification

DOCSIS[5] is an international standard developed by CableLabs that defines the communications and operation support interface requirements for a data-over-cable system. It permits the addition of high-speed data transfer to an existing cable TV (CATV) system. It is employed by many cable television operators to provide Internet access over their existing hybrid fiber coaxial (HFC) infrastructure. The first DOCSIS specification was version 1.0 [11], issued in March 1997, with revision 1.1 [12] following in April 1999. Owing to increased demand for symmetric, real-time services such as IP telephony, DOCSIS was again revised to enhance upstream transmission speeds and QoS capabilities; this revision—DOCSIS 2.0 [13]—was released in January 2002 (Fig. 48.3).

The International Telecommunications Union Telecommunications Standardization Sector (ITU-T)[6] has adopted two DOCSIS variants as international standards. DOCSIS 1.1 was ratified as ITU-T Recommendation J.112; subsequently, DOCSIS 2.0 was ratifed as ITU-T Recommendation J.122. DOCSIS 2.0/J.122 is backward-compatible with DOCSIS 1.1/J.112. As frequency allocation band plans differ between US and European CATV systems, DOCSIS standards have been modified for use in Europe;

[5]http://www.cablemodem.com/.
[6]http://www.itu.int/ITU-T/.

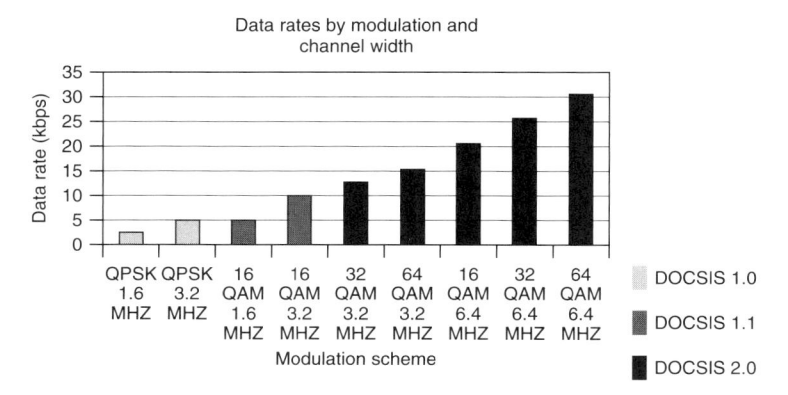

FIGURE 48.3 Comparison of the upstream modulation techniques employed in DOCSIS systems.

these are published under the name of "EuroDOCSIS." The main differences account for differing TV channel bandwidths; European cable channels conform to PAL TV standards and are 8 MHz wide, whereas in North America cable channels conform to NTSC standards, which specify 6 MHz. The wider bandwidth in EuroDOCSIS architectures permits more bandwidth to be allocated to the downstream data path (taken from a user's perspective, "downstream" is used to download data, while "upstream" is used to upload data). Japan employs other variants of DOCSIS.

The four successive versions of the DOCSIS cable modem specifications—DOCSIS 1.0, DOCSIS 1.1, and DOCSIS 2.0, and, now in development, DOCSIS 3.0 [14]—provide increasing levels of capabilities and functionality, while maintaining multivendor interoperability and full backward and forward compatibility of DOCSIS (http://www.itu.int/ITU-T/).

- DOCSIS 1.0 specifications include technology that was available in the 1995–1996 timeframe, and have become very widely deployed around the world. In DOCSIS 1.0 and 1.1, the upstream channels can be up to 3.2 MHz wide, and can deliver up to 10 Mbps per channel. DOCSIS 1.0 systems use quadrature phase-shift keying (QPSK) modulation across a 1.6-MHz channel, which in turn yields 2.56 Mbps throughput (2 bits/symbol × 1.28 Msymbols/s).
- DOCSIS 1.1 specifications provide improved operational flexibility, security, and QoS features that enable real-time services. DOCSIS 1.1 can utilize 16-level quadrature amplitude modulation (16-QAM) across a 3.2-MHz channel, increasing the upstream throughput by a factor of 4 (4 bits/symbol × 2.56 Msymbols/s). DOCSIS 1.1 enables provision of voice-over-IP telephony (VoIP), interactive gaming, and tier-based services.
- DOCSIS 2.0 triples the maximum upstream capacity of DOCSIS 1.1, by using S-CDMA (synchronous code-division multiple access) or A-TDMA (advanced time-division multiple access) and raising the upstream throughput to 30.72 Mbps by using 64-QAM or 128-QAM trellis-coded modulation (TCM) over a 6.4-MHz channel, resulting in an increase in the capacity to deliver high-speed data. A media access control (MAC) layer coordinates shared access to the upstream bandwidth.

- DOCSIS 3.0 specifications are currently in development at CableLabs and will include a number of enhancements, most notably, support for IPv6 and channel bonding (several downstream and several upstream channels will be "bonded" together to multiply the bandwidth delivered to each customer). Channel bonding provides cable operators with a flexible way to increase upstream by a minimum of 120 Mbps and downstream throughput to customers, and will increase the capacity to a minimum of 160 Mbps with data rates reaching into the future, at hundreds of megabits and potentially gigabits per second.

Although the physical layout and shared medium of the cable plant means that the data for each user pass by every other user on that section of the plant, the DOCSIS specifications ensure that every user's data are kept private through the use of encryption technology. Furthermore, DOCSIS 1.1, 2.0, and 3.0 provide additional security tools, including a mechanism for the operator to prevent theft of service by requiring that each modem authenticate itself using a digital certificate, a secure method to download new operational software to a modem, and a way to encrypt high-value "multicast" traffic and provide decryption keys only to those customers who are authorized for the service. Another significant change in DOCSIS 2.0 is the incorporation of trellis-coded modulation (TCM) for the upstream PHY. Upstream TCM FEC is available only in the S-CDMA modulation mode of DOCSIS 2.0 and will have a dramatic impact in reducing the affects of additive white Gaussian noise (AWGN). Primarily for implementation complexity concerns, the specification indicates that TCM FEC support by the CMTS receiver is optional.

Asynchronous time-division multiple access (ATDMA) is a direct evolution of DOCSIS 1.x physical layer (PHY), which uses TDMA multiplexing. DOCSIS 1.x upstream PHY uses a FDMA/TDMA burst multiplexing technique. FDMA accommodates simultaneous operation of multiple RF channels on different frequencies. TDMA allows multiple cable modems to share the same individual RF channel, because it allocates each cable modem its own timeslot in which to transmit. TDMA is carried over in DOCSIS 2.0, with numerous enhancements. SCDMA is a different approach, in which up to 128 symbols are transmitted simultaneously via 128 orthogonal codes. SCDMA multiplexing allows multiple modems to transmit in the same timeslot. Both ATDMA and SCDMA provide the same maximum data throughput, although one may outperform the other under specific operating conditions.

MoCA,[7] The Multimedia over Coax Alliance, has been formed as a nonprofit mutual benefit corporation to develop and promote specifications for the transport of digital entertainment and information content over in-home coaxial cable. The goal of MoCA is to create specifications and certify products that will tap into the vast amounts of unused bandwidth available on the in-home coax without the need for new connections, wiring, point-of-entry devices, or truck rolls.

More than 70% of homes in the United States have coax already installed into the home infrastructure. Many have existing coax in one or more primary entertainment consumption locations such as family rooms, media rooms, and master bedrooms—ideal for deploying networks. It has high speed (270 Mbps), quality of service (QoS), and the innate security of a shielded, wired connection combined with state-of-the art packet-level encryption. The MoCA network also can also be used as a backbone for multiple wireless access points used to extend the reach of wireless throughout a consumer's entire home.

[7] http://www.mocalliance.org/en/index.asp.

48.2.4 Wireless Networks

IEEE 802.11[8] is the WiFi (*Wi*reless *Fi*delity) standard, denotes a set of Wireless LAN/WLAN standards developed by working group 11 of the IEEE LAN/MAN Standards Committee (IEEE 802). The term *802.11x* is also used to denote this set of standards, and is not to be mistaken for any one of its elements. There is no single 802.11x standard. The term *IEEE 802.11* is also used to refer to the original 802.11, which is now sometimes called "802.11 legacy." IEEE 802.11 has been adopted for wireless connectivity in public places, college campuses, and the workplace, using the same network adapters that one would use in the home or in business.

The 802.11 family currently includes six over-the-air modulation techniques that all use the same protocol; the most popular (and prolific) techniques are those defined by the "b," "a," and "g" amendments to the original standard; security was originally included, and was later enhanced via the 802.11i amendment. Other standards in the family (c–f, h–j, n) are service enhancement and extensions, or corrections to previous specifications. 802.11b was the first widely accepted wireless networking standard, followed (somewhat counterintuitively) by 802.11a and 802.11 g. The 802.11b and 802.11 g standards use the 2.4-Gigahertz (GHz) band, operating under Part 15 of the FCC Rules and Regulations.

IEEE 802.16[9] is a new standard beyond the 802.11 specifications and is to offer many enhancements, anywhere from longer range to greater transfer speeds. The geographic region covered by one or several access points is called a "hotspot."

WiMAX[10] is an acronym that stands for *w*orldwide *i*nteroperability for *m*icrowave *a*ccess, with the mission to promote, certify, and mark for products that pass conformity and interoperability tests for the IEEE 802.16 standards. WiMAX can be used for a number of applications, including "last mile" broadband connections, hotspots, and cellular backhaul, and high-speed enterprise connectivity for business. Products that pass the conformity tests for WiMAX are capable of forming wireless connections between them to permit the carrying of Internet packet data. It is similar to WiFi in concept, but has certain improvements that are aimed at improving performance and should permit usage over much greater distances.

GSM[11] (Global System for Mobile Communications) is a European digital communications standard that provides full duplex data traffic to any device fitted with GSM capability, such as a phone, fax, or pager, at a rate of 9600 bps using the TDMA communications scheme. GSM is purely digital system and can easily interface with other digital communications systems, such as ISDN, and digital devices, such as Group 3 facsimile machines. Unlike any other service, GSM products require the use of a *subscriber identity module*, or SIM card that enables for greater security and also greater ease of use as this card may be transported from one phone to another, while maintaining the same information available to the user.

GPRS[12] (General Packet Radio Service) is a standardized part of GSM Phase 2+ and represents the first implementation of packet switching within GSM that is a circuit-switched technology. GPRS offers theoretical data speeds of up to 115 kbit/s (kps) using multislot techniques. GPRS is an essential precursor for 3G (third

---

[8] http://grouper.ieee.org/groups/802/11/.
[9] http://www.ieee802.org/16/.
[10] http://www.wimaxforum.org/home/.
[11] http://www.gsmworld.com/index.shtml.
[12] http://www.gsmworld.com/technology/gprs/index.shtml.

generation) as it introduces the packet-switched core required for UMTS. GPRS-enabled networks offer "always-on," higher-capacity, Internet-based content and packet-based data services. This enables services such as color Internet browsing, email on the move, powerful visual communications, multimedia messages, and location-based services.

UMTS[13] (Universal Mobile Telecommunications System) is the European entrant for 3G technologies. It has been subsumed into the IMT-2000 family as the WCDMA (wideband CDMA) technology. It provides excellent voice quality and easy-to-use data services across a broad range of devices and is providing significantly higher bit rates than with GSM. It can offer new, particularly innovative services in addition to second-generation mobile services such as voice, SMS, or certain mobile multimedia services, which are already available on GSM/GPRS networks. Video-based consumer services such as videotelephony (an association of telephone and television techniques that allows both users to see each other during their telephone conversation) and videostreaming (viewing uninterrupted video sequences on a telephone) are eagerly awaited. Professional customers will gain mobile access to the same tools available in the office environment, and in particular, access to data networks; the office will therefore become completely mobile.

3GPP[14]—*third-generation partnership project* is the generic term used for the next generation of mobile communications services. These new systems will provide enhanced services in comparison to those available today, namely, voice, text and data. The concepts for 3GSM services are currently being developed across the industry and by global groups such as GSM Association's vision of 3GSM, which is based on today's GSM standard, but evolved to include an additional radio air interface better suited to high-speed and multimedia data services. Services that will be offered by 3GSM are video on demand, high-speed multimedia, and Internet access, to name only a few.

48.2.4.1 3G UMTS/Satellite Interoperability

In the scope of the European Union MAESTRO [15], this R & D project is under EU Framework Program 6 with the strategic objective of "mobile and wireless system beyond 3G." It is an international consortium of 20 partners addressing the whole mobile multimedia value chain. This partnership will enable the development and implementation of the innovative satellite digital multimedia broadcast (SDMB) technology. Based on the UMTS standard, this SDMB system [16] will complement 3G mobile networks and provide the greatest broadband transmission capacity for multimedia services. It will utilize the natural assets of satellite systems and ensure that the envisaged SDMB system is fully interoperable with terrestrial UMTS standards in order to encourage multimedia usage adoption in Europe and contribute to the successful deployment of 3G.

48.2.4.2 Bluetooth

Bluetooth[15] is one of the latest protocols to enter the wireless arena. Imaginatively named after a Viking King, this short-range wireless protocol is not aimed solely at the home network but at the personal-area network (PAN). Bluetooth is intended primarily to reduce the number of cables required to interconnect small devices like mobile phones, PDAs, laptops, keyboards, and headsets to each other. The Bluetooth network can connect to

---

[13] http://www.umts-forum.org/servlet/dycon/ztumts/umts/Live/en/umts/Home.
[14] http://www.3gpp.org/.
[15] http://www.bluetooth.com/bluetooth/.

access points in preexisting networks within a range of ∼10 m (30 ft) with the data transmitted at a maximum of 1 Mbps. Radiofrequency operation is in the unlicensed industrial, scientific, and medical (ISM) band at 2.4–2.48 GHz, using a spread-spectrum, frequency-hopping, full-duplex signal at up to 1600 hops/s. The signal hops among 79 frequencies at 1 MHz intervals to give a high degree of interference immunity. RF output is specified as 0 dBm (1 mW) in the 10-m-range version and −30 to +20 dBm (100 mW) in the longer-range version.

The Bluetooth wireless technology comprises hardware, software, and interoperability requirements. Bluetooth wireless technology provides a universal bridge to existing data networks, a peripheral interface, and a mechanism for forming small, private ad hoc groupings of connected devices away from fixed network infrastructures. Bluetooth radio uses a fast acknowledgment and frequency-hopping scheme to make the link robust, even in noisy radio environments. The Bluetooth solution answers the need for short-range wireless connectivity within areas of data and voice access points, cable replacement, ad hoc networking, and data and voice access points. Bluetooth wireless technology facilitates real-time voice and data transmissions, which makes it possible to connect any portable and stationary communication device as easily as switching on the lights. In the future, Bluetooth is likely to be standard in tens of millions of mobile phones, PCs, laptops, and a wide range of other electronic devices. As a result, the market will demand new innovative applications, value-added services, end-to-end solutions, and much more. The possibilities opened up really are limitless, and because the radiofrequency used is globally available, Bluetooth can offer fast and secure access to wireless connectivity all over the world. With potential like that, it's no wonder that Bluetooth is set to become the fastest adopted technology in history.

The name *Bluetooth* derives from the tenth-century king of Denmark, King Harold Bluetooth, who engaged in diplomacy, which led warring parties to negotiate with each other. The inventors of the Bluetooth technology thought this a fitting name for their technology, which allowed different devices to talk to each other.

48.2.4.3 Other Technologies

The *HomeRF Wireless Technology*[16] Working Group developed a single specification [Shared Wireless Access Protocol (SWAP)] for a broad range of interoperable consumer devices. SWAP [17] is an open-industry specification that allows PCs, peripherals, cordless telephones, and other consumer devices to share and communicate voice and data in and around the home without the complication and expense of running new wires. The SWAP specification provides low-cost voice and data communications in the 2.4-GHz ISM band. Unlike other wireless LAN standards, the HomeRF protocol provides high-quality, multiuser voice capabilities. It combines the best of broadband wireless data-networking technology with the most prevalent digital cordless telephony standard in the world. In telecommunications, cable modems and xDSL are often referred to as being the "last mile." In that context, HomeRF could be referred to as the "last 50 meters."

ZigBee Alliance[17] is an association of companies working together to enable reliable, cost-effective, low-power, wirelessly networked, monitoring and control products based on an open global standard. The goal of the ZigBee Alliance is to provide the consumer with ultimate flexibility, mobility, and ease of use by building wireless intelligence and

---

[16] http://www.umts-forum.org/servlet/dycon/ztumts/umts/Live/en/umts/Home.
[17] http://www.zigbee.org/en/index.asp.

capabilities into everyday devices. ZigBee technology will be embedded in a wide range of products and applications across consumer, commercial, industrial, and government markets worldwide. ZigBee is providing a standards-based wireless platform optimised for the unique needs of remote monitoring and control applications, including simplicity, reliability, low cost, and low power, with the focus on defining the network, security, and application software layers; providing interoperability and conformance-testing specifications; promoting the ZigBee brand globally to build market-awareness; and managing the evolution of the technology.

The *KONNEX Association KNX standard*[18] is a system for home and building controls that is truly open (with no royalties for Konnex members) and platform-independent, guaranteeing multivendor and cross-discipline interoperability. Ensured via certification and symbolized by the KNX trademark, it supports many configuration methods (PC tools, device configurations, and plug-play), and media (TP, PL, RF, Ethernet). The KNX standard is fully compliant with the EN 50090 series, the European Standard for Home and Building Electronic Systems. The primary task for Konnex Association in the coming years will be the promotion of its *One Single Standard*, which is based on the communication stack of EIB but enlarged with the physical layers, configuration modes, and application experience of BatiBUS and EHS. The goal is to develop a standard that makes commands such as "start," "stop," "set spin speed," and "read actual temperature" uniform across all brands. However, the standard also needs to leave room for brand-specific features, as appliance companies still want to distinguish themselves.

In December 2003, CECED published CHAIN [18] (*CECED Home Appliances Interoperating Network*). This protocol allows domestic appliances of all brands to cooperate in a single automated home system. The technical layer of the communication is provided by the KONNEX field bus standard, which was developed more recently and was built on existing European standards for building automation. Of course, both developments must be synchronized; therefore, as an addition to the CHAIN standard, CECED and the KONNEX Association signed a contract to merge the command set into the current KONNEX standard, EHS 1.3a.

HAVi[19] (*Home Audio Video Interoperability*) is a standard that will allow all manner of digital consumer electronics and home appliances to communicate with each other. Eight of the world's leading manufacturers in this field have actually developed a standard that will bring you plug-and-enjoy convenience and easy interoperability to all your new digital home devices. Those companies are Grundig AG, Hitachi Ltd., Matsushita Electric Industrial Co. (Panasonic), Royal Philips Electronics, Sharp Corporation, Sony Corporation, Thomson Multimedia, and Toshiba Corporation. HAVi is a digital AV networking initiative that provides a home networking software specification for seamless interoperability among home entertainment products. The HAVi specification is AV-device-centric, so it has been designed to meet the particular demands of digital audio and video. It defines an operating-system-neutral middleware that manages multidirectional AV streams, event schedules, and registries, while providing APIs for the creation of a new generation of software applications.

IEEE 1394[20] (i.LINK® or FireWire®) has been chosen as the interconnection medium and has more than enough capacity to simultaneously carry multiple digital

---
[18] http://www.konnex.org/.
[19] http://www.havi.org/.
[20] http://www.1394ta.org/index.html.

audiovideostreams around the house, and provides support for digital copy protection. HAVi is the answer to the future of home networking. Each appliance added to the network automatically installs its own application and interface software. The complexity and sophistication has been built into the products in a way that simplifies control for the user. As each appliance is added to the HAVi networking system, it's automatically registered by the system so that other devices know what it is capable of. Applications may possess several functions, all supported by HAVi, which has standardized the application programming interfaces (APIs) of the most common AV functions. This means that a VCR (videocassette recorder) can search for an appliance that offers a clock with the time-of-day and automatically sets its own timers. HAVi is upgradable, which means that you'll be able to increase the functionality of devices as updates become available. Not even a home PC is required for a HAVi network to operate.

The *OSGi*[21] (Open Services Gateway initiative) Alliance was founded in March 1999, with the objective of providing a forum for the development of open specifications for the delivery of multiple services over wide-area networks to local networks and devices, and accelerating the demand for products and services based on those specifications worldwide through the sponsorship of market and user education programs. The original founders consisted of only 15 companies; currently more than 60 companies have committed to support the full incorporation and charter of the organization.

The OSGi Service Platform specification is a Java-based application-layer framework that gives service providers, network operators, and device and appliance manufacturers a vendor-neutral application and device layer APIs and functions, which will enable virtually all emerging home networking platforms, protocols, and services to seamlessly interoperate with back-end services, using existing residential telephone, cable TV, or electric wiring.

The key criteria for the Open Services Gateway Specification are

- The system must be platform-independent, so that it can be implemented on a variety of computing, communications, consumer electronic, and household products and platforms.
- It must be standards-based so that both vendors and service providers can have a standard platform to work from, and no single company controls the entire architecture and functionality.
- It must feature very advanced security and integrity technology as multiple service providers and network operators might manage objects or attributes in the OSGi gateway device or inside the facility to which it connects.
- Absolute or specific requirements must not be placed on downstream (in-house) network technologies, services, or protocols. Any vendor must be free to use whatever technology is applicable to its market.
- The management and operations of a network consisting of potentially millions of subscribers makes scalability and manageability a very major concern.
- The services gateway must be available at all times and not prone to crashes caused even by malicious applications.

As the OSGi Service Platform specification focuses on providing an open application layer and gateway interface for services gateways, complementing and enhancing

[21] http://www.osgi.org/

virtually all current residential networking standards and initiatives. Some of these include JINI, Bluetooth, CAL, CEBus, HAVi, Home API, HomePNA, HomePnP, HomeRF, and VESA. It also preserves consumer investments in future smart home devices.

UPnP[22] (Universal Plug and Play) is architecture for pervasive peer-to-peer network connectivity of PCs of all form factors, intelligent appliances, and wireless devices. UPnP is a distributed, open networking architecture that leverages TCP/IP and the Web to enable seamless proximity networking and in addition to control and transfer data among networked devices in the home, office, and everywhere in between. Universal Plug and Play is an evolving architecture that is designed to extend the zero-configuration mantra to a highly dynamic world of many networked devices supplied by many vendors.

48.3 ACCESS NETWORKS

Telecommunications today is probably the most rapidy evolving field of study. It is continuously offering new challenges and opportunities to telecommunications network planners. The basic idea of telecommunication is the exchange of information. The information may include voice, text, data, image, and video. A telecommunications network is therefore a system that can provide these services to a number of end users. From the end users' perspective, the network has several main tasks:

- Enable interconnection of end users
- Facilitate exchange of information in a form desired and suitable for their terminals
- Send and receive signals to/from the end users to facilitate the establishment, maintenance, and dismantling of connections
- Provide additional services such as wakeup calls and billing information

Demand and traffic patterns will change faster in the future than they do today. To cope with this, one important property that a network should have is flexibility. *Flexibility*, in simple terms, implies the ability to provide bandwidth on demand. If bandwidth can be provided on demand, then the network becomes capable of deploying and supporting a vide variety of services and with greater ease and speed. The ETSI NGN@HOME[23] standardization working group has been working on standardizing the area of in-home networking.

The residential gateway should support interfaces in such a way that the network termination requirements of the media are satisfied (Fig. 48.4). ETSI has the following standards for telecommunications network equipment:

- EN 300 386 [19], a harmonized standard for telecommunications network equipment
- ES 201 468 [20], a standard providing additional requirements for enhanced reliability of service in specific applications

There are multiple interfaces at the boundary to the home-area network and within it [21]. The interaction between the HAN and the access network has to be managed at several levels for

[22]http://www.upnp.org/.
[23]http://portal.etsi.org/Portal_Common/home.asp.

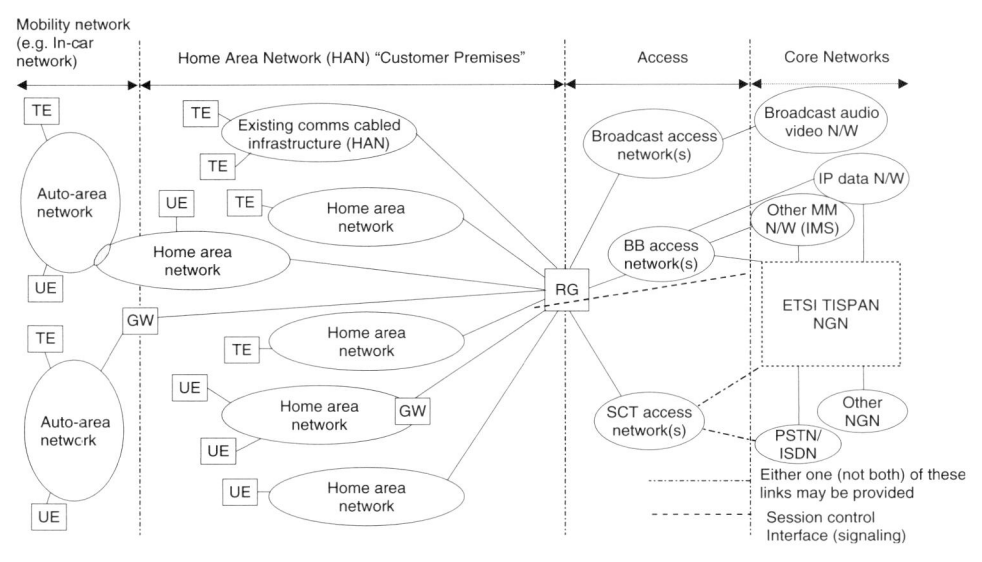

FIGURE 48.4 Access to home interfaces.

- Ensuring privacy within the home domain;
- Proving end devices that may be required for specific services
- Requesting resource allocation from end devices (QoS aspects)
- User profile management
- Service-level management

Next-generation home networks (NGN@Home)[24] will be required to support access networks of diverse technologies and capabilities. Regardless of the type of access network technology, the NGN in-home communications and services are required to support next-generation types of access technologies:

- Switched circuit technology (SCT)—PSTN/ISDN/GSM/GPRS/3GPP
- Digital subscriber line (xDSL)
- Powerline communications
- Hybrid fiber coax (HFC)
- Satellite and terrestrial broadcast
- WLAN (used in local loop)—IEEE 802.11x

All NGN-capable access types are required to offer IP connectivity.

The *home residential gateway* is an IP-based device that *enables* a service provider to offer enhanced set of home network services with QoS, device and service discovery, security, firewall, and provisioning and Management (Fig. 48.5). It also enables users *to connect* devices like PCs, kitchen appliances, audiovideo equipment, and security systems to high-speed Internet access. At the same time Home Residential Gateway enables users

[24]http://portal.etsi.org/at/ATNGNSummary.asp.

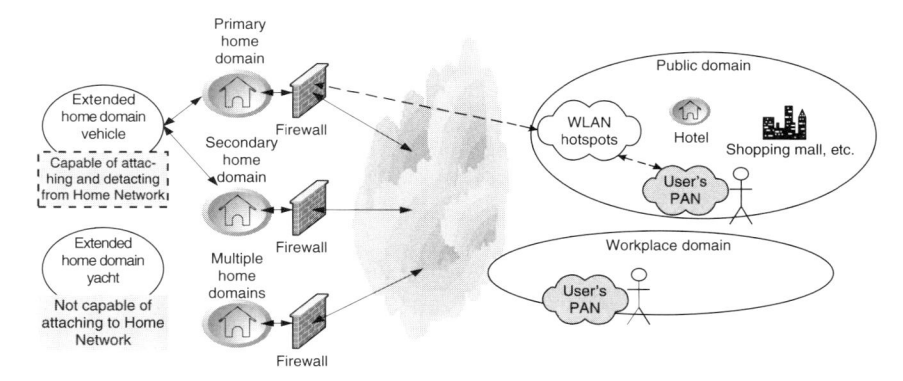

FIGURE 48.5 Multiple home domains.

to share a broadband connection for all PCs, by setting up home LANs, sharing files and printers, and playing interactive games, and is also able *to provide* solutions for automation in homes, buildings, and assisting people in their living environments.

48.3.1 Residential Gateway Architecture

The next generation of in-home network should support not only multiple different home networks based on IP but also other non-IP based networks, which should be interconnected into one overall structure, as shown in Figure 48.6. Connection to the wide-area network should be done through a single residential gateway architecture that on one side would support different access technologies and on the home side would connect to other home routers/switches and also legacy networks through separate gateways.

From the Figure 48.6 it is clear that there are four fundamental areas to the NGN in-home networking:

1. Multiple access networks (using both IP and non-IP native access technologies)

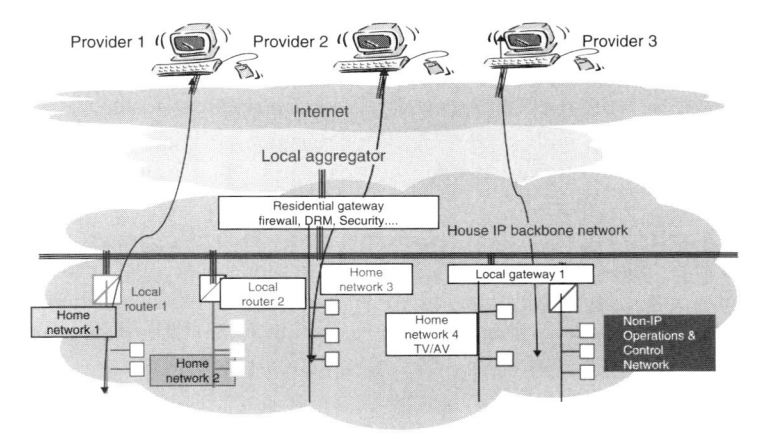

FIGURE 48.6 Home and access network model.

2. Multiple home-area networks (including the control domain, the transport domain, and the applications environment)
3. Multiple services and service providers (multiple content streams and formats)
4. Multiple end-user devices and terminal equipment connected within the home-area network

The NGN home networking and the Residential Gateway models have several areas of focus:

- *General Model.* The Home Network Architecture targets at supporting a wide range of services, from legacy telephony to new-generation services, such as audio, data, video broadcast and conversational services, streaming services, interactive gaming.
- *Functional Architecture Model.* A distributed functional architecture with the use of a new set of protocols to control user sessions (identification, authentication), resource allocations and QoS, traffic policing and enforcement, services and applications between various entities within the home network, packet filtering (depending on "IP address/port," i.e., firewall functionality), packet marking, resource allocation and bandwidth reservation, allocation and translation of IP addresses and port numbers (NAPT), throughput limitation, and optionally media ciphering/deciphering, media transcoding, media flow topology (conferencing, flow redirection, etc.), user authentication, usage metering, IP address allocation.
- *End-to-end Quality of Service.* Quality of Service is the ability to transmit in good conditions, a given type of traffic, in terms of availability, speed, time of transmission, rates of packet loss. It is a management concept which aims to optimize network resources (management information system) or a process (logistics) and ensure good performance for critical applications the organization. The Quality of Service can provide users with data rates and response times differentiated by applications (or activities) following the protocols implemented in the structure.
- *Service Platforms. (Including APIs)* That is collection of delivery and support Platforms, infrastructure capabilities and hardware requirements to support the construction, maintenance, and availability of a Service Component or capabilities.
- *Network Management.* Refers to the activities, methods, procedures, and tools that pertain to the operation, administration, maintenance, and provisioning of networked systems.

    Operation deals with keeping the network (and the services that the network provides) up and running smoothly. It includes monitoring the network to spot problems as soon as possible, ideally before users are affected.

    Administration deals with keeping track of resources in the network and how they are assigned. It includes all the "housekeeping" that is necessary to keep the network under control.

    Maintenance is concerned with performing repairs and upgrades—for example, when equipment must be replaced, when a router needs a patch for an operating system image, when a new switch is added to a network. Maintenance also involves corrective and preventive measures to make the managed network run "better", such as adjusting device configuration parameters.

    Provisioning is concerned with configuring resources in the network to support a given service. For example, this might include setting up the network so that a new customer can receive voice service.

- *Security& DRM/CA.* is the means of ensuring that data is kept safe from corruption and that access to it is suitably controlled. In such a way data security helps to ensure privacy and protection of personal data.

  DRM: Digital Rights Management refers to access control technologies used by publishers and copyright holders to limit usage of digital media or devices. It may also refer to restrictions associated with specific instances of digital works or devices.

  CA: Conditional Access is a system by which electronic transmission of digital media, especially satellite television signals through cable, is limited to subscribe clients. This is called conditional access. The signal is encrypted and is unavailable for unauthorized reception. A set-top box containing a conditional access module is required in the customer premises to receive and decrypt the signal.

- *Easy-to-Acquire/Store/Access Digital Music.* From anywhere in the home access to digital music collection stored on multiple, network-enabled devices, including PCs, "virtual jukeboxes," and portable audio players and for playback on any network-enabled playback device in the home.

- *Easy-to-Manage/View/Share Digital Photos.* The wireless download feature transfer all the photos to a media archive on a PC that will distribute the photos to photo frames, PC screensavers, TV adapters, and other devices throughout the home. It even securely sends the images across the Internet to friends or family.

- *Distributed, Multiuser Content Recording and Playback.* Using a universal remote, access to any of the network-enabled set-top boxes, PCs, or TVs in the home and select programs for viewing, or for recording and later playback, utilizing available tuner resources embedded in network-enabled TVs, dedicated PVRs, STBs, and PCs.

In order to deliver digital interoperability in the home, Residential Gateway is required to support:

- Fast Internet access and sharing
- QoS supported VoIP services
- Video delivery services broadcast quality
- Interoperable media formats and streaming protocols
- Interoperable media management and control framework
- Compatible authentication and authorization mechanisms for users and devices
- Transparent connectivity between devices inside the AV home network
- Security functions
- Network storage and remote access functions
- Remote device management functions
- Unified framework for device discovery, configuration, and control
- Home control, communication, and more advanced entertainment scenarios

End users can select the service provider independent of the access mechanism. Different end users within the same HAN can select different service providers. They could roam between different delivery networks, according to their subscription profiles with the selected service provider. For example, a user can register with the service provider for delivery of content when connected via a neighbor's HAN. So the objective is to

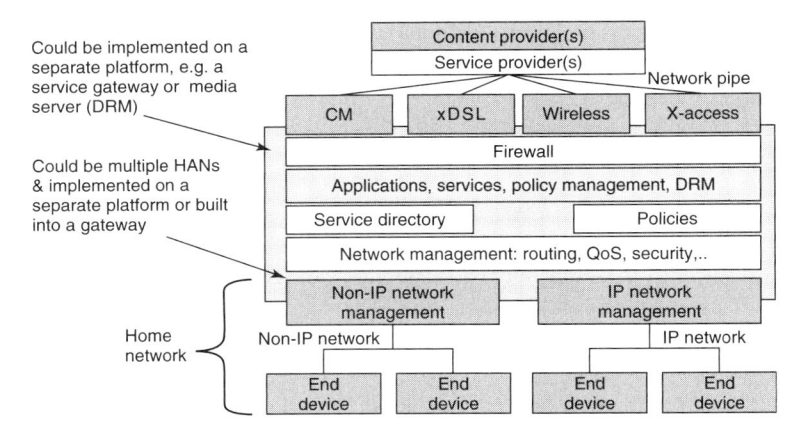

FIGURE 48.7 Home gateway architecture.

define an open network architecture enabling the provision of services to users in their homes and in other locations. A multiservice home network is based on a *home residential gateway* (HRG), which acts as a service platform for definition of end-user needs. The HRG has an embedded agent that could allow remote management of the home network by the home network service operator (Fig. 48.7).

While the HRG may be a single device [which is an objective of many groups, including the Home Gateway Initiative (HGI)[25]], because it is likely there will be legacy and service-specific gateways in a home, in many cases the residential gateway may consist of a number of logically connected gateway devices. Furthermore, the functionality of a HRG (its processing, control, and monitoring requirements) may also be dispersed either to management systems belonging to service providers or service aggregators or to secondary gateways or "half"-gateways within the home-area network.

There is a general assumption that, with the exception of "legacy" applications, IP will be the dominant protocol for information delivery between service providers and end-user applications, regardless of the physical access delivery method.

All end devices that HRG coordinates, have shared access to the Internet (Fig. 48.8). There are four physical/logical modules:

- *Access provider module* — provides access to Internet for the connection module(s) on the gateway, received via xDSL, HFC, PLC, xTTH, FWA, GPRS, UMTS, or any other new access technology. Local advertisement may appear on the end user's screen.
- *Connection module* — provides content to end devices, through access provider(s) and out-of-band broadcasters.
- *Policy coordination module* — coordinates changes among the other modules. It handles NAT, DHCP, IP routing, DRM and CA rights, multicast optimization, network address translation, quality of service, and security. It makes appropriate adjustments to the other modules as needed.
- *HAN module* — The home access network (HAN) module might be included in a separate hardware unit such as a hub, bridge, switch, or access point. It ties the various home networking media together. It should support Ethernet, PLC, IEEE

---
[25] http://www.homegatewayinitiative.org/info/whatis.html.

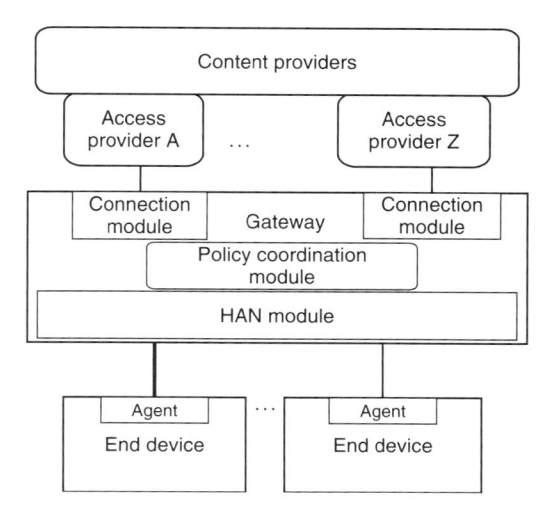

FIGURE 48.8 Home gateway architecture overview.

1394, 802.11, HPNA, Bluetooth, USB, and coaxial cable. Its role is to notify the policy coordination module of pertinent changes.

48.3.2 The Protocol Reference Model

The NGN@HOME & TISPAN[26] [Functional Architecture of the Resource and Admission Control Subsystem (RACS)] protocol reference model is shown in Figure 48.9–48.12. It consists of seven layers and three planes.

There are three planes:

- Data plane
- Control plane
- Management plane.

The IP layer at layer 3 is seen as a central layer in Figure 48.10. It has multiple branches on top (L4–L7 multiple stacks) and multiple roots below (L1–L2 multiple stacks).

The IP protocol is the crucial protocol on which everything is based and is located at layer 3. The protocol is either IP version 4 or IP version 6. The IP layer contains not only the IP protocol but also a number of other IP family protocols, (e.g. ARP, ICMP).

Below the IP layer there is always some form of Ethernet. It is there either (1) with its Ethernet cabling, physical interface, and the medium access convergence (MAC layer), and maybe some other sublayers on top of it or (2) with another physical transmission layer below it [e.g., asynchronous transfer mode (ATM)] and a transmission convergence layer to adapt to the MAC layer.

The following forms of Ethernet are supported:

- 802.3 wired Ethernet CSMA/CD
- 802.11 wireless Ethernet

[26] http://portal.etsi.org/Portal_Common/home.asp.

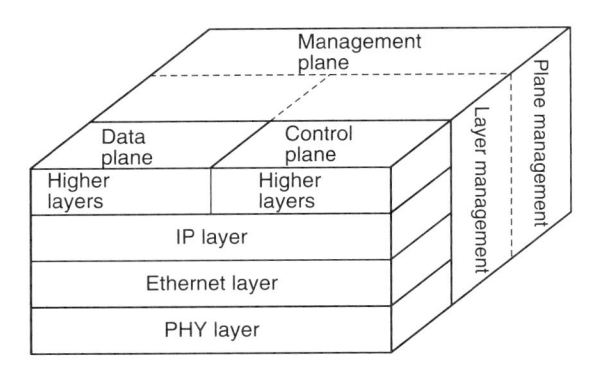

FIGURE 48.9 Home gateway protocol reference model.

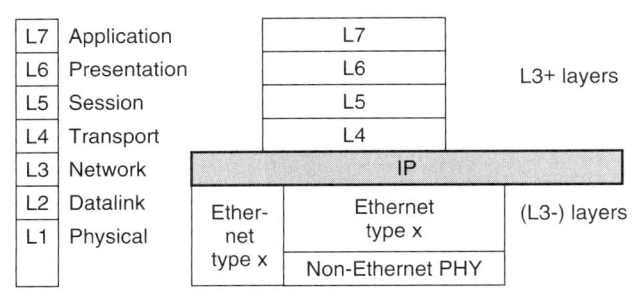

FIGURE 48.10 Home gateway protocol layers.

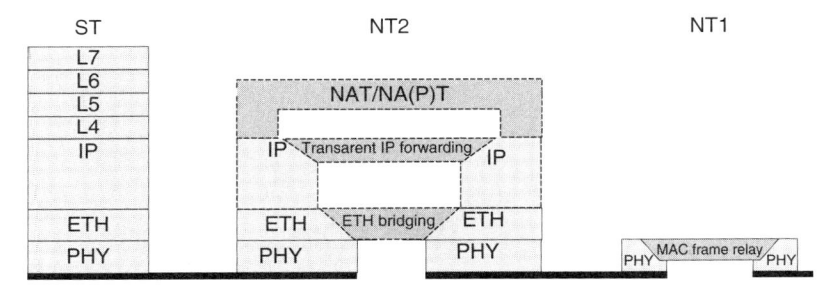

FIGURE 48.11 Data plane.

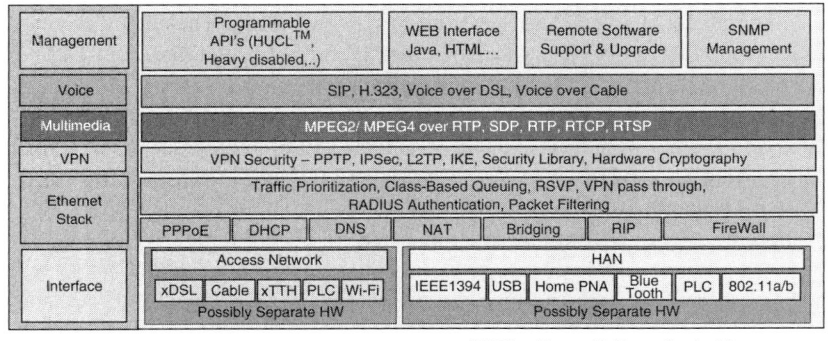

HUCL - Home Uniform Control Language

FIGURE 48.12 Home gateway stack (example).

Above the IP layer, in layer 4 there are TCP and UDP protocols; other L4 protocols may also be found there:

- The Transmission Control Protocol (TCP) enables two hosts to establish a connection and exchange streams of data. TCP **guarantees delivery** of data and also guarantees that packets will be delivered **in the same order** in which they were sent.
- The User Datagram Protocol (UDP) provides low error recovery services, offering a direct way to send and receive **datagrams** over an IP network.

48.3.2.1 The Data Plane

The *data plane* includes the transfer layers for the user-endpoint–user-endpoint transfer (Fig. 48.11). Within the network, transfer is up to the IP layer, although in some devices data traffic may be relayed at the physical or Ethernet layer. Within the home network protocol, stacks can be considered for the different functional entities.

48.3.2.2 The Control Plane

Control plane functions are related to a call containing connections. Within the packet-based network, a call is called a *session*, the instantiation of a service. The session can contain connection-oriented or connectionless connections. Multiple services can be used to form an application. From the protocol reference model, it is concluded that any communication function other than data plane commutation will pass through the control plane, whether it is for acquiring an IP address, authentication, signaling, management, or any other function that is not pure data transfer. Taking this into account avoids needless discussions on what control or management is. Stacks for the control plane go up to layer 7.

48.3.2.3 The Management Plane

The *management plane* relates to actions of setting parameters, which are of a more permanent nature then just a session communication. It provides two types of functions, layer management and plane management:

- *Plane management functions* perform management functions related to a system as a whole and provide coordination between all the planes. Plane management has no layered structure. The management plane handles internal system-handling functions.
- *Layer management functions* perform management functions (e.g., metasignaling) relating to resources and parameters residing in the system's protocol entities. Layer management handles the operation and maintenance (OM) information flows specific to the layer concerned.

The home residential gateway (Fig. 48.12) enables the delivery of new services to devices within the home with in order to interact with IP (and non-IP via specific gateways)-based home devices. This would give the service provider (SP) a management, provisioning, QoS and security to the home residential gateway together with the LAN messaging, prioritized QoS and simple remote diagnostics for all home devices in the SP's domain of management. The objective of the home residential gateway is to enable the delivery of new services to devices within the home, in order to interact with IP (and non-IP via specific gateways)-based home devices.

48.4 QUALITY-OF-SERVICE (QoS) REQUIREMENTS AND FUNCTIONS

Quality of service includes two aspects: service performance and service differentiation (ITU-T E.800) [22]. The key parameters of service performance are bandwidth, delay, jitter, and packet loss. The guarantee of service performance should be end-to-end, consistent, and predictable, at a level equal to or above a guaranteed minimum (RFC 2990) [23]. *Service differentiation* means providing different performance guarantees for different service applications. Some key services have to be carried with accurate and unaffected QoS guarantees even under heavy loads. Especially for voice services, the IP network should be capable of providing a carrier-class QoS that is equivalent to the legacy PSTN.

The end-to-end QoS architecture should encompass CPEs, be independent of access technology, and accommodate multiple administrative domains. QoS should support varying services, such as real-time multimedia communications and VPN, convergence of connectionless and connection-oriented networks and technology, and proactive (e.g., admission control) and reactive mechanisms (e.g., congestion control) based on measurements. The HRG enables home networking applications to utilize QoS resources that use management mechanisms to prioritize data flows and support real-time application traffic, such as VoIP, A/V streaming, and videogaming, by using prioritized media access and queuing.

- *Home Residential Gateway QoS.*

    Enables home networking applications to establish data transmission among hosts as well as between the hosts and the HRG using compliant messaging

    Enables home networking applications to establish data sessions between the access node and the HRG device

    Supports a transparent bridging functionality for QoS messaging from/to home-compliant applications

    Assigns traffic priorities (differentiated media access) to specific applications

    Prioritizes queuing in the HRG device in conjunction with the packet-handling functionality

- *Home Residential Gateway QoS-Enabled Services.* The NGN in-home architecture requires the support of a wide range of QoS-enabled services [24]. To offer these QoS services, it is necessary to define

    Bearer service QoS classes

    QoS control mechanisms

    QoS control architecture

    QoS control signalling

The provision of NGN in-home QoS mechanisms should account for different QoS control mechanisms corresponding to different technologies and possibly different business models. The following three scenarios have been identified:

- *Proxy QoS with Policy-Push.* The client's terminal or home gateway does not itself support native QoS signaling mechanisms. It requests a specific service to the application manager, which determines the QoS needs for this service (as in a xDSL network).

- *Client-Requested QoS with Policy-Push.* The client is able to request its QoS needs and the terminal, or the home gateway is capable of sending QoS requests over signaling and/or management protocols for its own QoS needs, but requires prior authorization from an application manager (as in a mobile network).
- *Client-Requested QoS with Policy-Pull.* The client terminal or home gateway is capable of sending QoS requests over signaling and management protocols for its own QoS needs, and does not require prior authorization.

48.4.1 VPN Service Requirements

Virtual Private Network (VPN) services constitute an important piece of the current service market for the service/network providers, and their value will continue to grow. It will also continue to grow with the evolution of application scenarios and enabling technologies and also looking at service providers' increasing variegated set of network and service environments.

Some significant evolving requirements are simultaneous data/voice/video support, multicast support, QoS support, enhanced security, mobility integration (nomadicity, roaming), increased access technology diversification, increased interworking scenarios, customer-on-demand capabilities, multilayer VPN services (L1/L2/L3) and related features (multilayer resource control), multiprovider and other complex connectivity scenarios, IPV6/IPV4 support, VPN OM, and ubiquitous user identification. A number of these requirements are common to other services whose support is required by future NGN in-home architectures. At the same time, some of the inherent characteristics of the VPN services, such as service–transport layer separation, virtualization of resources, multipoint connectivity, and autodiscovery capabilities, make them particularly interesting, looking at some general characteristics required by future NGN in-home architectures.

48.4.2 Managed and Unmanaged Services

There are two concepts: managed services and unmanaged services:

- *Managed service* is a service for which the broadband service provider guarantees the quality of service to the customer. The service can be offered by the broadband service provider or operated by the broadband service provider for the benefit of a third party. For example, this is the case for an IPTV service, which should provide QoS guarantee to the customer. A managed flow could also be local: reading on a PC the video recorded from the IPTV STB.
- *Unmanaged service* is a service for which the broadband service provider has no commitment to the customer in terms of quality of service. For example, photos upload service from the PC through the Internet. An unmanaged service could also be looking at the photos located on the PC hard drive from a wireless setup box.

Managed services must have a higher level of priority than unmanaged services as they are linked to a commitment of the broadband service provider to the customer.

48.4.3 User Involvement in Setting Quality of Service

For a user perspective, the QoS parameters should be set automatically with default settings, so that there is no need for a customer action to set up the default quality of service defined by the broadband operator. The user should not be able to change the

QoS settings for managed services. The risk of service unavailability must be avoided. Errors that occur when the customer sets incorrect QoS priorities and calls the hotline for support must be prevented; the user must not have access to these settings.

48.4.4 Fixed Mobile Convergence

Fixed mobile convergence is a complex issue that needs careful study. Expectations are that all triple play services will be available on nomadic (portable, roaming-enabled) devices within in the home provided that they have the capability to run those services. These devices will be able to move from the home environment to the mobile network hotspots and be able to connect to the services. The user's experience will depend on the context of his/her location. As an example, when the user is at home and a phone call is placed to the home phone number, all telephones in the home environment will ring (including the user's personal phone), but when the user is away from home and a call is placed to the home phone, the personal phone will not ring.

Services that are common in the mobile network, such as push-to-talk, presence, location, and messaging, will also work over the broadband network. Some services that may not work in the mobile network (such as VOD services) will work at home on the nomadic device. In all cases, when in the user's home, the nomadic device will be able to interact with other devices and services that are available there. It is also important to consider the user experience authentication mechanisms (phonebooks, etc.) that are reused when the nomadic device is placed in the home environment. The operator perspective is also important when analyzing fixed mobile convergence. Some technologies, like unlicensed mobile access (UMA),[27] extend the mobile operator's paradigm into the home. Other technologies, like WiFi, VoIP and GSM, could be considered as an extension of the fixed network operator paradigm in the mobile arena.

48.4.5 NGN In-Home Network Mobility Support

Mobility here is defined as the ability of the user to communicate and access services irrespective of changes in location or terminal, that is, independent of the network access point and of changes in the terminal type. The degree of service availability may depend on the access network capabilities and service-level agreements between the user's home network and the visited network.

- *Terminal mobility* is the ability of a terminal to access telecommunication services from different locations and while in motion, and the capability of the network to identify and locate that terminal.
- *Personal mobility* is the ability of the user to access telecommunication services at any terminal on the basis of a personal identifier, and the capability of the network to provide those services delineated in the user's service profile.
- *Service mobility* is applied for a specific service, such as the user's ability to use the particular (subscribed) service irrespective of the user's location and the terminal that is used for that purpose.

One crucial requirement for NGN is to provide the mobility management for users and terminals to ensure the roaming across the heterogeneous networks and the seamless mobility for ongoing sessions in the networks.

---

[27] http://www.umatechnology.org/.

Potential user requirements for mobility are as follows:

- Users should be able to gain access from any network access point. This includes all the access technologies (fixed, mobile radio, WLAN, WLL, etc.), and users are able to access their services through other networks (roaming). These possibilities may be limited by subscription and roaming arrangements among various service providers.
- Users should be able to get their services in a consistent manner, which is dependent on the constraints they experience in their current situations (e.g., terminal capabilities, bandwidth limitations). This is required for services provided by the network operator as well as services provided by a third party.
- Users' availability and reachability should be known to network functions and possibly to services and applications, including those provided by a third party.

48.5 SECURITY

The ability to guarantee secure communications and to block unwanted traffic or access to a terminal is beneficial for almost all types of basic service. To support the home user security requirements, certain security functions reside within the home residential gateway security domain, that is, on a per-home basis, including servers for key distribution, encryption, and authentication as well as some other client functions:

1. *Home Security Portal.* The home security portal (HSP) communicates with network or service provider security servers, and includes functions that provide client-side participation in the authentication, key exchange, and certificate management processes.
2. *Firewall.* The firewall (FW) provides functionality that protects the home network from malicious attack.
3. *Key Distribution Center Servers.* The key distribution center (KDC) servers provide security services to the CSP and include functions that participate in the authentication and key exchange processes.

Network security issues have changed very little since the mid-1990s. Protecting the confidentiality of information, preventing unauthorized access, and defending the network against attacks remain primary concerns for network security specialists. Network security is significantly more challenging, with widespread remote access and a high number of increasingly sophisticated attacks.

The network has been placed in a vulnerable position and will remain that way because of several key trends:

- *Changing levels of trust*—an ever-widening range of network access is being granted to different users, which is making the network increasingly vulnerable.
- *Ubiquitous access to the Internet*—the availability of the Internet has made every home, office, or business partner a potential entry point for an attack. This ubiquitous access allows sophisticated attacks to be launched against the corporate network by deliberate attackers or unknowingly by remote users logging onto the corporate network.

- *Attack sophistication*—new types of attack that target application vulnerabilities have been added to the long list of viruses, worms, and Trojan horse attacks that need to be prevented.

Security components, different security layers, and their intended uses are

- *Virtual Private Network (VPN)*—protects communications between sites and/or users with an encrypted and authenticated communications session.
- *Denial of Service (DoS)*—protects against denial of service type attacks.
- *Network Firewall*—protects the network by controlling who and what can have access to the network.
- *Application-aware firewall*—a combination of network and application protection detects and halts application attacks.
- *Intrusion prevention*—technology designed to protect against a wide range of sophisticated application-level attacks.
- *Antivirus protection*—protection against virus attacks at the desktop, gateway, and server level.
- *Personal firewall*—protects content on personal computers and, in turn, keeps corporate networks safe.

48.5.1 Security Authentication Requirements and Copy Protection

An NGN in-home network should provide security from the network operator and user perspectives. It should provide the possibility to establish trust relationships with other networks and with users. This includes the capability of the network to authenticate and authorize a single user and another network. A user should be able to authenticate the network. The IP multimedia applications should be provided in a secure manner. The NGN in-home Network should allow for a user to register with multiple terminals in parallel and multiple users to register with the same terminal. At any time the NGN home network should be able to verify the identity of users and terminals. It should also be able to check the authorization of the user to use resources of the NGN in-home Network and to access services offered by it.

A user profile, that is, a collection of user related data, is provided for support of

- Authentication
- Authorization
- Service subscription information
- Location
- Charging

The NGN in-home network should support mechanisms for the network operator to guarantee the authenticity of a user identity presented for an incoming call to a user where the call is entirely within that operator's network.

48.5.2 General Security Issues

Consumers will expect the intelligent home to provide good levels of security. This means physical security of the occupants and property and security of information and other electronic data. With the HRG reference model, it is possible to distinguish three main security rules/applications:

- The home gateway itself, border element between the network access and the home network.
- The fixed home devices (PC, home server, VoIP phones, etc.), which are always connected to the home network and access the public network through the Gateway.
- The portable home devices (portable PC, PDAs, tablet computers, etc.), which can be connected to the home network with access to the public network performed through the Gateway. They could also have other access interfaces to the mobile network where the gateway couldn't play any role, as they are using this second connection mode a different architecture; this is also a security issue.

The main security functionalities are firewall protection, VPN capabilities, cryptography (encryption and hashing) capabilities, virus protection, intrusion detection, authentication and authorization, code authentication/signature, and access control. *Security in remote management operations* is another key factor to be taken into account. In this sense, the support of additional security tools, such as authentication features embedded in some chipsets (TI OMAP [25], the Intel Trusted Platform Module [26]) or use of smart cards (which may contain passwords, digital certificates, etc.), and other configuration parameters can be provided. It must be possible to remotely configure and manage security policies with reference to the user access rights.

48.5.3 Firewall Protection

A firewall is considered a first line of defense in protecting private information; it is a system designed to prevent unauthorized access to or from the home network and the terminals. Without a firewall, other security mechanisms, such as VPNs, storage encryption, and authentication, remain vulnerable to attack. With respect to *static packet filtering*, which refers to a stateless filtering in which decisions are made only from the contents of the current packet and no context is kept; a firewall performs *dynamic packet filtering*, referring to a stateful inspection that tracks all connections crossing the firewall and ensuring that they are valid in relation to defined a set of rules. A stateful inspection firewall also monitors the state of the connection and compiles the information in a state table. This means that filtering decisions are also based on the context that has been established by prior packets that have passed through the firewall. The effectiveness of a stateful firewall could be diminished by applications that include IP addresses and TCP/UDP ports information in the payload (e.g., FTP, SIP protocols, peer-to-peer applications like as videoconferencing, online gaming, etc.). To properly filter these kinds of protocols, the firewall must be supported by a specific application-level gateway that recognizes the specific packet and analyzes the payload in order to obtain the required information.

48.5.4 Demilitarized Zone

A *demilitarized zone* (DMZ), a firewall configuration for securing local-area networks (LANs), is useful for users who want to host their own Internet services without allowing unauthorized access to the private home network. The DMZ is a subnet placed between the public network and the internal network's line of defense. Typically, the DMZ contains devices accessible to the Internet, such as Web (HTTP) servers, FTP servers, SMTP (email) servers, and DNS (Domain Name Service) servers.

48.5.5 Antispoofing

Internet Protocol (IP) *spoofing* is a hacking technique consisting in using the IP address of a machine, or equipment, in order to assume its identity. This technique allows the creation of IP packets with a source IP address belonging to someone else. This technique is used to attack networks while being disguised as someone else and makes it possible to carry out a DDoS (distributed denial of service). The SSH (Secure SHell) protocol relies on cryptography and authentication by password and checks that the used operating system generates sequence numbers that cannot be easily predicted or deciphered (RFC 1948) [27].

48.5.6 URL Filtering

The *URL filtering* mechanism—the possibility of denying a list of URLs or URLs that contain a specific pattern (e.g., parental control)—is an example of censorware functionalities that include all the mechanisms necessary to prevent another person from sending or receiving information to restrict access to objectionable material. To implement these features, a packet filter firewall can be used. In this case the firewall can examine not only the header information but also the content of the packet up through the application layer.

48.5.7 VPN Capabilities

The VPN (Virtual Private Network) is the main application in a network environment that can utilize authentication, confidentiality, and key exchange functionalities simultaneously. VPN is a network constructed by using public, not "trusted" (i.e., private, nonsecure), wiring to connect nodes and enable corporations or service providers to extend services to employees and partners without the risk of compromising their confidentiality and security policies. Different technologies (standard and proprietary solutions) can be adopted for VPN implementation: from level 2 solutions like PPTP and L2TP to application-level solutions like SSL, passing through the IP-level standard solution, namely, IPSEC. This last solution is considered here because it realizes a standard, flexible, and network-controllable architecture and allows working at the IP level regardless of the application (e.g., SSL cannot be used with applications based on UDP). The VPN IPSEC features to support are encryption algorithms (3DES and AES), encapsulation mode (tunnel, transport), key management, authentication algorithms (MD5 and SHA1 to support authenticated hash HMAC), and authentication methods (preshared key, IKE/PKI).

48.5.8 IPSEC NAT Traversal

One of the applications experiencing problems with network address translation (NAT) is the IPSEC protocol. A dedicated solution called *IPSec NAT Traversal* (NAT-T) is in the process of being standardized by the IPSec Working Group of the Internet Engineering Task Force (IETF).

IPSec NAT-T [28] capable peers during the IPSec negotiation process automatically to determine

1. Whether both the initiating IPSec peer (typically a client computer) and responding IPSec peer (typically a server) can perform IPSec NAT-T
2. Whether there are any NATs in the path between them.

If both of these conditions hold, the peers automatically use IPSec NAT-T to send IPSec-protected traffic across a NAT. If neither peer supports IPSec NAT-T, then normal IPSec negotiations and IPSec protection is performed. If both peers support IPSec NAT-T and there are no NATs between them, normal IPSec protection is performed.

48.5.9 Encryption Algorithms/Hashing

The encryption function can implement confidentiality of either communication data or stored data. Encryption algorithms may be classified into two types of encryption algorithm: symmetric or asymmetric. In public-key algorithms, there are two kinds of keys: the public key and the private key. Knowledge of the public key does not imply knowledge of the private key. A sender uses a public key of a receiver to encrypt the content. As a receiver has only a private key, it is capable of reading a message that is decrypted from a cipher text. In symmetric encryption, knowledge of the encryption key implies knowledge of the decipherment key and vice versa. The known algorithms can often be used for different purposes, such as key exchange or authentication, but they can be broadly categorized as follows:

- *Private (single, shared) key algorithms*—used for bulk data encryption, as they are comparatively fast. They do require a secret key to be known by both parties. Examples include DES, Blowfish, IDEA, LOKI, RC4, and AES.
- *Public (two) key algorithms*—used for key validation and distribution and for signature applications, which is advantageous because a public key is used, but disadvantageous because of the high computational cost compared to that of private-key schemes.

48.5.10 Virus Protection

Architecture of an antivirus system is involves an end-to-end network for the home, with the following components:

- The *Security operation center* (SOC) is devoted mainly to updating the antivirus (AV) signature; it makes the AV signature available for update to the SOC customer.
- User terminals and servers have an *antivirus (AV) engine*, which is used to find any malicious code (viruses, worm, Trojan horse) in the device, according to the signature downloaded in the user terminals/servers.
- An AV relay has all the functionality to interact between the AV facility in the user terminals/servers and the SOC that is able to synchronise the user terminal/server with the latest, more recently updated AV signature file. It can support the terminal with push functionality, delivering the updates directly to the terminal whenever they are made available without asking to the user terminal/server to poll the AV signature information at the SOC level.

48.5.11 Intrusion Detection

An *intrusion detection system* (IDS) monitors network traffic for suspicious activity and alerts the network administrator of possible security problems. Some IDS products can be configured to respond to malicious traffic by taking actions such as blocking a TCP connection, which may be used by an attacker to break into a protected system (e.g., a Web server). Network IDSs should be placed at strategic points within the network to monitor traffic to and from all devices on the network, such as the border between the private, secure, LAN, and the public (noninsecure) network (Internet), where the IDS system can scan all inbound and outbound traffic, with the HRG as a suitable location for the IDS.

48.5.12 Authentication

Authentication is the act of establishing or confirming something, or someone, as being authentic. Authentication of an object may involve confirming its provenance. Authentication of a person often consists in verifying their identity. In computer security, authentication is the process of attempting to verify the identity of the sender of a communication such as a request to log in. The sender being authenticated may be a person using a computer, an actual computer, or a computer program. A "blind" credential, in contrast, does not establish identity at all, only a narrow right or status of the user or program. Some security technologies that may be applied to authentication are

1. Use of authentication information—passwords supplied by a sending entity and checked by the receiving entity
2. Cryptographic technologies
3. Use of characteristics and/or possessions of the entity

The authentication function can be grouped into two categories: user authentication and message authentication. *Message authentication* can be provided by a device certificate or an ID certificate in the home network. *User authentication* function can be based on three factors: (1) what you know, (2) what you have, and (3) who you are. The authentication function may be incorporated in order to provide peer entity authentication. If the function does not succeed in authenticating the entity, this will result in rejection or termination of the connection and may lead to an entry in the security audit trail and/or a report to a security management center. When cryptographic techniques are used, they may be combined with "handshaking" protocols to protect against replay.

48.5.13 Code Authentication/Signature

A code authentication using a *hash message authentication code* (HMAC) [29] is defined as a public function with a input message and a secret key that produces a fixed-length value that serves as the authenticator in order authenticate a message and enable the receiver to verify the authenticity of that message. A MAC provides countermeasures against masquerade, content modification, sequence modification, and timing modification. A typical MAC function is HMAC (hash-based MAC). MAC is based on the symmetric encryption algorithm. The digital signature function defines two processes: a process for signing data, and a process for verifying signed data. The first process uses private-key functions (i.e., unique and confidential) to produce the signature. The second process uses public-key functions to verify the validity of signature. The signing process involves either encryption of the data, or the production of a cryptographic check value of the data, using the signatory's private information as a private key.

48.5.14 Access Control

The access control function may use the authenticated identity of an entity or information about or capabilities of the entity, in order to determine and enforce the access rights of the entity. If the entity attempts to use an unauthorized resource or an authorized resource with an improper type of access, then the access control function will reject the attempt and may additionally report the incident for the purposes of generating an alarm and/or recording it as part of a security audit trail.

The access control function may be based on the use of the following items:

- Access control information bases, where the access rights of peer entities are maintained in a database
- Authentication information such as passwords, the possession and subsequent presentation of which constitute evidence of the accessing entity's authorization
- Capabilities, the possession and subsequent presentation of which is evidence of the right to access the entity or resource defined by the capability
- An authorization certificate
- Security labels, which, when associated with an entity, may be used to grant or deny access, usually according to a security policy

The access control function may be applied either at peer entities of a communication association and/or at a secure home gateway. Access control involved at the origin entity or mobile security gateway is used to determine whether the sender is authorized to communicate with the recipient and/or to use the required communication resources. The access control function allows a home device to know what each authenticated device is allowed to do. There are predominant authorization mechanisms, such as an access control list (ACL), authorization server, and authorization certificate. A device can control access by an ACL alone. This allows an access control to be deleted with ease, given that one can edit the ACL of the device. It has the disadvantage of requiring a large amount of ACL. If a person has a home network containing a number of home devices and that ACL is very large, then it might make sense to move the ACL from each home device to a server, which is called an *authorization server*. Another way to administer authorization is to allow delegation by means of authorization certificates. An *authorization certificate* is a digitally signed ACL entry.

48.5.15 Electronic Data Security

Critical data entering or leaving the house, via the residential home gateway, should be secure. The electronic system should ensure that filtering of incoming data meets the consumers' requirement. The electronic system should ensure that critical outgoing data (e.g., credit card details, personal medical data, and information related to personal security) is secure and adequately encrypted.

48.5.16 Privacy

Privacy is the interest that individuals have in sustaining a "personal space," free from interference by other people and organizations. It is an interest that has several dimensions:

- *Privacy of the Person.* This is concerned with the integrity of the individual's body. Issues include compulsory immunization, blood transfusion, provision of samples of body fluids and body tissue, and sterilization.
- *Privacy of Personal Behavior.* This relates to all aspects of behavior, but especially to sensitive matters, such as sexual preferences and habits, political activities, and religious practices, both in private and in public places.
- *Privacy of Personal Communications.* Individuals claim an interest in being able to communicate among themselves, using various media, without routine monitoring of their communications by other persons or organizations.
- *Privacy of Personal Data.* Individuals claim that data about themselves should not be automatically available to other individuals and organizations, and even where data are possessed by another party, the individual must be able to exercise a substantial degree of control over those data and their use.
- *Information Privacy.* This is the interest individuals have in controlling, or at least significantly influencing, the handling of data about themselves.

These are the privacy aspects that are of primary concern in the intelligent home since the system "knows" about the occupants and is in a position to transmit this information to a third party.

48.5.16.1 Privacy Protection

Privacy protection is a process of finding appropriate balances between privacy and multiple competing interests. Important implication of this definition is *the interest to be balanced* against many other, often competing, interests. The privacy interest of one person may conflict with that of another person, groups of people, organisation, or society as a whole. It is impossible to ensure total privacy while at the same time monitoring the safety of vulnerable individuals.

48.6 OTHER CONCERNS

48.6.1 Emergency Services

Many existing intelligent home applications are concerned with the security of the home and its occupants, so access to emergency services, (police, fire, ambulance, etc.) is one of the major benefits. The mechanisms used by the applications may include alarm calls, or closed-circuit TV (CCTV) feeds to remote monitoring centers. Also, and traditionally, operators of voice services have been required to provide telephone numbers for phone-lines to be used exclusively by the user to communicate with the emergency services. The numbers vary from country to country. This requirement has been waived, or made optional, by some regulators for operators basing their services on IP. Where access to emergency services is offered to a consumer and the service is provided using an IP platform, the ISP must support emergency service access at least to the standard required for the PSTN. Such access is not normally available over commodity ISP networks.

48.6.2 Grade of Service

Grade of service typically refers to the overall performance of a network in terms of parameters related to traffic engineering and network capacity. This includes mean time to, or between, failure(s) (MTBF,[28] MTTF[29]), availability and serviceability, probability of blocking (user cannot make a call), or early termination. These are key parameters for 24/7 services, such as emergencies. Grade-of-service issues are also discussed in the ITU-T E series recommendations.

48.6.3 Personalization

Personalisation is a key "design for all" consideration for an intelligent home with various occupants, each with his/her own needs and flexibility to adapt new requirements. Personal recognition systems (e.g., contact-free smart cards or biometrics) should enable systems or services to automatically configure themselves to meet that individual's needs. Personalization can accommodate essential personal needs (e.g., medical, vision, hearing, language, general access to systems). It can also contribute to comfort and convenience by configuring home entertainment systems, newsgathering, personal communications, and other features to an individual's requirements. Personalisation systems should not compromise an occupant's privacy, compromise the security of the house or occupants, or represent any threat to others.

48.6.4 Comfort of the Intelligent Home

Comfort and convenience are consumer expectations of intelligent homes and smart living. These principals should be considered in both the design and implementations of an intelligent home with the ergonomics and design-for-all principals employed when designing components, systems, or services. The aspect of comfort is easily overlooked for the ambient noise level. Many of the devices that will be installed in the intelligent home will contain cooling fans. The combined noise should not be judged intrusive to the consumer.

48.6.5 Compatibility with Essential Services

The intelligent home will control and monitor the essential services for security; health; and use of gas, electricity, and water. The house system needs to report a problem or other information to a responsible body, other than the householder, such as police, medical services, or utility providers.

48.6.6 Energy Consumption

The intelligent house should be designed with intelligent power and heat management and low-power-consumption devices to provide significant energy savings, with a possibility of coupling a with a green energy sources like solar and wind energy.

---

[28] Mean time between failure(s); an "average" time between failures,

[29] Mean time to failure; an estimate of the average, or mean, time until a design's or component's first failure.

48.6.7 Healthcare Services

There are two categories of healthcare provision, each with its own requirements:

- *Elderly or sick people*—to offer health-monitoring health maintenance and "telecare" services. The service needs to be particularly reliable, as it will involve data transfer to remote medical services, including emergency services, better access to healthcare, provision of better healthcare, improved communication, cost saving, reduced waiting lists, increased standard of health, and better education and access to information.
- *Others*—particularly the young, and the more computer/Internet-literate population, will require a proactive and interactive healthcare service to allow self-management with emphasis on preventive medicine. This could include local monitoring and subscription services to send reports to healthcare consultants.

48.6.8 Access for People with Disabilities

An *adapted access* refers to the use of accessibility aids for the disabled with the specific goal of enabling them to effectively use the devices.[30] These accessibility aids technology with tools to help people with disabilities to use computers and other devices more effectively. Some general categories of disabilities, and some common aids include:

- *Motor impairments*—sticky keys and slow keys, hardware devices such as head-mounted eye-tracking systems
- *Visual impairments*—screen enlargement utilities, tactile and auditory output and text-to-speech systems
- *Hearing impairments*—visible alerts, speech-to-text systems, captioning

48.6.9 User Needs and Requirements

This area represents an entirely new system of using electric installations, appliances, and communication in a way that consumers are unaccustomed and unfamiliar with. If the technology is difficult for consumers to operate and maintain, some of them will be disadvantaged, as they will not be able to enjoy the potential benefits offered by the system. The elderly or disabled who would benefit from such systems might not be able to operate them. When designing intelligent homes, it is important that the provision of such services not be hindered, or consumers' choices restricted. This technology can mean increased comfort, enjoyment, convenience, security, and energy savings for most groups of consumers. Different groups of consumers may achieve different benefits (e.g., physically disabled people can use remote control to operate all devices in the home, as opposed to having to move to individual devices round the home to control them).

It is important that different consumer needs be addressed and standards put in place to ensure that intelligent homes can be adapted to changes in the householders' needs or multiple needs. The consumers of tomorrow are likely to be more dependent on service providers than those in the past. Many services will be offered by subscription, providing

---

[30] http://main.wgbh.org/wgbh/access/.

content, equipment maintenance, insurance, and other utilities. Consumers would look for the convenience of a one-stop solution to service provision and problem solving, which could be facilitated by offering bundled/aggregated services, which offer interoperability, reliability, and maintenance, all via a service agreement.

REFERENCES AND NOTES

1. EBU—European Standards for Broadcasting (http://www.ebu.ch/en/technical/publications/euro_standards/index.php).
2. *CableLabs DOCSIS Set-top Gateway (DSG) Spec* (http://www.cablemodem.com/specifications/gateway.html).
3. ITI-T Recommendation G-9954 (http://www.itu.int/itudoc/itu-t/aap/sg15aap/recaap/g.9954/g9954s.html).
4. ITI-T Recommendation G.989.1 (http://www.itu.int/itudoc/itu-t/com15/contr/01-04/018.html).
5. Federal Communications Commission: *Bulletin FO-10, Telephone Interference*, Field bulletin on radiofrequency interference.
6. *HomePlug® Powerline Alliance BPL Specification* (http://www.homeplug.org/en/news/press010705.asp).
7. EIA (Electronics Industry Association) CEBus standards (http://www.smarthomeforum.com/start/cebus.asp?ID=5).
8. *HomePlug 1.0 Powerline Communication LANs Protocol* (http://www.cise.ufl.edu/~nemo/papers/IJCS2003.pdf).
9. *HomePlug® AV Standard Announcement* (http://www.homeplug.org/en/news/press010505.asp).
10. *Wireless Local Loop (WLL) Definition and Overview* (http://www.iec.org/online/tutorials/wll/).
11. *Cablelabs DOCSIS 1.0 Interface Specifications* (http://www.cablemodem.com/specifications/specifications10.html).
12. *Cablelabs DOCSIS 1.1 Interface Specifications* (http://www.cablemodem.com/specifications/specifications11.html).
13. *Cablelabs DOCSIS 2.0 Interface Specifications* (http://www.cablemodem.com/specifications/specifications20.html).
14. *Cablelabs DOCSIS Project* (http://www.cablemodem.com/primer/).
15. The Mobile Applications and sEervices based on Satellite and Terrestrial inteRwOrking project (MAESTRO) technical implementations of innovative mobile satellite systems concepts with close integration and interworking with 3G and beyond 3G mobile terrestrial networks (http://ist-maestro.dyndns.org/maestro/).
16. *The SDMB Project System Objective* (http://telecom.esa.int/telecom/www/object/printfriendly.cfm?fobjectid=11985).
17. *Simple Workflow Access Protocol* (SWAP) Draft Proposal, May 6, 1998 (http://www.ifi.uni-klu.ac.at/Public/Raetsch/SWAP%20Simple%20Workflow%20Access%20Protocoll%20Draft%209805.pdf).
18. CHAIN (*Ceced Home Appliances Interoperating Network*) (http://www.ceced.org/ebusiness/CHAIN.html?r=1).
19. ETSI EN 300 386, ERM & EMC requirements (http://webapp.etsi.org/action/PU/20050412/en_300386v010303p.pdf).
20. ETSI ES 201 468, ERM & EMC requirements for enhanced availability of services (http://webapp.etsi.org/action/MV/MV20050819/es_201468v010301m.pdf).

21. ETSI NGN@HOME TR 102 160 series work program (http://webapp.etsi.org/Work Program/Report_WorkItem.asp?WKI_ID=16155).
22. E.800 Recommendation; Quality of service and dependability vocabulary (http://www.itu.int/ITU-T/studygroups/com02/e-series.html).
23. RFC 2990; Next Steps for the IP QoS Architecture (http://rfc.net/rfc2990.html).
24. This approach is in conformance with PacketCable multimedia Architecture Framework (PKT-TR-MM-ARCH-VO1-030627) as endorsed by ITU-T J.179.
25. OMAP™ is a Texas Instruments platform consisting of high-performance, power-efficient processors, a robust software infrastructure and comprehensive support network for the rapid development of differentiated Internet appliances, 2.5G and 3G wireless handsets and portable data terminals (PDAs), and other multimedia-enhanced devices (http://focus.ti.com/omap/docs/omaphomepage.tsp).
26. Trusted Platform Module FROM iNTEL is a component on the desktop board that is specifically designed to enhance platform security above and beyond the capabilities of today's software by providing a protected space for key operations and other security critical tasks (http://www.intel.com/support/motherboards/desktop/d915gmh/sb/cs-015012.htm).
27. RFC 1948: *Defending against Sequence Number Attacks* (http://www.faqs.org/rfcs/rfc1948.html).
28. RFC 3947: *Negotiation of NAT-Traversal in the IKE* (http://www.ietf.org/rfc/rfc3947.txt).
29. FIPS PUB 198 Federal Information Processing Standards Publication; *The Keyed-Hash Message Authentication Code* (HMAC) (http://csrc.nist.gov/publications/fips/fips198/fips-198a.pdf).

49

ICT Standardization for the Elderly and People with Disabilities in Japan

Hajime Yamada
Toyo University, Tokyo, Japan

49.1 BACKGROUND

The number of people using information/communication technology (ICT) equipment and services, which combine hardware, software, and network technologies, is increasing, as is the variety of ICT equipment and services. Our everyday lives are filled with such equipment and services.

As society becomes even more information-oriented, we are becoming increasingly dependent on ICT equipment and services. Currently available equipment and services, however, are not always user-friendly for all possible individuals.

Typically, the groups lacking accessibility are the people with disabilities and the elderly. However, they are not the only ones who are experiencing difficulty in operating ICT equipment, such as personal computers (PCs). Improved accessibility will have an impact on a greater range of users, and allow ICT equipment and services to penetrate deeper into our daily lives. There is no way to achieve a highly information-oriented society without first improving accessibility.

The Engineering Handbook of Smart Technology for Aging, Disability, and Independence,
Edited by A. Helal, M. Mokhtari and B. Abdulrazak
Copyright © 2008 John Wiley & Sons, Inc.

49.2 JAPAN AS AN AGING SOCIETY

Statistics of the Ministry of Health, Labor and Welfare (MHLW) show that the number of people with disabilities including disabled children, totaled 6.56 million as of fiscal 2005 [1]. The proportion of people with disabilities against the total national population is about 5%, which is less than that the United States and elsewhere, due to the strict criteria for registration in Japan. We can find people in difficulties who are not officially registered as disabled.

There is no doubt that Japan is a graying society. According to the 2005 edition of the *White Paper on the Aged Society*, Japanese people aged 65 years or older accounted for about 20% of the national population, and this figure is expected to top 26% (approximately 33 million people) by 2015 [2]. The elderly can be regarded as midlevel disabled people because various human abilities deteriorate over time.

With inclusion of the elderly, the size of the accessibility market is significantly increased, becoming large enough to encourage private (profitmaking) corporations to address its needs more aggressively rather than simply targeting the small market of registered people with disabilities. By providing appropriate accessibility standards to the public, the market will function more efficiently and effectively.

Discussions concerning accessibility for the elderly and people with disabilities are often held from a social welfare policy perspective. However, when the temporarily disabled are included, the Japanese population targeted by these policies numbers several tens of millions, constituting a large and certain market, under any criteria. In addition, given the massive population scale, it is unrealistic to treat these people as merely those requiring protection, like many traditional policies.

Through improved accessibility to ICT equipment and services, the elderly and people with disabilities will be able to contribute to and participate more fully in society. Improved realization and utilization of their abilities is essential for energizing and developing the whole of society.

49.3 ACCESSIBILITY

There are three approaches to improving the accessibility to ICT equipment and services [3]:

1. Providing people with a special aid that is specific for their individual disabilities, to enhance the usability of equipment and services.
2. Providing functions to change the input/output method or multiple input/output options, enabling a person with any kind of difficulty to use the equipment or service. For PCs, some operating systems and popular software applications include options with such capabilities.
3. Ensuring that accessibility is built into every ICT equipment and service (this is an expansion of approach 2). In other words, this represents the standardization of equipment and services. There are a number of activities underway globally toward the development of standards on how to provide ICT equipment and services with the needs of the elderly and people with disabilities in mind.

Assistive technologies must be developed (i.e., approach 1) for the severely disabled, and those whose needs cannot be fully covered by standard-compliant products (i.e., approach 3). When assistive technologies are expensive, social welfare concerns dictate that government support may be necessary. This mix of encouraging market mechanisms and social welfare policy should satisfy the needs of the largest number of people.

49.3.1 Development of Assistive Technology as a Means of Improving Accessibility

People with amyotrophic lateral sclerosis (ALS) are profoundly disabled and have difficulty even speaking. To assist with their communication, a sensor system that can detect the movement of their eyes and eyelids (blinking), the parts of the body they can manage to move slightly, has been developed. The system displays a large table of characters on its screen, on which the user can move the cursor through eye movements and select a character by blinking. Figure 49.1 shows the display designed for ALS patients.

Aside from this, a circular push-type input device is offered to allow disabled persons lacking sufficient muscular strength to perform complicated operations and enter characters in Morse code. Other products available are software that enables the numeric keys to substitute for mouse operations and alternatives to the mouse, such as trackballs and touch panels. This is also the case with output devices. Text reading software, a program that generates audio output of Webpages, is a typical product in this area, in addition to Braille output devices (Braille displays and printers). These represent part of the efforts to provide input/output devices specifically designed to address the needs of those with varying types and levels of disabilities.

Although the cases mentioned above are all PC-related, they do not represent the only type of technology designed for people with poor accessibility. Automated teller machines (ATMs) at post offices and banks, for example, now often employ only touch panels (touchscreens), which are user-unfriendly to the visually impaired. To cope with this problem, models accepting entry from both the touchscreen and keypad have appeared. This move can be categorized into the second approach (approach 2 in the list at beginning

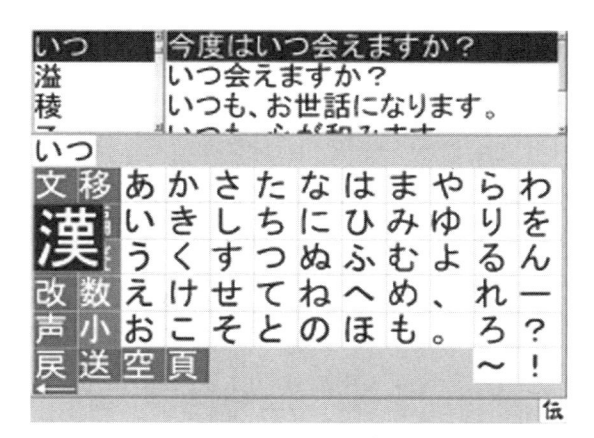

FIGURE 49.1 A display panel designed for ALS patients (from the Hitachi KE Systems Website: http://www.hke.jp/products/dennosin/denindex.htm).

of Section 49.3) for its provision of alternative input/output methods. However, these ATMs still have plenty of room for improvement, such as standardization of the key layout among different models.

It is necessary, as described in this section, to develop assistive technologies for people whose needs are not covered by standard technologies. However, it is also necessary to develop a set of national accessibility standards, so that the widest possible range of people may enjoy the usefulness of ICT economically.

49.3.2 Non-ICT-Related Accessibility Standardization in Japan

Japan began standardization activities for the elderly and people with disabilities in the mid-1980s.

The Ad-hoc Committee on Standardization for the Elderly and People with Disabilities in the Japanese Industrial Standards Committee (JISC) published a report in 1998 [4]. This report emphasized the importance of standardization, established the direction of japanese policy making in this area, and triggered various standardization activities.

Table 49.1 lists the Japan Industrial Standard (JIS) standards already authorized in this area. [This list does not include ICT-related standards, which are listed later (in Section 49.4) in Table 49.3.] Among them, JIS S0011, S0012, S0021 were authorized in 2000, 2 years after the Ad-hoc Committee's report [5].

While the JIS S0021 standard determines general requirements for packaging and receptacles, the JIS S0022 provides detailed specifications for opening such items. We call this structure a *two-tier standardization scheme*, consisting of upper-layer general requirements and lower-layer detailed specifications. The methodology is described in detail later.

49.3.3 ICT-Related Accessibility Standardization in Japan

Preparation of separate accessibility guidelines for information processing equipment and telecommunication facilities (listed in Table 49.2) began in the 1980s.

For information-processing equipment, the Ministry of International Trade and Industry (MITI) was at the center of activities and consequently, *Accessibility Guidelines for the Use of Computers by People with Disabilities* was published by MITI in 1995. In 2000 these guidelines were substituted by a revised MITI announcement, entitled *Accessibility Guidelines for the Use of Computers by People with Disabilities and the Elderly* [7].

For telecommunications facilities, *Accessibility Guidelines for the Use of Telecommunication Facilities by People with Disabilities* were announced by the Ministry of Posts and Telecommunications (MPT) in 1998. The Telecommunication Access Council announced its guidelines in 2000, in which details were added to the MPT Guidelines. Moreover, *Guidelines for the Creation of Internet Web Content Accessible by People with Disabilities* were jointly announced by MPT and the Ministry of Health and Welfare (MHW) in 1999, Ministry of Internal Affairs and Communications, *ICT Policy in Japan*, 2002 (in Japanese) [8,9].

Each of these guidelines provides abstract requirements for equipment and services rather than concrete standard specifications.

Guidelines for information-processing equipment and telecommunications facilities, which have been developed independently in each field, should remain consistent with

TABLE 49.1 Non-ICT JIS Standards for the Elderly and People with Disabilities

Number	Title
S0011	Guidelines for All People, Including the Elderly and People with Disabilities: Marking Tactile Dots on Consumer Products
S0012	Guidelines for All People, Including the Elderly and People with Disabilities: Usability of Consumer Products
S0013	Guidelines for All People, Including the Elderly and People with Disabilities: Auditory Signals on Consumer Products
S0014	Guidelines for all people, including the elderly and people with disabilities: Auditory Signals on Consumer Products — Sound Pressure Levels of Signals for the Elderly and in Noisy Conditions
S0021	Guidelines for all People, Including the Elderly and People with Disabilities: Packaging and Receptacles
S0022	Guidelines for All People, Including the Elderly and People with Disabilities: Packaging and Receptacles — Test Methods for Opening
S0023	Guidelines for Designing of Clothes in Consideration of the Elderly
S0024	Guidelines for the Elderly and People with Disabilities — Housing Equipment
S0025	Guidelines for All People, Including the Elderly and People with Disabilities: Packaging and Receptacles — Tactile Warnings of Danger — Requirements
S0031	Guidelines for the Elderly and People with Disabilities — Visual Signs and Displays — Specification of Age-Related Relative Luminance and Its Use in the Assessment of Light
S0032	Guidelines for the Elderly and People with Disabilities — Visual Signs and Displays — Estimation of the Minimum Legible Size for a Single Japanese Character
T0901	Guidelines of an Electronic Guide System, Using Audible Signage for the Visually Impaired
T9251	Dimensions and Patterns of Raised Parts of Tactile Ground Surface Indicators for the Blind
Z8071[6]	Guidelines for Standards Developers to Address the Needs of Older Persons and Persons with Disabilities
S0022-3	Guidelines for All People Including Elderly and People with Disabilities — Packaging and Receptacles — Tactile Indication for Identification
S0022-4	Guidelines for All People Including Elderly and People with Disabilities — Packaging and Receptacles — Evaluation Method by User
S0023-2	Guidelines for Designing of Clothes in Consideration of the Older Persons — How to Use ff Button
S0026	Guidelines for Older Persons and People with Disabilities — Shape, Color, and Arrangement of Toilet Operation Equipment and Appliance in Public Rest Room
S0033	Guidelines for the Elderly and People with Disabilities — Visual Signs and Displays — A Method for Color Combination Based on Categories of Fundamental Colors as a Function of Age
T0921	Guidelines for All People Including Elderly and People with Disabilities — Using Method of Braille Sign — Public Facility
T0922	Guidelines for Older Persons and Peoples with Disabilities — Methods of Displaying Tactile Guide Maps

each other as much as possible. More recent technologic advancements are increasingly blurring the distinction between information processing and telecommunications (ICT), and compliant products, with close but different standards, which may confuse consumers. Japan therefore decided to standardize accessibility guidelines by adopting a two-tier structure.

TABLE 49.2 Early Developments of Guidelines on Two Fields of Technology

Information-Processing Devices (Led Mainly by MITI)

1974–1976	Japan Electronic Industry Development Association (JEIDA): *Investigation of the Contribution Plan of Rehabilitation toward Disabled People*
1988	JEIDA: *Investigation for the Preparation of Electronic Product Accessibility Guidelines*
1990	JEIDA: *Computer Accessibility Guidelines*
1995	Notice 231: *Accessibility Guidelines for the Use of Computers by People with Disabilities*
2000	Revision and announcement of *Accessibility Guidelines for the Use of Computers by People with Disabilities and the Elderly*

Telecommunications Facilities (Led Mainly by MPT)

1998	Notice 515: *Accessibility Guidelines for the Use of Telecommunication Facilities by People with Disabilities*
1998	Establishment of the Telecommunication Access Council
1999	MPT and MHW: *Guidelines for the Creation of Internet Web Content Accessible by People with Disabilities*
2000	Telecommunication Access Council: *Accessibility Guidelines for the Use of Telecommunication Equipment by People with Disabilities*

49.4 ICT STANDARDIZATION IN JAPAN

49.4.1 The Two-Tier Structure of Standards

Japan has uniquely adopted a two-tier structure for national standardization for product accessibility.

Figure 49.2 summarizes the two-tier structure. A standard developed as upper-layer general requirements (common guidelines) identifies features common to all ICT equipment and services. A JIS standard has been prepared, which will be applied in common and positioned above the guidelines for individual equipment. Meanwhile, a series of lower-layer standards for individual categories of equipment and services (series standards), such as information-processing equipment, communication facilities, office

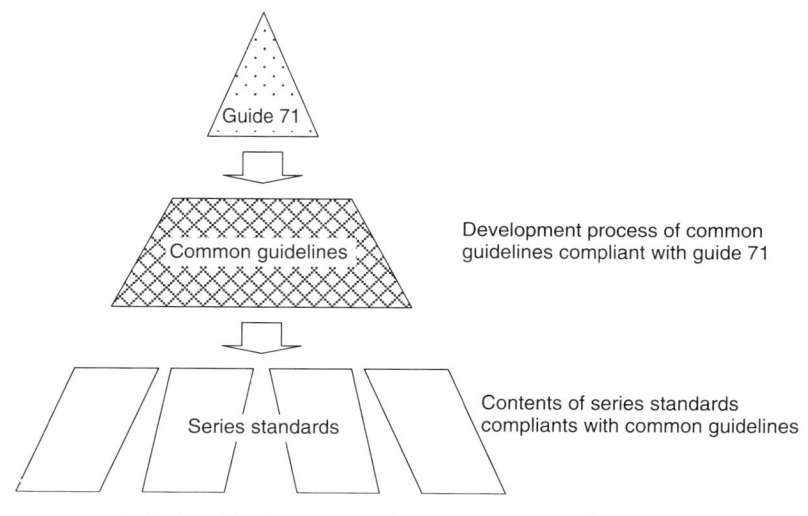

FIGURE 49.2 Two-tier structure of ICT accessibility standards.

machines, software, and the Internet, are being developed. These will comply with the upper-layer common standard.

The standards for accessibility will cover a wide area of products and services, and their complexity makes accessibility standardization processes both time- and resource-consuming. In order to ensure consistent standards, the adoption of a two-tier standardization scheme is recommended, in which the upper-layer standard determines general requirements while lower-layer standards provide detailed specifications.

ICT is developing very rapidly, and in such a changing environment, it is very difficult for standardization processes to keep pace with product developments. Consequently, general guidelines for all products, including equipment and services that do not exist at the time of standardization, are very helpful and welcome.

A two-tier structure is also adopted in the area of packaging and receptacles. This is a method for reducing the deviations in individual standards, developed in parallel by different organizations.

49.4.2 Common Standards Development

In 2000 activities to create guidelines common to all ICT fields began. In September 2000, an internal organization of the Japan Standards Association, namely, the Information Technology Research and Standardization Center (INSTAC), autonomously established the Standardization Investigation Committee for Realizing Barrier-Free Access to Information [10]. On the basis of the Committee's conclusions, the Standardization Investigation Committee for the Improvement of Accessibility Common to Areas of Information Technology and Software Products was organized in April 2001 within INSTAC, and launched its activities as a body to carry out state-entrusted investigations. (The author of this chapter, Hajime Yamada, is the chair of this committee.)

The committee structure is shown in Figure 49.3. Cooperation is required from various organizations to create the common standard, and the successful establishment of a cooperative committee affects the success of the work.

Two ministries (MPHPT and METI) both supported and participated in the committee's activities. In Japan, where government bureaucracies tend to compete against each other, it is remarkable that the two ministries formed a system together in cooperation and with understanding of the importance of providing JIS to meet the needs of the elderly and disabled. Other groups and organizations that had been independently preparing guidelines and promoting relevant activities on accessibility also came together in the committee [11–16]. In addition to the ministries and organizations, the committee

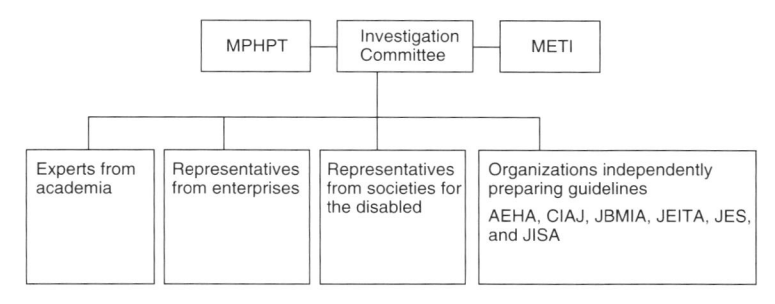

FIGURE 49.3 Structure of the Investigation Committee.

comprises accessibility experts from academia and representatives from enterprises and societies for the disabled.

The committee achieved a draft common standard in the autumn of 2003, which was approved by JISC in December 2003. This standard was published as JIS X8341-1 in May 2004.

49.4.3 Individual Standard Development

Guidelines for computers had been developed by the Japan Electronics and Information Technology Industries Association (JEITA), based on the aforementioned guidelines developed by MITI in 1995. JEITA also took the responsibility for standardization. These guidelines became the baseline document and were adopted as the JIS X8341-2 standard in December 2003 and published in May 2004.

In 1999 MPT and MHW published, as mentioned above, *Guidelines for the Creation of Internet Web Content Accessible by People with Disabilities*. The JIS draft, which is slated to become the JIS X8341-3 standard, was prepared in accordance with the Japanese guidelines as well as those of the World Wide Web Consortium (W3C) guidelines on accessibility [17]. The standard was published in June 2004, following the efforts of the Working Group under INSTAC.

For telecommunications facilities, *Accessibility Guidelines for the Use of Telecommunication Facilities by People with Disabilities* were announced by MPT in 1998 (described earlier). The document became the basis of the JIS X8341-4 standard. The Communications and Information Network Association of Japan (CIAJ) developed a draft, which was published in October 2005.

In addition, the JIS X8341-5 standard provides accessibility recommendations for office equipment. The Japan Business Machine and Information System Industries Association (JBMIA) took the leadership of standardization, and the standard was published in January 2006.

We find that the organizations that participated in the development of Common Guidelines took the responsibility for individual standard development. In this way, ICT accessibility standards were developed efficiently and in parallel. Table 49.3 summarizes the ICT accessibility standards.

49.4.4 Impacts on Industry

Standardization by JIS enhances the spread of accessible equipment and services.

Government procurement policies that require compliance with accessibility standards can be an incentive for manufacturers to develop and market accessible equipment and

TABLE 49.3 ICT-Related JIS Standards for the Elderly and People with Disabilities: X8341 Series

Number	Title	Published
X8341-1	Part 1: Common Guidelines	May 2004
X8341-2	Part 2: Information Processing Equipment	May 2004
X8341-3	Part 3: Web Content	June 2004
X8341-4	Part 4: Telecommunications Equipment	October 2005
X8341-5	Part 5: Office Equipment	January 2006

services. In 1995 the government announced guidelines for the criteria to be used in the general evaluation of contracts and tenders for the supply of computers and services to the government as an agreement among agencies and bureaus. A statement in the announcement reads: "Items to be evaluated shall be established in conformity with international and national standards." Therefore, equipment and services supplied to the government must have been designed with consideration for accessibility [18]. When the new series of JIS X8341 standards were published in 2004, government procurement processes had to check for conformity with this new national accessibility standard. It is anticipated that this may trigger an explosive spread of such accessible equipment and services in the private sector.

The other policy measure is the implementation of requirements in standards into e-government and e-local government. Such e-systems use Web technologies, indicating that compliance with JIS X8341-3 is necessary to allow everyone, including the elderly and disabled, to enjoy the advantages of e-systems. On the basis of guidelines developed jointly by MPT and MHW, a basic concept for providing administrative information through electronic means was approved through interministry meetings held during 2001. Subsequently, the Websites of administrative organizations (i.e., national, regional, and local government entities) had to conform to these guidelines [19]. This movement was accelerated by the amendment of the Fundamental Law for the People with Disabilities, which was done in May 2004.

Article 19—"Realization of information barrier free"—was added to the law and mandates the following:

> States and local authorities shall undertake the necessary measures to spread electronic computers and their related devices and other information and communications equipment that is user-friendly for people with disabilities, to enhance the convenience of the latter in their use of telecommunications and broadcasting services, and to equip facilities which provide information for people with disabilities, allowing them to make use of information in an efficient manner and express their own will.

Under this provision, consideration is stipulated for "promoting the computerization of administration and the use of information and communications technologies in public services."

One good example is the Website of Setagaya, a local city near Tokyo. Figure 49.4 displays its top page. Users can change the size and color of the text, as well as the background color. In addition, a voice synthesizer reads all the text on the Website. This reading system is very useful for the visually impaired. It is also useful for the staff who check the site to determine whether the contents are accessible. These functions are provided by the "Raku Raku Web Sansaku." Setagaya is not an exception but many cities are currently also striving to ensure their Websites are universally accessible.

Likewise, private companies are moving to provide accessible products for the market. Fujitsu's mobile phone, named the "Raku Raku phone," features a variety of accessibility functions; a larger button size, one-touch buttons for dedicated receiving parties, and the ability to alter the text color and the background and size of the text and other features. In addition, a voice synthesizer is installed, through which people can listen to emails received by the mobile phone. This function is very useful, of course, for people with impaired vision. In addition, young people watching TV or eating dinner may put their mobile units aside and "read" the email received without viewing the screen. More than 11 million Raku Raku phones have been sold, and this is only one example of where

FIGURE 49.4 Top page of Setagaya (http://www.city.setagaya.tokyo.jp/index.shtml).

a universally accessible product is accepted; not only by older and disabled persons but also by ordinary people with similar needs.

49.4.5 Need for International Harmonization

Similar standardization activities are also underway in Europe [20] and the United States [21]. The rapid aging of the Japanese population has compelled the national standards organization to consider strategies for accessibility standardization. The same is happening in most other developed countries, where populations are also aging. The more recent recognition of the problems of aging societies is the reason why standardization activities in this area have now emerged globally.

The international harmonization of ICT accessibility standards in various countries is necessary for a couple of reasons. One is the reduction in international trade barriers when domestic standards are harmonized. If Japanese standards differ from those in the United States, manufacturers need to manufacture different products for individual markets. The second reason is to reduce barriers to the international movement of people. Older and disabled persons travel frequently nowadays. If equipment and services differ from country to country, they become confused; hence product harmonization is also useful for ordinary (nondisabled/nonelderly) people.

Different national approaches to accessibility standardization are highlighted when we compare the JIS X8341-1 standard and the United States' Article 508 technical specifications:

1. *Conceptual or Practical.* The JIS standard demonstrates general accessibility requirements in ICT equipment and services. It is conceptual and can be applied

to products that do not exist at the time of its approval. On the other hand, the 508 technical specifications directly specify the requirements for currently available products; and make practical recommendations. It is necessary to decide which methodology to adopt when preparing harmonized international standards.

2. *Qualitative or Quantitative.* The JIS standard does not specify requirements in a quantitative manner. However, it issues general guidelines to industry, which are then used like ISO system management standards, i.e. the ISO 9000 and ISO 14000 series. In particular, Article 6.1, "Basic requirements for development and design," in the JIS standard is important because it asks corporations to establish internal management systems on accessibility. This article may have a great impact on industry's approach to accessibility issues [22]. On the other hand, by providing a standard in a quantitative manner, we can judge whether a product complies with the specifications in the standard. However, there is a problem that the 508 technical specifications include not scientific but empirical numbers [23].

There are several ways to achieve international harmonization. We decided to take the most active; namely, Japan decided to submit its national standards for international standardization.

Practical standards are useful for designing and evaluating contemporary equipment and services. However, there is a risk of such standards "soon becoming outdated," owing to the rapid and unpredictable development of ICT. We need a set of international standards that are effective and remain useful for more than 5 years; hence conceptual Japanese standards should be the basis of international standardization. We also decided to submit scientific data presented in Japanese standards such as JIS S0014, *Guidelines for All People, Including the Elderly and People with Disabilities—Auditory Signals on Consumer Products—Sound Pressure Levels of Signals for the Elderly and in Noisy Conditions*, for international standardization.

In order to reduce international trade barriers, the easiest option for Japanese manufacturers is to make domestic Japanese standards international. The internationalization strategy is taken now because Japan is one of the front-running countries, which already has national standards for ICT accessibility.

Furthermore, Japan has a historic record of initiating accessibility standardization in ISO/IEC.

49.4.6 Development of Guide 71 in ISO/IEC

In 1998, in response to a proposal from Japan, the Committee on Consumer Policy (COPOLCO) of the International Organization for Standardization (ISO) adopted a resolution at its general meeting to set up a taskforce to develop a policy statement on general principles and guidelines for the design of products and environments addressing the needs of older and people with disabilities. This resolution is based on "universal design," a concept of making all facilities, products, and services universally accessible, regardless of whether the person is older or disabled.

The ISO working group, chaired by Japan, produced general principles in the form of the ISO/IEC [24] Guide 71 (*Guidelines for Standards Developers to Address the Needs of Older Persons and Persons with Disabilities*) in 2001 [25]. This document serves as a comprehensive guide, applicable to all standardization activities [26].

However, we must note that the Guide showcases only "the best practice" in standardization activities and does not define any technical specification for the accessibility of any product and/or service.

ISO/IEC Guide 71 can be used as a general reference source for standardization work for the elderly and disabled, and in this sense, it is true that its adoption represents a starting point. However, adopting Guide 71 alone is insufficient. We need to start standardization activities to determine the accessibility requirements in a variety of product areas, based on the procedures described in Guide 71. Therefore, following the adoption of Guide 71, ISO and IEC sought to develop accessibility standards to be met by every piece of equipment and each service in respective areas such as ICT.

49.4.7 Proposals to ISO and Other International Standardization Organizations

Japan is contributing to international standardization by providing its national standards for international organizations as baseline documents.

The JIS X8341-1 was submitted to the ISO TC159/SC4/WG4 developed ISO 9241-20 "Ergonomics of human-system interaction - Part 20: Accessibility guidelines for information/communication technology (ICT) equipment and services." Japan also provided the Project Editor (Hajime Yamada) for ISO 9241-20. The ISO9241-20 was approved and published in 2008.

The JIS X8341-3 was submitted to the World Wide Web Consortium (W3C), which is the organization developing international Web accessibility standards, notably with the Web Accessibility Initiative (WAI). Web Content Accessibility Guidelines 2.0, in which Japanese contributions have been taken into account, are now being developed for WAI. The JIS X8341-4 is already approved in the ITU-T (Telecommunication Standardization Sector of International Telecommunication Union) as F.790 "Telecommunications accessibility guidelines for older persons and persons with disabilities: in 2007, with no substantial modifications from X8341-4.

The JIS X8341-5 is at the final ballot stage in ISO/IEC Joint Technical Committee 1 (JTC1) SC28 as ISO/IEC 10779 "Information technology — Office equipment accessibility guidelines for elderly persons and persons with disabilities." The JIS X8341-2 is under discussion in ISO/IEC JTC1 SC35.

Finally JIS S0014 is included in the TR 22411, "Ergonomics data and guidelines for the application of ISO/IEC Guide 71 to products and services to address the needs of older persons and persons with disabilities", in ISO TC159/WG2.

49.5 CONSIDERATIONS AND CONCLUSIONS

It is very important to expand the size of the accessible equipment and service markets. When governments develop national informatization strategies, the issue of accessibility should be taken into account. In Japan, the Strategic Headquarters for the Promotion of an Advanced Information and Telecommunications Network Society (IT Strategic Headquarters) was established within the Cabinet in January 2001. The homepage of the IT Strategic Headquarters explained two reasons for its establishment, including the following [27]:

In light of the urgency to adapt ourselves to rapid and drastic global changes in the socioeconomic structure, caused by the utilization of information and telecommunications technology.

In order to promote measures for forming an advanced information and telecommunications network society expeditiously and intensively.

The establishment was based on a law called the "Basic Law on the Formation of an Advanced Information and Telecommunications Network Society," enacted in January 2001. The law provides the definition of an "advanced information and telecommunications network society," namely: "a society in which people can develop themselves creatively and vigorously in all fields of activities by acquiring, sharing and transmitting a variety of information or knowledge on a global scale, freely and safely through the Internet and other advanced information and telecommunications networks." One of the policy measures is ICT accessibility to attain the objective of an advanced society, with networked information and telecommunications. Recommendations for other countries to follow this trend are also suggested.

Governments are encouraged to use their public procurement policies to promote ICT accessibility as an incentive to manufacturers to develop and market accessible products and services. Government procurement amounts to 5–20% of gross domestic product (GDP) in each country. The size of this market is clearly large enough to encourage businesses and manufacturers to move eagerly to meet accessibility requirements if they are a prerequisite to passing procurement procedures.

The amendment of the Fundamental Law for the People with Disabilities was a turning point in Japan. Fortunately, the national ICT accessibility standardization was synchronized. From then onward, government agencies, local governments, and industry began to consider ICT accessibility seriously. Other countries are also recommended to use public procurement as a tool to facilitate ICT accessibility, while international harmonization of this policy measure is also necessary.

This chapter has explained the standardization activities of ICT accessibility in Japan. Our society is moving toward a highly information-oriented society. Improved accessibility to realize a society inclusive of all, including the elderly and disabled, seems inevitable. To achieve ICT accessibility, Japan has developed national standards and submitted them to the international arena.

REFERENCES AND NOTES

1. Cabinet Office: *White Paper on People with Disabilities*, 2005 (in Japanese)
2. Cabinet Office: *White Paper on the Aging Society*, 2005 (in Japanese)
3. Yamada H, Yamazaki T: Trends in R&D and standardization on accessibility in the information and communications field: Toward barrier-free equipment and services of information and communications, *Science & Technology Trends*, Science and Technology Foresight Center of NISTEP, 2003.
4. Japanese Industrial Standards Committee: *Ad-hoc Committee on Standardization for the Elderly and People with Disabilities* (summary) (http://www.meti.go.jp/english/aboutmeti/data/a234201e.html).
5. An English translation of the JIS standards is searchable at the JSA Web Store: http://www.webstore.jsa.or.jp/webstore/Top/indexEn.jsp.
6. This standard was adopted and translated from ISO/IEC Guide 71.

7. Ministry of International Trade and Industry Notification No.362.
8. Related information can be found in the Ministry of Internal Affairs and Communications: *ICT Policy in Japan*, 2002 (in Japanese).
9. In 2001 administrative reforms prompted the merger of many Japanese Ministries; the Ministry of Posts and Telecommunications (MPT) became the Ministry of Public Management, Home Affairs, Posts and Telecommunications (MPHPT); the Ministry of Health and Welfare (MHW) became the Ministry of Health, Labour and Welfare (MHLW); and the Ministry of International Trade and Industry became the Ministry of Economy, Trade and Industry. In 2005 MPHPT changed its English name to the Ministry of Internal Affairs and Communications (MIC).
10. Yamada H: *Anyone Should be Accessible to the Information* (http://www.jsa.or.jp/stdz/instac/committe/barrier-free/bf-b.htm).
11. Communications and Information Network Association of Japan (CIAJ) (http://www.ciaj.or.jp/e.htm).
12. Japan Electronics and Information Technology Industries Association (JEITA) (http://www.jeita.or.jp/english/).
13. Japan Information Technology Services Industry Association (JISA) (http://www.jisa.or.jp/).
14. Japan Business Machine and Information System Industries Association (JBMIA) (http://www.jbmia.or.jp/english/index.htm).
15. Japan Ergonomics Society (JES) (http://www.ergonomics.jp/index_e.html).
16. Association for Electric Home Appliances (AEHA) (http://www.aeha.or.jp/).
17. World Wide Web Consortium: *Web Accessibility Initiative (WAI) Guidelines* (http://www.w3.org/WAI/).
18. Cabinet Office: *Standard Guide for the Overall Greatest Value Evaluation Methodology Concerning the Procurement of Computer Products and Services* (http://www.kantei.go.jp/foreign/procurement/2000/at/at2-9.html).
19. Government of Japan: *e-Japan Priority Program* (see, e.g., http://www.kantei.go.jp/foreign/it/network/priority-all/6.html).
20. European Committee for Standardization: *CEN/ISSS Workshop in Relation to Design-for-All and Assistive Technologies for ICT*; additional information is provided by ETSI, which organized a Workshop in 2003.
21. US Department of justice: *Department of Justice Section 508 Home Page* (http://www.usdoj.gov/crt/508/).
22. Article 6.1 reads as follows: Information accessibility developers should develop and design to ensure that information equipment and services meet the following basic requirements. Managers and administrators should be fully aware of the development and design of accessible information equipment and services, and have a concrete accessibility policy."
23. For example, in the 508 technical specifications, there is a requirement that "For transmitted voice signals, telecommunications products shall provide a gain adjustable up to a minimum of 20 dB. For incremental volume control, at least one intermediate step of 12dB of gain shall be provided." But we cannot find any scientific explanation for and 12dB.
24. International Electrotechnical Commission.
25. International Organization for Standardization: *Annual Report*, 2001.
26. International Organization for Standardization: Standards to address the needs of elderly and disabled, *Press Release of ISO*, Aug, 2001.
27. Further details on the IT Strategic Headquarters and the e-Japan program are available at http://www.kantei.go.jp/foreign/policy/it/index_e.html.

Index

Academic skills, 114. *See* Students with disabilities
Access control, telematics, 900–901. *See* Information access; Security and safety
Accessibility. *See* Computer platforms and operating systems; Workplace computer access
    Americans with Disabilities Act of 1990 (ADA), 45, 62, 74, 102, 103, 105, 138, 241, 521, 530, 533, 805, 808, 810
    client fitting, 34–35
    computer platforms and operating systems, 263–279
    definitions, 64–65
    information and communication technology (ICT), 908–912
    Japan, 908
    telematics, 904
    transportation services:
        Asia, 549–566
        Europe, 536–548
        U.S., 74–75, 521
    universal design, 808
Access networks, 883–891
    generally, 883–885
    protocol reference model, 888–891
    residential gateway architecture, 885–888

Accident avoidance experiments, traffic safety, 469–473
Active crash countermeasures, 464–468
Active-LeZi (ALZ) algorithm, 772–773. *See* Smart space algorithms
Activities of daily living (ADL), 1
    cognitive disabilities, 217–219
    ecologic model, 572–574
    motor and physical disabilities, 5
    summary chart, 130
Adaptive cruise control, collision warning systems and, 738
Aesthetics, user-centered design, 793
AFMASTER robot, 360
Africa, 58
Age level, United States, 66–67. *See* Demography; Elderly
AIDS, 58
Air Carrier Access Act, 530
Air transport, 530–532
Alarm(s). *See* Alerting systems; Information and communication technology (ICT); Pervasive computing and monitoring
    intelligent transportation systems (ITSs), 741, 743–744
    telecare applications, 721–723

The Engineering Handbook of Smart Technology for Aging, Disability, and Independence,
Edited by A. Helal, M. Mokhtari and B. Abdulrazak
Copyright © 2008 John Wiley & Sons, Inc.

Alarm(s). (*Continued*)
  visual disabilities, 175–176
Alarm-based automated medication devices, 639–640
Albrecht, Gary, 211
Alerting systems, hearing disabilities, 198–199
Algorithms. *See* Smart space algorithms
Alternative communication. *See* Augmentative-alternative communication (AAC) devices
Alzheimer's disease. *See* Cognitive disabilities; Dementia; Elderly
  demography, 1, 66–67, 217–218
  electronic and information systems, 209, 230
  low-tech assistive technologies, 136–137
  people with special needs (PwSN), 7
Ambient intelligence, telecare, technology trends, 715
Ambulatory aid, low-tech assistive technologies, 139–140
Ambulatory care, trends in, 713
Ambulatory monitoring, smart textiles, 674–676
American Association of Retired Persons (AARP), 67, 68, 768, 805
American Medical Association (AMA), 71
American National Standards Institute (ANSI), 37–38, 200
American sign language:
  augmentative-alternative communication (AAC) devices, 301–302
  wearable computer systems, 332–334
American Standard Code for Information Interchange (ASCII), 308
Americans with Disabilities Act of 1990 (ADA), 45, 62, 74, 102, 103, 105, 138, 241, 521, 530, 533, 805, 808, 810
Amplified telephone, hearing disabilities, 199–200
Amplitude, cutaneous perception, 340–341
Animal-assisted therapy (AAT), 405–407. *See* Robot therapy
Aniridia, 144–145
Antispoofing, security and safety, telematics, 897
Aphasia:
  communication disabilities, 6
  voice interactive systems, 292
Appliances (home):
  context awareness, 588
  visual disabilities, 163

Application layer, middleware architecture, smart house design, 700
Application programming interface (API), smart space middleware, 607–608
Architectural Barriers Act of 1968, 74–75
Arm (upper-limb prostheses), 424–432
  control systems, 426–432
  power systems, 424–426
ARPH robot, 368
Artificial arm, upper-limb prostheses, 424–432
  control systems, 426–432
  power systems, 424–426
Artificial hand, upper-limb prostheses, 422–424
Artificial limb. *See* Human limb prostheses
Assistive robotics, 355–374. *See* Mobile platform-based robot systems; Smart house design; Telecare; Telecare-robotics concept; Wheelchair(s); specific assistive robot devices
  history of, 357–359
  manipulator on base, 364–365
  MATS robot, 369
  mobile autonomous robot, 367–368
  overview, 355–357, 369–371
  telecare, 717–719
  unifunction robots, 363–364
  wheelchair-mounted, 365–367
  workstation robots, 359–363
    AFMASTER, 360
    DeVAR and ProVAR, 362–363
    MASTER1, 360
    RAID, 360
    RAID-MASTER, 361–362
Assistive technologies (AT), 1, 11–24. *See* International perspective; Low-tech assistive technologies; Optimal use; Technology evaluation; United States; Virtual companions; specific assistive technologies and devices
  classification, 15–18, 19–24
    cognitive disabilities, 23
    communication disabilities, 24
    hearing disabilities, 22
    motor disabilities, 19–20
    visual disabilities, 21
  context awareness, 588
  definitions, 13–14, 63–65
  design methods, 18, 23–24
  future prospects, 46–47
  growth in, 211

International Classification of Functioning, Disability and Health (ICF), 14
international perspective, 49–59
low-tech, 129–142
marketplace, 18
optimal use of, 29–48
overview, 12–13
rehabilitation, 804
security and safety, 624–627
United States, 61–80
workplace, 69
Assistive Technology Act of 1998, 13–14, 74, 102, 208
Association for the Advancement of Assistive Technology in Europe (AAATE), 94
ATLAS study (WHO), 205–206
Attendant-propelled wheelchair, 441
Audio:
  computer platforms and operating systems, 269–270
  visual disabilities, 171
  workplace computer access, visual disabilities, 253–254
Audit function, research function and, technology evaluation, 834–835
Auditory warnings, intelligent transportation systems (ITSs), 741, 743–744
Augmentative-alternative communication (AAC) devices, 137, 297–316
  communication assistant, 303–313
    caption format standard, 312–313
    design considerations, 305–311
    display options, 307–309
    font options, 309
    speech recognition, 310–311
    wireless transmission system, 306–307
    generally, 303–305
    user input and testing, 311–312
  mobile wireless technology integration, 300–301
  overview, 297–298
  sign language, 301–302
  target population, 298
  technology transfer, 313
  text messaging, 302
  traditional forms, 299–300
Aura, smart space middleware, 613–614
Authentication, 896, 900
Autism:
  communication disabilities, 6
  diagnosis of, wearable computer systems, 328–330

voice interactive systems, 292
Automated dispensing medication devices, 640
Automated medication management, 631–644. *See* Medication
  compliance, 631–632
  devices, 638–642
    alarm-based, 639–640
    automated dispensing, 640
    generally, 638–639
    monitoring, 640
    pillholders, 639
    user interfaces, 640–642
  noncompliance, 632–634
  overview, 631
  stakeholders, 634–635
  user requirements, 635–638
Automatic teller machines (ATMs):
  Japan, 909–912
  universal design, 810
  visual disabilities, 178–182
Automobile, car location, wearable computer systems, 324–328. *See* Intelligent transportation systems (ITSs); Traffic safety; Transportation services (Asia); Transportation services (Europe); Transportation services (U.S.)
Autonomously guided wheelchair, 451–454

Balance, lower-limb prostheses, 432–433
Bath wheelchair, 441
Beach wheelchair, 441
Best's disease, 159
Bickenbach, Jerome E., 81
Biosignal-based interfaces, wheelchair-based robotic system, 385–386
Blind navigation, 479–500. *See* Visual disabilities; Wayfinding
  devices in, 484–485
  factors in, 480–484
  future prospects, 493–494, 497–498
  global positioning system, 491–492
  indoor, 492–493
  infrared signage, 489–491
  optical (camera or laser-based) devices, 488–489
  overview, 479–480
  sonar-based devices, 485–487
  summary table of technology, 495–496
Bluetooth network, telematics, 879–880. *See* Telematics
Body-area network, telecare, technology trends, 714–715

Body location, cutaneous perception, 342
BPL (broadband powerline) access, powerline networks, telematics, 873–875
Braille:
 blind navigation, 480
 sensory substitution, 343–344
 visual disabilities, 171–172, 180
Brain damage. See Cognitive disabilities
 cognitive disabilities, 219
 wearable computer systems, 324–328
Brakes, manual wheelchair, 441
Broadband powerline (BPL) access, powerline networks, telematics, 873–875
Brundtland, Gro Harlem, 88

Camber angle, manual wheelchair, 441
Camera(s), telecare, technology trends, 716
Camera-based devices, blind navigation, 488–489
Cane(s):
 long, blind navigation, 484–485
 low-tech assistive technologies, 139
Caption format standard, communication assistant, 312–313
Captioning:
 hearing disability, 197–198
 wearable computer systems, 335–337
 workplace computer access, hearing disabilities, 255–256
Cardiac patients, smart textiles, 676–677
Care, cure and, 712
Caregivers, cognitive disabilities, 224–225
Care-O-Bot II walker system, 368, 514
Car location, wearable computer systems, 324–328. See Intelligent transportation systems (ITSs); Traffic safety; Transportation services (Asia); Transportation services(Europe); Transportation services (U.S.)
CARMEN navigation system, 511–512
Caster flutter, manual wheelchair, 441
Cataracts, 146
Center for Medicare Medicaid Services (CMS), 42, 63
Centers for Disease Control and Prevention, 93
Central American Free Trade Agreement (CAFTA), 10, 54
Central hearing loss, 6
Charge-coupled device (CCD) camera, eye-mouse system, 384–385
Charles Bonnet syndrome, 159
China, transportation services, 562–565

Civil rights issues. See Discrimination
 Americans with Disabilities Act of 1990 (ADA), 45, 62, 74, 102, 103, 105, 138, 241, 521, 530, 533, 805, 808, 810
 cognitive disabilities, 206–208
 model of, 50
 public transportation, 519
 Vocational Rehabilitation Act of 1973, 103
Classification:
 assistive technologies (AT), 15–18, 19–24
 cognitive disabilities, 230–232
 disability concept, 1–2
 international Standards Organization (ISO) 9999, 118, 119–122
Client-centered approach. See User-centered design
 optimal use, 41
 usability philosophy, 856–858
Client fitting, optimal use, 32–35
Client rejection, optimal use, 32
Client training, optimal use, 31–32, 35
Clinger Act of 1996, 208
Closed-circuit television (CCTV), visual disabilities, 170
Coats' disease, 159
Cochlear implants, 194–195
Code authorization/signature, telematics, 900
Cognitive disabilities. See Brain damage; Dementia; Elderly; Students with disabilities
 assistive devices, 217–236
  classification systems, 230–232
  dedicated activities, 225–230
  generally, 225–226
  handwashing, 226
  medication, 226–227
  mobility, 228
  social interaction, 228–230
  generally, 217–218
  generic orthotics, 219–225
  adaptive strategies, 225
  caregivers, 224–225
  generally, 219–220
  information organizer, 223–224
  multimedia procedure assistants, 222–223
  pagers, 221–222
  Personal Digital Assistants (PDAs), 220–221
 civil rights issues, 206–208
 classification assistive technologies, 23
 demography, 203–206, 211
 developed world, 203–204

developing world, 204–206
distance education technology, 109–110
independence needs, 218–219
low-tech assistive technologies, compensatory considerations, 136–137
overview, 203
people with special needs (PwSN), 7
technological categories, 208–211
  assistive, 208
  electronic and information systems, 208–209
  universal design, 209–211
traffic safety, 462
voice interactive systems, 292
wearable computer systems, 324–328
workplace computer access, 257–259
Collision warning systems, adaptive cruise control and, 738
Coloboma, 159
Colorblindness, 146–150
Comfort, telematics, 903
Common object request broker architecture (CORBA), 616, 770
Communication assistant, 303–313. *See* Augmentative-alternative communication (AAC) devices
  caption format standard, 312–313
  design considerations, 305–311
    display options, 307–309
    font options, 309
    speech recognition, 310–311
    wireless transmission system, 306–307
  generally, 303–305
  user input and testing, 311–312
Communication disabilities:
  classification of assistive technologies, 24
  cognitive disabilities, 228–230
  context awareness, 587
  International Standards Organization (ISO) 9999, 121
  low-tech assistive technologies, 137–138
  people with special needs (PwSN), 6–7
Communication performance experiments, traffic safety, 473–474
Compatibility, telematics, 903
Compliance, automated medication management, 631–632
Computer. *See* Interfaces; Voice interactive systems; Wearable computer systems; Workplace computer access
  cognitive disabilities, 229, 257–259
  visual disabilities, 173–174

voice interactive systems, 281–296
wearable systems, 317–338
Computer platforms and operating systems, 263–279
  components in, 264
  current technology, 275–277
    Java Swing API, 277
    Microsoft Active Accessibility (MSAA), 275–276
    Microsoft UI automation, 276
    SWT, 277
  device support, 266–275
    audio, 269–270
    display, 270–271
    element relationships, 273
    event protocols and event semantics, 273
    generally, 266
    introspection/discovery capability, 273
    keyboard, 267
    MVC design pattern, 271–272
    navigation, 274–275
    object model access, 272–273
    pointing device, 267–269
    roles and states, 273–274
  graphical user interfaces (GUIs), 265–266
  overview, 263
  platforms, 264–265
Confidentiality. *See* Security and safety
  smart space middleware, 610–611
  technology evaluation, 847–848
Congenital cataract, 159
Consumer empowerment, optimal use, 44–46
Context awareness, 585–605
  applications and systems, 588–590
  definitions, 586–587
  modeling, 590–600
    analysis, 599–600
    context modeling language, 598–599
    generally, 590–591
    markup scheme approaches, 593–594
    ontology-based approaches, 594–597
    requirements, 591–593
    requirements analysis model, 597
  overview, 585–586
  role of, 587–588
  smart house design, 700–702
  software infrastructure, 600–603
    context toolkit, 601–602
    PACE middleware, 602–603
    reference architecture, 600–601
    Solar platform, 602
Context fabric, smart space middleware, 614

Context management layer, middleware architecture, smart house design, 700
Context management services, smart space middleware, 616–617
Context-modeling language (CML), 598–599, 603
Context processing and management, smart space middleware, 609–610
Context toolkit, context awareness, software infrastructure, 601–602
Continuity, ICF, 88–89
Continuous quality improvement (CQI), total quality management (TQM) and, 39–40
Control interfaces. *See* Interfaces
Convergent systems, visual disabilities, 183–185
COOL AIDE walker system, 506–509
Cooltown, smart space middleware, 614
Copy protection, security and safety, telematics, 896
CORBA (common object request broker architecture), 616, 770
Corneal dystrophy, 159
Corneal graft, 159
Cranial arteritis, 161
Crash countermeasures, traffic safety, 463–468
Cruise control, collision warning systems and, 738
Cure, care and, 712
Customer needs, design for well-being (DfW), 826–829. *See* Client-centered approach; User-centered design
Cutaneous perception, 340–343. *See* Sensory substitution
  aging, 342–343
  amplitude, 340–341
  body location, 342
  duration, 341
  frequency, 341
  rhythm, 342
  waveform, 341

Data collection methods, 860–863
  objective, 862–863
  specific methodologies, 863
  subjective, 860–862
Data over cable service interface specification (DOCSIS), telematics, 875–877
Deafblindness, visual disabilities, 175
Decoder Circuitry Act of 1990, 62
Dementia. *See* Alzheimer's disease; Cognitive disabilities; Elderly
  demography, 1, 66–67, 217–218
  low-tech assistive technologies, 136–137
  people with special needs (PwSN), 7
Demilitarized zone, telematics, 897
Demography:
  Alzheimer's disease, 1, 66–67, 217–218
  cognitive disabilities, 203–206, 211
  disability, 132
  elderly, 501, 711–712, 727–728, 768, 908
  Europe, 528–529
  healthcare, 749–750
  Japan, 908
  people with special needs (PwSN), 1, 7–11
  student populations, 102–103
  transportation services (Asia), 550–551
  visual disabilities, 143–144, 174–175
Department of Health and Human Services (HHS), 63
Department of Housing and Urban Development (HUD), 73–74
Depot (institutional) wheelchair, 441
Depression, elderly, 579–580
Design for well-being (DfW), 819–832. *See* Client-centered approach; Design methods; Universal design; Usability; User-centered design; Well-being
  agenda, 821–824
  customer needs, 826–829
  overview, 819–820, 829–830
  values in, 824–826
Design methods, assistive technologies, 18, 23–24. *See* Client-centered approach; Design for well-being (DfW); Universal design; Usability; User-centered design
DeVAR robot, 362–363, 376
Diabetic retinopathy, 150–152
Digital hearing aids, 192–193
Digital technology, visual disabilities, 171
Disability-adjusted life-years (DALYs), 53
Disability concept, 1–7. *See* Elderly; People with special needs (PwSN); Students with disabilities; specific disabilities
  definitions and classifications, 1–2
  handicap and well-being, 2
  people with special needs (PwSN), 3–4
Disability resource center, students with disabilities, 104
Disability Support Services (DSS), students with disabilities, 104
Disabled People's International (DPI), 2

Discrimination. *See* Civil rights issues
  Americans with Disabilities Act of 1990
    (ADA), 45, 62, 74, 102, 103, 105, 138,
    241, 521, 530, 533, 805, 808, 810
  cognitive disabilities, 206–208
  students, 101–102
  United States, 65–66, 72–74
Discussion groups, usability data collection
    methods, 861
Display(s):
  communication assistant, 307–309
  computer platforms and operating systems,
    270–271
  visual disabilities, 181
Distance education technology:
  accessibility barriers, 109
  cognitive and learning impairments,
    109–110
  generally, 107–108
  handouts and resources, 110–111
  hearing, 109
  interactive tools, 111
  limitations of, 110
  motor impairments, 109
  universal design, 110
  vision, 109
DOCSIS (data over cable service interface
    specification), telematics, 875–877
Domestic appliances, visual disabilities, 163
Down syndrome, 210–211
Drive-by-wire, intelligent transportation
    systems (ITSs), 739
Drive-in facilities, 745
Driving abilities, client fitting, 34. *See*
    Intelligent transportation systems (ITSs);
    Traffic safety; Transportation services
    (Asia); Transportation services (Europe);
    Transportation services (U.S.)
Dry eye, 160
Duration, cutaneous perception, 341
Dynamic balance, lower-limb prostheses,
    432–433
Dyscalculia, communication disabilities,
    6–7
Dyslexia, communication disabilities, 6

Economic factors, 67
Education, 68. *See* Students with disabilities
Education for All Handicapped Children's Act
    of 1975, 102
Elderly, 569–584. *See* Alzheimer's disease;
    Cognitive disabilities; Dementia;
    Information and communication
    technology (ICT); Intelligent
    transportation systems (ITSs); Virtual
    companions
  context awareness, 587–588
  cutaneous perception, 342–343
  demography, 501, 711–712, 727–728, 768,
    908
  ecologic model, 572–574
  example, 579–580
  facet model, 574–579
  healthcare workers, 711–712
  information and communication technology
    (ICT), 907–920
  Japan, 908
  mobility, 501–502
  overview, 569–570, 581–583
  people with special needs (PwSN), 1
  pervasive computing and monitoring,
    570–571
  research and development, 571–572
  robot therapy, 405–418
  security and safety, 624–627
  traffic safety, 459–463 (*See* Traffic safety)
  universal design, 807–811
  usability testing, 863–864
  user-centered design, 790–793
  virtual companions, 645–671
Electrocardiography (ECG), smart textiles,
    674–676
Electronic and information technology (EIT),
    cognitive disabilities, 208–209
Electronic assistive technology (EAT). *See*
    Virtual companions
Electronic data security, telematics, 901
Electronic mail, cognitive disabilities, 229
Electronic purse, visual disabilities,
    183–185
Electronic textiles. *See* Smart textiles
Electronic toll collection, 745
Electronic travel aids, blind navigation, 484,
    485
Emergency services, telematics, 902
Emerging technologies, 65, 75–76
EMG interface. *See* Interfaces
  powered wheelchair, 446
  upper-limb prostheses, 427–430
  wheelchair-based robotic system, 395–396
Employment. *See* Workplace; Workplace
    computer access; Workstation robots
  cognitive disabilities, 218–219
  low-tech assistive technologies, 141

Employment. (*Continued*)
  students with disabilities, 113
  United States, 67–68
  work assistant mobile robot, 389–392, 397–399
Encryption algorithms/hashing, telematics, 898–899
End-user residence subsystem, telecare-robotics concept, 729
Energy consumption, telematics, 903
Engelberger, Joe, 368
Engineering and Physical Sciences Research Council (EPSRC, UK), 821
Episode discovery (ED) algorithm, mining sequential patterns, 771–772
Ergonomics:
  intelligent transportation systems (ITSs), 744–745
  universal design, 814
  usability philosophy, 856–858
E-textiles. *See* Smart textiles
Ethical concerns, technology evaluation, 847–848
Ethnography, user-centered design, 788
Europe. *See International Classification of Functioning, Disability and Health* (ICF)
  demography, 528–529
  standardization, 916
European Commission (EC), 14
European Union, 10
Evaluation. *See* Technology evaluation
Expressive language disorder, communication disabilities, 6
Eye. *See* Visual disabilities
Eye-mouse system, wheelchair-based robotic system, 383–385, 394–395

Fabrics. *See* Smart textiles
Facet model, elderly, 574–579
Fair Housing Act of 1988, 45, 73–74, 808
Family members, client training, 31
Fare payment, public transportation, 533
Federal Communications Commission (FCC), 75
Firewall protection, telematics, 897
Fitting, optimal use, 32–35
Fixed mobile convergence, telematics, 893–894
Floors, smart floor, 706–709
FM systems, hearing disabilities, 197
Focus groups:
  research design, technology evaluation, 846

  universal design, 811–813
  usability data collection methods, 861
Follow-up care, 31, 35
Font options, communication assistant, 309
Food and Drug Administration (FDA), 36, 37, 66, 194
Food preparation, visual disabilities, 164
Frequency, cutaneous perception, 341
FRIEND robot, 376

Gaia, smart space middleware, 613
Gastroesophageal reflux disease (GERD) diagnosis, 334–335
Gator Tech Smart House, 614, 695–709. *See* Smart house design
Gears, powered wheelchair, 447
General Agreement on Trade and Tariffs (GATT), 53–54
Genetic eye disease, 160
Genetic therapy, 12
George Mason University (Fairfax, Virginia), 105–107, 113–114
Giant cell arteritis, 161
Glaucoma, 152–153
Global positioning system (GPS):
  blind navigation, 480–481, 491–492
  cognitive disabilities, 228
  visual disabilities, 169
Grab bars, low-tech assistive technologies, 138–139
Grade of service, telematics, 902–903
Graphical user interfaces (GUIs), 251, 252. *See* Computer platforms and operating systems; Interfaces; Voice interactive systems
  computer platforms and operating systems, 265–266
  voice interactive systems, 281–282
Graphics, tactile, visual disabilities, 172, 187
Grasp/prehension, upper-limb prostheses, 422–424
Grateful acceptance, defined, 29
Guide 71 (ISO/IEC), 917–918
Guide dogs:
  blind navigation, 484–485
  public transportation (U.S.), 534
Guido walker, 503–505

Hand, upper-limb prostheses, 422–424
Handicap. *See* Elderly; People with special needs (PwSN); specific disabilities

International Classification of Functioning, Disability and Health (ICF), 2–3
  well-being and, disability concept, 2
Handrails, low-tech assistive technologies, 138–139
Handwashing, cognitive disabilities, 226
Handwriting, low-tech assistive technologies, 138
Handy robot, 365
Hashing, telematics, 898–899
HAVi (Home Audio Video Interoperability), telematics, 881
Head-shoulder interface, wheelchair-based robotic system, 386, 395
Head-up displays, intelligent transportation systems (ITSs), 740–741
Healthcare. *See* Automated medication management; Home health technologies; Smart textiles
  context awareness, 588
  demography, 749–750
  home health technologies, 749–766
  telematics, 903–904
  trends in, 711–713
Healthcare workers, shortage of, 711–712, 728
Health insurance, 43
Health-related quality of life (HRQL), technology assessment, 845. *See* Quality of life
Hearing disabilities:
  assistive devices, 191–202
    alerting and warning systems, 198–199
    personal systems, 191–195
    telecommunications, 199–201
    wide-area systems, 195–198
  classification of assistive technologies, 22
  distance education technology, 109
  intelligent transportation systems (ITSs), 743–744
  low-tech assistive technologies, 136, 137
  people with special needs (PwSN), 6
  universal design, 810
  voice interactive systems, 289–290
  wearable computer systems, 332–334
  workplace computer access, 254–256
Hemianopsia, 160
Heumann, Judith, 53
High-degree myopia, 160
HIV-AIDS, 58
Hoist, robotic, mobile platform-based robot systems, 386–389, 396–397
Holter monitoring, 675

Home appliances:
  context awareness, 588
  visual disabilities, 163
Home-area networks, telematics, 870–871. *See* Telematics
Home Audio Video Interoperability (HAVi), telematics, 881
Homecare delivery. *See* Assistive technologies (AT); Home health technologies; Smart house design; Telecare; Telecare-robotics concept; Wheelchair(s)
Home health technologies, 749–766
  overview, 749–751, 763–764
  PlaceLab, 751–757
    described, 752–753
    design goals, 755–756
    generally, 751–752
    MITes sensor kit research, 761–763
    rationale for, 753–755
    study structure, 756–757
  sensor kits, 757–764
    generally, 757–759
    MITes, 759–761
    MITes health research, 761–763
Home modification, United States, 68
HomePlug 1.0, 873
HomePlug AV, 873
Home residential gateway, telematics, 868–869. *See* Telematics
HomeRF wireless technology, telematics, 880
Hong Kong, transportation services, 562–565
Housing, smart, visual disabilities, 166. *See* Smart house design
Human activity assistive technology (HATT) model, 848
Human assistance, 12
Human limb prostheses, 419–436
  lower-limb, 432–433
  overview, 419
  upper-limb, 420–432
    arms, 424–432
    control systems, 426–432
    power systems, 424–426
    design, 421–422
    generally, 420
    prehension/grasp, 422–424
Human-robot interfaces, wheelchair-based robotic system, 383–386. *See* Interfaces

IBM WebSphere voice server, 294–295
IEEE 1394, telematics, 881–882

Illumination, public transportation, 533
IMP (intelligent mobility platform) walker, 509–511
Inclusive design:
    user-centered design, 788–789
    visual disabilities, 176–178
Income, United States, 67
INDEPENDENCE IBOT 3000 Transporter (IBOT) wheelchair, 449–450
India, transportation services, 552–553
Individuals with Disabilities Education Act of 1997, 111
Individuals with Disabilities in Education Act of 1990 (IDEA), 102
Individuals with Disabilities in Education Improvement Act of 2004 (IDEA), 102
Indoor blind navigation, 492–493
Inductance plethysmography, smart textiles, 685–686
Information access. *See* Security and safety
    telecare, 717, 720–721, 724
    telematics, 900–901
    visual disabilities, 169–174, 176
Information and communication technology (ICT), 907–920. *See* Alarm(s); Pervasive computing and monitoring
    accessibility, 908–912
    Japan, 908
    overview, 907
    policy implications, 918–919
    standardization, 912–918
Information organizer, 223–224
Information systems:
    cognitive disabilities, 208–209
    public transportation:
        Europe, 542
        U.S., 532–534
Infrared (IR) systems:
    hearing disability, 197
    orientation, 168–169
    signage, blind navigation, 489–491
In-home mobility support, telematics, 894. *See* Smart house design
Inspections, usability data collection methods, 861–862
Institutional (depot) wheelchair, 441
Integrated care, care trends, 712
Intellectual disabilities, students with disabilities, 111–114
Intelligent environment, defined, 768–769

Intelligent home, telematics, 869–870. *See* Smart house design; Telematics
Intelligent monitoring systems. *See* Elderly
Intelligent transportation systems (ITSs), 737–747. *See* Traffic safety
    collision warning systems and adaptive cruise control, 738
    drive-by-wire, 739
    ergonomics, 744–745
    head-up displays, 740–741
    hearing disabilities, 743–744
    in-vehicle navigation systems, 742
    lane-keeping assistance, 738
    multifunction controls, 743
    nonvisual warnings, 741
    overview, 737–738
    parking aids, 739–740
    telematics, 742–743
    universal design, 810
Interactive digital television, visual disabilities, 185
Interactive Workspaces, smart space middleware, 614–615
Intercity public transportation (U.S.), 528
Interfaces. *See* Computer platforms and operating systems; Telematics; Voice interactive systems
    application programming interface (API), 607–608
    automated medication management, 640–642
    human-robot interfaces, wheelchair-based robotic system, 383–386, 394–396
    ordinary and extraordinary human-machine interaction concept, 790
    powered wheelchair, 443–447
    upper-limb prostheses, EMG interface, 427–430
    usability, 856
Internal acceptance, defined, 29
International Classification of Functioning, Disability and Health (ICF), 2, 52, 57, 65, 81–100. *See* World Health Organization (WHO)
    applications, 93–96
    assistive technologies, 14
    handicap, 2–3
    International Standards Organization (ISO) 9999, 121–122
    overview, 83
    perspective of, 81–82
    principles of, 84–90, 833

interactional model, 86–87
multidimensionality, 84–86
neutrality, 89–90
spectrum continuity, 88–89
universality, 87–88
structure of, 90–93
International Classification of Impairment, Disease, and Handicap (ICIDH), 2, 52, 83, 85, 805
International disability policy research (IDPR), 49. *See* International perspective
International perspective, 49–59. *See* United States
demand side, 50–51
Japan, 907–920
overview, 49–50
people with special needs (PwSN), 10–11
policy framework, 55–57
research areas, 57–58
supply side, 51–54
International Standards Organization (ISO) 1999, user-centered design, 787
International Standards Organization (ISO) 9241, usability, 855, 858
International Standards Organization (ISO) 9999, 13, 15–18, 63, 117–126
application areas, 124
classification system, 118, 119–122
coding system, 119
future prospects, 124–125
history of, 122–124
overview, 117
scope of, 118
International Standards Organization (ISO) 13407, usability, 857
International Standards Organization (ISO/IEC) Guide 71, Japan, 917–918
International Statistical Classification of Diseases and Related Health Problems (ICD-10), 83
Internet:
cognitive disabilities, 210
smart space middleware, 612–617
telecare, technology trends, 716–717
visual disabilities, 174, 187
workplace computer access, 240–241
Internet residential gateway, 869. *See* Telematics
Interoperability:
context modeling requirements, 592–593
smart space middleware, 610
Interviews:

research design, technology evaluation, 846
usability data collection methods, 860–861
user-centered design, 796
Introspection/discovery capability, computer platforms and operating systems, 273
Intrusion detection system, telematics, 899
In-vehicle navigation systems, intelligent transportation systems (ITSs), 742
IP replay, hearing disabilities, 201
IPSEC NAT traversal, telematics, 898
IST-MATS robot, 376

Japan, 64. *See International Classification of Functioning, Disability and Health* (ICF)
elderly, 908
transportation services, 560–562
Java Swing API, 277
Jini architecture, smart space middleware, 611–612
Joystick, powered wheelchair, 443–445

KARES II robot, 368, 376, 377–386, 392–396. *See* Wheelchair-based robotic system
Keyboard. *See* Interfaces
augmentative-alternative communication (AAC) devices, 302
computer platforms and operating systems, 267
Keypads, visual disabilities, 181–182
Knops, Harry, 64
Knowledge layer, middleware architecture, smart house design, 700
Konnex (KNX), telematics, 881
Korea, transportation services, 557

Labor force, United States, 67–68. *See* Employment; Workplace
Laissez-faire model, 50
Lane-keeping assistance, intelligent transportation systems (ITSs), 738
Language disorders, cognitive disabilities, 7
Laser-based devices:
blind navigation, 488–489
Pearl robotic walking assistant, 511–514
Learning impairments, distance education technology, 109–110. *See* Students with disabilities
Leisure:
low-tech assistive technologies, 140
students with disabilities, 114

Lifespan design, 805
Lifestyle, care trends, 713
Lighting:
   public transportation (U.S.), 533
   visual disabilities, 170–171
Limb prostheses. *See* Human limb prostheses
Literacy, workplace computer access, 258
Living laboratories. *See* Home health technologies
Long cane, blind navigation, 484–485
Loudness control, hearing aids, 193
Lower-limb prostheses, 432–433
Low-tech assistive technologies, 129–142
   assessment and selection considerations, 132–134
      availability/affordability, 134
      desired tasks and activities, 133
      device characteristics, 134
      environment and context, 134
      functional limitations, 132–133
      residual abilities and skills, 133
   compensatory considerations, 134–141
      cognitive disabilities, 136–137
      communication disabilities, 137–138
      employment, 141
      hearing disabilities, 136
      mobility, 138–140
      physical limitations, 135
      recreation and leisure, 140
      visual disabilities, 135–136
   overview, 129–132

Mace, Ron, 64
Macular degeneration, 153–154
Macular dystrophy, 160
Macular hole, 160
Magnetic induction, hearing disabilities, 196
Malaysia, transportation services, 553–555
Managed and unmanaged services, telematics, 893
Manipulator on base robotic, 364–365
Manual wheelchair, 440–442
MANUS robot, 366–367, 376
Maps, visual disabilities, 168
Marketplace:
   assistive technologies, 18
   international perspective, 50–54
Markhov decision process (MDP), smart space algorithms, 774–776
Markup scheme, context modeling requirements, 593–594

Maslow model of needs, people with special needs (PwSN) concept, 3–4
MASTER1 robot, 360
Matching Person and Technology (MPT) tool, 845
Matching requirements:
   International Classification of Functioning, Disability and Health (ICF), 94–95
   optimal use, 32
MATS robot, 369
MavHome, 614, 767–769, 777–781. *See* Smart space algorithms
Maximal policy model, 50
Mechanical system, powered wheelchair, 447–449
Medicaid, 43, 62, 63, 71–72
Medical records, telecare, information access, 720–721
Medicare, 42, 63, 70–71
Medication. *See* Automated medication management
   cognitive disabilities, 226–227
   visual disabilities, 164–165
Mercosur (Mercado Comun del Sur), 54
Microsoft Active Accessibility (MSAA), 275–276
Microsoft Speech Server, 293–294, 295
Microsoft UI automation, 276
Middleware architecture (smart house design), 698–700. *See* Smart space middleware
   application layer, 700
   context management layer, 700
   knowledge layer, 700
   physical layer, 698
   sensor platform layer, 699
   service layer, 699–700
Minimum description length (MDL), mining sequential patterns, 772
Mining sequential patterns, smart space algorithms, 771–772
Mixed receptive-expressive language disorder, communication disabilities, 6
Mobile autonomous robot, 367–368
Mobile phones. *See* Mobile telephones
Mobile platform-based robot systems, 375–403. *See* Assistive robotics; Wheelchair-mounted assistive robots
   overview, 375–377
   robotic hoist, 386–389
   user trials, 392–399
      KARES II, 392–396

robotic hoist, 396–397
wheelchair-based robotic system, 377–386
  generally, 377–381
  human-robot interfaces, 383–386
  robotic arm, 382–383
wheelchair-mounted assistive robots, 377–386
work assistant for manufacturing, 389–392, 397–399
Mobile telephones. *See* Telephone
universal design, 809–810
visual disabilities, 183
Mobile wireless technology, augmentative-alternative communication (AAC) integration, 300–301. *See* Telematics
Mobility. *See* Motor disabilities
cognitive disabilities, 228
elderly, 501–502
low-tech assistive technologies, 138–140
visual disabilities, 167–169
Mobility aids, blind navigation, 484, 485
Model-view-controller (MVC) design pattern, computer platforms and operating systems, 271–272
Monitoring:
  automated medication devices, 640
  context awareness, applications and systems, 588–590
  pervasive computing and monitoring, 570–571
  smart textiles, 674–676
  telecare applications, 721–723
  video, technology trends, 716
Motor disabilities:
  classification of assistive technologies, 19–20
  distance education technology, 109
  low-tech assistive technologies, 134–135
  people with special needs (PwSN), 4–5
  traffic safety, 462
  voice interactive systems, 290–291
  workplace computer access, 242–250
Motors, powered wheelchair, 447
MOVAID robot, 367–368
MoVAR robot, 367
Multidimensionality, ICF, 84–86
Multifunction controls, intelligent transportation systems (ITSs), 743
Multimedia procedure assistants, 222–223

MVC (model-view-controller) design pattern, computer platforms and operating systems, 271–272
Myoelectric control, upper-limb prostheses, 427
MySpoon robot, 363–364

National Center for Accessible Transportation (NCAT), 519
National Center for Medical Rehabilitation Research (NCMRR), 65
National Health Interview Survey on Disability (NHIS-D), 132
National Institute on Disability and Rehabilitation Research (NIDRR), 65, 66, 68
National Institutes of Health (NIH), 65, 66
National Science and Technology Policy Organization and Priorities Act of 1976, 61, 62
National Science Foundation (NSF), 821, 824
Naturally occurring retirement communities (NORCs), 807
Navigation, computer platforms and operating systems, 274–275
Navigation systems, in-vehicle, intelligent transportation systems (ITSs), 742
Needs:
  design for well-being (DfW), 823–824
  people with special needs (PwSN) concept, 3–4
  policy models, 50–51
  research and development, elderly, 571–572
  telematics, 904
Negative policy model, 50
Networks. *See* Telematics
Neuroelectric control, upper-limb prostheses, 427–430
Neutrality, ICF, 89–90
Ninja project, smart space middleware, 614
Noise reduction, hearing aids, 193–194
Noncompliance, automated medication management, 632–634
Nongovernmental organizations (NGOs), 10
Nonvisual warnings, intelligent transportation systems (ITSs), 741
North American Free Trade Agreement (NAFTA), 10, 54
Nursing home residents, 502
Nystagmus, 155–157

Objective data collection methods, usability, 862–863
Object-role-modeling (ORM), 598–599
Observational studies, research design, technology evaluation, 846–847
Observations, usability data collection methods, 862
Office of Equity and Diversity Services (George Mason University), 105–107
Office of Vocational Rehabilitation (OVR), 43
Older Americans Act of 1965, 14, 63, 72–73
OnStar, telematics, 742–743
Ontology-based approaches, context modeling requirements, 594–597
Open Services Gateway Initiative (OSGi), telematics, 882–883
Operating systems. *See* Computer platforms and operating systems
Optical (camera or laser-based) devices, blind navigation, 488–489
Optimal use, 29–48
  client-centered approach, 41
  client fitting, 32–35
  client rejection, 32
  client training, 31–32
  consumer empowerment, 44–46
  future prospects, 46–47
  matching requirements, 32
  overview, 31
  participatory action design (PAD), 35–36
  quality assurance, 37–38
  reimbursement and payment, 41–44
  service delivery models, 40–41
  total quality management (TQM) and continuous quality improvement (CQI), 39–40
Ordinary and extraordinary human-machine interaction concept, user-centered design, 790
Organization for Economic Cooperation and Development (OECD), 51
Orientation:
  cognitive disabilities, 228
  visual disabilities, 167–169, 187
Orientation and mobility (OM) training, 482
Orphan technology, 64
OSGi (Open Services Gateway Initiative), telematics, 882–883
OSGi Service Platform, smart space middleware, 612, 616
Over-the-road buses, public transportation (U.S.), 529–530
Oxygen project, smart space middleware, 613

PACE middleware, context awareness, 602–603. *See* Smart space middleware
Packaging, visual disabilities, 164
Pagers, 221–222
PAMM walking aid system, 505–506
Parking aids, intelligent transportation systems (ITSs), 739–740
Parkinson's disease, voice interactive systems, 292
Paro (seal robot), robot therapy, 407–409. *See* Robot therapy
Participatory action design (PAD), 35–36, 788. *See* User-centered design
Passenger ferry service, public transportation (U.S.), 526, 530
Passenger rail, public transportation (U.S.), 528–529
Payment, optimal use, 41–44
People with special needs (PwSN). *See* Disability concept; Elderly; specific disabilities
  assistive technologies, 11–24
  demography, 1, 7–11
  disability concept, 3–4
  impairment types, 4–7
    cognitive disabilities, 7
    communication disabilities, 6–7
    hearing, 6
    motor and physical disabilities, 4–5
    vision, 5
  user-centered design, 790–793
Personal Digital Assistants (PDAs), 65, 113, 130, 209, 220–221, 308, 492
Personalization, telematics, 903
Personal transportation. *See* Intelligent transportation systems (ITSs); Traffic safety; Transportation services (Asia); Transportation services (Europe); Transportation services (U.S.)
Pervasive computing and monitoring. *See* Alarm(s); Information and communication technology (ICT)
  defined, 76
  elderly, 570–571
Philippines, transportation services, 556–557
Phoneline networks, existing communications infrastructure, telematics, 871

Physical disabilities, people with special needs (PwSN), 4–5. *See* Elderly; Motor disabilities; specific physical disabilities
Physical layer, middleware architecture, smart house design, 698
Piecemeal approach model, 50
Piezoresistive sensors, smart textiles, 684–685
Pillholders, automated medication devices, 639
Pin arrays, sensory substitution, 344–346
PlaceLab, 751–757
 described, 752–753
 design goals, 755–756
 generally, 751–752
 MITes sensor kit research, 761–763
 rationale for, 753–755
 study structure, 756–757
Platforms. *See* Computer platforms and operating systems
Plethysmography, smart textiles, 684–686
Pneumography, smart textiles, 686–687
Positioning systems:
 cognitive disabilities, 228
 visual disabilities, 169
Posterior vitreous detachment, 161
Poverty, United States, 67
Powered wheelchair, 443–450
 innovations, 449–450
 interfaces, 443–447
 mechanical system, 447–449
 motors and gears, 447
Powerline networks (telematics), 871–875
 broadband powerline (BPL) access, 873–875
 generally, 871–873
 HomePlug 1.0, 873
 HomePlug AV, 873
Prehension/grasp, upper-limb prostheses, 422–424
Pressure sore prevention, wearable computer systems, 330–332
Printed receipts, visual disabilities, 182
Privacy. *See* Security and safety
 smart space middleware, 610–611
 technology evaluation, 847–848
 telecare, 723–724
 telematics, 901–902
Proactive healthcare. *See* Home health technologies
ProPHeT decisionmaking, smart space algorithms, 774–776
Proposal writing, research design, technology evaluation, 836–838

Prostheses. *See* Human limb prostheses
Prosthetic design, 804
Protocol reference model, access networks, 888–891
ProVAR robot, 362–363, 377
Psychosocial Impact of Assistive Device Scale (PIADS), 845
Public terminals, visual disabilities, 178–182
Pushrim-activated power-assisted wheelchair (PAPAW), 449

Qualitative data, research design, technology evaluation, 846
Qualitative-quantitative combined study design, technology evaluation, 840–842
Qualitative study design, technology evaluation, 838–840
Quality assurance:
 continuous quality improvement (CQI), total quality management (TQM) and, 39–40
 optimal use, 37–40
Quality function deployment (QFD), 827
Quality of life:
 ecologic model, 572–574
 facet model, 574–579
 technology assessment, 845
Quality-of-service requirements (telematics), 891–894
 fixed mobile convergence, 893–894
 generally, 891–892
 in-home mobility support, 894
 managed and unmanaged services, 893
 user involvement, 893
 Virtual Private Network (VPN), 892–893
Quantitative data, research design, technology evaluation, 845
Quantitative study design, technology evaluation, 838
Quebec User Evaluation Satisfaction 2.0 (QUEST) with Assistive Technology, 845
Questionnaires:
 usability data collection methods, 861
 user-centered design, 796

Radabaugh, Mary Pat, 317
RAID-MASTER robot, 361–362
RAID robot, 361, 376, 377
Raised-paper diagrams, sensory substitution, 343–344
Randomization types, research design, technology evaluation, 843–844

Randomized controlled trials (RCTs), 66
RAPTOR robot, 376
Reading machine, visual disabilities, 172
Recreation, low-tech assistive technologies, 140
Reference architecture, context awareness, software infrastructure, 600–601
Rehabilitation, 12
   assistive technology, 804
   telecare, 723
   voice interactive systems, 292
Rehabilitation Act of 1973, 44, 62, 79, 101, 103
Rehabilitation Act of 1998, 208, 858–859
Rehabilitation and therapy, voice interactive systems, 292
Rehabilitation Engineering Society of North America (RESNA), 37–38
Reimbursement, optimal use, 41–44
Relay services, hearing disabilities, 200–201
Reluctant acceptance, defined, 29
Remote caregiver operation center subsystem, telecare-robotics concept, 730–731
Requirements analysis model, context modeling, 597
Research design (technology evaluation), 836–847
   focus groups, 846
   generally, 836
   interviews, 846
   materials and procedures, 844–846
      qualitative data, 846
      quantitative data, 845
   observational studies, 846–847
   proposal writing, 836–838
   qualitative-quantitative combined study design, 840–842
   qualitative study design, 838–840
   quantitative study design, 838
   randomization types, 843–844
   sampling types, 842–843
   subjects and participants, 842
Research & development (R&D), 65–66, 69–70, 571–572
Research function, audit function and, technology evaluation, 834–835
Research process, technology evaluation, 835
Research subjects and participants, research design, technology evaluation, 842
Residential gateway architecture:
   access networks, 885–888
   telematics, 868–869 (*See* Telematics)

Residual abilities and skills, low-tech assistive technologies, 133
Retinal detachment, 161
Retinitis pigmentosa (RP), 157–159
Retinopathy of prematurity, 161
Rhythm, cutaneous perception, 342
Road intersection accidents, traffic safety, 468
Robotic arm, wheelchair-based robotic system, 382–383, 393–394
Robotic hoist, mobile platform-based robot systems, 386–389, 396–397
Robotics, telecare, 717–719
Robotic walkers. *See* Walker systems
Robots. *See* Assistive robotics; Mobile platform-based robot systems; Workstation robots; specific robots
Robot therapy, 405–418
   applications and evaluation, 409–415
   overview, 405–407
   seal robot (Paro), 407–409
Rubber-tired vehicles, public transportation (U.S.), 523–524
Runtime querying, context modeling requirements, 592

Safety. *See* Security and safety
SALSA middleware, 615
SALT standards, voice interactive systems, 295
Sampling types, research design, technology evaluation, 842–843
Scalability, smart space middleware, 611
Scenarios, usability data collection methods, 862
Schloss, Irving P., 61
School districts, 43
Scooters, low-tech assistive technologies, 139–140
Screens, visual disabilities, 181. *See* Display(s)
Seal robot (Paro), robot therapy, 407–409. *See* Robot therapy
Security and safety, 619–629
   automated medication management, 636–637
   concepts, 620–621
   elderly, 624–627
   future prospects, 627–628
   overview, 619
   privacy needs, 622–623
   safety needs, 624
   security needs, 621–622
   smart space middleware, 610–611

technology evaluation, 847–848
telecare, 723–724, 734–735
telematics, 894–902
  access control, 900–901
    antispoofing, 897
    authentication, 900
    authentication requirements and copy protection, 896
    code authorization/signature, 900
    demilitarized zone, 897
    electronic data security, 901
    encryption algorithms/hashing, 898–899
    firewall protection, 897
    generally, 894–896
    intrusion detection system, 899
    IPSEC NAT traversal, 898
    main applications, 896–897
    privacy, 901–902
    URL filtering, 898
    Virtual Private Network (VPN) capabilities, 898
    virus protection, 899
  trust needs, 623–624
  virtual companions, 655–656
Security services gateway, 869. *See* Telematics
Self-care, trends in, 712–713
Sensor development, telecare, technology trends, 713–714
Sensor kits:
  generally, 757–759
  home health technologies, 757–764
  MITes, 759–761
Sensor platform, smart house design, 702–703
Sensor platform layer, middleware architecture, smart house design, 699
Sensors, smart textiles, 678–681
Sensory substitution, 343–349. *See* Cutaneous perception
  Braille and raised-paper diagrams, 343–344
  pin arrays, 344–346
  vibrotactile displays, 346–349
Sensory translation rules, blind navigation, 482–483
Sequential patterns, mining, smart space algorithms, 771–772
Service animals. *See* Guide dogs
Service delivery models, optimal use, 40–41
Service layer, middleware architecture, smart house design, 699–700
Service-oriented architecture (SOA), smart space middleware, 610

Set-top box gateway, 869. *See* Telematics
Shopping, 165–166
Signage, infrared, blind navigation, 489–491
Signals, visual disabilities, 175–176
Sign language:
  augmentative-alternative communication (AAC) devices, 301–302
  wearable computer systems, 332–334
SIMBAD project, pervasive computing and monitoring, 570
Smart environments. *See* Context awareness; Elderly; Security and safety; Smart house design; Smart space algorithms
Smart floor, smart house design, 706–709
Smart house design, 695–709. *See* Context awareness; Smart space algorithms; Telecare; Telecare-robotics concept; Telematics; Wheelchair(s)
  context-awareness, 588, 700–702
  middleware architecture, 698–700
    application layer, 700
    context management layer, 700
    knowledge layer, 700
    physical layer, 698
    sensor platform layer, 699
    service layer, 699–700
  overview, 695–696
  sensor platform, 702–703
  smart floor, 706–709
  smart plugs, 703–706
  technologies, 696–698
  virtual companions, 647
  visual disabilities, 166
  wheelchairs, 439–440, 450–454
Smart plugs, smart house design, 703–706
Smart space algorithms, 767–783
  case study, 776–777
  living environment applications, 777–781
  MavHome, 768–769
  motivation, 767–768
  overview, 767
  technologies, 771–776
    active-LeZi (ALZ) algorithm, 772–773
    mining sequential patterns, 771–772
    ProPHeT decisionmaking, 774–776
Smart space middleware, 607–618. *See* Middleware architecture (smart house design)
  context processing and management, 609–610
  device interaction and integration, 608–609
  interoperability, 610

Smart space middleware (*Continued*)
   overview, 607–608
   scalability, 611
   security and privacy, 610–611
   standards and technology, 611–613
      Jini architecture, 611–612
      OSGi Service Platform, 612
      Universal Plug and Play (UPnP), 612
      web services, 612–613
   systems, 613–617
Smart textiles, 673–692. *See* Wearable computer systems
   ambulatory monitoring, 674–676
   chronic disease:
      at-risk individuals, 677
      at-risk professionals, 677–678
      cardiac patients, 676–677
      variables monitored, 678
   future prospects, 690
   overview, 673–674, 690–691
   sensors, 678–681
   transducer, 682–684
   WEALTHY system example, 687–689
   wearable systems, 684–687
SMART^{wheel}, 34
SOCAM, smart space middleware, 614
Social interaction:
   cognitive disabilities, 228–230
   context awareness, 588
Social rights model, 50. *See* Civil rights issues; Discrimination
Social Security Act of 1935, 70
Social Security Disability Insurance (SSDI), 63, 70, 71
Software engineering, context modeling requirements, 592, 598–599
Software infrastructure, context awareness, 600–603
Solar platform, context awareness, software infrastructure, 602
Sonar-based devices, blind navigation, 485–487
Spectrum continuity, ICF, 88–89
Speech disorders:
   communication disabilities, 6
   low-tech assistive technologies, 137
   voice interactive systems, 291–292
Speech output, visual disabilities, 181
Speech recognition:
   communication assistant, 310–311
   visual disabilities, 173
   voice interactive systems, 284–286

Spoofing, security and safety, telematics, 897
Sports wheelchair, 441
Standards and standardization. *See* Information and communication technology (ICT); specific standards and codes
   information and communication technology (ICT), 907–920
   usability, 858–859
   visual disabilities, 178
   voice interactive systems, 292–296
Standing poles, low-tech assistive technologies, 138–139
Stargardt's macular dystrophy, 161
Static balance, lower-limb prostheses, 432–433
Steel-tired vehicles, public transportation (U.S.), 524–526
Stroke, cognitive disabilities, 7
Students with disabilities, 101–116. *See* Brain damage; Cognitive disabilities
   application process case study, 105–107
      access, 106
      assistive technology initiative, 106
      consultation and screening, 106
      text access, 106–107
      Web access, 107
   distance education technology, 107–111
      accessibility barriers, 109
      cognitive and learning impairments, 109–110
      generally, 107–108
      handouts and resources, 110–111
      hearing, 109
      interactive tools, 111
      limitations of, 110
      motor impairments, 109
      universal design, 110
      vision, 109
   intellectual disabilities, 111–114
   overview, 101–102
   rights and services, 102–105
      legislation, 105
      organizational structure, 103–105
Subjective data collection methods, usability, 860–862
Supplementary Security Income (SSI), 63, 71
Supply side, international perspective, 51–54
Surgery, 11
SWT accessibility API, 277

Tactile displays, 339–352
   cutaneous perception, 340–343

aging, 342–343
amplitude, 340–341
body location, 342
duration, 341
frequency, 341
rhythm, 342
waveform, 341
overview, 339–340, 349–351
sensory substitution, 343–349
Braille and raised-paper diagrams, 343–344
pin arrays, 344–346
vibrotactile displays, 346–349
visual disabilities, 172, 187
workplace computer access, visual disabilities, 254
Taiwan, transportation services, 558–560
Tape recorders, visual disabilities, 171
TAURO robot, 368
Technology Act of 1988, 74
Technology evaluation, 833–853
audit and research functions, 834–835
ethical concerns, 847–848
overview, 833–834
research design, 836–847
focus groups, 846
generally, 836
interviews, 846
materials and procedures, 844–846
qualitative data, 846
quantitative data, 845
observational studies, 846–847
proposal writing, 836–838
qualitative-quantitative combined study design, 840–842
qualitative study design, 838–840
quantitative study design, 838
randomization types, 843–844
sampling types, 842–843
subjects and participants, 842
research process, 835
Technology Related Assistance for Individuals with Disabilities Act of 1988 (Tech Act), 13–14, 63, 74, 101–102, 129, 208, 218
Technology transfer, augmentative-alternative communication (AAC) devices, 313
Telecare, 76, 711–725. *See* Smart house design; Telecare-robotics concept
applications, 721–723
care trends, 711–713
information access, 720–721
innovation, 719

overview, 711
security and safety, 723–724
technology trends, 713–719
ambient intelligence, 715
body-area network, 714–715
information access, 717
Internet, 716–717
robotics, 717–719
sensor development, 713–714
video, 716, 717
virtual reality, 717
wireless connectivity, 714
Telecare-robotics concept, 727–736. *See* Telecare
end-user residence subsystem, 729
functional characteristics, 734
overview, 727–729
remote caregiver operation center subsystem, 730–731
scenarios, 731–734
technical characteristics, 734–735
Telecommunications Act of 1996, 62, 75
Telecommunications relay service (TRS), hearing disabilities, 200
Telehealth, 76
Telematics, 867–906. *See* Interfaces
access, 904
access networks, 883–891
generally, 883–885
protocol reference model, 888–891
residential gateway architecture, 885–888
comfort, 903
compatibility, 903
emergency services, 902
energy consumption, 903
existing communications infrastructure, 871–883
data over cable service interface specification (DOCSIS), 875–877
phoneline networks, 871
powerline networks, 871–875
broadband powerline (BPL) access, 873–875
generally, 871–873
HomePlug 1.0, 873
HomePlug AV, 873
wireless networks, 878–883
Bluetooth network, 879–880
generally, 878–879
Home Audio Video Interoperability (HAVi), 881
HomeRF wireless technology, 880

Telematics (*Continued*)
    IEEE 1394, 881–882
    Konnex (KNX), 881
    OSGi (Open Services Gateway Initiative), 882–883
    UMTS/satellite interoperability, 879
    ZigBee Alliance, 880–881
  grade of service, 902–903
  healthcare services, 903–904
  intelligent transportation systems (ITSs), 742–743
  overview, 867
  personalization, 903
  quality-of-service requirements, 891–894
    fixed mobile convergence, 893–894
    generally, 891–892
    in-home mobility support, 894
    managed and unmanaged services, 893
    user involvement, 893
    Virtual Private Network (VPN), 892–893
  security and safety, 894–902
    access control, 900–901
    antispoofing, 897
    authentication, 900
    authentication requirements and copy protection, 896
    code authorization/signature, 900
    demilitarized zone, 897
    electronic data security, 901
    encryption algorithms/hashing, 898–899
    firewall protection, 897
    generally, 894–896
    intrusion detection system, 899
    IPSEC NAT traversal, 898
    main applications, 896–897
    privacy, 901–902
    URL filtering, 898
    Virtual Private Network (VPN) capabilities, 898
    virus protection, 899
  trends, 867–871
    generally, 867–868
    home-area networks, 870–871
    intelligent home, 869–870
    residential gateway architecture, 868–869
  user needs, 904
Telephone. *See* Mobile telephones
  hearing disabilities, 196, 199–200
  low-tech assistive technologies, 137
  visual disabilities, 178–182, 183
Telesign, wearable computer systems, 332–334

Television:
  captioning, hearing disability, 197–198
  closed-circuit television, visual disabilities, 170
  Interactive digital television, visual disabilities, 170
  visual disabilities, 166
  warning systems, hearing disability, 198–199
Television Decoder Circuitry Act, 198
Temporal arteritis, 161
Textiles. *See* Smart textiles
Text messaging, AAC devices, 302
Text-to-speech synthesis, voice interactive systems, 282–284
Thailand, transportation services, 558
Theaters, user-centered design, 797–799
Therapy. *See* Robot therapy
  robot therapy, 405–418
  voice interactive systems, 292
Thyroid eye disease, 161
Ticket to Work and Work Incentives Improvement Act of 1999, 72
TIDE-MOVAID robot, 376
TIDE-RAID robot, 376
Tinnitus, 6
Toll collection, electronic, 745
Tongue-controlled powered wheelchair, 445–446
Total quality management (TQM), continuous quality improvement (CQI) and, 39–40
Touch screens, visual disabilities, 181–182
Trade-Related Aspects of Intellectual Property Rights (TRIPPS), 54
Traffic safety, 459–477. *See* Intelligent transportation systems (ITSs); Transportation services (Asia); Transportation services (Europe); Transportation services (U.S.)
  countermeasure applications, 474–475
  countermeasure studies, 468–477
    accident avoidance experiments, 469–473
    communication performance experiments, 473–474
    road intersection accidents, 468
  crash countermeasures, 463–468
  elderly, 459–463
  overview, 475–476
  statistics on, 459, 460–462
  universal design, 810
Training, optimal use, 31–32
Transducer, smart textiles, 682–684

Transgenerational design, 805
Transient ischemic attack (TIA), cognitive disabilities, 7
Transnational organizations, 51–54
Transportation services (Asia), 549–566. *See* Intelligent transportation systems (ITSs); Traffic safety
  China, 562–565
  demography, 550–551
  India, 552–553
  Japan, 560–562
  Korea, 557
  Malaysia, 553–555
  overview, 549
  Philippines, 556–557
  Taiwan, 558–560
  Thailand, 558
  Vietnam, 557–558
Transportation services (Europe), 535–548. *See* Intelligent transportation systems (ITSs); Traffic safety
  accessibility policy, 536–537
  definitions, 538–539
  legislation, 538, 539–545
  local measures, 545–548
  member state role, 543–545
  overview, 535–536
Transportation services (U.S.), 519–534. *See* Intelligent transportation systems (ITSs); Traffic safety
  information systems, 532–534
  infrastructure, 521
  overview, 519–520
  system features, 520
  types of, 521–532
    air transport, 530–532
    intercity modes, 528
    over-the-road buses, 529–530
    passenger ferry service, 526, 530
    passenger rail, 528–529
    rubber-tired vehicles, 523–524
    steel-tired vehicles, 524–526
    surface modes, 528
    urban modes, 521–522
    vehicle accommodation, 522
  universal design, 810
Trust management services, smart space middleware, 617
Trust needs, security and safety, 623–624
  Y system,D
    200, 810, 813

UMTS/satellite interoperability, telematics, 879
Unifunction robots, 363–364
United Nations, 10, 51–52, 206
United States, 61–80. *See* International perspective; Transportation services (U.S.)
  access, 74–75
  age level, 66–67
  benefits, 70–72
  cognitive disabilities, 207
  context of, 62
  definitions and classifications, 63–65
  discrimination, 65–66, 72–74
  economic factors, 67
  emerging technologies, 75–76
  employment, 67–68
  overview, 61–62
  science and technology, 69–70
  studies of, 63
  trends in, 68–69
  universal design, 75
United States Department of Health and Human Services (HHS), 63
United States Department of Housing and Urban Development (HUD), 73–74
United States Food and Drug Administration (FDA), 36, 37, 66, 194
Universal design, 803–818
  assistive technologies, 24, 64
  cognitive disabilities, 209–211
  distance education technology, 110
  elderly, 807–811
  future prospects, 813–815
  methods, 811–813
  overview, 803–806, 815–816
  tools, 806–807
  United States, 75
  usability philosophy, 857–858
  wearable computer systems, 321–322
  workplace computer access, 241–242
Universality, ICF, 87–88
Universal Mobile Telecommunications System (UMTS), 176
Universal Plug and Play (UPnP), smart space middleware, 612
Unmanaged and managed services, telematics, 893
UPnP (Universal Plug and Play), smart space middleware, 612
Upper-extremity impairments, workplace computer access, 242–250
Upper-limb prostheses, 420–432
  arms, 424–432

Upper-limb prostheses, (*Continued*)
    control systems, 426–432
        power systems, 424–426
    design, 421–422
    generally, 420
    prehension/grasp, 422–424
Urban public transportation (U.S.), 521–522
URL filtering, telematics, 898
URMAD robot, 367
Usability, 855–866. *See* Client-centered approach; User-based testing; User-centered design
    criteria in, 859
    data collection methods, 860–863
        objective, 862–863
        specific methodologies, 863
        subjective, 860–862
    elderly, 863–864
    interfaces, 856
    norms and standards, 858–859
    overview, 855–856
    philosophies in, 856–858
    workplace, 864–865
User-based testing. *See* Client-centered approach
    communication assistant, 311–312
    usability data collection methods, 862–863
User-centered design, 787–802. *See* Client-centered approach
    aesthetics, 793
    disabled user involvement in design process, 793–795
    inclusive design, 788–789
    methodology, 795–799
        interviews, 796
        mutuality, 795–796
        questionnaires, 796
        theater use, 797–799
    ordinary and extraordinary human-machine interaction concept, 790
    overview, 787–788
    people with special needs, 790–793
    universal design, 811–813
User involvement, telematics, 893
User needs, telematics, 904
User profile management, security and safety, 626–627, 628
Utilities gateway, 869. *See* Telematics
Uveitis, 162

Veterans Administration (VA), 43, 65, 70
Vibrating signals, visual disabilities, 175–176

Vibrotactile displays, sensory substitution, 346–349
Video, telecare, 716, 717, 722–723
Video relay service (VRS), hearing disabilities, 201
Vietnam, transportation services, 557–558
Virtual communities, context awareness, 588
Virtual companions, 645–671
    assistive interaction, 665–666
    dependability, 647–649
    design, 649–652
    framework evaluation, 652–657
        method, 652–653
        prototype implementation, 653–654
        refinement, 656–657
        testing, scenario-based, 654–656
    as metaphor, 647
    needs assessment, 657–668
    overview, 645–646
Virtual Private Network (VPN), telematics, 892–893, 898
Virtual reality:
    telecare, Internet, 717
    visual disabilities, 187–188
Virus protection, telematics, 899
Visitability concept, universal design, 808–809
Visual disabilities, 143–162. *See* Blind navigation; Wayfinding
    assistive devices, 163–189
        convergent systems, 183–185
        domestic appliances, 163
        food preparation, 164
        future prospects, 185–188
        inclusive design, 176–178
        information access, 169–174
        medicines, 164–165
        mobility and orientation, 167–169
        multiple impairments, 174–176
        packaging, 164
        public terminals, 178–182
        shopping, 165–166
        smart housing, 166
        television, 166
    classification of assistive technologies, 21
    demography, 143–144, 174–175
    distance education technology, 109, 110–111
    Guido walker, 503–505
    low-tech assistive technologies, 135–136
    pathologies, 144–162
        aniridia, 144–145
        Best's disease, 159

cataracts, 146
Charles Bonnet syndrome, 159
Coats' disease, 159
coloboma, 159
colorblindness, 146–150
congenital cataract, 159
corneal dystrophy, 159
corneal graft, 159
diabetic retinopathy, 150–152
dry eye, 160
genetic eye disease, 160
glaucoma, 152–153
hemianopsia, 160
high-degree myopia, 160
macular degeneration, 153–154
macular dystrophy, 160
macular hole, 160
nystagmus, 155–157
posterior vitreous detachment, 161
retinal detachment, 161
retinitis pigmentosa (RP), 157–159
retinopathy of prematurity, 161
Stargardt's macular dystrophy, 161
temporal arteritis, 161
thyroid eye disease, 161
uveitis, 162
people with special needs (PwSN), 5
traffic safety, 462
universal design, 810
user-centered design, 791–792
voice interactive systems, 287–289
workplace computer access, 250–254
Vocational assistive mobile robot system, work assistant mobile robot, 389–392, 397–399
Vocational Rehabilitation Act Amendments of 1998, 103
Vocational Rehabilitation Act of 1973, 103, 105
Voice carryover (VCO) systems, hearing disabilities, 200–201
Voice interactive systems, 281–296. See Interfaces
  assistive technologies, 286–292
    generally, 286
    hearing disabilities, 289–290
    motor disabilities, 290–291
    rehabilitation and therapy, 292
    speech impairment, 291–292
    visual disabilities, 287–289
  IBM WebSphere voice server, 294–295
  Microsoft Speech Server, 293–294, 295
  overview, 281–282
  SALT and VXML standards, 295
  speech recognition, 284–286
  standards, 292–296
  text-to-speech synthesis, 282–284
Volume control, hearing aids, 193
Voting machines, universal design, 810
VPN (Virtual Private Network capabilities), telematics, 898
VXML standards, voice interactive systems, 295

Walkers, low-tech assistive technologies, 139
Walker systems, 501–518
  Care-O-bot II, 514
  COOL AIDE, 506–509
  future prospects, 514–515
  Guido, 503–505
  IMP (intelligent mobility platform), 509–511
  overview, 501–503
  PAMM walking aid system, 505–506
  Pearl robotic walking assistant, 511–514
Walking chairs, 450
WALKY robot, 367, 376, 377
Warning systems, hearing disabilities, 198–199. See Alarm(s); Information and communication technology (ICT); Pervasive computing and monitoring
Waveform, cutaneous perception, 341
Wayfinding, 228. See Blind navigation
WEALTHY system, 687–689
Wearable computer systems, 317–338. See Smart textiles
  autism diagnosis, 328–330
  captioning, 335–337
  cognitive disabilities, 324–328
  design issues, 319–321
  design process factors, 322–324
  gastroesophageal reflux disease diagnosis, 334–335
  overview, 317–319
  pressure sore prevention, 330–332
  sign language, 332–334
  smart textiles, 684–687
  user needs, 321–322
Web Content Accessibility Guidelines, 241
Web services, smart space middleware, 612–617
Well-being. See Design for well-being (DfW)
  defined, 571

Well-being. (*Continued*)
  ecologic model, 572–574
  facet model, 574–579
  handicap and, disability concept, 2
Wheelchair(s), 439–457
  manual, 440–442
  powered, 443–450
    innovations, 449–450
    interfaces, 443–447
    mechanical system, 447–449
    motors and gears, 447
  pressure sore prevention, wearable computer systems, 330–332
  quality assurance, 37–38
  smart house design, 439–440, 450–454
Wheelchair-based robotic system, 377–386
  generally, 377–381
  human-robot interfaces, 383–386
  robotic arm, 382–383
  user trials, 392–396
Wheelchair-mounted assistive robots, 365–367. *See* Wheelchair-based robotic system
Wide-area assistive listening, 195–198
Wireless connectivity, telecare, technology trends, 714
Wireless networks (telematics), 878–883
  Bluetooth network, 879–880
  generally, 878–879
  Home Audio Video Interoperability (HAVi), 881
  HomeRF wireless technology, 880
  IEEE 1394, 881–882
  Konnex (KNX), 881
  OSGi (Open Services Gateway Initiative), 882–883
  UMTS/satellite interoperability, 879
  ZigBee Alliance, 880–881
Wireless transmission system, communication assistant, 306–307

Work assistant mobile robot, 389–392, 397–399
Workers' Compensation, 43
Workplace. *See* Employment
  United States, 67–68, 69
  usability, 864–865
  work assistant mobile robot, 389–392, 397–399
Workplace computer access, 239–261
  cognitive disabilities, 257–259
  future prospects, 259–260
  hearing disabilities, 254–256
  legislation, 240–241
  overview, 239–240
  universal design, 241–242
  upper-extremity impairments, 242–250
  visual disabilities, 250–254
Workstation robots, 359–363
  AFMASTER, 360
  DeVAR and ProVAR, 362–363
  MASTER1, 360
  RAID, 360
  RAID-MASTER, 361–362
World Bank, 10, 51, 52–53
World Health Organization (WHO), 1, 2–3, 10, 14, 15–18, 51, 52, 53, 57, 65, 81, 121, 143, 205, 805, 823, 833. *See International Classification of Functioning, Disability and Health* (ICF)
World Trade Organization (WTO), 10, 51, 53–54
World Wide Web Accessibility Initiative (WAI), 210
Writing, low-tech assistive technologies, 138

Yarns, biomonitoring smart textiles, 678–681

Zero configuration technology, 770
ZigBee Alliance, telematics, 880–881
Zola, Irving, 88